The
PACIFIC WAR
Encyclopedia

James F. Dunnigan and Albert A. Nofi

Checkmark Books®

An imprint of Facts On File, Inc.

THE PACIFIC WAR ENCYCLOPEDIA

Checkmark Books
An imprint of Facts On File, Inc.
11 Penn Plaza
New York NY 10001

Library of Congress Cataloging-in-Publication Data

Dunnigan, James F.
    The Pacific war encyclopedia / James F. Dunnigan and Albert A. Nofi.
        p.   cm.
    Includes bibliographical references and index.
    ISBN 0-8160-4393-0
    1. World War, 1939-1945—Pacific Area-Encyclopedias.   I. Nofi, Albert A.   II. Title.
D767.9.D86   1998
940.54'099—dc2 1   97-15634

You can find Facts On File on the World Wide Web at http://www.factsonfile.com

Text design by Cathy Rincon
Cover design by Robert Yaffe
All photographic reproductions are from the National Archives.
Diagrams on pages 95 and 486 copyright © 1995 Combined Books, used with permission.
All other illustrations are from the authors' collections.
Maps by Karen Little and Dale Williams.

This book is printed on acid-free paper.

Printed in the United States of America

MP FOF 10 9 8 7 6 5 4 3 2 1

Contents

To

Chief Petty Officer William Howell

USN 1941–45

USS *Monterey* (CVL 26), 1943–45

ACKNOWLEDGMENTS

The authors wish to acknowledge the following for their contributions to this work:

Dennis Casey, Ted Cook, Fun Fong, Norman Friedman, Mark Herman, Kay Larsen;
Philip K. Lundeberg, curator emeritus, National Museum of American History;
Kathleen Williams, Shelby Stanton, US Army Center of Military History;
US Army Military History Institute; US Air Force Historical Research Agency;
US Marine Corps Historical Reference Section; US Navy Historical Center;
and Mary S. Nofi, who has to put up with one of us.

INTRODUCTION

The *Pacific War Encyclopedia* is a unique reference book. Most of the entries are longer than is customary in works of this nature. These long entries are both more discursive and analytic than is usual in reference works. In addition, in many entries the reader will find unusual approaches to the presentation of the material, such as statistical analyses of subjects not normally quantifiable, for example, the relative effectiveness of Japanese troops vis-à-vis American or British ones.

Although this is a work about the Pacific War, frequent comparisons have been made with other theaters in order more effectively to establish the global framework within which the Pacific War unfolded.

Another unusual aspect of this work is that we have kept descriptions of campaigns and battles to a minimum. There are numerous excellent treatments of the details of these, and we wanted to focus this book on matters not usually covered in standard histories.

We have covered the technical and human aspects of the war in great detail. All ship classes and aircraft types are covered, as are the techniques of naval and amphibious warfare. There are more than a thousand separate items covering a vast amount of information about the War in the Pacific.

It should be borne in mind that no work, regardless of size, can fully examine a phenomenon so enormous and complex as the Pacific War. We have left a great deal out of this work. We tend to focus more on an American perspective, if only because the authors are Americans. Moreover, although every effort has been made to ensure accuracy, this work is unlikely to be free of error or oversight. Despite the passage of more than 50 years since Douglas MacArthur pronounced the words "These proceedings are closed," on the deck of the battleship *Missouri*, new and interesting information—reports, orders, analyses, diaries—is still turning up and innovative perspectives and interpretations are still being generated, developments that will undoubtedly continue for at least another 50 years.

The authors may be reached via Internet e-mail at jfdunnigan@aol.com and anofi@aol.com.

Terms and Conventions Used in the Work

Times and Dates: It is important to recall that the International Date Line runs through the center of the Pacific Ocean, roughly along the 180th line of longitude. The date advances by one day when moving west across the line, but declines by one day when moving east. So the Japanese attack on PEARL HARBOR occurred on Sunday, 7 December 1941, in the United States and HAWAII, but on Monday, 8 December 1941, in Australia, Japan, and China. In addition, once the war began the United States went on "double daylight savings," or War Time, which further complicates reconciling the sequence of events. In this work all references to date and time will be made on the basis of the local situation.

Names: The spelling and forms of the names of persons and places are given in the style in which they appeared during the war. With the exception of particularly well-known persons (CHIANG KAI-SHEK, for example), East Asian names are usually in the European fashion, with family name second. For the more modern forms of some World War II place-names, see the Appendix.

Cross-references: Items mentioned in the text that are the subject of entries in this book have been indicated by SMALL CAPITAL LETTERS. At the end of many entries will be the names of entries of related interest.

References to specific military units (e.g., Seventh Infantry Division) should be checked under the main reference of the army in question: for example, US Army, Divisions, or Marine Corps, Divisions.

Aircraft References: Since Japanese aircraft were always referred to by their Allied code names, they have been referenced using these. Consult the table in "Aircraft, Japanese, Allied Code Names," for the appropriate entries. Technical details on the various aircraft—Allied and Japanese—are included in the Aircraft Tables.

Bibliographic References: Many entries include references to published materials, in abbreviated form. These should be checked against the bibliography and recommended reading list at the end of the volume. In the case of multivolume official histories, the reference entry includes only the series title. In most cases these references are to unusual or particularly valuable materials. Between the official histories and popular treatments, there are so many works on most operations that we have elected not to include references to them. References to campaigns are found in the bibliography. Similarly, there are usually no bibliographic references for individuals, ships, aircraft, and geographic locations.

Ship Descriptions: All major classes of warships have their own entries. In addition, there are master tables for each of the major categories of warship: aircraft carrier, battleship, cruiser, and destroyer. Submarines have been grouped under single entries for each of the principal nations. Most of the numerous classes of smaller vessels have been omitted.

In entries for particular classes of major warships there are short descriptions of the activities and fate of the most prominent members of the class. The years of laying down (when construction began), launching (when construction was sufficiently advanced for the still-incomplete vessel to be put into the water), and completion are given in parentheses, such as (1934–1936–1937). The date of laying down gives some idea as to the time the ship was designed, usually a year or so earlier. Launch date is important because at that point it is not likely that significant changes can be made in the ship without a virtual rebuilding. Completion date merely indicates the moment at which the ship is officially ready for service, after which a ship would normally spend a month or more on a "shakedown" cruise to determine any technical problems. In wartime, however, this cruise was sometimes omitted, or took place en route to the war zone. In descriptions of classes of minor warships the year of the laying down of the first vessels in the class is given, followed by that of the completion of the last to be built.

Abbreviations:

AA:	antiaircraft
A/C:	aircraft
Adm:	admiral
AFV:	armored fighting vehicles (tanks, APCs, etc.)
APC:	armored personnel carrier
Arm.:	armored
Art.:	artillery
ASW:	antisubmarine warfare
A/T:	antitank
BB:	battleship, including battle cruisers
Bde.:	brigade
BG:	brigadier general
Br.:	British/Britain
c.:	circa, about
CA:	heavy cruiser
CAP:	combat air patrol (aircraft maintained over a carrier, for defensive purposes)
Capt.:	captain
Cav.:	cavalry
CB:	large cruiser
CBI:	China-Burma-India Theater of Operations
Cdr.:	commander
CINCPAC:	Commander in Chief, Pacific (US Navy)
CL:	light cruiser
CLAA:	antiaircraft light cruiser (not introduced until after World War II)
CNO:	US Chief of Naval Operations
COL:	colonel
CPL:	corporal
CV:	aircraft carrier
CVE:	escort aircraft carrier
CVL:	light aircraft carrier
DD:	destroyer
DE:	destroyer escort
Div.:	division
Ens.:	ensign
ETO:	European Theater of Operations
Fr.:	French/France
Gen.:	general
Ger.:	German/Germany
GHQ:	general headquarters
GRT:	gross register ton, describes size of non-warships
HIJMS:	"His Imperial Japanese Majesty's Ship"
HMAS:	"His Majesty's Australian Ship"
HMNZ:	"His Majesty's New Zealand Ship"
HMS:	"His [Britannic] Majesty's Ship"
HNMS:	"Her Netherlands' Majesty's Ship"
IJN:	Imperial Japanese Navy
Inf.:	infantry
IX-:	US Navy type designation for a "miscellaneous" vessel, such as an historic relic or one performing a highly unusual mission, such as an "Aircraft Carrier, Training"
Jap.:	Japanese/Japan
JCS:	US Joint Chiefs of Staff

KIA:	killed in action	Recon:	reconnaissance
Knot:	KTS.; nautical mile per hour, equal to 1.15 land miles or 1.85 kilometers	RN:	Britain's Royal Navy
		SGT:	sergeant
LG:	lieutenant general	SNLF:	special naval landing force, Japanese "Marines"
Lt:	lieutenant (1Lt, first lieutenant; 2Lt, second lieutenant)		
		Sov.:	Soviet
LtCdr:	lieutenant commander	SS:	submarine
LTC:	lieutenant colonel	Staff Sgt.:	staff sergeant
Maj.:	major	TF:	task force, group of warships traveling together
MG:	major general		
mg.:	machine gun	TG:	task group, portion of a naval TF
Mtr.:	mortar	T/O&E:	table of organization and equipment, the officially prescribed organization of the allotments of troops and equipment in a military formation
MPH:	miles per hour		
na:	not available		
Neth.:	Netherlands		
PFC:	private first class	US:	the United States
PBY:	Catalina multiengine floatplane used for reconnaissance	USAAF:	the United States Army Air Forces— more correctly, the Army Air Corps in the early part of the war, a change of nomenclature that we largely ignore
POW:	prisoner of war		
PTO:	Pacific Theater of Operations		
RAdm:	rear admiral	USAT:	"United States Army Transport"
RAF:	Britain's Royal Air Force	USMC:	the US Marine Corps
RCT:	regimental combat team, a US task force consisting of an infantry regiment, an artillery battalion, and sundry support forces, about a third of a division	USN:	the US Navy
		USS:	"United States' Ship"
		VAdm:	vice admiral

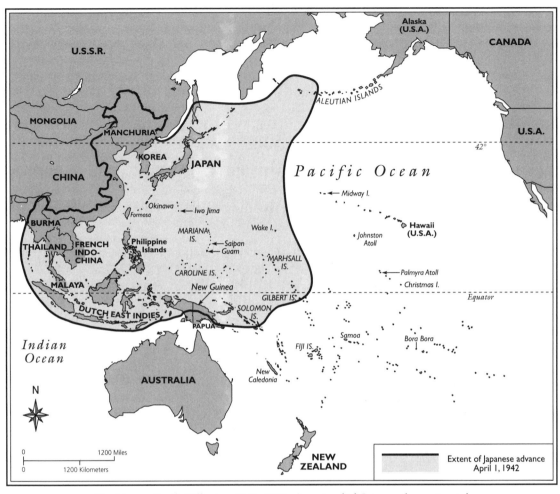

The Japanese Pacific Offensive, 1941–1942. Areas in which Japanese forces operated
December 7, 1941 through April 1, 1942 are indicated by the lines.

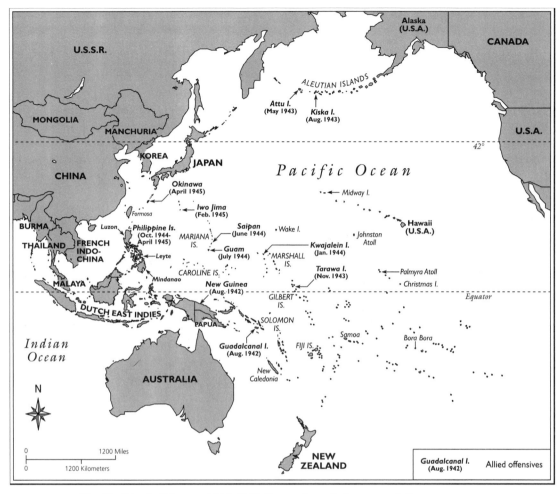

The Allied Pacific Offensive, 1942–1945. Dates indicate the beginning of offensive operations.

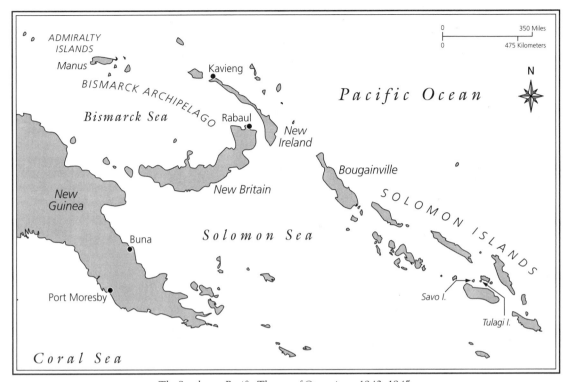

The Southwest Pacific Theater of Operations, 1942–1945.

A-20 Havoc/Boston, US Attack Bomber

The A-20 Havoc (or Boston, as it was known to the British) was originally built mainly for export, although the US Army Air Corps began to receive A-20s in 1941. Several were present during the PEARL HARBOR attack and A-20s saw action in New Guinea during the dark days of 1942.

The A-20 was an odd duck. Although it looked like a twin-engine medium bomber, it performed

Nose canopies for the A-20 Havoc, at the Long Beach, California, plant of Douglas Aircraft. Note the women aircraft workers.

like a single-engine light bomber and was actually quite small compared to the B-25 or B-26 twin-engine bombers. The crew was usually two (pilot and a machine gunner, who faced the rear), although some aircraft were modified to add a bombardier. The A-20 was so narrow that there was no room for the crew to move from their seats. It was nimble and fast, but sacrificed range for payload, which could be up to 4,000 pounds of bombs. As the war went on, more .50 caliber machine guns were added. This made the A-20 a potent strafing (low-flying machine gun) aircraft. The short range, compared to that of the two-engine B-25 and B-26, made the A-20 less desirable in the Pacific. As a result, most served in Europe. Russia eagerly received 3,000 and Britain 1,800 of the nearly 7,000 produced, and even the Dutch got several, a few of which were captured intact by the Japanese in 1942 in JAVA. The United States used 2,000, including some converted to night fighters in late 1942 (the P-70) and some for photo reconnaissance.

See also AIRCRAFT TYPES, DEVELOPMENT.

A-26 Invader, US Attack Bomber

The A-26 Invader was a much improved A-20 that closely resembled the A-20, but was considered a new aircraft. It was faster (the fastest US bomber of the war) more heavily armed (up to 22 .50 caliber machine guns, although 12 was standard) and armored than the A-20. With that many machine guns, and a 4,000-pound load, low-flying A-26s were the terror of German troops in late 1944. In the Pacific, the A-26 obliterated Japanese shipping. The concentrated fire of a dozen or more .50 caliber machine guns quickly shredded merchant ships and even destroyers. The A-26 also used rockets; these caused problems when the fast moving A-26 flew over a target seconds after its rockets hit, so that debris from the explosions was hurled into the underside of the aircraft. Approximately 2,500 A-26s were built.

See also AIRCRAFT TYPES, DEVELOPMENT.

A-28 Hudson, US Attack Bomber

The unique A-28 Hudson was originally designed as a civilian airliner (the Lockheed 14) in 1937. When the British sought combat aircraft in the United States during 1938 Lockheed quickly modified its airliner to produce the Hudson, a light bomber, in 1939. Some 2,800 were eventually built, with about 80% of them being used by the British. The US Army Air Corps called its version the A-28 or A-29, depending upon details of design. The US Navy used a few A-28s for recon work, calling them the PBO.

The A-28 weighed 10 tons, not large for a two-engine aircraft. Its top speed was 246 MPH, and it could fly over 2,000 miles. Because of its range, it was often used as an armed patrol aircraft. Armament consisted of seven .30 caliber machine guns and 750 pounds of bombs. During the early years of the war the Hudson was a vital weapon in the Allied air arsenal and many were present in the Pacific during 1942.

See also AIRCRAFT TYPES, DEVELOPMENT; RECONNAISSANCE, NAVAL.

A-35 Vengeance, US Dive Bomber

The A-35 Vengeance was a US dive bomber built to British specifications by the American Vultee company. After it entered service in 1942, several hundred were used in the Burma area. Production ended in late 1944, after 1,500 had been manufactured. The A-35 (American name) Vengeance (British name) was a reasonably efficient bomber for 1942. It had a top speed of 279 MPH and carried half a ton of bombs.

See also AIRCRAFT TYPES, DEVELOPMENT.

A5M Claude, Japanese Fighter

The first modern Japanese aircraft carrier fighter, the A5M Claude was introduced in 1936. Like the equally hapless US F2A Brewster F2A BUFFALO, the A5M was too slow, underarmed, and, particularly for a carrier plane, short-ranged. However, in

1936 the A5M was quite an able interceptor. The superb Japanese prewar pilots were able to rack up a good combat record with the A5M in China. Fortunately for the Japanese, the new A6M ZERO had replaced the Claude on most Japanese carriers by late 1941. Aircraft technology moved quickly in the late 1930s. The US F2A Buffalo, entering service only two years after the A5M, was already obsolete. By 1941 about 1,000 A5Ms had been manufactured; production was resumed toward the end of the war, for KAMIKAZE service, since the Claude was cheaper to produce than the Zero.

See also AIRCRAFT TYPES, DEVELOPMENT;

A6M Zero/Zeke, Japanese Fighter

More A6M Zero/Zekes were manufactured than any other Japanese fighter of the war (over 10,000) and, for its first year, it was one of the most lethal in the Pacific. The A6M was very fast, could climb to 13,000 feet in 4.3 minutes, and had exceptional range because of its light construction and correspondingly small engine. But this performance was not achieved without cost. While the A6M was fast and nimble, it was not as sturdy as American fighters. The large fuel supply was not protected by self-sealing fuel tanks, turning what for an American fighter would be a non-fatal hit into a fiery inferno for an A6M. American pilots soon learned how to avoid the A6M's advantages. After the first year of the war, more maneuverable US fighters appeared, and by 1943 the A6M was no longer a fearsome opponent. The Zero did undergo upgrades throughout the war, and the 1944 model was about 20% more capable than the 1941 version. "Zeke" was the initial American code name for the airplane. The designation "Zero" has nothing to do with American contempt for things Japanese, as has been suggested, but rather was the name the Japanese themselves gave the airplane from its year of introduction, 1940—2600 in the imperial calendar.

See also A6M2-N RUFE; AIRCRAFT TYPES, DEVELOPMENT; CARRIERS, DESIGNING AIRCRAFT FOR.

A6M2-N Rufe, Japanese Floatplane Fighter

The A6M2-N Rufe was a floatplane version of the Japanese A6M ZERO carrier fighter. Because of the floats suspended underneath the aircraft, the Rufe had about 20% less combat capability than the original Zero. The idea behind this aircraft (of which only 327 were built) was to base it in forward areas where airfields had not yet been built. Operating from coves and bays, the Rufe could attack enemy reconnaissance aircraft and give protection to Japanese recon planes. The Rufe had some success operating in this fashion but was generally outfought by most Allied fighters.

See also AIRCRAFT TYPES, DEVELOPMENT; CARRIERS, DESIGNING AIRCRAFT FOR; RECONNAISSANCE, NAVAL.

ABDA

Acronym for the "American-British-Dutch-Australian" command organized to oversee operations in Malaya and the NETHERLANDS EAST INDIES in the opening months of the Pacific War in early 1942. It lasted only a few weeks.

See also DOORMAN, KAREL; JAVA SEA, BATTLE OF; WAVELL, ARCHIBALD.

Aces, Allied

Traditionally an "ace" is a pilot who has shot down at least five enemy airplanes. Some nations made more of this than others. However, in general the number of aircraft a pilot kills can be taken as a rough indication of his skill. Although Australian, New Zealand, and British pilots served in the Pacific and related areas, the top aces were all American.

Aces, Japanese

The Japanese did not regard individual accomplishment in the same way that Western air forces did. The number of aircraft shot down by a unit was considered more worthy of attention than how many aircraft were downed by individual pilots. Records were kept of what individual pilots thought they had shot down, if only so the records of squadrons could be compiled and intelligence data on enemy losses cataloged. After the war, the records of Japanese naval aces were sorted out and given wider distribution than during the war. Army records remain very confusing.

Of the top 10 aces, four were commissioned officers, two were warrant officers, and four were enlisted men (petty officers). Only three survived the war, mainly because Japanese pilots were kept in action until killed or disabled. The American practice was to withdraw experienced pilots after a time for use as instructors. Not only did this policy provide better training for new pilots, it also prevented pilots from developing a fatal case of combat fatigue. After a number of combat sorties, anywhere from a handful to over a hundred, a pilot's nerves became frazzled and he began to make mistakes.

Exceptionally "productive" pilots were recognized by the Japanese, usually in the form of promotions. If a pilot had a very good day, shooting down several enemy aircraft, he might be "mentioned in dispatches" (the All Units Bulletin, a report to higher headquarters and the public) and often given a "double promotion" as well. Since most Japanese pilots were enlisted men who were

TOP TEN IMPERIAL JAPANESE NAVY ACES

Rank	Pilot	Enemy Planes Shot Down	Notes
1	Hiroyoshi Nishizawa	87+	KIA 1944; claimed 102
2	Tetsuzo Iwamoto	c. 80	Survived
3	Shoichi Sugita	c. 70	KIA 1945
4	Saburo Sakai	64	Survived
5	Takeo Okumura	54	KIA 1943
6	Toshio Ota	34	KIA 1942
7	Kazuo Sugino	32	Survived
8	Shizuo Ishii	29	KIA 1943
9	Kaneyoshi Muto	28	KIA 1945
10	Jun-ichi Sasai	27	KIA 1942

not qualified to become officers, the double promotion was in effect a hefty pay raise. Officers commanded the aircraft units, and if they got too many promotions they would be too senior to continue to command flying units.

The highest scoring Japanese fighter ace, Hiroyoshi Nishizawa, had an attitude toward combat typical of most Japanese soldiers, sailors, and airmen. During the summer of 1942, Nishizawa was engaged in an air battle over the SOLOMONS. In the course of downing six American F4F WILDCATS, his aircraft was hit. Thinking he would not be able to make it back to base in his smoking aircraft, he

THE TWELVE TOP ALLIED ACES OF THE PACIFIC WAR

Rank	Pilot	Service	Enemy Planes Shot Down	Notes
1	Richard I. Bong	Army	40	Killed, flying accident, '45
2	Thomas McGuire Jr.	Army	38	KIA '45, by ace Soichi Sugita
3	David McCampbell	Navy	34	Survived
4	Gregory Boyington	Marines	28	Six in China, '41–'42; POW, '43
5	Charles W. MacDonald	Army	27	Survived
6	Joseph J. Foss	Marines	26	Survived
7	Robert M. Hanson	Marines	25	Survived
8	Cecil E. Harris	Navy	24	Survived
9	Eugene A. Valencia	Navy	23	Survived
10	Gerald R. Johnson	Army	22	Survived
10	Neil E. Kearby	Army	22	Survived
10	Jay T. Robbins	Army	22	Survived

decided to get one more American aircraft by ramming. Finding no American aircraft nearby, he limped homeward, barely making it back to a Japanese airfield. Many Japanese pilots in damaged aircraft did succeed in "getting one more American" by ramming. Nishizawa, with over 80 kills, eventually died while a passenger in a Japanese transport aircraft shot down by US fighters. Nishizawa, who had always maintained that he would never be bested in combat, was right.

One reason for the higher number of "kills" by Japanese aces was that many of them had seen extensive combat service in China from 1937 on, against Chinese pilots who were often poorly trained and usually flying inferior aircraft. Then they added to their scores in the opening months of the war, against Allied pilots in the Philippines, MALAYA, the NETHERLANDS EAST INDIES, and Burma, who were often flying obsolete aircraft like the Brewster F2A BUFFALO.

AD Skyraider, Carrier Bomber

The US AD Skyraider was the ultimate World War II carrier bomber. But because design work wasn't begun until 1944, and the first flight took place only in early 1945, the Skyraider didn't see action in the Pacific War. Proof of its effectiveness can be seen in its combat record during the Korean and Vietnam wars. The Skyraider remained in production until 1957, with nearly 3,200 being built. The most remarkable aspect of the aircraft was its armament (four 20mm cannon, 8,000 pounds of bombs) and endurance (over four hours). The Skyraider could "loiter" over a battlefield until it was needed, just the kind of service the troops most wanted. With a top speed of only 318 MPH, the Skyraider was slow enough to find its target and hit it accurately. Also quite robust, the aircraft could take a lot of damage, and could land almost anywhere that was relatively flat and long enough. Although originally designed as a dive and torpedo bomber, it spent all of its career hitting land targets.

See also: AIRCRAFT TYPES, DEVELOPMENT.

Adachi, Hatazo (1884–1947)

Hatazo Adachi entered the Japanese Army in 1910, and saw no action thereafter until the 1930s. By the bombing of PEARL HARBOR he was the chief of staff of the Japanese North China Area Army. In late 1942 he commanded the 18th Army, concentrated at RABAUL and in northeastern New Guinea, where he continued to serve as an army commander for the remainder of the war. Although Adachi was constantly defeated, he was not relieved. This was fairly typical in the Japanese Army, where social connections often counted for more than battlefield performance.

Addu Atoll, Maldive Islands

Located just a few hundred miles southwest of India, in the northern part of the bleak Maldive Islands, Addu Atoll had an ample natural harbor. As is typical for the area, the atoll does not offer much protection from genuinely foul weather (its highest point is only about 20 feet above sea level). The ROYAL NAVY decided to develop the atoll as an advanced fleet base shortly before the Pacific War began. Known as Base T, the Japanese never learned of its existence, and the Royal Navy continued to use the atoll to support operations in the Eastern Indian Ocean, despite its limited facilities.

Adelaide, Australia

A large port, supported by a moderately large city with a modest industrial base and considerable agricultural resources, Adelaide, on the southern coast of Australia, was not well located for a naval base. It served as an entry port for Allied supplies during the war.

Adelaide, Australian Light Cruiser

Although completed in the early 1920s, *Adelaide* (1915–1918–1922) was actually built to a 1912 design, somewhat updated to incorporate the experience of World War I. She was quite slow for a cruiser, only 24.5 knots, due largely to having originally been designed to burn coal. As a result, she was obsolete long before the Pacific War began, and was quickly relegated to escort duties in the Indian Ocean. In this role she proved adequate. On 26 November 1942, in company with the Dutch cruiser JACOB VAN HEEMSKERCK, *Adelaide* intercepted a German BLOCKADE RUNNER bound for France from the Netherlands East Indies. Scrapped in 1949.

Admiralty Islands

A chain of nearly 20 mostly volcanic islands (c. 800 square miles), the largest of which is MANUS (c. 600 square miles), in the BISMARCK ARCHIPELAGO between New Guinea and the equator. Although rugged and extremely humid, the thinly populated, jungle-clad islands were ideally suited for air bases.

Aftereffects of the Pacific War

The Pacific War left an enormous impression on the US Navy, the US Marine Corps, and the resuscitated Japanese armed forces. These were the military legacies of the Pacific War.

The US Navy fervently embraced aircraft carriers, underway replenishment, and long-range amphibious operations, concepts that have defined the US Navy and Marine Corps since 1945. These war-based concepts did not really suit postwar conditions. While the navy used its carrier aviation extensively during the Korean, Vietnam, and Gulf wars, this was not how carrier aviation was meant to operate. In those three wars, carriers were merely substitutes for additional airfields that could have been built on nearby friendly territory. But the carriers were available, even though they were more expensive to operate. Moreover, there has not been another carrier versus carrier naval battle since June 1944. With the collapse of the Soviet Union in 1991, there is no longer even a viable carrier force to face US flattops in battle.

Similarly, since 1945 the Marines have had only one opportunity (Inchon, Korea, 1950) to practice the amphibious operations they engaged in so frequently and successfully during World War II. With the demise of the Soviet empire in 1991, the US Navy and Marine Corps have had a hard time hanging on to their powerful, and expensive, World War II legacy of carriers and amphibious shipping.

The effect of the war on the Japanese armed forces is another story, however. As a result of Japan's defeat, the Japanese armed forces were discredited. They were also all but outlawed in Japan's post–World War II constitution. Once seen as a most noble career, military service is now looked down on. However, the post-World War II Japanese who do choose to serve in the "Self Defense Forces" are even more diligent and efficient than their wartime predecessors, and have gained a deserved reputation for excellence in spite of the fact that the best men no longer flock to the colors. In addition, although Japan's defense budget is held to 1% of GNP, that 1% grows with Japan's huge GNP. As Russia's military spending rapidly shrinks, we face the prospect that Japan will shortly have the world's second largest defense budget.

Ref: Dunnigan and Nofi, *Shooting Blanks*.

Agano Class, Japanese Light Cruisers

Like all Japanese light cruisers, the Agano Class ships were designed to serve as flotilla leaders. As a result, they were much more lightly armed than contemporary foreign light cruisers, even considering their relatively small displacement. They were, however, good sea boats, fast and handy. With OYODO they were Japan's only modern light cruisers, but saw surprisingly little action.

Agano (1940–1941–1942) was TORPEDOED near TRUK by *Skate* (SS–305) on 17 February 1944, while serving with the Combined Fleet.

Yahagi (1941–1942–1943), skippered by Tameichi Hara, formerly of *Shigure*, took part in YA-

MATO's last sortie and was sunk by carrier aircraft northwest of OKINAWA on April 7, 1945.

Sakawa (1942–1944–1944) was taken as a war prize by the United States and expended in the Bikini ATOMIC BOMB tests.

Noshiro (1941–1942–1943) formed part of the force that tangled with the US escort carriers off SAMAR, on October 25, 1944, helping to sink *Gambier Bay*. She was sunk the next day by carrier aircraft.

See also SHIRATSUYU CLASS.

Ref: Hara, *Japanese Destroyer Captain.*

AGC (Amphibious Command Ship)

AGCs were American ships especially configured to serve as the flagships for amphibious invasion forces. By the end of the war there were 24 AGCs in service. Of these, 16 had been specifically built as AGCs between 1943 and 1945, using standard merchant-type hulls. Of the other eight, two were converted from prewar cargo-passenger ships and six from former Coast Guard cutters. Over 600 men were needed to man the elaborate communications arrangements for air control, fire support coordination, and the like. AGCs were the nerve centers of amphibious operations. The specially built ones were 435 feet long and displaced 7,430 tons. Top speed was 16 knots and they were armed with two 5-inch guns and eight 40mm antiaircraft guns. The two conversions were a bit smaller, and the Coast Guard cutters were only 2,200 tons. The AGC was a small, but key, element of the amphibious armadas formed during the war. Simply having hundreds of specialized amphibious craft for an operation was not enough. All of these ships had to be carefully organized and supervised during the landing and "over the beach" support operations that followed. The Japanese never realized how crucial the one or two AGCs in each invasion fleet were. The loss of an AGC during a landing would have been catastrophic, as the resulting confusion would have made the landing force much less effective.

Air Combat Tactics

When the Pacific War began, Allied pilots quickly discovered that their fighters were quite different than those the Japanese used. While the Japanese Zero weighed 2.7 tons, the American F4F WILDCAT was 33% heavier, at 3.6 tons; the Japanese stressed speed and maneuverability at all costs, US aircraft were built to take more punishment, at the cost of speed and maneuverability. The Zero had a top speed of 305 MPH, the F4F Wildcat, 276. American pilots quickly learned new air combat tactics, such as the diving attack. F4F Wildcats would promptly fly as high as they could, so that the Zeros would be below them. Then the F4F Wildcats would dive and get off a few shots. Since they were diving, and were heavier, they could temporarily obtain a speed advantage over the Zeros. Unfortunately, the Zeros would follow the F4F Wildcats down and, if they caught up, nail the American aircraft.

A more elegant, and effective, tactic was the "Thach Weave," (named after USN pilot John Thach). The tactic required two less maneuverable (but better armed and armored) US F4F fighters to fly side-by-side about 1,000 feet apart. When "bounced" (caught from behind) by a more nimble Japanese "Zero," the two airplanes would immediately turn toward the enemy aircraft. This meant that one of the American aircraft would probably end up coming head-on at the Zero with guns blazing. Because of the superior firepower and protection of the F4F, the American plane would likely come out ahead. If that attack failed, the two US aircraft would continue to turn toward the Japanese aircraft until it was shot down or ran short on fuel and had to leave the battle. This was very frustrating for the Japanese, and rather boring for the Americans, but it negated Japanese fighter superiority in 1942, a time when the Japanese needed every advantage they could get.

By late 1942, more capable US aircraft came on the scene. The F6F HELLCAT was much heavier, at 5.7 tons, but was about 20 MPH faster than the F4F Wildcat and nearly as maneuverable as the Zero. At about the same time, the 5.7-ton F4U COR-

SAIR appeared, with a top speed of over 400 MPH. The Japanese were unable to counter these fighters.

Air Defense, Ships

On balance, ships were usually not very safe in the presence of airplanes, particularly early in the war when air defenses were relatively weak. There were several factors at work in determining the survivability of a ship under air attack. The first was the number of friendly fighters put over the ships, since these can defend at some distance. Failing the presence of friendly fighters, or if the enemy gets past them, a ship must defend itself with individual ship antiaircraft armament. Prewar estimates of the antiaircraft requirements of warships were uniformly inadequate. In practice throughout the war, all navies continuously increased the antiaircraft capacity of all their ships, not only adding guns, but also developing new and more effective ones.

Consider the AA firepower of the US battleship South Dakota.

Date	5"/38	40mm	1.1"	20mm	.50 MG
Mar. '42	16	—	28	16	8
Sept. '42	16	16	20	36+	—
Feb. '43	16	68	—	35	—
Dec. '44	16	68	—	72	—
Mar. '45	16	68	—	77	—

South Dakota was designed in the mid-1930s, laid down in 1939, launched in 1941, and commissioned in March of 1942. Designed with one of the heaviest allotments of antiaircraft guns of any ship, her three sisters had four additional 5-inch guns. This enormous antiaircraft capacity was continuously upgraded throughout the war. The additional firepower added to *South Dakota* in September of 1942 enabled her to survive the Battle of the SANTA CRUZ ISLANDS (26 October 1942) during which she was attacked by at least 65 Japanese dive bombers and torpedo bombers, downing 26, the world's record for a single warship in a single engagement. Attackers hit with three bombs

and a near miss, resulting in one death and 50 wounded, plus damage to one 16-inch gun turret.

The success of *South Dakota* at Santa Cruz was due not only to the volume of AA fire, but also to:

1. Effective radar fire direction;
2. The resiliency and maneuverability of the ship;
3. The introduction of proximity fuzed ammunition for her 5-inch guns.

With sturdy construction and efficient American damage control techniques, *South Dakota* was probably a lot more survivable than any other ship in the fleet at the time. But her volume of AA fire was still considered inadequate, and, as is the case with other ships in various navies, her antiaircraft defenses were repeatedly enhanced. Reporting for repairs or an overhaul generally meant receiving additional antiaircraft firepower.

Consider some other examples:

US Ships

CV *Enterprise*	5"	40mm	1.1"	20mm	.50 MG
Dec. '41	8	—	16	—	24
Jan. '45	8	60	—	32	—

CL *Brooklyn*	5"	40mm	1.1"	20mm	.5 MG
Dec. '41	8	—	—	—	8
Jan. '45	8	28	—	20	—

DD *Benson*	5"	40mm	1.1"	20mm	.50 MG
Dec. '40	5	—	—	—	6
Dec. '41	4	4	—	7	—
Dec. '45	4	12	—	4	—

Japanese Ships

BB *Yamato*	5"	25mm	13.2mm
Dec. '41	12	24	4
Jun. '43	24	36	—
Apr. '44	24	98	—
Jull. '44	24	113	—
Jan. '45	24	150	—

CV *Shokaku*	5"	25mm	13.2mm
Dec. '41	16	42	—
Jun. '43	16	70	—
Jul. '44	16	96	—

DD *Kisumi* (Asashio Class)	5"	25mm	13.2mm
Dec. '41	6	—	4
Dec. '43	4	12	—
Jun. '44	4	28	4

The Japanese added more antiaircraft weapons to their ships than did the Americans. However, US and Allied ships usually started out with more, and better quality, AA guns than did Japanese ships, and also tended to acquire air defense radar, radar fire direction, and the proximity fuze, which proved immensely important. Lacking these, as the war went on Japanese ships became relatively much more vulnerable to US air attacks than US ships were to Japanese air attacks, particularly as the quality of Japanese pilots declined.

The formation in which a ship found itself also affected air defense capability. Ships were safer traveling in relatively tight groups than in looser formations or singly. This is a simple matter of geometry: A group of ships has a smaller defensive perimeter than the sum of the defensive perimeters of the individual vessels. In groups they could share defensive responsibility, particularly if they had the doctrine, communications facilities, and training to do so.

The larger the formation, the more secure the ships at its center, albeit that very large formations made captains and admirals nervous, which is probably why they never used huge task forces. The most typical task force had three to five carriers plus escorts, despite the fact that some airmen were thinking in terms of task forces of eight carriers.

Aside from the PEARL HARBOR Strike Force, the Japanese were never able to come close to emulating the virtually impregnable US fast carrier task forces of '44–'45. As Japanese air defense capacity proved inadequate, it is impossible to assess what a Japanese fast carrier task force might have been capable of.

However, despite the enormous volume of AA firepower generated by US warships, a matter in which they were more or less emulated by the British and even the Japanese, the primary reasons US

A Japanese torpedo bomber explodes after a direct hit by a 5-inch shell from the second USS Yorktown (CV-10) during a US carrier raid on Kwajalein and other nearby islands, December 4, 1943. Note the black smoke from air bursts, and the splashes made by shell fragments on the water.

surface forces were relatively immune from air attack after mid–1944 were:

1. The precipitous decline in the quality of Japanese pilots;
2. The development of radar-controlled centralized air defense fire direction;
3. The proximity fuze (officially designated the "VT" or "Variable Telemetry" fuze, but more commonly called the "funny fuze").

The proximity fuze contained a miniature radar set. A proximity fuzed shell would explode when the returning radar signal indicated that there was an airplane within lethal range. This turned near misses into hits and made antiaircraft fire by large

(5-inch) guns much more effective. By mid-1943, although only about 25% of AA ammo issued to the fleet had proximity fuzes, these accounted for about 50% of Japanese aircraft shot down, making the fuze about 300% more effective than the old timed or impact fuzes. By 1945 this had risen to nearly 600%, and this despite the fact that perhaps 30% percent of proximity fuzed rounds were duds!

However, proximity fuzed ammunition was in relatively short supply, so that even in 1945 the "mix" of AA ammo aboard ships was roughly 1:1

between proximity fuzed and old-fashioned timed projectiles.

Air Force, Japanese, Growth

The development of Japan's air forces and aircraft industry in the 1920s was an extraordinary event. Japan was the only non-Western nation to develop its own aircraft industry before World War II. Moreover, Japan did not begin industrializing until the late 19th century, making its leap into aircraft production even more remarkable.

A good view of some of the antiaircraft armament aboard a US cruiser—probably USS Portland (CA-33)—showing two 5"/25 dual-purpose guns, plus a number of 20mm and 40mm pieces, from a photograph taken during the landings on Mindoro, the Philippines, December 15, 1944. Note helmeted seamen on full alert and inflatable life rafts secured to the bulkheads.

A Japanese airplane bursts into flames after being struck by antiaircraft fire while attacking USS Kitkun Bay (CVE-71) in the Marianas, in June 1944, in an image taken from a sister escort carrier.

Japan was, from the 1860s, eager to catch up with the West, and by the 1890s had its own arms industry. While some weapons and equipment were still bought from Western firms, Japan was increasingly self-sufficient in the construction of all modern weapons. Going into the 1920s, Japan required no outside assistance and was developing weapons and equipment that were in some cases superior to anything in the West.

Then, as now, the Japanese had a talent for taking existing technology and producing superior versions. In the five years following the Wright Brothers demonstration of powered flight, most of the world's major armed forces, including Japan,

expressed interest. The army was the first service to look into air operations. In the 1870s a balloon unit was established, and these balloons (used for reconnaissance) were employed throughout the late 19th century; it was this experience that led to the sending of the two army officers to Europe in 1910 to learn to fly. They brought back to Japan two aircraft. In 1912, Japan built its first aircraft, an improved version of one of the aircraft brought back from Europe. The first airplane of purely Japanese design was built in 1916. World War I demonstrated the value of aircraft, and a French military mission came to Japan in 1919 with pilot instructors and World War I aircraft. By the early

1930s, the Japanese aircraft industry was essentially independent of foreign technology and assistance. Annual Japanese aircraft PRODUCTION went from 445 in 1930 to 952 in 1935, and 4,768 in 1940.

By 1925 the army had established the Army Air Corps (on a par with the other branches like infantry and artillery). By the early 1930s, the army was using nothing but Japanese-designed and -manufactured aircraft. Because of ongoing operations in China, Japanese Army pilots were probably the most capable in the world at the time. However, the army had decided that the Soviet Union was likely to be its most dangerous future enemy, and new aircraft designs were adjusted to most effectively deal with this threat. As a result, going into World War II, Japanese Army aircraft were optimized for relatively short-range missions in cold weather. This meant that the Japanese Army Air Force was less well equipped to deal with fighting in the Pacific than the navy. The navy had investigated the use of aircraft a year after the army. In 1921, a British naval mission came to Japan with aircraft and instructors, and from that beginning the Japanese Naval Air Service began. Later that same year, Japan's first aircraft carrier (HOSHO) was launched. During the 1920s, British designers working in Japan helped develop many of Japan's early, domestically produced aircraft.

More carriers were built in the 1920s. As in America, these carriers were reactions to the Washington Naval DISARMAMENT TREATY, which reduced the number of battleships the major powers could have. Rather than scrap battleships being built, Japan was allowed to convert some of them to aircraft carriers. Additional carriers were built in the 1930s, and fully modern carrier aircraft were designed and built in the late 1930s. Two of Japan's most modern carriers didn't enter service until 1941. Japanese naval aviators were able to pick up valuable experience in China during the 1930s, although these operations were minor until 1937. After that year, naval aircraft were heavily used in China, giving Japanese Navy pilots valuable experience that provided them with a decisive edge in the early battles against Western forces.

Had Western leaders paid more attention to the development of Japanese aviation, there would have been fewer unpleasant surprises in the months after PEARL HARBOR. The evidence was available, and Western military attaches sent accurate reports about the advanced state of Japanese air forces. But preconceived ideas about the Japanese led to ideas of inept Japanese pilots barely getting into the air aboard poorly built aircraft.

Ref: Overy, *The Air War*.

Air Groups, Aircraft Carriers

The contingent of aircraft assigned to a carrier is called its "air group." An air group usually consisted of several squadrons, each of one type of aircraft. There was a mix of fighters, torpedo bombers, and dive bombers. The authorized number of aircraft in an air group varied a great deal during the war, as experience dictated various changes, newer types of aircraft became available, and newer carriers came into service. And of course, actual numbers of aircraft carried at any given moment would be affected by combat or administrative loss.

A number of unusual air groups were formed during the war. Three US carriers were eventually equipped primarily for night operations. In June of 1944 CVL INDEPENDENCE was converted to this role, followed in January of 1945 by CV *Enterprise* and the following June by CV *Bon Homme Richard*. These carriers had aircraft of all types fitted with special equipment for night flying and fighting, although they also regularly performed daytime missions.

From time to time it was proposed to equip one or two carriers entirely with fighters, so that they could assume the task of Combat Air Patrol over the fleet, freeing up the fighters of the regular carriers to escort their bombers. This was actually tried out experimentally in the spring of 1943, where there were only two Allied carriers operating in the Pacific, USS *Saratoga* and HMS *Victorious* (on loan from the ROYAL NAVY). The two carriers shared their air groups, both of which were equipped with American aircraft, so that *Saratoga* ended up with

COMPOSITION OF US CARRIER AIR GROUPS

Month	Type	Ftrs.	DBmrs.	TBmrs.	Total	Note
Dec. '41	CV	18	36	18	72	A
Jun. '42	CV	24	36	18	78	B
Aug. '42	CVE	12	9	9	30	
Sept. '42	CV	36	36	18	90	
Dec. '42	CVL	21	9	0	30	
Jun. '43	CVE	12	6	0	20	C
Sept. '43	CV	38	28	18	84	D
Jan. '44	CVL	24	—9—		33	
Jan. '44	CVE	16	—12—		28	E
Jan. '44	CVE	15	—15—		30	F
Jun. '44	CV	54	24	18	96	
Dec. '44	CV	71	15	15	101	G

Key: Month, that in which a new formula for air group composition was instituted; CV, fleet carrier; CVE, escort carrier; CVL, light carrier; Ftrs., fighters; DBmrs., dive bombers; TBmrs., torpedo bombers. Note refers to the lettered comments that appear below.

Several trends are noticeable in these figures. Not only did the number of aircraft on carriers generally rise, but also the proportion of fighters increased markedly, from 25% of the air group at the start of the war to 70% by its end. In addition, note that by early 1944 the advent of the Grumman TBF AVENGER, officially a dive bomber, had tended to blur the differences between torpedo bombers and dive bombers. A very good airplane, the TBF Avenger could be employed in either role, or as a level bomber, or even, with some modifications, as a light cargo and passenger transport. Aircraft totals exclude the two or three so called "utility" aircraft on all carriers, usually light cargo/passenger planes.

A. At the time of PEARL HARBOR, LEXINGTON actually had only 63 aircraft embarked and *Enterprise* only 68, both ships having left some of their own planes behind in order to take on aircraft that they had just delivered to Wake and MIDWAY respectively.

B. Actual totals at Midway were: *Enterprise*, 79 aircraft (27 Ftr., 37 DBmr., 15 TBmr.); *Hornet*, 69 (17 Ftr., 38 DBmr., 14 TBmr.); and YORKTOWN, 75 (25 Ftr., 37 DBmr., 13 TBmr.); plus a couple of utility aircraft each.

C. BOGUE CLASS, converted from merchant ships.

D. This was the authorized number, but many ships managed to have 2–3 additional combat aircraft.

E. Bogue and CASABLANCA CLASSES, displacing under 14,000 tons full load.

F. SANGAMON and COMMENCEMENT BAY CLASSES, displacing more than 20,000 tons full load.

G. Actually, the official figure for fighters reads something like "to capacity," so that most carriers had many more than is indicated here—*Saratoga*, for example, apparently carried 96 fighters. This was possible due to deck stowage, a practice not favored in the economy-minded prewar navy, since the aircraft deteriorated rapidly with extended exposure to the elements. But deck storage was eminently practical once aircraft production had reached flood proportions, and heavy combat and operational losses would prevent any planes getting old enough to develop saltwater damage. In addition, while older aircraft had often possessed only folding wing tips, later US naval aircraft had wings that folded tightly alongside the fuselage, permitting the aircraft to be stored overhead,

leaving the floor of the hangar deck available for additional airplanes. Four fighters on each carrier were equipped for nighttime Combat Air Patrol, supported by a specially equipped TBF Avenger, which served as a night air control aircraft.

72 TBF Avenger and SBD DAUNTLESS bombers and 12 F4F WILDCAT fighters, while *Victorious* had 36 Wildcats and only 12 TBF Avengers. The experiment was not judged a success and was never repeated. However, it was by no means unusual for escort carriers to be equipped entirely with fighters or bombers, especially when operating in support of amphibious landings.

Escort carriers were also often used as aircraft transports, in which role they were capable of carrying as many as 74 airplanes, if they were folding-wing navy types. They could not operate these aircraft, which had to be loaded and offloaded by cranes.

Japanese carrier air groups tended to be much less uniform than American ones, partially because Japanese carriers tended to be much less uniform in their basic characteristics than American ones. In addition, the Japanese Navy tended to "marry" air groups to particular carriers, so that when the carrier was out of action so too was its air group. In contrast, the US Navy viewed air groups and carriers as separate entities that could be mixed and matched as needed. When *Saratoga* was TORPEDOED in early 1942, her pilots and aircraft were immediately transferred to other carriers, whereas when SHOKAKU was put out of action at CORAL SEA, her air group was grounded until she was restored to service. As with American air groups, the Imperial Navy's also underwent evolution.

It is interesting to note that while there was a general increase in air group size of Japanese carriers, overall it was relatively minor. Similarly, although the tendency was to increase the proportion of fighters in air groups, this was not as marked as in the case of the US air groups. One reason for this is that the Japanese did not adopt deck stowage of aircraft. Moreover, their poorly conceived folding wing designs (basically the wings formed a triangle over the fuselage) consumed overhead space that prevented overhead stowage. In addition, due to technical problems concerning hangar deck stowage space and service area design, Japanese carriers were generally incapable of operating their full rated complements of aircraft, usually carrying some in a dismantled state. Most of the Japanese carriers appear to have been able to operate at only about 85% of their rated aircraft

COMPOSITION OF JAPANESE CARRIER AIR GROUPS

Month	Type	Ftrs.	DBmrs.	TBmrs.	Total	Note
Dec. '41	CV	18	18	18–27	54–63	A
Dec. '41	CVL	16–24	21–0	0–21	37–45	B
Dec. '41	CVE	12	0	12–15	24–27	C
Jun. '42	CV	21	21	21	63	D
Aug. '42	CV	27	27	18	72	E
Aug. '42	CVL	16	21	0	37	
Oct. '42	CV	18–27	20–27	10–23	55–72	F
Oct. '42	CVL	18	0	6	22	G
May '44	CV	26–27	26–25	17	69	
May '44	CVL	20–21	0	9–10	29–30	

A. This despite the rated complements of the carriers; AKAGI and KAGA, c. 90; SORYU and HIRYU, c. 70; and Shokaku and Zuikaku, c. 85. At Midway Kaga does seem to have had 83 aircraft (30 Ftrs., 23 DBmrs., 30 TBmrs.), although whether she managed to operate all of them is unclear.

B. ZUIHO, Shoho, and RYUJO.

C. RYUHO and HOSHO. Strictly speaking, these were not escort carriers, merely very small carriers. The Imperial Navy built a few escort carriers, which saw limited service. The Imperial Army built some aircraft transports, which looked like escort carriers and are sometimes so classified, but they had very limited aircraft operating capabilities, and in some cases none whatsoever (see AIRCRAFT CARRIERS, IMPERIAL JAPANESE ARMY).

D. Kaga, however, had an additional 9 torpedo bombers.

E. However, at EASTERN SOLOMONS Shokaku had only 14 dive bombers.

F. JUNYO, 55; Shokaku, 61; Zuikaku, 72.

G. Zuiho.

No information is available for 1943, during which the Japanese were desperately trying to rebuild their carrier fleet and air groups and undertook no combat operations. Although the Japanese did commit carriers in the Battle of LEYTE GULF in October of 1944, the composition of their air groups is unclear. The four carriers (Zuikaku, Zuiho, Chiyoda, and CHITOSE), could operate about 170 aircraft, but actually had a total of 116 among them (80 Ftrs., 36 TBmrs.). However, even before the battle was joined most of these aircraft were flown off to land bases, leaving only 29 with the fleet, none of which did anything during the ensuing fighting. There were also two hybrid "battleship/carriers," which had no aircraft.

COMPOSITION OF BRITISH CARRIER AIR GROUPS

Date	Type	Ftrs.	DBmrs.	TBmrs.	Total	Note
Feb. '42	CV	21	—	24	45	A
Feb. '42	CV	12	—	21	33	B
Feb. '42	CVL	—	—	12	12	C
May '42	CV	21–29	—	20–18	41–47	D
Nov. '42	CV	30	—	12	42	E
May '43	CV	36	12	—	48	F
May '44	CV	28–42	18–0	21–15	57	G
Mar. '45	CV	29	18	—	47	H
May '45	CV	36–37	16–14	—	52–51	I
May '45	CV	49	20	—	69	J
Jul. '45	CV	42	12	—	54	K
Jul. '45	CV	60	18	—	78	L

A. INDOMITABLE, with 12 FULMAR and 9 Sea HURRICANE fighters, and 24 ALBACORE torpedo bombers.

B. Formidable, with 12 "Martlet" fighters (F4F Wildcats) and 21 Albacores—a very small airgroup, even for a British carrier. Note her aircraft complement for July 1945, in Note K, below.

C. HERMES, a dozen Swordfish torpedo bombers.

D. ILLUSTRIOUS. The fighters were F4F Wildcats, plus 1–6 Fulmars equipped for night patrol; the bombers were Swordfish.

E. Victorious as equipped for the North Africa landings. She had 12 F4F Wildcat and 6 SEAFIRE ("navalized" SPITFIRE) fighters, plus 6 Fulmar night fighters and 18 Albacore bombers.

F. Victorious, while operating in company with Saratoga in the Pacific, was equipped with 36 F4F Wildcats and a dozen TBF Avengers.

G. Illustrious, with F4U CORSAIR fighters, TBF Avenger dive bombers, and BARRACUDA torpedo bombers, as available, a very unsatisfactory airgroup.

H. Indomitable, F6F HELLCATS and TBF Avengers.

I. Illustrious, F4U Corsairs and TBF Avengers, and Victorious with F6F Hellcats and TBF Avengers.

J. Indefatigable, 40 Seafire and 9 FIREFLY fighters, plus 20 TBF Avengers.

K. Formidable, sister ship to Illustrious, and Victorious, with 36 F4U Corsairs and 6 F6F Hellcats, plus a dozen TBF Avengers.

L. IMPLACABLE, 48 Seafires and a dozen Fireflys, plus 18 TBF Avengers.

capacity. The worst case seems to have been TAIHO, at only 65%.

British carrier air groups lacked uniformity throughout the war. There were many reasons for this. The Royal Air Force was responsible for procuring aircraft and pilots for carriers, while the Royal Navy was responsible for operating them, reserving their command to navy surface warfare officers. The result was airplanes that were either obsolete or wholly unsuited to carrier operations, pilots lacking adequate understanding of naval operations, and skippers much preferring to command battleships. Given such handicaps it's a wonder that the Fleet Air Arm managed to garner a good deal of glory, its most notable success being the airstrike against Taranto harbor by 21 very obsolete SWORDFISH biplanes on the night of November 11–12, 1940, which put an important part of the Italian battlefleet out of action for several months. In the Indian Ocean and in the Pacific the Royal Navy's carriers were less effective, until reequipped with American aircraft.

British carriers operated mostly in the Indian Ocean, but there were none there from about May of 1942 until about May of 1944. When *Victorious* operated in the South Pacific from May through August of 1943, she did so only after several months of reequipping and retraining in HAWAII with US aircraft. In early 1945 a British carrier task force began operating with the Third/Fifth Fleet, continuing until the surrender of Japan.

Aircraft, Damage

A study conducted by the US Navy concerning causes of aircraft damage in combat between September 1944 and August 1945 proved rather interesting, although not necessarily conclusive, as it was based on aircraft for which it was possible to determine the cause of loss.

It comes as no surprise that multi-engine aircraft (B-24 LIBERATORS; in the Navy, Privateers) were more survivable than single-engine ones (TBF AVENGERS, F4U CORSAIRS, F6F HELICATS, and F4F WILDCATS). After all, multi-engine aircraft have a lot of built-in redundancy. What is interesting is that for both types of aircraft, fuel system hits were less fatal than oil system hits.

Aircraft, Japanese, Allied Code Names

In order to make it easier for US personnel to quickly identify Japanese aircraft, the Armed Forces adopted a system of code names that gave each type of airplane a distinct but simple name. This did not arise without some acrimony, as the army and the navy each initially had a different system, neither of which was particularly useful.

ALLIED CODE NAMES OF JAPANESE AIRCRAFT TYPES	
Type	**Codenamed After**
Bombers	Women
Fighters	Men
Gliders	Birds
Reconnaissance	
Single-engine	Men
Multi-engine	Women
Trainers	Trees
Transports	Women's names beginning with T

In mid-1942 an Army Air Force intelligence officer in the Southwest Pacific began using common, English given names to identify each distinct type of airplane. The idea was so sensible that with some minor refinements it was almost immediately adopted by US forces in the Southwest Pacific. By late 1942 the practice was formally adopted for all American forces in the Pacific. Not long after that, British Commonwealth forces began using it as well.

The names were assigned by a small staff in Australia. Initially the men involved used "Hill Billy"

System Damaged	Single-engine			Multi-engine		
	Cases	Lost	(%)	Cases	Lost	(%)
Control Surfaces	27	0	(0)	20	0	(0)
Electricals	6	0	(0)	57	21	(37)
Engine	37	23	(62)	9	1	(11)
Fuel System	30	21	(80)	31	2	(6)
Hydraulics	35	21	(60)	17	2	(12)
Oil System	27	23	(85)	9	3	(33)
Pilot and Controls	97	74	(76)	29	6	(20)
Propeller	9	0	(0)	7	0	(0)
Structure	215	23	(11)	135	5	(4)
Other	18	5	(28)	0	0	—

ALLIED CODE NAMES OF JAPANESE AIRCRAFT

Name	Airplane
Abdul	Early designation for Nate
Adam	Nakajima SK, Navy Type 97 seaplane fighter*
Alf	Kawanishi E7K, Navy Type 94 recon floatplane
Ann	Mitsubishi Ki–30, Army Type 97 light bomber
Babs	Mitsubishi Ki–15, Army Type 97 recon plane, and Mitsubishi C5M, Navy Type 98 recon plane—the same aircraft (see Norma)
Baka	Yokosuka MXY7 Ohka, Navy special (suicide) attack plane
Belle	Kawanishi H3K1, Navy Type 90–2 biplane flying boat
Ben	Nagoya-Sento Ki–1, Navy carrier fighter
Bess	Heinkel He–111, Army bomber
Betty	Mitsubishi G4M1/G4M3, Navy Type 1 bomber, and the Mitsubishi G6M1, a variant with several models used as a night fighter, trainer, and transport
Bob	Aichi, Navy Type 97 recon seaplane#, later assigned to the Kawasaki Ki–28, experimental Army Type 97 fighter.
Buzzard	Kokusai Ku–7, army experimental transport glider
Cedar	Tachikawa Ki–17, Army Type 95 primary trainer
Cherry	Yokosuka H5Y, Navy Type 99 flying boat
Clara	Tachikawa Ki–70, Army experimental recon plane
Claude	Mitsubishi A5M, Navy Type 96 carrier fighter
Cypress	Kyushu K9W, Navy Type 2 primary trainer, and the Kokusai Ki–86, Army Type 4 primary trainer version
Dave	Nakajima E8N, Navy recon seaplane
Dick	Seversky A8V1, Navy Type S fighter
Dinah	Mitsubishi Ki46, Army Type 100 recon plane
Doc	Messerschmitt Bf–110 fighter#
Doris	Mitsubishi B–97, medium bomber
Dot	Yokosuka D4Y, navy carrier bomber; also Judy
Edna	Mansyu Ki–71, army experimental recon plane
Emily	Kawanishi H8K, Navy Type 2 flying boat
Eve/Eva	Bomber version of Mitsubishi Ohtori civil aircraft#
Frances	Yokosuka P1Y, navy bomber, and night fighter derivatives
Frank	Mitsubishi TK–4, Army Type 0 fighter# (also Harry), designation later given to the purported Nakajima K–84, Army Type 4 Fighter#
Fred	Focke-Wulf Fw–190 fighter#
Gander	later designation for Goose
George	Kawanishi N1K1-J, navy interceptor, the Shiden, and Kawanishi N1K5-J, navy interceptor Shiden Kai
Glen	Yokosuka E14Y, Navy Type 0 recon plane

ALLIED CODE NAMES OF JAPANESE AIRCRAFT

Name	Airplane
Goose	Kokusai Ku–8, Army Type 4 transport glider, later Gander
Grace	Aichi B7A, navy carrier bomber
Gus	Nakajima AT–27, twin-engine fighter#
Gwen	Mitsubishi Ki–21–IIB, Army Type 97 heavy bomber (later Sally III)
Hamp	Early designation for the Zeke, formerly Hap
Hank	Aichi E10A, Navy Type 96 night recon plane
Hap	First designation of the Zeke, later Hamp
Harry	See Frank
Helen	Nakajima Ki–49, Army Type 100 heavy bomber
Hickory	Tachikawa Ki–54, Army Type 1 trainer/transport (see Joyce)
Ida	Tachikawa Ki–36, Army Type 98 liaison airplane, and the Tachikawa Ki–54, Army Type 99 trainer version
Ione	Aichi AI–104, Navy Type 98 recon seaplane#
Irene	Junkers Ju–87A, dive bomber#
Irving	Nakajima J1N1–C and J1N1–R, Navy Type 2 recon plane, and Nakajima J1N1–S, navy night fighter
Jack	Mitsubishi J2M, navy interceptor (the Raiden fighter)
Jake	Aichi E13A, Navy Type 0 recon seaplane
Jane	Early designation for Sally
Janice	Junkers Ju88, medium bomber#
Jean	Yokosuka B4Y, Navy Type 96 carrier bomber
Jerry	Heinkel He–112, Navy Type He fighter
Jill	Nakajima B6N, navy carrier bomber
Jim	Alternative designation for Oscar, briefly used in China
Joe	TK19, experimental fighter#
Joyce	Light bomber version of Hickory
Judy	Yokosuka D4Y, Navy Type 2 carrier bomber, and derivatives
Julia	Heavy bomber version of Lily#
June	Floatplane version of Val#
Kate	Nakajima B5N, Navy Type 97 carrier bomber
Kate 61	Later designation for Mabel
Laura	Aichi E11A, Navy Type 98 night recon seaplane
Lily	Kawasaki Ki–48, Army Type 99 light bomber (see Julia)
Liz	Nakajima G5N, navy experimental bomber
Lorna	Kyushu Q1W, navy maritime patrol plane
Louise	Mitsubishi Ki–2, Army Type 93 light bomber (also Loise)
Luke	Mitsubishi J4M, navy experimental interceptor
Mabel	Mitsubishi B5M, Navy Type 97 carrier bomber (later called Kate 61)

ALLIED CODE NAMES OF JAPANESE AIRCRAFT

Name	Airplane
Mary	Kawasaki Ki–32, Army Type 98 light bomber
Mavis	Kawanishi H6K, Navy Type 97 flying boat
Mike	Messerschmitt Bf–109E#
Millie	Vultee V–11GB, Type 98 light bomber#
Myrt	Nakajima C6N, navy carrier recon plane
Nate	Nakajima Ki–27, army fighter (see Abdul)
Nell	Mitsubishi G3M, Navy Type 96 bomber, and the variant Yokosuka L3Y, Navy Type 96 transport (see Tina)
Nick	Kawasaki Ki–45, Army Type 2 fighter
Norm	Kawanishi E15K, Navy Type 2, recon seaplane
Norma	Believed to be light bomber version of the Mitsubishi Ki–15, Army Type 97 recon plane# (see Babs)
Oak	Kyushu K10W, Navy Type 2 trainer
Omar	Susukaze 20, twin-engine fighter#
Oscar	Nakajima Ki–43, Army Type 1 fighter (see Jim)
Pat	Tachikawa Ki–74, army fighter# (see Patsy)
Patsy	Tachikawa Ki–74, army experimental long-range bomber (see Pat)
Paul	Aichi E16A, navy recon seaplane
Peggy	Mitsubishi Ki–67, Army Type 4 heavy bomber
Pete	Mitsubishi F1M, Navy Type 0 observation floatplane
Pine	Mitsubishi K3M, Navy Type 90 trainer
Randy	Kawasaki Ki–102B, Army Type 4 attack aircraft
Ray	Mitsubishi Type 1 fighter# (probably a misreported Zeke)
Rex	Kawanishi N1K, navy seaplane fighter
Rita	Nakajima G8N, navy experimental attack bomber
Rob	Kawasaki Ki–64, army experimental fighter
Rufe	Nakajima A6M2–N, Navy Type 2 fighter floatplane (a floatplane version of the Zeke)
Ruth	Fiat BR 20 Army Type 1 heavy bomber
Sally	Mitsubishi Ki–21, Army Type 97 heavy bomber (original designation Jane; see also Gwen)
Sam	Mitsubishi A7M, navy experimental carrier fighter
Sandy	Duplicated designation for Claude
Slim	Watanabe E9W, Navy Type 96 recon biplane
Sonia	Mitsubishi Ki–51, Army Type 99 attack aircraft
Spruce	Tachikawa Ki–9, Army Type 95 intermediate trainer
Stella	Kokusai Ki–76, Army Type 2 liaison aircraft
Steve	Mitsubishi Ki–73, army experimental fighter
Susie	Aichi D1A1 and D1A2, Navy Type 94 and Type 96 carrier bombers
Tabby	Douglas L2D (DC–3), Navy Type 0 transport
Teresa	Kokusai Ki–59, Army Type 1 transport (also Theresa)

ALLIED CODE NAMES OF JAPANESE AIRCRAFT

Name	Airplane
Tess	Douglas DC–2, commercial transport*
Thalia	Kawasaki Ki–56, Army Type 1 transport
Thelma	Lockheed 14, Army Type L0 transport
Thora	Nakajima Ki–34, Army Type 97 transport, and the Nakajima L1N, Navy Type 97 transport—the same aircraft
Tillie	Yokosuka H7Y, navy experimental flying boat
Tina	Mitsubishi Ki–33, Army Type 96 transport# (error for the Yokosuka L3Y Nell)
Toby	Lockheed 14, commercial transport (see Thelma)
Tojo	Nakajima Ki–44, Army Type 2 fighter
Tony	Kawasaki Ki–61, Army Type 3 fighter (the Hien)
Topsy	Mitsubishi Ki–57, Army Type 100 transport, and the Mitsubishi L4M, Navy Type 0 transport—the same aircraft
Trixie	Junkers Ju–52, commercial transport#
Trudy	Focke-Wulf, FW 200, long-range reconnaissance plane#
Val	Aichi D3A, Navy Type 99 carrier bomber
Willow	Yokosuka K5Y, Navy Type 95 trainer
Zeke	Mitsubishi A6M, Navy Type 0 carrier fighter, generally known as the Zero (earlier designations Hap and Hamp; see also Ray, Rufe)

*Erroneously reported. The aircraft was believed in service, but was either never built, misidentified, or not in use as indicated.

names, allegedly because one of them came from Tennessee. They soon ran out of these, and then went on to use their own names and those of their wives and friends. As the number of aircraft grew, they became more resourceful, and began using the names of prominent people, such as "Hap," after Hap Arnold, head of the Army Air Forces (an "honor" to which Arnold objected, leading to a change in designation to "Hamp").

Most aircraft have individual entries, found under their Japanese designation, e.g., A5M or Ki-61.

See also AIRCRAFT, JAPANESE, FALSE REPORTS.

Ref: Francillon, *Japanese Aircraft*.

Aircraft, Japanese, False Reports

Collecting information on the Japanese military was difficult before the outbreak of the war, and became almost impossible during it. As a result, a great many errors were made. Considering the surprise with which the Zero took the world, there developed a tendency to believe that Japanese aircraft engineering and industry were extremely advanced and versatile. As a result of fragmentary information often gathered from inept agents or unreliable sources, the Allies were led to believe that the Japanese were diligently designing and building flocks of new and spectacularly effective airplanes. Many of these notional aircraft eventually found their way into Allied recognition books and intelligence briefings, complete with specifications, nicknames, and occasional "triviews" (pictures showing the airplane from various directions).

None of the aircraft indicated as "Erroneously Reported" on the table in the preceding section, "Aircraft, Japanese, Allied Code Names," were used by the Japanese. They were, however, reported in use by Allied intelligence.

There were actually several categories of such aircraft.

1. Misidentification: An existing airplane was sighted but taken for a new and different aircraft, either because the observer was poorly trained or surprised, or because minor modifications in the airplane led it to appear somewhat different, as in the case of the Ray. Another source of error in this regard was the assumption that a new role or model was a logical development of an existing aircraft, such as the Norma. This was a quite common error. Indeed, considering the enormous difficulties under which intelligence collection proceeded, it is rather surprising that this sort of thing did not occur more often.

2. Foreign: The Japanese had received test models of certain German and other foreign aircraft, and it was widely believed that some of these had been put into service, such as the Fred or the Tess. In fact, the Japanese did produce several foreign aircraft types under (prewar) license during the war. With one exception, these were all American models.

Chief among these were the DC-3 transport, of which the Japanese produced over 500 under a prewar license. Allied pilots were often unaware of this, and when a DC-3 in Japanese colors was spotted, it gave rise to stories (largely false) of the Japanese using "captured DC-3s." The Japanese also produced the Lockheed 14 under license, and a German biplane trainer.

3. Imaginary: A wholly fictitious aircraft was reported. This sometimes was the result of relying on very inept agents. However, the origins of some of the imaginary aircraft were rather amusing. For example, the Nakajima SKT-97 "Gus" and the Suzukaze 20 "Omar" first appeared in Allied aviation literature around the beginning of the Pacific War, in the American aviation reference book *Aerosphere*, with full descriptions of their specifications. Along with lots of other technicalese, we are told that the Nakajima SKT-97 was an "enclosed cockpit low wing cantilever monoplane," in which the "pilot sits between two engines, one forward and one to the rear, with armor plate protection for both pilot and engines." The airplane was purportedly capable of traveling 410 miles per hour with range of 1,250 miles. The Suzukaze 20 was also a "low-wing cantilever monoplane," with an "enclosed cockpit to the rear of wing." It was supposedly capable of 478 MPH.

The actual origins of the two aircraft is an interesting lesson in how erroneous information can come to be taken as accurate, particularly in wartime. *Aerosphere* had merely copied the material from *Flight*, a British aviation magazine. The British magazine, in turn, had copied its information from a German publication. And the Germans had derived their information as a result of a mistranslation of an article that had appeared in the Japanese aviation magazine *Sora* ("Sky"). *Sora* was popular with young aviation enthusiasts and model builders. It had a monthly feature, "Dreams of Future Designers," which presented the fanciful designs of aspiring aviation engineers. The April 1941 issue of *Sora* contained two of these designs, the Nakajima STK-97 and the Suzukaze 20.

So the daydreams of a couple of Japanese teenagers ended up giving nightmares to Allied soldiers, sailors, and airmen who had to memorize all sorts of information about aircraft that never existed.

Aircraft, Losses

Although the air war in the Pacific did not reach the proportions of that in Europe, it was still an extraordinary undertaking, involving literally tens of thousands of aircraft, millions of tons of supplies, and hundreds of thousands of pilots and ground support personnel.

US figures, of course, include aircraft committed to the war against Germany and Italy, as well as to that with Japan, and Japanese figures include aircraft involved in operations against China, the Netherlands, the British Commonwealth, and, right at the end, the Soviet Union. So the two sets are not totally comparable.

By the end of the war, over half of American aircraft were either in the Pacific or on their way there. Most Japanese aircraft losses, particularly naval aircraft losses, were inflicted by the United States, particularly the US Navy.

Adding the "Wartime Losses" to the August 15, 1945, figures will not give a total for the number of aircraft available during the war, as obsolete types were withdrawn from service and scrapped, even by the Japanese.

AIRCRAFT AVAILABILITY AND EXPENDITURE: THE UNITED STATES AND JAPAN IN WORLD WAR II

	Service	On Hand 7 Dec. '41	Wartime Losses	On Hand 15 Aug. '45
U.S.	Army	12,300	13,055	66,000
	Navy/Marines	5,300	8,500	41,000
	Total U.S.	17,600	21,555	107,000
Jap.	Army	4,826	15,935	8,920
	Navy	2,120	27,190	7,307
	Total Japan	6,946	43,125	16,227

Ref: Overy, *The Air War*; Roscoe, *On the Seas and in the Skies.*

Aircraft, Non-combat Losses

The War in the Pacific was notable for the high number of aircraft destroyed by "non-combat causes." Overall, only 25% of the aircraft lost were due to enemy action, a lower rate than in Europe. The others were destroyed by weather, the difficulty of operating from aircraft carriers and hastily built airfields, and the insidious effect of the tropical climate on machines. In the 14-month ALEUTIAN ISLANDS campaign in Alaska, 87% of aircraft losses were to non-combat causes. Although the climate was not tropical, the arctic weather proved even more ruinous to an aircraft's life span.

Ref: Overy, *The Air War, 1939–1945.*

Aircraft, Still Flying in the 1990s

Several World War II–era aircraft are still in use today, and one is a most unlikely candidate. The DC-3 (or C-47 in military usage) continues to fly in commercial service well into the 1990s. Nearly 1,000 DC-3s are still flying worldwide, mostly owned by small domestic carriers in the United States and by some Third World air transport companies. The Japanese had a prewar license to produce the DC-3, and were so impressed that they went on to produce 485 of their own version, called the L2D. The Soviets also produced 2,000 of their own license built version (the Li-2). Rugged, versatile and much beloved by its two- or three-man crews (who affectionately nicknamed it "Flying Dumbo" and "Gooney Bird"), the DC-3 is one old soldier of World War II that refuses to fade away. Some will still be in commercial service into the 21st century. The only other aircraft that approaches the DC-3 in longevity is the Russian Po-2 biplane. First produced in 1920, it saw service as a light night bomber during World War II, and is used as a crop duster these days. It is simple, robust and slow enough to continue its agricultural chores. Many World War II-era transports served on for decades after the war. The two-engine C-46 and four-engine C-54 served into the 1980s, and a few are still around in the 1990s. The only other World War II airplane that has seen a great deal of service is the AT-6 Texan. The principal US basic training airplane during the war, some were still in service as trainers with the South African Air Force as late as 1995.

Aircraft Carriers

The aircraft carrier was the newest, and ultimately the most decisive type of warship in World War II. Essentially a fast moving, floating airstrip, the carrier had been invented during World War I. The very earliest carriers were converted from vessels of various types, colliers, ferries, and the like. By the 1920s several nations had carriers, mostly converted from partially completed battleships or battlecruisers. Since they lacked the big guns and, usually, the heavy armor protection of the battlewagons, the newer carriers were often about as fast as cruisers or destroyers.

As carriers began to be built from scratch, the principal navies (British, American, and Japanese) incorporated improvements based on their experience with the converted vessels. As a result, conversions aside, most prewar carriers were larger than heavy cruisers but smaller than battleships, between 14,000–24,000 tons displacement, although there were a few that were smaller, notably several Japanese ones. Size was not so important as speed (higher speed vessels being better able to get into and out of combat quickly) and capacity to carry and operate aircraft, two rather different functions, affected by but not totally dependent upon size.

Several of the converted carriers, being essentially experimental vessels, had poor aircraft capacities. The United States was lucky in this regard, as its two converted carriers, LEXINGTON and Saratoga, were roomy vessels, as were most subsequent American "purpose built" carriers. In contrast, the Japanese adopted some unusual design elements, so that even the carriers they built from the keel up could not operate all the aircraft they could carry, due to poorly laid-out hangar decks and aircraft stowage facilities. In addition, the Japanese had a policy of not storing aircraft on deck, a practice that the US Navy adopted before the war, and embraced enthusiastically during it. As a result, US carriers of comparable size usually could operate as many as 65% more aircraft (90–100 as against 55–65). British carriers tended to have a smaller aircraft capacity (55–65), due to a decision to provide relatively heavy armor. In compensation, British carriers were much more survivable ships.

A second critical factor in carrier effectiveness, and more important than carrier size, was the ship's capacity to carry avgas (aviation fuel) and fuel, which determined operational endurance. While this was, of course, partially connected to the size of the vessel, once again policy decisions and design were a factor. In consequence, US carriers tended to have greater fuel capacity than either Japanese or British ones, which meant American carriers could generate more missions between trips to the barn.

The pressures of the war led to several variations on the aircraft carrier. The larger ships (CVs) soon became the primary weapon of sea power, and were in extremely short supply during the first 18 months of the war. This shortage had been anticipated even before the Pacific War broke out, as prescient observers of naval affairs noted the value of aircraft in antisubmarine warfare. As a result, in 1941, under prodding from President Franklin D. ROOSEVELT, the US Navy authorized the experimental conversion of a merchant ship into an escort carrier (CVE), a type that the ROYAL NAVY was finding of some value. CVEs were smallish vessels, often less than half the size of CVs, rather slow (12–18 knots), relatively unmaneuverable, and able to carry only a handful of aircraft (15–36). Despite their limitations, they proved so useful not only as convoy escorts, but also as supports for the fleet in offensive operations, that the United States

AIRCRAFT CARRIERS

Fleet Carriers & Light Carriers (CV, CVL)

Navy	Class	Year	Tot.	Displacement Full	Crew	Combat Surf	Combat AAA	A/C	Main	Sec.	DP	AAA	TT	Length	Beam	Draft	HP	Spd.	Armor Belt	Armor Deck
Jp	Akagi	1927	1	42.8	2,000	9	3	72	6x8	None	None	12x4	0	235.0	29.0	8.1	133.0	31.0	10.0	1.0
Br	Centaur	MHB	8	24.0	1,390	2	2	42	None	None	8x4.5	None	0	198.1	27.4	7.5	76.0	29.5	0.0	0.0
Jp	Chitose	1943	2	15.3	800	2	1	30	None	None	8x5	None	0	174.0	20.8	7.5	44.0	28.9	0.0	0.0
Br	Colossus	1944	10	18.0	1,300	1	0	37	None	None	None	None	0	190.0	24.4	7.1	40.0	25.0	0.0	0.0
Br	Eagle II	1945	2	46.0	2,740	2	6	78	None	None	16x4.5	None	0	245.0	34.4	9.5	152.0	23.0	4.5	4.0
US	Essex	1942	26	34.9	2,686	4	7	91	None	None	12x5	None	0	249.9	28.3	8.4	150.0	32.7	4.0	4.0
Br	Furious	1925	1	22.5	1,218	2	1	36	10x5.5	None	2x4	None	0	224.0	27.5	8.6	90.0	30.0	3.0	1.0
Br	Hermes	1923	1	13.0	664	2	1	20	6x5.5	None	None	4x4	0	166.1	27.3	5.7	40.0	25.0	3.0	1.0
Jp	Hiryu	1939	1	21.9	1,100	3	3	64	None	None	12x5	None	0	210.0	22.3	7.8	153.0	34.3	5.9	2.2
Jp	Hosho	1922	1	10.0	550	0	0	22	4x5.5	None	None	None	0	155.5	18.0	6.2	30.0	25.0	0.0	0.0
Jp	Ibuki	1945	1	14.6	1,015	1	1	27	None	None	None	4x3	0	187.8	21.2	6.3	72.0	29.0	0.0	0.0
Br	Illustrious	1940	3	28.6	1,229	4	6	33	None	None	16x4.5	None	0	205.1	29.2	8.7	111.0	30.5	4.5	3.0
Br	Implacable	1944	2	32.1	1,585	4	6	60	None	None	16x4.5	None	0	205.1	29.2	8.8	148.0	32.0	4.5	3.0
US	Independence	1943	9	14.8	1,569	1	1	30	None	None	None	None	0	182.9	21.8	7.4	100.0	31.6	5.6	2.0
Br	Indomitable	1941	1	29.7	1,392	4	6	45	None	None	16x4.5	None	0	205.1	29.2	8.8	111.0	30.5	4.5	3.0
Jp	Junyo	1942	2	28.3	1,200	3	2	53	None	None	12x5	None	0	206.0	26.7	8.2	56.3	23.0	0.0	0.0
Jp	Kaga	1928	1	43.7	2,016	10	3	81	10x8	None	16x5	None	0	240.3	32.5	9.5	127.4	28.3	11.0	1.0
US	Lexington	1926	2	43.1	2,330	17	6	63	8x8	None	None	12x5	0	259.1	32.1	10.2	180.0	33.3	7.0	2.0
Br	Magnificent	MHB	6	17.8	1,300	1	0	37	None	None	None	None	0	192.0	24.4	7.0	40.0	25.0	0.0	0.0
Br	Malta	MHB	4	56.8	2,780	4	6	81	None	None	16x4.5	None	0	249.9	35.4	10.5	200.0	32.5	4.5	4.0
US	Midway	1945	3	59.9	4,104	6	11	137	None	None	18x5	None	0	274.3	34.4	10.5	212.0	33.0	7.0	7.5
US	Ranger	1934	1	17.6	1,788	3	4	76	None	None	8x5	8x5	0	222.5	24.4	6.8	53.5	29.3	2.0	1.0
Jp	Ryuho	1942	1	16.7	990	2	2	31	None	None	8x5	None	0	197.3	19.6	6.7	52.0	26.5	0.0	0.0
Jp	Ryujo	1933	1	13.7	924	2	2	37	None	None	8x5	None	0	167.0	20.8	7.1	65.0	29.0	0.0	0.0
US	Saipan	1946	2	17.8	1,821	1	1	48	None	None	None	None	0	202.4	23.4	8.2	120.0	33.0	4.6	2.5
Jp	Shinano	1944	1	71.9	2,400	5	6	70	None	None	16x5	None	0	244.0	36.3	10.3	150.0	27.0	8.1	10.6
Jp	Shokaku	1941	2	32.1	1,660	4	4	72	None	None	16x5	None	0	236.1	26.0	8.9	160.0	34.2	6.5	5.1
Jp	Soryu	1937	1	19.8	1,100	3	3	63	None	None	12x5	None	0	210.0	21.3	7.6	152.0	34.5	1.8	2.2

AIRCRAFT CARRIERS (Continued)

Navy	Class	Year	Tot.	Displacement Full	Crew	Combat Surf	Combat AAA	A/C	Guns Main	Sec.	DP	AAA	TT	Length	Beam	Draft	HP	Spd.	Armor Belt	Deck
Jp	Taiho	1944	1	37.7	1,751	2	2	53	None	None	None	12x3.9	0	238.0	27.7	9.6	160.0	33.0	5.9	8.0
Br	Unicorn	1943	1	20.3	1,200	2	2	35	None	None	8x4	None	0	171.9	27.4	7.3	40.0	24.0	0.0	0.0
Jp	Unryu	1944	6	20.0	1,550	3	3	65	None	None	12x5	None	0	207.0	22.0	7.8	152.0	34.0	5.9	3.2
US	Wasp	1940	1	18.5	2,167	3	4	76	None	None	8x5	None	0	210.3	24.9	7.1	70.0	29.5	0.6	1.3
US	Yorktown	1937	3	25.5	220	3	5	96	None	None	8x5	None	0	234.7	25.3	7.9	120.0	32.5	4.8	1.5
Jp	Zuiho	1940	2	14.3	785	1	2	30	None	None	8x5	None	0	185.0	18.2	6.6	523.0	28.0	0.0	0.0
Escort Carriers (CVE)																				
US	Bogue	1942	11	13.9	890	1	1	28	None	None	2x5	None	0	151.1	34.0	7.1	8.5	16.5	0.0	0.0
US	Casablanca	1943	50	10.9	860	1	0	27	None	None	1x5	None	0	149.4	19.9	6.3	9.0	19.0	0.0	0.0
US	Commencement Bay	1944	22	21.4	1,066	2	1	33	None	None	2x5	None	0	169.9	32.1	8.5	16.0	19.0	0.0	0.0
Jp	Kaiyo	1943	1	16.5	829	2	2	24	None	None	8x5	None	0	155.0	21.9	8.0	52.0	23.0	0.0	0.0
US	Long Island	1942	1	15.0	856	1	1	16	None	None	1x4, 2x3	None	0	141.7	21.2	7.7	8.5	16.5	0.0	0.0
US	Sangamon	1942	4	23.9	1,080	6	0	31	None	None	1x5	None	0	160.0	22.9	9.3	13.5	18.0	0.0	0.0
Jp	Shinyo	1943	1	20.6	942	2	1	33	None	None	8x5	None	0	185.0	25.6	8.2	26.0	22.0	0.0	0.0
Jp	Taiyo	1941	3	19.7	850	2	2	27	None	None	None	6x4.7	0	168.0	22.5	7.7	25.5	21.0	0.0	0.0

Key to the Table: **Navy** = nation the ship belongs to: Au = Australia, Br = Britain, Cn = Canada, Fr = France, Nth = Netherlands, NZ = New Zealand, Jp = Japan, US = US. **Class** = name of the lead ship in the class. **Year** = when the first ship in the class entered service. MHB = might have been, a class that was not, but could have been, in action. Tot. = total number of ships in that class. **Displacement** is the amount of water the ship displaces (i.e., the weight of the water that would occupy the space occupied by the ship), expressed in thousands of tons. **Full** = "fighting weight," or weight with basic crew, fuel, munitions and other supplies, all the items needed to go to war. **Crew** = number normally carried. **Combat** = relative combat value for each ship in the following areas: **Surf** = value in surface engagements; **AAA** = value against attacking aircraft. A group of ships would combine their values, which was particularly effective when defending against enemy aircraft. **A/C** = aircraft carried. **Guns** = there are many different types: **Main** = the largest guns, which on battleships can be from 11 to 18 inches in bore diameter; **Sec.** = secondary guns for use against smaller surface targets (these became obsolete during World War II, usually converted to AAA use); **DP** = dual purpose, for use against surface and air targets; **AAA** = antiaircraft artillery, generally the same caliber as the DP guns, but whose only purpose is to attack aircraft. Most ships also carried as many anti-aircraft heavy machine guns as they could. The caliber varying from 12.7mm to 40mm, the latter (20mm and up) were actually automatic cannon, as they fired explosive shells. **TT** = torpedo tubes carried. **Dimensions** are expressed in meters. There are three of them: **Length** = how long the ship was; **Beam** = width of the ship; **Draft** = how deep into the water the bottom of the ship is at full load. HP = maximum horsepower generated by the ship's engines. **Spd.** = top speed in knots (nautical miles per hour). **Armor** = the protection many ships had against enemy fire. Given in inches for the following positions on the ship: **Belt** = an area along the waterline to protect engines and ammo magazines; **Deck** = for protection from "plunging" shells (fired from a great distance away) or bombs.

eventually built scores from scratch. They were also cheap and could be made available quickly. Through the war the United States commissioned some 77 escort carriers, the British Commonwealth 43 (many built in the United States), some of which were operated by Canada, and Japan five. Escort carriers served in many roles: antisubmarine patrol, support of ground forces, fleet defense, flight deck training, and particularly as aircraft transports. During the OKINAWA Campaign 25 US CVEs were engaged in this role: four carrying replacement aircraft for the fast carriers, 17 supporting distant bases, and four carrying aircraft to Okinawa for the army. Escort carriers were cramped and uncomfortable and highly inflammable, prompting sailors to joke that CVE stood for "Combustible, Vulnerable, and Expendable."

In addition, the shortage of carriers early in the war led the United States and Japan to convert unfinished vessels of other types to light aircraft carriers (CVLs). These were rather larger than escort carriers. CVLs were generally capable of operating only about 30 aircraft, the same as CVEs, but had much better engines, enabling them to keep up with the CVs and other fast elements of the fleet, making them an important element in the fast carrier task forces.

Altogether there were 60 different classes of aircraft carrier in service or building during World War II, excluding several classes of "merchant aircraft carriers" operated by the British and Dutch in the Atlantic, and the Japanese Army's so-called "aircraft carriers," all of which had very limited aircraft capacities and operational capabilities.

While the aircraft carrier was the premier naval weapon of World War II, it wasn't until the late 1930s that aircraft carriers became capable enough to rule the seas. Through the mid-1930s, carrier aircraft were unable to carry a sufficient weight of bombs to present a threat to battleships. As long as battleships were capable of withstanding attacks by carrier bombers, the carriers themselves could be hunted down and sunk by battleships and cruisers. But in the mid-1930s, new and more powerful carrier aircraft began to appear.

Carriers were also among the most vulnerable of ships. While they could inflict enormous damage, they could take much less than any other ship their size because of their relative lack of armor and all the aviation gas and aircraft munitions they carried. Plus, the big flight deck made a wonderful target for attacking aircraft.

Aircraft carriers can be considered weapons that "expend" aircraft for ammunition. As a result, although the most significant datum about carriers is the number of aircraft they can operate, some aircraft "carriers" were extraordinarily inefficient at even carrying aircraft. Consider the relationship between the size of carriers and their aircraft complements (see table, pages 24–25).

British carriers had a low Index because they tended to be more heavily armored, including an armored flight deck. While there were obviously some advantages in terms of stability and survivability to a relatively low Index, such ships were not very cost effective; you had a huge vessel (and an enormous crew) with low firepower. Generally, the higher the Index the better the carrier was, operationally.

There were some disadvantages to a high Index. For example, RANGER, which proved to be the only US fleet carrier that did not operate in the Pacific, was rather overcrowded, and WASP not much better.

In addition to carrying the aircraft, you had to keep them flying. This required aviation fuel (avgas), a very volatile commodity that aircraft consumed in enormous amounts, 300 gallons, roughly a ton, per sortie on average. As the war progressed, larger and thirstier aircraft were introduced. The newer planes had longer range, largely because they carried a lot more fuel.

If we rank the carriers on the basis of thousands of gallons of avgas (actually, just high-grade gasoline) per aircraft, we get a somewhat different perspective (see page 26).

All other things being equal, like being able to carry a useful number of aircraft, it is interesting to note that most American and Japanese carriers had a sortie figure of about 6 or better, allowing a rel-

AIRCRAFT CARRYING CAPACITY

Class	Aircraft			Efficiency			
	Navy	Type	Com.	Displ.	A/C	Index	Rank
Activity	Br.	CVE	'42	14.5	10	0.7	59
Akagi	Jap.	CV	'27	42.8	72	1.7	33
Ameer	Br.	CVE	'43	15.6	20	1.3	45
Aquila	It.	CV	'43+	27.8	66	2.4	12
Archer	Br.	CVE	'41	13.0	16	1.2	48
Argus	Br.	CV	'18	17.7	18	1.0	54
Ark Royal	Br.	CV	'38	28.1	60	2.1	17
Attacker	Br.	CVE	'42	10.4	20	1.9	23
Audacity	Br.	CVE	'41	10.4	6	0.6	60
Avenger	Br.	CVE	'42	10.4	15	1.4	39
Bearn	Fr.	CV	'27	28.4	40	1.4	40
Bogue	U.S.	CVE	'42	14.1	28	2.0	21
Campania	Br.	CVE	'44	16.2	18	1.1	53
Casablanca	U.S.	CVE	'43	10.9	27	2.5	11
Centaur	Br.	CVL	'46	24.9	42	1.7	32
Chitose	Jap.	CVL	'44	15.3	30	2.0	22
Colossus	Br.	CVL	'44	18.3	48	2.6	9
Commencement Bay	U.S.	CVE	'44	21.7	33	1.5	37
Courageous	Br.	CV	'28	26.5	48	1.8	28
Eagle	Br.	CV	'23	27.2	20	0.7	58
Eagle II	Br.	CV	'45+	46.5	80	1.7	30
Essex	U.S.	CV	'42	34.9	91	2.6	10
Furious	Br.	CV	'25	22.5	36	1.6	36
Graf Zeppelin	Ger.	CV	'42+	37.0	42	1.1	51
Hermes	Br.	CVL	'23	13.2	12	0.9	56
Hiryu	Jap.	CV	'39	21.9	64	2.9	5
Hosho	Jap.	CVL	'22	10.0	12	1.2	50
Ibuki	Jap.	CVL	'45+	14.6	27	1.8	27
Illustrious	Br.	CV	'40	28.7	36	1.3	46
Implacable	Br.	CV	'44	32.6	54	1.7	34
Independence	U.S.	CVL	'43	14.8	30	2.0	20
Indomitable	Br.	CV	'41	29.7	52	1.8	29
Joffre	Fr.	CV	'42+	28.7	40	1.4	43
Junyo	Jap.	CV	'42	28.3	53	1.9	24
Kaga	Jap.	CV	'28	43.7	81	1.9	26
Kaiyo	Jap.	CVE	'43	16.5	24	1.5	38
Lexington	U.S.	CV	'27	43.1	96	2.2	16
Long Island	U.S.	CVE	'41	14.3	16	1.1	52
Majestic	Br.	CVL	'45+	18.1	37	2.0	19
Malta	Br.	CV	'46+	57.7	81	1.4	42
Midway	U.S.	CV	'45	59.9	137	2.3	14
Pretoria Castle	Br.	CVE	'43	23.8	21	0.9	57
Ranger	U.S.	CV	'34	17.6	76	4.3	1
Ryuho	Jap.	CVL	'42	16.7	31	1.9	25
Ryujo	Jap.	CVL	'33	13.7	37	2.7	7

Class	Aircraft			Efficiency			
	Navy	Type	Com.	Displ.	A/C	Index	Rank
Saipan	U.S.	CVL	'46	17.8	48	2.7	8
Sangamon	U.S.	CVE	'42	24.3	30	1.2	47
Shinano	Jap.	CV	'44	71.9	70	1.0	55
Shinyo	Jap.	CVE	'43	20.6	33	1.6	35
Shokaku	Jap.	CV	'41	32.1	72	2.2	15
Soryu	Jap.	CV	'37	19.8	63	3.2	4
Taiho	Jap.	CV	'44	37.7	53	1.4	41
Taiyo	Jap.	CVE	'41	19.7	27	1.4	44
Unicorn	Br.	CVL	'43	20.6	35	1.7	31
Unryu	Jap.	CV	'44	22.9	65	2.8	6
Vindex	Br.	CVE	'43	17.3	21	1.2	49
Wasp	U.S.	CV	'40	18.5	76	4.1	2
Yorktown	U.S.	CV	'37	25.5	96	3.8	3
Zuiho	Jap.	CVL	'40	14.3	30	2.1	18

This table lists alphabetically all classes of carriers in service or that might have been in service during World War II. Classes that saw no service in the Pacific do not have individual entries in this encyclopedia. **Class** is the name of the first ship in a group (class) of ships built more or less to the same design. **Navy** is the nation that built and used the ship: U.S. is United States, Jap. is Japan, and Br. is British. **Type:** fleet carriers (CV), light carriers (CVL), and escort carriers (originally ACV and later CVE). **Com.** is the year of commissioning, as a carrier in the case of other types converted to carrier; + indicates the probable year of completion of ships that never entered service during the war. **Displ.** is the full load (i.e., war capacity) displacement in thousands of tons. **A/C** indicates the maximum number of aircraft the carrier could carry, excluding the 12–15 disassembled aircraft often found on Japanese carriers, since they could not operate all aircraft for which they were rated. **Index** is the number of aircraft per thousand tons of displacement, an indication of how efficient the ship was in terms of carrying the maximum number of aircraft. **Rank** gives the relative standing of the carriers, based on Index figure, with "1" indicating the greatest efficiency; obviously, the more aircraft a carrier could carry the better she was.

atively high actual sortie rate, while British carriers were much worse off, a further consequence of their preference for armoring their carriers. Escort carriers usually had a very high fuel capacity because they were all built on commercial hulls, often tanker designs. Their very high sortie ratings must be compared with their limited aircraft capacity and their very low speed. Interestingly, the ship with the greatest amount of fuel available per aircraft was the Japanese HOSHO, which was already obsolete at the start of the war and could carry only a handful of airplanes.

Carriers were almost always short of fuel due to constant aircraft operations, most of which were noncombatant in nature (patrolling, training, administrative movements, and so forth). Prudence dictated that a carrier always have sufficient avgas on hand for combat operations, during which the number of sorties would climb rapidly. Thus they were always slowing down to take on additional avgas from fleet tankers. Carrier captains constantly kept a close eye on their avgas supply, and much time and effort went into getting back to a port for refueling, or meeting up with a tanker for underway replenishment.

Another interesting aspect of carrier operations often overlooked is the number of men available to operate the ship and the aircraft (pages 27–28).

Combat operations, particularly early in the war, usually resulted in the loss of most of a carrier's aircraft, either destroyed outright or damaged beyond repair. It was also normal to lose more aircraft from non-combat accidents than from enemy fire. Thus carriers constantly had to replenish their supply of aircraft. Pilots tended to be more durable than aircraft, but these highly trained men also had

AVIATION FUEL CAPACITY EFFICIENCY

Class	Navy	Type	Com.	Displ.	A/C	Avgas Data Full	Load	Sorties	Rank
Activity	Br.	CVE	'42	14.5	10	20.0	2.0	6.7	24
Akagi	Jap.	CV	'27	42.8	72	255.0	3.5	11.8	8
Ameer	Br.	CVE	'43	15.6	20	35.0	1.8	5.8	30
Aquila	It.	CV	'43+	27.8	66	72.0	1.1	3.6	41
Archer	Br.	CVE	'41	13.0	16	42.0	2.6	8.8	13
Ark Royal	Br.	CV	'38	28.1	60	100.0	1.7	5.6	32
Attacker	Br.	CVE	'42	10.4	20	50.0	2.5	8.3	17
Audacity	Br.	CVE	'41	10.4	6	10.0	1.7	5.6	33
Avenger	Br.	CVE	'42	10.4	15	36.0	2.4	8.0	21
Bearn	Fr.	CV	'27	28.4	40	26.0	0.7	2.2	44
Bogue	U.S.	CVE	'42	14.1	28	100.0	3.6	11.9	7
Casablanca	U.S.	CVE	'43	10.9	27	100.0	3.7	12.3	5
Centaur	Br.	CVL	'46	24.9	42	75.0	1.8	6.0	27
Colossus	Br.	CVL	'44	18.3	48	80.0	1.7	5.6	31
Commencement Bay	U.S.	CVE	'44	21.7	33	120.0	3.6	12.1	6
Courageous	Br.	CV	'28	26.5	48	34.5	0.7	2.4	43
Eagle II	Br.	CV	'45+	46.5	80	103.3	1.3	4.3	39
Essex	U.S.	CV	'42	34.9	91	240.0	2.6	8.8	12
Furious	Br.	CV	'25	22.5	36	22.0	0.6	2.0	45
Graf Zeppelin	Ger.	CV	'42+	37.0	42	65.0	1.5	5.2	34
Hiryu	Jap.	CV	'39	21.9	64	150.0	2.3	7.8	22
Hosho	Jap.	CVL	'22	10.0	12	98.0	8.2	27.2	1
Illustrious	Br.	CV	'40	28.7	36	50.5	1.4	4.7	38
Implacable	Br.	CV	'44	32.6	54	94.7	1.8	5.8	29
Independence	U.S.	CVL	'43	14.8	30	120.0	4.0	13.3	4
Indomitable	Br.	CV	'41	29.7	52	75.1	1.4	4.8	36
Kaga	Jap.	CV	'28	43.7	81	225.0	2.8	9.3	11
Lexington	U.S.	CV	'27	43.1	96	137.5	1.4	4.8	37
Long Island	U.S.	CVE	'41	14.3	16	100.0	6.3	20.8	2
Majestic	Br.	CVL	'45	18.1	37	75.0	2.0	6.8	23
Malta	Br.	CV	'46+	57.7	81	160.0	2.0	6.6	25
Midway	U.S.	CV	'45	59.9	137	350.0	2.6	8.5	15
Ranger	U.S.	CV	'34	17.6	76	135.0	1.8	5.9	28
Ryujo	Jap.	CVL	'33	13.7	37	47.0	1.3	4.2	40
Saipan	U.S.	CVL	'46	17.8	48	140.0	2.9	9.7	10
Sangamon	U.S.	CVE	'42	24.3	30	120.0	4.0	13.3	3
Shinano	Jap.	CV	'44	71.9	70	171.0	2.4	8.1	20
Shokaku	Jap.	CV	'41	32.1	72	187.0	2.6	8.7	14
Soryu	Jap.	CV	'37	19.8	63	96.0	1.5	5.1	35
Taiho	Jap.	CV	'44	37.7	53	176.0	3.3	11.1	9
Unicorn	Br.	CVL	'43	20.6	35	36.0	1.0	3.4	42
Unryu	Jap.	CV	'44	22.9	65	162.0	2.5	8.3	18
Vindex	Br.	CVE	'43	17.3	21	52.0	2.5	8.3	19
Yorktown	U.S.	CV	'37	25.5	96	178.0	1.9	6.2	26

Class, Navy, Com., Displ., and **A/C** are the same as for the previous chart. This list is somewhat shorter than the previous one, due primarily to the extreme difficulty of securing information on the avgas capacity of some carriers, even a half-century after the war. **Full** is the carrier's avgas capacity in thousands of gallons. **Load** gives the thousands of gallons available per aircraft carrier. **Sorties** indicates the number of missions each airplane could undertake on the basis of the ship's avgas supply, using a notional average of about 300 gallons per mission. The higher the sortie figure the better the carrier. **Rank** indicates the relative efficiency of the carrier, in terms of the number of sorties, the highest being "1."

MANPOWER EFFICIENCY

Class	Navy	Type	Com.	Displ.	A/C	Crew	Ratio	Rank
Activity	Br.	CVE	'42	14.5	10	700	70.0	58
Akagi	Jap.	CV	'27	42.8	72	1,600	22.2	11
Ameer	Br.	CVE	'43	15.6	20	646	32.3	35
Aquila	It.	CV	'43+	27.8	66	1,420	21.5	8
Archer	Br.	CVE	'41	13.0	16	555	34.7	45
Argus	Br.	CV	'18	17.7	18	373	20.7	7
Ark Royal	Br.	CV	'38	28.1	60	1,600	26.7	21
Attacker	Br.	CVE	'42	10.4	20	646	32.3	34
Avenger	Br.	CVE	'42	10.4	15	555	37.0	47
Bearn	Fr.	CV	'27	28.4	40	865	21.6	9
Bogue	U.S.	CVE	'42	14.1	28	890	31.8	31
Campania	Br.	CVE	'44	16.2	18	700	38.9	50
Casablanca	U.S.	CVE	'43	10.9	27	860	31.9	32
Chitose	Jap.	CVL	'44	15.3	30	800	26.7	20
Colossus	Br.	CVL	'44	18.3	48	1,300	27.1	22
Commencement Bay	U.S.	CVE	'44	21.7	33	1,066	32.3	36
Courageous	Br.	CV	'28	26.5	48	1,200	25.0	17
Eagle	Br.	CV	'23	27.2	20	834	41.7	51
Eagle II	Br.	CV	'45+	46.5	80	2,250	28.1	24
Essex	U.S.	CV	'42	34.9	91	2,682	29.5	27
Furious	Br.	CV	'25	22.5	36	1,218	33.8	42
Graf Zeppelin	Ger.	CV	'42+	37.0	42	1,760	41.9	52
Hermes	Br.	CVL	'23	13.2	12	664	55.3	56
Hiryu	Jap.	CV	'39	21.9	64	1,100	17.2	3
Hosho	Jap.	CVL	'22	10.0	12	550	45.8	54
Ibuki	Jap.	CVL	'45+	14.6	27	1,015	37.6	48
Illustrious	Br.	CV	'40	28.7	36	1,200	33.3	40
Implacable	Br.	CV	'44	32.6	54	1,400	25.9	18
Independence	U.S.	CVL	'43	14.8	30	1,569	52.3	55
Indomitable	Br.	CV	'41	29.7	52	2,000	38.5	49
Joffre	Fr.	CV	'42	28.7	40	1,250	31.3	29
Junyo	Jap.	CV	'42	28.3	53	1,200	22.6	12
Kaga	Jap.	CV	'28	43.7	81	1,340	16.5	2
Kaiyo	Jap.	CVE	'43	16.5	24	829	34.5	44
Lexington	U.S.	CV	'27	43.1	96	2,122	22.1	10
Long Island	U.S.	CVE	'41	14.3	16	970	60.6	57
Majestic	Br.	CVL	'45	18.1	37	1,100	29.7	28
Malta	Br.	CV	'46+	57.7	81	3,520	43.5	53
Midway	U.S.	CV	'45	59.9	137	2,510	18.3	5
Ranger	U.S.	CV	'34	17.6	76	1,788	23.5	14
Ryuho	Jap.	CVL	'42	16.7	31	989	31.9	33
Ryujo	Jap.	CVL	'33	13.7	37	600	16.2	1
Saipan	U.S.	CVL	'46	17.8	48	1,553	32.4	37
Sangamon	U.S.	CVE	'42	24.3	30	1,080	36.0	46
Shinano	Jap.	CV	'44	71.9	70	2,400	34.3	43
Shinyo	Jap.	CVE	'43	20.6	33	942	28.5	26

				MANPOWER EFFICIENCY (*Continued*)					
Class	Navy	Type	Com.	Displ.	A/C	Crew	Ratio	Rank
Shokaku	Jap.	CV	'41	32.1	72	1,660	23.1	13
Soryu	Jap.	CV	'37	19.8	63	1,100	17.5	4
Taiho	Jap.	CV	'44	37.7	53	1,751	33.0	38
Taiyo	Jap.	CVE	'41	19.7	27	747	27.7	23
Unicorn	Br.	CVL	'43	20.6	35	1,094	31.3	30
Unryu	Jap.	CV	'44	22.9	65	1,595	24.5	16
Vindex	Br.	CVE	'43	17.3	21	700	33.3	41
Wasp	U.S.	CV	'40	18.5	76	2,167	28.5	25
Yorktown	U.S.	CV	'37	25.5	96	1,890	19.7	6
Zuiho	Jap.	CVL	'40	14.3	30	785	26.2	19

Class, Navy, Type, Com., Displ., and **A/C** are the same as for the previous table. Warships are notorious for having large crews. Not only do the crewmen have to operate the ship, which almost always has more powerful and more complex engines than merchant vessels, but also they have to maintain and operate extensive electrical systems, communications networks, damage control facilities, and, of course, weapons. As a result, aircraft carriers have even larger crews than most warships of comparable size. This table compares virtually all of the World War II-era carriers on the basis of their manpower-to-aircraft ratio. **Crew** is the normal complement, including airgroup. **Ratio** is the number of crewmen per aircraft. **Rank** rates the carriers on the basis of the lowest to highest ratios, with "1" being lowest. It is interesting to note that escort carriers have relatively poor ratios, while purpose-built carriers have relatively good ones.

to be replaced as their numbers dwindled. Thus the carriers with larger capacity for aircraft, avgas, and crews were much better prepared for combat than larger carriers that were not.

Ref: Blair, *The Fast Carriers*; Chesneua, *Aircraft Carriers of the World*; Friedman, *United States Aircraft Carriers*; Roscoe, *On the Seas and in the Skies*.

Aircraft Carriers, Imperial Japanese Army

In order to ferry airplanes to distant theaters, the Imperial Army converted merchant ships to serve as aircraft transports. Although these vessels looked like escort carriers, their appearance was deceiving. They carried 8 to 35 aircraft, depending upon type. But they weren't designed to serve as convoy escorts. Their principal function was to move airplanes from one place to another. These ships are occasionally listed as escort carriers in some works on the Pacific War, and this has given rise to the legend that the Imperial Army built its own aircraft carriers to spite the Imperial Navy.

The real story is quite amusing. From an operational perspective it is cheaper and more efficient to move aircraft fully assembled, than crated up. Indeed, American experience demonstrated that disassembled fighter aircraft required up to 250 manhours to put back together, and the job required trained technicians. However, unlike the US Navy, the Imperial Navy refused to provide the aircraft transportation services that the Imperial Army required. So the army procured its own transports, which looked like carriers, each with a short flight deck. The Japanese Army "carriers" had a limited capability to operate aircraft, to the extent that lightly loaded airplanes could fly off to nearby land bases, but their flight decks were too short to permit aircraft to land. This was enough, since many airbases were on islands that lacked port facilities to unload the aircraft the traditional way. The Allies used true escort carriers for the same purpose, allowing army pilots to make one carrier takeoff in order to reach their island air base.

Akitsu Maru (11,800 tons standard, 20 aircraft capacity, 403-foot flight deck) began as an ocean liner in 1939, but was taken over incomplete by the army while still on the ways, and converted to a "landing ship with flight deck" in 1941–42. She had facilities to store and service 20 landing craft, as well as her aircraft, and could make 20 knots. She was torpedoed by *Queenfish* (SS-393) on 15 November 1944 off Kyushu.

Nigitsu Maru was a sistership to *Akitsu Maru*, laid down in 1941 and converted in 1942–43. She succumbed to a TORPEDO from *Hake* (SS-256) some 700 miles east of FORMOSA on January 12, 1944.

Shimane Maru (11,800 tons standard, 12 aircraft capacity, 508-foot flight deck) was converted from a tanker 1944–45, but was shortly ordered converted into a coal burning freighter, which work was in hand when she was sunk by US carrier aircraft on 24 July 1945.

Otakisan Maru, sister to *Shimane Maru*, was still under conversion when the war ended. Her incomplete hull was accidentally mined shortly after the armistice.

Yamashiro Maru (10,100 tons standard, 8 aircraft capacity, 410–foot flight deck) was converted from a tanker in 1944, on an even more austere plan than *Shimane Maru*. She was sunk by US carrier aircraft on February 17, 1945, shortly after work had been ordered to convert her into a coal-burning freighter.

Chigusa Maru, a sister to *Yamashiro Maru*, was taken over for conversion in 1944, but the work was still incomplete when the war ended. She was subsequently rebuilt as a tanker and entered commercial service.

Kumano Maru (8,000 tons standard, up to 35 aircraft capacity, 360–foot flight deck) was converted from a freighter still on the ways in 1944–45. Classed as a "landing ship with flight deck," she could operate up to 25 landing craft, the exact number affecting the number of aircraft she could carry. She survived the war and was converted to a freighter.

The Imperial Army had plans to convert three more vessels, two of which would have been sisters to *Shimane Maru*, but work was never begun.

Aircraft Carriers, Training, US Navy

Training pilots to operate from aircraft carriers requires the use of aircraft carriers. Even before PEARL HARBOR, anticipating that in wartime there might be a serious shortage of operational carriers—at one point in late 1942 only three were available worldwide—the US Navy made a remarkable decision, one that resulted in the commissioning of the only sweet (non-salt) water, coal-fired, paddlewheel aircraft carriers ever. In early 1942 the navy requisitioned the Great Lakes excursion steamer *Seeandbee*, completed shortly before World War I, for conversion into a training carrier at Buffalo, New York. The ship's superstructure was completely removed, and she was provided with a wooden flight deck, a set of arrester wires, and a small island. The ship's original coal-burning boilers and paddle wheels were retained. Mounting no armament, the ship had no facilities to service aircraft, and could not even refuel them. The result was the USS *Sable*, classed as a "miscellaneous vessel," IX-64. A very austere "aircraft carrier," *Sable* could be used to train pilots to land and take off. So successful was the experiment that, shortly after *Sable* entered service in August 1942, the excursion steamer *Greater Buffalo*, which had entered service in the 1920s, was taken in hand for conversion, completing in March 1943 as USS *Wolverine* (IX-81). (See page 30.)

The two ships operated throughout the war, and were even provided with advanced landing aids to assist the young pilots in learning their craft. It is not known how many men trained aboard the two vessels, but the figure is certainly in the tens of thousands. Both were scrapped after the war.

Aircraft Carriers, US Shortage of, 1942–1943

At the beginning of the Pacific War the United States had eight aircraft carriers of all types, of which only three were in the Pacific (LEXINGTON, *Saratoga*, and *Enterprise*), facing 10 Japanese carri-

THE PADDLE WHEEL CARRIERS						
Ship	Displ.	Dimensions	HP	Speed	Crew	Scrapped
Sable	7,200	484.5'x58.25'x15.5'	8,000	16 kts.	270	1947
Wolverine	8,000	519'x58'x15.5'	10,000	18 kts.	300	1948

ers. Although reinforcements arrived from the Atlantic, the number of carriers available remained low through 1942 due to loss (*Lexington*, YORKTOWN, WASP, *Hornet*) or damage (*Saratoga*, *Enterprise*). As a result, at the conclusion of the Battle of SANTA CRUZ in October 1942, the US carrier fleet was down to three active vessels, *Enterprise*, which remained in service despite some damage; the escort carrier LONG ISLAND, in the Pacific; and the little RANGER, in the Atlantic. The only other carrier available was *Saratoga*, undergoing repairs from a TORPEDO hit. Although the Japanese actually had more carriers available at that time, their aircrews had been so badly depleted that they were unable to capitalize on their advantage.

Desperate to increase its carrier strength in the Pacific, the US Navy—with great reluctance—asked the ROYAL NAVY for the loan of a carrier shortly after Santa Cruz. The Royal Navy—with equally great reluctance—arranged for HMS *Victorious* to be made available in March of 1943. As the ship had to be reequipped with American aircraft and trained to operate with US forces, she did not enter service until May of 1943, and was returned to British control that August. Even before *Victorious* reached the Pacific *Enterprise* and *Saratoga* were back in full service, and before she joined the fleet, in May, several SANGAMON CLASS escort carriers were operating in the Pacific as well, while the new fleet carrier ESSEX and seven new escort carriers were available in the Atlantic.

The carrier shortage might have been fatal had the Imperial Navy possessed a realistic pilot training program before the war. However, although the Imperial Navy had a lot of carriers during this period (*Shokaku*, *Zuikaku*, *Hiyo*, *Junyo*, ZUIHO, *Ryuho*, and *Hosho*, plus several escorts), it didn't have many well-trained pilots. Had the Japanese essayed operations with the partially trained air crews that they had by early 1943, they might have seriously affected Allied operations. As it was, the carrier shortage greatly slowed the tempo of Allied operations in the Pacific.

Aircraft Squadrons, US Navy Designations

The US Navy and Marines used letter codes to designate aviation squadrons. There were two types of squadrons: heavier than air, denoted with a V, and lighter than air (i.e., blimps, barrage balloons, and, in the early 1930s, zeppelins), denoted by a Z. The initial letter was followed by one or more letters to indicate the specific function of the aircraft in that squadron. Following the letters was a number, to identify a specific squadron. The most commonly used letter designations during World War II were:

VB	Bombing Squadron
VC	Composite Squadron (bombers, fighters, etc., mixed)
VD	Photo Reconnaissance
VF	Fighting Squadron (fighter aircraft)
VP	Patrol Squadron
VPB	Patrol Bombing Squadron
VR	Transport Squadron
VS	Scouting Squadron
VT	Torpedo Squadron

A Marine Corps squadron was indicated by the addition of an M to the code: VMF, Marine fighter squadron; VMB, Marine bomber squadron; and so forth.

Aircraft Table

The Pacific War was truly the Air War, with virtually every type of Allied aircraft serving there.

This included several prominent types that did not see service in Europe, such as the F4U CORSAIR fighter and the B-29 heavy bomber, not to mention less well known types like the P-26, B-10, B-18, WIRRAWAY, B-32, and others. Both carrier and the more numerous land-based aircraft played vital roles in the Pacific. The table on pages 32–34 includes the more numerous types.

Aircraft Types, Development

At best, airplane designers are ultimately reduced to making a series of compromises among a number of mutually desirable, and mutually exclusive, characteristics, such as speed, range, durability, climb rate, and munitions load. Designing airplanes capable of operating from aircraft carriers requires even more compromises. An aircraft designer must understand certain basic assumptions about the way in which the airplane is to be used in order to determine which characteristics are most desirable.

These assumptions vary between nations, and even between sister services of the same nation, each of which may have its own design philosophy. And that philosophy may be rooted not only in perceived military necessity but also in political expedience, interservice rivalry, and sheer obstinacy. The carrier aircraft that saw service in World War II, most spectacularly in the Pacific, reflected three very different design philosophies: British, American, and Japanese.

Britain's ROYAL NAVY had pioneered the development of the aircraft carrier, and made the first carrier air strikes as early as 1917. However, with the formation of the Royal Air Force (RAF) in 1918, the Royal Navy began to fall behind in the evolution of naval aviation. The RAF was given control over naval aircraft. Dependent as it was upon the heavy bomber-oriented Royal Air Force for its aircraft designs and pilots, the Royal Navy's air arm ended up decidedly inferior to the US or Japanese naval air service. With the RAF largely indifferent to the unique problems of carrier aviation, British carriers, in many ways excellent vessels, went to sea with equally indifferent aircraft. For example, the performance characteristics of the FULMAR, introduced in 1940, were actually inferior to those of the Japanese Claude or the American F2A BUFFALO, which entered service in 1936 and 1938 respectively and were both considered obsolete by 1940. Further complicating matters was the fact that the Royal Navy never permitted an aviation officer to command one of its carriers, thereby failing to develop a critical mass of aviation-oriented officers, who might have been able to go to bat for the Senior Service.

Despite these handicaps, Royal Navy carriers performed yeoman service on numerous occasions, most spectacularly at Taranto Harbor on the night of November 11–12, 1940, when several Italian battleships were sunk or disabled in a nighttime airstrike that forecast PEARL HARBOR. British carriers that operated in the Indian Ocean during 1942–45, often with striking success against Japanese land and naval targets, were fortunate in not having to meet any of their Japanese cousins. Had this been the case, the outcome would have been a foregone conclusion, at least in 1942. Indeed, when Britain sent a carrier task force to the central Pacific in early 1945 it was equipped largely with American-made aircraft.

The US Navy got into the aircraft carrier business in the early 1920s, at about the same time as the Imperial Navy and nearly a decade after the Royal Navy. Several factors fostered the development of American carrier aviation. Quite early, command of aircraft carriers was reserved to aviation-qualified officers, providing flyers with a career path to high rank. This caused a flock of mid-level and even fairly senior officers to get their wings. William F. HALSEY got his at age 52. Moreover, despite occasional acrimony, relations between "brown-shoe" officers (i.e., aviation) and "black-shoe" officers (i.e., battleship) were friendlier than those prevailing in the British or Japanese navies. Although they squabbled over the details, American carrier and battleship admirals more or less agreed that carriers might have an important role to play in a major Pacific War, albeit disagreeing

AIRCRAFT TABLE

Nation	Type	Designation/Name	Builder	Year	Built	AA	AS	Speed	Reach	Wght.	Armament	Load	Crew	Range	CV?	Service
U.S.	BmrM	A-20 Havoc/Bosto	Douglas	1940	6,800	2	6	282	405	10.9	5x12.7mm	4,000	2	890	N	Air
U.S.	BmrM	A-26 Invader	Douglas	1944	2,500	3	11	324	550	15.8	12x12.7mm	4,000	2	1,210	N	Air
U.S.	BmrM	A-28 Hudson	Lockheed	1939	2,800	3	2	246	955	8.3	7x7.62mm	1,400	6	2,100	N	Air
U.S.	BmrL	A-35 Vengeance	Vultee	1942	1,528	2	3	279	236	6.1	4x12.7mm	1,000	2	520	N	Air
Jap.	Ftr	A5M Claude	Mitsubishi	1936	1,000	5	0	237	295	1.6	2x7.7mm	60	1	650	Y	Navy
Jap.	Ftr	A6M Zero/Zeke	Mitsubishi	1941	10,937	6	3	307	386	2.7	2x20mm, 2x7.7mm	550	1	850	Y	Navy
Jap.	Ftr	A6M2-N Rufe	Mitsubishi	1942	327	3	3	307	364	3.1	2x20mm, 2x7.7mm	550	1	800	N	Navy
U.S.	BmrT	AD Skyraider	Douglas	1946	3,200	3	14	318	500	11.3	4x20mm	8,000	1	1,100	Y	Navy
Br.	BmrT	Albacore	Fairey	1940	803	2	2	140	364	4.7	3x7.62mm	2,000	2	800	Y	Navy
U.S.	BmrT	AM-1 Mauler	Martin	1946	750	3	13	319	500	12.0	4x20mm	7,000	1	1,100	Y	Navy
U.S.	BmrL	B-10	Martin	1934	300	2	0	260	909	6.9	3x7.62mm	2,260	4	2,000	N	Air
U.S.	BmrH	B-17 Flying Fort	Boeing	1939	12,731	4	13	249	773	29.0	13x12.7mm	8,000	10	1,700	N	Air
U.S.	BmrM	B-18 Bolo	Douglas	1937	375	3	3	197	393	12.5	6x12.7mm	2,500	7	865	N	Air
U.S.	BmrH	B-24 Liberator	Consolidated	1941	18,800	4	13	261	818	29.2	10x12.7mm	8,000	9	1,800	N	Air
U.S.	BmrM	B-25 Mitchell	North American	1940	9,800	4	7	239	500	18.9	3x7.62mm, 4+12.7mm	3,200	5	1,100	N	Air
U.S.	BmrM	B-26 Marauder	Martin	1941	5,150	3	7	249	477	17.3	5x7.62mm	5,800	5	1,050	N	Air
U.S.	BmrH	B-29 Superfortre	Boeing	1944	3,100	4	28	355	1,614	64.0	11x12.7mm	20,000	13	3,550	N	Air
U.S.	BmrH	B-36	Convair	1947	382	5	100	450	4,545	162.0	16x20mm	84,000	15	10,000	N	Air
Jap.	BmrT	B5N Kate	Nakajima	1937	1,150	2	2	205	241	4.1	3-4x7.7mm	1,750	2	530	Y	Navy
Jap.	BmrT	B6N Jill	Nakajima	1944	1,270	2	4	259	409	5.4	2-3x7.7mm	1,750	2	900	Y	Navy
Jap.	BmrT	B7A Grace	Aichi	1944	100	2	5	305	455	6.5	2x20mm, 7.92mm	2,200	2	1,000	Y	Navy
Br.	BmrT	Barracuda	Fairey	1941	2,500	2	2	198	250	6.5	2x7.7mm	1,500	2	550	Y	Navy
Br.	BmrL	Battle	Fairey	1935	2,400	2	0	209	409	4.8	2x7.7mm	1,000	3	900	N	Air
Br.	FtrN	Beaufighter	Bristol	1940	5,560	3	4	287	591	11.5	4x20mm	2,100	2	1,300	N	Air
Br.	BmrT	Beaufort	Bristol	1939	2,100	2	2	230	405	9.6	5x7.7mm	1,500	3	890	N	Air
Br.	BmrL	Blenheim	Bristol	1936	5,400	2	0	266	1,045	6.5	5x7.7mm	1,300	3	2,300	N	Air
Jap.	DBmr	D3A Val	Aichi	1938	816	2	0	231	382	3.8	3x7.7mm	816	2	840	Y	Navy
Jap.	DBmr	D4Y Judy	Yokosuk	1942	2,319	3	3	313	518	3.9	2x7.7mm, 1x7.9mm	1,300	2	1,140	Y	Navy
Br.	BmrL	DH 98 Mosquito	de Havilland	1940	7,781	3	2	369	1,364	11.5	nil	2,000	2	3,000	N	Air
Br.	Ftr	DH 100 Vampire	de Havilland	1946	1,100	9	7	469	477	5.6	4x20mm	2,000	1	1,050	N	Air
Br.	Ftr	DH 103 Hornet	de Havilland	1945	420	8	7	472	1,182	9.4	4x20mm	2,000	1	2,600	N	Air
Jap.	Boat	E13A Jake	Aichi	1939	1,400	1	0	203	500	4.0	1x7.7mm	816	3	1,100	N	Navy
Jap.	Float	E16A Paul	Aichi	1944	252	1	3	250	341	4.1	1x7.7mm	1,000	3	750	N	Navy
Jap.	Float	E7K	Kawanishi	1934	530	1	0	149	455	3.3	1x7.7mm	500	3	1,000	N	Navy
Jap.	Float	F1M2 Pete	Mitsubishi	1940	1,114	3	0	200	409	2.5	3x7.7mm	120	2	900	N	Navy
U.S.	Ftr	F2A Buffalo	Brewster	1940	500	5	1	297	391	3.2	4x12.7mm	200	1	860	N	Navy
U.S.	Ftr	F4F Wildcat	Grumman	1939	7,900	5	2	276	305	3.6	6x12.7mm	500	1	670	Y	Navy
U.S.	Ftr	F4U Corsair	Chance-Vought	1943	11,100	8	7	408	441	6.3	4x20mm	3,000	1	970	Y	Navy
U.S.	Ftr	F6F Hellcat	Grumman	1942	12,275	6	5	322	373	6.3	6x12.7mm	2,000	1	820	Y	Navy

Nation	Type	Designation/Name	Builder	Year	Built	AA	AS	Speed	Reach	Wght.	Armament	Load	Crew	Range	CV?	Service
U.S.	Ftr	F6U Pirate	Chance-Vought	1948	30	8	7	521	545	11.1	4x12.7mm	2,000	1	1,200	Y	Navy
U.S.	Ftr	F7F Tigercat	Grumman	1945	210	9	8	371	432	11.6	4x20mm or 12.7mm	4,000	2	950	Y	Navy
U.S.	Ftr	F8F Bearcat	Grumman	1945	730	9	6	366	436	5.8	4x12.7mm	2,000	1	960	Y	Navy
U.S.	Ftr	FH-1 Phantom	McDonnell	1946	61	8	6	439	273	5.1	4x12.7mm	2,000	1	600	N	Navy
Br.	Ftr	Firefly	Fairey	1943	600	4	3	335	500	7.3	2x20mm	500	2	1,100	N	Air
U.S.	Ftr	FJ-1 Fury	Hawker	1946	31	8	6	391	273	5.6	4x20mm	2,000	1	600	Y	Navy
U.S.	Ftr	FR-1 Fireball	Ryan	1946	66	7	6	369	545	5.2	4x12.7mm	1,000	1	1,200	Y	Navy
Br.	Ftr	Fulmar	Fairey	1940	600	3	1	243	316	4.4	6x7.7mm	500	2	695	Y	Navy
Jap.	BmrM	G3M Nell	Mitsubishi	1936	1,050	2	1	200	636	8.0	1x20mm, 4x7.7mm	1,700	4	1,400	N	Navy
Jap.	BmrM	G4M Betty	Mitsubishi	1941	2,400	2	6	237	1,682	12.5	4x20mm, 1x7.7mm	2,200	4	3,700	N	Navy
Jap.	Boat	H6K Mavis	Kawanishi	1937	217	2	1	183	1,000	21.5	4x7.62mm	2,200	5	2,200	N	Navy
Jap.	Boat	H8K Emily	Kawanishi	1942	131	2	8	252	1,761	32.5	2x20mm, 4x7.7mm	4,400	10	3,875	N	Navy
Br.	Ftr	Hurricane	Hawker	1937	12,800	5	0	290	182	3.7	6x7.7mm	1,000	1	400	N	Air
Jap.	Ftr	J2M Jack	Mitsubishi	1943	450	7	3	370	257	3.3	2x20mm, 2x7.7mm	550	1	565	N	Air
Jap.	Ftr	J8M Shusui	Mitsubishi	1945	1	6	3	521	23	3.8	2x20mm		1	50	N	Air
Jap.	BmrM	Ki-21 Sally	Mitsubishi	1938	2,064	3	2	262	534	9.7	6x7.7mm	2,200	5	1,175	N	Air
Jap.	Ftr	Ki-27 Nate	Nakajima	1937	3,400	4	0	248	132	1.7	2x7.7mm	440	1	290	N	Air
Jap.	BmrL	Ki-30 Ann	Mitsubishi	1938	704	2	0	233	364	3.3	2x7.7mm	660	2	800	N	Air
Jap.	Ftr	Ki-43 Oscar	Nakajima	1941	5,900	5	2	287	409	2.6	2x12.7mm	550	1	900	N	Air
Jap.	Ftr	Ki-44 Tojo	Nakajima	1942	1,200	6	3	330	318	2.7	4x12.7mm	550	1	700	N	Air
Jap.	Ftr	Ki-45 Nick	Kawasaki	1942	1,701	4	2	295	364	5.2	1x20mm, 2x7.7mm	550	2	800	N	Air
Jap.	BmrM	Ki-46 Dinah	Mitsubishi	1941	1,700	3	1	370	814	5.0	1x7.7mm	0	5	1,790	N	Air
Jap.	BmrL	Ki-48 Lily	Kawasaki	1940	1,977	2	2	273	589	6.7	3x7.7mm	1,750	2	1,295	N	Air
Jap.	BmrM	Ki-49 Helen	Nakajima	1942	800	3	5	265	589	10.6	1x20mm, 6x7.7/12.7mm	2,200	8	1,295	N	Air
Jap.	BmrL	Ki-51 Sonia	Mitsubishi	1940	2,385	5	0	228	260	2.9	2x7.7mm	440	2	572	N	Air
Jap.	Ftr	Ki-61 Tony	Kawasaki	1942	2,791	5	2	320	289	3.2	2x12.7, 2x7.7mm	550	1	635	N	Air
Jap.	BmrM	Ki-67 Peggy	Mitsubishi	1944	700	4	6	291	932	13.7	1x20mm, 4x12.7mm	2,600	7	2,050	N	Air
Jap.	Ftr	Ki-84 Frank	Nakajima	1944	3,480	7	5	337	416	3.6	4x20mm	550	1	915	N	Air
Jap.	Ftr	Ki-100	Kawasaki	1945	396	6	4	341	491	3.5	2x12.7, 2x7.7mm	550	1	1,080	N	Air
Jap.	Ftr	Ki-102 Randy	Kawasaki	1944	238	4	5	313	491	7.3	1x57mm, 2x20mm, 1x12.5mm	1,100	2	1,080	N	Air
Jap.	Ftr	Ki-108	Kawasaki	1945	4	7	5	324	545	7.6	1x57mm, 2x20mm, 1x12.5mm	550	1	1,200	N	Air
Jap.	Ftr	Ki-109	Mitsubishi	1945	22	5	6	291	932	10.8	1x75mm, 4x12.7mm	550	2	2,050	N	Air
Br.	Ftr	Meteor	Gloster	1944	3,550	7	6	514	273	7.1	4x20mm	2,000	1	600	N	Navy
Jap.	BmrL	MXY-7 Baka	Yokosuka	1945	852	1	4	403	50	2.1	nil	1,700	1	50	N	Air
Jap.	Ftr	N1K1 George	Kawanishi	1944	1,417	6	6	321	409	4.8	2x20mm, 2x7.7mm	2,200	1	900	N	Air
U.S.	Ftr	P-26 Peashooter	Boeing	1934	147	3	0	203	142	1.3	2x7.62mm/12.7mm	240	1	313	N	Air
U.S.	Ftr	P-35	Severski	1941	76	3	1	245	455	2.8	1x7.62mm, 1x12.7mm	100	1	1,000	N	Air
Br.	Ftr	P-36 Hawk	Curtis	1936	350	3	0	261	326	2.7	2x7.62mm	250	1	718	N	Air
U.S.	Ftr	P-38 Lightning	Lockheed	1942	8,600	7	4	360	177	9.7	1x20mm, 4x12.7mm	1,600	1	390	N	Air

AIRCRAFT TABLE (Continued)

Nation	Type	Designation/Name	Builder	Year	Built	AA	AS	Speed	Reach	Wght.	Armament	Load	Crew	Range	CV?	Service
U.S.	Ftr	P-39 Airacobra	Bell	1941	7,500	4	2	334	268	3.8	1x37mm, 4x12.7mm	500	1	590	N	Air
U.S.	Ftr	P-40 Tomahawk	Curtis	1939	13,200	4	2	328	95	4.0	6x12.7mm	500	1	208	N	Air
U.S.	Ftr	P-47 Thunderbolt	Republic	1942	15,660	7	7	372	233	8.8	8x12.7mm	3,000	1	512	N	Air
U.S.	Ftr	P-51 Mustang	North American	1942	15,586	9	5	380	491	5.2	4x20mm	2,000	1	1,080	N	Air
U.S.	Ftr	P-59 Aircomet	Bell	1945	190	6	5	359	273	6.2	1x37mm, 3x12.7mm	1,500	1	600	N	Air
U.S.	Ftr	P-61 Black Widow	Northrop	1943	691	7	6	326	395	17.2	4x20mm, 4x12.7mm	1,000	3	868	N	Air
U.S.	Ftr	P-63 Kingcobra	Bell	1943	3,303	6	4	354	177	4.8	1x37mm, 4x12.7mm	1,500	1	390	N	Air
U.S.	Ftr	P-66	Vultee	1941	144	5	1	340	386	7.3	4x7.62mm, 2x12.7mm	100	1	850	N	Air
Jap.	BmrM	P1Y1 Frances	Yokosuka	1943	1,082	2	4	307	491	10.5	2x20mm	2,000	7	1,080	N	Navy
U.S.	Boat	PB2Y Coronado	Consolidated	1942	210	2	5	298	409	30.3	8x12.7mm	1,200	11	900	N	Navy
U.S.	Boat	PBM Mariner	Martin	1941	1,600	2	6	195	1,000	27.3	8x12.7mm	4,000	9	2,200	N	Navy
U.S.	Boat	PBY Catalina	Consolidated	1936	3,300	2	3	152	909	16.0	3x7.62mm, 2x12.7mm	4,000	7	2,000	N	Navy
U.S.	BmrM	PV-1 Ventura	Lockheed	1942	2,145	2	5	271	636	14.0	2x12.7mm	3,000	6	1,400	N	Air
U.S.	DBmr	SB2A Buccaneer	Brewster	1941	750	1	2	200	409		2x7.62mm	1,000	1	900	Y	Navy
U.S.	DBmr	SB2C Helldiver	Curtis	1943	5,000	3	4	255	759	6.3	5x12.7mm	1,000	2	1,670	Y	Navy
U.S.	DBmr	SBD Dauntless	Douglas	1940	5,936	2	2	221	440	4.3	4x.30/12.7mm	1,000	2	968	Y	Navy
U.S.	Float	SC Seahawk	Curtis	1944	9	1	4	272	247	4.0	2x12.7mm	1,000	2	543	N	Navy
Br.	Ftr	Seafire	Supermarine	1942	2,000	6	3	339	273	7.0	8x7.7mm	500	1	600	Y	Navy
U.S.	Float	SO3C Seamew	Curtis	1942	800	1	0	275	455		2x7.62mm	0	2	1,000	N	Navy
U.S.	Float	SOC Seagull	Curtis	1935	258	1	0	250	455		2x7.62mm	200	2	1,000	N	Navy
Br.	Ftr	Spitfire	Supermarine	1935	20,500	6	0	330	273	7.0	8x7.7mm	500	1	600	N	Air
Br.	BmrT	Swordfish	Fairey	1935	2,391	2	0	139	455	4.1	2x7.62mm	1,500	2	1,000	Y	Navy
U.S.	BmrT	TBD-1 Devastator	Douglas	1937	1,000	2	0	179	282	4.6	2x7.62mm	1,000	2	620	Y	Navy
U.S.	BmrT	TBF Avenger	Grumman	1942	9,830	3	4	240	399	8.1	1x7.62mm, 3x12.7mm	2,000	3	877	Y	Navy
Br.	FBmr	Tempest	Hawker	1944	920	6	5	384	332	6.2	4x20mm	2,000	1	730	N	Air
Br.	FBmr	Typhoon	Hawker	1941	3,330	6	4	358	200	6.0	4x20mm	2,000	1	440	N	Air
Br.	BmrT	Vildebeeste	Vickers	1937	202	2	0	156	284	3.8	2x7.62mm	1,500	2	625	N	Air
Au.	BmrL	Wirraway	Commonwealth	1937	755	1	0	200	282	2.8	2x7.62mm	200	2	620	N	Air

Nation = nation of origin. **Type** = type of aircraft. Ftr = fighter; DBmr = dive bomber (one engine, dives down on target); BmrH = heavy bomber (usually four engines); BmrL = light bomber (one engine); BmrM = medium bomber (two engines); BmrT = torpedo bomber; Boat = flying boat; Float = float plane; FrB = fighter-bomber; FrN = night fighter. **Designation/Name** = official designation and name; Allied nickname for Japanese aircraft. **Year** = year first in service. **Built** = number manufactured during World War II. **AA** = air combat capability, ranked from 9 (the best) to 1 (the worst). Pilot quality has the most influence on the outcome of air-to-air combat since the best pilots in the worst fighters can beat the worst pilots in the best planes. **AS** = anti-surface capability on a scale of 100 (the most bombs carried over the longest distance and dropped with the most accuracy) to 0 (no bombing capability at all). Basically the ability to put a lot of bombs on a surface (land or sea) target. In practice, the crews have to be specifically trained for hitting land and/or sea targets, as a different set of skills is required to handle moving ships at sea. Bombers operating from carriers usually had crews trained to bomb ships. **Speed** = speed, maximum, in miles per hour. **Reach** = maximum one-way trip possible, in miles. **Wght.** = weight. **Armament** = machine guns or cannon carried, number of each weapon and the caliber of the weapon in millimeters (25.4mm = one inch). **Load** = bomb/torpedo load possible, in kilograms. **Crew** = crew size. **Range** = maximum operational round-trip range, in miles. **CV?** Does the aircraft normally operate from carriers—Y = Yes, N = No. **Service** = branch of the military that is the primary user of the aircraft. Air = army or air force, while Navy = navy.

on whether they might be decisive. The speed with which carriers took over as the principal arm of sea power after Pearl Harbor was one result of this attitude.

Virtually from the moment airplanes were invented, the Japanese Navy was very air-minded. Having carefully observed the development of British naval aviation during World War I, Japan promptly built the first genuine aircraft carrier, HOSHO (completed 1922). The evolution of carrier aviation in the Imperial Navy closely paralleled that in the US Navy. There were, however, critical differences. Japanese aircraft design policy, for example, stressed speed, range, and maneuverability, while the US Navy stressed pilot safety and aircraft reliability and durability.

In some ways the Japanese attitude was superior to the American, for it recognized the essentially offensive character of carrier warfare. Aircraft carriers are purely offensive weapons. Thus, the greater operational reach of Japanese carrier aircraft was of considerable advantage.

However, although unlike the British the Japanese developed a crop of senior naval officers who appreciated carrier capabilities, they produced few who were completely able to break free from traditional notions of the battleship as the ultimate arbiter of sea power. This is, perhaps, a moot point, since their basic problem was one of quantity. The critical flaw in Japanese naval aviation was Japan's limited ability to mass produce, in increasing order of importance, carriers, aircraft, and pilots. As a result, once losses began to mount, as they did even during the victorious months from Pearl Harbor to the CORAL SEA, the quality of Japan's naval air arm began to decline. The Japanese effectively admitted that they couldn't resolve this problem when they resorted to KAMIKAZE tactics. By March 1945 all of Japan's remaining aircraft carriers had been laid up, partially due to a fuel shortage, but primarily for lack of pilots.

Although the Japanese were able to expand aircraft and aircraft carrier production by a consider-able margin, through new construction and the conversion of other types of vessels, they were unable to develop engines to compete with the higher powered aircraft that the United States began introducing in mid-1942. By late 1942 the Japanese, who had the best carrier aircraft at the time of Pearl Harbor, were beginning to fall behind as newer and better American aircraft became increasingly available. And, of course, they were never able to solve their pilot production problems.

The marked differences among American and Japanese carrier aircraft design philosophies make it difficult to compare aircraft. Although the greater operational reach of Japanese carrier aircraft was theoretically a decisive advantage, it was offset by American radar and superior antiaircraft capacity. Moreover, US pilots learned to cope tactically with the speedier and more maneuverable Zeros.

Japanese aircraft advantages began to evaporate after 1942. With that, attrition and industrial potential became the ultimate arbiters of victory. Since the United States was able not only to expand aircraft and carrier production far more rapidly than Japan (while simultaneously introducing more advanced aircraft), but also to expand pilot production enormously, the decision was inevitable.

But it wasn't just carrier-borne aircraft that ruled the seas. Land-based bombers also played a decisive role.

Although the American and British air forces favored the four-engined heavy bomber as the decisive arm of air power, most other air forces looked to the smaller two-engined medium bomber.

These had the disadvantage of a relatively low bomb capacity (one or two tons as against four or five), but were usually faster, more maneuverable, and much cheaper to build.

Operationally, the two-engined bomber was supposed to do the same things that the heavy bombers could do, inflict decisive damage on the enemy by means of massive bombing attacks from high altitude. Like the heavy bombers, they did not prove very successful in this role. However, their greater maneuverability ultimately led them to success in a variety of other roles, especially anti-shipping and ground attack, which they performed at very low altitudes, often coming in "on the deck" to strike not only with bombs but also with heavy machine guns, light cannon, rockets, and even light field pieces. In this role aircraft such as the B-25 Mitchell proved enormously effective against shipping and other surface targets. The medium bomber could carry sufficient firepower to devastate a freighter or small warship in one pass. This enabled the medium bomber to achieve surprise, as any subsequent passes would find the target ship thoroughly alerted and desperately evading and resisting.

Although in the prewar period several nations developed single-engined bombers, most of these did not prove of great value in the war, since they proved incapable of coping with even moderate fighter resistance. Even two-engine medium bombers didn't carry enough firepower to defend themselves.

The two single-engine types that proved most successful were the dive bomber and the torpedo bomber, highly specialized aircraft. Although initially neither type was particularly safe in the presence of fighters, by war's end the United States had come up with a superbly versatile bomber, the TBF AVENGER, carrier-capable, suitable for service as a dive bomber, torpedo bomber, ground attack aircraft, antisubmarine patrol bomber, and even light transport.

See also AIR COMBAT TACTICS; AIRCRAFT TABLES; CARRIERS, DESIGNING AIRCRAFT FOR.

Ref: Francillon, *Japanese Aircraft*; Hezlet, *Aircraft and Sea Power*; Roscoe, *On the Seas and in the Skies*.

Airsols

Abbreviation for Air Command Solomons. In a rare example of inter-service and international cooperation, all the army, navy, Marine Corps, and some New Zealand aircraft in the Solomons were combined under the control of one headquarters. Command of the unit was rotated and aircraft were efficiently used without the usual duplication of effort and confusion that result from separate commands for each service. The origins of AIRSOLS could be seen at Henderson Field on GUADALCANAL. The Marine Corps seized this unfinished airstrip from the Japanese in August 1942, quickly finished it, and then welcomed warplanes from the army, navy, Marine Corps, and Royal New Zealand Air Force. All planes that could reach Henderson were welcome to come in and join the fight.

Aitape, New Guinea

One of the few good harbors on the northern coast of New Guinea, Aitape had a safe anchorage, but virtually no port facilities. Strategically, however, a base there, whether air or naval, could enable one to project power not only along the New Guinea coast, but also well into the PHILIPPINE SEA, to the north.

AKA (Attack Cargo Ship)

US merchant vessels of about 4,000–8,000 GRT specialized for the rapid unloading of military cargo in a war zone. In addition to landing craft and machinery, the cargo was loaded so that those items needed first could be unloaded first. This was called "combat loading." Not all of these carried LCVPS, LCTS and LCMs. Those that did had a dozen or so LCVPs, up to eight LCMs and one LCP. AKAs also used the small craft from the APAs or LSDs to land supplies. Crew size (100–400) and armament (several 3-inch or 5-inch guns and up to eight 40mm antiaircraft guns) varied with ship size. While some were special built as AKs, many of the early ones were merchantmen quickly taken into service. Top speed varied between 12 and 20 knots. Over 200 were put into service between 1942 and 1945.

Akagi, Japanese Aircraft Carrier

Japan's first large carrier, *Akagi* (1920–1925–1927) had been laid down as a 41,000–ton battle cruiser.

She was converted to a carrier under the terms of the Naval Disarmament Treaty of 1922. Fast and rather well protected for a carrier, she could operate only about two-thirds of the aircraft that she was capable of storing. With KAGA she formed Carrier Division One. *Akagi* saw action in the Sino-Japanese War, and she served as flagship of the First Air Fleet from PEARL HARBOR to MIDWAY, where she had to be scuttled after US dive bombers turned her into a burning wreck.

Akatsuki Class, Japanese Destroyers

Built 1930–33, the four Akatsukis were modified versions of FUBUKI, slightly smaller but with virtually the same capabilities. Rebuilt in the late–1930s to improve stability, they gained displacement but lost some speed. They saw considerable service, particularly in the SOLOMONS, where *Akatsuki* was sunk during the night action off GUADALCANAL on 12–13 November 1942. Only one survived the war.

Akitsuki Class, Japanese Destroyers

Japan ordered 16 destroyers of the Akitsuki Class in 1939–41, but only 13 were actually laid down and 12 completed 1942–45. A further 37 ordered in 1942 were never begun. Large vessels, designed as escorts for carrier task forces, the Akitsukis had an unusual main armament oriented primarily toward antiaircraft protection: eight 3.9"/65 dual purpose (anti-ship and antiaircraft) guns, rather than the usual six 5"/50 dual purpose guns of most recent Japanese destroyers. They proved very successful ships, but came along much too late to affect the course of the war. Six were war losses: three to surface ships, one to a submarine, and two to air attack.

Alaska Class, US Large Cruisers

Although a very fine design, combining high speed with considerable firepower, excellent protection, great endurance, and fine sea keeping qualities, the Alaskas were white elephants. Although frequently termed battlecruisers, they were not really similar to those World War I–era vessels that were supposed to serve as scouts for the battlefleet. They were really super-heavy cruisers, evolving out of a concern that 8–inch-gunned heavy cruisers were inadequate to meet the demands of modern warfare, and because Japan seemed to be building something similar (the " B-64 Type Super Heavy Cruisers"). Despite their rather odd origins, and their lack of a true role, the Alaskas proved excellent ships, helping to escort carrier task forces and providing amphibious fire support in the last months of the war. They were enormously expensive, at about $70 million each (nearly $400 million in current dollars). These ships were so expensive because the navy spent a lot of time working out their design, among other things experimenting with new patterns of 10-inch, 11-inch, and 12-inch guns in double and triple turrets before settling upon the final design. The needs of the service would have been better served by building another pair of ESSEX CLASS carriers, which would have been available much sooner, done a lot more work, and cost a lot less.

Alaska, CB-1 (1941–1943–1944), joined the Pacific Fleet in early 1945, helping to screen carriers from air attack and bombarding Japanese installations until the end of the war. Scrapped 1961.

Guam, CB-2 (1942–1943–1944), served with fast carriers from late March 1945 until the end of the war. Scrapped 1961.

A third unit, *Hawaii*, CB-3 (1943–1945–), was never completed, and her hull was scrapped in 1960. *Samoa*, *Puerto Rico*, and *Philippines* were never laid down.

Alaska Territory

A vast, sparsely inhabited territory, Alaska had been largely neglected by the United States until the possibility of war with Japan loomed. A modest effort was made to develop bases in the territory, but little had been accomplished by the time the Pacific War broke out.

Alaska was the scene of some fighting in 1942–43, with Japanese attacks on DUTCH HARBOR and several other installations, and occupation of Attu and KISKA, from which they were ejected by mid-1943.

Alaska served as transshipment route for Lend-Lease aircraft bound for the Soviet Union, and as a base for American operations against the KURILE ISLANDS.

The enormous wartime effort to develop the defenses of Alaska resulted in a tremendous spur to the economic growth of the territory.

Albacore, British Carrier Torpedo Bomber

The Albacore was one of several obsolete 1930s aircraft that the British used in the Indian Ocean early in the war. A biplane torpedo bomber, the Albacore had a decent range and carrying capacity, but was woefully slow (140 MPH). Nevertheless, it served into 1943.

See also AIRCRAFT TYPES, DEVELOPMENT.

ALCAN Highway

Also known as the Alaska-Canada Highway, this was a 1,450-mile-long all-weather, paved two-lane road from Dawson Creek, British Columbia, to Big Delta, Alaska, establishing an overland link between the United States and Alaska. Proposed by some Americans and Canadians long before the outbreak of the Pacific War, the project was deemed too expensive until PEARL HARBOR. On the recommendation of the War, Navy, and Interior Departments, it was approved by President ROOSEVELT in mid-January 1942, and accepted by Canada's Prime Minister William MacKenzie King at the end of February. The work was to be performed in two stages. The first project was a roughly built "pioneer" track, to be put through as quickly as possible by Army Engineers. The second stage would increasingly be turned over to civilian agencies and contractors to complete a proper road. Construction began in mid-March, with the arrival

of the first of what would eventually number 10,607 Army Engineer and support troops, about a third of whom were BLACK AMERICANS. Despite numerous difficulties caused by the peculiarities of subarctic climate (temperature variations that rose from below freezing to above 80° in 12 hours, quaking bogs, and permafrost) and by the Continental Divide, the work progressed rapidly. By November a "pioneer" road had been pushed through, complete with numerous bridges. From the time construction began to the completion of this phase of the project, only eight months and 12 days were required. Although for most of its course this was only a rough-cut track, it could be used by motor vehicles, and the first trucks from Dawson Creek reached Fairbanks, about 100 miles northwest of Big Delta over connecting roads, on November 21. Construction to complete the road continued through the winter, despite severe weather conditions. By spring 1943 civilian agencies began taking over the work, and the last army construction troops left in July. Thereafter about 7,500 civilian workers labored to complete the project. By the time it was completed, in late 1943, it had long since lost any military utility.

At approximately the same time the highway was being built, a small oil pipeline was laid alongside it. Although the "Canol" pipeline—actually an interconnected series of three lines that converged across the Yukon to join the highway—proved an extremely inexpensive way of transporting fuel to Alaska, it was eventually abandoned because of its limited capacity and the waning Japanese threat in the North Pacific area.

Aleutian Islands, Alaska

This chain of islands stretches about 1,100 miles westward from Alaska, between the Bering Sea and the North Pacific. A desperately bleak, rugged place, there are 70 large and numerous smaller volcanic islands in five major groupings, totaling about 6,800 square miles. They have some of the worst weather in the world. In 1942 the population was extremely thin.

In June of 1942, while Japanese carriers were being hammered in the battle of MIDWAY, another Japanese task force was landing troops on two Aleutian Islands: Attu and KISKA. Hundreds of miles from the nearest US base at DUTCH HARBOR, the landings were not discovered by American aircraft for four days. Not much usually happened this far north, but in June 1942 the war came to Alaska.

All but one of the Pacific War campaigns were fought in tropical areas. The one exception was the battle for control of two islands in the Aleutians where the climate is decidedly arctic.

The Japanese expected to smash US carrier forces at Midway, and to support that expected victory, they sent occupation forces to the Aleutians, the idea being to lure some US strength away from the main event. There they would establish airbases, guarded by ground troops. These bases, plus the one to be established on Midway, would prevent another DOOLITTLE-type raid like that on Tokyo two months earlier. The westernmost of the American Aleutian Islands were less than 650 miles from the Japanese KURILE ISLANDS. Throughout World War II, Japan feared that the Americans would take this, the shortest route from US to Japanese territory, to launch an amphibious invasion of their Home Islands. The Doolittle Raid made this fear more tangible, thus the decision to invade the Aleutians.

On 7 June 1942, Japanese forces began landing in the Aleutians, at Kiska and Attu, two of the westernmost islands in the chain. Neither island had more than a handful of people on it, and these offered no resistance to the approximately 1,200 Japanese troops who landed on each. Over the next 11 months, the garrisons were built up so that by May 1943 Attu was occupied by 2,500 Japanese and Kiska by 5,400. Attu Island was only 650 miles from the airbase on Paramushiru, the northernmost of the Japanese Kuriles.

The US and Canadian response to this Japanese invasion of their home waters was swift and considerable. The public was in an uproar and elected officials responded to the clamor to "throw the Japs out." For the next year, about a third of all Allied

shipping in the Pacific went toward supporting the Aleutians campaign. Airfields were built on islands west of Dutch Harbor, a minor US base at the time of the invasion. Hundreds of aircraft were sent north and US and Canadian warships patrolled the area and threw a naval blockade around the Japanese bases. Over 100,000 troops were sent to this inhospitable corner of Alaska to take the islands back, at a time when the population of all of Alaska was only about 75,000 people.

This Allied buildup put the Japanese at a severe disadvantage. With so many land-based Allied aircraft in the area, they could no longer risk their few remaining carriers to escort supply ships into the area. Besides, the weather was abominable, all year round. Carrier operations would have been too risky even without the presence of Allied bombers. While the Japanese had put fighters and bombers on their own Aleutian airfields, the Allied aircraft were more numerous and held the advantage. Without a steady stream of supply ships bringing in fuel and ammunition, the Japanese air strength could never be increased to the point where it could take control of the Aleutian skies.

In the first three months of 1943, the Japanese tried to break the Allied blockade by escorting their supply ships with cruisers and destroyers. This effort ended with the Battle of the KOMANDORSKI ISLANDS, when the Japanese warships were fought to a standstill by Allied ships. The Japanese withdrew their ships and supplied their Aleutian bases with SUBMARINES.

In May of 1943, the Allied counterattack began. Jumping past Kiska, in the first example of the "leapfrog" STRATEGY that would come to characterize operations in the Pacific, on 12 May, 10,000 American troops assaulted Attu. The Japanese were cleared out by the 28th. As would all Japanese garrisons in the future, the 2,500 Japanese troops in this one fought to the death. The battle ended with the remaining 600 Japanese troops making a final assault that almost reached the American artillery positions. The Japanese troops that survived this attack, and saw that they could not breach the new American defense line, promptly committed suicide. Twenty-eight Japanese were taken prisoner, none of them officers.

American CASUALTIES were heavy, with 549 dead, 1,148 wounded, and 2,132 non-combat casualties. The arctic climate and rugged geography had a lot to do with the non-combat casualties. Because it was the army's first amphibious assault in the Pacific, a lot of mistakes were made. Moreover, in a tactic the Japanese would forget and rediscover later in the war, their troops withdrew to fortified positions away from the coast. Thus three US battleships and many cruisers supporting the invasion were unable to pummel the defenders.

The Japanese still had 5,400 troops on Kiska, 200 miles east of Attu. What the Japanese feared more than losing Kiska was that this Allied move was the first step toward invading the northernmost Japanese Home Islands. The Japanese had already assembled a large force of warships to support their Aleutian garrison, but after Attu fell, they decided to use the assembled naval forces to evacuate Kiska and use the troops taken out to reinforce the garrison in the Japanese Kuriles 600 miles to the west.

At first the Japanese tried to evacuate the Kiska garrison with submarines. But after three subs were sunk by Allied forces, they decided to wait for foggy weather and do it with warships. They finally got their chance at the end of July 1943. Two light cruisers and 10 destroyers worked their way into Kiska harbor and, still shrouded by fog, took aboard the surviving 5,100 men of the garrison in a few hours, and then made their way back to the Kuriles. Part of this was accomplished with some luck. The American task force blockading Kiska was off refueling when the Japanese warships slipped into Kiska. The foggy weather kept Allied aircraft at bay. Previous Allied air reconnaissance had interpreted Japanese troop movements (preparing for the evacuation) as a redeployment for the coming Allied amphibious assault.

The Allies did not learn of the Japanese evacuation of Kiska for weeks. Indeed, on 16 August 1943, 34,000 American and Canadian troops assaulted Kiska. Prepared for a fight, it took them several days to realize that the Japanese were gone, and in the process there were 313 casualties, including 24 deaths from FRIENDLY FIRE and four from Japanese MINES and booby traps, while a US destroyer was lost to a Japanese mine, with about 70 fatalities. Most of the rest of the casualties were from non-combat causes, mainly trench foot.

The Allied effort was not wasted, as the Japanese were certain that the Kurile Islands were next. By the summer of 1944, the Kuriles garrison had been increased to 41,000 troops. Moreover, 500 warplanes were assigned to the area. However, save for raids by aircraft or naval vessels operating out of the Aleutians, the Americans never came that way. Nevertheless, the Japanese deployed substantial scarce resources in fear that something might happen up north. Also, by clearing the Aleutians of Japanese bases, the United States was able to fly over 6,000 Lend-Lease aircraft directly to the Soviet Union.

The Japanese had about 4,000 fatalities in the Aleutian campaign, four times the Allied losses. Their equipment losses included three destroyers, five submarines, nine transports, and over 200 aircraft (most to non-combat causes, among them a Zero that was captured virtually intact and proved immensely educational to US aviation engineers). US losses were much less, except in terms of aircraft. Over 600 aircraft were lost, but only about 100 due to enemy action. The bad weather and arctic conditions, accounted for the rest of the losses. The Aleutians were a bad place to fly. The US Navy lost three destroyers and one submarine.

From the Japanese point of view, the campaign was not a total disaster. The operation involved about 10,000 Japanese ground troops, plus some air and naval forces for about 14 months. Over 300,000 Allied troops were tied up in the Aleutians and Alaska, including an infantry division (the Seventh) that would have otherwise been sent to the South Pacific. A third of the Allied Pacific shipping was tied up supporting the Aleutians, as well as thousands of scarce engineer troops building the ALCAN HIGHWAY through Canada to Alaska. Three American battleships, half a dozen cruisers, and as many destroyers were diverted from the South Pacific to the Aleutians.

See also EVACUATIONS, JAPANESE ARMED FORCES; FALSE BATTLES OF THE PACIFIC WAR.

Ref: Garfield, *The Thousand Mile War*; Hutchison, *World War II in the North Pacific*.

Alexander, Harold (1891–1969)

Field Marshal Sir Harold Alexander entered the British Army in 1911 as a Guards officer, rising to lieutenant colonel during World War I, during which he commanded an infantry battalion at the front. After the war he was for a time military adviser to Latvia during its border war with Russia in 1919. By the outbreak of World War II he was commander of the British First Infantry Division, among the first units dispatched to France, in which role he greatly distinguished himself while commanding the rearguard during the Dunkirk operation. Thereafter he held a variety of commands in Britain, until March of 1942, when he was put in command in Burma, where he made it possible for William SLIM to withdraw with some semblance of order in the face of the Japanese tide. Although he failed in the impossible mission of saving Burma, Alexander once again distinguished himself as a rearguard fighter. In August 1942, he was sent to replace Claude Auchinleck as commander in chief in the Middle East, where Erwin Rommel's Italo-German forces had just been halted on the Alamein line. In his new command, Alexander oversaw Bernard Law Montgomery's successful defense at Alam Halfa and his Alamein offensive, and, after the Anglo-American landings in northwestern Africa, the Tunisian Campaign, the Sicilian operation, and the Italian Campaign. An extremely good officer, like many commanders Alexander tended to see his theater as the most critical one. Unwilling to see that the Italian Campaign was essentially a strategic diversion, he continuously argued for more troops when the focus of Allied operations had shifted to northwestern Europe, the most decisive theater. After the war, by which time he had been promoted to field

marshal, Alexander served in a variety of civil and military posts until his retirement.

Allen M. Sumner Class, US Destroyers

A US wartime development, 47 destroyers of this class were built 1943–45 (of an order of 58, of which five were canceled and the rest completed postwar). They proved somewhat disappointing in service. Of virtually the same physical dimensions as the very successful FLETCHER CLASS, they mounted a heavier armament, including three double 5"/38 dual-purpose turrets, rather than five single mounts. As a result, the Sumners were overweight, slow, and top-heavy; a "top-heavy" ship has a high center of gravity, causing her to roll badly, and presents an increased danger of capsizing if broadsided by heavy seas. Despite their limitations, the Sumners saw considerable service and took a lot of damage. None became war losses. The most famous unit of the class was the USS *Laffey* (DD-724), the second of that name in the war

See also DESTROYERS, PICKET DUTY.

Altitude Sickness

World War II aircraft were the first to fly high enough to cause physical problems for the crews. The most obvious problem was lack of oxygen. Flying higher than 15,000 feet would cause loss of mental ability and, if you went high enough, you could pass out. So aircrews were equipped with face masks to supply additional oxygen. If, for whatever reason, this oxygen supply were lost, the pilot had to take the aircraft promptly to a lower altitude before the crew became unconscious or incapable of flying their aircraft. Since most World War II aircraft were not pressurized, crews also discovered (the hard way) that gas in the intestines expanded several times over when they were flying at altitudes of 20,000 feet and up. The thinner air caused the higher-pressure intestinal gas to expand, at great discomfort to the victim. Normally the lower air pressure was not a problem, due to oxygen masks, but passing gas could be very painful, often debilitating, and sometimes fatal. With thousands of bombers and fighters flying at those altitudes, something had to be done. The solution was in the diet. Fliers solved the problem by removing or reducing from their diets whenever possible beans, cabbage, corn, onions, and many other foods that normally cause gas in humans.

AM-1 Mauler, US Carrier Bomber

The AM-1 Mauler, a carrier bomber, began development during the war, but did not reach the US fleet until 1946. It's an example of what the navy might have had if the war had started later, lasted longer, or if the United States had begun developing new aircraft more quickly. The first flight was in the summer of 1944. The AM-1 was faster than the TBF AVENGER, had a longer range, and carried over three times as much weight in bombs (7,000 pounds). Its firepower was also considerable: four 20mm cannon.

See also AIRCRAFT TYPES, DEVELOPMENT.

Amboina, Ceram, Netherlands East Indies

Although not extensively appointed, Amboina had a good harbor, with modestly extensive port facilities, as well as a modestly good airport for the East Indies in 1941. Its excellent location in the eastern NETHERLANDS EAST INDIES made it a potentially valuable naval and air base, particularly for anyone interested in control of western New Guinea, within easy flying distance.

American Citizens, Relocation of

America's most shameful moment in World War II was the internment of Japanese Americans in concentration camps during the war. This has been considered a shamelessly racist attack on Japanese Americans in the aftermath of the PEARL HARBOR attack.

Or was it?

The Japanese Americans were caught up in what was the ancient practice of rounding up in wartime enemy citizens and others thought to be of dubious loyalty. Some 16,810 enemy aliens (non-citizens who were not permanent residents) were rounded up, of whom 36% were Japanese. These "internees" were imprisoned in what we would today call medium-security prisons. This was normal in wartime. The only exceptions were Americans of Japanese or German ancestry caught in those respective nations when war was declared. In these cases, the Japanese and German governments coerced (where needed) these Americans to fight against their adopted country.

The more controversial program was the relocation of Japanese Americans (legally resident aliens and citizens alike) from the West Coast. This began in late February 1942, when, on the basis of Executive Order Number 9066, signed by President ROOSEVELT on February 19, 1942, the West Coast was declared an "Exclusion Zone." This meant that any one of questionable loyalty to the United States was ordered to move to another part of the country. Rather than try to separate loyal from disloyal Japanese Americans, all persons of Japanese ancestry were removed from the zone. The program was mandatory and, beginning in April, 110,000 Japanese Americans were sent to relocation centers. About 40% of these people were long-term residents who were excluded by law from becoming US citizens.

The 40,000 adult non-citizen Japanese-American legal residents being relocated were questioned about their loyalty to the United States. Some 18,000 of them refused to renounce the emperor of Japan or swear allegiance to the United States and were promptly interned.

It should be kept in mind that most Japanese immigration to the United States occurred before the 1930s, a time when life was quite hard in Japan. But from the 1930s on, while the rest of the world was mired in the Great Depression, Japan prospered and Japanese at home and abroad took pride in their country's accomplishments. The improved situation in Japan, plus the usual racism immigrants

A Japanese-American girl awaits "evacuation" at Arcadia, California, April 5, 1942, among over 100,000 persons of Japanese ancestry who would be "relocated" from their West Coast homes in 1942.

suffered in their new country, caused many Japanese to return home during the 1930s. This was why there were 20,000 Japanese with American citizenship in Japan when the war broke out.

Japanese intelligence officials were well aware of the changed attitudes of overseas Japanese, and they set about creating networks of spies and informers to take advantage of it. The coded messages Japanese diplomats sent home were decrypted by American codebreakers and it was this information, the shock of Pearl Harbor, the invasion of the Philippines, and the public's perception that the West Coast would be attacked that led to the relocation program.

Once in the camps, those who did profess their loyalty did not have to sit out the war in the "con-

centration camps." If they could find jobs and housing in another part of the country, they could go there and live freely until the war was over. The West Coast was still off limits because it was deemed particularly vulnerable due to the many military bases and war factories located there. These facilities would provide much of the support for the war effort in the Pacific. If Japanese agents were in place, radio messages could be sent to Japan detailing what was where and in what shape. A lot of information could be picked up from talkative defense workers and sailors.

The Japanese were reluctant to trust a non-Japanese as an agent. The Japanese Americans were a perfect population from which to recruit agents, and this was exactly what the Japanese did.

Moreover, many Japanese Americans made no secret of their loyalties before the war. It was the ones who kept quiet that had the FBI worried.

The FBI had been keeping tabs on various Japanese-American organizations. Some of these were criminal organizations, such as the Tokyo Club and the Toyo Club, known to have ties with the Yakuza (Japanese gangsters involved in organized crime) back in Japan. Others were military, such as the Society of the Black Dragon (more properly the Amur River Society), the Imperial Comradeship Society, and the Japanese Military Servicemen's League, allegedly composed of Japanese veterans living in the United States, which were secretly funded by the Imperial Army. Indeed, it was feared that there were as many as 10,000 secret Japanese reservists living in the United States. During the CHINA INCIDENT, Japanese reservists living in SHANGHAI and other cities had proven a major asset during military operations. Some Japanese-American groups had ties to groups like the German-American Bund and one notoriously pro-fascist Italian-American fraternal organization that still exists.

Japanese Americans in other parts of the country were not affected by the exclusion order and went on with their lives. By the middle of 1944, over 40,000 of the interned Japanese Americans from the West Coast had found new homes and were living freely outside the camps. Nearly 10,000 Japanese Americans got away from the camps by going off to college or joining the military. While most who enlisted were sent to Europe, many of those who spoke Japanese were sent to the Pacific where they served as intelligence specialists and translators, often on high-level staffs.

Most of those who remained in the camps were either too old, or too young, to find jobs. Many of those who remained also could not speak English. People of suspect loyalty were also kept in the camps. While most of the people in the camps were loyal Americans, many were not. Loyalists provided information on pro-Japanese activity among detainees, and there was quite a lot of it. The pro-Japanese internees were often quite fanatical about

their beliefs and would terrorize and badger those who were patriotic Americans. After the war, many of the detainees refused to believe that Japan had been defeated. And even after being presented with irrefutable proof, some 6,000 of them requested REPATRIATION to Japan.

Some, but not many, Japanese Americans living outside the exclusion zone moved to the camps to be close to relatives. Others who had found housing and work in other parts of the country voluntarily returned to the camps, although the government charged them a dollar a day (about $10 in 1996 dollars) for room and board if they did so. The government soon realized that it did not want to be in the camp business.

Occupants of the camps were paid for work they did to help run the camps, and most were eventually free to leave on a temporary or permanent basis under increasingly liberal conditions. There were still restrictions on movement, as Japanese Americans were still forbidden to enter the West Coast exclusion zone until after the war. The camps contained a range of amenities like schools for the children (and adults), libraries, stores, banks, and medical facilities. Food was plentiful, as was medical care and education. That said, they were still detention camps, hastily built in the wilderness and closely guarded. There was a good deal of hardship, though no deliberate abuse.

Of course, the most contentious issue in all this was the reasoning behind the relocation. Fear of a Japanese invasion and the presence of Japanese sympathizers was not all driven by racism against Japanese. Americans had watched in horror as the Nazis overran Europe during the last two years, often with the aid of local sympathizers. Before Pearl Harbor, there were numerous active groups of German, Italian, and Japanese Americans who openly supported the aggressive ambitions of their erstwhile motherlands. But among German Americans and Italian Americans and exiles there were many prominent voices condemning Nazi and Fascist aggression (Bertolt Brecht, Willy Ley, Marlene Dietrich, Fiorello LaGuardia, Arturo Toscanini), while there was no vocal opposition to

Japanese aggression in the Japanese-American community—which to some suggested grounds for suspicion.

Some say that the Japanese should not have been treated any differently than Germans or Italians. In fact, to a great extent they weren't. Despite the "better" image of Italian and German Americans, the government actually began to round some of them up even before it began rounding up Japanese Americans. The *first* persons "relocated" under Executive Order 9066 were over 10,000 German and Italian Americans, beginning in February of 1942. These people were forcibly removed from the West Coast—yes, the West Coast—since the commanding general on the West Coast, LG John L. DEWITT, believed there were Axis agents among them who would provide material aid to a Japanese invasion. This was supposed to have been only the initial stage in the evacuation of several hundred thousand Italian and German Americans, but in the end the army was overruled. Nevertheless, several hundred thousand additional Italian and German Americans had severe restrictions placed on their activities and movements: Italian-born persons, for example, could no longer work as fishermen or live within a certain distance of the coast, a matter that proved particularly embarrassing in the case of the Italian-American mayor of SAN FRANCISCO. Several hundred members of other ethnic minorities, notably Hungarian and Romanian Americans, were also relocated. Thousands of people—by one estimate as many as 700,000—had restrictions placed on their activities.

What caused the panic that led to the Japanese-American roundup on the West Coast was the fact that Japan was seen as threatening an invasion of the West Coast, while at worst the European Axis was a threat to shipping, with their SUBMARINES in the Atlantic.

The Pearl Harbor attack was also a major factor, as it was seen as treacherous because, at the same time, Japanese diplomats in Washington were attempting to resolve the differences between the two nations. Germany and Italy declared war after Pearl Harbor, without benefit of any sneak attacks or other real, or apparent, treachery.

Fears that Japanese Americans might represent a potential "fifth column" were also fanned by the Niihau incident. His airplane damaged by American antiaircraft fire over Pearl Harbor on 7 December 1941, Japanese fighter pilot Shigenori Nishikaichi managed to crash-land on Niihau, the smallest of the inhabited Hawaiian islands. Convincing a local Japanese American that the arrival of the emperor's forces was imminent, the pair embarked upon a violent rampage, terrorizing the island until killed several days later, leaving behind a trail of dead and injured people. In addition, the collaboration of many locally resident Japanese with Japanese occupation forces in the Philippines and other areas only strengthened the hand of those who advocated relocation of Japanese Americans.

While an actual invasion of the West Coast was beyond Japanese capabilities, public opinion in 1942 thought otherwise. "Something had to be done," and if that something meant trampling on the Bill of Rights in the process, it was done. And regretted later. But the government knew something they dared not reveal at the time.

There were Japanese espionage networks on the West Coast, and much crucial information regarding these activities remained secret for many years because this data was obtained by cryptanalysis (the MAGIC system). What MAGIC seemed to reveal was that Japanese diplomats had established an extensive system of Japanese American agents on the West Coast. As with many German Americans and Italian Americans, there were many Japanese Americans who were still loyal to "the Old Country."

Indeed, virtually all of the 20,000 Japanese Americans in Japan at the beginning of the war renounced their American citizenship and joined the Japanese war effort. Given the nature of Japanese society and the war fever then present in Japan, it is doubtful many of these Japanese Americans had much choice in the matter. But many of them promptly joined the Japanese armed forces or enthusiastically supported the Japanese war effort. Several Japanese-American women, known collectively as TOKYO ROSE, became prominent delivering English-language radio broadcasts to American troops. One of these women was later convicted of treason, though subsequently pardoned.

Many of those who remained in the camps during the war, even if they had declared their allegiance to the United States, were known to truly loyal Japanese Americans as having pro-Japanese sympathies. The MAGIC intercepts did not detail every Japanese-American agent, because not all the messages could be deciphered; even when they could, the Japanese diplomats in America did not always use names that could be traced to a specific individual in the United States. But the FBI had picked up on some of this activity. What the MAGIC intercepts confirmed was that the extent of the Japanese support was larger than anyone had previously suspected, and there was no way to assure that the majority of these traitors would be picked up even if the MAGIC information was used in a roundup.

So it was not all black and white. While the "invasion panic" on the West Coast, along with anti-Japanese attitudes stemming from Pearl Harbor and the well publicized Japanese ATROCI-TIES in China before the war, were a major cause of the exclusion zone, the main reason was the evidence of Japanese espionage activities. The Germans and Italians also had thousands of pro-fascist supporters in America, and thousands of these were also rounded up. The same could have been done among Japanese Americans on the West Coast, but the added invasion hysteria and bad feelings because of Pearl Harbor, led to one of the less flattering incidents in US history.

The removal was not a unanimous decision. Many Americans protested, including FBI director J. Edgar Hoover, hardly an adamant civil libertarian. It was pointed out that the same kind of hysteria was directed against German Americans 25 years earlier during World War I. Of course, there was no removal of German Americans then,

mainly because there was much less likelihood of a German invasion of America. But Americans of German extraction were persecuted, and apologized to, after a fashion, later. Now there was another war scare, and the speculative future garnered more attention than unambiguous past events. It took a Supreme Court decision to affirm the removal, and thousands of Japanese Americans endured their lot through the war.

There were also a few Japanese Americans removed from HAWAII, where they comprised a large minority of the population. The main reason why the removals were not on the same scale as on the West Coast was that Hawaii was under martial law early in the war, and the West Coast was not. The Hawaiian wartime labor shortage, the logistical nightmare early in the war of moving that many people back to the mainland, along with the fact that the Hawaiian population was rather less paranoid about their Japanese-American neighbors than were those on the mainland, were all factors in minimizing the removal.

The American people, and government, began to regret the removal even before the war was over. Japanese Americans fought bravely in Europe and the Pacific. The accounts of their uncommon courage in the defense of their country, despite their shabby treatment, began to make headlines in 1944.

From the beginning, there was no official policy of punishing the Japanese Americans beyond removing them from what was then considered a war zone. The officials in charge of supervising the removal were instructed to be generous in making necessary financial arrangements. While many of the Japanese Americans were farmers, few owned their land, most leased it. These farmers were paid for their crops in the ground and arrangements were made for leases to be taken over for the duration of the "emergency." After the war, the returning Japanese Americans were able to make claims for losses that occurred in any event, and over a quarter-billion dollars (in current money) was paid by the government to satisfy these terms. About three dozen German and Italian Americans also received reparations for their losses due to internment, despite the fact that over 10,000 were moved, and scores of thousands more had restrictions placed on their activities.

Over the years, the myth has grown up that an entirely innocent Japanese-American population was thoughtlessly uprooted and tossed into concentration camps in a fit of racist hysteria. The truth was a bit more complex. Many of the Japanese Americans so interned were disloyal. Of those military-age males who spent the war in the camps, only 6% volunteered for military service. And many of those interned were, by their own admission, loyal to Japan. But most Japanese Americans did not spend the war in the internment camps. Ironically, the guilt among Americans built up in the decades after the war. The Civil Liberties Act of 1988 provided $20,000 in further reparations to all surviving Japanese Americans who had spent time in the camps. This was paid to those who were loyal, as well as those who weren't. No similar "compensation" was paid to Italian and German Americans whose liberties had been interfered with.

See also FALSE BATTLES OF THE PACIFIC WAR; FUJITA, FRANK; JAPANESE-AMERICANS, IMPERIAL ARMED FORCES; SAKAKIDA, RICHARD.

Ref: Collins, *Native American Aliens*; Crost, *Honor by Fire*; Fox, *The Unknown Internment*; Harrington, *Yankee Samurai*; Smith, *Democracy on Trial*; Stephan, *Hawaii under the Rising Sun*.

American President Line

The American President Line was a US-flag shipping company, which conducted transpacific and 'round the world cruises. Organized in the 1930s, through the merger of several Depression-wracked companies, the line had a fleet of 27 cargo-passenger ships on the eve of the Pacific War, virtually all of which were named after US presidents. All of them ended up in US service, several even before the war began, either requisitioned for the navy or the army, or under charter. At least seven were lost in the war. These were large ships, from 9,300 to 21,900 GRT, roomy vessels able to make 14 knots or better, and thus ideally suited for use as troop transports or hospital ships. The larger ones were capable of lifting more than 4,000 troops, with their equipment, a full infantry regimental combat team. Several had interesting wartime histories.

President Coolidge. Completed in 1931, she was 21,900 GRT and could make 20 knots. The navy requisitioned her with the intention of converting her into an aircraft carrier (a proposal that it also advanced for the liners *America* and NORMANDIE), but the army quickly convinced the president that large, fast troop ships were just as desperately needed as aircraft carriers. She served as a troop transport in the South Pacific in 1942. On October 26, 1942 she struck a mine at ESPIRITU SANTO. With great presence of mind, her skipper promptly ran her up on a reef to keep her from sinking. As a result, all but two of the c. 5,440 troops aboard were saved, albeit without their equipment. Although salvage was planned, the ship shortly slid off the reef and sank in deep water.

President Grant. A 10,500-GRT vessel completed in 1921 and capable of 14 knots, she was being used as a transport when she grounded on Ulumo Reef, New Guinea, on February 26, 1944. Although CASUALTIES were few, the ship was a total loss.

President Harrison. Completed in 1921, she was 10,500 GRT. She brought the Fourth Marines to the Philippines from SHANGHAI on 4 December 1941, and then sailed immediately for TIENTSIN, the port of Peking, to evacuate the US legation guards there. Early on 8 December (Pearl Harbor Day, west of the International Date Line), she was strafed by Japanese aircraft off the Yangtze estuary. Her skipper tried to wreck her in shoal water, but she grounded relatively safely. Captured by the Japanese, she was renamed *Kakko Maru*, and later *Kachidoki Maru*. On September 12, 1944, while carrying over 1,000 Australian and British PRISONERS OF WAR from MALAYA to Japan, she was sunk by the US submarine *Pampanito* (SS-383) off the Philippines, with great loss of life

President Taylor. A sister to *President Grant*, also completed in 1921, she accidentally grounded at CANTON ISLAND on 14 February 1942. There was no loss of life, and there were hopes of salvaging the ship, but some days later she was hit by a Japanese air raid from the GILBERT ISLANDS and destroyed.

Three other ships, *President Cleveland* (renamed USS *Trasker H. Bliss)*, *President Pierce* (USAT *Hugh L. Scott*), and *President Van Buren* (USS *Thomas R. Stone)* were lost in the first five days of the North African invasion, 7–12 November 1942.

See also FRIENDLY FIRE, ALLIED PRISONER OF WAR DEATHS BY.

Ref: Niven, *The American President Line.*

Ammunition Availability, US Aircraft Carriers

In order to inflict damage upon the enemy, carriers had to carry ammunition as well as airplanes and fuel. Surprisingly, although they expended it in enormous amounts (in late 1942 a full US Navy carrier AIR GROUP of 36 fighters, 36 dive bombers, and 18 torpedo bombers could deliver about 50 tons of ammunition in a single sortie), it was rare that a carrier exhausted its ordnance stocks, which were quite ample for extended combat operations.

Some idea of how long these ammo loads could last may be gained by noting that the 325 tons that ESSEX carried in December 1942 provided sufficient TORPEDOES for two sorties by each of the ship's 18 torpedo bombers and enough heavy bombs (500–pounders and above) for 17 or 18 sorties by each of her 36 dive bombers, not to mention the smaller ammunition, suitable for use by fighters (see p. 49).

Changes in the types and amounts of ammunition were dictated by the changing military situation and the missions that the ships were being called upon to perform. For example, on the one hand, the 1942–43 allocations for *Essex* and *Enter-prise* occurred at a time when a clash with a Japanese carrier task force was still possible, hence the large stocks of heavier ordnance; there was also a shortage of destroyers and escort carriers to keep an eye out for Japanese SUBMARINES, thus the large supply of depth charges. On the other hand, the 1945 allocation for *Bunker Hill* was an acknowledgment that the Imperial Navy was finished, but that a lot of work had to be done supporting soldiers and Marines on hostile beaches.

See also BOMBS, CARRIER AIRCRAFT.

Ref: Friedman, *United States Aircraft Carriers.*

Amoy, China

An important river port on the Chinese coast, Amoy had extensive facilities to accommodate vessels of moderate size. Its location made it valuable for control of Fukien Province.

Amphibious Assaults

Amphibious warfare, putting troops ashore on enemy territory, is as old as naval warfare itself. And in the thousands of years of amphibious operations, up until the early years of World War II, the techniques did not change much. The same ancient methods were being used to get the troops ashore. That is, merchantmen were commandeered to carry the men and weapons, and an impromptu arrangement of barges and smaller boats were used to get the infantry and their equipment from the ships onto the enemy beaches. It was slow and clumsy, but for thousands of years it had worked. After PEARL HARBOR, all that began to change.

During the 1920s and '30s, American and British officers began developing new ideas on amphibious operations. The basic thrust of this work was to do for amphibious warfare what mechanization had done for ground combat in the form of the "blitzkrieg." This meant getting a lot of motor vehicles, including TANKS, onto the beach in the early stages of an assault. To this end, the British

CARRIER AMMUNITION ALLOCATIONS

Item	CV *Essex* 12/42	CV *Essex* 10/43	CV *Enterp.* 10/43	CV *Bunker H.* 1/45	CVL *Indep.* mid–43	CVE *Sang.* 8/42	CvE *Comm. Bay* 11/44
Bombs							
100–lb. GP	0	504	504	300	162	150	180
100–lb. HE	500	0	0	0	0	0	0
100–lb. In	300	296	288	240	180	175	121
220–lb. Fr	0	0	0	300	0	0	0
250–lb. GP	0	0	0	50	0	0	0
500–lb. AP	0	0	288	460	0	0	0
500–lb. GP	0	296	288	0	72	85	120
500–lb. HE	300	0	0	0	0	0	0
1,000–lb. AP	0	239	756	0	73	40	75
1,000–lb. GP	400	146	378	75	36	40	30
1,600–lb. AP	20	19	18	0	0	24	15
2,000–lb. GP	20	19	18	15	0	0	15
Rockets							
3.5"	0	0	0	300	0	0	132
5.0"	0	0	0	1,700	0	0	1,180
11.75"	0	0	0	108	0	0	0
Other							
Torpedoes	36	36	36	0	24	46	9
DC	300	296	288	48	36	110	120

Carrier names have been abbreviated: *Enterp., Enterprise; Bunker H., Bunker Hill*, both Essex Class; *Indep., Independence; Sang., Sangamon; Comm. Bay, Commencement Bay*. Key: AP, armor piercing, usually half were semi-armor piercing, useful against less heavily protected targets; DC, depth charges; Fr. fragmentation; GP, general purpose; HE, high explosive; In, incendiary.

invented the LST (landing ship tank), which literally ran itself up on the beach, let down a ramp in its bow, and allowed the trucks and armored vehicles to roll right onto the shore.

The American contribution came from Marine and army officers who developed new techniques for getting the troops ashore in LST-type vessels and keeping the supplies coming at a volume befitting the Americans' "pile it on" style of warfare.

Once America was in the war, the American and British ideas fused and what we now think of as amphibious warfare became a reality.

These new techniques were needed, in both Europe and the Pacific, and for quite different reasons. In Europe, one had to get ashore quickly and in force in order to avoid being shoved back into the sea by the nimble and experienced German mechanized divisions.

In the Pacific, the problems were quite different. Many of the islands to be assaulted were so small that heavy enemy fortifications were right on the beach. This was also a problem in Europe, although troops could often attack somewhere that was not heavily defended on the shoreline. But in the Pacific, an old-fashioned amphibious assault would not make much progress against the strong Japanese beach defenses. Even on the larger islands where, later in the war, the Japanese did not defend the beaches, it was essential to get the maximum amount of troops and firepower ashore quickly in order to disrupt the strong Japanese defenses inland. The new amphibious warfare did not see its full potential until 1944, but even in 1943 the new equipment and techniques began to have an effect.

The Allied revolution in amphibious warfare depended, like its land counterpart, on mechanization and organization. Three items comprised most of what is now considered "modern amphibious warfare." Specialized amphibious warfare ships—not just the LST, but also the many smaller amphibious ships and boats. Thousands of these had to be built and proper tactics had to be developed. AMPHIBIOUS VEHICLES that could quickly swim ashore and thereafter operate as land vehicles. These were the DUKWS, LVTs, and armored vehicles that could be floated ashore. Logistical arrangements were necessary to support this new equipment once it got ashore. The US Army took the lead in this area, with its amphibious engineer (actually logistical) units. The USN and the British adopted most of the techniques the US Army pioneered.

By the end of World War II, Allied amphibious operations reached a peak of capability that has not been equaled since.

Ref: Dyer, *The Amphibians Came to Conquer*; Isely and Crowl, *The U.S. Marines and Amphibious War*.

Amphibious Operations, Attrition

Most of the fighting in the Pacific took place close to water and sand. While this may have been rather picturesque, it was hard on the vehicles. Those who had to use and take care of the many trucks that were constantly hauling supplies and troops off the beach, soon learned that the combination of salt water and fine sand drastically shortened the life of the normally robust army trucks everyone used. Among other depredations, the brake shoes wore out in 10 days and the tires had to be replaced weekly if the vehicles were constantly on the beach. More than a month of use under these conditions would reduce many trucks to a state of uselessness. Even off the beach, the rigors of constantly driving across the generally roadless island terrain drastically shortened a vehicle's normal useful life. By the end of the war, most supply officers accepted the fact that a truck with more than 25,000 miles on it was more trouble than it was worth in the combat zone. Under peacetime conditions these same trucks were still useful after the 100,000 mile mark. But in wartime, and especially on the Pacific islands, the rust, dust, and fatigue wore the trucks out a lot more quickly.

Amphibious Operations, Building Up Shipping

As successful as American amphibious capabilities were, they did have limitations. There were never enough resources for all of the attacks the generals and admirals wanted to make. Limited resources was nothing new in warfare, but this was a new weapon and no one knew exactly the benefits of amphibious shipping in any particular situation. Amphibious operations were an essential item both in Europe and the Pacific. While the European war needed amphibious shipping from time to time, in the Pacific there was a constant need for landing on enemy islands. However, since the Allies had early on agreed that the European war would be settled first, Europe got first call on the scarce amphibious shipping.

In late 1942, North Africa was invaded by American and British forces, tying up just about all of the Allied amphibious shipping. In the Pacific the Marines were holding out against the Japanese on GUADALCANAL while the army fought on in New Guinea. Amphibious shipping began heading to the Pacific early in 1943, but this changed as summer approached. Europe had first call on amphibious shipping from the summer of 1943, as Sicily (July) and Italy (September) were invaded, and then the largest amphibious fleet in history was assembled for the cross-channel attack in June of 1944.

Through 1944, the Pacific had sporadic access to amphibious shipping and had to be careful using it. Until the invasion of France, Europe would have first call on landing ships to replace those that were inevitably lost running up on beaches. After the Normandy landings in June 1944, the Pacific got the shipping, the main reason so many major Pacific landings occurred from late 1944 through early 1945. After the summer of 1944, Europe had little need for amphibious shipping and much of what they had used for Normandy got sent to the Pacific

Over four million tons of amphibious shipping (LST, LSM, LCI, LCT) were built during the war and over a third of that was lost, mostly to wear and tear. By the end of the war, nearly all of it was in the Pacific. The APA are listed because, although they don't run up on the beach, they have to approach closely to load and land the troops in the LCVPS.

Ref: Dyer, *The Amphibians Came to Conquer*; Isely and Crowl, *The U.S. Marines and Amphibious War*.

Amphibious Operations, Logistical Arrangements

Getting the troops ashore in strength was one thing, and not an easy one. But it wasn't enough. The fighting on the beachhead often went on for weeks. All that time, supplies and reinforcements had to come across the beach, while numerous CASUALTIES had to be evacuated in the other direction.

The US Army first recognized and solved the potential logistical problems of modern amphibious operations. In 1942, the army began organizing Engineer Amphibious Brigades, one of which would support each assault division. A 7,400-man Engineer Amphibious Brigade had two battalions operating over a hundred small amphibious craft and another two staffed with engineers trained to get the supplies off the beach and to the right destination as quickly as possible. In addition, the brigade had a small artillery detachment to protect itself (all the engineers were, as was customary,

SEAGOING AMPHIBIOUS SHIPPING AVAILABILITY PACIFIC THEATER OF OPERATIONS VS. ALL OTHERS

Type	Sept. 1943 PTO	Other	Jan. 1944 PTO	Other	May 1944 PTO	Other
LST	67	159	117	127	125	198
LCT	103	638	130	687	150	853
LSM	60	143	105	115	113	188 estimated
LCI	62	268	101	196	115	162
APA	22	35	30	31	40	40
Tonnage	0.4	1.1	0.66	0.94	0.71	1.29 in millions
% Pacific	26%		42%		35%	

"Other" includes the Indian Ocean, as well as training establishments and the ETO.

armed and trained to serve as infantry when needed). There were also two ordnance companies, to perform on-the-spot repair of weapons, a maintenance battalion to keep all the brigade's equipment in working order, a quartermaster battalion to run the supply dumps, a LVT or DUKW company to help move supplies around on the beach, and a medical battalion, to care for the wounded troops coming back from the fighting and then evacuating them from the beach.

The navy had been less energetic in dealing with the logistics (supplies) of amphibious operations, partially because the Marines took care of the assault and the navy did all the support (gunfire, ships) chores. Although the Marines were part of the navy, this was one example of the problems their increasing independence could cause. The Marines tried to take care of beachhead logistics themselves and the navy ignored any problems unless the Marines made an issue of it. The navy was most sensitive about protecting its turf. When the admirals saw that the army had organized these Engineer Amphibious Brigades, protests were made.

Typical of many of these inter-service squabbles, a compromise was reached. The army was allowed to keep the brigades it had created in 1942, but promised not to create any more. Meanwhile, the navy copied the army's idea to beef up its own logistic support for amphibious operations. The army made extensive use of these Engineer Amphibious Brigades in the Pacific, particularly during the New Guinea and Philippines campaigns.

The navy was not without innovations in the logistics of amphibious operations, creating dozens of Naval Construction Battalions (the SEABEES), crucial in rebuilding (or creating from scratch) airfields and ship support facilities on islands. The Seabees were fast, carving operational airfields out of tropical jungle in days, often while beating off Japanese attacks in the bargain. This capability shocked the Japanese, except for those who had been to America and saw what the extensive use of bulldozers and other forms of mechanization could do to speed up construction.

The combination of improved amphibious logistics and fast construction of new facilities made the fast pace of the American Pacific offensive possible. These innovations had not been foreseen by the Japanese, who were dismayed to see heavily fortified islands assaulted, conquered, and then begin operating as air and fleet bases within weeks. This was a radically new approach to amphibious warfare. Neither the Japanese, nor anyone else since, has come up with an antidote for this "other" blitzkrieg of World War II—American fast-paced island-hopping offensive across the Pacific.

See also UNITED STATES ARMY, ENGINEER SPECIAL BRIGADES.

Ref: Dyer, *The Amphibians Came to Conquer*; Isely and Crowl, *The U.S. Marines and Amphibious War*; Stanton, *Order of Battle*.

Amphibious Operations, Naval Gunfire Support

The Japanese quickly learned that US amphibious operations were accompanied by unprecedented quantities of naval gunfire support. In addition to the battleships (12-, 14- and 16-inch guns) and cruisers (8-, and 6-inch guns), there were a lot of destroyers (5-inch guns). The "hardest" (most fortified) targets were assigned to the largest guns, which plastered them with quarter-ton, half-ton,

and one-ton shells from comfortable ranges before the landing craft beached. When the troops hit the beach, the destroyers (which fired smaller 55-pound rounds) could come in close for all sorts of direct-fire support missions. During preliminary bombardments, destroyers were usually assigned low-priority targets. And thereby hangs a tale.

During the invasion of GUAM in July 1944, one destroyer was assigned to fire on some Japanese latrines. The destroyermen were disappointed at being given so lowly an assignment, but all the other targets were covered by larger ships. However, unbeknownst to Naval Intelligence, the local Japanese troops, thinking the Americans would not waste shells on latrines, stored much of their reserve ammunition in what looked like a latrine. The destroyer sailors, upon firing at their target, began wondering if they had been secretly issued some new, extremely powerful, 5-inch shells. Each shell they fired at the latrines resulted in a huge explosion. Later reports confirmed that the Japanese had hidden behind the outhouse. Incidentally, the Japanese were late in catching on to the notion of camouflaging their latrines, which was why the destroyer was assigned to them in the first place. One result of this, aside from a lot of destroyed outhouses, was that it was for a time relatively easy to estimate the number of Japanese troops in an area. One had merely to count the latrines and consult the standard Japanese Army regulations on the ratio of outhouses to troops.

The enormous amount of ammunition expended in "preparatory bombardments" of beaches was never enough to wholly obliterate the defenses, particularly if the enemy's CAMOUFLAGE efforts were effective. Although the Marines and soldiers hitting the beach still faced voluminous enemy firepower, the "softening up" by battlewagons, cruisers, destroyers, and rocket-firing vessels made their task a lot easier.

Ref: Dyer, *The Amphibians Came to Conquer*; Isely and Crowl, *The U.S. Marines and Amphibious War*.

Amphibious Operations, Surprise

Amphibious landings are always tricky undertakings, complicated mostly by the sea and the weather. But the troops on the receiving end of these assaults developed some lethal DECEPTIONS to further confound the attacking troops. Both the Germans and the Japanese quickly figured out that they could further complicate, and perhaps compromise, amphibious landings by adding hazards patterned after those nature already provided.

The most effective were underwater obstacles, often nothing more than poles driven into the beach underwater at heights just below the water during high tide (when landing craft would most likely approach the beach). The landing craft would run into them and sink, taking the troops or vehicles they were carrying to the bottom of the sea. Although these underwater obstacles were visible at low tide, they could be covered by gunfire.

The solution to the underwater obstacle problem was solved by yet another deception. The Allies trained underwater swimmers (UDTs) equipped with scuba gear and explosives to go in before a beach assault and destroy enough of the obstacles to allow for a landing. This usually worked, although the Japanese sometimes ambushed the frogmen. Although the Japanese also planned to train their own divers—to swim underwater toward the landing craft and destroy them with explosives—this was rather akin to underwater kamikaze and never really worked. Another favorite tactic was to plant MINES near the high-tide line. The troops coming off the landing craft would walk right into an unseen minefield. Shelling the mined beaches before the landing was one solution, but too much shelling tore up the ground and made it difficult for troops to maneuver. And even heavy shelling was not guaranteed to get all the mines, leaving the attacking troops to deal with one more unknown as they worked their way inland. This lethal beach game between defender and attacker went on throughout World War II, and continues to this day.

Amphibious Operations, Task Forces

The shipping needed for a landing depended, of course, on the size of the landing force. The chart below shows two landing operations of the Pacific War. One was relatively small, the other quite large.

Operation	Guam July '44	Leyte October '44
Divisions	1.3	4
AGC	1	5
APA	34	32
AKA	7	10
LSD	6	10
LST	30	67
LCI	0	9
LCT	0	23

Note that each operation used a quite different combination of specialized shipping. There were several other differences between the two landings that explain this. GUAM was a navy operation deep in the central Pacific. Leyte was an army operation within range of several land bases. Thus the army could use shorter-range LCIs and LCTs. Indeed, these smaller ships were preferred by the army in the southwest Pacific, where there were many relatively small landings performed within range of land-based aircraft and nearby naval bases. Another major difference between the two operations was the size of the island being assaulted. Leyte was much larger than Guam and contained a larger Japanese garrison. Thus the Leyte assault required more TANKS and trucks, which is seen in the greater number of LSTs and LCTs.

The above chart does not show all the shipping used, for example, the cargo and tanker ships involved. Generally, 15–20 LIBERTY SHIPS (or their equivalents) were necessary to support a division-sized landing. The Liberty ship was quite large for its time, being about 16,000 GRT. A division also required 12–15 LSTs and LSDs to carry vehicles. LCTs, LCIs and LSMs could be used instead of LSTs if the invasion did not require a long ocean voyage. Of course, several of these smaller vessels hauled the load one LST could handle. As a rule of thumb, an amphibious operation required about one seagoing vessel for every 1,100 men to be put on the beach.

There were many other types of support ships. These included repair and hospital ships, to care for equipment and men injured during the operation. Each amphibious task force also included dozens of escorts (destroyers and escort carriers) as well as bombardment ships (cruisers and battleships). The larger aircraft carriers normally operated in their own task forces and, being juicy targets, tried to stay away from enemy land-based aircraft. Moreover, enemy SUBMARINES could be expected to head for an invasion site, and this was yet another reason to keep the big carriers far out to sea. The carrier task forces often did come by to launch air strikes on the invasion site, but did not stick around, like the escorts assigned to the amphibious task force.

Amphibious Operations, Technique

It wasn't until 1943 that the Allies got a chance to use their new amphibious techniques fully. Special amphibious ships began to appear in 1942, but it took another year and a few false starts before many of the kinks were worked out of the system. In its final form, the new "blitzkrieg from the sea" went through the following drill when executing assaults.

Careful Planning. In addition to finding out as much as possible about the enemy troops in the target area, the new "beaching" ships required detailed data on local tides and underwater geography. This requirement gave rise to the use of scuba divers to sneak in to obtain this information. Later, these "beach jumpers" evolved into UDT (underwater demolition teams) that went in to demolish any man-made or natural obstacles off the coast to be invaded. Based on all this information, plans would be made stipulating where each ship and

boat would be, and when, in order to get the hundreds of ships and boats onto the right part of the beach. The basic assault plan included destroying enemy air power in the area and driving away or destroying enemy warships. Then began several days of air attacks on the enemy units on the beach and behind it, usually executed by aircraft from the large (or "fast") carriers. The amphibious task force was several hundred miles away during most of this, moving at a speed of only 200–300 miles a day. When the preliminary bombardment was over, the amphibious task force appeared off the enemy shore. First minesweepers, protected by small warships, went in to clear lanes for the more vulnerable (and valuable) landing ships and transports.

Flexible Execution. Plans never work out precisely, once forces encounter an armed enemy. The troops have to be trained to deal with the unexpected, and the support forces (gunships, aircraft, and logistics units) have to be drilled on the many changes in plans that will occur once the shooting begins. They had to be ready to deal with anything unusual the enemy might come up with. A good example of the necessity of flexible execution was the Japanese use of KAMIKAZE suicide aircraft in the Philippines. US commanders had to deal with this radical new tactic while still moving forward with the amphibious attack.

The Assault. Several miles off the coast (out of machine-gun, but not artillery, range) the APAs got their infantry into the LCVPs for the actual assault. This would be launched in waves, of which there might be half a dozen or more. The LCVPs and LVTs spent a half an hour or more getting to the beach. Before, and during this time, destroyers, cruisers, and battleships shelled enemy fortifications and blasted any functioning enemy artillery. The Japanese learned to hold their artillery fire until the landing craft were very close and then blast them at point-blank range. In response, navy destroyers would come in as close as they could (without going aground, often only a few hundred yards offshore) and shoot it out with the enemy artillery. Landing plans made provision for destroyers running back and forth without getting mixed up with the hundred or more LCVPs and LVTs making their way to the beach. Once the assault troops cleared beaches of enemy troops (not an easy task), larger ships carrying TANKS and, eventually, logistical units and supplies could come in.

Vigorous Follow-up. Getting ashore is, literally, only half the battle. The assault troops will run out of ammunition, water, and food if not resupplied. CASUALTIES have to be taken off the beach to hospital ships. Once the troops get a few miles inland, artillery and engineer troops are brought in to provide fire support and build roads and airfields. Soon, the landing force will have land-based aircraft and a lot of artillery to help finish off the enemy force. But artillery and aircraft require mountains of supply. Thus the landing beaches remain hectic places for the duration of the battle. All day long, LSTs and other ships beach themselves and unload vehicles and supplies. These are driven inland to supply dumps. This immense logistical support was a major innovation in amphibious operations and provided the additional firepower that saved many lives among the fighting troops.

Allied amphibious tactics and techniques changed constantly during the war. After each landing, the experience was carefully examined and lessons learned were applied to the next assault. The enemy was also learning from his mistakes, so one had to adapt quickly just to avoid running into more formidable resistance during the next operation.

Amphibious Operations, Unloading Ships

Moving men, equipment, and supplies from ship to shore in the Pacific was, particularly for the Allies, little different than an amphibious invasion. They had little choice, as the Japanese grabbed most of the good ports in the Central and South Pacific early in the war. The Allies were never able to build their own ports and, instead, relied heavily

Marines boarding LCVPs from a Coast Guard-manned attack transport in preparation for the landing at Empress Augusta Bay, Bougainville, November 1, 1943. Techniques of loading and landing troops and supplies had been tested by the Marine Corps throughout the 1930s and were refined during the war by constant rehearsal and combat experience.

on amphibious vessels to bring material from freighters to land bases. But rather than use their valuable amphibious shipping, thousands of "lighters" (flat-bottomed coastal boats) were brought in to get the supplies from the freighters anchored in the deeper water to the easily built shallow-water wharves on the coast. While practical, this method doubled the time to unload a ship, as the cargo had to be unloaded twice (once to the lighter and then from the lighter to the wharf or beach). The Japanese did not have the resources to build many lighters, or the engineering equipment and trucks to quickly build the many wharves, storage areas, roads, and other cargo-handling facilities to handle numerous amphibious operations. They did use a lot of barges, not just to bring cargo ashore but also to move it between nearby islands. Overall, however, the Allies had more to unload, and greater means to unload it faster.

Amphibious Vehicles

Getting to the beach in force was a major accomplishment of World War II amphibious technique, but often it wasn't enough. Getting across the beach and inland quickly, during the first moments of the landing, was soon seen as a crucial task. Landings were at most risk in the first hours, and just being able to land vehicles from LSTs and such was not always sufficient. Two solutions were versions of land vehicles modified so they could swim ashore on their own.

In late 1943 the US Army started using the DUKW (called "duck"), essentially a standard army truck that could swim, developed by Roderick Stephens, a noted boat designer who went on to design the winners of three America's Cup races. The components of the army "deuce and a half" truck, a 6 by 6 (power to all six wheels) vehicle with a 5,000–pound (2.5–ton) carrying capacity, were fitted into a metal box. In effect the DUKW was a cross between a truck and a flat-bottomed boat. A fully loaded DUKW weighed 8.8 tons and was 31 feet long, 8.3 feet wide, and 7.1 feet high. It could go as fast as 45 miles an hour on roads, and about 6 miles an hour in the water. One tank of fuel would carry it 220 miles on roads and 50 miles in water. There was also a smaller DUKW (a "jeep" version weighing two tons), but few were manufactured or used. DUKWs spent most of their time ferrying supplies and troops (up to 25 men) from ships offshore.

The total of 21,147 DUKWs proved invaluable getting men and material ashore more quickly than via larger boats that had to beach themselves. Moreover, the DUKW could go places the beaching boats couldn't. Coasts often had mudflats, sandbars, and reefs that only the DUKW could get over. The DUKW could also swim up to a sand spit,

drive across, and then continue swimming. The DUKW suffered less damage coming ashore than those ships that threw themselves onto a beach.

The sand and salt water did considerable damage to the DUKWs. As with ships and carrier aircraft, the DUKWs were constructed of sturdier materials than ordinary vehicles. But even so, the tires and brake shoes had to be replaced frequently and a DUKW didn't last as long (100,000 miles or more) as a regular army truck.

By 1944, the DUKW were moved to the combat area by LSTs and then used to move supplies quickly from LSTs and cargo ships offshore to the beach and then inland to the front line. This became a remarkably efficient system, with infantry regiments being able to radio the LST-based "DUKW Motor Pool Headquarters," request specific supplies, and then see them arrive within hours. CASUALTIES could be evacuated with equal dispatch to hospital ships offshore. This was unprecedented in warfare and a truly revolutionary step in amphibious operations. However, as useful as it was, the DUKW was basically an unarmored truck and was not capable of standing up to the enemy fire encountered during the initial landing. The US Marines came up with another amphibious vehicle for that task: the "Alligator" (or LVT, for landing vehicle, tracked).

The LVT was a originally a prewar civilian vehicle developed for use in the marshlands of Florida. It was tracked (like a TANK) and could swim. By late 1942, the Marines had them in service. Over 10,000 were produced before the war was over. Larger (several feet wider and higher, although a few feet shorter) and heavier (up to 16 tons for the armored version) than a DUKW, the LVT also cost over twice as much to build and required more effort to maintain. Moreover, it was not as fast as the DUKW. This is a common difference between wheeled and tracked vehicles. The first LVTs were very slow, with maximum speeds of 12 MPH on land and 3-4 MPH in the water. The definitive version of the LVT, which came out in 1944, had a top land speed of 20 MPH and 5 MPH in the water. The 1944 model was still

Marines using an LVT during the assault on Tinian, 24 June 1944. In addition to its amphibious capabilities, the LVT served as a surrogate tank.

slower than the DUKW, but the LVT had several key advantages. For one thing, its tracks enabled it to cross obstacles more easily than the wheeled DUKW. This was very important on the day of an assault when the beach was torn up by combat. The Marines, more than the army, hit the most heavily defended beaches. The LVT's ability to crawl over just about anything, and relatively quickly, was often the difference between life and death in those first hours of a landing.

Like the DUKW, the original LVT was not a combat vehicle. Lacking armor and heavy weapons, it was as vulnerable as the DUKW to enemy fire. Moreover, both the DUKW and LVT were slower getting to the beach than the existing "slide

up on the beach" landing craft. What the assault troops needed, an armed and armored LVT, appeared as early as 1943.

The first "assault LVTs" were simply regular LVTs with armor bolted on to give the troops some protection from machine-gun fire and shell fragments. By the end of 1943, some of these LVTs had a turret-mounted 37mm gun added. What the Marines really wanted, a fully armored and heavily armed LVT, appeared in 1944. This, the LVT(A), was for all practical purposes an amphibious light tank. Built as such, it had a turret with a 75mm cannon plus up to four machine guns. The armor made it virtually immune to machine-gun fire and shell fragments. Several tons heavier, the 16-ton

LVT(A) was also slower (17 MPH on land and 5–6 MPH at sea) than the unarmored LVT. Since enemy tanks were not expected on the beach, and the LVT(A) couldn't carry a large antitank gun anyway, the 75mm cannon was intended for use against enemy troops and fortifications. The LVT(A)'s machine guns were to give the assault troops additional firepower.

Less than a thousand LVT(A)s were built and they were organized into nine "Amphibian Tank" battalions (each with 75 LVT(A)s, 12 LVTs, and 700 men). Three of these were Marine units and all were used in the Pacific. Of the six Army battalions, only one was used in the Pacific. The other five Army battalions were to be used in Europe, in support of river-crossing assaults, but the war in Europe ended before they could get into action.

Had the Army paid more attention to Marine experience with the LTV earlier, it might have had several battalions available for D-day, which would have prevented the near disaster on Omaha Beach. As the future of amphibious vehicles, the LVT(A) became the model of the post–World War II versions of the LVT which continues in use to this day.

Anami, Korechika (1887–1945)

Korechika Anami served in several posts in China, Japan, and elsewhere before becoming an army commander in China in early 1941. Moved with some of these China-based units to New Guinea in late 1943, he commanded for less than a year with little success. He then went on to various other posts in the Pacific and was eventually moved back to staff posts in Tokyo. By the end of the war he was the minister of war. Refusing to aid the coup to overthrow the government when the surrender was announced, he committed suicide on the day of the surrender.

Anchorage, Alaska

The principal city of Alaska, a small town of limited resources and poor port facilities, albeit with a decent airfield. Its location, however, nearly 800 miles northeast of DUTCH HARBOR, made it only marginally useful as a base.

Andaman Islands

These islands number over 200, in the eastern Bay of Bengal, about 300 miles southwest of RANGOON, and total about 2,500 square miles. Fairly hot and humid, with few inhabitants, the islands are hilly and forested. The Japanese took them from the British with little effort in early 1942, and the Allies left them there for the rest of the war, undisturbed save for an occasional air raid. For a time the Japanese attempted to make PORT BLAIR, the principal town, into a base.

Ando, Rikichi

Rikichi Ando joined the Japanese Army in 1914 and quickly rose through the ranks. He was one of the hot-headed generals in China who inexorably dragged Japan deeper into conflict with the West. In early 1940 he became commander of the South China Area Army. It was Ando who made an unauthorized move into French INDO-CHINA after Germany had defeated France. It was this move that caused the confrontation with the West, which led to the oil embargo and, soon thereafter, PEARL HARBOR. If there was any one act that led inevitably to war with America, it was this incursion into Vietnam. As a result, America embargoed Japan and Japan went to war. General Ando was responsible, and he acted against orders. The Japanese government was not pleased with all the trouble Ando had caused, and recalled and retired him as punishment. However, once the decision was made (in the fall of 1941) to go to war against the West, Ando was recalled to service, promoted to full general, and given command of the 10th Area Army in FORMOSA. This was a crucial post, as the Japanese always feared that the Allies might invade Formosa and thus cut off Japanese access to the oil and other raw materials to the south.

Anguar, Palau

Although wholly undeveloped, and with poor possibilities as a port, Anguar had some strategic value as an airbase, lying about 600 miles east of the Philippines and a few dozen miles southwest of PELELIU. It was invaded by US troops in conjunction with the Peleliu operation in late–1944.

ANGAU (Australian New Guinea Administrative Unit)

A quasi-military organization, the ANGAU followed the troops, with the intention of completely restoring the prewar colonial relationship between Australians and the aboriginal peoples. Noted for a less than friendly attitude toward the local inhabitants, representatives of the ANGAU often confiscated goods given the natives by friendly American and even Australian troops, with whom they were often at odds for not treating the aborigines with the proper degree of arrogance and brutality. They also took a dim view of anything resembling native collaboration with the Japanese, a phenomenon that was, in fact, not particularly common.

Ref: Sinclair, *To Find a Path*; White and Lindstrom, *The Pacific Theater*.

Anti-Comintern Pact (November 1936)

Germany, Japan, and Italy concluded this pact—it was not a proper alliance—for the alleged purpose of countering communist influence. This was the beginning of what Italian dictator Benito Mussolini called "the Axis" (because the world would revolve around them), against which the "Allies" later fought. The treaty was mostly for show, but starkly divided the world. The Soviet "Comintern" was the "Communist International," an organization of Marxist parties preparing for the "Red Crusade" that would spread the world revolution. This had caused a lot of nervousness in the 1920s, but had become only something for fascists to rail against. The "communist threat" would not become a big issue again until the late 1940s. The Soviets formally dissolved the Comintern as a favor to the Allies before World War II was over, to very little notice.

The Anti-Comintern Pact pledged the signatory powers only to cooperate, not necessarily to go to each other's defense. As a result, in early 1939 HITLER tried to get Japan to conclude a real alliance. The Japanese realized that he meant to have a war with Britain, and wanted their support. Although the Imperial Army was for the treaty, the Court, the navy, and other influential elements were opposed, since they feared being dragged into a war before Japan was ready. The anti-treaty faction won. This was one reason that Hitler concluded his non-aggression deal with Stalin in August of that year.

Deciding that Hitler's pact with Stalin precluded a Soviet-German War, the Japanese made a non-aggression pact with the Russians as well, and began considering their options in the Pacific. Of course, Hitler did not inform them of his plans for Russia.

In September 1940, while heavily engaged against Britain and still more than six months before he invaded Russia, Hitler arranged for the Tripartite Treaty, among Italy, Germany, and Japan. This was a defensive alliance. Japan was pledged to assist Germany and Italy if a third party became involved in their war with Britain, while Germany and Italy pledged to assist Japan if a third party intervened in her war with China. To Hitler's great chagrin, Japan refused to attack Russia when he did, on the grounds that the Tripartite Pact did not cover a third party entering the war by being attacked.

Meanwhile, that November the Anti-Comintern Pact of 25 November 1936 was renewed for five years at Berlin, by Germany, Japan, Italy, Hungary, Spain, MANCHUKUO (a Japanese puppet state), Bulgaria, Croatia (an Italian puppet state), Denmark (under German control), Finland, Romania, Slovakia (a German puppet), and (curiously) the Nationalist government in China (which fought local communists throughout the

1930s). Although the Anti-Comintern Pact had little effect on the war, the Tripartite Treaty was invoked by Hitler when he declared war on the United States shortly after Pearl Harbor. He did so at least partially in the belief that Japan would then loyally support him in his war against Russia. The Japanese, however, had sampled war with Russia at Nomonhan and were shy of a rematch.

See also GERMANY IN THE PACIFIC WAR; ITALY IN THE PACIFIC WAR.

Aoba Class, Japanese Heavy Cruisers

Essentially improved FURUTAKAS, mounting their 8-inch guns in twin turrets from the start, the two Aobas saw extensive service, notably in the SOL-OMONS. Very durable ships, at one point in her career AOBA was reduced to a total wreck above the main deck, yet was still able to make speed and ultimately returned to service. Both were sunk by US carrier aircraft. With the Furutakas, they were the smallest heavy cruisers ever built.

Aoba (1924–1926–1927) fought in the CORAL SEA, at SAVO ISLAND, and CAPE ESPERANCE, where she was almost lost, not returning to service for nearly a year. She was sunk by US carrier aircraft on July 28, 1945 in Honshu's KURE harbor.

Kinugasa (1924–1926–1927) was with *Aoba* until Cape Esperance, and went on to take part in the protracted Naval Battle of GUADALCANAL, being sunk on 14 November 1942 by US carrier aircraft.

Benito Mussolini, the Duce of fascist Italy, and Adolph Hitler, the Führer of Nazi Germany, Japan's partners in the Axis, at Munich shortly after the fall of France in 1940.

APA (attack transport)

In addition to those amphibious warfare ships that literally "hit the beach," there were a number of other more conventional ship types that did not run up on the beach.

Merchant ships of about 6,800 to 21,000 GRT were modified (or built from scratch) for the transport and landing of assault troops. Most carried 1,500 troops, plus 15–33 LCVPs and 2–4 LCMs. These were the ships from which the troops climbed down the cargo nets to get into the LCVPs. Nearly 150 were built or modified for APA service between 1942 and 1945. Landing a division required about a dozen APAs. Crew size was about 500 men, speed was 15–20 knots, and armament varied, but usually included one or more 5-inch or 3-inch guns plus up to a dozen 40mm antiaircraft guns.

Apia, Western Samoa

The principal port of British-controlled Western SAMOA, with limited facilities and only a modest anchorage, although with a fair airfield. Apia's principal value was as a base location on the long route from the Americas to Australia.

Arkansas, US Battleship

The oldest American battleship, designed when Theodore Roosevelt was in the White House, and indeed the oldest American combatant in the war, *Arkansas*, BB-33 (1910–1911–1912), saw some service in the Pacific, providing fire support for amphibious landings during the last year of the war, after turning in a virtuoso performance during amphibious assaults all over the European Theater. After the war she was expended during the Bikini ATOMIC BOMB tests, being virtually at ground zero. Her sistership, *Wyoming*, BB-32 (1910–1911–1912), had been partially disarmed under terms of the Naval DISARMAMENT TREATIES, and served as a gunnery training ship throughout the war. At one

point it was proposed to refit her for war service, but saner minds prevailed.

Artillery

Called by Stalin the "God of War," artillery, the principal killer in the European Theater, was brought down a notch or two in the Pacific. The frequent dense jungles, and the intense use of shovels, soil, CORAL, and trees to build shell-proof dugouts greatly reduced the effectiveness of artillery. However, except for the opening campaign in the Philippines in 1941–42, the United States main-

ARTILLERY OF THE PACIFIC WAR				
Country	Caliber	Type	Range	RPM
U.S.	37mm	A/T Gun	5,000	6.0
	75mm	A/T Gun	8,500	2.5
	75mm	Pack Howitzer	9,800	2.5
	105mm	Howitzer	12,500	2.0
	155mm	Howitzer	16,500	1.0
Britain	40mm	A/T Gun	5,000	6.0
	57mm	A/T Gun	5,000	5.0
	88mm	Howitzer	12,100	10.0
	140mm	Gun	16,500	1.0
Japan	37mm	A/T Gun	5,000	6.0
	70mm	Inf. Howitzer	3,000	3.0
	75mm	Inf. Howitzer	8,000	2.5
	75mm	Howitzer	9,000	2.5
	150mm	Howitzer	15,000	1.0

Country = the nation that manufactured and used this weapon. **Caliber** = the diameter of the gun's shell in millimeters (25.4mm equals one inch). **Type** = the type of artillery weapon. **A/T Gun** = antitank gun, which was the same type of gun mounted on TANKS. **Howitzer** = a short-barreled weapon capable of relatively high-angled fire. **Pack** = howitzer capable of being disassembled into several more manageable pieces, for transportation on muleback. **Inf.** = infantry howitzer, a shorter range than a regular howitzer, but lighter. **Gun** = a long-range piece, with little ability to execute high-angle fire. In the later stages of the war some US 105mm howitzers were self-propelled. **Range** = in meters, with 1,600 meters equaling a mile. **RPM** = rounds per minute that the weapon can fire on a sustained basis. The RPM can be more than doubled for a few minutes, but this leads to barrel overheating. The proper designations of the British weapons, used by most Commonwealth forces, were: 37mm A/T, 2–pounder; 57mm, 6–pounder; 88mm, 25–pounder; 140mm, 5.5–inch gun.

tained the artillery advantage over the Japanese throughout the Pacific War.

The advantage was far more than merely quantitative. There were more pieces in an American division, army (72, plus about 100 antitank guns) or Marine (60, plus 54 antitank guns), than in a Japanese one (48, plus 18 small antitank guns), not to mention a more generous allocation of artillery to higher commands.

Moreover, while US Army divisional artillery was largely 105mm and 155mm guns and howitzers (Marine divisions began with 75mm and 105mm pieces, with some 155mms, but soon graduated to heavier ones), most Japanese artillery was 75mm and 150mm. In addition, all US artillery was motorized while most Japanese artillery was horse-drawn (see HORSES AND MULES IN THE PACIFIC), which frequently meant manhandled. US artillery had an elaborate and flexible fire-control system while, the Japanese fire control was more rigid and unresponsive to urgent troop needs. Finally, US artillery had several times more ammunition per gun than did the Japanese. In practical terms, US divisions had anywhere from three to ten times as much artillery firepower at their disposal than Japanese divisions.

Having captured a Japanese Model 92 70mm howitzer on Saipan, these Marines are using it against its former owners during the attack on Garapan, the island's principal town, July 1944. Note that one of the men is covering his ears, while another is shouting to cope with the overpressure as the gun is fired; the other two men appear to have stuffed cotton in their ears.

Chinese forces used a variety of mostly obsolete artillery pieces, although some units received US 75mm pack howitzers. Artillery units of the PHILIPPINE ARMY were mostly equipped with obsolete 2.95-inch howitzers and 75mm guns, all of pre–World War I manufacture.

Not only was Japanese artillery lighter than US artillery, it was distributed differently. The United States emphasized centralized coordination of artillery, while the Japanese relied rather heavily on the 70mm and 75mm infantry howitzers. There were 10 of these in each infantry regiment, in contrast to none in the comparable US regiment. Japanese training and doctrine stressed the use of these for close support of their infantry, a role in which they proved very valuable. However, in very dense environments, such as the jungles of GUADALCANAL or Burma, the infantry howitzers often could not be brought close enough to the front to be effective. In such situations the troops often had to attack without any artillery support, since the Japanese were unable to coordinate divisional artillery with infantry attacks. The US practice was to pool artillery assets at division level and deliver fire on call from the front-line units. Sophisticated communications and coordination techniques permitted all guns within range to fire in coordination, often with all the rounds landing on the target at the same time, a devastating experience for the troops on the receiving end. As the war progressed it was found useful to provide some light artillery firepower to the troops right up on the front lines, in the form of bazookas (portable rocket launchers) and light antitank guns, which proved useful for breaking into fortifications.

An experiment in allocating a battery of 105mm howitzers to each infantry regiment proved less than successful, however, and it was customary for these to be sent up to division artillery, where they formed an extra battalion on an ad hoc basis. As the war went on US troops also benefited from the presence of "flying artillery," aircraft equipped for ground support operations. Marine pilots were particularly good at this, since all of them were trained as infantry officers before getting their wings. An-

"Red Legs"—artillerymen—of C Battery, 90th Field Artillery Battalion, 25th Infantry Division, firing a 105mm howitzer in a nocturnal bombardment of Japanese positions at Balete Pass, Luzon April 19, 1945. Note the ready ammunition, and the fact that the gunners are preparing to load a fresh round even as the piece is discharging. The speed, accuracy, and effectiveness of American artillery was a major factor in minimizing US casualties in all theaters.

tiaircraft artillery played an important part in the war, as air attacks on ground troops were used by both sides until near the end of the war. Where the Japanese had lost air superiority, they usually still had aircraft and these could be sent in to attack at night. Although not very accurate, this kept the troops from getting their much needed sleep and would do some damage.

The principal defense against air attacks was a variety of antiaircraft guns. Japanese and American varieties were similar in caliber, but not in quality. For example, the Japanese heavy machine gun was a 13.2mm weapon with a 450 rounds per minute (RPM) rate of fire. The equivalent US weapon was the .50 caliber (12.7mm) machine gun with a 540 RPM rate of fire. The Japanese weapon had a higher effective altitude (13,000 feet versus 10,000), but this was less important than rate of fire for a machine gun that typically fired at aircraft a few thousand, or a few hundred, feet away. For a weapon of that caliber, it was also important to put a lot of bullets into the aircraft to have any effect. While the Japanese used a larger caliber (13.2mm versus 12.7mm) bullet, American aircraft were far more resistant to such damage than their Japanese counterparts.

Medium caliber antiaircraft guns showed the same discrepancies in quality. Both sides had a 40mm gun, but the Japanese used an older British design that had a meager 250 RPM rate of fire and a ceiling of 14,000 feet. The US 40mm had a 420 RPM and 22,000-foot ceiling. US troops were also more liberally supplied with ammunition. Nevertheless, the Japanese managed to keep some antiaircraft guns operating until the end of the war, causing steady losses among attacking American aircraft.

Ref: *Handbook on Japanese Military Forces*; Harries and Harries, *Soldiers of the Sun*; Perret, *There's a War to Be Won*.

Asashio Class, Japanese Destroyers

Built 1935–1938, once some technical problems with their steering had been worked out, the 10 Asashios proved to be good ships, specialized for surface actions. As with all vessels, during the war their armament was steadily upgraded. All were war losses, two to SUBMARINES, four to air attack, and four to surface ships, including three during the Battle of SURIGAO STRAIT.

Atlanta Class, US Antiaircraft Cruisers

A highly successful design, the Atlanta Class proved so valuable that even before the first batch of four had been completed a second batch had been ordered, to a slightly different design (sometimes known as the Oakland Class), and later a third batch, of three ships, was laid down, not to be completed until after the war. They were very expensive ships, running about $23 million each, more than any prewar cruisers, all of which were larger. Although fast, they were lightly protected. Designed to shoot down airplanes, they did some of their hardest fighting in surface actions in the SOLOMON ISLANDS, where their numerous rapid-fire 5-inch guns proved remarkably valuable, and they had one of the heaviest TORPEDO armaments in the fleet.

Atlanta, CLAA-51 (1940–1941–1942), put in an excellent performance defending the carriers in the Battle of the EASTERN SOLOMONS, and then went down under the pounding of Japanese battleships and destroyers in the Naval Battle of GUADALCANAL on November 12–13, 1942.

Juneau, CLAA-52 (1940–1941–1942), helped defend the fleet in the Battle of SANTA CRUZ, and went on to fight in the first Naval Battle of Guadalcanal (November 12–13, 1942), which she survived only to be torpedoed the next morning by the Japanese submarine I-26, sinking quickly. Among the 676 men lost were the five SULLIVAN BROTHERS.

San Diego, CLAA-53 (1940–1941–1942), had a busy but relatively undistinguished war, covering the carriers in a number of actions. Scrapped in 1960.

San Juan, CLAA-54 (1940–1941–1942), saw considerable service and was lightly damaged during the Battle of the Santa Cruz Islands. Scrapped in 1962.

The four ships of the Oakland group, *Oakland* CLAA-95 (1941–1942–1942), *Reno* CLAA-96 (1941–1942–1943), *Flint* CLAA-97 (1942–1944–1944), and *Tucson* CLAA-98 (1942–1944–1945) saw much less action than the first batch. Indeed, the completion of the last two was deliberately delayed to permit work to be done on more desperately needed types of vessels, such as destroyers and escort carriers. The final group, *Juneau* (CLAA-119), *Spokane* (CLAA-120), and *Fresno* (CLAA-

121), were laid down 1944–45 and completed in 1946. All were scrapped in the 1960s.

The Oakland and Juneau groups differed from the four original ships; they had four fewer 5"/38 guns, mounted differently, which led to improved stability.

Atomic Bomb

France, Britain, the United States, Germany, Japan, and the Soviet Union all tried to build an atomic bomb during World War II. Only the United States succeeded.

The potential for producing nuclear bombs was widely known, at least among scientists, before World War II. The American government took note of warnings from scientists and began work in earnest the summer before PEARL HARBOR. The US program, code-named the Manhattan Project, required four years and over $20 billion (in 1996 dollars) to produce the first successful detonation of an atomic bomb on 16 July 1945. Within days, the components of two more bombs were on their way, carried by a heavy cruiser, to the B-29 base at TINIAN. Nine months earlier, a special B-29 unit (the 509th Composite Group) had begun training to drop the bombs. The B-29s had to be modified to drop one five-ton bomb, rather than dozens of 500-pound bombs. Engineers on Tinian were ordered to prepare special facilities for loading the single large bomb into the modified bomb bay of the "atomic B-29's." In July 1945, the special B-29s began making practice runs over Japan. No one was told about the atomic bomb until the first one was dropped.

On 6 August, the first atomic bomb used in combat was dropped on HIROSHIMA, Japan, by a B-29 called the *Enola Gay*.

Hiroshima and NAGASAKI were two of a number of cities that were kept as pristine targets, in order to illustrate better the awesome power of the A-bombs. Both Hiroshima and Nagasaki were major seaports and had a number of military installations and industrial complexes. By the standards of the day, they were excellent strategic targets. Had they not been saved for this purpose, they would have been obliterated earlier, along with most of the major cities of Japan. The target committee suggested cities based on psychological factors, not military value. The "aim points" were the city centers, not the military installations. Hiroshima, for example, had an army base with 40,000 soldiers, and a population of about 275,000, but the aim point was the city center.

The bomb used on Hiroshima was called "Little Boy" or "Thin Man." It was a gun-assembled U-235 (uranium) bomb; this means that two pieces of uranium 235 are literally shot against each other. When the two chunks of metal meet they form a critical mass. So much uranium is in one place that a fission reaction occurs, that is, the neutrons that escape a "splitting" uranium atom cause more than one other uranium atom to split also in what is called a chain reaction. During this process much of the energy that binds the nucleus of atoms is converted into other energy forms such as heat and radiation. The same reaction occurs in nuclear power plants, but is more controlled and slower. The Manhattan Project first achieved this controlled chain reaction, then built a device that would create an uncontrolled chain reaction, an atomic bomb. While the 1945 atomic bombs were not mechanically complicated, the hard part was obtaining the necessary uranium 235 or plutonium. In nature uranium 235 is always found mixed with uranium 238, which cannot be used for a fission reaction (that is, a bomb). In nature the ratio between U235 and U238 is less than one part in a hundred, so building a bomb requires uranium that is more than 60% U235. Both uranium isotopes are very similar chemically and extremely hard to separate. Once the Manhattan Project scientists overcame this problem, and did it via several techniques, the rest was much less daunting.

Hiroshima had not been firebombed previously because its geography, namely a flat area containing the city and surrounded by hills, made it a good target for an atomic bomb. Tokyo wasn't selected because it had already been firebombed so many times it was no longer worthy of further attention.

Moreover, an atomic bomb on Tokyo would have destroyed the government and prevented an organized surrender of the Japanese.

Between the Hiroshima and Nagasaki bombings, American aircraft dropped millions of leaflets that said:

TO THE JAPANESE PEOPLE

America asks that you take immediate heed of what we say in this leaflet. We are in possession of the most destructive explosive ever devised by man. A single one of our newly developed Atomic Bombs is actually the equivalent in explosive power to what 2,000 of our giant B-29s can carry on a single mission. This awful fact is one for you to ponder and we solemnly assure you it is grimly accurate.

We have just begun to use this weapon against your homeland. If you still have any doubt, make inquiry as to what happened to Hiroshima when just one Atomic Bomb fell on that city.

The mushroom cloud from the atomic bomb dropped on Nagasaki on 9 August 1945.

YIELD OF THE FIRST THREE ATOMIC BOMBS	
Bomb	Kilotons
Trinity Test	19
Hiroshima	15
Nagasaki	21

Before using this bomb to destroy every resource of the military by which they are prolonging this useless war, we ask that you now petition the Emperor to end the war. Our President has outlined for you the thirteen consequences of an honorable surrender. We urge that you accept these consequences and begin the work of building a new, better and peace-loving Japan.

You should take steps now to cease military resistance. Otherwise, we shall employ the bomb and all our other superior weapons to promptly and forcefully end the war.

No answer was forthcoming from the Japanese, so on August 9 a second B-29 was sent out with an atomic bomb. This one bomb was called the Fat Man. It was an implosion bomb using Pu-239 (plutonium).

The city of Kokura had been spared firebombing so that it could serve as an atomic target, and was the primary target. When Kokura was hidden by overcast, the target was changed to Nagasaki, the secondary target. Nagasaki had been bombed prior to the atomic bombing, but not heavily. It was a secondary target for the atomic bomb because it was on the way to IWO JIMA, where the B-29 (*Bock's Car*) was headed after finding Kokura clouded over. *Bock's Car* was low on fuel due to a problem with its fuel tanks. The Fat Man bomb design did not allow for disabling the fuse in flight, so the bomb had to be dropped somewhere. Nagasaki became the target.

The two atomic bombs killed about 200,000 people, some 70% in the Hiroshima attack. The exact number is still a matter of some dispute because many Japanese claim that just about anyone in the two cities at the time of the bombing, who later died, did so as a result of radiation from the bombs. Studies of the survivors indicate a somewhat raised incidence of certain cancers from bomb radiation. Of those who were flash blinded many recovered their sight. No genetic damage has been found. The most probable explanation for the lack of evidence of genetic damage is that those who were close enough to be damaged genetically were killed.

American PRISONERS OF WAR working in Japan reported the Japanese attitude suddenly changed after 6 August. The Japanese told the prisoners that a big bomb had struck Hiroshima. Many Japanese officials then provided food and Red Cross parcels and excused the prisoners from going to work. This was more likely the closer the Americans were to Hiroshima and Nagasaki. Japanese records are somewhat vague on this point, but it appears that at least a dozen or so Americans were killed by the nuclear attacks, as well as some 20,000 Koreans, who had been enticed or drafted to work in Japan.

See also HIROSHIMA, THE PLOT.

Ref: Armstrong, *Unconditional Surrender*; Butow, *Japan's Decision to Surrender*; Feis, *The Atomic Bomb and the End of World War II*; Sigal, *Fighting to the Finish*.

COL *Paul Tibbets Jr. in the cockpit of his B-29,* Enola Gay, *shortly before taking off to drop the atomic bomb on Hiroshima, August 6, 1945.*

Atomic Bomb, Aircraft and Aircrew

The aircraft involved in the dropping of the atomic bombs on HIROSHIMA and Nagasaki were B-29s. The Hiroshima bomb, known as "Little Boy" or "Thin Man," was dropped on August 6, 1945 by the bomber *Enola Gay*. The aircraft was commanded by Col. Paul W. Tibbets Jr., who had named it after his mother. The copilot was Capt. Robert A. Lewis, the navigator Capt. Theodore Van Kirk, the flight engineer was 1Lt Wyatt E. Duzenberry, the electronics officer 2Lt Maurice Jeppson, the bombardier Maj. Thomas W. Ferebee. US Navy Capt. William S. Parsons was the armorer, who actually prepared the bomb for use. Enlisted personnel aboard were Staff Sergeant George R. Ceron, Sergeant Robert R. Shumand, and Private First Class Richard H. Nelson. After the war *Enola Gay* was retained as a relic, but neglected, even after being turned over to the Smithsonian

Institution. In the late 1980s a restoration project began, in anticipation of exhibiting the airplane for the 50th anniversary of the bombing. When this came to pass, the presentation was so biased as to argue that the war had been forced upon Japan by the United States. This led to an outcry by veterans and historians, which resulted in a more balanced presentation.

The NAGASAKI bomb, known as "Fat Man" and "Fat Boy," was dropped by *Bock's Car*, flown by Maj. Charles Sweeney. The bombardier was Capt. Kermin K. Beahan. Navy Cdr. Frederick L. Ashworth performed the final assembly and arming of the bomb.

Maj. Charles Sweeney had also been at Hiroshima, as pilot of *The Great Artiste*, one of several B-29s serving as chase planes taking photographs and making scientific observations.

Apparently *The Great Artiste* and *Straight Flush* were the only airplanes to take part in both attacks, serving as chase planes both times.

Legend to the contrary notwithstanding, neither the pilots, the bombardiers, the armorers, nor any of the crew members of either *Enola Gay* or *Bock's Car* ever suffered any mental disorders as a result of their role in the bombing. All considered, and continue to consider, their missions essential to bringing the war to a speedy end.

Atomic Bomb, the Bikini Tests

Less than a year after the surrender of Japan, a great task force once again dropped anchor in a Pacific lagoon. The lagoon was that of Bikini Atoll, one of the CAROLINE ISLANDS, a pleasant place inhabited by little more than a hundred people who were rather unceremoniously moved to another atoll.

The fleet was an odd one, 95 mostly obsolete vessels: a fleet carrier, a light carrier, four battleships, two heavy cruisers, 17 destroyers, eight SUBMARINES, 27 LSTs, LCIs, and LCTs, and 25 attack transports and cargo ships. Odder still, although most of the ships were American, there were also several former Japanese ones and even a former German heavy cruiser. The occasion was "Operation Crossroads," a pair of tests designed to determine the probable effects of nuclear weapons on a task force at sea.

As closely as possible the ships were fitted out as if for war. The aircraft carriers had airplanes on their hangar decks, avgas in their fuel tank, and bombs in their magazines. The battleships, cruisers, and destroyers had full magazines as well. The idea was to have everything as "normal" as possible, so that maximum benefit could be gained from the test.

The first test took place on July 1, 1946. A nuclear weapon was dropped from a B-29, to detonate in the air just above the fleet. The results were marginal. Although there was extensive damage to the upper works of many of the ships, few of the

larger ones suffered significant damage, although the former Japanese light cruiser *Sakawa* sank the next day.

The second test, on July 25, 1946, was quite another matter. A nuclear device was suspended underwater beneath a specially equipped LCI in the middle of the anchored vessels. The results were striking. Many smaller ships and craft went down immediately; the old battleship ARKANSAS and the carrier *Saratoga*, both within a few hundred yards of "ground Zero," were extensively damaged and sank within hours. Other vessels took longer to succumb. For example, the former Japanese battleship NAGATO finally capsized on the 29th. Surprisingly, a number of the ships involved in the test were salvable, particularly the old battlewagons *New York*, *Nevada*, and PENNSYLVANIA, and even the light carrier INDEPENDENCE. These were towed to various naval bases for study, and later expended as targets.

A lot was learned from the Bikini nuclear weapons tests, resulting in innovative developments in the design of ships built afterward. There was a negative side as well. Little was known about radiation poisoning and even less about the tolerable limits. Although some ships were deemed too "hot" to be boarded, and were sunk by a few well placed rounds, most of the others were repeatedly visited by military and scientific personnel. The resulting effects on the health of these people are still being debated, although the radiation monitoring methods then in use did do a good job of warning sailors and technicians away from particularly "hot" areas.

After nearly five decades the Bikinians (who have grown in number to nearly 2,000) are now permitted to visit their native atoll, but it will be many years before they will be able to return permanently, as certain plants and animals traditional in their diet have been found to contain higher than normal concentrations of several radioactive isotopes. In addition, there are the ships lying at the bottom of their lagoon, most of them with ammunition still in their magazines. In the meantime, the Bikini islanders have been paid $100 million in compensation. With this, ironically, the islanders have managed to cope somewhat better than neighboring islanders who did not have their ancestral atolls nuked.

It isn't true, as some Japanese assert, that *Nagato* was included as a final insult to the Imperial Navy. She was included because she was available, and constructed on different principles and using different techniques than were comparable American battleships. Indeed, the presence of such former enemy vessels as *Nagato, Sakawa*, and the German heavy cruiser *Prinz Eugen* could just as easily be regarded as rather insulting to the American warships present that had fought so gallantly to oppose Japanese and German aggression.

Atomic Bomb, Japanese

The Japanese atomic bomb research program was designated "Project A." Directed by noted nuclear physicist Hideki Yukawa, the scientists working on the project had a very difficult time securing support from the Imperial Army. At one point a request for a mere 50,000 yen (about $12,000 in money of 1941) was literally laughed off by one high army officer. Only when an accidental explosion—certainly non-nuclear in origin—destroyed a Tokyo laboratory and an adjacent building, killing several scientists and technicians, did the army suddenly become more interested. Even then the number of scientists working on the project never exceeded 50.

Aside from the difficulty of obtaining official support, Japanese nuclear weapons researchers were hampered by a general lack of resources. In addition, like their German counterparts, the Japanese scientists never hit upon the notion of critical mass. There was some cooperation between Germany and Japan in terms of nuclear weapons development, once each decided to inform the other of its work. This was quite late. Almost literally in the last hours of the Third Reich, on 25 March 1945, a submarine, U-234, was sent to Japan with a cargo of technical information and samples of various innovative weapons, plus 1,200 pounds of uranium oxide. Still at sea when Germany surrendered on 8 May, U-234 turned herself over to the US Navy. Although it was carefully inventoried at the time, the fate of the uranium oxide aboard the submarine has never been established, and it has long been rumored that it was processed to extract the critical isotope U-235, which was used to help make the bombs dropped on Japan.

Although the Japanese atomic bomb program was officially halted in early 1945, it continued covertly until 1947, when it was discovered by the Occupation authorities.

See also HIROSHIMA, THE PLOT.

Ref: Wilcox, *Japan's Secret War.*

Atrocities, Japanese

The list of Japanese atrocities during World War II is a long and gruesome one. Here is a random sample of some of the more ghastly incidents.

BATAAN DEATH MARCH: 60,000 Philippine and American PRISONERS were forced to march 70 miles to prison camps. The Japanese killed thousands of POWs who stumbled and fell along the way.

Japan's Unit 731 conducted biological experiments on Allied prisoners of war and medical experiments on more than 30,000 men, women, and children. Unit 731 was also responsible for releasing thousands of bubonic plague-carrying rats at the end of the war, resulting in an epidemic that killed thousands of Chinese.

Japanese soldiers cannibalized American prisoners in the Philippines and on some other Pacific islands, as well as 100 Australian POWs and many more natives in Papua New Guinea.

Sixteen thousand Allied prisoners of war and 70,000 native workers were killed in 14 months, on the Burma/Siam railroad (immortalized in the novel and motion picture *The Bridge on the River Kwai*).

Captured women were forced into prostitution as COMFORT WOMEN in colonies and conquered territories.

Thirty-three Australian nurses were machine-gunned on the island of Bangka.

Survivors of the sinking USS *Houston* were machine-gunned in the water, leaving only 368 out of a crew of almost 1,100.

Hundreds of Indian prisoners of war were massacred in North BORNEO, in 1942.

Twenty-five hundred Australian and British prisoners of war were massacred in Borneo in 1945.

More than 100,000 Chinese residents of SINGAPORE were massacred after the capture of that city from the British in February 1942.

Twenty thousand people were massacred at Mandor, Borneo.

More than 200 American prisoners of war were burned to death in a cave (including Manning Kimmel, son of Husband KIMMEL, former commander in chief, US Fleet) in the Palawan massacre.

The surprise attack on PEARL HARBOR left over 2,400 Americans dead. At the time, Japanese officials were discussing peace in Washington, D.C.

The remains of eight people massacred by Japanese troops at Tapel, Cagayan Province, Luzon, on July 1, 1945. The man in the picture is Pedro Cerono, who located the site for US officials on November 23, 1945.

Rape of Nanking: 300,000 men, women, and children were raped, slaughtered, and mutilated. Untold numbers of prisoners were murdered, and some 20,000 young men of military age were machine-gunned to death.

"Practice" surgery on Allied prisoners was routine. The few "patients" who did survive the procedures were killed, as the Japanese did not see any reason to practice postoperative skills. Surgery was usually performed without anesthesia, as the scarce medicines were saved for Japanese patients. This macabre form of medical training was common in China, but American and Allied prisoners were subjected to it on GUADALCANAL and other battlefields. For the Japanese whose feeling was "better suicide than capture," this was a valuable opportunity to better their own medical capability.

All Japanese prisoner of war camp commanders were instructed in written orders to massacre Allied prisoners of war immediately if Japan itself were invaded. None were to be liberated.

Auckland, New Zealand

An excellent harbor, albeit with relatively limited repair facilities and lacking in a strong industrial base to support such, Auckland was the principal port of New Zealand, and an important air transport center as well.

Aung San (1895–1947)

A Burmese nationalist leader, Aung San had initially been a communist, but later collaborated with the Japanese. Together with a number of other young Burmese nationalists he attended a Japanese military training program in FORMOSA in the 1930s. He worked closely with Keiji Suzuki to create the Patriot Burma Forces, served as chief of staff to the Burma Independence Army in 1941–42, and was named head of the Burma Defense Force, which later became the Burmese National Army. Although he attempted to cooperate with the Japanese, the divergent objectives of Japanese

imperialism and Burmese nationalism made matters difficult. By late 1944 his disillusionment, certainly fueled at least in part by Japanese defeat in the field, was such that he began making covert peace overtures to the British, breaking with Ba Maw, the formal head of the Japanese-sponsored independent Burma. In May 1945 he even traveled secretly to India to meet with MOUNTBATTEN and plan STRATEGY.

After the war Aung San became active in the politics of independent Burma, but was assassinated in 1947. His daughter, Aung San Suu Kyi, is the noted Burmese democratic leader, winner of the Nobel Prize for peace.

Australia, Commonwealth of

Relatively flat and very dry, except for the eastern and northern coastal regions, Australia is about two million square miles in area. The smallest continent was in 1941 a member of the British Commonwealth. Internal communications were poor, in some regions very poor. To reach the northwestern part of the country from the eastern or southern areas one had to go by airplane or ship. Most of the population of about seven million was concentrated in the southeastern part of the country. The Australian economy was primarily agricultural. Although its industry was advanced for the Pacific region, it was ill-suited to the needs of modern war production. Despite these limitations, with some time and money, Australia proved a welcome source of many useful goods (canteens, mess kits, some spare parts), and a valuable source of food for Allied forces in the South Pacific. Excluding the Soviet Union, Australia probably was the most militarized of all the Allied powers during the war. Under the premiership of John CURTIN the economy was rigorously centralized. Personnel management reached extraordinary proportions. Many businesses and services, such as bank branches, were merged or closed to conserve manpower. Both men and women were subjected to CONSCRIPTION not only for military but also for labor service. Even food, although never in short supply, was so rigidly controlled for military use that there were actual shortages of some items.

The Japanese bombed DARWIN in northwestern Australia in early 1942. This, and the ongoing series of Allied defeats in the NETHERLANDS EAST INDIES, New Guinea, and the SOLOMONS through mid–1942, caused an invasion scare that prompted the Commonwealth government to make extensive provision for scorched earth (destroy everything) resistance. Despite the near panic in some circles, the Japanese never contemplated an invasion of Australia. Even if they had, their resources, and the character of the country, would have limited them to a lodgment on the northern or northwestern coasts, where they would have had little impact.

Nearly 900,000 Australians served during the war, including some 40,000 women, nearly 14% of the population, a remarkable turnout. Over half a million were sent out of Australia. About 27,100 Australian military personnel died in the war, 17,500 of them in the Pacific, of whom about 9,500 were killed or mortally wounded in action. Some 8,000 Australians were killed or died of starvation or disease while PRISONERS of the Japanese.

Ref: *Australia in the Second World War*; Long, *The Six Years War*.

Australia Class, Australian Heavy Cruisers

The Australia-class heavy cruisers shared with their half-sisters of the British KENT CLASS, a general lack of handiness at sea, having a very wide turning circle. As in all British-designed heavy cruisers, they had minimal protection in the form of an armored box. They were well-built and resilient.

Australia (1925–1927–1928) saw extensive service throughout the war, from the CORAL SEA to the OKINAWA Campaign. She was repeatedly hit: damaged off FORMOSA on 16 October 1944, she was almost abandoned when a typhoon blew up; off Luzon, when she took a KAMIKAZE in January 1945; and during the Okinawa Campaign, when she took six kamikazes over several days. She was back in service for operations off Japan in the closing weeks of the war, and was scrapped in 1955.

Canberra (1925–1927–1928) served in the southwest Pacific from the Coral Sea to SAVO ISLAND, when she had to be scuttled after taking about 20 4.7-inch to 8-inch shells, plus possibly two TORPEDOES, in three minutes.

Australian Army

Australia, a vast land of some 2 million square miles but only some 7.2 million inhabitants, was virtually bereft of military resources in the homeland at the outbreak of the Pacific War. Several fine divisions were serving with British forces in North Africa, but only one fully equipped and trained (albeit green) division remained in the South Pacific, and this was promptly lost through inept British generalship in MALAYA.

There were also several partially trained divisions, and the national militia, which consisted of five divisions of World War I veterans (men in their 40s and 50s). Although the Australian government successfully pressured the British to return their divisions from the Middle East, they were slow in coming home and arrived much too late to prevent the Japanese from overrunning most of New Guinea.

Although the best Australian manpower had already been invested in the North African campaign, units raised later gave a good account of themselves during the horrors of the New Guinea Campaign. In was in this hellhole that most Australian units fought until the end of the war.

The Australian Army was organized and equipped on the British model, although as the war went on it received more and more US equipment. Australia produced some of its own weapons, equipment, and ammunition, but was dependent on imports for the most part. While the Australian leadership was eager to fulfill their Commonwealth obligations to Britain, many Australians became increasingly war weary as the fighting went on year after year.

General Douglas MACARTHUR never cared much for the Australians, and the feeling was reciprocated. MacArthur's arrogant ways did not go down well with the more freewheeling Australians. The situation was not helped much by the caustic personality of Australia's senior military officer, General Sir Thomas BLAMEY. Already a veteran of campaigns in Greece and North Africa by the end of 1941, Blamey was forced to accept MacArthur as his commander. This arrangement was in recognition of the fact that, in early 1942, it was the US fleet (and American supplies and reinforcements) that would keep the Japanese from descending on Australia itself. This was a real fear among the Australians, who suffered Japanese air raids along their northern coast. The Japanese did consider an invasion of Australia, but even they had to face the fact that Australia was too large and Japanese troop commitments too vast to make such an operation practicable.

Despite their mutual dislike, MacArthur and Blamey were both competent combat leaders. Australian troops did much of the jungle fighting in steamy New Guinea and the SOLOMONS. This later led to a controversy that still lingers. In late 1944, MacArthur ordered Australian units into battle against isolated Japanese forces in the Solomons, NEW BRITAIN, and BORNEO. The war was obviously coming to an end, and the Australians had been involved since 1939. It seemed a waste of Australian lives to go after the still fanatical Japanese in these out-of-the-way places. Although the subsequent fighting used tactics that minimized CASUALTIES among the nearly 100,000 Australians involved, bad feelings about the campaign continue to this day.

Ref: *Australia in the Second World War*; Long, *The Six Years War*.

Australian Army, Divisions

Australian divisions generally conformed to the standard "Commonwealth" pattern of ORGANI-ZATION, with some minor modifications. By the eve of the Pacific War the best units, composed entirely of volunteers, had been sent to fight in North Africa. Prying these fine units loose from the British required an enormous amount of political pressure.

Meanwhile, back home the Australian Army raised new units through CONSCRIPTION into the militia. These conscripts were not liable for overseas service. Only in mid–1942 were the limitations on "overseas" service modified to permit conscripts in Papua and Northeast New Guinea, the one an outright Australian possession and the other mandated to Australia by the League of Nations.

First Australian Armored Division. Formed in Australia in the autumn of 1941 with an eye toward service in North Africa, on the outbreak of the Pacific War the division still lacked TANKS but was otherwise well equipped. It remained a critical component of MacArthur's reserve during the winter and spring of 1942, when the possibility of a Japanese invasion of Australia caused come concern. It thereafter gradually ran down and was disbanded in mid–1944.

First Australian Division. A militia unit, composed of World War I veterans and conscripts. Activated in December 1941, for much of the first half of the war the division performed garrison and security duties in Australia, and was eventually turned into a training formation.

First Australian Cavalry Division. A militia unit activated in December 1941, the division performed garrison and security duties. In March 1942 it was reorganized as the 1st Australian Motorized Division, and was disbanded in mid-1943.

Second Australian Division. A militia unit activated in December 1941, the 2nd Australian Division performed garrison and security duties. It was later reorganized as the second 2nd Australian Motorized Division, but was disbanded in mid–1944.

Second Australian Cavalry Division. A militia unit activated in December 1941, the division performed garrison and security duties. Reorganized as the first 2nd Australian Motorized Division in March 1942, it was disbanded later that year.

Third Australian Armored Division. Formed in late 1941 for possible service in North Africa, on the outbreak of the Pacific War the division lacked its tanks and some other critical equipment, but was otherwise fairly well trained. It formed part of the garrison of Australia until disbanded in mid–1944.

Third Australian Division. Composed of militiamen, the division was activated in December 1941. For a time it performed garrison and security duties, but beginning in mid-1942 it was reinforced, reequipped, and retrained, and was shortly committed to operations in New Guinea, where it performed well.

Fourth Australian Division. As with the 3rd Australian Division, the 4th was a militia unit activated in December 1941. In mid-1942 it was reorganized for offensive operations, and eventually served in New Guinea.

Fifth Australian Division. A militia unit activated in December 1941, the division was reinforced with a brigade of regular troops, retrained, and reequipped for active service, and went to New Guinea in August 1942.

Sixth Australian Division. A veteran outfit with a glorious record in North Africa from June 1940, the division returned to Australia in February 1942. Although some elements served on Java in the final weeks of the NETHERLANDS EAST INDIES Campaign, the division as a whole was shortly committed to New Guinea, where it served for most of the war.

Seventh Australian Division. In North Africa from February 1941, the veteran division returned home in February and March 1942. It was soon committed to operations in New Guinea. In July 1945 the division conducted an amphibious assault at BALIKPAPAN in BORNEO, and there it ended the war.

Eighth Australian Division. A new unit, incomplete and not at full strength, the division was sent to MALAYA in July 1941. Caught up in the British disaster there, it joined the retreat to SINGAPORE, where it was overwhelmed on the beaches by the Japanese. The remnants surrendered on 15 February 1942.

Ninth Australian Division. The finest of the Australian divisions, the 9th had seen almost continuous action in North Africa from February 1941 to December 1942, when it returned home. After a short period of rest and retraining for jungle warfare, the division went into action in New Guinea. In June 1945 the division undertook an amphibious landing at BRUNEI, in northwestern Borneo. The end of the war found it advancing south into Sarawak.

10th Australian Division. Organized shortly before the Pacific War broke out, the division was disbanded in early 1943, having never left Australia.

11th Australian Division. Organized from the forces garrisoning PORT MORESBY, Papua, in late 1942, the division saw service in New Guinea throughout the war.

12th Australian Division. Organized from the garrison of the Northern Territories, the division saw limited combat service in New Guinea toward the end of the war.

Ref: *Australia in the Second World War*; Long, *The Six Years War.*

Australian Navy, Royal

At the outbreak of the Pacific War the main strength of the Royal Australian Navy comprised two heavy and three light cruisers, one of which was obsolete, plus a few destroyers. The men were well trained, and many had seen active service against the European Axis powers. Although their numbers were and remained small, Australian naval forces took part in virtually all of the operations in the Pacific. By 1945, Australian ships were operationally almost completely integrated into the US Navy.

Ref: *Australia in the Second World War*; Long, *The Six Years War*.

Australian-American Relations

The presence of large numbers of US troops in Australia from early 1942 onward led to occasional difficulties between Americans and Australians. The worst incidents occurred in BRISBANE, on November 26–27, 1942. On the night of November 26, Australian civilians and some military personnel became involved in a riot with American troops at a canteen. An American MP opened fire, wounding nine Australians, one of whom subsequently died. The following night several mobs of Australians, mostly servicemen, roamed the streets and roughed up American personnel, particularly those whom they encountered with Australian women. The Australian authorities brought in some infantrymen and restored order without injury.

The incident prompted a major campaign by both US and Australian authorities to "Know our Allies," which greatly reduced tensions. Nevertheless, incidents continued to the end of the war. The tension was caused by a variety of factors. American troops were much better paid than Australians. Many Australians also resented the fact that the US troops were enjoying life in the safety of Australia, while most of Australia's military personnel were abroad. Differing attitudes concerning propriety in dating were also at work. Some Americans adopted patronizing attitudes toward the Australians, viewing themselves as having come to their rescue.

Relations at higher levels were often almost as bad. General MACARTHUR did not like Australians, and managed to freeze Australia's General BLAMEY out of any serious influence in operations and STRATEGY, despite the fact that, officially Blamey was commander of all Allied ground forces.

These tensions tended to disappear closer to the front.

Ref: *Australia in the Second World War*.

Awa Maru

Awa Maru was a Japanese transport with an official safe conduct from the US Navy to serve as a REPATRIATION ship and to carry Red Cross supplies to PRISONERS OF WAR, as provided for under the terms of the GENEVA CONVENTION. Although she bore the proper identification markings, on 28 March 1945 she was sunk by the US submarine *Queenfish* (SS-393). A diplomatic stir resulted, and the United States promised to replace the ship. However, it transpired that the Japanese had been using her to carry contraband items between the Home Islands and Southeast Asia. As a result, the United States procrastinated in replacing the vessel. Japan used the incident to end the repatriation of Allied personnel.

The skipper of *Queenfish* was subject to a court-martial and received a letter of reprimand. Japanese nationalists have on occasion used this incident, and the sinking of several hospital ships by American forces, to accuse the United States of violating the Geneva Convention. The sinking of *Awa Maru* was one of a number of accidental sinkings of immune or neutral vessels in the Pacific War.

See also SHIP SINKINGS, ACCIDENTAL.

Ref: Corbett, *Quiet Passages*.

B

B-10, US Bomber

Billed as the "first genuine strategic bomber," the B-10 was an early 1930s American design. The Army Air Corps received 103 in 1935 and 1936, some of which were passed on to the PHILIPPINE ARMY Air Force in the late '30s. The airplane was also exported, with 120 going to Dutch forces in the East Indies (INDONESIA). The Dutch B-10s played a minor role in the first few months of fighting in the Pacific War. By 1930s standards, the B-10 was a rather good bomber. It had a top speed of 260 MPH and a range of 2,000 miles. However, it had only three .30 caliber machine guns for defense and carried only a ton of bombs. The B-10 was an easy target for Japanese fighters.

See also AIRCRAFT TYPES, DEVELOPMENT.

B-17 Flying Fortress, US Bomber

The US B-17 Flying Fortress was the first modern four-engine heavy bomber, entering combat in 1941. Although it promised more than it delivered, its combat accomplishments were significant in the Pacific War. The prototype first flew in the mid-1930s, but there were a lot of bugs to work out before the B-17 actually entered service in 1939. Although the ostensible reason for building the plane was to find and destroy warships far out at sea, the initial experience with B-17s in the Pacific War was not encouraging. Many B-17s were destroyed on the ground by the Japanese at PEARL HARBOR and in the Philippines. B-17 attacks on ships at sea were rarely successful (although the Air

Corps made certain the newspapers printed otherwise). But the B-17 soon began to prove useful as a long-range reconnaissance aircraft that could fight its way past enemy interceptors. Japanese fighters were not as lethal to B-17s as were the Germans. Although the vast majority of the 12,000 B-17s served in Europe, over a thousand were in the Pacific during the war, serving as armed reconnaissance aircraft and bombers.

See also AIRCRAFT TYPES, DEVELOPMENT; RECONNAISSANCE, NAVAL.

B-18 Bolo, US Bomber

The B-18 Bolo was a DC-3 transport redesigned as a US bomber. Although relatively respectable when it came into use in 1936, bomber technology advanced rapidly in the next few years. Most of the 375 B-18s built were converted to maritime reconnaissance use, and in this guise served in the early months of the Pacific War, particularly off HAWAII, in the Philippines, and on the west coast of the United States, Canada, and Alaska. By WW II standards, the B-18 was slow (about 200 MPH top speed), poorly armed, and could carry, at most, a ton of bombs, but it did manage to sink a few German SUBMARINES off the East Coast.

See also AIRCRAFT TYPES, DEVELOPMENT: RECONNAISSANCE, NAVAL.

B-24 Liberator, US Bomber

The B-24 Liberator was America's second-generation heavy bomber. Often unfavorably compared to the B-17, the B-24 was actually a superior aircraft and was produced in greater numbers than the B-17 (19,000 versus 12,000). The B-24 beat the B-17 by about 10% in range, speed, and payload. The longer range of the B-24 made it better suited for Pacific use. The navy used modified B-24 (the PB4Y-2 Privateer) with even longer range as patrol aircraft. The B-24 was a terrific antisubmarine aircraft, able to carry as many as 24 depth charges at ranges up to 1,000 miles. Over a thousand B-24s constantly scoured the vast Pacific for enemy ships. Because of this patrol coverage, the Japanese were unable to stage many surprise attacks. There were also several hundred B-24s converted to transports, as the C-109 tanker (carrying nearly nine tons of fuel) and the C-87 freighter (hauling over eight tons of freight or passengers). Several C-87s were fitted out for the use of various dignitaries who had to travel great distances.

See also AIRCRAFT TYPES, DEVELOPMENT; RECONNAISSANCE, NAVAL.

B-25 Mitchell, US Bomber

The US Mitchell was the most produced (nearly 10,000) twin-engine bomber of the war. Many considered it the most effective. The B-25 was particularly lethal in the Pacific, where many carried a 75mm gun and eight .50 caliber machine guns facing forward, plus six .50 calibers pointed in other directions. This "ship buster" version could also carry a TORPEDO or 3,200 pounds of bombs. A thousand of this anti-shipping version were built, a quarter of them flying under navy or Marine colors. Coming in at low altitude, these aircraft, with heavier armament than a tank, were the scourge of Japanese merchantmen and their escorts. B-25s entered combat in the Pacific when they flew off the deck of the carrier *Hornet* for the DOOLITTLE Raid in 1942, and continued to fly in combat until the end of the war. As it had entered service in 1940, the B-25 was a major component of American air power from the very beginning. Thousands were given to various allied air forces, particularly Russia

and Britain. Designed for use against land targets, the B-25 proved that bombers could take on warships, but only if they came down to sea level.

See also AIRCRAFT TYPES, DEVELOPMENT.

B-26 Marauder, US Bomber

The B-26 Marauder entered US service a year after the B-25, and the two twin-engine bombers were often confused with each other, despite the fact that the B-25 had a twin tail and the B-26 the more common single-tail rudder. Because the B-25 got to the Pacific first, and performed well, few B-26s were sent. The aircraft were about equal in performance, with the more modern B-26 having a slight edge. Both weighed 15–16 tons fully loaded for a typical mission. Although the B-26 had a reputation for being difficult to land, it had the lowest loss rate of any American combat aircraft. There were two groups of B-26s in the Pacific; these generally performed the conventional bombing missions while the B-25 got down low and did the glamorous work. Only about 5,000 B-26s were produced, and many remained in service into the late 1940s.

See also AIRCRAFT TYPES, DEVELOPMENT.

B-29 Superfortress, US Bomber

The US B-29 Superfortress was the world's first truly strategic bomber. Weighing over 60 tons fully loaded, it could fly over 3,000 miles carrying five tons of bombs. It was fast, with a top speed of 355 MPH and a cruising speed of 290 MPH. It normally flew over five miles high, and the crew spaces were pressurized and heated. This was a big plus for the crew, who often suffered frostbite and oxygen starvation in B-17s and B-24s at those altitudes. It was the Fall of France in June 1940 that spurred development of the B-29. Fearing that England would be next and needing a way to attack Nazi targets in Europe, the United States conceived the B-29 as a bomber with sufficient reach to hit European targets from North America or Iceland. In fact, this proved unnecessary, as Britain held and the Germans turned their attentions to Russia in 1941.

By early 1942, the United States was faced with a war against Japan, and the Japanese were winning. An aircraft like the B-29 was now needed to bomb Japan across the even vaster Pacific Ocean. The prototype B-29 flew in late 1942. Regular production began in early 1943. After training crews and sending units overseas, the first B-29 saw combat in June 1944. Over 3,000 B-29s were eventually produced, and the entire B-29 program cost more than the Manhattan Project, which built the ATOMIC BOMB. By early 1945, up to 600 B-29s at a time were flying against Japanese cities from bases in the MARIANAS Islands. The last B-29 was produced in 1946. They served in the Korean War and in foreign air forces until the late 1950s.

See also AIRCRAFT TYPES, DEVELOPMENT.

B-32 Dominator, US Bomber

As a form of insurance in case the B-29 program did not work out, another super heavy bomber, the B-32, was designed and built. A derivative of the B-24, the B-32 was not nearly as capable as the B-29, weighing only 50 tons and carrying only 10 tons of bombs for 2,400 miles. Only 115 were built. They were sent to the Pacific before the end of the war, and were taken out of service in 1947. Several B-32s undertook bombing raids over Japan in the closing weeks of the war. On 18 August 1945 a pair of B-32s were on a reconnaissance mission over Tokyo when they were jumped by more than a dozen Japanese fighters. In the ensuing action, one of the bombers, *Hobo Queen*, was hit, suffering one man killed and two wounded, while apparently one or more of the attackers were shot down. This was probably the last combat action by US aircraft in the war (some ground fighting continued on outlying islands until much later). It occurred well after the armistice.

See also AIRCRAFT TYPES, DEVELOPMENT; RECONNAISSANCE, NAVAL.

B-36 Peacemaker, US Bomber

Design work for the US B-36 began in 1942. It was the most ambitious World War II heavy bomber project, designed to bomb Germany from bases in North America. The first prototype flew a year after the Japanese surrendered, and production models didn't appear until 1948. This could have been speeded up had the war in the Pacific lasted longer. With a longer reach (over 6,000 miles) than the B-29 and a bigger bomb load (38 tons, max), it could have pounded the Japanese Home Islands from halfway across the Pacific. Only 382 were built, and production ended in 1951 (as the B-47 and B-52 were approaching production). Later ("D") versions had four jet engines added to the standard six piston engines, which worked double "pusher" propellers (i.e., the props were on the rear edge of the wing). The B-36 was the last World War II bomber.

See also AIRCRAFT TYPES, DEVELOPMENT.

B5N Kate, Japanese Carrier Torpedo Bomber

The B5N Kate, Japan's premier carrier torpedo bomber early in World War II, carried the TORPEDOES at PEARL HARBOR. Although considered obsolete by 1941, they were superior to the US TBD-1 DEVASTATOR, but not nearly as good as the TBF AVENGER. Entering service in 1937, with production continuing until 1942, some 1,100 were manufactured, and some were still in service in 1944.

See also AIRCRAFT TYPES, DEVELOPMENT; CARRIERS, DESIGNING AIRCRAFT FOR.

B64, Japanese "Super Heavy Cruisers"

In the late 1930s the Imperial Navy proposed the construction of several "super heavy cruisers," to be armed with nine 12.2–inch guns. Various test designs and technical experiments were begun in 1939, and in 1941 final plans began to be put together. Word of this reached the US Navy, which promptly decided to build some super heavy cruisers of its own, the Alaska Class large cruisers. Learning of the American proposal, the Japanese promptly revised their plans. The new plans, designated B65, were approved in 1942 under provisional designations *No. 795* and *No. 796* but were never actually begun.

B6N Jill, Japanese Torpedo Bomber

The B6N Jill carrier torpedo bomber was the replacement for the B5N and didn't enter service until early 1943. The B6N, slightly superior to the two-years-older TBF AVENGER, its American counterpart, arrived at a bad time for Japanese carrier aviation. During 1944, most of Japan's carriers had been destroyed. The B6N ended its career in 1945 operating from land bases and making KAMIKAZE attacks.

See also AIRCRAFT TYPES, DEVELOPMENT; CARRIERS, DESIGNING AIRCRAFT FOR.

B7A Grace, Japanese Torpedo Bomber

The B7A Grace was the last-generation Japanese torpedo bomber. Problems with its engine delayed delivery from 1943 to 1944. Although only 114 were produced, it was probably the best torpedo bomber of the war. As fast as many fighters (over 300 MPH) and quite maneuverable, it arrived too late to operate from carriers and flew from land bases until the end of the war.

See also AIRCRAFT TYPES, DEVELOPMENT; CARRIERS, DESIGNING AIRCRAFT FOR.

Bagley Class, US Destroyers

The Bagley class was designed in response to questions raised about the capabilities of the MAHAN CLASS. Unlike their half-sisters, the GRIDLEYS, they were built by the navy in its own yards from 1935 to 1937, with no corners cut. As a result, although superficially not much different from the Gridleys, they were much better ships, sturdier and more stable. Like the Gridleys, they had only four 5"/38

dual-purpose guns, plus 16 TORPEDO tubes. But they were much more stable, and during the war proved capable of mounting greatly enhanced antiaircraft batteries with no difficulties. The eight Bagleys saw considerable service in the Pacific, notably in the SOLOMONS and New Guinea areas. Three were sunk: *Jarvis* (DD-393) by air attack off GUADALCANAL on 9 August 1942; *Blue* (DD-387) scuttled off TULAGI on 23 August 1942 after being torpedoed by the Japanese destroyer *Kawakaze* the previous night; and *Henley* (DD-391) by a Japanese submarine in New Guinea's Gulf of Huon on October 3, 1943. The surviving members of the class were scrapped or expended as targets in the late 1940s.

Baker Island

About a square mile of barren land, Baker Island lies near the equator southwest of HAWAII and about 300 miles east of the GILBERTS. The small US radio facility there was evacuated in early 1942. It remained unoccupied thereafter until September 1943, when, in preparation for the TARAWA and MAKIN landings, US troops landed on the island and established an air base, from which B-24S could reach the eastern parts of the MARSHALL ISLANDS.

Balikpapan, Borneo, Netherlands East Indies

A modest harbor, on the southeastern coast of Borneo, with few facilities for docking or repairing ships, Balikpapan was important for its oil loading facilities and its refinery. It was the scene of some of the first fighting in the war, when the Japanese landed there in late January of 1942, and again when the Australians landed there on July 1, 1945, in the last amphibious operation of the war.

Baltimore Class, US Heavy Cruisers

The best American heavy cruisers of the war, and the largest class of heavy cruisers ever built, 18 of an order of 24 were completed, only six in time to see action in the war. There were two somewhat different designs (*Baltimore* and *Oregon City*). Free of the restrictions of the naval DISARMAMENT TREATIES, the Baltimores displaced over 40% more than the older American heavy cruisers. They were also quite expensive at about $40 million a ship, more than twice the cost of the older heavy cruisers. Although not particularly better armored than the experimental WICHITA, they were better constructed, had superior antiaircraft defenses, were much more stable, and far more comfortable. Despite this the navy still considered them inadequate, and the follow-on Newport News Class was larger still. Although all saw considerable service from late 1943 on, this was primarily as escorts for fast carrier task forces, and they were never tested in action against Japanese surface forces.

Baltimore, CA-68 (1941–1942–1943), began her service in the Pacific by bringing President ROOSEVELT to HAWAII in July 1943, and then went on to serve with the fast carriers until the end of the war. Scrapped in the 1970s.

Boston, CA-69 (1941–1943–1943), served in the Pacific from late 1943, usually with the fast carriers. With *Canberra*, she became one of the navy's first guided missile cruisers in the late 1950s and was scrapped in the 1970s.

Canberra, CA-70 (1941–1943–1943) (ex-*Pittsburgh*), was named to commemorate the Australian cruiser sunk at SAVO ISLAND. She entered service in early 1944. She took a KAMIKAZE off Leyte in October 1944 and a TORPEDO off FORMOSA later that year, but was back in service in time for the surrender of Japan. Converted to a missile cruiser in the late 1950s, she was scrapped in the 1970s.

Quincy, CA-71 (1941–1943–1943) (ex-*St. Paul*), was named to honor the cruiser sunk at Savo Island. She entered service in early 1944, and spent most of her war in European waters, reaching the Pacific too late to see much action. She was scrapped in the 1970s.

Pittsburgh, CA-72 (1943–1944–1944), went to the Pacific in early 1945, and put in a heroic performance assisting the carrier *Franklin* following the disastrous Japanese attack on her on 19 March. She later lost her bow in the typhoon of June 1945, and returned to service too late to be in at the surrender of Japan. She was scrapped in the 1970s.

Eight additional units were completed before the surrender of Japan, but saw no action in the war: *St. Paul*, CA-73; *Columbus*, CA-74; *Helena*, CA-75; *Bremerton*, CA-130; *Fall River*, CA-131; *Macon*, CA-132; *Los Angeles*, CA-135; and *Chicago*, CA-136. Five more units were completed after the war, one as late as 1953. Six units were canceled.

Bangkok, Siam

The capital and principal port of SIAM (Thailand), Bangkok lies quite far upriver from the sea, but can accommodate vessels of considerable size. Although it lacked extensive support and service facilities, it did have a good airport.

Banzai Charges

Many people imagine the Japanese Army during World War II as a mass of soldiers launching a hopeless charge led by officers waving *katana* (samurai swords). This was the banzai charge, and when one occurred, it made a vivid impression on the defending troops.

Most of these attacks were more an expression of frustration and despair than a tactic of the Japanese infantry. When the Japanese launched a banzai attack they were announcing that they were in a hopeless situation and would rather die fighting than surrender. It took time for the Allied troops to realize this. Meanwhile, these assaults were terrifying. Standard Japanese infantry tactics emphasized DECEPTION, not straight ahead assaults. The Japanese were very fond of night operations and CAMOUFLAGE. They believed that a battle won by stealth, subterfuge, and surprise was more worthy than a victory soaked in blood. The Japanese Army trained hard, and more than any other army, at night. No other army was as strict as the Japanese, who enforced an extremely strict discipline in the ranks. The Japanese made death and suffering a patriotic duty, and the troops tended to be enthusiastic about their soldiering.

So when it was time to pull off a deception, Japanese officers could depend on their troops to perform their tasks diligently, even unto certain death. The troops were hard-working, and did not think it unusual to be literally worked to death. The extent and thoroughness of Japanese fortifications was indicative of this. Not only were Japanese field works stoutly built, but they were also generally very well camouflaged. What made the Japanese somewhat less than supermen on the battlefield was a lack of logistical support, and overconfidence resulting from years of fighting the rather lackadaisical Chinese. Their early victories over the British also led them to believe that Western troops in general would be pushovers.

Although the Japanese had been badly defeated by the Soviets in two 1939 border battles, they excused this away as a "special case." Once the Japanese had acquired some firsthand experience with US soldiers and Marines they shaped up fast. Their logistical problems were more intractable. The Japanese depended on superhuman effort from their troops because Japan went into World War II a poor country. And things went downhill after PEARL HARBOR. Japanese soldiers never had enough ammunition, food, or fuel. Thousands starved to death on GUADALCANAL, for example, and many more suffered the same fate elsewhere. Yet there were never any major discipline problems. Starving soldiers simply kept going until they dropped.

During the war, Americans called the Japanese soldiers "sneaky." The Japanese would have considered that a compliment, as would any competent soldier. But when all their deceptions and carefully prepared maneuvers failed, Japanese officers and soldiers were expected to go down fighting. Surrender was not something covered in Japanese training. Surrender was unthinkable. Enemy troops that surrendered were considered dishonored and no longer worth the respect one gives a worthy foe.

This is one of the reasons why the Japanese often treated PRISONERS so barbarically. For the Japanese, a hopeless situation required desperate measures, and surrender wasn't one of the options. The result was usually one final "give them all we've got" infantry assault or banzai attack. It was understood that this was going to be (literally) a do-or-die attack. Before the attack, officers and troops said their goodbyes to one another, for none expected to survive. And few did.

Ref: *Handbook on Japanese Military Forces*; Harries and Harries, *Soldiers of the Sun*; Hayashi and Coox, *Kogun*.

Barracuda, British Torpedo Bomber

The Barracuda was the successor to the ROYAL NAVY's ALBACORE torpedo bomber. It was faster but had a shorter range. Coming into service in 1941, it was already obsolete by World War II standards and would not have fared well had it been used heavily in the Pacific.

See also AIRCRAFT TYPES, DEVELOPMENT; CARRIERS, DESIGNING AIRCRAFT FOR.

Basilone, John (1916–1945)

Basilone, a Marine sergeant, earned the MEDAL OF HONOR on GUADALCANAL, for actions in October 1942. As the first ground soldier to win the Medal of Honor in an American offensive, "Manila John" became rather famous. Brought to the United States to participate in War Bond drives, he later voluntarily returned to combat duties and won a Navy Cross posthumously on IWO JIMA, according to some accounts while trying to win another Medal of Honor.

Bat Bomb, The

The "Bat Bomb" was an experimental US program to determine whether bats could be used to carry incendiary devices. The project, formally known as Project X-Ray and informally as the Adams Plan, after its originator, Lyle S. Adams, an inventor and entrepreneur, began in early 1942, with the blessings of President ROOSEVELT. The basic premise was simple, to use bats to carry incendiaries to set fire to the notoriously flammable Japanese cities. Bombers would carry large numbers of hibernating bats; an estimated 200,000 could be carried in a B-29. Several hundred bats could be stored and transported in a large metallic canister, which would break apart after a suitable interval upon being dropped from 10,000 feet. These would be released over Japanese cities. When dropped, the bats, each equipped with a small incendiary device, would revive as they passed through warmer air, and seek refuge in houses and other buildings, where, after a timed interval, the incendiaries would ignite, which would kill the bats and start numerous fires in hard-to-reach places.

Despite a small staff and a minuscule budget, a great deal of progress was made. It was determined that the Mexican free-tailed bat, which weighed some 10–12 grams (about half an ounce) could carry a "payload" of roughly 175% of its own weight. The technical problems of devising an effective incendiary device complete with timer and igniter weighing only 17.5 grams were resolved through the use of napalm encapsulated in a small celluloid vial, with a tiny mechanical timer and igniter.

Although initial military reaction to the Bat Bomb was skeptical, feasibility demonstrations soon brought the project support from the army air force, the navy (which helped produce the incendiary devices), and the Marine Corps.

The project was canceled in mid–1944, by which time the seizure of the MARIANAS made conventional bombing of Japan possible, and, unbeknownst to the experimenters and most of their supporters, progress on the ATOMIC BOMB had reached the point where its practicality was certain.

Ref: Couffer, *Bat Bomb*.

Bataan, Philippines

Bataan is a heavily forested, mountainous peninsula on the north side of the entrance to Manila Bay. For many years US plans for the defense of the Philippines from a Japanese invasion presupposed that American and Philippine forces would immediately retire to defensive positions on the Bataan Peninsula, there to hold out until relieved by the US fleet. However, little was actually done to prepare the peninsula for defense. No combat positions were surveyed, no food and ammunition stockpiled, and no efforts made to improve internal communications. As a result, when the Japanese did invade in 1941, they were eventually able to batter their way into Bataan.

See also PHILIPPINES, CAMPAIGN FOR 1941–1942.

Bataan Death March

Shortly after the surrender of US and Philippine forces on Bataan in April 1942, the Japanese force-marched 70,000 PRISONERS 70 miles to prison camps. The men were denied medical treatment, food, and water. Men who fell out, or failed to keep up, were usually killed, often by their own comrades, acting under coercion. Filipino civilians who attempted to succor them were frequently killed.

The ATROCITIES to which these troops were subject were contrary to instructions from the Japanese commander, General Masaharu HOMMA, who wished to abide by the GENEVA CONVENTION. However, he had been effectively removed from command in all but name.

Some of the suffering was caused by Japanese misunderstanding of the condition of the American and Philippine troops on Bataan: They were unaware of the degree to which the defenders were suffering from malnutrition, and believed that there were sufficient supplies available to sustain the prisoners until they reached the POW camps. However, much of it was merely casual brutality,

The Bataan Death March. Note that the men have their hands bound and that one has an untreated injury to the face. The figure at far right appears to be a Japanese guard.

partially a reflection of how Japanese troops had been wont to treat prisoners of war in China.

The mistreatment of the prisoners was not uniform. To a large extent it depended upon the officers and guards accompanying the marchers. Some of the marchers were relatively well treated by their guards.

See also TOKYO CRIMES TRIBUNAL.

Batavia, Java, Netherlands East Indies.

The capital of the NETHERLANDS EAST INDIES, located in western Java, Batavia has a fine harbor, with modestly extensive facilities to service ships,

a small naval base, and an important airport, by the standards of the region.

Battle, British Light Bomber

The Battle was an obsolete British single-engined light bomber. A few were still in Southeast Asia at the end of 1941, but all disappeared in 1942.

See also AIRCRAFT TYPES, DEVELOPMENT.

Battles, Carrier versus Carrier

While the Pacific War is known as the "war of the carriers" and the "beginning of the carrier age," only five carrier-to-carrier battles were fought during the entire war.

- ❂ Coral Sea (7–8 May 1942)
- ❂ Midway (3–4 June 1942)
- ❂ Eastern Solomons (24 August 1942)
- ❂ Santa Cruz Islands (26–27 October 1942)
- ❂ Philippine Sea (19–21 June 1944)

There hasn't been another carrier versus carrier battle since the Battle of the PHILIPPINE SEA in June 1944, and it is unlikely that there will be another one any time soon. The "carrier versus carrier" era lasted only 25 months, from the CORAL SEA to the Philippine Sea. And the Philippine Sea was so one-sided it became known as the GREAT MARIANAS TURKEY SHOOT. In fact, the last evenly matched carrier-to-carrier combat was the Battle of SANTA CRUZ ISLANDS. This was also the last time an American carrier was sunk in a carrier battle. In effect, the "Golden Age of Carrier Battles" lasted five months and four battles from May to October 1942.

The protracted Naval Battle of GUADALCANAL (11–15 November 1942) was the only other occasion during the war when carrier-borne aircraft fought each other, as US carrier aircraft and Japanese carrier aircraft tangled repeatedly in the skies over the lower SOLOMONS. Since the carriers themselves stayed safely out of range that was hardly a "carrier battle."

American and Filipino troops on the Bataan Death March, using improvised litters to carry badly injured or ill comrades. The experiences of the men on the march varied greatly. These men appear to have been relatively well treated; often, ill or wounded men were killed by the guards.

Carriers proved to be more useful against everything other than carriers. Attacks on enemy bases, shipping, and in support of amphibious landings comprised the bulk of carrier activity throughout the war. Although land-based aircraft were two to three times as effective as carrier planes, the carriers could move swiftly across the vast expanse of the Pacific. It was this mobility that made carriers less effective. The carriers could not lug around as much avgas or munitions as a land base could stockpile. Operating at sea caused more damage to the aircraft, and the shortage of space on a carrier made aircraft maintenance more difficult. Despite these limitations, the aircraft carrier reigned supreme across the Pacific. As long as the carriers stayed away from more numerous land-based aircraft (something the Japanese weren't able to muster by 1944), the carriers could slug it out with anything they came up against. Note that the last American carrier lost in combat was a victim of land-based aircraft. The second most dangerous foe of carriers was SUBMARINES. Thus, since late 1942, the carrier situation hasn't changed. The US carrier fleet is supreme and its only foe is large numbers of land-based aircraft and submarines.

Ref: Hezlet, *Aircraft and Sea Power*; Reynolds, *The Fast Carriers*; Roscoe, *On the Seas and in the Skies*.

Battles, Naval, Distance from Shore

As vast as the Pacific was, most large groups of ships endeavored to move in such a way that they were always within a few hundred miles of land, especially land with an airbase full of friendly fighters and bombers. This was an ancient custom, and the world record for distance from the site of a sea battle to shore is still the British victory known as the "Glorious First of June" (1 June 1794), fought some 400 miles from the nearest land and decidedly in the age of sail.

But having the protection of friendly air power, or avoiding enemy land-based aircraft, was seen as crucial during World War II. Moreover, aircraft could spot and attack lurking SUBMARINES or ap-

proaching enemy task forces. Friendly aircraft patrols provided weather reports, which were often a protection against a more formidable foe than enemy TORPEDOES and bombs. Nearby land bases also provided anchorage and repair facilities for ships that broke down or were damaged in combat. Such nearby succor was often the difference between saving, or losing, a valuable ship.

Battleship, Battlecruiser, and Large Cruiser Tables

See pages 86 and 87.

Battleships, Encounters, World War II, All Theaters

There were 10 battleship-to-battleship slugouts during World War II, most of which took place in the Atlantic or Mediterranean.

- April 9, 1940: off the Lofoten Islands, Norwegian Sea. The German battleships *Gneisenau* and *Scharnhorst* engage the old British battlecruiser RENOWN in an indecisive action.

- July 3, 1940: at Mers el Kebir, Algeria. The old British battleships *Resolution* and *Valiant*, with the battlecruiser *Hood* and other ships, attack the French fleet in port, sinking the old battleship *Bretagne*, severely damaging her sister *Provence*, and less seriously damaging the new *Dunkerque*, while the latter's sister *Strasbourg* managed to escape unscathed.

- July 9, 1940: off Calabria, Italy. An Italian squadron including the reconstructed old battleships *Giulio Cesare* and *Conte di Cavour* was intercepted by a British squadron including the older battleship *Warspite*, resulting in an indecisive but often intense action of about 50 minutes. (HM Battleships ROYAL SOVEREIGN and *Malaya* were also present, but did not engage.)

- September 24–25, 1940: at Dakar, French West Africa. A British and Free French attempt to seize the port involved two clashes between the

BATTLESHIPS, BATTLECRUISERS, LARGE CRUISERS (BB)

Navy	Class	Year	Tot.	Displacement Full	Crew	Combat Surf.	AAA	A/C	Guns Main
U.S.	*Alaska*	1944	6	34.3	1,571	24	10	2	9x12
U.S.	*Arkansas*	1912	1	30.1	1,242	26	9	2	12x12
U.S.	*California*	1921	2	40.3	2,375	36	14	2	12x14
Jp.	*Fuso*	1915	2	38.5	1,396	34	4	3	12x14
U.S.	*Iowa*	1943	6	57.5	1,921	50	16	3	9x16
Jp.	*Ise* (A)	1917	2	39.5	1,376	34	4	3	12x14
Jp.	*Ise* (B)	1943	2	38.1	1,463	22	6	22	8x14
Br.	*King George V*	1940	5	42.1	1,422	30	9	2	10x14
Jp.	*Kongo*	1913	4	32.2	1,220	23	3	3	8x14
Br.	*Lion*	MHB	4	46.3	1,680	38	9	2	9x16
U.S.	*Maryland*	1923	3	40.3	2,375	40	13	2	8x16
U.S.	*Montana*	MHB	5	70.5	2,150	62	16	3	12x16
Jp.	*Nagato*	1920	2	42.8	1,368	36	5	3	8x16
Br.	*Nelson*	1927	2	44.3	1,314	38	7	2	9x16
U.S.	*Nevada*	1916	2	31.7	1,374	30	14	2	10x14
U.S.	*New Mexico*	1918	3	36.2	1,443	34	14	2	12x14
U.S.	*New York*	1914	2	31.9	1,290	30	10	2	10x14
U.S.	*North Carolina*	1941	2	44.4	1,880	48	15	3	9x16
U.S.	*Pennsylvania*	1916	2	35.9	1,052	34	12	2	12x14
Br.	*Queen Elizabeth*	1915	5	37.0	1,150	21	11	2	8x15
Br.	*Renown*	1916	2	37.0	1,200	21	6	2	6x15
Fr.	*Richelieu*	1940	4	43.3	1,670	28	13	3	8x15
Br.	*Royal Sovereign*	1916	5	33.5	1,100	28	10	2	8x15
U.S.	*South Dakota*	1942	4	44.5	1,793	48	14	3	9x16
Br.	*Vanguard*	1946	1	51.4	1,893	28	9	2	8x15
Jp.	*Yamato*	1941	4	70.0	2,500	45	6	7	9x18.1

Navy = nation the ship belongs to: Br. = Britain, Fr. = France, Jp = Japan, US = United States. **Class** = names of the lead ship in the class. **Year** = when the first ship in the class entered service; MHB = might have been, a class that was not, but could have been in action. **Tot.** = total number of ships in that class. **Displacement** = the amount of water the ship displaces (i.e., the weight of the water that would occupy the space occupied by the ship), expressed in thousands of tons. There are two values for this: **Std.** = standard, or weight with basic crew, fuel, munitions and other supplies; **Full** = "fighting weight," loaded with all the items needed to go to war. **Crew** = number normally carried. **Combat** = relative combat value for each ship in the following areas: **Surf.** = value in surface engagements, **AAA** = value against attacking aircraft. A group of ships would combine their values, which was particularly effective when defending against enemy aircraft. **A/C** = aircraft carried. **Guns** = many different types: **Main** = the largest guns, on battleships. These can be from 11 to 18 inches in bore diameter; **Sec.** = secondary guns for use against smaller surface targets (these became obsolete during World War II, usually converted to AAA use); **DP** =

BATTLESHIPS, BATTLECRUISERS, LARGE CRUISERS (BB)

Sec.	DP	AAA	TT	Length	Dimensions Beam	Draft	HP	Spd.	Armor Belt	Deck
None	12x5	None	0	241.3	27.0	9.7	150.0	33.0	9.0	5.2
16x5	None	8x3	0	168.9	32.3	9.1	28.0	21.0	11.0	4.3
14x5	None	8x5	0	182.9	34.8	10.1	29.5	20.5	13.5	5.5
14x6	8x5	None	0	210.0	30.6	9.7	75.0	24.8	12.0	7.0
None	20x5	None	0	262.1	33.0	11.0	212.0	32.5	13.0	8.1
16x5.5	8x5	None	0	213.4	31.7	9.2	80.0	25.3	12.0	8.0
16x5.5	16x5	None	0	219.6	31.7	9.0	80.0	25.3	12.0	8.0
None	16x5.25	None	0	213.4	31.4	8.8	110.0	28.0	15.0	3.0
14x6	8x5	None	0	214.5	28.0	8.4	136.0	30.5	8.0	2.3
None	16x5.25	None	0	225.6	31.7	9.1	130.0	30.0	15.0	4.0
14x5	None	8x5	0	182.9	34.8	10.1	30.0	21.0	13.5	5.5
None	20x5	None	0	271.3	36.9	11.2	172.0	28.0	24.3	9.0
18x5.5	8x5	None	0	221.1	33.0	9.5	82.0	25.0	11.8	7.7
12x6	6x4.7	None	2	201.2	32.3	8.6	45.0	23.0	14.0	3.0
12x5	None	8x5	0	175.3	32.9	9.0	25.0	20.5	13.5	5.0
12x5	None	8x5	0	182.9	32.4	9.4	40.0	22.0	13.5	5.5
16x5	None	8x3	0	172.2	32.3	9.2	28.1	21.0	12.0	6.3
None	20x5	None	0	217.8	33.0	10.0	121.0	28.0	12.8	7.6
12x5	None	8x5	0	182.9	32.4	9.2	33.4	21.0	13.5	4.8
None	20x4.5	None	0	181.8	31.5	9.3	80.0	24.0	13.0	3.0
12x4	8x4.5	6x4	2	227.3	31.1	8.1	120.0	29.0	9.0	11.0
None	9x6	12x3.9	0	242.0	33.0	9.6	150.0	30.0	13.5	8.8
12x6	None	8x4	2	175.8	31.1	8.6	40.0	21.0	13.0	1.5
None	16x5	None	0	203.0	33.0	10.7	130.0	27.5	13.1	7.9
None	16x5.25	None	0	231.6	32.9	9.4	130.0	30.0	14.0	4.0
12x6.1	12x5	None	0	244.0	36.9	10.4	150.0	27.0	16.1	9.1

dual purpose, for use against surface and air targets; **AAA** = antiaircraft artillery, generally the same caliber as the DP guns, but whose only purpose is to attack aircraft; **HMG** = heavy machine guns, caliber varying from 12.7mm to 40mm, the latter (20mm and up) were actually automatic cannon, as they fired explosive shells. **TT** = torpedo tubes carried. **DC** = depth charges carried (for use against submarines). **Dimensions** = expressed in meters. There are three of them: **Length** = how long the ship was; **Beam** = width of the ship; **Draft** = how deep into the water the bottom of the ship is at full load. **HP** = maximum horsepower generated by the ship's engines. **Spd.** = top speed in knots (nautical miles per hour). **Armor** = the protection many ships had against enemy fire. Given in inches for the following positions on the ship: **Belt** = an area along the waterline to protect engines and ammo magazines; **Turret** = rotating structures containing the main guns; **Deck** = for protection from "plunging" shells (fired from a great distance away) or bombs; **Tower** = a tower in which the fire control crew operates.

incomplete Vichy French battleship RICHELIEU and the British battlewagons *Barham* and *Resolution*. On the 24th *Richelieu* was damaged by near-misses from 15-inch shells, and was unable to reply due to malfunctions in her untested 15-inch guns. The next day *Richelieu* managed to get off a few rounds, scoring one 15-inch hit on *Barham*, while none of the 250 15-inch rounds fired back injured her. The British and Free French broke off the attempt to seize Dakar when a Vichyite submarine put a TORPEDO into *Resolution*.

- May 24, 1941: in the Denmark Straits, between Iceland and Greenland. In a brief morning encounter, the new German battleship *Bismarck* with the escorting heavy cruiser *Prinz Eugen* took several hits while sinking the British battlecruiser *Hood* and damaging the very new British battleship *Prince of Wales*. Later that afternoon *Bismarck* and *Prince of Wales* briefly clashed again, with no ill effects to either.
- May 27, 1941: in the North Atlantic, about 500 miles northwest of Brest, France. After a wide-ranging chase across the Atlantic, *Bismarck*, slowed by several fortuitous aerial torpedo hits, was pounded to pieces by the new British battleship KING GEORGE V and the older *Rodney*, reducing the German battleship to a burning wreck, which was finished off by several torpedoes.
- November 8, 1942: at Casablanca, Morocco. The new USS *Massachusetts* exchanged several hundred rounds of heavy caliber shells with the partially completed French *Jean Bart*, tied up at a dock at Casablanca, with the latter (which had only half of her guns mounted and was not yet fully operational for sea) coming off poorly.
- November 14–15, 1942: off GUADALCANAL, Solomon Islands. A confused encounter off Guadalcanal, in which the USS *Washington* got the better of HIJMS *Kirishima*, after the USS *South Dakota* had been temporarily put out of action, in a battle sometimes known as the Second Naval Battle of Guadalcanal.

- December 26, 1943: off North Cape, Norway (the northernmost point in Europe). A British squadron including the new battleship *Duke of York* encountered the German *Scharnhorst*, resulting in the latter's sinking after a protracted slugfest.
- October 25, 1944: SURIGAO STRAIT, the Philippines. Essentially an ambush by a squadron of US battlewagons, mostly veterans of PEARL HARBOR, who piled on the Japanese battleship *Yamashiro*, with the aid of flocks of cruisers, destroyers, and smaller warships (which had already accounted for *Yamashiro*'s sister FUSO) (see LEYTE GULF, BATTLE OF).

Despite the air power pundits, there were a lot of battleship slugouts during World War II, indeed more than there were carrier battles (ten to five). Of course, most of these were in the European theater, but then the Pacific was most eminently a carrier theater. On the other hand, the battleship actions off Guadalcanal and in the Surigao Strait were both considerably more important strategically than were the ones in the European War.

Battleships, the Ultimate Battle

The Imperial Navy's YAMATO and *Musashi* were the largest battlewagons ever built, displacing almost 70,000 tons at full load. They also toted the heaviest guns ever to put to sea, nine pieces of 460mm caliber, a bore diameter of 18.11 inches, capable of throwing a 3,219-pound shell a maximum distance of slightly over 45,000 yards. In contrast, the largest American battleships, IOWA and her sisters *New Jersey*, *Wisconsin*, and *Missouri*, displaced only about 57,000 tons at full load, and mounted nine 16-inch guns (406mm), which fired a 2,700–pound shell to about 42,000 yards.

There was one moment in the war when Yamato- and IOWA-CLASS ships might have clashed, during the Battle of LEYTE GULF, in the Philippines, on October 25, 1944. With a squadron consisting of *Yamato*, three older battleships, some cruisers, and several destroyers Admiral Takeo KURITA had managed to elude US aerial reconnaissance and, slipping through the San Bernardino Strait, had emerged off SAMAR to fall on a clutch of escort carriers. The running fight that ensued turned into a moral victory for the Americans, when, despite losing an escort carrier and three destroyer-type ships to Japanese gunfire, they managed to put up such a fight that the Japanese decided to withdraw. As the faster enemy ships began steaming off one US bluejacket is supposed to have cried out, "They're getting away!" US planning for the invasion of the Philippines had envisioned the possibility that the Japanese might threaten the landings with surface forces. Admiral William F. HALSEY had seven fast battleships helping to escort the carriers of his Third Fleet. In an emergency he was supposed to form these into Task Force 34 under Admiral Willis LEE, the navy's best battleship man, and leave them to guard the large concentration of shipping in Leyte Gulf. However, when Halsey took his fleet north to pursue the Japanese carriers, he took the battlewagons with him. Had he not done so, or had he heeded the initial warnings to dispatch them southward, the result might have been a slug out in which *Yamato*, NAGATO, *Haruna*, and KONGO would have been pitted against *Iowa*, *New Jersey*, *Massachusetts*, SOUTH DAKOTA, *Washington*, and *Alabama*. As Samuel Eliot MORISON would later write, "What a brawl that would have been . . . !"

However, aside from *Yamato*, the Japanese ships were all old and slow in comparison with the American ones. A true test would have pitted a squadron of Iowas against a squadron of Yamatos.

The differences between the two classes are interesting. Since speed in a ship is partially a factor of hull length and fineness, between her more powerful engines and her finer lines *Iowa* was about 20% faster than *Yamato*. In addition, *Iowa*'s deeper draft made for greater stability, making her a better "gun platform" than her rival. Both of these factors would have been important in an engagement at sea. Moreover, *Iowa* was a much handier ship, re-

COMPARISON OF JAPANESE YAMATO-CLASS AND AMERICAN IOWA-CLASS BATTLESHIPS

	Yamato	Iowa
Displacement (tons)		
Standard	64,000	48,110
Full Load	69,988	57,540
Dimensions		
Length: Waterline	839'11"	860'
Overall	862' 9"	887' 3"
Beam (width)	121' 1"	108' 2"
Draft (depth)	34' 1"	36' 2.25"
Machinery		
Boilers	12	8
Turbines	4	4
Horsepower	150,000	212,000
Speed (Maximum)	27 knots	32.5 knots
	(31.2 MPH)	(37.6 MPH)
Armor (Maximums)		
Belt	16.1"	12.9"
Deck	9"	8.1"
Barbettes (turret bases)	21.5"	17.3"
Turret Faces	25.6"	19.7"
Conning Tower	19.7"	17.5"
Armament		
Main Battery	9 x 18.11"/45	9 x 16"/50
Secondary Battery	12 x 6.1"/60	—
Dual Purpose	12 x 5"/40	20 x 5"/38
Light AA	(omitted)	
Crew	2,500	1,921

sponding to the helm more rapidly, with a smaller tactical diameter (the minimum diameter necessary to make a full circle), which made her more maneuverable.

On paper, of course, *Yamato*'s thicker armor suggests a much better protected ship, but this is rather deceptive. Thickness of plate must make an allowance for quality. In the years before World War II the US Navy had made considerable strides in armor technology. As a result, the protection offered by its new armor plate was equivalent to about 25% more thickness in terms of the older type of armor carried by *Yamato*. Barbettes are the rounded bases on which rest the turrets; the conning tower is an armored citadel from which the skipper and steersman can fight the ship in comparative safety.

An additional important factor was that *Iowa* appears to have been much better constructed than *Yamato*. On 25 December 1943, for example, *Yamato* took a TORPEDO, which demonstrated that the jointing between the hull and her armor belt was faulty. As a full repair would have entailed the addition of over 5,000 tons to the ship's displacement, the Imperial Navy merely patched up the damaged section and pretended there was no problem. When a similar incident occurred to *Musashi* in March 1944, the Imperial Navy continued to pretend.

Of course the big difference was in the main batteries, *Yamato*'s 18.11-inch rifles making *Iowa*'s 16-inchers seem puny by comparison, with an armor-piercing shell weight nearly 20% more and with almost 7% more range. But this is a superficial comparison. A deeper look proves more interesting.

The 16"/50 was about 66.6 feet long. Longer barrel length lends stability to the shell in flight, which increases range, which is one reason why, although the Japanese gun has a bore diameter 13%

greater than the American piece, its maximum range was only 7% greater.

Other factors of importance were the propellant used (the gunpowder) and shell aerodynamics. On this score the US piece was better, with a slightly higher muzzle velocity, the speed with which the shell leaves the barrel, measured in feet per second (fps).

Incidentally, the marginally greater maximum range of the Japanese gun would have been of no consequence. The greatest range at which a land-based heavy artillery piece ever hit a target deliberately aimed at appears to have been about 17.4 nautical miles (c. 35,200 yards, 20 land miles), a feat accomplished by a US Army model 16"/45 coast defense gun at Fort Weaver, HAWAII, in August of 1938, under absolutely wonderful conditions of weather and sea. The longest range deliberate hit at sea in naval combat occurred on 9 July 1940, off Calabria, Italy, in the Mediterranean, when the British battleship *Warspite* put a single 15-inch round into the Italian battleship *Giulio Cesare* at 26,000 yards, about 12.8 nautical miles. Of course, this was before fire control (FC) radar. Using FC radar in a test conducted in February 1944 the Iowa-class ship *New Jersey* was able to straddle a radio-controlled target destroyer at ranges varying from 34,000 to 39,000 yards, while both were moving at 30 knots.

It may seem odd to measure the penetrability of a gun at zero range (i.e., at the instant the projectile leaves the barrel), but it actually is of some value for comparison purposes. The number of rounds per minute that the pieces were capable of firing is a rather optimistic figure, since it was dangerous and exhausting to attempt to sustain maximum rates of fire for more than a few minutes. Of course, this still gave the US gun a higher rate of fire.

In effect, on technical grounds, the US 16"/50 battleship gun (traditionally called a "rifle") was by no means inferior in performance to the Japanese 18.11"/45. And in action, that performance would have been enhanced by fire control radar, a development with which the Japanese had very little success.

MAIN BATTERY GUN PERFORMANCE COMPARISON

	American 16"/50	Japanese 18.11"/45
Muzzle Velocity	2,559 fps	2,600 fps
Penetration at		
0 yards	34"	32.62"
20,000 yards	c. 20.4"	20.04"
30,000 yards	c. 14.7"	14.97"
Rounds Per Minute	2	1

Gun caliber is given in inches and barrel length. Thus, if a piece is described as 18.11"/45 it means that the bore is 18.11 inches in diameter and the barrel is 45 times that in length, or slightly less than 70 feet.

So in the ultimate battleship brawl of all time, a squadron of four Iowas would probably have defeated a squadron of four Yamatos.

Ref: Friedman, *United States Battleships*; Garzke and Dulin, *Battleships*.

Battleships and Battlecruisers

Until well into the 20th century battleships (BBs) were the principal arbiters of sea power. By World War I they were already large vessels, 20,000 tons or more, heavily armored (for example, belts of 12 inches or more of specially hardened steel along their sides), and armed with eight to a dozen of the heaviest caliber cannon possible, from 11–inch (firing 750–pound shells) on up to 18.1 inch (3,200-pound shells). Their job was to fight similar ships in large, decisive battles.

Battleships were the lineal descendants of the old wooden ships-of-the-line of Horatio Nelson's day, changed by an evolving technology. The threat of surface attack by light forces—TORPEDO boats and destroyers—led to the introduction of rapid-fire secondary armament, and the introduction of the submarine led to changes in tactics and great increases in the role of the destroyer; but on the eve of World War I the battleship was the undisputed capital ship.

The battleship emerged from the First World War with its reputation intact. Of the approximately 70 modern "battlewagons" that saw service in the war, only two were sunk, one by a mine (planted by a submarine) and the other by an internal explosion, probably caused by deterioration of ammunition. The record of the two dozen or so battlecruisers (CC), large ships that toted battleship artillery but sacrificed armor protection for superior speed, was less impressive, four being lost in action, all to enemy gunfire. Although this confirmed the relative invulnerability of the battlewagons, it was also rather surprising. After all, the admirals of the age were perfectly aware that their ships could be sunk, by gunfire, MINES, or torpedoes, whether launched by surface vessels or submarines. Of course, by the end of World War I

aviation enthusiasts like BG William "Billy" Mitchell were claiming that the battleship was vulnerable to the airplane. Although much has been made of their alleged foresight, these people were overstating the case a great deal, considering the capabilities of aircraft at the time. Even the famous sinking of the obsolete German prize *Ostfriesland* by United States Army bombers on July 21, 1921, was not a particularly valid test. The trial had been rigged in favor of the airmen. It was a clear, calm day and the ship was firmly anchored in Chesapeake Bay. The air enthusiasts cheated in the bargain. The rules of the test required that after each bomb hit, engineers were to board the ship to evaluate the damage. The flyboys ignored this provision and attacked in waves, dropping more bombs and heavier bombs than they could have carried in actual war. In addition, they came in at such low speed and altitude that had the ship been maneuvering they would certainly not have hit it, and had it been firing back all the aircraft would probably have been shot down. An observer from the RAF commented, "This proves nothing."

Fortunately for the navy, the air attack on *Ostfriesland* was not the only such test.

BATTLESHIPS SUNK IN WEAPONS TRIALS, 1915–33

Type	Britain	France	Japan	US
Trials Held	'25–'31	'22–'31	'15–'33	'20–'24
Pre-Dreadnought	0	1	3	6
Dreadnought	2	0	0	1
Incomplete	0	0	1	1
Total	2	1	4	8

The table includes all battleships sunk in weapons trials in the period, including air attacks, battleships and coast defense gunfire, torpedoes, and mines. Pre-dreadnought battleships were small (10,000–18,000 tons) ships launched 1885–1909, and very obsolete even before World War I. Dreadnought battleships (the German *Ostfriesland*, sunk by the US, and Britain's *Monarch* and *Emperor of India*) were newer, and larger (22,000–25,000 tons), but essentially obsolete by 1920. The two incomplete vessels, Japan's *Tosa* and the American *Washington* were very modern ships. *Tosa* was about 75% complete (c. 30,000 of a planned 39,900 tons) when sunk in gunfire, torpedo, and mine trials; her sister became the famous aircraft carrier *Akagi*. *Washington*, a unit of the Maryland Class, was about 76% complete (c. 28,000 tons of 32,600), when sunk by a combination of battleship gunfire and naval aircraft.

Battleships and Battlecruisers

Aside from the *Ostfriesland* fiasco, other trials were conducted on a scientific basis, with engineers surveying the damage at each stage in the procedure. Given the large number of warships the major navies had to dispose of due to the DISARMAMENT TREATIES, it is rather surprising that other navies did not emulate the extensive American and Japanese tests. These tests provided some valuable clues as to the vulnerability of battleships. The sailors asserted that a battleship underway and fully manned could avoid or shoot down attacking aircraft. And if, per chance, a battleship were hit, the armor would protect it. Finally, the large crews of the battlewagons could surely bring any damage under control. In all this the sailors were correct, but not correct enough.

During the 1920s and 1930s all navies considered the battleship the principal arm of sea power. But the bigger ones—the ROYAL NAVY, the Imperial Japanese Navy, and the US Navy—also invested their money in aircraft carriers. This was partially out of concern that the new weapon had potential and partially because various naval disarmament treaties restricted the number of battleships, which made it attractive to have some aircraft carriers around, if only to provide billets for senior officers. These navies began to debate the ways in which the future of naval warfare would develop.

Ultimately, they all came to assume that the battleship and the carrier were complementary. In fleet actions, carrier aircraft would scout ahead of the battleline, feeling for the enemy, and, having found him, soften him up with air attacks. Then the battleships would go in to fight. Afterward the carrier aircraft would follow up victory by harrying the retiring enemy, or cover defeat by serving as the rear guard.

Meanwhile, of course, bigger and better battleships were being built. By the mid-1930s, when large-scale battleship construction was resumed after the naval disarmament treaties, displacements and guns were growing very large, 35,000 tons and 14–inch guns minimal. Battlewagons were also growing faster.

Earlier generations of battlewagons had been quite slow, usually able to make little more than two-thirds the 30 knots that light cruisers and destroyers could manage. By the late 1930s technology had reached the point where even the slowest of the newer battlewagons could approach the vicinity of 30 knots. Their earlier slowness had fostered the development of the battlecruiser, which was as large as a battleship, and carried virtually the same armament, but traded armor protection for higher speed. The battlecruiser had not worked out very well in combat, and by the late 1930s the surviving battlecruisers were even more obsolete than the older battleships, although they often found themselves in the company of the newer battlewagons, still being able to keep up. Then came World War II, and the aircraft carrier took a while to establish itself as the primary warship.

Despite the predictions of the air-minded, the primacy of the airplane—and the carrier—did not occur suddenly. Battleships several times came under air attack early in the war with little ill-effect. Nor were the British air raid on Taranto (November 11–12, 1940) and the Japanese one at PEARL HARBOR (December 7, 1941) particularly good tests of the survivability of the battleship against air power, in as much as in both instances the ships were surprised while at anchor in port, and only partially manned.

The sinking of "Force Z"—HMS *Prince of Wales* and HMS *Repulse*—by Japanese aircraft on the high seas off MALAYA on December 10, 1941, was a much clearer demonstration that battleships were vulnerable to air power. However, even this was not necessarily a decisive demonstration, given the limited antiaircraft ability of both vessels. In fact, the importance of the battleship still seemed so critical that for a time after Pearl Harbor the US Navy seriously considered purchasing Chile's only battlewagon, a ship in many ways comparable to the USS NEVADA.

Moreover, despite the disaster to Force Z, later in the war American and British battleships would survive even more intensive attacks as they became almost literally floating antiaircraft fortresses. In fact, battlewagons proved immensely valuable in helping to defend carriers—which were even more vulnerable than battleships—from air attack, while protecting themselves. On one occasion, USS *South Dakota* shot down over two dozen attacking aircraft in about five minutes, incurring only minor damage. And their heavy guns were extremely useful in covering amphibious assaults all over the world, not a few landings being largely decided by the support of battleship gunfire. During the protracted ground struggle for OKINAWA, for example, US battleships and large cruisers expended 23,157 rounds of 16-inch, 14-inch, and 12-inch ammunition, a weight of metal of over 12,000 tons.

Ref: Friedman, *United States Battleships*; Garzke and Dulin, *Battleships*; O'Connell, *Sacred Vessels*.

Beaufighter, British Fighter

The Beaufighter was a British heavy fighter originally designed as a long-range bomber escort and night fighter. Deliveries began in the summer of 1940 and those that reached the Pacific the next year soon became formidable tactical bombers (using TORPEDOES, bombs and rockets). Also carried were four forward-firing 20mm cannon. The Japanese called the Beaufighter "Whispering Death" because of its relatively quiet engine. Nearly 6,000 were built and the last ones in the Far East were not withdrawn from service until 1960.

See also AIRCRAFT TYPES, DEVELOPMENT.

Beaufort, British Torpedo Bomber

The Beaufort was a land-based British torpedo bomber. Although a 1930s design, it stayed in use well into 1944. Australia used a third of the 2,100 produced, so the Beaufort was well represented in the Pacific.

See also AIRCRAFT TYPES, DEVELOPMENT; CARRIERS DEVELOPING AIRCRAFT.

Benham Class, US Destroyers

Although they were a derivative of the BAGLEY CLASS destroyers, the 10 ships of this class, constructed 1936–39, incorporated numerous lessons learned from the navy's experience with the FARRAGUT CLASS, which had proven somewhat unsatisfactory in service. As a result, they were larger, but had a smaller main battery, and more TORPEDO tubes, with more powerful engines and a somewhat higher speed. Several Benhams were assigned to Neutrality Patrol in 1940, and were modified to enhance their antisubmarine capability, losing half their torpedo tubes in the process, while gaining a y-gun (depth charge thrower) and more antiaircraft guns, alterations that proved so successful that they were soon effected on the Pacific Fleet units as well. All units later had further improvements made to their air defense capacity. They saw considerable service, and two were lost in action.

Bennett, Henry Gordon (1887–1962)

Australian Army officer. In World War I Bennett served as a battalion and later brigade commander on the Western Front. Like virtually all Australian officers, between the wars he was a civilian, being by profession an actuary, at which he became quite wealthy. In 1940 he was made commander of the newly raised 8th Australian Division. For all his efforts, the division never completed its training, as men were continuously drafted away for service with the Australian divisions in North Africa. Despite this, in 1941 the division was sent to bolster the defenses of MALAYA, where it took part in the British disaster of December 1941–February 1942, surrendering at SINGAPORE.

Bennett managed to elude capture, making his way back to Australia. His public denunciations of British military leadership made him a political liability, and although he was eventually given a corps command, he saw no combat service for the rest of the war. Unlike most Commonwealth senior officers, he was never knighted.

Benson/Gleaves Classes, US Destroyers

The 96 ships of the Benson and Gleaves classes built 1938–43 were the last prewar-designed destroyers to enter service. Essentially somewhat smaller versions of the SIMS CLASS, they had four smaller boilers, rather than three large ones, plus 10 TORPEDO tubes in two banks of five, rather than eight in two banks of four. There were numerous versions of the basic design, and, in fact, on paper about 40 of the 96 units belonged to the Gleaves class, which was officially a few tons heavier and had some minor differences in appearance. To a great extent these were differences of no consequence. More important was the fact that the later units of the group—regardless of official class—were built to a modified wartime version, which had one less 5-inch gun and far more antiaircraft guns, changes that were effected to previously completed vessels as time and the exigencies of war permitted.

Biak, Battle of

Biak is an extensive island in the Schouten group, on Geelink Bay, a large gulf on the northwestern coast of New Guinea. A rugged, rather waterless, thinly populated place, Biak was very undeveloped in 1941. Although there were no places suitable for a naval base, there were a number of areas with great potential as air bases, from which a large part of the Philippine Sea and all of western New Guinea could be reached.

Biak became a valuable military objective for the Allies only when they discovered, in early 1944, that it was the only place along the coast of New Guinea that had ground suitable for building airfields quickly for heavy bombers like the B-24s. New Guinea, especially northwest New Guinea, was mainly mountains and swamps, not the kind of terrain favored by airfield builders.

On 27 May 1944, 12,000 troops of the American 41st Infantry Division (less one of its three infantry regiments) invaded Biak. This island provided air bases only 900 miles from the Philippines,

as well as access to vital Japanese shipping lanes west of New Guinea. The Japanese were keen to hang onto Biak. The American invasion was a rather hasty affair, but this had the benefit of catching the Japanese by surprise.

The Japanese garrison was 11,000 strong and in the midst of preparing extensive fortifications inland from the invasion beaches. The American troops soon came up against the partially completed fortifications. The Japanese also had some of their small, nine-ton TANKS on Biak, and they used them in the first tank battle of the Pacific War. The larger and more powerful American M-4 Sherman tanks were clearly superior and the Japanese tank force lost its first and last battle. The six American infantry battalions on the island were soon reinforced by two more and the Japanese systematically cleared from their fortifications.

In June 1944, the Japanese made two attempts to reinforce their beleaguered garrison on Biak. First, a heavily escorted convoy, carrying a 2,500-man brigade, was turned back by US bombers flying from newly built airfields. The Japanese then tried to slip in 600 troops on six destroyers. These were also caught by US bombers and forced back. A third attempt was about to be mounted, using battleships, when the US invasion of SAIPAN occurred on 11 June. This caused the Japanese to divert their attention from Biak, although there was some shooting when US warships went in pursuit of the Japanese surface ships. The subsequent relief attempt of Saipan and Battle of the PHILIPPINE SEA (the GREAT MARIANAS TURKEY SHOOT) off the MARIANAS was a disaster for the Japanese. Moreover, had they gone through with their attempted relief of Biak (with three battleships plus cruisers and destroyers), they might have succeeded. All the Americans had in the area were US Army Air Force bombers and fighters, plus some light surface forces and possibly not enough to stop the Japanese super-battleships *Musashi* and YAMATO. But the Japanese suspected that the Americans had carriers in the Biak area (they did not) and decided against the third attempt at relieving Biak.

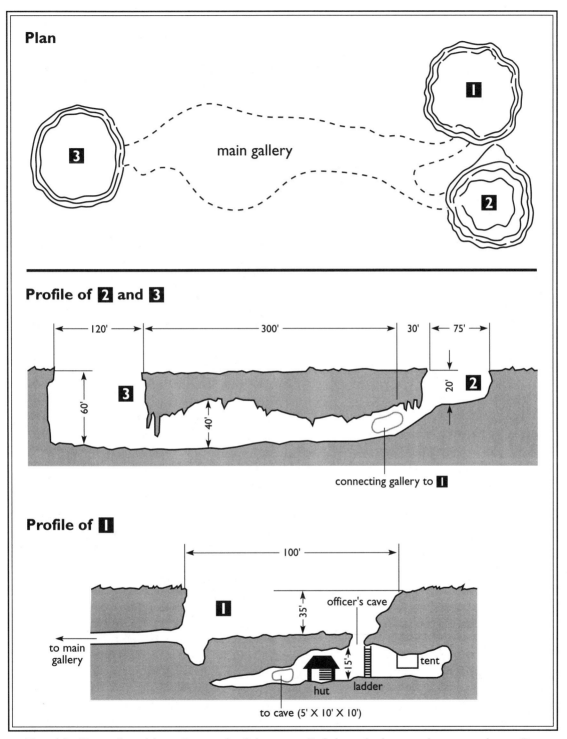

Plan

3

main gallery

1

2

Profile of 2 and 3

120'

300'

30'

75'

3

60'

40'

2

20'

connecting gallery to 1

Profile of 1

100'

officer's cave

1

35'

to main gallery

15'

tent

hut

ladder

to cave (5' X 10' X 10')

Plan of the "Sumps," an elaborate Japanese fortified system on Biak that took advantage of some natural caves. First assaulted by US troops on June 22, 1944, the position was not secured until the 27th. From MacArthur's New Guinea Campaign by Nathan Prefer (Conshohocken, Pa.: 1995); used with permission.

By the end of June, Biak was secured and air-fields under construction to support the final drive on the Philippines.

Biological Warfare

Although most major powers engaged in some bacteriological warfare research during World War II (if only to figure out how to cope with the possible use of germ warfare by the enemy), Japan was the only one to employ biological agents in the field. The Japanese germ warfare program was first suggested, then developed, and eventually carried out by Lieutenant General Shiro Ishii, a physician in the Japanese Army. Ishii began promoting the idea in the 1930s, inspired by the fact that biological weapons had been banned by the GENEVA CONVENTIONS. Ishii reasoned that if the Western nations were that concerned about biological weapons, then Japan must have them. He ended up commanding the germ warfare centers in MANCHURIA during the 1930s, including the infamous Detachment 731 (outside of Harbin). Major General Masaji Kitano was his deputy. Over 3,000 technicians and support personnel were assigned to Detachment 731. Four sub-detachments were set up during the war in China. Over 3,000 Chinese, Koreans, Russians, and Americans were killed during experiments by Detachment 731. POWs and detainees who tried to escape or otherwise caused trouble were sent to Detachment 731 as punishment, and the result was usually lethal, or at least quite painful, for the victim. Starting with relatively simple weapons, like cholera and typhoid cultures that could be dropped in wells by Japanese troops, work advanced to more exotic diseases that could be delivered by air.

The principal weapon developed from all this was the "Plague Bomb" (containers of fleas infected with plague that could be dropped from aircraft). Bombs were tested in central China (Nimpo) in 1940. There was no dramatic effect, if only because plague was actually difficult to spread. The fleas needed a host (such as rats) in order to survive long enough to spread the disease. The Japanese tried infestation on the ground in July 1942 to halt Chinese Army advances at Chekiang. Again, there was no dramatic effect. But there were deaths from the persistent Japanese attempts to make biological warfare work. The Japanese got better at it and by the end of the war had killed about 170,000 Chinese civilians. Another 30,000 deaths from these experiments occurred until the infections finally disappeared by 1948.

The Japanese also planned to send high-altitude balloons carrying plague-infected rats to North America (where plague already existed in parts of the western deserts), and toward the very end of the war there was a project to use submarine-launched aircraft to spread plague on the West Coast. In the summer of 1944, there was a fierce debate in the Japanese high command over the use of biological weapons to assist in the defense of Japanese-held islands. Although a submarine was sent to SAIPAN with biological weapons for the defender (and was sunk on the way), the high command ultimately agreed not to use biological weapons. The reasoning was that, since the Americans were apparently going to win the war, it was more likely that American biological or chemical weapons would be used on Japan if Japan were the first to use such devices. But a year later, this thinking changed. In July of 1945, Detachment 731 was enlisted to work with the navy to equip an aircraft carried by a submarine. Such aircraft had been flown off subs earlier in the war on recon missions. Such aircraft could carry small bombs, in this case bombs carrying fleas infected with Bubonic Plague. The war ended before the sub could depart for SAN DIEGO, where it was supposed to drop the plague bombs on 22 September 1945.

Detachment 731 conducted experiments on communicability in humans of many infectious disease. They also conducted frostbite research on the effects of cold on humans, using PRISONERS as test subjects. Chinese prisoners were also used to test the effectiveness of POISON GAS in the open, under realistic conditions. The Japanese used men, women, and children for all these tests, and often dissected the victim while still alive, and without any painkillers. Films were made of the experiments, so that senior officials back in Japan, including the emperor, could keep up on the Japanese Army's work in medical research. And it was the Japanese Army in general, not just Detachment 731, that routinely abused and murdered Chinese and Allied prisoners and civilians in the name of "medical research." For the most part it was just "practice surgery," but if any Japanese Army surgeon felt like doing what he considered "medical research," he generally could ask the local Japanese police for a subject and a prisoner (usually Chinese, often a Chinese communist, the preferred victims) would be sent over.

When the Russians invaded Manchuria in the summer of 1945, Ishii ordered Detachment 731's facilities destroyed, with over 400 of the remaining prisoners executed. Much equipment was shipped to Korea. Ishii and his senior staff fled south into China, but were captured in Nanking during September and turned over to US forces. Ishii negotiated immunity from prosecution in return for his research material. He later lectured at army bases in the United States in 1948, describing his experience with human testing of infectious organisms. Major General Kitano also struck a deal with the Americans and went on to become president of a Japanese drug company (Green Cross). He lived into the 1980s as a respected member of the Japanese medical community. The Russians captured many Japanese officers and MDs who participated in human experimentation and tried all as war criminals. Most were sentenced to 25 years hard labor but many were released in the 1950s.

See also: ATROCITIES, JAPANESE

Bismarck Archipelago

An island group just northeast of New Guinea, in the southwest Pacific, including NEW BRITAIN, New Ireland, and several other large islands, as well as the Admiralty group, for a total of about 19,000

rather rugged, jungle covered, but thinly inhabited square miles.

Bismarck Sea, Battle of the

The Bismarck Sea is a body of water just northeast of New Guinea, in the southwest Pacific, between the Bismarck Archipelago, the Solomons, and New Guinea, with some small islets and atolls separating it from the Coral Sea.

On March 1–4, 1943, a rather small, if protracted air-sea battle took place there. What made the "Battle of the Bismarck Sea" interesting was that it pitted land-based air power against sea power and demonstrated that aircraft ruled the seas. This was not done by high-altitude bombardment, however, but by aircraft using the right tactics and weapons, low-level attacks with high firepower.

In early 1943, the Allies were fighting their way across the northeast coast of New Guinea. To the northeast was the major Japanese base of RABAUL and a powerful fleet of cruisers and destroyers. The Allies had established themselves on this coast of New Guinea with several hundred fighters and bombers. An American and three Australian divisions were closing in on the Japanese base at LAE. On March 1, the Japanese sent a convoy of eight destroyers and nine transports to Lae, carrying an infantry division. Overhead, the Japanese had dozens of fighters flying escort, and bombers at the ready in case the Allies should send in warships.

Alerted by an intelligence coup and some lucky reconnaissance, the American air forces had a nasty surprise in store for the Japanese. Over the previous six months, General George KENNEY, commander of the US Army Air Force in the area, had developed new anti-shipping tactics. B-25 twin-engine bombers had more machine guns added, so that they could now rake enemy ships with 10/.50 caliber machine guns at once. This was often enough to sink smaller transports. A few passes by these B-25 "gunships" could leave even destroyers smoldering wrecks. In addition, the B-25s and other twin-engine bombers practiced and perfected "skip bombing." With this method, the aircraft came in low and released a bomb with a delay fuse. The bomb was skipped off the water and into the target, hitting the ship in the side like a TORPEDO, doing maximum damage to the usual targets, destroyers and transports. Allied fighters flew above to keep Japanese fighters at bay. And just to mop up, the navy sent a PT-BOAT squadron. Between the gunships and skip bombing, the Japanese could never again run convoys across contested waters in daylight. The battle ran its course March 1–4, 1943. The 17-ship Japanese convoy was demolished, with only four of the destroyers escaping. The Japanese lost 25 aircraft and over 3,500 sailors and soldiers. US and Australian losses were three fighters and two bombers of the 335 aircraft committed.

See also SAKAKIDA, RICHARD.

Black Americans in the Pacific War

Well over 800,000 black men and women served in the armed forces during World War II. Blacks, who totaled about 10% of the population, constituted about 7% of the armed forces. Restrictive policies and institutional discrimination kept most blacks out of combat jobs. Nevertheless, African Americans served in every theater and in every branch, in a variety of duties.

In all theaters the most significant role performed by black troops was in the rear. Many quartermaster and engineer construction units were composed primarily of black troops, who usually served under white officers. Over a third of the engineering troops who worked on the BURMA ROAD and the ALCAN Highway were black, as were most of the personnel of the famed "Red Ball Express" (a collection of truck battalions), which sustained the army's drive across France in the summer of 1944.

Only about 3% of the armed forces' combat personnel were black, comprising two infantry divisions (92nd and 93rd), plus several independent regiments, battalions, and fighter squadrons. The experience of black troops was satisfactory, and often distinguished, but generally reported negatively. For example, when the 25th Regimental Combat Team (93rd Division) first went into action in the South Pacific there was some confusion in one company (not an unusual occurrence when a green unit enters combat for the first time), which was widely reported as panic in the ranks. Similar discriminatory treatment plagued reporting of the performance of black units throughout the war.

About 200,000 African Americans served in the Asiatic-Pacific Theater. American racism, combined with the character of the theater, with numerous island needing garrisons, limited the participation of black troops in the Pacific War. Far more African-American troops saw action in the European-North African-Middle Eastern Theater than in the Pacific. So while many African-American fighter pilots, artillerymen, tankers, tank destroyers, and infantrymen rendered yeoman service in Europe, very few black troops entered combat in the Pacific, at least deliberately. The two largest, mostly black combat units in the Pacific were the 93rd Infantry Division and the 24th Regimental Combat Team. Neither unit was ever committed to anything other than rear-area security and mopping-up operations, and as a result neither was ever actually tested under fire: The 93rd Division, for example, took fewer than 200 casualties.

However, many black soldiers served in combat support roles in the Asiatic-Pacific Theater. For example, several Army Amphtrak (Amphibious Tractor) battalions, which supported the OKINAWA and IWO JIMA landings, were manned by black personnel, and their performance under fire was comparable to that of their white counterparts.

If the army was openly racist, the navy and Marines were even more so, at least initially. The navy had been relatively integrated, at least up to the rank of chief petty officer, until the presidency of Woodrow Wilson, who, despite his progressive reputation, was a blatant racist. Along with prohibiting alcoholic beverages aboard ship, the Wilson administration decided that the navy should be lily

Troops of the 93rd Infantry Division on a "mopping-up" mission near Numa Numa on Bougainville, May 1, 1944. Note the dense jungle.

white. As a result, by the late 1920s blacks had virtually been excluded from the service, even as mess boys, that role having been given to Filipinos: In 1932 there were only 441 black men in the navy, down from 10,000 in 1918. As the Marines had never recruited blacks, they had no problem with this policy. However, by the eve of the war, potential wartime manpower shortages soon suggested to even the most hard-nosed senior navy and Marine officers that obtaining some black personnel might be useful, if only to free up some whites for "important" positions.

The navy quietly began recruiting African Americans again in the early 1930s, but numbers remained small until shortly after the outbreak of

the European War, in 1939. By bringing back to service some of the senior petty officers who had been thrown out during the so-called "Progressive Era," the navy was able to suggest to potential black recruits that it was not as racist as its reputation would have it. The most notable of these men was CPO John Henry Turpin, who had enlisted as a boy in 1883. Turpin's service was long and varied, and he had actually been aboard the USS *Maine* when she blew up in 1898. By World War I Turpin was something of a legend in the navy, despite his color. He retired in 1925 as a chief gunner's mate. Although pushing 70, he was recalled in 1938, and served on recruiting duty, one of the oldest men in uniform. However, the navy also discovered that using chief petty officers, of any color, for recruiting did not always produce the desired results. These crusty old salts were more likely to frighten than entice potential recruits. Despite this, many blacks did join the navy. Most ended up working as mess boys. But in the Navy, even mess boys had an important combat role. On ships, everyone is in combat during battle. Everyone has a "battle station." A black sailor might be a waiter in the officers' mess most of the time, but when "general quarters" sounded, he put on a steel HELMET and manned a gun along with the white boys, as did Dorie MILLER, one of the heroes at PEARL HARBOR. By the end of the war there were few US warships without some black seamen, and many of them gained at least grudging respect from their white comrades. By that time, black men were beginning to be assigned to duties other than service in the mess, a few young men even being accepted for training as combat pilots.

The Marines addressed the novel problem of having to accept black recruits by assuming that a black Marine was still a Marine. In the Marines every man was an infantryman and was expected to turn out for that duty on short notice. So, although the Corps trained only a small number of African Americans specifically as combat troops, and assigned them to units that were unlikely to see combat (the 51st and 52nd Defense Battalions, one of which performed mopping-up duties on several islands, the other never left California), black Marines were expected to be able to join the firing

US Navy steward's mates polishing silverware in the officers' mess aboard the carrier Ticonderoga *(CV-14), November 1944. Most African Americans in the navy performed similar tasks.*

Somewhere behind the lines: black Marines preparing to move up on Peleliu, September 15, 1944.

line if necessary, and were trained appropriately. On SAIPAN black Marines first served under fire as ammunition carriers; on Peleliu they often ended up supporting their white comrades on the front lines, a tale repeated at Iwo Jima and on Okinawa. By the end of the war, General VANDEGRIFT, the Marine Corps commandant admitted publicly that blacks made splendid Marines.

The third branch of the sea services, the Coast Guard, had little problem accommodating black recruits. From its creation as the Revenue Cutter Service, under George Washington, the Coast Guard had a record of recruiting black men on a more or less equal footing with whites. Although there was a great deal of racism in the service, there were even occasional black officers, including sev-

eral ships' captains in the late 19th century. Although it too was affected by Wilsonian racism, the Coast Guard managed to retain some black personnel right through the 1940s. In this regard it's worth noting that the last persons ever executed for piracy as a result of a US court decision were two white rumrunners in the 1920s who had killed a black coastguardsman. During World War II many black men served in the Coast Guard, in which capacity they performed a wide range of military duties.

The status of black troops off duty was often worse than when they were on duty. Although post-exchanges (general stores) were not racially segregated (to save money, not to promote equality), leisure-time facilities were often limited. On those islands with black populations, the black troops were often welcome in local establishments. However, in Australia and New Zealand, which had "whites only" immigration policies, a number of serious incidents occurred that were never satisfactorily resolved. Generally the black victims of Australian or American racism were considered at fault whenever a fight broke out. Some attempts were made to establish special clubs for black troops, often with aboriginal or mixed race women serving as hostesses, in Australia and New Guinea, but quite often black troops had to make do with set-aside hours at clubs or none at all.

Despite the limited opportunities for distinction that their status offered, the performance of black personnel in World War II was extremely important in the ultimate decision to end segregation in the armed forces, which was issued by President TRUMAN in 1948. Even the most convinced racists had to accept the testimony of white combat veterans on this point, and this eliminated what had long been the primary argument against putting blacks and whites in the same units.

See also BURAKUMI; PACIFIC ISLANDERS, RESISTANCE TO THE JAPANESE.

Black Coast Guardsmen with their 20mm antiaircraft gun somewhere in the South Pacific. Although rated as Steward's Mates, these men, like all sailors, were assigned a combat post during "general quarters."

Ref: MacGregor, *Integration of the Armed Forces*; Nelson, *The Integration of the Negro into the United States Navy*.

Blamey, Thomas (1884–1951)

Thomas A. Blamey, the son of a shopkeeper, worked as a teacher before being commissioned in the Australian militia in 1906. He distinguished himself as a staff officer during World War I, rising to colonel. After the war Blamey resigned from active service. Between the wars he rose to become chief commissioner of police for the State of Victoria. His appointment as commander of Australia's ground forces in 1940, primarily on the basis of his considerable administrative skills, caused a good deal of protest. Not only did Blamey lack serious combat experience, but he was also, in the bargain, tactless, often rude, and very self-aggrandizing: His nickname was "Typhoid Tom." As a lieutenant general, in April of 1941 he was briefly second in command to Sir Archibald WAVELL in the Mediterranean-Middle Eastern Theater, and performed yeoman service in organizing the Allied withdrawal from Greece. Recalled from the Middle East after PEARL HARBOR, Blamey was made commander of all Allied ground forces in Australia under the overall command of Douglas MACARTHUR. This was a difficult task, as MacArthur constantly ignored proper channels to communicate directly with units, and essentially denied Blamey any control over American troops. Blamey directed the defeat of the Japanese offensive over the OWEN STANLEY MOUNTAINS in New Guinea, and the Allied offensive to the BUNA-GONA position, until early 1943. After the fall of Buna, Blamey was increasingly ignored by MacArthur, so that by the end of the war his effective authority was limited to Australian troops in Australia. Despite this he was eventually made a field marshal, the only Australian to achieve such rank. A good officer, Blamey performed well in command, but did not "work and play well with others," which was one reason his active influence on Allied op-

erations was limited, another being MacArthur's extraordinary hostility toward non-American troops and commanders.

Blenheim, British Bomber

The Blenheim was the first modern British "fast bomber." When the first ones entered service in 1936, they were indeed able to outrun many fighters. This situation did not last and the Blenheim went through several different versions until production ceased in the summer of 1943. Some 5,400 were produced. Several hundred of the Mark V version served in the Far East as light bombers until late 1943.

See also AIRCRAFT TYPES, DEVELOPMENT.

Blockade Runners

The definitive history of blockade-running during the Second World War has yet to be written. When Britain declared war on Germany in September 1939, it also imposed a tight maritime blockade. As the war spread, the Allies extended the blockade to additional powers, culminating in December of 1941 with its imposition against Japan. Almost as soon as the blockade began, attempts were made to run it. Although it was run numerous times—both by warships attempting to get to sea in order to raid Allied commerce and by merchantmen carrying contraband—the Allied blockade of the Axis powers was probably the tightest ever imposed, a situation fostered by the fact that even when Allied fortunes were at their lowest point, they still controlled most of the world's seas.

Blockade-runners were either vessels on war missions or those carrying goods, documents, and personnel.

German warships—including battleships—and armed merchant raiders ran the British blockade of the North Sea several times, with considerable success. However, despite the injury and panic they often caused, these missions were of limited importance in terms of their overall impact on the course of the war. More critical to the Axis war effort were the ships attempting to carry goods, technical equipment, documents, and critical personnel through the blockade.

The cargo carried by blockade-runners was usually critical materials. Typical cargo for a vessel running from Europe to the Far East might include mercury, ball bearings, or medicines. A vessel going from the Far East to Europe would likely carry rubber, tin, or other raw materials, or specialized goods such as silk. For example, when the Italian blockade-runner *Pietro Orseolo* made the last of her three trips through the blockade, from Kobe to Bordeaux in 65 days, from January 25, 1943 to April 2, 1942, she carried 1,988 tons of crude rubber, plus 28 tons of rubber tires, as well as 4,486 tons of tropical cooking oils, 83 of tin, and 21 of special lubricating oils. Three German blockade-runners sunk in South American waters as a result of ULTRA intercepts on 2–4 January 1944, *Weserland, Bergenland*, and *Rio Grande*, were carrying sufficient rubber to provide tires for 5,000 heavy bombers, which they did upon being salvaged. The Italian submarine *Cappellini*, which made a run from La Pallice, France, to SABANG Sumatra, in about 60 days during the spring and summer of 1943, mostly on the surface, carried, among other things, 90 tons of mercury—sufficient to manufacture fulminate of mercury for some 30 million rounds of ammunition. On her return voyage she was to carry 155 tons of cargo: 92 of rubber, 54 of tin, 5 of tungsten, and 4 of medicinals. In one famous case, that of the German submarine U-234, the cargo consisted of 1,200 pounds of uranium oxide, which found its way into Allied hands when Germany surrendered, and may have been used in one of the ATOMIC BOMBS.

Blockade-runners also carried samples of new equipment, such as radar and proximity fuzes, which the Axis partners thought to share with each other. Documents that were transferred by blockade-runners included plans for special weapons and equipment. The transfer of personnel involved diplomatic officials and military officers, and, in one

notable case, the Indian nationalist leader Subhas Chandra BOSE.

Several dozen Axis ships appear to have made successful voyages between ports in the Far East and Bordeaux, or from Bordeaux to the Far East. The fastest voyage appears to have been that of the German freighter *Orsone*, which carried 6,950 tons of mixed cargo from Kobe to Bordeaux between December 24, 1941 and February 19, 1942, 57 days. While a few ships managed the trip in 60–65 days, most required more than 70.

Although the Italians and Germans used both SUBMARINES and surface ships in their blockade-running attempts, the Japanese appear to have confined their efforts solely to submarines, a number of which made the run between the Far East and Europe.

Losses among blockade-runners were heavy, although actual statistics are uncertain.

In addition to Axis attempts to run the Allied blockade, there were Allied attempts to run the blockade the Japanese imposed on the Philippines and East Indies during the fighting in late 1941 and early 1942. Although some success was achieved, particularly in getting troops into the East Indies and some supplies into BATAAN, mostly by submarine but occasionally by surface ship, overall these operations were insufficient to affect the outcome of operations there.

See also GERMANY IN THE PACIFIC WAR; I-52; ITALY IN THE PACIFIC WAR.

Ref: Brice, *Axis Blockade Runners*.

Bloody Ridge, Battle of

This battle, also called the battle of Edson's Ridge, was the closest the Japanese ever came to retaking GUADALCANAL from US Marines in 1942. On the night of 13 September 1942, the Japanese Kawaguchi Brigade attacked Marines defending Henderson Field. The Marine positions were on a series of low ridges about a kilometer south of the vital airfield. The Japanese brigade had landed two weeks earlier at night, via destroyer transports (American aircraft operating from Henderson Field prevented slower merchant ships from getting close enough to Guadalcanal). About half of Kawaguchi's force arrived outside the Marine positions, which were held by 840 men of the combined 1st Raider/1st Parachute Battalions, commanded by LTC Merritt Edson (1897–1955). The Japanese made 12 attacks that night. Although the Marines fell back to new positions, the line held. The Japanese lost half their force, the Marines suffered 30% CASUALTIES. Most of the Japanese losses were from artillery fire, or US warplanes attacking them in the days before the attack was launched.

The Japanese lost the battle for a number of reasons. They were too impetuous and over-ambitious. General Kawaguchi sent his assault battalions into the jungle, to march around the Marine position, without much preparation. Half of the assault forces got lost and only 1,700 Japanese troops actually made the attack on time. Other Japanese troops blundered into the American lines in the dark. This led to some Japanese troops wandering around the airfield area, but not enough Japanese got through to make a difference.

This battle made quite an impression on many Japanese commanders. The Americans were not going to be as easy to push around as the Chinese or anyone else the Japanese had tangled with in the past year.

Bogue Class, US Escort Carriers

The Bogue-class ships were converted from reciprocating steam-engined C3 merchant hulls under construction when the United States entered the war. The work was done quickly, so that they were all launched in 1942, and entered service between June of that year and April of 1943: One actually took only 11 months, from keel laying to completion. The 21 ships (of which 10 were built for Britain) displaced less than the LONG ISLAND (about 14,000 tons full load as against about 15,000) and were no faster, but were more responsive to their helms, had a much greater aircraft complement (initially 16 fighters and 12 torpedo bombers), and possessed an island superstructure. Like *Long Island*,

they were very cramped internally. They saw extensive antisubmarine service in the Atlantic, where one was lost, and several were employed in a variety of roles in the Pacific.

Bombers, Heavy

Mention strategic bombing in World War II, and most people will think of the B-17 Flying Fortress. The B-17 was the first four-engine heavy bomber to enter service (in 1939). But the B-17 was only second in terms of numbers built, with 12,731 produced. There were 18,325 B-24 Liberators built. Number three in this list was the British Lancaster (7,377). The B-29, the biggest four-engine bomber of the war and the only one to drop an ATOMIC BOMB, appeared in 1944 and only 3,000 were built.

More B-24s were produced because they were more effective aircraft than B-17s. The B-24 could fly higher, faster, and carry more bombs than the B-17. B-24s, however, were more difficult aircraft to fly than B-17s. The overall superiority of the B-24 over the B-17 wasn't huge, but in wartime, every little bit helps.

Quantity deliveries of the B-17 began in 1939, the B-24 in 1942. Thus the B-17 had time to implant itself on the public consciousness even while larger numbers of B-24s were appearing and doing more of the work. Some missions, like hitting key targets just a little too far away for the B-17, went to the B-24. Naval reconnaissance was also a favorite task for the B-24. The B-24 was also an extraordinary escort aircraft. By one estimate, during the Battle of the Atlantic a B-24 saved one merchant ship for every five escort missions it flew.

Like all airplanes, the B-24 had its faults, and these were amplified in the public's mind as a means of resisting the thought that the popular "Fortress" was being replaced. Along those lines, the B-29 was called the "Super Fortress" and designated a new generation of bombers and a worthy successor to the B-17.

See also AIRCRAFT TYPES, DEVELOPMENT.

Bombing, Deaths From

World War II was the first conflict in which a substantial number of deaths were inflicted by aircraft. In some cases, the numbers were enormous.

At least several million civilian and military deaths can be attributed to air attacks. In addition, the British suffered 2,754 deaths from ballistic missiles (V-2s), a record that stood until the 1980s, when Iraq and Iran rained SCUD missiles (derived from the V-2 design) on each other's cities. Over 10,000 deaths resulted. Britain also suffered 6,184 deaths from German V-1 cruise missiles. This record still stands.

Nation	Civilian Deaths from Air Raids
Japan	668,000
Germany	593,000
Britain	60,400

Bombing, Difficulties of Hitting Ships

Before the war, air power enthusiasts claimed that they could disable warships with heavy bombers from considerable altitudes. In practice, this proved wholly impossible. Indeed, so few underway ships were hit by high-level bombers that the probability of hitting was actually less than chance.

The problem was one of the relative size of the target when viewed from high altitude, and the fact that the target was usually moving in an unpredictable fashion. The farther up one went, the smaller the target became, and the more significant became even minor changes in course, speed, and position. Consider the aircraft carrier MIDWAY. Although she was actually commissioned too late to see action in the war, *Midway* had the largest target area of any ship of the day, her length of 968 feet and beam of 136 feet giving a total deck area of roughly 14,700 square yards. By chance, this is proportionally and roughly the same dimensions as a dollar bill. A paper dollar is 6 inches by about 2.5 inches, which gives a surface area of about 15 square inches, or very roughly about one square inch for each of the carrier's thousand square yards.

Place a dollar bill at your feet, then stand up and look down at it. The apparent size of the dollar as you look at it is roughly the same size that the carrier *Midway* would have been if you had viewed her from about 10,000 feet.

So the principal reason that high-level bombers found it "difficult" to hit surface ships was that they were very, very small targets. Add to that the fact that the ships were usually somewhat CAMOUFLAGED, were almost always moving, often making evasive maneuvers and probably shooting like mad, or that the attacking aircraft were also moving and might even be the object of unfriendly fighter aircraft, not to mention that there might be smoke or clouds obscuring the view, and it's no surprise that the number of ships actually hit by high-level bombers was negligible. Indeed, considering the lack of success that strategic bombers had in hitting factories and such, it's remarkable that in postwar literature the bomber enthusiasts repeatedly argued that wartime experience vindicated their prewar claims to be able to hit ships under way at sea from altitude.

After the Battle of Midway, for example, the Army Air Corps reported that as a result of 16 separate air raids by groups of B-17s which expended 314 500- and 600-pound bombs, 22 direct hits and numerous near-misses had been scored on "carriers, battleships, cruisers, and destroyers," with several sinkings resulting. One of the ships attacked was the submarine USS *Grayling* (SS-209). On June 7, 1942 she was beset by 12 B-17s and had to submerge to escape their attentions. Although she suffered no ill effects in the attack, the bomber pilots claimed to have sunk a Japanese cruiser. In fact, despite grand claims that made it into the headlines back home, during the Battle of Midway not a single Japanese ship appears to have been hit by a B-17. So unlikely was it that a high-level bomber could sink an underway ship that on the only occasion when it occurred, the Japanese destroyer *Mochitzuki* off BOUGAINVILLE on October 24, 1943, the ship's crew at first thought that she had struck a mine or been hit by a TORPEDO. At the official inquiry into the ship's loss, her skipper ascribed the incident to ill-fortune, allegedly commenting "even the B-17s can get a lucky hit once in a while."

Ref: Dunnigan and Nofi, *Victory at Sea.*

Bombing, Ineffectiveness of

Dropping a lot of bombs doesn't do much damage. This phenomenon was first encountered in a bombing campaign against enemy forces on American territory. In June 1942, the Japanese occupied two of the ALEUTIAN ISLANDS off the coast of Alaska. They held these islands for 14 months during which hundreds of American aircraft were brought forward to conduct an intense bombing campaign. Some 7,300 attack sorties were flown and 4,300 tons of bombs were dropped (in addition to tons of machine-gun bullets during strafing runs). After the war, when Japanese records could be examined, it was discovered that only 450 Japanese troops were killed by all these raids (about 6% of the troops being attacked), or about one soldier for each ton of ammunition expended. Perhaps if more of the pilots had served in the ground forces, they would have realized how resourceful their targets could be.

This pattern was found again and again during the Pacific War. Part of it was due to the thoroughness with which the Japanese prepared fortified positions. Japanese artillery fire and bombing was equally ineffective against well dug in American troops, but there was a lot more US firepower used in the Pacific, so despite the odds American firepower was more effective.

Bombing, North America, Japanese Attacks

While the Allies dropped millions of tons of bombs on Germany and Japan, the Axis powers had little opportunity to retaliate. In particular, the United States was practically immune to such attacks. The Japanese launched some 6,000 balloons eastward, each carrying five small incendiary bombs. At least 316 of these reached the West Coast (about 300 were located during the war, and the rest afterward). Several forest fires were started and several deaths occurred, when a picnicking family came upon one. Information on the balloon bombs was largely suppressed during the war to prevent panic and to keep the Japanese in the dark as to how their balloon operation was going.

But both Germany and Japan did make long-range aircraft that could reach North America. Fortunately, they didn't make many of these aircraft, nor make a strenuous effort to bomb North America until near the end of the war. In late 1942 a Japanese submarine, modified to carry a single-engine reconnaissance plane, launched its E14Y1 "Glenn" off the coast of Oregon. Four 167-pound incendiary bombs were dropped in forests, but no major fire was started. Earlier in 1942, Japan put the first of its four-engine float planes, the H8K, into service. The H8K was a very large aircraft (124-foot wingspan, 92 feet long). Its defensive armament consisted of four 7.7 mm and six 20mm machine guns. It had a range of 4,400 miles. It could carry over four tons of bombs and had a top speed of 289 miles per hour. Japan's Admiral Kinsei did a little math and concluded that half a dozen H8Ks could fly to the California coast, land on the water, be refueled by SUBMARINES, bomb Los Angeles, and then fly back to Japanese-held territory. This plan was approved before the Battle of MIDWAY, and scaled back after the battle to three H8Ks being sent out to bomb HAWAII. Bad weather forced the H8Ks to drop their bombs blindly. Undiscouraged, the Japanese planned to take 30 H8Ks, refuel them from submarines off Baja, California, and then fly cross-country to bomb the Texas oil fields. Then, in cooperation with German U-boats (some of which would be tankers), the H8Ks would range up and down the East Coast of the United States, making air raids on major cities, mainly for terror and propaganda value. The Germans were eager to cooperate and prepared the tanker subs needed. Fortunately, American victories in the Pacific forced the Japanese to use their

H8Ks for the more mundane task of patrolling before this scheme could be carried out. Thus while there were bombs over Tokyo, despite strenuous Japanese efforts, there were no bombs over Brooklyn.

See also I-26.

Ref: Mikesh, *Japan's World War II Balloon Bomb Attack on North America*; Webber, *Retaliation* and *Silent Siege*.

Bombing, Strategic

Until 1941, it was thought by both American and Japanese strategists that attacks on the Japanese Home Islands would be by ship bombardment and carrier aircraft. The new B-17 bomber did not have the range to reach Japan from any nearby islands. Although the army had started building the longer-range B-29 bomber in late 1940, that plane did not make its first flight until September 1942 (by which time the even larger and longer-ranged B-36 was already on the drawing board) and would not be available in large quantities until late 1944. After PEARL HARBOR, it became obvious that the decades-old war plans for attacking the Home Islands would have to be scrapped because of the danger from Japanese land-based aircraft. The B-29, designed to attack European targets from North America (with 2.5-ton bomb loads), could also carry 10 tons of bombs against targets 1,500 miles distant. This would make it ideal for use against Japan, flying from small islands in the central Pacific.

See also BOMBING JAPAN.

Bombing Japan

One thing the Japanese didn't expect was to see waves of American bombers over their cities. To the east there was the vast Pacific Ocean, with no nearby islands to support airfields. To the west were Korea and China, occupied by dozens of Japanese divisions. The Japanese thought their cities were safe from air attack.

The 1942 DOOLITTLE Raid was a shock, but was soon seen as a special case. The Japanese did thereafter maintain hundreds of interceptors to guard against future carrier raids. But they knew these raids could do little damage because Japan's cities were vast and the bomb capacity of carrier aircraft limited.

What the Japanese didn't foresee was the B-29 bomber. They were familiar with the smaller B-17, as it had gone into service in the late 1930s. The B-17, and subsequent B-24, didn't have the range to reach Japan from the nearest Pacific islands, the MARIANAS, 1,500 miles distant. The B-17 could, at most, fly nearly a thousand miles with a minuscule bomb load.

In 1940, the United States began designing the B-29, an aircraft with a 3,500 mile range, and the ability to reach a target 1,500 miles distant while carrying several tons of bombs. The B-29 first flew in 1942. The aircraft was originally conceived as a "worst-case" weapon, a bomber that could bomb Germany from North America or Iceland if the Nazis took Britain. By the time the B-29 was ready for mass production in late 1943, it was clear that it would see service in the Pacific.

The Marianas were not taken until the summer of 1944. The first B-29 units were formed in September 1943. So it was decided to send the first B-29s to India. From there they could operate against Japanese targets in southeast Asia. The first raid was on 27 May 1944, as 16 B-29s hit the railroad repair shops in BANGKOK, Siam. But India was just a staging area for bases in China.

The first major B-29 raids operated from Chinese bases. But because China was cut off from sea or land access, all fuel and bombs for these raids had to be flown in from India. Two tons of fuel were required to fly in one ton of supplies. Some B-29 raids were made on Japan from Chinese bases, but there was no hope of flying in sufficient supplies to mount a significant air assault. The largest raids from Chinese bases were about a hundred aircraft. Raids from China continued into early 1945 (when Japanese troops captured the bases), hitting targets all over the region, from Burma to MANCHURIA and southern Japan. However, an effective bombing campaign against Japan would have to wait for the Marianas to be captured and bases built there (particularly on SAIPAN).

In October 1944, the first B-29s landed on Saipan. In November, the first B-29 raids hit Tokyo—all this while the battle for the Philippines was still raging and most of southeast Asia and China was still under Japanese control.

After the first few months of bombing, it was noted that the European style of high-altitude precision daylight bombing wasn't having the desired effect. There had long been plans to eventually switch to firebombing of cities, after industrial targets (steel mills and aircraft factories) had been destroyed. But intelligence information indicated that many key weapons components were made by small shops in urban residential neighborhoods. These shops employed about one-sixth of the workforce. Moreover, it was known that largely wood Japanese housing was much easier to burn than the typically brick or stone buildings found in Europe. After a few tests of firebombing and the adoption of low-level flying tactics, the B-29s switched to this form of attack. Japan's urban areas began to burn, and with them went their industrial capacity. The damage to Japanese cities was immense. In major areas like Tokyo (equal in population to New York City, but with only about a third the land area) 50% of the buildings were destroyed. Many smaller cities suffered over 60% destruction. Over 2.2 million homes were destroyed and 668,000 civilians died in these raids. Although more than twice as much bomb tonnage was dropped on Germany, the losses in homes (255,000) and lives (593,000) were lower there, due to the German brick and masonry construction. The bombing campaign against Germany went on for over two years, compared to less than a year in Japan. The two ATOMIC BOMBS combined with incendiary bombs used against exceptionally vulnerable Japanese housing were devastating. And, unlike the air war against Germany, it was bombing that brought Japan to its knees. The atomic bombs were the final blow from the air, pre-

DESTRUCTION IN SELECTED JAPANESE URBAN CENTERS		
City	Area	% Devastated
Kobe	15.7 sq. mi.	8.8
Nagoya	39.7	12.4
Osaka	59.8	15.6
Tokyo	110.8	56.3
Yokohama	20.2	9.9

ceded by the firebombs and naval MINES dropped by B-29s. By the end of the war there were six B-29 wings (each with 192 B-29s and 12,000 troops). One was based in India, the others in the Marianas (Saipan, GUAM, and TINIAN). Most raids were small, with 25–50 aircraft. But every two weeks or so there were larger raids of 500–600 B-29s. The bombing of Japan cost about $3 million for each square mile devastated; in 1995 dollars, this destruction cost about 50 cents a square foot.

In general, the effectiveness of attacks from the air tended to be much overestimated by the Americans. It was one thing to go after ships with low-flying bombers, where results could be instantly seen. Attacks on land targets were another matter. One reason firebomb raids were popular in the air assault on Japan was because the resulting damage (hundreds of acres of blackened ruins) was unambiguous.

Bombers were also used to attack Japanese forces in the field, which was quite different than bombing urban areas, as was first noted in the Aleutians in 1943. After the Japanese bases at Attu and KISKA were captured, it was possible to assess the effectiveness of the 7,300 bombing and strafing sorties flown (and 4,300 tons of bombs dropped). Most of the Japanese bomb shelters were unharmed. After the war, when Japanese records could be examined, it was discovered that only 6% (450 men) of the Japanese troops subjected to these attacks were killed (and about three times as many injured to one degree or another). The same result was seen on the central Pacific islands, where US Navy and Marine aircraft flew thousands of sorties against Japanese defenders. Interrogation of PRISONERS indicated that it was the Marines on the ground who did the most damage, followed by the big guns on the ships and, least feared of all, the aircraft attacks.

The Japanese were well aware of the problems with air attacks. Their pilots, most of whom had died by 1943, were much more intensively trained in bombing and, as a result, were far more accurate.

Ref: Edoin, *The Night Tokyo Burned*; Kerr, *Flames Over Tokyo*.

Bombs, Carrier Aircraft

At the beginning of the war, there was not much to choose from in aircraft ordnance. There were bombs available in different weights, from a few pounds to more than a ton. There were several different types in each weight class, distinguished by armor-piercing ability, percentage of weight devoted to explosives, and type of fuze. The armor-piercing bombs were often converted naval gun shells, with as little as 5% of their weight comprising explosives. These bombs used delayed action fuzes to penetrate deep inside a ship before exploding.

The United States introduced an armor-piercing bomb in May 1942 that was specifically designed for this purpose (the AP Mk 1). It weighed 1,600 pounds, of which 209 pounds were explosive. This bomb could penetrate five inches of deck armor. Because so few enemy ships with armored decks (battleships) were encountered, most carriers had perhaps 20 of these bombs on hand. As the war went on, most of the bombs dropped were non-armor-piercing (or "light case") types. These bombs (500 and 1,000 pounds being the most common) had 30–50% of their weight devoted to explosives. From 1943 on, US forces began to use more air-to-surface rockets. The 3.5-inch (55-pound) rocket was developed for use against SUB-MARINES. German U-boats would often be submerged by the time an approaching aircraft got close enough to drop a bomb, so the rocket solved that problem. A larger version, the 5-inch (90-pound) rocket was developed for use in the Pacific

against surface (and land) targets. Both types were in wide use by 1944.

Two other unconventional bombs deserve mention. The ATOMIC BOMB is well known, but only two were dropped. Another type of bomb that did more damage to Japanese cities, and killed more people, was the Mk 69 incendiary bomb. Weighing only six pounds, millions were dropped, destroying Japan's industrial power and most of the cities' housing factories.

See also AMMUNITION AVAILABILITY; BOMBING JAPAN; BOMBING, STRATEGIC.

Bong, Richard I. (1920–1945)

Top-scoring US ACE in the war, Bong, an army pilot, was officially credited with downing 40 Japanese aircraft, which he attained in a P-38. He served in the southwest Pacific and was personally awarded a MEDAL OF HONOR by Douglas MACARTHUR. Bong was killed test-flying a P-80 jet on 6 August 1945.

Bonin Islands

Located about 500 miles south of Tokyo, just north of the VOLCANO ISLANDS, these are more than 25 islands that total only about 40 square miles. Thinly populated, the Japanese extensively fortified and garrisoned them during World War II, but they were ignored by the United States except for occasional air raids and naval bombardments.

Borneo, Battles of, 1942 and 1945

The large island of Borneo, situated between the Philippines and the Dutch East Indies, was notable primarily for its oil fields, the principal source of oil in Asia. In 1940, the Borneo fields produced 65 million barrels of oil, most of it coming from the BALIKPAPAN area, which had been producing for over 40 years. The Dutch-controlled oil fields of Balikpapan and TARAKAN on the east coast, and

British-controlled Miri on the west coast, were key Japanese targets.

The Japanese invasion came over a seven-week period, from the middle of December 1941 (Miri, on the British west coast) to February 10, 1942, when they defeated the Dutch garrison on the southern end of the island. The major objective was Balikpapan, on the southeast coast.

There was less than a division of Allied troops on Borneo, spread out in battalion-sized garrisons holding the few coastal towns. The interior of the island was a tropical jungle populated by stone age tribes. Using their superior air power and naval superiority, the Japanese were able to use about a division of troops to pick off the Allied-held towns one by one. The Allies were aware of the importance of the Borneo oil to future Japanese plans and made strenuous efforts to impede the offensive.

When the Japanese invasion force approached Balikpapan in late January 1942, several naval battles resulted. On January 23, 1941, US destroyers and a Dutch submarine attacked Japanese shipping off Balikpapan. While the Japanese took losses, they kept on coming and on January 24, 1942 the Japanese began landings at Balikpapan.

In late February 1942, the Japanese 48th Division arrived at Balikpapan from the Philippines, providing more manpower to complete the destruction of remaining Allied forces on the island and support additional operations to the south in the NETHERLANDS EAST INDIES.

The Japanese garrisoned Borneo with infantry and aircraft, but this did not prevent American air raids beginning in August 1943. At that point, B-24 bombers were available and could make it to Balikpapan from Australia. Allied advances into western New Guinea provided air bases close enough for more regular air raids by 1944.

In late April 1945, US and Australian warships began four days of bombarding the Japanese-held oil facilities on Tarakan Island (off the northeast coast of Borneo). In early May 1945, Australian forces landed on Tarakan, off Borneo. In early July 1945, Australian troops invaded Balikpapan and retook the oil fields. Fighting in Borneo was still going on when the war ended.

Bose, Subhas Chandra (1897–1945)

A radical Indian nationalist, Bose urged a more violent approach in Indian resistance to the British than Ghandi. Although on the fringes of the independence movement, like most nationalist leaders he saw the outbreak of World War II as an opportunity for India. Imprisoned before the war, in 1940 he managed to escape, and made his way to Germany. The Germans feted him, and permitted him to raise a contingent of Indian troops from among PRISONERS OF WAR captured in North Africa. When Japan entered the war, the Germans shipped him east on a submarine, which rendezvoused with a Japanese submarine in the Indian Ocean. He played an active role in recruiting the INDIAN NATIONAL ARMY, and in October of 1943 was proclaimed the head of a "Provisional Government of Free India." With the collapse of Japanese fortunes in Burma in early 1945 he attempted to flee by air, only to die in a plane crash.

Bougainville, Campaign for

Largest of the Solomon Islands, Bougainville is the most northerly (except for the much smaller Buka) island in the SOLOMONS chain. It totals nearly 4,000 square miles, and in 1941 had some 45,000 inhabitants, mostly Melanesians who spoke about 18 different languages. A rugged place, with a convoluted coastline, Bougainville was hot, humid, and jungle-covered.

The Japanese moved into Bougainville in early 1942, against light resistance from the sparse Australian forces available.

The Japanese were determined to hold on to it as they saw that its loss would provide the Allies with a base for an assault on the major Japanese base in the area; RABAUL. By mid-1943, the Allies decided to bypass Rabaul and its 100,000 man garrison in favor of conquering Bougainville, which would provide airbases for advances to islands north of Rabaul, and would complete the encirclement of Rabaul.

Bougainville had long been subjected to air and warship attacks, ever since American troops established themselves on GUADALCANAL in August of 1942. Allied troops had landed on islands adjacent to Guadalcanal, and fought much smaller Japanese garrisons. In a pattern that would be repeated until the end of the war, these smaller Japanese forces just kept on fighting, waging what amounted to a GUERRILLA war against the larger Allied forces guarding the new airfields and bases.

The Japanese had garrisoned Bougainville with the Sixth Infantry Division. The bulk of the unit's troops were deployed on the southern part of the island, where there were five Japanese airfields. The battle for Bougainville began when a New Zealand brigade landed on Treasury Island, just south of Bougainville on October 27, 1943. This would provide a site for another airbase. A Marine parachute battalion then made an amphibious raid on Choiseul Island, just to the south of Bougainville, to make the Japanese think the next American invasion was coming there. Meanwhile, Allied aircraft hammered the Japanese airbases on Bougainville. On 1 November 1943, 14,000 troops of the US Third Marine Division landed at Cape Torokina, on EMPRESS AUGUSTA BAY, in the middle of Bougainville's southwestern coast. This was far from any Japanese ground troops and in an area suitable for the rapid construction of airfields. The next night, the Japanese sent a task force of four cruisers and eight destroyers to attack Allied shipping in Empress Augusta Bay. Allied ships (four cruisers, eight destroyers) met the Japanese and defeated the enemy, sinking a cruiser and destroyer in the process.

Determined to stop the Bougainville invasion, the Japanese ordered eight cruisers and four destroyers south from the main fleet base at TRUK. American codebreakers intercepted this order. As there were no additional surface ships in the area to defend the Empress Augusta Bay beachhead against such a large force, American carriers (two

CVs and one CVL) were called in. It was risky to bring carriers in so close to Rabaul, as that base now held some 150 Japanese aircraft. But luck was with the Americans. Over several days and several raids, three Japanese cruisers were damaged, as were three destroyers. One destroyer was also sunk. Moreover, the Japanese lost 55 aircraft, four times as many as the Americans lost. The carriers escaped damage and the Japanese withdrew their cruisers, along with the threat to Empress Augusta Bay.

Meanwhile, on Bougainville, the US 37th Infantry Division joined the Marines. The Japanese tried to reinforce their garrison on Bougainville, but Allied control of the air meant that the Japanese could move at sea only by night, usually along the coast and slowly at that.

Three airfields were built in the Empress Augusta Bay area, and the 62,000 US troops there prepared for any Japanese counterattack. The Third Marine Division had been replaced by the army's Americal Division. The Japanese attack came in early March 1944, when 15,000 troops, backed by artillery, hit the American lines. The attacks failed, and the Japanese lost several thousand troops.

The Japanese maintained a presence on Bougainville until the end of the war. But with Rabaul isolated by the end of 1944, there were few supplies available for Japanese troops fighting on in the SOLOMONS. American garrisons were reduced, and a low-level guerrilla war went on until the war ended.

See also CARTWHEEL.

Ref: Gailey, *Bougainville*; *History of United States Marine Corps Operations*, vol. 1 (Hugh and Ludwig, *Pearl Harbor to Guadalcanal*).

Boyington, Gregory "Pappy" (1912–)

Marine Corps ace Boyington was one of several "retired" pilots who served in the AVG, shooting down six Japanese aircraft before he returned to the Corps and shot down 28 more while commanding Marine Fighter Squadron 214, the "Black Sheep," in the GUADALCANAL and SOLOMONS campaigns, for which he was awarded a MEDAL OF HONOR. Shot down in late 1943, he spent 20 months as a prisoner of war.

Ref: Boyington, *Baa, Baa, Black Sheep*.

Bremerton, Washington, United States

With nearby Seattle, a world-class port, having important ship repair facilities and a major naval shipyard. Because of the curvature of the Earth, Bremerton was the closest continental US base to Japan.

Brererton, Lewis Hyde (1890–1967)

A US Army general commanding air force and airborne units in many theaters. Sent to the Philippines in 1941 to be General MACARTHUR's air force commander, he did badly at first, and a Japanese attack destroyed many of his aircraft on the ground; he did better later, with limited resources. Before the Philippines fell he was pulled out and sent to India to organize the new US Middle East Air Force. This he did with great success. In October 1942 he was transferred to command the newly formed Ninth Air Force, for service in the upcoming Tunisian campaign in North Africa. He spent the rest of the war commanding air and airborne forces in the European theater.

Brisbane, Australia

One of the larger cities in Australia, Brisbane, on the central portion of the east coast, had a good harbor, with good facilities, some industrial capacity, and an excellent airbase. It was a major entry port for US forces and munitions during the war.

See also AUSTRALIAN-AMERICAN RELATIONS.

British Army

By the outbreak of the Pacific War the British Army had already been at war for more than two years, and had experienced some particularly trying times in France, North Africa, and Greece. Despite

some bright moments (Dunkirk, O'Connor's Offensive in North Africa), things had not gone well for the British Army. There were a number of things wrong, not least of which was leadership, which tended to be poor at the middle levels. Doctrine was somewhat inflexible, training sometimes inadequate, equipment not always the best, and manpower, which was generally of good quality, in increasingly short supply. The generation that was decimated in Flanders fields during World War I had not left enough sons to fill the ranks for World War II.

Some of the leadership and materiel problems were resolved with time, as doctrine and training were improved, better leaders came to the fore, and superior equipment was procured. Nothing could resolve the manpower crisis, however, and although Britain had actually mobilized something like 40 divisions by late 1942, as time went on some divisions had to be broken up in order to keep the balance at full strength.

With her resources stretched quite thinly, Britain could spare few units for the Pacific War. Nearly all British troops in the Pacific theater served in Burma, alongside Indian and East African divisions, which had substantial British cadres. The Burma Campaign, conducted largely to keep the Japanese out of India, was a hard-fought infantry war similar to the British operations in North Africa (albeit on a smaller scale). Burma was a sideshow, but one in which the British Army eventually prevailed.

In order to secure the enthusiastic (or at least willing) help of the Indians, Britain promised, soon after Japan entered the war, that India would have its independence after the war was won. Although disliked as a colonial power, the British had behaved well enough in India to be taken at their word. Thus most of the fighting in Burma was undertaken willingly and competently by Indian troops (and by some from other colonies in Africa). Operations in India and Burma were complicated by the fact that during the early stages of the Pacific War, British naval power in the Indian Ocean was shattered by the Japanese. Although MIDWAY, and growing American naval power, kept the Japanese from returning to the Indian Ocean in force, the British had their hands full dealing with enemy SUBMARINES (German and Italian as well as Japanese) that operated out of Dutch East Indies bases. Eventually, the same aircraft-based tactics that worked so well against submarines in the Atlantic provided the same winning edge in the Indian Ocean. Britain was able to speed the Burma offensive along with amphibious operations along the exposed Burmese coast from 1944 on.

The biggest ally, and most formidable opponent, the British faced in Burma was not the Japanese, but the climate (tropical) and geography (mountainous and soggy). The Japanese faced these same obstacles and were never able to overcome both the British and the natural obstacles. The Burmese war went on for over three years. Neither side was ever close to any kind of dramatic breakthrough, but neither could afford to stop fighting. The British had to keep the Japanese out of India, and the Japanese had to keep the British from getting too close to their vital oil supplies in the Dutch East Indies.

Peak wartime strength of the British Army was 4.6 million troops, of whom about 10% saw service in the Pacific and related areas. Additional British troops served in the Indian Army.

British Army, Divisions and Other Notable Formations in the Pacific War

Second Infantry Division. A prewar regular division stationed in Britain, the division served in France and Belgium, September 1939–May 1940, being one of the units rescued at Dunkirk. On garrison duty in Britain thereafter, it was shipped to India in April–June 1942. Heavily engaged during the battles for Kohima in 1944 and in the liberation of central Burma in early 1945, in March of that year the division was pulled back to India for reorganization and retraining in anticipation of commitment to the proposed campaigns in Thailand and MALAYA.

11th (East African) Division. Formed in February of 1943, the division was composed of troops recruited in East Africa under British officers, with British artillery. It served in Burma June 1944–April 1945. Among its personnel was a Sgt. Idi Amin, who acquired a reputation for brutality toward Japanese PRISONERS.

18th Infantry Division. A Second Line Territorial Division (the equivalent of a Reserve NATIONAL GUARD division, if such existed) from East Anglia, the division was activated in September 1939. Although trained and equipped for service in North Africa, rising tensions in Asia caused the division to be shipped to the Far East in October 1941. The division arrived in India in late December, after the Japanese began the Pacific War. Although some senior officers urged that the division be retained for the defense of India, the British Far Eastern Command sent it on to SINGAPORE, where it arrived on 29 January 1942, even as the Japanese were closing in on the city. It surrendered to the Japanese on 15 February, a tremendous waste of scarce manpower and equipment.

36th Infantry Division. Originally organized in the Indian Army as the 36th Indian Division, by mid–1944 the division was almost completely composed of British personnel (there was only one Indian battalion, the First of the Seventh Rajput Regiment) and was transferred to the British Army. In British service the division fought in the liberation of MANDALAY and RANGOON, February–May 1945, and was resting and reorganizing for the proposed offensive into Thailand and Malaya when the war ended.

70th Division. Formed in Egypt as the Sixth Division in November 1939, and redesignated the 70th in October 1941. The division took part in operations in the Western Desert and Syria (including the defense of Tobruk in April–December 1941), before being shipped to India in September 1943. In India the division was broken up to help form the CHINDITS.

81st (West African) Division. Formed in March 1943 in Nigeria, it was composed of African personnel under British officers, with additional British troops in the artillery and specialized elements. The division served in India, August–December 1943, and then in Burma until March 1945, taking part in the British landings in the Arakan.

82nd (West African) Division. Formed in Nigeria in August 1943, it comprised mostly African enlisted personnel serving under British officers and specialists. The division served in India August–November 1944, and then in Burma until the end of the war, participating in the Arakan Campaign.

Burma Division. The prewar garrison of Burma, the division comprised two brigades, one of one British, Burmese, and Indian battalion, and one of Indians and British. It was incomplete, poorly equipped, and poorly trained, and actually existed primarily as an administrative unit, rather than an operational one, until the Japanese invasion. Hastily concentrated when the Japanese invaded, it was destroyed in the general collapse of British fortunes in April of 1942.

First Malaya Infantry Brigade. A prewar active army unit on permanent garrison duty in Fortress Singapore, at the outbreak of the Pacific War the First Malaya Brigade comprised a battalion each of regular British, Indian, and Malay troops. It surrendered to the Japanese on 14 February 1942.

Second Malaya Infantry Brigade. Formed in Malaya in September 1940 from British and Indian troops, the Second Malaya Brigade formed part of the garrison of Fortress Singapore, and was captured by the Japanese on 14 February 1942.

Seventh Armoured Brigade. Organized in Egypt in 1939, the brigade served in the famous Seventh Armoured Division ("The Desert Rats") during the North African Campaign, from December 1940 through November 1941. It was then transferred to the Far East, landing in Burma in February 1942. With the 17th Indian Division it formed the backbone of British resistance in Burma, and was even briefly attached to the Chinese 38th Division, before being withdrawn to India in May 1942. After a period of garrison duty in India, the brigade was transferred to occupation duties in the Middle East. In May 1944 it was committed to action with the British Eighth Army in Italy. The Seventh Armoured Brigade ended the war in Austria.

Force 136. Organized in India by honorary MG Colin MacKenzie, Force 136 conducted special warfare operations in Burma and Southeast Asia from 1943 to the end of the war. Among its more successful operations were its clandestine contacts with the Siamese government, technically allied with the Japanese, and the Japanese-puppet Burmese government.

British Navy; British Far Eastern Fleet; British Pacific Fleet

See ROYAL NAVY.

Brooke, Alan (1883–1963)

Brooke, later known as Field Marshal Viscount Alanbrooke, the senior British military officer for most of World War II, entered the British Army as an artilleryman, in which capacity he served with great distinction for much of World War I.

Between the wars he held a variety of posts, and in 1940 commanded the British II Corps with great skill during the retreat to Dunkirk. He was appointed chief of the Imperial General Staff in 1941 and is generally credited with the markedly improved British performance that characterized the rest of the war.

Brooklyn Class, US Light Cruisers

The Brooklyn class was designed to counter the Japanese MOGAMI CLASS, which originally had 15 6-inch guns (later converted to 10 8–inchers). The ships were only partially satisfactory. They were relatively expensive, at about $18.5 million apiece.

Experience gained from them proved valuable in the design of subsequent American cruisers, both heavy and light.

Brooklyn, CL-40 (1935–1936–1938), spent most of the war in European waters and was sold to Chile in 1951.

Philadelphia, CL-41 (1935–1936–1938), spent most of the war in European waters. Sold to Brazil in 1951.

Savannah, CL-42 (1934–1937–1938), spent most of the war in European waters, having the dubious distinction of being one of the first ships hit by a GUIDED MISSILE, which almost sank her off Salerno. Scrapped in 1960.

Nashville, CL-43 (1935–1937–1938), served throughout the Pacific, from the Aleutians to the southern Philippines, surviving a KAMIKAZE in the process. Sold to Chile in 1951.

Phoenix, CL-44 (1935–1938–1939), survived PEARL HARBOR without a scratch, and 20 other fights nearly as well, losing only one man to enemy action in the course of the war, while accumulating nine battle stars. In 1951 she was sold to Argentina. Renamed *General Belgrano*, on May 2, 1982 during the Argentine-British War she took two TORPEDOES from the nuclear submarine HMS *Conqueror* and sank in about 45 minutes with heavy loss of life. She thus achieved the dubious distinction of being the first ship ever sunk by a nuclear submarine. World War II–era torpedoes were used.

Boise, CL-47 (1935–1936–1939), began the war as part of the Asiatic Fleet, went on to fight at the Battle of CAPE ESPERANCE, where she took some damage. She supported the landings in Sicily and at Salerno, and then returned to the Pacific in time for the liberation of the Philippines. Sold to Argentina in 1951.

Honolulu, CL-48 (1935–1937–1938), fought in the Solomons Campaign (TASSAFARONGA and KOLOMBANGARA), and then went on to escort carrier task forces. Scrapped in 1960.

St. Louis, CL-49 (1936–1938–1939), took part in numerous actions in the Solomons and in support of landings throughout the southwest Pacific. Sold to Brazil 1951.

Helena, CL-50 (1936–1938–1939), was heavily damaged at Pearl Harbor and took nearly six months to return to service. She fought in the battles of Cape Esperance and GUADALCANAL, both times being the first US ship to open fire. She was sunk by three torpedoes at the Battle of KULA GULF, July 6, 1943. Among the survivors was the husband of the eventual typing teacher of one of the authors.

St. Louis and *Helena* had eight 5"/38 dual-purpose secondary guns in double mounts, rather than eight 5"/25s in single mounts, and the two are sometimes lumped together as the St. Louis class.

Brown, Wilson, Jr. (1882–1959)

One of the oldest American officers to serve afloat during the Pacific War, Wilson Brown Jr. graduated from the US Naval Academy in 1902. During World War I he was on the staff of Admiral William S. Sims, commander of US naval forces in Europe, and later commanded a destroyer. After the war he held various staff and line positions and attended several navy schools. For a time during the 1930s he was naval aide to President ROOSEVELT, who got him assigned as superintendent of the Naval Academy. On the eve of the Pacific War he was commander of the LEXINGTON task force. In this capacity he took part in the abortive WAKE ISLAND relief operation (which, but for the faint-heartedness of some higher-ups, might have resulted in the first American victory at sea as early as mid-December 1941), in the raids on the MANDATES, and in the daring Lae-Salamaua raid over New Guinea's OWEN STANLEY MOUNTAINS in March of 1942. On 3 April 1942 Brown, already overage by navy regulations, yielded command of his task force to RAdm Aubrey FITCH and saw no further combat service in the war. Although a "black shoe" officer (surface warfare), Brown performed well in command of a carrier task force. This was because, aside from being a capable strategist in his own right, he was aware of his lack of flying credentials, and so he listened to, and usually accepted, the advice of several of his air-qualified subordinates, such as Captain Frederick SHERMAN of the carrier *Lexington*. How he might have fared in a carrier battle remains an unanswerable question of the Pacific War, but he demonstrated that able admirals of the Old School could apply their talents with new technology.

Brunei, Borneo

On the northwestern coast of BORNEO, about 700 miles northeast of SINGAPORE, Brunei was a modest oil port with a fair harbor but few facilities. Its primary function was to pump oil into tankers and to bring in drilling equipment.

Buckley Class, US Destroyer Escorts

The Buckleys, which totaled 102 ships, were the second generation of US destroyer escorts. Built 1942–44 on the basis of experience with the earlier EVARTS CLASS, they saw considerable service. They proved quite satisfactory, most being retained in reserve by the navy into the 1960s. They were sometimes referred to as the "TE" Class, because of their electric turbine engines. They were good ships, and lucky: Only four became war losses.

Buckner, Simon B. (1886–1945)

The son of Confederate LG Simon B. Buckner Sr., Buckner attended VMI and West Point, being commissioned in the infantry in 1908. Before World War I he saw service in the Philippines and on the Mexican Border. When the United States entered World War I he became a flight instructor, in which assignment he spent most of the war. He afterward held a variety of posts, while rising steadily through the ranks. In July of 1940 he was named commander of all army personnel in ALASKA, where he thoroughly reorganized the defenses. Buckner remained in Alaska, while rising to lieutenant general, until

March of 1944 (in the meantime having recovered KISKA and ATTU from the Japanese). Ordered to HAWAII, Buckner took command of the Tenth Army (XXIV Corps and III Marine Amphibious Corps), which he took to OKINAWA the following spring. Buckner's operations on Okinawa were not brilliant, and he was severely criticized by his Marine subordinates for not making use of their amphibious capabilities. The general was killed in action by Japanese artillery on 18 June 1945, three days before the island was declared secure. He was the second-highest ranking American army officer killed in action during the war.

Buna, Papua New Guinea

A small trading post on the northeastern coast of New Guinea, with a very limited port. It was of value to the Japanese in order to supply their advance from nearby GONA over the KOKODA TRAIL and was the scene of heavy fighting in 1942 and 1943.

Buna-Gona Campaign

One of the most horrendous campaigns of the Pacific War, this one was fought virtually from the beaches on the south shore of New Guinea, up through the tropical mountains running down the spine of the island, and down to the beaches and swamps of the north shore. The Japanese had first landed in New Guinea in early March 1942, on the northeast coast at Salamaua and LAE. In one of the earliest American counterattacks, two US carriers south of New Guinea launched an air attack, over the OWEN STANLEY MOUNTAINS, at the Japanese transports still unloading troops and material. Three ships were sunk and four damaged. This slowed, but did not stop, Japanese construction of airfields at these two sites. Some 3,000 construction troops, protected by a thousand SNLF troops, worked on the airfields. Japanese airfield construction proceeded more slowly than American efforts. The Japanese airfields on New Guinea were planned to support further cross-country advances to the south coast of New Guinea. In late July the Japanese landed a battalion-sized unit (the "Yokoyama Force") at the adjacent villages of BUNA and GONA. This was the northern terminus of the KOKODA TRAIL, a narrow track—often less than a yard wide—that went over the Owen Stanley Mountains to a point 30 miles north of PORT MORESBY, the main and indeed the only Allied base on New Guinea. The Japanese promptly began advancing along the Kokoda Trail. The Australians had a battalion-sized force in the Port Moresby area, and part of it was sent up the Kokoda Trail, to guard the approach from the north. The Australian forces fell back through and over the Owen Stanleys as the Japanese approached. The Japanese themselves then halted and waited for reinforcements. In August, things heated up. The Japanese brought forward a brigade, and the Australians moved two brigades into Port Moresby and one to MILNE BAY, on the far eastern tip of New Guinea, where an airfield was being built. In late August, 1,500 Japanese troops landed at Milne Bay, but after a week of fighting, were forced to withdraw.

At the same time, the battle along the Kokoda Trail raged. Two Japanese brigades fought their way over the Owen Stanleys and to within 25 miles of Port Moresby by the middle of September. There, the Japanese supplies ran out and the Australians began to push them back across the mountains. An American infantry regiment was sent to reinforce the Australians, advancing up another trail over the Owen Stanleys. Allied aircraft kept the Japanese troops out of supplies, while they used transport aircraft to fly supplies and reinforcements over the Owen Stanleys to sustain their own troops. Hasty airfields were prepared in several places for this. By October, two regiments of the US 32nd Infantry Division had been brought to the north coast of New Guinea, by aircraft or boat, from the Australian base at Milne Bay. The Japanese resisted this sea movement along the north coast of New Guinea, but were able to sink only some supply barges. All the troops got through, al-

though without much ammunition or heavy weapons.

By November, the Japanese troops were starving, outnumbered, and falling back to their coastal bases. There, the remaining 5,000 Japanese troops fortified themselves in three separate areas along a 10-mile stretch of coast (from west to east): Gona, Sanananda, and Buna. The Australian Seventh and US 32nd Infantry Divisions, both at about half-strength, were ordered to clear the Japanese out of their coastal refuges. This turned out to be even more difficult than fighting across the Owen Stanleys.

The Allied troops lacked heavy weapons and the Americans in particular were short of artillery. None of the troops were trained to conduct offensive operations in jungles. Allied pilots were not experienced in providing close air support. There were so many cases of Allied aircraft bombing or strafing friendly troops that after a while the troops tended to avoid calling for air support. Lacking TANKS or much artillery, the attacks were very costly. Over half the Allied CASUALTIES in this campaign were taken during the assaults on these Japanese coastal redoubts. The Japanese were well dug in and much of the surrounding terrain was swampy. Further complicating matters was the fact that none of the Allied troops were acclimated to the environment. This was a particular problem for the Americans, who were mostly National Guardsmen from Michigan and Wisconsin, on average older than the norm for infantry combat. Casualties from disease and heat were very high.

Gona fell to Australian troops on December 9, 1942, the first probing attack having been made on November 7. It took a lot of hard fighting to clear the Japanese out of the smallest of their three enclaves. The Australians also had the benefit of delayed action fuzes for their artillery. These allowed shells to penetrate the dirt and logs of the Japanese fortifications before exploding, enabling the Australians to work their way into the Japanese fortress methodically. Even so, they suffered some 500 dead taking Gona.

Buna didn't fall until January 2, 1943, and not before some ugly events on and off the battlefield. Unlike the Australians, the American troops didn't have much artillery or a lot of ammunition. Much of their ammo had gone down with barges shot up by Japanese aircraft. The American infantry were forced to go after the Japanese fortifications with rifles and grenades, and many of their grenades proved defective. General MACARTHUR, far to the rear, saw the Australians take Gona and his Americans fail to take Buna. He sent a team of officers to the front to find out what was wrong. The inspection team failed to note the woeful supply situation of the American troops and simply reported that the division commander and his officers were not providing proper leadership. This was not the case; the division commander, Ed Harding, had requested tanks and artillery as well as more ammunition, including grenades that worked. These supplies were on the way, but MacArthur would not wait. He sent a new division commander, Bob EICHELBERGER ("Take Buna or don't come back alive,"), who launched a major attack on 5 December. Again, the Americans failed. Eichelberger then noted that American airpower had effectively cut off the Japanese Buna garrison from resupply or reinforcement, so he decided to wait for the tanks and artillery. On December 18, the tanks arrived, as well as an Australian brigade. It took two weeks of fighting, but Buna fell on January 2, 1943. Allied troops suffered 2,800 casualties.

Meanwhile, the Australians had been hammering away at Sanananda, the most heavily fortified of the Japanese positions, for two months. With Gona and Buna taken, both the Australian Seventh and American 32nd Divisions combined to reduce Sanananda, which fell on 13 January, at the cost of another 3,500 Allied casualties.

The six months of hard campaigning over the Owen Stanley Mountains had cost the Allies 8,500 casualties, including 3,000 dead. Japanese losses had been much higher, with some 15,000 dying. But then, the Japanese fought to the death and, more importantly, were never able to get their supply system functioning properly. The Japanese lost more troops to starvation and disease than to Allied weapons, a situation that was repeating itself at the same time on GUADALCANAL. Not only were the Allied supply efforts superior, but the speed with which Allied troops built airfields enabled Allied aircraft to frustrate Japanese attempts to reinforce their troops in New Guinea. As was the case at Guadalcanal, Allied aircraft controlled the sea approaches to New Guinea and few Japanese ships got through. Cut off from supply and reinforcement, it was only a matter of time before the Japanese forces were wiped out.

Finally, the Japanese headquarters was forced to deal with two Allied advances simultaneously. Japanese forces in New Guinea and Guadalcanal were calling for help at the same time, and there were not enough resources to go around. Allied superiority in material resources was beginning to assert itself.

One historian said of the struggle for Buna-Gona that it may not have been tougher than any other in the war, "but it was certainly the nastiest."

Burakumi

The Japanese underclass, a large (several million strong) socially disadvantaged group of outcasts relegated to the most menial occupations for centuries. Although recruited into the Imperial Army, the Burakumi were almost always used as service troops, and many were in the Transportation Corps.

See also BLACK AMERICANS IN THE PACIFIC WAR.

Burke, Arleigh (1901–1996)

Arleigh Burke graduated from Annapolis in 1923 and held a variety of posts in the peacetime navy. In 1940 he was assigned to the Bureau of Ordnance, where he languished until May of 1943, when, promoted to captain, he was sent to the Pacific to command a destroyer squadron. Burke greatly distinguished himself during the fighting for the northern SOLOMONS, earning the nickname "Thirty-one Knot Burke" after having made an unusual maneuver during an action; a superior asked him what he was doing and he replied, "Thirty-one knots." In 1945 he became an acting commodore and, although a non-flyer, chief of staff to Marc MITSCHER, commander of Task Force 38/58. He ended the war as chief of staff to the commander, Atlantic Fleet. Burke's postwar career was equally impressive, concluding with an unprecedented six-year term as chief of naval operations (1955–61), for which post he was jumped over nearly 100 more senior officers. He retired to an active career in business.

Burma

A large country, with a very diverse population, Burma had been under British control for nearly a century. Until 1937 it was administered as part of India. In 1937 it was set up as a semi-autonomous federation, with some degree of internal self-government and its own prime minister. The Japanese occupied the country in early 1942 and quickly established a puppet regime, with considerable support from some local elements. Burma was formally granted "independence" by the Japanese on 1 August 1943. The leaders of this independent government were more interested in Burmese objectives than Japanese ones, and relations between the two were increasingly tense. By 1945 representatives of the Burmese puppet government were in contact with the British, and for the most part cooperated in the British return to power. There was one segment of the Burmese population that did resist the Japanese actively and gave substantial armed assistance to the British. These were the Kachins, and other tribal peoples, in northern Burma. The "tribes" had long experienced bad relations with the mainstream Burmese, and found the Japanese to be even worse. The British, having extensive experience dealing with tribal cultures, came off looking much better and thus were able to enlist irregular troops from among the tribes. Actual independence within the British

Commonwealth was secured in 1947. Soon after achieving independence the country fell under the control of one ethnic faction, the "majority" Burmese group, which imposed an authoritarian regime that still continues; the country has been continuously plagued by ethnic and regional insurgencies.

See also AUNG SAN; GUERRILLA WARS; UNITED STATES ARMY, OTHER NOTABLE UNITS.

Burma Campaign, 1942–1945

Japanese forces invaded Burma, a British colony, in January 1942. The Japanese came across the Siam/Burma border with two reinforced infantry divisions and air superiority. The British had two understrength divisions, of mixed British, Indian, and Burmese troops. By March 1942, the surviving British forces were retreating into the jungles of northern Burma and toward the border with India, along with a handful of Americans who had managed to get into action in the theater under Joseph STILWELL.

Burma was crucial for the Allied war effort because the BURMA ROAD, from Burma into China, was the only practical way of supplying Chinese forces. The Japanese had earlier seized the coastal areas of China and now the Japanese fleet controlled the western Pacific. But the Indian Ocean remained under Allied control and supplies could be sent into China over the Burma Road. Unfortunately, by April the Japanese had advanced into central Burma and cut the Burma Road. This route over the mountains would not be reopened until the Japanese were driven out of northern Burma in late 1944.

The Chinese saw the danger to their supply route and sent several of their best divisions south to stop the Japanese. But the Japanese also received two more divisions in April and proceeded to clear Chinese and British forces from Burma by May. The British retreated west into India, the Chinese north into China. The Allies still held about a fifth of Burma as the monsoon rains began in May, but it was a remote, mountainous, and jungle covered part of the country, largely in the northernmost region. The Japanese controlled all that was worthwhile. Despite 42,000 British and 95,000 Chinese troops, the Japanese Army of some 50,000 men had triumphed. The Japanese lost some 7,000 soldiers, the Allies nearly 100,000. The Japanese were confident that after some rest and rebuilding, they could advance into India.

The Japanese spent the rest of 1942 nailing down their control of Burma, taking over the civil government and rebuilding their supply system so they could continue their offensive into India. The British were rushing in troops and supplies to their positions in the jungles of eastern India. To assure Indian cooperation in the face of Japanese calls for rebellion and Indian independence, the British promised Indians sovereignty after the war. This kept things quiet in the rear, but did nothing to stay the upcoming Japanese attacks.

During 1943, the British had additional resources, and used some of their superior strength to launch a counterattack down the Burmese coast, in the Arakan. Although Japanese forces there were small, the British advance was so cautious and slow that the Japanese were able to move in reinforcements and stop the British cold. The Japanese then counterattacked and sent the British back to their original lines. This hurt British troop morale, as the Japanese were perceived as masters of jungle warfare.

China was now cut off, except via supply by air. For the rest of the war, hundreds of bombers and transport aircraft in eastern India lifted men and supplies "over the HUMP" (the 20,000-foot-high peaks of the eastern Himalayan "foothills"). This wasn't much, but it kept the Chinese in the fight and tied down Japanese forces in China.

To tie down the Japanese further and gain time to prepare for a return to the offensive, the British began to employ special warfare forces, notably Orde WINGATE's CHINDITS. Chindit operations were effective in annoying the Japanese but at enormous cost.

During 1944, both sides attacked. Japan massed three divisions and 100,000 troops in northwest Burma for an attack into India, which initially ran into a British attack. Farther to the north, five American-trained and -equipped Chinese divisions advanced south, supported by MERRILL'S MARAUDERS, an American special warfare unit, to keep the Japanese from advancing north into China and, if possible, to begin retaking parts of the Burma Road. These two campaigns ended in Japanese defeats, but not before some truly desperate fighting. The Japanese offensive into India was conducted with slender logistic resources, on the assumption that the troops would be able to sustain their advance through the capture of British supplies. The Japanese commander ordered his troops forward with the admonition that few could be expected to survive. This attitude was meant to encourage the troops. It did. The Japanese fought their way into Assam, eastern India, and were halted only in desperate fighting by the largely Indian garrisons at Imphal and Kohima. Although surrounded, the Commonwealth troops held on and were supplied from the air. This stubborn resistance left an insufficient number of Japanese troops to continue the offensive. By the summer of 1944, the poorly supplied Japanese offensive collapsed and the broken Japanese force straggled back into Burma. The British pursued and advanced into central Burma. The Japanese had gambled everything on their 1944 offensive. When it failed, and the invasion force was destroyed in the process, there was little left with which to defend Burma.

In the midst of all this, throughout 1943 and 1944, the special Allied "raider" units like the British Chindits and American Merrill's Marauders moved through the Japanese rear area, attacking support units, tearing up rail lines, and blowing up bridges. While heralded in the Western media as a heroic effort against the Japanese, these operations cost more than they were worth. But these operations did demonstrate that it was possible to supply combat units comprising several thousand troops by air. The Allies had enormous aircraft resources compared to the Japanese and thus were able to do things that otherwise made no economic sense.

As 1945 opened, British forces advanced through central Burma, along the north Burmese coast, and by sea with amphibious forces aimed at southern Burma. The Chinese continued their advance from the north, opening the Burma Road once more by February. By May, RANGOON and the major population areas of Burma were retaken. From then, until the end of the war, Allied troops pursued Japanese forces through the bush and back toward Thailand.

Ref: Masters, *The Road Past Mandalay*.

Burma National Army

Prior to World War II, the Burmese had become increasingly restless under British rule, a restlessness fostered by Japanese agents.

The most notable Japanese operative in Burma was COL Keiji Suzuki. Suzuki undertook several missions to Burma in the 1930s and early 1940s, disguised as a journalist. He developed extensive contacts with nationalist elements, whom he supplied with money. With his help some young nationalists, including AUNG SAN, received military training in FORMOSA. Just prior to the Japanese invasion of Burma he helped organize the Patriot Burmese Forces, which were shortly renamed the Burma Independence Army (BIA), in INDOCHINA; these forces initially numbered about 2,500 men, mostly exiles associated with the Burma Independence Movement (BIM), a small anti-British nationalist group that had been formed in the late 1930s.

Using the *nom de guerre* Bo Mogyoe ("General Lightning"), Suzuki led the Burma Independence Army into combat in Burma on December 10, 1941, with Aung San as his chief of staff. Support for the Japanese invaders proved widespread, and by summer of 1942 the BIA numbered 20,000 men, of whom about 12,000 were reasonably well-armed and trained, and proved rather effective in combat against British and Chinese troops. However, Japanese imperialist objectives and Burmese nationalist objectives differed and the occupiers and the BIM soon had a falling out. Since Suzuki was one of the few Japanese officers who sincerely believed in the Asian brotherhood line being preached by Japanese propaganda, he was promoted to major general and shipped out of the country. The BIM was disbanded by force, and a more amenable set of puppets put into power. Meanwhile, the Japanese recruited the Burma Defense Force, under General Aung San. This became the Burma National Army in August 1943, when the Japanese proclaimed the "independence" of Burma under Dr. Ba Maw (1893–1977), who had formerly been the prime minister of the British colonial government. The BNA was recruited mostly from dissident elements in the highly fragmented Burmese population (there is no "majority" in Burma, where ethnic and political rivalries are fierce). Although the Burma National Army fielded several notional divisions, it was never committed to serious combat. By mid-1944 the Burmese leaders and the BNA were in clandestine contact with the British, and in early 1945 began a GUERRILLA resistance against the Japanese.

Burma Road

With the outbreak of the CHINA INCIDENT in 1937, China quickly found itself unable to import materials from abroad, as the Japanese occupied much of the country's coast, and imposed a fairly tight blockade on those ports remaining in Chinese hands. In an effort to get around the Japanese blockade the Chinese undertook to build a road from southern China into northern Burma, where it would tie into existing roads and railroads that connected with MANDALAY and other ports. Although planned since the 1920s, little work had been done until the Japanese invasion. The road ran 700 miles through jungles and mountains, from Kunming in Yunan to Lashio, and was completed in the remarkably short time of about 18 months. Most of the work was done with simple hand tools, wielded by an estimated 150,000–200,000 coolies, many of whom died from disease and injury.

Traffic began moving along the "Burma Road" in 1938. Although of limited capacity—in most

A US Army truck convoy, somewhere on the Burma Road in 1945.

places only one lane wide—and expensive to operate, the road proved a vital conduit of supplies to the Chinese. In early 1940 the British government closed down the road in an effort to placate the Japanese, but this decision was reversed not long after Winston CHURCHILL came to power.

In April of 1942, Chinese forces in Burma desperately tried to defend Lashio from the Japanese, but its fall on April 29 cut the Burma Road. To prevent the Japanese from using it to continue their advance northward into China the Chinese forces then sabotaged sections of the road. Thereafter the principal objective of American and Chinese military forces in Burma was the reopening of the Burma Road. In pursuit of this objective, those portions of the road still in Chinese hands were improved, again mostly using hand tools, while US Army Engineers—about a third of whom were BLACK AMERICANS—used modern construction equipment to build a new road from Allied-

held territory on the Indian frontier across the grain of the mountain and river lines in northwestern Burma, a virtually untouched wilderness. The road ran about 230 miles from Ledo in Assam, to Myitkyina, which was liberated by Allied forces in mid-1944. This permitted the reopening of the Burma Road after the Allies retook Lashio in the spring of 1945. The Ledo Road was later renamed the STILWELL Road.

There was also a pipeline, from CALCUTTA to Kunming, running alongside the Ledo Road, to connect with the Burma Road. Built in 1944–45, it was nearly 1,900 miles long and was later extended to Chungking.

Bush, George (1924–)

After enlisting in the navy on his 18th birthday (June 12, 1942) and undergoing basic training, Bush entered flight school (one of his classmates was baseball great Ted Williams), graduating as an ensign in June 1943, the youngest pilot in the navy at the time. Assigned to Torpedo Squadron 51, aboard the light carrier *San Jacinto* in early 1944, he flew 58 combat missions in TBF AVENGER torpedo bombers. In September 1944 his airplane was badly shot up over Chichi Jima, but he did not ditch until after completing his bomb run. Although his tail-gunner was killed, Bush and his belly-gunner managed to bail out successfully, but the belly-gunner was killed in the fall. Despite being injured during his bail out and by the sting of a jellyfish (Portuguese Man-'o-War), Bush was able to inflate his life raft. He was rescued by the submarine *Finback* (SS-230) about three hours later. Rotated stateside in December 1944, Bush was discharged as a naval lieutenant shortly after the surrender of Japan. During his military career he had logged more than 1,200 hours in the air, and, in addition to having been shot down once, survived two crashes. Later, he entered politics, served as director of the CIA, then vice president under REAGAN (1981–89), and was himself elected president, serving 1989–93.

Bwagaoia, Louisiades

The principal, indeed only, town in the LOUISIADE ARCHIPELAGO, just off the northeastern tip of New Guinea, Bwagaoia had a fair harbor but little else to recommend it.

Byrd, Richard E. (1887–1957)

Already famous as an arctic explorer, Byrd was a rear admiral when the Pacific War began. He was promptly assigned the task of conducting a survey of islands in the south and southeastern Pacific for prospective sites for air and naval bases, and served in various other technical posts throughout the war. After the war he resumed his arctic adventures.

Bywater, Hector (1884–1940)

A British journalist whose novel *The Great Pacific War* (1925) allegedly predicted the principal events of the Second World War in the Pacific, from an attack on PEARL HARBOR in conjunction with simultaneous assaults on other places across the Pacific, to a US counteroffensive through the central Pacific.

Actually, Bywater's novel was not as prescient as is often claimed, nor was it adopted as a textbook by the Japanese Naval War College.

The broad outline of the probable course of a naval war between the United States and Japan had been discussed in the professional literature for many years, and was readily accessible to Bywater, who specialized in military reporting. In fact, Bywater had actually written a "serious" book on the subject, *Sea Power in the Pacific: A Study of the American-Japanese Naval Problem* (London: 1921). The novel was not very prescient. It did include a "surprise attack" on Pearl Harbor, but this was by combined air and sea forces. Bywater almost entirely missed the dominant role that air power would have in the war, so that all of his naval battles are decided largely by surface gunnery duels. He wholly underestimated the requirements for amphibious operations, missed entirely Japan's vulnerability to the submarine, and assumed that there would be only one line of advance against the Japanese, rather than the multiple offensives (major ones in the Central and Southwest Pacific, and smaller ones in Southeast Asia, China, and, if only as a threat, in the Aleutians).

C

C-46 Commando, US Transport Aircraft

A contemporary of the C-47/DC-3, this was a more ambitious two-engine design, and production versions were not ready until 1942. The US military bought 3,144, and they remained on active service into the Vietnam War, the last retiring in 1969. In effect, the C-46 was an "improved C-47." A slightly higher cruise speed (185 miles an hour) and better high-altitude performance made it more suited for Pacific service. It was also 10 tons heavier than the C-47. Range was about the same, although the C-46 could carry a slightly heavier cargo over the same distance. Because of its ruggedness, C-46s were kept in military service longer after World War II than the more numerous C-47s. In the Pacific it was particularly useful for the airlift from India to China. However, it was considered a "troublesome" aircraft by pilots who much preferred the more reliable C-47.

See also AIRCRAFT TYPES, DEVELOPMENT.

C-47 (DC-3) Skytrain, US Transport Aircraft

The most commonly used air transport of World War II. A state-of-the-art aircraft in the mid-1930s (during which only 500 were built), over 13,000 DC-3s were produced for use during World War II. The DC-3 was the most widely manufactured transport aircraft of the war. When allied paratroopers jumped, it was usually from the twin-engine DC-3 (the aircraft could carry 28 troops, but over 60 people were squeezed in during emergencies). With a maximum range of 2,100 miles

and a top speed of 240 miles per hour, the DC-3 usually cruised at a speed of 170 miles per hour. The 13-ton DC-3 was the common cargo carrier (up to five tons) and general purpose "flying truck." There were many minor variations, usually with engines of varying horsepower (850–1,400). This had an effect on lifting power and range (bigger engines could lift more), but used more fuel and could not fly as far. The usual DC-3 sortie was to fly 500–1,000 miles with a three-ton load. The aircraft was nicknamed "Flying Dumbo" and "Gooney Bird."

See also AIRCRAFT TYPES, DEVELOPMENT; B-18.

C-54 (DC-4A) Skymaster, US Transport Aircraft

The Douglas Corporation designed the DC-4A as a four-engine transcontinental transport during the 1930s. It first flew in 1938. But after only 24 commercial versions were built, the military appropriated the aircraft and designated it the C-54. The 1,163 produced for military use weighed 33 tons and had a range of 3,900 miles with 50 passengers on board. The C-54 cruised at a swift 225 miles an hour and could carry up to 10 tons of cargo. During World War II, the C-54 made 79,642 ocean crossings with only two aircraft lost to accidents. This was not nearly as safe as modern transports, but excellent by World War II standards. The C-54 made the flying boat obsolete as a transport. Many were converted to commercial passenger service right after World War II. Some served on after the war, into the 1960s.

See also AIRCRAFT TYPES, DEVELOPMENT.

C-87 Liberator, US Transport Aircraft

A transport version of the B-24 heavy bomber. One of the few transport aircraft capable of transoceanic flight, only a limited number of C-87s were built. Several were requisitioned by senior officers for their personal use.

See also AIRCRAFT TYPES, DEVELOPMENT.

Calcutta, India

A major port, with extensive facilities for repairing and servicing ships, Calcutta lacked the capacity to handle warships and, being a river port, was unsuited as a naval base, but did have several airports and air bases nearby. It was occasionally subject to Japanese air attack from Burma.

California Class, US Battleships

Like all the older US battleships, the "Prune Barge" and her sister ship were rather slow, but were powerful, well protected vessels. In practical terms they were half-sisters to the NEW MEXICO CLASS and the MARYLAND CLASS, which they greatly resembled.

California, BB-45 (1916–1919–1921), the largest American warship ever built on the West Coast (and with the old *Oregon* of 1896, one of only two American capital ships ever built there), was "unbuttoned" on the morning of 7 December 1941, with her watertight doors opened in anticipation of an inspection. She took two TORPEDOES and one bomb, which set off a magazine explosion. A fast-thinking ensign instituted counterflooding measures, which prevented her from capsizing, and she sank on an even keel. Raised, she required major reconstruction, which included widening her to 114 feet and making her even more closely like *West Virginia*, of the Maryland class. She rejoined the fleet in mid-1944 and served in support of amphibious landings to the end of the war. With *Tennessee*, *West Virginia*, *Mississippi* she played a major role in the night battleship action off SURIGAO STRAIT in October of 1944, when they collectively fired 225 14-inch and 16-inch rounds at the Japanese fleet. *California* was scrapped in the early 1960s.

Tennessee, BB-43 (1917–1919–1920), was tied up between *West Virginia* and Ford Island on December 7, 1941, and was only lightly damaged, by two Japanese bombs and by a great deal of debris when *Arizona*, tied up astern, exploded. She was back in service within weeks, operating with the remnants of the battlefleet until late 1942. Modernized, though not as much as *California*, she emerged in mid-1943 in time to support the KISKA landings. She went on to support operations through to the end of the war, and was scrapped in the early 1960s

Callaghan, Daniel (1890–1942)

"Uncle Dan" Callaghan graduated from the Naval Academy in 1911. He had a long and varied career, but saw little action. Naval aide to FDR in 1938, in 1941 he was given command of the heavy cruiser *San Francisco*, among the first US ships to get to sea during the PEARL HARBOR attack. He served as chief of staff to Admiral Robert I. GHORMLEY during the opening phase of the GUADALCANAL Campaign. Promoted to rear admiral, Callaghan returned to sea in time to command the US squadron in the First Naval Battle of Guadalcanal (November 12–13, 1942), a major reverse for the United States, during which he was killed in action and won a MEDAL OF HONOR in the process.

Although a good officer, Callaghan's appointment to command the cruiser-destroyer squadron off Guadalcanal in November 1942 was dictated solely by the rigidity of naval regulations: Norman SCOTT had already encountered the Japanese several times, and bested them at CAPE ESPERANCE, but Callaghan was senior and therefore automatically in command.

Cam Ranh Bay, Indo-China

Although one of the best natural harbors in the world, Cam Ranh Bay lacked all but the most rudimentary facilities to service and repair shipping. However, its fine location on the central southern curve of the Indo-Chinese coast gave it great potential as a naval and air base for the domination of the East China Sea. The Japanese made use of Cam Ranh Bay several times, most notably early in the war, when some of their operations in the NETHERLANDS EAST INDIES were staged from there. It received several courtesy calls from American bombers and carrier aircraft in 1944–45.

Camouflage

The special jungle camouflage suit used by US troops in the CBI and the South Pacific was designed by Norvell Gillespie (1914–73), a horticulturist who was for a time an editor of *Better Homes and Gardens*. Gillespie also designed a camouflage suit for Europe (predecessor to the modern "tree suit"), but its use was spurned by the troops, who felt it made them look like Nazi SS men.

The Japanese did not have camouflage uniforms, but were well trained in the use of local materials to disguise themselves and their equipment. The one camouflage item sometimes issued to troops was the camouflage netting cape. This was a net, itself dyed a dark pattern, which the troops wore over their shoulders and "garnished" with local vegetation. A similar net was available for the HELMET, and more vegetation was attached here. All this was very effective, for the cape broke up the distinctive outline of the human form, and all that local vegetation blended right in. When the netting was not available, the troops used locally procured material to sew strips of cloth on their uniforms, and then could attach leaves and grass. Troops were also well trained on how to hide bunkers, camps, airfields, and even transport ships with similar types of camouflage.

Toward the end of the war, when the Japanese were getting pounded heavily, their already well-developed skill and effective use of camouflage kept increasing. In the last year of the Pacific War, American troops encountered very effective camouflage. The encounter was often fatal for all of those involved, for the Japanese could put their troops in well concealed positions that were also suicidal. For example, the Japanese would dig small, round holes, just big enough for one soldier and his rifle or machine gun, then cover it with underbrush and dirt. When American troops passed by, the Japanese soldier would raise his head, shoulders, and weapon out of the hole and start shooting or throwing grenades. The surprise of this was very effective, but the American counterattack was invariably fatal for the lone Japanese soldier.

Since Americans were generally on the attack for the second half of the Pacific War, they had less incentive to use camouflage. Depending on where they were and how strong the local Japanese (especially air forces) were, Allied troops would adjust their attitude toward using camouflage accordingly. If the Japanese were likely to attack, especially from the air, Allied soldiers used camouflage more.

Even people on the home front became aware of the need for camouflage as protection from enemy air attack. This sometimes had humorous consequences. For example, after Louis B. Mayer, the head of MGM, kept pestering the army's camouflage people to "do something" to conceal his studio in Hollywood to protect it from possible enemy bombing, they eventually responded with an elaborate scheme that shielded the entire installation from view. Only after the war did Mayer learn that the studio was disguised to resemble a nearby aircraft factory. The nearby aircraft factory was in turn camouflaged to resemble a suburban development, complete with streets, swimming pools, and parks.

See also DECEPTION.

Canadian Armed Forces

Few Canadian military personnel saw action in the Pacific Theater, but those who did fought well.

The prewar Canadian Army was quite small, less than 4,000 men on active duty, among the smallest in the world. Standards were high, however, and quality suffered little as a result of wartime expansion. In some ways the Canadian Army combined the best features of both the American and the British armies, being more flexible than the British but better disciplined and trained than the American.

The Canadian Army took part in two major ground operations in the Pacific. On 16 November 1941 two infantry battalions, the Royal Rifles of Canada and the Winnipeg Grenadiers, arrived in HONG KONG to strengthen the local garrison. Just three weeks later they found themselves in a desperate fight against overwhelmingly superior Japanese forces. Although the troops were neither well equipped nor fully trained, they gave a good account of themselves for three weeks, before surrendering on Christmas Day. They suffered considerably while PRISONERS of the Japanese.

The second and last time Canadian ground forces were committed to action in the Pacific was at KISKA in the summer of 1943, as part of the First Special Service Force, a unique commando brigade organized for special operations, consisting of several battalions each of American and Canadian troops. That operation was, in fact, unnecessary, since the Japanese had already evacuated the island. In any case, Canada's primary strategic interests lay in the European theater, rather than in the Pacific. Canadian ground troops did not fight again in the Pacific.

However, beginning in November 1944, Canadian observers were attached to US Army and Marine units fighting in the Pacific. A total of 95 officers served in this capacity, three of whom were wounded in action. In addition, shortly after the surrender of Germany, Canada began seeking a role in the invasion of Honshu (Operation Coronet), and the new Canadian Sixth Division (30,000 men, including supply and support elements) was being trained to take part in that operation when Japan surrendered.

The Royal Canadian Air Force and the Royal Canadian Navy were much more active in the Pacific than was the army. Both took part in operations in the Aleutians and Gulf of Alaska throughout the war. In addition, the light cruiser UGANDA and the TRIBAL CLASS destroyer *Algon-*

quin served with the British Pacific Fleet in the last months of the war. However, as with the army, the bulk of Canada's air and naval forces (the third largest navy in the world by the end of the war) were committed to the war against Germany.

See also ROYAL NAVY; UNITED STATES ARMY, OTHER NOTABLE UNITS.

Cannon/Edsall Classes, US Destroyer Escorts

Ordered at the same time as the BUCKLEYS, the 66 vessels of the Cannon Class (Type "DET") and the 85 ships of the Edsall Class ("FMR") were built 1942–44. They were essentially enlarged EVARTS, with about 200 tons more displacement at full load, on a longer and wider hull, with slightly more powerful engines and a touch more speed. They had virtually the same main armament, but added three TORPEDO tubes. As with all ships, they saw their antiaircraft armament enhanced during the war. "DET" referred to DEs with diesel electric turbine power plants, "FMR" to geared turbine diesels.

Canopus, USS, at Bataan

Among the US Navy ships in Manila Bay when Japan bombed PEARL HARBOR was the submarine tender *Canopus*, affectionately nicknamed "The Old Lady" by her crew. Her duties were mundane, to supply and repair SUBMARINES, which were to do the actual work of war. But by Christmas of 1941, all of her charges were gone, transferred south to Australia, from whence they could carry on the war more effectively. Meanwhile, of course, the Japanese had overrun most of the Philippines. As they were closing in on Manila, American and Filipino troops retreated to the BATAAN Peninsula for a desperate last stand. On Christmas night *Canopus* went with them, steaming the few miles across Manila Bay to tie up at the dock at Mariveles, a small port at the southern tip of the rugged peninsula. There, covered with vines and brush, she set up shop as a general repair facility to support the troops at the front. Despite her jungle CAMOUFLAGE, Japanese aviators managed to spot her, and on 29 December 1941 she was subjected to a serious air attack. Working hard, the ship's crew was able to put out the fires and repair most of the damage, so that within a few days she was seaworthy again. On 5 January 1942, she was hit again, albeit lightly. Once again the damage was quickly repaired.

However, recognizing that the ship was an easy target, her skipper, Cdr. Earl L. Sackett, decided that a little DECEPTION was in order. By judicious flooding of some bilge spaces, Sackett caused the ship to acquire what naval historian Samuel Eliot MORISON termed a "pathetic list." Some of the ship's most visible injuries (those that would not affect her seaworthiness or operability) were left unrepaired. Her cargo booms were slued around as if broken or jammed. A few smudge pots were sited here and there on her decks, to give the impression that the ship was slowly smoldering below. No attempt was made to restore most of the ship's camouflage of brush and vines, and, most telling of all, she was allowed to rust. Finally, as much as possible the ship's company assumed a nocturnal routine. These measures soon gave the ship the look of an abandoned hulk. As a result, although Japanese aircraft striking at installations in and around Mariveles Harbor repeatedly overflew the ship, none of them bothered to attack the obvious derelict.

Safe from Japanese attack, *Canopus* played an important role in the defense of Bataan. While her magazines supplied munitions and spare parts to the defenders, her machine shops kept weapons and equipment in good repair and converted several motor launches into improvised gunboats ("Mickey Mouse battleships" the troops called them), and her bluejackets turned out with rifles for combat duty from time to time. In this fashion *Canopus* helped prolong the defense of Bataan until the end. It must have come as a surprise to Japanese observers when, on 9 April 1942, that terrible night of surrender, the "destroyed" *Canopus* suddenly came to life, cast off from the dock,

and under her own power backed out of Mariveles Harbor into the dark waters of the South China Sea, where her crew promptly scuttled her.

See also SEAPLANE TENDERS.

Canton, China

A major river port, Canton had only limited facilities to repair ships, and none at all to support warships. Canton was occupied by the Japanese prior to PEARL HARBOR, and it was the base from which the Japanese assault on HONG KONG was launched. Throughout the war Canton served as an important port of embarkation for Japanese forces being shifted from China to other parts of the Asiatic-Pacific Theater. It was not liberated until after the Japanese surrender.

Canton Island, Phoenix Group

Slightly over three square miles, Canton is one of the Phoenix Islands, lying to the south of HAWAII. It was an important link in the chain of air bases that the United States began establishing on the route to Australia even before PEARL HARBOR. Aside from its importance for aerial reconnaissance, Canton figured in the war during the campaign for the GILBERTS, in late 1943, when bombers based there raided MAKIN and other islands.

Cape Esperance, Battle of

A naval battle fought 11–13 October 1942, during the GUADALCANAL Campaign. This was one of many surface combats waged to establish naval superiority around Guadalcanal during the second half of 1942. What made this battle unique was that it was fought by the escorts of Japanese and American convoys bringing supplies to their respective forces on the island. During October of 1942, the Japanese were trying to isolate the US forces on Guadalcanal, but were hampered by the American airfield on the island, and the fighters and bombers it contained. These American aircraft made life very costly for Japanese transports during the daylight hours. The Japanese could also fly bombers, but they had come a long way and were unable to patrol the area as well as the local American aircraft. American aircraft and Allied COAST-WATCHERS on the islands north of Guadalcanal usually spotted Japanese ships coming south, and in this case the approaching American convoy was alerted that the Japanese were approaching Guadalcanal. On the night of 11 October US warships (five cruisers and five destroyers) under Norman SCOTT intercepted the Japanese convoy (two transports and six destroyers serving as fast cargo ships, plus three cruisers and two destroyers) off Cape Esperance, the northern tip of Guadalcanal. Superior numbers and the element of surprise gave the US ships their first nighttime naval victory of the war. The Japanese lost a cruiser and a destroyer, with two other cruisers damaged. American losses were one destroyer, plus two cruisers and two destroyers damaged. While the entire American convoy was landed, only part of the Japanese reinforcements made it ashore and several of the transports were sunk or damaged. The American ships quickly departed from Guadalcanal, as the Japanese had many combat aircraft over the island the next day and more warships headed south.

Ref: Cook, *The Battle of Cape Esperance*.

Cape St. George, Battle of

On 25 November 1943 the Japanese sent another TOKYO EXPRESS down "The Slot," in an attempt to bring reinforcements to their forces in the central SOLOMONS. Three Japanese destroyer transports, escorted by two other destroyers, were intercepted by five US destroyers, under the redoubtable Arleigh "31 Knot" BURKE. The ensuing battle was decidedly one-sided. Both Japanese escorts were sunk, as was one of the three destroyer transports. None of the US ships was hit.

Caroline Islands

A large archipelago of small islands in the western Pacific, totaling about 450 square miles spread over several hundred thousand square miles of ocean. Thinly populated, the literally hundreds of islands, islets, and atolls fall into several distinct groups. Most of the islands are low-lying CORAL atolls, but there are also many "high" islands, formed by combinations of volcanism, earthquakes, and coral. Inhabited by Melanesians, the islands were under Spanish control until 1898, when they were sold to Germany. In 1914 the Japanese occupied them, and held them under the terms of a League of Nations Mandate granted in 1919. The Japanese made some investment in economic development, and in the late 1930s began to develop the islands for military purposes. During World War II some of them were heavily fortified and became the scene of desperate fighting.

Caroline Islands, Campaign for

The Caroline Islands sit right in the middle of the Pacific Ocean, and, after World War I were controlled by the Japanese under a League of Nations Mandate. Despite Allied suspicions, Japan did little to fortify the islands until the late 1930s. Then they got to work. TRUK, in particular, was built up into a major air (four airfields) and naval base. Until early 1944, Truk was the main base for the Japanese fleet. Because of the large size of the Truk garrison, and the out-of-the-way location of the Carolines (there wasn't anything of military importance right in the middle of the Pacific), the Allies decided to bypass Truk and most of the Carolines. The Japanese hadn't considered this option, and maintained their garrison until the end of the war. The Japanese attitude was largely driven by pride. The Japanese Army leadership saw the untenable situation of Truk, but to the navy the island was its premier naval base in the Pacific and could not be abandoned. In the end, the navy's ships were sunk or forced to seek bases elsewhere, and the island's aircraft were destroyed. All that was left was the underfed garrison.

The invasion of the GILBERTS (TARAWA) in late 1943, and especially the accompanying carrier raids on Japanese bases in adjacent areas, made it clear to the Japanese that Truk was in danger. By early 1944, the United States had numerous carriers roaming the Pacific. American SUBMARINES were a persistent problem around Truk, and other Japanese island bases. But the situation was particularly difficult at Truk, where numerous warships and hundreds of aircraft required constant supplies of fuel, ammunition, and spare parts to keep them combat worthy. American subs, and now the threat of carrier raids, made Truk more expensive than it was worth. This was what the Japanese Army saw more clearly than the navy. Through the second half of 1943, the admirals resisted army suggestions that Truk, and other central Pacific bases, be abandoned, or that at least fewer resources be sent out to reinforce them. In early February 1944, the navy bowed to the inevitable and began moving its main fleet base from Truk to Japan. They were just in time, for in February the first of two major carrier attacks on Truk took place.

On February 17–18, US Task Force 58 (six battleships, nine carriers, and many other ships) launched 30 raids on Truk, each by 150 aircraft or more. The Japanese lost most of their aircraft on Truk, with 270 planes destroyed on the ground or in the air. Most of the ships still in Truk harbor were hit; 24 transports, two cruisers, four destroyers, two submarines, and several smaller ships. Another two dozen transports and over a dozen warships escaped. But Truk now had only a hundred aircraft, and little fuel or ammunition to make them operational. The Japanese naturally saw this as a prelude to an amphibious attack, but instead the United States shortly invaded the MARSHALL ISLANDS (to the east of Truk) and then the MARIANAS (to the north) in June. Before that happened, US carriers hit Truk again, on April 29–30, 1944 in an attack that was followed up by gunfire from battleships and cruisers. Over a hundred aircraft were destroyed, and the few remaining ships sunk or chased away. Most importantly, the airbase facilities were destroyed. Truk ceased to function as a military base, and became little more than a prison camp for its large garrison.

Truk would be visited one more time before the end of the war. In June of 1945, a British task force bombarded the island with its guns. Truk was no longer worth an air raid.

Carrier Aircraft Tactics

One of the significant developments of the Pacific War was the use of mission packaging in air warfare. "Mission packaging" refers to the process of tailoring groups of aircraft for particular operations. While the terminology is post-World War II, the notion of mixing and matching fighters, bombers, and air control aircraft to come up with a "package" best suited to the mission at hand was one that carrier AIR GROUP commanders certainly understood.

The prewar theory in the US Navy was that an entire air group would make a "coordinated" attack. The fighters would escort the bombers to the target. There, the dive-bombers would go in first, with the fighters covering them from enemy interception. This would draw the enemy's attention (and defensive fighters) upward, permitting the torpedo bombers to go in virtually on the deck, covered by the fighters, which would descend to lower altitudes in company with the dive-bombers.

In practice this didn't work out too well. The three types of aircraft had differing speeds and ranges and often arrived over the target at different times, if at all, with frequently fatal results to the bomber pilots. At MIDWAY only Ensign GAY survived of over 40 men in Torpedo Squadron Eight, and none of their TORPEDOES hit anything.

Moreover, there weren't enough fighters to go around. Initially, the theory was that a strike force required about one escort for every three attacking aircraft, and in theory a carrier had just enough aircraft to do this. Unfortunately, since a typical prewar US carrier air group had about 54 strike aircraft (TBDs and SBDs) and only 18 fighters, this meant that a carrier commander didn't have enough resources to provide fighters both to escort his strike aircraft and to maintain a CAP (combat air patrol) over the carrier. Experience demonstrated that the demands for escorts and CAP pretty much reversed the prewar ratio of fighters to strike aircraft, so that by late–1944 a carrier had mostly fighters and only about a third of a quarter bombers, albeit by then the fighters were capable of carrying out light bombing missions of their own. By then, missions were regularly composed of from one to three fighters for each bomber, depending upon the expected opposition.

Initially CAP had not been a major concern. Early war practice was to put two to eight fighters over a carrier, depending upon circumstances. This ran afoul of limited resources, there not being enough fighters on board to keep many in the air for any length of time. As fighter contingents increased, the number of fighters allocated to CAP increased. Eventually, by mid-1944, when the Third/Fifth Fleet was operating with 15–16 CVs and CVLs, not to mention supporting CVEs, the fighter contingents from a whole carrier would occasionally be earmarked for CAP. It was even suggested that some carriers be designated as CAP carriers and assigned only fighters, with the mission of fleet defense. Alternately, it was proposed that CVEs be mostly equipped with fighters to provide cover for the CVs, which could then use all of their fighters to escort strike missions. These proposals were rejected. The main reason for this appears to have been that carriermen preferred to be defended by their "own" men. Nevertheless, both suggestions seem reasonable, at least retrospectively.

One reason that the British were willing to accept the loss of aircraft capacity as a result of using armored flight decks is that they believed this would make a CAP less essential. The British also put a lot of resources into carrier defense via anti-aircraft gunfire. British carriers did survive hits more handily than anyone else because of the armored flight decks, and managed to get by with smaller CAPs.

During the war, mission packages tended to get larger and larger. Of course, during major battles missions were flown by whole air groups (all the aircraft on one carrier). But this was not the case when air strikes were being conducted against ground targets or enemy shipping early in the war, when it was not unusual for a strike to consist of literally a handful of aircraft, say a half-dozen bombers and four fighters. As time went by strikes got larger, often comprising whole air groups and sometimes several air groups in coordination. This was particularly the case when carriers were supporting ground operations.

Ref: Reynolds, *The Fast Carriers*; Roscoe, *On the Seas and in the Skies*.

Carrier Losses

The first aircraft carrier to be sunk in action was HMS *Courageous*, a converted World War I "lite" battlecruiser that took two TORPEDOES from the German submarine *U-29* on 17 September 1939, going down in 15 minutes. Curiously, her sister ship HMS *Glorious* was the second carrier to be lost in action when she had the misfortune to encounter the German battleships *Scharnhorst* and *Gneisenau* off Norway on June 8, 1940. Despite a heroic, and ultimately fatal, defense by the destroyer HMS *Acasta*, the unlucky carrier was pounded with 11–inch shells for over an hour before she went down.

The first carrier killed in the Pacific War was also British: HMS HERMES, the only British carrier lost in the war with Japan, was sunk by Japanese carrier aircraft near CEYLON on 9 March 1942. While the first US carrier, *Langley*, was sunk by Japanese aircraft south of JAVA in February 1942, she was no longer officially an aircraft "carrier," having been demoted to the status of an aircraft "tender" some years before the war. In this role the very slow *Langley*, which had a very short flight deck, was used to deliver aircraft, which was what she was doing when sunk.

The first Japanese carrier sunk in the war was HIJMS *Shoho*, done in by US carrier aircraft at the CORAL SEA on May 8, 1942, shortly before the loss of the first American carrier, USS LEXINGTON. The last American fleet carrier lost in action was *Hornet*, during the Battle of the SANTA CRUZ ISLANDS, October 24, 1942. However the light carrier *Prince-*

ton was lost during the Battle of LEYTE GULF, on October 24, 1944, and the escort carrier BISMARCK SEA on February 21, 1945, off IWO JIMA—all to Japanese air attack.

The first Japanese carrier to be sunk by a US submarine was HIJMS *Chuyo* on 4 December 1943 by the USS *Sailfish* (SS-192), which, as *Squalus*, had been sunk in an accident before the war, to be salvaged and recommissioned under another name.

The last of the 20 aircraft carriers lost by the Imperial Japanese Navy was *Amagi*, pounded to death by US carrier aircraft in KURE harbor on July 24, 1945.

Ref: Brown, *Warship Losses of World War Two.*

Carrier Raids, US, 1942

Immediately after PEARL HARBOR, there wasn't much the United States could do in the Pacific. The Japanese quickly seized most of the major Allied bases in the region, and the shock of this rapid conquest left the Allies in need of some morale building. This needed boost came in the form of a series of raids by the US carriers, including the two ships that had escaped destruction at Pearl Harbor.

The Japanese cooperated by committing their dozen carriers to supporting ground operations and a largely unnecessary sortie into the Indian Ocean. They made no effort to follow up their success at Pearl Harbor by tracking down and destroying the numerically fewer US Pacific carriers.

After Pearl Harbor the United States quickly added two carriers from the Atlantic (*Hornet* and YORKTOWN) to the three already in the Pacific (*Enterprise*, LEXINGTON, and *Saratoga*). However, on 11 January 1942 *Saratoga* was TORPEDOED by a Japanese sub 500 miles south of HAWAII, forcing her back to a West Coast shipyard for several months of repairs and modernization. Since *Saratoga*'s pilots and aircraft were distributed to the other carriers and training centers, this gave the United States four fully staffed carriers for use against the Japanese.

Despite the risk of losing more carriers, a policy of raiding was adopted. The first two attempts involved WAKE ISLAND. In mid-December 1941 an attempt was made to aid the hard-pressed US garrison there, and if successful might have resulted in the first carrier-to-carrier battle ever. Then, in January 1942 an attempt was made to hit the newly installed Japanese garrison on the island. Both attempts failed through a combination of inexperience, excessive caution, and bad luck.

In early February, however, the MARSHALL ISLANDS were hit in the first successful raid. In late February, a raid on RABAUL (in the BISMARCKS) was called off when the US carrier was spotted by Japanese recon aircraft. Early March saw a successful raid on MARCUS ISLAND, only 1,000 miles from the Japanese Home Islands. In mid-March came Wilson BROWN's spectacular raid against Japanese forces landing on the north coast of New Guinea: *Lexington* and *Yorktown* launched 104 aircraft from the Gulf of Papua, which, by taking advantage of favorable thermals, managed to cross the OWEN STANLEY MOUNTAINS to hit LAE and Salamaua, sinking or damaging several Japanese transports, all but one of the aircraft then returning safely. Then in mid-April came the even more spectacular DOOLITTLE Raid, when 16 Army B-25 bombers launched from *Hornet* bombed Tokyo.

At this point the Japanese decided to make a decisive attempt to crush the USN, resulting in the battles of CORAL SEA (May 7–8) and MIDWAY (June 3–5). The two battles evened up the carrier situation in the Pacific, when the Japanese lost five carriers (*Shoho* at Coral Sea, and AKAGI, *Kaga*, SORYU, and HIRYU at Midway) at a cost of two American ones (*Lexington* and *Yorktown*). This ended the period of carrier raids by the United States.

By allowing these raids, the Japanese enabled the American carriers to gain valuable experience. As with all their ships and sailors, the Japanese carriers and AIR GROUPS began the war better trained than their Allied counterparts. Without these raids, and their opportunity for relatively risk-free practice, the Battle of Midway might easily have gone the other way.

Carrier Task Forces, Composition, Japanese

Even before the war broke out, the Japanese Navy had figured out that carriers operating in groups were many times more effective than carriers operating singly. Right at the start of the war the Japanese created the world's first operational fast carrier task force, grouping six carriers together with some fast battleships, cruisers, and destroyers, and sending it against PEARL HARBOR with devastating effect. This force operated for about five months, roaming the western Pacific in support of Japanese operations, and even raiding into the Indian Ocean. The "First Air Fleet" carried all before it and appeared invincible. At the time, it was. But then the Japanese broke it up, just in time for the battles of the CORAL SEA and MIDWAY. The Imperial Navy was never again able to put together so many fleet carriers, and its carriers were never again to be nearly as effective. Despite this, the Japanese clearly understood that larger carrier task forces were better carrier task forces, in contrast to the US Navy, which remained uncertain as to the optimal size of a carrier task force until well into 1943.

Carrier Task Forces, Composition, United States

The United States began the Pacific War with a poverty of carriers and a plethora of missions. There were only three carriers in the Pacific at the time of PEARL HARBOR, and only three more were to trickle in from the Atlantic over the first year of the war, mostly to replace losses. So carriers had to operate singly, with small escorts, in order to accomplish everything that had to be done. Gradually, as more and more carriers became available,

JAPANESE CARRIER TASK FORCES

Year	Operation	CV/CVL	BB/CA/CL	DD	Note
1941	Pearl Harbor	6	5	9	
	Wake	2	2	2	A
	Rabaul	4	4	7	B
1942	Indian Ocean	6	7	11	C
	Coral Sea	2	4	6	D
	Midway	4	5	12	E
	Aleutians	2	2	4	
	Eastern Solomons	2	6	17	F
	Santa Cruz	3	7	15	G
1944	Philippine Sea				
	Heavy TG	3	3	9–20	H
	Light TG	1	3–4	3	

A. This task force comprised one division of the Pearl Harbor Strike Force (the "First Air Fleet"). Note the extremely thin escort with which these carriers operated.   B. Two divisions of the Pearl Harbor Strike Force.   C. The reunited First Air Fleet.   D. Excludes invasion force with one light carrier.   E. Excludes invasion force and battle fleet, with one light carrier.   F. Excludes a light carrier and supporting vessels serving as a bombardment group and bait.   G. Excludes forces earmarked for surface action. The total Japanese force available was two fleet and two light carriers, five battleships, 15 cruisers, and 44 destroyers.   H. There were two heavy task groups and three light ones, totaling five fleet and four light carriers, plus five battleships, nine cruisers, and 28 destroyers.

US CARRIER TASK FORCES

Year	Operation	CV/CVL	BB/CA/CL	DD	Note
1941	Raids	1	3–4	5–9	A
1942	Raids	1–2	4–6	5–10	B
	Coral Sea	2	7	12	C
	Midway: TF 16	2	6	11	D
	TF 17	1	2	6	D
	Eastern Solomons	1	2–3	5–7	E
	Santa Cruz	1	3–4	6–8	F
1944					
	Philippine Sea	3–4	3–5	9–12	G

A. The task forces that attempted to relieve WAKE ISLAND and then raided Jaluit in the MANDATES.

B. Raids on the Mandates in early 1942 were by one-carrier task forces, but that which hit the Japanese in New Guinea had two carriers.

C. Actually there were two separate task forces operating cooperatively.

D. These operated in cooperation.

E. There were three task forces operating under a single command and totaling three carriers, eight battleships and cruisers, and 18 destroyers.

F. The two-carrier task forces were supported by a surface combat group, for a total of two carriers, 12 battleships and cruisers, and 18 destroyers.

G. The four-carrier task forces (one of them with three carriers, the others with four) operated in conjunction with a battleship task force, for a total of 15 carriers, seven battleships, 21 cruisers, and 69 destroyers. This was basically the pattern to which the Third/Fifth Fleet adhered through to the end of the war, a model that was also adopted by the ROYAL NAVY task force that served in the Pacific in 1945.

task forces grew larger, with consequent improvements in effectiveness.

Despite this, going into 1943, several American admirals still believed that single-carrier, or two-carrier, task forces were best. The most air-minded, however, thought "more is better," holding out for the largest possible task forces. In fact they were correct. Operationally, the effectiveness of a carrier task force increases geometrically as the number of carriers increases arithmetically: A two-carrier task force is four times more effective than a one-carrier task force, a three-carrier task force is nine times more effective, etc. This is because the larger formations permit a concentration of the striking power of the carriers, and of their defensive firepower. Gradually the "more is better" admirals won out, so that by mid-1943 task forces of three and four carriers were considered best, and some were advocating even larger groupings.

Carrier Task Forces, Tactical Formations, Japanese

Tactical formations in the early period of the Pacific War were based on single-ship defense. At CORAL SEA, each carrier was covered by four to five cruisers and destroyers standing about 1,600 yards away. At MIDWAY the Japanese grouped the carriers together and surrounded them with a screen of battleships, cruisers, and destroyers at less than a nautical mile distance. For the defense of HIRYU, their last carrier at Midway, they grouped two battleships, one heavy cruiser, and five destroyers within about a nautical mile. Neither arrangement provided sufficient coverage, and this certainly contributed to the demise of the "First Air Fleet." Even this early in the war US escorts were routinely getting to within a half-mile of friendly carriers.

After SANTA CRUZ the Japanese carrier fleet was withdrawn from action for over a year, due largely to the enormous loss of trained pilots. This ought to have given them enough time to train more pilots and study the continuing carrier operations, in support of landings and in attacks on Japanese ba-

ses. They failed to do either very well. For the battle of the PHILIPPINE SEA VAdm Jisaburo OZAWA formed two-carrier task forces, one composed of three CVLs and one of five CVs and a CVL. He then proceeded to separate them by about 100 miles, sending the light carriers ahead of the main body, disposed in three task groups, each of one CVL plus escorts deployed on a front of about 12 miles, while the main body formed two task groups, fleet deployed roughly thus:

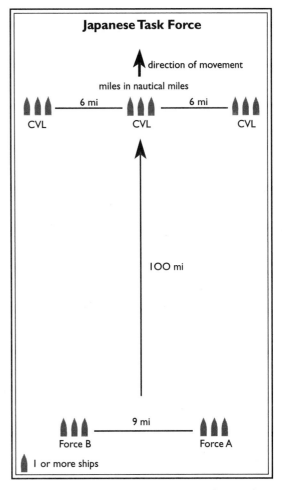

Ozawa intended the light carriers as bait, to lure SPRUANCE into a strike against them, so that he could in turn locate the US carriers and hit them using his longer-range aircraft. Although the "bait"

was rather far ahead of the main body, this might have worked had his pilots been adequately trained. However, despite the longer range of his aircraft, he probably put too much distance between his striking force and his bait. In any case his resources were not adequate to the needs of the moment.

In grouping their carriers for the PEARL HARBOR operation, the Japanese inadvertently hit upon the ideal size for a carrier task force. However, they failed to maintain it. As a result they frittered away their superiority through dispersal, leading to their disaster at MIDWAY, where they committed only four of their nine available carriers, even granting that several of those sent off on unnecessary missions were relatively light. After Midway, their ability to build large carrier task forces was not as great as that of the United States, and steadily declined.

Carrier Task Forces, Tactical Formations, US

In each of the 1942 carrier task forces, the carriers were actually operating in small task groups, each with its own dedicated escorts, but with the group usually operating under a single higher command. At EASTERN SOLOMONS and SANTA CRUZ, the carriers were deployed about 10 miles apart, each at the center of a ring composed of battleships, cruisers, and destroyers about 1,800 to 2,500 yards distant. This did not permit mutual support among the three task forces, and made it impossible to provide adequate CAP (carrier air patrol—fighters protecting their ships). In contrast, at the PHILIPPINE SEA, the fleet deployed in five task groups (TGs), one composed primarily of battleships. Each carrier TG formed a circle about 4 miles across, with the carriers in the middle, closely accompanied by two to three destroyers and surrounded by cruisers and still more destroyers: Intervals between escorts and carriers were often as little as a half mile. The battleship TG formed a larger circle, about 6 miles across, with all of the

ships save the flagship deployed on the perimeter. The relative disposition of the TGs was:

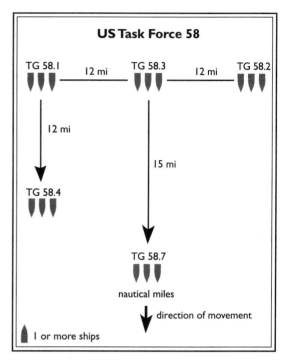

A picket of destroyers was deployed in a wide circle several miles out from the fleet, to provide early warning. This formation was adopted to maximize antiaircraft firepower. Normally the battleships comprising TG 58.7 were dispersed among the carrier task groups. However, VAdm Raymond SPRUANCE formed TG 58.7 and deployed it between his carriers and the Japanese, figuring that the battlewagons would likely prove irresistible to attacking enemy aircraft, while being both more able to defend themselves and more survivable than the carriers.

This sort of formation remained the norm through to the end of the war, by which time most TGs were composed of four heavy carriers plus one light carrier, for a total of about 430 aircraft. Some carrier admirals were by then thinking in terms of even larger task groups, with up to eight carriers, a development that would almost certainly have occurred had the war lasted into 1946. The organization of the carriers into task groups had other operational advantages besides enhancing the striking power and flexibility of the Fast Carrier Task Force. Even with the extraordinary logistical capabilities of the Servrons (SERVICE SQUADRONS) it was difficult for a carrier to sustain operations continuously for more than three to four weeks without a break of a week or so, if only to rest the men. Once the fleet was organized into four-carrier task groups it could operate almost uninterruptedly, with individual task groups pulling out for a week's rest every few weeks.

Carriers, Designing Aircraft for

When the aircraft carrier was first developed, by the ROYAL NAVY during World War I, there was no differentiation between carrier-capable and other types of aircraft. However, the rigors of carrier operations soon caused the Royal Naval Air Service to modify existing aircraft to make them better suited to carrier operations. By the end of World War I, aircraft specially modified or designed for carrier operations were the norm on Britain's small fleet of carriers. As more nations got into the carrier business (Japan, the United States, and even France), the differences between carrier aircraft and land-based aircraft began to multiply. Carrier aircraft had to have sturdier frames, and particularly sturdy landing gear, to enable them to take the punishment inherent in carrier landings, described by some pilots as "controlled crashes." This made carrier planes heavier, and consequently slower and generally less maneuverable than land planes, and usually of much shorter range. Other differences resulted from differing national attitudes toward the importance of carrier warfare and the ways in which carriers should be operated. The US Navy designed its carrier aircraft to have folding wings, to improve stowage, which resulted in greater weight due to the machinery and complex bracing necessary to make folding wings work. In addition, the US Navy wanted to be able to stow aircraft on deck in all sorts of weather, which meant planes had to be more weather proof than aircraft routinely stowed below decks. As a result, US carrier aircraft were much heavier than Japanese or British ones, and in consequence rather slow and of shorter range. In compensation, they were able to take much more punishment, and US carriers were able to take many more aircraft to sea with them.

While the Japanese Navy did not wholly dispense with folding wings, it made limited use of this potentially valuable technology, preferring to save weight. In addition, the Japanese insisted on stowing all aircraft below decks. While this reduced the aircraft contingents of their carriers, they had lighter, and hence faster and more agile carrier aircraft than did the US Navy, at least until American industry came up with far more powerful aircraft engines.

The Royal Navy had the worst carrier aircraft in the world. This was primarily because the design of carrier aircraft was in the hands of the Royal Air Force, which had little interest in the matter. As a result, British carrier aircraft never rivaled either Japanese or American planes. Since for the first two years of its war the Royal Navy was fighting Germans and Italians, the flaws of its carrier aircraft were not obvious. Moreover, the Royal Navy never clashed with the Imperial Navy in an air-sea battle, and so escaped the consequences of its inferiority in aircraft design. When the Royal Navy sent a carrier task force to fight alongside the Third/Fifth Fleet in early 1945, it was largely equipped with American aircraft plus "navalized" versions of RAF aircraft, which, however good their tactical performance, were structurally unsuited to carrier duty at sea.

See also AIRCRAFT TYPES, DEVELOPMENT.

Carriers, Flightdeck Operations

For a carrier to be useful it had to be able to launch and recover airplanes. There was no "normal" time prescribed to arm, fuel, and launch a deckload strike by a fleet carrier. Prewar training demonstrated that this could be done in about 90 minutes, assuming all aircraft were already on deck, which was US Navy policy for most of the war, even when operations were not going on. This made fueling, arming, and launching a lot easier, as bringing aircraft up from the hangar deck was a slow, tedious, and rather dangerous procedure.

Surprisingly, during the war it turned out that the 90–minute figure was regularly bettered. Normally, a carrier always had some aircraft ready for action. These were either fighters to replace CAP or SBDs and fighters to replace aircraft on reconnaissance and antisubmarine patrol. In addition, since the ship's skipper and the air group commander usually knew what they were doing in a particular neighborhood, they had some idea of the type of missions that they would most probably be called upon to launch. Moreover, preparing for a major mission did not require particularly much more time than preparing for a minor one. For example, the 16 B-25 that undertook the Tokyo Raid were armed, fueled, and away in about an hour.

As carrier "ground crews" became more skillful, the time it took to launch got shorter. In addition, in mid–1943 US carriers began using jeeps to haul aircraft around their decks, which further reduced the time necessary to get off a strike, as airplanes had hitherto been manhandled from place to place. As a result, in practice, a deckload strike could get clear in 30 minutes, if some of the aircraft were armed and ready at the start—and provided there were no aircraft to recover and the winds and seas were favorable.

Also, as radar improved, the carriers had more time to prepare to receive an attack, so they could spot and launch aircraft at relative leisure, disarming, defueling, and stowing below all those not needed to defend the ship.

In this regard it's worth recalling that at MIDWAY Admiral Chuichi NAGUMO, Japan's most experienced carrierman, thought he had enough time to rearm, and then to re-rearm his aircraft, about 30–45 minutes. He was wrong, but only by about 10 minutes. His best course would have been to stick with his original decision to arm his aircraft for another go at Midway Island and launch them, retaining the fighters to cover the fleet. The strike on Midway would have been a waste of ammunition, though probably not of planes, but the enhanced CAP might have saved the carriers, particularly given the fact that there would have been no fueled and ammunitioned aircraft to blow up when C. Wade McClusky showed up with his *Enterprise* dive-bombers.

In the later Pacific air battles US carriers routinely launched armed TORPEDO and dive-bombers into the blue rather than try to take a Japanese attack with them on deck.

Assuming that there were no CASUALTIES among the aircrew or damage to the aircraft, in an optimal situation, recovery from an airstrike could take about one to two minutes per plane. Damaged planes and wounded pilots made recovery much more difficult, as can be seen in some extraordinarily graphic newsreel footage. On some critical occasions the wounded men were told to wait, so that undamaged aircraft could be recovered first, lest the flight deck be smashed so badly that operations would have to cease entirely. There were also occasions on which injured pilots bulled their way to the head of the line. As the number of carriers multiplied, the practice of waving off the damaged aircraft fell into disuse, because there were always other carriers that could help take up the slack.

Carter, James E. (1924–)

The son of a peanut farmer, Jimmy Carter entered Annapolis in 1943. During the summer of 1944 he saw active service aboard the battleship *New York* on convoy duty off the East Coast and in the Caribbean. In June of 1946 his class was graduated a year ahead of schedule, with Carter standing 59th out of 820. He served in the navy until 1953, transferring to SUBMARINES in 1948, and was for a time the engineering officer aboard a nuclear-powered boat. Resigning from the navy in 1953 to enter the family business, he became active in politics, and was elected president in 1976. In 1980 he lost a bid for reelection to RONALD REAGAN.

CARTWHEEL, the Rabaul Campaign

CARTWHEEL was the campaign to isolate, but not capture, RABAUL, one of the largest Japanese bases in the Pacific. As such, it was the most far ranging encirclement battle of the war, with the two Allied pincers advancing over a thousand miles. It all began in the spring of 1942, when the Japanese occupied the Bismarck island group (northeast of New Guinea) and began turning it into their principal bastion in the southwest Pacific. The spacious natural harbor of Rabaul was the center of this complex.

The Japanese put over 100,000 troops and hundreds of aircraft into Rabaul. The port generally held the second largest concentration of Japanese warships in the Pacific (after TRUK, the main base). Rabaul's cruisers and destroyers escorted transports feeding troops and supplies to sustain the protracted battles in New Guinea and the SOLOMONS.

General MACARTHUR, the Allied commander for the southwest Pacific, decided that it would be easier to encircle Rabaul with Allied-held islands than it would be to directly assault so heavily fortified a place. This encircling operation was called CARTWHEEL. The offensive took place between September of 1943 and early 1944. The key attack was a series of carrier air raids on Rabaul that destroyed local Japanese airpower. These raids also destroyed the viability of Rabaul as a base for warships, thus leaving over 100,000 Japanese troops isolated and starving by mid-1944.

The last link in the fence thrown around Rabaul was put into place when two island groups north of Rabaul were taken in early 1944 (the ADMIRALTY ISLANDS in February and the St. Matthias Islands in March). Once Rabaul was surrounded by Allied-held islands, few reinforcements or supplies could reach these Japanese, thus making them relatively harmless.

Casablanca Class, US Escort Carriers

Based on experience gained from LONG ISLAND and other escort carriers converted from merchant hulls, the 49 ships of the Casablanca class were ordered as purpose built escort carriers in early 1942, laid down between March 1942 and March 1943; each took only three to four months to complete due to innovative mass PRODUCTION construction methods introduced by the Kaiser Industries shipyard in Vancouver, Washington. They saw extensive service in the Pacific.

Some of the more notable vessels in the class were:

Liscome Bay, CVE-56 (1942–1943–1943), was lost on 24 November 1943 (Thanksgiving Day), on her first major operation (she had been completed only four months earlier). Torpedoed by the Japanese submarine *I-175* off MAKIN ISLAND, she went down in about 30 minutes, with the loss of more than 650 lives, among them PEARL HARBOR hero Dorie MILLER.

Anzio, CVE-57 (1942–1943–1943), was the premier submarine-killing escort carrier of the Pacific War, her aircraft accounting for I-13, I-41, I-361, and I-368.

St. Lo, CVE-63 (1943–1943–1943), was originally to have been named *Chapin Bay*, but was launched as *Midway*. As *Midway* she saw considerable service as an aircraft transport, carrying army and Marine aircraft to bases established on newly secured islands. In September 1944 she was renamed again, becoming *St. Lo*, the name *Midway* being needed for a new fleet carrier. Renaming warships is traditionally considered bad luck; off Leyte, a KAMIKAZE plane went through her flight deck setting off the bombs and TORPEDOES on her hangar deck and sinking her on 25 October 1944, just after she had survived the onslaught of the Japanese battlefleet off SAMAR. She had the dubious distinction of being the first ship ever sunk by kamikaze attack.

Gambier Bay, CVE-73 (1943–1943–1943), formed part of Taffy Three, supporting the landings at LEYTE GULF on 25 October 1944, when the Japanese battlefleet turned up. After more than an hour of trying to outrun the faster Japanese ships, she was caught by heavy cruisers *Chokai* and *Haguro* and light cruiser *Noshiro*, which proceeded to pound her until she capsized.

Omanney Bay, CVE-79 (1943–1943–1943), initially served as an aircraft transport. She survived the onslaught of the Japanese battlefleet off Samar in October 1944, but was severely crippled off Panay by a kamikaze on January 4, 1945, while steaming northward to take part in the landings at Lingayen Gulf, and was purposely sunk by torpedoes from the USS *Burns* (DD-588).

The other members of the class had varying experiences during the war. Several took kamikaze or other damage. After the war the more heavily damaged units were scrapped. The surviving units served in a variety of roles into the 1960s, when they were scrapped.

Casualties, Army Versus Marine

The US Marines undertook some of the bloodiest amphibious assaults of the war. But their overall casualty rates were not as high as many army units that engaged in less intense combat in the Euro-

An unusual view of the escort carrier USS Casablanca, *April 19, 1945. The LCVP in the foreground, from which the image was taken, is returning a "liberty party" from Rara Island, near Manus.*

pean Theater of Operations over longer periods. For example, the 29th Marines sustained the highest losses of any Marine regiment in one battle, 2,821 dead and wounded in 82 days of combat during the OKINAWA Campaign in 1945. This was less than 100% of T/O strength. In contrast, by early 1945, 47 infantry regiments in 19 army divisions had suffered at least 100% losses, and in some cases over 200% casualties. All of these regiments were in the European Theater, and all of these regiments had been in action over three months, many for eight months or more. Marines tended to be in combat for short, intense, island assaults. The army

THE TWENTY DIVISIONS WITH THE HIGHEST CASUALTIES

Rank	Division	Theater	Combat Deaths	Other Losses	Total	Ratio
1	3rd Inf.	ETO	5,558	20,419	25,977	3.7
2	9th Inf.	ETO	4,504	18,773	23,277	4.2
3	4th Inf.	ETO	4,836	17,824	22,660	3.7
4	45th Inf.	ETO	4,080	16,913	20,993	4.1
5	1st Inf.	ETO	4,280	16,379	20,659	3.8
6	29th Inf.	ETO	4,786	15,834	20,620	3.3
7	36th Inf.	ETO	3,637	15,829	19,466	4.4
8	1st Mar.	PTO	5,435	13,849	19,284	2.5
9	90th Inf.	ETO	3,930	15,270	19,200	3.9
10	30th Inf.	ETO	3,516	14,930	18,446	4.2
11	80th Inf.	ETO	3,480	13,607	17,087	3.9
12	2nd Inf.	ETO	3,488	13,307	16,795	3.8
13	28th Inf.	ETO	2,683	14,079	16,762	5.2
14	34th Inf.	ETO	3,350	13,051	16,401	3.9
15	4th Mar.	PTO	3,317	13,006	16,323	3.9
16	83rd Inf.	ETO	3,620	12,290	15,910	3.4
17	35th Inf.	ETO	2,947	12,935	15,882	4.4
18	79th Inf.	ETO	2,943	12,260	15,203	4.2
19	8th Inf.	ETO	2,820	11,166	13,986	4.0
20	88th Inf.	ETO	2,556	10,555	13,111	4.1

The figures under *Combat Dead* include only troops killed or mortally wounded in action. Those under *Other Losses* include men not mortally wounded, PRISONERS and non-combat deaths. *Ratio* is the number of other losses to combat dead. Note that these tables omit reference to the Regular Army's Philippine Division, and the divisions of the PHILIPPINE ARMY, which were largely destroyed in combat in 1941–42.

THE TWENTY DIVISIONS WITH THE HIGHEST PROPORTION OF COMBAT DEATHS

Rank	Division	Theater	Combat Deaths	Other Losses	Total	Ratio
1	66th Inf.	ETO	800	652	1,452	0.8
2	20th Arm.	ETO	59	121	180	2.1
3	89th Inf.	ETO	325	704	1,029	2.2
4	American	PTO	1,157	2,893	4,050	2.5
5	27th Inf.	PTO	1,844	4,689	6,533	2.5
6	1st Mar.	PTO	5,435	13,849	19,284	2.5
7	25th Inf.	PTO	1,497	3,935	5,432	2.6
8	32nd Inf.	PTO	1,985	5,283	7,268	2.7
9	101st A/B	ETO	2,090	6,064	8,154	2.9
10	69th Inf.	ETO	383	1,123	1,506	2.9
11	11th A/B	PTO	614	1,806	2,420	2.9
12	7th Inf.	PTO	2,334	6,878	9,212	2.9
13	71st Inf.	ETO	278	836	1,114	3.0
14	77th Inf.	PTO	1,850	5,611	7,461	3.0
15	40th Inf.	PTO	748	2,277	3,025	3.0
16	5th Mar.	PTO	2,113	6,450	8,563	3.1
17	9th Arm.	ETO	693	2,157	2,850	3.1
18	3rd Arm.	ETO	2,126	6,647	8,773	3.1
19	24th Inf.	PTO	1,689	5,323	7,012	3.2
20	1st Cav.	PTO	970	3,085	4,055	3.2

Omits divisions with fewer than 50 combat dead. The figures under *Combat Dead* include only troops killed or mortally wounded in action. Those under *Other Losses* include men not mortally wounded, PRISONERS and non-combat deaths. *Ratio* is the number of other losses to combat dead. Note that these tables omit reference to the Regular Army's Philippine Division, and the divisions of the PHILIPPINE ARMY, which were largely destroyed in combat in 1941–42.

regiments endured generally less concentrated combat but for much longer periods.

Unlike the situation in World War I, no formal tally of "days in combat" was made for US divisions in World War II, due to the differing nature of the two wars. Unofficially, the highest number of days in combat claimed for a US division is apparently 305, for the Second Infantry Division in the ETO. The First Marine Division probably had the highest number of days in contact with the enemy in the Pacific Theater, about 225, a figure that was certainly exceeded by several divisions in the ETO, notably the First, Second, Third, 29th, 36th, and

45th Infantry Divisions and the First and Second Armored Divisions. Overall casualties in Marine divisions and army divisions in the Pacific were lower than those for divisions in the ETO, as can be seen on the tables on pages 142–143.

So most divisions in the Pacific had fewer casualties overall than those in the European Theater. However, if one compares the divisions only on the basis of the number of men killed in action or mortally wounded as a proportion of total casualties, a very different picture emerges.

While overall casualties in divisions fighting in the Pacific were lower than those of divisions fighting in Europe, the proportion of casualties killed or mortally wounded was much higher. On the average, Pacific divisions lost one man killed for every 3.1 other casualties, while European Theater divisions lost one man killed for every 3.9 other losses. Twelve out of the 20 divisions with the highest proportion of men killed in combat to wounded were Pacific divisions, which constituted about a quarter of US divisions. This was a consequence of the often fanatical resistance encountered and the difficulties of assaulting enemy-held beaches. Omitting the first three divisions, all committed to action in the last weeks of the European War, and only lightly engaged, the mortality rates of Pacific divisions become even more obvious. Since Marine divisions generally took the toughest beaches, they tended to have the heaviest losses in the Pacific Theater.

The navy's ratio of killed to wounded was worse than that for either the army or the Marines. Almost half of navy losses were killed or died of wounds, 36,950 men and women, of approximately 75,000 casualties, 49.5%, a ratio of almost 1:1. The Coast Guard suffered 575 killed or dead of wounds, out of approximately 1,000 casualties, over 57%, a ratio of more than 1:1.

See also MARINE CORPS, US, DIVISIONS AND OTHER NOTABLE FORMATIONS; UNITED STATES ARMY, DIVISIONS.

Ref: *Army Battle Casualties and Nonbattle Deaths in World War II*; Stanton, *Order of Battle*.

DIVISIONS IN THE PACIFIC RANKED BY CASUALTIES

Rank	Division	Combat Deaths	Other Losses	Total	Ratio
1	1st Mar.	5,435	13,849	19,284	2.5
2	4th Mar.	3,317	13,006	16,323	3.9
3	2nd Mar.	2,729	8,753	11,482	3.2
4	7th Inf.	2,334	6,878	9,212	2.9
5	5th Mar.	2,113	6,450	8,563	3.1
6	96th Inf.	2,036	6,776	8,812	3.3
7	3rd Mar.	1,932	6,744	8,676	3.5
8	6th Mar.	1,637	6,590	8,227	4.0
9	77th Inf.	1,850	5,611	7,461	3.0
10	32nd Inf.	1,985	5,283	7,268	2.7
11	24th Inf.	1,689	5,323	7,012	3.2
12	27th Inf.	1,844	4,689	6,533	2.5
13	43rd Inf.	1,406	4,620	6,026	3.3
14	37th Inf.	1,344	4,616	5,960	3.4
15	25th Inf.	1,497	3,935	5,432	2.6
16	1st Cav.	970	3,085	4,055	3.2
17	Americal	1,157	2,893	4,050	2.5
18	41st Inf.	960	3,300	4,260	3.4
19	38th Inf.	784	2,680	3,464	3.4
20	40th Inf.	748	2,277	3,025	3.0
21	33rd Inf.	524	1,902	2,426	3.6
22	11th A/B	614	1,806	2,420	2.9
23	6th Inf.	514	1,856	2,370	3.6
24	81st Inf.	515	1,799	2,314	3.5
25	31st Inf.	414	1,319	1,733	3.2
26	93rd Inf.	17	116	133	6.8
27	98th Inf.	0	0	0	0.0

The figures under *Combat Dead* include only troops killed or mortally wounded in action. Those under *Other Losses* include men not mortally wounded, PRISONERS and non-combat deaths. *Ratio* is the number of other losses to combat dead. Note that these tables omit reference to the Regular Army's Philippine Division, and the divisions of the PHILIPPINE ARMY, which were largely destroyed in combat in 1941–42.

Casualties, Deaths, Medical Analysis of Mortal Wounds

There were apparently about 52,000 US Army combat deaths in the Pacific, exclusive of PHILIPPINE ARMY troops. During the Leyte Campaign personnel of the US Sixth Army conducted a survey of the causes of deaths among men who were mortally wounded. The results give some idea of the nature of the fighting, at least on Leyte.

Battle-weary leatherneck of the 22nd Regiment, returning aboard an attack transport after the assault on Eniwetok, late February 1944. Marine units in the Pacific incurred high casualty rates, a consequence of getting many of the toughest amphibious assignments.

CAUSES OF 519 MORTAL WOUNDS

Agent	Cases	Percent
Bayonet	1	0.19
Blast	2	0.39
Fragmentation	170	32.76
Gunshot	249	47.98
Other	97	18.69

Notes on the above chart: **Agent** = the type of weapon causing the death. **Bayonet** = the long knife carried by infantry, which can be fitted to the end of a rifle, but is sometimes used in combat as a knife, wielded by hand. **Blast** = wounds caused by the concussive effects of explosions. **Fragmentation** = wounds made by metal, rock, and other debris driven into the flesh by explosions. **Gunshot** = bullets from pistols, rifles, or machine guns. **Other** = includes wounds caused by multiple agents or undetermined agents, and by other causes, such as fire, drowning, and the collapse of buildings or bunkers (common in combat) when hit by shells or bombs.

DISTRIBUTION OF 249 MORTAL GUNSHOT WOUNDS

Area	Cases	Percent
Abdomen	66	26.5
Back	21	8.4
Buttocks	7	2.8
Chest	67	26.9
Extremities, Lower	18	7.2
Extremities, Upper	9	3.6
Head	49	19.7
Multiple	3	1.2
Unknown	9	3.6

DISTRIBUTION OF 170 MORTAL FRAGMENTATION WOUNDS

Area	Cases	Percent
Abdomen	25	14.7
Back	7	4.1
Buttocks	6	3.5
Chest	30	17.6
Extremities, Lower	37	21.8
Extremities, Upper	11	6.5
Head	33	19.4
Multiple	12	7.1
Unknown	9	5.3

It is probable that the nature and distribution of the wounds in other areas similar to Leyte more or less conformed to the patterns found there. Leyte is hilly and naturally forested, with some large, open agricultural land but few urban areas of note. In that regard it is more or less similar to most of the other islands in the Philippines, and even to NEW GUINEA, the SOLOMONS, and other nearby areas, such as BIAK or PELELIU, although these were even less urbanized. Were such statistics available for CORAL atolls, they would probably be somewhat different, due to the open nature of most such islands.

Figures for Japanese troops would show even greater difference. Fragmentation wounds would certainly be higher, as US forces were more plentifully supplied with artillery. In addition, burn wounds would be numerous enough to require a separate category, given US troops' use of flamethrowers, white phosphorus, and napalm.

Casualties, Disease and Other Causes of Non-effectiveness in Armies

At any moment during the war an average of 4.22% of US Army personnel were classified as "Non-effective," and most of those were non-combat related. Of nearly 18 million hospital admissions of army personnel during the war, 15 million were for disease and two million for non-combat-related injuries, while less than a million were combat related.

Chances of getting hurt by enemy action in the Pacific were much less than the risk of being laid low by disease or heat. Prior to the 20th century, all wars had seen more troops killed by disease than enemy weapons. In this century, weapons have become more lethal, and the tools to deal with disease more effective. But no one had fought a major war in the Pacific before, so all concerned received a rude shock when they confronted the unhealthy climate and abundance of tropical diseases.

Early in the war, before the full extent of tropical diseases was evident, Allied troops suffered up to a hundred (or more) disease and heat casualties for every combat casualty. Quickly realizing how serious the problem was, this ratio was reduced to 60 to 1 in 1944 and 40 to 1 by the end of the war. While most of these injuries were not fatal, they did put the affected soldiers out of action for days, weeks, or longer. Thus more personnel were needed in the tropics to do the same work performed in healthier climates. Moreover, the tropical diseases often had severe effects; many infected soldiers were discharged from the service to suffer the rest of their lives from diseases that are, to this day, incurable. Many of these infections are chronic and shorten victims' lives in the bargain. Many veterans of World War II still suffer from tropical bugs they picked up during their service in the tropics.

In Europe, which was a relatively "healthy" battlefield, the number of man-days lost to disease and non-combat injuries was roughly the same as that from combat injuries (which, while fewer, tended to cause greater damage, and required longer to recover from). In Europe during 1944–45 the army experienced the loss of 101,698,977 man-days due to non-effectiveness.

These figures include long periods of relative inactivity. During periods of intensive combat, battle injuries could soar dramatically. For example, during the approximately 55-day-long Normandy Campaign (from D-day to the end of July) about 80% of "non-effectives" among the British forces were the result of combat. In addition, relatively speaking, the ETO was a healthy theater, free of such interesting afflictions as jungle rot, elephantiasis, dengue fever, and other exciting tropical ailments.

In contrast, in the Pacific, combat caused less than 20% of the days lost. Don't be misled by the seemingly lower combat casualties in the Pacific. Other enemies were going after the troops out there, and the bugs and microbes were far more effective than the Japanese.

The most troublesome disease in the Pacific was malaria. This infection came in many varieties, some worse than others, all incurable. Fully half the US casualties in the Pacific were caused by malaria. Although not usually fatal, it was debilitating. At any given time during the war, three out of every thousand troops in the Pacific were out of action because of malaria; many more would have the disease but be able to function on some level. In some areas the disease was worse than in others. An attempt to build an airbase at NDENI in the SANTA CRUZ ISLANDS had to be abandoned due to malaria; at MILNE BAY, in New Guinea, the disease was only slightly less virulent, with an annual hospitalization rate of 2,236 cases per thousand men! Since sailors aboard ships on the high seas were safely away from the mosquitoes that carried the disease, and most rear area bases had exterminated the local mosquitoes, their rate of infection was much lower. But the combat units in the jungle were hit very

NON-EFFECTIVENESS IN THE ETO		
Cause	Lost Man Days	Percent
Battle Injury	49,726,067	48.9
Disease	37,533,605	36.9
Other	14,439,305	14.2

hard. Over 10% of the combat troops would be out of action because of malaria in good times, and in some places, like BURMA, close to half the men in a unit would be laid low.

Note that these figures do not tell the whole story, since they relate only to men sick enough to require hospitalization. Many men with mild cases of malaria and other ailments remained in the field. In contrast to their losses from disease, Commonwealth troops in the serpent-haunted jungles of Assam and Burma suffered only three men dead of snake bite for the whole war.

So serious was the danger from malaria that all troops in the South and southwest Pacific were given four hours of instruction in dealing with the disease, a program that appears to have had only marginal success. If the troops in malarial areas took their quinine medication daily, they had a much better chance of avoiding infection. But quinine was considered by many troops to be nearly as unpleasant as the disease, so many were not religious about taking it. Atabrine, essentially a stronger synthetic quinine, was more effective, but gave the skin a yellow tint and had a bad taste, reasons enough for the troops to be reluctant to use it, augmented by rumors that the stuff impaired virility. The most effective anti-malarial measure was the use of DDT to eliminate the mosquitoes. DDT has since been outlawed (because it is toxic to humans and other species when swallowed or absorbed through the skin), and the death and disability toll due to malaria has risen back to its normally high levels.

While malaria was the biggest health problem, there were plenty of others. One of the more obvious ones was heat. Most Pacific fighting was done in tropical conditions, and the summers were bru-

tal. In the first year or so of the war, before the troops were trained to deal with the heat, about one in six suffered from heat exhaustion and similar disabilities, and about 2% of those died. This fell hardest on the combat troops who, unlike their rear area brethren, could not always stop and cool down, or get prompt life-saving aid when heat problems laid them low.

The one bright spot in all this was that the horrendous tropical living conditions hurt the Japanese even more. While the Allies had numerous highly trained doctors and medics, as well as plentiful medical supplies, the Japanese were much less well off. This was first seen clearly during the 1942 battle for GUADALCANAL. American infantry battalions would lose about 25% of their strength to disease after three months in the jungle. Japanese battalions lost 50%. While the Americans improved their techniques for dealing with tropical diseases, the Japanese did not do so to the same degree. Were it not for the Japanese custom of not surrendering and fighting to the death, they would not have been able to hold out for as long as they did in the Pacific jungles.

While US practice was to get soldiers incapacitated (by wound or disease) back to a field hospital within hours, the Japanese often had no hospital to evacuate their injured troops to. Japanese soldiers were expected to grit their teeth and endure the pain of wounds or debility of disease. Japanese soldiers would literally lie down and die without complaint. As much as Allied troops despised the heat and the diseases, these afflictions turned out to be remarkably effective auxiliaries in the war against Japan.

The British experience in Burma, one of two candidates for the distinction of being the least healthy theater of operations (the other being New Guinea), is interesting in this regard. For every man evacuated to the rear by reason of wounds in 1943, there were 120 evacuated for non-battle-related conditions, mostly malaria and other even more gruesome tropical diseases, a figure that fell to 60 in 1944 due to aggressive preventive measures and the introduction of new medicines, and to 40 in 1945, still extraordinarily high.

HOSPITALIZATION RATE PER THOUSAND MEN COMMONWEALTH FORCES IN BURMA, 1944	
Disease	Rate
Diarrhea	84.9
Dysentery	92.5
Malaria	364.2
Unknown	151.6
Venereal	59.0

In the whole US Army is considered, including the several million troops who never left the United States or were stationed in other non-combat areas, the proportion of battle injuries as a cause of non-effectiveness drops to only 18%. In addition, the accident rate in the ZI, or Zone of the Interior (i.e., the 48 states), was extremely high. In 1943 alone fully 5,000 people were killed in military-related aviation accidents.

Ref: *ARMY BATTLE CASUALTIES AND NONBATTLE DEATHS IN WORLD WAR II*; Stone, *CRISIS FLEETING*.

Casualties, Proportions, Japanese and US Compared

During the war about 16% of the personnel of the Imperial Japanese Navy became casualties, as did some 20% of the men in the Imperial Army, and more than 30% of those in the Imperial Merchant Marine.

In contrast, only about 7% of the personnel in the US Army (including the Army Air Forces) became casualties, about 3% of naval personnel (including the Coast Guard), about 17% of Marine personnel, and less than 0.5% of American merchant mariners.

Cavalry

The general utility of the HORSE in warfare began to decline in the mid–19th century. The introduc-

tion of the rifle and then the machine gun made the use of horses on the battlefield highly dangerous. World War I, with its endless lines of trenches, doomed the cavalry as an effective tactical arm forever. But horses still soldiered on in a number of ways, most notably for transport purposes. Indeed, the horse made something of a comeback during World War II, albeit not in its traditional roles. So unexpected was this development that it caught most armies by surprise. This occurred in all theaters, including the Pacific.

The United States, which had six cavalry divisions on the eve of the war, four in the NATIONAL GUARD, committed some horse cavalry units to operations overseas. Although the National Guard cavalry divisions were inactivated, and the First Cavalry Division converted to infantry, the entire Second Cavalry Division, composed primarily of BLACK AMERICAN troops, served in North Africa in 1943–44, where it performed security and occupation duties until it was inactivated. In the Pacific, one of the first US units to go into action was the 26th Cavalry (PHILIPPINE SCOUTS), a partially horsed and partially mechanized unit stationed on Luzon in December 1941, which performed heroically during the retreat to BATAAN. The 112th Cavalry Regiment, Texas National Guard, served mounted for a time on NEW CALEDONIA until converted to infantry in May 1943, but the 124th Cavalry, also from Texas, which fought in Burma, continued to use horses for some duties in 1944–45.

The Soviet Union maintained thousands of horse troopers in the Far East throughout the war, the better to keep an eye on their Japanese counterparts across the border. Mongolia was a Soviet satellite at the time, and many Mongolian cavalrymen, direct descendants of the ancient "Mongol Horde," served throughout the war. Just before the war began, in 1939, there were several multi-division clashes between Japanese and Soviet forces on the Russo-Manchurian border that featured the extensive use of horse cavalry.

Japan began the war with several cavalry brigades in China, where it was also common for divisional reconnaissance regiments to be mounted. There was also a lot of horse cavalry in the Chinese collaborationist and MANCHUKUOAN armies. Japanese cavalry brigades were eventually mechanized, but the rest served mounted to the end of the war. Likewise, the Chinese Nationalists and communists both made extensive use of cavalry.

Although the British Army converted its cavalry regiments to mechanized reconnaissance units prior to World War II, the British Indian Army maintained some cavalry, which performed occupation duties in the Middle East, and went into action several times in MALAYA and Burma in 1942, not always with success. Even the US Navy used cavalry, SACO raising a regiment from local manpower in Inner Mongolia, while the Coast Guard, which used horse patrols to help guard East Coast beaches against the landing of German agents by submarine, was actually called upon to lend instructors in mounted patrolling to the Chinese Nationalists at the end of the war.

So the horse cavalry soldiered on with surprising effectiveness in an otherwise mechanized war.

Cavite

A small city (c. 35,000 inhabitants) on a peninsula jutting into Manila Bay, less than 10 miles southwest of Manila. The site of a naval base since Spanish times, Cavite was the principal US Navy installation in the Philippines, with extensive workshops and warehouses, though no major ship repair facilities. The base was heavily bombed by the Japanese on 12 December 1941, rendering it an almost complete loss. It was occupied by the Japanese at the end of December. US forces recaptured Cavite in February 1945.

CBI (China, Burma, India)

One of the more obscure theaters of World War II was "the CBI" (China-Burma-India). This was an area that was ignored for good reason, as there was little chance of anything happening here that would likely change the outcome of the war. Most of the crucial military action in the CBI was in Burma, which the Japanese invaded in early 1942. Throughout the war, fighting continued in this area, mainly because it was the "gateway to India." The British were concerned about Japan instigating further unrest in an already unstable India, especially if Japanese forces battled their way across the Indian border.

Burma also provided land access to China. The BURMA ROAD was the only way to get significant aid to Chinese troops within China. In 1942, the Japanese stopped just short of the Indian border, cutting the Burma Road. For the next three years, British, African, Indian, US and Chinese troops prosecuted a series of campaigns against dogged Japanese resistance. The CBI consumed Allied resources, but also tied up some first-line Japanese divisions.

The war in Burma began in January 1942, with a Japanese invasion of this British colony. The Japanese had two large, quite capable divisions to face two lower quality British divisions (containing a mix of British, Indian, and Burmese troops). The fighting proceeded slowly, the opposing forces being infantry units operating in jungle and rice paddy terrain. By April, the Japanese held the southern part of the country. The Chinese were alarmed at this development, as much Allied military aid to China came in over the Burma Road. This route went from Burmese ports via a long twisting road, over the mountains into southern China. The Nationalist Chinese sent two "armies" (each the size of a US corps) south along the Burma Road. About half of these troops were veterans, the rest less reliable, untrained soldiers. The Japanese responded by sending two more divisions into Burma and diverting troops from the retreating British toward the oncoming Chinese. This stopped the Chinese cold and sent them reeling back into China (most of the 95,000 troops were lost to desertion and sickness). The British were forced back into India, with the Japanese in possession of all of Burma.

The battles in Burma, like those in the rest of the Pacific Theater, were defined by the inhospitable terrain. Most of the subsequent fighting took place in the northern part of the country and that area was largely mountains and jungle. Disease and logistical difficulties were a constant problem for both sides.

For the rest of 1942, both sides rebuilt their forces and prepared to go on the offensive. The British got going first, and began advancing down the Burmese coast, in a region called the Arakan, during December. The Japanese fell back. By March 1943, the British attack had faltered, after

US Army truck convoys negotiating the road between Chen-Yi and Kweiyang, China, had to cope with an infamous series of 21 hairpin turns at Annan, shown here in a photograph taken March 26, 1945. Arguably the most important function of US forces in the CBI was maintaining the supply lines to China.

advancing some hundred miles down the Burmese coast. The Japanese, now reinforced, began their own attack. By May, the Japanese had recovered half of the lost coastline. Then came the monsoon rains, and combat had to slow down because of the nasty weather.

While the Japanese were pushing the British back up the Arakan coast, one of the more striking operations of the Burma war took place. Orde WINGATE, a British artillery officer, convinced his superiors that he could train British soldiers to operate in the jungle. Thus prepared, he would send groups of several hundred men each behind Japanese lines in order to attack rear area installations (particularly railroads). Wingate's troops were called CHINDITS after a mispronunciation of the Burmese word for "lion" (*chinthe*) and introduced a new form of warfare. Wingate wasn't just unleashing light infantry to terrorize the enemy rear area (an ancient tactic), he was using modern technology (radios to coordinate the raids and aircraft to supply them) to do the job in a more effective manner. While the Chindits caused the Japanese a lot of trouble, this was not of much assistance to the main British operations on the coast. There, the Japanese regained the initiative while the Chindits were rampaging through their rear area. But in the long run, the Chindits had a noticeable effect. The Japanese logistical arrangements were threadbare to begin with, and the operations of the Chindits (and later, the American MERRILL'S MARAUDERS) caused the Japanese supply situation to fail during later operations. This effect was a big help to the major British offensives. Lastly, there was the propaganda value of Allied troops going into the Japanese rear area.

Overall, 1943 did not go very well for the Allies. The Japanese were poised to invade India, and prospects of substantial reinforcements were meager. Throughout the year, however, the Chinese had been encouraged to renew operations in northern Burma. There, from the town of Ledo, a new road was being built into China, over which to carry military material. The Chinese had a vested interest in seeing the "Ledo Road" completed, thus they were enthusiastic about providing the troops to protect it from possible Japanese interference.

In 1944 the Burmese fighting developed into three different campaigns. In the north were the Chinese, fighting against Japanese efforts to disrupt work on the Ledo Road. On the coast, preparations went ahead for an Allied advance south, assisted by amphibious operations (if enough ships could be pried away from other theaters). In the center, the Japanese were getting ready to move into India, firmly believing that this would cause the Indian people to rise up in rebellion against the British. This was not entirely out of the question, but the British had been aware of the danger for several years and had made political moves (promising India independence after the war) to keep the peace. The battle in north Burma developed well for the Chinese throughout 1944. But in November they were forced to withdraw two divisions to deal with a major Japanese offensive in central China. Thus the Chinese were not able to inflict any decisive damage on the Japanese, although the Ledo Road remained secure. Farther south, the Japanese began an offensive in March that led to the sieges of Imphal and Kohima, just across the border in India. The Japanese logistical plan depended on the British retreating and leaving Allied supplies behind, but the British stayed and fought even when surrounded. Increased Allied airpower gave the Allies air superiority by mid-1944 and enabled isolated forces to be regularly resupplied by air. This was something the Japanese had not expected either. By the end of summer, the Japanese offensive collapsed. The lack of supplies led to enormous Japanese losses due to disease and starvation. Less than half their 65,000 dead were from combat causes.

Down along the coast, the fighting was desultory, with little progress being made by the Allies.

In early 1945, the Japanese paid for the desperate offensives they had launched in 1944. The Allies—mostly Indians—advanced on all fronts and by May were driving across all of Burma. RANGOON fell and the fighting became more a hunt for the many Japanese units that were still in the bush and unwilling to surrender. Looming behind all the ac-

tion in Burma, whose main purpose was to keep the Japanese out of India, was the war in China.

Cebu, Philippines

Although possessed of a decent small harbor, Cebu had only limited facilities to support shipping, and none at all to serve as a naval base, which would have been of marginal use anyway, given its location, virtually in the heart of the Philippine archipelago. On the eve of the war an attempt was made to turn the island's rugged interior into a "last-ditch" bastion, but little equipment had been stockpiled by the time the Japanese arrived, and the defenders surrendered upon the capitulation of CORREGIDOR. There was some Filipino GUERRILLA activity on Cebu during the war, and the island was liberated by elements of the Americal Division in March 1945.

Central Pacific Campaign

TARAWA, SAIPAN, GUAM, TINIAN, IWO JIMA, OKINAWA. The image most people have of the war in the Pacific is of amphibious assaults on these islands in the central Pacific. While the island assaults took place, they were not the centerpiece of the Pacific War. The Central Pacific Campaign didn't really get underway until late 1943. Until, and after that time, most of the fighting took place in the SOLOMONS then NEW GUINEA, on the road to the Philippines. Several of the epic island assaults weren't actually part of the central Pacific offensive but rather further stops on the road that went from New Guinea to the Philippines.

The campaign that began in New Guinea during early 1942 could have been the sole offensive that eventually would fight its way north to the islands just south of Japan. From bases there, the B-29s could (and ultimately did) fly north to hit Japan's cities. But the American warship building program had begun only in 1940 and would not begin to fill the fleet with new ships until 1943. By 1944 the fleet would be much larger than anything the Japanese could muster. The naval battles in

1942, particularly at MIDWAY and in defense of GUADALCANAL, had crippled Japanese carrier power and made the enemy vulnerable to an American naval offensive. So it was decided that, rather than risk all these new US carriers in the New Guinea area (where the Japanese had substantial land-based aircraft), a second offensive would be launched across the vast central Pacific.

To a certain extent, this second offensive was suggested by the admirals so that the navy could play a major, and singular, role in the Pacific fighting. In New Guinea, General MACARTHUR was capable of advancing north with minimal navy support. The army actually made more amphibious landings than the navy's Marines in the Pacific. The army also had ample land-based aircraft (and effective tactics for attacking enemy ships) as well as a lot of shipping under its control.

MacArthur suggested that all resources be devoted to his drive north to the Philippines and Japan itself. He felt that a navy offensive through the central Pacific would delay the taking of FORMOSA and the isolation of Japan from its vital oil supplies to the south. MacArthur also made the point, later proven to be true, that the amphibious assaults in the central Pacific would be far bloodier than the ones he was undertaking in the larger, and less widely scattered, island groups between Australia and the Philippines.

The navy won the argument. MacArthur eventually did make it to the Philippines, and Japan lost access to its oil not because Formosa was taken (it wasn't) but because USN subs sank most of Japan's oil tankers by 1944.

The Central Pacific Campaign did ensure that the remaining Japanese fleet, which included a lot of battleships and smaller warships, as well as thousands of aircraft, was tied up in the central Pacific and not sent south to oppose MacArthur. The USN offensive also stretched Japanese resources so thin that they were weaker everywhere and thus speeded up the destruction of Japanese military power. We'll never know if MacArthur's STRATEGY would have been more effective, but the dual offensive approach did annihilate Japanese military power in the Pacific.

All of the central Pacific invasions were undertaken over unprecedented distances. The troops embarked thousands of miles away in places like HAWAII, the west coast of the United States, and the Solomons. The invasion fleets stayed at sea for months at a time, supplied by hundreds of tankers and freighters. While the fighting was usually over in less than a month, CASUALTIES were high and the divisions involved were sent back to their bases for rest, retraining, and replacements. Then these divisions went out for yet another invasion. These divisions, with their usual specialist units for amphibious operations, numbered 15,000–20,000 men.

In 11 months, the US Navy advanced 4,200 (statute) miles, from Hawaii to Peleliu. This was unheard of in military history. The advance averaged nearly 400 miles a month. The first jump, from Hawaii to the GILBERTS, took US forces 1,600 miles from Hawaii. The next advance, to the MARSHALLS, increased the distance to 2,400 miles. The third operation, to the MARIANAS, was 3,700 miles from Hawaii. The final leg, to the PALAUS, part of the CAROLINES, completed the drive, some 4,200 miles from where it began 11 months earlier. By way of comparison, the distance from New Guinea to the Philippines was only some 2,000 miles. And while it was only 4,000 miles from Hawaii to Tokyo, there were no islands along that northern Pacific route. The islands were the key, as they provided unsinkable aircraft carriers and land bases to support the fleet. The central Pacific offensive got started in November 1943 when the Second Marine Division and the army's 27th Infantry Division stormed Tarawa and MAKIN islands in the Gilberts. These atolls (little island groups created by CORAL) were the closest to Allied-held territory and would provide air and naval bases for further advances. Tarawa was controlled by the Japanese Navy and garrisoned by naval infantry (SNLF) troops. Tarawa itself contained only two battalions of combat troops, the rest of the personnel belonged to various support units. This was typical of

Supported by rifle-toting comrades, a soldier of the Seventh Infantry Division uses a flamethrower against Japanese fortifications on Kwajalein, February 4, 1944.

the Japanese island garrisons, although the many support troops could be just as lethal as trained infantrymen when armed with a rifle and secure in a bunker. All Japanese troops would fight to the death no matter what their military specialty.

Tarawa set the tone for future operations. The Japanese would not surrender, so all but 146 of the 4,836-man garrison died. The United States suffered 3,300 CASUALTIES (including 900 dead). Tarawa was the first of the classic "island assaults" of the Pacific War. Much went wrong and it was a bloody lesson for the Marines, who changed tactics and techniques before undertaking their next invasion.

The next phase of the central Pacific drive came two months later. In January 1944, the Marshall

Islands, several hundred miles north of the Gilberts (KWAJALEIN and two smaller atolls), were attacked by the Fourth Marine Division and the army's Seventh Infantry Division. The Japanese garrison of some 10,000 men was wiped out, with the Americans suffering 1,700 casualties. The Japanese learned some lessons from the loss of Tarawa, but this next assault came so quickly that there was not sufficient time to radically change the existing defenses in the Marshalls. Not only were the Americans faster in making this next attack, but they were also able to incorporate lessons from Tarawa. These landings in the Marshalls went much more smoothly.

So successful were the Marshall Islands operations that it was decided to go straight for the Mariana Islands. MacArthur still urged that all available resources be directed toward the liberation of the Philippines. But continuing US carrier raids on the main Japanese fleet base of TRUK (in the Carolines) had been so devastating to enemy air and naval forces in the area that it appeared Truk could be bypassed. Moreover, the army's new B-29 bomber was entering mass PRODUCTION and bases in the Marianas were needed for the bombing of Japan to begin.

In June and July 1944, the Marianas Islands (Guam, Saipan, and Tinian, and their 50,000-man garrison, several hundred miles northeast of the main Japanese fleet base of Truk) were invaded by the Second, Third, and Fourth Marine Divisions, a Marine brigade, and the army's 27th and 77th Infantry Divisions.

This was the largest transoceanic invasion ever launched. The 105,000 assault troops were supported by 29 carriers of various kinds (carrying 891 aircraft), 14 battleships, 25 cruisers, and 152 destroyers plus hundreds of freighters, tankers, and amphibious ships. The Marianas were truly in the middle of nowhere and the US armada gathered from as far away as the west coast of North America and the east coast of Australia.

As usual, nearly all Japanese fought to the death and the struggle went on into August. Nearly 23,000 Americans became casualties. The Japanese Army was in charge of defending the Marianas, and they deployed four infantry divisions to the defense of Guam, Saipan, and Tinian. More troops were on the way, but US SUBMARINES were intercepting many of these reinforcement convoys. Meanwhile the Japanese could not ignore MacArthur's steady progress from Allied bases in eastern New Guinea. The Allied capture of western New Guinea would endanger Japan's oil supplies. Thus, just before the American invasion fleet appeared in the Marianas, Japan had sent off aircraft and ships to deal with MacArthur, unaware that the US fleet was fast approaching the Marianas. As a result, the Japanese got beaten by MacArthur in the south and by the US fleet in the Marianas. The defeat in the Mari-

anas was made more catastrophic by the Japanese decision to offer battle with their rebuilt carrier fleet. This resulted in the GREAT MARIANAS TUR-KEY SHOOT (Battle of the PHILIPPINE SEA) as more experienced and better trained US pilots chopped their Japanese counterparts to pieces. The Japanese not only lost the Marianas, they also saw their fleet reduced to near impotence. During the summer of 1944, MacArthur gained control of western New Guinea and began moving north to take island bases within aircraft range of the Philippines. With the Marianas now in American hands, MacArthur urged an immediate drive on the Philippines.

Earlier in the year it had been agreed that the Palau Islands would be taken in the fall to provide further airbases and to complete the encirclement of the Japanese base at TRUK. Some navy commanders urged that Palau be bypassed and all resources put into the Philippines assault. But prudence took precedence and a slightly scaled back Palau operation went forward while the Philippines invasion was moved up to October 1944.

In September, Peleliu Island (in the Palaus, a thousand miles west of Truk) was assaulted by the First Marine Division and the army's 81st Infantry Division. The 10,500 Japanese were well fortified and turned the battle into something nearly as bloody as TARAWA, with 10,000 Americans becoming casualties. In hindsight, the Peleliu attack could have been dropped. The Japanese threat in the area was not nearly as powerful as was thought at the time. But that's hindsight. At the time, Peleliu seemed necessary and so the assault went forward.

These operations in the Gilberts, Marshalls, Marianas, and Palaus completed the encirclement, and neutralization of, the main Japanese naval base at Truk. Now surrounded by US-held islands (crammed with bombers and fighters) the Japanese were forced to withdraw their fleet from Truk. This, in turn, made it easier for MacArthur's forces coming up from the south to invade the Philippines during November of 1944.

Peleliu was also, in effect, the end of the central Pacific offensive. For shortly after Peleliu, Mac-

Arthur invaded the Philippines and the two separate offensives merged. The next island assaults to the north were, for all practical purposes, the combined American offensive toward Japan.

By early 1945, the Philippines were pretty much under Allied control, although thousands of Japanese fought on in jungles and mountains, while several hundred thousand more were isolated in places like RABAUL and the Caroline Islands (especially Truk). Meanwhile, B-29 bombers were operating from the Marianas and systematically burning down Japan's urban areas.

The remaining island assaults were for the purpose of providing forward bases for land-based aircraft and the late 1945 invasion of Japan itself.

In February 1945, the Third, Fourth, and Fifth Marine Divisions attacked Iwo Jima. This small, volcanic island just south of the Japanese Home Islands was an important part of the Japanese defense system against B-29 raids. In American hands, it would provide an emergency airfield for damaged or crippled aircraft (the B-29 had a lot of engine trouble) returning from raids. Some 20,000 Japanese were dug in to resist an invasion. A third of the invading American force was killed or wounded (23,000 troops) in five weeks of fighting to secure the island.

In April 1945, the First, Second, and Sixth Marine Divisions and the army's 27th, 7th, 77th, and 96th Infantry Divisions attacked Okinawa and some smaller outlying islands. The island, considered by the Japanese as a part of Japan, was garrisoned by 110,000 troops, including many recently conscripted Okinawans. The fighting was the toughest yet seen in the Pacific. The island was not conquered until the end of June. Nearly 110,000 Japanese troops were killed on Okinawa, plus possibly as many civilians. It was somewhat encouraging to note that 7,000 Japanese surrendered, but many of these were recently conscripted civilians. Thousands of civilians committed suicide rather than be "conquered." America suffered a record number of combat deaths (12,281, including 4,907 navy). Over 50,000 Americans were wounded.

There were also over 14,000 combat fatigue casualties and nearly 30,000 non-combat casualties. It was a rough campaign. During the protracted ground fighting on Okinawa, the Japanese made heavy use of KAMIKAZE suicide aircraft, losing over 1,900 of them (plus 2,300 other aircraft) in attacks against the fleet. There were 36 Allied ships sunk (26 by kamikaze) and 368 damaged (164 by kamikaze).

The stubborn and bloody resistance at Okinawa gave rise to the very real fears that it would be repeated if the Allies had to proceed with their invasion of the Japanese Home Islands. The ATOMIC BOMBS, and the Soviet invasion of MANCHURIA in August, caused the Japanese to surrender before the planned amphibious invasion came off.

The invasion of Japan itself, scheduled for November 1, never happened, leaving Okinawa as the last major amphibious operation of the war. The central Pacific offensive lasted only 11 months (from Tarawa in November 1943, to Peleliu in September 1944). Most of the amphibious operations in the Pacific were launched by MacArthur's American, Australian, and New Zealand army troops rather than Marines. But the boldest and bloodiest island assaults were carried off by the Marines during the 11-month central Pacific offensive. The audacity and ferocity of these amphibious operations made an impression on the American memory of the Pacific War far more than the less glamorous island-hopping and years of jungle fighting endured by MacArthur's army troops.

Ceylon

A large (c. 25,000 square miles) tear-shaped island just southeast of India and well sited for a major base to dominate the Bay of Bengal. By 1942 the British had done little to develop Ceylon, and it was extremely exposed to Japanese attack, as was demonstrated in the spring of that year. Now known as Sri Lanka, for most of the war light naval and air forces were based there to patrol the Bay of

Bengal and Indian Ocean, and keep an eye on Japanese forces in the ANDAMAN and NICOBAR Islands.

Changsha, China

Although very far from the sea, Changsha was at the head of navigation for small oceangoing vessels, and had surprisingly extensive port facilities, although only a limited capacity to service ships. It was an important regional center, and was stoutly defended by the Chinese, 1939–1941.

See also, CHINA, ARMIES.

Chefoo, China

An important coastal city, Chefoo had some port facilities and a small airfield, and was the administrative center for the surrounding region.

Chemulpo/Inchon, Korea

The port of Seoul (which was some miles up the Han River), the principal city of Korea (called Chosen by the Japanese), Chemulpo (the Japanese name for Inchon) was of only limited importance. Plagued by unusually severe tides, it was very unsuited for use as a naval base.

Chennault, Claire Lee (1890–1958)

Claire Chennault was a teacher in Texas when he joined the army by way of a reserve officers' training camp in 1917, soon becoming a pilot and flight instructor. He passed to the Regular Army in 1920 and remained in the Air Corps, becoming an outspoken advocate of fighter aircraft and something of a critic of the bomber-ring that dominated the Air Corps. He was retired in 1937, ostensibly for deafness (a common problem among open-cockpit pilots). Invited by CHIANG KAI-SHEK to reorganize the Chinese Republican Air Force and establish an air defense system, Chennault proved surprisingly successful, creating an effective system of air observers (using telephones) to provide early warning of Japanese bomber raids. In 1940 he came to the

United States to recruit the American Volunteer Group (AVG) and returned to China in 1941 with new pilots and aircraft for the Chinese. Most of these were still being trained in Burma in early December, and it was there that the FLYING TIGERS got their baptism of fire. Quickly moving into China, the AVG was soon made a part of the US Army Air Corps, as was Chennault, who was promoted to general rank. The AVG became the 14th Air Force and Chennault remained its commander for the rest of the war. It is widely believed that the general personally shot down over 40 Japanese aircraft during his many years in China, but he never formally claimed any such victories.

Chennault was an excellent organizer and commander of air forces, but as a member of the "air power can do everything" school, he greatly exaggerated the effectiveness of his forces (at one point he claimed that with fewer than 50 medium and heavy bombers he could defeat Japan). His obsession with air power led him to denigrate STILWELL's efforts to create an effective Chinese ground force. Although he possessed considerable influence with Chiang Kai-Shek, he made no effort to support Stilwell's proposals for the reorganization of the Chinese Army. In fact, the two men cordially despised each other.

The general's son Jack commanded a fighter squadron in the ALEUTIANS for much of the war, which used the distinctive "Tiger's Grin" insignia of the 14th Air Force.

Chiang Kai-shek (1887–1975)

Born into a comfortable middle-class family and given a classical Chinese education, Chiang, who became a Methodist, studied at a Chinese military academy 1906–07 before attending the Japanese academy from 1907 to 1911 (Japan being the model on which many Chinese nationalists wished to reform their own country), graduating and receiving a commission. On the outbreak of the Chinese Revolution in October 1911 he deserted from the Japanese Army to return home, where he shortly put himself at the head of the revolutionary movement in his native Chekiang. Over the next dozen years he was in or out of power, generally struggling against reactionary forces, and usually supportive of Sun Yat-sen, his brother-in-law. In 1923 he joined Sun's KUOMINTANG Party, became a major general, and spent some time studying at the Frunze Academy in Russia. Head of the famous WHAMPOA MILITARY ACADEMY (1923–25), he also helped reform the KMT army, with Soviet assistance, and commanded the Northern Expedition, 1925–27, with the goal of bringing northern China under Republican control. In July 1927 Chiang broke with the USSR and defeated the Chinese communists, but shortly resigned to permit the KMT to try a more conciliatory approach in establishing a single regime. Back in power in 1928, as chairman of the KMT executive committee and commander-in-chief, he resumed the Northern Expedition, capturing Peking. Over the next few years he tried to centralize control with only moderate success, since warlords and communists controlled large areas.

From 1930 through 1934 he undertook five campaigns to eliminate the communists, with only moderate success. With the rising threat of Japanese aggression, strongly nationalist elements in the KMT forced him to conclude an alliance with the communists (by kidnapping him, in the famous Sian Incident), which was more or less maintained, if chillingly, through to nearly the end of World War II.

With open Japanese invasion in 1937, Chiang led the Chinese armies with little skill but occasional success, greatly protracting the war. More adept at politics and diplomacy, Chiang was able to gain US sympathy and some aid for the Chinese cause, which was one factor in the rising tensions between Japan and America. The US entry into the war was of considerable help to Chiang, as American aid increased. Although Nationalist Chinese armies conducted operations against the Japanese, particularly in Burma, the war tended to be one of stalemate, punctuated by occasional Japanese advances (ICHI GO and "rice" offensives), as both Chiang and the communists conserved their resources for the future.

The surrender of Japan briefly put Chiang, who had assumed the presidency of China in 1943, in control of most of China, but the resumption of civil war with the communists proved his undoing. Unable to resolve the political and social problems of the Chinese people, or to root out corruption in his army, he was gradually driven out of China, and by 1949 had retreated to FORMOSA (Taiwan), where he remained in power until his death in 1975 at age 87.

Despite his numerous shortcomings, it is difficult to see who would have been better able to lead China through the war.

See also CHIANG KAI-SHEK, MADAME.

Chiang Kai-shek, Madame (1899–   )

Born Mayling Soong, one of six children of Charles Soong, a prosperous Chinese American, Mme. Chiang was an important asset to her husband. A Christian, and fluent in several languages, she was not only politically astute, but her family connections also greatly furthered his career. Her eldest sister Cingling was married to Sun Yat-sen, and was later a high official in the Chinese Communist Party. Her second sister, Ailing, had served for a time as Sun's secretary before going on to marry the financier H. H. Kung. Ailing and her husband did very well in business, both in China and the United States, and he served for a time as finance minister of China. All three of her brothers became very wealthy in banking and finance, in both China and the United States, and one of them, T. V. Soong, had served variously as a diplomat, foreign minister, and prime minister. Talented and attractive, Mme. Chiang greatly influenced American views on the KMT movement, suggesting, with help from the powerful Luce family (owners of *Time*, *Life*, and *Fortune*), that it was a modernizing, democratic force. She left Taiwan not long after her husband's death and went to live in America, where she still resides at the time of this writing, in 1997.

China

See also CHIANG KAI-SHEK.
Ref: Seagrave, *The Soong Dynasty*.

China

The most populous country in the world, with some 400 million people, China was poor, disorganized, and weak. The poverty stemmed from a variety of causes, most notably an inability to establish a stable political regime following the collapse of the Qing Dynasty and the establishment of a republic in 1911. The KUOMINTANG Party, which attained power in central China by the mid–1920s, undertook a program of unification and modernization, but was stymied in its efforts by the problem of overcoming local warlords and a very strong communist opposition. Nevertheless, by the mid–1930s the country was more united than it had been at any time over the previous quarter-century. The Japanese invasion of 1937 led to a temporary reconciliation of the Kuomintang regime with the Chinese communists, but this was too little, too late. China was barely able to survive being overwhelmed by the Japanese, at an enormous human cost.

The war did much to discredit the leadership of CHIANG KAI-SHEK and strengthen the image of the communists as a coherent, patriotic force, which ultimately led to the triumph of the communists in the Civil War of 1945–49.

Ref: Ch'i, *Nationalist China at War*; Eastman, "Nationalist China during the Sino-Japanese War, 1937–1945"; Iriye, Akira, "Japanese Aggression and China's International Position, 1931–1945."

China, Air Force

During the 1930s the KMT regime had attempted to build up an air force with only mixed results. Training missions were arranged from several different countries, aircraft were procured on a rather disorganized basis (not many of them, either), and the personnel selected for aviation training were not always the best. The Japanese invasion in 1937 effectively smashed this tiny air force, and the Chinese were never able to recover.

Chinese pilots were initially of only mediocre quality. The sons of prominent KMT officials and warlords were qualified as pilots, no matter how inept they were. However, some Chinese pilots were very good, and there were some good volunteer pilots as well. Although American pilots with the Chinese Air Force received the greatest attention, the largest contingent of foreign "volunteers" came from the Soviet Union. Between 1937 and 1939, when the Russians cut off aid to the Nationalists, some 2,000 Red Air Force pilots served with the Chinese Air Force. Russia also supplied about a thousand aircraft, including many I-15 and I-16 fighters, and about 500 other military advisers, for a total aid package estimated at about $250 million.

Claire CHENNAULT's American Volunteer Group began operating in late 1941, after PEARL HARBOR. It gave the Chinese Air Force a much needed boost. And as time passed Chinese pilots, and even whole squadrons and AIR GROUPS, were trained in the United States, to American standards. Meanwhile, increasingly modern equipment was made available. Thus, as the war went on the Chinese Air Force became more proficient.

In 1937 Chinese pilots were flying Gloucester Gladiators, Hawk 3s, and I-15s, but by 1945 they were flying P-51s, which were more than a match for their Japanese opponents, and B-25s, albeit not in great numbers.

AIRCRAFT AVAILABLE	
1937	305
1939	135
1940	215
1941	364
1942	337
1943	c. 200
1944	na
1945	na

Figures are mostly as of December 31. That for 1937 is as of the Japanese invasion; 1943 includes only operational aircraft.

China, Armies

There was no single Chinese Army. There were actually several: CHIANG KAI-SHEK's Kuomintang (KMT) Nationalist Army, sometimes called the "Central Army," various warlord armies, the Communist Party's army, and even an army of Chinese serving the Japanese. Quality varied tremendously. At their best, some Chinese units were able to stand up to and slug it out with Japanese units of comparable size, for example, several of the Nationalist divisions sent into Burma in early 1942. However, in most of the army, equipment was always scarce, training often nonexistent, morale abysmal, rations in short supply, leadership a joke, and corruption the order of the day, which last was most responsible for the other problems.

The problems of the KMT army ran deep. The country was poor and politically fragmented, its leadership inadequate, and its armed forces undisciplined, poorly equipped, overly numerous, and suffered from low morale. Nevertheless, in the early 1920s the KMT had begun a serious effort to build a disciplined, modern force. Making effective use of Soviet advisers and aid, the central army—the forces directly under KMT control—had gotten off to a good start by the late 1920s, when Chiang Kai-shek undertook the "Northern Expedition," to wrest control of northern China and MANCHURIA from the warlords, and the "Bandit Suppression Campaign," to crush the communists. Both undertakings proceeded with considerable success. Beginning in 1928 the Nationalist government had secured the services of a German military mission, headed by the brilliant organizer General Hans von Seekt, who was later succeeded by Alexander von Falkenhausen. The German mission did excellent work, for the 380,000 troops that it was able to train. Of these, about 80,000 were more or less directly under German control, and even partially armed with German equipment (even to the famous "coal scuttle" HELMETS). However, these forces comprised only 31 of the Chinese Army's 176 divisions—those directly controlled by Chiang Kai-shek and the KMT. The other 145 divisions belonged to more than a dozen different regional warlords and the communists, all of whom had managed to take advantage of the increasing tensions with the Japanese in the period from 1931 to 1935 to avoid being overwhelmed by the central government. While some of the warlord armies and the communist forces were fairly effective, others were not. Then the CHINA INCIDENT began, in 1937, when Japanese forces invaded China from their colonial territories in Manchuria.

Chiang committed the cream of his forces to the defense of SHANGHAI, in August-November 1937. He gathered some 71 divisions (c. 460,000 men), composed of his own units, forces he could pry loose from the warlords, and newly raised formations. The best unit in the army, the German-trained 88th Division, successfully held up the 200,000 Japanese attackers for weeks, although in the process it was ground to pieces. Interestingly, the first German soldier to die in World War II was a Lt von Schmeling, killed commanding a battalion in this division. The fall of Shanghai (in which the Chinese lost about 270,000 men, against Japanese CASUALTIES of about 40,000) led to a protracted struggle for Nanking (November-December 1937), which led to yet another for Wuhan (January-April 1938). The ultimate Chinese success in halting the Japanese at the Battle of Taierchuang, in March 1938 (see JAPAN, FIRST DEFEAT), could not compensate for the damage done to the Chinese armies; losses in these three campaigns amounted to between 400,000 and 500,000 men, including about 60% of the German-trained troops, among them over 10,000 of the best officers.

Through 1938 and into 1939 the Chinese cobbled together a shaky united political front against the Japanese, and expanded their army enormously. By October 1939, when the Japanese were beaten off from CHANGSHA, the Chinese Army had 308 divisions. But only 82 of these had eight months or more of training, while the Japanese had 25 divisions and 20 separate brigades in China at the time, and were regularly rotating tired formations back home and bringing in fresh ones. Moreover, Chinese units were always desperately short of equipment: By 1939 most divisions had only about half of their proper allotments of arms and equipment. And casualties were horrendous.

Battle losses of course created an ongoing manpower drain. But they were by no means the only cause of the Chinese Army's problems. Manpower management was disastrous. From 1937 through 1945 some 14 million men were drafted in China. But about 75% were lost even before they completed training. Disease was a big problem. Inadequate food, clothing, and shelter (often caused by grafting generals) were major contributing factors to losses from disease. Poor medical care made matters worse. In 1937 there were only 8,000 medical officers in the army, of whom only 2,000 were proper physicians, the rest being essentially first-aid technicians. Nor did the number of medical personnel increase very much, in proportion to the size of the army. Many men merely deserted, fleeing to the hills and often resorting to banditry. So the Chinese Army had to fight most of its battles with inadequate numbers of poorly trained troops, who tended to get killed before they could acquire much experience.

The loss of officers in the 1937–38 battles was particularly serious. There were only about 90,000 officers in the army in 1937, and the loss of over 10% of them in less than a year was a blow from which the Chinese Army never fully recovered. The prewar officer corps had been quite well trained, at least in the company grades. Since the mid–1920s, the WHAMPOA MILITARY ACADEMY (later reorganized as the Central Military Academy) had produced about 3,000 good junior officers each year. A further 176 army cadets—and a handful from the air force and navy as well—had been sent each year to various foreign military schools, notably in Germany (where Chiang Kai-shek sent his favorite son, Chiang Wei-kuo, during the mid–1930s), but also in Britain, the United States, and for a time even in the Soviet Union. In addition, the German military mission had created a number of effective officer training programs, a university reserve officer training corps had been established, and even a staff college, which had graduated about 2,000 officers by 1937. Even relatively poor officers generally led by example, since it was often the only way they could get their forces to fight. As a result, officers tended to be killed off in great numbers. A Japanese estimate put the Chinese annual loss of officers at 54,000. Since the Chinese Army was producing only about that many new officers each year (42,000–43,000 graduates of officer training programs, plus about 12,000 men commissioned directly from the ranks), the leadership shortage only got worse as the war dragged on. In 1937 an average of 80% of the 16–20 officers in each infantry battalion were academy graduates, a figure that fell to 10% by 1945. Meanwhile the army kept expanding, and the proportion of officers to enlisted men fell. In 1937 the army had 2.2 million men (1.7 million active troops plus 0.5 million reservists) with about 90,000 officers, a ratio of about 24 men to one officer; by 1945 the army numbered about five million men, with only about 180,000 officers, a ratio of about 28 to 1, and these officers were much less well trained than those of 1937.

Higher-level Chinese officers tended to be even less well-trained than junior officers, even those trained during the war. Many of the field grade and general officers had received most of their training

CHINESE ARMY COMBAT LOSSES, WORLD WAR II		
Year	Chinese Official Figure	Japanese Estimated Figure
	(Numbers in Thousands)	
1937	367.4	NA
1938	735.0	823.2
1939	346.5	395.2
1940	661.9	847.0
1941	299.5	708.0
1942	247.2	NA
1943	162.9	NA
1944	210.7	NA
1945	168.9	NA
Total	3,200.0	NA

NA = not available

on the job during the revolutionary and civil wars of 1911–31. Then, too, many of the most senior officers owed their positions to their political influence rather than their military skills. Many of the political generals were corrupt. The administrative apparatus of the Chinese Army was rudimentary, senior officers were generally given lump sums, which they were supposed to disburse for rations, pay, and other expenses. A lot of the money simply disappeared. Nevertheless, there were a number of excellent Chinese generals. Probably the best of the lot was Hseuh Yueh, who successfully defended Changsha against three Japanese attempts in 1939–41, and did a good job of holding Hengyung in June-August 1944, during ICHI GO. Tai An-lan, who organized, trained, and commanded the 200th Division, was another capable commander, who died at the head of his division in Burma in 1942, a not unusual fate for a Chinese general. In fact, China appears to have lost more generals in combat during World War II than any other combatant, apparently several hundred.

Ultimately, it was a combination of stubborn, if usually unskilled Chinese resistance, plus the vastness of the country and Japanese logistical limitations that prevented the emperor's forces from overrunning China.

The advent of LEND-LEASE, once the United States was in the war, brought about a concerted effort to strengthen the Chinese Army. But it was not particularly successful. Desperately trying to keep together a feeble coalition, Chiang had to carefully allocate the arms and equipment that did reach China, through Burma until the Japanese overran that country in early 1942, and then over the HUMP from India until the reopening of the BURMA ROAD. This was one reason for the oft-repeated charges that Chiang was hoarding new equipment toward that day when he would have a showdown with the communists. In fact, while he was trying to keep some of it on the side, a lot of new equipment tended to be spread thinly throughout the army so that every warlord received his "fair share," a practice that did little for combat efficiency. Some contingents in the army used these supplies wisely, while others did not. Moreover, the Chinese purchasing missions tended to request the most modern and impressive equipment, rather than equipment that was better suited to use by Chinese troops, who tended to be technologically unsophisticated. China, which lacked an infrastructure suitable to the employment and maintenance of much modern equipment, had a much harder time maintaining high-tech gear. The Chinese made repeated attempts to procure medium TANKS, despite the fact that there were few bridges in China capable of bearing their weight. The American entry into the war did lead to some improvement in the Chinese Army, but by no means as much as might have been expected. Given the political situation in China, however, it's unlikely that much more could have been done.

A number of attempts were made to remedy this situation, particularly after America's LG Joseph STILWELL became Chiang's chief-of-staff (one of several "hats" Stilwell wore) in 1942. Stilwell developed several plans to reorganize the Chinese Army. The simplest was based on the fact that although the army had literally hundreds of divisions, most of them were woefully understrength—often with no more than 3,500 men—and very poorly equipped. Stilwell proposed abolishing most of the divisions, regrouping the manpower and equipment into 60 full-sized formations, plus army and corps service and support troops. This was not practical given the political realities of wartime China. Chiang could not afford to alienate so many warlords. Chinese generals who felt that they had suffered insults at the hands of the government had more than once taken their troops over to the enemy. In fact, between 1937 and 1945 apparently as many as a hundred Chinese generals and warlords went over to the Japanese, bringing with them some 500,000 troops. So Stilwell came up with an elaborate plan to raise a Chinese Army in India (it being cheaper to fly the men to India to be armed, equipped, trained, and maintained, than to fly everything over the Hump to China), providing them with modern organization and equipment, and then fly them over the Himalayas to form the striking force of the KMT armies. This was done, albeit not to the extent planned. Ultimately there were supposed to be 30 such divisions raised in several increments, with 30 more to follow, but less than 10 were formed in this way. When tested in action, the new units proved excellent. But they were rarely used properly.

The Chinese Communist Army was created from the survivors of the famous "Long March." Under almost constant pressure from the Nationalists during the mid–1930s, by 1937 there were only about 80,000 men in the Chinese communist forces in Shansi in northern China, about 40% of whom were militiamen, and perhaps 12,000 in Fukien and Kiangsi, most of whom were militia. When the China Incident began, Chiang Kai-shek was forced by some of his subordinates to adopt a "united front" against the Japanese. As a result, the Chinese communist forces in Shansi were reorganized as the Eighth Route Army, under Chu Teh, while those in Fukien and Kiangsi became the New Fourth Army under Yeh T'ing. A period of considerable growth began.

Chinese communist forces were generally of good quality, although GUERRILLA forces often did not cooperate with higher headquarters. Chinese communist leaders concentrated on building up their forces during the war, acutely aware that sooner or later there would be a reckoning with Chiang and the KMT. Clashes between communist and Nationalist forces occurred several times during the war. The most notable incident occurred in February 1941, when the New Fourth Army was roughly handled by Nationalist forces. However, an open break was avoided until after the surrender of Japan. Although their propaganda asserted that 84% of the Japanese Army in China was committed against them, in fact the communists and Japanese were never continuously engaged against each other, and in 1944 the two groups actually concluded an informal truce so that the Japanese could concentrate forces for the Ichi Go offensive. As a result, the quality of Chinese communist forces tended to increase as the war went on, while Nationalist forces did the bulk of the fighting and took the bulk of the losses. The surrender of the Japanese provided an enormous boost to the Chinese communists, who acquired large stocks of equipment, to which was subsequently added the equipment that the Soviets captured in Manchuria. This left them in an excellent position when full-scale civil war broke out anew in 1946.

Ultimately, neither the Nationalists nor the communists were as much interested in fighting the Japanese (who they realized were going to lose the war in the Pacific to the Americans regardless of what was accomplished in China) as in getting ready to fight each other. While the Nationalists always had half a dozen or so excellent divisions available, these units constituted their strategic reserve. The Allies constantly demanded that these units be sent south into Burma. But the Nationalists knew that they would need these units to ward off any sudden moves by the Japanese or communists. This was at the heart of the argument over what the Chinese army should be doing. The Allies wanted help in Burma, the Nationalists and communists wanted to fight each other. The Japanese were content to leave all Chinese troops alone most of the time.

Arguably, had the Chinese leadership provided more effective direction in the war against Japan, they might have been able to affect the outcome, as Japan ultimately used her enormous armies in

GROWTH OF CHINESE COMMUNIST FORCES (THOUSANDS OF TROOPS)

Year	Eighth Route Army	New Fourth Army	Total CCF
1937	80	12	92
1938	157	25	181
1939	270	50	320
1940	400	100	500
1941	305	135	440
1942	340	111	451
1943	339	126	465
1944	321	154	475
1945	614	296	910

China as a pool from which to draw units for duty elsewhere. But as a practical matter, the Chinese were virtually cut off from outside military aid for most of the war. Although there was some domestic manufacture of arms (about 800,000 rifles, 87,000 machine guns, and 12,000 light mortars between 1942 and 1944), most of the weapons and supply they had was flown in over the Himalaya Mountains, and about 48% of what did come over the mountains (only some 3,000 tons a month in 1943) was consumed by US advisers and units. The principal weapon the Chinese used to fight the Japanese was sheer manpower. Millions of Chinese troops spent most of their time just being in front of the Japanese. There were always too many Chinese troops for the Japanese to destroy, even if they were often more or less unarmed: In late 1943 there were about three million troops in the Chinese Army, who were armed with only a million rifles, 83,000 machine guns, 7,800 mortars, and 1,300 pieces of artillery. These tied up about 1.2 million Japanese troops, plus several hundred thousand less efficient collaborationist troops.

Although never as bad as that for the Chinese, the Japanese supply situation was also rather poor. When the Japanese launched Ichi Go, several large offensives designed to overrun US airbases in southern and central China during 1944, they were able to keep advancing (despite heavy troop losses) until they ran out of supplies in early 1945. The resources for this offensive against the KMT armies were gathered largely by suspending operations against the Chinese communist forces from 1943 onward. The beating the KMT units took during Ichi Go, coupled with the two-year respite it allowed the communists, was partially responsible for communist military success in the civil war that followed the departure of Japanese forces in 1945.

On paper, peak wartime strength of the Chinese Army was about 6 million men. In practice, at the end of the war there were about 3.8 million Nationalists and warlord troops and 1.2 million communists—a total of about 5 million.

Ref: Ch'i, *Nationalist China at War*; Liu, *A Military History of Modern China*; Van Slyle, "The Chinese Communist Movement during the Sino-Japanese War, 1937–1945."

China, Armies, Some Notable Formations

(Note: see, Organization, Ground Combat Divisions, for an explanation of the several types of Chinese divisions.)

Eighth Route Army. The principal Chinese communist force, commanded by Chu Teh, the founder of the Chinese People's Liberation Army. Created from the survivors of the Long March in Shansi in August of 1937, from the outbreak of the CHINA INCIDENT, the Eighth Route Army grew from about 80,000 troops to over 600,000 by 1945. Most of these forces were militia and part-time GUERRILLAS, rather than front-line troops. The main subordinate units of the army were initially the 115th, 120th, and 129th Divisions. A well-trained, skillful force, the Eighth Route Army engaged the Japanese on several occasions during the war, not always successfully, nor did it always fare well in occasional clashes with Nationalist troops. Its most spectacular feat of arms occurred on September 25, 1937, when the 115th Division, under Lin Piao, ambushed the Japanese 5th Division, severely injuring it before disengaging and making its escape. During the "Hundred Regiments Offensive" of August-October 1940, the Eighth Route Army undertook a widespread series of attacks (initially with 22 regiments, but ultimately involving 104) against Japanese communications with some success, provoking violent reprisals by the Japanese against the civilian population.

New 22nd Division. A "triangular" division trained by the German Military Mission, the division fought in Southern Kiangsi in late 1939–early 1940, then was sent into Burma with the Chinese Expeditionary Force in early 1942, taking part in some of the heaviest fighting of that campaign before retreating into India. Reorganized, retrained, and reequipped in India, along with the New 38th Division, it took part in the operations to open the Ledo Road in late 1943, and in the Allied 1944 offensive, helping to recover Myitkyina. In December 1944 it was transferred to China by air, and joined additional Chinese forces in attacking southward to help liberate the BURMA ROAD in early 1945. At the end of the war it formed part of the GHQ reserve, in southern China.

38th Division. A pre–1937 unit, the division was heavily engaged in operations in the Peking-Tientsin area in the summer of 1937, fought all through the China Incident, retaking Nan-yang from the Japanese Third Division in early 1941. Remaining active in central China throughout the war, the division was generally in the Sixth War Area (Hupei-Wuhan). In the spring of 1944 it retook Feng-cheng from the Japanese. It took part in the Chinese offensive in Western Honan and Northern Hupei in early 1945, but was destroyed in a Japanese counteroffensive near Hsiang–yang, 24–30 March 1945.

New 38th Division. A "triangular" division, one of the series trained by the German Military Mission, the division was sent into Burma in early 1942 with the Chinese Expeditionary Force. It performed well, relieving British troops in danger of being surrounded at Yenangyaung, and helping to cover the retreat into India. With the New 22nd Division, it was reorganized, reequipped, and retrained in India. It took part in the Allied operations to open the Ledo Road in late 1943–early 1944, and had an important role in the Allied 1944 offensive in Burma; fighting at Myitkyina, it was the unit that linked up with Chinese forces driving down from northern Burma to reestablish land communications with China.

57th Division. A prewar central army unit, the division fought in most of the campaigns of the China Incident. From December 1941 it was mostly in the Hunan area. It took 90% CASUALTIES defending Ch'ang-te in November-December 1943, after which it was only partially rebuilt.

88th Division. A German-trained unit of the KMT central army, the division made an heroic defense of SHANGHAI in mid–1937. Although it lost heavily at Shanghai, it then took part in the defense of Nanking later that year and was later heavily engaged in the June-November 1938 battle for Wuhan. By then effectively burned out, the division was not in combat for some time afterward. In the spring of 1942 it fought the Japanese in Yunan, along the Salween River, toward the end of the first Burma Campaign. It remained active in southern China throughout the war. The end of the war found it back in Shanghai, helping to disarm surrendering Japanese forces.

93rd Division. A unit of the GHQ reserve in 1937, the division fought in Kwangsi in late 1939 and early 1940, helping to eject the Japanese from Ling-Shan in March of that year. In early 1942 it went into Burma with the Chinese Expeditionary Force, and was heavily engaged against the Japanese 18th and 56th Divisions in April. It fell back into China with the collapse of the Allied defense in Burma. It thereafter formed part of the GHQ reserve, fighting on through to the end of the war.

200th Division. A "triangular" division organized in the Ninth War Area (Hunan) after the Japanese invasion of 1937. Its commander, Gen. Tai An-lan, was unusually energetic and the division was well trained and reasonably well cared for by Chinese standards. One of the few motorized divisions in the Chinese Army, it included a tank regiment and one of motorized infantry, equipped with Soviet material purchased in 1938–39. The division saw active service in the defense of CHANGSHA in the late summer of 1939, fought in southern Kwangsi from November 1939 through February 1940. In early 1942 the division was sent from Yunan into Burma with the Chinese Expeditionary Force. It proved the most effective Chinese division in Burma, being heavily engaged on several occasions, during one of which Tai An-lan was killed in action. The division retreated across the Salween River into Yunan in May 1942. Never rebuilt as a motorized formation, it remained in southern China for most of the next two years, helping garrison Kunming. In mid–1944 the division was again committed to action along the Yunan-Burma border, to help beat off a Japanese offensive, but was then withdrawn to the Kunming area once again, where it remained for the rest of the war.

First Provisional Tank Group (Chinese-American). Organized in India in October 1943, the group consisted mostly of Chinese troops with a small contingent of American advisers and technicians. It entered combat in Burma in January 1944, and in particular supported the Chinese 22nd Division and MERRILL'S MARAUDERS in operations from March 1944 through the capture of Myitkyina in August. It later supported the operations of Task Force Mars. In mid–1945 it was disbanded in southern China. Although the number of Americans in the group gradually rose from a few dozen to over 200, it nevertheless remained essentially a Chinese force.

See also ORGANIZATION, GROUND COMBAT DIVISIONS 1942;

China, Army, Japanese Collaborationist

By 1941 Japan controlled much of the population and most of the economic resources of China. A puppet government under Ching-wei Wang, a former KUOMINTANG member and erstwhile cabinet minister, was installed, and a considerable army recruited, eventually amounting to some 20 divisions (about a million troops by some estimates). These troops were not of the best quality. Nearly 500,000 were former Chinese troops, Nationalist or warlord forces brought over by capture or desertion of their generals. About 300,000 had been directly recruited by the Wang government, picking over what was left after the Nationalists had been through the region. The balance of the collaborationist army was composed of police troops and militiamen, many of whom were indistinguishable from bandits, but were refraining from attacking the Japanese. These forces proved adequate for oc-

cupation duty and combat against equally inept Chinese Nationalist troops, but did less well against Chinese communist main force troops, or those Nationalist units that had the benefit of American training and equipment. After the war most of these troops ended up in the Nationalist or the communist Chinese Army. These units were kept on a short leash in terms of weapons and ammunition. The Japanese did not entirely trust them, as one can imagine, and used Japanese units for all crucial combat tasks.

China, Army in India

After the collapse of Allied forces in Burma in mid–1942, two Chinese divisions, the New 22nd and the New 38th, withdrew to India. There, at the urging of Gen. Joseph STILWELL, who commanded all Chinese forces in Burma and India, they were reorganized, retrained, and reequipped by the United States. Chinese forces in India eventually included the New 30th Division, flown in over the HUMP in 1943, and the 14th and 50th Divisions, transferred by air in April 1944 (when they were flown into India these divisions actually consisted mostly of troops with virtually no equipment). In December of 1944 the New 22nd and the 14th Divisions were flown back to China, with all their equipment, where they became part of the GHQ reserve. These divisions supported the Allied offensive in Burma by attacking southward from Yunan, helping to clear the BURMA ROAD in January 1945. Another unit organized in India was the Sino-American First Provisional Tank Group, which supported American and Chinese operations in Burma. With the liberation of most of Burma in early 1945, the Chinese forces in that country and in India returned to their homeland.

China, Campaigns in

Most Americans don't think of the war in China as part of the Pacific War. In fact, the fighting in China was much more intense and bloody than what Americans faced in the Pacific. CASUALTIES were in the millions, both before and after PEARL HARBOR.

It was Japan's invasion of China (which began in 1931 or 1932 or 1933 or 1937, depending on how one wishes to count various "incidents") that eventually got the United States into World War II in the first place. And it was in China, not Poland, that the earliest battles of World War II were fought.

Japan had been making steady inroads in China and KOREA since the 1880s. Initially, the Japanese saw themselves as competing on equal terms with European powers (particularly Britain and Russia) that struggled for colonial trading privileges in China. But the Japanese soon realized that they could attempt to conquer China, one piece at a time.

Their war with China in 1894–95 got Japan a free hand in Korea, control of some of MANCHURIA, and all of FORMOSA. A war with Russia in 1904–05 left them in control of all of Korea and more of Manchuria. Note that the Russians had already grabbed much of Manchuria before the 1904–05 war (partly to keep the Japanese out), and this was used as Japan's justification for expanding its control in the area.

After World War I, the Japanese were given more leeway in China because the Japanese had sided with the Allies against the Germans during the war. As a result of that cooperation, the Japanese received some of the German colonies in the Pacific, including many well placed islands in the central Pacific, and wanted the German concessions on the large Shantung Peninsula southeast of Peking.

Meanwhile the Chinese had begun to organize themselves. A revolution had deposed the monarchy just before World War I, and the rebels were attempting to weld the various warlords into a cohesive government. But during the 1920s there came a communist revolution. This actually helped the Japanese, who played one Chinese faction against another through the 1920s. Meanwhile, the

Japanese increased their military strength in Korea and parts of Manchuria. More importantly, they increased their economic presence which meant access to raw materials and markets, as well as favorable trading terms. The Japanese built railroads and other facilities and staffed them with Japanese colonists.

The Japanese generals running the show in China became more and more independent of the government back in Tokyo. Using subversion and threats, Japanese military leaders gained control over larger portions of Manchuria. In 1931, the Japanese Army staged the "Manchurian Incident" with local Chinese troops, giving them an excuse to conquer all of Manchuria. This took about a year, after which they promptly declared Manchuria an independent nation. Over the next year the Japanese Army occupied additional portions of northern China. While the Japanese government was not happy with this freelancing by the army commanders in China, it was not about to risk a military coup by attempting to assert civilian control over the army. Through the 1930s, over a million Japanese settlers moved into Manchuria.

Although the Japanese government never made any serious attempts to rein in its ambitious generals in China, this did not satisfy the increasingly bold Japanese Army officer corps. In 1936 there was an attempted coup in Tokyo by junior army officers. Several senior civilian officials were assassinated before the coup was suppressed. The junior officers wanted even more support for the Chinese war, and although the coup failed, they had made their point.

In 1937, Japan began large-scale warfare against China. Attacking from enclaves in Manchuria and along the coast, the Japanese advanced into central China. Japan had 300,000 troops in China at the time, plus 150,000 Manchurian and Mongolian troops under Japanese officers. The Chinese had over two million troops under arms, but these were much less well equipped, trained, and led than the Japanese invaders. For two years the Japanese advanced deeper into China. But progress was slow and casualties mounted.

Gradually, the Japanese came to control much of northern China and nearly all the coastal areas. In 1939 they decided to return to their earlier subversion and attrition tactics. With control of all Chinese ports, the Japanese felt that Chinese military resistance would soon wither. But there were still two supply routes open to the Chinese. One was the railroad from French INDO-CHINA (Vietnam) and the other the BURMA ROAD that went from Burmese ports into southern China. America, and other Western nations, were still willing to support China, and these two routes kept the Chinese armed forces going. The Japanese, naturally, sought to shut down these two routes, and they would once they were at war with the United States and Britain (which controlled Burma).

Many Western nations were not happy with Japanese attempts to conquer China. Diplomatic protests had no effect. In the summer of 1941, the Western nations raised the ante by freezing Japanese assets and then invoking a trade embargo. Because Japan was dependent on Western-controlled raw materials (particularly oil) to keep its economy going, the embargo gave it a choice of getting out of China, seeing its economy (and military power) collapse, or going to war with America, Britain, and Holland (which controlled the oil supplies).

At the start of the Pacific War, most of the Japanese Army was in China. Thirteen divisions were in Manchuria, keeping an eye on Russia. Another 23 divisions were in China, not to mention a goodly number of independent brigades. There were also about 20 divisions of Japanese-controlled Chinese troops representing the government of the "independent Manchuria" the Japanese had set up. The Japanese had only about 10 divisions to spare for the conquest of the Pacific, including MALAYA and Burma. It was very much a shoestring operation in the Pacific because of the massive number of troops needed to keep an eye on China. While China got the bulk of the troops, the Japanese effort in the Pacific got most of everything else. As

a result, the Japanese Army in China spent the rest of the war fighting a poor man's war. The most common offensive operations were short, local advances for the purpose of stealing the rice crops at harvest time. This helped feed the Japanese troops and made the Chinese weaker.

After their supply lines from Indo-China and Burma were cut in late 1941, the Chinese received only a trickle of supplies flown in over the Himalayan Mountains by US aircraft. Thus neither side had the ammunition or other supplies to sustain any major operations. For most of the war, the Chinese front was a stalemate. Moreover, the Nationalist Chinese (who received all the support from the Allies) devoted over a third of their troops to watching the communist armies. Despite the threat of Japanese conquest, the Chinese civil war went on.

In 1944 the Japanese took advantage of this situation by establishing a truce with the Chinese communists. This allowed the communists to strengthen their hold over the northwestern Chinese territory they controlled, and enabled the Japanese to send troops south for their 1944 offensive against American airfields.

From May through November of 1944, the Japanese again advanced, overrunning US airfields in central China. Much of the supplies flown in by American transports went to support US combat aircraft. As small as this air force was, it bothered the Japanese a great deal, and they scraped together what resources they had to knock out the American airfields.

As with the 1937 campaign, the 1944 operation was hampered by logistical problems and constant resistance from the Chinese population. Moreover, the Chinese Nationalist Army had been receiving more military aid and training from the United States since 1941 and had become a more competent force.

However, the American commanders in China were convinced that airpower could stop the Japanese if there was a major offensive. Thus the Chinese ground troops were not as well equipped as they could have been if a lot of the airlifted supply had gone to building up the Chinese Army instead of the bombing campaign. Despite the obstacles, the Japanese managed to capture the airfields and link up with their forces in Indo-China. This cut Nationalist Chinese-controlled territory in half, making the Nationalist situation much worse.

The 1944 offensive went on for a year and exhausted Japanese forces in China, making them ripe for rapid defeat by the Russians in the summer of 1945. In April of 1945, the Russians made clear their intentions by abrogating the non-aggression treaty with Japan. Realizing that their Manchurian army had been bled dry to support the Pacific and Chinese operations, Japanese commanders were ordered to send troops from China to Manchuria. This evened up the situation sufficiently for the Chinese to recover a lot of the territory the Japanese had earlier taken. When the Russians attacked in August 1945, the Japanese, even reinforced, were not able to stop them. When Japan surrendered on August 15, the communists and Nationalists were quick to grab the surrendered weapons and continue their civil war (which the communists won by 1949).

Throughout the Pacific War, most of the Japanese Army was in China. While the Chinese troops were not active much of the time, many of Japan's best troops were thus occupied, rather than being sent against Allied troops in the Pacific or in Burma. China's role, though generally neglected, was critical to the Allied victory.

See also CHINA INCIDENT.

Ref: Ch'l, *Nationalist China at War*; Eastman, "Nationalist China during the Sino-Japanese War, 1937–1945"; Iriye, Akira, "Japanese Aggression and China's International Position, 1931–1945."

China, Navy

In 1937 the Chinese Navy was quite small, less than 70 vessels, totaling only about 60,000 tons. Of modern vessels there were two light cruisers, NING HAI and *Ping Hai*, plus 16 large gunboats, and a flotilla of smaller gunboats and motor torpedo boats. The navy had ordered a number of SUBMARINES in Europe, but none of these had been delivered by the outbreak of the CHINA INCIDENT. There were also many older vessels, most virtually useless, but retained for prestige purposes, including eight cruisers, three destroyers, eight torpedo boats, and 10 large and several small gunboats, virtually all completed before World War I. Only about six vessels survived the initial Japanese invasion in 1937. Many were scuttled to avoid capture, the rest sunk by Japanese aircraft.

As the Japanese spread themselves over much of the coastal area of China, the Chinese Navy was increasingly confined to the upper reaches of the major rivers. By 1939 the principal occupation of the Chinese Navy was laying and clearing mines, and sustaining four regiments of naval infantry.

China, Resistance to the Japanese

The Sino-Japanese theater in World War II was arguably the largest GUERRILLA war of the 20th century. Because the Chinese were largely cut off from outside support after 1942, they could not afford to fight a conventional war. So several million Chinese troops played cat and mouse with over 50 Japanese divisions (including 20 composed of Chinese in the pay of the Japanese). The Japanese were not much better off, having limited resources to begin with and most of that being devoted to the war with the Americans in the Pacific. There were actually three guerrilla wars going on at the same time. There was the obvious one, Chinese versus Japanese. Then there was the ongoing conflict between Chinese Nationalists and Chinese communists. Finally, there was still a fair amount of free-lance fighting by brigands and sundry warlords. While there were a number of large battles and some wide-scale offensives by the Japanese, much of the action was between small groups of armed men (and sometimes women) sneaking around and shooting at each other. While there were front lines and many organized Chinese units, the front lines were long and porous, while the Chinese had many armed supporters behind the Japanese lines. Not much has been heard about this war in the West. It was especially ugly, with ATROCITIES the norm and loyalty in short supply. Americans became increasingly frustrated by the deceit they encountered from both the communists and the Nationalists (who were more interested in fighting each other than the Japanese). It was a large war that continued into the early 1950s as the communists first defeated the Nationalists and then, after establishing control over the entire country, went after sundry non-Chinese minorities. Some of these conflicts continue to the present.

Ref: Ch'i, *Nationalist China at War*; Eastman, "Nationalist China during the Sino-Japanese War, 1937–1945"; Iriye, Akira, "Japanese Aggression and China's International Position, 1931–1945."

China, Separate Peace with Japan

On at least one occasion during the war, CHIANG KAI-SHEK, the leader of Nationalist China, appears to have attempted to negotiate a separate peace with the Japanese. This seems to have been one of the sources of friction between Chiang and his principal American military adviser, Gen. Joseph STILWELL. Moreover, Chiang's chief of intelligence (called by Stilwell "the head of Chiang's Gestapo") did maintain contact with Chinese officials working in the Japanese puppet government in China and MANCHURIA. What exactly was discussed via these contacts is not known completely. Very likely it was nothing more than the ancient Chinese custom of keeping in touch with one's enemies.

China Incident

A euphemism used to describe the Sino-Japanese War, so as to pretend that Japan was not invading China. Arguably the first "incident" was the "Tsinan Incident" in 1928. Here Japanese troops, stationed in northern China by international agreement to protect certain rail lines, attempted to interfere in CHIANG KAI-SHEK's "Northern Expedition," a drive to bring the warlords of North China under the control of the Nationalist government. This failed, after a week of desultory fighting, and the Nationalists were able to bring most of the northern warlords to heel (aided by the fact that the Japanese assassinated the most effective of the warlords, Chang Tso-lin, the "Old Marshal"). Three years later, in the fall of 1931, in the "Manchurian Incident" or "Mukden Incident," the Japanese seized control of MANCHURIA on the pretext that Chinese Nationalists had blown up a train on the Japanese-owned PORT ARTHUR-Mukden railroad (the blast was apparently the work of Japanese agents provocateur). The Chinese, unable to react militarily, instituted a surprisingly effective boycott of Japanese goods and businesses in China. The result, in January of 1932, was the "Shanghai Incident," in which the Japanese made an amphibious attack on SHANGHAI with some 70,000 troops, in an effort to coerce the Chinese into giving up the boycott. The Chinese fought stubbornly, with a good deal of success, but were driven back: They agreed to end the boycott in March and the Japanese withdrew. Meanwhile the Japanese proclaimed Manchuria independent as MANCHUKUO, under the former Chinese emperor, Pu-yi. A League of Nations commission headed by Britain's Viscount Lytton spent six weeks in April, May, and June of 1932 investigating the "Manchurian Incident," and then proceeded to spend eight months preparing its report. Meanwhile, in January of 1933 came the "Jehol Incident," when the Japanese occupied that province, legally part of Inner Mongolia, claiming it was actually a part of MANCHURIA, and thus of Manchukuo, which they claimed included everything north of the Great Wall. Although the Chinese fought back, Japanese troops soon threatened Peking, and an armistice was arranged whereby China agreed to Japanese occupation of Jehol and the demilitarization of large areas along the Manchukuoan-Chinese frontier and in Hopei. During the Jehol Incident, the Lytton Commission finally produced its report, a 180,000-word document that concluded that "although there was no official declaration of war, without doubt vast areas of China have been captured by Japan." The report was approved by the League of Nations membership by a vote of 42 to 1 (Japan) in February 1933, and Japan withdrew from the league.

Over the next few years there occurred the Northern Kalgan, Chahar, and Suiyuan Incidents, in which Japanese forces found pretexts to attack Chinese forces and eject them from additional territories, notably Inner Mongolia. These were on a smaller scale than the previous incidents, and attracted less international notice, but had the net effect of increasing Japanese power in northern China.

In mid-1937 the final "China Incident" began. On the night of July 7–8, elements of the Japanese Kwantung Army were allegedly on maneuvers at Lukouchiao, near Peking, when they claimed to have been attacked by Chinese security forces. They promptly stormed across the Marco Polo Bridge, touching off a full-scale Sino-Japanese War.

See also CHINA, CAMPAIGNS IN.

Ref: Ch'i, *Nationalist China at War*; Eastman, "Nationalist China during the Sino-Japanese War, 1937–1945,"; Iriye, Akira, "Japanese Aggression and China's International Position, 1931–1945,"; Liu, *A Military History of Modern China*.

Chindits

A noted special warfare force, raised in India by British general Orde WINGATE. Deriving their name from a mispronunciation of *Chinthe*, the statues that serve as guardians of Burmese temples, the Chindits specialized in making air assaults deep into the Japanese rear in Burma, and then fighting their way back toward British lines, destroying everything in their path, while being resupplied by air. Highly successful in disrupting Japanese operations, the Chindits were

also extremely expensive. Not only did their operations tie up an enormous amount of air transport, but they were also very wasteful of men, since all but the most lightly wounded were usually abandoned.

There were eventually six Chindit brigades, the Third West African, the 14th, 16th, and 23rd British, and the 77th and 111th Indian. Each brigade fielded several columns, created by breaking up the component battalions.

Chindit column organization varied depending upon whether the infantry company around which the column was built was composed of British, Indian, Gurkha, or African troops. Chindit operations were extremely costly in manpower. Wingate's first operation resulted in the loss of about a third of the troops involved. During the Myitkyina operation the 11th Brigade lost over 700 men and the 77th nearly 1,600, while MERRILL'S MARAUDERS, a US unit organized along the same lines as the Chindits, lost nearly 500.

EXAMPLES OF CHINDIT ORGANIZATION

	Type of Column	
	British	Gurkha
Element		
Headquarters Detachment	8	8
Medical Detachment	5	5
RAF Detachment	5	5
Signal Troops	11	12
Sabotage Team	29	29
Burma Rifles Detachment	45	45
Infantry Company	115	167
Support Group	31	41
Transport Group	57	57
Total	306	369
Manpower Profile		
British Commissioned Officers	14	10
Indian Commissioned Officers	3	8
British Enlisted Men	176	30
Indian Enlisted Men	72	280
Burmese Enlisted Men	41	41

Chitose Class, Japanese Light Aircraft Carriers

The Imperial Navy designed and built these two ships as seaplane carriers, with provision for rapid conversion into proper aircraft carriers, in a move to get around the limitations on carrier tonnage imposed by the Naval DISARMAMENT TREATIES. As seaplane carriers, *Chitose* (1934–1936–1938) and *Chiyoda* (1936–1937–1938) supported Japanese offensive operations in the South Pacific in 1941–42, the former being seriously damaged in the Battle of the Eastern SOLOMONS. Taken in hand for conversion to light carriers 1942–43 and 1943–44 respectively, they emerged with surprisingly good characteristics, in many ways comparable to the IN-DEPENDENCE-class light carriers, and might have made a formidable record for themselves were it not for the fact that by 1944 the quality of Japanese carrier pilots was extremely poor. Both ships took part in the Battle of the PHILIPPINE SEA, each forming the core of two of KURITA's three "bait" light carrier task forces, and were later sunk by US carrier aircraft and surface vessels off Cape Engaño during the Battle of LEYTE GULF in October of 1944.

Chittagong, India

Although possessed of a small airfield and a good harbor, Chittagong, on the northeastern coast of the Bay of Bengal, had only limited port facilities and no industrial capacity. It was several times bombed by the Japanese.

Christmas Island (Indian Ocean)

The small (60 square mile) volcanic island south of JAVA and west of Australia provided some phosphates (or raw material for explosives) and was a useful anchorage for Allied vessels. On 7 March 1942 a Japanese squadron led by battleships KONGO and *Haruna* conducted a short bombardment of the island. On 31 March Japanese naval troops occupied the island, which was undefended.

They confiscated the phosphate stockpile, looted the small civilian settlement, and left on 3 April. Australian forces reoccupied the island soon afterward and held it until the end of the war. Aside from an occasional reconnaissance flight, the Japanese left it alone.

Christmas Island (Pacific Ocean)

The Pacific Christmas Island lies almost directly south of HAWAII, in the Line Islands, near the GILBERTS. The largest atoll in the world in terms of land area (c. 200 square miles), it was virtually uninhabited at the outbreak of the war (there were fewer than 50 people living in two settlements, called London and Paris, at opposite ends of the lagoon entrance). Even before PEARL HARBOR the United States began developing the island as an air base. Christmas was an important link in the chain of air bases that the United States established to help protect communications with the south Pacific.

Chungking, China

Some modest industrial facilities and the presence of the Nationalist Chinese government made Chungking of considerable importance, as did its relative inaccessibility to Japanese attack, deep in the interior of China. It was repeatedly bombed by Japanese aircraft.

Churchill, Winston Leonard Spencer (1874–1965)

Winston Churchill was the son of Lord Randolph Churchill, the distinguished British politician, and the American socialite Jenny Jerome. He graduated from Sandhurst, the British military academy, in 1895 and had a successful career as an officer and journalist (on the Spanish side) during the Cuban War for Independence, on the Northwest Frontier of India, in the Sudan (where he took part in the charge of the 21st Lancers of Omdurman), and in South Africa, before entering politics. He began World War I as First Lord of the Admiralty, finding time to promote the invention of the tank, before commanding the Sixth Battalion, Royal Scots Fusiliers, on the Western Front for several months after the disastrous Gallipoli Campaign, of which he had been a major promoter. He later became minister of munitions and secretary of state for war. For most of the years between the wars he was politically on the sidelines, but was again made First Lord of the Admiralty on the eve of World War II and became prime minister upon the collapse of France in 1940.

A man of enormous ego and numerous faults, nevertheless his drive, organizational abilities, oratorical skills, and vision were indispensable to the success of Allied arms in the war.

Clemson and Wickes Classes, US Destroyers

Completed soon after World War I, the Clemson and Wickes Classes were famous as the "four-stack" destroyers that constituted about a third of the US Navy's assets in that type of warship at the start of World War II. Although obsolete almost as soon as they were completed, they saw significant service during World War II. The 50 given to the ROYAL NAVY, in exchange for basing rights at British colonies in the Americas in 1940, saw much action in Atlantic and European waters, as did additional units given to Canada and Russia. Many others fought through the war in US service, including the battles of the Asiatic Fleet. A large number were converted to serve as high-speed transports and mine warfare vessels. Twenty were lost in US service, and seven in British. A Clemson-class ship was the first US warship to be sunk in World War II, when *Reuben James*, DD-245 (1918–1919–1920), was TORPEDOED by *U-562* in the Atlantic on 31 October 1941, going down with the loss of 115 men.

See also WARSHIPS, US, CAPTURED.

Cleveland Class, US Light Cruisers

The best American light cruisers of the war, and the most numerous class of light cruisers ever built,

29 were commissioned out of an order of 52 (not including nine other hulls completed as light aircraft carriers). Although the Clevelands had three fewer 6–inch guns than the preceding BROOKLYNS, they were decidedly superior to their predecessors, despite having been designed in some haste, when the treaty limitations on light cruisers were lifted in 1939. They were also much more expensive, at $31 million to $42 million each. However, they were rather top-heavy and cramped. The ships were ordered in three slightly different batches, so that there were some variations in dimensions, armament, and appearance. They rendered excellent service in the war, none becoming CASUALTIES although several were in the thick of surface actions in the southwest Pacific. Perhaps their most notable moment in the war occurred during the Battle of EMPRESS AUGUSTA BAY (2 November 1943), when a squadron of four Clevelands with eight destroyers (four of them commanded by the redoubtable Arleigh "31 Knot" BURKE) ambushed a Japanese force consisting of two heavy cruisers, two light cruisers, and six destroyers, sinking a light cruiser and a destroyer with virtually no damage to themselves. The more notable members of the class were:

Cleveland, CL-55 (1940–1941–1942), the name ship of the class, saw considerable service, notably in the southwest Pacific (Empress Augusta Bay, etc.).

Columbia, CL-56 (1940–1941–1942), was heavily engaged from late 1942 to the end of the war, fighting at Empress Augusta Bay and SURIGAO STRAIT, and taking two KAMIKAZE off Luzon in January 1945.

Montpelier, CL-57 (1940–1942–1942), took part in a number of actions in the SOLOMONS, including Empress Augusta Bay, and went on to support the liberation of the Philippines.

Denver, CL-58 (1940–1942–1942), took part in Empress Augusta Bay (she was the only American ship hit, and then only by several dud 8-inch shells) and Surigao Strait, and ended the war supporting operations for the liberation of the southern Philippines.

Santa Fe, CL-60 (1941–1942–1942), escorted fast carrier task forces from early 1943, but took part in one of the last surface actions of the war when she helped sink the damaged Japanese carrier *Chiyoda* and several of her escorts off Cape Engaño, October 25, 1944.

Birmingham, CL-62 (1941–1942–1943), supported the landings in Sicily and Salerno, and then passed to the Pacific to help escort carrier task forces. On October 24, 1944, off Leyte, she was almost lost when, attempting to go to the support of the sinking light carrier *Princeton*, she was severely damaged when the latter's torpedo magazine detonated.

Mobile, CL-63 (1941–1942–1943), escorted carrier task forces, taking part in the surface action off Cape Engaño on October 25, 1944.

Houston, CL-81 (1941–1943–1943), originally to have been named *Flint*, but renamed to honor the heavy cruiser sunk in the Sunda Strait early in 1942. She spent her war escorting the fast carriers. Torpedoed on October 14 and 16, 1944, during the Third Fleet's three-day raid on FORMOSA, *Houston* took 6,500 tons of water, equal to 45% of her displacement, an extraordinary amount of water. There was some fear that she might have to be abandoned due to a typhoon, but she was towed clear, repaired, and returned to service.

Of these, *Birmingham* was scrapped in 1959, all the rest in 1960.

See also INDEPENDENCE CLASS, US LIGHT AIRCRAFT CARRIERS.

Climate, Effect on Health

The health of troops can be greatly affected by the climate in which they operate. In tropical areas, the heat was a significant danger. Among Allied troops operating in tropical areas during 1942 and 1943, between 15% and 20% were victims of heat prostration and similar afflictions. Of these, about 2% died. This problem even affected naval forces, particularly SUBMARINES traveling on the surface, which are very poorly ventilated, the principal rea-

son the US Navy began experimenting with air conditioning on subs during the 1930s.

At the other climatic extreme, in sub-arctic and arctic environments, the situation is not quite so bad, provided reasonable care is taken to provide the necessary specialized clothing and equipment. Based on its experience operating in higher latitudes, the US Army determined that men from southern states were 3–5% more likely to succumb to cold weather-induced problems (ranging from colds to frostbite) than were men from northern states. On this basis it seems reasonable to assume that Japanese troops, who generally came from a milder environment, suffered greatly during the ALEUTIANS Campaign.

Coastwatchers

Coastwatchers were Britons, Australians, and New Zealanders who stayed on South Pacific islands after the withdrawal of Commonwealth forces in the face of the Japanese advance in early and mid-1942, to provide intelligence to Allied forces. The idea predated the war. It was created in the late 1930s, at the urging of LtCdr Eric Feldt, RAN, who had concluded that the extensive activity of Japanese fishing and pearling vessels in the islands during the 1920s and 1930s masked an intensive reconnaissance effort, which suggested the probability that the Japanese would attempt to invade the islands in the event of war. Coastwatchers were recruited before the outbreak of the Pacific War, mostly from among European traders and government officials with long experience in the islands. Feldt code named the coastwatcher system "Ferdinand," after the passive bull of the children's tale, and stressed that coastwatchers were not supposed to act aggressively, but merely collect information. Given commissions and small detachments of men from the Solomon Islands Defence Force, 16 of these men went into hiding in the Solomon Islands when the Japanese came. More coastwatchers were recruited during the war, largely from among Europeans who had remained behind when the Japanese came, and they eventually covered the

SOLOMONS, the BISMARCKS, and portions of Papua-New Guinea. Coastwatchers were on many islands that the Japanese never occupied, and even on some of the ones they only partially occupied, such as GUADALCANAL. In some areas new coastwatchers recruited from former residents were landed from SUBMARINES, aircraft, or even small boats.

Coastwatchers proved invaluable during the protracted fighting in the lower Solomons. They provided timely warnings of Japanese air raids from the RABAUL area, and of the movements of Japanese warships and merchantmen in the Slot, enabling Allied forces to cope more readily with enemy attacks.

Coastwatchers also proved very helpful in rescuing downed Allied pilots. For example, Geoffrey Kuper, of mixed British and Solomons descent, and his detachment of 12 men on Santa Isabel rescued 28 Allied pilots, about a quarter of all those rescued by the local people in all of the northern Solomons. Because of his racial background, Kuper was the only coastwatcher not granted a commission.

Despite Feldt's dictum that coastwatchers were not to act in an aggressive fashion, some did. Precise numbers are not known, but Cdr. Feldt himself claimed that 5,414 Japanese troops had been killed by coastwatchers and their security personnel, a further 1,492 wounded, and 74 taken prisoner. Coastwatchers and their security detachments rescued 75 European and 260 Asian PRISONERS of the Japanese, plus 321 aviators who had been shot down, 280 naval personnel who had lost their ships, and 190 missionaries and their families, plus thousands of natives. CASUALTIES among the coastwatchers were 33 Europeans and about 60 Solomon Islanders.

See also KENNEDY'S ARMY.

Ref: Feldt, *The Coastwatchers*; Lord, *Lonely Vigil*.

Collins, J. Lawton (1896–1992)

J. Lawton Collins graduated from West Point in 1917, but saw no service overseas in World War I. Between the wars he held a variety of posts, and attended most of the army's higher academic institutions (Command and General Staff College, War College, Industrial College). Immediately after PEARL HARBOR he was named chief of staff to the commanding general of the Hawaiian Department, and within a few months was promoted to major general and given the 25th Infantry Division. He took his division to GUADALCANAL in December and later led it on New Georgia, each time distinguishing himself. In March of 1944 he was sent to Europe, where he took command of VII Corps, leading it during the Normandy landings, the breakout from the beachhead, the drive across France, the Rhineland Campaign, and on to the Elbe by the surrender of Germany, earning the nickname "Lightning Joe" in the process. Promoted to lieutenant general, Collins and his VII Corps were awaiting transfer to the Pacific when Japan surrendered. After the war he held a variety of increasingly important administrative and command assignments, culminating in chief of staff of the army, while becoming involved in a scheme to abolish the Marine Corps, a perennial project among some officers in the Old Army. After his retirement he continued in public service and served on the boards of various corporations, including Pfizer Chemicals, of Brooklyn, New York, which had been the principal developer of penicillin, arguably one of the most important weapons to be introduced during the war.

Colombo, Ceylon

A medium-sized port on the west coast of CEYLON, with some facilities to service shipping, and a small naval base, Colombo proved too exposed to Japanese carrier raids to be of much use in the spring of 1942. Its importance grew later, once the Japanese Navy withdrew its carriers from the Indian Ocean.

Colonies, Asian and Pacific

Save in China and Siam, all of the territory that Japan seized during the war was controlled by distant colonial powers, specifically Britain, France, the Netherlands, Portugal, and the United States. One element in Japanese STRATEGY was its ability to manipulate the downtrodden victims of Western imperialism, by pointing out that Japan was the only Asian nation numbered among the Great Powers.

India was in ferment throughout the 1930s. The Indians wanted the British out ("Quit India"), but the British were in no hurry to leave. Japan's call of "Asia for the Asiatics" fell on receptive ears throughout India, especially during the war (some of the first US troops to reach India were greeted by hostile demonstrators bearing "US Quit India" signs). Britain also controlled Burma and MALAYA, while Holland controlled INDONESIA (the NETHERLANDS EAST INDIES), France controlled INDO-CHINA (Vietnam, Laos, and Cambodia), and the United States controlled the Philippines. All of these nations were eager to get rid of their colonial rulers. When the Japanese came, many people in most of these areas at least tacitly supported them.

The exception was the Philippines; already promised independence by 1946, the Filipinos generally preferred to remain loyal to the United States. In between, a nervously independent SIAM worried about her future.

After the German conquest of France in 1940, Japan took over control of French Indo-China. Following PEARL HARBOR, Siam cooperated with Japan, if only to protect its fragile sovereignty, allowing Japanese troops to use its territory to support operations in Malaya and Burma. By early 1942, the British were being chased out of Burma by advancing Japanese troops. The Japanese carrier fleet rampaged through the Indian Ocean in March and April, bombing naval bases and sinking British warships. Although Japanese ground forces never reached densely populated Indian territory, the British diverted substantial resources to ensure that India remained British. At the end of March 1942, Britain announced that India would have its independence as soon as Germany and Japan were defeated. Burma was also liberated voluntarily, as was Malaya, albeit later. Indonesia and Vietnam

had to fight for their independence when the colonial powers returned, and the United States was drawn into the latter struggle.

The Japanese victories had a profound effect on the colonial populations. Until the Japanese came along, the Westerners were considered invincible. However, the Japanese occupation was much harsher than Western rule, no one who went through it has forgotten or forgiven the treatment meted out by the Japanese.

Colossus Class, British Aircraft Carriers

Classed as light fleet carriers by the ROYAL NAVY, *Colossus* and her nine sisters (four of which reached the Pacific late in the war but saw no combat service there) were built 1942–46. They actually carried slightly more aircraft than did the much larger ILLUSTRIOUS CLASS fleet carriers, and had a superior avgas (aircraft fuel) capacity as well (c. 2,600 gallons per plane against c. 1,500). This was due to their almost complete lack of armor and their inferior machinery, which made them about five knots slower.

Combat Effectiveness

Wars test nations in various ways, socially, economically, and politically as well as militarily. Generally the military test attracts the most attention. Although in World War II Japanese military forces conquered far more territory and people than the German military forces, it's the Germans who were most respected as warriors.

Allied troops invariably developed a grudging respect for the German troops they faced. Even during the last months of the war, German troops were still winning battlefield victories because of their better training and tactics. In the Pacific, Japanese troops certainly overcame all comers with their superior training and tactics in the early part of the war, and remained formidable opponents right to the end. Determining which army was better is difficult. The designers of the hundreds of World War II wargames published in the past thirty years had to deal with this situation in concrete terms. These historical games had to re-create the situations they dealt with accurately by calculating the relative degree of competency of the different armies under different circumstances at various times. However, there was no way the casual reader of World War II history could easily grasp this relationship until the late American military historian Trevor N. DuPuy came along.

DuPuy's specialty was collecting information on hundreds of World War II battles, in some of which he had himself fought. He organized the data and reduced it to easily understood values. DuPuy called his technique the Quantified Judgment Method, because he realized not all factors could be quantified, and some professional judgment had to be used. This leaves a good deal of room for criticism, but does not necessarily negate DuPuy's basic conclusions. What he came up with, and published in several books, was the following overall set of relationships among the major combatants of World War II:

RELATIVE SUPERIORITY OF ARMIES

Opponents	Period	Superior	Superiority
Germans vs. Allies	late 1942–1945	Germans	26%
Germans vs. Russians	1941–1945	Germans	58%
Allies vs. Japanese	late 1942–1945	Allies	30%

These are, of course, summary figures, based on the overall experience of the war. They changed throughout the war. In 1941 the German superiority over the Russians was sometimes over 200%. The Japanese were much better than the Allies (United States and Commonwealth) in 1941 and early 1942. The experience of war changed the armies. In general they all improved, some faster than others. US troops adapted rather quickly to fighting in the Pacific. The Japanese adapted rather less quickly to dealing with American innovations.

It's also important to note that there were considerable differences between units of all armies. Among the Allies, the best divisions were about 50% better than the worst, a phenomenon demon-

strable in other armies as well. This was usually the effect of a superior (or inferior) division commander, but was sometimes due to the quality of the personnel, the amount of equipment, and the degree of training the division possessed.

Ref: DuPuy, *Numbers, Predictions, and War.*

Combat Psychology, Japan

American troops were shocked by the seeming fanaticism of the Japanese soldiers, sailors, and pilots they encountered. Early in the war, it simply appeared that the Japanese were better soldiers than prewar estimates had assumed. Rapid victories in MALAYA and Burma gave rise to the long-lasting rumor that the Japanese were natural jungle fighters (in reality, few Japanese had ever seen a jungle until they joined the army). But when the Japanese began losing, it became apparent that something else was at work. This was first noticed on GUADALCANAL where the Japanese persistently attacked in unfavorable situations. When trapped, they would not surrender. When successful, they were quite vicious and ruthless. When an occasional Japanese prisoner was taken, he was quite docile. What to make of all this? As we now know, conformity, eagerness, dedication, and a never-say-die attitude serve the Japanese well—in business. Japanese culture in World War II emphasized, and rewarded, these same qualities, especially demonstrations of "spirit." Basically, "spirit" was similar to religious faith combined with the group spirit of an athletic team. Japanese culture used rituals to maintain this spirit and faith in the all-powerful emperor. While there were non-conformists and non-believers among the Japanese, the majority did believe, or simply found it convenient to conform. When fighting was at hand, Japanese soldiers eagerly united to engage in what was, for them, a quasi-religious experience. Moreover, they had one advantage every general attempts to get: They were resigned to death. Fortunately, the Japanese were not as well trained, led, or supported as the US soldiers and Marines. Japanese military doctrine, because it did not recognize surrender as a viable option, gave Japanese troops caught in an untenable situation little choice but to attack and die. Neither their training, nor their leaders, knew how to deal with the hopelessness of their situation. Thus, the Japanese would simply form up and make a suicidal attack (the BANZAI CHARGE) on the Americans. This was always an impressive display of spirit, but it was no protection from American bullets, bombs, and shells.

Comfort Women

These were women conscripted by the Japanese Army for service as prostitutes in military brothels. The practice began during the CHINA INCIDENT as a method of reducing rape. At first only prostitutes were recruited, apparently voluntarily. By 1945 well over 130,000 young women had been recruited into prostitution, the overwhelming majority of them involuntarily. About 80% of the women were Koreans, the rest Chinese, Indonesian, Papuan, Filipino, Dutch, and even Japanese. Many were brought in by the *Jungshindae*, the WOMEN'S VOLUNTARY SERVICE CORPS. Other women were merely taken from internment camps, schools, or right out of the local population.

Conditions under which the women worked varied from poor to abominable, depending upon the location, whether they were reserved for officers, and the people managing the brothels, often civilian contractors. Some women were forced to service as many as 50 men a day, in 12-hour shifts, seven days a week. Others fared relatively better. Women who contracted venereal disease were often beaten.

After the war, former "comfort women" received no reparations until they began to organize in the 1980s, bringing international attention to their plight. Not only had most suffered severe emotional trauma as a result of their experiences, but also many suffered lifelong physical effects from beatings, venereal disease, and sexual abuse. Most of the women considered themselves a disgrace to their families, and few established normal lives. Not until 1993 did the Japanese government acknowledge its involvement in the recruitment of "comfort women," and it still refuses to undertake any form of compensation.

The actual number of women who were forced to become "comfort women" is not known with any certainty, nor is the number who died as a result of their experience.

In addition to providing comfort women for their own troops during the war, after it the Japanese government also recruited women to serve the American occupation forces. Documents that became available only in the early 1990s revealed that in the days following the formal surrender of Japan, the Japanese government recruited 55,000 Japanese women, often using coercion, to serve in the "Recreation and Amusement Association," which hastily organized hundreds of brothels for the expected American occupation forces, in order to provide a "sexual dike" to protect Japanese womankind from the sort of large-scale molestation and rape that Japanese troops had commonly inflicted upon occupied populations. The extent to which the US occupation forces were aware of this program is unclear. In March 1946, concerned about a soaring venereal disease rate, the US authorities declared Recreation and Amusement Association brothels off limits.

Ref: Hicks, *The Comfort Women*.

Commandos, Unofficial

In March 1943, a ship full of British commandos steamed into a port in Portuguese Goa (on the west coast of India). The commandos then assaulted and destroyed an interned German freighter that had been using a powerful radio transmitter to let nearby German SUBMARINES know the comings and goings of British merchant ships in the Indian Ocean. For diplomatic reasons, the operation was never officially acknowledged by the British government. Although neutral in World War II, Portugal and its territories were hotbeds of Allied and Axis spies. Many Portuguese officials were pliant, and their cooperation could often be bought. But a major British military operation on Portuguese territory would cause many Portuguese to be more pro-Axis, harming Allied espionage efforts. Thus middle-aged members of a paramilitary British social organization, the Calcutta Light Horse, were asked to volunteer for an unofficial mission. The volunteers were told that, for diplomatic reasons, they could receive no official recognition. If captured, they were to be considered freelancers acting on their own. The raid was a success, largely due to some preliminary diplomacy. One volunteer visited the port before the raid and paid off a Portuguese official to throw a lavish party the night of the raid and invite the officers of the German and Italian ships in port. Arrangements were then made to make the town's brothels free for the entire week before the raid. As a result, few of the officers and sailors were on the ship the commandos attacked. Though the raid was never officially recognized, many of the volunteers and their uniformed trainers spoke freely about it. A film about the incident starred David Niven, a graduate of the Royal Military Academy at Sandhurst with a distinguished war record.

Ref: Leasor, *Boarding Party*.

Commencement Bay Class, US Escort Aircraft Carriers

A large class of 23 units, laid down from 1943 through 1945, only eight were in commission before the war ended, and these saw only limited service. Based on the very successful SANGAMON Class escort carriers, they were slightly smaller (about 21,400 tons to 23,800) and somewhat faster (19 knots to 18) than their predecessors, and able to operate slightly more (33 to 31) aircraft. They were also more reliable, better sea boats, and much better armed (58 antiaircraft barrels as against 30 on *Sangamon*). *Commencement Bay* and her sisters were built in improvised Pacific Coast shipyards using mass PRODUCTION techniques, which proved enormously successful. The completed vessels (six were canceled) served in various capacities until scrapped beginning in the 1960s.

Conferences, Allied

The heads of the Allied governments met several times during the war to plan political and military STRATEGY and the postwar world.

In addition to these "summit" meetings, there are numerous lower level political conferences throughout the war, such the Rio Conference, in January 1942, at which most—but not all—of the American republics agreed to support the war effort against Japan. In addition there were numerous combined (i.e., inter-Allied) and joint (i.e., army-navy) military staff conferences, such as the "Pacific Military Conference" held in Washington in March 1943, to hammer out strategy.

Dates	Code Name	Location	Participants
Aug. '41	—	Argentia Bay	FDR, Churchill
Dec. '41–Jan. '42	Arcadia	Washington	FDR, Churchill
Jan. '43	Symbol	Casablanca	FDR, Churchill
May '43	Trident	Washington	FDR, Churchill
Aug. '43	Quadrant	Quebec	FDR, Churchill
Nov. '43	Sextant	Cairo	FDR, Churchill, Chiang
Nov.–Dec. '43	Eureka	Teheran	FDR, Churchill, Stalin
Sept. '44	Octagon	Quebec	FDR, Churchill
Oct. '44	Tolstoy	Moscow	Churchill, Stalin
Jan.–Feb. '45	Argonaut	Malta and Yalta	FDR, Churchill, Stalin
Jan. '45	Cricket	Malta	FDR, Churchill
Feb. '45	Magneto	Yalta	FDR, Churchill, Stalin
Jul.–Aug. '45	Terminal	Potsdam	Truman, Attlee, Stalin

Conscription

All the belligerents in World War II used conscription to fill their ranks, as did all of the prominent neutrals. Conscription is the most efficient way of managing a nation's manpower in a major war. It allows a nation to make optimal use of the skills of its citizens by organizing the assignment of all personnel. In addition, it ensures that the burden of service is fairly well distributed among all sectors of the population.

While a voluntary military system appears attractive, it is in fact extremely wasteful. In wartime the most highly motivated people—who are generally the better educated and possess the greatest leadership skills—are most likely to join first. As a result, they tend to end up serving in military jobs below their mental and technical capabilities, while important jobs in the industrial sector may go unfilled. For example, a tool and die maker toting a rifle is making a smaller contribution to the war effort than if he had remained at home working in an aircraft factory, albeit that he may get greater personal satisfaction out of soldiering.

Of course, compulsory military service was unknown in the English-speaking world, at least in peacetime, until the eve of World War II. For the rest of the world, industrialized or not, conscription was the norm. Many countries, including Britain and several of the Commonwealth nations, drafted people—women as well as men—for service in war industries, and several, including Britain, used drafted women in the military services. Australia, New Zealand, Canada, and South Africa began the war with a mixed military system, putting restrictions on the use of conscripts abroad. In Canada such conscripts were called "Zombies." As the war went on and the casualty lists grew, these restrictions were at first modified, and later generally abolished entirely. Australia, for example, initially used conscripts only within the Commonwealth itself. This was later construed to include Papua-New Guinea, which were Australian territories. Similarly, South Africa limited the use of conscripts to "southern Africa," a geographic region that was stretched to include Ethiopia by 1941, while the "southern" was shortly afterward dropped so that conscripts could serve in North Africa. Still later, all restrictions were entirely eliminated.

In the case of the United States, responding to the increasing threat of war, the ROOSEVELT administration proposed a "selective service" plan

This famous James Montgomery Flagg recruiting poster from World War I was recycled for use during World War II. Despite commendable levels of voluntary enlistments, only conscription was capable of mobilizing the nation's manpower in an orderly fashion.

("selective" because the intention was to take only some of the eligible men) shortly after the fall of France in the summer of 1940. The resulting political battle was a bruising one, as pacifists, communists, fascists, conservatives, and liberals all jumped on the president's "warmongering." Nevertheless, on 16 September 1940 the United States enacted its first peacetime military draft. The intention was to draft up to 900,000 men annually for one year's service, in order to create a pool of trained men in the event of a national emergency. Only men between 20 and 26 years of age were eligible under the terms of the Selective Service Act. Registration began on 16 October, the first names were drawn in a lottery held on 29 October, and the first batch of "selectees" were inducted on 25 November. Since the first draftees were to be discharged in October of 1941, the men joked that they were in the army on the "OHIO Plan" ("Over the Hill in October"). Most of them served until 1945, some until early 1946.

In the summer of 1941, with the German invasion of Russia and the desperate desert battles in North Africa, the president requested that the Selective Service Act be amended to extend tours of duty to as much as 30 months. Despite renewed bitter opposition from a broad if peculiar range of groups from the far right to the far left (with the communists suddenly becoming pro-conscription when HITLER invaded Russia), the amendment passed on 18 August 1941, squeaking through the House of Representatives by just one vote. (Convinced by the narrow margin of the vote that the American people lacked the will to fight, a number of senior Japanese officers who had hitherto been hesitant about a conflict with the United States joined the war party.)

Initially all of the draftees were assigned to the army, so joining the navy, the Marines, or the coast guard was one way a young man could "dodge" the draft. The reluctance of the sea services to accept draftees actually worked against them. For example, the navy missed the many thousands of bargees, fishermen, ferrymen, and weekend sailors who were drafted in the first two years of the war, men who would have required much less training to become small boat and landing craft operators than Iowa farm boys. Of course, wartime pressures on manpower eventually caused the sea services to dip into the pool of draftees as well.

From the enactment of the draft to the surrender of Japan, about 30 million American men were registered with the Selective Service System.

When a man registered for the draft, he was given a series of tests to determine his eligibility, and placed into one of 13 categories.

Class Explanation

I-A	Fit for military service
I-B	Fit for limited military service
I-C	Already in armed forces
I-D	Student, fit for military service, temporarily deferred
I-E	Student, fit for limited military service, temporarily deferred
II-A	Deferred, essential war worker
III-A	Deferred due to dependents
IV-A	Already served in the armed forces
IV-B	Deferred by law; government officials, and some others
IV-C	Alien disqualified from service (usually an Axis national)
IV-D	Clergyman
IV-E	Conscientious objector (several categories)
IV-F	Unfit for military service due to physical, mental, or moral (i.e., criminal record) condition

A man's draft status could change. Many men classified IV-F due to physical shortcomings worked to overcome their problems and requested reclassification. In addition, as time went on and casualty lists grew longer, physical, mental, and moral standards were modified (for example, men missing a few teeth were initially IV-F, but were later accepted for service, as were men with minor felony convictions).

Of the 30 million men who registered for the draft only 18 million received the famous letter that began "Greetings . . ." Of these, 6.5 million were rejected for physical, mental, or moral shortcomings, so that only 11.5 million men were taken into the service. In addition to the drafted men, some 300,000 men came into the service from the NATIONAL GUARD, and nearly six million men and 350,000 women volunteered, so that nearly 18 million men and women saw service during the war, exclusive of Filipino personnel serving in the PHILIPPINE ARMY. Had the war dragged on into 1946, not only were additional young men to be drafted as they came of age, but there were also plans afoot to draft as many as 1.5 million women, although a major congressional battle might have erupted over the latter proposal.

Without Selective Service, the United States would have been even less prepared for war than was actually the case.

Coral

Corals are tiny invertebrate tropical animals with limestone-like exoskeletons. Coral islands are composed of the skeletal remains of literally millions of these animals. Individually virtually microscopic, millions of generations of these animals can build up enormous structures, such as reefs and atolls, and sometimes, with the aid of a little volcanic activity, even mountains. Coral islands in the Central Pacific are generally flat, often no more than four or five feet above sea level, while those in the volcanic western Pacific are often high and rugged.

An excellent construction material, dead or alive, coral is usually soft enough to be dug out without explosives. If packed, rolled, and wet regularly, coral forms a hard, firm surface suitable for runways and roads.

Coral presents special problems in combat. Coral dust is very fine and gets in the nose and throat, which, combined with the tropical environment, caused considerable privation among the troops serving in the Pacific. Live coral is often sharp, and coral fragments can cause serious injury. Some corals are also poisonous. Just another little problem for the troops to worry about.

Coral Sea, Battle of

The Battle of the Coral Sea—northeast of Australia, southeast of Japan, and southwest of the Solomons—was the first battle between aircraft carriers. As such, it was the first naval battle in which neither side could see each other. All the fighting involved carrier aircraft attacking enemy ships, including their carriers. The engagement, fought on May 7–8, 1942, set the pattern for all the other 1942 carrier actions. The Coral Sea operation was the result of Japan's desire to occupy New Guinea and the Solomon Islands.

In March, US carrier aircraft carried out a daring attack on Japanese ships landing troops on the north coast of New Guinea. Flying over the supposedly too high OWEN STANLEY MOUNTAINS by taking advantage of favorable thermals to catch the Japanese completely off guard, the US aircraft struck when the Japanese were not expecting it. The raid was only moderately successful, as the ships had already discharged their troops and cargoes. In response to this raid, the Japanese decided to occupy the balance of New Guinea.

Japanese forces, concentrated at RABAUL, were to sortie by ship into the CORAL SEA and secure PORT MORESBY on the south coast of New Guinea and TULAGI in the EASTERN SOLOMONS. As with most Japanese plans, many task forces were involved. The principal striking element was a task force built around the carriers SHOKAKU and *Zuikaku*, plus two heavy cruisers and six destroyers. Earmarked for the occupation of Port Moresby were three light cruisers, five destroyers, a seaplane tender, a flotilla of smaller warships, and 11 troop transports, plus various supply ships, all covered by a light carrier, four heavy cruisers, and a destroyer. Finally there was the Tulagi occupation force, two destroyers, a troop transport, and various small warships. The plan was for the carrier task force, under VAdm Takeo TAKAGI, to enter the Coral Sea from the east and engage and destroy any Allied warships encountered, thereby enabling the landing forces to go about their business.

This did not seem an overly difficult assignment, as the Allies were believed to have only slender resources. This was true. Allied forces comprised RAdm Frank Jack FLETCHER's Task Force 17, carriers YORKTOWN and LEXINGTON, with eight American and Australian cruisers and 11 destroyers, supported by a fueling group of two oilers and two destroyers. Both sides, of course, committed SUBMARINES and long-range reconnaissance aircraft to the operation, and land-based fighters and bombers were within range.

The battle ranged over the Solomon Sea and the northern portions of the Coral Sea. On 3 May the Japanese occupied Tulagi unopposed, and a raid from *Yorktown* the next day did little damage. This gave away Fletcher's position, but the Japanese were unable to take advantage of the situation since their carriers had been ordered to drop off fighters at Rabaul. Over the next two days each fleet maneuvered cautiously, trying to locate its opponent without revealing its own location. Reconnaissance was poor, and despite the fact that the two task forces passed within about 70 miles of each other at one point, neither spotted the other. Not until the 7th was first blood drawn between the two fleets.

Early on 7 May, the dawn patrol from *Shokaku* and *Zuikaku* located the American oiler *Neosho* and destroyer SIMS. Acting on an erroneous report that the two ships were a carrier and cruiser, Admiral Takagi ordered an airstrike, which quickly sent the two vessels to the bottom, at the cost of six aircraft lost. Meanwhile, US carrier planes were also acting on a false lead, a *Yorktown* scout having reported "two carriers and four heavy cruisers" some 175 miles northwest of TF 17. Not until both American carriers had launched full deckloads of aircraft was it discovered that the scout had intended to say "two heavy cruisers and two destroyers" but miscoded his message. So the airstrike was aborted. Then Lady Luck, the true goddess of war, took a hand. Just as the American aircraft were preparing to return to their ships, they came upon the Port Moresby support group, steaming southeastward in the Solomon Sea. They promptly jumped the light carrier *Soho*. It required only 10 minutes before the cry "Scratch one flattop" went out over the radio waves for the first time. This so upset VAdm Shigeyoshi Inoue, overall Japanese commander in the area, that he effectively aborted the Port Moresby operation.

Meanwhile, Fletcher, realizing that he had located the Port Moresby invasion force, ordered a cruiser squadron under Britain's RAdm J. G. GRACE to go after it, thereby weakening his defensive screen. Grace's mission turned into a wild-goose chase, but he did successfully beat off an attack by 31 land-based Japanese aircraft, immediately after which he had to endure another by

USAAF B-17s, which tried a high-altitude bomb run on him; fortunately his squadron suffered no loss either time. The Japanese airmen reported two battleships and a heavy cruiser sunk; the American flyboys were almost as optimistic (even though they had attacked friendly ships).

Toward evening, Takagi sent out an offensive scouting mission, with orders to sink Fletcher's carriers. Intercepted by Fletcher's CAP (combat air patrol), they were roughly handled, losing nine. Attempting to return to their ships after dark, six tried to land on *Yorktown* and were duly shot down, while 11 others splashed making night landings on their own carriers.

As of the end of 7 May both sides had little to brag about, the United States having accounted for a light carrier and about 20 enemy aircraft and the Japanese for an oiler and a destroyer. Then came the 8th.

Each side sent out predawn reconnaissance patrols on 8 May, and each managed to locate the other's carriers. Each immediately launched massive strikes, the Japanese of 121 aircraft and the Americans of 122. Although the air strikes were of virtually identical size, and indeed the two task forces were quite closely matched as well (United States: two carriers, five cruisers, seven destroyers; Japanese, two carriers, four cruisers, six destroyers), meteorological conditions favored the Japanese. They were operating from the Solomon Sea, just then overcast and subject to occasional rain squalls, while the Americans were to the southwest in the bright and sunny Coral Sea, one of the calmest expanses of water in the world.

The American air strikes went in first. At about 1057 hours, *Yorktown*'s bombers, having failed to locate *Zuikaku*, took on *Shokaku*, scoring only two hits but damaging her flight deck sufficiently to prevent further air operations. Half of *Lexington*'s bombers missed the Japanese entirely, while the other half put another bomb into *Shokaku* at about 1240 hours; Takagi immediately ordered her to retire on TRUK. By this time Japanese air strikes were working over Task Force 17. Between 1118 hours and 1140 hours *Yorktown* took a bomb hit, but *Lex-*

ington took a real pounding, two TORPEDOES and two bombs, which left her listing and on fire. As both sides recovered aircraft, Takagi decided to leave the area, conceding a strategic victory to Fletcher, despite his heavier loss in ships (fleet carrier *Lexington*, which went down despite heroic damage control efforts, oiler *Neosho*, and destroyer *Sims*, against only light carrier *Shoho*). In addition to having their strategic intention frustrated in this action, the Japanese lost the services of two fleet carriers, for *Shokaku*'s damage required about two months to repair, while *Zuikaku*'s plane and PILOT losses required a month to make up. As a result, neither carrier was present for MIDWAY.

The Coral Sea also revealed both navies' bad habits and inexperience at this new form of warfare. Japanese communications were sloppy, with admirals being in the habit of not passing on vital information, a trait they were never able to overcome throughout the war. Their admirals tended to fight as if they were the only Japanese force engaged and constantly missed opportunities to coordinate with other Japanese forces, a real problem given their propensity to scatter offensive elements, apparently in order to deceive the US forces as to where the main blow was to fall. The Japanese also lacked the rapid repair techniques of the Americans. While the heavily damaged *Yorktown* was repaired in time for the Battle of Midway, the less heavily damaged *Shokaku* was not ready until a week after Midway was over.

The major US errors were largely due to inexperience. The Japanese had more experience in carrier operations and were able to attack American carriers more efficiently, expertly maneuvering their aircraft groups to search out and attack enemy ships. American officers closed this experience gap by the end of 1942.

Corregidor, Philippines

A tadpole-shaped rocky island blocking the entrance to Manila Bay, Corregidor was heavily fortified in the decades before the Naval DISARMAMENT TREATIES. Properly stocked with

US troops on Corregidor surrender to the Japanese, May 6, 1942.

food and ammunition, it was capable of holding out under intensive attack for long periods. However, by the early 1940s it was vulnerable to air attack, most of the fortifications lacking overhead protection. One of the most important defensive installations on the island was Malinta Tunnel, which had a main corridor 1,400 feet long, off which were a number of side tunnels fitted out for various purposes, such as offices, barracks, hospital, and so forth.

During the fighting on BATAAN, Corregidor came under frequent air attack. With the surrender of Bataan on April 9, 1942 Corregidor became the object of increasingly intensive air and artillery bombardment, which gradually disabled most of the heavy coast artillery guns and mortars on the island. Some personnel were evacuated by submarine, but it proved impossible to bring out more than a handful. On May 5, Japanese troops effected a landing in battalion strength on the island. Although resistance was tenacious, the Japanese brought several light TANKS ashore, and these proved decisive, the defenders having no way to cope with them. Corregidor surrendered on 6 May. Many of the wounded in Malinta Tunnel were massacred in their beds.

By 1945 the Japanese had made some repairs to the defenses, and added elaborate field works of their own. As American forces approached Manila, the Japanese beefed up the garrison to some 6,000 men. In February 1945, covered by an intensive artillery and aerial bombardment, the 503rd Parachute Infantry Regiment made a combat jump onto Corregidor. Reinforced by a battalion of the 34th Infantry, which arrived by amphibious craft, the paratroopers retook the island after several days of heavy fighting. Virtually all of the Japanese troops on the island were killed, some of them sealed up in Malinta Tunnel when they refused to surrender. US CASUALTIES amounted to nearly a third of the troops committed, 223 killed and 1,107 wounded.

Cruisers

As originally conceived, in the late 19th century, cruisers were the descendants of the frigates of the age of sail, their duties being to "show the flag" in remote areas, in order to keep the locals from stirring up trouble, and, in wartime, to provide scouts with some firepower for the fleet. Cruisers were large enough for these tasks, but not so large and expensive as battleships. Many cruisers were effectively large destroyers, equipped with TORPEDOES and capable of doing most of the jobs destroyers were designed for. Indeed, in the Japanese Navy light cruisers were normally used as leaders of destroyer squadrons. But cruisers usually had larger, and longer-ranged guns than destroyers. Cruisers also had some armor so they could usually defeat destroyers, unless the DDs got in a spread of torpedoes first. Cruisers were relatively valuable, and merited protection by destroyers, but were sometimes sent out on missions unescorted. The vague

role of cruisers led to experimentation in their design.

Light cruisers (CL) were between 2,500 and 12,000 tons in displacement, usually carrying six to a dozen five-inch or six-inch guns, but occasionally more, plus one or two banks of torpedoes and some antiaircraft armament. Lightly armored, they were usually fast and relatively cheap, and could outshoot most things they couldn't outrun. Heavy cruisers (CA) were from 8,000 to 18,000 tons displacement, toting six to ten guns of eight-inch caliber plus antiaircraft weapons. Although the US Navy dispensed with torpedoes on its heavy cruisers, the Japanese continued to include them, which proved a considerable asset. Ideally, the light cruisers were supposed to "show the flag" in peacetime, and in war serve as anti-destroyer protection for fleets, provide firepower to help defend convoys from surface attack, and, in some navies, serve as flagships for destroyer squadrons.

During the late 1930s, with aircraft looming larger as an anti-ship threat, a new variety of light cruiser was developed to protect the fleet from air attack, the antiaircraft cruiser (CLAA). The first few were created by the simple expedient of reequipping older light cruisers with a copious battery of four-inch or five-inch antiaircraft or dual-purpose guns and some radar, sometimes with a healthy allocation of torpedoes as well. Later purpose-built antiaircraft cruisers appeared in several navies. Although very light, these vessels proved immensely valuable in combat, and not only in an antiaircraft role.

Generally much better armored than light cruisers, heavy cruisers were usually slower. They were supposed to serve as muscular scouts, able to locate enemy fleets, fight off enemy scouts, and, in battle, add their firepower to that of the battlewagons.

Unfortunately, by World War II a lot had changed and the role of the cruiser had become somewhat uncertain, particularly that of the heavy cruiser, since its scouting function had been usurped by aircraft and radar. Moreover, since one had to fight with what one had on hand, it was not uncommon in the numerous battles among the islands of the South and southwest Pacific for heavy cruisers, light cruisers, and even antiaircraft cruisers to find themselves slugging it out in surface melees against enemy vessels of like type or even battleships.

Late in the war the United States introduced the large cruiser (CB), which was a sort of super heavy cruiser. These ships were sometimes called battlecruisers due to their considerable size (over 34,000 tons at full load, as much as a fleet carrier) and heavier armament (nine 12-inch guns). They had the least well-defined role of any category of warship.

The seven US heavy cruisers and three light cruisers sunk in the war were lost to ship- or submarine-launched torpedoes, or to a combination of torpedoes and surface gunfire, except one, which was lost to an aircraft torpedo. Of the 16 Japanese heavy cruisers and 24 light cruisers lost in the war, 15 succumbed to submarine torpedoes (two from British SUBMARINES), four to guns or torpedoes in surface combat (one by the British), six by a combination of surface combat and air combat, and 15 by air attack.

JAPANESE CRUISER ATTRITION	
Year	Lost
1942	6
1943	2
1944	24
1945	8

Crutchley, V.A.C. (1893–1986)

Victor Alexander Charles Crutchley joined the ROYAL NAVY shortly before World War I, during which he won the Victoria Cross. He rose steadily though the ranks thereafter, and by the outbreak of World War II was a captain. He had a distinguished combat career, the most spectacular moment being when, as skipper of the battleship *Warspite*, he led some destroyers into the narrow waters of Narvik Fjord in Norway early in 1940, to wipe out an entire German destroyer squadron. Appointed commander of the Australian cruiser squadron in mid-1942, and placed in command of part of the task force that supported the GUADALCANAL landings, he was in command, though not present, at the disastrous Battle of SAVO ISLAND, for which he was found faultless, in as much as he was absent on orders. Crutchley continued to command the Australian squadron for most of the rest of the war, and saw considerable service in support of the Seventh Fleet. He retired as a full admiral in 1946.

Cunningham, Andrew Browne (1883–1963)

The most distinguished British sea dog since Nelson, Cunningham was born in Scotland. He entered the ROYAL NAVY via Dartmouth Academy in 1898, served in various ships thereafter, seeing action at the Dardanelles and in the Zeebrugge Raid during World War I, winning considerable distinction. After the war he held various posts ashore and afloat, and in 1939 was named commander of the Mediterranean Fleet. During World War II Cunningham took part in numerous operations in the Mediterranean (Cape Spartivento, the Taranto Raid, Cape Matapan, Torch, etc.), and upon the death of Sir Dudley Pound in 1943 was made first sea lord, from which post he supervised all British naval operations worldwide.

Curtin, John (1885–1945)

Born into a poor Australian family, John Curtin left school at the age of 12 to work as a printer's apprentice. He became active in the trade union movement, and eventually became editor of a leading Labour Party newspaper. His long political career culminated in October 1941, when he became Labour prime minister of Australia with the ouster of Robert Menzies. A deft politician and capable

CRUISERS

Navy	Class	Year	Tot.	Displacement Full	Std.	Crew	Combat Surf.	AAA	A/C	Guns Main	Sec.	DP	AAA	HMG	TT	DC	Dimension Length	Beam	Draft	HP	Spd.	Armor Belt	Turret	Deck	Tower
Heavy Cruisers (CA)																									
Jp.	Aoba	1927	2	10.7	9.0	625	12	1	2	6x8	None	None	4x4.7	12	12	0	177.5	17.6	5.7	102.0	33.0	3.0	1.0	1.4	3.0
Au.	Australia	1942	2	14.5	10.9	698	14	2	3	8x8	None	8x4	None	4	0	0	179.8	20.8	6.3	80.0	31.5	4.5	1.0	1.0	0.0
U.S.	Baltimore	1943	24	17.0	14.5	2,039	16	7	4	9x8	None	12x5	None	72	0	0	202.4	21.6	7.3	120.0	33.0	6.0	8.0	2.5	6.0
U.S.	Des Moines	MHB	4	20.9	17.2	1,799	16	8	4	9x8	None	12x5	None	72	0	0	213.4	23.0	7.9	120.0	33.0	6.0	8.0	3.5	6.5
Br.	Exeter	1930	1	10.5	8.4	630	11	3	2	6x8	None	8x4	None	16	6	0	164.6	17.7	6.2	80.0	32.0	3.0	1.0	1.0	3.0
Jp.	Furutaka	1926	2	10.3	8.7	625	12	1	2	6x8	None	None	4x4.7	12	8	0	176.8	16.9	5.6	102.0	33.0	3.0	1.0	1.4	3.0
Br.	Kent	1928	5	14.5	10.9	698	14	3	3	8x8	None	8x4	None	8	8	0	179.8	20.8	6.3	80.0	31.5	4.5	1.0	1.0	3.0
Br.	London	1929	4	14.4	10.8	700	14	3	3	8x8	None	8x4	None	16	8	0	181.4	20.1	6.3	80.0	32.3	3.5	1.0	1.0	3.0
Jp.	Mogami (B)	1940	4	15.5	12.4	850	14	2	3	8x8	None	8x5	None	12	12	0	198.0	20.2	5.9	152.0	34.9	4.9	1.0	2.4	3.0
Jp.	Mogami (C)	1943	4	15.5	12.2	850	7	2	11	4x8	None	8x5	None	30	12	0	198.0	20.2	5.9	152.0	35.0	4.9	1.0	2.4	3.0
Jp.	Nachi	1928	4	16.5	13.0	773	16	2	3	10x8	None	8x5	None	10	16	0	201.7	20.7	6.3	130.0	33.0	3.9	1.0	1.4	3.0
U.S.	New Orleans	1934	7	12.5	10.1	868	15	7	4	9x8	None	None	8x5	8	0	0	176.2	18.8	6.9	107.0	32.7	5.8	6.0	2.5	6.0
Br.	Norfolk	1930	2	13.4	10.0	710	14	3	1	8x8	None	8x4	None	16	8	0	181.4	20.1	6.4	80.0	32.3	1.0	1.0	1.0	3.0
U.S.	Northampton	1930	6	11.4	9.0	740	15	5	4	9x8	None	None	8x5	8	0	0	177.4	20.1	5.9	107.0	32.5	3.8	2.5	2.0	2.5
U.S.	Pensacola	1930	2	11.5	9.1	631	16	5	4	10x8	None	None	8x5	8	0	0	173.7	19.9	5.9	107.0	32.5	4.0	2.5	1.8	2.5
U.S.	Portland	1933	2	12.8	10.3	807	15	5	4	9x8	None	None	8x5	8	0	0	180.4	20.1	6.4	107.0	32.5	3.0	2.5	2.5	2.5
Jp.	Takao	1932	4	16.5	13.4	773	16	2	3	10x8	None	8x5	None	12	16	0	201.7	20.7	6.3	130.0	34.2	4.9	1.0	1.4	3.0
Jp.	Tone	1938	2	15.2	11.2	850	14	2	6	8x8	None	8x5	None	12	12	0	189.1	18.5	6.5	152.0	35.0	4.9	1.0	2.4	3.0
U.S.	Wichita	1939	1	13.0	10.6	929	15	6	4	9x8	None	8x5	None	8	0	0	182.9	18.8	7.2	100.0	33.0	6.0	8.0	2.5	6.0
Light Cruisers (CL)																									
N.Z.	Achilles	1933	2	9.2	7.1	570	4	2	1	8x6	None	4x4	None	8	8	0	159.1	17.0	5.8	72.0	32.5	4.0	1.0	1.3	1.0
Au.	Adelaide	1922	1	6.1	5.1	470	6	2	0	8x6	None	4x4	None	None	None	0	140.2	15.1	5.4	25.0	25.5	0.0	0.0	2.0	0.0
Jp.	Agano	1942	4	8.5	6.7	730	4	1	2	6x6	None	None	4x3	32	8	16	162.0	15.2	5.6	100.0	35.0	2.2	1.0	0.7	3.0
Br.	Arethusa	1935	4	6.7	5.3	500	4	3	1	6x6	None	8x4	None	6	6	0	146.3	15.5	5.0	64.0	32.3	2.3	1.0	1.0	3.0
U.S.	Brooklyn	1938	9	12.2	9.8	686	14	5	4	15x6	None	8x5	None	24	0	0	182.9	18.8	6.9	100.0	32.5	5.0	6.5	2.0	5.0
U.S.	Cleveland	1942	29	14.1	11.7	1285	6	7	4	12x6	None	12x5	None	38	0	0	182.9	20.2	7.5	100.0	32.5	5.0	6.5	2.0	5.0
Nth.	De Ruyter	1935	1	7.5	6.0	435	4	1	1	7x5.9	None	None	None	18	0	0	168.3	15.7	5.1	76.0	33.5	2.0	1.2	1.0	1.2
Fr.	Duguay Trouin	1926	3	9.4	7.2	578	4	1	2	8x6.1	None	4x3	4x3	4	12	0	175.3	17.2	5.2	100.0	33.0	0.8	1.0	0.	1.0
Br.	Edinburgh	1939	2	13.2	10.6	850	6	4	3	12x6	None	12x4	None	16	6	0	176.5	19.3	6.5	80.0	32.5	4.5	4.0	2.	3.0
Br.	Enterprise	1926	2	9.2	7.6	972	4	2	0	7x6	None	None	5x4	6	16	0	162.1	16.5	5.0	80.0	32.0	3.0	1.0	1.	0.0
Br.	Fiji	1940	8	10.5	8.5	920	5	2	2	12x6	None	8x4	None	8	6	0	164.0	18.9	6.0	72.5	31.5	3.5	2.0	2	0.0
Br.	Gloucester	1939	3	11.7	9.4	800	5	2	2	12x6	None	8x4	None	8	6	0	170.1	19.0	6.3	82.5	32.3	4.5	4.0	2	0.0
Nth.	Java	1925	2	7.2	6.7	525	3	4	0	10x5.9	None	None	None	10	0	0	155.3	16.0	5.5	72.0	31.0	3.0	4.0	2	5.0

Navy	Class	Year	Tot.	Std.	Full	Crew	A/C	Main	Sec.	DP	AAA	HMG	TT	DC	Length	Beam	Draft	HP	Spd.	Belt	Deck	Surf.	AAA
Jp.	Katori	1940	4	5.9	6.2	400	1	4x5.5	None	2x5	None	4	4	0	123.5	16.0	5.8	8.0	18.0	0.0	0.0	2.0	0.0
Jp.	Kitakami (Kuma)	1920	2	5.9	7.5	450?	0	4x5.5	None	None	None	8	40	0	162.1	17.5	4.8	90.0	33.6	2.5	1.0	1.0	0.0
Jp.	Kuma	1919	3	5.6	7.0	450	0	7x5.5	None	None	2x3.1	2	8	0	162.1	14.2	4.8	90.0	33.6	2.5	1.0	1.3	0.0
Fr.	La Galissonnière	1935	6	7.6	9.1	764	4	9x6	None	None	8x3.5	8	4	0	172.0	17.5	5.4	84.0	31.0	4.0	4.0	1.5	3.8
N.Z.	Leander	1933	3	7.1	9.2	570	1	8x6	4x4	None	None	8	8	0	159.1	17.0	5.8	72.0	32.5	4.0	1.0	1.3	0.0
Jp.	Mogami (A)	1935	4	11.2	15.0	850	3	15x6	8x5	None	None	12	12	0	198.1	19.2	5.9	152.0	35.0	4.9	1.0	2.4	3.0
Jp.	Nagara	1921	6	5.6	6.5	450	1	7x5.5	None	None	2x3.1	8	8	0	162.1	14.2	4.8	90.0	34.5	2.5	1.0	1.3	0.0
U.S.	Omaha	1922	10	7.1	9.5	458	0	12x6	None	2x3	None	10	10	0	169.4	16.9	4.1	90.0	34.0	3.0	0.0	1.5	?
Jp.	Oyodo	1943	1	8.2	11.4	750	2	6x6	8x4	None	None	12	0	0	180.0	16.6	6.0	110.0	35.0	2.0	1.0	1.0	0.0
Au.	Perth	1936	3	7.1	9.1	570	1	8x6	None	8x4	None	12	8	0	159.1	17.3	5.7	72.0	32.5	4.0	1.0	1.4	0.0
Jp.	Sendai	1924	3	5.2	7.1	450	1	7x5.5	None	None	2x3	12	8	0	152.4	14.2	4.9	75.0	35.2	2.5	1.0	1.0	0.0
Br.	Southampton	1937	5	9.1	11.4	748	3	12x6	8x4	None	None	6	6	0	170.1	18.8	6.2	75.0	32.0	4.5	2.0	1.1	3.0
Br.	Swiftsure	1944	5	8.8	11.1	960	1	9x6	10x4	None	None	6	6	0	164.0	19.2	6.4	72.5	31.5	3.5	1.0	2.0	3.0
Jp.	Tenryu	1919	2	3.9	4.4	327	0	4x5.5	None	None	3x3.1	6	6	0	142.9	12.3	4.0	51.0	33.0	2.0	0.6	2.0	0.0
Nth.	Tromp	1940	1	3.8	4.8	309	0	6x5.9	None	None	None	6	6	0	125.0	12.4	4.2	56.0	33.5	0.6	0.6	1.0	0.5
Br.	Uganda	1943	3	8.5	10.5	920	2	9x6	8x4	None	None	6	6	0	164.0	18.9	6.0	72.5	31.5	3.5	2.0	2.0	0.0
Jp.	Yubari	1923	1	3.4	4.4	328	0	6x5.5	None	None	1x3	4	0	0	132.6	12.0	3.6	57.5	33.0	2.3	1.0	1.0	0.0
Antiaircraft Cruisers (CLAA)																							
U.S.	Atlanta	1942	11	6.7	8.3	623	0	None	None	16x5	None	24	8	8	161.6	16.2	6.3	75.0	32.5	3.8	1.3	0.3	3.8
Br.	Bellona	1943	5	6.0	7.8	530	0	None	None	8x5.25	None	12	0	8	147.8	15.4	5.4	62.0	32.0	3.0	1.0	1.0	3.0
Br.	Charybdis	1941	1	5.6	7.3	500	0	None	None	8x4.5	None	8	6	6	147.8	15.4	5.1	62.0	32.2	3.0	0.5	1.0	3.0
Br.	Cleopatra	1941	6	5.6	7.3	530	0	None	None	10x5.25	None	8	6	6	147.8	15.4	5.1	62.0	32.2	3.0	0.5	1.0	3.0
Br.	Dido	1940	3	5.6	7.3	500	0	None	None	8x5.25	None	8	6	6	147.8	15.4	5.1	62.0	32.2	3.0	0.5	1.0	3.0
Nth.	Jacob van Heemskerck	1942	1	3.8	4.8	309	0	None	None	10x4	None	10	6	6	125.0	12.4	4.2	56.0	33.5	0.6	0.0	1.0	0.5
Br.	Scylla	1942	1	5.6	7.3	500	0	None	None	8x4.5	None	8	6	6	147.8	15.4	5.1	62.0	32.2	3.0	0.5	1.0	3.0
U.S.	Worcester	1948	2	14.7	18.0	1,401	4	None	None	12x6	24x3	12	0	0	202.4	21.5	7.5	120.0	33.0	5.0	6.5	3.5	5.0

Key to the table: **Navy** = nation the ship belongs to: Au. = Australia, Br. = Britain, Cn. = Canada, Fr. = France, Nth. = Netherlands, N.Z. = New Zealand, Jp. = Japan, U.S. = United States. **Class** = names of the lead ship in the class. **Year** = when the first ship in the class entered service; MHB = might have been, a class that was not, but could have been in action. **Tot.** = total number of ships in that class. **Displacement** = the amount of water that the ship displaces (i.e., the weight of the water that would occupy the space occupied by the ship), expressed in thousands of tons. There are two values for this: **Std.** = standard, or weight with basic crew, fuel, munitions and other supplies; **Full** = "fighting weight," loaded with all the items needed to go to war. **Crew** = number normally carried. **Combat** = relative combat value for each ship in the following areas: **Surf.** = value in surface engagements; **AAA** = value against attacking aircraft. A group of ships would combine their values, which was particularly effective when defending against enemy aircraft. **A/C** = aircraft carried. **Guns** = many different types: **Main** = the largest guns, on battleships. These can be from 11 to 18 inches in bore diameter; **Sec.** = secondary guns for use against smaller surface targets (these became obsolete during World War II, usually converted to AAA use); **DP** = dual purpose, for use against surface and air targets; **AAA** = antiaircraft artillery, generally the same caliber as the DP guns, but whose only purpose is to attack aircraft; **HMG** = heavy machine guns, caliber varying from 12.7mm to 40mm, the latter (20mm and up) were actually automatic cannon, as they fired explosive shells. **DC** = depth charges carried. **TT** = torpedo tubes carried. **Dimensions** = three of them, expressed in meters: **Length** = how long the ship was, **Beam** = width of the ship, **Draft** = how deep into the water the bottom of the ship is at full load. **Spd.** = top speed in knots (nautical miles per hour). **Armor** = the protection many ships had against enemy fire. Given in inches for the following positions on the ship: **Belt** = an area along the waterline to protect engines and ammo magazines; **Turret** = rotating structures containing the main guns; **Deck** = for protection from "plunging" shells (fired from a great distance away) or bombs; **HP** = maximum horsepower generated by the ship's engines. **Tower** = in which the fire control crew operates.

diplomat, he successfully pressed for the return of Australia's three divisions in British service in North Africa, a matter of considerable importance in the difficult days after PEARL HARBOR that culminated in the Japanese occupation of much of New Guinea and air attacks on northwestern Australian cities. Equally hard-nosed at home, Curtin subjected Australia's economy, society, and population to remarkably rigid controls, and remained immensely popular while doing so. He died of natural causes on 5 July 1945, just weeks before the surrender of Japan.

D

D3A Val, Japanese Carrier Dive Bomber

The D3A Val was the primary Japanese carrier dive bomber for the first year of the war. While not particularly outstanding in the speed, bombload, or range departments, in the hands of well trained crews the Val did an outstanding job. The aircraft was quite maneuverable and the D3A could tangle with enemy fighters once its bombs had been dropped. PRODUCTION of the D3A continued until January 1944, with 816 being delivered. The D3A ended its career as a trainer and KAMIKAZE.

See also AIRCRAFT TYPES, DEVELOPMENT; CARRIERS, DESIGNING AIRCRAFT FOR.

D4Y Judy, Japanese Carrier Dive Bomber

The D4Y Judy was a new Japanese carrier dive bomber that began replacing the older Val during the summer of 1942. By early 1943 the replacement was complete. Unfortunately, most of the well trained prewar crews were now dead, and the Judy ended up operating mainly from land bases with less skillful crews. In comparison to the older Val, the Judy was superior in nearly all aspects (speed, range, bombload).

See also AIRCRAFT TYPES, DEVELOPMENT; CARRIERS, DESIGNING AIRCRAFT FOR.

Da Nang, Indo-China

Aside from some facilities to support coastal shipping, the fine harbor at Da Nang was of limited consequence as a port, but shared with CAM RANH BAY great potential value as a naval or air base.

Used as a base by the Japanese during the opening operations in the South China Sea in December 1941, it became familiar to Americans in a later war.

Dalny, Manchuria/Manchukuo

Formerly known as Dairen, Dalny had a small, somewhat cramped harbor, with some port facilities, and served as a local base for the Imperial Navy in the Yellow Sea.

Damage, Sinking Ships

Sinking a warship is not as easy as it may seem. Among the factors that come into play are the nature of the basic structure of the ship (compartmentalization, armor, machinery spacing, etc.); size of the vessel; location of hits; time of day; CASUALTIES; damage control techniques, equipment, training, and experience; weather; type of ammunition used; and plain dumb luck. Small-caliber hits can sometimes cause enormous damage, while major-caliber hits can sometimes be of little consequence.

For example, three of the four US carriers lost in 1942—LEXINGTON, YORKTOWN, and *Hornet*—were considerably less damaged at the time they were abandoned than were a number of carriers that were saved despite severe damage in '44–'45, such as *Bunker Hill* or *Franklin* (see ESSEX CLASS). The difference lay in experience and in improved damage control techniques and equipment. Of the carriers lost in '42, only WASP, which succumbed to a spread of three TORPEDOES, would have been lost if late war damage control techniques had been available.

The Japanese never caught on to some of the tricks that saved US carriers later in the war. For example, while they carefully drained avgas lines during air attacks, they didn't hit upon the idea of filling these pipes and hoses with carbon dioxide. This removed volatile fumes from these elaborate plumbing systems, further reducing the danger of explosion.

Different types of ships endured damage in different ways.

Battleships. Since they were designed to "take it," battleships generally did. In fact, relatively speaking, battleships usually took more damage than any other type of vessel before succumbing, as can be seen by some examples.

USS Bunker Hill (CV-17), burning after taking two kamikaze hits in 30 seconds off Okinawa on May 11, 1945. Despite enormous damage and very heavy casualties, the ship was saved and returned to service.

The Japanese battleship *Hiei* was lost after the night action off GUADALCANAL on November 12–13, during which she took about 50 hits from 5- and 8-inch shells. Although these did little direct damage to the ship structurally, they started uncontrollable fires. Since these left her dead in the water, the Japanese scuttled her rather than leave her to be finished off by US aircraft the next morning.

The US battleship SOUTH DAKOTA took one 5-inch, six 6-inch (including one armor piercer or AP), 18 8-inch (of which five were AP), one 14-inch, and one unknown-sized shell, for a total of 27, during the night action off Guadalcanal on November 14–15, 1942. Two hits, both 8-inch AP, affected flotation, resulting in a list of about 0.75%, virtually imperceptible without instruments. Eighteen of the hits were in soft parts of the ship, one of which knocked out her search radar, and some of which caused a temporary loss of electrical power. This last might have been fatal, were it not for the presence of USS *Washington*, which shot up the Japanese sufficiently as to discourage them from continuing the fight. Total casualties were 38 killed and 60 wounded.

On the same occasion that *South Dakota* was seriously injured, *Washington* turned the Japanese battleship *Kirishima* into a burning wreck with nine 16-inch and about 40 5-inch hits in a very few minutes. Despite this damage, the Japanese ship remained afloat, and had to be scuttled the next morning.

The German battleship *Bismarck* absorbed an enormous amount of damage during her May 1941 raid into the Atlantic. On 24 May she took three 14-inch shell hits, causing some flooding and reducing speed from 30 to 28 knots, plus one aerial torpedo several hours later, which reduced speed to 20 knots. On 26 May two or three aerial torpedoes jammed her rudder, making her very slow and very difficult to steer. On 27 May she was hit by scores—if not hundreds—of 14- and 16-inch, plus hundreds of 6- and 8-inch shells, plus at least one torpedo. The last of the shells were taken at ranges as short as 2,200 yards. This turned the ship into a burning wreck, wracked by internal explosions and unable to maneuver or return fire. Despite this damage, she remained afloat, and the British had to pump three more torpedoes into her before she sank, a process already begun by the Germans, who had ordered her scuttled.

The Japanese battleships *Musashi* and YAMATO, the largest warships in the world until the 1960s, both absorbed an extraordinary amount of damage before going down. *Musashi* took an estimated 19 aerial torpedoes and 17 bombs during the Battle of LEYTE GULF on 24 October 1944. *Yamato* absorbed about a dozen torpedoes and six bombs north of OKINAWA on 7 April 1945.

Of course, even a battleship could succumb to a lucky hit. The Italian battleship *Roma* was lost in September 1943 when a single unmanned German Felix guided MISSILE (actually a pilotless, radio-controlled glide bomb) penetrated a magazine. This is the closest thing to a KAMIKAZE kill of a battleship in the war.

Carriers. Carriers were relatively frail vessels, not well protected, offering huge target areas and full of volatile aviation fuel.

The US carrier *Franklin* was almost lost when a Japanese bomber put two 500-pound armor piercing bombs through her flight deck off Okinawa in 1945. These penetrated to the hangar deck, where they set off fueled and ammunitioned aircraft. The resulting series of explosions killed over 700 and wounded more than 200 of her crew within minutes, while causing a nearly fatal list and extensive fires. Despite this, within hours she was able, with some assistance, to overcome the fires, restart her engines, and get out of the battle area. She then made a 12,000-mile voyage to the Brooklyn Navy Yard under her own power, stopping only once to take on stores and spare parts.

The US light carrier *Princeton* was lost to a single bomb, which penetrated several decks to detonate in a magazine, off Leyte in 1944.

The Japanese carrier TAIHO was lost to a single submarine torpedo on the eve of the Battle of the PHILIPPINE SEA. The hit, a relatively minor one, caused aviation fuel to leak into the ship's bilges. There it vaporized and eventually detonated, causing the ship to blow up.

Cruisers. The distinction between heavy and light cruisers appears to have been of lesser importance than that between larger and smaller ones, and the degree of protection. Most US cruisers were relatively large, only the ATLANTA CLASS being under 10,000 tons, whereas most Japanese light cruisers and four of their heavy cruisers were below that figure. Many British-designed light cruisers were also below that figure.

The Australian heavy cruiser AUSTRALIA managed to survive a half-dozen kamikaze hits over several days off Okinawa in early 1945.

The Japanese heavy cruiser MOGAMI was virtually a total wreck after the Battle of MIDWAY (June 6–7, 1942), having been repeatedly bombed by US aircraft, yet managed to keep under way, get her engines back in order, and make it home safely, to be repaired and returned to service.

The upperworks of the Japanese heavy cruiser AOBA, a small ship, were turned into a total wreck by US cruiser and destroyer gunfire during the Battle of CAPE ESPERANCE (October 11–12, 1942), yet within a couple of hours the ship was able to make 25 knots, getting away and living to fight another day.

The US heavy cruiser *San Francisco* survived a dozen hits by 14-inch high-explosive (not armor-piercing) shells, plus 33 more of 5-inch to 6-inch shells, off Guadalcanal on the night of November 12–13, 1942, in an action which saw three of the crew awarded the MEDAL OF HONOR (RAdm Dan CALLAGHAN and two commanders).

The US light cruiser *Houston* (the second of the name in the war) was hit by two Japanese aerial torpedoes in October 1944. These caused her to take on 6,500 tons of water, over 45% of her normal full load displacement, yet she survived. No other vessel in history ever shipped proportionally so much water without sinking.

Destroyers. Despite being quite small vessels, destroyers tended to be pretty resilient. While the

HITS BY DISPLACEMENT NEEDED TO SINK A HEAVY WARSHIP

Ship Type	Type of Ammunition					
	Shells			Other		
	Heavy	Medium	Light	Bomb	Torp	Kamikaze
BB	1–2	5–8	50+	1+	2+	2–4?
CA	1–2	2–3	5–8	1–2	1–2	1–2?
CL	1	1–2	3–5	1–2	1–2	1?

American destroyer *William D. Porter* (DD-579) succumbed to a single kamikaze hit on 10 June 1945, the destroyer *Laffey* (DD-724) survived six on 16 April. The very new destroyer *Aaron Ward* (DD-771) survived five kamikaze hits that same May, but was never repaired and was scrapped shortly after the war.

From anecdotal information such as this, it is possible to develop some rough guidelines as to the amount of damage various types of ships can absorb before sinking.

For any ship, and especially the smaller ones, a single hit in a vital area (the ammunition magazine, for example) could blow the vessel apart im-

TOTAL HITS NEEDED TO SINK A LIGHTER WARSHIP

Ship Type	Type of Ammunition					
	Shells			Other		
	Heavy	Medium	Light	Bomb	Torp	Kamikaze
CV/CVL	8–10	15–25	50+	1–10	1–2	1–3?
CVE	1–6	3–10	15–40	1–2	1–2	1
DD/DE	1–3	1–10	5–20	1–2	1–2	1
Merchant	1–2	2–3	5–10	1–3	1–2	1

"Heavy" refers to shells of 11-inch caliber or greater, "medium" to shells 5.5-inch to 8-inch, and "light" to those of 3-inch to 5-inch. Bombs are assumed to be of 500 pounds or more. The question marks indicate that no ship of the indicated type was ever actually sunk by kamikaze. Figures for the numbers of shells and bombs for heavier ships are per thousand tons of displacement. Figures for lighter warships are absolute. Thus a 32,000-ton battleship (BB) would probably require 32 to 64 heavy shell hits to sink, or two or more torpedoes or kamikaze, while a carrier of like displacement would probably absorb no more than 10 heavy shells before sinking. Older Japanese light cruisers were more likely to match the profile for destroyers than the larger light cruisers favored by the United States.

mediately. In fact, the figures given above are only a rough guide. There are many factors that influence whether a ship will sink. Indeed, perhaps the most important thing is not so much the amount of damage that is inflicted on the ship as the rate at which it is inflicted: A lot of damage suffered over several hours may not be as deadly as a relatively small amount inflicted all at once, since the latter short-circuits the ship's damage control systems. Basically, if a ship doesn't sink at once, and is not a blazing inferno, her chances are good, especially if her power plant is relatively unscathed.

See also DESTROYERS, PICKET DUTY.

Ref: Friedman, *United States Aircraft Carriers*; ———, *United States Battleships*; ———, *United States Destroyers*; Garzke and Dulin, *Battleships*.

Darwin, Australia

The most important city in northwestern Australia, with a roomy, sheltered harbor, fair port facilities, a small naval base, and a large airfield. However, its limited access to other parts of Australia and its relative isolation made it rather exposed for a base, if nearby portions of the NETHERLANDS EAST INDIES were in hostile hands, since it had to be supplied by sea.

On 19 February 1942 Darwin suffered what turned out to be the most devastating Japanese attack on Australia. Aircraft from the First Air Fleet (the Pearl Harbor Task Force) sank seven merchant ships totaling 43,000 GRT, while damaging six other merchant vessels and several small craft. The destroyer USS *Peary* (DD-226) was sunk and two others damaged. In addition to damage to port facilities, some $4 million worth of damage was done to the local airfield and hundreds of people were killed.

This attack caused a considerable reorganization and strengthening of Allied air defenses in the area. Darwin played an important role in the defense of northwestern Australia throughout the war.

Death, Japanese Attitudes Toward

The Japanese saw death in battle somewhat differently than Western troops. This can best be seen by the many terms they used for a soldier lost in battle. They had a term for "killed in action" (*senbotsu*), but they also had terms for the various ways one could be killed. Each of these was associated with varying degrees of military honor. All cultures recognize a concept of "honor" in military operations and the ways in which a soldier may be killed, but only the Japanese had the term *gyokusai*, which meant "to seek death rather than dishonor." For the Japanese this meant a soldier would rather be killed in a hopeless situation than surrender. Japanese culture did not expect a soldier to waste his life uselessly in a hopeless situation, thus there was the term *tai-atari* (literally "body crashing," or ram-

ming one's aircraft or ship into the enemy). Wounded soldiers would explode a grenade when enemy troops came near, thus performing a *jibaku* (self-destruction, while also hurting the enemy). If all hope were lost and no enemy were around, there was always *jiketsu* (usually called "hara-kiri" in the West). This form of suicide was not to be confused with *jisatsu* (garden-variety suicide).

Deaths, World War II

The number of people who were killed in or died as a consequence of World War II cannot be determined with any reasonable degree of accuracy.

Most navy dead were buried at sea. Here, two victims of the sinking of the escort carrier Liscome Bay *are given a formal burial from a Coast Guard attack transport (APA), somewhere off the Gilbert Islands. Most of the approximately 640 men lost when the ship was torpedoed remained entombed in her.*

DEATHS IN WORLD WAR II

Nation	Military	Civilian	Total Notes
Allies			
Australia	37.6	2.5	40.1
Belgium	22.7	76.0	98.7
Brazil	1.5	1.0	2.5+
Britain	403.0	92.7	495.7
British Colonies	7.0	0.0	7.0 A
Canada	42.7	1.0	43.7
China	1,900.0	20,000.0	21,400.0 B
Czechoslovakia	6.6	315.0	321.6+
Denmark	6.4	1.0	7.4
France	245.0	350.0	595.0
Greece	88.3	325.0	413.3
India	48.7	3,000.0	3,048.7
Indo-China	0.0	2,000.0	2,000.0+
Luxembourg	0.1	1.0	1.1
Malaya	0.0	50.0	50.0+
Mexico	0.0	0.1	0.1+
Netherlands	13.7	236.0	249.7
Netherlands East Indies	0.0	100.0	100.0+
New Zealand	8.7	0.0	8.7
Norway	3.0	7.0	10.0
Philippines (US)	40.0	100.0	140.0 C
Poland	597.3	5,675.0	6,272.3
Russia	13,600.0	16,000.0	29,600.0 D
South Africa	8.5	0.0	8.5
United States	407.0	6.0	413.0
Yugoslavia	305.0	1,355.0	1,660.0
Allied Total	17,792.8	49,786.8	67,079.7
Axis			
Bulgaria	18.8	140.0	158.8
Finland	82.0	12.0	94.0
Germany	3,250.0	2,445.0	5,695.0 E
Hungary	200.0	600.0	800.0+
Italy	380.0	152.9	532.9
Japan	2,565.9	672.0	3,237.9
Korea	50	250.0	250.0 F
Romania	450.0	465.0	915.0
Axis Total	6,996.7	4,436.9	11,683.6
Grand Total	24,789.5	54,523.8	79,263.3

+Figures partially estimated.

Notes: All figures are in thousands. British Colonies includes all places not otherwise mentioned.

A. Territories not otherwise enumerated.

B. Includes casualties from 1937 onward.

C. Estimate for civilian casualties probably too low.

D. Includes Latvia, Estonia, and Lithuania, and people shot by Stalin for various reasons, including the misfortune of having become prisoners of war.

E. Excludes Austria.

F. Korea was a Japanese colony during the war. Some Korean military dead are apparently included in Japanese military dead. Figures for civilians are a minimum, as there was widespread hunger in Korea during the war.

Traditional estimates range from a low of 30 million to high of 55 million, yet with some merely cursory research we readily arrived at a figure of nearly 80 million.

The figures published by some countries are very incomplete. For example, generally published figures for civilian losses in Hungary are about 200,000, yet about 90% of Hungary's 400,000 Jews perished in HITLER's death camps. Civilian deaths in Russia are based on recently published documents, which have greatly increased the numbers admitted in the late 1980s (c. 25 million), which were themselves higher than the previous official figures (c. 20 million). There is a similar problem with regard to China, where record keeping was so bad the army was unable to determine the fate of nearly 1.9 million recruits, many of whom may have died of disease, hunger, and exposure even before they were properly enlisted. The enormous civilian losses in India were due to starvation, caused by a combination of the global shipping shortage and the callousness of some British officials. Starvation was also the big killer in Indo-China, where the Japanese requisitioned most of the coastal shipping needed to move rice from the south to the north, and then confiscated a substantial portion of the rice crop as well. There seem to be no reliable figures for civilian losses in MALAYA, SINGAPORE, British BORNEO, or the Philippines, nor any at all for CASUALTIES suffered by the people of Burma, Thailand, Morocco, Algeria, Tunisia, Libya, Ethiopia, Egypt, Syria, Iraq, and Persia, in which there was fighting to a greater or lesser degree, as well as Switzerland and Sweden, which suffered several accidental air attacks in the course of the war, nor a proper tally of losses among neutral merchant seamen. The war-related deaths in those nations should easily add several million to the death count.

Note also that the figures do not include people killed during industrial accidents contingent upon the increased workload in many countries: About 300,000 Americans died in such mishaps during the war, many of them war-related. And then there are the people who died after the war, often long after, from the lingering effects of wounds or privation, and from the civil disorders, insurrections, and anti-colonial revolutions engendered by the war.

So it is not unreasonable to say that nearly a hundred million people perished as a result of World War II. This was about 5% of the planet's population at the time.

A US military cemetery in the Ryukyu Islands, spring 1945.

Deception

Deception has long played a role in warfare. More so in the East than in the West, winning a military advantage through deception was considered an admirable goal. There were many cases of successful deception in the Pacific War, on both sides. Here are a few of the more notable ones.

For America, World War II began with a brilliant subterfuge. The Japanese attack on PEARL HARBOR could not have succeeded without a series of successful deceptions. The Japanese were great believers in surprise generally, and deceptions in particular. Moving a fleet across the Pacific undetected was no mean feat. The Japanese did not normally operate at that great a distance. American admirals knew this, and the Japanese took advantage of it. The planners of the attack realized that the distance problem could be turned to their advantage. The shortest route that could be taken covered some of the stormiest, and least traveled, waters in the world. This route would be a key element in the Pearl Harbor deceptions. The first step was to examine the shipping lanes between Japan and Pearl Harbor. Sure enough, the route that saw the least shipping traffic ran from the KURILE ISLANDS (in northern Japan) to Pearl Harbor. If the fleet steamed north of MIDWAY Island before turning south toward HAWAII, it would traverse an area that was rarely traveled by any ships. The main reason this route was bereft of traffic was not because it was out of the way, but because the North Pacific, like the North Atlantic, suffers from wretched weather. In the winter, the weather is at its worst. That was when the Japanese planned to pass through this stormy region. As a test, the Japanese sent a merchant vessel along the course in October of 1941. Not a single ship was spotted.

But the fleet's passage would not be entirely uncontested. Storms were fierce and bad weather was the norm. While none of the two dozen Japanese ships was lost during the trip, some were damaged and many crewmen were washed overboard. Refueling was difficult. It can be truly said that the most difficult portion of the Pearl Harbor operation was the struggle to get through the stormy North Pacific in one piece. The Americans knew what the North Pacific was like in winter, but they also kept track of the Japanese fleet by monitoring its radio broadcasts, which yielded the general location of the transmitter. Americans were also breaking Japanese codes, but that took longer. Monitoring the coded (and sometimes uncoded) radio traffic of the fleet was called "traffic analysis," and most navies used this technique to good effect. Knowing that, the Japanese used it against the American traffic analysts. Twice before in the previous year, the Japanese carrier fleet had "gone silent" (ceased all radio use) and, it was later discovered, headed south toward the NETHERLANDS EAST INDIES.

In November 1941, the ships involved in the Pearl Harbor operation went silent. Other radio stations began transmitting the messages that the now silent ships would normally send. Individually or in small groups, these ships moved from the INLAND SEA, through the Sea of Japan, and concentrated in a Kurile Island anchorage. On November 26th, the six carriers of the Pearl Harbor task force, plus their escorts and tankers, set out into the murky, storm-tossed North Pacific. As expected, the ships were not spotted crossing the North Pacific. They encountered one ship, but it was Japanese. Maintaining radio silence, even the sailors in the ships were not told what their mission was until 2 December (while still 3,200 miles from Hawaii). The Japanese refueled again on the 3rd, sent the tankers home, and then picked up speed to cover the remaining 2,500 miles to their launching position. Right on schedule, the Japanese arrived at a point 500 miles from Pearl Harbor at 2100 hours on 6 December. The next day was a Sunday, and that was yet another part of the Japanese deception. The Japanese knew that Sunday was the day that the US military was least prepared, especially during peacetime. American recon aircraft were scouting out 400 miles from Pearl Harbor, covering an arc ranging from northwest to south, the direction a weather-wise defender would expect a Japanese fleet to come from. But the Japanese were coming from the north.

Knowing what was in Pearl Harbor was a crucial part of the attack. The Japanese had to know which ships were normally berthed where as well as details on US combat aircraft in the area and the location of military facilities. Moreover, they had to know when it was likely that the maximum number of ships would be in port. Ships at sea on training exercises would be impossible to find, and they would be alerted by the attack on Pearl Harbor. Only the ships tied up in port could be hit by the surprise attack. The Japanese collected the information using local agents, plus a naval officer sent in as a civilian to make sure nothing was missed. Photos were taken and the movement and berthing routines of the fleet noted.

One important item that made the Pearl Harbor attack possible was the 1940 decision to move the Pacific Fleet battleships from SAN DIEGO to Pearl Harbor. This was intended to "send the Japanese a message." That it did, but the message was "bomb me." In 1941 both Japanese and American admirals still considered the battleship to be the key naval weapon and the aircraft carriers just another support system. The Japanese were thus looking for battleships and they expected to find nine or ten, plus two or three carriers, and dozens of cruisers, destroyers, and SUBMARINES sitting in Pearl Harbor on Sunday morning. Except for the missing carriers, which were off on various missions, they were not disappointed. Their spies had done their job well. So well that the Japanese were able to build a scale model of the harbor back in Japan to aid in the attack planning. The attacking Japanese pilots knew more about the layout of Pearl Harbor than most of the people stationed there. One of the technical issues that lulled the Americans into thinking such an attack wouldn't happen was the depth of the water in Pearl Harbor. For TORPEDO carrying aircraft to launch their weapons, the water had to be deep enough for the torpedoes to sink quite a bit before coming to the surface and moving toward their target. The water depth in Pearl

Harbor (only 40 feet where the battleships were berthed) was too shallow for any known torpedo. What the Americans missed, and the Japanese didn't, was that in late 1940 the British had used modified torpedoes (and bombing techniques) to overcome the same problem when they made an air attack on Italian ships in Taranto harbor. The Japanese duplicated the British techniques with their own aircraft and torpedoes. This was all kept quite secret, and even the sailors involved in the project were not told what particular operation it was for.

Another technical problem, how to get at battleships that were berthed between another ship and the pier, was solved by turning some 16–inch naval gun shells into bombs. These shells were designed to devastate a battleship if they came down through the deck at a sharp angle ("plunging fire"), and it was straight into the ship's thinly armored deck that the bombers would drop their modified shells. While the Japanese pulled off a magnificent series of deceptions at Pearl Harbor, they also stumbled into one. Thinking that sinking battleships would cripple the American fleet, they later found out that they had actually rescued these battleships from certain destruction early in the war. Only two of the eight battleships at Pearl were a total loss. Three others were sunk in the shallow harbor, but were raised and restored to duty. The damaged battleships could not be used in the first few months of the war when Japanese carriers reigned supreme. Any of these battleships caught by Japanese carriers on the open seas would have been sent to the bottom, beyond recovery. This is exactly what happened to two British battleships on 10 December. The six repaired US battleships later returned to service and survived the war.

A larger feat of Japanese self-deception was their decision not to bomb the fuel reserves at Pearl Harbor, nor the ship repair facilities. Hitting these two targets would have caused fleet maintenance to be moved back to the West Coast for over a year until the damage could be repaired. The Japanese failed to appreciate the logistical problems of fighting a Pacific war, and the importance of the fuel and repair facilities at Pearl Harbor. But even more fatal was the Japanese self-deception on what targets to hit at Pearl Harbor. The attack was magnificent but, like the Charge of the Light Brigade, it did not aid the attackers' cause. America was in the war, it was angry, it was forced to depend on the weapon of the future, carrier aviation, and, worst of all, the Japanese thought they had a victory.

After the embarrassing failure to anticipate the attack on Pearl Harbor, Americans were quick to take up on deception. In order to convince the Japanese that the United States was planning an invasion of the Kurile Islands from the ALEUTIANS, American troops shipping out from West Coast ports for the South Pacific were occasionally issued winter underwear, and the shoulder patches of units stationed in Alaska.

Since the Japanese eventually grew to realize that just prior to American amphibious landings "Frogmen" would be sent in to reconnoiter the beaches and blow up obstacles, the US Navy began employing Frogmen to make bogus reconnaissances of literally scores of beaches on which it had absolutely no intention of landing.

While US Marines stormed ashore, Japanese "marines" sneaked ashore, in another form of deception. There were good reasons for both approaches. One vivid image many people have of World War II in the Pacific is US Marines coming from the sea against fierce Japanese resistance. This was indeed often the case, and the Marines had to use such straight-ahead methods because the islands to be taken were often small and usually heavily fortified. The Japanese also had amphibious forces, as well as specially designed amphibious shipping. They did not have an elite assault force like the US Marine Corps (USMC), but they did have sailors armed and trained as amphibious infantry. These Special Naval Landing Forces (SNLF) made the initial landing, followed by regular army troops. The Japanese made several successful amphibious landings early in the war (and many before Pearl Harbor). But the Japanese landing methods were quite different from the USMC tactics. Japanese amphibious operations depended on deception to succeed. Japan was a poor nation, especially compared to the United States, and the cheapest, yet still effective, methods of accomplishing military goals often involved deception. Moreover, most objectives for Japanese amphibious assaults were not on small islands but on the mainland of Asia or larger islands. The Japanese would scout the enemy-held shore thoroughly and find the area that was least likely to be defended or reinforced. If necessary, they would make a feint or demonstration somewhere else to draw enemy troops away from the actual landing site. What the Japanese sought, usually successfully, was an unopposed landing. Once the SNLF troops were ashore, they would fan out and ensure that no enemy troops were in the area. Then, more numerous army troops would come ashore and proceed to carry out the mission (usually taking a nearby port or city). The Japanese used warships to provide fire support, and carrier aircraft to obtain air superiority and provide air support for ground troops. Since their army aircraft had exceptional range, the Japanese were often able to use land-based aircraft to support landings.

When they were not able to use deception, the Japanese tended to have problems. An excellent example of this was the first Japanese attempt to take WAKE ISLAND from the Americans. The Japanese bombarded tiny Wake Island on 7 December 1941 and on the 11th attempted a landing. The American garrison was not large, but it had artillery and Marines and drove the Japanese off. On the 23rd, reinforced by more warships and two aircraft carriers (from the group that had attacked Pearl Harbor), the Japanese hit the island with a lot more firepower. Troops got ashore and soon the island was taken. This taught the Japanese that, where deception could not be used, overwhelming force was the only alternative. But as the war went on, the Americans had the overwhelming force. The USMC used it, and was never driven off a beach it had landed on.

In furtherance of Allied operations in northeastern New Guinea during mid–1943, MG George KENNEY, commander of the Fifth Air Force, wanted to advance his forward fighter bases closer to WEWAK (on the north-central coast of the big island some 400 miles northwest of LAE and the other Japanese bases on the Huon Peninsula), the Allied objective and the principal Japanese air base in the area. If he could put his fighters closer to Wewak, he could escort heavy bomber missions against the major Japanese base, thereby furthering the isolation of those farther to the east. As there were a number of old air strips (left by miners and missionaries) in the region, there was no shortage of potential sites at which a major base might be developed. But there were some problems nonetheless. First, the possible sites for air bases could not be reached by overland movement. Construction engineers and equipment would have to be flown in. However, since the Japanese still retained considerable air strength in the region, and since they could reasonably be expected to object to the Fifth Air Force setting up shop on their doorstep, it was also reasonable to assume that the airfields would be subjected to devastating enemy air attacks from the start. How to resolve this dilemma occupied the Americans for some time. However, Kenney soon came up with a creative solution. Not very far from Lae there was an old airstrip at a place called Bena Bena, once used by gold miners but now so overgrown that the Japanese had not thought it worth the effort to rehabilitate. In short order, and with some carelessness, airborne troops were dropped at Bena Bena. Rapidly securing the area (which was wholly undefended) the troops quickly cleared enough of the strip for construction engineers and equipment to be flown in. With that, work began in earnest.

Of course, the Japanese soon got wind of this, as the work was ill-concealed from aerial reconnaissance. In short order the "Emperor's eagles" began paying regular calls on Bena Bena, bombing and strafing to their hearts' content. But despite the devastation, the tenacious construction troops kept at it. Although the regular news communiqués issued from Kenney's headquarters put a positive spin on the raids ("Seventeen enemy bombers attacked Bena Bena yesterday. No damage was reported."), the Japanese were pleased to note that their attacks seemed to have virtually halted progress on the air base. This was precisely what Kenney wanted them to think, for Bena Bena was never intended to be an air base at all. In fact, it was a ruse, a trick designed to draw the attention of the Japanese from the real air base, which was just then under construction 40 miles from Lae. Only a handful of engineers had actually been landed at Bena Bena, and they were instructed to do the minimum amount of work necessary to attract the attention of the enemy, most obviously by clearing the airstrip of brush and by creating lots of dust. While the Japanese were blasting Bena Bena, construction troops had been less spectacularly inserted into Tsili Tsili, another abandoned airstrip, some 40 miles from Lae, on 16 June 1943. Working quickly, and with excellent CAMOU-FLAGE discipline (they left the clearing of the brush-covered airstrip for last) the troops managed to have the strip ready to receive aircraft within 10 days, a remarkable achievement. Kenney immediately laid on a series of heavy bomber raids against Wewak, with fighters from Tsili Tsili providing escorts. The destruction wrought at Wewak (a probably optimistic estimate of over 400 aircraft destroyed or damaged in the first two days alone) greatly interfered with the Japanese ability to support their bases on the Huon Peninsula. And, to add insult to injury, Bena Bena was eventually developed as an air base after all.

General Kenney was an unusually active trickster. Noticing that by late 1943, the Japanese were increasingly reluctant to commit their air forces in the face of growing US air power, he sought ways to entice them into a major air battle, one in which his fighter pilots could have a field day. The problem was that in order to do so he had to offer the Japanese a prize worth the risk of their precious airplanes. After thinking on the matter, he came up with an interesting scheme, one with which he approached Chief of Staff General George C. MAR-SHALL when he ran into him at a high-level STRATEGY conference. Would it be possible, Kenney asked for an "old or new boat fixed up with a painted wooden or other cheap deck and smokestack so that she looks like a carrier. . . ." Kenney went on to explain that he would run this "aircraft carrier" around in Japanese patrolled areas, with several layers of fighter cover stacked high above her, and ambush any Japanese aircraft that attempted to attack her. Marshall's reaction was that he had no ships to spare, and that Kenney had best try "to get the boat locally." Kenney next tried the Army Service Forces, which controlled a lot of shipping, but they had none to spare. He then approached the navy, but Seventh Fleet commander Admiral Thomas KINKAID demurred. It is easy to see why the navy was reluctant to take part in the deception. Not only would it have to provide the ship, at a time when shipping was very tight, but it would also have to provide the crews, who might be exposed to considerable danger. And for Kenney's trick to be convincing, the "carrier" would have to operate with a realistic escort, destroyers and the like, which were also in short supply. With that Kenney dropped the idea.

The feint that the US Second Marine Division conducted against a beach on the southern coast of OKINAWA, in an effort to draw Japanese attention away from the actual landing sites in the spring of 1945, was so convincing that Japan's LG Mitsuru USHIJIMA, commander of the defenses of the island, believed he had beaten off a major amphibious assault.

Another aspect of deception is that a wholly innocent act can have the same effect as a deliberate deception. Faced with increasing difficulties in maintaining the supply of fuel oil for their ships, in early 1944 the Japanese decided to base a major portion of the Combined Fleet at SINGA-PORE, so that it would be closer to the oil producing Netherlands East Indies. As this occurred at about the time same time the Japanese Army in

Burma undertook the Imphal-Kohima offensive, it convinced the British that they were planning a naval offensive in the Indian Ocean, in support of that operation. As a result, the ROYAL NAVY shelved plans to send a part of its British Far Eastern Fleet to support MACARTHUR in the southwest Pacific.

See also: CAMOUFLAGE.

Ref: Dunnigan and Nofi, *Victory and Deceit*; Dwyer, *Seaborne Deception*; Reit, *Masquerade*.

Demobilization

When wars end, the armies go home. Different countries do this in different ways. For the United States, demobilization planning began even as the army and navy struggled to find ways to get the maximum number of troops to the fighting fronts in 1942–43. The intention was that the troops be returned to the United States and demobilized in an orderly fashion. As the demobilization plan finally evolved in 1944, it was assumed that the war in Europe would be over around mid–1945 and that in the Pacific about a year later. Events overtook planning; the war in Europe ended a couple of months sooner than expected, and the Pacific fighting was over nearly a year earlier than expected. Moreover, while the officers planning the return of the troops tried to account for everything, they forgot the folks back home, who, almost as soon as the fighting ended in Europe, began clamoring to "bring the boys home."

The army had wanted to bring the troops home in organized formations, particularly in divisions. There were several reasons for this. Some divisions were to be transferred to the Pacific, in anticipation of the invasion of Japan, scheduled for November, and it seemed a good idea to keep a few additional ones together as long as possible as a strategic reserve. Also, veteran formations were thought best for occupation duties, since no one was quite certain that the Germans had not established a vast secret resistance, which would rise up if the Allies let down their guard. Then too, there was increasing concern over Soviet intentions in the postwar world.

There were also logistical and managerial considerations. Bringing the troops home in their divisions would allow equipment to be collected, serviced, and stockpiled with the least pain to the army. And, of course, there was the lure of marching up Broadway in triumph, to the cheers of the crowd, the way the Doughboys had after World War I. But the 1918 victory parade meant that some men who had been in the service a short time were demobilized before some who had gone "over there" with Pershing in June of 1917. America's mothers were not going to stand for that again, particularly those whose sons had been in the army since late 1940.

The nation's political leadership could not buck the tide. President ROOSEVELT died shortly before Germany surrendered, and his successor, former vice president TRUMAN, did not have Roosevelt's stature, clout, or skill at communicating unpleasantries to the public. In office less than a month when Germany surrendered, Truman ordered all existing demobilization plans to be discarded and all possible efforts made to get the troops home as quickly as possible.

So the army's elaborate planning pretty much went by the board, and there were few great victory parades. Most of the troops came home as individuals, based on an elaborate system of "points." A man received a point for each month he was in the army, another for each month he was overseas, five for each battle star he had been awarded, and additional ones for being married and having dependents, and so forth. The higher one's points, the sooner one was supposed to be put on the road home.

While fair in a sense, the point system eviscerated some units, severely affecting their combat abilities. For example, the 45th Infantry Division, originally scheduled to return home in August of 1945 (for retraining and redeployment to the Pacific), had lost 600 officers and 11,000 enlisted men by then, about 65% of its manpower. The artillery staff ended up with only one officer, the divisional artillery commander himself! All this was very scary to the officers who would have to command in the invasion of Japan, with less experienced troops. Moreover, while the Germans had been tough, at least they knew when to surrender, while the diehard spirit of the Japanese had become well known. Since late 1944 tales of the suicidal KAMIKAZE pilots and the havoc they wreaked had been received with grim foreboding by GIs in Europe. Orders to redeploy to the Pacific were seen by many of these men as a virtual death sentence. Cases of indiscipline increased markedly in the European Theater after the surrender of Germany. Of course the ATOMIC BOMB ended the war before very many troops from the ETO had reached the Pacific. It was for this reason that V-J Day was a much more joyous occasion than V-E Day. And why low-point veterans of the war in Europe considered the bomb a lifesaver.

At first the movement of troops home was purely an army affair, as the navy, happy to be rid of the unwanted war in Europe, was rushing everything afloat to the Pacific. The initial movement involved nearly 600 vessels of the War Shipping Board, plus some additional hired ships, most notably the two superliners QUEEN MARY and *Queen Elizabeth*, each of which could accommodate up to 15,000 men. Then Japan collapsed, nearly a year ahead of schedule. With Japan out of the war, the pressure to "bring the boys home" became enormous. The Truman administration ordered the troops brought home forthwith. Everything afloat was pressed into service to help bring them back. LIBERTY SHIPS, Victory ships, attack transports, and scores of warships (even battleships!) were converted to troop transports for "Operation Magic Carpet." Best of all were carriers, for bunks could be stacked as many as five high in their spacious hangar decks. *Lake Champlain*, a newly commissioned ESSEX CLASS carrier, was converted to carry some 3,300 troops. Some lucky guys were flown home in C-54, C-47s, and even heavy bombers, which could carry one or two men in addition to their crews. And so the boys came home. Of some 5.5 million US Army personnel (about two-thirds of total army personnel) abroad in the respective theaters at the end of operations in Europe, about

REPATRIATION OF ARMY PERSONNEL	
Period	Number
V-E Day to Sept. '45	1,216,750
Oct. 45 to Apr. '46	3,123,394
May 46 to Sept. '46	127,233

4 million were still overseas by V-J Day. By the end of December 1946 only 870,000 army personnel were still overseas. Many of these troops were fresh draftees hastily sent overseas to take up occupation duties, so that the veterans could go home. The average movement overseas had been about 157,000 troops a month for the 41 months of the war, while movement home over the next 14 months averaged about 430,000 men per month, with the peak month being December of 1945, when 695,486 army personnel came home.

In this rush to get home, there was little thought of equipment. Thousands of airplanes, trucks, and TANKS, and many tons of supplies and ammunition, were simply dumped into the ocean or just abandoned where they sat. Thousands of buildings, docks, airfields, and other facilities were turned over to the local people, if there were any, or, in the many places where there weren't any people, simply left unattended. Veterans returning decades later to visit the battlefields of their youth found many bases just as they had left them at the end of the war. In most cases, aside from the ravages of time, weather, and jungle growth, nothing had changed. (When the Korean War broke out, in 1950, someone in the Pentagon remembered all that materiel abandoned in odd little places all across the Pacific and salvaged much of it for use in the new conflict.)

In the words of George C. MARSHALL, "It was not a demobilization, it was a rout."

There were millions of Japanese military and civilian personnel outside of the Home Islands at the time of the surrender, plus enormous numbers of Koreans and other former subjects of the emperor who had been displaced in his service. Japanese demobilization was supervised by the US occupation authorities. The actual management of the demobilization was in the hands of Japanese army and navy officers. For the purpose of managing the orderly discharge of all the troops, the Japanese Army Ministry was reorganized as the "First Demobilization Bureau," while some of the Navy Ministry became the "Second Demobilization Bureau." Each bureau managed the repatriation and demobilization of its own former personnel.

The process of returning the several million troops from overseas was a difficult one. In a number of cases returning colonial powers had coopted Japanese troops for service against recalcitrant locals, notably in French INDO-CHINA and the NETHERLANDS EAST INDIES, and these troops were actually engaged in military operations against local rebels for some months. Demobilizing troops were usually investigated for possible war crime charges, treated for any ailments they might have contracted (malnutrition was the primary problem), and then organized for movement home. Shipment of personnel back to the Home Islands was initially in surviving Japanese vessels, including warships (a number of carriers served in this role). As it soon became obvious that there were fewer than 200 vessels suitable for such duties, and that these could move less than 100,000 men at a time, by early 1946 the United States was lending a hand with LSTs and other vessels. Despite this, repatriation proceeded slowly. Moreover, since there was not a lot that demobilized troops could do in Japan, unemployment being extraordinarily high, some troops were left abroad in POW camps, their keep being paid partially by the Allies and partially by Japan. As late as 1947 troops were still coming home, the last large group being from Burma.

In fact, not all Japanese military personnel were actually demobilized. In addition to those who served as managers of the demobilization, a number of officers were retained to assist the staff of the United States Strategic Bombing Survey in the performance of their duties; many officers were detailed to assist Allied forces in convincing hold-out Japanese troops to surrender, a process that went

on into the late 1940s; and other personnel were active in assisting US military historians. In addition, although officially serving as civilians, many former Imperial Navy officers and men performed military duties aboard minesweepers, helping to clear the enormous numbers of MINES planted in Japanese waters. During the Korean War many of these men served under fire, for example, assisting US Navy minesweepers off WONSAN in late 1950, and during the evacuation of that port after the Chinese communist intervention. These forces later became the cadre about which the Maritime Self-Defense Force was organized.

See also JAPAN, FORCES ABROAD AT THE SURRENDER; MORISON, SAMUEL ELIOT; TOKYO WAR CRIMES TRIBUNAL.

DeRuyter, Netherlands Light Cruiser

Designed under severe financial limitations and size restrictions, *DeRuyter* (1932–1935–1936) was primarily suited only for showing the Dutch flag in the Far East. Although outclassed by American and British ships in the ABDA squadron, she served as its flagship in the early months of the war in the NETHERLANDS EAST INDIES, and went down fighting in the JAVA SEA on 28 February 1942, having absorbed at least one TORPEDO and numerous 8–inch shells from the Japanese heavy cruiser *Haguro.*

Des Moines Class, US Heavy Cruisers

A derivative of the BALTIMORE CLASS, the three Des Moines Class ships were the culmination of US heavy cruiser design, and the largest heavy cruisers ever built. They were superior to all previous heavy cruisers, having a fully automatic 8–inch gun, enormous displacement, extensive protection, and much better sea-keeping qualities. Laid down in 1945, they were completed in 1948–49. They would have been deadly opponents in a surface action, but they never saw action. Assigned to various duties after the war, such as serving as flagships, the Des Moines Class ships were eventually relegated to reserve status, and later slated for disposal, although a campaign to preserve *Des Moines* herself as a memorial may save her from the scrap heap.

Destroyers

Destroyers (DDs) were the real workhorses of all of the fleets. They did everything. Destroyers were created in the late 19th century to defend heavier ships against attacks by torpedo boats, from which role they derived their name, "torpedo-boat destroyers." Originally rather small vessels (150–300 tons), destroyers gradually grew in size and capability, and by World War II displaced from about 1,000 tons to about 2,500 with some exceptional designs even reaching the vicinity of 3,000 tons. Meanwhile their mission expanded.

Through World War I destroyers continued to protect larger ships against TORPEDOES, although increasingly the torpedoes came from SUBMARINES rather than torpedo boats. Between the wars, as destroyers continued to be general purpose bodyguards for larger ships, they came to be equipped to defend against aircraft as well. Destroyers were usually also armed with torpedoes, which they could use against enemy surface ships.

Destroyers were fast, so they could keep up with any other type of ship and still maneuver around as they sought to head off any enemy threats, or to deliver torpedo attacks. They were also small, cramped, and rather uncomfortable, particularly in heavy weather or cold climates. Because of their high fuel consumption, destroyers had to be refueled frequently. At full steam the typical US DD ran out of fuel in about four days. Operationally, although enemy attacks were generally against larger ships, destroyers took their "screening" role seriously and as a result took a disproportionate amount of losses.

One consequence of World War II was the creation of a variety of destroyer types. The destroyer escort (DE) was a sort of pocket variety destroyer, with lighter surface armament and lower speed on a smaller hull, specialized for antisubmarine duties. There were also destroyers that, through the fitting of additional radars and antiaircraft armament, became specialized in the antiaircraft defense of fleets. Later in the war such vessels were often posted at some distance from the main body of a fleet as "radar picket ships," to give early warning of the approach of enemy aircraft.

Destroyers, particularly older models, were also frequently converted for service as high-speed transports (ADPs), being able to carry modest but sometimes critical quantities of men and supplies to isolated garrisons on remote islands. Even before the war the United States and Japan began converting older destroyers to a variety of odd jobs, such as minesweeping (DMSs) and mine laying (DMLs), or general purpose patrol boats and escorts.

Ref: Friedman, *United States Destroyers.*

Destroyers, Picket Duty

During the last 10 months of the war, and particularly during the protracted struggle for OKINAWA, many destroyers were placed on "picket duty," posted at some distance from the fleet in order to try and keep Japanese suicide aircraft from the carriers and transports. This was no easy task, for many of the "Emperor's Eagles" were very anxious to demonstrate their belief that "duty is a heavy burden, but death is lighter than a feather." In consequence, they would frequently attack the pickets rather than pass them by to try for the larger warships and transports farther on. As a result, destroyer-type vessels (DDs, DEs, DMSs) bore the brunt of the KAMIKAZE onslaught; 16 were sunk by kamikaze attack (19.3% of the 83 vessels sunk by kamikaze) and 139 were damaged (39.7% of the 285 damaged vessels). What is surprising about this is the battering some ships survived. Take the case of the destroyer USS *Laffey.*

On the morning of 16 April 1945, *Laffey* (DD-724), an ALLEN M. SUMNER CLASS destroyer commissioned in early 1944, was on radar picket patrol off Okinawa. From about 0827 to 0947 she was subject to the attentions of about 50 Japanese aircraft. Although many of the attackers were downed by friendly fighters flying combat air patrol, at least

DESTROYERS, DESTROYER ESCOERTS, AND TROPEDO BOATS

Navy	Class	Year	Displacement		Crew	Combat			Guns				TT	Length	Beam	Draft	HP	Spd.	Armor	
			Tot.	Full		Surf	AAA	A/C	Main	Sec.	DP	AAA							Belt	Deck

Destroyers (DE)

Navy	Class	Year	Tot.	Full	Crew	Surf	AAA	A/C	Main	Sec.	DP	AAA	TT	Length	Beam	Draft	HP	Spd.	Belt	Deck
Br.	Acasta	1929	1	1.8	138	1	1	0	None	None	4x4.7	1x3	4	95.1	9.8	3.7	34.0	35.3	0.0	0.0
Jp.	Akatsuke	1931	4	2.0	200	2	1	0	None	None	4x5	None	9	106.7	10.4	3.3	50.0	34.0	0.0	0.0
Jp.	Akitsuki	1941	13	3.7	300	2	2	0	None	None	8x3.9	None	4	126.0	11.6	4.2	52.0	33.0	0.0	0.0
U.S.	Allen M. Sumner	1944	58	3.2	336	2	2	0	None	None	6x5	None	10	112.5	12.5	4.3	60.0	36.5	0.0	0.0
Au.	Arunta	1942	3	2.5	220	2	2	0	None	None	8x4.7	None	4	108.4	11.1	4.0	44.0	36.4	0.0	0.0
Jp.	Asashio	1937	10	2.3	200	2	1	0	None	None	6x5	None	8	111.0	10.4	3.7	50.0	35.0	0.0	0.0
U.S.	Bagley	1936	8	2.3	192	2	2	0	None	None	5x5	None	8	103.9	11.0	3.9	50.0	35.0	0.0	0.0
U.S.	Benham	1938	10	2.3	184	4	2	0	None	None	4x5	None	16	103.9	10.8	3.9	50.0	38.5	0.0	0.0
U.S.	Benson/Gleaves	1939	96	2.4	208	2	2	0	None	None	5x5	None	10	106.2	11.0	4.0	50.0	35.0	0.0	0.0
U.S.	Clemson/Wickes	1919	67	1.3	114	1	0	0	4x4	None	None	1x3	12	95.8	9.4	3.0	27.0	35.0	0.0	0.0
U.S.	Farragut	1934	8	2.3	192	2	2	0	None	None	5x5	None	8	103.9	11.0	3.9	50.0	35.0	0.0	0.0
U.S.	Fletcher	1942	175	2.9	273	2	2	0	None	None	5x5	None	10	112.5	12.1	4.2	60.0	33.0	0.0	0.0
Jp.	Fubuki	1928	19	2.1	197	2	1	0	None	None	6x5	None	9	111.9	10.4	3.2	50.0	34.0	0.0	0.0
U.S.	Gearing	1945	105	3.5	336	2	2	0	None	None	6x5	None	10	119.0	12.5	4.4	60.0	36.8	0.0	0.0
U.S.	Gridley	1936	4	2.2	158	2	2	0	None	None	4x5	None	16	103.9	10.7	3.9	50.0	38.5	0.0	0.0
Jp.	Hatsuharu	1932	6	2.1	200	2	1	0	None	None	5x5	None	9	103.5	10.0	3.0	42.0	33.0	0.0	0.0
Jp.	Kagero	1938	18	2.5	240	2	1	0	None	None	6x5	None	8	111.0	10.8	3.8	52.0	35.0	0.0	0.0
Jp.	Kamikaze	1923	9	1.7	148	2	1	0	None	None	3x4.7	None	6	102.6	9.1	2.9	38.5	34.0	0.0	0.0
Fr.	L'Adroit	1927	14	2.0	142	2	0	0	4x5.1	None	None	None	6	107.2	9.8	4.3	34.0	33.0	0.0	0.0
U.S.	Mahan	1935	18	2.3	192	2	2	0	None	None	5x5	None	8	103.9	11.0	3.9	50.0	35.0	0.0	0.0
Jp.	Minekaze	1919	13	2.9	148	2	1	0	None	None	3x4.7	None	6	111.9	10.4	3.2	50.0	34.0	0.0	0.0
Jp.	Mutsuki	1925	12	1.9	150	2	1	0	None	None	4x4.7	None	6	97.5	9.2	3.0	38.5	34.0	0.0	0.0
U.S.	Porter	1935	8	2.3	192	2	2	0	None	None	5x5	None	8	103.9	11.0	3.9	50.0	35.0	0.0	0.0
Cn.	Saguenay	1929	1	1.8	138	1	1	0	None	None	4x4.7	1x3	4	95.1	9.8	3.7	34.0	35.3	0.0	0.0
Br.	Saumarez	1943	16	2.5	200	2	1	0	None	None	4x4.7	None	8	103.5	10.9	4.3	40.0	36.8	0.0	0.0
Jp.	Shimakaze	1942	1	3.0	250	2	1	0	None	None	6x5	None	15	120.5	11.2	4.1	75.0	39.0	0.0	0.0
Jp.	Shiratsuyu	1935	10	2.3	200	2	2	0	None	None	5x5	None	8	103.5	9.9	3.5	42.0	34.0	0.0	0.0
U.S.	Sims	1938	12	2.3	192	2	2	0	None	None	5x5	None	8	103.9	11.0	3.9	50.0	35.0	0.0	0.0
U.S.	Somers	1937	5	2.8	294	2	3	0	None	None	8x5	None	12	116.1	11.3	3.8	52.0	37.0	0.0	0.0
Br.	Tribal	1937	16	2.5	220	2	1	0	None	None	7x4.7	1x4	4	108.4	11.1	4.0	44.0	36.4	0.0	0.0
Nth.	Van Ghent	1926	4	1.6	129	2	2	0	4x4.9	None	None	2x3*	6	93.6	9.5	2.9	31.0	36.0	0.0	0.0
Jp.	Yugumo	1941	20	2.9	228	2	1	0	None	None	6x5	None	8	111.6	10.8	3.8	52.0	35.0	0.0	0.0

Destroyer Escorts (DE)

Navy	Class	Year	Tot	Displ	Crew	Full	Combat	A/C	Surf	Sec	Main	AAA	TT	Length	Beam	Draft	HP	Spd	Belt	Deck
U.S.	Buckley	1943	102	1.8	186	1	1	0	None	None	3x3	None	2	91.4	11.3	3.4	12.0	23.0	0.0	0.0
U.S.	Cannon	1943	157	1.6	186	1	1	0	None	None	3x3	None	3	93.3	11.2	3.2	6.0	21.0	0.0	0.0
U.S.	Evarts	1942	68	1.4	156	1	1	0	None	None	3x3	None	0	88.2	10.7	3.1	6.0	19.5	0.0	0.0
Jp.	Matsu	1944	18	1.9	200	1	1	0	None	None	3x5	None	4	92.2	9.4	3.3	19.0	27.8	0.0	0.0
U.S.	Rudderow	1943	109	1.8	156	1	1	0	None	None	2x5	None	3	93.3	11.3	3.4	12.0	23.0	0.0	0.0
Jp.	Tachibana	1944	18	1.6	?	1	1	0	None	None	3x5	None	4	100.0	9.4	3.4	19.0	27.8	0.0	0.0

Torpedo Boats

Navy	Class	Year	Tot	Displ	Crew	Full	Combat	A/C	Surf	Sec	Main	AAA	TT	Length	Beam	Draft	HP	Spd	Belt	Deck
Jp.	Otori	1935	8	1.0	113	1	1	0	None	None	3x4.7	None	3	88.5	8.2	2.8	19.0	30.5	0.0	0.0
Jp.	Tomozuru	1935	4	0.8	120	1	1	0	None	None	3x4.7	None	2	77.5	7.4	2.5	11.0	28.0	0.0	0.0

Navy = nation the ship belongs to; Au = Australia, Br = Britain, Cn = Canada, Fr = France, Nth = Netherlands, Jp = Japan, US = United States. **Class** = names of the lead ship in the class. **Year** = when the first ship in the class entered service; MHB = might have been, a class that was not, but could have been in action. **Tot.** = total number of ships in that class. **Displacement** = the amount of water the ship displaces (i.e., the weight of the water that would occupy the space occupied by the ship), expressed in thousands of tons. **Full** = "fighting weight," or weight with basic crew, fuel, munitions and other supplies, all the items needed to go to war. **Crew** = number normally carried. **Combat** = relative combat value for each ship in the following areas: **Surf.** = value in surface engagements; **AAA** = value against attacking aircraft. **A/C** = aircraft carried. **Guns** = many different types: **Main** = the largest guns, on battleships from 11 to 18 inches in bore diameter; **Sec.** = secondary guns for use against smaller surface targets (these became obsolete during World War II, usually converted to AAA use); **DP** = dual purpose, for use against surface and air targets; **AAA** = antiaircraft artillery, generally the same caliber as the DP guns, but whose only purpose is to attack aircraft. Most ships also carried as many anti-aircraft heavy machine guns as they could. The caliber varying from 12.7mm to 40mm, the latter (20mm and up) were actually automatic cannon, as they fired explosive shells. **TT** = torpedo tubes carried. **Dimensions** = expressed in meters. There are three of them: **Length** = how long the ship was; **Beam** = width of the ship; **Draft** = how deep into the water the bottom of the ship is at full load. **HP** = maximum horsepower generated by the ship's engines. **Spd.** = top speed in knots (nautical miles per hour). **Armor** = the protection many ships had against enemy fire. Given in inches for the following positions on the ship: **Belt** = an area along the waterline to protect engines and ammo magazines; **Deck** = for protection from "plunging" shells (fired from a great distance away) or bombs.

22 of the enemy managed to get through to make attacks on the ship herself. Altogether, *Laffey* was hit by seven kamikaze (five Vals, a Judy, and an Oscar), six of which blew up spectacularly while the seventh (a Val) bounced off to explode in the sea hard by her port quarter, which jammed the ship's rudder. In addition she was struck by four bombs and strafed several times by other Japanese aircraft.

Aside from the kamikaze that actually struck her, *Laffey* managed to shoot down eight of her attackers. When the ordeal was over, *Laffey* had suffered 31 crewmen killed and 72 wounded, about 30% of her complement. She was down at the stern and unable to steer due to the jammed rudder. Her fire control director was gone and her only working guns were four 20mm antiaircraft pieces (out of six 5-inch, 12 40mm, and 11 20mm). Despite her damage, *Laffey* was repaired. After many years on active duty, *Laffey* was retired in 1977. She is today preserved as a war memorial in Charleston, South Carolina, along with the ESSEX CLASS carrier *Yorktown*, second of that name in the war.

As can be seen, the destroyerman's lot off Okinawa was not a pleasant one. Thus it is understandable that one day during the long watch, the crew of one of the "Tin Cans" grew frustrated at the many Japanese pilots who persisted in attacking them rather than continuing on to try for bigger targets. Knowing that the Japanese were supposed to be looking to sink carriers, the destroyermen erected a large sign proclaiming "Carriers This Way."

It's doubtful that any of the attacking Japanese ever saw the sign, or if they did could even read it, and hardly likely that had they done so they would have paid it much heed, but it may have made the destroyermen feel better.

Ref: Becton, *The Ship That Would Not Die*.

DeWitt, John L. (1880–1962)

After two years at Princeton, DeWitt was commissioned a second lieutenant during the Spanish-American War. He saw action in the Philippine Insurrection, served in garrison for a time, and by 1917 was a captain on the staff of the quartermaster general. After serving at the Plattsburg Officers' Training Camp for a time, he went to France as a staff officer with the 42nd Division. He ended the war as assistant chief of staff for supply of the I Corps. By 1934 he had served in various military academic, staff, and line posts, rising to quartermaster general of the army. DeWitt was then given a series of operational commands, rising from brigade to the Philippine Department. Later commandant of the Army War College, in 1939 he was promoted to temporary lieutenant general and given command of the Fourth Army, an administrative—and later operational—command on the West Coast. Shortly after PEARL HARBOR DeWitt added his voice to those demanding the removal of suspected disloyal elements from the West Coast. By February of 1942 he had secured authorization to detain and remove persons of Italian, German, and Japanese nationality and Americans of such descent. Under this authority DeWitt relocated about 125,000 persons, mostly of Japanese descent, and many of them American citizens, while placing restrictions on many more. In September 1943 DeWitt was relieved of command of the Fourth Army and became commandant of the joint Army-Navy Staff College. From late 1945 until his retirement in 1947 he was on the staff of the chief of staff of the army. One of the few high-ranking officers who received no promotion during the war, upon his retirement he reverted to his permanent rank of major general.

See also AMERICAN CITIZENS, RELOCATION OF; FALSE BATTLES OF THE PACIFIC WAR.

DH 98 Mosquito, British Light Bomber

The British DH 98 Mosquito was one of the more remarkable aircraft of the war. Designed and built by DeHavilland in 1940, it entered service in 1941. Most of the 7,800 built were used in Europe. Those that appeared in the Pacific served as recon, night fighter, and bomber aircraft. The DH 98 was very fast, difficult to spot using radar (much of the fuselage was plywood), and had very long range. In effect, it was the first "stealth bomber." Production and use continued after the war.

See also AIRCRAFT TYPES DEVELOPMENT.

DH 100 Vampire, British Jet Fighter

Development work on the British DH 100 Vampire began in 1941, at the same time the manufacturer DeHavilland, was getting its famous DH 98 MOSQUITO bomber into PRODUCTION. Although the DH 100 was jet-powered, it borrowed many design concepts from the DH 98, including the extensive use of wood in the structure. This made for a light aircraft that could be easily propelled by the low-thrust jet engines available in the early 1940s. The DH 100 had only one engine, unlike the other early jets, which all had two. Only about 40 production aircraft were ready in early 1945, too late to have much effect on the war. However, if the Pacific War had gone on longer, DH 100s would have showed up in Burma. Over a thousand DH 100s were built, many serving into the early 1950s. With a top speed of over 500 MPH, it was heavily armed (four 20mm cannon and a ton of bombs).

See also AIRCRAFT TYPES, DEVELOPMENT.

DH 103 Hornet, British Carrier Fighter

The British DH 103 Hornet was a two-engine fighter that entered service in early 1945. It also saw service on carriers such as the *Sea Hornet*. Over 400 were built (half for the ROYAL NAVY, in the late 1940s), and it served into the 1950s. Had the Pacific War gone on longer, more DH 103s would have been built and sent east. The DH 103 had a top speed of 472 MPH and was armed with four 20mm cannon and a ton of bombs or rockets.

See also AIRCRAFT TYPES, DEVELOPMENT; CARRIERS, DESIGNING AIRCRAFT FOR.

Dido Class, British Antiaircraft Cruisers

A good antiaircraft cruiser design, modified through several subsequent versions as the ROYAL NAVY gained experience with this type of vessel. They had fine sea-keeping qualities. Although they were designed for an antiaircraft role, they lacked an efficient fire control system and were not suited to a surface slugfest, as were their American counterparts, designed later. The class totaled 16 vessels, in five different groups (*Dido, Charybdis, Scylla, Cleopatra,* and *Bellona,* listed separately on the cruiser tables), which differed primarily in details of armament. For example, the five ships of the Bellona Group, the last and arguably best of the lot, had eight rather than 10 5.25-inch dual purpose guns, but more light antiaircraft armament, on a hull that displaced about 300 tons more than the original units. Aside from some design changes, one reason for the numerous variations on the basic *Dido* design was Britain's great shortage of resources, which made it difficult to mass produce ships to a single design. There is some controversy as to their fragility. Three succumbed to a single TORPEDO each, two went down after taking two torpedoes, and one was rendered a constructive total loss by a single mine, all in the European Theater, where a sixth unit was also sunk by a German guided missile. On the other hand several units survived equally serious torpedo and bomb hits. Several units of this class operated in the Indian Ocean during the war. *Euryalus* (1937–1939–1941) and *Argonaut* (1939–1941–1942), of the original design, and *Black Prince* (1939–1942–1943), of the Bellona Group, served with the British Pacific Fleet in 1945. The first pair were scrapped in the 1950s, the third in 1962.

Dili, Timor

The principal port of Portuguese East TIMOR, Dili was virtually bereft of facilities to service and support shipping, but was quite conveniently located with regard to Australia, less than 400 miles to the southeast.

Disarmament Treaties, Prewar

The end of World War I led to an immediate reduction in armies worldwide, as both victors and vanquished alike rapidly demobilized the enormous hosts they had raised since 1914.

The reductions went far beyond the level of the "normal" peacetime establishments maintained prior to the outbreak of the war, if only because no one seriously believed there would be another major war, particularly since Germany's armed forces had been reduced to little more than a constabulary.

The end of the war also took care of two of the principal navies in the world, those of Germany and Russia, the one reduced to insignificance by the Treaty of Versailles and the other reduced by revolution and civil war. Two others, those of France and Italy, fell decisively into the second rank of naval power, if only for lack of funds. Three navies remained strong, the American, the Japanese, and the British. All three seemed intent on further increasing the size of their fleets.

THE CAPITAL SHIP BALANCE, 1920–1922

Country	Period Completed 1905–1914	Period Completed 1914–1920	Building	Total
Britain	23	19	9	51
Japan	2	8	16	26
United States	8	9	18	35

Only Dreadnought-type "all big gun" battleships and battlecruisers have been included in the table. Ships completed before 1914 were more or less obsolete by the early 1920s, while those completed between 1914 and 1920 were still effective but, having been designed before 1915, did not benefit from wartime experience, and so were at least marginally out of date. The category "Building" includes vessels actually under construction or already ordered but not yet laid down.

Aside from eliminating several first-class navies, the Great War substantially altered the balance of naval power in another way, for it threatened to dethrone Britain from its traditional naval supremacy. Subtracting the obsolete vessels from her inventory, Britain's margin of superiority over either

of the two other major navies was so slender as to be nonexistent, and considering the number of capital ships being built, the prognosis was not good for the ROYAL NAVY.

The strain of the war had prevented Britain from ordering very many new capital ships, while both Japan and the United States had been busy indeed. Moreover, the wily newcomers had delayed the actual start of construction of many of their new ships so that they were able to incorporate the lessons of the war. As if that were not enough, Japan had announced that it planned to build its navy on the basis of the "8-8-8" Plan, which stated that the first-line strength of the fleet would always be maintained at eight battleships and eight battlecruisers no more than eight years old, plus older vessels. One did not need a degree in advanced math to realize that this meant the Japanese would add two capital ships to their fleet every year, shortly giving them the largest battlefleet in the world, a matter of concern to the United States.

The United States responded by planning to expand its navy as well. In the face of the Japanese and American threats to their naval primacy, the British reluctantly began planning to expand too. A major naval arms race loomed, with all the attendant expense. The cost would be heavy for the United States, heavier still for Britain, and heaviest of all for Japan.

If the Japanese actually did try to implement the "8-8-8" Plan, they would be able to bear the expense for only six or eight years before running out of money and credit, by which time (c. 1928–30) they would have about 40 serviceable battleships and battlecruisers, almost all less than 15 years old. At that point the Japanese would have had either to abandon the "8-8-8" program, thereby admitting that Japan was not a first-class power, or go to war to secure the resources necessary to become a first-class power. In American and British naval circles, it was presumed that the latter course would be more likely.

In an effort to halt the incipient naval arms race, in 1921 the British suggested a naval disarmament conference, in compliance with the disarmament provisions of the Treaty of Versailles. The response was surprisingly warm, and led to one of the most successful instances of international disarmament in history, the Naval Disarmament Treaties of 1922 and 1930.

On 12 November 1921 delegates from the United States, Britain, and Japan convened in Washington (chosen to ease isolationist fears that Uncle Sam was being hustled), with France and Italy invited out of politeness. On the very first day the American secretary of state dropped a bombshell. Subtly observing that the United States had the economic wherewithal to outbuild both its rivals, Charles Evans Hughes announced that America would be willing to scrap a significant portion of its existing fleet and of vessels still under construction, if the other powers would do the same and agree to limitations on the size of their fleets. The offer was accepted "with almost indecent haste," as one naval historian put it.

The Washington (1921–22) naval disarmament treaty was worked out in a remarkably short time, and implemented with considerable goodwill. As modified by a later conference in London in 1930, it made a real difference.

When all the wheeling and dealing was over, Britain, which had only one capital ship completed since 1916 (in contrast to eight for the United States and five for Japan) was allowed to lay down and complete two wholly new battleships, of the NELSON CLASS, while the United States and Japan were permitted to convert two incomplete ships each into aircraft carriers, and France one. Further restrictions were imposed on the replacement of existing vessels, and on the displacement (35,000 tons "standard") and guns (16–inch) that future battleships could tote.

In addition the three major powers agreed that the United States and Britain, each of which had interests in both the Atlantic and the Pacific, "needed" more capital ships than did Japan, which had interests only in the Pacific. The Japanese accepted this deal when the other powers sweetened

CAPITAL SHIPS "SUNK" BY THE NAVAL DISARMAMENT TREATIES, 1922–1931

Navy	Old BB	Newer BB	Building	Ordered	Total
British	3	27	0	4	34
French	9	0	5	0	14
Italian	6	1	4	0	11
Japanese	9	4	6	8	27
United States	21	7	13	0	41

Old BBs covers pre-dreadnought battleships (smaller vessels with only four main guns), which were obsolete. *Newer BBs* includes all dreadnoughts, most of which were built from 1905 to 1914. *Building* covers ships actually laid down and in various stages of construction at the time the disarmament conference was convened. *Ordered* covers vessels officially authorized for construction, but not yet laid down. Note that in the immediate aftermath of World War I, the British had already disposed of 24 even older pre-dreadnoughts, plus six dreadnoughts built between 1905 and 1915, and had indicated that they wanted to convert three unsuccessful battlecruisers into aircraft carriers, so their real reduction was 61. The French and Italians had also disposed of many older ships in the immediate aftermath of the war, but none of these were of any real combat value.

it by barring new fortifications in the Pacific between Japan and SINGAPORE, west of HAWAII, and giving Japan a better ratio in some other categories of warship.

A total tonnage limitation was placed on the size of the navies of all the signatories in the ratio 5:5:3:1.75:1.¾ for Britain, the United States, Japan, France, and Italy. Design restrictions were placed on other classes of warship as well, which were rigidly defined as to size and armament, including the introduction of the distinction between the "heavy cruiser" and the "light cruiser," a matter of gun caliber (6-inch or under, as opposed to anything over and up to 10-inch). In addition, the treaties specified the "life span" of each category of warship, so that what amounted to a "battleship holiday" was established, with no power being allowed to build new ships for nearly 10 years, when France was scheduled to lay down two new vessels as replacements for her two oldest ones. Further "refinements" of the treaties conceded to Japan a slight increase in its allowance for cruisers, and parity in SUBMARINES.

Although Britain failed to ban submarines, these agreements did make a difference, as fleets actually were reduced. However, the treaty had some unintended results. Perhaps the most important was that Japanese militarists would later use the treaty to argue that the Japanese Empire had been insulted by relegation to a state of inferiority. Efforts at further significant reductions in naval armaments, which were made well into the 1930s, came to grief due to demands for "parity" by a militarized Japan and a resurgent Germany. Thus a treaty aimed at reducing tensions and armaments eventually increased both.

At the time, and afterward, particularly during World War II, many American navalists argued—indeed, some still argue—that the Disarmament Treaties strengthened Japan, with disastrous results in 1941. This was hardly the case. In fact, had the United States adhered to the letter of the treaties, building up to allowable limits, its margin of superiority over the Japanese would have been much greater than was actually the case in 1941. However, fiscal conservatives, pacifists, and isolationists on both left and right combined to reduce the fleet further than as prescribed by the treaties.

For example, a 1927 proposal by the Coolidge administration to build five aircraft carriers and 25 cruisers, as permitted by the treaty, was cut down to one carrier and 15 cruisers. This was passed by Congress in 1928, but no moneys were appropriated. The first ships were not actually laid down until 1930, and some as late as 1936. Not until 1934 did Congress agree to build the navy up to the United States' treaty allowance, and so little money was appropriated that it would have taken until 1944 to achieve that goal. Even that limited goal was achieved only after enormous pressure from the White House. As a result, on 7 December 1941 the Imperial Navy was not about 60% the size of the US Navy, as prescribed by the disarmament treaties, but around 80%, and that only after President ROOSEVELT had been fighting for several years to strengthen the fleet.

THE NAVAL BALANCE, 1922–1941 (THOUSANDS OF STANDARD TONS)

Year	Britain	Japan	United States	Ratio	Situation
1922	1,361	547	1,134	1:0.4:0.8	Treaties in force
1936	1,192	784	1,078	1:0.7:0.9	Treaties expire
1941	1,398	1,085	1,352	1:0.8:1.0	No limitations

The table gives some idea of the impact of the failure of the United States to build up to treaty limits by comparing the actual strength of the three principal navies at different periods from 1922 on.

Ref: Pelz, *Race to Pearl Harbor*.

Dohihara, Kenji (1883–1948)

Dohihara (or Doihara) graduated from the Japanese military academy in 1904, and served on various staffs, as an intelligence officer, and as a military adviser to several pro-Japanese warlords in China for much of his career. One of the "wild men" in China, pressing for increased Japanese intervention, Western journalists dubbed him "Lawrence of Manchuria" for his exploits in establishing Japanese rule in northern China during the early 1930s. After leading the Army Secret Police in Manchuria for a time while being regularly promoted he was posted back to Japan in 1940 and commanded the Eastern Military District of Japan. Sent to command army troops in MALAYA from March 1944 to April 1945, he returned to Japan to command part of the forces to oppose the expected invasion. After surrender Dohihara commanded Japanese troops during DEMOBILIZATION. He was arrested, tried, convicted, and hanged as a war criminal in 1948.

Doolittle, James H. (1896–1993)

James H. Doolittle was a college student when he enlisted in the army in 1917. Assigned to the Air

A USAAF B-25 takes off from the deck of the USS Hornet *(CV-8) on April 18, 1942, bound for Tokyo on the Doolittle Raid. Note that the men on the signal bridge are wearing the US 1917 helmet.*

Service, he served as a flight instructor, and remained in the service after the war, while pursuing several advanced academic degrees in science and engineering. Much of his career was spent in experimentation and in often spectacular test flights. Resigning from the army in 1930, he went into business, while still racing (Harmon Trophy, 1930; Bendix, 1931; world air speed record, 1932) and serving as an adviser to government and industry on aviation.

Recalled to active duty in 1940, he helped plan the expansion of the Air Corps for the coming war. A very progressive thinker for his day, Doolittle advocated the abolition of separate facilities for BLACK AMERICANS, on the grounds that segrega-

tion impeded the war effort. In April of 1942, he led the spectacular raid that bears his name, when 16 B-25s took off from the carrier *Hornet* to bomb Tokyo and other targets in Japan. This feat, which he suggested and planned, brought him a promotion to brigadier general, a MEDAL OF HONOR, and command of the Twelfth Air Force in England. He led this command into action during the North African Campaign in November 1942, and thereafter held a variety of increasingly important posts in the air war against Germany, ending with command of the Eighth Air Force. Soon after the war in Europe ended, Doolittle began transferring his command to OKINAWA, in anticipation of the invasion of Japan. After the war he returned to the reserves, working in industry and as an adviser to government on numerous projects. He died in 1993, one of the last of the larger than life legends of the Pacific War.

Doorman, Karel W. (1889–1942)

The senior Dutch naval officer afloat in the Far East at the beginning of the Pacific War, Doorman had a distinguished but peaceful career. Nevertheless, in the interests of inter-Allied cooperation, he was appointed commander of ABDA force, the "American-British-Dutch-Australian" naval command in the Far East in February of 1942, as the Allies faced an overwhelmingly superior Japanese offensive. It was a hopeless command, for not only were the forces available of greatly differing capabilities, but they had also never trained together, lacked a common doctrine, and could not even communicate with each other readily. Despite these handicaps, Doorman and his Allied subordinates were game, and did the only thing they could in such a situation, go down fighting in the Battle of the JAVA SEA.

Doss, Desmond T. (1919–   )

A conscientious objector (CO), he served in the army as a medical corpsman, and served with the 77th Division on GUAM, Leyte, and OKINAWA, where he became the first CO ever to earn the MEDAL OF HONOR.

DUKW

The DUKW, pronounced "Duck," was a standard US Army 2.5–ton truck that could swim. Amphibious operations during World War II were different from earlier ones in that there were now motor vehicles (trucks and TANKS) and a lot more weapons. Special ships were developed that could deliver vehicles right on to the beach. What was missing was a way to move sufficient ammunition

and fuel to keep all these vehicles and weapons functioning once they were off the beach. This problem was quickly noticed, and by the end of 1942 an elegant and simple solution had been reached. A steel, flat-bottom boat hull was built that was large enough to have the mechanical parts of the 2.5-ton truck built into it. A small propeller was added aft to provide propulsion while floating. Sundry other adjustments were made, and by 1943 hundreds of DUKWs were in service. More than 20,000 were built before the war ended, and some served on into the early 1950s before being replaced by tracked LVT-type vehicles. The letters DUKW are the army equipment code describing an amphibious cargo vehicle with a 6-by-6 wheel arrangement and a 5,000-pound (2.5 ton) carrying capacity. A fully loaded DUKW weighed 8.8 tons and was 31 feet long, 8.3 feet wide, and 7.1 feet high. It could go as fast as 45 MPH on roads, and about 6 MPH in the water. One tank of fuel would carry them 220 miles on roads and 50 miles in water. There was also a smaller version of the DUKW weighing 2 tons, but few were manufactured or used. DUKWs spent most of their time ferrying supplies and troops (up to 25 men) from ships offshore, over the beach to locations inland.

See also AMPHIBIOUS ASSAULTS; AMPHIBIOUS VEHICLES.

Dutch Harbor, Aleutians, Alaska

Although it was the principal American naval base in Alaska, Dutch Harbor had very limited facilities to repair and service shipping, and only a tiny airfield. The most extensive American base in the north Pacific, and the farthest west, it was nevertheless a thousand miles east of the westernmost islands in the Aleutian chain. Heavily bombed by the Japanese in June 1942, it was subsequently built up into a fairly substantial base, which supported operations in the ALEUTIANS and against the KURILE ISLANDS.

E

E and F Class, British Destroyers

Several units of these virtually identical classes, built 1932–35, served with the ABDA squadron in the struggle for the East Indies in early 1942, during which two were sunk.

E7K Alf, Japanese Reconnaissance Floatplane

The E7K was the original Japanese floatplane equipping cruisers and battleships. It was in the process of being replaced by the F1M2 when the war broke out. By the end of 1942 it had been withdrawn from front-line service. Like all Japanese floatplanes, its primary mission was scouting for the fleet.

See: AIRCRAFT TYPES, DEVELOPMENT; RECONNAISSANCE, NAVAL.

E13A Jake, Japanese Reconnaissance Floatplane

The E13A Jake was the principal floatplane of the fleet. Some 1,400 were built, and they were sitting ducks for any Allied fighter (even bombers or flying boats) they came across.

See also AIRCRAFT TYPES, DEVELOPMENT: RECONNAISSANCE, NAVAL.

E16A Paul, Japanese Floatplane Divebomber

The E16A Paul was the third Japanese floatplane introduced during the war. Entering service in the summer of 1944, the E16A could carry a thousand pounds of bombs, making it capable of effective divebombing. This was rarely possible, however, because most Allied ships now operated in conjunction with aircraft carriers. While faster (250 MPH) than previous floatplanes, the E16A was still an easy target for Allied fighters (and most other combat aircraft).

See also AIRCRAFT TYPES, DEVELOPMENT; RECONNAISSANCE, NAVAL.

Eastern Solomons, Battle of

The late August 1942 Battle of the Eastern Solomons was a consequence of the American landing on GUADALCANAL on August 7, 1942. On the night of August 9, a Japanese cruiser-destroyer squadron inflicted a serious defeat on American and Australian cruisers off SAVO ISLAND, in an effort to gain control of the waters around Guadalcanal, to land reinforcements, and at the same time strangle the Marines' tentative hold on the island. Meanwhile, from his headquarters at TRUK, Admiral Isoroku YAMAMOTO began concentrating a major force for a decisive blow against the US fleet in the south Pacific, an operation that would also cover the landing of additional reinforcements on Guadalcanal.

In late August, Yamamoto concentrated two battleships, three carriers, a seaplane carrier, eight heavy cruisers, three light cruisers, 23 destroyers, two dozen SUBMARINES, and a number of smaller warships and auxiliary vessels at Truk, while three heavy cruisers, a light cruiser, eight destroyers, and three submarines concentrated at RABAUL to escort the reinforcements to Guadalcanal.

As was usual with Japanese plans, their forces were divided into numerous subordinate groups scattered rather widely over the ocean. The Truk-based task force comprised five groups organized into two task forces, all under VAdm Nobutake KONDO, while the Rabaul force, under RAdm Raizo TANAKA ("Tenacious Tanaka"), comprised no less than four task groups. The plan called for the submarines to spread out ahead of the fleet in order to ambush American warships. Then light carrier RYUJO, accompanied by a heavy cruiser and two destroyers, would serve as bait, steaming well ahead of VAdm Chuichi NAGUMO's two fleet carriers to provoke an American reaction both by her presence and by airstrikes on the Marines at Henderson Field. When the American carriers took the bait, they would in turn be jumped and annihilated by massive airstrikes from SHOKAKU and *Zuikaku*.

When the Japanese began to move, reconnaissance aircraft and Australian COASTWATCHERS quickly apprised VAdm Robert Lee GHORMLEY of the fact. As a result, he ordered VAdm Frank FLETCHER into action.

Fletcher had three carrier task forces, each built around a single carrier plus two or three cruisers (and in one case a fast battleship) and five to seven destroyers. By dawn on 23 August Fletcher was about 150 miles northeast of Henderson Field, actually on the Pacific side of the Solomons. Misinformed by fleet intelligence that the Japanese carriers had not yet passed Truk, Fletcher decided that he had a few days' grace, and promptly dispatched Task Force 18, WASP and her escorts, southward to refuel, thereby reducing his effectives by a third. The next morning a PBY spotted *Ryujo*, Kondo's "bait," about 280 miles northwest of Fletcher's position. Fletcher took the bait. At 1345 (1:45 P.M.) on August 24 he launched 38 bombers plus escorts. As these aircraft were on their way, one of Fletcher's scouts came across *Zuikaku* and *Shokaku*, just 60 miles beyond *Ryujo*. Although Fletcher tried to switch the air strike to the more valuable targets, communications problems inter-

fered. *Ryujo* was hit hard, and went down at about 2000. By then Nagumo had already launched two strikes, one at 1507 and the other at 1600.

Aware that the Japanese air strike was coming, Fletcher deployed his two carriers about 10 miles apart, each closely surrounded by its escorts. He also put up 51 F4F WILDCATS as CAP and flew off bombers that could not be defueled and demunitioned in time to be struck below. CAP intercepted the first Japanese strike at 1629. Although the US Navy fighters accounted for a good many of the attackers, 24 Japanese dive bombers got through, concentrating on carrier *Enterprise* and battleship NORTH CAROLINA. *Enterprise* took three bombs, which caused considerable damage, including a steering problem that plagued her for several hours.

By 1647 the survivors of the first Japanese air strike were winging their way home. The second Japanese air strike went totally astray and returned to its carriers.

During the Japanese attack, carrier *Saratoga* had received only minimal attention. As a result, she was able to organize an air strike of her own, albeit a modest one (seven bombers with no escorts). At 1745 *Saratoga*'s planes hit Kondo's main body, severely damaging a seaplane carrier. By the time these planes returned to *Saratoga*, Fletcher had decided to break off the action, and the fleet was soon steaming southward. Although Kondo attempted to pursue with his battleships and heavy cruisers, he soon gave up the effort.

Both sides made serious errors during this battle. Yamamoto could have committed heavier forces, and Fletcher sent a third of his force off to refuel on the very eve of battle. Strategically and tactically it was an American victory, for at the loss of just 17 aircraft Fletcher had killed a light carrier, a destroyer, and several dozen aircraft, while the Japanese had not even come close to annihilating American sea power in the South Pacific.

Economic Resources, Japan

Japan was critically short of every kind of raw material, including food, from the first day of the war.

THE JAPANESE ECONOMY, 1940	
Importation Requirements	
Commodity	**% Imported***
Cotton	100
Jute	100
Mercury	100
Nickel	100
Rubber	100
Wool	100
Tropical Gums	95
Petroleum	92
Scrap Iron	92 (85)
Lead	90 (65)
Iron Ore	84 (65)
Zinc	80
Aluminum	77 (60)
Alloying Ores	62
Machine Tool	50
Copper	40
Coal	15 (0)
Food	0

Figures count as domestic production commodities produced in Korea and Formosa. The occasional figure in parentheses includes Manchurian production as domestic production.
*All figures have been rounded to the nearest whole percentage point.

The Allied situation was much better, despite problems with things like rubber and tin.

Japan could feed itself only with imports from Korea and FORMOSA. The Home Islands had to import 20% of their rice and other grains, 65% of their soybeans, and 100% of their sugar.

Korea was a major source of iron ore and coal, as well as food, Formosa produced aluminum ore, a little oil, some food, and most of Japan's sugar. The United States was a major source of scrap iron, essential in the PRODUCTION of steel, and was virtually Japan's only supplier of machine tools. Alloying ores include zinc, nickel, tin, and manganese, used to make metal alloys so essential to the manufacture of military equipment (note that zinc and nickel are listed separately as well). Although its contribution in terms of all commodities cannot be determined, the importance of

MANCHURIA to the Japanese economy can be seen from the figures that can be determined.

Upon securing the "Southern Resources Area," the Japanese no longer had a problem with regard to access to raw materials, save in the matter of food. Existing prewar stockpiles (for example, they had 4.2 million tons of iron ore on hand at the start of the war) and output in the conquered territories were more than they required. There was enough tin stockpiled in Burma when it was overrun in '42 to keep Japanese industry going for at least a year, and there was more tin in INDONESIA.

The critical problem was not the supply of materials, but sealift, since between 80% and 90% of the industry in the "Greater East Asia Co-Prosperity Sphere" was in the Home Islands. Since they had difficulties with shipping availability even before the submarine campaign began to bite, they were never able to import as much as they needed.

This once led to an interesting staff dust-up in the CBI, when Allied economic warfare experts tried to convince air power aficionados that bombing tin mines that the Japanese were trying to expand was counterproductive: The Japanese were actually wasting more resources in trying to expand output than they were gaining in increased production, since they were already unable to find enough ships to export all the ore they were digging up.

Food was actually in short supply even before PEARL HARBOR. Full rationing was introduced in April of 1941. Rationing of many other commodities had actually begun as early as 1938. Korea was the big source of rice, the Japanese taking a major portion of the annual 2.5 million-ton Korean crop. However, Korean harvests were bad in 1939–41, about 20% lower than normal (c. 2.0 million tons), and they continued so during the war, even as Japanese agricultural output fell due to mobilization. So although the Japanese just took a larger share of the Korean crop (leaving the Koreans to eat feed-quality wheat or starve), they still found themselves with serious shortages, a situation exacerbated by their increasing shortage of shipping.

Incidentally, during the 1930s the United States accounted for $148 million (31%) of Japan's annual exports, and about $170 million of Japan's imports. And US investment in Japan totaled some $420 million. So when Japan went to war with the United States, it attacked its largest trading partner.

Ref: Barnhart, *Japan Prepares for Total War*.

Eichelberger, Robert L. (1886–1961)

One of the most successful, and least known, US corps and army commanders in World War II. Graduating from West Point in 1909, he served on the staff of the Siberian Expedition in 1918–19, and later spent several years in the Far East. The outbreak of World War II found him as superintendent of West Point, from which post in March of 1942 he went on to command various divisions and corps in training. That October, he took command of I Corps, in Australia, which he took into action in New Guinea. He was then put on the shelf for over a year, and continued to suffer relative obscurity because of favorable publicity that greatly annoyed MACARTHUR, who would not tolerate subordinates getting any attention in the press.

However, early in 1944 he returned to operational command and thereafter held important posts in all of Douglas MacArthur's offensives, culminating in the occupation of Japan by his Eighth Army in August–September of 1945.

Eisenhower, Dwight David (1890–1969)

A poor farm boy from Kansas (albeit born in Texas), Eisenhower graduated from West Point in 1915 (61st in a class of 164), having acquired a "football knee." During World War I he served in the Tank Corps as a temporary LTC, but despite strenuous efforts was unable to get overseas. Reverting to captain at the end of the war, he made major in 1920, in which rank he remained for the next 16 years. In the interim he served in Panama, graduated first in the Command and General Staff

School class of 1926, went on to the Army War College, and in 1933 was attached to the office of the chief of staff, General Douglas MACARTHUR. For the next six years Eisenhower served as an aide to MacArthur. When MacArthur went to the Philippines as military adviser to the new commonwealth government in 1935, Eisenhower went with him and played an important role in planning the development of the PHILIPPINE ARMY. In 1939 LTC Eisenhower returned to stateside duty. His years with the touchy, erratic, egocentric MacArthur seem to have fitted Eisenhower well to work with such notoriously difficult men as Winston CHURCHILL, Bernard Law Montgomery, and George S. Patton. Shortly after PEARL HARBOR, Eisenhower, by then a brigadier general, was made chief of war plans, in which post he made strenuous efforts to organize the flow of supplies to the beleaguered American and Filipino forces in the Philippines, with only marginal success. In April 1942 he went to Europe to command US Army forces there, then led the campaigns in North Africa, Sicily, and Italy, before gong to England to direct the liberation of northwestern Europe. After the war he served as 34th president of the United States, from 1953 to 1961. Eisenhower's friendly, easygoing attitude tended to mask his considerable intellect and great integrity.

Ellice Islands

A group of nine islands totaling about 26 square miles, inhabited by several thousand Polynesians. Located just south of the GILBERTS, this made them an important Allied base during the war. When the Japanese had the chance to take them, in early 1942, they failed to do so. FUNAFATI was later developed into a major air base by the United States, from which heavy bombers ranged over the Gilberts until they were taken in late 1943.

Empress Augusta Bay, Battle of

On 2 November 1943, US surface forces stopped four Japanese cruisers and six destroyers from interfering with an Allied amphibious landing on BOUGAINVILLE, in the northern SOLOMONS. The Americans had four cruisers and eight destroyers. More importantly, the US sailors were well trained and experienced and made excellent use of their superior radar equipment. The Japanese were good night fighters, but the Americans had learned since their defeats in the summer of 1942. The Japanese lost one cruiser and one destroyer, plus damage to all their other ships. One US destroyer suffered significant damage.

Enderbury Island

This is a small Pacific island, about four square miles, near CANTON in the Phoenix Group. The United States established an airstrip there in the late 1930s, which served to protect the long supply lines to the South Pacific.

England, USS (DE-635)

England (built in 250 days, 4 April–10 December 1943!), a BUCKLEY CLASS ship, was the most successful submarine-killing DE of the war. Skippered by LtCdr Walton V. Pendleton, she was part of an antisubmarine hunter-killer group, when, between 19 and 31 May 1944, she sank six Japanese SUBMARINES. By taking advantage of Ultra decrypts of Japanese radio traffic, the hunter-killer group was able to determine the location of a Japanese submarine patrol line in the central Pacific, just north of the ADMIRALTY ISLANDS.

After her impressive achievement (she accounted for nearly 5% of all Japanese submarines sunk in the war), *England* served on picket duty off OKINAWA, where she took a KAMIKAZE on 9 May 1945. *England* was scrapped in 1946, but in accordance with Admiral King's remark that "There will always be an *England* in the US Navy," in 1963 a new guided missile destroyer leader was commissioned with the name, and later rerated as a cruiser.

JAPANESE SUBMARINES DESTROYED BY USS *ENGLAND*	
Date	Boat
19 May	*I–16*
22 May	*Ro–106*
23 May	*Ro–104*
24 May	*Ro–116*
26 May	*Ro–108*
31 May	*Ro–105*

Eniwetok, Marshall Islands

A lovely atoll, with lots of room for ships but no facilities to service them. Eniwetok is nicely located to serve as a base for the domination of the other islands in the MARSHALLS group, many of which shared its natural assets, including strategic location. The US took the atoll early in 1944 and used it as a base.

See also CENTRAL PACIFIC CAMPAIGN.

Espionage, Japanese in the United States

Even before PEARL HARBOR, Japanese espionage networks in the United States had been compromised. Decryption of the principal Japanese diplomatic codes in the years before the war had given US counterintelligence agencies, most notably the FBI, a good notion of who was supplying information to the Japanese government. Despite some resistance from F.B.I. director J. Edgar Hoover, President ROOSEVELT permitted British intelligence to operate with considerable freedom in the United States long before Pearl Harbor; while the principal focus of their attention was on the Germans, they also worked against the Japanese.

Japanese intelligence also attempted to secure support from potentially subversive elements in the United States. Money was funneled to Japanese-American cultural and social organizations, some of which maintained contacts with German-American and Italian-American groups of dubious loyalty, and some went to a few black radical organizations, including one that has since attained some prominence.

The belief that the Japanese-American community was riddled with espionage networks proved largely false, although there were some individuals who supplied information to Japanese officials on an informal basis before the war.

See also AMERICAN CITIZENS, RELOCATION OF.

Espiritu Santo, New Hebrides

The principal island of the NEW HEBRIDES, Espiritu Santo had an excellent harbor, with limited facilities to service ships, and a small airfield, located about 450 miles southeast of the easternmost tip of the SOLOMON ISLANDS.

Its proximity to the Solomon Islands, and its location athwart the main line of communications between the United States and Australia and New Zealand, prompted the United States to develop Espiritu Santo into a major base from mid–1942. It served as the principal operational base for the GUADALCANAL Campaign, including the great naval battles in the South Pacific (SAVO ISLAND, Eastern Solomons, CAPE ESPERANCE, SANTA CRUZ, Guadalcanal, and so forth) and for operations in the central Solomons into 1943.

Essex Class, US Aircraft Carriers

Essex was the name ship of the largest and most successful class of carriers ever built. Of 32 ordered to two somewhat differing designs, 16 were completed in time to serve in the war and 10 more over the next few years, mostly to modified designs. The Essex Class was designed on the basis of all previous US experience with carriers. They were large, fast, roomy ships, well protected and with an enormous capacity to operate aircraft. From the time they began to enter service, at the end of 1942, they dominated events in the Pacific. Intensively involved in combat, not one was sunk despite often horrendous damage. With periodic modifications and reconstruction, elements of the class formed part of the navy's first-line forces until the early 1980s.

The more notable members of the class were:

Essex, CV-9 (1941–1942–1942), began operating in the Pacific in mid–1943, and saw extensive service thereafter. In the course of the war she took a KAMIKAZE off Luzon in November 1944. She was scrapped in 1975.

Yorktown, CV-10 (1941–1943–1943), originally to have been named *Bon Homme Richard*, she was renamed before launching to commemorate the famous carrier sunk at MIDWAY. She operated throughout the Pacific, being damaged only once, and that lightly. Her aircraft helped sink the battleship YAMATO. She is preserved as a war memorial at Charleston, South Carolina.

Intrepid, CV-11 (1941–1943–1944), earned the nickname "The Evil Eye" because of the number of times she was damaged by enemy action, being hit by one TORPEDO and four kamikaze, plus a near-miss by a fifth. She is preserved as a war memorial on New York's North River.

Hornet, CV-12 (1942–1943–1943), originally to have been named *Kearsarge*, was renamed while still on the way to commemorate the YORKTOWN CLASS carrier sunk in 1942. She was given only a two-week shakedown cruise and rushed off to war in early 1944. *Hornet* was under attack on 42 separate days, but the only damage she sustained was from the typhoon of 5 June 1945, when a portion of her flight deck collapsed. After lengthy postwar service, she was slated for scrapping in 1996, but had a last-minute stay of execution to gain more time for the securing of the necessary funds to preserve her as a war memorial.

Franklin, CV-13 (1942–1943–1944), was the most heavily damaged carrier to survive the war. On 19 March 1945 she was hit by two 500-pound bombs that caused massive explosions throughout her hanger deck. Over 700 men were killed and nearly 300 wounded (some 40% of her crew), and the ship developed a pronounced list and lost all power. However, after being towed clear and hastily repaired, she managed to make the 12,000-mile voyage back to New York with only one stop. Repaired, she was never recommissioned and was scrapped in 1964. Although she was actually named after the 1864 Civil War battle in Tennessee, the crew nicknamed her "Big Ben," after Benjamin Franklin.

Ticonderoga, CV-14 (1943–1944–1944), entered combat in November 1944 in the Philippines. She took two kamikaze off Luzon in January 1945, which caused dangerous fires, requiring extensive flooding. She was back in action in April to take part in the final operations against Japan. She was scrapped in 1973.

Randolph, CV-15 (1943–1944–1944), saw considerable service but was damaged only once, by a kamikaze while lying anchored at ULITHI Atoll in March 1945. Only lightly damaged, she was soon back in service, and took part in the final operations against Japan. Scrapped in 1973.

Lexington, CV-16 (1941–1942–1943), originally to have been named *Cabot*, but renamed before being launched to commemorate the original LEXINGTON, sunk at the CORAL SEA. She took part in numerous operations, most notably the Battle of the PHILIPPINE SEA and LEYTE GULF, but was damaged by enemy action only three times: by a torpedo in the MARSHALL ISLANDS in December 1943, by a kamikaze off Luzon in January 1945, and by a Japanese bomb in March 1945. This last was not repaired in time to return to combat before the war ended. She is preserved as a war memorial at Corpus Christi, Texas.

Bunker Hill, CV-17 (1941–1942–1943), reached the Pacific late in 1943 and fought through to 11 March 1945, when she was hit by two kamikazes. These caused extensive fires and severely damaged the flight deck. Although repaired by July 1945, the ship saw no further action in the war. Scrapped in 1966.

Wasp, CV-18 (1942–1943–1943), was originally to have been named *Oriskany*, but was renamed to commemorate the old WASP, sunk in September 1942. She reached the war zone in early 1944, and served through to the end of the war, being damaged only once, and that lightly. Scrapped in 1973.

Hancock, CV-19 (1943–1943–1944), began operating with the Fast Carrier Task Force in late 1944, and served until the end of the war. She was

damaged once by a kamikaze and once by an accidental fuel explosion, but neither required extensive repairs. Scrapped in 1976.

Bennington, CV-20 (1942–1944–1944), arrived in the Pacific early in 1945. She supported the OKINAWA landings, helped sink YAMATO, and took part in the final operations against Japan. The only damage she sustained was from the 5 June 1945 typhoon, which collapsed her flight deck forward. She was scrapped in the 1980s.

Bon Homme Richard, CV-31 (1943–1944–1944), took part in the Okinawa operation and in the final assault on Japan, incurring no damage. Scrapped in the 1980s.

Shangri-La, CV-38 (1943–1944–1944), began combat operations in the Pacific only in the spring of 1945, taking part in raids against Japan, during which she suffered no damage. She was the last new carrier to see action in the war. Her name came about in a curious fashion. Asked by some journalists where the DOOLITTLE Raiders had taken off from, President ROOSEVELT replied by saying "Shangri-La," the name of a fictional Asian country in the popular novel and film *Lost Horizon*, and the name was shortly given to the new carrier. Scrapped in the 1980s.

Three other units of the Essex Class were completed before the end of the Pacific War, but saw no action: *Boxer* (CV-21), *Antietam* (CV-36), and *Lake Champlain* (CV-39). A further six units were completed after the war, one as late as 1950: *Leyte* (CV-32), *Kearsarge* (CV-33), *Oriskany* (CV-34), *Princeton* (CV-37), *Tarawa* (CV-40), *Valley Forge* (CV-45), and *Philippine Sea* (CV-47). Two units were canceled after being laid down, *Reprisal* (CV-35) and *Iwo Jima* (CV-46).

Evacuations, Japanese Armed Forces

While the Japanese had a reputation for fighting to the last man, they were also quite capable of withdrawing from a hopeless situation. They often did this so cleverly that the Allies attacked where the Japanese last were, thinking the foe remained dug in to receive the attack. This tactic became increasingly difficult to sustain after 1943, when the Allies had great naval and air superiority and could interfere in any attempt at evacuation. But in that year, the Japanese pulled two of their most notable disappearing acts. On GUADALCANAL, where the fighting had been going on since August 1942, the Japanese decided to quit the island and evacuated 10,000 surviving troops by night in February 1943. The Allied troops weren't sure the Japanese were gone until American troops reached the north end of the island and found evidence of the final evacuation. A more embarrassing example took place in May 1943, in the ALEUTIANS off Alaska where the Japanese had been dug in since June 1942. After a bitter struggle for Attu Island in May, the Allies prepared to take KISKA Island. In August a force of 35,000 American and Canadian troops began coming ashore, after the usual intensive naval and air bombardment, only to discover that the Japanese had evacuated their 6,000 troops two weeks previously. This discovery was a painful one, as the navy lost a destroyer and 70 men to a Japanese mine, and the ground troops lost 21 of their number to FRIENDLY FIRE.

By this time the Japanese had refined the art of evacuation, and practiced it—or attempted to do so—quite often during the Solomons campaign, sparking a number of surface fights.

See also KOLOMBANGARA, BATTLE OF; VELLA LAVELLA, BATTLE OF.

Evarts Class, US Destroyer Escorts

The first PRODUCTION model US destroyer escorts, 68 units of the Evarts Class were completed 1943–44 (five more were canceled). They were small, cramped, slow, and underarmed, and came into service only after the U-boat menace had been beaten, but they performed a variety of useful duties. All were disposed of immediately after the war. Officially they were the "GMT Class," referring to their General Motors diesel electric tandem drive.

Exeter, British Heavy Cruiser

Exeter (1928–1929–1931) was a British attempt to design a "lite" heavy cruiser, the larger eight-gunned vessels having proven unsatisfactory for Britain's peacetime naval requirements. A successful ship, though undergunned by the standards of the Pacific War, she was extremely sturdy. In the action with the German pocket battleship *Graf Spee* in December of 1939 she survived seven 11-inch hits (over 5,000 pounds of explosive shell), albeit that they put her out of action. In the Far East when the Pacific War began, she served with the ABDA squadron. In the Battle of the JAVA SEA, severe damage by a Japanese 8-inch shell greatly reduced her speed. At the Battle of Sunda Strait, March 1, 1942, she took numerous hits from NACHI CLASS heavy cruisers. Ordered abandoned, scuttling charges were fired, but the ship did not sink until TORPEDOED by a Japanese destroyer.

F

F1M2 Pete, Japanese Reconnaissance Floatplane

The F1M2 Pete was the principal Japanese float-plane for cruisers and battleships. Introduced in 1940, some 1,100 were built. It had some attack capability, with a 120-pound bomb load. However, its slow speed (200 MPH) and meager armament (one machine gun) made it an easy target for Allied fighters.

See also AIRCRAFT TYPES, DEVELOPMENT; RE-CONNAISSANCE, NAVAL.

F2A Buffalo, Brewster, US Fighter

The Buffalo was the first modern US carrier fighter, reaching the fleet in 1940, when it was already out-performed by the Japanese A5M and A6M. The next generation, the F4F WILDCAT, was much su-perior, and by late 1941 the Buffalo was being re-placed. Some F2As were still on carriers at the time of PEARL HARBOR, and many also served with Dutch and British forces from land bases in the East Indies. The former were quickly withdrawn, while the latter were torn up in combat. Only 500 were produced, the last in June 1941. Most ended up serving with European nations desperate for any kind of combat aircraft.

See also AIRCRAFT TYPES, DEVELOPMENT; CAR-RIERS, DESIGNING AIRCRAFT FOR.

F4F Wildcat, US Carrier Fighter

The F4F Wildcat, in its original design as a biplane, lost out to the F2A BUFFALO in a flyoff competi-tion. Redesigned as a monoplane, the F4F was clearly superior to the F2A and production began immediately. Ironically, the F4F first entered com-bat in British colors. An order of F4Fs for France ended up in Britain when France fell in June 1940. The ROYAL NAVY put the aircraft into service as the "Martlet." In December of 1940, a Martlet shot down a German bomber, scoring the F4F's first kill. The British ultimately took delivery of 1,100 F4Fs. Meanwhile, the US Navy was rapidly replacing all its older carrier fighters (biplanes or F2As) with Wildcats. By the end of 1941, nearly all carrier fighters were F4Fs, and by early 1942, all of the older fighters were gone. The Wildcat was not the best fighter but it was good enough. In particular, it was rugged, being able to take more punishment than its opponents. By the end of 1942, Wildcats had downed 5.9 enemy aircraft for each F4F lost.

See also AIRCRAFT TYPES, DEVELOPMENT; CAR-RIERS, DESIGNING AIRCRAFT FOR.

F4U Corsair, US Carrier Fighter

The US F4U Corsair, something of a dark horse in the "best fighter of World War II" competition, managed to move to the front of the pack. Origi-nally designed as a carrier fighter, it first flew in May 1940. The navy was dubious of its ability to operate from carriers because the pilot's view of the flight deck was quite restricted during landing, and the airplane had a relatively weak undercarriage. Admitting that, the F4U was a very capable aircraft regardless; mass PRODUCTION was begun in June 1941. The navy decided to have Marine pilots fly the F4U from land bases only.

Entering combat in early 1943, the F4U quickly established its superiority. Through the end of the war, 2,140 enemy aircraft were shot down by the F4U, which lost only 189 in return. There were, as with all combat aircraft, other ways to lose F4Us. Of approximately 1,400 F4Us lost to other causes, 349 went to enemy antiaircraft fire, 164 to landing accidents, and the rest to other operational mishaps. While about one in 300 F4U landings resulted in damage or loss of the aircraft, this was not unusual by World War II standards. Indeed, until quite recently, getting shot down in combat was less likely than losing aircraft through non-combat accidents.

The F4U also found work as a fighter-bomber, being able to carry 3,000 pounds of bombs. It was a big airplane, weighing up to six tons fully loaded. By early 1944, British (who received 2,000 F4Us)

A Marine Corps F4U Corsair in action in support of Marines on Okinawa, June 1945. Tough and versatile, the Corsair proved enormously effective in ground support.

and US F4U pilots convinced the navy that the aircraft could safely operate on carriers. By the end of the war, 15% of F4U sorties had been flown from carriers. Some 5,000 F4Us were built during the war, with even more built into the 1950s. The F4U served into the 1960s with foreign air forces.

See also AIRCRAFT TYPES, DEVELOPMENT; CARRIERS, DESIGNING AIRCRAFT FOR.

F6F Hellcat, US Carrier Fighter

The Hellcat was the US Navy's successor to the F4F WILDCAT carrier fighter. Although the F6F didn't enter service until early 1943 (after all the crucial carrier battles of 1942 were over), it performed admirably for the rest of the war. Some 12,000 F6Fs were produced, and those that got into action downed 6,477 enemy aircraft, while losing only 270 of their own in air combat. While not as capable as the F4U CORSAIR, the Hellcat was more than a match for any Japanese aircraft it encountered from 1943 on. This was partly because the Japanese were unable to produce quality pilots as quickly as the Allies. No matter how much Japanese aircraft improved, the more skillful Allied pilots more than made up for any equipment advantages.

See also AIRCRAFT TYPES, DEVELOPMENT; CARRIERS, DESIGNING AIRCRAFT FOR.

F6U Pirate, US Carrier Fighter

The F6U Pirate was one of several jet fighter projects the US Navy began during World War II. It was not a success. Development began in 1944 and it was not ready for production until 1949. At that point, the other jet fighter projects looked more promising, and the F6U was abandoned after only 30 were built. It might have turned out otherwise, although the navy would not have had a carrier-based jet fighter until 1946 at the earliest.

See also AIRCRAFT TYPES, DEVELOPMENT; CARRIERS, DEVELOPING AIRCRAFT FOR.

An F6F Hellcat preparing to take off from the deck of the second USS Yorktown (CV-10), November 1945. The rotation of the propeller combined with the forward motion of the airplane creates the illusion of an "aura" in this image

F7F Tigercat, US Carrier Fighter

The F7F Tigercat was developed as a twin-engine multi-role fighter bomber for the US Navy's new 45,000-ton "super carriers." The first F7Fs arrived in the combat zone on 15 August 1945, the day Japan surrendered. Only about 100 F7Fs were produced before the war ended and most of these were the night fighter version. While the 9-ton F7F was not the best interceptor, it was capable of many other tasks. It was the first navy fighter that could carry a TORPEDO. Its maximum bomb load was 2,000 pounds, and its four 20mm cannon gave it substantial air-to-air firepower. Had the war continued, many more F7Fs would have been pro-

duced. As it was, the introduction of jet aircraft after World War II cut short the F7F's career. Only about 200 more were produced and it was withdrawn from service by 1952.

See also AIRCRAFT TYPES, DEVELOPMENT; CARRIERS, DESIGNING AIRCRAFT FOR.

F8F Bearcat, US Carrier Fighter

The US F8F Bearcat was the replacement for the F6F HELLCAT. Work began in 1943 and it was in production by early 1945. The F8F was lighter, smaller, and more capable than its predecessor, the F6F. The F8F was, without doubt, the most capable

221

propeller-driven carrier fighter ever produced. However, it never got into combat from US carriers, as the first F8F unit was in transit to the Pacific when the war ended. Over 700 were eventually produced, as the F8F was to be the main navy carrier fighter until the jets were ready in the late 1940s. Production continued until 1948, and the F8F was withdrawn from US service in the early 1950s. At that point, many of the F8Fs were given to foreign governments. The French used F8Fs in their Vietnam war, the South Vietnamese government inherited some, and some were sold to Thailand.

See also AIRCRAFT TYPES, DEVELOPMENT; CARRIERS, DESIGNING AIRCRAFT FOR.

False Battles of the Pacific War

There were numerous occasions during the Pacific War when Allied forces erroneously believed they were under attack. On several occasions this caused severe dislocation of civilian life. Worse, in a number of instances troops actually opened fire without anyone being on the receiving end. Some of the more infamous instances were large enough to be considered battles.

December 8 and 10, 1941: The first and second "Battles of San Francisco" were caused by nervous civilians, who reported suspicious aircraft overhead. When LTG John L. DEWITT gave credence to these rumors, the city and environs were blacked out. As army aircraft went aloft in search of the aircraft carriers that DeWitt and others swore were somewhere off the coast, there was considerable panic among civilians.

December 9, 1941: The "Battle of Los Angeles" was sparked by erroneous reports of Japanese aircraft over the city and of SUBMARINES offshore. The city was blacked out, troops took up positions to repel invasion, antiaircraft batteries were manned, and aircraft took to the skies, while there was some panic among the populace.

Spring 1943: The "Battle of the Pribiloff Islands" is an incident that the air force still prefers not to discuss. A number of B-24s were vectored in on a reported Japanese fleet approaching the ALEUTIANS from the northwest. It later transpired that the "fleet" was actually the Pribiloff Islands, dimly seen through overcast skies, and the bombers appear to have wrought enormous carnage among the resident seal population.

July 1943: The "Battle of the Pips" was based on a very strong series of radar contacts ("pips"). On July 27, US battleships, cruisers, and destroyers expended several hundred rounds of ammunition at what they thought was a Japanese squadron attempting to relieve the KISKA garrison. In fact, the pips were false returns, probably engendered by the peculiar meteorological conditions prevailing in such high latitudes.

Normally, false battles are much smaller affairs. Troops operating in the jungle, particularly green troops, can easily be panicked into wild firing by unfamiliar noises in the night (land crabs were a notable culprit in this regard, as they rustled about in the underbrush after dark). Interestingly, while the navy came clean about the Battle of the Pips (S. E. MORISON devotes several pages to it in his semi-official history), no official air force treatments of the war mention the Pribiloff Islands affair, although the air force official history of the war devotes several pages to the Battle of the Pips.

Farragut Class, US Destroyers

The Farraguts, built 1933–36, were the first destroyers added to the US Navy since the early 1920s, their construction being advocated by President ROOSEVELT as a "pump priming" measure to help get the economy going again during the Great Depression, not to mention help rebuild the fleet. The eight ships more or less set the model for American destroyers in the early part of World War II. They had a high forecastle, to improve seakeeping capacity, and they introduced the 5"/38 dual-purpose gun as their main armament. But they lacked adequate protection for the 5-inch guns, and were rather cramped, due to the necessity of adhering to the limitations of the naval DISARMAMENT TREATIES. They saw heavy service during the war, yet not one was lost to enemy action. Three were lost to hazards of the sea: *Hull* (DD-350) and *Monaghan* (DD-354) to the great typhoon of 18 December 1944, and *Worden* (DD-352) by grounding in a fog in the ALEUTIANS on 12 January 1943. The surviving units, all heavily modified by the end of the war, were scrapped in 1947.

Ferrying Aircraft

Moving aircraft from one place to another was much easier, and more efficient, on one-way trips with friendly airbases at both ends. Because such aircraft could use nearly all their fuel for movement (keeping a small reserve in case bad weather was encountered), a ferry flight could cover at least three times the distance an airplane would normally fly on a combat mission. For combat missions, an aircraft had to fly out and back, while maintaining a third of its fuel load for combat itself. Even bombers would burn more fuel over the combat zone in order to dodge flak or enemy fighters. As the war went on, aircraft were equipped with extra fuel tanks. These were often drop tanks (that could be dropped like a bomb when no longer needed), and during a ferry mission the normal weapons load was usually replaced with fuel. These techniques enabled normally short-range aircraft to be ferried long distances. The biggest danger during these operations was getting lost, so a larger aircraft with a navigator on board usually accompanied groups of fighters being ferried over large expanses of open water.

FH-1 Phantom, US Carrier Jet Fighter

The FH-1 Phantom was another of the US Navy's jet fighter projects and probably the most successful. Work began in 1943 and the first flight took place in early 1945. In the summer of 1947, the first unit received its FH-1s. Because the war was over, only 61 were produced. Work went ahead on more advanced designs, although if the war in the Pacific had gone on long enough, the capable FH-1 would have been the most likely navy jet the Japanese would have had to face.

See also AIRCRAFT TYPES, DEVELOPMENT; CARRIERS, DESIGNING AIRCRAFT FOR.

Fighter Aircraft

Fighters developed out of reconnaissance aircraft during World War I, initially to prevent enemy reconnaissance aircraft from doing their jobs. A logical consequence of this was that they assumed the duty of escorting friendly reconnaissance aircraft, which meant that they often had to tangle with enemy fighters intent on downing the recon planes. When bombers come along, also developed out of reconnaissance aircraft, the fighters assumed the escort/intercept role for them as well.

Fighters were very difficult aircraft to design, combining agility, speed, endurance, and toughness in a relatively small airframe. Not until the late 1930s had technology advanced sufficiently to provide engines that could give fighters the same speed as the more advanced multi-engined bombers. This development also permitted the introduction of the monoplane fighter. It was in this period that many of the most famous fighters of World War II were designed, the A6M ZERO, the Bf-109, the SPITFIRE, the F4F WILDCAT, and so forth.

As with all weapons, various nations had different notions of what was most desirable in a fighter. The Japanese, for example, went in for fast, maneuverable aircraft with considerable range, such as the Zero, which were relatively lightly built, offering little protection to the pilot: In effect, the Zero was an "all offense" fighter. At least initially, the Americans also favored "long legged" (great range) aircraft, but theirs were slower and less maneuverable, because they preferred providing the maximum possible protection for the pilot, with armor plate and selfsealing gas tanks. The war accelerated engine design, so that by mid-war it became possible to build fighters that were not only fast, maneuverable, and "long legged," but also provided maximum protection for the pilot. Due to economic factors, only the Allies were able to take full advantage of these developments.

Virtually all fighters were designed to intercept and attack bombers and tangle with enemy fighters. During the war several specialized roles developed, such as ground attack, night fighter, photoreconnaissance, and even antisubmarine fighters. Initially aircraft assigned such roles were older types, bordering on obsolescence, and those newer aircraft that proved less than effective as first-line fighters, such as the P-39 or the Me-110.

The Allies, with their enormous industrial strength, soon developed specialized variants of virtually all their fighter aircraft. The Axis, with limited ability to produce aircraft, tended to relegate older models to such specialized roles.

Fighters proved to be the most versatile aircraft of the war.

See also AIRCRAFT TYPES, DEVELOPMENT; CARRIERS, DESIGNING AIRCRAFT FOR.

Fiji Class, British Light Cruisers

A large class, initially of 11 units, the Fijis were smaller than previous British light cruisers mounting 12 6-inch guns. As a result, they proved rather unstable, and the three last units were completed to a modified design as the UGANDA CLASS. They saw considerable action, mostly in the Atlantic and European waters, where one was sunk. *Gambia* (1939–1940–1942) was lent to the Royal New Zealand Navy, from 1944 until after the war, and saw service with the British Pacific Fleet in 1945.

See also ROYAL NAVY.

Fiji Islands

A large island group in southwestern Polynesia, in 1941 Fiji was a protectorate of the British Empire. Located about 1,300 miles north of New Zealand, the colony comprised more than 800 islands (of which only 105 were inhabited) totaling about 7,000 square miles, scattered over nearly a million square miles of ocean. The islands were on Japan's list of objectives to be seized following the capture of MIDWAY.

Although few in number, the native Fijians were tough troops, and the Fiji Defence Force eventually totaled about 8,500 men, serving under New Zealand officers. Over 6,000 of the Fiji troops were native Fijians, slightly more than a thousand were of mixed European-Fijian descent, and the balance were Europeans (mostly New Zealanders) and Indians (who comprised nearly half the population, but were kept out of military service by the British for fear of offending the Fijians). In mid-1942 the bulk of the Fiji Defence Force was formed into a brigade group. At peak strength it consisted of three infantry battalions, three commandos, an artillery battery, an engineer company, a service company, a transport company, a signals section, and small ordnance, medical, pay, and records detachments. There was also a territorial battalion and two labor battalions, which were not included in the brigade group. Of these forces, two commandos and two infantry battalions served in combat.

First Commando: Organized in 1942, a "Special Detachment" of about 30 men served alongside US Marines on GUADALCANAL later that same year, and the entire commando went on to fight on New Georgia and VELLA LAVELLA.

Second Commando: Organized in 1943, the Second Commando performed mopping up and security operations in the Solomon Islands in conjunction with the Solomon Islands Defence Force.

1st Battalion: Organized in 1942, in early 1943 it cleared Florida Island, north of Guadalcanal, of Japanese stragglers, and went on to fight on BOUGAINVILLE, where it had a rough initiation into sustained combat, and KOLOMBANGARA from mid-1943 into 1944.

3rd Battalion: Organized in 1943, it served on Bougainville in 1944–45.

About 2,500 Fijian troops saw combat in the South Pacific, of whom 29 were killed in action or died of wounds. Fijian troops earned one Victoria Cross and two Silver Stars.

See also TONGA.

Ref: Gillespie, *Official History of New Zealand in the Second World War, 1939–1945, The Pacific*; Ravuvu, *Fijians at War*; Ready, *Forgotten Allies*; White and Lindstrom, *The Pacific Theater*.

Firefly, British Carrier Aircraft

The Firefly was originally designed by the British as a two-seat carrier fighter. Entering service in late 1942, it was soon apparent that the Firefly was most effective as a carrier bomber. Some 600 were built and were quite successful. The Firefly was rebuilt after the war and continued to serve into the 1950s, seeing combat service in Korea and Malaya.

See also AIRCRAFT TYPES, DEVELOPMENT; CARRIERS, DESIGNING AIRCRAFT FOR.

Fitch, Aubrey W. (1883–1978)

Aubrey Fitch graduated from the Naval Academy at Annapolis in 1906, and during World War I served aboard a battleship with the British Grand Fleet. After a variety of assignments in the peacetime navy, he took flight training in 1929 and subsequently commanded an aircraft tender and the carriers *Langley*, *Saratoga*, and LEXINGTON. On the eve of World War II he was commander, Carrier Division 1, with his flag in *Saratoga*. In the opening months of the war, he commanded in the carrier raids on the MANDATES and New Guinea, and was aboard *Lexington* at CORAL SEA. He thereafter commanded all Allied land-based air forces in the South Pacific, then became deputy chief of naval operations for air, and at the end of the war superintendent of Annapolis. Retiring as an admiral, he served for a time as an adviser to industry.

FJ-1 Fury, US Carrier Jet Fighter

The FJ-1 Fury was the third US Navy project to produce a jet fighter. This one was begun in 1944, by the company that was working on what would eventually become the highly successful Air Force F-86. The FJ-1 didn't make its first flight until 1946 and it was not all that impressive. Only 30 were produced and one unit was equipped with it. More advanced designs were used for the navy's post-World War II jet fighter.

See also AIRCRAFT TYPES, DEVELOPMENT; CARRIERS, DESIGNING AIRCRAFT FOR.

Flags

The use of flags has long been obsolete in land combat, but continues in naval warfare. One reason for this is tradition. Even more important is telling friend from foe. Even to the trained eye all ships tend to look alike, and are painted virtually the same, gray or some similar nondescript color, specifically to reduce visibility. Once in action, however, it is crucial to be able to tell the good guys from the bad, something radar was not very useful for in the 1940s. Besides, radar didn't always work. Naval actions usually occurred at night, and after even a few minutes firing there tended to be a lot of smoke. So when in action warships wear their largest ensigns, usually more than one.

Flags were also used extensively for signals, despite the availability of radio and searchlights, which can readily give away one's position.

Several flags used during the Pacific War are of historic interest.

The Z Flag: A Japanese naval ensign worn by the great Admiral Count Heihachiro Togo's flagship, the battleship *Mikasa*, at the Battle of Tsushima Strait (May 27–28 1905), in which the Japanese smashed the Russian Fleet. It was called the Z Flag because shortly before the battle Togo had displayed a Nelsonian message coded Z ("The rise or fall of the Empire depend upon this battle . . ."). The same flag was hoisted up the mast of NAGUMO's flagship AKAGI at 0600 on the morning of December 7, 1941, just before aircraft began taking off to attack Pearl Harbor.

The Capitol Flag: The flag that was flying over the Capitol building in Washington on December 7, 1941 became the first American flag to fly over

Rome on June 4, 1944, over Berlin on July 20, 1945, and over Tokyo on September 7, 1945. It was worn by the battleship *Missouri* on September 2, 1945, when the formal instrument of surrender of Japan was signed.

The Perry Flag: The flag worn by Commodore Matthew C. Perry's flagship USS *Mississippi* when he sailed into Tokyo harbor in July of 1853 was prominently displayed in a case overlooking the spot aboard the USS *Missouri* where the Japanese instrument of surrender was formally signed.

The Tarawa Flag: A flag that the Marines raised over Tarawa on November 20, 1943 was the first flag hoisted aboard the ESSEX CLASS carrier *Tarawa* (CV-40) when she was commissioned on December 8, 1945.

See also IWO JIMA, BATTLE OF.

Fleet, US Army

Over 100,000 US Army troops spent most of World War II serving as sailors. In an army tradition going back to the American Revolution, the army supplied most of its own ships for moving troops and supplies, as well as for launching over a hundred amphibious assaults. As a result, the army ended up operating more ships and boats than the US Navy during the war.

During the 1930s, it was agreed that the navy would control all shipping in any future war. This was more efficient, even though it flew in the face of historical experience. In the past, the army was reluctant to entrust its shipping to another service. There was always a fair amount of rivalry between the army and navy, and, until the eve of World War II, the navy had tolerated this situation. But with a pro-navy president in the White House and logic on its side, the navy got its way. The navy soon regretted it. As the army began handing over its many ships in 1941, the navy realized that it could not provide crews for these vessels as well as all the new warships it was putting into service. So for the moment the navy agreed to let the army keep many of its ships.

After PEARL HARBOR, the situation became even more confused. In early 1942, army commanders operating out of AUSTRALIA were told to grab shipping any which way they could. The battle with the Japanese was desperate at that point, and the navy had more important things to do than argue with the army about who controlled what ship. Moreover, the situation was so chaotic in the southwest Pacific that, to this day, no one is sure exactly how many ships General MACARTHUR controlled. Back in Washington, the generals and admirals went at each other throughout 1942 over who would control what ships. A compromise of sorts was reached—in actuality a victory for the generals. However, although the army went on to control more ships than the navy by the end of the war, it would be inaccurate to say that the US Army had the largest fleet during World War II. While the army had some 1,600 large ships (over 1,000 tons displacement), the rest of its vessels were much smaller. While the navy put to sea with over 12 million tons of ships, the army had only about two-thirds as much.

THE ARMY AND NAVY FLEETS COMPARED		
Type	**Army**	**Navy**
Over 1,000 tons	1,665	3,436
Under 1,000 tons	1,225	6,228 seagoing vessels
Under 1,000 tons	19,750	4,070 coastal or harbor craft
Small Amphibious Assault	88,366	60,974
Total	111,006	74,708

In addition, and not counted above, the army also had 16,787 pontoon "boats" that were used to build bridges across rivers and, in a pinch, to ferry troops across rivers or other bodies of water. Since these pontoons are not very handy (or useful) in ocean waters, they are not counted. Moreover, the army did have a lot of seagoing barges (8,596) that are counted above because these vessels were used at sea, being pulled by the 4,434 tugs the army operated.

As you can see, the army "fleet" was basically a logistical support outfit that did most of its work in coastal waters. The navy fleet was a high seas combat organization. What combat ships the army did maintain were for coastal operations, mainly for laying MINES to defend army-controlled ports.

The other major combat mission of the army "fleet" was amphibious assaults. The army conducted more of these than the navy, if only because there were only six Marine divisions in the Pacific and more than three times as many army divisions. All of the fighting in the Pacific was on islands of one sort of another, and this made amphibious capability a necessity no matter what uniform the troops wore.

The army fleet was thus heavy on troop transports and small ships that could keep the cargo moving from ship to shore. The army also maintained its own hospital ships and vessels needed to keep all its floating equipment in good repair.

After World War II, the navy finally did get control of everything that floats. But not before the army presided over the largest fleet in history.

See also AMPHIBIOUS VEHICLES.

Ref: Grover, *U.S. Army Ships and Watercraft of World War II.*

Fletcher, Frank J. (1885–1973)

Frank Jack Fletcher graduated from Annapolis in 1906, and had a varied and interesting career thereafter. He won a MEDAL OF HONOR at Vera Cruz in 1914. During World War I he commanded a destroyer on antisubmarine patrol, and afterward he served in various line, staff, and academic posts. In late 1941 he was given command of the YORKTOWN task force by Admiral Husband KIMMEL, another non-flyer who thought Fletcher had better qualifications to command than Aubrey FITCH, a flyer. Fletcher took his command into action in the raids on the MANDATES and New Guinea. In overall command at the CORAL SEA and MIDWAY (where he gallantly conceded command to Raymond SPRUANCE after *Yorktown* was hit), during the GUADALCANAL landings, and in the Battle of the EASTERN SOLOMONS. He later commanded all naval forces in the north Pacific, overseeing the

occupation of northern Japan. Fletcher commanded in three of the five carrier battles of the war, a distinction no other officer on either side can claim. While not an outstanding commander, Fletcher was competent, and he won most of his battles.

Fletcher Class, US Destroyers

Save for the 1936 SOMERS CLASS, the Fletchers were the first US destroyers to displace more than 1,800 standard tons, being over 25% larger than their predecessors. The US Navy's mobilization destroyer, they were the largest class of destroyer ever built, totaling 175 ships (of over 180 ordered), all completed 1942–44. There were a number of differences among various units, since their basic design was modified in the light of wartime experience. Excellent ships, they were versatile and tough and actually superior in several ways to the succeeding ALLEN M. SUMNER CLASS. They saw extensive service, and 19 became war losses. Some continued in service with the United States and with foreign navies into the 1970s.

Flying Tigers

One of the oddest organizations of the Pacific War was the American Volunteer Group (AVG), better known as the Flying Tigers. Quite a number of myths have grown up around this organization, most of then created by enthusiastic, and ill-informed, journalists.

The popular perception that the Flying Tigers were volunteer American pilots fighting for the Chinese before the United States entered the war was wrong on all counts. While the pilots were officially volunteers, they were in fact funded by the US government and recruited with the assistance of the American government from the ranks of army, navy, and Marine pilots on active duty. The Nationalist Chinese government was using foreign pilots in an attempt to blunt increasingly effective Japanese air power. This effort had not worked so well initially, and the American government decided to try a little unofficial military assistance. American public opinion was against any direct US involvement in the China war, so the AVG was put together as if it were a private initiative with no connection to the US government. Recruiting of pilots and shipment of American fighters (bought with US foreign aid provided to China) went on through 1941. By December of that year, the pilots and aircraft had reached Burma, where unit training would take place before the AVG moved on to China. It was here that the Flying Tigers found themselves on December 7. Although it wasn't formally activated yet (that occurred on December 18), the AVG promptly went into combat against the Japanese invasion of

Burma, inflicting heavy losses on the Japanese. Later the AVG moved on to China, where it continued flying and fighting to good effect.

By late December 1941, the American media had discovered the AVG and promptly christened them the "Flying Tigers." The Walt Disney studios created the snappy "shark's grin" logo, and all the hoopla went on until 4 July 1942 when the AVG was disbanded and its pilots and aircraft incorporated into the US Army Air Force. But the AVG was as good as its reputation. From the beginning of the war until it was taken into the USAAF, the AVG destroyed a confirmed 296 Japanese aircraft of nearly 600 claimed, while losing only 12 of its own in combat (another 74 were lost to accidents

P-40s with the distinctive emblem of the Fourteenth Air Force—"The Flying Tigers"—somewhere in China in 1942. Note the kit of the Chinese guard, typical of better equipped Nationalist troops.

and other causes). CASUALTIES were eight killed in combat, four missing, three killed by Japanese bombers, and nine killed in accidents.

The Flying Tiger pilots were a select group of odd, but extraordinarily effective men. After the war, some of them were among the founders of the Hell's Angels Motorcycle Club.

Ref: Ford, *Flying Tigers*.

Foochow, China

An important city in southeastern China, Foochow's river port was adequate for small ships. The city lacked any extensive facilities to service vessels or to repair them. There was a small airfield.

Food, Rations, Japanese

The normal Japanese diet was quite austere, based largely on rice, barley, vegetables, and a bit of fish or meat. In garrison conditions, each soldier was provided with a daily ration of 20 ounces of rice and barley, plus a cash allowance to purchase meat, fish, and vegetables. Soldiers would pool their money for bulk purchases that would then be cooked by members of their "mess group." The standard field ration was nominally 66 ounces per man per day.

Item	Weight
Rice or grain or hardtack	600–690 grams
Canned beef or fish	150
Dehydrated vegetables	120
Pickled plums or vegetables	45
Confection bar*	45
Powdered soy sauce	30
Powdered bean paste	30
Sugar	20
Salt	5
Tea	3

*The confection was made from tea, butter, milk, sugar, eggs, and flour.

The Japanese also supplied their troops with a special combat (or "iron") ration, which consisted of a half-pound of biscuits and extracts per meal, providing about a thousand calories.

Overall, the Japanese rations were about two-thirds the size of Allied rations. This was sufficient for the smaller Japanese, but led to malnutrition when Allied PRISONERS were fed this ration (as stipulated by the GENEVA CONVENTION, which specified that POWs had to be fed what capturing troops got).

When supply from the Home Islands was available, the Japanese had a wide variety of foods available in canned form, albeit that much of it was not to American tastes, such as seaweed, crabmeat, rice cakes, and bean paste. Even so, Japanese troops fighting in the SOLOMONS and NEW GUINEA often got no food at all, or at best got the "emergency" rations, which were one-third or one-half the size of the standard ration. Attempts to forage in the jungle were a mixed success, and thousands of Japanese troops literally starved to death. Many thousands more died of diseases made worse by malnutrition.

On bypassed islands, the Japanese grew their own food as much as possible, but it is known that a number of downed Allied fliers and island natives were eaten. The Japanese Army issued special instructions on the preparation of human flesh for consumption, even specifying the parts to be allocated to the officers' mess.

So desperate were Japanese troops for food at times, that often, when they overran an Allied position, the first "loot" they went for was the food, which was often consumed on the spot. Japanese troops found Allied rations strange but palatable, save for cheese, which was unknown to them, and which they tended to discard. Although during the early weeks on GUADALCANAL Marines had their limited rations supplemented by items captured from the Japanese, Allied troops overrunning Japanese positions much preferred inedible souvenirs, such as officers' swords, flags, bits of clothing, and small weapons. Of course, the Allied troops would just as often trade these battle souvenirs to rear area troops and ship crews for rare (on the battlefield) delicacies such as ice cream, steaks, and whiskey. It is for this reason that so many sailors and army non-combat types came home with battlefield souvenirs, while the combat troops returned only with the memories of those rare battlefield feasts—of ice cream, fresh meat, and strong drink.

Food, Rations, US

The United States provided a wide range of different types of rations for distribution depending upon circumstances.

A *Rations* consisted of cooked meals made with fresh or frozen ingredients. They were served at bases and on ships.

B *Rations* were cooked meals with all perishables provided in cans, even butter. Where fresh vegetables or refrigeration were not available, troops would subsist on the B Ration. Sometimes they would do this for many months.

C *Rations* were for use in combat. They came in packets that provided 3,000 calories, a full day's meals, in the form of three cans containing various combinations of "meat" (which could include Spam or poultry) and vegetables, which could be eaten cold, plus three cans containing cigarettes, sweets, and other consumables. The pound cake was quite good and troops would trade the more popular items for larger quantities of the less favored ones.

D *Rations* consisted of "Logan Bars," a confection made from chocolate, oatmeal, and sugar. Three bars provided about 1,800 calories. They were effective as an "iron ration" but were not particularly tasty and the troops disliked them intensely.

K *Rations* were supposed to be issued to troops in combat. They consisted of 3,000–3,400 calories of food packed in a 6-inch by 2-inch by 2-inch container weighing a pound and a half. The ration comprised "meat" (actually preserved meat, whether pemmican, Spam, chicken, beef, or pork), crackers, a 2-ounce Logan Bar, beverage mixes, and cigarettes. To many of the troops, the processed meat seemed like a form of "cheese" and was not considered good eating.

There was also a special "Assault Ration." It was discovered that during the first few days of an amphibious operation the troops often discarded most of the items in their K Rations, keeping only the candy and the cigarettes. As a result, the Armed Forces developed a special packet that contained only candy and cigarettes, which was issued to troops preparing to make an assault landing.

On the morning of an amphibious assault it was also common to feed the troops a breakfast of steak and eggs, occasionally with a shot of whisky "for medicinal purposes." This was arguably counterproductive, since it was heavy, but it pleased the troops.

There was one item that was a guaranteed morale booster, fresh bread. In all theaters, regardless of circumstances, the Quartermaster Corps made strenuous efforts to supply fresh bread to the troops on a regular basis.

This was by no means easy. Supplies of flour, yeast, sugar, and salt were not always available. When available, the raw materials were not always of the best quality; Australian wheat, for example, had a lower gluten content than did standard American wheat, resulting in a smaller and poorer quality loaf. Nor was bakery equipment always available. Although the troops sometimes grumbled about the quality of their bread, army bakers did a remarkable job. Improvisation was common. One bakery unit, finding that the tropical environment quickly made fresh yeast unusable, improvised a leavening agent out of fermented coconut milk (why they were fermenting coconut milk is another matter). Another unit, short of ovens, discovered that with a little work they could improvise using standard 55-gallon barrels. The resulting "ovens" consumed more fuel than proper ones did, and could only be used for a few days before the metal burned through, but the product was tasty and well received. In mid-1943, working on the theory that, since the American household had given up making bread for buying it, the army sought to do so too, and suggested that bread be supplied in cans from contractors in the United States. This was shot down pretty quickly. Not only would the quality of the canned product have been much lower than fresh bread, but it would also require considerably more shipping. And, of course, there was nothing like the smell of freshly made bread to make a soldier feel like Uncle Sam cared about him, at least a little.

Efforts to procure rations in Australia and New Zealand initially met with only limited success. Australian rations were based on only 24 different food items, while American ones were based on 39 items. Moreover, the most abundant meat available in the Antipodes was mutton, which was not highly thought of among Americans. US troops were known to cry "Baa!" when they saw rations marked "Made in New Zealand." Vegetable preferences were also different, squash, onions, pumpkin, and turnips being more common in Australia and New Zealand than American favorites such as carrots, tomatoes, sweet potatoes, or corn ("maize" or "Indian corn" as the Aussies or Kiwis would say), while the staple starch was invariably potatoes, where Americans preferred rice or macaroni on occasion. Nor were food processing and canning facilities in either Dominion up to American standards. Many of these problems were overcome, and eventually a great deal of the rations consumed by American troops in the South Pacific were produced in New Zealand or Australia, although the tendency to grumble about mutton continued throughout the war.

Although Uncle Sam endeavored to provide a varied diet, as the battle fronts drew closer to Japan, rations tended to become monotonous because the global shipping shortage was never resolved during the war. Indeed, even during the initial phases of the occupation of Japan most troops continued to eat packaged rations, due partially to the shipping shortage and partially to the desperate food shortage that existed in the Home Islands.

Sailors always eat better than soldiers. After fuel oil, the most precious fluid in the navy was coffee. The fleet lived on coffee, consuming it in endless gallons. There was usually a pot brewing almost anywhere one could be installed. Taste, of course, varied, but strong and black was not unusual, and the black gang (the engine room hands) often put a little salt in theirs, to help them retain body salt in the extreme heat of their work areas. A cup of hot coffee was particularly appreciated by bluejackets standing watch on cold nights in northern latitudes, such as the Atlantic convoy routes or the ALEUTIANS, and special heavy mugs were even issued, without handles, so that the men could grip them with mittens.

In normal circumstances a battleship used about 250 pounds of coffee a day, nearly two tons a week, nearly two pounds a man, at a time when civilians back home were being rationed to a fifth of a pound a week. But the demand for coffee rose precipitously when a ship went into action, and it was not unusual for daily consumption to double in combat. During the protracted struggle with the KAMIKAZE off OKINAWA, coffee was often the only sustenance many of the men on the picket ships bothered with for days on end.

As Samuel Eliot MORISON said, "The U.S. Navy could probably win a war without coffee, but would prefer not to try." Of course, the men didn't live on coffee alone; there were other staples, such as lemon pie. Lemon pie was very popular in the navy, and on many ships was available virtually every night. This was one reason the navy supplied larger ships, such as battlewagons, with more than a half-ton of lemons a week.

And then there was ice cream. Most of the bigger ships in the fleet had their own ice cream and soda fountains, affectionately known as the "gedunk bar." British tars often joked about the American addiction to ice cream, claiming that their grog ration was a superior privilege, but they always seemed to head straight for the "gedunk bar" whenever they were guests on an American vessel. There was an unwritten law in the fleet that on specific occasions (such as after duty on Sundays) a sailor had the right to eat as much ice cream as he wanted, in any combination. These indulgent concoctions were obtained from the ship's "gedunk bar." The "gedunk line" was a busy place, as men awaited their turn to whip up some fanciful concoction. On one occasion legend has it that the gedunk line became the scene of a classic encounter, when Admiral William F. HALSEY allegedly dressed down two ensigns who were trying to jump to the head of the line, considering that he himself was patiently waiting his turn. Alas for folklore, the incident appears never to have taken place, but it was part of the oral tradition of the war.

The navy also supplied proper food for its men. In contrast to the army, in which the troops often had to subsist for weeks and months out of cans, the navy provided a quite varied and balanced diet. A large ship, such as a battlewagon or flattop, with a crew of about 2,000 officers and men, was usually provided with over 20 tons of food a week. A typical week's fare might consist of:

Asparagus	900 pounds
Beef, frozen	10,000 pounds
Carrots	1,500 pounds
Celery	600 pounds
Cucumbers	850 pounds
Eggs	1,500 dozen
Fish, frozen	500 pounds
Ham, smoked	750 pounds
Lemons	1,200 pounds
Lettuce, iceberg	1,200 pounds
Luncheon meat ("Spam")	250 pounds
Oranges	1,900 pounds
Potatoes, sweet	900 pounds
Potatoes, white	9,000 pounds
Rhubarb	500 pounds
Tomatoes	900 pounds
Veal, frozen	2,000 pounds

There were also several tons of flour and baking supplies, and milk (fresh, condensed, and powdered) and other dairy products, as well as hundreds of pounds of seasonings and condiments, plus about a ton of ice cream and several tons of coffee.

Forces Overseas, US

Including those who got there and were killed or who were wounded and sent home, nearly 12 million Americans served overseas during World War II. This was 73% of the 16.8 million that entered service. While the average time in uniform was 33 months, the average time overseas was 16 months. Most went to Europe, but over three million served in the Pacific. Getting them there, and keeping them supplied, was no easy task.

Before the war, a large proportion of the active personnel of the armed forces were stationed in places like HAWAII (not yet a state), Panama, and the PHILIPPINES. In 1940, CONSCRIPTION was begun and manpower in uniform in the 48 states (the "Zone of the Interior") grew enormously, reducing the proportion of troops overseas.

In 1940, the distribution of troops among the branches of the service still followed a peacetime pattern. The army had 59%, the navy 35%, and the Marines 6% of total personnel, with the Army Air Corps at a bit less than 10% of army strength. In December 1941, the army was still the largest service, with 75% of the troops, plus another 5% in the Air Corps. The navy had 17% of manpower, and the Marines only 3%. Since the Marines were part of the navy, this brought the navy total to 20%. As building programs for aircraft and ships produced more equipment, the relative size of the Army Air Corps and navy grew. By 1945, the army (ground and service forces) had 48% of troops, the Army Air Corps 20%, the navy 28%, plus 4% in the Marines.

Until 1943, nearly half of the navy was operating in the Atlantic, to battle the German submarine offensive. Many of these sailors were operating out of US ports and were thus not overseas (although they were often at sea for weeks at a time). But the Battle of the Atlantic was won

US ARMED FORCES AND TROOPS OVERSEAS (THOUSANDS)						
	1940	1941	1942	1943	1944	1945
Total Troops	458	1,801	3,859	9,045	11,451	12,123
Overseas	164	281	940	2,494	5,512	7,447
% Overseas	36%	16%	24%	28%	48%	61%

U.S. ARMY AND MARINE DIVISIONS IN THE PACIFIC WAR

Year	Army All	Army Pacific	Marine All	Marine Pacific	USA Total	USA Pacific
Prewar	8	2	0	0	8	2
1940	24	2	0	0	24	2
1941	37	3	2	0	39	3
1942	73	3	3	2	76	5
1943	90	9	5	3	95	12
1944	89	13	6	4	95	17
1945	89	21	6	6	95	27

during the spring of 1943, and from that point on a greater proportion of ships and sailors went to the Pacific.

The navy had little problem getting to the Pacific, as the sailors had their ships. Ground forces had to obtain shipping to get them to where they were needed. Because of the German SUBMARINES in the Atlantic, and the need to send supplies to the Allies (Britain and Russia), there was, at first, not enough shipping to get the ground forces overseas in great numbers.

Before the war, the United States had divisions in Hawaii and the Philippines. Although it was decided early on to give priority to defeating the Germans first, most of the divisions initially sent overseas went to the Pacific. This changed by mid-1943, when more divisions began going to Europe. By the end of the war, all US divisions were overseas. If the invasion of Japan had gone forward, there would have been over 50 American divisions in the Pacific, including the six Marine divisions. Note that the table omits the Philippine Army, 1941–42.

See also MARINE CORPS, US DIVISIONS; US ARMY, DIVISIONS.

Ford, Gerald R. (1913–)

Commissioned an ensign in the navy in April 1942, Ford served as a gunnery officer aboard the light carrier *Monterey* from 1943 to the end of the war, earning 10 battle stars. He was discharged in February 1946 as a lieutenant commander. Ford entered politics, and in 1973 was appointed to replace the resigned Spiro Agnew as vice president. Succeeding to the presidency upon the resignation of Nixon in 1974, he lost the election of 1976. Ford thus became the first, and so far only, president under the terms of the 25th Amendment. Among Ford's shipmates was Bill Howell (see the individual history in the chronology).

Formosa

Now called Taiwan, this is a large island (c. 14,000 square miles) about 115 miles east of China. Held by the Japanese since 1896, the island had been turned into a major air and naval base. For a time it figured in American plans, the navy wanting to capture the place in 1944. But it was bypassed in favor of OKINAWA, probably a wise move considering the size of Formosa and of its garrison.

Formosa, Carrier Raids, 1944–45

Formosa (Taiwan) had been a Japanese possession since the late 19th century and was given a large ground and air garrison early in the war. Its position off the east China coast made the island an essential piece of real estate. Whoever held Formosa, controlled the flow of oil from the NETHERLANDS EAST INDIES to Japan. While the Allies never actually invaded Formosa, mainly because sinking most Japanese tankers and occupying the Philippines had the same effect on Japan's oil supply, the Japanese were never sure that the United States would not invade. Moreover, Formosa contained several major (and dozens of minor) Japanese airfields. It was from Formosa that Japanese bombers flew when they supported the Philippines invasion the week after Pearl Harbor.

The presence of these air bases, and the hundreds of combat aircraft they usually contained, became more of a concern as American forces got closer to Japan. The position of Formosa, far from any Allied land bases, made it necessary to hit the island with carrier aircraft. This approach required

A basketball game in the aft elevator well of USS Monterey *(CVL-26), June or July 1944. Cdr. Gerald R. Ford is believed to be the jumper to the left. Yeoman Bill Howell, whose wartime career is followed in the Chronology, is either the other man going for the jump shot or the one in the right foreground.*

a lot of carriers, as Formosa's land-based aircraft would have to be smothered before they could strike at the vulnerable carriers.

The Allies did manage to launch their first attack on Formosan air bases from Chinese bases. Aircraft and supplies flown over the Himalaya Mountains into China provided America with sufficient bombers to launch such an attack on November 25, 1943. Some 42 Japanese aircraft were

destroyed, mostly on the ground. This attack, and others like it against Japanese targets in China, prompted the Japanese to stage a major ground offensive in early 1944. This offensive eventually overran most of the American air bases. Thus it was up to the carrier-based aircraft to shut Formosa down, and keep it shut down.

On October 9, 1944 US Navy carriers began a three-day raid on Formosa. Carrier aircraft flew some 2,500 sorties over three days. On the last day, a hundred B-29 sorties were flown from Chinese bases. When it was over, the Japanese had lost over 500 aircraft, over three dozen ships sunk, and much of their repair and support facilities on the island bombed. US losses were 79 aircraft and three ships damaged.

Three months later, another series of carrier aircraft sweeps was launched. On 10 January, US carriers began a sweep of the South China Sea. After about a week of this, Formosa was hit again, with the Japanese losing a dozen ships and 110 aircraft.

Finally, on April 9, 1945, a British carrier task force made another raid on Formosa, mainly against the airfields that were supporting KAMIKAZE attacks against Allied ships off OKINAWA.

While Formosa was never invaded, its air facilities were in ruins by the end of the war, with the bulk of the damage being done by carrier aircraft. This achievement led American admirals to believe, after the war, that carrier air power could take on land-based aircraft and win.

Forrestal, James (1892–1949)

James V. Forrestal began life in modest circumstances, became a journalist and later a lawyer. During World War I he left a lucrative Wall Street law firm to serve as a naval aviator, winning the Navy Cross. After the war he returned to the law, rising to presidency of his firm. In 1940, after a brief stint as an aide to President ROOSEVELT, he was appointed the first undersecretary of the navy, in which post he proved immensely effective, far more so than his immediate superior, Secretary Frank Knox, whose principal qualification for the job was that he was a former Rough Rider and a well-connected Republican. On Knox's death in 1944, Forrestal became secretary of the navy. After the war he was influential in bringing about the creation of the Department of Defense, and was the first secretary thereof. He committed suicide shortly after resigning from this post at the president's request in 1949.

Fort Stevens, Oregon

The only military post in the continental United States to come under direct enemy attack during World War II, Fort Stevens, a coast defense installation, lay near the mouth of the Columbia River. On June 22, 1942 the Japanese SUBMARINE I-27 surfaced just off Tillamook Head and proceeded to get into position to shell the fort. The submarine fired a number of 5.5-inch rounds, beginning at 2300 hours. Despite the fact that it was over six months since PEARL HARBOR, the garrison evidenced a certain lack of readiness.

Indeed, not until the second round landed did the garrison realize it was under attack: "After the second round was fired, we knew someone was shooting at us," said one soldier. Nor did the garrison ever fire a shot in reply. Confusion among the senior officers present, a breakdown in communications, and an inability to locate the source of the attack all combined to keep the fort's admittedly obsolete coast defense mortars silent. As a result, the submarine got clean away.

There were several other occasions on which Japanese submarines attacked the North American mainland during the war.

Date	Place	Boat	Note
13 Feb. '42	Goleta, Calif.	I–17	Shelling
23 Feb. '42	Elwood, Calif.	I–17	Shelling
20 Jun. '42	Point Estevan, B.C.	I–26	Shelling
22 Jun. '42	Fort Stevens, Oreg.	I–27	Shelling
10 Sep. '42	Mt. Emily, Oreg.	I–25	Floatplane attack

Ref: Boyd and Yoshida, *The Japanese Submarine Force and World War II.*

FR-1 Fireball, US Carrier Prop/Jet Fighter

The US FR-1 Fireball was unique in the history of fighter aircraft. From a distance, the FR-1 looked like the F6F HELLCAT. Indeed, the FR-1 was about the same size and weight as the F6F. But the FR-1 had a jet engine in addition to the conventional piston engine driving a prop. The jet engine would quickly give the FR-1 additional speed and power. This combination was desirable in general, and after the KAMIKAZE aircraft appeared, something as perky as the FR-1 was seen as a solution. With its long range and "speed on demand" from the jet engine, the FR-1s could get out there and destroy kamikazes before they got close to their targets. As the prospects of an invasion of Japan became more likely, the need for the FR-1 increased. Although development didn't begin until late 1942, the first FR-1 flew in June 1944 and the first deliveries of production aircraft were in March 1945. The war ended before the first FR-1 squadron could complete its training. Only 66 were built. The FR-1 was taken out of service in 1947, as by then it was obvious that more capable pure jet aircraft were on the way. However, if the war had continued, FR-1s would have played a major role in defending the fleet from kamikaze.

See also AIRCRAFT TYPES, DEVELOPMENT; CARRIERS, DESIGNING AIRCRAFT FOR.

Fraser, Bruce A. (1888–1981)

Bruce Fraser, the son of a general, joined the ROYAL NAVY as a cadet in 1902. He specialized in gunnery and served in various posts, mostly on battleships, and emerged from World War I as a commander. During 1919 he performed a secret mission in Russia, and was imprisoned by the communists for about eight months. Returning to duty, he developed an innovative fire control system during the 1920s. Meanwhile, he held various posts afloat and ashore, and on the outbreak of World War II was a rear admiral and Third Sea Lord of the Admiralty (equivalent to a bureau chief in the Navy Department). He served as second in command of the Home Fleet in 1942, and commander from 1943. On Christmas Eve of 1943 a squadron under his command defeated the German battleship *Scharnhorst* off North Cape, Norway, in the Arctic Ocean. Promoted to admiral in 1944, that August he relieved Somerville as commander of the British Far

Eastern Fleet, in the Indian Ocean. In November he was named commander of the British Pacific Fleet, a largely administrative post (Philip VIAN was the actual operational commander). After the war he was knighted, created a viscount, promoted to admiral of the fleet, and served for a time as First Sea Lord (CNO).

Fremantle/Perth, Australia

The port of Perth, Fremantle was the principal port on the western coast of Australia, with some facilities to service shipping and a modest naval shipyard. Perth itself, an extensive city, had some industrial facilities and was a major air base. During the war Fremantle served as a base for US SUBMARINES operating in the Indian Ocean and East Indies.

French Frigate Shoal, Hawaiian Islands

A sprawling, uninhabitable atoll surrounding a shallow lagoon in the Pacific, about halfway between Oahu and MIDWAY in the Hawaiian chain, French Frigate Shoal figured in Japanese war plans several times. On March 5, 1942, two Japanese Emily flying boats staged out of WOTJE, in the MANDATES, landed at French Frigate Shoal and were refueled by three SUBMARINES, which had arrived there several days earlier. They then attempted an air raid on PEARL HARBOR. Although they failed to hit their objective (one's bombs fell in the open sea and the other's on a hillside six miles from the naval base) due to poor visibility caused by light rain and overcast skies, they caused quite a stir among senior military personnel. Subsequent Japanese efforts to use the place were frustrated by regular US Navy surface and air patrols, and the occasional stationing of a destroyer or other small warship. Several atolls in the area were made into emergency landing strips—and from the air looked like aircraft carriers.

Friendly Fire

Often called "own fire" during World War II, "Friendly Fire" occurs when troops come under the fire of their own side, usually accidentally. Friendly Fire was a particular problem in the Pacific, especially in the jungles and at sea. The infantry often found themselves doing battle under conditions where lush vegetation limited visibility to a few feet. Friendly and enemy troops often got mixed up, and surgery often found American bullets inside American soldiers. Artillery was always indiscriminate, and in the Pacific land battles it frequently fell on soldiers of both sides. Night fighting was very common in the Pacific War, as the Japanese favored it. Under these circumstances, Friendly Fire was even more likely. To prevent revealing one's position at night, soldiers of both sides avoided using firearms and resorted to hand grenades. With all of these explosive objects being tossed around during a night action, one can imagine how many American troops got hit by fragments that were "Made in USA." Interviews held after the war indicated that up to 20% of combat CASUALTIES may have been from Friendly Fire, although officially it was only about 2%.

Another area where Friendly Fire was quite common was during air attacks on surface targets, particularly at sea. There were numerous occasions during the Pacific War in which army aircraft mistakenly attacked navy vessels, fortunately with minimal casualties, since the AAF was not only weak in ship recognition but was also notoriously unable to hit ships.

During many of the massive air-sea battles in the Pacific, the United States suffered some casualties from friendly antiaircraft fire, falling on ships often some distance from the firing vessel.

Considering the amount of antiaircraft fire that was expended during Allied attacks on Axis cities and Axis attacks on Allied cities, the casualty rate from Friendly Fire must have been enormous. Most of the civilian casualties during the PEARL HARBOR attack were the result of civilians being hit by antiaircraft bullets falling back to earth. The bullets from .50 caliber (half-inch in diameter) machine guns were a principal cause, as these falling rounds could injure or kill no matter where they hit someone.

Naval combat, especially conducted at night, often resulted in Friendly Fire problems. Several of the GUADALCANAL naval actions were quite chaotic, with ship captains knowing at the time that they might be firing at friendly ships.

There were at least two cases of US subs being sunk by their own TORPEDOES, which circled around, after missing the enemy target, to sink the firing submarine.

Friendly Fire, Allied Prisoner of War Deaths by

Tens of thousands of Allied troops and civilians found themselves involuntary guests of the Japanese government during the war. A lot of these people, upwards of 30%, did not survive the war. Most died as a result of ATROCITIES or neglect by the Japanese. Thousands, however, were killed by Allied forces. The principal cause of such deaths among Allied PRISONERS was submarine attacks, the Japanese tending to ship prisoners from outlying areas to the Home Islands as the war dragged on. Some examples:

- July 1, 1942: Off Luzon, the 10,000-ton Japanese transport *Montevideo Maru*, carrying 850 Australian troops and 160 civilians who had been captured in New Guinea, was TORPEDOED by *Sturgeon* (SS-187). There were no survivors.
- December 3, 1943: Off Honshu, the US submarine *Sailfish* (SS-192) torpedoed the Japanese escort carrier *Chuyo*, which sank taking with her a number of prisoners of war whom she was transporting to Japan, including survivors of the US submarine *Sculpin* (SS-191).
- September 7, 1944: Off Mindanao US submarine *Barb* (SS-220) torpedoed the Japanese transport *Shinyo Maru*, which was carrying 710 US prisoners to Japan. Only 81 men survived, pulled from the sea by Filipino GUERRILLAS,

who arranged for them to be picked up by *Narwhal* (SS-167).

- September 11, 1944: Off Hainan Island, in the South China Sea, the Japanese transports *Rokyu Maru* and *Kachidoki Maru* (formerly SS *President Harrison*), carrying 1,300–1,600 British and Australian prisoners of war from SINGAPORE to Japan, were torpedoed by US submarines *Sea Lion* (SS-195) and *Pampanito* (SS-383), respectively. *Rokyu Maru* sank slowly, and no one aboard was seriously injured, while the Japanese crew abandoned ship, to be rescued by some escorts. *Kachidoki Maru* went down rather quickly, the crew also abandoning ship. Many of the prisoners managed to escape the sinking ships, using lifeboats, rafts, and debris. A good many were rescued by Japanese destroyers, and about 160 others by US submarines the following day, the rest, over 300 men, were lost, either drowned or machine-gunned by Japanese seamen.
- October 29, 1944: Off the coast of China the US submarine *Shark* (SS-314) torpedoed the transport *Arisan Maru*, which was carrying about 1,790 American and Filipino prisoners, of whom only five survived.
- December 15, 1944: US aircraft attacked the Japanese transport *Oryoku Maru* in Subic Bay, the Philippines, killing about half of the 1,800 American and Filipino prisoners aboard.
- January 9, 1945: US carrier aircraft sank the transport *Fukuyama Maru*, carrying prisoners of war en route to Japan off Formosa. Among those killed was Capt. Willibald C. Bianchi, who had won a MEDAL OF HONOR on BATAAN.

Other allied prisoners of war were killed in air attacks on Japanese cities, including five Army Air Force personnel in the ATOMIC BOMBING of HIROSHIMA, and several more at NAGASAKI.

No figures are available on the total number of Americans held prisoner by the Japanese who were killed by Friendly Fire.

Frobisher, British Heavy Cruiser

The only unit of the Hawkins Class to serve in the Pacific War, *Frobisher* (1916–1920–1924) was designed in 1915 to pursue German surface raiders in the Indian and Pacific Oceans. Only lightly reconstructed between the wars, by 1939 she was largely disarmed and serving as a training ship. Confronted with a desperate shortage of warships, in 1942 the ROYAL NAVY rearmed her for convoy escort and patrol duty. In this role she served with the British Far Eastern Fleet, 1942–44, when she was relegated to the reserve. She mounted five 7.5 guns in single-gun shields; they were much older and lighter pieces than the 8-inch guns carried in pairs in turrets on more modern heavy cruisers. She would not have fared well in a surface action. She was scrapped in 1949.

Fubuki Class, Japanese Destroyers

The 19 units of the Fubuki Class (one of the original 20 having been lost in a prewar accident) were in many ways the "typical" Japanese destroyers of the war. When built, between 1925 and 1931, they were the most heavily armed destroyers in the world, superior in many ways to those in American or British service. Reconstructed in the late '30s, they emerged somewhat larger, with somewhat less speed than before, but with improved seaworthiness. They saw extensive service in the war, during which all but one were lost—two to MINES, three by US surface ships, six by SUBMARINES, and seven by US aircraft. *Isonami* (1926–1927–1928) was the first Japanese warship of note sunk in the war, when a Dutch submarine sank her off Celebes on December 8, 1941.

Fuchida, Mitsuo (1902–1976)

A Japanese Navy pilot, Fuchida helped plan the PEARL HARBOR attack and was the tactical commander of the air strike. It was he who sent the famous message *Tora! Tora! Tora!* ("Tiger! Tiger!

Tiger!") as the air strike arrived over the US fleet, to signal that complete surprise had been achieved. Upon his return to the flagship AKAGI, he pressed Admiral Chuichi NAGUMO to launch a third strike, which the latter overruled. Ill, and unable to fly at MIDWAY, he was wounded when *Akagi* was attacked. He later served on Admiral Koga's staff. After the war he became a Protestant minister and pacifist, and moved to the United States, where he eventually became a citizen.

See also GENDA, MINORU.

Fugu Plan

The Fugu Plan was a Japanese scheme, developed during the 1930s, to settle exiled German Jews in MANCHUKUO. The plan was rooted in Japanese admiration for the accomplishments of the Jewish People as attributed to them by anti-Semites. In effect, the Japanese bought the notion that the Jewish people had unusual business acumen and controlled banking in the Western world. Unlike Westerners who believed this notion—as embodied, for example, in the notorious *The Protocols of the Elders of Zion*—the Japanese thought this admirable, the more so because some Japanese leaders also accepted the notion that the Jewish people were somehow related to the Japanese.

The idea was to settle at least 50,000, and possibly as many as a million, German Jews in Manchukuo, where their business skill, coupled with generous support from "Jewish bankers," would lead to rapid economic development, turning Manchukuo into a bulwark against Russia. A not unnoticed benefit of the plan assumed that Jews persecuted in Russia, would support Japanese interests.

Although the plan made little headway, a surprising number of European Jews did manage to make their way to the Far East by various means. For example, in 1940 the Japanese consul in Lithuania, Chiune (or Senpo) Sugihara, issued some 10,000 visas to Jews seeking to leave Lithuania, which authorized them to pass through Japan en route to other countries. This enabled them to leave Lithuania, then occupied by the Soviets, and they eventually arrived in Japan, where they settled for a time in KOBE, where the Japanese were offended by attacks on them by resident Germans. Leaders of this community, as well as leaders of some other Far Eastern Jewish colonies, met several times with Japanese military leaders to discuss cooperation. Nothing came of this, however, and by mid-1941 most of the Jewish people in Japan had relocated to SHANGHAI, where there was already a substantial Jewish community. This community found itself little disturbed by the outbreak of World War II.

Meanwhile, the Nazis got wind of the existence of a large Jewish population under Japanese control. SS Colonel Josef Meisinger, the chief Nazi party official in the Far East, who had supervised the occupation of Warsaw in 1939–41, killing thousands of Poles, Jews and non-Jews alike, approached the Japanese with various schemes to "relocate" the Jewish population of Shanghai. These were frustrated by Japanese officials sympathetic to the Jewish residents, and by their very impracticality. One of Meisinger's schemes was to entice the Jews aboard ships, which could then be sunk, a proposal that, considering the increasingly desperate shipping shortage confronting Japan, was easily evaded.

Although they suffered considerable privation, as did all residents of the city during the war, the Jews of Shanghai survived, and most migrated to Israel after the war. Meisinger was arrested in Japan by the Allied occupation forces in late 1945, and was later tried and executed for crimes against humanity.

See also GERMANY IN THE PACIFIC WAR.

Ref: Tokayer, *The Fugu Plan*.

Fujita, Frank, Jr. (1921–)

Of European- and Japanese-American ancestry, Frank Fujita Jr. was a sergeant in the Texas National Guard aboard the PENSACOLA CONVOY when the Pacific War broke out. His unit, the Second Battalion, 131st Artillery, found its way to JAVA in early 1942, where it was captured by the Japanese on 10 March. One of only two Japanese Americans captured by the Japanese during World War II (the other was Richard SAKAKIDA), Fujita was transferred to Japan in December 1942. Not until June 1943 did his captors realize he was half-Japanese. Although subject to considerable pressure to make propaganda broadcasts for the emperor, Fujita was otherwise treated more or less as badly as all other PRISONERS OF WAR. He did, however, manage to keep a diary and make some sketches, which provide a valuable insight into prisoner-of-war life under Japanese control. He was liberated August 29, 1945. Only 300 of the 500 men in his battalion survived imprisonment, a death rate of 45%.

See also AMERICAN CITIZENS, RELOCATION OF.
Ref: Fujita, *Foo*.

Fulmar, British Carrier Fighter

The Fulmar was a specially built British carrier fighter. Not as effective as American and Japanese carrier aircraft, it did most of its fighting against the Italians in the Mediterranean and German U-boats in the Atlantic. Armament was eight .30 caliber machine guns and 500 pounds of bombs. Some 600 were produced, with production ending in early 1943.

See also AIRCRAFT TYPES, DEVELOPMENT; CARRIERS, DESIGNING AIRCRAFT FOR.

Funafati, Ellice Islands

A pleasant atoll, with considerable room for ships, Funafati was large enough to make an air base possible, if anyone cared to build one. Strategically, Funafati's principal value in the war was that it is the southernmost island in the ELLICE group, with SAMOA about 600 miles to the east and FIJI the same to the south. The United States began an airfield even before the war, and it became a major air base, although it figured directly in operations only briefly, during the GILBERTS campaign.

Furious, British Aircraft Carrier

One of the very first carriers, *Furious* was designed as a very light battlecruiser (very fast, wholly unprotected, with two 18-inch guns). She was laid down in 1915 and launched in 1916, but then completed as a partial seaplane carrier (one 18-inch gun aft, plus a hangar and "flying off" deck forward) in 1917. *Furious* was shortly converted into a full seaplane carrier (with limited landing capabilities) by March 1918, and she undertook the first genuine carrier air attack in history on July 19, 1918, when her aircraft raided the Zeppelin works at Tondern, in Schleswig. In 1919 she was put into reserve. In mid-1922 she began a complete reconstruction, emerging in 1922 as a full-deck aircraft carrier. She was not a successful carrier, having too few aircraft (36) and a limited avgas storage capacity (c. 575 gallons per airplane, enough for perhaps two sorties) for her size. Nevertheless, she performed well throughout most of the war, in a variety of roles, operating against Japanese land targets and coastal shipping in the Indian Ocean in 1942 and 1943. She was retired from front-line service in 1944 as newer carriers became available. The only prewar British carrier to survive the war, she was scrapped in 1948.

Furutaka Class, Japanese Heavy Cruisers

Japan's first "Treaty" cruisers, the two Furutakas were quite small for heavy cruisers. As completed they mounted their six 8-inch guns in single turrets, converting to double turrets only after extensive refits in the mid-1930s, when their protection, quite light, was somewhat improved, with a concomitant reduction in speed. Both saw extensive service, beginning the war with the South Seas Force, and fought at the CORAL SEA and then in the SOLOMONS—SAVO ISLAND among other actions—until lost.

Furutaka (1922–1925–1926) was sunk by a TOR-PEDO from a US cruiser in the Battle of CAPE ESPERANCE, October 11, 1942.

Kako (1922–1926–1926) was torpedoed by the US submarine *S44* (SS-155) in the BISMARCK ARCHIPELAGO on August 10, 1942.

Fusan, Korea

The principal port of Korea, Fusan (Pusan in Korean) had limited but satisfactory facilities to support and repair shipping, especially small coastal vessels. It was a major node in the movement of Korean goods to Japan, and served as one of the ports through which US forces entered Korea after the surrender of Japan.

Fuso Class, Japanese Battleships

The first dreadnought battleships designed by the Imperial Navy, the Fusos were good ships, reasonably well protected and relatively fast for their day, but very obsolete by World War II standards, despite extensive reconstruction in the early 1930s that added about 50% more armor, yet saw a modest speed increase due to new engines. They op-erated together throughout the war, providing distant cover and support to lighter forces and carrier task forces. Like all Japanese battleships they saw little action. A plan to convert them into battleship-carriers, like the ISE CLASS, was considered but rejected. Both were sunk by US battleships, cruisers, destroyers, and torpedo boats during a night action in SURIGAO STRAIT on October 25, 1944.

Fuso (1912–1914–1915) took only one torpedo from a US destroyer at Surigao Strait, which caused internal explosions, leaving her burning and sinking.

Yamashiro (1913–1915–1917) took at least two torpedoes from US destroyers at Surigao, before running into the massed fire of five battleships and numerous cruisers and destroyers. After about seven minutes, during which she gamely fired back with all her guns, she attempted to turn away, and was shortly hit by two torpedoes from the destroyer *Newcomb* (DD-586). She capsized and sank about eight minutes later. She was the last battleship to be fired upon by another battleship, and the last to be injured by one, when she was struck by some rounds from USS *Mississippi* just as the action was ending, at about 0415 hours on October 25, 1944.

G

G3M Nell, Japanese Bomber

The G3M Nell was the Japanese Navy's first modern, land-based bomber. The G3M entered service in late 1936. These two-engine bombers were excellent, making raids over a thousand miles from their bases. Although their bomb load was only 1,700 pounds (or one TORPEDO), the highly trained crews made the most of it. It was G3Ms that sank the British battleship *Prince of Wales* and battlecruiser *Repulse* off MALAYA on December 10, 1941. The British thought they were out of range of Japanese bombers. Early in World War II it was replaced by the G4M, which carried more fuel in the same light-type airframe, thus making it even more dangerous for the crew than the 8-ton G3M.

See also AIRCRAFT TYPES, DEVELOPMENT.

G4M Betty, Japanese Bomber

The G4M Betty was the Japanese Navy's principal heavy bomber. The G4M had a very long range (over 3,000 miles) for a two-engine bomber, achieved at the expense of any protection for the aircraft or crew. Carrying over three tons of fuel in unprotected tanks, the G4M tended to erupt in a ball of flame after taking a few hits from Allied fighters or antiaircraft guns. This made the G4M very unpopular with its crews. But deliveries began in early 1941, and the G4M was heavily used in the first year of the war. Nearly 2,500 were produced, and 250 were prominently used during the first six months of the war. The G4M had a max bomb load of 2,200 pounds. It could also carry a single TORPEDO and was effective as a torpedo bomber. Typical takeoff weight was 12 tons or more. Initially, the G4M had only three 7.7mm machine guns for defense. Later versions had two 20mm cannon and two machine guns.

See also AIRCRAFT TYPES, DEVELOPMENT.

Gay, George H., Jr. (1917–1994)

US Navy pilot. On 4 June 1942, Gay, then an ensign flying a TBD1 DEVASTATOR torpedo bomber off the carrier *Hornet*, was the only survivor of Torpedo Squadron 8, in its unsuccessful attempt to attack the Japanese carriers at MIDWAY. Ditching in the middle of the Japanese fleet, Gay was an eyewitness to the devastating attack on the Japanese fleet by US Navy dive bombers, which sank three of the four Japanese carriers in a few minutes, an attack made possible by the sacrifice of "Torpedo 8." Rescued, Gay, a tall, handsome man, became a popular hero. After the war, he was for many years a pilot for TWA, and often lectured on his experiences at Midway.

Gearing Class, US Destroyers

The culmination of US destroyer development in World War II, most of the 116 Gearings ordered were not completed until after the surrender of Japan, but about 40 entered service during the war. Very successful ships, much better designed than ALLEN M. SUMNER, and her sisters, which they closely resembled (save for being longer and thus more stable), none were lost in action. A number of units were modified as "radar picket" ships, designed to provide early warning for carrier task forces, with additional radar and antiaircraft armament. The Gearings continued in service after the war, some even surviving into the 1980s in reserve status in the US Navy, and on active duty in other navies.

Geiger, Roy (1885–1947)

Roy Geiger took a degree in law, but after practicing for several years enlisted in the US Marines in 1907. Commissioned two years later, he served aboard ship, in Panama, in Nicaragua, and China, before taking flight training, and, by late 1918, was leading a Marine bomber squadron in France, garnering a Navy Cross in the process. After World War I he was actively involved in the development of both Marine aviation and amphibious doctrine. Shortly before PEARL HARBOR he became commander of the First Marine Aircraft Wing, which he later led during the GUADALCANAL Campaign. For a time director of Marine Aviation, "flying a desk" in Washington, in late 1943 he assumed command of III Marine Amphibious Corps. Geiger led this outfit in the invasions of GUAM, PELELIU, and OKINAWA, where, on the death of LG Simon B. Bolivar, he assumed command of the 10th Army, thereby becoming the only Marine ever to command a field army. He died shortly before he was scheduled to retire, and was posthumously promoted to full general.

Genda, Minoru (1904–1989)

A Japanese naval aviation officer, Genda was a tactical innovator and excellent planner. His analysis of the British air attack on the Italian Fleet at Taranto on November 11–12, 1940, was a factor in the evolution of Isoruku YAMAMOTO's scheme to attack PEARL HARBOR, an operation that Genda helped to plan. He took part in the Pearl Harbor operation with the First Air Fleet and was present at MIDWAY, which, like FUCHIDA, he survived by mere chance (both men were ill during the battle, but had gone AWOL from sick bay on AKAGI to observe the attack of Torpedo Squadron 8, and thus were on deck when the US dive bombers arrived overhead). He spent most of the rest of the war as a staff officer in Japan or other rear areas. In the 1950s he became an officer in Japan's "Self-Defense Force," and rose to the seniormost ranks before retiring.

See also GAY, GEORGE H., JR.

Generals, Proportions in the Service, Allied, 1944

Some armies are more generous with rank than others. As a result, they have a higher proportion of senior commanders to troops. Figures for the principal Allied armies in the Pacific in 1944 suggest that the US Army and Marine Corps actually were much more top-heavy than the British Army, while the Australian Army was extremely lean at the top.

These figures exclude women, which would not materially affect their magnitude in any case. The US Army figure includes the Army Air Forces. If one counts all personnel and all branches of the service, the US figure for generals and admirals to lower ranking personnel was about 1:5,580.

In World War II, the US Army Ground and Service Forces had 14 generals per combat division (two with the division and the rest "supporting" it, all the way up to the chief of staff, GENERAL MARSHALL). Interestingly, the supposedly "lean" Marines had 13 generals per combat division.

The Army Air Forces had 244 aircraft per general, but this figure omits general officers of the

Army	Generals to Troops
Australia	1:14,953
Britain	1: 8,333
United States Army	1: 6,460
Marines	1: 6,089

Army Service Forces who were working for the AAF.

The navy had 1.8 combat ships (statistically an average of 7.9 thousand tons) and 53 aircraft per admiral.

Comparable figures for the Japanese Armed Forces cannot be determined.

Geneva Convention

A collective term for the "rules of war," which have been codified in a series of international conferences beginning in the middle of the 19th century. The formal agreement in force during World War II was the Geneva Convention of 1929, which strengthened arrangements made at the Hague in 1899 and 1907, and at Geneva in 1904.

Basically, these agreements ban the use of certain weapons, such as explosive bullets and poison, prescribe the status of belligerents and non-belligerents and of combatants and noncombatants, require the wearing of uniforms, detail the rights and immunities of medical personnel, and detail the proper treatment of PRISONERS OF WAR. The earlier agreements had held up relatively well during World War I, but some refinement was thought necessary, and thus the 1929 agreement was concluded.

In World War II the Geneva Convention again held up, outside of the Russian Front and the Pacific. In Russia, both the Germans and the Russians blatantly violated the convention on an enormous scale, but the Germans generally adhered to it with regard to Western European and American prisoners. In the Pacific, while there were some violations by American and British Commonwealth troops, these were rare and were often subject to at least administrative, if not legal, penalties: Officers who failed to protect prisoners of war often found their prospects for promotion evaporate. The Japanese, however, consistently violated the provisions of the Geneva Convention with regard to the treatment of enemy civilians and prisoners of war. In an attempt to excuse this violation of the rules of war, defense lawyers for Japanese personnel ac-

cused of war crimes—and some postwar apologists for Japan—argued that Japan was not bound by the rules, since it had never ratified the 1929 Geneva Convention. However, Japan had ratified the agreements of 1899, 1904, and 1907, and had observed them during the Russo-Japanese War and World War I. Moreover, in early 1942 the Japanese Government had announced that, although Japan had not ratified the 1929 Geneva conventions, it would consider itself bound by them. Despite this, the Japanese used chemical weapons before and during World War II. These weapons were explicitly forbidden by the 1929 Geneva Convention agreements, at least their "first use." The Japanese used chemical and BIOLOGICAL WARFARE only on the Chinese, of course, since the Chinese did not have the means to retaliate.

Based on their record, Japanese violations of the rules of war were certainly actionable. Several hundred Japanese officers and soldiers were convicted by the TOKYO WAR CRIMES TRIBUNAL in the late 1940s, and hanged.

George VI, King of Great Britain (1895–1952)

The second son of King George V, George VI entered the ROYAL NAVY on the eve of World War I, intending to make it a career. He saw extensive service as a junior officer during World War I, serving under fire during the Battle of Jutland (1916). After the war he engaged in activities normal to the second son of the king, but was thrust onto the throne by the abrupt abdication of his brother, Edward VIII, in 1936. Although his role in policy and STRATEGY was constitutionally limited, he was kept constantly informed and occasionally consulted on vital matters, and is generally believed to have been a reliable source of common sense.

German-American Commanders in the Pacific War

A surprising number of prominent US military and naval officers during World War II were of German descent. At the outbreak of the Pacific War the senior-most US naval officer, Admiral Harold Stark, was of German-American ancestry. The navy also had Admiral Chester W. NIMITZ, as well as Marc MITSCHER, who commanded the fast carriers for most of the last two years in the Pacific. In the army were generals Walter KRUEGER (who had actually been born in Germany), Robert L. EICHELBERGER, and Albert C. WEDEMEYER (who trained at the *Kriegsakademie* in the late–1930s!), not to mention Henry Arnold, chief of the Army Air Forces, Dwight D. EISENHOWER, who helped plan the Pacific War before being sent off to command the war against Germany, and General Carl Spaatz, who was responsible for bombing Germany. Even the Marine Corps had some Germans, notably MG Harry Schmidt.

It should not be surprising that there were so many American commanders of German ancestry, for the Germans are the most numerous ethnic group in the United States, after those who migrated from the British Isles.

Germany First

Within a few months of the PEARL HARBOR attack, the three principal nations opposing Germany and Japan (America, Britain, and Russia) agreed that the defeat of Germany should be given priority over the defeat of Japan. Actually, British and American officials had agreed to this earlier, in 1941. But any talk of war with Germany was an unpopular topic with the American voters. Most Americans, before Pearl Harbor, wanted no part of World War II. Yet before Pearl Harbor, the United States had been getting more and more involved with the war against Germany. The war in Europe had been going on since September 1939, and German SUBMARINES were a growing threat to Britain's vital shipping. Britain had to import much of its food and other goods. Worse yet, from the summer of 1940 Great Britain was the only nation actively opposing the Germans. A year later, with the German invasion of Russia, some of the pressure was off Britain, but those German submarines were still getting closer to shutting down the British economy, and war effort.

President ROOSEVELT bent the rules to help the British battle German submarines in the Atlantic. But American public opinion wanted no part of the war. Pearl Harbor changed all that. Yet Roosevelt still saw Germany as the principal threat. He had a good case, for the German armed forces were larger and more deadly than those of Japan. Moreover, Germany in early 1942 occupied most of Europe and controlled nearly half the world's industrial production. In the first two months of 1942, American and British officers and government officials met and worked out the details of how Germany would be defeated first. The Pacific Theater was divided into British (MALAYA and everything to the west) and American (everything else) zones. Putting AUSTRALIA and NEW ZEALAND under American protection was politically embarrassing for the British, as these nations were members of the British Commonwealth. But Roosevelt declared General MACARTHUR a hero for his losing battle against the Japanese in the PHILIPPINES and announced that MacArthur would be brought out of the Philippines to command Allied troops in the defense of Australia and adjacent areas.

Roosevelt could not ignore the effect Pearl Harbor had on the American electorate. Although he preached "Germany First" to his British and Russian allies, in practice the Pacific never really suffered much from this policy. The US Navy never had less than two-thirds of its strength in the Pacific. The entire Marine Corps was in the Pacific throughout the war. In the first year of the war, the army had more troops in the Pacific than in Europe. The Pacific felt the pinch when the June 1944 D-day invasion of France grabbed most of the worldwide supply of Allied amphibious shipping. But aside from the few months of operation in France, the Pacific got the lion's share of amphibious ships. Europe did get most of the US Army troops and aircraft. But the US Navy had plenty of aircraft, and all those warships. Roosevelt could not afford to look bad in the Pacific, for this was the primary focus of Americans during World War

II. After all, it was the attack on Pearl Harbor that got America into the war. There was no thought of declaring war on Germany even after Pearl Harbor. Roosevelt had a nervous four days right after Pearl Harbor, for the Germans did not immediately come to the aid of their ally Japan. Roosevelt had good reason to fear that the Germans would not declare war. The Japanese had signed a non-aggression pact with Russia in 1941, and refused to attack Russia when Germany invaded the Soviet Union five months earlier. If Germany reciprocated and did not declare war on America, Roosevelt would have had a hard time getting a US declaration of war against Germany. But four days after Pearl Harbor, HITLER made one of the worst mistakes of his career, and declared war on the United States.

Germany in the Pacific War

While Japan conducted no military operations in the Atlantic nor in the European Theater, German—and Italian—forces played a role in the Indian Ocean and the Pacific, using SUBMARINES and merchant cruiser raids.

Germany sent 10 armed merchant cruisers to sea during World War II. A typical raider was equipped with six 150mm guns, about a dozen lighter pieces, some machine guns, four to six 21-inch TORPEDO tubes, and a couple of hundred MINES. Several carried one or two light seaplanes for reconnaissance and attack missions, and a couple even carried a motor torpedo boat. Disguised as neutral or even Allied vessels, they sneaked through the British blockade of German waters, and ranged the seas, attacking Allied shipping. The raiders accounted for some 590,000 GRT. Five of the raiders operated in the Indian Ocean or the Pacific, mostly prior to PEARL HARBOR.

Komet (3,300 GRT), reached the Pacific via Soviet arctic waters in the spring of 1940 (the first and only non-Russian ship ever to make the passage) and returned to Germany via the Indian Ocean and the Atlantic, having sunk 10 ships, totaling about 21,000 GRT.

Atlantis (7,900 GRT) accounted for 22 vessels (c. 150,000 GRT), several in the Indian Ocean, before being sunk in the South Atlantic by HMS *Dorsetshire* in November 1941.

Kormoran (8,700 GRT) conducted a 350-day voyage from Germany, which took her into the Indian Ocean. On 19 November 1941 she tangled with the Australian light cruiser *Sydney*, turning the warship into a burning wreck, which drifted away and was never seen again. However, *Kormoran* had incurred so much damage in the exchange that she had to be abandoned. In addition to *Sydney* she had accounted for 11 merchant ships, totaling 68,274 GRT.

Thor (3,900 GRT) conducted two raids during the war, one before Pearl Harbor in which she accounted for 12 ships (96,500 GRT). Her second raid took her into the Indian Ocean and then the Pacific, reaching Yokohama in late 1942 after sinking 10 ships (55,600 GRT). In November 1942 she was destroyed by fire when a German supply ship tied up alongside her in Yokohama blew up.

Michel (4,750 GRT) sortied from Germany shortly before Pearl Harbor, and conducted a 373-day cruise in the Atlantic, the Indian Ocean, and the Pacific, culminating at Yokohama in March 1943, having accounted for 15 ships (c. 99,400 GRT). In early June 1943 she began a second raid from Batavia, in the NETHERLANDS EAST INDIES, operating in the Indian Ocean and South Pacific. On 17 October 1943 she was sunk by the USS *Tarpon* (SS-175). In her 149-day second voyage she accounted for only three vessels (27,632 GRT).

Many German submarines operated in the Indian Ocean, accounting for most Allied shipping losses in that area. Although most of the U-boats that operated in the Indian Ocean did so from bases in France, making the long voyage there and back, a number were officially based at SABANG and at some other Japanese-held ports in the East Indies. The German U-boat flotilla in the Indian Ocean was reinforced in late 1943 when Japan turned over three Italian boats that it had seized at Sabang when Italy surrendered, one of which was shortly returned to the Japanese.

Altogether 11 German submarines were lost in the Indian Ocean, plus two former Italian ones (one of which had been taken over in France and was being employed as a BLOCKADE RUNNER).

Four German submarines that were in Japanese ports when Germany surrendered were taken into Japanese service, including one former Italian boat.

There were some German ground troops in the Pacific Theater, although they saw no combat. In SINGAPORE, MALAYA, China, and some other Japanese occupied areas, as well as in Japan itself, resident Germans of military age were conscripted for military service, through the Nazi Party Ausland Organization. Save for a handful who reached Europe aboard blockade runners or submarines, none of these "soldiers" saw combat.

See also FUGU PLAN; HITLER, GERMANY, AND THE PACIFIC WAR.

Ghormley, Robert L. (1883–1958)

Robert Lee Ghormley graduated from the US Naval Academy in 1906, after already having taken a bachelor's degree at the University of Idaho. His career was varied, including service in Nicaragua and with the battle force of the Atlantic Fleet during World War I. Between the wars he held a variety of posts, mostly staff (he commanded only two ships in his career). From 1940 he was the navy's special observer in Britain, from which post he was transferred in April of 1942 to command in the southwest Pacific as a vice admiral. Ghormley planned and commanded the GUADALCANAL landings, about which he appears to have had serious personal doubts. Although he performed adequately, he can hardly be said to have been an inspiring or aggressive commander. In mid-October he was relieved by William F. HALSEY, a close friend. Thereafter he held a variety of administrative posts, culminating in May of 1945 in being assigned to oversee the demobilization of the German Navy. He retired a year later. Ghormley was not a bad officer, but suffered from several handicaps, not least of which was his own pessimism and lack of command experience. In addi-

tion, he had to operate on limited resources, against an enemy who for a long time had a considerable psychological advantage, with subordinates who were often contentious, and in a type of battle that had never been fought before, a combined land-sea-air operation in three dimensions.

Gibbs, William Francis (1886–1967)

A graduate of Harvard and of Columbia Law School, Gibbs eschewed the bar and spent 1913–17 traveling to study naval engineering and architecture. From 1917 to 1919 he worked as a naval architect for the Navy Department, and in 1919 was an adviser to the American delegation at the Versailles Peace Conference. From 1919 to 1922 he worked as chief constructor for International Mercantile Marine, which eventually became the United States Lines. In 1922 with Frederic H. Gibbs he formed Gibbs Brothers, an independent naval architecture firm, which became Gibbs & Cox in 1929 with the addition of another partner. Gibbs, who was the principal innovator and idea man in the firm, remained president of Gibbs & Cox until his death, by which time it was the most successful naval architecture firm in the world.

Gibbs was responsible for numerous technical advances in merchant ship design in the 1920s and 1930s. Although particularly noted for his liners, such as *America* in 1937 (later the troop ship *West Point*), Gibbs's greatest work was the creation of the fleets that won the war. From 1933 onward he helped introduce high-pressure steam turbines to the navy, designed numerous new warships, introduced modularized design to warship construction (which is one reason most US ships looked a lot alike), and helped design the LIBERTY SHIP. By one reckoning, barring SUBMARINES, Gibbs & Cox was responsible for something like 60% of major ship construction in the United States during the war. In addition to his services as a naval architect, Gibbs also served as adviser to the Office of War Mobilization, as shipbuilding czar for the War Production Board (1941–43), and later as head of the shipbuilding committee of the Combined Chiefs of Staff (1943–45).

After the war Gibbs produced the liner *United States* (1952), which still holds the speed record for an Atlantic crossing, 35 knots, and that in foul weather. Although designed as a luxury liner, Gibbs so laid out the ship that she could easily be converted into a troop transport, hospital ship, or even aircraft carrier. On her many voyages up and down the North (Hudson) River, *United States* always gave a long toot on her whistle when she passed Gibbs's office, near the Battery at the southern tip of Manhattan Island.

Gilbert Islands

The Gilberts—now the Republic of Kiribati—straddle both the equator and the International Date Line. Although the numerous islands and islets are sprawled across over a million square miles, their total land area is only about 275 square miles. Thinly populated, they were under British control when the Japanese arrived in early 1942.

The Gilberts were the closest Japanese-held island group to Hawaii (1,600 miles southeastward) and thus the prime target for an early American counteroffensive. Beyond the Gilberts were the MARSHALLS (800 miles farther west), and beyond them the MARIANAS (yet another 1,100 miles to the west). With the Marianas, the United States would have island air bases from which B-29 bombers could strike Japan itself. But first the Gilberts had to be taken and they would prove more difficult than anticipated. This was to be the first of the US Navy's transoceanic amphibious operations, with 108,000 soldiers, sailors, and Marines steaming over a thousand miles to attack the Japanese-held Gilberts. Save for the November 1942 landings in North Africa, partially staged from Gibraltar, this had never been done before. Two islands were invaded. Elements of the army's 27th Division went after MAKIN, while the Second Marine Division took on the more heavily garrisoned TARAWA.

Months before the invasion, American aircraft operating out of the ELLICE ISLANDS, 500 miles to the south, scrutinized and bombed the objectives and other Japanese-held islands in the area. In September 1943, unoccupied BAKER ISLAND, 300 miles to the east of the Gilberts, was captured by American troops and airfields were quickly built. This base, and those in the ELLICE ISLANDS, provided the aircraft that hit Tarawa and Makin daily from November 12 until the amphibious landings took place on the 20th.

The army had a problem with speed. Army tactics emphasized minimizing friendly CASUALTIES. This was fine for regular ground combat. But when you are taking an enemy-held island with hostile subs in the area, speed is of the essence. The soldiers took longer than expected, and as a result a Japanese sub, one of nine sent into action as soon as word of the invasion reached Tokyo, TORPEDOED a US escort carrier, *Liscome Bay*. Thus the capture of Makin cost the army 64 soldiers, and the navy 642 sailors when the carrier went down.

Less than a hundred miles from Makin the Marines were having their own problems. While the army faced only 800 Japanese troops (most of them laborers), the Marines took on 4,600 well entrenched infantry. Over 1,100 Marines died, and twice as many were wounded; only 17 Japanese survived. A landing on Abemama Atoll, the third objective in the Gilberts operation, proved much less bloody for the United States. The small Japanese garrison there—about a platoon—committed mass suicide before the first Marine set foot ashore.

The Tarawa and Makin operations revealed many flaws in amphibious doctrine, planning, and equipment. It was clear that more reconnaissance was needed: At Tarawa the Marines had suffered enormously because faulty intelligence had forced thousands of them to wade through neck-high water under withering fire from the enemy. The operations proved the need for closer coordination between air and ground forces, for an amphibious tank, more training, and more demolition equipment.

Troops of the 165th Infantry (New York's "Fighting 69th"), 27th Infantry Division, land on Butaritari, Makin Atoll, on November 20, 1943. Despite a heavy preliminary gunfire and air bombardment, evidenced by the heavy smoke in the background, the Japanese put up a stout defense.

By the invasion of the Marshalls, just two months later, many of these mistakes had been corrected.

Gona, New Guinea

Gona is located on the northeastern coast of New Guinea, with a modest anchorage; its principal value was that it lay at one end of the KOKODA TRAIL, a barely negotiable path from the northern to southern coasts of New Guinea, over the OWEN STANLEY MOUNTAINS.

Goto, Aritomo (1890–1942)

RAdm Aritomo Goto was commander of the Japanese Sixth Cruiser Squadron at the onset of the Pacific War. He was constantly in action from the initial seizure of RABAUL and the SOLOMONS. After the US invasion of GUADALCANAL in August

1942, Goto and his squadron were active in resisting the American presence. Goto was killed in action during the Battle of CAPE ESPERANCE in October 1942.

Graves Registration

The Pacific campaign had some unique problems with the dead. All theaters generated a lot of dead bodies. But the Pacific was unique in that there were more bodies in a short period, it was always hot, the Japanese tended to keep sniping right to the end, and, until late 1943, few senior commanders paid much attention to the situation. This led to morale problems, which forced many local commanders to improvise. Initially, the dead were often buried where they lay, and this led to a higher proportion of unidentified dead or lost graves in the wilderness that most Pacific battlefields consisted of. It was impossible to erect permanent markers in the jungle, and subsequent construction activity often unearthed the now anonymous remains. The American military had developed an efficient "Graves Registration" system during World War I, but after 1918 most of this knowledge was lost. Graves Registration units were raised early in the Second World War, but most went to Europe.

Even before Japan attacked PEARL HARBOR, American leaders agreed that once the United States was in the war, defeating Germany would be the priority. Therefore the Pacific was starved for support units. However, it was in the Pacific that American troops first got into ground combat in battles that tended to be spread out over enormous ocean distances. These early battles were often desperate affairs, and the living naturally got priority over the dead. But the situation could not be ignored.

Commanders had learned in earlier wars that it was better for morale to have specially trained Graves Registration troops recover, identify, and bury both friendly and enemy dead. Without such troops, commanders improvised. Some units simply asked around to find troops who had been morticians. They usually found some. These impromptu Graves Registration specialists were then assigned a few more troops and given the challenging task of taking care of the dead. In the tropical climate, bodies decomposed quickly. While the stench was bad enough, there were also health problems arising from unburied corpses. Graves Registration troops tried to get to the bodies as quickly as possible, for taking fingerprints was one way to identify a corpse that had lost its ID tags ("dog tags"). A less certain method was to simply note physical features (height, hair color, tattoos, and scars). But all these methods (save an examination for dental work) became more difficult if the body had begun to rot. The next step was to lay out cemeteries and supervise the digging of graves. Even if soldiers had to be hastily buried in a combat zone, a Graves Registration specialist knew what information to record, including a careful note of the location of the temporary grave. By the time more Graves Registration units arrived in 1944, the problem was under control, at least for friendly dead.

The Japanese corpses were another matter, for the enemy had a tendency to die to the last man. While this was less of a problem when they died in a bunker or cave (which was simply sealed), there were often thousands of Japanese dead piled up in front of American positions. Getting these bodies buried in a hurry was always a formidable chore. Moreover, the Japanese who were still alive continued to snipe at the Graves Registration troops while the bodies were being attended to. Another oddity of this situation was that the GENEVA CONVENTION stipulated that enemy and friendly dead were supposed to be given equal treatment. Basically, this was meant to obtain confirmation, for the next of kin, that a loved one had died and was not going to be eternally "missing in action." For the Japanese dead, final rites usually consisted of a head count and then burial in a mass grave. For a nation devoted to ancestor worship, this was particularly painful to the families of the Japanese dead. Indeed, to this day, Japanese still visit the most remote Pacific battlefields in generally vain attempts to locate the remains of their ancestors. Thousands of American troops "missing in action" still remain in unmarked graves beneath the lush vegetation of Pacific islands.

Great Marianas Turkey Shoot

The last carrier-versus-carrier battle of World War II—there have been no such battles since. This action was fought as the Japanese sent their carrier fleet, rebuilt after MIDWAY and the SOLOMONS, against the American fleet invading the MARIANA Islands.

"Turkey Shoot" was the popular name given to the air battle between US and Japanese carrier aircraft during the June 19–20, 1944 Battle of the PHILIPPINE SEA. All was not as it appeared during the "Great Marianas Turkey Shoot." It is commonly accepted that the cause of the inequality of the battle was the relative quality of the pilots. A look at trends in pilot training during the war reveals that the quality of Japanese pilots, perhaps the best in the world at the onset of the war, declined steadily during it. However, it turns out that this was not the principal reason for the poor pilot performance against the Americans in 1944. A host of other factors resulted in a disaster for Japanese carrier aviation for example:

Lack of fuel. Japan had been short of oil since the beginning of the war and her inability to boost production at captured oil fields, or to produce enough tankers to carry the oil, made it impossible for ships to stay at sea long, or for pilots to fly much. The lack of sea and air time led to less capable sailors and pilots. Practice makes perfect and after 1942 the Americans had had a lot more practice.

American Submarines. US SUBMARINES not only made steady inroads on the available Japanese tankers and merchant ships, but also limited the amount of time carriers could spend at sea. One, SHINANO, was 10 hours into her maiden voyage when she was sent to the bottom by a prowling US sub. Carriers could not be risked when too many US subs were in the area, and the Japanese never had enough land-based aircraft and destroyers to keep large areas free of US subs. In the Philippine

Sea, the Japanese lost their newest, and arguably best, carrier, TAIHO, and several heavy cruisers to US subs even before the battle was joined.

Better Coordination by the Americans. The US Navy had developed the CIC (combat information center). Because of the wide use of radios in aircraft, and powerful shipboard radars, the admiral in the CIC (on his flagship) could thus control hundreds of aircraft at once and coordinate them against large Japanese attacks. The Japanese had nothing quite as effective as the CIC, and suffered much from the efficient American CICs.

Better AntiAircraft on US Ships. American heavy (5–inch) antiaircraft shells were equipped with proximity fuzes (which had a small radar set in them, causing the shell to detonate when it was close to a target), and there were literally thousands of efficient smaller caliber (20mm and 40mm) automatic antiaircraft guns in the American fleet as well. The CIC, using the reports from radar, would activate the long-range fire of relatively large caliber shipboard AA guns (mostly 5-inch) against those Japanese aircraft that got past the CIC-controlled US fighters. The proximity fuze would cause the shells to explode whenever they came close to an aircraft or when they made a direct hit. The CIC directed thousands of shells into the path of approaching Japanese aircraft, forming a wall of radar-equipped shells that the approaching Japanese aircraft would have to fly through. Those Japanese aircraft that survived the "wall" then had to face the thousands of 20mm and 40mm automatic cannon on the defending ships. As a result, in one case an attack of over 300 Japanese aircraft was practically annihilated.

During the Battle of the Philippine Sea the Japanese lost two carriers, two destroyers, a tanker, and over 400 aircraft, with another three carriers, a battleship, three cruisers, a destroyer, and a few dozen other ships damaged. US losses amounted to 17 aircraft, with some of the crewmen being rescued by submarine, plus one man killed and several wounded on a battleship that was hit by a bomb causing minimal damage. An additional US casualty was Raymond SPRUANCE, who suffered from possibly unwarranted criticism when he did not pursue the Japanese, having decided that his primary mission was to cover the Marines and soldiers fighting to secure the Marianas.

Gridley Class, US Destroyers

Even before the MAHAN CLASS was completed, a debate over the ships' effectiveness resulted in a new design, with an order for a dozen ships. Construction of four of the ships was allocated to the Bethlehem Shipbuilding Company, while the other eight went to various Navy Yards. Although the basic design and appearance was virtually the same, the two groups are generally regarded as separate classes, the four Bethlehem ships being known as the Gridley Class and the eight Navy Yard vessels as the BAGLEY CLASS, a development dictated by the actual characteristics of the ships upon completion. In order to save money, Bethlehem cut a lot of corners in construction. As a result, they were rather lightly built, and somewhat overloaded at full load. They proved a disappointment in service, particularly as they could not be fitted with an adequate antiaircraft allotment without extensive reduction in their TORPEDO armament, and were relegated to the Atlantic Fleet, as soon as enough FLETCHERS became available in the Pacific. None of the Gridleys were lost in action, and all four were scrapped soon after the war.

Gripsholm, Swedish Ocean Liner

Gripsholm saw extensive service during the war as a REPATRIATION ship for civilians and diplomatic personnel, including military attaches, who found themselves trapped in enemy countries by the outbreak of war. This was a time-consuming affair, as elaborate arrangements had to be made to ensure the safety of the ship, beginning with the securing of a safe-conduct from Germany, so that she could leave the Baltic. It was also expensive, as charter and operating fees for the ship ran to about $15,000

a day. Sailing from New York in 1942–43, *Gripsholm* made several trips between the United States, Japan, and various neutral ports where personnel exchanges were made; in 1943, she brought German and Italian internees from the United States to Europe in exchange for several hundred American noncombatants held by the Axis. With the breakdown in repatriation arrangements after the sinking of the Japanese AWA MARU in the spring of 1945, *Gripsholm* was pressed into service as a troop transport.

Guadalcanal, Solomons

Pretty when seen from the sea, the large island of Guadalcanal had an abominable climate, was home to numerous diseases, and had not a single town, nor even a large village. There were no port facilities to speak of, nor anything resembling a proper harbor, but there were several beaches and coves suitable for landing troops (Lunga Point, CAPE ESPERANCE, etc.) and lots of room for building air bases. Strategically, Guadalcanal is the easternmost large island in the SOLOMONS chain, which, if held in strength, would prevent advances by an enemy up the Solomons, or farther eastward.

Guadalcanal, Campaign for

The Guadalcanal Campaign, from August 1942 to February 1943, was neither the biggest nor the longest battle of the Pacific War. Its main claim to fame was not as "the turning point" in the Pacific War, but rather as history's first three-dimensional campaign. For the first time in history, sea, land, and air forces were combined as never before.

In May 1942, the Japanese landed construction troops on Guadalcanal, in the southern Solomon Islands, in order to build an airstrip. This field would enable them to interdict Allied supply convoys going to Australia and provide a springboard for further advances to the south. Recognizing the danger, the United States decided to make Guadalcanal the site of the first Allied offensive in the

Pacific. In August, the First Marine Division made a virtually unopposed landing on Guadalcanal and on nearby TULAGI, where there was some heavy fighting. The Marines cleared the Japanese troops away from the incomplete airfield and quickly completed it.

For the next six months, Japanese ground, naval, and air forces fought desperately to take the airfield back. Two carrier battles, four major and some 30 smaller naval surface battles, eight major land battles and over 30 major air or air-sea battles, not to mention hundreds of ordinary air raids, were conducted in that six-month period. By early 1943, the Japanese had abandoned attempts to retake the airfield, and left Guadalcanal.

This was the first of many three-dimensional battles in the Pacific War. Crucial and often desperate combat was seen on land, sea, and air. It was also the only campaign in which the Japanese had virtual parity in resources with the Allies, which is why it was such "a near run thing."

The Guadalcanal campaign consisted of four rather distinct series of battles: air combats in defense of the Marine beachhead and base; ground fighting on the island; carrier battles in the vicinity; and surface naval clashes in waters near the island.

The series of nearly 40 surface engagements in the waters between Guadalcanal and Florida Islands in the SOLOMONS (IRON BOTTOM SOUND) in 1942 set a number of records for the US Navy. To begin with, Guadalcanal was the navy's first major amphibious operation since 1898. And (barring the JAVA SEA battles, which were under Allied command) the Battle of SAVO ISLAND August 9) was the US Navy's first fleet action since 1898 (and only about the fifth in its entire history), its first-ever night fleet engagement, its first-ever defeat in a fleet action, and its worst-ever defeat (after PEARL HARBOR), with four heavy cruisers (one of them Australian) and a destroyer sunk, 1,270 men killed, and 709 wounded in an action lasting little more than a half hour, at virtually no loss to the enemy. The Battle of CAPE ESPERANCE (October 11–12,

1942) provided three firsts, the navy's first victory in a fleet action since 1898, its first victory in a night fleet action, and its first surface victory against a Japanese squadron.

A month later a less fortunate "first" occurred, the first death of an American admiral in a fleet action, when RAdm Norman SCOTT was killed on the bridge of his flagship in the opening moments of the First Naval Battle of Guadalcanal (November 12–13), followed within minutes by the death of RAdm Dan CALLAGHAN, the task force commander, the two men immediately becoming the first and second admirals ever to receive posthumous MEDALS OF HONOR in a fleet action. (One MOH had been posthumously awarded to an admiral for Pearl Harbor, a very different kind of battle.) The Second Naval Battle of Guadalcanal (November 14–15, 1942) saw four American battleship firsts. Very early on 15 November there occurred the first encounter between battleships in the Pacific War, when the American battlewagons SOUTH DAKOTA and Washington took on HIJMS Kirishima, which was also the first time American battleships had ever encountered enemy battleship at sea (and only the second encounter between a US and enemy battleship ever). The action was also the occasion of the first (and last) time a US battleship was hit by fire from an enemy battleship, when South Dakota took one 14-inch round from Kirishima, plus possibly a 5-incher. And a few minutes later occurred the first time a US battlewagon "sank" an enemy battleship, when Washington turned Kirishima into a burning wreck, her big guns scoring with nine 16-inch hits, followed up by about 40 5-inch shells. Most of these surface actions took place at night between August and November 1942.

There were also two carrier battles (EASTERN SOLOMONS, August 23–25, and SANTA CRUZ, 26 October), many minor surface actions, and numerous encounters between land-based aircraft and ships. Losses among ships were considerable. The United States lost two carriers, five heavy cruisers, two light cruisers, and 14 destroyers, which, with an Australian heavy cruiser, came to 24 major warships—over 126,000 tons; Japan lost two battleships, a light carrier, three heavy cruisers, a light cruiser, 11 destroyers, and six SUBMARINES, also totaling 24 major warships—for nearly 135,000 tons.

Never before, or since, has the US Navy engaged in such a furious round of surface combat. As hard-fought as the ground fighting on Guadalcanal was, four times as many sailors as Marines and soldiers lost their lives in the naval battles fought in support of the ground and air forces on the island.

There was another unique dimension to the American experience at Guadalcanal. It was the first genuinely joint services operation in American history. There was virtually no distinction among the services in staffs or operations, and little interservice squabbling. In some of the desperate ground actions, GIs and Marines literally fought shoulder-to-shoulder against fierce Japanese attacks. Even in the air, there was no distinction as to service, or even nationality. A Japanese air strike might be met by aircraft being flown by army, navy, or Marine pilots, or even New Zealanders or Australians, rather indiscriminately, and occasionally all at once, sometimes even flying very different aircraft. Guadalcanal was just about the only such battle during World War II, and there have been few others since.

Guadalcanal, Naval Battles of

Collective name for a series of naval and air battles off Guadalcanal island on November 12–15, 1942. A complex series of events led up to these actions. In early November 1942, the Japanese had landed just barely enough troops (65 destroyer and two cruiser loads) to outnumber the Marines on Guadalcanal. American reinforcements were also coming in, and these had to worry about sudden appearances of the Tokyo Express destroyers and cruisers at night. During daylight hours Japanese air raids were spotted by COASTWATCHERS long before they reached Guadalcanal, thus providing

US ships with time to stop unloading and escape. To overcome this American advantage, the Japanese decided to send battleships to Guadalcanal, to bombard the American airfield and shut it down once and for all. The battleships would also sweep away any US cruisers and destroyers attempting to stop this beefed up version of the Tokyo Express bringing Japanese reinforcements. The Japanese had used two battleships to bombard Henderson Field on Guadalcanal in October and noted that this had disrupted American air operations. So the Japanese sought to bombard the airfield further, perhaps even shut it down, and make it easier to bring their transports south.

On the night of November 12–13, 1942, two Japanese battleships, two cruisers, and 14 destroyers came down the Slot from RABAUL to blast the Guadalcanal airfield. The Japanese warships were also covering a convoy of 11 transports escorted by another 11 destroyers. The Japanese were not looking for a naval battle, for they felt that bringing battleships would cause any American cruisers and destroyers in the area to flee. Alerted by coastwatchers that the Japanese ships were coming, the US transports stopped unloading and fled south. The American force of five cruisers and eight destroyers, under Dan CALLAGHAN and Norman SCOTT, waited to confront the Japanese warships. At about 0124 hours on the 13th (a Friday), American radar spotted the Japanese ships approaching the Guadalcanal airfield. The Americans should have had surprise in their favor, but a combination of poor ship handling and a delay in giving the order to open fire allowed the Japanese to gain a tactical edge. A near collision between an American and Japanese destroyer at 0141 alerted the Japanese. The Americans had lost a tremendous advantage, for the Japanese battleships had high-explosive shells on their decks to speed up the bombardment of the airfield. The American confusion and delay in opening fire gave the Japanese time to clear their decks and switch to armor-piercing shells. The shooting began at 0150 and continued for about half an hour. The United

States lost three cruisers and five destroyers, as well as both admirals. Another cruiser, *Juneau*, was sunk by a Japanese submarine just before noon the next day, as it limped away with the other surviving cruiser and three destroyers. But the Japanese actually lost more heavily. One of their battleships, *Hiei*, was so badly shot up that it could not get away and was sunk the following day by US aircraft operating from Guadalcanal, who went on to sink the two Japanese cruisers, and managed to damage all the other ships as well. Most importantly, the US airfield was not bombarded, which allowed these aircraft to go after the retreating Japanese ships. Moreover, the Japanese transports failed to reach Guadalcanal. This, and his failure to bombard the airfield, led to the relief of the Japanese admiral, who never received another seagoing command.

On November 13, Allied and Japanese aircraft, both land- and carrier-based, clashed over Guadalcanal and surrounding waters, with the Americans sinking the already badly damaged battleship *Hiei*.

That night, November 13–14, the Japanese convoy again moved south. This time, two Japanese cruisers entered the waters off Henderson Field and bombarded the vital American airfield on Guadalcanal. Damage was not sufficient to shut down air operations.

On the morning of November 14 American aircraft were up and after Japanese ships, sinking two cruisers and seven transports. A newly approaching force was detected and attacked, but steamed on. The Japanese proved to be moving another bombardment force down from Rabaul, with one battleship, four cruisers, and nine destroyers. But this time, there was a force of two American battleships and four destroyers to meet them.

On the night of November 14–15, the four US destroyers were quickly sunk or disabled and one of the American battleships was temporarily disabled when Japanese fire caused her electrical system to fail. But the other US battleship, *Washington*, went after the Japanese battleship *Kirishima*. *Washington* pounded the modernized *Kirishima* (nine 16-inch hits in the first couple of minutes) into a burn-ing hulk that had to be scuttled the next morning. Another Japanese destroyer was wrecked and the remainder of the Japanese ships withdrew.

This major Japanese naval offensive was an overall failure. Two battleships were lost and, more importantly, only 4,000 of the 10,000 troops sent to Guadalcanal got through. Another 5,000 were rescued after their transports were sunk, but these had to be returned to Rabaul. The United States lost many ships, but with its much larger shipbuilding industry was able to replace them. The Japanese losses were usually not replaced.

Guam, Battle for, 1944

The Japanese turned Guam into a rather important base. Aside from its prestige value to the United States, Guam had to be recaptured because it was the principal island of the MARIANAS, which were needed as B-29 bases that could carry the war to Japan.

On July 21, 1944, 39,000 American troops (First Marine Division and the army's 77th Infantry Division, later reinforced by a Marine brigade) landed on Guam. Their opposition consisted of 18,000 Japanese troops. Nearly all the defenders were dead by the time the battle ended on 11 August. Some 1,400 Americans died and another 5,600 were wounded. It could have been worse, but lessons were learned from the previous month's fighting on nearby SAIPAN. The initial naval bombardment was longer, heavier, and better directed. Much more attention was paid to what the enemy was up to, and friendly CASUALTIES were lower as a result.

Guam, Marianas

Only about a thousand miles south of Tokyo, Guam had been a US possession since 1898, while the surrounding MARIANAS Islands, of which at 200 square miles Guam forms the largest, had been in Japanese hands since 1914. Although one of the largest islands in the central Pacific, Guam had a

Beneath the after 16-inch turret of USS South Dakota *(BB-49), Chaplain N. D. Lindner (USN) conducts a memorial service for those killed in a Japanese air attack off Guam on 19 June 1944.*

small, cramped harbor with few facilities, at Agana, but there were several large, deep sheltered bays along the island's periphery that were very suitable for anchorage. The island was valuable for supporting air bases. In late 1941, Guam was garrisoned by only 500 US military personnel, plus some Chamorro (native Guamanian) militiamen armed with nothing larger than machine guns. Two days after PEARL HARBOR was attacked, a Japanese invasion force showed up off Guam. The next day the US garrison surrendered to the 6,000 invading Japanese troops. US losses were 17 dead, Japanese losses 10.

The US effort to recapture Guam in mid–1944 sparked the Battle of the PHILIPPINE SEA.

Guerrilla Wars

Although the Japanese actively promoted their conquests as "liberations" of Asians from European colonial rule, many of the victims saw the change as just another alien occupation. Japanese attitudes toward non-Japanese were extremely callous. Moreover, the Japanese never developed effective anti-guerrilla techniques. Their response to partisan activity was brute force. Entire villages were destroyed and the inhabitants killed. This created more hatred of the Japanese and, naturally, more guerrillas. The Japanese never learned to fight the guerrillas on equal terms. Instead they favored large-scale "search and destroy" operations that

Using a flag lashed to a boat hook, two Marine officers raise "Old Glory" on Guam, July 20, 1944, within eight minutes of landing.

rarely found much but destroyed whatever goodwill the Japanese had obtained by expelling the colonial powers.

As a result, there were guerrilla wars in every country the Japanese occupied, offering varying degrees of resistance. Moreover, the wartime anti-Japanese partisans usually became post-World War II anti-Western freedom fighters. The later conflict in Vietnam actually began as an anti-Japanese resistance in the early 1940s. A number of World War II resistance efforts continue to this day, with the Japanese and the Europeans replaced by local "occupiers," that is, the ethnic group that dominates the now-independent country. Nearly all of the Asian nations liberated from Japanese occupation, which subsequently won their independence from foreign rule, were multiethnic. A majority group, or collection of the larger minorities, rule, and the minorities left out are often engaged in some form of resistance to what they see as "foreign occupation." Some of the more rambunctious minorities are BURMA, INDONESIA, and China.

See also CHINA, ARMIES; INDONESIA, RESISTANCE TO THE JAPANESE; KOREA, RESISTANCE TO THE JAPANESE; MALAYA, RESISTANCE TO THE JAPANESE; PACIFIC ISLANDERS, RESISTANCE TO THE JAPANESE; PHILIPPINES, RESISTANCE TO THE JAPANESE; TIMOR; VIETNAM, RESISTANCE TO THE JAPANESE.

Guided Missiles

The concept of a pilotless guided weapon dates back to the earliest years of heavier-than-air flight, and experimental models existed in World War I. During World War II guided missiles began operational use with varying degrees of success. The most effective guided missile was the German Felix, actually a guided glide bomb, which accounted for an Italian battleship and several smaller vessels in the Mediterranean in 1943–45.

The United States deployed several guided missiles in the Pacific War.

Azon Bomb. Also known as the VB1 (Vertical Bomb 1), once dropped this could be partially guided by the bombardier, who was able to make horizontal corrections to its flight (hence "Azon," from "Azimuth Only"). First used against a railroad bridge in Burma in late December 1944, it was moderately successful. Some 3,000 Azon glide bombs were used in Europe. Since the Azon could adjust the fall of the bomb only laterally, the bomber generals in Europe did not think that they were worth the trouble. The bomber had to hang around for a few minutes until the bomb guidance operator was finished, in Europe this left it vulnerable to flak or fighters. In the Pacific, it was a different story. There were no huge fleets of friendly bombers available to deliver conventional bombs, nor masses of enemy interceptors, nor large quantities of antiaircraft guns, and there were lots of difficult Japanese targets in places like Southeast Asia. In Asia some 500 Azons were used to knock out 27 bridges, several of which had resisted repeated attacks with conventional bombs.

As World War II was ending, two improved models (Razon and Tarzon) were completed. But with the end of the war, development was halted and the existing weapons were put into storage. When the Korean War began in 1950, the stored bombs were taken out and used. Half of them were defective after years in storage. Even so, the Razons proved twice as effective as conventional bombing. The heavier, and more reliable, Tarzon was used with spectacular success. Six targets were destroyed using only 28 bombs. This was 10 times as effective as conventional bombs.

The Bat. A fairly successful US Navy anti-ship missile with a thousand-pound warhead. Using a radar homing system, the Bat was essentially a powered glide bomb. A PB4Y Privateer (the navy designation for the B-24) could carry two under its wings. The missile would be launched in the general direction of an enemy ship, and its internal radar would guide it to the target. Its range was 15–20 miles. Although not very reliable (a lot of them plunged harmlessly into the sea), the Bat accounted for a number of Japanese ship losses from its introduction in April 1945 to the end of the war, including one destroyer. It is to be distinguished from the "BAT BOMB."

Glomb, Gorgon, and Gargoyle. These similar air-to-surface missiles, effectively glide bombs (hence "Glomb," from "Glide Bomb") with television guidance systems, were under development by the navy at the end of the war. Glomb could carry 9 tons of bombs or 10 tons of napalm. It was designed to be towed to the vicinity of a target and then released, with a television guidance system used to guide it to its objective. Some prototype designs involved the use of pigeons as guidance systems. A pigeon fitted with a special harness was housed in the missile, in front of a television monitor. The television camera in the missile would transmit an image of the target to the monitor, and the pigeon was supposedly trained to peck at the principal object in the image. As it moved its head, its harness would relay to the missile course and altitude changes. None of these missiles reached much beyond the prototype stage. Work began in 1941, Glomb was canceled in 1944, and the other projects died after the war.

Little Joe. An experimental, 400 MPH, radio-controlled rocket-propelled surface-to-air missile, the Little Joe was intended to defeat the Japanese Baka-piloted kamikaze rocket. Launched from shipboard, it had a 100–pound warhead, which detonated by means of a proximity fuze.

Japan experimented with several guided missiles, but none ever reached PRODUCTION, and none was used in combat. The Imperial Army developed a series of air-launched anti-ship missiles, intending to use them to beat off amphibious attacks.

Igo-I-A: A large (c. 3,300 pounds) radio-controlled, hydrogen peroxide fueled air-to-surface missile with a nearly 1,800–pound warhead, designed by Mitsubishi to be delivered by the KI-67 PEGGY bomber. The missile began testing in late 1944, but was never approved for production.

Igo-I-B: A 1,500-pound, radio-controlled, liquid fueled air-to-surface missile with a 660-pound warhead designed by Kawasaka for delivery by the KI-102B RANDY bomber. The Igo-I-B was rather successful in tests in late 1944, and about 180 were actually produced, but none was ever used operationally.

Igo-I-C: A very experimental system devised by scientists from Tokyo University, the missile was designed to home in on the shock waves produced by the firing of heavy naval guns. Some tests were made in early and mid–1945, with mixed results.

The Imperial Navy devised a family of missiles, under the designation Funryu ("Raging Dragon"). Two of the projects showed some promise, Funryu 2 and 4.

Funryu 1: A radio-controlled air-to-surface anti-shipping missile, it did not get to the experimental stage.

Funryu 2: A gyro-stabilized, solid-fueled surface-to-air missile, able to deliver a 110-pound warhead to 16,000 feet at about 525 miles per hour.

Funryu 3: A liquid-fueled version of the Funryu 2, which was not proceeded with.

Funryu 4: A radar-controlled, liquid fueled surface-to-air missile able to deliver a 440-pound warhead to about 49,000 feet.

Arguably, the Japanese Navy's Okha or "Baka" rocket-powered aircraft was a guided missile as well, with a human guidance system.

See also KAMIKAZE.

Gun Crews, Response Time

Within seven minutes after the onset of the Japanese attack on PEARL HARBOR, nearly all navy shipboard antiaircraft guns were manned and in action. The US Army had 31 antiaircraft batteries at Pearl Harbor and only four got into action during the attack. There is some mitigation for the soldiers' slow performance. Sailors live in the ship, near their guns, while soldiers live in barracks some distance away from their weapons and ammunition. Sailors have a well practiced drill ("General Quarters") wherein all hands drop what they are doing and rush topside to their battle stations. It made a difference. Moreover, both soldiers and sailors had to take special measures to get at the ammunition, which is kept under lock and key in peacetime. The soldiers had to find tools to break the locks on the magazines. The sailors had many damage control tools (designed for breaking and entering) with which to remove the locks on their ammunition containers.

H

H6K Mavis, Japanese Flying Boat

The H6K Mavis was a Japanese contemporary of the American PBY flying boat. Larger than the PBY, it was roughly equal in performance. However, the limited industrial resources of Japan resulted in production of only about 200 of these naval reconnaissance aircraft. Reliability and vulnerability problems caused the Mavis to be withdrawn from front-line service by late 1942.

See also AIRCRAFT TYPES, DEVELOPMENT; RECONNAISSANCE, NAVAL.

H8K Emily, Japanese Flying Boat

The H8K Emily was a rather huge flying boat that first appeared in early 1942. An excellent recon aircraft, only 131 were produced. With a one-way range of 3,800 miles, the Japanese made all sorts of interesting plans for using the H8K to bomb targets in North America. These schemes involved H8Ks being refueled by Japanese and German tanker submarines. Limited resources prevented any of these operations from being carried out.

See also AIRCRAFT TYPES, DEVELOPMENT; RECONNAISSANCE, NAVAL.

Haiphong, Indo-China

The principal port of French INDO-CHINA, Haiphong had modest facilities to support shipping, and, being several miles up the Red River, was unsuited for use as a naval base. There was a French air base nearby.

Hakodate, Hokkaido, Japan

A small but modern port, with considerable facilities to service minor warships of all types, up to destroyers and light cruisers.

Halsey, William F. (1882–1959)

Bill (never "Bull" except in the headlines) Halsey, a navy brat, graduated from Annapolis in 1904 and shortly was assigned to various battleships, sailing with the "Great White Fleet." He alternated command of several destroyers with a tour on the staff of the Naval Academy from 1911 through 1921, winning a Navy Cross during World War I for action in the North Atlantic. In 1921 he was posted to the Office of Naval Intelligence, serving as a naval attaché in Germany and several other European countries until 1924. He returned to sea duty, commanding various destroyers and serving in battleships until 1927. He then had a round of academic posts and school assignments, emerging in 1935 as a 52-year-old naval aviator. Over the next few years he commanded the carrier *Saratoga*, the Pensacola Naval Air Station, Carrier Division 2, Carrier Division 1, all air units of the Pacific Battle Force, and Carrier Division 2 again (LEXINGTON and YORKTOWN).

Shortly before the PEARL HARBOR attack his CarDiv was returning from delivering aircraft to WAKE ISLAND, already on full war alert (Halsey was one of several officers who understood the meaning of "this is to be considered a war warning"). During the war he had an active, varied, and distinguished career: the raids on the MANDATES, the DOOLITTLE

Raid, the GUADALCANAL Campaign, the SOLOMONS Campaign, and finally as leader of the Third Fleet in the Central Pacific. After the war he retired as a fleet admiral, and entered business. Shortly before his death he led an ultimately futile campaign to preserve the carrier *Enterprise* as a war memorial. Halsey was a tough, aggressive officer who made surprisingly few mistakes (the most glaring being his failure to adequately cover the "jeep carriers" off SAMAR during the Battle of LEYTE GULF).

Hara, Chuichi (1889–1964)

RAdm Chuichi Hara was one of the more successful, or at least luckier, of the Japanese carrier admirals. He began the war commanding the Fifth Carrier Division (SHOKAKU and *Zuikaku*), which was the busiest carrier division for the first months of the war. Because Hara's carriers fought in the Battle of the CORAL SEA (May 1942) where *Shokaku* was damaged, they did not participate in the debacle at MIDWAY a month later. His division was given a light carrier and a number of escorts and used extensively during the battles over GUADALCANAL. Once Guadalcanal was abandoned, Hara and his ships retired to the main fleet base at TRUK. In June 1944, Hara was made commander of the Fourth ("Mandates") Fleet (which guarded the Central Pacific MANDATES awarded Japan after World War I by the League of Nations), a post he held until the end of the war.

Hart, Thomas C. (1877–1971)

Thomas C. Hart graduated from the US Naval Academy in 1897, and served aboard the old battleship *Massachusetts* during the Battle of Santiago in the Spanish-American War. Thereafter he had a fairly routine peacetime career, while rising steadily through the ranks and becoming a submariner. During World War I he commanded a submarine squadron based in Ireland, and later served as a staff officer. After the war he held a variety of commands, attended both the Navy and Army War Colleges, held several staff positions, and in mid-1939 was appointed commander of the Asiatic Fleet, based in the Philippines.

One of the oldest officers still on active duty, in the months before PEARL HARBOR, Hart did what he could to prepare for war. This included "stealing" a cruiser from the Pacific Fleet, conducting officially unofficial staff talks with British and Dutch naval officers, and dispersing his forces beyond the range of Japanese air power based on FORMOSA (a matter in which he proved far more prescient than his army counterpart, Douglas MACARTHUR). When war came Hart shifted his headquarters to the Netherlands East Indies, and assumed command of all Allied naval forces under Archibald WAVELL.

Relieved in February, shortly before the Japanese overwhelmed the greatly outnumbered Allied surface forces, he retired (he was already past retirement age) but was immediately recalled to active duty as a member of the navy's General Board, which advised the CNO on STRATEGY and policy. In 1945 he returned to inactive status. Shortly thereafter, the governor of Connecticut appointed him to a US Senate seat left vacant by a death. He retired from the Senate in 1946 and lived quietly thereafter. One of the oldest officers to see action in the war, Hart proved surprisingly good in a desperate situation.

Hata, Shunroku (1885–1962)

Shunroku Hata joined the Japanese Army in 1901 and quickly moved up in rank. During the 1930s he commanded many of the Japanese troops fighting in China. Returning to Japan in 1938 he held a number of senior government posts until early 1942, when he returned to the command of the Central China Area Army. He held this position until late 1944. Hata was promoted to field marshal in 1943, and returned to Japan to command forces against the expected Allied invasion. Arrested, tried, convicted, and sentenced to life imprisonment as a war criminal, he was released within a few years.

Hatsuharu Class, Japanese Destroyers

Considerably smaller than the FUBUKI and AKAT-SUKI CLASS destroyers that preceded them, the Hatsuharus, built 1931–35, carried virtually the same armament. This made them top-heavy, and after the torpedo boat TOMOZURU capsized in 1933, the completed Hatsuharus were extensively modified, while those still building were finished to the new design. This increased displacement to about that of the Fubuki Class, while speed fell considerably. They saw a lot of service, were several times rearmed, and all six became war losses, one to a US submarine, one to a mine, and four to aircraft.

Hawaii

A long chain of islands in the mid-Pacific, about 2,100 miles southwest of San Francisco. The hundreds of islands and islets stretch over a thousand miles roughly norwestward from Hawaii proper to KURE, some 60 miles northwest of Midway. Total land area is only about 11,000 square miles, virtually all of it in the eight main islands (one of which was a US military target range). Of some 420,000 civilian residents, approximately half lived on Oahu, the principal American military base in the Pacific for the entire war.

Hawaii, Planned Japanese Invasion of

Despite the Japanese attack, PEARL HARBOR was still the most important American base in the Pacific, sustaining the offensives that ultimately brought Japan to its knees. The Japanese actually planned a Hawaiian invasion and alerted two infantry divisions for that purpose early in 1942. The loss of four aircraft carriers at MIDWAY killed these plans, and the divisions were sent to other battles in the Pacific.

A successful Japanese occupation of the Hawaiian Islands would have seriously hampered America's ability to carry on the war. Almost certainly the "Germany first" doctrine would have been tossed out, and a major reshuffling of American resources to the Pacific would have begun, even more so than that engendered by Pearl Harbor. The principal US effort in the Pacific would have been focused on recovering Hawaii, which would have given the Japanese something of a free hand in the south and southwest Pacific, with dire consequences for Australia and New Zealand. However, the possibility of a successful Japanese seizure of the Hawaiian Islands was low.

Even on December 7, 1941 the United States already had two infantry divisions on Oahu, the 24th and 25th, albeit understrength, plus the Hawaiian National Guard (two regiments), and various auxiliary and Army Air Force troops, for a total of about 42,000 army personnel, plus numerous sailors and Marines, not to mention some rather elaborate coast defense installations.

Shortly after the Japanese attack, additional forces began to arrive in considerable numbers, including several battalions of light TANKS and antiaircraft artillery, and the entire 27th Infantry Division, an oversized prewar NATIONAL GUARD formation (it still had four infantry regiments).

By March of 1942 there were nearly 75,000 army and Marine combat troops on Oahu, plus many more soldiers, sailors, and Marines performing noncombat duties, most of whom had some infantry training. There were also new aircraft, which were rapidly funneled into the islands. In order to seize Oahu, the Japanese would have had to first attain control of the surrounding seas and skies. They could do this in most of the Pacific, with their "First Air Fleet" of six carriers, but would have had trouble going up against the considerably enhanced American resources in airplanes and antiaircraft defenses in Hawaii in early 1942. Since it's unlikely that they would have been able to duplicate their 7 December 1941 feat of destroying American air power on the ground, they would have been at a distinct disadvantage, particularly since US carriers would have been lurking in the neighborhood as well. Of course they would have attempted to grab one or two of the less well-defended islands first, in order to establish air bases from which to over-

The Japanese never seriously considered occupying Hawaii, which was heavily garrisoned throughout the war. Silhouetted against the sky, PFC Angelo B. Reina, 391st Infantry Regiment, stands guard on Oahu in early 1945.

whelm the defenses of Oahu, but that would have tied up a lot of the troops needed for the main assault. Such a move would also have delayed the attack on Oahu, putting a severe strain on their already overstretched logistical resources, possibly forcing them to curtail offensive operations in other areas, and subjecting them to the attentions of US SUBMARINES, a marginal but very real threat.

Finally, the Japanese were not too successful when landing against opposition, and were several times beaten off beaches in 1942, operations in which the defenders were not particularly well-prepared, such as at MILNE BAY in New Guinea. So

it seems likely that the Japanese would have suffered a severe reverse.

The major obstacle the Japanese faced in attacking Hawaii was logistical. There were not enough cargo ships available to sustain a major operation as far away as Hawaii. The offensives the Japanese did undertake required so much shipping that industry on the Home Islands was deprived of essential transport. An invasion of Hawaii would have required more sea transport than any previous Japanese operation. Moreover, to keep a garrison supplied in far off Hawaii would have continued this drain on Japanese shipping. However, even an unsuccessful Japanese attempt to take Oahu might have had interesting and negative effects on the course of the Pacific War. Defeating such an effort would certainly have drawn US resources rather decisively into the central Pacific, with the possibility of offensive movements against the MANDATES in mid-1942, particularly if the Philippines were still holding out. This would have been a dangerous proposition given that carrier and amphibious warfare doctrines were both still in the formative stages. At the same time, the lessened attention given over to the south and southwest Pacific might have permitted the Japanese to secure control of New Guinea and the SOLOMONS (GUADALCANAL), making the defense of Australia and New Zealand more difficult. In the end, the United States would still have won, but just possibly at greater cost.

See also AMERICAN CITIZENS, RELOCATION OF.
Ref: Stephan, *Hawaii under the Rising Sun*.

Heavy Weapons

Most of the firepower available to the infantry is found in its "heavy weapons." Machine guns, mortars, and light artillery were the principal heavy weapons. Later in the war, rocket launchers, flamethrowers, and some even more exotic devices were added to this arsenal of gear the troops had to carry around the battlefield.

"Heavy weapons" are so called not only because they generate heavier firepower, but also because they are literally heavy. US infantrymen—whether army or Marine—had a 33-pound .30 caliber (7.62mm) "light" machine gun, as well as a heavier, water-cooled .30 caliber (7.62mm) version of this machine gun for defensive situations (in which the gun would be fired at a more sustained rate than the air-cooled version, which is why it had a water jacket around the barrel, to keep it cool). A soldier could lighten this weapon by taking the water out of the "water jacket." In addition there was the 17-pound BAR (Browning automatic rifle), a successful World War I weapon. It was basically the

equivalent of a fully automatic M-1 with a 20-round magazine and was immensely popular. The favorite infantry machine gun was the .50 caliber (12.7mm). This weapon weighed 128 pounds and was best used in defensive situations where it could be brought forward by vehicle, or, as often happened, manhandled forward by the troops. The .50 caliber bullet could still be lethal at a range of three miles (although it couldn't be aimed that far).

British Commonwealth forces had two machine guns. The Vickers 7.7mm machine gun was heavy (30 pounds) but had excellent range (c. 1,100 yards). The Bren gun, of the same caliber, was lighter (23 pounds) but had less range (c. 750 yards). Commonwealth troops were supplied with two mortars, a 51mm light infantry piece (21 pounds) that fired a 2.75-pound shell, with less than 500 yards range, and a heavier (112 pounds) 81mm weapon, which fired a 10-pound shell to somewhat more than 2,500 yards.

The Chinese had a variety of machine guns, having procured them from many sources, including captured Japanese equipment. The most common was probably the old Maxim, a pre–World War I design still found in Chinese communist units into the Korean War. They also had a variety of mortars. They manufactured several of their own models, made extensive use of captured Japanese equipment, and had some supplied by the United States as well.

The principal Japanese machine gun was the Model 11 Light Machine Gun (the "Nambu Light"). This was a 6.5mm weapon based on a French design. Nambu was the name of the designer, a Japanese general who was responsible for many Japanese weapons design. The Model 11 weighed 22 pounds, with a 30-round magazine. The Japanese had not yet mastered quality mass PRODUCTION, and this was the cause of frequent reliability problems with the Model 11 (and most other Japanese machine guns).

A more recent (1936) version of the Nambu Light also existed (the Model 96). There was also a 7.7mm version (the Model 99), that weighed 22 pounds. It also had reliability problems and, like the 6.5mm models, had to use slightly weaker ammo to cut down on jamming. Since machine guns are most likely to fail when they are used a lot, as in the middle of a battle, the poorly manufactured Japanese machine guns spared many American soldiers death and injury.

Because of less plentiful and capable artillery, the Japanese equipped their infantry with more mortars. One of the more common models was the 50mm "knee mortar." This was so named because at first it was thought that the concave base plate meant it was fired while resting on a soldier's thigh, an impression furthered by pictures of Japanese troops posed in this fashion. This was found to be untrue after a few Allied soldiers broke their legs while trying it. The Japanese pictures had been made because the troops looked tough that way. Weighing 11 pounds and firing 20- to 30-ounce projectiles, the "knee mortar" was widely used by the infantry because of its accuracy and 120- to 600-meter range. The Japanese 52-pound 81mm medium mortar (Model 99) was more conventional and could even use the ammunition of the US 81mm mortar. The mortar could be broken down to three 17-pound loads for easy battlefield mobility. The shells weighed seven pounds each. A heavier (145 pounds) 81mm mortar (Model 97) had a longer range (3,000 meters versus 2,000 meters for the Model 99).

The Japanese had an assortment of other, generally larger, mortars that were used as artillery and not carried around by the infantry.

US mortars were of 60mm and 81mm variety. The 81mm was similar to the Japanese Model 97. The 60mm mortar weighed 42 pounds and fired three-pound shells as far as 1,800 meters.

Both sides used "infantry guns." These were artillery guns that were customized for direct fire. That is, these guns had sights and additional armor shields so that they could be used up front with the infantry to fire at enemy positions from close range. The idea behind this was that the fire would be more accurate, and it was. It was also difficult to haul these guns through the jungle and keep them supplied with ammunition.

The Japanese had a 500-pound 70mm gun for battalion level support and a 1,200-pound 75mm gun for regimental support. Both had a range of 3,000 meters. The United States used a modified version of its standard 105mm artillery piece. This weapon still weighed nearly 2 tons but had a range of 9,000 meters and was often used like conventional artillery (fired "over the hill" at targets the crew could not see). Some US units also used the old 75mm pack howitzer, which had a lighter shell and shorter reach, but theoretically could be broken down into manhandleable elements.

Ref: *Handbook on Japanese Military Forces.*

Heering, Edmund Francis (1898–1982)

In civil life an attorney, Heering entered the Australian Army in World War I and served with some distinction. Between the wars he returned to his profession and eventually became a judge. Reentering the army in 1939, he served as commander of the Sixth Australian Division in North Africa in 1941, bringing it home to Australia in February 1942. For a time commander of various corps in Australia, in late 1942 he was named commander of Australian troops on New Guinea, and subsequently of I Corps. In 1944 he was appointed chief justice of Victoria.

Helicopters

Helicopters were a very new technology in World War II, and barely got into use before the end of the war. The Germans had a two-seater early in the war, but used it only on a few warships for scouting. The United States developed the R-4 helicopter early in the war. This aircraft weighed 1.2 tons, had a rotor diameter of 38 feet, and an enclosed cockpit for a crew of two. With a max speed of 82 miles an hour, the R-4 was further limited by a range of about a hundred miles (depending on the weather).

Although the first flight was made in January 1942, only 130 were built during the war. The idea was to test this model thoroughly before building the next generation of helicopters for battlefield use. Thus 45 R-4s were sent to Britain for evaluation, while the US Army Air Force took 35. The US Navy took 20, one of which made the first landing on a US ship in 1943 (a tanker, not a warship). The rest of the R-4s were spread around to various other organizations for evaluation.

The army sent some R-4s to Alaska for testing in cold weather, and others were shipped to the war zone in Burma to see how helicopters worked in the tropics. There, on April 15, 1945, the first use of helicopters in a combat zone rescue mission took place. The crew of a transport plane had to bail out high in the mountain jungles of Burma. A search plane crashed during the search. When a patrol reached the injured search plane survivor on foot, they radioed back that he was too ill to move. The US base at Shinbwiyang had an experimental Sikorsky YR-4 helicopter on hand for testing, and the helicopter pilot, Lt R. F. Murdock, decided to attempt the risky mission in an area where no aircraft could land. He succeeded, and thus effected the first use of a helicopter as a rescue aircraft, with Capt. James L. Green, USAAF, the first man rescued.

More powerful models were used extensively in the Korean War (1950–53) and in Vietnam (1964–75) the third generation of choppers came of age as battlefield weapons (mainly the legendary UH-1 "Huey").

Helmets

The first US troops to see action in the war wore the WWI style M1917A1 helmet. It was designed in 1917, based on the British Mark 1 helmet, and modified in 1919. Troops on Wake, GUAM, the Philippines, JAVA, and MIDWAY during the opening months of the war used it, as did the sailors in the fleet into mid-1942. In some obscure corners of the war it was not replaced until late 1943.

The M1 helmet, *the* US WWII helmet, was officially adopted on June 9, 1941. Although several senior officers, including George S. Patton, wore it during the famous "Louisiana Maneuvers" later that year, it began being issued only in early 1942. Although some naval personnel used it at Midway, the Marines on GUADALCANAL were the first to use it in ground combat. It was used by all services, even bomber crewmen, who donned them when encountering enemy fighters or flak. The helmet had been designed during World War I, by specialists in medieval armor from the Metropolitan Museum of Art. It was not issued at that time, however, since the British helmet was already being manufactured in the United States.

The navy had a special helmet for telephone talkers, a large, uncomfortable thing that is often seen in pictures, making the navy "talkers" look like Darth Vader with the face showing.

Although some PHILIPPINE ARMY troops were issued the M1917A1 helmet, most Filipino soldiers who had helmets—and many did not—wore a locally produced version made from densely woven tropical fibers, which proved almost as effective as a steel one.

For most of the war British Empire and Commonwealth forces used the Mark 1 helmet, designed by a committee in 1916. A modified version, known as the Mark 4, was introduced in 1944 and saw some use in Burma. However, Commonwealth troops in jungles often preferred to dispense with the helmet, taking their chances in exchange for greater comfort and a lighter load. Many Indian Army troops, particularly Sikhs, did not use the helmet for religious reasons, adhering to their traditional turbans.

Some Chinese troops used the German "coal scuttle" helmet, acquired under the aegis of the German Military Mission in the 1930s, or the very high-quality Czech helmet, procured through commercial channels. Those Chinese troops trained and equipped by the United States were usually issued the M1 helmet. Most Chinese troops wore no helmet at all.

CK3/c Richard Salter, a navy "gun talker" who relayed commands from fire control to the gunners, wearing the helmet characteristic of his trade. Aboard USS Tulagi (CVE-72), August 1944.

The Japanese issued millions of steel helmets. Very similar in design to the US M1, it was developed in a pragmatic and cheap-to-produce shape for protecting combat troops. Unfortunately, the metal used was of very poor quality and the helmet provided very little protection. In the Pacific, Japanese troops frequently discarded the helmet, or were not even issued one. They preferred the woolen field cap, which in colder climates could be worn under the steel helmet.

The Japanese did design a fiber helmet (using rice or, more often, sorghum). This unique item weighed one-third as much as the steel helmet and provided better protection against shell fragments. Few were made. In rare instances, body armor—canvas vest with pockets for metal plates—was issued to officers.

Hermes, British Aircraft Carrier

Hermes (1918–1919–1923) was the first purpose-built aircraft carrier to be laid down, but was completed about six months after the Japanese HOSHO. She was relatively fast and an excellent sea boat, but obsolete by World War II. Despite this, and her limited aircraft complement (12), she saw service against Axis forces in East Africa and the Mediterranean. With the outbreak of the Pacific War she was sent to bolster the British Far Eastern Fleet. On 9 April 1942, while operating with a light escort, she was overwhelmed by Japanese carrier-based dive bombers off Ceylon.

See also ROYAL NAVY.

Hershey, Lewis B. (1893–1977)

The man who sent "Greetings" to several generations of American youth, Lewis B. Hershey joined the NATIONAL GUARD in 1911. He served as a captain for a time in France in 1918, and later entered the Regular Army as an artilleryman. Hershey held a variety of posts in the 1920s and '30s, becoming secretary to the Joint Army-Navy Selective Service Committee, a planning body, in 1936. In October of 1940, promoted to temporary brigadier general, he became deputy head of the Selective Service System, being named director the following July. From then until his final retirement in 1970 (with a brief interval during which there was no draft in the late 1940s), Hershey oversaw the CONSCRIPTION of literally tens of millions of men for the US Armed Forces.

Higashikuni, Prince Naruhiko (1870–1965)

Prince Naruhiko Higashikuni was one of Emperor Hirohito's uncles. He joined the army in 1908 and rose through the ranks until he achieved command of the Second Army in China in 1938. Heavily involved in combat operations there, by early 1939 Higashikuni was back in Japan as adviser to the emperor and head of the Defense Command for the

Home Islands. He became a field marshal in 1945 and agreed with the emperor that surrender was a viable option. Higashikuni was made prime minister to speed the surrender along. He went into retailing after the war, and founded a new religion, which was banned.

Higgins, Andrew Jackson, Jr. (1885–1952)

A noted motorboat builder, Higgins gained some fame designing racing motorboats and rum-running boats during Prohibition, as well as fast patrol boats for the Coast Guard, so they could intercept rum-runners. He designed the Higgins Boat, an early landing craft used by the Marines at GUADAL-CANAL. Although fast, it lacked a bow ramp: To disembark the troops had to jump over the bows. The Higgins Boat was shortly superseded by the standard LCVP, which had a bow ramp. Higgins was a multifaceted technical genius who made important contributions not only in boat building (he had some input in the design of PT-BOATS, for example), but also in shipbuilding (AKAs and LIBERTY SHIPS), portable bridges, explosives, and even aircraft design.

Higuchi, Kiichiro (1888–1970)

Kiichiro Higuchi joined the Japanese Army in 1908. He served in Siberia during the Allied intervention in Russia in 1918–22, and in a variety of posts. Promoted to lieutenant general in 1939. Commanded an army-size unit in northern Japan until the end of the war. Despite a varied career, Higuchi saw little combat, most of his duties having been as a staff officer.

Hirohito (1901–1989)

Hirohito was the eldest son of Emperor Taisho (reigned 1912–26) and grandson of the great Emperor Meiji (1867–1912). He had only ceremonial military experience. A small child during the Russo-Japanese War, he was a carefully sheltered student during World War I. A keen anglophile, he visited Britain while still crown prince, and was impressed by what he saw. Although he came to the throne in 1926, for several years he had been serving as regent since his father was mentally unstable. Although he came to power during a period of growing democracy in Japan, his generally superior understanding of the West did not stiffen his resolve sufficiently to put him into direct conflict with the generals and admirals who began to slowly take over Japan, preferring to confine himself to scientific pursuits (he was probably the world's premier amateur biologist). Although constitutionally he had enormous power, he failed to exercise it despite personal misgivings about the prospects for war.

Hirohito's regnal name was "Showa," signifying "Enlightened Peace" or "Bright Peace," and the nationalists and militarists were fond of referring to the age of Japanese imperial dominance toward which they were working as the "Showa Era."

See also JAPAN, THE EMPEROR.

Ref: Bergamini, *Japan's Imperial Conspiracy*; Hoyt, *Hirohito*; Irokawa, *The Age of Hirohito*.

Hirohito, the Emperor's Treasure

When Japan accepted defeat in August 1945, it went to great lengths to preserve its emperor from harm, or diminution in status. General Douglas MACARTHUR, the American officer in charge of postwar Japan, was willing to accommodate these Japanese desires. After all, an emperor in debt to America would prove useful in keeping the peace among the emperor-worshipping Japanese. But the emperor had another reason to work closely with the American conquerors, he wanted to keep the emperor's treasure under Japanese control. Allied investigators were seizing control of all Japanese government assets, and the emperor was considered part of the government. The personal fortune of the emperor was immense, and a large chunk of it had been transferred to Swiss bank accounts during the war. The Swiss, then and now, were noted for preserving money in their banks from the prying eyes, and hands, of foreign governments. The emperor had over $100 billion (in 1990s terms) sequestered in these Swiss accounts. He was not inclined to bring it back to Japan until, shall we say, "it was safe." The money had been steadily transferred to the Swiss accounts during the war, and the flow of these foreign currencies to Switzerland increased as the tide of battle turned against the Japanese. Much of the Imperial wealth had long been tied up in Japanese banks and financial institutions. The Japanese always had a knack for planning ahead, and there were many Japanese bankers, and imperial advisers, who could see beyond the catastrophe of Japan losing a war.

In the postwar years, Allied investigators were only dimly aware of this offshore wealth, and the Japanese were not about to enlighten them. As long as the emperor maintained good relations with the occupying powers (particularly MacArthur), there was little danger of the treasure being discovered, much less seized. If the Swiss bank accounts were uncovered, the lawyers might still be fighting the issue out in court. In the early 1950s, it was considered safe to bring this wealth back to Japan. The money certainly was needed. Although MacArthur was gone (to Korea, and then retirement after an argument with President TRUMAN), the Japanese economy was beginning to boom. A large part of this boom was due to the orders for goods and services to support the war raging in Korea. Because of the need for a stronger Japanese industry, and because Americans had a new enemy in Asia (the Chinese communists), restrictions on Japanese banking were relaxed. The emperor's treasure began returning to Japan, often through the same prewar Japanese banks that had arranged its transfer to Switzerland in the first place. Today, the Japanese imperial family is still quite wealthy. While the Japanese are quite secretive about the extent of the emperor's treasure, a substantial amount of this wealth is probably still sitting in Swiss bank accounts.

Ref: Bergamini, *Japan's Imperial Conspiracy*; Hoyt, *Hirohito*; Irokawa, *The Age of Hirohito*.

Hiroshima, Japan

Hiroshima lies at the mouth of the Ota River, by the INLAND SEA on southwestern Honshu. In 1940 its population was approximately 350,000. The city was an important manufacturing center, with commercial shipyards and engineering installations, as well as textile plants and other light industries, and was also the commercial hub of an important agricultural region. In addition the city housed extensive military installations, being the headquarters of the 59th Army and several divisions and brigades. The presence of large number of troops, and of war workers, particularly many Koreans, considerably raised the number of people in the city by mid–1945.

On 6 August 1945 the USAAF B-29 *Enola Gay* dropped an ATOMIC BOMB on Hiroshima, which devastated about four square miles—c. 60%—of the city. Postwar analysis indicates that approximately 130,000 persons were killed in the attack, nearly a third of whom were military personnel. About 20,000 Korean laborers and factory workers were among the dead. Additional deaths from fallout, burns, and other injuries have never been reliably calculated.

Hiroshima, the Plot

The ATOMIC BOMB attacks on HIROSHIMA and NAGASAKI (August 6 and 9, 1945) have spawned a number of interesting conspiracy theories. The first is that senior military officers, fearful that President Harry S TRUMAN might not let them use their new toy, falsely argued that the invasion of Japan (tentatively scheduled to begin on 1 November 1945) would result in "a million American dead," which convinced the president to use the bomb.

A variant of this has the president himself deciding to use the bomb not to bring Japan to a speedy surrender, but to "send a message to the

Russians." This argument has recently been re-vived as part of a conspiracy theory accusing Tru-man of having deliberately started the Cold War in order to justify a greater degree of government control over the American people and to sustain the Military-Industrial Complex.

In fact, neither tale holds much water. No one in the armed forces ever suggested that the inva-sion of Japan would cost a million American lives. The military staff estimated there would be 250,000–500,000 CASUALTIES. After the war, some senior nonmilitary officials and journalists ca-sually made this a "half million dead" and then "a million dead." In any event, any estimate of casu-alties includes killed, wounded, and missing. The original estimates were a not unreasonable figure based on recent American experience with fanat-ical Japanese defenders of IWO JIMA and OKINAWA and borne out by a postwar examination of Japa-nese plans for the defense of the Home Islands. There was no indication the Japanese would fight any less strenuously if their Home Islands were in-vaded. Indeed, it was a safe bet that the fighting would have been even more costly.

As for the Truman "message" theory, this rests on the assumption that no one seriously believed Japan would have to be invaded, which is patently untrue. The Russians knew of the atomic bomb (both officially and unofficially) and the Western Allies knew of Russia's plans to invade MANCHU-RIA. The main consideration was ending the war and saving American lives, not playing diplomatic games or doing warm-up exercises for the Cold War. The Japanese consistently demonstrated a marked reluctance to surrender, either on the bat-tlefield or at the negotiating table. The American people, in light of Germany's surrender in May of 1945, were eager to end the war in the Pacific as soon as possible. The voters were making this wish quite clear to their elected officials and the chief among these, President Harry Truman, was listen-ing intently. He had been told that a blockade of Japan might have to go on for a year or more before Japan finally gave in. The American people wanted something done. The atomic bomb was simply an-other incentive for the Japanese to surrender, and no one was sure it would be any more persuasive than the recent firebomb raids (which killed more people than the atomic bombs).

A third conspiracy theory is that the United States used the bomb on Japan because the Japa-nese were not white, the proof being that it was not used on Germany. Actually, research on the atomic bomb was aimed specifically at having it available for use against Germany. In 1942 the Al-lies agreed that Germany must be defeated first and priority in resources was given to achieve that goal. In fact the B-36 bomber was designed specifically to deliver the bomb to Germany from bases in North America, should the Germans manage to conquer Britain. The only reason it wasn't so used was that Germany surrendered more than two months be-fore the first bomb was even tested. Anyone who doubts that the United States would not have used the bomb on Germany if it was available should consider the firebomb raids on Hamburg and Dres-den, each of which was more deadly than the com-bined CASUALTIES of the atomic bombings of Hiroshima and Nagasaki. Despite this reality, the racial interpretation of the use of the bomb on Ja-pan has proven extremely durable.

Ref: Giangreco, "Casualty Projections. . . .".

Hiryu, Japanese Aircraft Carrier

Although sometimes inaccurately called a sister of SORYU, *Hiryu* (1936–1937–1939) was somewhat larger and had different dimensions and a greater operating range, with marginally more aircraft op-erating capacity. Paired with *Soryu* in Carrier Di-vision Two, she served during the CHINA INCIDENT and with the First Air Fleet from PEARL HARBOR to MIDWAY, where she took four bombs from US dive bombers, which caused extensive fires and forced her to be scuttled. She was the last of the four Japanese carriers to be fatally stricken during the battle, and before she sank her AIR GROUP ac-counted for the USS YORKTOWN.

Hitler, Germany, and the Pacific War

Adolf Hitler's elation upon receiving word of the successful Japanese attack on Pearl Harbor, soon turned to anger when he discovered that not one of his senior military advisers knew where the place was. Hitler soon recovered, and honored the German treaty with Japan by declaring war on the United States. Or perhaps he did it in an effort to entice the Japanese to join in his war on Russia. Certainly in the summer of 1942 he openly suggested that the Japanese attack Russia. The Japanese, however, also had a treaty with the Soviet Union and honored that. Japan was well aware of Soviet military might, having lost several border battles with Soviet forces in 1939.

One result of Japanese neutrality was that Japanese officials, military officers, and businessmen could sometimes travel to or from Germany via the Soviet Union: Taking the Trans-Siberian Railroad, they could make connections to neutral Turkey, and take its rail system to Bulgaria and thence on to Germany.

Despite Japan's neutrality toward the Soviet Union, Germany maintained active relations with its Far Eastern ally throughout the war. A U-boat flotilla was sent to operate in the Indian Ocean. These subs were based in the NETHERLANDS EAST INDIES. Germany also sent surface ships to act as commerce raiders but, again, the action was limited to the Indian Ocean. There was a fair amount of trade conducted between Germany and Japan, using surface ships and cargo SUBMARINES as BLOCKADE RUNNERS. Most of the trade consisted of rare raw materials from Japan and military technology from Germany. Among the more notable technology items supplied were plans and sample parts for the Me-262 jet aircraft, the V-1 rocket (the Japanese copy became the Cherry Blossom rocket), and several tank models. Despite their status as "honorary Aryans," Hitler still considered the Japanese *untermenschen*, and reportedly washed his hands several times immediately after shaking hands with Japanese diplomats.

See also ANTI-COMINTERN TREATY; GERMANY IN THE PACIFIC WAR; OSHIMA, HIROSHI.

Ho Chi Minh (1890–1969)

Born into a traditional scholarly family, Ho—who had an enormous number of pen names, party names, and other aliases—had a classical Confucian education and then went to Europe. On the eve of World War I he was a waiter at the Hotel Carleton in London. During the war he moved to Paris, where he joined the French Socialist Party, tried to bring up Vietnam at the Versailles Conference, and later helped form the French Communist Party. He thereafter worked tirelessly for international communism and Vietnamese independence. During World War II he returned to Vietnam to help organize resistance against the Japanese, a project in which he was aided by the OSS (his code name was Lucius). With the surrender of Japan, the French returned and the resistance promptly began fighting them. The result was a divided Vietnam by 1954. By the early '60s communist GUERRILLAS were active in Ho's name in South Vietnam, leading to American intervention, which ended with the achievement of Ho's goal of a unified Vietnam in 1975, six years after his death.

Hobart, Tasmania, Australia

Extensive facilities and a small naval base made Hobart of some value, assuming a threat to Australia from the southeast, the least likely direction. It was, however, an important port for Allied goods and troops arriving in Australia.

Hollandia, New Guinea

The capital and principal port of Netherlands NEW GUINEA, Hollandia had nothing particularly noteworthy going for it as a base, aside from an airstrip and a roomy, well protected harbor almost totally lacking in port facilities. Strategically, its possession gives one the opportunity to develop naval and air domination over the southern half of the

Philippine Sea, and air control over much of New Guinea, provided one has the resources.

Homma, Masaharu (1887–1946)

Masaharu Homma began his Japanese army career in 1907, and later served with a British battalion on the Western Front during World War I, winning a Military Cross. As a result of this, he had a reputation for being pro-British. A bright and capable officer, he held many staff and command positions during the 1920s. He commanded the 14th Army that invaded the Philippines in late 1941. While successful in conquering the Philippines in less than six months, this was longer than the General Staff felt was necessary. Even before the last American resistance ended on May 6, 1942, Homma was already in trouble with his superiors. As a result, the last months of fighting in the Philippines were under his control in name only. Subordinate officers were given authority by the General Staff to run operations in Homma's name, even disregarding his orders to treat PRISONERS humanely. Homma, being a good Japanese soldier, went along with it. One of Homma's greatest transgressions in the eyes of superiors was not making suicidal attacks with inadequate forces (a practice most other Japanese generals followed energetically). Having served in Europe during World War I, Homma knew how futile such attacks were. In Japanese eyes, he had been "tainted" by Western military thinking. As a result, he returned to Tokyo in disgrace (despite a "victory celebration" in his "honor") and spent the rest of the war on the reserve list.

Because of the BATAAN DEATH MARCH (for which insubordinate junior officers were responsible) and other ATROCITIES by troops under his command in 1942, he was condemned as a war criminal and sentenced to death. That he was one of the few Japanese commanders who spoke fluent (British) English and was rather compassionate in military matters, no doubt made the Allied prosecutors uncomfortable in railroading the "Butcher of Bataan," but popular opinion demanded Homma's head, and Homma, the career soldier to the end, accepted responsibility. Unlike the other condemned war criminals, Homma was not hanged, but faced a firing squad (a "soldier's death"). Homma was cleared of his war criminal conviction by the Japanese government in 1952, it being an open secret (even to the Allied prosecutors) that Homma was not responsible for the atrocities in the Philippines. Homma was quite intelligent, a "thinker," so to speak. He was also several inches taller (at 5 feet 10 inches) than the average Japanese officer. But, as the old Japanese saying goes, "the nail that stands out must be hammered down." That Homma lasted so long in the Japanese army, and advanced so far, is a tribute to his talents.

Ref: Whittam, *Bataan*.

Honda, Masaki (1889–1964)

Masaki Honda joined the Japanese Army in 1910, beginning his career in the prestigious Imperial Guards Division. He held a series of command and staff positions in China during the 1930s and early 1940s. Honda commanded the Thirty-third Army in Burma from early 1944 until the end of the war, and was in charge of all Japanese troops in Burma from the surrender to their repatriation in 1947. He died in 1964.

Hong Kong, China

A British Crown Colony, Hong Kong was one of the largest and best equipped ports in the world, and an important international center of commerce and finance long before World War II. However, its value as a naval base depended totally on who controlled the surrounding portions of China, as these territories controlled access to the port and supply into the city itself. The Japanese had long controlled the Chinese hinterland of Hong Kong, and on 8 December 1941 (December 7 in the Western Hemisphere), their 38th Infantry Division attacked the principal defensive position on the mainland portion of the colony, the Gin Drinker's Line. The defenders, a brigade of three infantry battalions (two Indian and one British), supported by local defense volunteers, were quickly driven back. On December 11–13 the defenders were concentrated on Hong Kong Island, garrisoned by a brigade of three battalions (one Indian battalion and two of recently arrived CANADIAN reservists) and some local defense forces. The Japanese bombarded the island for five days (13–18 December), while issuing demands for surrender, which were repeatedly rejected. Then, on the night of 18–19 December the Japanese undertook landings on the island, and by nightfall on the 19th had split the defenders into two pockets at opposite ends of the island. Despite desperate fighting, the Japanese continued to make gains. On Christmas Day the defenders surrendered.

While a successful defense of Hong Kong was not possible, British MG C. M. Maltby did not prove an intelligent or effective commander. In the prewar period he had made no effort to disperse supplies and had done little to prepare the populace for defense. Most local volunteers were of European background, Asian volunteers not being considered reliable. Once the battle was joined, he missed a number of opportunities to undertake counterattacks, and those he did execute were badly timed. Despite the fact that Britain had been at war in Europe and Africa for over two years, an extraordinary peacetime mindset prevailed in Hong Kong. At one point during the defense, objections were raised by British officers when a platoon of Canadian infantry sought to take up certain defensive positions during the fighting for the Stanley Barracks, because enlisted men were prohibited from entering the officers' mess.

Hong Kong remained under Japanese occupation for the rest of the war. In late 1944 and 1945 its dockyards were increasingly subject to American air raids, including some by B-29s flying from Burma, and naval aircraft off of carriers raiding into the South China Sea. The city was liberated by the ROYAL NAVY on 30 August 1945, but the formal surrender of the Japanese forces there did not take place until 16 September, when Admiral Bruce FRASER accepted it in the name of the Crown.

Honolulu, Oahu, Hawaii

The principal city in Hawaii, Honolulu had only a modest harbor with some facilities to service cargo and merchant shipping, wholly overshadowed as a military base by PEARL HARBOR, nearly 20 miles to the west. A prewar luxury tourist spot, during the war Honolulu's tourist business underwent considerable expansion, not all of it well regarded, since it primarily involved delivering services to soldiers, sailors, and Marines.

Horii, Tomitaro (1890–1942)

Tomitaro Horii began his Japanese Army career in 1911 and served in staff and command positions in China during the 1930s, including the battle for SHANGHAI in 1932. He commanded the key South Seas Detachment that took GUAM, RABAUL, and portions of New Guinea and he commanded the PORT MORESBY invasion force that was turned back during the battle of the CORAL SEA. Horii led the overland assault on Port Moresby and drowned crossing a river in late 1942. Had Horii survived the war, he would have been tried as a war criminal for the torture and execution of Australian PRISONERS at Rabaul.

Horn Island, Australia

Located in the Torres Strait, between the mainland of Australia and New Guinea, Horn Island had only limited value as a port, with a poor anchorage and no facilities. However, it was well suited for use as a forward air base, being essentially the northernmost point in Australia. Although there was only a modest strip in 1941, it was an important stopover for aircraft bound for New Guinea, and more elaborate facilities were developed during the war.

Horses and Mules in the Pacific

The image of World War II as a struggle between mechanized forces is an enduring one. It is also erroneous. In all theaters CAVALRY played some role, but it was in terms of their abilities as beasts of burden that horses and their illegitimate kin, mules, played a surprisingly important role in the war, even in the Pacific.

Only two armies planned to fight the war entirely with motor transport, the British and the American. Indeed, the only horses with the British Army that went to France in late 1939 were polo ponies and riding horses brought along for officers' entertainment. But in practice both the British and the US armies found it impossible to entirely dispense with the equine race for transportation purposes. British and American troops in Burma found horses and mules indispensable for the movement of supplies, and the long-range penetration operations practiced by the CHINDITS and MERRILL'S MARAUDERS would have been impossible without pack mules. Similarly pack trains, at first improvised but later more or less formally organized, were found useful during operations in Italy from 1943 through 1945. Even in the Pacific horses and mules were often found invaluable. On many a tropic isle, local animals were pressed into service by US and Australian troops in order to transport supplies along narrow tracks through jungles and over mountains. For example, Australian troops used mules extensively during the fighting along the KOKODA TRAIL in 1942. Similarly, in the Philippines in early 1945, during the protracted fighting for Baguio, a highland resort town in northern Luzon, the 33rd Infantry Division improvised a pack train of 48 horses, which were outfitted with captured Japanese horse furniture.

Other armies made much greater use of horses than did the United States or the British. Germany and Russia used literally hundreds of thousands of horses for transport, since they were never able to fully mechanize their forces.

Although they possessed a number of fully motorized divisions, most of the Japanese Army's transport was hippotrain (horsedrawn) for the entire war, even in the South Pacific, at least for as long as the horses managed to survive. And all of the armies in China—whether Japanese, Japanese satellite, Nationalist, or communist—relied very heavily upon animal transport.

Hosho, Japanese Aircraft Carrier

Although laid down after the British HERMES, *Hosho* (1919–1921–1922) was completed about six months earlier, and thus became the first aircraft carrier specifically designed and built as such from the keel up. *Hosho* served as an important test bed in the development of Japanese naval aviation. She took part in some operations against China, but by World War II she was useless as a first-line vessel. Despite this she saw active service providing air cover for the battlefleet during 1942, though never in combat. She also served as a training carrier. Although damaged by US carrier aircraft at KURE in July 1945, she survived the war, to serve as a repatriation ship for troops before being scrapped in 1947.

Hosogaya, Boshiro (1884–1964)

Japanese naval officer. From late 1941 VAdm Hosogaya commanded the Fifth Fleet, in northern waters. He directed the occupation of Attu and KISKA, and fought the Battle of the KOMANDORSKI ISLANDS, March 26, 1943, after which he was relieved. He held no further posts during the war.

Housing Destroyed

More firepower was used in World War II than in any other conflict and the heaviest fighting was in heavily populated areas. One of the big losses (aside from the civilians themselves) were homes. Many of these homes were centuries old, and often the loss of a family's house led to some of the inhabi-

Nation	Dwellings Destroyed
Soviet Union	3,000,000
Japan	2,251,900
Poland	516,000
Britain	456,000
France	255,500
Germany	255,000
Netherlands	82,530

tants dying of exposure. The greatest destruction of housing units is shown in the table above.

The figure for the Soviet Union is a conservative estimate. The other nations mentioned actually kept track of the destruction: It was probably just as extensive in several other countries, but the records are sparser. For every home destroyed, there were two to four or more that were damaged to some extent. As in Japan, the highly flammable construction of most homes and the use of firebombs, resulted in twice as many homes destroyed as were damaged. Naturally, there was equal (if not more) destruction to businesses and government structures. Not all of this was from aircraft attack; TANKS and artillery generally tore up the landscape and anything that was built on it.

Hump, The

The Hump was what pilots called a 500 mile route over a series of Himalayan foothills, 14,000–16,000 feet high, from Dinjan, India, to Yonan in China. After early 1942, when the Japanese cut the land route (the BURMA ROAD) into China, the only way in was by air. So began a regular air service between India and China until the land route was opened again in 1945. During some 40 months of operation, the Allied airlift took some 650,000 tons of cargo into China. The return flights carried Chinese hog bristle and silk for export, as well as Chinese troops (brought to India for training) and Allied personnel.

Going in, aircraft were almost always heavily laden, flying over some of the most inhospitable terrain in the world. In addition to the mountains, the region received over 200 inches of rain a year. At the higher altitudes, this rain often turned to ice, making flying very difficult and often fatal. The Chinese end of the flight was on a high plateau (6,300 feet above sea level), which made flying even more difficult for those not used to landing in the thinner air. It was dangerous work, with 155 accidents (and 168 dead) in the second half of 1944, an accident rate of two per thousand hours in the air. By mid-1945, the accident rate had been reduced to 0.36 per thousand hours. There was also some risk from Japanese warplanes, especially from bombing raids on the Chinese airfields.

The workhorse of the airlift was the C-47, the military version of the DC-3 transport (nearly a thousand still flying in the 1990s). The C-47 was not a fast aircraft, taking about three hours for the trip, but it had a fuel capacity that allowed a round trip without refueling. The weather and high altitude saw to it that each C-47 sortie delivered only a few tons. In order to get the cargo through, it was often necessary to fly at night, a dangerous option for 1940s aircraft.

Airlifts began in May 1942, with only about 80 tons making the trip. Nearly half of the materials airlifted were for the use of US forces in China, particularly air forces, but over 330,000 tons were delivered for the Chinese. The weapons, ammunition, and military equipment sent in were the only outside source of aid the Chinese received during the darkest days of their war with the Japanese. These supplies kept China in the war, and the bulk of Japanese ground forces occupied. This was the greatest airlift operation of World War II.

AVERAGE AIRLIFT OVER THE HUMP	
Month	Tons
June 1942	106
June 1943	3,000
June 1944	18,200
June 1945	73,700

Hurricane, British Fighter

The Hurricane, Britain's first modern fighter, entered service in 1937. Production ended in 1944 after nearly 13,000 had been built. Several thousand were sent to Russia, and other allies received as many. After 1941, the Hurricane was the principal British fighter in the Far East. The Hurricane had a rough time against the Zero, but Japanese Army fighters and especially bombers were less of a problem. However, the Hurricane, like most Allied fighters, had tremendous firepower and was well protected. This made a difference even when faced with the Zero. There was also a "navalized" version, the "Sea Hurricane," of lesser capabilities, for use on carriers.

See also AIRCRAFT TYPES, DEVELOPMENT; CARRIERS, DEVELOPING AIRCRAFT FOR.

Hyakutake, Seikichi (1888–1947)

Seikichi Hyakutake entered the Japanese Army in 1909. Originally an infantryman, he later became a noted cryptanalyst. Passing between command and staff during the 1920s and '30s, on the eve of the war he was in charge of signal training for the entire Japanese Army. Made a lieutenant general in 1939, in early 1942 he assumed command of the Seventeenth Army in New Guinea. After the American invasion of GUADALCANAL in August 1942, he was ordered to retake it. This effort failed and he withdrew with his remaining forces to BOUGAINVILLE, far to the northwest of Guadalcanal. There he and his now reinforced army remained until the end of the war, even though he suffered an incapacitating stroke in early 1945.

I

I-26, Japanese Submarine

I-26 was one of 20 units of the B-1 Class built 1939–41. These were large boats, displacing nearly 2,200 tons standard on the surface, and over 3,600 submerged. Armed with a 5.5-inch deck cannon and two 25mm machine guns, plus six 21-inch TORPEDO tubes, they were also equipped with a small floatplane, which was hoisted onto and off of the water for takeoff and landing. Because of this, these boats were normally assigned long-range reconnaissance missions as far afield as the west coast of North America and the east coast of Africa, and blockade-running missions to German-occupied Europe. All 20 were lost in action during the war.

I-26 was arguably the most active Japanese submarine of the war. In the first 10 months, while commanded by Minoru Yokota, she:

- sank the USAT *Cynthia Olsen* on December 7, 1941, about 700 miles northeast of Hawaii, thus scoring the first submarine victory of the Pacific War.
- shelled Point Estevan, British Columbia, June 20, 1942.
- torpedoed the USS *Saratoga* west of the SANTA CRUZ ISLANDS on August 31, 1942.
- sank the USS *Juneau* on November 13, 1942.

Thereafter the boat's career was still busy, but less spectacular. In September 1943, for example, her floatplane conducted a reconnaissance over the Fiji Islands. She was lost on October 24, 1944, during the Battle of LEYTE GULF, when she was caught on the surface by several US ships and tried to shoot her way out.

See also BOMBING, NORTH AMERICA, JAPANESE ATTACKS; FORT STEVENS, OREGON; SYDNEY.

Ref: Boyd and Yoshida, *The Japanese Submarine Force and World War II.*

I-52, Japanese Submarine

I-52 was a unit of the C3 Class, laid down at the KURE Navy Yard in 1942, launched in 1943, and commissioned that December. A large boat, displacing over 3,500 tons when submerged at full load, she had enormous range, 21,000 nautical miles when traveling on the surface at 16 knots. Converted into a BLOCKADE RUNNER, *I-52* set out from Kure in March of 1944, loaded with two metric tons of gold (i.e., 4,409 pounds), bound for Germany on a blockade-running mission, with a crew of 95, plus 14 passengers, mostly technicians who were to study recent German developments in several fields. At SINGAPORE she loaded 228 tons of alloying metals (tin, tungsten, and molybdenum), plus 54 tons of rubber and three tons of quinine. By remaining submerged during the day and running on the surface by night, *I-52* was able to elude Allied maritime and air patrols until the night of 22–23 June 1944, when she was located in the mid-Atlantic, about 1,400 miles west of the Cape Verde Islands, by a TBF AVENGER off the escort carrier USS BOGUE. Although it was a moonless night, LtCdr Jesse D. Taylor was able to locate the submarine and put a single TORPEDO into her. She sank in 17,000 feet of water.

Slightly more than 50 years later, *I-52* was located by an American treasure hunter, Paul R. Tidwell, using a Russian undersea research vessel.

Salvage value of the submarine is estimated at more than $25 million.

Not counting vessels ordered but never laid down, there were three boats (*I-52, I-53, I-54*) in the C3 class, all built 1942–44, plus five in the very similar C1 Class (*I-16, I-18, I-20, I-22,* and *I-24*), built 1937–41, and three in the equally similar C2 Class (*I-46, I-47, I-48*), built 1942–44. They had a very long operational range, 21,000 nautical miles at 16 knots in the case of the C3 design. All of these boats had interesting careers during the war, several being converted to carry the Kaiten "human torpedo" and one into a troop transport. Nine were sunk in the war, including one (*I-16*) by the famous USS ENGLAND.

Ref: Brice, *Axis Blockade Runners*; Boyd and Yoshida, *The Japanese Submarine Force and World War II*.

Ibuki, Japanese Light Aircraft Carrier

Ordered by the Imperial Navy as a heavy cruiser of a new design (12,200 tons standard, with 10 8-inch guns), *Ibuki* was laid down in April of 1942 and launched in May 1943. As the Japanese carrier situation was desperate, in November of '43 the still incomplete cruiser was taken in hand for conversion to a carrier. Construction lagged, however, due to wartime shortages, and work was halted in March of 1945, when the ship was about 80% complete. She was scrapped in 1947.

Ichi Go ("Operation Ichi")

A major Japanese offensive in China in 1944, probably the largest of the Pacific War. Ichi Go was intended to capture US airbases in south and central China, from which B-29s were raiding southern Japan. Preparations for the operation were protracted, due to severe shortages of supplies. There were basically three phases to the offensive.

Honan (April–May 1944) involved some 400,000 Japanese troops, including a tank division, initially against only about 100,000 Chinese, a fig-

ure greatly increased during the fighting. Japanese losses were some 7,000–10,000 killed and wounded, Chinese losses were reportedly over 50,000 killed and more than 100,000 wounded.

Hunan (June–August 1944) involved some 360,000 Japanese troops against an eventual 800,000 Chinese troops. Japanese CASUALTIES totaled about 20,000, Chinese casualties over 100,000.

Kwangsi (August–December 1944) saw over 100,000 Japanese troops engage an initial Chinese force of about equal strength, which was rapidly reinforced. Japanese losses were relatively low, but the Chinese suffered nearly 40,000 casualties.

Ichi Go was the last major Japanese offensive success of the war. At the cost of about 50,000 casualties, the Japanese occupied major areas of southern China, including about a half-dozen US air bases, and inflicted some 300,000 casualties on the Chinese, a loss to the Nationalists of about 10% of their forces, and those the best troops available. In addition, the area overrun by the Japanese included about 25% of Nationalist China's remaining industrial plant.

Ie Shima, Ryukyu Islands

A large island west of OKINAWA. Invaded by elements of the US 77th Division on April 16, 1945 and declared secure several days later. On April 18, the famous war correspondent Ernie PYLE was killed there by Japanese machine-gun fire. On August 19, 1945 the island served as an intermediate landing site for the Japanese delegation en route to Manila to settle details of the surrender of Japan.

See also JAPAN, SURRENDER OF, PROTOCOLS AND CEREMONY.

Illustrious Class, British Aircraft Carriers

A derivative of the very successful *Ark Royal, Illustrious* and her sisters were Britain's best carriers, and the first carriers to have a fully armored hangar deck. Of course, this limited aircraft capacity to that of an escort or light fleet carrier. Nevertheless, they were successful ships, handy and good in heavy seas as a result of their innovative "hurricane" bows, which brought the hull right up to the forward edge of the flight deck, and very tough, all three surviving KAMIKAZE attacks with little damage.

Illustrious (1937–1939–1940) had an extremely active career, launching the Taranto Raid, November 11–12, 1940, making several runs to supply Malta, participating in the occupation of Madagascar, and generally supporting British operations in European waters, during which she was heavily damaged by German air attack, requiring nearly a year to repair (June 1941–May 1942). Joining the Far East Fleet in January 1944, she took part in raids on Japanese forces in the NETHERLANDS EAST INDIES and Burma, before passing into the Pacific in early 1945 to participate in attacks on Formosa and Japan. She took a kamikaze in April and May 1945 off OKINAWA, with little effect. Scrapped in 1956.

Victorious (1937–1939–1941) was commissioned on 15 May 1941, and within nine days was in action during the pursuit of the German battleship *Bismarck*, which was damaged by one of her aircraft. She repeatedly attacked German targets in Norway, including the battleship *Tirpitz*, escorted convoys to northern Russia and Malta, served with the US Pacific Fleet for a time in early and mid-1943, and by mid-1944 was serving with the British Far Eastern Fleet. She joined the British Pacific Fleet in early 1945, taking two kamikaze, which required considerable repair. Rebuilt in the 1950s, she served into the 1960s, until seriously damaged by a fire. Scrapped in 1969.

Formidable (1937–1939–1941) served in the Mediterranean from early 1941 through late 1944, helping to win the Battle of Cape Matapan (March 28–29, 1941) and supporting numerous landings and ground actions, being seriously damaged on only one occasion. Joined the British Pacific Fleet in early 1945, took a kamikaze off Okinawa in May,

but was back in service almost immediately. Scrapped 1956.

HMS INDOMITABLE and HMS IMPLACABLE were originally to have been sisters to *Illustrious*, but were completed to modified designs.

See also ROYAL NAVY.

Imamura, Hitoshi (1886–1968)

Imamura graduated from the Japanese military academy in 1907 and served in many military attaché posts (including England and India) through the 1920s and 1930s. Also active in staff and training posts. He received a series of troop commands in Japan and China during the 1930s, leading to command of the Sixteenth Army, which would conquer JAVA and the Dutch East Indies. Used a uncharacteristically lenient policy in ruling the area, which seemed to pacify the locals and led to his promotion to command of all troops in the southeast Pacific in early 1943. From his headquarters in RABAUL, Imamura directed the fighting in the SOLOMONS and New Guinea until the end of the war, when he surrendered Japanese forces in the area.

Implacable Class, British Aircraft Carriers

A further refinement of the ILLUSTRIOUS design, incorporating lessons learned from INDOMITABLE, in some ways the Implacables were less successful than the earlier classes, their hangar deck not being suitable for some of the taller late-war aircraft, and their fuel capacity being too low. However, they could carry heavier aircraft than the earlier ships, and could operate 81 aircraft when using deck storage.

Implacable (1939–1942–1944) joined the British Pacific Fleet in late 1944, shortly after completing her training. Off OKINAWA she took a kamikaze with a 550-pound bomb, on the flight deck at the base of her island, with no significant effect. Scrapped 1955.

Indefatigable (1939–1942–1944) made a raid on the German battleship *Tirpitz* in Norway in mid-1944, before joining the British Pacific Fleet. She took a kamikaze off Okinawa, but was not seriously injured. Scrapped 1956.

See also ROYAL NAVY.

Independence Class, US Light Aircraft Carriers

When the "Two Ocean Navy" Act (see REARMAMENT, US, 1930s) was passed in 1940, President ROOSEVELT observed that despite the bill, the navy was not going to get any new carriers before 1944. He made two suggestions, to convert merchant ships to auxiliary aircraft carriers and to convert some of the cruisers under construction to light aircraft carriers. The navy reluctantly adopted the first suggestion, which led to the very successful LONG ISLAND, but resisted the second for over a year. However, by mid-1942 it was clear that the aircraft carrier was the new weapon of decision in naval warfare, and that there were not enough of them. At that point the president stopped suggesting and ordered nine partially completed CLEVELAND CLASS light cruisers to be converted to light aircraft carriers. The work was done quickly and the first ships began to enter service in January of 1943, with the last ready by the end of that year. The Independence Class ships were very successful improvisations, despite being cramped, uncomfortable, and unattractive. About half the size of a fleet carrier, they operated about a third as many aircraft. Fast, they remained in active first-line service with the fast carrier task force until the end of the war. When serving as aircraft transports, they could carry, though not operate, over 100 airplanes.

Independence, CVL-22 (1941–1942–1943) (ex-*Amsterdam*, CL-59), first went into action in the MARCUS ISLAND raid in September 1943 and took a TORPEDO off TARAWA that November. She returned to service in mid-1944 and stayed with the Fast Carrier Task Force until the end of the war. Afterward she was used in the Bikini ATOMIC BOMB tests, and was sunk as a target in 1951.

Princeton, CVL-23 (1941–1942–1943) (ex-*Tallahassee*, CL-61), joined the Fast Carrier Task Force in late 1943 and served with it until October 24, 1944; during the Battle of LEYTE GULF, she was struck by a 500-pound bomb that penetrated into her torpedo storage, setting off a series of explosions, causing her to be abandoned. She was sunk by torpedoes from the USS *Reno* (CLAA-96). Her nickname was "Peerless P."

Belleau Wood, CVL-24 (1941–1942–1943) (ex-*New Haven*, CL-76), joined the fleet in late 1943 and helped sink the Japanese carrier *Hiyo* during the Battle of the PHILIPPINE SEA, before taking a KAMIKAZE off Leyte in October 1944. She returned to the Fast Carrier Task Force early in 1945 and served to the end of the war. Lent to France in 1947, she saw service in the Indo-China war. She was returned and scrapped in 1960.

Cowpens, CVL-25 (1941–1943–1943) (ex-*Huntington*, CL-77), served with the Fast Carrier Task Force from early 1943, but the only damage she took was during the December 1944 typhoon. Scrapped 1959.

Monterey, CVL-26 (1941–1943–1943) (ex-*Dayton*, CL-78), reached the fleet in the fall of 1944 and was heavily engaged, but like *Cowpens* was damaged only in the December 1944 typhoon, when several aircraft on her hangar deck broke loose, causing potentially disastrous fires, which were put out with some difficulty. Future president Gerald R. FORD was later decorated for his part in the damage control effort. After the war she served for a time as a training carrier but was scrapped in 1970. In addition to the future president, her crew included Bill Howell, a navy enlisted man whose wartime services are followed in the Chronology.

Langley, CVL-27 (1942–1943–1943) (ex-*Fargo*, CL-85), was named after the navy's first carrier, which had been lost while serving as an aircraft transport south of JAVA in early 1942. CVL-27 served in the Pacific from early 1944 and was just completing a refit in the United States when the war ended. Although she had taken part in numerous operations, she had never suffered any damage. Transferred to France in 1951, she saw service in Indochina. She was returned in 1963 and scrapped.

Cabot, CVL-28 (1942–1943–1943) (ex-*Wilmington*, CL-79), took a kamikaze off Leyte in October 1944 and another off OKINAWA. Transferred to Spain in 1959, she served as a helicopter carrier until scrapped in the 1980s.

Bataan, CVL-29 (1942–1943–1943) (ex-*Buffalo*, CL-99), joined the fleet in early 1944 and served 18 months with the fast carriers without incurring any damage. After the war she was placed in reserve, but returned to duty during the Korean War. Scrapped in 1960.

San Jacinto, CVL-30 (1942–1943–1943) (ex-*Newark*, CL-100), served with the fast carriers from early 1944, participating in numerous operations yet incurring only minor damage. Among her aircrew was George BUSH. Scrapped 1959.

India

On the eve of World War II the British Indian Empire, which included the present countries of India, Pakistan, Bangladesh, and Sri Lanka, was a vast, extremely diverse region with some 300 million people. Beginning in the 17th century India had increasingly come under British control, which was more or less complete by the late 19th century. There were two types of territories in India, those controlled directly by Britain and those ruled by various kings and princes, which were in effect subject-allies of the British. Unlike most colonies, which had relatively sparse populations, India could not be ruled by Britons alone. A relatively small staff of British officials and civil servants supervised an enormous native Indian bureaucracy, which functioned with considerable efficiency. A similar situation prevailed in the Indian Army.

From early in the 20th century India became increasingly restless under British rule. By the 1920s the nationalist Congress Party, inspired by Mohandas Ghandi, led an increasingly effective nonviolent protest campaign against British rule. When World War II broke out, India proved an enormously important reservoir of manpower and wealth for the British Empire. Due to their resistance to cooperation with the British, Ghandi and some other Indian leaders were imprisoned. However, ultimately the only way that the British were able to secure peace in India was to promise independence as soon as the war ended. A few extremist leaders advocated violent revolution and cooperation with the Japanese, but most Indian nationalists rejected their position.

Northeastern India was the scene of some of the most savage fighting in the war. This caused a considerable increase in support for the British, and it was mostly Indian troops that fought and defeated the Japanese on the Burmese frontier and beyond.

The war had important effects on India. In addition to strengthening and modernizing the Indian Armed Forces, which shortly were divided between India and Pakistan, it also led to a considerable expansion of the infrastructure, with the building of numerous airfields, improvements in ports, and the development of whole new industries.

See also BOSE, SUBHAS CHANDRA.

Ref: Prasad, *Official History of the Indian Armed Forces in the Second World War, 1939–1945.*

Indian Armed Forces

In origin essentially a colonial auxiliary to the British Army, on the eve of World War II the Indian Army was a thoroughly professional, very modern military force. It was also quite small, in the mid-1930s running to only about 160,000 men and three divisions. By the outbreak of the European War in 1939 there were somewhat over 200,000 men, in six divisions, albeit not all at full strength or fully trained. During the war expansion was rapid, peaking at over two million men, all more or less volunteers, making it the largest purely volunteer army ever raised to that time. India was poor and rife with unemployment at the start of the war, and the armed forces offered the only prospect of employment for many men. Thus the military could be selective and the quality of the troops was quite high.

Although at first virtually all of the officers in the Indian Army were British, as time went on an increasing number of Indians were given commissions: In 1939 there were about 400 Indian line officers, a figure that grew to about 8,000 by the end of the war. Most Indian divisions contained about 30% British personnel, generally about a third of the infantry and all of the artillerymen. As the war went on, and British manpower became strained, the British contingents declined, and Indians began turning up as artillerymen. During the war Indian units served in all theaters except northwestern Europe. The quality of the early units was quite high, but the rapid expansion of the army in 1940–41 caused some problems with quality among the units that served in MALAYA and Burma in 1942. To some extent the difficulties lay in hasty training, poor manpower management, and equipment shortages. These problems were gradually resolved, so that when the Indian Army undertook its final offensives against the Japanese in Burma in 1944–45, it was a highly skilled, flexible, and effective force. It was this battle-hardened, well trained, professional force that provided the stable and effective armed forces of India and Pakistan when these two nations became independent shortly after World War II.

On the eve of World War II the Royal Indian Navy (originally named the "Royal Indian Marine") had only a handful of vessels, the largest of which was a sloop (a sort-of destroyer escort). During the war it expanded into an efficient force, equipped mostly with smaller vessels and landing craft.

The Royal Indian Air Force began the war with only a single squadron, and that a general purpose one geared primarily to noncombat duties. By early 1944 it possessed 10 squadrons, several of which were equipped with fighters or light bombers.

Ref: Prasad, *Official History of the Indian Armed Forces in the Second World War, 1939–1945.*

Indian Army, Divisions

In December 1941 there were 14 divisions in the Indian Army. The best five of these (among them an armored division) were committed to operations in North Africa or to occupation duty in the Middle East. The rest were all only partially trained and equipped. Six were scattered all across India, two—plus some miscellaneous brigades—were in MALAYA and one was in Burma. By the end of the war the Indian Army was maintaining 18 divisions on active duty, despite the loss of two in Malaya.

Indian divisions were more or less modeled on British lines. About 30% of their personnel were usually British, normally one battalion in each brigade, plus the artillery and many of the technical service troops. As time went on, however, shortages of British personnel led to the introduction of an increasing number of Indian troops to the artillery and technical service.

Third Indian Division. A prewar division, it was committed to the Burma Front in 1942. In 1943 it was disbanded to help form the CHINDITS.

Fifth Indian Division. A regular prewar formation, in 1940 the division served against the Italians in East Africa, then performed garrison duties in Cyprus through 1941, fought in North Africa in 1942 and 1943, after which it returned to India. There it was reorganized as a light division, with few motor vehicles and hundreds of mules, especially equipped to operate in the extremely mountainous, jungle-covered terrain of Burma. It was committed to action in Burma in early 1944. It was

INDIAN ARMED FORCES IN WORLD WAR II		
	1939	1945
Army	200,000	2,080,000
Air Force	285	29,200
Navy	1,850	30,500

Figures exclude British personnel, but include Indian State Forces (i.e., troops of the various princely states of India, about 16,000 of whom actually served in the field by the end of the war).

flown into Imphal to help break the Japanese siege, and fought on in Burma until the end of the war.

Seventh Indian Division. Raised in 1940, the division was not committed to action until September 1943, when it entered the fighting on the Burma Front, where it remained until the end of the war.

Ninth Indian Division. Although raised in early 1941, the division was relatively ill-trained, ill-equipped, and understrength when it was sent to Malaya on the eve of the Pacific War. During the retreat to SINGAPORE it was seriously mauled in an attempt to defend Kuala Lumpur. The remnants of the division surrendered on Singapore, February 15, 1942.

11th Indian Division. A new unit, green, ill-trained, poorly equipped, and missing one brigade, the division formed part of the garrison of Malaya in December 1941. It took part in the retreat to Singapore, where it surrendered on 15 February 1942.

14th Indian Division. Raised in 1941, the division was in northern India at the outbreak of the Pacific War. It was not committed to action on the India-Burma front until September 1942, which gave time for it to be properly trained and equipped. It proved a good unit in combat, fighting throughout the protracted struggle for Burma.

17th Indian Division. Raised in 1941, the division was only partially trained and ill-equipped when the Pacific War began. Worse, one brigade, with the division reconnaissance, artillery, and service elements, was in northeastern India, while the other two brigades were in Malaya, where they were eventually captured by the Japanese. The main body of the division, hastily strengthened by equally ill-prepared reinforcements, moved from India to Burma shortly after war broke out. Despite its limitations, with the British Seventh Armoured Brigade the division formed the backbone of resistance to the Japanese invaders, putting up impressive resistance at the Salween and Sittang Rivers

and at Prome, before its remnants retreated into India in May 1942. Rebuilt, it served thereafter in the defense of India and throughout the liberation of Burma.

19th Indian Division. Raised in 1941, the division was in southern India at the outbreak of the war, still in training and only partially equipped. Not committed to operations until late 1944, it fought in Burma from then until the end of the war.

20th Indian Division. Raised in 1941, the division was in southern India at the outbreak of the war, completing its training. It was deployed to Burma in February 1942, and served on the Burma Front until the end of the war.

21st Indian Division. Raised in 1942, the division went into action in Burma in October 1943, and fought on until the end of the war.

23rd Indian Division. Raised in late 1941 in southern India, the division entered Burma in February 1942, and thereafter served almost continuously on the Burma Front.

25th Indian Division. Raised in 1942, the division did not complete its training until early 1944, being repeatedly drained of manpower and equipment to sustain the troops in Burma. It was then transferred to Burma, where it fought until the end of the war.

26th Indian Division. In northern India in December 1941, the division went into action on the Burma Front in the spring of 1943. In September 1943 the division was withdrawn from combat. Although it remained under the British 14th Army, it was not employed again.

36th Indian Division. A "light" division (with only two brigades) organized in India in 1943, for amphibious operations it was eventually reorganized so that it consisted entirely of British troops. In mid–1944 it was transferred to the British Army, becoming the 36th Infantry Division.

44th Indian Airborne Division. Formed in 1944 from the 44th Indian Armoured Division (itself having been formed through the merger of the 32nd and 43rd Indian Armoured Divisions) and served as a headquarters and training command. Individual battalions saw some combat in Burma, but the division itself was never committed to action.

The Fourth, Fifth, Eighth, and 10th Indian Divisions saw service in the war against Germany and Italy. The Second, Sixth, 12th, and 39th Indian Divisions, and the 31st, 42nd, and 43rd Indian Armoured Divisions performed occupation duties in the Middle East or garrison duties in India during the war.

Ref: Prasad, *Official History of the Indian Armed Forces in the Second World War, 1939–1945.*

Indian National Army

As part of their "Asia for the Asiatics" campaign, the Japanese supported independence movements in a number of countries, not least of all India. Since India was generally regarded as the font of all British power, Japanese intelligence had been interested in stimulating greater unrest there than actually existed, and Japanese agents were already in contact with the more radical elements among Indian nationalists. After overrunning Malaya and Burma, the Japanese found themselves with about 55,000 Indian PRISONERS OF WAR, a total that reached some 75,000 by the end of 1942. As a result, quite early in 1942 the Japanese helped radical Indian exiles and disaffected prisoners of war organize the "Indian National Army" (INA). The head of this body was General Mohan Singh, a 30-year-old Indian major who had surrendered early in the Malaya Campaign.

Singh proved a surprisingly able organizer, and by June of 1942 had managed to put together a brigade group, gradually expanding it into a division, which on paper numbered about 16,000 men by late 1942. However, Singh and his principal supporters proved most interested in pursuing purely Indian objectives. A falling out occurred

that December. Rather than submit to Japanese domination, Singh ordered the INA to disband. The Japanese acted quickly, and in what can only be termed a coup, installed a new head of the INA, Subhas Chandra BOSE.

Bose was a much more radical Indian nationalist than Singh had been, but was also more amenable to Japanese interests. On the run from the British, Bose had spent the early war years in Germany, unsuccessfully trying to entice Indian POWs to join the collaborationist Free Indian Legion, which ultimately amounted to less than a thousand men. When Japan attacked the British Empire, HITLER had Bose put on a submarine and delivered him to Germany's "Honorary Aryan" allies, the Japanese. Bose purged the INA of Singh and about 4,000 of his supporters, and then began to reorganize it in early 1943.

By May 1943, the First Division of the INA had some 12,000 troops on paper, while two more divisions were in the process of formation. Although most of the troops were recruited from among the POWs held by the Japanese, some genuine volunteers did come forward from the large Indian expatriate communities throughout East Asia, including enough women to form the "Rani of Jhansi" Regiment. The INA went into combat for the first time in Burma in January 1944, when some small units supported the Japanese 55th Division in the Arakan Campaign. That April the INA's First Division, effectively 7,000–8,000 men strong, joined the Japanese 15th Army's offensive against Imphal and Kohima, in northeastern India.

For a variety of reasons, the results were not impressive. The Japanese had not been generous to the INA in terms of equipment (one of the reasons for their falling out with Mohan Singh), and the First Division was organized as a light infantry force, with virtually no artillery. In addition, training was poor, having been neglected apparently on the theory that the troops had already been trained by the British. There were also serious problems with leadership and manpower. The INA had a severe shortage of officers. Although several thousand Indian Army "Viceroy's Commissioned Officers" (i.e., native Indian officers) were among the prisoners in Japanese hands, only about 400 volunteered for the INA, of whom about 250 were medical personnel. As a result, the INA had to create officers on the spot, promoting men up through the ranks to the highest levels, in many cases men with few qualifications for their new positions.

In addition, most of the men who did join the INA appear to have done so because it seemed preferable to being starved or beaten to death in a Japanese prisoner of war camp, making their dedication to the cause somewhat suspect. Desertion was a serious problem: At least 700 men reportedly managed to make their way into the British lines during the Imphal-Kohima Campaign, some 10% of those engaged, and that in the midst of a very hot fight in a dense jungle. During the Imphal-Kohima Campaign the INA First Division lost between 4,500 and 5,500 men, of whom only about 400 were killed in action or died of wounds. As a result, Imphal-Kohima was not only the debut, but also the finale of the INA's combat role in World War II. Although some INA volunteers fought alongside the Japanese through to the end of the war, in terms of formal units the INA saw no further active service.

INA sympathizers among Indian ultra-nationalists have claimed that some 40,000 men volunteered for service, which would amount to over half of all Indian prisoners in Japanese hands. A more likely figure is between 20,000 and 25,000, most of whom appear to have joined in order to get better treatment: 25% of the Indian prisoners in Japanese hands who did not join the INA died before the end of the war, mostly from disease or malnutrition, as opposed to only about 1,500 (less than 6%) of the men in the INA. The 20,000–25,000 figure is confirmed by the fact that after the war the British detained about 20,000 Indians who had formerly been prisoners of the Japanese, on suspicion of collaboration. Strengthening the suggestion that most of the INA volunteers were more or less coerced into the organization is the fact that 19,000 of the detainees were released within a

short time with no stain on their military records. The remainder were subjected to rather intensive investigation, but once again most were soon released. In the end, a number of men were tried by courts-martial, with the result that several dozen were imprisoned and nine hanged as traitors.

Indian Ocean, Japanese Carrier Raids

After briefly returning to Japan following the PEARL HARBOR raid, Japan's First Air Fleet (six carriers, several battleships, plus cruisers and destroyers) steamed to its new central Pacific base at TRUK (in the CAROLINES). There was still some concern about the remaining American carrier force, and when these carriers raided Japanese bases in the MARSHALL ISLANDS, the First Air Fleet sortied unsuccessfully to try and catch them. After two months of this, the Japanese decided that the Americans would not venture out enough to be caught, so the First Air Fleet was sent to Southeast Asia, where the battles for Burma and the Dutch East Indies were still going on.

Japan had another naval foe in the form of the British Far East Fleet (three carriers, five old battleships, and smaller warships). Despite the sinking of two British battleships off MALAYA on 10 December, the Japanese knew that the remaining British fleet (many ships were on their way to the Far East) could interfere with their advance into the Dutch East Indies, and movement of Japanese transports. By March, the First Air Fleet, plus the Malay Force under Admiral OZAWA (two light carriers, five battleships), moved toward the Indian Ocean in search of the British fleet. Throughout April, the Japanese warships scoured the eastern Indian Ocean looking for the British.

Unable to bring the enemy to battle, the Japanese were content to stage air raids on British bases in India and Ceylon and to sink merchant shipping. Raids were also made on northern Australian ports. Although unable to destroy the British fleet, the Japanese did make it clear that Japan ruled the seas in this part of the world. In the space of five months, the First Air Fleet steamed over 50,000 miles from Pearl Harbor while destroying hundreds of Allied aircraft and sinking one British carrier, five American battleships, several cruisers, and numerous lesser ships. The Japanese fleet had proved to the British, the Americans, and most importantly to the Japanese and the people of Asia, that Japan was a major military power.

Ref: Barnett, *Engage the Enemy More Closely*; Marder, *Old Friends, New Enemies*; Roskill, *The United Kingdom Military Series: The War at Sea, 1939–1945*; *White Ensign*.

Indo-China, French

The French began taking control of Indo-China in the mid-19th century. By the eve of World War II it comprised the colonies and protectorates of Annam, Cochin-China, and Tonkin, which today form Vietnam, Cambodia, and Laos. When France fell to the Germans in 1940, the colonial administration adhered to the Vichy regime. In September 1940 Vichy acceded to Japanese pressure, and allowed Japanese troops to occupy the northern part of the colony. In protest, the United States put an embargo on shipments of scrap metal to Japan (America was a primary source of scrap metal for the Japanese), which had little effect on Japanese policy in Indo-China.

In late 1940–early 1941 SIAM attacked Indo-China in an effort to secure control of several frontier provinces. Although the French readily defeated the invaders on both land and sea (Battle of the Gulf of Siam, 17 January 1941), the Japanese pressured them into ceding the affected provinces anyway. By late 1941 the Japanese were in effective occupation of all of French Indo-China, although the colonial administration and garrison remained in place. In December 1941 Indo-China proved an important base from which the Japanese undertook operations against Burma, MALAYA, and the NETHERLANDS EAST INDIES.

As elsewhere, Japanese occupation policies were not gentle. Much of the colony's rice was exported, leading to severe privation: An estimated two million people starved to death in Indo-China during the Japanese occupation. This caused the Vietnamese nationalists, under the communist HO CHI MINH, already engaged in a desultory struggle with the French, to shift their attention to the new occupiers. A small but serious insurrection resulted, punctuated by occasional truces. The GUERRILLAS received some aid from the OSS. The next time the colony was directly affected by the war was in late 1944, when the US fleet sortied into the South China Sea and proceeded to make airstrikes against military and economic targets.

In early 1945, the Japanese decided to get rid of the French. In a well executed coup on 9 March they managed to capture virtually all important French civil and military personnel, who were promptly massacred. At least 4,500 Europeans died. One Foreign Legion officer, BG Marcel Alessandri, managed to avoid the disaster. Sensing something in the wind, on 9 March he put his command of some 2,000 men, including the Fifth Foreign Legion Regiment, on the march for Nationalist-occupied territory in southern China, about a thousand miles to the north. After an epic march of 98 days, during which it was subject to repeated harassment by Japanese forces totaling about 10,000 men, the column, reduced to about a thousand men, reached safety.

Upon the surrender of Japan, Ho Chi Minh and his communist-nationalist forces attempted to take control of Indo-China, which the Japanese had declared independent under a prince of the former imperial family, Bao Dai. The Japanese would have none of this, and fighting continued. When British forces arrived, some weeks after the formal surrender, the Japanese laid down their arms. However, the British soon ran into problems with Ho. Finding their own forces insufficient to keep the guerrillas in check, they rearmed the Japanese and turned them loose. Meanwhile, a French expedition arrived, to relieve the British and the Japanese. After a short period of tentative negotiations, the French and Ho fell out, and the First Indo-China War began.

Indomitable, British Aircraft Carrier

Originally to have been a sister to Britain's ILLUS-
TRIOUS, *Indomitable* (1937–1940–1941) was completed to a somewhat different design, which left
her less well protected but able to carry nearly 50%
more aircraft (48 as against 33). She had a very
active life, mostly in the Mediterranean (where she
was heavily damaged by bombs on a Malta convoy
in mid-1942, and again by a TORPEDO during the
invasion of Sicily in mid-1943). Intended to be
sent to the Far East in late 1941, with the battleship *Prince of Wales* and battlecruiser *Repulse, Indomitable* ran aground at Kingston, Jamaica. She
incurred some damage, and so could not accompany the two dreadnoughts, which probably saved
her from being sunk along with them off Malaya
on December 10. She joined the British Far Eastern
Fleet just over a month later, and subsequently
passed to the British Pacific Fleet, taking a KAMI-
KAZE with few ill effects in May of 1945. Scrapped
1956.

See also ROYAL NAVY.

Indonesia (the Netherlands East Indies), Campaign for

The Japanese had to conquer Southeast Asia in
stages, as the area to be taken was too vast to be
taken at once. The most distant, and last, area sub-
jugated was the Dutch East Indies (also known as
the NETHERLANDS EAST INDIES and today as Indonesia). Accordingly, the Japanese invaded MA-
LAYA, the Philippines, and SIAM first, on the same
day that PEARL HARBOR was bombed.

The invasion of the Netherlands East Indies did
not get underway until early January, a month after
Pearl Harbor. The invasion was conducted by three
task forces, each containing some warships (largely
cruisers and destroyers) and troop ships. The western convoy left from INDO-CHINA and made its first
landing on eastern Sumatra in mid-February. The
eastern convoy began landing in the Celebes in
early January. The central and east convoys had air

cover from the First Air Fleet carriers, which had
recently returned from the Pearl Harbor raid. In
all, the Japanese ground forces equaled about three
divisions of experienced troops. Since there were
dozens of different landings, the Japanese soldiers
operated in regimental or battalion size forces. The
85,000 Allied troops defending the area were
spread over a large area. Most of them were Dutch,
but there were many locals of dubious loyalty to
the Allied cause. While there was some hard fighting here and there, the Japanese superiority on the
ground was never in doubt. Nor did the Japanese
have any trouble in the air, with their carrier- and
land-based aircraft proving superior to what little
the Allies had in the area.

At sea it was a slightly different story. The Japanese Navy, while superior overall, was spread out
over a wide area escorting the numerous Japanese
convoys. The smaller Allied naval forces always
posed the threat that they would concentrate their
cruisers and destroyers to attack one of the Japanese convoys. Moreover, the numerous small islands and straits in the area made nighttime naval
ambushes a constant threat. Such proved to be the
case for the series of naval battles that accompanied the Japanese invasion. First blood went to a
force of four American destroyers that launched a
night attack on a Japanese convoy on 23 January
in the Macassar Strait. Sinking one small escort
and four loaded troop transports, the Americans
got away with little damage to themselves. On February 4, Japanese aircraft caught an Allied squadron in the Madoera Strait and damaged two
American cruisers. A similar battle was fought off
PALEMBANG on February 13–14, when Japanese
aircraft forced an Allied squadron to turn back
from its attempt to stop a Japanese landing.

On February 19–20 there was a hard-fought surface battle at Bandung Strait in which the Allies
came off second best and lost one destroyer. All
this led up to a major naval battle on February 27
in the Java Sea. An Allied force of five cruisers
and 10 destroyers took on a Japanese force of four
cruisers and 13 destroyers. The fighting went on

for seven hours. The Allies lost two cruisers and five destroyers, as well as the battle. The Allied units that survived the battle of the JAVA SEA were caught the following night (February 28–March 1) off Banten Bay on the Sunda Strait and took another beating. In the end, only four Allied destroyers made their way back to Australia. During these sea fights, Japanese troops were landing on more and more islands, quickly overcoming the resistance of usually greatly outnumbered Allied forces (US and Australian troops managed to get to some islands, to be swept up by the Japanese along with the Dutch). On 9 March the Dutch surrendered the Netherlands East Indies to the Japanese.

See also ABDA; FUJITA, FRANK; JAPAN, ATTITUDE TOWARD THE ENEMY.

Indonesia, Resistance to the Japanese

Even before the Japanese invasion in early 1942, there was some armed resistance to Dutch colonial rule in the NETHERLANDS EAST INDIES. Once the Japanese were there, the Allies were eager to supply more weapons to anyone who would fight the Japanese. The Indonesians realized this, and in a masterful political move the resistance leaders agreed among themselves that some Indonesians would become "freedom fighters" and receive aid from the Allies for resisting the Japanese, while some would become "collaborators" and gain aid from the Japanese. When the Dutch returned after V-J Day, they found both "pro" and "anti" Japanese groups united and ready to fight for independence. These two groups had also equipped themselves with much of the weapons and equipment the Japanese had surrendered on the islands. After a short but bloody struggle, the Dutch gave in.

See also GUERRILLA WARS.

Inland Sea, Japan

A large (c. 240 miles by 10–40 miles), extremely scenic, very sheltered body of water in the Japanese

Home Islands, bounded by Kyushu and Shikoku on the south and southeast, and by Honshu on the north and northwest. A valuable source of seafood, it is navigable by the largest ships, and was a major highway for the numerous small vessels that made up an enormous part of the Japanese merchant marine. The largest port on the Inland Sea, KURE, was also a major naval base. The difficulty of entering the Inland Sea by submarine made it valuable as a base area for the Imperial Navy, at least until US subs developed ways to breech the Japanese minefields guarding the entrances to the Inland Sea.

Inouye, Shigeyoshi

Shigeyoshi Inouye was one of the more original thinkers among Japanese admirals. Graduated from the naval academy in 1909, he studied in Switzerland and France 1918–21, before returning to Japan for various school and staff assignments, leading to command of a battleship in the early '30s.

Inouye (sometimes spelled Inoue) became a rear admiral in 1936 and soon began speaking out on the need for Japan to get along with the other world powers and not put itself in a position of getting into a war it could not win. Inouye opposed the army's aggressive actions in China and was an enthusiastic supporter of carrier aviation. His opinions did not damage his career, as he became a vice admiral in 1939 and chief of naval aviation in 1940. At that point he addressed the potential war with America and correctly predicted the island-hopping STRATEGY the United States would eventually pursue. Inouye urged that carrier aviation be given more resources than battleship building but was ignored. He finally got into trouble for stating, in early 1941, that the Japanese fleet was not capable of defeating the US Navy. For this he was transferred to the command of the Fourth Fleet in the Central Pacific Mandates. This fleet was comprised of light cruisers and destroyers, but was active in the seizure of GUAM, WAKE ISLAND, and RABAUL. He was later in charge of the forces used in the abortive attempt to seize PORT MORESBY on the south coast of New Guinea. The resulting defeat in the Battle of the CORAL SEA led to his recall to Tokyo and command of the Naval College for the remainder of the war. Toward the end of the war he encouraged making peace. While not a great combat commander, he was an excellent administrator and quite intelligent. He was also an accomplished musician. Something of an intellectual in uniform, Inouye was typical of the several admirals who saw the world situation, and Japan's place in it, more clearly than the army generals who controlled the government.

Iowa Class, US Battleships

The ultimate manifestation of US battleship design, the Iowas were quite possibly the most powerful battleships ever built. Their new model 16–inch guns gave them a range only a few hundred yards less than that of the Japanese 18.1–inch gun, with virtually the same penetrability and a considerably higher rate of fire. That, coupled with radar fire control, much higher ship speed (33 knots to 27, about 20%) and greater maneuverability would have made them more than a match for an equal number of YAMATOs.

The fastest battleships ever built, the Iowas were the only battleships fast enough to accompany the fast carrier task forces when they put on all speed.

Interestingly, when built, their armor belt was described as 16 inches thick, although it was actually only 12 inches. The navy's armor specialists had come up with a better quality of plate, and a better system for armoring the ships, so that 12 inches under the new system theoretically gave the same degree of protection as 16 inches under the old. Rather than give venal—or merely ill-informed—politicians and journalists another weapon with which to bewail the incompetence of the fleet's leadership, the navy decided to announce that the ships had thicker armor than was actually the case.

Iowa, BB-61 (1940–1942–1943), had a rough first year of life, grounding once in July 1943 and then being almost hit by an accidentally fired "friendly" TORPEDO while carrying FDR to the Casablanca Conference later that year. She entered the Pacific in early 1944 and helped raid the MARSHALL ISLANDS (taking two Japanese 6-inch shells, which caused little damage and only minor injuries). The ship served with the fast carriers during all major operations, and was in Tokyo Bay for the surrender of Japan.

New Jersey, BB-62 (1940–1941–1942), began active service in the Pacific in early 1944, supporting the fast carriers, often as flagship to HALSEY. She fired antiaircraft barrages, shelled enemy-held islands, and conducted preliminary bombardments, while steaming 220,000 miles and downing 20 enemy aircraft.

Missouri, BB-63 (1941–1944–1944), was the last American battleship to be completed, her construction being delayed in favor of more pressing needs. She joined the fleet in the CAROLINE ISLANDS in early 1945, and supported operations against IWO JIMA, OKINAWA, and the Home Islands. In April 1945 she took one KAMIKAZE and one near-miss off Kyushu, with little damage. In September 1945 she was chosen to host the surrender of Japan, since she was named after President TRUMAN's home state.

Wisconsin, BB-64 (1941–1943–1944), joined the Pacific Fleet in December 1944 and took part in all subsequent operations until the surrender of Japan.

Two additional units were laid down in 1942, *Illinois* (BB-65) and *Kentucky* (BB-66). *Illinois* was scrapped on the ways when only 22% complete. *Kentucky* was launched in 1950 to clear the slipway, and was scrapped in 1959, when about 85% complete.

After the war the four ships spent a lot of time mothballed, being occasionally hauled out for various wars (Korea, Vietnam, the Persian Gulf). Since the introduction of ironclads no other battleship class has seen such long and active combat

USS Iowa (BB-61) at battle drill in the Pacific sometime during 1944, firing a salvo from B turret, in which there would be a major accident in 1989.

service, spanning nearly 50 years. With the return of the last of the class to reserve status in 1992, the era of the gun-armed ship of the line seemingly came to an end, after a run of over four centuries. Maybe. Various proposals have been advanced to preserve the ships as war memorials.

See also BATTLESHIPS, THE ULTIMATE BATTLE.

Iron Bottom Sound

A nickname for the channel running between GUADALCANAL and Florida Island in the SOLOMONS. Including its extension northwestward, it was sometimes called the "Slot." It was called "Iron

Bottom Sound" from the enormous number of ships and aircraft that went to the bottom during the struggle for Guadalcanal in 1942–43.

The first ship to pave the sound is indeterminate, but it was certainly British or Australian as Japanese aircraft sank several small vessels during their initial occupation of TULAGI in early May 1942. The first warship sunk in the sound was certainly Japanese. On May 4 US carrier aircraft sank several Japanese vessels off Tulagi, the largest of which was the MUTSUKI CLASS destroyer *Kikudsuki*. The first American ship to go down in Iron Bottom Sound was apparently the transport *George F. El-*

liot, struck by a damaged Japanese G4M BETTY bomber on August 8, 1942.

The larger warships on the bottom of Iron Bottom Sound can be readily tabulated.

Australia: heavy cruiser *Canberra*.

United States: heavy cruisers *Astoria*, *Quincy*, NORTHAMPTON, and *Vincennes*, antiaircraft cruisers ATLANTA and *Juneau*, and 10 destroyers.

Japan: battleships *Kirishima* and *Hiei*, heavy cruisers FURUTAKA and *Kinugasa*, eight destroyers, and seven SUBMARINES.

There were also numerous smaller warcraft, including destroyer-transports, a corvette (HMNZS *Moa*), patrol boats, PT-BOATS, and landing vessels, as well as numerous merchantships, coastal traders, motorized barges, and native craft.

Ise Class, Japanese Battleships

A somewhat improved version of the FUSO CLASS battleships, *Ise* (1915–1916–1917) and *Hyuga* (1915–1917–1918) saw little action in World War II. They provided distant support for naval forces in the Philippines and the NETHERLANDS EAST INDIES during the initial phase of the war, and with the Combined Fleet battleships for the First Air Fleet during the MIDWAY Campaign. After Midway they were taken in hand for conversion to battleship/aircraft carriers (the "A" and "B" on the BATTLESHIP TABLE give the particulars of the original and the rebuilt designs). The conversion tied up precious shipyard space and consumed valuable materials for nearly two years. The after pair of turrets were removed and replaced by a hangar deck and short flight deck with catapults, which permitted them to operate about 22 aircraft each. Actually, they were glorified seaplane tenders, as they could only launch aircraft, which then had to land on the sea, from whence they were recovered by cranes. In fact, no aircraft ever seems to have been allocated to either ship, and their only operational mission as battleship-carriers was as "bait" in the Northern Force during the Battle of LEYTE GULF.

They retired to Japanese home waters, and were both sunk by US carrier aircraft in KURE, *Hyuga* on July 24, 1945 and *Ise* on the 28th.

Itagaki, Seishiro (1885–1946)

Seishiro Itagaki joined the Japanese Army in 1904 and served in China during the 1930s. He was in command of forces defeated by the Soviets at Nomonhan. This sidetracked his career, and he spent most of the rest of the war commanding Japanese troops in Korea as a full general. In early 1945, he became commander of Japanese forces in MALAYA and surrounding areas and held that post until the end of the war. He was hanged as a war criminal.

Italy in the Pacific War

Like Germany, Italy conducted some operations in the Asiatic-Pacific Theater during the war. Five specially modified SUBMARINES (*Da Vinci*, *Cagni*, *Cappellini*, *Giuliani*, and *Torelli*) made several patrols in the Indian Ocean from an Italian naval base near Bordeaux, in France. Of these, *Da Vinci's* was particularly successful, sinking six ships for a total of nearly 60,000 GRT in a 120-day patrol that ended on 23 May 1943, when she was sunk off the Azores while returning to base. *Cagni* made two war patrols into the Indian Ocean, one of 137 days, with only modest success. She was only 19 days into her second patrol when Italy concluded an armistice with the Allies, and she turned herself in at Durban, South Africa.

Several Italian merchant ships in Eritrea when Italy entered World War II attempted to run the blockade through to Italy; they proved singularly ineffective, only one ship actually reaching Europe, by crossing the Indian Ocean and the Pacific, to enter the Atlantic. The colonial sloop *Eritrea*, a 2,200-ton gunboat armed more or less like a destroyer, escaped from Massawa, Eritrea, shortly before the British captured the port in 1940. In an impressive voyage she made her way across the British-controlled Indian Ocean, through the Dutch East Indies, and into the China Seas in order to intern herself in Japan. In 1942, as part of Japan's agreement to allow Italian submarines basing rights in Sumatra, she was transferred to SABANG to serve as a floating headquarters. When the Italian armistice was concluded, *Eritrea* slipped out of port, eluded the Japanese and the British, to turn herself in at Colombo, in CEYLON.

A number of Italian surface ships and submarines operated as BLOCKADE RUNNERS during the war, carrying cargo between the Far East and European ports. By the spring of 1943 Italy began converting several long-range submarines (*Tazzoli, Cappellini, Giuliani, Bognolini, Finzi, Barbarigo,* and *Torelli*) into blockade runners, in a cooperative venture with the German Navy. Although these could carry only about 100–190 tons of cargo, they had several advantages over the surface ships. Their small size when on the surface, and their ability to avoid detection by submerging, made them more stealthy than surface vessels. They were also actually faster, able to sustain relatively high surface speeds of 12–15 knots when most merchant ships were making 8–10 knots. Two of the blockade-running submarines (*Barbarigo* and *Tazzoli*) were lost, en route. Three (*Cappellini, Giuliani,* and *Torelli*) made it to Sabang, in INDONESIA, after voyages of about 60 days each. There they rendezvoused with the sloop *Eritrea*. They were preparing for their return voyages at the time of the armistice. They were taken over by the Japanese, who turned two of them over to the Germans. Two boats still at Bordeaux when the Italian armistice was concluded were taken over by the Germans.

See: GERMANY IN THE PACIFIC WAR.

Ito, Seiichi (1890–1945)

Seiichi Ito entered the Japanese naval academy in 1908, and later attended Yale, graduating in the 1920s. A vice admiral by 1941, he served on the Navy Staff for most of the war. Appointed commander of the Second Fleet in late 1944, Ito sailed with the superbattleship YAMATO on its death ride in April 1945 and went down with the ship on April 6.

Iwo Jima, Battle of

Iwo Jima is a desolate place, with low-level volcanic activity producing noxious gases and a generally unpleasant atmosphere. One of the VOLCANO ISLANDS, the place literally reeked of sulfur. Iwo Jima had no harbor and not even a secure anchorage. It was, however, only 660 miles south of Tokyo and, despite its eight square miles, was capable of supporting several airfields. By early 1945 the island was heavily garrisoned and fortified by the Japanese, and had two complete airstrips with another building. This is what made Iwo Jima important. The Japanese were using Iwo to base fighters to attack the B-29s that had to pass by on their way north to bomb Japanese cities.

US bombers destroyed the Japanese airfields, but the island still harbored observers with radios who alerted Japan when B-29s passed over. Taking Iwo Jima would do more than eliminate a Japanese air base and air defense early warning station. The MARIANAS bases used by the B-29s were too far away from their Japanese targets for fighter escorts to accompany the bombers the entire distance. With fighter escorts, B-29 losses would be much lower. Moreover, the B-29 was still having trouble with its large, powerful cutting-edge engines. Many a B-29 developed engine trouble over Japan and could not make it all the way back to base. The same thing happened with aircraft that suffered battle damage. Thousands of lives could be saved if Iwo Jima were an American base. Lastly, the island would have to be taken anyway if the United States had to proceed with the invasion of Japan later in 1945. So the decision was made to invade Iwo Jima in early 1945.

The Japanese had been rushing troops and material to Iwo Jima since late 1944. They also activated the 109th Infantry Division there, as the core of the island's defense forces. By February, the island's garrison was 22,000 men and the place was filled with underground bunkers and fortifications. All civilians had been evacuated.

On February 19, 1945, the Third, Fourth, and Fifth Marine Divisions attacked Iwo Jima. A third

As leathernecks of the Fifth Marine Division form a firing line on the crest of a sandy slope above Beach Red 1, Iwo Jima, February 19, 1945, other Marines, on the extreme left of the beachhead, prepare to move up behind them. The fine volcanic sand made movement difficult, complicating the business of coping with the extensive and well sited Japanese defenses. Note the casualties among the men in the foreground.

of the invading American troops were killed or wounded (23,000 troops) in five weeks of fighting to secure the island. At first it was thought that only four days would be needed to take the Iwo. But the Japanese had learned from earlier encounters with American amphibious assaults and were determined to kill as many soldiers, sailors, and Marines as they could.

Thirty thousand US troops were put ashore on the first day, at a cost of 560 dead. Unlike previous island battles, the Japanese held most of their fire until the troops were ashore, and did not make any suicidal infantry assaults. The Japanese were carefully dug into the sides of hills and mountains, wait-

ing for Marines to walk into their gunsights. Bad as it was, the American losses could have been worse. What kept the American casualty rate down was the plentiful use of firepower at all stages of the protracted battle for the island. During daylight hours, each Marine infantry battalion had the exclusive use of the 5-inch guns from one or two destroyers, five to a dozen 127mm guns. The firepower from bigger ships (cruisers and battleships) was allocated as needed. At night, the larger ships would also pound previously selected targets in preparation for a Marine advance the next day. Hundreds of bombers were also available. In all, it was the fiercest battle of the Pacific War. The Japanese would not surrender, the Americans would not stop. By 16 March 1945, the United States declared Iwo Jima "secure." On March 26 the Iwo Jima operation was declared "completed." This was cutting it rather fine, as just before dawn on March 26, 350 Japanese troops tried to overrun an Army Air Force camp. Fierce fighting ensued. All the Japanese were killed, along with 53 Americans (plus another 119 wounded).

During the battle, Marines accounted for 20,703 Japanese killed. Another 216 Japanese troops were taken prisoner, many of them while wounded and unconscious. Resistance continued on the island for many months thereafter. At first, at the end of March, the Marines estimated there were no more than 300 Japanese left alive on the island. But during April and May the army troops who relieved the Marines, killed a further 1,602 Japanese troops and took 867 prisoner; and Japanese hold-outs kept turning up long after the war ended.

While the Japanese were wiped out, the US Marines suffered exceptional, by American standards, CASUALTIES. The entire landing force suffered 30% killed, wounded, and missing. For the six infantry regiments of the Fourth and Fifth Marine Divisions, the casualty rate was 75%. The navy also suffered 880 dead and 1,917 wounded. The KAMI-KAZE were active during the Iwo Jima assault. Be-

The wreckage of war litters the beach on Iwo Jima, with the base of Mount Suribachi looming in the background. The site appears to be Beach Red, the Fifth Marine Division beach, sometime in late February 1945. Note that the troops visible seem to be engaged in salvage operations.

Six men of the 28th Marines, Fifth Marine Division, raise the Stars and Stripes on the summit of Mount Suribachi, Iwo Jima, c. 1230 hours, February 23, 1945. Shown in Associated Press photographer Joe Rosenthal's famous picture are Cpl. Charles Block, the man at the base; Pharmacist's Mate John Bradley (USN), partially hidden by Cpl. René Gagnon; PFC Franklin Sousley, partially obscured by Sgt. Michael Strank; and Cpl. Ira Hayes, the last man to the left.

cause the attacking aircraft had to fly in over open water, the attacks were not as devastating as those in the Philippines. Several ships were hit, but the only significant damage was to one CV and to a CVE that sank.

The battle had one bright moment, and it was caught in a photograph. The ultimate image of American courage, power, and triumph in World War II is certainly Associated Press photographer Joe Rosenthal's shot of five Marines and a Navy Medical Corpsman raising Old Glory atop Iwo Jima's Mount Suribachi on February 23, 1945. This was actually the second flag raising that morning.

On the fourth day of the battle for Iwo Jima, the 28th Marines were pressing the Japanese defenses at the base on the eastern side of Mount Suribachi, a 550–foot volcanic cone that dominated the largely low-lying island. At about 0800 hours on 23 February 1944 the commander of the Second Battalion, LTC Chandler Johnson, pointed out a path located by scouts, to Ernest Thomas, platoon sergeant of the Third Platoon, E Company, 28th Marines. Ordering Thomas to tell platoon commander 1Lt Harold G. Schrier to take his platoon up the trail, Johnson handed him the battalion's 54–by–24-inch national color, and told him to raise it at the top. Schrier immediately set out with 40 men, who were accompanied by Marine photographer Louis Lowery. At about 1020 hours, Schrier and his men reached the summit of Mount Suribachi, after an arduous climb but little fighting, the Japanese not having fortified the slopes. A brief, hot firefight developed at the summit until the handful of Japanese troops holding the crater were wiped out. As they searched Japanese positions, two of the Marines found a 10-foot-long piece of pipe and fastened the flag to it. At about 1035, as the other members of the platoon stood guard, the flag was raised at the highest point on the summit, by 1Lt Harold G. Schrier, Sergeants Thomas and Henry O. Hansen, and Corporal Charles W. Lindberg, while Lowery took a picture.

Meanwhile, lower down the slope, Lieutenant Colonel Johnson spotted the flag. Realizing that it was too small to be seen from very far, and wanting to make sure that it stayed with the regiment rather than ended up as a souvenir for some senior officer, he dispatched an officer to secure a larger one from a nearby LST. The officer returned with a larger flag, the 96-by-50-inch battle ensign of *LST-779*. Johnson sent this up the mountain, with orders to raise it at the summit, and to bring the original flag back. A few minutes later photographers Robert Campbell, of the Marines, and Joseph Rosenthal, of the Associated Press, began to ascend the mountain, accompanied by Marine cameraman William Genaust. As the three climbed, they encountered Marine photographer Lowery coming down, who chided them for missing the flag raising.

As the three men reached the summit at about 1230, they found that the Marines were fastening the larger flag to another piece of pipe, about 20 feet long. As the three got into position to take pictures, Rosenthal, who was standing some 35 feet from the Marines readying the pipe, glanced around at the panoramic view of the battle. Suddenly, Genaust called out "Joe." Rosenthal turned, and there were six Marines already in the process of raising the flag. Rosenthal instantly snapped a picture, while Genaust's camera whirled away.

Meanwhile, Campbell took a photograph as several Marines lowered the original flag.

The large flag flying from the summit of Mount Suribachi could easily been seen, and almost as soon as it went up Marines on the ground below began cheering, while ships and landing craft sounded off with horns and whistles.

Rosenthal's photograph of the six Marines (Cpl. Charles Block, the man at the base; Navy Pharmacist's Mate John Bradley; Cpl. René Gagnon; PFC Franklin Sousley; Sgt. Michael Strank; and Cpl. Ira Hayes, the last man to the left) quickly became an inspiration to the nation, and a potent symbol of Marine courage and determination.

In the early 1990s, it was claimed that the second flag raising on Mount Suribachi was deliberately staged as a "photo opportunity" by the Marine brass, to garner more prestige for the Corps, and ultimately a bigger share of the postwar budget.

In fact, the entire affair was unplanned. Both flag raisings were prompted by LTC Chandler Johnson, the man on the spot, who was killed several days later, as were several of the other men involved (Thomas, Hansen, Block, Strank, Sousley, and Genaust). All standard histories of the battle—including the official Marine Corps and navy accounts—mention the circumstances of the flag raisings. Both flags are prominently displayed in the Marine Corps Museum, in Washington, D.C., with an explanation of the circumstances (and photographs) of both events, and Genaust's film of the second flag raising may be viewed on request.

Interestingly, perpetrators of this conspiratorial interpretation of the events failed to consult any of the surviving participants or witnesses to the two flag raisings, among whom is Joe Rosenthal himself. Although Rosenthal and the other men involved were very forthcoming when the tale that the events had been staged was circulated, their numerous letters to newspapers and magazines seem not to have made much of an impression. As a result, the story that the flag raising was staged "long after" the island was secured has received considerable circulation.

During the preparations for the invasion of Iwo Jima, where it was known that there were no civilians, the subject of using chemical weapons came up. On consideration, it was decided that the possible savings in American lives was not worth the bad press that was sure to result, which in this instance remains a highly debatable point.

Ref: Albee and Freeman, *Shadow of Suribachi.*

J

J2M Jack, Japanese Fighter

The J2M Jack was a new Japanese design that flew for the first time in early 1942. Called the *Raiden* (Thunderbolt) by the Japanese, this was to be a more powerful land-based interceptor. The beginning of the war threw Japanese aircraft production into turmoil, and it was believed to be more efficient to turn out more of the older designs than to expend the resources to switch to more modern designs. In any event, the J2M was nimble, fast (370 MPH), and well armed (two machine guns and two 20mm cannon). It also had a lot of problems getting a reliable engine. Fewer than 500 were produced.

See also AIRCRAFT TYPES, DEVELOPMENT.

J8M Shusui, Japanese Fighter

The J8M Shusui ("Sword Stroke") was a Japanese copy of the German Me 163 Komet, a crude, rocket-powered, short-range interceptor. The Germans were unable to do much with the Me 163 design in combat and the Japanese were able to do even less. The Germans sent plans and component samples to Japan in 1943. However, one of the two cargo SUBMARINES involved in this effort sank en route. The J8M got only as far as the prototype stage, with the engine still being perfected when the war ended. The liquid fuel rocket engine could run for only five to six minutes, producing a top speed of 560 MPH. But since the J8M could climb to 30,000 feet in less than four minutes, the aircraft had time to make a pass at a B-29 formation. Armed with two 30mm cannon, the J8M could inflict damage. After its fuel was spent, the aircraft became a glider and landed in that mode. The concept was viable and the J8M could have turned into a formidable interceptor, or KAMIKAZE.

See also AIRCRAFT TYPES, DEVELOPMENT.

Jacob van Heemskerck, Netherlands Antiaircraft Cruiser

Designed by the Royal Netherlands Navy as a sister ship to *Tromp, Van Heemskerck* (1937–1939–1941) was intended to be a very small, very fast light cruiser (really an enlarged flotilla leader) for service in the East Indies. Fitting out in the Netherlands when the Nazis invaded, both ships were towed to England and completed there. *Tromp* (1935–1937–1940), much further along in construction, was completed to the original design and saw extensive service in the Atlantic. *Van Heemskerck*, having only recently been launched when the Germans arrived, was completed as an antiaircraft cruiser. She saw considerable service with the British Far Eastern Fleet in the Indian Ocean. In company with the old Australian cruiser ADELAIDE, she intercepted a German BLOCKADE RUNNER in the Indian Ocean on 26 November 1942. Her abilities as an antiaircraft cruiser were never tested. She was scrapped in the late 1950s, although portions of the ship were preserved in the national war memorial.

See also ROYAL NAVY.

Japan

On the eve of World War II Japan had about 73 million people, 100 million if Korea and Formosa were included. The Home Islands had a land area of only about 375,000 square kilometers, slightly smaller than California.

The Home Islands are resource poor, rugged, and prone to earthquakes. This was one reason for Japan's rapid embrace of a policy of expansion after it had been "opened" in the 1850s.

Japan was a complex mixture of the traditional and the modern. Essentially an agricultural, feudal society in the mid-19th century, the country had modernized in some sectors with remarkable speed and efficiency, while remaining substantially unchanged in others, notably in the virtually religious veneration of the emperor, respect for hierarchy, and obedience to orders.

Although the Meiji Constitution created a centralized, authoritarian regime, the country had made considerable progress toward a democratic society by the mid-1920s. The accession of HIRO-HITO, however, coincided with the rise of fascistic national sentiments in some segments of society, most notably in the army, which proceeded to indulge in a series of assassinations of those whom it considered opponents. By the early 1930s the army was effectively beyond the control of the civil authorities, and even of military leaders opposed to its more extreme elements. By 1941 the extremists were in control of the government.

Japan, Attitude Toward the Enemy

The Japanese attitude toward the enemy was peculiar in many ways. While the Japanese would admire foes who fought fanatically, they would also treat with utmost cruelty enemy troops who surrendered rather than fight on and kill more Japanese troops.

Japanese officers and soldiers were perfectly willing to admire the enemy's ferocity in battle and devotion unto death. Several anecdotes illustrate this very well.

On August 17, 1937, at the beginning of the CHINA INCIDENT, 44 Chinese aircraft undertook a bombing raid against Japanese forces near SHANG-HAI. During the raid, one Chinese airplane was shot down by antiaircraft fire, and its pilot, Yen Hai-wen, bailed out. He landed behind Japanese lines. As Japanese troops closed in on him, Yen drew his pistol, killed several of his would-be captors, and then committed suicide. The Japanese deemed him so brave that his heroism was reported in newspapers in the Home Islands, and he was buried with the honors of war, beneath a monument that read "Tomb of a Gallant Chinese Air Warrior."

Just two days after Yen's heroic shoot-out with Japanese troops, another Chinese pilot, Shen Chung-hui, crashed his airplane into a Japanese ship off the China coast. Although the incident may well have been an accident, since Shen's plane had been hit by antiaircraft fire, many Japanese believed it was a deliberate act, and expressed admiration for his dedication.

At about 2320 hours on the night of February 28, 1942 the heavy cruiser USS *Houston* and light cruiser HMAS PERTH ran into superior Japanese forces off JAVA. The two vessels put up a tough fight. At 0005 on March 1, *Perth*, already hit several times, took a TORPEDO, then another, and went down. Already damaged from previous encounters with the Japanese, *Houston* had been absorbing enemy fire for some time, and was by then listing seriously. Still she fought on. At about 0010 hours she was hit hard in the engine room, then she took a torpedo, then more shells, some of which started fires. Then three more torpedoes tore into her. Still she kept firing. But she was in sinking condition, and at 0033 the word was passed to abandon ship. Within minutes, her battle ensign still streaming, the ship rolled over and plunged beneath the waves, with some holdout crewmen still firing at the enemy. The Japanese squadron, two heavy cruisers and several destroyers, formed line ahead, passed by the spot where she had gone down, and their skippers saluted her for a gallant foe.

During the final phase of the Battle of MIDWAY, Marine Capt. Richard E. Fleming (1917–42) made a glide bomb attack on the heavy cruiser *Mikuma*. He pressed the attack so desperately that when he was hit by antiaircraft fire, his Vindicator bomber crashed into one of the ship's turrets. Although the incident was probably an accident, it was taken as an example of heroic self-sacrifice by the Japanese, one of whom remarked "He was very brave," a conclusion in which the US Navy concurred, awarding him a MEDAL OF HONOR.

These incidents certainly demonstrate a considerable degree of admiration for the enemy's courage. But that admiration had its limits. It stopped when the fighting stopped. During their battle with *Houston* and *Perth* the Japanese repeatedly machine-gunned survivors in the water, and, having saluted the sunken *Houston*, the Japanese ships steamed away, leaving hundreds of survivors to drown, although in the end some were rescued. And had Yen, Shen, or Fleming been captured, they would almost certainly have been shot out of hand, after being pumped for information, or even tortured, as happened to numerous Allied airmen who fell into Japanese hands.

Japanese admiration after battle extended only to the heroic dead. PRISONERS OF WAR, even badly wounded men, were considered dishonorable, a major factor in the neglect of, and often outright brutality toward, them.

These Japanese attitudes were somewhat unique to World War II. In Japan's war with the Russians (1904–05) their attitude was much more like that of the European powers, and their treatment of prisoners of war was favorably commented upon. In the process of taking over the government in the 1920s and 1930s, the Japanese militarists instilled a much more fanatical attitude toward any enemy of Japan. While Japanese troops had long been quite determined in battle, the callous regard for enemy prisoners and civilians was of recent vintage. The implied blood lust the militarists preached was a minority attitude in Japanese culture, one that was made large by the need to encourage a warlike attitude among the general population. It worked, but it disappeared as quickly as it arrived once the war was over.

Japan, Attitude Toward Warfare

Before the Pacific War began, Western nations had adopted a rather superior attitude toward the capabilities of the Japanese armed forces. While this is often blamed on racism, there were numerous historical reasons for such a perspective. For one thing, the combat experience of Japanese forces through the late 1930s had not indicated that the Japanese were capable of extraordinary battlefield performance. Western military observers had witnessed Japanese troops in action during the Sino-Japanese War (1895–96) and the Russo-Japanese War (1904–05), and against German forces at Tsing-tao, in China, in 1914. The Japanese had exhibited suicidal bravery and a lack of tactical competence. Although the Japanese won these wars, the consensus in the West was that victory was more the result of enemy ineptitude or inferior numbers than Japanese excellence.

Few Western observers bothered to look closely at exactly how the Japanese military operated. After all, every Asian army Western troops had faced in more than a century had exhibited considerable ineptitude. Despite the fact that the Japanese were more diligent in following the instruction of their Western (mainly French and German) military advisers, the general attitude was that the result was just another mediocre army. There were Western military attachés in Japan during the 1930s who did note the skill possessed by Japanese troops. But their reports formed a distinctly minority opinion back home.

The Japanese saw little combat during World War I, and the Western nations felt that their own massive dose of combat experience simply increased the qualitative difference between Western and Japanese armed forces. When the Japanese became heavily involved fighting the Chinese during the 1930s, many Western observers explained away Japanese success by noting the very poor quality of Chinese troops.

The Japanese Navy was held in somewhat higher esteem, but it was still thought that Western ships would prove superior. The Japanese had been building all their own ships since the eve of World War I, and there had been no chance to see how these vessels would perform in combat. It was assumed that the Japanese would not soon overcome several centuries of Western experience in designing and using warships.

Combat aircraft were still relatively new, and it wasn't until World War II began that it became clear what air power could do. The Japanese had quickly adopted military aircraft before World War I (1914–18) and had begun to design and build their own during the 1920s. The resulting aircraft were quite different than those built in the West. This led foreign observers to believe that the Japanese had simply made inept copies of Western designs.

The Japanese also fought and lost a series of division-size battles with the Soviets in 1939, before war broke out in Europe. The details of these battles were not widely known in the West, but some word did get out. To many Western officers who heard of these battles in MANCHURIA, it simply confirmed what they already believed.

Overall, it was thought that the Japanese armed forces could not long withstand combat with Western troops and equipment. This attitude was quite wrong, as the events of December 1941 were to demonstrate. In fact, the Japanese armed forces were quite effective. Each of the historical examples Westerners used to downgrade the Japanese had to be hastily revisited and revised once the Japanese entered the war.

The first four months in the Pacific War were an endless string of dramatic Japanese victories. How did they do it with what were thought to be second-rate troops and equipment? Quite simply, the Japanese adapted techniques and equipment from other nations and applied them in a typically Japanese fashion. Always a nation apart, the Japanese had developed a collection of traits that they still possess. Disciplined, diligent, fearless, and convinced of their innate superiority, the Japanese spent the early part of the 20th century

building armed forces that looked Western but were uniquely Japanese. The key elements of this force, and why each was misinterpreted, were as follows.

Highly disciplined and well trained troops.

Westerners were accustomed to seeing Asian troops whipped into shape and made at least to appear disciplined and battle ready. But it had been noted that these troops usually performed well in combat only if they had Western officers (and often Western NCOs as well). It was felt that Asian armies were unable to provide effective training for their soldiers. This, until the Japanese were encountered, proved to be the case most of the time.

The Japanese troops were well disciplined. This was a Japanese characteristic. The normal discipline of Japanese civilians was even more pronounced in their armed forces. And the Japanese were also well trained. The problem, for Westerners, was the difficulty of telling how effective training is before troops go into combat. For the Western troops that had to face the Japanese in combat during the early months of the war, this was too late.

Japan managed to get a lot of combat experience out of World War I without doing a lot of fighting. Japanese officers were present at the front during World War I and they took notes. What they grasped was what the Germans invented, and everyone called, *blitzkrieg*. The Japanese version, called *den giki sen* (i.e., blitzkrieg), involved careful planning, fast movement, and vigorous attacks, when you must attack, and, above all, breaking the enemy's will to fight. This was consistent with the traditional Japanese approach to warfare.

In effect, the Japanese practiced blitzkrieg without the TANKS. This was not so much because the Japanese didn't believe in tanks, but because they often operated in areas that tanks could not operate in, against opponents for whom tanks would be overkill. Moreover, the relatively weak Japanese economy could neither build not support many tanks. Or, put another way, the Japanese adopted the quite successful "shock troop" infantry tactics the Germans developed in the last years of World War I. They added naval support and extensive use of aircraft, in effect, all the elements of blitzkrieg except the tanks.

The Japanese had also adopted the Western approach to training officers, and added a few uniquely Japanese elements. Their officer cadet schools were much harsher than anything in the West and were dedicated to turning out leaders who personified the stern traditions of the ancient samurai warrior. These officers were indoctrinated with the idea that spirit was superior to material matters. At the same time, these officers were thoroughly professional and fearless leaders. Their training was so Spartan that they regularly endured, and accepted, a poor diet. As a result, the officers were often smaller than their troops. Small, but tough.

Training, as most Western officers knew, is not very visible off the battlefield. But they assumed that Japanese troops were not very good troops, if only because they did not look very "smart" on the parade ground and frequently wore ill-fitting uniforms. In fact, the Japanese were drilled and instructed on how to be very effective in combat, rather than on the parade ground. Learning from past experience, they performed much of their training at night. This was a very modern attitude, but, as the Japanese had long observed, the night attack was the most likely to achieve surprise. Training was also conducted under very realistic, and dangerous, conditions. This better prepared the troops for combat, and, because of the Japanese attitude toward death, lethal training accidents did not cause any commotion as they would in the West. Japanese soldiers, sailors, and airmen were all much better trained, disciplined, and mentally prepared for combat than their Western counterparts. The shock of discovering this was played out in the spectacular Japanese victories in the first six months of the war.

Effective use of air power.   The Japanese built all their own aircraft after World War I, and they developed designs that reflected their own attitudes toward warfare. Key among these traits was the primacy of the offense. Attack was everything and defense was a bothersome, but sometimes necessary, detail. Thus their aircraft stressed offensive performance at the expense of protection. Japanese fighters were more nimble, carried heavier armament, and had a longer range than their Western counterparts. Their bombers had heavier bombloads and longer range. But both fighters and bombers were more prone to explode into flames if they were hit. Lacking armor and self-sealing fuel tanks, Japanese aircraft were lighter, but they were quickly put out of action if hit. Western pilots soon noted this and, by the end of 1942, were able to take advantage of it.

But this was not much help during the first six months of the war. The Japanese also had a very elitist attitude toward pilot selection and training. Their pilots were probably the most capable in the world when they entered combat. Thus, when the war began, Japanese fighters were able to sweep enemy fighters from the sky, while their bombers came in and hit targets with an accuracy unknown in the West. As the Germans discovered with their own blitzkrieg, air superiority not only added to combat power but also went far to demoralize the enemy troops.

While the highly capable Japanese air forces (army and navy) were initially a shock for their opponents, the Allies promptly learned to adapt. Moreover, the Allies (particularly the United States) had the ability to produce far more aircraft than the Japanese. By 1943, Japanese air power was no longer superior, but Allied air superiority was not as decisive as it had been for the Japanese earlier in the war. During 1941–42, Japan's foes were disorganized and not well prepared to fight. Air superiority then allowed Japan's capable forces to rapidly seize millions of square miles of land and sea. However, once the Allies secured air superiority, they found that controlling the air did little to unnerve Japan's do or die troops on the ground. Air power helped, but it never caused many Japanese defenders to give up without a fight.

Surprise. As the Japanese had demonstrated throughout their history, they believed wars were best begun with surprise attacks. This they had done during their wars with China in 1894, Russia in 1904, and China again in 1931. PEARL HARBOR was not the only swift, unexpected attack the Japanese carried out in the first weeks of the war. Their use of long-range, hard-hitting aircraft contributed considerably to the effect of surprise.

While surprise was an asset for the Japanese early in the war, it became a liability later on. Their desire to achieve surprise, coupled with their belief that the "spirit" of their soldiers could overcome material shortages, led to hastily organized and unsuccessful operations later on. Moreover, America had a technological edge that made surprise even more difficult to achieve. One American specialty was radar, which actually spotted the Pearl Harbor air strike coming in—but no one in charge believed it. All were believers after that. By 1943, all American task forces had several radar-equipped ships, which made it nearly impossible for Japanese aircraft to achieve surprise. The Allies also learned to break Japan's radio codes and thereby destroy Japanese hope of achieving surprise. This was particularly important because the Japanese never seriously suspected that their codes were being read by the enemy. Thus surprise was a one-time advantage for Japan, and repeated surprise attempts later in the war only gave aid and comfort to the enemy.

The American preference, and capability, for using massive amounts of firepower on the battlefield—coupled with the best communications systems any World War II armed force fielded—found the Japanese running into a hail of shells and bombs soon after one of their surprise attacks was launched. December 1941 was the high point for Japanese surprise attacks. After that, it was the Japanese who were being brought up short by events they didn't expect.

Not Afraid to Die. Or, as the Japanese put it, "To die for the Emperor Is to Live Forever."

This trait is something all generals wish their troops possessed. A soldier that has resigned himself to death is far more clearheaded in combat. But usually, the bulk of the troops have no desire whatsoever to die. Fear of death tends to be paralyzing and, ironically, makes it more likely that one will be killed. The Japanese armed forces were unique in that most of the troops were quite accepting of the fact that they were going to die. Japanese generals tended to see that their troops did just that if those deaths would win a battle. This was part of the Japanese attitude toward war. Part of a Japanese soldier's training was constant reminders about his new relationship with death.

Until they obtained some experience fighting Japanese troops, Western officers thought many Japanese soldiers were simply quite brave. It was a chilling experience when Allied soldiers realized they were facing a foe that, almost to a man, did not fear death. Throughout the war, the Japanese used this fear to good advantage, and the Allies had to adjust their tactics to deal with it. For one thing, there was no such thing as scaring Japanese troops into surrendering. With few exceptions, Japanese troops did not surrender. It was, quite literally, death before dishonor, as the Japanese saw defeat as the ultimate disgrace. The Japanese had, over the centuries, developed a large repertoire of ways to kill oneself in combat. So it was a matter not only of accepting the fact that one could get killed in combat, but also of contemplating the numerous ways one could accelerate the process in order to do the most damage to the enemy. The recognized methods ranged from looking for a way to kill as many enemy troops as possible, getting in one last shot after you have been wounded, or doing yourself in because you have been defeated and all that remains is to atone for your failure. While suicide was not considered a goal for all soldiers, it was accepted as an inevitable event in certain circumstances. Allied troops soon saw ample evidence that the Japanese view toward suicide was different than anything they had known before.

But there was, from the Japanese point of view, a dark side to all this. Their dependence on thoroughly trained and properly indoctrinated troops meant that replacements could not be had quickly. Their pilot training, in particular, was never up to the needs of prolonged war losses. Japanese pilots, while highly skilled, were often enthusiastic to the point of ramming enemy aircraft if they found themselves out of ammunition. While this was admirable from the pilots' point of view, it took years to train replacements, and Japan soon ran out of skilled pilots. The pilot attrition situation was made worse by the lack of protection in their aircraft. There were also heavy aircraft losses, but aircraft were easier to replace. By 1943 Japan had lost air superiority to better Allied pilots flying better designed aircraft built by the more numerous Western factories.

On the ground, the steady loss of infantry units was less of a problem because the Japanese plan always intended that their offensives would stop after six months or so. Then the Japanese would dig in and inflict such losses on the attacking Americans that a peace could be negotiated. The negotiated peace never came, but the American infantry and the prodigious output of US arms factories did. The Americans found ways to accommodate the Japanese soldiers' willingness to die. Many Japanese garrisons were simply bypassed. When Japanese troops had to be fought, firepower was used as much as possible. American losses were still heavier than if they had been fighting an opponent who would surrender when the situation was hopeless. But once the Japanese attitudes were confirmed, tactics were modified to minimize US losses and accommodate the Japanese desire to die rather than surrender. The Japanese were not relentlessly suicidal. They would withdraw their forces if that was possible and they felt that they had no chance of accomplishing anything useful. They successfully withdrew their defeated forces from GUADALCANAL and the ALEUTIANS. But when they were cornered, and withdrawal was not possible, the typical Japanese reaction was to make one last attack and sell their lives dearly. This was the fierce BANZAI attack that Allied troops came

to expect when the battle seemed to be just about over.

While the Japanese were not devoted to self-destruction, they did have a cavalier attitude toward the non-spiritual aspects of soldiering. While the troops often had excellent attitudes and high morale, they just as frequently had no ammunition and were starving. This was first noted on Guadalcanal. Here, American aircraft and warships made it difficult for the Japanese to supply their troops. More troops died from starvation and lack of medical care than from enemy action. The troops died without complaint and surrender was never considered an option. In addition to being the first battle of the American counteroffensive in the Pacific, Guadalcanal was also the most lopsided battle in terms of losses. There were 1,600 American dead on the island, and some 21,000 Japanese. This was largely a result of the length of the battle (six months) and the inability of the Japanese to supply their troops.

A Western commander in the same situation would never have let the battle go on so long. This was not the only battle where a Japanese commander deliberately allowed his troops to keep going unto certain death. The fighting in Burma included several operations where Japanese generals sent their troops to certain death from starvation and disease on the slim chance of victory.

Japanese attitudes toward death influenced their treatment of enemy soldiers and civilians. In general, the troops treated PRISONERS and civilians callously. Prisoners were despised for having done what Japanese soldiers would not think of doing—surrendering. Civilians were abused simply because they were foreigners. Summary executions of prisoners and enemy civilians were common, rape was generally unpunished, as were looting and other forms of misbehavior. Japanese military physicians would practice their surgical skills on enemy civilians and POWs. The victims were usually not given any painkillers and were killed after the procedures were completed. While most of the surgery practice was done on Chinese, Western POWs were sometimes used. The most gruesome operations involved the development and use of biological weapons against the Chinese. These biological devices were created in Manchuria by a special unit given the innocuous name "Detachment 731." In addition to developing a (bubonic) plague bomb, Detachment 731 conducted sundry forms of "medical research" on Chinese and Western prisoners.

The plague bomb never really worked. The basic idea was to spread the plague (the medieval "Black Death") in Chinese-held territory. The first field experiments were conducted in 1940. No discernible effect was noted. The weapon itself was an aircraft bomb containing plague-infected fleas instead of explosives. In 1942, the fleas were released near the front to halt the advance of Chinese troops. Again, there was no particular impact on the Chinese. This may have been due to the fact that the plague was endemic in China and that there were other diseases going around at the same time. Moreover, the fleas could not survive long without a host (usually a rodent). Even attempts to spread the plague by releasing flea infested rats had no effect. The 3,000 members of Detachment 731 and its four sub-detachments did manage to kill several thousand people with their medical experiments. These included "experimental surgery" and equally grim procedures performed in the name of "medical research." Perhaps the only practical effect of Detachment 731 was letting prisoners and captives held for interrogation know that if they didn't cooperate, they would be sent to Detachment 731 for "processing." The word got around China during the war that the detachment existed and that being sent there was worse than any of the more mundane ATROCITIES the Japanese committed on their victims.

Not all of these atrocities were officially condoned, but neither was there strong direction from the top against such beastly behavior. Many prisoners, especially Westerners, were treated according to the accepted (GENEVA CONVENTION) rules of war. Because prisoners were to be fed on the same scale as captors' troops, this left the generally larger Western soldiers quite starved on the Japanese soldier's skimpy rations. But prisoners were still brutalized and forced (despite Geneva Convention prohibitions) to work on war-related projects.

Like their Nazi allies, the Japanese used their fearsome reputation for brutality and atrocity, and their own disdain for death, as another weapon. It was not a decisive weapon, but it helped their cause and gave them one more reason not to improve their treatment of foreigners.

The Japanese war criminals were not rounded up and punished to the extent that the German ones were. Part of this was due to the fact that many of the countries the Japanese operated in promptly erupted in civil war and rebellion after World War II ended. In the chaos this created, many Japanese war criminals were able to cover their tracks and make their escape. There were other reasons, but the fact remains that many Japanese atrocities went unpunished.

Speed. The Japanese knew that if they could move faster than their opponents, they could control the action and more easily win the battle. When they were able to use their fleet, and had air superiority, their non-mechanized infantry could move along quite swiftly. One thing many Western officers didn't realize was that infantry forces could move as rapidly as mechanized forces if the opposition was cleared away by bombers or warships. The Japanese were also quite adept at impromptu amphibious operations. Their infantry units could get on and off the ships quickly, and sea movement was several times faster than going overland in trucks and armored vehicles. This combination was the key to their lightning conquest of the Pacific islands early in the Pacific War.

Speed, however, rarely worked for the Japanese when they did not have time to plan their operations carefully. After 1942, the Allies had the initiative and all the Japanese could do was react to the increasing number of Allied offensives. Under these conditions the Japanese still tried to operate quickly, but now their haste merely yielded sloppiness and errors the enemy was quick to take advantage of. But the Japanese changed their style of warfare slowly and their changes came too late.

For the first six months of the war, the skill, speed, and surprise tactics of Japanese troops carried all before them in the Pacific. The Japanese were not supermen, nor did they have any spectacular new weapons. They simply did what they did very well and, most importantly, did it much better than their opponents expected.

In a final irony, those Japanese who were taken prisoner (often while disabled by wounds) responded by talking freely. Japanese soldiers were not given any instruction on how to behave as prisoners because it was unthinkable that one would be taken alive. Of course, Japanese officers knew that there was a possibility that some of their troops would be taken alive while they were incapacitated by wounds. But it was felt best to ignore any possibility of surrender and to not discuss it under any circumstances. This proved to be an incorrect assessment of the situation, for as the war went on and the situation became more hopeless, an increasing number of Japanese overcame their conditioning and surrendered voluntarily. The number of prisoners was never that great, but in the final battles they totaled in the thousands.

Initially, only a handful of prisoners were taken. Most were seriously wounded and had to undergo extensive medical care before they could be interrogated in depth. After all possible information was obtained, the Japanese POWs were sent back to camps in the United States. Some of these prisoners refused to return to Japan after the war for fear of what would become of soldiers who had dishonored themselves by surrendering. Many of these apprehensive POWs were allowed to remain in America, where some still live too ashamed to let their families know that they survived when so many of their comrades perished. Hundreds of other defeated Japanese not only refused to surrender when defeated but also would not believe that the war ended at all. On battlefields far from Japan, these troops fought on, or at least avoided any contact with the local populations. From the 1950s onward, every few years one or two would surrender to teams of Japanese officials who made regular trips to these old battlefields. There, the officials would tramp through the jungle with loudspeakers, announcing in Japanese that the war was over and it was safe to come home now. Some old soldiers may still be out there, resourceful and unbending old men, loyal to their emperor to the end.

See also JAPAN, FIRST DEFEAT.

Ref: Dunnigan and Nofi, *Shooting Blanks*; *Handbook on Japanese Military Forces*; Harries and Harries, *Soldiers of the Sun*; Hayashi and Coox, *Kogun*.

Japan, Colonial Administration

Japanese colonial administration was based on the objective of gaining the maximum benefit for Japan from the colonial territory. In this regard, Japan's attitude was not too different from that of any other colonial power. However, while most Western powers—or at least Britain and the United States—were becoming uncomfortable with imperialism and making tentative steps toward liberalizing their colonial policies, the Japanese acted very much out of self-interest.

Despite the urgings of some officers who truly believed that Japan had a mission to liberate its Asian brothers, little attempt was made to reconcile the inhabitants of Japanese colonies and occupied territories with imperial rule. Unlike the British in India or the Americans in the Philippines, the local people had at best menial roles in the colonial administration. Even in the NETHERLANDS EAST INDIES, which the Japanese promised would become independent after the war, there were over 23,000 Japanese officials working in civil administration, more representatives of the new "mother country" than had been the case under Dutch rule. Not even symbolic concessions were made to local sensibilities, even in areas that were technically independent: Japanese soldiers were not obliged to obey commands of satellite country officers, or even sentries.

One objective of Japanese colonial policy was to "Japanize" the native population. In Korea and the MANDATES, for example, education was in Japanese, and all residents were required to adopt Japanese names. The colonial peoples were considered distinctly second class.

Japan, the Emperor

The Japanese shared many cultural traits with the Chinese. One was that they, the Japanese, were a chosen people who were born to rule. Even during centuries of isolation, Japan saw itself as an empire waiting for the opportune time to assert its foreordained role as a world leader.

The head of the Japanese government was the emperor, in this case Hirohito, who assumed the throne in 1926 at age 25. But although the constitution formally gave him considerable power, the emperor usually reigned as did a modern European monarch; he did not generally rule, although he technically had the authority to do so.

An ancient institution in Japan, the emperors never had as much power as they possessed in the 75 years prior to the surrender of Japan in 1945. Then, and now, the emperor was considered a divine creature, the direct descendant of the ancient gods of Japan, but more directly of a warrior, Jimmu Tenno, who allegedly lived in the seventh century B.C. (but more probably about a thousand years later).

Japan was long governed by feudal tribes (or clans, as the Japanese put it) that over the centuries came to be dominated by one feudal clan leader, who became known as the shogun. The emperor's clan was recognized as the most exalted in rank, and the keeper of important religious functions. But the emperor never ruled; a succession of shoguns did. From the 17th century to the 1860s, the undisputed shoguns of the Tokugawa clan led a peaceful, united, generally prosperous, and quite insular Japan.

But American and European warships barged into Japan in the 1850s, making the Japanese aware that their isolation had put them way behind in crucial areas of technology. A reform movement arose in Japan and, in a series of civil conflicts in the 1860s, deposed the shogunate and instituted a Western-style government, installing the emperor as a head of state. In effect, the quasi-religious figure of the emperor was something the reformers and conservatives could agree on as a unifying force in Japan.

A major samurai revolt against the reformers in the 1870s was put down by a new conscript army, and Japan began its rapid march into the Industrial Age. The imperial family and clan was brought along, but over a thousand years of submitting to the will of the ruling shogun was a habit not easily discarded. While the shoguns and their hordes of samurai warriors were gone, they had, in effect, been replaced by generals and a modern army. Non-Japanese never knew quite what to make of the emperor.

The Japanese people were unrestrained in their adoration and respect for the emperor, and this gave foreigners the impression that all the emperor had to do was issue an order and it would be done. Although Japan had a parliamentary system of government before 1945, it was a government dominated by a small number of powerful groups. The emperor had influence, but not the ability to act like an autocrat.

Japan, today a nation of manners and custom, was even more so before 1945. Although the emperor's power was theoretically unlimited, in practice it was constrained by a mass of custom and obligation. Many things are "simply not done," or at least not done without considerable consensus building and negotiation. This approach was developed over the centuries as the dozens of warring clans in Japan learned to resolve their differences and become a unified country.

An example of the power of consensus building and custom can be seen in the outlawing of firearms in the 17th century. This order actually worked, banning firearms from Japan for over two centuries. When the permanent unification of Japan occurred in the 17th century, and when all the fighting and talking were over, the new shogun declared that firearms made it too easy for someone to raise a peasant army and overthrow the samurai ("knights") who traditionally defended and ruled Japan. A samurai took years to train in the use of the sword and bow, and his devotion to his feudal lord, and the emperor, were considered the glue that would keep Japan together. A peasant could be trained in the use of firearms within a few weeks, and could be controlled by whoever paid him. So the shogun ordered all but a few government-owned firearms destroyed. And it was done.

The modern (post-1860s) Japanese emperors have been acutely aware that their elevated status could be quickly changed back to "national historical shrine" if the imperial household stepped out of line. This did not prevent the modern emperors from grabbing all the power they could. Yet, most of the emperor's power came from being in the middle of things.

A major branch of the pre-1945 government was the "Palace Institutions." The "institutions" enabled the emperor to have thousands of civil servants, family members, and retainers on the payroll serving only the emperor. Thus the emperor had experts in all areas of government at his disposal. While this still did not actually allow the emperor to issue orders to the government, it did keep him informed on what was going on and, in particular, on what the many strong personalities running the government were up to.

The emperor could order government officials to report to him on what their departments were doing. An "audience with the emperor" was either a gift to bestow on a cooperative government official, or a means to punish an official with whom the emperor was at odds. All of this was done according to an immense tradition of protocol and procedure. After all, the emperor was, to the Japanese, a god who walked the earth.

Much has been written about whether or not Hirohito should have been treated as a war criminal and punished for his role in starting (or at least for not trying to prevent) the war in the Pacific. Hirohito was not blameless. He could have refused to approve the army's aggressive policies in the 1920s and 1930s. But the emperor was well aware of the fact that past emperors who overstepped

their bounds were simply ignored. A too rambunctious emperor could be put into a form of exile, shut up in the imperial palace (which was normal anyway) and guarded by soldiers in order to "protect" him.

Thus, while Hirohito did not order the aggression that led to the war with America, he didn't make a bold move to stop it either. At least not until August 1945. At that point the emperor did stick his neck out and order the surrender. That act no doubt saved the imperial institution in Japan. And no doubt it was this result that crossed Hirohito's mind when he made his move.

See also JAPAN, MEIJI CONSTITUTION.

Ref: Bergamini, *Japan's Imperial Conspiracy*; Hoyt, *Hirohito*; Irokawa, *The Age of Hirohito*.

Japan, First Defeat

The Japanese were much chagrined when they suffered their defeat at MIDWAY in mid-1942. This was thought to be the first Japanese defeat of the war. It wasn't, however, as the Chinese had defeated the Japanese at the Battle of Taierchuang in March of 1938. The Chinese began by attacking a Japanese garrison in the walled town of that name. After two weeks of fierce fighting, and heavy reinforcements by both sides, 16,000 Japanese and 15,000 Chinese were dead, and the Chinese held the town. This was one of the few Chinese victories in their war against the Japanese, which began in 1931 and went on until the summer of 1945. This was the first Japanese battlefield defeat in several centuries. The Japanese later lost several more battles to the Chinese, and were ultimately smashed by a Russian blitzkrieg on the Siberian and Mongolian frontier in 1938–39. However, although the Imperial Army had, in fact, been bested several times before the Pacific War began, Midway was the first defeat ever, regardless of the size of the action, in the history of the Imperial Navy, since its foundation in the mid-19th century, and this may have been of considerable psychological importance.

Japan, Forces Abroad at the Surrender

The STRATEGY of "bypassing" or "leap-frogging" Japanese concentrations, to leave them isolated and relatively harmless in the rear, enabled the Allies to greatly reduce their CASUALTIES, while permitting them to advance great distances. But it also created a security problem. All of those bypassed Japanese forces did have to be contained, an activity that involved a great many Allied troops: Indeed, by the end of the war most of the Australian and New Zealand forces, and substantial American forces, were primarily involved in keeping isolated Japanese forces entertained.

Allied intelligence estimates as to the number of Japanese troops in these places was in several cases very inaccurate. For example, MACARTHUR's intelligence staff believed there were only about 80,000 Japanese isolated in the RABAUL Pocket, that is, Papua New Guinea, the Solomons, and the Bismarcks. In fact, there were actually nearly 140,000, plus some 20,000–25,000 civilians.

In addition there were 1,356,400 Koreans working in Japan, plus 1,152,650 non-Japanese personnel (Micronesians, Koreans, Chinese, Formosans, Indonesians, and others) outside of their native places and in company with the imperial forces.

Ref: *Report of General MacArthur.*

JAPANESE FORCES ABROAD AT SURRENDER

Areas	Personnel
China	1,501,200+
Formosa	479,050+
Hong Kong	19,200
Indian Ocean-Malaya-Netherlands Indies	710,670
Indo-China	32,000
Korea	750,000+
Manchuria	1,105,200+
Mandates and other Pacific Islands	171,000
Papua-New Guinea, the Solomons and Bismarcks	138,200
Philippines	152,400
Ryukyu Islands	69,200

+Figures include Japanese civilians

Japan, Government

At the head of the Japanese government was the emperor, but he was the head of state, not the head of government. From the early 1930s to the end of the war the military was responsible for giving most (but not all) of the orders. This was accomplished by having a general as the prime minister and by using the government to cow the population and any other organizations that might threaten military control.

Prime Minister   The most powerful person in Japan, the prime minister was appointed by the emperor on the advice of his principal advisers (especially senior princes) and elder statesmen. Until the armed forces forced its will on the nation in 1932, the prime minister was usually the head of the largest party in the Diet (parliament). Through the 1920s and early 1930s, the armed forces became more of a dominant force (with the aid of nationalist and expansionist civilians). Japan's overseas empire in China, FORMOSA, and Korea was popular with many, but not all, Japanese. The military made the overseas empire a matter of national honor and cast those in opposition as traitors. The armed forces flexed their muscles in 1932 (after assassinating two civilian prime ministers) and forced the emperor to appoint the first of a succession (with a few short-term civilians) of generals or admirals as prime minister. While the military met with resistance, it was using guns and its opponents, by and large, were not. Still, by having the emperor's appointment the military had, in a sense, accommodated its largely civilian opposition. Thus the Diet remained in session and civilians still headed many of the ministries. The prime minister presided over the following ministries:

Foreign Ministry   The Japanese State Department.

Home Ministry   Controlled all the police in the nation as well as the prefectural (provincial) governors. There were no "states" as in America. The Japanese were very centralized. There was also a special national police force whose name can best be translated as "Thought Police." This force served both as a secret police for the government and as a protection against the spread of any "un-Japanese" thought or behavior.

Finance Ministry The Treasury Department, controlled the national banking system and national finances.

War Ministry This was the department that controlled the army's support services. This included logistics, recruiting, and so on. This ministry also controlled the semiautonomous secret police (which served mainly overseas at the behest of local commanders). This ministry was always headed by an army officer, usually nominated by the General Staff.

Navy Ministry Served the same function as the War Ministry, for the Navy. This ministry was always headed by a naval officer, nominated by the Naval Staff.

Justice Ministry The court system.

Education Ministry Controlled all schools in the nation, as well as propaganda and government publications.

Commerce and Industry Ministry Controlled smaller businesses and worked with (and sometimes for) the larger businesses.

Agricultural and Forestry Ministry Controlled raw materials PRODUCTION within Japan.

Transportation Ministry In charge of the national road and railroad network as well as ports and coastal shipping.

Overseas Affairs Ministry Controlled the overseas colonies (China, Korea, Formosa, and, later, new territories conquered by Japan).

Welfare Ministry Controlled national health and, more importantly, the rationing system (which was in force long before PEARL HARBOR).

Munitions Ministry Coordinated (not very effectively) munitions and weapons production.

Cabinet Planning Board Controlled the mobilization of Japan's resources for the war effort.

Military General Staffs There were two of these, one for the army and one for the navy. The army was the larger and more powerful, but the navy always managed to maintain its independence. Each of the General Staffs controlled all the military units of its respective service. The General Staffs each had a chief of staff who was, in effect, the head of that service. The war and navy ministries were subordinate (in practice) to their respective chiefs of staff.

The Diet (Parliament) Set up in the previous century, the Diet was to make Japan a constitutional monarchy, and, until the military took over, this system more or less worked. The Diet had two chambers. The lower chamber was the House of Representatives. This comprised 466 members elected by the 14 million males who had the franchise (out of a total of 70 million Japanese citizens; women didn't get the vote, nor did all men, until after World War II).

There was a multiplicity of parties, and this annoyed the military (and many conservatives and nationalists). The Diet continued to exist through the period of military rule, but all it did was approve the budget increases and discuss legislation introduced by the prime minister. The lower chamber was kept under control by the secret police and various political and economic pressures.

The upper chamber was the House of Peers, whose role was to "guide" the House of Representatives. And this the House of Peers did, especially during the period of military rule. The Peers were organized in a uniquely Japanese fashion. Of the nearly 400 members, 66 were wealthy individuals elected by the 6,000 biggest taxpayers in Japan. Another 150 were nobles elected by the thousand or so adult male members of the nobility. The emperor selected another 125 members, based on the selectees' high achievements in the service of Japan. All princes and marquises (senior nobles) were automatically members.

Japan, Imperial Ambitions

The cause of the war in the Pacific was not Japan itself, but that segment of the population that was fanatically devoted to expanding the Japanese "empire." Until Japan threw off its centuries of isolationism in the late 19th century, Japan had an emperor, but no empire. The reforms that transformed Japan from a feudal society to a modern nation-state also created a segment of the population that saw Japan's role as expansionistic and militaristic. These attitudes were the result of three influences;

Economics   Japan was overpopulated, and the introduction of new technology from the West made the situation worse by improving living standards, increasing the birth rate, and creating a need for more resources. One solution was to seize foreign territory and send Japanese colonists overseas to the new lands. This was done, and continued until the end of World War II. Naturally, the colonists would be enthusiastic about their new opportunities and their families became supporters of this expansion. This group included millions of Japanese from every social class.

Culture   The old feudal nobility and their samurai warriors now had better weapons, which they wanted to put to use. The Japanese were quite confident of their military ability, the nation never having been conquered by a foreign power. Military success against China, Korea, and Russia from 1880 to 1910 added to this sense of power. The militarists could not be denied as they piled success upon success. The military classes had lost much in the 19th-century reforms and saw overseas expansion as a means to recover their position.

Colonialism   Japan quickly became aware of how rapidly the Western nations were taking over the world. Japan realized, especially after defeating Russia in the 1905 war, that it was the only non-Western nation that was holding its own. These successes appealed to nearly all Japanese. The Western nations had colonies, and now Japan also

had them. During World War I, the Allies treated Japan as an equal (in order to obtain Japanese support in the Pacific), and this gave the Japanese a greater sense that Asia and the Pacific was their bailiwick and that Japan should be supreme in the region.

Although Japan's military expansion had broad appeal in the general population, it was the tacit acceptance of the extremists that caused the problems. When moderate politicians were assassinated or overseas military commanders went to war without permission, there was a tendency to indulge these acts. The perpetrators were either not punished or not punished severely. While moderate politicians held sway in Japan through the early 1930s, the hundreds of thousands of troops and colonists in Korea, MANCHURIA, and China became increasingly independent. This was not an unusual situation for colonies, but it ultimately proved disastrous as the aggressive actions of the colonial armies dragged Japan into a war with the West that it could not win. Not content to operate independently in the overseas colonies, the military pushed for control of the government at home. The politicians (and much of the population) opposed this. But the expansionists/militarists/nationalists had weapons and will. Assassination, and the threat of assassination, cowed most politicians and the population, and by the early 1930s the generals and admirals were running the government. What made this situation worse was that most of the fanatics were junior- and middle-level officers and their civilian allies. Bit by bit, like-minded generals and admirals assumed positions of power. The emperor would protest against the violence and militarization of the government, and after one round of assassinations in 1936 even responded forcibly to supress a coup attempt. But the emperor knew his power was limited. Seventy years earlier the emperor had been a puppet of the feudal overlords, and there was fear that this relationship would be revived.

Ref: Hoyt *Japan's War*; Ienaga, *The Pacific War*.

Japan, the Imperial Conspiracy

It has been suggested that Emperor HIROHITO played an active, indeed a key, role in preparing and planning for Japan's aggression in China and against the Western powers, even taking a personal interest in germ warfare experimentation. Actually, there is something to this, but not as much as has been averred. The 19th-century Meiji Constitution did not create a constitutional monarchy in Japan, with a figurehead sovereign. Behind a facade of parliamentary rule, Japan was essentially an authoritarian monarchy, much like Imperial Germany or Czarist Russia had been before World War I. The emperor retained enormous power, albeit that he usually refrained from exercising it.

This is where Hirohito's responsibility for the war lay. Not only did he fail to oppose the imposition of a militaristic regime on Japan during the early 1930s, but he also raised no objections to the militarists' adventurism in China. And when the armed forces asked him for a declaration of war against the Western powers, he did not hesitate. It is worth recalling in this regard that when, in mid-August of 1945 and in the aftermath of HIROSHIMA, the Russian invasion of MANCHURIA, and NAGASAKI, the emperor ordered Japan to surrender ("The war not having developed entirely to Japan's satisfaction . . ."), the country and its armed forces did so quickly and efficiently, despite the efforts of some militaristic fanatics to prevent it. So Hirohito's responsibility for the war was a sin of omission, rather than one of commission. That said, it is well to remember that for most of Japan's history, the emperor was kept as a puppet by the military strongmen who actually ran the country. For the emperor to go against the generals was to risk all of his power.

Japan, Imperial Institutions

The list of organizations that comprised the emperor's palace institutions is a long one.

Imperial Family Council   All adult males of the imperial family in descent from an emperor (to the fifth generation). Imperial family councilors were the princes of Japan, and there were about 25 of them through most of HIROHITO's reign. While this group was to advise the emperor on family matters (money, marriages, indiscretions among the royal kin), it also served as a means for the emperor to get advice from family members concerning affairs of state. Adult princes would have some high government job. Even if some of these posts were largely ceremonial (it was prestigious to have a prince around), they did allow the princes to be aware of what was going on in the organizations. A few princes did hold powerful posts, and used these councilors meetings to give the emperor frank advice.

Privy Council   This was composed of 26 elder statesmen (known as the privy councilors, or *jushin*) appointed by the emperor to offer advice on any situation the emperor wanted advice on. While the prime minister "advised" the emperor on who should join this council, all of the Jushin were devoted to the emperor (although some had markedly different ideas on how Japan should be governed). The *jushin* were not as intimate as the family councilors, but the Privy Council was a better way to nudge the government to do something the emperor wanted, but the government didn't (like surrendering at the end of the war).

Lord Privy Seal   This post was held by a loyal aristocrat. Technically, the job entailed supervising Japanese royalty. This included duties like maintaining imperial archives, tombs, and shrines, training young nobles in protocol, and keeping track of all the documents that passed before the emperor (and especially those that had to obtain an imperial seal, the "privy seal"). In practice, the Lord Privy Seal was the emperor's chief adviser on domestic politics. To assist in this function, the Lord Privy Seal also supervised the Spy Service Directorate (which had access to all Japanese espionage and would prepare analysis for the emperor and his advisers). Again, in Japanese fashion, having access to all this information did little more than keep the emperor informed. He could not order the many espionage agencies to do anything. This setup did enable the emperor to dare to defy the "fight to the last" government in August 1945 and broadcast his surrender announcement. In typical Japanese fashion, the emperor would not have done this unless he was relatively certain that most Japanese would accept it.

Grand Chamberlain In charge of the emperor's personal living arrangements, this office encompassed a vast bureaucracy that maintained dozens of imperial residences. The chamberlain was also in charge of the many ceremonies the emperor had to participate in, and looked after the living arrangements of the crown prince, the empress, and the emperor's mother (the empress dowager). In practice, the chamberlain was also the emperor's adviser on foreign affairs.

Aides-de-camp The emperor's personal military advisers were senior military officers assigned to keep the emperor informed on military affairs. There was a chief imperial aide-de-camp and dozens of assistants.

Supreme War Council A military version of the Privy Council. It comprised senior military officers selected by the emperor (with the cooperation of the army and navy leaders). There was also an advisory group (the Board of Field Marshals and Fleet Admirals) that was consulted from time to time. The Supreme War Council was a means of communication between the emperor and the generals who were running the country. It was not a decision-making body, except in the sense that any policy that seemed to "displease" the emperor would give succor to those generals or admirals who opposed it.

Imperial Headquarters This was formed in 1937, when it became clear that operations in China had reached wartime intensity. In effect, the establishment of this organization marked the entry of Japan (by Japanese reckoning) into a state of war. The permanent staff of the Imperial Headquarters (located in Tokyo) were staff and support personnel. Meetings with the emperor at Imperial Headquarters comprised the most senior military officials (army chief of staff, navy chief of staff, war minister, and navy minister). While decisions were talked about at the Supreme War Council, they were confirmed at Imperial Headquarters.

Imperial Household Ministry Managed (and still manages) the emperor's wealth, which was (and still is) immense. Tens of billions of dollars of assets included millions of acres of crown lands (from which rents were and still are collected) and two dozen palaces. In effect, this ministry (answerable to the emperor, not the prime minister) was the emperor's business manager and treasurer. The emperor held equity positions in many of Japan's largest companies, giving him a certain amount of control over the economy.

Japan, Meiji Constitution

The constitution under which the Japanese Empire operated during World War II was instituted in 1889. It was not composed by representatives of the people. Rather, it was written by the Meiji emperor (Mutsuhito, reigned 1867–1912) and his advisers. Mutsuhito then presented it to the nation, with the prefatory comment that "The rights of sovereignty of the Empire We have inherited from Our ancestors, and We bequeath them to Our descendants." Although it gave Japan the veneer of being a constitutional monarchy, the Meiji Constitution reserved far more power to the sovereign than did the constitutions of such European monarchies as Britain, Sweden, or the Netherlands. It more closely resembled the constitutions of Imperial Germany (defunct after World War I) or the Kingdom of Italy (ditto after World War II), in that the sovereign retained enormous power, particularly over the armed forces.

HIROHITO's father, the Taisho emperor (Yoshihito, reigned 1912–26), was a weak ruler and mentally unstable. During his reign the government evolved toward a more European-style of monarchy. However, by 1924 Hirohito had to take over as regent for his father. Hirohito made little effort to foster the democratic trend, and by the early 1930s the militaristic nationalists were on the rise. Under the constitution he clearly had the power to prevent that.

The Meiji Constitution was divided into several chapters, of which the first three were the most important.

Chapter I dealt with the emperor. Its first article read "The Empire of Japan shall be reigned over and ruled by a line of Emperors unbroken for ages eternal." The next three articles defined who was eligible to become emperor and established that he was "sacred and inviolable" and embodied "in Himself the rights of sovereignty." The succeeding articles outlined the emperor's power. Among other things he had the power to enact laws, "with the consent of the Diet," which he could dissolve at will. He could appoint or dismiss all civil and military officers, and could even restructure most government agencies. He was supreme commander of the army and navy, established their organization and size, and had the power to declare war and make peace, with no reference to the Diet.

Chapter II dealt with the subjects of the emperor. Rather than a "Bill of Rights," this chapter was essentially a "Bill of Obligations." Several articles established that subjects had the right to serve in civil and military capacities, and that they were liable to pay taxes and serve in the armed forces. In addition, subjects "within the limits of the law, shall enjoy freedom of speech, writing, press, public assemblies, and association" and "have freedom of residence and of changing their residence." One article read "All provisions contained in the preceding articles of this chapter that are not in conflict with the law or the rules and discipline of the Army and the Navy shall apply to the officers and the men of the Army and the Navy."

Chapter III established the Imperial Diet, to consist of two houses. The upper house ("of Peers") consisted of members of the imperial family, the nobles, and anyone the emperor chose to appoint to it. The lower house ("of Representatives") was chosen by election "according to the provisions of the Election Law," which so severely limited the franchise that most Japanese men could not vote. Laws were proposed by the government, and had to be voted upon by both houses.

The remaining chapters of the constitution dealt with technical matters, such as the political organization of the country into prefectures, the organization of the courts, and so forth.

Japan, Occupation of

Planning for the Occupation of Japan actually began in 1943, despite the contemporary estimate that the war was likely to drag on into 1947 or even 1948. By early 1945 it was clear that the war was going to end much sooner, perhaps in 1946. By the summer of 1945 planning was well advanced, with minor differences based on whether Japan would have to be invaded or would surrender. The plan, dubbed Blacklist, was put into force when Japan actually surrendered.

US troops began landing in Japan even before the signing of the final surrender on September 2, 1945. By the end of September there were nearly a dozen divisions in the country, including a combined British Commonwealth task force.

The Japanese proved enormously cooperative in defeat. Initial projections had been that the occupation of Japan would require about 500,000 troops for several years, but within little more than a year the garrison was down to four divisions and a total of about 100,000 men.

The occupation was supposed to be supervised by the Allied Control Commission, which included representatives of all of the Allied powers, including the Soviet Union. In practice, however, the commission was merely a nod to Allied solidarity, and the occupation was headed by General of the Army Douglas MACARTHUR. MacArthur established an almost imperial presence, even to the point of humiliating the diminutive HIROHITO by towering over him in a widely distributed photograph of the pair. The occupation of Japan was different from that of Germany. In Germany the Allied occupation authorities completely abolished the government, and hence the sovereignty of the country. In contrast, during the occupation, although Japan's sovereignty was restricted in many ways, the country retained a civil government, including a foreign ministry (which continued to use the wartime PURPLE Code for some time after the surrender, wholly unaware of the fact that US cryptanalysts had cracked this code in 1941 and that MacArthur was reading Japanese communications).

The immediate postwar years were very difficult in Japan. Food was very scarce, unemployment was very high, and the country's industry was in ruins. A major factor in the economic recovery of Japan was the US occupation. American personnel in Japan spent an enormous amount of money, which helped fuel the economy: US troops were estimated to have spent some $200 million a year on prostitutes alone. At first this particular industry was officially unofficial, and young Japanese women were exhorted to become COMFORT WOMEN for the good of the country. When the US occupation authorities found out about this, they forced the Japanese to abolish the organization, but prostitution flourished anyway. Other industries were slower to recover.

During the Korean War a lot of defense procurement contracts were let in Japan, and US warships were routinely refitted and repaired in dockyards originally built for the Imperial Navy, which had been idle since 1945. This was good for US taxpayers, since the cost of labor in Japan was extraordinarily low. It also gave a major stimulus to the Japanese economy. The postwar fortunes of several major Japanese corporations were more or less derived from this war work.

The government and business leadership carefully gathered together investment capital in the late 1940s, waiting for the day when they could operate without the supervision of American occupation officials. In 1952, Japan was again allowed to run its own affairs. US military occupation would continue until 1955, but as of 1952 America had no direct role in Japanese internal affairs. This, coupled with the flood of American contracts associated with the Korean War effort, put Japan on the road to recovery.

Progress was slow. Most of Japan's cities had to be rebuilt. But Japan had experience in this, for Tokyo had been devastated during a 1923 earthquake and the Japanese had quickly rebuilt their capital and largest city. Now they had to do it again. Japanese industry adopted wholesale American ideas on marketing and manufacturing. Many of these were gradually modified, and often improved, to suit Japanese tastes. After numerous false starts in the 1950s and 1960s, Japanese began to produce world-class manufactured goods at competitive prices. By the 1980s, Japan had the second largest economy in the world.

Prewar investment in naval shipyards paid off particularly in the boom that affected Japanese shipbuilding in the late 1950s and 1960s. The experience gained in the construction and repair of the YAMATO CLASS battleships, and the shipyard facilities that were constructed to build them, proved enormously valuable when the supertanker boom developed, in the late 1950s.

The Korean War also marked the rebirth, albeit unofficially, of the Japanese Navy. Although officially completely disarmed after her surrender, Japan still maintained a small naval capability with American blessings. There was a pressing need for this, as the United States had laid an extraordinary number of MINES in Japanese waters late in the war in order to strangle shipping. The Japanese had engaged in extensive mining as well, in anticipation of an American invasion.

So even as the Imperial Army and Navy were being disbanded from 1945 onward, some former naval officers (even a former battleship skipper) and ratings were hired, officially as civilians, to man a large number of minesweepers. When the Korean War came, a lot of these vessels were pressed into service, crews and all, to support the US amphibious landing at Inchon (see CHEMULPO/

INCHON) and the evacuation of WONSAN. Soon afterward the "Maritime Self-Defense Agency" was created.

Japan, Proposed Invasion of, 1945–46

The United States began making plans for the eventual invasion of Japan surprisingly early in the war. By early 1943, it was felt that the first phase of this assault would take place in late 1946 or even 1947, with the fighting continuing into 1948. As the war developed, the target date was brought forward until, at the time of the Japanese surrender on 15 August 1945, the date was set for November 1, and troops, aircraft, ships, and supplies were already being concentrated for the operation known as "Downfall." Because Japan was a collection of major islands, the invasion would take place in phases.

First, there would be some preliminary operations involving the seizure of various small islands off the Japanese Home Islands, to provide bases for air, naval, and logistical support. Then would come "Operation Olympic," wherein the southernmost of the principal Japanese islands, Kyushu, would be hit with 10 infantry, three Marine, and one parachute division. There would also be 2,458 ocean-going ships, plus 8,000 aircraft adding their firepower to the attack. But the bulk of the CASUALTIES would be taken by the 250,000 ground combat troops going ashore in the first waves. Resistance was expected to be so heavy that one Marine division was not even mentioned in the tentative plans for operations following the securing of the beachheads, as it was assumed that it would be so depleted by losses it would no longer be fit for action. This was to be a larger and far more complex amphibious operation than the D-day assault against Normandy. Securing Kyushu was believed to require some 750,000 ground troops.

Until the day they surrendered, the Japanese went ahead with their preparations for resisting the expected Allied invasion. By the end of 1945, the Japanese planned to have 2.5 million troops under

arms in the Home Islands. These would be organized into over 50 divisions and numerous smaller units. Japan's aircraft factories were still operating, although just barely, and planes were being held back for the final defense of the Home Islands. Thus Japan would have had nearly 9,000 aircraft to resist the invasion with. About half of these would be used in KAMIKAZE suicide attacks. Unlike the earliest kamikaze, not all the pilots were volunteers and few had much flying experience. The veteran, or at least trained, pilots were now reserved for interceptor and bomber aircraft.

The Japanese were confident that they could do serious damage with their kamikaze, and they were probably right. Through the end of the war, for each 15 kamikaze aircraft lost, one Allied ship was damaged and for every hundred kamikaze shot down, one Allied ship was sunk. American defenses against kamikaze were getting better as the war went on, but these attacks would still be effective. During the first kamikaze attacks in late 1944, one in six aircraft hit something. By the time of the OKINAWA campaign in early 1945, only one in nine kamikaze were doing any damage. Both sides calculated that only one in 12–20 kamikaze would connect during the Downfall operation. But the Japanese also decided to change their kamikaze tactics, going for troopships and landing craft rather than carriers and battleships. By this method they expected to be able to destroy the equivalent of two divisions (over 30,000 soldiers and sailors) before the troops even got ashore.

To defend Kyushu, the Japanese would have had some 600,000 troops available by November. This may have been overly optimistic, as by August 1945 Allied naval and air power had effectively sealed off each of the Japanese Home Islands. But despite the lack of reinforcements from the main island of Honshu, there would still have been some 400,000 Japanese troops on Kyushu.

For the Allies, the battle was expected to revolve around air power to destroy Japanese mobility on Kyushu. The Allies expected the battle to resemble more the fighting on the Philippines than on the smaller islands in the Pacific. Moreover, most of the newly raised Japanese divisions were spending most of their time building coastal fortifications, not training. These "static divisions" were expected to stay in their entrenchments and keep shooting until killed. Not much training was required for this, and the Japanese had regularly shown a preference for fighting to the death. American troops had developed better tactics for destroying troops holding out in fortifications, but these new methods did not eliminate all risk to the attackers. It would still be a bloody battle.

In the Philippines, the Japanese withdrew when there was an opportunity, and strong Japanese units were still holding out when the war ended. There would be some of this on Kyushu and these Japanese troops would have to be hunted down. In the Philippines, this "hunting" was greatly aided by local Filipino GUERRILLAS. But in the Philippines, the local population was pro-American. On Kyushu, the locals were not only going to be hostile, but were also organized to resist.

Nearly a quarter of the Japanese population (including many women) were conscripted or volunteered for local defense forces. While these irregulars were not well armed, they were nearly as determined as the uniformed troops. So there would be no friendly locals giving information about where the Japanese troops were or what shape they were in. Indeed, the locals could be expected to attack you when your back was turned, or perhaps when it wasn't. Allied planners foresaw widespread resistance and great slaughter. So did the Japanese, but they were the people who had coined the phrase "death is lighter than a feather."

The second phase of "Downfall" was "Coronet." This was to be the invasion of the main island, Honshu, in March of 1946. The Allies were transferring troops from Europe for this. At the time Japan surrendered, two infantry divisions from Europe were already in the Pacific, while two armored divisions, nine infantry divisions, and two amphibious brigades were retraining in the United States for deployment to the Pacific (see UNITED STATES ARMY, FORCES IN TRANSIT). Coronet would involve 19 infantry divisions, three Marine divisions,

one airborne division, and, in a first for the Pacific War, two armored divisions.

The objective of this invasion was Tokyo and the surrounding Kanto Plain. The landings were to be close to Tokyo, on several beaches to the southwest, southeast, east, and northeast of the Japanese capital. It was expected to be the final battle, and a bloodier one than that for Kyushu (where fighting would probably still be going on when "Coronet" kicked off).

Despite their unbroken string of victories, Allied troops did not look forward to an invasion of Japan with any enthusiasm. They were pretty sure what would happen, mainly because two Japanese-populated islands (SAIPAN and Okinawa) had already been invaded and the reactions of Japanese civilians were now known. The Japanese civilians on these islands actively assisted the Japanese troops. Moreover, many of the civilians committed suicide when it was clear that the battle was lost. On Saipan, two-thirds of the civilian population died and, as usual, nearly all the troops fought to the death. On Saipan, 30,000 Japanese troops caused 14,000 American casualties. On Okinawa, nearly 110,000 Japanese troops died (and at least 75,000 civilians), but there were over 60,000 US combat casualties and over 40,000 noncombat injuries. On Iwo Jima the ratio had been even worse, approximately one American killed or injured for every Japanese soldier killed.

The Kyushu invasion (Operation Olympic) would be more like the Philippines fighting, which had cost the United States 60,000 casualties, including 13,000 dead. Based on this experience, and taking into account the differences between the campaigns, US Army planners estimated that the Kyushu fighting would cause 125,000 American casualties, including 31,000 dead. The Honshu invasion (Operation Coronet) in early 1946 would involve about twice as many troops, and was expected to cause about twice as many casualties. Thus, if Japan were to be conquered by invasion, the American casualties, based on contemporary experience, would be about 370,000, including about 80,000 dead. This would amount to a 27%

increase in US casualties for the war, including the ETO.

In the face of this, US commanders contemplated the use of chemical weapons and (for the senior officers who knew about it) ATOMIC BOMBS. It was decided to not use chemical weapons because the Japanese could respond in kind. With atomic bombs, there were doubts about how many would be available by the November invasion date. There was also uncertainty as to how this new weapon should actually be used: Some generals urged that it be withheld for use in a tactical mode, to obliterate Japanese troop concentrations. Some of the effects of radiation were known, and this complicated any plans to use atomic bombs anywhere near friendly troops. In the end, more mundane new techniques, like flamethrower TANKS and point-blank fire from 155mm and 8-inch guns were seen as a more practical way of digging diehard Japanese troops out of their fortifications.

What was certain was that the Japanese would resist fiercely, as they had done consistently throughout the war. While the Okinawa battle had, for the first time, featured Japanese civilians organized to resist US troops, there had also been an increase in the number of Japanese that surrendered. But this increase in PRISONERS was not all that encouraging, as it amounted to only a few percent of the enemy soldiers in the area. The rest had fought to the death. In the defense of their own homeland, Japanese resistance could be expected to be even more determined. Nor was such a suicidal policy by an entire nation unknown. In the 1860s, Paraguay attacked three of its neighbors, with the result that most of Paraguay's population died in a protracted and hopeless defensive struggle.

The oft quoted figure of "one million American dead" if Japan were invaded appeared after the war in the memoirs of politicians who were depending on fragile memories, or trying too hard to make their case for the use of the atomic bomb. This mythical million deaths began as an exaggeration of the 370,000 casualties figure, sometimes given

by staff officers as "250,000 to 500,000." Half a million soon became a million and casualties became deaths. The actual staff estimates have been sitting in unclassified archives, and in the memories of those staff officers who calculated them, since 1945, but the media picked up on the "million American dead" figure because it made more compelling reading. While the "million dead" is a myth, the expected 80,000 dead and 290,000 wounded were very real, based as they were on recent experience. An invasion of Japan would have caused a significant increase in American deaths in World War II, by more than a quarter, and would have nearly doubled the number of combat deaths to date in the Pacific. Avoiding this invasion by any means possible was no trivial matter.

Fortunately, other factors were working to bring the Japanese to terms before the nation dragged itself into an epic of suicidal resistance. Since the spring of 1945, the naval blockade of Japan had been growing tighter. Food was tightly rationed, with the average citizen getting about 75% of the minimal caloric intake. The winter of 1945–46 would have been one of starvation and general weakening of the entire population. Keep in mind, however, that Japan was minimally self-sufficient in food production. While some would starve, most could survive indefinitely. The food shortage would hurt the Japanese, but would not necessarily lead to social disintegration. Starvation would not guarantee a Japanese surrender, and the Allies could not, for political reasons (the voters wanted the war over, now) keep over a million soldiers and sailors under arms for a year or more blockading Japan, while fighting dragged on in China, the South Pacific, and Southeast Asia.

The problem that faced the Allies was how to get Japan to surrender as soon as possible. Japan had been decisively defeated by mid-1944, as many Japanese leaders knew. But none wanted to admit defeat, particularly in view of what some of the more fanatical military leaders might do. By mid-1945 some Japanese—the "peace" party—were making indirect offers to surrender, but on terms very favorable to Japan: no occupation and with

Japanese supervision of demobilization and war crimes trials. This was like the German surrender in 1918. It would go badly for Japan, to be sure, but the army would survive as an institution, which was what the Imperial Army (still in control of the Japanese government) wanted. This was refused. After all, leaving the German Army intact after World War I had played a part in the reemergence of the German Army in World War II.

Going into August, the negotiations came down to whether or not the Japanese emperor would be able to remain on the throne. The Allies were willing to give way on this point. The reasoning was that the emperor, and his authority, would be needed to keep the population under control after the war. Unfortunately, the Japanese made the mistake of sending their surrender proposals through their ambassador in Moscow, hoping to use the Soviets as an intermediary. The Russians weren't ready for Japan to surrender just yet; Stalin needed time to redeploy the Red Army for a real estate grab in the Far East. Diplomats and politicians in Washington were still debating exactly how to understand and approach the Japanese government. This, as we have seen in the subsequent 50 years, is a difficult task that has still not been mastered.

A naval and air blockade was the only other alternative to an invasion, and no one was sure how long this would take to bring the Japanese to terms. Most estimates had a blockade bringing a surrender at the end of 1945 or sometime in 1946. But it was also pointed out that the Japanese could drag the process out for several years. In America, this was politically unacceptable. The United States had now been at war for over three years. Germany had been defeated. The American people wanted peace. While some troops had been demobilized, many others had not, and there were already signs of unrest in the ranks. Mutinous behavior was becoming increasingly common through the summer of 1945 as troops were transferred from Europe to the Pacific. The government could not deal too harshly with these reluctant soldiers, the voters would not stand for it. The troops had done their job, the people wanted peace. Japan

MAJOR ALLIED NAVAL FORCES FOR THE INVASION OF JAPAN	
Aircraft Carriers	c. 80 (including 8 British) with c. 3,500 A/C
Battleships	c. 30 (including 6 British)
Cruisers	c. 85 (including c. 12 British Commonwealth)
Destroyers	c. 480 (including c. 30 British Commonwealth)
Amphibious Warfare	c. 1,400

must be defeated as soon as possible, by whatever means available.

The atomic bomb, which was not successfully tested until July 1945, was seen as one more weapon to induce surrender. In strictly military terms, the atomic bomb was not a decisive weapon. There were only two of these bombs available after the first one was tested. While only one B-29 was required to deliver an atomic bomb, the damage caused would be less than that already inflicted by raids using 600 B-29s carrying explosive and incendiary bombs. What the atomic bomb did have going for it was the shock of one bomb doing the work of hundreds of bombers. The Japanese didn't know how many atomic bombs we had, and we left it to their imaginations how many we might have and how quickly we would use them. Against a people who seemed to disdain death, there was doubt that even the atomic bomb would bring the Japanese to surrender: Indeed, some leaders still opposed surrender after NAGASAKI.

On August 6, 1945, came the atomic bombing of HIROSHIMA, with its enormous destruction. Two days later, the Soviets invaded MANCHURIA and began to sweep away the million-man Japanese garrison. Millions of Japanese colonists were also at risk, as were the Japanese armies to the south in China proper and INDO-CHINA. It was to maintain their position in China that Japan had gone to war with America in the first place. Soviet intervention meant China was lost. Then, on August 9 came the atomic bombing of Nagasaki. There seemed no end to the calamities that were to befall Japan. And the American bombers still came over nightly in devastating air raids. Although many Japanese preferred to fight to the death, the emperor issued the order for surrender on August 15. This wasn't actually the last word, as elements of the "war party" were opposed to surrender (preferring "*Ichioku gyokusai*—A Hundred Million Die Together") and attempted a coup, which was put down only with some difficulty and bloodshed. Then Japan was ready to surrender, and "Olympic" and "Coronet" joined the long list of historical "what ifs."

In hindsight, some historians have questioned the need for the atomic bombs. At the time, nothing seemed likely to dissuade the Japanese from making a suicidal last stand on their Home Islands. The Japanese had already demonstrated their stubbornness in dozens of battles. Saipan and Okinawa merely confirmed that Japanese civilians were every bit as determined as their soldiers. Japan had

JAPANESE ARMY GROUND TROOPS

	Kyushu	Honshu	Tokyo Area	Shikoku	Hokkaido	Total
Infantry Divisions	10	34	(16)	4	5	53
Tank Divisions		2	(2)			2
Infantry Brigades	7	22	(12)	1	3	33
Tank Brigades	3	4	(2)			7

JAPANESE ARMY AND NAVY AIR FORCES

	Army	Navy	Total
Conventional Combat Aircraft	1,100	3,200	4,300
Suicide Attack Aircraft	2,100	2,000	4,100

JAPANESE NAVAL FORCES

Conventional Surface Warships	34
Conventional Submarines	21
Suicide Attack Boats	2,850
Suicide Submarines	450

About half of the infantry divisions were virtually immobile coast defense formations. No estimate can be made for ground forces of the Imperial Navy. Figures for aircraft and naval forces are partially estimated. Conventional surface warships were mostly destroyer escorts and torpedo boats, with one light cruiser and three or four destroyers. Not all were in operational condition. Several of the surviving conventional submarines had been converted into Kaiten carriers.

ALLIED GROUND FORCES FOR THE INVASION OF JAPAN

	Assault	Reserves	Follow On
Operation Olympic			
Airborne Division		1	
Infantry Divisions	7.3	3	
Marine Divisions	3		
Engineer Special Brigades	3		
Operation Coronet			
Airborne Division			1
Armored Divisions		2	
Infantry Divisions	6	9	18
Marine Divisions	2	1	
Engineer Special Brigades	4		

Divisions committed to Olympic, the attack on Kyushu scheduled for about 1 November 1945, were all Pacific-seasoned American units, except one, which had seen no combat (the 98th). Divisions assigned to the assault phase of Coronet, the attack on Tokyo scheduled for about 1 March 1946, were all veterans of the Pacific as well. Reserve forces for Coronet included five US infantry divisions that were veterans of the Pacific War, plus one veteran Australian Pacific division, and one US division from the ETO. In addition, there were two US armored divisions that had seen some action in the ETO, plus a British Division from the ETO, and a new Canadian infantry division. Among the Follow On divisions, the airborne unit (the 11th) was a veteran of Kyushu, three divisions were veterans of other Pacific fighting, two were British Commonwealth, one Philippine Army, and 12 US divisions transferred from Europe. There were also to be token French and Dutch contingents.

never surrendered, the nation had never been defeated.

Japan required an unprecedented series of calamities before surrender became possible. Destruction of her fleet, isolation of millions of troops overseas, most of her cities burned to the ground, blockade, atomic bombs, and destruction of the greatest of her remaining armies (in Manchuria) was what it finally took. Fortunately, the invasion was not needed. On 15 August, the emperor of Japan did something Japanese emperors rarely did. He overrode all opposing counsel and broadcast the order to surrender. With no assurances that the Allies would respect the imperial institutions of Japan, the emperor threw himself, and his people, upon the uncertain mercies of the same peoples Japan had savagely fought for the past four years.

Ref: Allen and Polmar, *Codename Downfall*; Hayashi and Coox, *Kogun*; Sigal, *Fighting to the Finish*; Skates, *The Invasion of Japan*.

Japan, Surrender Holdouts

When the emperor announced the surrender of Japan on August 15 1945, not all Japanese troops obeyed. The Allies suspected that this would happen, although the scope of the refusals was not as high as they feared. At first, there were thousands of individual Japanese soldiers, sailors, and airmen who refused to surrender, and even a few entire units. Senior Japanese officers were sent out to convince leaders of combat units to lay down their arms, and this generally worked. There were a few cases of aircraft or small warships that attempted to continue the fight, but these were quickly and sharply dealt with by superior Allied force.

Individuals were another matter. Particularly in areas overseas where there were extensive forests or jungles to flee to, thousands of individual soldiers did just that. Some went in small groups, others singly. Many of these individuals and small groups had gotten the surrender news secondhand (by word of mouth or rumor). They did not believe that the emperor they worshipped could ever do such a thing. It had to be an Allied trick. So they fought on, or at least maintained themselves and their weapons in the wilderness until they "received new orders." As a result, for several years Japanese officials went to countries like the Philippines, to drop leaflets or to wander through the forests with megaphones, trying to convince the diehards to pack it in. By the late 1940s, most of these troops had been convinced to surrender. But hundreds fought on for decades. The vast majority of these renegades were ill-educated enlisted men tremendously loyal to their emperor. On March 10, 1974 Lt Onodo Hiro surrendered on Lubang, a small island off Luzon. In 1945 he had been ordered to carry on GUERRILLA resistance to the Americans, and over the years he had killed several civilians. He was located by a Japanese tourist, but refused to believe that the war was over until his former regimental commander was brought to Lubang. Given a tumultuous welcome in Japan, the old veteran wrote a book about his adventures, received back pay for all his years in the jungle, and was the object of numerous offers of marriage.

As late as 1990, two former soldiers (now in their 70s) surrendered in Thailand. These two, however, were an unusual case. After the war, they had joined the communist guerrillas (as had many Axis soldiers in Europe) and fought on in MALAYA and Thailand until the Thai government offered an amnesty for communist guerrillas in the 1970s. These two knew that Japan had lost the war, but knew that they were again in trouble once the British suppressed the Malayan communists in the 1940s and 50s. So the two old soldiers stayed where they were and adapted to the local culture.

Japan, Surrender of, Protocols and Ceremony

Under the terms communicated to the Japanese after they indicated their willingness to surrender, their armed forces were to lay down their arms immediately. To permit effective communication with outlying garrisons, the Allies allowed the Japanese to use specially marked aircraft—white with green crosses on their wings, fuselage, and tail—from August 15 through 25 (this also permitted the Japanese to repatriate some officers and officials wanted for war crimes, and for still others to use these flights to arrange their escape).

Using the password "Bataan," the Japanese armistice negotiating team headed by General Masakazu Kawabe arrived on IE SHIMA in an appropriately marked airplane early on August 19, where they transplanted to an American aircraft also codenamed "Bataan" for the final flight to Manila. At Manila the only objection to the American terms was a request that the onset of the occupation be postponed from the 23rd to the 26th, as this was necessary to ensure that the government would be able to enforce compliance by all military commanders. This was done. The Japanese delegation flew back to Japan by the same route it had come.

The surrender ceremony was held on September 2, 1945, in Tokyo Bay, which was crammed with Allied warships, while clouds of naval aircraft flew overhead. The ceremony took place aboard the battleship USS *Missouri*, chosen because she was named after President TRUMAN's home state. For the occasion the ship was wearing a FLAG that had been flying over the Capitol Building on December 7, 1941, and also had the flag that Commodore Perry used when he "opened" Japan—secured to a

Japanese prisoners of war on Guam hear the emperor's surrender message, 15 August 1945.

Navy and Marine F4U Corsair and F6F Hellcat fighters flying over the USS Missouri and other elements of the Third Fleet, Tokyo Bay, September 2, 1945.

bulkhead overlooking the table on which the surrender documents were placed.

The Allied representatives gathered on the battlewagon early. The Japanese delegation set out from land by tugboat, there being nothing more dignified left afloat. This rendezvoused with the destroyer *Lansdowne* (DD-486), which actually brought the delegation into the midst of the fleet. *Lansdowne* approached *Missouri*, and the Japanese delegation entered an admiral's barge (a sort-of seagoing limousine), which carried them to the battleship.

The Japanese party, nine men (three to sign for the imperial government and various government agencies, three to sign for the imperial armed forces, and three serving as witnesses and aides) climbed the ladder to the battlewagon's main deck. Still officially enemies, they were neither piped aboard nor saluted.

General of the Army Douglas MACARTHUR served as master of ceremonies. He delivered a brief introductory address, and then directed the Japanese delegates to sign. They did so in turn, at the places indicated by MacArthur's aide. The general then signed for the Allies as a whole, first asking LG Sir Arthur E. PERCIVAL and Gen. Jonathan WAINWRIGHT who had been flown to Tokyo from a POW camp in MANCHURIA, to stand by him as witnesses. He then invited the representatives of the individual Allied powers to sign in turn.

Aboard the USS Missouri, anchored in Tokyo Bay on September 2, 1945, General of the Army Douglas MacArthur signs the Japanese Instrument of Surrender. Looking on are General Johnathan Wainwright and Lieutenant General Sir Arthur E. Percival, the American and British commanders who had surrendered in the Philippines and at Singapore in 1942. They were flown to the ceremony from a POW camp in Manchuria.

SIGNATORIES TO THE INSTRUMENT OF SURRENDER

The Allies		The Japanese	
The Allied Command	General of the Army Douglas MacArthur	**Government Delegates**	
Australia	Gen. Sir Thomas Blamey	Central Liaison Office	Katsuo Okezaki
Canada	Gen. Moore-Cosgrave	Foreign Ministry	Mamoru Shigemitsu
China	Gen. Hsu Yung-cheng	Information Bureau	Sunichi Kase
Britain	Adm Sir Bruce Fraser		
France	Gen. Jacques F. Leclerc		
Netherlands	Adm C.E.L. Helfrich	**Military Delegates**	
New Zealand	VAdm Leonard M. Isitt	Imperial GHQ	Gen. Yoshijiro Umezo
Soviet Union	LG Kuzma N. Derevyanko	Army GHQ	LG Shuichi Miyakozi
United States	Fleet Admiral Chester W. Nimitz	Navy GHQ	RAdm Todatoshi Tomioka

At the end of the ceremony MacArthur made another short address and then said "These proceedings are closed." The Japanese were now formally piped over the side, with salutes, signifying that they were no longer enemies.

Japan, War Aims

The long-term cause of the Pacific War was Japan's rampant militarism and the consequent Japanese attitude that, as Asians, they should run Asia without interference from Western powers.

The dark side of this concept was that the Japanese felt that they should be the "elder brother" to the other Asians and, in general, in charge of any part of Asia that Japanese troops could control. This point of view met with resistance from other Asians, particularly the Koreans and Chinese who were Japan's first victims. This Japanese aggression, under way since the 1870s, came under increasing criticism from Western powers. The desire of the Western nations (particularly the United States and Britain) to rein in Japanese aggression led to an embargo on Japan when Japanese troops entered French-controlled Indo-China (Vietnam and adjacent areas) in 1941 and took over. The embargo was the short-term cause of the war. Japan had few raw materials of its own. While it could get coal and mineral ores from its Chinese and Korean territories, oil was available only from Western-controlled sources (INDONESIA). Japan's navy and air force were useless without oil, so the embargo would eventually disarm Japan. Faced with the choice of surrender or striking back, Japan chose the action her history dictated. To many Japanese, the PEARL HARBOR attack was an act of self-defense.

Japan's expansionist war aims were established half a century before Pearl Harbor. Nothing was able to dissuade Japan from these goals short of a full-scale war. Curiously, the Japanese still hold the view that "they couldn't help themselves" and that the war, and its consequences, made Japan a victim as much as anyone else. This is what is taught in Japanese schools today and is the opinion held by many Japanese.

Ref: Ienaga, *The Pacific War*.

One of the most famous images of the Second World War: A sailor kisses a nurse as New York's Times Square celebrates the end of the war.

Japanese Americans, Imperial Armed Forces

Hundreds—perhaps thousands—of Japanese Americans who were visiting or studying in Japan at the time of PEARL HARBOR eventually found themselves drafted into the Japanese Army or Navy, many serving as junior officers: One was a lieutenant aboard HIJMS YAMATO at the time of her sinking. Neither the identities nor the numbers of these men have ever been officially published, since they were not given much of a choice in the matter. A similar policy has been followed with regard to German-American and Italian-American men who found themselves serving against the United States. This has occurred in most American wars of this century, including the 1991 Gulf War with Iraq. Usually, these Americans in enemy uniform were reluctant warriors. However, many Japanese Americans caught in Japan at the start of the war remained in Japan after the war.

Only one Japanese American serving in the Imperial Armed Forces was ever brought to trial. Tomaya Kawakita, an American citizen residing in Japan, joined the Imperial Army when the war broke out. An interpreter at a prisoner of war camp in Japan, his brutality toward US PRISONERS earned him a lengthy prison sentence after the war.

See also AMERICAN CITIZENS, RELOCATION OF.

Japanese Army

The Japanese Army was the largest organization in Japan until the end of the war. At its peak, over 10% of the adult population was in uniform, or on an army civilian payroll. There were three major organizations in the army: the General Staff, the General Bureau, and the War Ministry.

The General Staff was organized along the German model. It had five "bureaus," which, while comprising only a few thousand people each, controlled the rest of the army.

The General Bureau took care of personnel affairs, organization, and mobilization. The First Bureau was the most important, as it planned and organized military operations. The Second Bureau was for intelligence. Within the Second Bureau there was one section for American and European armed forces and another for Asiatic forces. A third section controlled secret service operations. The Third Bureau oversaw transport and communications. The Fourth Bureau was the Historical Bureau. It collected records of events for later reconstruction to support future operations.

The War Ministry was larger (in personnel) than the General Staff, but much less powerful. The War Ministry basically controlled all the civilian organizations (especially those in Japan proper) that supported the army. There were eight bureaus in the War Ministry and the title of each accurately reflected its function.

The Personnel Bureau looked after senior military personnel, including awards for meritorious

service. The Military Affairs Bureau kept track of the military budget, and other items like ideology. The Military Administration Bureau took charge of such details as ceremonies, duty regulations, discipline, and the like. It controlled who was liable for military service and when they would be called to service. Within Japan, this bureau was responsible for the defense of installations, and state secrets. The Economic Mobilization Bureau coordinated the military's control over Japanese industry and economic resources. By the end of the war, this bureau was running what was left of the Japanese economy. The Ordnance Bureau controlled the disposition of weapons and ammunition. As the war went on, this bureau spent most of its time explaining to the military why there were no more weapons and munitions. The Judicial Bureau provided legal services. The Medical Bureau organized the nation's medical resources to support the war effort. The Intendance Bureau saw to the more mundane matters of meeting payrolls and supplying food and clothing.

The field forces were the actual fighting forces and were organized somewhat similarly to those in the West, but there were some differences that can cause some confusion.

The smallest independent operational army unit was the "independent brigade" (5,000–6,000 troops) commanded by a major general. Sometimes this was actually a reinforced regiment taken from a division. The most common unit in the army (as with most armies) was the division, commanded by a lieutenant general. The normal strength of divisions was 10,000–15,000 troops (and much less as the war went on), even though the official full strength was 18,000–20,000. Transportation problems, and steady losses to enemy action or disease, kept divisions in the Pacific understrength nearly all the time.

The Japanese didn't use the "corps" as did most Western armies, but called a unit with two or more divisions an "army." These armies were commanded by a lieutenant general (as were the divisions). Just to confuse matters, the next highest level was the "area army," which contained two or more armies and an air army. These area armies were commanded by a full general or a lieutenant general. Unlike most smaller units, the zarea armies sometimes had a name (North China Area Army or Burma Area Army) rather than a number.

Finally, there were the army groups, which comprised two or more area armies and were commanded by a general or field marshal. To further confuse matters, the Burma Area Army was considered an army group, but usually the name army group meant just that. The Southern Army Group controlled all army forces in Southeast Asia and the Pacific (except, at times, the Burma Area Army).

The army had its own air force (as did the navy). The basic organization of the air force was the *sentai* (group), commanded by a colonel. A *sentai* had three or more *chutai* (company, or squadron in US parlance) of 9–12 aircraft each and was commanded by a lieutenant colonel or major. A *hikodan* (air brigade or "wing"), commanded by a major general or colonel, had four or more *sentai*, one of which was comprised of reconnaissance aircraft. Larger units were *hikoshidan* (air divisions) with two or more *hikodan*, and *kokugun* (air army) with two or more *hikoshidan*. These were considered equivalent to other division-and army-size units for command purposes. There were often independent groups and squadrons, especially on out-of-the-way islands in the Pacific.

Ref: *Handbook on Japanese Military Forces*; Harries and Harries, *Soldiers of the Sun*; Hayashi and Coox, *Kogun*.

Japanese Army, Notable Divisions

When the Pacific War began, Japan already had over 50 divisions on active duty. In addition, there were a great many separate brigades and other large formations. Most of these forces were committed to operations in China. In fact, only about 10 divisions were used in the offensive operations that saw Japan overrun everything from HONG KONG south to JAVA, and from GUADALCANAL west to Burma. Many of the small separate units were eventually upgraded to the status of divisions, often with little or no increase in manpower or equipment allocations. At the time of its surrender the Japanese Army had 169 infantry divisions, plus four tank divisions, as well as a plethora of large independent brigades and similar formations. About 70 of the divisions—50 in the Home Islands and 20 elsewhere—had seen no combat during the war. Many of the units outside the Home Islands were in bad shape, either from having taken heavy CASUALTIES, from having been deprived of logistical support, or from having troops drawn off to support operations elsewhere. Further complicating any study of the Japanese order of battle is the fact that there were many, many different tables of organization and equipment (T/O&Es) in use in the Imperial Army, certainly far more than in the US Army.

It would be impossible to give even an outline history of so many units, nor would it be particularly profitable: Many of the divisions raised in 1943 and 1944 served on occupation duty in China, MANCHURIA, Korea, and elsewhere, with little notice or distinction. Most of the divisions in the Home Islands in August 1945 had been raised in 1944 and 1945. What follows provides an outline of the careers of the Japanese divisions active at the start of the war, and of those raised after PEARL HARBOR that had some importance in the war.

The 1st through the 57th Divisions were Type I formations, more or less organized on the "triangular" model. Most of those with higher numbers were Type II formations, organized on the "square" model (see ORGANIZATION, GROUND COMBAT DIVISIONS, 1942). The Japanese themselves did not use these classifications. Instead they classified units into three categories, based on their combat capabilities rather than their organizational structure: "A" units were fully prepared for any mission; "B" units were less well equipped, but still retained some flexibility; and "C" units were usually bereft of artillery and transport, and suitable only for occupation duties or static defense.

Imperial Guards Division. A prewar regular unit, normally stationed in Tokyo, the division was located in French Indo-China in December 1941. A triangular division, with about 12,500 men, with fully motorized transport, it took part in the MALAYA Campaign and the invasion of Sumatra, where it remained until the end of the war. In June 1943 it was redesignated the Second Imperial Guards Division.

First Imperial Guards Division. Organized in June 1943 from an independent Imperial Guards Brigade formed in 1941, when the Imperial Guards Division was shipped to Indo-China. The division formed part of the garrison of Tokyo until the end of the war.

Second Imperial Guards Division. The original Imperial Guards Division, as redesignated in June 1943.

Third Imperial Guards Division. Formed in April 1944 at Tokyo, where it remained until the end of the war.

First Division. In Manchuria in December 1941, the division was shipped to the Philippines in September 1944, and deployed to Leyte in October. Seriously mauled during the Leyte Campaign, its remnants retired on Luzon in January 1945, where they were destroyed.

Second Division. Located in Japan in December 1941, the division was committed to the invasion of Java in January 1942. Transferred to Guadalcanal in October 1942, the division was virtually destroyed there. Rebuilt in the Philippines, the Second Division served in Burma in 1944. Early in 1945 the division was transferred to occupation duty in French Indo-China, where it ended the war.

Third Division. The division was in China throughout the war.

Fourth Division. In China at the start of the war, the division arrived in the Philippines in February 1942. Transferred to Japan in July 1942, the division remained there until September 1943, when it was sent to Sumatra. In April 1945 it was transferred to BANGKOK, Thailand, where it ended the war.

Fifth Division. The division had been heavily involved in operations in China in 1937 and 1938, not always successfully, as when it was ambushed by the Chinese communist 115th Division in September 1939 (see CHINA ARMIES, SOME NOTABLE FORMATIONS). Probably the best trained and equipped division in the Imperial Army on the eve of the war, the Fifth was a motorized unit of about 15,000 and had an additional infantry regiment attached. In December 1941 it deployed from Hainan Island, off the south China coast, to Malaya, where it spearheaded the Japanese offensive against the British. The superb quality of this division had a lot to do with the rapid defeat of the British forces. The Allies did not take this into account in early 1942 when assessments of Japanese Army capabilities were made. By late 1942 and the fighting on Guadalcanal and New Guinea, a more accurate picture of Japanese Army competence appeared. In late 1942 the Fifth Division was transferred to Amboina in the NETHERLANDS EAST INDIES, where it remained until the end of the war.

Sixth Division. In China at the outbreak of the war, in December 1942 the division was transferred to New Georgia, in the Solomon Islands. It subsequently served on KOLOMBANGARA and BOUGAINVILLE, where it remained until the Japanese surrender.

Seventh Division. Remained in Japan throughout the war. Its 28th Infantry Regiment was detached in early 1942 for the invasion of MIDWAY. This regiment was the first Japanese combat unit committed to Guadalcanal (the Ichiki Detachment), where it was destroyed in August 1942.

Eighth Division. In Manchuria at the beginning of the Pacific War, in September 1944 the division was transferred to the Philippines, where it ended the war.

Ninth Division. In China in December 1941, the division was transferred to OKINAWA in mid-1944, and then later that same year to FORMOSA, where it served until the Japanese surrender.

10th Division. The division had seen service in China since the Shanghai-Nanking Campaign of 1937. In Manchuria for most of World War II, it was transferred to Luzon, the Philippines, in late 1944, and was still fighting when the war ended.

11th Division. Remained in Manchuria until the spring of 1945, when it was transferred to Japan. It saw no combat.

12th Division. In Manchuria at the outbreak of the war, in January 1945 the division was transferred to Formosa, where it remained until the Japanese surrender. It saw no combat.

13th Division. Committed to central China during the Shanghai-Nanking Campaign of 1937, the division was heavily involved in the Japanese defeat at Taierchuang in early 1938. It remained in central China until the surrender of Japan.

14th Division. Heavily involved in the fighting in China since 1937, the outbreak of the Pacific War found the division in Manchuria. In May 1944 it was transferred to PELELIU, in the PALAU ISLANDS, where it was destroyed in a grueling battle with the First Marine Division later that year.

15th Division. At Nanking, in central China, when the war began, in July 1943 the division was ordered transferred to Burma, a movement that it completed only in January 1944. Almost eliminated in the Imphal-Kohima Campaign of March–July 1944, the remnants of the division were destroyed in the final British offensive in Burma in May 1945.

16th Division. In December 1941 the division took part in the invasion of the Philippines from bases in Okinawa and the Palaus. After taking part in the BATAAN Campaign, the division remained

on occupation duty in the Philippines, and was destroyed on Leyte in November 1944.

17th Division. In central China at the beginning of the Pacific War, in August 1943 the division was transferred to RABAUL, and thence to NEW BRITAIN, where it remained until the end of the war.

18th Division. Committed to the Malaya Campaign from Hainan and south China in December 1941, the division went on to fight in Burma, from early 1942 to the end of the war.

19th Division. Stationed in Korea from the start of the war, in late 1944 the 19th Division was transferred to Luzon, where its remnants were still fighting when Japan surrendered.

20th Division. In Korea at the beginning of the war, in early 1943 the division was transferred to New Guinea, where it was virtually destroyed in the fighting for WEWAK in mid-1944.

21st Division. Save for its 62nd Infantry Regiment, which served in the Philippines in early and mid-1942, the division spent the entire war in Hanoi, in French Indo-China.

22nd Division. Spent most of the war in China; in early 1945 it was transferred to Indo-China, where it remained until the surrender of Japan.

23rd Division. The division was on occupation duty in Manchuria until October 1944, when it was ordered to Luzon, where it arrived in December, and was virtually eliminated in combat in January 1945.

24th Division. On occupation duty in Manchuria at the start of the war, in mid-1944 the division was transferred to Okinawa, where it was destroyed in the fighting there in the spring of 1945.

25th Division. In Manchuria for the entire war.

26th Division. In northern China from the start of the war, in mid-1944 the division was sent to the Philippines, where it was destroyed in the fighting on Leyte later that year.

27th Division.   The division remained in China throughout the war.

28th Division.   On occupation duty in Manchuria for the entire war, save for the 36th Infantry Regiment, which was detached to the RYUKYU IS-LANDS, where it was destroyed in the spring of 1945.

29th Division.   On duty in Manchuria at the start of the war, in early 1944 the division was transferred to the MARIANAS, where it was destroyed in combat on GUAM and TINIAN that summer.

30th Division.   Activated in Korea in June 1943, the division was sent to the Philippines, where it was destroyed on Leyte Island in late 1944.

31st Division.   Activated in China in March 1943, the division was sent to Burma where it arrived in October 1943. It took part in the Imphal-Kohima Campaign in March–July 1944, and in the final collapse of the Japanese Army in Burma in 1945.

32nd Division.   Stationed in China throughout the war.

33rd Division.   In Indo-China at the start of the war, the division took part in the occupation of Thailand and the invasion of Burma, capturing RANGOON in March 1942. It remained in Burma for the entire war, participating in the Imphal-Kohima Campaign and the final Japanese debacle.

34th Division.   Remained in China for the entire war.

35th Division.   In China in December 1942, the division was transferred to New Guinea during 1944, where it was destroyed.

36th Division.   In northern China at the start of the war, in early 1943 the division was transferred to New Guinea, where it was destroyed in the fighting for Halembera.

37th Division.   On duty in northern China before the war, in February 1945 the division was transferred to Indochina, where it remained until the end of hostilities.

38th Division.   A large unit (c. 20,000 men), with motorized transport, the division began the war with the attack on Hong Kong. Early in 1942 it took part in operations in the Netherlands East Indies, elements fighting on Java, Amboina, TI-MOR, and Sumatra. By October 1942 it was at Rabaul, and then went to Guadalcanal, where it was virtually destroyed. The division was rebuilt at Rabaul in mid-1943, and it remained in the great CARTWHEEL pocket until the end of the war.

39th Division.   Largely recruited in the HIRO-SHIMA area, the division was sent to central China in 1937, where it played a major role in the massacre of Chinese civilians in the CHANGSHA area. It remained in central China until the end of the war.

40th Division.   In central China throughout the war.

41st Division.   In China at the outbreak of the war, the division was transferred to New Guinea in early 1943. It took part in the fighting at Madang, AITAPE, HOLLANDIA, and Wewak, and was virtually eliminated by the end of 1944.

42nd Division.   Formed in Japan in June 1943, from the 63rd Independent Infantry Group, and sent to the KURILE ISLANDS in early 1944, it remained there until the end of the war.

43rd Division.   Activated in Japan in June 1943, from the 62nd Independent Infantry Group, the division was sent to SAIPAN in early 1944, where it was destroyed in the American invasion that June.

44th Division.   Formed in April 1944, at Osaka, Japan, where it remained until the end of the war.

46th Division.   Formed in Japan in June 1943, the bulk of the division was sent on occupation duty to the Lesser Sunda Islands, in the Netherlands East Indies, in early 1944, while one regiment

(143rd Infantry) was sent to the BONIN ISLANDS. The division ended the war in these locations.

47th Division. Formed in Japan in June 1943 from the 67th Independent Infantry Group, in September 1944 the division was sent to China, where it remained until the end of the war.

48th Division. Invaded the Philippines from Formosa in December 1942. It was transferred to the Netherlands East Indies in March 1943, and ended the war on Timor.

49th Division. Formed in Korea in January 1944, from the 64th Independent Infantry Group, the division was transferred to Burma in mid-1944, where it served until the end of the war.

50th Division. Activated on Formosa in May 1944, the division remained there for the rest of the war. It saw no combat.

51st Division. In Manchuria at the start of the war, the division was transferred to south China early in 1942. Later that year it was sent to Rabaul. Subsequently ordered to LAE, on March 3–5, 1943, the division's 115th Infantry and most of its artillery were sent to the bottom in the Battle of the BISMARCK SEA. The balance of the division was virtually destroyed in the fighting around Lae in the spring of 1943.

52nd Division. Stationed in Japan from the beginning of the war, in November 1943 the division was transferred to the CAROLINE ISLANDS, where it remained at the end of the war, having been bypassed by US forces.

53rd Division. At Kyoto in December 1941, the division was transferred to Burma in early 1944, where it was heavily engaged until the end of the war.

54th Division. In Japan at the start of the war, the division was sent to Java in early 1942, and in September was in Burma, where it served until the surrender of Japan.

55th Division. The bulk of the division was stationed in Indo-China in December 1941. It invaded Thailand at the start of the war, and then went on to fight in Burma until the end of the war. Meanwhile, the division's 144th Infantry Regiment began the war in the Marianas, as the "South Seas Detachment," and occupied Guam in December 1941 and Rabaul in January 1942, formed the PORT MORESBY landing force that was turned back in the Battle of the CORAL SEA, and was eliminated in action on New Guinea that August. The regiment was reactivated in Burma in mid-1944.

56th Division. Less one regiment (146th Infantry) left behind in Japan, the division landed on Mindanao, the Philippines, in December 1941, went on to fight on Java in February, and thence to Burma by mid-1942, there it was reunited with the 146th Infantry and there it remained for the rest of the war.

57th Division. Served in Manchuria throughout the war.

62nd Division. Formed from the Fourth Independent Mixed Brigade in China in June 1943, and transferred to Okinawa in mid-1944, where it was destroyed in the spring of 1945.

79th Division. Formed on Luzon in 1944, the division was only lightly engaged during the fighting there in January 1945. Retiring into the eastern mountains, when it surrendered at the end of the war it was still relatively intact

91st Division. Formed on Shimushu, in the Kurile Islands, in April 1944 from miscellaneous small garrison units, the division performed local defense duties until August 1945, when it put up a stiff resistance to Russian forces, which had invaded in violation of the armistice.

100th Division. Raised from the 30th Independent Mixed Brigade in the Philippines in mid-1944 and destroyed by the US Army in early 1945.

102nd Division. Activated from the 31st Independent Mixed Brigade in the Central Visayan Islands of the Philippines in mid-1944, and destroyed there by US and Philippines troops in early 1945.

103rd Division. Formed from the 32nd Independent Mixed Brigade on Luzon, the Philippines, in mid-1944. During the initial part of the Luzon Campaign, in early 1945, the division was only lightly engaged. Retiring into the eastern mountains, it fought on until the end of the war, surrendering while still relatively intact.

105th Division. Formed in the summer of 1944 from the 33rd Independent Mixed Brigade, on Luzon, in the Philippines, its remnants were still active there at the end of the war.

109th Division. Formed on IWO JIMA in late 1944, and there destroyed by the US Marines in early 1945.

First Tank Division. Activated in Manchuria from the 1st Tank Group and the 1st Cavalry Brigade Group in August 1942. The division was later transferred to the Home Islands in anticipation of an American invasion. It was disbanded at the end of the war.

Second Tank Division. Formed in Manchuria from the Second Tank Group and Second Cavalry Brigade Group in August 1942, the division was transferred to the Philippines in mid-1944, and took part in the defense of Luzon in early 1945, in which it was virtually destroyed.

Third Tank Division. Raised in August 1942 in Manchuria, on the basis of the Third Tank Group, the division was disbanded shortly before the end of the war.

Fourth Tank Division. Raised in Manchuria in mid-1944, the division was shortly committed to the Japanese "Airfields" offensive in south China. It was transferred to Japan in anticipation of a US invasion, and it remained there until the end of the war. Had an invasion of Honshu proven necessary, the Fourth Tank Division would probably have encountered the US 13th and 20th Armored Divisions, which were designated to take part in Operation Coronet.

Ref: *Handbook on Japanese Military Forces*; Hayashi and Coox, *Kogun*.

Japanese Army, Notable Separate Brigades and Groups

As with the numerous divisions in the Imperial Army, so too it would be impossible to outline the history of all the numerous separate brigades and groups formed during the war. Most were formed for occupation purposes and saw little action, save in GUERRILLA suppression operations and in the perpetration of ATROCITIES on local residents. Some, however, played important roles in the war, while others became the cadres for the formation of divisions.

There were several types of these organizations.

Amphibious Brigade: 3,200 men, in three 1,035-strong battalions plus small headquarters and support units.

Cavalry Brigade Group: 5,000–6,000 troops, in two or three 1,200-man CAVALRY regiments, a 350-man HORSE artillery regiment (eight guns), a 350-man light tank battalion, plus other support units.

Garrison Brigade: 2,000–3,000 troops in three or four infantry battalions and few, if any, support units. These were used in rear areas to keep the locals under control.

Independent Infantry Brigade: About 4,900 troops in four infantry battalions and a signal unit.

Independent Infantry Group. About 7,600 men in three infantry regiments, with some additional logistical services. This was essentially the infantry element of a division, without the artillery, reconnaissance, and other elements.

Independent Mixed Brigade: Usually about 5,500–10,000 men in five or more infantry battalions, plus one or more battalions each of artillery and engineers, plus some support and service troops. Called "mixed" because they were composed of more than one type of combat troops. Many were somewhat strengthened and redesignated as divisions later in the war.

Parachute Force: About 1,700 men in two parachute battalions and an artillery unit.

Separate Infantry Brigade: Essentially a regiment of infantry with a battalion of engineers and some support and service troops attached.

Tank Group: 3,000–4,000 troops, in one or more tank regiments (850 men, 85 to 95 light and medium TANKS), plus an infantry battalion, some artillery and support units. Later expanded into small divisions.

Examples of these unit types are:

24th Independent Mixed Brigade. A small unit, with only four infantry battalions, the 24th Independent Mixed Brigade was activated in Burma in February 1944 from miscellaneous forces. It took part in the Imphal-Kohima Campaign and was destroyed during the final British offensive in Burma in early and mid-1945.

55th Independent Mixed Brigade. Activated in the Philippines from miscellaneous forces in June 1944, the brigade, only about 3,000 strong, was committed to combat on Leyte that October, and was essentially destroyed by the end of the campaign.

57th Independent Mixed Brigade. Formed in Japan in the spring of 1944, the brigade was sent to the Philippines and committed to the Leyte Campaign, in which it was destroyed.

58th Independent Mixed Brigade. Activated in the Philippines in June 1944 and lost during the fighting on Leyte later that year.

65th Separate Infantry Brigade. Formed from older reservists shortly before PEARL HARBOR, the brigade was committed to the fighting in the Philippines in December 1941. It did not perform well in the sustained fighting on BATAAN. Shortly after

the end of the fighting in the Philippines, the brigade was disbanded.

Raider Detachments (Teishintai). In an attempt to imitate the success of the CHINDITS in Burma, the Japanese created a brigade-sized force in 1943–44. Three small battalions were formed, with some auxiliary services. Raider detachments were small, some 30–40 officers and men, and supposed to infiltrate Allied lines to engage in sabotage and harassment. Although a number of these missions were undertaken, the success rate was not great, the troops and their officers lacking the training, equipment, and individual initiative necessary for such tactics to succeed.

Ref: *Handbook on Japanese Military Forces;* Hayashi and Coox, *Kogun.*

Japanese Assets in the United States, Freezing of, 1941

In July 1941 the United States froze Japanese assets, as did Britain and the Netherlands, since Japan was still trying to conquer China and had now occupied all of French INDO-CHINA. All previous protests and sanctions had not made any impression on the Japanese. The asset freeze, however, had the effect of prohibiting exports of British-, Dutch-, and American-controlled oil to Japan (without government issued permits). As Japan was entirely dependent on these oil imports to keep its industry and military going, the embargo would have eventually crippled Japan's war effort, as well as its economy. The Japanese had a choice between getting out of China, and thus avoiding the bad effects of the embargo, or going to war and hoping that would break the embargo. The Japanese decided on war.

Japanese Navy, Administration

The Japanese Navy organization was similar to the army in terms of the Navy General Staff and the Navy Ministry. The Navy General Staff used the term "Department" rather than "Bureau" (as the army called subdivisions of its General Staff). Like the army, the navy adopted many organizational and command practices from European nations (particularly Germany, Britain, and France). Navy combat units were, of course, organized quite differently than those in the army. All navy combat units were under the command of the Combined Fleet.

Subordinate to the Combined Fleet were the area fleets, which were responsible for a geographical area. These fleets usually had a large local port as a main base (SINGAPORE, TRUK, or a base in Japan) and often many other smaller land bases. Area fleets had some major fleet units (battleships and carriers), but most of these were assigned to mobile fleets for major operations. Area fleets contained one or more fleets and air fleets. These controlled the smaller units containing individual ships and aircraft.

The largest subdivision of a fleet was the group (containing two or more smaller units containing individual ships). Fleets also had separate base forces, which were ports with land-based sailors (some serving as a defense garrison), small ships, and float planes for reconnaissance.

Individual ships were organized into divisions (two or more of one type of capital ships such as battleships or carriers), flotillas (three to four cruisers or up to 12–20 destroyers, SUBMARINES, or smaller ships). Flotillas were also subdivided into divisions (two cruisers or two to four destroyers).

All submarines belonged to the Sixth Fleet.

A mobile fleet was a temporary organization for specific operations. Subdivisions of a mobile fleet were called striking forces, and these were equivalents to US task forces. Sometimes a mobile fleet would be sent to assist an operation being staged by an area fleet.

Aircraft were organized into air fleets (*koku kantai*). Two or more groups (*koku sentai*) comprised an air fleet. Squadrons (*kokutai*) contained 18–36 of one type of aircraft. Groups contained two or more squadrons. Carriers had an AIR GROUP attached, usually containing three squadrons (one

each of fighters, dive bombers, and torpedo bombers).

Japanese Satellite Forces

The Japanese made extensive attempts to supplement their own forces by raising troops in the territories they occupied, with some degree of success. Although none of these forces possessed any great combat power, nor played any significant role in the war, some of them were at least of use locally, by relieving Japanese troops of some security duties.

The forces raised in China, MANCHUKUO, Burma, and the Philippines belonged to the collaborationist governments that the Japanese created. On paper the Indian and Indonesian forces were created by what might be termed committees of national liberation, which were cooperating with the Japanese toward the day when, at the end of the war, they would secure independence. The Mongolian force was recruited by the occupation forces from disaffected elements in Inner Mongolia. The Russian contingent was recruited for special operations from among White Russian exiles in MANCHURIA but it apparently was never employed.

In practically all cases the manpower was more or less dragooned into the ranks. Training was poor, equipment limited, and leadership generally inept. Moreover, it is impossible to gain any reli-

Contingent	Divisions	Manpower
British Borneo	—	c. 1,500 (Dayak tribesmen)
Burma	2	c. 20.000
China	20	c. 1,000,000
French Indo-China	—	c. 3,000
India	3	20,000–25,000
Indonesia	12	c. 50,000, and 50,000 paramilitary
Malaya	—	c. 5,000
Manchukuo	40	c. 500,000
Mongolia	9	c. 45,000
Philippines	—	c. 4,000–5,000, and 10,000 constabulary
Russia	—	several hundred

able idea as to the numbers of men involved. It seems likely that the total number of men recruited into satellite formations by the Japanese may have reached 1.5 million.

See also BURMA NATIONAL ARMY; CHINA, ARMY, JAPANESE COLLABORATIONIST; INDIAN NATIONAL ARMY; PHILIPPINES, REPUBLIC OF THE; SIAMESE ARMED FORCES.

Java Class, Netherlands Light Cruisers

Although completed in the mid-1920s, the Netherlands' Java Class light cruisers were designed and laid down during World War I. Despite some modernization, they were very outdated by the Second World War, and were actually slated to be replaced when the war began.

Java (1916–1921–1925) formed part of Karel DOORMAN's ABDA squadron during the Battle of the JAVA SEA on February 27, 1942. In company with DERUYTER, she took several shell hits, and was then struck by at least one TORPEDO from the Japanese heavy cruiser NACHI. She burst into flames, was wracked by explosions, went dead in the water, and sank within five minutes.

Sumatra (1916–1920–1926) was under refit at Soerabaya when the war began. Unfit for duty, she managed to escape, making her way to England. There she was laid up and later scuttled to form part of the Normandy-beach breakwaters in 1944.

Java Sea, Battle of

One of the few ship-to-ship naval battles between Allied and Japanese forces during the initial Japanese expansion occurred in the Java Sea. On February 27, 1942, five cruisers and nine destroyers (the ABDA—American-British-Dutch-Australian—Force), commanded by a Dutch admiral, sallied forth to prevent further Japanese landings in what was then the NETHERLANDS EAST INDIES (INDONESIA). Over the next three days, most of this force was sunk by Japanese ships and aircraft. Slight damage was done to the Japanese. But it was only some bad luck that prevented this Allied force from doing significant harm to the Japanese invasion force. The Japanese were fairly reckless in pushing their troop-laden transports forward. Several times the Allied warships came quite close to sinking these vulnerable transports. As it was, the presence of Allied warships in the area threw the tight Japanese schedule into a state of confusion.

The reason the Japanese were moving so quickly was that they had to seize the oil fields and refineries on Sumatra before they could be destroyed beyond recovery. The Japanese oil situation was desperate and was the primary reason Japan went to war in the first place. As it turned out, the Japanese were luckier than the Allies. The oil field defenders were surprised by Japanese paratroopers, who were soon reinforced by forces landed from the sea. Had the ABDA force gotten a few of those Japanese transports, the Sumatra oil fields would have remained in Allied hands long enough to be devastated beyond repair (at least with the resources Japan had available). That done, Japan would have been out of fuel by 1944, and suffered severe oil shortages for over a year before that. Japanese resistance to the Allied advance would have been weaker. In short, a little bit of luck in the Java Sea during February 1942 would have changed the course of the war.

Johnson, Lyndon B. (1908–1973)

A member of the House of Representatives, Johnson joined the Naval Reserve in 1940 and went on active duty as a lieutenant commander after PEARL HARBOR, although not resigning his seat. He served briefly as an aviation observer. By some accounts he was nearly killed in action over New Guinea on 9 June 1942, in an incident that resulted in his being awarded a Silver Star. However, the aircraft, a B-25 named "The Heckling Hare," had incurred no damage, and none of the other personnel aboard were decorated. In mid-1942 Johnson requested a discharge, when President ROOSEVELT asked that all members of Congress return to their legislative duties. He subsequently rose in politics to become vice president under John F. KENNEDY, rising to the presidency on the latter's assassination, and was elected in 1964 for a single term.

Johnston Island

A tiny place, 700 miles southwest of HAWAII. Johnston had no anchorage or port facilities, but was useful as an air base, particularly for patrol planes, since it neatly covered the southwestern approaches to Hawaii. Although it was built up into a respectable air base, the war essentially passed Johnston by. Today it houses the US Army's principal experimental facility for the incineration of poison gas.

Junyo Class, Japanese Aircraft Carriers

The two ships of the Junyo—or Hiyo—Class were converted from the hulls of ocean liners that were still on the stocks when taken over in 1940. They were not successful ships, being slow, crowded, virtually unprotected, and poorly subdivided. Rushed into combat too soon to have had a proper shake-down, they appear to have been mechanically unreliable. They saw only limited combat service.

Junyo (1939–1941–1942) (ex-*Kashiwara Maru*) took part in the Japanese attack on the ALEUTIANS in June 1942, fought in the Battle of SANTA CRUZ, covered the Japanese evacuation of GUADAL-CANAL, and was heavily damaged in the Battle of the PHILIPPINE SEA. Late that same year, she was seriously damaged near NAGASAKI by TORPEDOES from *Sea Devil* (SS-400) and *Redfin* (SS-272). Not repaired, she survived the war, served for a time as a transport returning Japanese troops home, and was scrapped in 1947.

Hiyo (1939–1941–1942) (ex-*Izumo Maru*) took part in skirmishing that preceded the Battle of the Santa Cruz Islands, which she missed due to engine trouble. She was back in service later that year, covering "Tokyo Express" operations and making attacks on US forces in the Guadalcanal area. Hiyo was sunk by a single torpedo from a *Yorktown* (CV-10) or a *Belleau Wood* (CVL-24) TBF AVENGER on 20 June 1944, during the Battle of the Philippine Sea.

K

Kaga, Japanese Aircraft Carrier

Kaga (1920–1921–1928) was originally designed as a battleship, and was scheduled to be scrapped on the ways under the Washington Naval DISARMAMENT TREATY. She was reprieved and converted to a carrier when AKAGI's sister ship was wrecked abuilding by the great Tokyo earthquake of 1923. More or less a half-sister of *Akagi, Kaga* was rather slower. Like all older carriers, she was modernized during the 1930s. *Kaga* took part in operations against China 1932–39, and with *Akagi* she formed Carrier Division One and roamed the Pacific from PEARL HARBOR to MIDWAY, where US dive bombers put four bombs into her, starting fires that caused her to blow up and sink eight hours later.

Kagero Class, Japanese Destroyers

Built 1937–41, the Kageros were regarded in the Imperial Japanese Navy as "ideal" fleet destroyers, fast, heavily armed, and maneuverable. They saw extensive service in the war, during which they were modified to enhance antiaircraft capability at the cost of surface firepower. They had a busy war, some beginning it at Pearl Harbor. All but one of the 18 units in the class became war losses, five in surface actions, one to MINES, three to US SUBMARINES, and eight to aircraft.

Kaiyo, Japanese Escort Carrier

In late 1941 the Imperial Navy requisitioned the passenger liner *Argentina Maru* (1938–1938–1939)

for use as a troop transport. With the shortage of carriers after MIDWAY, she was converted 1942–43 into the escort carrier *Kaiyo.* The ship spent her first year as an aircraft transport, and from mid-1944 as a training carrier. On July 24, 1945 she was seriously damaged by aircraft from HMS *Formidable, Indefatigable,* and *Victorious* off Kyushu. She survived and was scrapped in 1948. A sister ship, *Brazil Maru,* had also been requisitioned in 1941 for conversion into an escort carrier, but the work was not proceeded with and she was later sunk.

Kamikaze

Most of what happened during the Pacific War was anticipated by American admirals and generals during the 1930s. One thing was not foreseen, the Japanese use of suicide aircraft. Even the Japanese did not expect to take such an extreme measure. But after the disastrous Battle of the PHILIPPINE SEA (the GREAT MARIANAS TURKEY SHOOT) of June 1944, it was obvious that American carrier aircraft ruled the skies. Moreover, American ships now had formidable arrays of 20mm and 40mm antiaircraft guns as well as radar fuzes for their 5-inch guns. Between these guns and the formidable F6F HELLCAT fighters, it was nearly impossible for Japanese bombers to make normal attacks on ships. Since aircraft were the best (and often only) way to attack enemy ships, the Japanese came up with the concept of one-way suicide attacks by their bombers.

The Imperial Navy called the new attack method *kamikaze,* a Japanese term for "divine," or "heavenly," "wind" (army suicide pilots were called *Tokkatai*, "Special Attack Units"). The term had a prominent place in Japanese history, as timely storms had saved Japan from invasion by Mongol fleets during the medieval period. Moreover, Japanese pilots were already accustomed to making suicide attacks when all else failed. This was part of Japan's military tradition, something Americans had witnessed time after time as Japanese ground troops fought to the death and refused to surrender in the most hopeless situations.

The first kamikaze units were organized in the Philippines in the fall of 1944. There was no problem in getting pilots to volunteer for such duty.

A quad-40mm antiaircraft gun aboard the second USS Hornet (CV-12), in action against Japanese aircraft off Japan on 16 February 1945, during the Fifth Fleet's raid on Tokyo. By this time in the war the increasing effectiveness of US air defenses and the declining abilities of Japanese pilots made conventional attacks against American warships so risky that kamikaze attacks were only a little more suicidal.

From the beginning, the Japanese sought to make as much as they could of their kamikaze. These attackers would allow them to use even obsolete aircraft. Pilot training could be minimal and often was, with many pilots receiving only a weeks flight training. Precious aviation fuel would be saved, as aircraft need be given only enough for going out and (if no enemy ships were found) coming back. The third of a plane's fuel usually reserved for maneuvering and a margin of safety could be dispensed with.

The first kamikaze attacks took place on October 25, 1944 off SAMAR island in the southern Philippines. Shortly after American destroyers and escort carriers had fought off a Japanese battleship force, the kamikaze struck. The results were encouraging, with two escort carriers damaged and one sunk. Between October and December, kamikaze made more successful attacks on supply convoys steaming north to support further operations in the Philippines. Thus encouraged, the Japanese continued to expand their kamikaze force and prepared to use it against the expected US invasion of the main Philippine island of Luzon. In December, small groups of kamikaze made successful attacks on American ships moving in to invade outlying islands. The major attacks, however, would come once the American invasion fleet was sitting off the coast in support of the amphibious assault.

In early January the kamikaze were unleashed on the first warships to arrive at Lingayen Gulf to shell the beaches before the amphibious ships arrived. Hundreds of kamikaze flew out to meet the Americans, and inflicted losses the USN had not experienced since late 1942. While carrier fighters and numerous antiaircraft guns took their toll, many ships were hit. Since nearly all these were warships, sinkings were few but American CASUALTIES were high. Because many of the injuries were from the aircrafts' gasoline, the experience came as quite a shock to those sailors that survived. Previous Japanese air attacks had tried to put only bombs on their targets. Kamikaze put the entire aircraft on the target, and the exploding aircraft

The flight deck of USS Bunker Hill (CV-17), looking aft, moments after she had been struck by kamikaze aircraft.

gas tanks added to the normal mayhem of an exploding bomb.

Fortunately, the Japanese had a limited number of aircraft. From the first kamikaze attack on October 24, 1944, to the departure of the last Japanese aircraft from Luzon at the end of January, 378 kamikaze were sent out. All were lost, as well as 102 escorting fighters. For this effort, 16 US vessels were sunk (two CVEs, three DDs, one DMS, plus 10 smaller vessels) and another 87 damaged (including seven CVs, two CVLs, 13 CVEs, five BBs, three CAs, seven CLs, 23 DDs, five DEs, one DMS). On the American ships there were thousands of casualties. Fortunately, this was the most effective the kamikaze ever got. The element

of surprise was now lost; the American defenders, now thoroughly alerted to how the kamikaze operated, began to change their defensive procedures to limit the damage from suicide aircraft.

The following month, February 1945, the kamikaze were again encountered during the IWO JIMA assault. Because the attacking aircraft had to fly in over open water, the attacks were not as devastating as those in the Philippines. Several ships were hit, but the only significant damage was to one CV and a CVE that was sunk. Worse was yet to come.

In April, the United States invaded OKINAWA. In addition to the usual fanatic resistance on the ground, the Japanese launched over 1,500 kamikaze and nearly as many regular aircraft at the American ships. Ship losses were heavy, with 21 sunk and 43 damaged so severely that repairs were not complete when the war ended; another 23 were damaged and required at least 30 days to repair. A further 151 ships received lesser damage. Worst of all, the crews sustained 9,700 casualties, 4,300 of which were fatal. For the navy, this campaign was the most costly of the war. Seven percent of all the navy's crew casualties for the Pacific War were incurred during the battles with the kamikaze off Okinawa. And this was despite the many measures the fleet had taken to counter kamikaze. In addition to better control of fighters and antiaircraft guns, there was more crew training in damage-control techniques. There were also radar-equipped destroyers serving as a "picket line" to give early warning of the attacks and absorb some of the punishment. The destroyers contained air control parties that would direct fighters to the incoming kamikaze as quickly as possible. But it was never enough.

The problem with Okinawa was that the island, and nearby ones, were large enough to support many airfields. Kamikaze could also fly in from Taiwan and Japan itself (Kyushu). This amounted to over 200 enemy airfields, too many for even the vast airpower of America to shut down. Moreover, the airfields in distant Taiwan and Kyushu proved no problem for the kamikaze. Since they did not have to return, they could nearly double their range.

The Japanese still allowed for a certain number of kamikaze to turn back due to mechanical problems or a lack of targets. There were also fighter escorts for the kamikaze, to prevent the inexperienced suicide pilots from being shot down before getting to their targets. The more experienced fighter pilots also served as navigators for the kamikaze, who barely knew how to fly and were rarely up to the difficult task of navigating over open water.

The invasion fleet also had to worry about attacks by Japanese SUBMARINES, surface ships, and smaller suicide boats. Patrol aircraft and destroyers kept Japanese subs, as well as the smaller suicide boats, at bay. But the kamikaze came in by the hundreds. During the Okinawa campaign 1,900 kamikaze aircraft attacked 587 US and Commonwealth ships, of which 320 were warships. Eight of the attacks were massed strikes by an average of 150 aircraft. One had 350 planes. Despite all the interceptors and antiaircraft fire, 7% of the kamikaze hit something.

After Okinawa, the next Allied assault would have been on Japan itself. For this eventuality the Japanese had 3,000 to 5,000 kamikaze ready, more than twice as many as were used during the Okinawa battle. Moreover, these would be coming over the hills of Kyushu, not over open water. Radar pickets and fighters would be less effective. The US Navy could expect to take more than 10,000 casualties and see more than 300 ships hit during this battle. It was not something any sailor was looking forward to.

The atomic bombs on HIROSHIMA and NAGASAKI ended the war without an invasion of Japan. This came as a relief to some of the kamikaze pilots, for after the initial use of these suicide aircraft, fewer Japanese volunteered. Toward the end, army and navy pilots were simply ordered to join kamikaze units. Japanese morale was weakening toward the end of the war, although it didn't seem that way in mid-1945, as American sailors watched yet another swarm of suicide bombers headed right for them.

Kamikaze tactics evolved between the initial attacks off Leyte and the great wave attacks at Okinawa. The attacks off Leyte were conducted by small numbers of aircraft simulating conventional attacks until the last possible moment. As time went on, it was realized that larger numbers of aircraft, swarming in from different directions and at different altitudes, were more effective.

Kamikaze aircraft were sometimes accompanied by aircraft intended to make conventional attacks, and were often escorted by fighters, for the purpose of beating off Allied combat air patrols. Clever kamikaze pilots often resorted to elaborate ruses to enable them to get close to ships, feigning damage, for example, and making it look like they were

VICTIMS OF KAMIKAZE ATTACKS		
Type	Sunk	Damaged
CV	0	16
CVL	0	3
CVE	3	17
BB	0	15
CA	0	5
CL	0	10
DD	13	87
DE	1	24
DMS/DML	2	28
SS	0	1
Other	64	144
TOTAL	83	350

eral times rearmed and refitted during the war, in which seven were lost: Two succumbed to carrier aircraft, four to SUBMARINES, and one, *Hayate* (1923–1925–1925), had the dubious distinction of being one of the few ships lost in the war to shore batteries, when the Marines on WAKE ISLAND sank her on 11 December 1941.

Kamikaze, Rocket Powered

As bad as the KAMIKAZE aircraft attacks were, the Japanese developed even more effective weapons for this form of combat. Because the kamikaze program was under way only during the last year of the war, the Japanese did not have time to mass-produce specialized weapons for these attacks. One system that did get into production was the MXY7 *Okha* (Cherry Blossom), nicknamed the *Baka* (Fool) by American sailors. This was a small, rocket-powered aircraft that was launched from a bomber. The Okha was made of wood, consisted largely of a 2,600–pound warhead, and had a minuscule cockpit and very simple controls. But because of its shape and rocket propulsion it would dive into an American formation at over 500 miles an hour. This made it very difficult for US interceptors or antiaircraft guns to catch it. Fortunately, the ill-trained pilots had trouble controlling the Okha. Of some 2,000 built, only about 50 were ever used to attack US ships, and only three vessels were sunk in Okha attacks. But if the Japanese had thought to use the kamikaze tactic earlier, and built a lot more Okha, the results of the attacks would have been far worse.

Katori Class, Japanese Light Cruisers

A peculiar class, the Katori were designed as training cruisers, escorts, and flotilla leaders for SUBMARINES. They were under-armed (no better than a destroyer) and under-engined (their maximum speed was 18 knots, less even than the slowest battleships), and do not seem to have been particularly useful vessels. The construction of these ships demonstrates some of the muddle that prevailed in

crashing into the sea, until the last moment, when they tried to alter course to hit their targets. This was one reason that naval antiaircraft gunners often kept firing on a damaged plane until it hit the water. Another interesting trick was observed by naval historian Samuel Eliot MORISON off Okinawa, when two aircraft apparently locked in a deadly dogfight suddenly broke off the fight, to dive on US warships. The dogfight had been a clever, and successful, ruse to keep American fighters from interfering with the two kamikaze, and to keep ships' antiaircraft gunners from taking the risk of shooting down a "friendly" airplane. Kamikaze aircraft were most effective in conditions of reduced visibility, mist, twilight, and the like. Morning twilight was apparently the best time to attack, since much of their approach could be made under cover of darkness, while their final plunge would occur when there was some light.

See also JAPAN, ATTITUDE TOWARD THE ENEMY; KELLY, COLIN.

Kamikaze Class, Japanese Destroyers

A Japanese World War I design, the nine Kamikaze Class destroyers (all named after various winds, such as the "divine wind," *kamikaze*) had been built from 1920 to 1925 and were obsolescent by 1941. Despite this, they saw extensive service, being sev-

Japanese military circles prior to the war. Amazingly, the Imperial Navy proposed to build eight of these vessels. They saw limited service during the war.

Katori (1938–1939–1940) was damaged by carrier aircraft off TRUK on 17 January 1944, and then finished off by gunfire from cruisers and destroyers.

Kashima (1938–1939–1940) served as titular flagship for the Fourth Fleet in the MANDATES; she survived the war and saw service bringing Japanese troops back to the Home Islands after the surrender. Scrapped in 1947.

Kashiii (1940–1941–1941) was sunk by US carrier aircraft in the China Seas on January 12, 1945.

A fourth unit, *Kashiwara*, was laid down in 1941 but canceled and scrapped while still on the ways. Four other units were proposed in 1942 but were never ordered.

Kavieng, New Ireland, Bismarck Archipelago

Although its somewhat sheltered anchorage served as a port for the shipment of copra and other tropical products, Kavieng had little else to commend itself to the curious, although there was an extensive hinterland, which could be used for air bases, provided port facilities were developed to support them.

Kawabe, Masakazu (1886–1965)

Masakazu Kawabe graduated from the Japanese military academy in 1907. From late in World War I to 1921 he served in a diplomatic capacity in Switzerland and later traveled extensively in Europe and America. Military attaché in Berlin in the late 1920s, during the 1930s he held a variety of increasingly important posts in China. He commanded the Third Army in China at the beginning of the Pacific War, and then the Burma Area Army from early 1943 until September 1944. He returned to Japan to command forces to oppose an expected Allied invasion. On 19 August 1945 he led the Japanese delegation to Manila to negotiate details

of the surrender of the Home Islands. His brother Torashiro was also a general.

See also JAPAN, SURRENDER OF, PROTOCOLS AND CEREMONY.

Kawabe, Torashiro (1890–1960)

Brother of Masakazu KAWABE, Torashiro was also a general, with a distinguished career and one of a handful of senior army personnel who attempted to limit Japanese involvement in China.

Kelly, Colin (1915–1941)

Properly Colin Kelly II, a US Army captain and early war hero. On 10 December 1941 Kelly was piloting a B-17 in an attack on Japanese shipping northwest of the Philippines. After making its bomb run, the plane was attacked by a Japanese Zero flown by ACE Saburo SAKAI. Kelly held the damaged bomber steady until the crew could bail out, but could not get out himself and was killed when the plane crashed. He was awarded the Distinguished Flying Cross, and President ROOSEVELT wrote a letter to "The President of the United States in 1956" requesting a presidential appointment to West Point for Kelly's son.

Kelly quickly became a popular hero, with his exploit inflated beyond recognition: He was widely believed to have been awarded a MEDAL OF HONOR for sinking the battleship *Haruna*, with one variant of the tale having it that he crashed his injured B-17 into the vessel, a feat that met with much admiration in contrast to the contempt that greeted the Japanese introduction of KAMIKAZE tactics. His son, Colin Kelly III, graduated from West Point in 1963 and later entered the ministry.

See also SUICIDE, US OFFICERS; JAPAN, ATTITUDE TOWARD THE ENEMY.

Kendori, Celebes, Netherlands East Indies

The principal port of the Celebes Islands ("The Spice Islands"), Kendori could accommodate and service small merchant ships, and, if developed as a naval and air base, could permit one to dominate the eastern and central NETHERLANDS EAST INDIES. The Japanese used it as a base during the First Air Fleet's foray into the Indian Ocean, in March 1942.

Kennedy, John F. (1917–1963)

Son of the influential and wealthy Joseph Kennedy, for a time ambassador to Britain, Kennedy was commissioned an ensign in the navy in September 1941, after being rejected by the army because of a bad back. In 1943, by then a lieutenant, he was made commander of *PT-109*, in the Solomon Islands. He saw a great deal of action. On the night of 2 August 1943 *PT-109* was rammed and sunk by the Japanese destroyer *Amagiri*. Kennedy managed to swim four miles to a nearby island, while pulling a wounded shipmate. Rescued several days later through the assistance of some Solomon Islanders, Kennedy was awarded a Purple Heart and the Navy-Marine Corps Medal. Partially on the strength of his war record, he was elected president in 1960. Shortly after his election, *Amagiri*'s wartime skipper apologized for sinking the PT-BOAT.

Kennedy's Army

A contingent of the SOLOMON ISLANDS DEFENCE FORCE, under the command of Maj. Donald G. Kennedy, a big, brutal, eccentric, womanizing New Zealander who had served in the Solomons colonial administration since mid-1940. With the evacuation of most white residents of the Solomons from February to May 1942, Kennedy was for a long time the only representative of the Crown in the Solomons north of GUADALCANAL. He was responsible for upholding the authority of the Crown on Santa Isabel, the New Georgias, the Rennell Islands, Florida, and the Shortlands, often meting out rough punishment to district leaders and village headmen who went astray, while also serving as a COASTWATCHER.

Kennedy's "army" consisted of a detail of some 30 men from the Solomon Islands Defence Force.

These men not only provided for his personal security, but also undertook reconnaissance missions, rescued Allied PILOTS, captured Japanese personnel for Allied intelligence, and waged GUERRILLA warfare against the Japanese with surprising success, considering that many of the islands were heavily garrisoned by the enemy: There were some 4,000–5,000 Japanese troops on Santa Isabel alone, slightly more than the total native population.

Kennedy gradually extended his intelligence gathering network by recruiting additional coastwatchers from among European residents of the Solomons who had stayed behind. His most successful subordinate was Geoffrey Kuper, a medical practitioner of mixed European and Melanesian descent, who worked on Santa Isabel.

Although Kennedy became the object of intensive search by the Japanese, he survived the war, in no small measure due to the support and devotion of his "army."

Ref. Feldt, *The Coastwatchers*; Walter Lord, *Lonely Vigil*.

Kenney, George C. (1889–1977)

George C. Kenney graduated from MIT in 1911 and began a career as an engineer. In World War I he entered the Air Service (75 missions, 2 "kills") and remained in the Air Corps after the war. Between the wars he held a variety of posts in the Air Corps and attended most of the army's higher institutions, rising to brigadier general in early 1941. In early 1942 he was promoted to major general, and that August was sent to command the newly formed Fifth Air Force, in the southwest Pacific, with a concurrent command of all Allied air forces in MACARTHUR's theater, a post in which he served with considerable distinction to the end of the war.

Kenney was excessively optimistic about the effectiveness of airpower. Some of the difficulties experienced in the BUNA-GONA CAMPAIGN can be attributed to his belief that airpower could substitute for artillery. He also tended to believe what his pilots told him, so that after the Battle of the

Kent Class, British Heavy Cruisers

BISMARCK SEA he claimed his planes had sunk 22 ships, downed 55 aircraft, and killed 15,000 of the enemy, considerably more than the actual figures. However, he was an extremely good administrator, an excellent commander of air forces, and a technical innovator. He devised the "Kenney Cocktail," a 100-pound white phosphorous bomb, as well as the idea of arming B-25s with quad .50-caliber machine guns for anti-ship operations and the notion of skip bombing. He was certainly not a member of the heavy bomber ring that tended to dominate USAAF thinking in most theaters. He was also able to conceive and implement some of the most imaginative DECEPTIONS of the war.

Kent Class, British Heavy Cruisers

Britain's first "Treaty" cruisers, the five Kents were sisters to the AUSTRALIAS. Although not the handiest ships, and relatively lightly protected, they were well-designed and rather resilient, several surviving considerable damage during the war. Despite this they were not well liked in the British fleet, since they had large crews and were unsuited to the "showing the flag" missions that the ROYAL NAVY performed in peacetime. They all saw considerable service, particularly in the war against Germany and Italy, and several served against Japan in the Indian Ocean, during which *Cornwall* (1924–1926–1928) was lost. While in company with HMS *Dorsetshire* she was caught by Japanese carrier aircraft off CEYLON on April 5, 1942, taking nine hits and six near-misses by Japanese 250–550-pound bombs in 12 minutes.

Khota Baru, Malaya

The principal British base in northern MALAYA, some 400 miles north of SINGAPORE, Khota Baru had an elaborate air base. It was also virtually impossible to defend without a large garrison and an air force, Thailand being to the north, INDO-CHINA to the northeast, and the South China Sea to the east. Khota Baru was the first place the Japanese

attacked when they invaded Malaya on 8 December 1941. Indian troops guarding the place were greatly outnumbered, and after putting up a token resistance, retreated.

Ki-21 Sally, Japanese Bomber

The Ki-21 Sally was the standard army medium bomber until 1944. First introduced in 1938, it could carry a ton of bombs and travel no faster than 262 MPH. Used mostly in China, those that did appear in the Pacific were very vulnerable to the heavily armed Allied fighters. Like most Japanese bombers of the period, the Ki-21 was lightly constructed and lacked self-sealing fuel tanks.

See also AIRCRAFT TYPES, DEVELOPMENT.

Ki-27 Nate, Japanese Fighter

The Ki-27 Nate was the first modern Japanese Army fighter, introduced in 1937 and produced un-

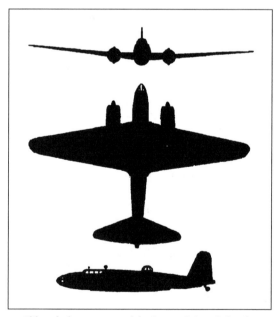

Although the mainstay of the Imperial Army's bomber squadrons into 1944, the Ki-21 Sally was inferior to its navy counterpart, the G4M Betty.

til 1940. It was used primarily in China, where it remained in service until 1943. While slow and fragile, it was possibly the most maneuverable fighter of World War II. Some 3,400 were built, and at the beginning of the war, it was the most numerous Japanese fighter. Some were encountered in the Pacific in areas where the army was responsible for air defense.

See also AIRCRAFT TYPES, DEVELOPMENT.

Ki-30 Ann, Japanese Bomber

The Ki-30 Ann was the oldest Japanese Army light bomber to appear in the war, having first appeared in 1938. Production ceased before PEARL HARBOR, as the Ki-48 and Ki-50 went into production to replace it. An unsuccessful design, used mainly in China.

See also AIRCRAFT TYPES, DEVELOPMENT.

Ki-43 Oscar, Japanese Fighter

The Ki-43 Oscar was the Japanese Army equivalent of the navy's A6M ZERO. Entering service in 1940, it was the most heavily produced aircraft after the Zero (5,900 produced). Not as capable as the Zero, mainly because of lower speed and inadequate armament (usually just two 7.7mm machine guns). Still, the Ki-43 was very maneuverable and a deadly dogfighter. After seeing the more heavily armed and armored Allied aircraft in action, late-model Ki-43s received self-sealing fuel tanks and some armor. Attempts were made to upgrade armament, but these were less successful.

See also AIRCRAFT TYPES, DEVELOPMENT.

Ki-44 Tojo, Japanese Fighter

The Japanese Ki-44 Tojo was the replacement for the Ki-43. Production was delayed until 1942 so as not to interrupt the mass production of the Ki-43. The Ki-44 recognized the need for greater speed and rate of climb. Pilots new to the aircraft missed the maneuverability of the Ki-43, but came to appreciate the Ki-44's qualities when in combat

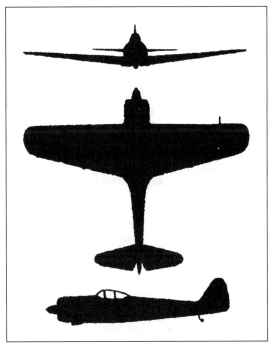

The best Japanese army fighter of the early period of the war, the Ki-43 Oscar was not as good as the navy's A6M Zero, but was still superior to most Allied fighters until 1943.

against Allied aircraft. The Ki-44 saw heavy action in New Guinea during 1942 and 1943. In 1944, cannon were added and from then through the end of the war, the Ki-44 was deadly against US heavy bombers. Some 1,200 were built.

See also AIRCRAFT TYPES, DEVELOPMENT.

Ki-45 Nick, Japanese Fighter

The Ki-45 Nick was the first Japanese Army twin-engine fighter and was intended as a long-range escort for bombers. At the time, Zeros were used for this duty, but the Zeros had little fuel for fighting enemy interceptors once over the target. The Ki-45 entered service in 1941, but it never performed in its designed role. Although speedy and maneuverable, it was no real match for most Allied fighters. It was first used as a long-range

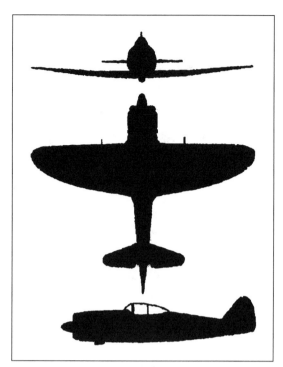

Introduced in late 1942, the Ki–44 Tojo—originally the Hap—was the best Japanese Army fighter in general use during the war.

fighter and reconnaissance aircraft. It could have been used in support of the long-range bombing attacks against GUADALCANAL in 1942, but the air attacks were a navy operation and the two Japanese services rarely cooperated early in the war. By 1944, the Ki-45 found its role as a night-fighter (against B-29s) and as a KAMIKAZE (during the daytime). Against bombers, the heavier armament of the Ki-45 was crucial. As a kamikaze, the heavy weight of the Ki-45 was telling. Only 1,700 Ki-45s were produced.

See also AIRCRAFT TYPES, DEVELOPMENT.

Ki-46 Dinah, Japanese Reconnaissance Aircraft

All but a few (which served as interceptors) were reconnaissance aircraft, one of the best in the war.

See also AIRCRAFT TYPES, DEVELOPMENT; RECONNAISSANCE, NAVAL.

Ki-48 Lily, Japanese Bomber

The Ki-48 Lily was a Japanese light bomber that entered service in 1940. A failure in combat, it was too slow and had neither exceptional range nor bombload to make up for its operation deficiencies. Nearly 2,000 were produced, most being used in China.

See also AIRCRAFT TYPES, DEVELOPMENT.

Ki-49 Helen, Japanese Bomber

The Ki-49 Helen was the Japanese Army's most modern bomber, introduced in 1942. While faster than the earlier Japanese bomber designs, it did not

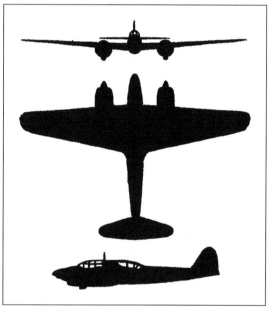

Intended as a strategic (i.e., long-range escort) fighter, the Imperial Army's Ki-45 Nick proved inadequate in this—or any other role—due partially to its poor qualities and partially to inter-service rivalry.

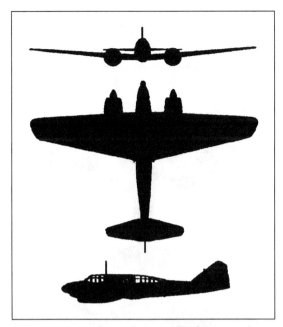

Very fast—370 miles per hour—and with a range of over 800 miles, the Ki-46 Dinah was an effective reconnaissance airplane, and proved useful as an interceptor as well.

have the carrying capacity or robustness of US medium bombers.

See also AIRCRAFT TYPES, DEVELOPMENT.

Ki-51 Sonia, Japanese Bomber

The Ki-51 Sonia was a Japanese Army light bomber that first appeared in 1940. A more successful design than the Ki-49 of the same period. Nearly 2,400 were produced.

See also AIRCRAFT TYPES, DEVELOPMENT.

Ki-61 Tony, Japanese Fighter

The Ki-61 Tony was one of the better all-around Japanese fighters of the war. An army aircraft, it was built with the help of some German technology. Entering service in 1943, it was used until the end of the war. Profiting from the experience of earlier generations of fighters, the Ki-61 was more robust, with self-sealing fuel tanks and some armor. In 1945, several hundred were fitted with a new type of engine, and the performance improvement was so dramatic that this version was called the Ki-100.

See also AIRCRAFT TYPES, DEVELOPMENT.

Ki-67 Peggy, Japanese Bomber

The Ki-67 Peggy was a good Japanese Army medium bomber, unfortunately appearing in early 1944. Only 700 were built and most served to provide Allied fighters with sturdier targets than previous Japanese bombers.

See also AIRCRAFT TYPES, DEVELOPMENT.

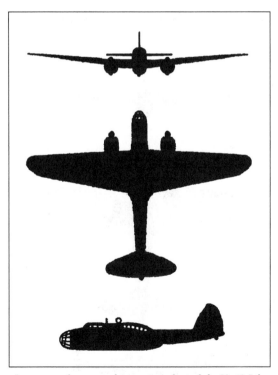

Its poor performance characteristics limited the Ki-48 Lily army light bomber to operations in China for the duration of the war.

Ki-84 Frank, Japanese Fighter

The Ki-84 Frank was the best Japanese fighter to enter production. But this new army aircraft didn't arrive until early 1944. At that point, the US submarine offensive against Japanese shipping was making a noticeable dent in raw materials supplies. This meant that factories cut corners in producing the high-quality parts the Ki-84 needed (the Japanese didn't get into high-quality manufacturing until the 1950s). Consequently, the high performance components, especially the powerful engine, were prone to frequent breakdowns. When everything was working, a Ki-84 could outfly the American P-51 or P-47. But all too often, something would fail, and the Ki-84 pilot would find himself at a grave disadvantage. Even when returning from a successful mission, the Ki-84's landing gear frequently failed from the stress of landing. The Ki-84 was more stoutly built (in theory) than previous

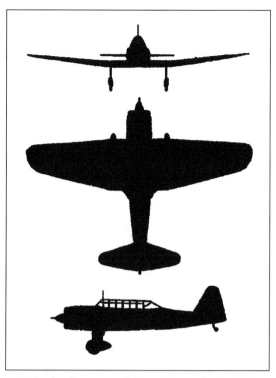

With a bomb capacity of about 440 pounds, the Ki-51 Sonia was essentially a ground attack aircraft rather than a light bomber.

Japanese fighters, and required higher quality metals than Japanese industry was accustomed to producing. Some 3,500 were produced, but as quantities increased, quality steadily declined. To this, many Allied pilots owed their lives.

See also AIRCRAFT TYPES DEVELOPMENT.

Ki-100, Japanese Fighter

The Ki-100 was the last fighter produced for the Japanese Army and it was by far the best. The Ki-100 was actually a redesigned and reengined Ki-61, a successful older fighter. The more powerful and reliable engine of the Ki-100 made a big difference. Fortunately for the Allies, the Ki-100 didn't enter service until March 1945. Only 396 were built (including 275 Ki-61 conversions). With a maximum speed of 360 MPH, great maneuverability, and

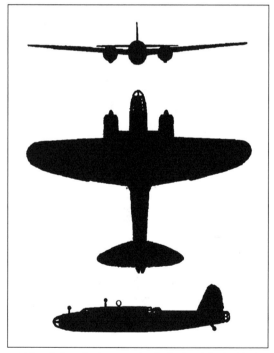

Although fast, the Ki-49 Helen had a bomb load of little more than a ton, limiting its usefulness.

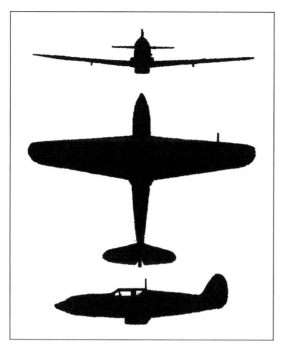

One of the best Japanese Army fighters, the Ki-61 Tony was tougher and had better pilot protection than earlier Japanese fighters.

heavy armament (two 20mm cannon and two 12.7mm machine guns), the Ki-100 proved lethal to B-29s and their P-51 escorts. The US Navy's F6F HELLCATS (which were used on numerous carrier raids against the Japanese Home Islands) took a beating from the superior Ki-100. Had the Japanese managed to improve their engine technology and quality control earlier, the Ki-100 would have been available in quantity earlier, and that would have caused far more US CASUALTIES.

See also AIRCRAFT TYPES, DEVELOPMENT.

Ki-102 Randy, Japanese Attack Aircraft

The Ki-102 Randy was a ground attack version of the Ki-96 Japanese Army heavy (two-engine) fighter. Development work began in 1943, production began in late 1944, and 238 were built before the war ended. The Ki-102 had better protection (armor and self-sealing fuel tanks) and armament (a 57mm gun, two 20mm cannon, and a rear-facing 12.7mm machine gun, plus half a ton of bombs or drop tanks) than older Japanese fighters. Fifteen high-altitude interceptor versions were also produced before the war ended. Most of these aircraft were kept in Japan, and only a few were involved during the battle for OKINAWA. The Ki-102 was an effective aircraft that would have been a considerable threat to Allied troops if there had been an invasion of Japan.

See also AIRCRAFT TYPES, DEVELOPMENT.

Ki-108, Japanese Fighter

The Ki-108 was a Ki-96 redesigned as a high-altitude fighter (to oppose heavy bomber raids). Work began in 1943, but the difficulty in perfecting the pressurized cabin delayed production. Testing was still going on with the four prototypes when the war ended. Had the Ki-108 gotten into service, its armament of one 37mm and two 20mm cannon would have been lethal to the B-29. Ironically, the Americans found (in early 1945) that low-altitude B-29 raids were more effective than high-altitude ones. Since these low-altitude raids tended to be at night, what the Japanese needed was a radar-equipped night fighter. Attempts to build these met with little success as the Ki-108 demonstrated.

See also AIRCRAFT TYPES, DEVELOPMENT.

Ki-109, Japanese Fighter

The Ki-109 was a Japanese Army Ki-67 heavy bomber redesigned as a heavy fighter. The project began in early 1943, when the Japanese became aware of the B-29's existence and pondered how to deal with its nighttime raids. The initial concept had two versions of the Ki-109. One would be a "hunter" equipped with radar and a 40cm (15.8-inch) searchlight, which would find the B-29s. The second version would be the "killer," having two 37mm cannon firing upward at an angle. This was soon dropped for a single version mounting a 75mm gun in its nose (and 15 shells, to be loaded by the copilot). This would keep the Ki-109 out of range of the B-29's defensive armament; at the time, it was thought that the B-29s would not have fighter escorts (a false hope, as it turned out). Only 22 of these aircraft were built before the war ended, not enough to have any noticeable effect on the B-29 raids.

See also AIRCRAFT TYPES, DEVELOPMENT.

Kieta, Bougainville

A copra (dried coconut meat) port, Kieta had no facilities beyond a modestly sheltered anchorage, not even a proper dock. Control of Kieta, however, did bring with it domination of the northern SOL-OMON ISLANDS. Occupied by the Japanese for most of the war, from mid-1943, it was virtually isolated.

Kimmel, Husband E. (1882–1968)

The son of a Confederate officer (who had not re-signed from the US Army until after fighting against the Confederacy at Bull Run!), Husband E. Kimmel graduated from the Naval Academy in 1904. Before World War I he served in various bat-tleships, took part in the Great White Fleet's world cruise, and was wounded during the occupation of Vera Cruz in 1914. The following year he served as an aide-de-camp to Assistant Secretary of the Navy Franklin D. ROOSEVELT, an assignment that would have a positive effect on his career. During World War I Kimmel served as a gunnery officer in the Sixth Battle Squadron, the American rein-forcement to Britain's Grand Fleet, and as a tech-nical adviser to the ROYAL NAVY. He rose rapidly during the years of peace, and in early 1941 FDR jumped him over the heads of numerous other of-ficers to command the entire US Fleet. Making his headquarters with the Pacific Fleet, Kimmel was at PEARL HARBOR when the Japanese attacked, and was relieved of duty 10 days later. Beached, he held no further commands until retirement. Although several congressional investigations concluded that Kimmel, and his army counterpart LTG Walter C. Short, were guilty of dereliction of duty and had

committed errors of judgment, a postwar inquiry reduced the conclusions to errors of judgment, a more accurate assessment.

Kimmel was a good officer, and his actions after the Japanese attack were commendable. He organ-ized a carrier sortie, which might have caught two Japanese carriers unawares off Wake; he dispatched his SUBMARINES on aggressive war patrols; and re-organized what surface and air forces remained. But all of this was after the fact. Other officers in the Pacific (HART and HALSEY, for example) perceived that war was imminent on the basis of the same communications from the Navy Department that Kimmel received. Kimmel lacked aviation creden-tials and had not attended the war college. He ap-pears to have been lulled into complacency by the strength of his forces, the apparent impregnability of the Hawaiian Islands, and his own contempt for the Japanese.

The argument as to the extent of Kimmel's re-sponsibility for the disaster at Pearl Harbor is nev-erending. Halsey appears to have thought him lax. Kimmel made things worse by demanding a court-martial (which he could not be given, since it would reveal that the Japanese PURPLE Code had been broken, albeit this would not have strength-ened his case) and by hurling accusations in all directions, specifically that his former patron Pres-ident Roosevelt and other high officials had "de-nied" him access to information they had that would have caused him to place his forces on alert. Arguably a case can be made that he did not re-ceive certain information, although how much more warning he needed than the communiqué of 27 November ("This is to be considered a war warning") and that of 28 November ("Hostile ac-tion is possible at any moment . . .") is difficult to understand.

Kimmel was the brother-in-law of Admiral Thomas KINKAID, after whom he named his second son. The two older of his three sons were Naval Academy graduates and submariners. The eldest, Manning E. Kimmel, Annapolis '35, survived the sinking of his boat, USS *Robalo* (SS-273), on 26 July 1944, and made it ashore on PALAWAN in the Philippines with some of his crew, only to be captured by Japanese troops and later burned to death. When word of this reached NIMITZ, Kimmel's replacement, he ordered the admiral's second son, Thomas Kinkaid Kimmel, to shore duty.

Kimura, Heitaro (1888–1948).

Heitaro Kimura graduated from the military academy in 1908. After serving in Siberia (1918–19) he held a diplomatic post in Germany for a time. During the 1920s he held various posts, and in 1930 went to London as a technical delegate to the disarmament conference. During the 1930s he rose through various staff appointments and was vice minister of war in December of 1941, TOJO being the minister. He became commander of the Burma Area Army in September 1944, was arrested in 1945, and tried and hanged as a war criminal in 1948.

King, Ernest J. (1878–1956)

Ernest J. King graduated from Annapolis in 1901, after serving in action as a midshipman aboard the protected cruiser *San Francisco* during the war with Spain in 1898. Until World War I he was assigned to various ships and staffs, serving as an observer with the Japanese during the Russo-Japanese War and taking part in the occupation of Vera Cruz in 1914. When the United States entered World War I he was assigned to the staff of the Atlantic Fleet. After the war he specialized in SUBMARINES, but in 1928, at the age of 49, he qualified as a naval aviator. King thereafter became closely identified with naval aviation. In 1933 President ROOSEVELT jumped him to rear admiral when he discovered that none of the candidates for chief of the Bureau of Aviation was flight qualified. On the eve of World War II King was serving as commander of the Atlantic Fleet, from which assignment a few days after PEARL HARBOR he replaced KIMMEL as commander in chief, US Fleet, and in March the president made him chief of naval operations as well, under the terms of some special legislation.

King's role in the war was indispensable. He not only oversaw the expansion of the navy, but he was also involved in plotting military STRATEGY, directing the antisubmarine effort (he created the Tenth Fleet, a paper organization with himself as its head, to coordinate the antisubmarine war in the Atlantic), and helping coordinate American strategy and operations with those of the Allies. King retired in late 1945, shortly after promotion to five-star rank. For several years thereafter he served as an adviser to the secretary of the navy and to the president.

King Bay, Australia

A small town, with access to a large, fairly protected inlet on Australia's western coast, King Bay had limited facilities but was the most important anchorage between FREMANTLE and DARWIN.

King George V Class, British Battleships

The "KGVs" were good battleships, albeit undergunned. They had been designed in the early 1930s, when Britain was attempting to secure a newer and more restrictive naval limitation treaty. Their peculiar gun arrangement (two quadruple turrets and one double) was dictated by the need to scale back from a planned main battery of 12 guns in three turrets. The quadruple turrets proved rather successful in action. Although they saw extensive service, they were never tested to their limits. Despite this they seem to have been reasonably resilient ships. They were quite reliable as well, *King George V* herself at one point spending 52 consecutive days underway during the final months of the Pacific War.

King George V (1937–1939–1940) had a very active wartime career, raiding targets on German-held islands in Arctic waters, helping to sink the German battleship *Bismarck* on 27 May 1941, waiting in vain for a sortie by *Bismarck*'s sister ship *Tirpitz*, supporting the landings in Sicily and Italy, and then serving with the British Pacific Fleet from early 1945, conducting shore bombardments and escorting British carriers until the surrender of Japan, at which she was present in Tokyo Harbor. Scrapped in 1957.

Prince of Wales (1937–1939–1941) was seriously damaged while fitting out in August 1940, during a German air raid on Liverpool. This delayed her completion by several months. She had an active career of only 216 days. Commissioned on March 31, 1941, she completed on May 8, and on the 22nd went to sea (with some workmen still aboard making final adjustments) in pursuit of the German *Bismarck*. On the 24th she swapped salvoes with *Bismarck*, and the accompanying heavy cruiser *Prinz Eugen*, putting three rounds into her but taking seven hits in return. Repaired, in August she carried Winston CHURCHILL to Argentia Bay for the conference that resulted in the Atlantic Charter. In October she was ordered to the Far East, where she was lost off MALAYA on 10 December 1942 after taking six aerial TORPEDO hits and at least one bomb. It was nearly two hours after the first torpedo hit before the ship rolled over and sank.

Duke of York (1937–1940–1941) had just entered service when the Japanese attacked PEARL HARBOR. She ferried Winston Churchill to the United States for the Arcadia Conference. She spent much of her war in northern waters, escorting convoys to Russia in the hope that German battleships might sortie from Norwegian bases. On Boxing Day (December 26), 1943 she shot it out with the German battleship *Scharnhorst*, taking some damage while heavily damaging her opponent with 10 14–inch hits; *Scharnhorst* was shortly sunk by a torpedo. She reached the Pacific in late spring 1945. She saw no action before the armistice but served as flagship of the British Pacific Fleet (TF 37) in Tokyo Bay. Scrapped in 1957.

Anson (1937–1940–1942) spent most of the war on guard for German battleships based in Norway. In the spring of 1945 she accompanied *Duke of York* to the Pacific, where the war ended before she could see action. Scrapped in 1957.

Howe (1937–1940–1942) spent 1942–43 on guard against sorties by German battleships based in Norway, supported the invasion of Sicily in mid-1943, and in August 1944, after a refit during which her antiaircraft capacity was considerably increased, joined the British Far Eastern Fleet. She shortly became the flagship of the new British Pacific Fleet, and escorted TF37/57 (the ROYAL NAVY component of the Fast Carrier Task Force) in operations against OKINAWA and Japan. Scrapped in 1957.

Like all British ships, the KGVs had an inadequate antiaircraft fire control system; nevertheless *King George V* and *Howe* were able to beat off serious Japanese air attacks.

Kinkaid, Thomas (1888–1972)

Thomas C. Kinkaid graduated from Annapolis in 1908. He served mostly in battleships until 1917, when he was assigned as a liaison officer to the British Admiralty. After World War I he held various assignments, commanded several ships, held several diplomatic posts, and attended the Naval War College. Shortly after PEARL HARBOR he took command of the *Enterprise* Task Force, which he commanded during the raids on the MANDATES, at MIDWAY, and at SANTA CRUZ. In early 1943 he became commander of naval forces in the North Pacific, overseeing the recovery of the ALEUTIANS. Later that year, by then a vice admiral, he was assigned to command the Seventh Fleet ("MacArthur's Navy"), which he led during the fighting for the northern SOLOMONS, the BISMARCKS, New Guinea, and the Philippines. On the surrender of Japan he oversaw the occupation of Korea and the movement of Chinese Nationalist troops to northern China. After the war he held several administrative posts until his retirement in 1950. One of the most successful US naval officers of the war, Kinkaid, who conducted more amphibious operations than any other commander in history, was little noticed by the public, overshadowed by having to work under Douglas MacArthur and by the admirals of the more glamorous fast carriers.

He was the brother-in-law of Admiral Husband KIMMEL.

Kiska, Aleutians, Alaska

Rarely visited, even by Aleut hunters and fishermen, Kiska did possess some ground suitable for use as an air base, should someone have wanted to try to build one there. Even then, it had little offensive value, as there was nothing within striking distance. However, as a forward defensive position it might have some value under certain circumstances. The climate was atrocious, possibly the worst on the planet for aircraft operations.

Kiska was occupied by the Japanese in mid-1942, during the MIDWAY Campaign. Although they attempted to develop it as a base, US sea and air power gradually isolated the island. They abandoned Kiska shortly after the United States retook Attu, in mid-1943.

Kobe, Japan

A major port and naval base with extensive facilities, located on Honshu, in the heart of Japan.

Koga, Mineichi (1885–1944)

Mineichi Koga graduated from the naval academy in 1906 and rose quickly through the ranks, aided by family connections with the Imperial Household. He became a rear admiral in the 1930s, when he became a major force on the Naval General Staff. Koga thought battleships could hold their own against aircraft, which put him in sync with the mainstream of Japanese naval thought. But he also believed that the Japanese Navy could not succeed against the American fleet. This caused his removal from the General Staff, followed by a succession of fleet commands. He commanded the China Area Fleet early in the war. Later in 1942 he went to command the Yokosuka Naval Base. When Admiral YAMAMOTO, the commander of the Combined Fleet, was killed in early 1943, Koga took his place. Proving an able and energetic commander, Koga sought to reorganize the fleet along the obviously more efficient American lines. Koga planned to pull back Japanese naval forces and conserve them to inflict maximum damage when the Americans began to close in. Before Koga could complete these plans, he was killed in an airplane crash in March 1944.

Kokoda Trail, Papua-New Guinea

A jungle track stretching from the road head some 30 miles north of PORT MORESBY, on the southern coast of Papua, over the OWEN STANLEY MOUNTAINS, at an altitude of some 7,000 feet, to the vicinity of GONA on the northwest coast. Literally only a few feet wide in most places, its worst sector was the so-called "Golden Stairway," a series of some 2,000 log and mud steps ascending the Owen Stanleys for several miles. The trail, which cut through dense jungle and was often no more than a muddy path, was the scene of heavy fighting in 1942. Overall, it was little more than 100 miles long.

Kolombangara, Battle of

A naval engagement in the Solomons, fought on the night of 12–13 July 1943. US light cruisers *Honolulu* and *St. Louis* plus the New Zealand *Leander* and 10 destroyers ran up the Slot to interfere in a "Tokyo Express" led by the light cruiser *Jintsu*, with five destroyers and four destroyer-transports. The two squadrons made contact at 0108 on July 13, and opened fire almost simultaneously. *Jintsu* blew up under a hail of 6-inch shells, while *Leander* took a TORPEDO in the first few seconds. The Japanese destroyers made a second torpedo run, sinking the destroyer *Gwin* and putting "fish" into both remaining Allied light cruisers. Both sides then drew off.

Despite the heavy odds against them, at Kolombangara the Japanese again demonstrated their superiority at night tactics.

See also KULA GULF, BATTLE OF; MORISON S. E.

Komandorski Islands, Battle of

On March 26, 1943 there occurred the last daylight gun battle between major surface ships that did not involve aircraft or SUBMARINES. It was also the longest naval gun battle in this century. What's more, it ended when the Japanese, who were at the point of defeating the American force, suddenly withdrew because they mistakenly thought they were under attack by American aircraft.

In a desperate effort to resupply their bases on Attu and KISKA in the ALEUTIAN ISLANDS (seized in June 1942), a Japanese convoy was dispatched consisting of four transports, escorted by elements of the Fifth Fleet, two heavy and two light cruisers, and four destroyers under VAdm Boshiro HOSO-GAYA. This was intercepted by an American force of one heavy and one light cruiser and four destroyers, under RAdm Charles H. MCMORRIS. The battle came down to a long-range gunnery duel between the heavy cruisers. Although outgunned, the American cruisers outfought the Japanese for over three hours. Then, a few hits by Japanese shells in vital areas left the US heavy cruiser *Salt Lake City* (nicknamed "Swayback Maru" by her devoted crew) dead in the water. At this point, it looked like the Americans were finished, as the Japanese could now pound the US heavy cruiser to pieces and then move in and crush the smaller American vessels.

Fortunately, the overcast weather and the fact that the US cruiser was running low on ammo saved the day. *Salt Lake City* had to use high explosive (HE) shells, as it had no more armor piercing (AP) ones. The HE shells, coming in through the overcast and exploding on the water like aircraft bombs, made the Japanese commander think that American aircraft had arrived and that he was

now under air attack, especially since the dye used to color the explosion for observation purposes was of a different color than that used in *Salt Lake City*'s AP shells. Both sides had called for aircraft support as soon as the battle began. But the changeable weather in those northern waters had prevented either side's aircraft from taking off. The Japanese commander didn't know the US aircraft were not able to fly, but he knew their imminent arrival was a possibility. Seeing what he thought were bombs, he ordered his ships and the convoy to turn back. Although US destroyers essayed a TORPEDO attack on the retiring Japanese, the battle was over. The amazed, and relieved, American commander signaled his base that the Japanese had withdrawn and that he would bring in his damaged cruiser as soon as emergency repairs could be made. McMorris was rightly hailed as a hero. Hosogaya was relieved.

Ref: Hutchison, *World War II in the North Pacific*; Lorelli, *The Battle of the Komandorski Islands*.

Kondo, Nobutake (1886–1953)

Marked early as a potential Japanese admiral, Nobutake Kondo fulfilled that promise. Graduating from the naval academy in 1907, he served in staff positions. He had a lot of foreign travel, including duty in Russia in 1919–20, and studied in Germany, becoming pro-German. Despite this, he did not believe Japan could successfully take on America. By 1939 he was a vice admiral. He commanded the naval strike force that assisted the invasion of MALAYA in December 1941 and then the Dutch East Indies in early 1942. While he disagreed with the wisdom of the MIDWAY operation, he commanded the Second Fleet in the campaign there (the invasion covering force of battleships, a light carrier, and lighter units, providing extra firepower in the event of intervention by Allied surface warships). He took over command of the surviving units of the demolished carrier forces and led heavy units in battles for GUADALCANAL during 1942. Kondo lost his flagship (battleship *Kirishima*) in a

BATTLE OF THE KOMANDORSKI ISLANDS AMMUNITION EXPENDITURE

Caliber	US	Japan
8–inch	832	1,611
6–inch	271	—
Smaller	2,314	300+
Torpedoes	5	47

US smaller guns were 3-inch and 5-inch, Japanese 5.5-inch and 5.1-inch.

night surface action off Guadalcanal in November 1942. He proceeded to command naval aviation (25th Air Fleet) in the GILBERT ISLANDS until the American invasion in 1943. He then moved to command the China Area Fleet until the end of the war. After the surrender, he remained in command of Japanese naval forces in INDO-CHINA for several months to assist the British in fighting communist GUERRILLAS (the Vietminh). After the war, he became a successful businessman. Kondo was an extremely likable officer, partly because he always allowed subordinates to speak their piece. A very efficient officer and excellent bureaucrat, he became friends with many of his former enemies after the war.

Kongo Class, Japanese Battleships

HIJMS *Kongo* was built in a British shipyard, to a British design. Her sisters were built in Japanese yards, to the same design. They were the last Japanese warships to be designed by foreign naval architects. Originally built as battlecruisers (at 27.5 knots, fast for their day), during the 1930s they were extensively reconstructed. They were given additional armor, while their engines were replaced with more modern ones, bringing their speed up to about 30 knots. These upgrades permitted them to be reclassed as "fast battleships," and they accompanied carrier task forces in the early part of the war. As a result, they saw much more action than all other Japanese battleships together.

Kongo (1911–1912–1913) was the last Japanese warship ordered from a foreign shipyard. In December 1941 she supported Second Fleet operations in the Philippines and NETHERLANDS EAST INDIES. She served in the Solomons, where she bombarded GUADALCANAL on one occasion. Like most Japanese battleships she was inactive for most of 1943–44, but was part of the battle squadron that shot up the US escort carriers off SAMAR on October 25, 1944. She was sunk by a single TORPEDO from USS *Sealion* (SS-315, the second boat of that name) on November 21, 1944, in the East China Sea.

Hiei (1911–1912–1914) was partially disarmed in the late 1920s and serving as a training ship under the terms of the naval DISARMAMENT TREATIES. In the late 1930s she was secretly modernized and rearmed, joining the fleet in time to help escort the First Air Fleet in its operations from PEARL HARBOR to the Indian Ocean. She then served in the Solomons, where she became the first Japanese battleship to be lost in the war, when she was turned into a burning wreck by about 50 shells of 5-inch to 8-inch caliber off GUADALCANAL on November 12–13, 1942, her shattered hulk being sunk that morning by US aircraft.

Haruna (1912–1913–1915) served with *Kongo* for much of the war, initially in the Second Fleet, then during operations against Guadalcanal and later at Samar. Reported sunk on five occasions (including one attributed to Colin KELLY) *Haruna* survived until 28 July 1945, when she was sunk in KURE Harbor by US carrier aircraft.

Kirishima (1912–1913–1915) accompanied *Hiei* for much of the war, serving with the First Air Fleet at Pearl Harbor and in the Indian Ocean. She took part in both major night actions off Guadalcanal on November 12–12 and 14–15, 1942, during the second of which she absorbed nine 16-inch and about 40 to 50 5-inch shells, which turned her into a burning wreck, causing her to be scuttled.

Korea

Called Chosen by the Japanese, Korea is a large (c. 85,000 square miles) peninsula jutting southward from the Asian mainland just west of Japan, inhabited by a people culturally and racially distinct from the Chinese but related to the Japanese. Korea was under Japanese occupation after the Russo-Japanese War (1904–05). After Japanese annexation in 1909, the Koreans suffered considerable oppression. Not only did the Japanese institute a systematic campaign to obliterate Korean culture (for example, use of the Korean language was virtually prohibited and all Koreans were forced to adopt Japanese names), but they undertook a determined program to stamp out Christianity in the peninsula, with considerable success, the number of practicing Christians falling from about 700,000 to 250,000 by 1941. Although Koreans were legally Japanese citizens as well as subjects of the emperor, they were definitely second-class citizens. For example, while Korean men with the appropriate financial qualifications had the right to vote, no election was ever held in Korea. Nearly 60% of the 87,600 jobs in government administration in Korea in the late 1930s were held by Japanese, Koreans mostly occupying lower level positions. Of 3,000 physicians in the country, only about 150 were Koreans. The highest ranking Korean in the railroad system was an assistant station master.

On the eve of World War II Korea's population comprised approximately 22.2 million Koreans, plus about 650,000 resident Japanese (a figure that rose to nearly a million by the end of the Pacific War). By 1945 there were some 2.4 million Koreans in Japan, and another 1.6 million in China and MANCHURIA, mostly as workers: Perhaps as many as 20,000 of the people killed by the ATOMIC BOMB at HIROSHIMA were Koreans. In addition to a substantial military garrison, there were some 60,000 police, mostly recruited from among Koreans. This was about one police officer for every 441 inhabitants.

Koreans were subject to Japanese CONSCRIPTION. Men were drafted into the Japanese armed forces, hundreds of thousands serving as labor troops, and beginning in 1943 as combat troops as well, although only about 35,000 were actually taken for combat service. Women were drafted into the WOMEN'S VOLUNTARY SERVICE CORPS, which primarily supplied laborers for factories and agriculture, but also provided tens of thousands of COMFORT WOMEN to the Imperial Army.

The Japanese did foster some industrialization in the north, where there are various significant mineral deposits, and agriculture in the south, a region intensively exploited to help feed Japan.

During World War II Korea was occasionally bombed, but was largely spared the horrors of battle, although Soviet troops penetrated the northern areas of the country in the last weeks of the war.

Korea, Resistance to the Japanese

Unlike the other nations occupied by the Japanese, Korea had been under Japanese rule since 1904. Thus the Japanese had more than 30 years to enforce their rule. Many Koreans had fled to China and joined the communist GUERRILLAS there. A large Korean population existed in MANCHURIA, and many men from this group also fled deeper into China to join the fight. Many Koreans who stayed behind joined Japanese-controlled army units and many more were conscripted for service as labor troops overseas. These Koreans at first confused American troops (who could not tell the difference between a Korean and a Japanese soldier) by quickly running away or surrendering rather than fighting to the death as Japanese usually did. The Koreans were not enthusiastic about supporting the Japanese war effort; most of their guerrilla activities were in the form of sabotage and lackadaisical attitudes on the job. The North Korean invasion of South Korea in 1950 was spearheaded by 100,000 Korean veterans of the war in China, while many of the South Korean officers had formerly served in the Japanese Army.

Krueger, Walter (1881–1967)

Born in Germany, Krueger came to America with his family when he was eight. In 1898 he enlisted in the volunteers for the Spanish-American War, seeing action in Cuba. Passing to the Regular Army, he served during the Philippine Insurrection, being commissioned in 1901. His career thereafter included the staff college and troop duty, and accompanying Pershing's Mexican Expedition. In 1918 he served as a staff officer with various divisions and corps in France. After the war he held various staff and line assignments, attended the Army and Navy War Colleges (he returned to the latter as an instructor), and by late 1941 was an acting lieutenant general in command of the Third Army.

Stateside for the first 18 months of the war, in mid-1943 Krueger took command of the Sixth Army, organizing in Australia. He led the Sixth Army in numerous operations, including the Woodlark Island, NEW BRITAIN, the ADMIRALTY ISLANDS, New Guinea, BIAK, Leyte, and ultimately Luzon, ending the war on occupation duty in Japan. Krueger managed the often difficult task of working in the shadow of Douglas MACARTHUR. He had many fine qualities: A meticulous planner and trainer, he was also a fairly good military historian and linguist, translating several military classics from his native German to English. However, Krueger was not a particularly great commander. His principal virtue as a soldier was that he had no interest in publicity, which made him an excellent subordinate for MacArthur, who wanted it all.

Kuching, Borneo

A small port on the northwestern coast of BORNEO, mostly for coastal traders, with no significant facilities to service or repair ships, but of some value for projecting airpower into the South China Sea. The Japanese occupied it early in 1942, but it remained a backwater throughout the war.

Kula Gulf, Battle of

A night encounter on July 5–6, 1943 between an American light cruiser/destroyer squadron and a "Tokyo Express" of 10 destroyers attempting to land reinforcements on Munda. The Japanese lost destroyers *Nagatsuki* and *Niizuki* to US gunfire, but managed to torpedo the light cruiser USS *Helena*, which sank after a series of internal explosions.

See also KOLOMBANGARA, BATTLE OF; MORISON, S. E.

Kuma Class, Japanese Light Cruisers

Like all Japanese light cruisers the Kumas were designed primarily as flotilla leaders. Although very old by World War II standards, they performed well in this role. Shortly before the war began two units of the class were converted to torpedo cruisers, mounting three fewer 5.5-inch guns, but with a record 40 TORPEDO tubes. In this mode they might have proven an enormously powerful opponent in a surface action, but they were never tested in a battle where they could use this tremendous torpedo capacity. The other units in the class were less extensively modified.

Kuma (1918–1919–1920) led a destroyer flotilla during the invasion of the Philippines, and later in the NETHERLANDS EAST INDIES. Sunk off PENANG by the British T-Class submarine *Tally-Ho* on 11 January 1944.

Tama (1918–1919–1921) served initially in the Philippines and Netherlands East Indies, and was later at the KOMANDORSKI ISLANDS. While escorting the "bait" task force during the Battle of LEYTE GULF, she was bombed off Cape Engaño on 25 October 1944, and finished off that same day by USS *Jallao* (SS-368).

Kitikami (1919–1920–1921), one of the units converted into a torpedo cruiser, served in the South China Sea and East Indian waters. In January 1944 she took a British torpedo in her after engine room, causing considerable damage. During repairs *Kitikami* was converted into a transport for the Kaiten suicide submarine, with greatly reduced speed (c. 23 knots). Severely damaged in the carrier air strikes against KURE on July 24 and 28, 1945, she survived, to be scrapped in 1947.

Oi (1919–1920–1921) was one of the units converted into a torpedo cruiser in 1940–41. She saw a good deal of service, mostly in the Netherlands East Indies and China Seas, but no serious action until sunk on 19 July 1944 by USS *Flasher* (SS-249) in the South China Sea.

Kiso (1919–1920–1921) served primarily in Southeast Asian waters, and was sunk in Manila Bay by US carrier aircraft on November 13, 1944.

Note that *Kitikami* and *Oi* are listed separately on the cruiser table.

Kuomintang (KMT)

Founded by Chinese republican leader Dr. Sun Yat-sen in 1911, the Kuomintang (Nationalist Peoples' Party, abbreviated KMT) began as a liberal, more or less democratic party with a vaguely socialist program. The party—and Sun—were in and out of government from the Revolution of 1911 until the mid-1920s, when the KMT established a separate government from the warlord-dominated one in Peking. A national congress in 1924 created a coalition with many other groups, including the Chinese communists. The better disciplined communists exercised increasing influence over the KMT until 1928, when General CHIANG KAI-SHEK and the more conservative elements in the party ousted them. This began the long Chinese Civil War, which combined KMT campaigns against the communists with operations against the warlords, most notably the "Northern Offensive," which brought most of China under KMT rule. Attempts to crush the communists were only partially successful, and resulted in the "Long March," which established the communists in Shensi Province.

Despite this failure, and ongoing problems with Japan, by the mid-1930s the KMT had established a stable, moderately progressive regime throughout much of China. Although not strictly democratic, the KMT probably represented the political aspirations of most of the Chinese people better than the communists. The Japanese invasion of 1937 was undoubtedly the single most serious cause of the failure of the KMT. The party proved unable to wage an effective war against the Japanese, and grew increasingly corrupt and authoritarian. Although Chiang and the KMT held China together long enough to win the war, they proved unable to win the renewed civil war with the communists that broke out soon afterward.

Ref: Ch'i, *Nationalist China at War*; Eastman, "Nationalist China during the Sino-Japanese War, 1937–1945."

Kure, Honshu, Japan

The principal base of the Imperial Navy, with extensive construction and repair installations, important air bases, and excellent access to the rest of Japan by rail; securely located on the interior of the INLAND SEA. Kure was capable of building or repairing warships of any size. It was the site of the Eta Jima Naval Academy for line officers (other branches went to MAIZURU or Tokyo) and of the Kure SNLF. In July 1945, while sheltering the remnants of the Imperial Navy, Kure was twice raided (24th and 28th) by aircraft from the US Third Fleet. Japanese losses were three battleships (ISE, *Hyuga, Haruna*), one carrier (*Amagi*), one escort carrier (KAIYO), two heavy cruisers (TONE, AOBA), one light cruiser (OYODO), a submarine, two obsolete coast defense ships, and three smaller warships sunk, plus three carriers and numerous smaller vessels badly damaged.

Kure Atoll, Hawaiian Islands

The northwesternmost islets in the Hawaiian chain, some 60 miles from MIDWAY, Kure figured in the war several times. During the Battle of Midway PT-BOATS patrolled the area to ensure that the Japanese would not try using it as an advanced seaplane base. Later one islet was bulldozed into an emergency landing strip, and it still looks like an aircraft carrier from the air.

Kuribayashi, Tadamichi (1891–1945)

Scion of a family that had produced samurai for generations, Kuribayashi graduated from the military academy in 1914, entering the army as a cavalryman. He served as an assistant military attaché in the United States, and later as military attaché to Canada, and in the process decided that "America was the last country that Japan should go to war with." He commanded a cavalry regiment during the CHINA INCIDENT, was chief of staff to the Twenty-first Army in China, 1941–43, during which he planned the capture of HONG KONG, and from 1943 to 1944 he was commander of the First Imperial Guards Division, in Tokyo. Given command of the 109th Division and IWO JIMA in mid-1944, he was chiefly responsible for planning the defenses that proved so difficult to break in early 1945. Kuribayashi, who was quite tall for a Japanese, 5'9", was apparently killed in action late in February 1945.

Kurile Islands

A chain of hundreds of islands, islets, and rocky outcrops stretching about 750 miles southwestward from Kamchatka in Russia to Hokkaido, the northernmost island of Japan. Only about 30 of the islands are of any size, and the total area is only about 6,000 square miles. The Kuriles, which were largely Russian before the Russo-Japanese War (1904–05), were thinly populated, mostly by hunting and fishing tribes. Despite some of the foulest weather in the world, they were an important strategic base for the Japanese: It was from the Kuriles that the PEARL HARBOR Striking Force set sail in November of 1941.

During the war the islands provided the bases from which the Japanese conducted their operations in the ALEUTIANS. Several of the ports were bombed by US aircraft during the latter period of the war, and there were even several raids by US surface ships.

On August 17, 1945, after the formal establishment of the armistice, Soviet troops undertook an offensive to occupy the Kuriles. Using their 10th Rifle Division, two independent rifle regiments, and three naval infantry battalions, supported by the 124th Air Division and the North Pacific Flotilla, based out of Petropavlovsk on the Kamchatka Peninsula, the Soviets, under MG A. R. Grechko, began operations against the islands. The Japanese government formally protested the violation of the armistice to MACARTHUR, who passed the protest on to his political superiors. However, the Soviets ignored US protests and pressed on.

Japanese resistance was relatively light, although the 91st Division, on Shimushu, put up a tough fight, and the Russians soon overran most of the islands.

See also MANCHURIA, CAMPAIGN FOR, 1945.

Ref: Hutchison, *World War II in the North Pacific*.

Kurita, Takeo (1889–1977)

Takeo Kurita graduated from the Japanese naval academy in 1910 and specialized in TORPEDO warfare thereafter, while commanding successively more important vessels. By PEARL HARBOR he was rear admiral commanding the Seventh Cruiser Squadron. He became vice admiral in 1942 and that year commanded surface forces battling to recover GUADALCANAL. Commander of Second Fleet as of early 1944, he lost most of his ships in the naval battles to defend the Philippines during that year. Relieved of command in late 1944, he returned to Japan.

Kusaka, Junichi (1889–1972)

Junichi Kusaka entered the Imperial Navy shortly before World War I. He rose steadily thereafter, and in 1942 was made a vice admiral, commanding the South East Area Fleet at RABAUL, a post that he held until the end of the war. He was the principal Japanese commander in the BISMARCKS area for the entire war. His cousin was Admiral Ryunosuke KUSAKA.

Kusaka, Ryunosuke (1892–1971)

Ryunosuke Kusaka, cousin of Junichi KUSAKA, graduated from the naval academy during World War I. A naval aviator, he commanded carriers HOSHO and AKAGI. A rear admiral and staff officer at the start of the Pacific War, he remained a staff officer for the entire war, although he became a vice admiral. He was more pragmatic than most of the fleet commanders, which may be why he never got a major command. He also opposed suicide attacks.

Kwajalein, Marshall Islands

The largest lagoon in the world, on the most sprawling atoll in the world, Kwajalein had an extensive protected anchorage and ample space for the establishment of naval and air base facilities. This could be used to dominate the entire region. The potential utility of Kwajalein in this regard had been noted by the US Navy even before World War I. Surprisingly, the Japanese, who had owned the place since taking it from Germany in 1914, gave little thought to developing it as a base. Captured by the United States in early 1944, the atoll was developed into an important base.

See also CENTRAL PACIFIC CAMPAIGN; MARSHALL ISLANDS CAMPAIGN.

L

La Gallissonier Class, French Light Cruisers

The best French light cruisers of World War II, these six vessels, built from 1931 to 1937, were too small, too undergunned, and too lightly protected to be suitable for the Pacific War. Three were scuttled with the French Fleet at Toulon on November 27, 1942, the other three saw some service "showing the flag" with the British Far Eastern Fleet in 1943–45.

See also ROYAL NAVY.

Labuan, Borneo

A small port suitable for coastwise shipping, with no facilities to repair or service vessels. As a base, nearby BRUNEI was more suitable.

L'Adroit Class, French Destroyers

An older class, L'Adroit and her 13 sisters (built 1924–30) were the last French destroyers of ordinary proportions for a decade (after them came the "monster" classes, the French developing a predilection for destroyers that approached the size of small light cruisers). Nine were lost in the ETO, but some of the survivors served with the ROYAL NAVY in the Indian Ocean and one was in the South Pacific during the GUADALCANAL Campaign. The survivors were scrapped in the 1950s.

Lae, New Guinea

A fairly large town, by local standards, on the east coast of New Guinea, with a good harbor but with limited facilities, with some potential as a base for dominating the local area. Lae was taken by the Japanese in early 1942 and became the object of major Allied operations during the New Guinea Campaign.

Lamotte-Picquet, French Light Cruiser

Lamotte-Picquet (1923–1924–1926) was one of three ships of the Duguay-Trouin class, the first new cruisers built for France since 1908. Technically rated as heavy cruisers under the terms of the DISARMAMENT TREATIES, since they carried 6.1-inch guns, they were good ships, reliable, fast, and seaworthy, but very lightly armed and not well protected—their thickest armor was one inch. Lamotte-Picquet was stationed in INDO-CHINA throughout the Pacific War, under Vichyite control. She performed well during the brief Siamese-French War of 1940–41 (see SIAMESE ARMED FORCES). Thereafter inactive for the rest of the war, she was sunk by US carrier aircraft near SAIGON on January 12, 1945. Her sister Primauguet was active in the Mediterranean under Vichy control until she was lost during the Allied landings in North Africa in late 1942. Duguay-Trouin was interned by the British at Alexandria after the Fall of France in 1940, but returned to duty under Free French control in mid-1943 and survived the war.

Lanikai, US Schooner

On 4 December 1941 the schooner Lanikai was commissioned in the US Navy by personal order of President ROOSEVELT. Commanded by Lieutenant Kemp Tolley, she was sent into the South China Sea in the last days of peace to observe Japanese movements out of CAM RANH BAY, in Indo-China. Tolley later claimed the purpose of the mission was to provoke a Japanese attack, so that Roosevelt would have a pretext to go to war. Considering that the president and his principal political and military advisers already believed that Japan intended to attack the United States and other Western powers, and that Japanese shipping movements toward this end had been under observation for several days already, the charge falls into the category of yet another anti-Roosevelt conspiracy theory.

LCI (Landing Craft, Infantry), Allied Landing Vessels

Smaller still than the LSM, LCIs were only 153 feet long and 246 tons (387 tons full load). About a thousand were built, plus 300 gunship versions and 49 used as flotilla flagships. LCIs could carry about 200–250 infantrymen with their equipment. After running aground, two ramps were let down allowing a single file of troops to walk down each ramp onto the beach. Depending on beach conditions, the troops might still have to wade through ankle-to knee-deep water. Crew size was 25–30 sailors. Top speed was 14 knots, making them a bit faster than LSTS and LSMs. Armament was four or five 20mm antiaircraft guns. Some were specialized for fire-support missions, with crews of 78 men, armed with three 40mm antiaircraft guns and a 10-tube, 5-inch rocket launcher. LCIs were ideal for operations such as the TINIAN landings or the many short-range assaults in the southwest Pacific, since they could be loaded in friendly ports and make the short sea voyage necessary to get to their objectives. While the LCI was seagoing, its fuel supply was too meager to get very far over open seas.

LCT (Landing Craft, Tank), Allied Landing Vessels

Similar in size to the LCI, but designed to carry vehicles over short distances, up to a hundred miles or so. There were two main designs: average length of both was 115 feet, full-load weight 290 tons. LCTs had a bow ramp for discharging three to four TANKS, or several more trucks and jeeps, or about 150 tons of cargo. They were slow, with a top speed of 8–10 knots. The crew consisted of a dozen officers and men. About a thousand were built, and some were converted to gunships (firing rockets.)

LCVP (Landing Craft, Vehicle and Personnel), Allied Landing Vessels

These were the amphibious assault vessels most frequently seen, especially in photos and or film, landing troops and vehicles. Basically a boxy boat with a hinged front ramp, it was run up on the beach to disgorge 36 assaulting infantrymen directly into action; one or two jeeps or trucks, depending on size and load; or a tank. Numerous types existed, but all were very small (about 8–12 tons empty, and 36 feet long) and capable of being carried aboard AKAs, APAs, LSTs, and just about anything else. Somewhat larger versions were known as LCMs (Landing Craft, Motorized), running about 23 tons empty, with a length of 50 feet and a capacity to lift 60 armed troops or a tank into action, or carry over 25 tons of cargo. LCVPs had a crew of three, LCMs of four. Other nations, including Japan, had developed similar vessels before World War II. But only America and Britain went on to develop a wide variety of larger "run them up on the beach and unload" craft.

Leander Class, New Zealand Light Cruisers

Good light cruisers in a European context, New Zealand's Leanders (sisters to Britain's Ajax class) were of only limited value in the Pacific, having relatively short range and rather light armament. Nevertheless, they saw considerable action.

Leander (1930–1931–1933) fought in a number of the surface actions in the SOLOMONS, being so badly damaged by a Japanese 24-inch TORPEDO at KOLOMBANGARA that she nearly sank.

Achilles (1931–1932–1933) fought in World War II's first surface action, when, in company with her British sister *Ajax* (1933–1934–1935) and the heavy cruiser HMS EXETER, she took on the German "pocket battleship" *Graf Spee* in December of 1939. *Achilles* went on to fight in the Pacific, notably in the Solomons and New Guinea Campaigns.

As both ships were actually on loan to New Zealand from the ROYAL NAVY, they were returned to British control in 1945 and 1946 respectively. *Leander* was scrapped in 1949, but *Achilles* was sold to India in 1948, and remained in service for many years, until she was scrapped in 1978.

Lee, Willis (1888–1945)

Willis "Ching Chong China" Lee, the premier American battleship admiral of the war, graduated from Annapolis in 1908. He had an active career in surface ships, took part in the Vera Cruz operation in 1914, and commanded destroyers during World War I, while finding time to win a medal as part of the US Olympic rifle team. Between the wars he held various command and staff assignments, and on the eve of the Pacific War was director of fleet training. In mid-1942 he was sent to command the fast battleships in the southwest Pacific, a post he held for virtually the rest of the war. Lee, a deceptively scholarly looking man with wire-rimmed glasses, developed innovative techniques for the cooperation of modern battleships with carriers in air battles (SANTA CRUZ ISLAND, for example), defeated a Japanese squadron in a night slug-out off GUADALCANAL on November 4–15, 1942, took part in the battles of the PHILIPPINE SEA and Leyte (where he just missed a possible battleship action off SAMAR by bad luck and poor guessing on HALSEY's part), and went right on to OKINAWA (where he was denied the chance to shoot it out with YAMATO because the carrier admirals wanted to strut their stuff, this resulted in weakening the air cover over the fleet, possibly per-

mitting the KAMIKAZE some additional degree of success). Although he served most of the war subordinate to carrier admirals, he also demonstrated some ability to handle independent commands, overseeing the occupation of BAKER ISLAND (during which he had no battleships, but several carriers) and the raid on NAURU in late 1943. On leave after Okinawa, he was temporarily assigned to Task Force 69, in the Atlantic, a special command organized to develop techniques for coping with kamikaze attacks, an extremely critical assignment given that the navy was then involved in planning for Operation Olympic, the invasion of Japan, scheduled for November 1, 1945. While still acting in this capacity, Lee died of a heart attack in August of 1945.

LeMay, Curtis E. (1906–1990)

Curtis E. LeMay failed to get into West Point but managed to secure a commission in the army through ROTC. After flight training he served with various bomber units. LeMay's rise was rapid, and by the time of PEARL HARBOR he was a major. Jumped to colonel the following March, LeMay was given command of the 305th Bombardment Group, which deployed to England the following month. LeMay engaged in many missions over Germany in the following months, rising to major general by early 1944, at the comparatively young age of 38. In August of 1944 he was assigned to command the bomber elements of the Twentieth Air Force, operating in the CBI and later the Marianas, rising to its command by mid-1945. In this capacity LeMay oversaw the bombing of Japan, including the use of the ATOMIC BOMB. After the war LeMay held a variety of staff posts, created the Strategic Air Command, and ultimately became chief of staff of the air force, retiring in 1965. He afterward dabbled in business and right-wing politics. An excellent pilot and officer equally capable in both combat and staff, LeMay was typical of the bomber-minded generals who emerged from World War II to dominate the air force during the Cold War.

Lend-Lease

Lend-Lease was a program under which the president was authorized to "lend or lease" surplus military equipment to certain countries under certain circumstances. It was created because by early 1941, Britain, China, and various governments-in-exile were running out of money with which to purchase munitions and other assistance from the United States. As a result, President Franklin D. ROOSEVELT proposed this innovative arrangement under which he would be authorized to "lend" military equipment and other materials to nations whose defense was considered vital to that of the United States. It was enacted as Public Law 1776 on March 11, 1941, over often hysterical ("This bill will guarantee that every fourth American boy is plowed under!") opposition from isolationist groups ranging from the German-American Bund to the Communist Party, then still faithfully following the Moscow line of friendship with HITLER. Lend-Lease had an enormous impact on the war. Military equipment, foodstuffs, and in some cases cash totaling nearly $51 billion of very uninflated 1940s money was dispensed to nearly 45 countries (including the USSR, beginning within days of Hitler's invasion, to the praises of the suddenly interventionist American Communist Party).

In terms of 1998 dollars, the $51 billion spent during the war would be worth over $600 billion. The range of materials covered by Lend-Lease was extraordinary. Russia, for example, received over 430,000 trucks, nearly 7,000 fighters, and over 340,000 field telephones, as well as samples of unusual equipment such as the M-1 rifle, the T-10 heavy tank, and the B-17, not to mention a lot of gold braid, which was found useful in raising the morale of Red Army officers (who wore it) and men (who saluted it).

Most Lend-Lease money was allocated to European countries, reasonable given that the Nazis posed a greater threat to American security than the Japanese. Considering the allocations to what would eventually be known as "Third World" countries, some Lend-Lease aid seems more likely

LEND-LEASE AID	
Country	Sum ($1940s)
Belgium	148,394,457.76
Bolivia	5,633,989.02
Brazil	332,545,226.43
British Empire	31,267,240,530.63
Chile	21,817,478.16
China	1,548,794,965.99
Colombia	7,809,732.58
Costa Rica	155,022.73
Cuba	5,739,133.33
Czechoslovakia	413,398.78
Dominican Republic	1,610,590.38
Ecuador	7,063,079.96
Egypt	1,019,169.14
El Salvador	892,358.28
Ethiopia	5,151,163.25
France	3,207,608,188.75
Greece	75,475,880.30
Guatemala	1,819,403.19
Haiti	1,449,096.40
Honduras	732,358.11
Iceland	4,795,027.90
Iran	4,795,092.50
Iraq	4,144.14
Liberia	6,408,240.13
Mexico	36,287,010.67
Netherlands	230,127,717.63
Nicaragua	872,841.73
Norway	51,524,124.36
Panama	83,555.92
Paraguay	1,933,302.00
Peru	18,525,771.19
Poland	16,934,163.60
Saudi Arabia	17,417,878.70
Turkey	26,640,031.50
Uruguay	7,148,610.13
USSR	11,260,343,603.02
Venezuela	4,336,079.35
Yugoslavia	32,026,355.58
Total Payments to Nations	$48,213,174,315.42
Other Expenditures +	2,578,827,000.00
Grand Total	$50,792,001,315.42

+Materials not charged to the recipient nations, including goods lost in shipment, items consumed by American forces, and administrative costs.

to have been made to keep the local leadership happy than as an investment in the defense of the Free World. Certainly no other explanation seems reasonable for the fact that the Polish government-in-exile, which had several divisions fighting fascism, received less money than Peru, Saudi Arabia, or Turkey, which had none at all.

Several countries provided the United States with what was termed "Reverse Lend-Lease," goods and equipment of use to American forces and the US war effort. For example, Belgium kicked in a lot of then seemingly useless uranium ore (from its African colonies), while Australia and New Zealand contributed a lot of rations to US forces in the South Pacific, a form of payment not always appreciated by the troops (see FOOD, RATIONS, US). Reverse Lend-Lease amounted to about $10 billion, leaving a deficit of some $41 billion. However, it is worth recalling that virtually all the money involved in Lend-Lease was spent in the United States, buying those TANKS and planes and uniforms that were then shipped to the receiving nations. And in any case, the balance may be considered to have been paid in blood at places like Alamein, Stalingrad, and Imphal.

Lexington Class, US Aircraft Carriers

Laid down as battlecruisers, the Lexingtons were converted to carriers under the terms of the naval DISARMAMENT TREATIES. The largest, most impressive looking carriers in the US Navy during the war, they had the most powerful engines in the fleet, until the advent of the IOWA CLASS battleships, and the longest flight decks (888 feet), until the MIDWAY CLASS entered service. They used a very successful but very expensive electric turbine drive, so powerful that Lexington was once able to jump-start a municipal power plant after a blackout. The two ships were central to the development of American naval airpower doctrine, serving as test beds for numerous experiments in STRATEGY, tactics, and even logistics. Initially operating only about 65 aircraft, it was eventually realized that they could comfortably function with over 100.

Lexington, CV-2 (1921–1925–1927), was one of the most beloved ships ever to wear the American flag. At sea when PEARL HARBOR was attacked, she took part in all the early carrier operations, from the abortive WAKE ISLAND relief mission to the MANDATES raids and Wilson BROWN's strike across the Owen Stanley Mountains in Papua, before fighting in the Battle of the CORAL SEA. On May 8, 1942, she was damaged by two TORPEDOES and two bombs, which caused a list and some fires. Her damage control parties appeared to have had everything under control when two severe internal explosions caused by the accumulation of fumes from avgas wracked the ship. The ship had to be abandoned and sunk by torpedoes from the USS *Phelps* (DD-360). Adjustments were made to all other carriers to limit future incidents of the same sort.

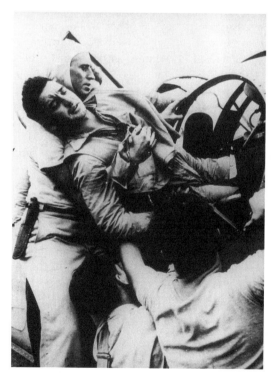

Badly wounded gunner Kenneth Bratton is lifted out of the turret of a Saratoga *(CV-3) TBF Avenger after a raid on Rabaul, November 1943.*

Saratoga, CV-3 (1920–1925–1927), was at SAN DIEGO when Pearl Harbor was attacked. She took part in the abortive Wake Island relief mission, was torpedoed on 11 January 1942 south of HAWAII, took part in the raids on the Mandates in the spring of 1942, helped cover the GUADALCANAL landings, took another torpedo 31 August 1942 off Guadalcanal, fought in the Battle of the EASTERN SOLOMONS, supported landings all cross the Pacific, served with the ROYAL NAVY in the Indian Ocean for a time in 1944, then returned to the Pacific in time to take a KAMIKAZE off IWO JIMA. Although repaired, she saw no further combat service in the war, and was expended as a target at Bikini (see ATOMIC BOMB, THE BIKINI TESTS).

Leyte Gulf, Battle of

The greatest naval battle in history, Leyte Gulf was the Imperial Navy's last attempt to engage in a decisive battle with the US Navy. It was actually a series of interrelated engagements fought over tens of thousands of square miles of ocean in October 1944.

Aware that the next major American move in the Pacific was almost certainly a landing in the Philippines, the Imperial Navy developed a series of possible defensive plans, the precise one to be used depending upon the actual site of the American landings. The plan recognized several serious obstacles to Japanese success, the most significant being the virtual incompetence of their naval aviators by this point in the war. So the plan envisioned the use of Japan's remaining carriers (with minimal AIR GROUPS) as "bait" to lure the main American strength northward, away from the invasion beaches, which would then be in a position to be hit by surface forces, which had quietly made their way through the numerous small seas and straits in the Philippine archipelago. The version of Operation "Sho" ("Victory") that was put into effect was that designed to cope with an American landing on Leyte, in the central part of the eastern Philippines. This envisioned four main task forces, all under VAdm Jisaburo OZAWA. Ozawa's Main Body of the Mobile Force, concentrated in the INLAND SEA and comprising four carriers and two hybrid battleship/carriers, would steam southward from Japan into the western PHILIPPINE SEA, constituting the "bait" for the trap. The actual offensive elements were "A Force," "C Force," and the "Second Striking Force."

"A Force"—five battleships, including the behemoths YAMATO and *Musashi*, with nine heavy cruisers and accompanying destroyers—concentrated at BRUNEI Bay (where it was easy to get fuel). They would then thread their way through the Sibuyan Sea, in the central Philippines, debouch from San Bernardino Strait, and speed south to shoot up American transports off Leyte.

The "Second Striking Force"—two heavy cruisers, a light cruiser, and four destroyers in the Inland Sea—would sail south through the China Sea and into the Sulu Sea, where it would unite with "C Force."

"C Force," which had two old battleships, a heavy cruiser, and four destroyers, was to start from Brunei Bay. Once the "Second Striking Force" and "C Force" united, in the Sulu Sea, the two squadrons would thread their way through the many islands and debouch from SURIGAO STRAIT right into Leyte Gulf, to devastate American shipping off the beaches.

"Operation Sho" was put into effect on 20 October, as various elements began to steam for their objectives. Meanwhile, the US Navy had brought over 200 warships (including two Australian) into action off the Philippines, supporting over 400 transports and hundreds of other smaller vessels, which were actually effecting the landings on Leyte Island.

The fleet was widely dispersed. The Fast Carrier Task Force, still under Marc MITSCHER, was deployed about 100 miles east of Leyte, with the individual task groups rotating into and out of action in order to refuel and remunition. With Mitscher was Third Fleet Commander William F. HALSEY, over 15 carriers, seven fast battleships, and dozens of cruisers and destroyers. Between Mitscher and Leyte were three escort carrier task groups, assigned to support the beachhead. And in Leyte Gulf itself was Seventh Fleet, six old battleships (five of them Pearl Harbor veterans), eight cruisers, nearly 20 destroyers, and numerous PT-BOATS, protecting the transports and lending fire support to the combat troops on Leyte itself.

Not until 23 October did Halsey learn that the Japanese fleet was on the move. At 0630 that day, two US SUBMARINES sank two and disabled one of the heavy cruisers accompanying VAdm Takeo KURITA's "A Force." Although he had to cope with attacks from Japanese land-based aircraft, which sank light carrier *Princeton*, Mitscher launched a major strike against Kurita's squadron, 259 aircraft. These intercepted Kurita in the Sibuyan Sea and heavily worked him over. Superbattleship *Musashi* went down, after taking enormous punishment, and the other ships turned back. So one of the Japanese attack forces had been defeated by the evening of 24 October.

Meanwhile, before noon on 24 October, carrier reconnaissance aircraft had spotted the combined "C Force" and the "Second Striking Force." VAdm Thomas KINKAID, commanding Seventh Fleet, actually inside Leyte Gulf, correctly concluded that these ships were headed for Surigao Strait, and ordered the old battleships off Leyte to intercept.

RAdm Jesse Oldendorf, commanding the fire support vessels, deployed his old battleships, cruisers, destroyers, and torpedo boats in a massive ambush at the northern end of Surigao Strait, not 50 miles south of the invasion beaches. Oldendorf's torpedo boats began harassing VAdm Shoji Nishimura's ships shortly before midnight. Around 0200 Oldendorf's destroyers began getting their licks in, and at 0300 battleship FUSO, struck by several TORPEDOES, began to burn and then blew up, while *Yamashiro* took one, and then a second torpedo.

But the surviving ships of the Japanese squadron kept coming, firing on whatever targets they could locate. The American battleships opened fire at 0353. By 0411 only a wounded cruiser and destroyer *Shigure* (see SHIRATSUYR CLASS) were left and fleeing south past the second Japanese squad-

ron, "C Force," which shortly retired, having already taken some damage. So the Japanese had now lost two rounds.

Meanwhile, shortly after 1500 on 24 October, reconnaissance aircraft from Task Force 38 had spotted the Japanese carriers coming south. Now that Halsey knew where the enemy was he went after him. By midnight on October 24, Admiral Halsey was steaming north with the fast carriers and battleships, intent upon intercepting Ozawa's carriers. This was precisely what the Japanese wanted, as their carriers were worthless anyway. By his action, Halsey exposed the landings to terrible danger.

During that same night, Kurita's "A Force," having turned eastward, seemingly in abandonment of its mission, reversed course once more to steam for San Bernardino Strait. Early on 25 October, Kurita debouched into the broad waters of the Philippine Sea and began racing southward, wholly undetected by American air reconnaissance. Actually, a recon plane had spotted them shortly before midnight, but Halsey dismissed the contact. False contacts were a common problem during World War II. At 0646 Kurita's four battleships, six heavy cruisers, and dozen or so destroyers blundered into "Taffy 3," a group of six escort carriers, three destroyers, and four destroyer escorts. A wild melee ensued, as Kurita's heavy ships strove to overwhelm the American vessels. Since Kurita thought the American vessels were fleet carriers and cruisers, he moved somewhat cautiously, which worked against him.

Straining hopelessly to pile on speed, the "jeep" carriers and their escorts fought back with air attacks (some made without ammunition), gunfire, and torpedo attacks. American losses were heavy, two escort carriers, a destroyer, and two destroyer escorts. Kurita might have done more damage, but other escort carrier groups in the area began lending a hand, and then he received word that the "Second Striking Force" had been annihilated at Surigao Strait. He lost his nerve, and at 1236 began steaming northward.

During Taffy 3's ordeal off SAMAR, the bulk of Task Force 38 was steaming northward in the hope of intercepting and destroying Ozawa's carriers. The first air strikes were launched at dawn, and by 0800 Ozawa's carriers were being heavily worked over. This continued throughout the day, so that by early afternoon Ozawa had lost four carriers and a destroyer, some finished off by gunfire from Halsey's heavy cruisers. Halsey, by that time apprised of his error in leaving San Bernardino Strait unguarded, dispatched his fast battleships southward, to arrive off Samar just in time to sink a damaged Japanese destroyer, the battleships having gotten clean away.

Thus ended the Battle of Leyte Gulf, the greatest naval battle in history. It was an overwhelming American victory, and marked the virtual death of the Imperial Navy.

Liberty Ships

Even before the United States entered the war, the navy began to consider the problem of maintaining an adequate supply of shipping in the face of a global war and the depredations of the German U-boats. The solution was to mass-produce merchant vessels to a standard design. After examining various designs, including a special-order British merchantman under construction in US shipyards, the navy came up with what was eventually named the "Liberty Ship." The Liberty ship was essentially a modified version of a standard prewar Maritime Commission design. Liberty ships, of which there were several versions (including a tanker model), were relatively large for their day, some 440 feet long by 50 in the beam (or width). They were rated at between 10,000 and 14,000 GRT, about twice the size of the average prewar merchant ship. The comparable tanker was about 16,000 tons, roughly 60% larger than the normal American prewar tanker. Liberty ships were also relatively slow, being able to make only about 10 knots. But they were easy to build, and lots of short cuts were employed in their construction, such as the use of electric welding rather than rivets, prefabrication of engines, superstructures, bows, and sterns, as-

sembly-line PRODUCTION, and modification to traditional shipbuilding techniques to allow unskilled labor to perform the work. All of these techniques reduced construction time to such an extent that, at least for propaganda purposes, it was possible for the SS *Robert E. Perry* to be built in four days, 15 hours, and 27 minutes, and sail with a full cargo five days later, whereas the first Liberty ship, *Patrick Henry*, required 244 days to complete. More normally, several weeks were required, that itself being quite an accomplishment.

Construction of Liberty ships began before the United States entered the war, and *Patrick Henry* was launched in September of 1941. Although construction of Liberty ships ended in 1944 (the last was *Benjamin Warner*), construction of the larger, faster (15 knots), and better built derivative, the Victory ship, continued into 1945. Altogether

Nearly a dozen Victory ships fitting out at a West Coast shipyard in mid-1944.

LIBERTY/VICTORY SHIP CONSTRUCTION	
Year	Number
1941	c. 20
1942	746
1943	2,242
1944	2,161
1945	c. 500

nearly 6,000 copies of these two designs were built, at a total cost of about $13 billion. Liberty ships were a wartime expedient, designed to last at most five years. This, plus their hasty, sometimes overly hasty, construction, resulted in as many as a third of all Liberty ships having technical problems, some of them serious, as when poorly welded seams parted in heavy seas or substandard materials resulted in ruptured fuel lines. However, overall, Liberty ships were an immensely valuable improvisation and greatly extended Allied shipping resources. Surprisingly, some were still in merchant service in the 1960s.

Most Liberty ships were named after famous Americans, including various members of the Confederacy, several notable persons of African descent, including Booker T. Washington and Frederick Douglass, and even the actress Carole Lombard, who died in an airplane crash during a war bond drive.

See also GIBBS, WILLIAM FRANCIS; SHIPBUILDING, WARSHIPS.

Ref: Lane, *Ships for Victory*.

Lindbergh, Charles (1902–1974)

The first man to fly solo across the Atlantic (1927), Lindbergh was of German descent, and the son of a former member of Congress who opposed the US declaration of war against Germany in 1917. In the 1930s Lindbergh several times visited Germany and was given the royal treatment by HITLER and particularly Hermann Göring, head of the Luftwaffe. Through some simple DECEPTIONS, Göring

managed to convince Lindbergh that the German air force was far larger than was actually the case. When World War II broke out in 1939, Lindbergh quickly became prominent in the "America First Committee," which opposed not only US entry into the war but also any suggestion of assistance to Britain (unbeknownst to Lindbergh, the America First Committee was being covertly financed by Germany).

Lindbergh resigned his reserve commission as a colonel in the Air Corps in 1940. His offer to return to duty after PEARL HARBOR was rejected by President Roosevelt. An employee of United Aircraft, he was hired as a technical adviser by the AAF, teaching PILOTS fuel conservation techniques and over-water navigation. While visiting the front in the South Pacific, he unofficially—and as a civilian in violation of the GENEVA CONVENTION—undertook at least 50 combat missions, mostly in P-38s, shooting down at least one Japanese aircraft and, by some accounts, enough to put him in the "ace" category.

Line Islands

The Line Islands comprise two chains, one on each side of the equator (the "line"), totaling 10 atolls, including Palmyra and CHRISTMAS, over a thousand miles south of Hawaii. Small in area (less than 400 square miles, half of it being Christmas) and thinly populated (fewer than 100 inhabitants), they provided important sites for aircraft patrolling the vulnerable Allied lines of communication from North America to the South Pacific.

Lingayen, Luzon, Philippines

Aside from a somewhat sheltered bay, the only port facilities at Lingayen, on the northwestern coast of Luzon, were a couple of simple jetties. But the local beach was broad and relatively free of obstacles, making it ideal for amphibious landings, which took place twice, once in December of 1941, when the Japanese arrived, and again in January of 1945, when the Americans returned.

Logistics, Allocations and Consumption, General

To facilitate the flow of supplies to the troops, long before World War II the US Army adopted a system of dividing all supplies into five basic classes, refined, postwar, into the present ten classes.

Since consumption of supplies was to a great extent predictable (after all, the troops have to eat, whether in combat or not), a unit's needs in each category could be calculated by determining the number of men and consulting fairly standard reference tables.

Class	Character
I.	Rations
II.	Clothing, personal equipment and supplies, administrative supplies
III.	Petroleum products, chemicals
IV.	Heavy equipment, construction supplies
V.	Ammunition

However, despite the most careful attention to sustaining the flow of supplies to the front-line troops, there were often shortages the closer one got to the enemy. As an example, consider the daily consumption rate in XIV Corps on New Georgia, in December of 1943.

DAILY INDIVIDUAL CONSUMPTION OF PRINCIPAL SUPPLIES XIV CORPS, NEW GEORGIA, DECEMBER 1943

	25th Div.	43rd Div.	Corps Troops
Class I	4.0 lbs.	5.7 lbs.	6.98 lbs
Class II	0.3	0.5	4.86
Class III	3.8	4.0	5.70
Class IV	0.0	0.0	0.14

With the exception of Class III (Petroleum, Oils, and Lubricants–POLs), the categories of supply in question are not combat critical. After all, in combat many troops don't eat much anyway

(Class I). In fact, the closer to the firing line, the lower the rate of consumption, at least of these categories of supply. During the New Georgia operation the 24th Infantry Division was more heavily engaged than the 43rd Division, while corps troops were generally rear echelon types with greater access to supplies, not to mention more leisure time in which to consume them. Note how much less supply the combat units were getting. The surprisingly high consumption of POLs by the corps troops was also a consequence of being in the rear. REMFs ("Rear Echelon Mother Fuckers") might "borrow" a jeep for a ride to visit some buddies a few miles down the road, a luxury unavailable to the guys on the front lines.

Logistics, Allocations and Consumption, Petroleum

One of the most crucial resources in modern warfare is the availability of POLs (petroleum, oils, and lubricants). Prewar army estimates of the probable consumption rates of what are termed Class III supplies proved unrealistic in several ways and were repeatedly modified on the basis of experience throughout the war. The basic unit of calculation for probable POL consumption, and in fact for all supply consumption, was the individual soldier. As a result, the allotments indicated may seem rather odd.

US ARMY ESTIMATED POL REQUIREMENTS PER MAN PER DAY

	Sept. '44	Feb. '45
Gasoline	1.080 gal.	0.98000 gal.
Diesel	0.300	0.32000
Kerosene	0.038	0.02800
Engine Oils	0.046	0.04500
Lubricating Oils	0.016	0.01200
Greases	0.003	0.00341
Total	1.483	1.38841

The differences in allocations were caused by a variety of factors. As new equipment became available and old equipment passed out of service, requirements changed to suit the changed needs of the equipment. Different operational requirements might also effect the statistics. Operations in an area with limited water supply might boost the requirements for diesel fuel, necessary to run water pumps. The greater precision with which the February 1945 allotments were laid out was due to a refinement of the supply system. Where in September 1944 the formula had merely listed "greases" and "engine oils," that for February 1945 specified greases and oils of different weight, which appear to be rounded in the case of the latter.

The idea of allocating the supplies in such great detail on a per-man-per-day basis may seem odd, but is actually quite reasonable. The quartermasters were not assuming that each man would use the allotted gallon plus of POL each day, but rather that consumption in a given unit would average out to that figure. So in September 1944 a division of 14,000 men would have required 20,786.2 gallons of POL per day, while in February of 1945 the same division would have needed only 19,436.34 gallons per day, a difference of 1,325.86 gallons, about 6.5%. Multiply that several times to account for the number of divisions in an army, and then add the requirements for non-divisional forces, and then calculate the savings in shipping, arguably the most critical resource in the Pacific War.

Logistics, Australian Unions

During the dark days of mid-1942, Australian stevedores very often refused to modify their union contracts in order to aid the war effort, even when it appeared the Japanese were about to descend on Australia itself. In 1942, American and Australian forces were fighting a desperate battle to the north in New Guinea. Lack of adequate rail and road systems in Australia forced heavy dependence on sea transport along the Australian coast. The Australian government was unable (because of growing war weariness among the population for a war they had been in since 1939) or unwilling (it was a La-

bour government) to abrogate the union contracts the stevedores insisted on maintaining. In addition to limiting hours of work and detailing safety requirements, these contracts allowed the laborers to refuse to work when it was raining. In fairness to the stevedores, it's worth recalling that they were mostly older men, as virtually all of Australia's young men were in uniform. Still, there was some measure of a more than natural self-interest in overzealous adherence to the contracts. Because they received double- and triple-time pay for weekend work, many stevedores would show up only on weekends so they got a week's pay for two days work. Often, American troops had to be put to work unloading ships, and it was found that, on average, the troops could unload cargo two to three times more quickly than the Australian stevedores. Moreover, the Australians often didn't show up when they were supposed to, with absenteeism of close to 20% on occasion. When the Americans tried to automate the process (more cranes and fork lifts), the civilian workers threatened, and then staged, a few strikes. These problems were not fully resolved until the shipping operations could be shifted to ports in New Guinea and the Philippines in 1943 and 1944.

Logistics, Fleet Train

Warships were of little value without an enormous logistical tail to move forward fuel, munitions, and other supplies. This was provided by the fleet trains, composed of numerous different types of highly specialized vessels: fleet oilers for the warships, avgas tankers for the aircraft, ammunition ships, destroyer tenders, general cargo vessels, provision ships, seaplane tenders, heavy repair ships, hospital ships, submarine tenders, floating dry docks, and a host of others, down to net tenders, water lighters, and "honey bucket" (excrement) barges.

Prior to World War II, all navies had come up with methods for sustaining a fleet at a distance from its base. These techniques consisted of ships designed to accompany the fleet and provide it the necessities. But nearly all navies had thought of this function as of secondary importance. It was the US Navy that gave the matter the most thought, and solved it by organizing the fleet train in much the same fashion as it organized the fleet—in task forces.

Although it took time to implement, since initially there was a shortage of all types of logistical support vessels, by early 1943 the US Navy had a number of "servrons" or "service squadrons." A typical servron might consist of some two dozen fleet oilers and avgas (aircraft fuel) tankers, four ammunition ships, three hospital ships, six provision ships, and four general cargo vessels, all escorted by a handful of destroyers and perhaps even an escort carrier. Such a squadron could sustain a modest task force for some weeks, until, nearing depletion, it was replaced by another, and could go "back to the barn" to replenish.

By early 1944 Pacific Fleet servrons totaled some 450 vessels. Later in the war servrons had become specialized, so that there were several that provided only fuel, and one that was in the business of sustaining the aircraft of the fleet, providing replacement aircraft, spare parts, aviation fuel, and the like.

The Japanese were never able to duplicate this effort, even in the early part of the war, when they were winning. Even the British found the task difficult. One reason for the relatively modest size of the ROYAL NAVY task force that served with the Third/Fifth Fleet during 1945 was Britain's inability to sustain a larger force with its own fleet train.

Long before the war broke out the US Navy had devoted considerable attention to the logistical problems involved in supporting fleet operations in a theater as vast as the Pacific. In earlier wars the navy had mostly relied on chartered civilian vessels for logistical support, as did all other navies. But that approach was not considered workable in the event of a protracted naval war in the Pacific. So it was intended that the navy acquire and operate ships crewed by naval personnel to meet the needs of the fleet. During the years of peace the navy did acquire some vessels for logistical support, but much preferred spending its money on warships. In the event of a national emergency it intended to acquire vessels from the merchant marine, whether through purchase or hire, or through requisition of vessels subsidized by the US Maritime Commission.

Meanwhile, the navy perfected several techniques that would stand it in good stead during the war. Perhaps the most important of these was underway refueling. Most navies used a method whereby a tanker passed cables over her stern to take a tow on the ship being refueled, and then passed a fuel line. This was a slow, clumsy procedure, which, since the tow had to be done at very low speed, exposed the ships to possible attack by SUBMARINES. The US Navy decided to try doing it with the tanker and the ship to be refueled running alongside, at a fair speed, 12 to 15 knots. Specialized equipment was developed to permit fuel lines to be passed between the ships, and personnel were trained to "play" the lines, so that as the ships moved they would remain relatively slack—an elaborate ballet that surprised and impressed foreign naval officers. Not only was this method faster than the towing method, but it was also possible to refuel two ships from one tanker simultaneously, an even greater savings in time. This method also permitted larger warships to top off the fuel tanks of smaller ones when necessary. Similar, though less spectacular, advances were made in the transfer of stores between underway ships.

When the war came, the navy was ready. Well, almost ready. The problem was that the navy didn't begin acquiring merchant ships for the fleet train until relatively late. As a result, when the war began the navy was forced to operate with relatively slender logistical support. However, the navy soon began acquiring ships, which were organized into special fleet service squadrons, the servrons.

A servron might be considered a logistical task force. Early versions were relatively small, but then there were relatively few ships out there battling the Japanese. By early 1943, servrons were getting larger. For example, around the end of March 1943 Servron 8 consisted of about 62 ships, excluding escorts.

4 ammunition ships
6 provision ships
3 general cargo ships
1 general stores ship
3 hospital ships
45 tankers (mostly fuel oil, but some avgas)

A year later Servron 8 consisted of some 430 ships, with warships (including one or two escort carriers, to provide extra security), and was operating in four divisions of 100–120 ships each. As the combat forces got larger, the servrons continued to grow. In 1944 the servrons were reorganized and specialized. One, for example, was assigned the job of supporting the AIR GROUPS of the fast carrier task forces. It was provided with ships that served as floating warehouses for aircraft parts, avgas tankers, an aircraft repair ship, and several escort carriers laden with replacement aircraft and pilots.

Other servrons specialized in fueling the fleet, and still others in bringing up food and other stores. Two examples from the MARIANAS CAMPAIGN (late spring 1944) are illustrative of the nature of this specialization. Task Group 52.7 (Service and Repair) comprised one net tender (to keep submarines out of anchorages), three ocean tugs, one seaplane tender, one repair ship, two salvage vessels, one landing vessel repair ship, and eight miscellaneous yard craft, plus escorts. Task Group 50.17 (Fueling Group) comprised 24 oilers, three hospital ships, and four escort carriers (two to supply aircraft to the fast carriers and two carrying Army Air Force P-47s, which were subsequently flown to land bases). There were also 21 destroyers and destroyer escorts, and the whole task group was organized into seven oiler groups, a hospital ship group, and three escort carrier groups.

The servron system had broad strategic implications. Early in the war combat ships, and particularly carriers, had to return to a major base after each operation to replenish their ammunition and stores. With the servron system, on the eve of a major operation the carrier task forces could rendezvous with a servron. After stocking up on fuel, stores, spares, aircraft, and aircrew, the carriers could go into action. During the operation, individual task forces, by mid-1944 usually of three or four carriers, could fall back as necessary to rendezvous with a servron and replenish while their sister task forces carried on the war. In this fashion operations could be conducted continuously, with task forces rotating into and out of action as necessary. The strategic benefits of this were tremendous, since it kept the Japanese continuously under pressure.

As efficient as they were, the navy's logistical arrangements were strained mightily in the latter part of the war. The enormous size of the forces operating afloat and ashore in the Pacific created so extraordinary a demand for fuel, munitions, rations, and all the other necessities of war that, during the protracted operations off OKINAWA and Japan itself in the spring and summer of 1945, there developed serious shortages of some supplies, and rations became boring. Politics and pride aside, this logistical strain was one reason the US Navy preferred not to have the ROYAL NAVY participate in the final campaigns in the Pacific. The Royal Navy, however, managed to scrape together a fairly effective version of the servron for its own use, totaling 92 ships, of which 17 were tankers and 13 ammunition ships.

In contrast to the efficient, if ultimately very strained, arrangements of the US Navy, the Japanese Navy had a wholly inadequate fleet train virtually from the start of the war. Even as late as the Marianas Campaign, the total fleet train for the Mobile Fleet, which fought the Battle of the PHILIPPINE SEA, was two refueling groups, totaling six smallish tankers, escorted by as many destroyers. Most of the ships were taken up from the merchant marine, operated by their civilian crews, and pressed into service without any modifications, to permit efficient replenishment at sea. As a result, the Japanese never really mastered underway refueling, a matter that greatly hampered operations.

Logistics, Ice Cream

Navy slang for ice cream was "gedunk" (a term that was often used to refer to other tooth-rotting pleasures). Aircraft carriers were large enough to provide crew amenities like an ice cream shop. But to supply ice cream to the rest of the fleet, the navy took one of the concrete transports built early in the war (when there was a steel shortage) and turned it into a floating ice cream factory. The ship itself was a turkey (most of the concrete ships were fobbed off on the army), but the Gedunk Cruiser could produce up to 5,000 gallons of ice cream an hour, making her one of the most popular ships in the fleet.

See also FOOD, RATIONS, US.

Logistics, Starvation

The Japanese soldiers on GUADALCANAL came to call the place "Starvation Island" because of the difficulty their leaders had in getting food delivered to the place. This situation was not unique to the Japanese. Islands in general, and the Pacific islands in particular, were not bountiful sources of food for the soldiers that fought there. The first case of starving soldiers on Pacific islands was found among American and Philippine troops in the Philippines. Much to the dismay of the Japanese invaders, the American and Philippine defenders didn't just roll over and quit. The fighting went on for over four months. The Japanese controlled the seas, and attempts to run this blockade were generally unsuccessful. Many of the civilian crews of the Allied BLOCKADE RUNNERS forced their ships back as they approached the Philippines, and the Japanese sank most of the ships that pressed on. Three runners did get through, but it wasn't enough. Although the food wasn't completely gone by the time the Japanese military action beat down the defenders, there wasn't much left. American troops had been getting less than a third of the food

required for several months (and some of their Filipino comrades even less).

The second case of "Starvation Island" was another American situation. The Hawaiian Islands could not feed themselves. When the Japanese struck on December 7, 1941, the 42,000 US troops in the islands had a 60-day supply of food. The 420,000 civilians on the island were worse off, with less than a 40-day supply. Most of the food consumed on the islands was imported. While the islands contained much fertile land, most had been turned over to plantations growing crops like pineapples. There was a great fear that the Japanese would blockade the islands and starve them into submission, or invade first. The Japanese didn't come, although several divisions were trained for that task. It was the Japanese who next suffered from the "Starvation Island" syndrome, thousands of their troops starved to death on Pacific islands before the war was over.

Logistics, Troop Movements

All of the divisions sent to the Pacific were infantry units, even the First Cavalry Division, which was reorganized as footsloggers. This helped a lot, because transportation of an armored division required twice as much shipping as did that of an infantry division. While armored divisions had fewer troops, they also had several hundred TANKS and about 10% more motor vehicles of other types.

Shipping requirements could be cut by over 40% if a division's equipment was broken down as much as possible and "boxed." This method, however, required a fully equipped (with piers and cranes) port at the other end to unload the equipment. Moreover, it took several extra weeks at either end to box or unbox the equipment.

Amphibious landings required four times as much shipping as the boxed method because the gear had to be stored in the order it would be needed and had to be ready to operate as soon as it left the ship. This was called "combat loading." As a result of this, it was preferable to send divisions to the Pacific boxed, unload them at a port,

**SHIPPING REQUIREMENTS
(THOUSANDS OF MEASUREMENT TONS)**

Year	Loading	Inf. Div.	Inf. RCT
1942	Boxed	54.8	18.3
	Normal	101.2	34.7
	Combat	200.0	66.7
1943	Boxed	69.9	23.3
	Normal	100.4	33.5
	Combat	200.0	67.0
1945	Boxed	44.9	14.9
	Normal	100.9	33.6
	Combat	200.0	66.7

and then reload them in the combat loading manner.

The 1942 infantry division had about 15,500 men and 2,100 motor vehicles, the 1943 version about 14,250 and 2,000 motor vehicles, and the 1945 one about 14,000 men and 2,100 vehicles. Since the First Cavalry Division was smaller than the standard infantry division, with only about 80% of the manpower and equipment, these figures do not apply to it. An "RCT" or "Regimental Combat Team" usually comprised an infantry regiment, an artillery battalion, and an engineer company, plus some miscellaneous organizations, more or less approximating a third of an infantry division, organized for an independent mission. A CAVALRY RCT was smaller.

In the examples given here it is assumed that each unit has all necessary equipment, plus three units of fire (full ammunition loads for three days for each weapon). Figures for 1942–43 assume 60 days' maintenance, including POLs (petroleum, oils, and lubricants); those for 1945 assume only 30 days' maintenance and POLs.

Actually these figures are approximations, as different situations might require different arrangements. A division making an amphibious landing might easily use more cargo capacity. The importance of combat loading was discovered the hard way, during the GUADALCANAL landing of August 1942. There, the American transports had to withdraw (because of Japanese attacks) before the ships

were unloaded. A lot of cargo sailed away with the half-empty ships, and the cargo that did get unloaded was not the most vital.

As a rule of thumb, along with every soldier, airman, or Marine sent overseas, the United States shipped 12 tons of equipment, and thereafter, for each man—or woman—overseas, one ton of supplies had to be shipped abroad each month.

In simpler terms, to send an infantry division's equipment overseas boxed required about six LIBERTY SHIPS (the most common type of ship used by the Allies). To move that same division into a combat zone for an amphibious assault took about 20 ships of various sizes. A dozen of these would be APA (cargo ships, often Liberty types, modified to carry combat-ready troops and landing craft), the rest would be LSTS and other specialized amphibious ships. Marine divisions were about a third larger than army divisions. But army divisions usually went into battle with a few additional specialized battalions (armor, artillery, etc.). While only 27 divisions fought in the Pacific (out of 95), this represented 27 out of 71 infantry divisions available to the United States, or 38% of the infantry units. The Marine support requirements were similar to those of the army, and were provided by the navy. Thus those 27 divisions required nearly two million troops (including replacements for dead, sick, and wounded) to be shipped to the Pacific and then supplied while there. That meant over 20 million tons of shipping to get them there, and then as much as 1.5 million tons of shipping a month to keep every one supplied. Toward the end of the war, many of the ships had to make 12,000-mile round trips to reach distant Pacific bases.

Logistics, Units of Measurement

Although the term "ton" is used frequently with reference to both merchant ships and warships, it has a very different meaning in each case. In fact, its meaning can vary considerably. And that meaning is not necessarily related to the familiar "ton." To begin, there is the ordinary "ton," by weight 2,000 English pounds, also known as the "short" ton in the United States and several other countries. Then there's the "long" ton or English ton or shipping ton, of 2,240 pounds. And there's the metric ton (or tonne), which is a thousand kilograms, or 2,204.6 pounds. When discussing cargo weight the US Armed Forces sometimes used the short ton and sometimes the long, while the British always used the long ton, and the Germans, the Italians, the French, the Japanese, the Russians, and practically everyone else in the world used the metric ton. So when dealing with particularly large figures, such as thousands of tons of ammunition expended, knowing which ton is meant can be extremely important.

Merchant ships are measured in three different sorts of "ton." Gross registered tonnage (GRT) is a measure of the cubic internal volume of the ship in notional "tons" of 100 cubic feet or 2.8 cubic meters, a measurement that includes all interior spaces of the ship. The GRT is actually not a particularly good guide to the cargo capacity of a ship. For example, the liner QUEEN ELIZABETH, the largest commercial ship in the world during the war, was about 83,000 GRT, but actually carried very little cargo. By enclosing a veranda deck she once added several thousand "tons" to her GRT.

Cargo is measured in measurement tons or freight tons. These are also units of volume rather than weight, amounting to 40 cubic feet of cargo stowage capacity. Thus one long ton of general military cargo ran about 2.1 measurement tons. Deadweight tons measure the actual weight of everything carried in the ship, including supplies, miscellaneous equipment, fuel, and even crew, expressed in long tons: As a rule, for every 1,500 deadweight tons, a cargo ship could carry about 1,775 measurement tons.

Warship tonnage is measured differently, in terms of "displacement tons." Each 35 cubic feet of seawater displaced by the vessel is a "displacement ton." As the volume of sea water in question actually weighs approximately one long ton, displacement gives a rough indication of the actual weight of the vessel. However, as established by various naval DISARMAMENT TREATIES, there are several different ways to measure the displacement of a warship, depending upon the amount of stores, ammunition, fuel, and crew carried. "Light Displacement" is measured taking the bare ship, without movables such as stores, fuel, ammunition, or crew. "Standard Displacement" is measured with normal stores, ammunition, fuel, and crew necessary for peacetime operations. "Full Load Displacement" measures the ship when fully loaded with all possible stores, ammunition, fuel, and crewmen, ready for a wartime mission. The differences among the three can be considerable. As completed, the battleship IOWA was approximately 44,000 tons light displacement, 48,500 tons standard, and 57,500 tons full load, while the Japanese YAMATO ran about 59,200 tons light displacement, 64,000 tons standard, and almost 70,000 tons full load.

A similar problem exists with regard to the transportation of oil. Since the US and British gallon are slightly different, what is known as a 55-gallon oil barrel in US parlance is only a 50-gallon drum in British usage.

Logistics, US Troops Overseas

For millions of Americans, World War II was an unprecedented opportunity to travel. However, these were not tourists, but heavily armed soldiers, sailors, airmen, and Marines. As the US armed forces increased from 1940 on, so did the number serving outside North America.

Year	Total Forces	Percentage in			Number Overseas	Percent
		Army	Navy	Marines		
1940	458	59%	35%	6%	164	36%
1941	1,801	81%	16%	3%	281	16%
1942	3,859	80%	17%	3%	940	24%
1943	9,045	77%	19%	4%	2,494	28%
1944	11,451	70%	26%	4%	5,512	48%
1945	12,123	68%	28%	4%	7,447	61%

All figures in thousands (except percentages)

During World War II, the air force belonged to the army (as the Army Air Forces) and had a peak size of 2.4 million troops (20% of all US military personnel), leaving the army proper (including Ground Forces and Service Forces, which also supported the AAF) with 48%. The navy buildup was not as swift as the army's because the navy first had to build ships. In 1940 an enormous SHIPBUILDING program was begun, and many of these vessels were completed and ready for crews in 1943 and 1944. Aircraft and TANKS for the army could be built much more quickly. The total number of men and women ever enrolled in the armed forces during the war was about 16.4 million, of whom about 11.3 million were in the army, 4.2 million in the navy, 0.67 million in the Marines, and 0.24 million in the Coast Guard. The average member of the service spent 33 months in uniform, while the average overseas tour was about 16.2 months. Throughout it all, despite casualties, the US population still increased. So, although there was a war going on, not everyone was spending all their time fighting.

Logistics and Distance

Merchant shipping had to go to a great variety of destinations. The Japanese in particular had to ship supplies to a widely scattered array of destinations. While SUBMARINES were not a threat to either side's shipping in the first year of the war, the long distances were. The weather in the Pacific could be treacherous, particularly since normal weather reporting was interrupted because neither side had weather stations in enemy territory. Without accurate weather reports, merchant shipping was more likely to run into bad weather, and often never be heard from again.

Japanese shipping was particularly inefficient, as each ship could belong to one of three different organizations (army, navy, or an industrial organization), which didn't coordinate the use of their shipping. As a result, Japanese shipping moved at an average rate of 60–70 miles a day. This included

AVERAGE DISTANCES FROM JAPANESE PORTS, 1942

Destination	Distance (Miles)	Voyage (Days)
Japanese-held Areas		
North China, Manchuria	900	15
South China	1,600	27
Indonesia	3,200	52
Burma	4,000	65
Truk	2,600	42
New Guinea, Solomons	2,900	48
Philippines	1,800	28
Potential Japanese Objectives		
Fiji, Samoa	4,500	73
Hawaii	3,700	60
Alaska	2,500	40
Panama	8,000	129

Distance is in nautical miles, **Voyage** gives the number of days a typical Japanese merchant ship would take to get to that area in the latter half of the war.

a lot of time sitting around port waiting for a cargo, even when there was something from one of the other organizations to be carried. Often, ships simply returned empty because of this lack of coordination.

If operated efficiently, merchant shipping could steam 200-300 miles a day (making allowances for time spent in port moving cargo, or waiting to load or unload). The "Potential Japanese Objectives" are those areas that the Japanese considered going after, or the Allies feared might be attacked. However, as can be seen from the distances those areas were from Japan these targets would have been very difficult to support. Supplying Hawaii would have required nearly 50% more shipping than that required for the Japanese bases in the central Pacific. Panama was so far away that it would have taken a large fraction of the Japanese tanker fleet just to support a naval attack against the canal. Alaska, on the other hand, was not that far away from Japan. This is not always evident because most maps do not take into account the fact that the Earth is

AVERAGE DISTANCES FROM US PORTS		
Destination	Distance (Miles)	Voyage (Days)
Brisbane	7,700	28
Dutch Harbor	2,400	9
Guadalcanal	7,200	26
Pago Pago, Samoa	5,150	19

Figures for Dutch Harbor are from Seattle, those for Guadalcanal, Pago Pago, and Brisbane are from San Francisco.

a globe and thus do not accurately portray the nearness of Alaska and Japan. This is one reason why Japan attacked and occupied some of the Aleutrans off the coast of Alaska in 1942. This also explains why the United States fought back energetically to retake these Japanese bases.

Allied shipping was far more efficient, and this enabled the Allies to bring far more men and materiel to bear.

Most of the resources Japan imported (raw materials and food) came from China and Korea. These areas were relatively close to Japan. However, rare (but vital) ores (like tin) and oil from Indonesia had to be moved longer distances. More importantly, fuel, food, other supplies, and reinforcements had to be regularly shipped to the distant Japanese military garrisons.

London Class, British Heavy Cruisers

Although apparently even less handy than the KENT CLASS heavy cruisers, which they greatly resembled, the four Londons, built 1926–29, were otherwise satisfactory ships. Several saw service in the Indian Ocean and one, *Shropshire* (1927–1928–1929), was transferred to the Royal Australian Navy in 1943 and gave good service in the southwest Pacific and the Philippines. They were scrapped 1950–55.

Long Beach, California, West Coast

Including the naval base at San Pedro and the relatively new facilities at Los Angeles and other local ports, Long Beach was one of the principal American bases on the West Coast, connected to the rest of the United States by an extensive rail system, and well within range of numerous air bases.

Long Island, US Escort Carrier

The first American escort carrier, *Long Island*, CVE-1 (?–1940–1941), was a pet project of President ROOSEVELT, partially inspired by British efforts to build such vessels. Converted from an incomplete, standard diesel-powered C3 cargo ship, M/S *Mormacmail,* in about a year. Although slow (16.5 knots), somewhat unresponsive to her helm, and with limited aircraft capacity (her first air group was 10 observation planes and six scout bombers), *Long Island* proved very satisfactory. Shortly after PEARL HARBOR she was transferred to the Pacific, where she supported the battleline (composed of Pearl Harbor survivors and other old battleships transferred from the Atlantic) during the MIDWAY Campaign. She was later used as a training ship and aircraft transport. Unlike later US escort carriers, she had no island superstructure. Her near-sister *Charger*, CVE-30 (?–1941–1942), was converted later, to a somewhat different plan. Both ships were sold in the late 1940s, to be reconverted to merchantmen. The four units of the British Archer Class were essentially sister ships.

Losses, Warships

The greatest sea war in history, World War II saw more warships sunk than any other.

All warships from SUBMARINES on up lost during the war by the belligerents are included in the table on page 379, regardless of what caused the loss, including accidents and the hazards of the sea. Neutral losses (Sweden) are included only in cases where they were caused by the actions of one of the belligerents. Ships sunk but subsequently raised and restored to active service have been omitted,

Country	CV	CVL	CVE	BB	CA	CL	DD	DE	SS
Australia						1	2	4	
Brazil						1			
Britain	5		4	5	5	24	100	42	75
Canada			1				8	1	
China						2			
Denmark									9
Estonia									1
France				5	4	6	57	1	65
Germany				4	5	4	53		994
Greece						1	4	1	4
Italy				2	7	8	86	13	116
Japan	13	2	4	11	17	27	← 160 →		133
Latvia									2
Netherlands						3	11		15
Norway							5		2
Poland						1	3	1	2
Romania							4		2
Russia				1		2	34		95
Sweden									1
United States	4	1	6	2	7	3	71	11	52
Yugoslavia						1	4		2

Key: **CV** = aircraft carrier; **CVL** = light aircraft carrier; **CVE** = escort carrier; **BB** = battleships and battlecruisers; **CA** = heavy cruisers; **CL** = light cruisers; **DD** = destroyer; **DE** = destroyer escort; **SS** = submarine.

as have all the numerous vessels smaller than submarines and destroyer escorts. Ships lost while still building have not been included. Vessels scuttled are included (c. 60% of French losses were due to scuttling, as were Danish losses shown), as are those captured during hostilities (i.e., omitting those captured upon the surrender of various of the Axis powers). Note that since many captured vessels were put into service by their captors and subsequently lost, there would be some double counting if totals were taken (e.g., several Yugoslav destroyers were commissioned in the Italian Navy, one being lost and two being in turn captured by the Germans, who put them into service and subsequently lost them as well). British battleship figures include two battlecruisers. German heavy cruiser figures include three "pocket battleships." German and Greek figures omit two very obsolete battleships each. Norwegian ones omit four coast defense ships, sort of third-class battleships, while Danish figures omit two; Finland also lost a coast defense ship, as did the Netherlands and Siam. Some idea of the losses among lesser ships may be gained by noting that the US Navy lost 142 smaller warships, that is, motor torpedo boats, mine warfare vessels, Coast Guard cutters, sub chasers, and gunboats. Losses to seaplane and destroyer tenders, transports, tankers, fleet auxiliaries (such as the floating dock *Dewey*, which was scuttled to prevent capture by the Japanese), and landing craft totaled 243. Losses to yard craft and other miscellaneous small vessels totaled nearly 150.

Ref: Brown, *Warship Losses of World War Two.*

Louisiade Archipelago

A collection of numerous very small islands streaming southeastward from New Guinea, separating the Solomon Sea from the CORAL SEA. They were thinly populated, by a surprisingly large number of different, if related, tribes all living close to nature. Economic resources were slight, but the islands were of some strategic value, enabling their occupiers to project airpower over a wide area.

LSD (Landing Ship, Dock), Allied Landing Vessels

Twenty-two of these 454-foot, 4,500-ton ships were built between 1942 and 1945. Each literally had a "dock" inside its stern, so that preloaded landing craft could be carried long distances. An LSD could carry two or three loaded LCTs or LCMs or as many as 14 loaded LCVPs/LCMs. But this was not their principal value. Their internal dock allowed them to provide on-the-spot repair facilities for LCTs, LCMs, and LCVPs (and any other small boats, like PT-BOATS). Given the beating these smaller craft took going up on a beach, it was quite an advantage to have an LSD handy after a landing. The amphibious craft were used heavily after an initial landing to bring supplies and reinforcements ashore. LSDs had a crew of 240, a top speed of 15 knots, and were armed with one 5-inch gun and 12 40mm antiaircraft guns. The LSD became the model for many post–World War II amphibious ships.

LSM (Landing Ship, Medium), Allied Landing Vessels

These were smaller versions of the LST, of which nearly 600 were built during 1944–45. They were, in fact, the smallest oceangoing vessels capable of making beach landings. At full load, these vessels displaced 1,000 tons, but had to be only 740 tons to run up on a beach. Some 200 feet long and with a crew of 50–60, they were armed with only two 40mm antiaircraft guns and had the same speed (8–12 knots) as LSTs. An LSM could carry several TANKS, trucks, and jeeps. Although their carrying capacity was about the same as that of an LCT, LSMs had much superior seagoing qualities. This

made them useful for small, short-range, transoceanic amphibious operations, particularly in places like the southwest Pacific. Their smaller size allowed them to get into some places LSTs couldn't reach. There were also many cases where only a few vehicles had to be delivered somewhere; thus it was cheaper to risk an LSM going up on the beach rather than a larger LST. Some LSMs were converted into inshore fire support vessels, armed, for example, with a 5-inch gun, several mortars or AA guns, and several score rocket launchers. The most preferred armament was the 5-inch rocket, the LSM being capable of getting off 30 rockets a minute when equipped with an automatic loader. Nearly 50 of this version were put into service, some of them being modified during construction for rocket launching duty.

LST (Landing Ship, Tank), Allied Landing Vessels

Nearly a thousand of these 300-foot ships were built from 1942 to 1945. They could carry as many as 20 TANKS, and put them right onto a beach. The beaching process was not without its shortcomings. While the ship had a full load displacement of 4,000 tons, it could only be at 2,400 tons when running up on the beach. Even at that, there was usually damage done to the LST. The average landing operation would render 10% of the LSTs involved unfit for further service. Moreover, the wear and tear on those that survived the run up onto the beach was such that, during the war, only about 85% of the LSTs still operational after a loading were actually fit enough for another landing. In effect, after about 10 beachings, an LST was a wreck and no longer useable. This was typical of all ships that ran up on beaches to disgorge their cargo. The LST was basically a modified transport and, as such, was rather slow (8 knots normally, with a max speed of 11–12 knots). Normally they carried a crew of some 100 and were armed with eight 40mm antiaircraft guns. LSTs were often converted to other uses, especially when they had only a few more beach landings left in their tortured hulls. Some ended up serving as repair ships, PT-boat tenders, floating barracks and supply dumps, casualty evacuation ships, and even improvised aircraft carriers for light reconnaissance planes (eight of which could be operated off a portable airstrip set up on deck). It was often said that "LST" referred to "Large Slow Target" because of their slow speed and weak antiaircraft armament.

Heavily laden with Marines and the "instrumentalities of war," a Coast Guard LST heads into the beach at Cape Gloucester, New Britain, 24 December 1943, in a picture taken by Don C. Hansen.

M

MacArthur, Douglas (1880–1964)

The son of Civil War hero Arthur MacArthur, who was awarded a MEDAL OF HONOR for bravery at Missionary Ridge, Douglas MacArthur graduated from West Point in 1903 with some of the highest grades ever recorded (as well as having the rather dubious distinction of being one of a handful of cadets in the history of the academy whose mother lived right outside the gate for four years). An engineer, he held a variety of staff and academic posts, but no troop commands (albeit that he got into action at Vera Cruz in 1914) until World War I, when he helped organize the 42nd "Rainbow" Division, composed of NATIONAL GUARD units from 26 states. As a staff officer, later deputy division commander, and for two days right at the end of the war acting division commander, MacArthur proved an able soldier, often going into action with the troops. After the war he reorganized West Point's academic and cadet discipline programs (and made a concerted effort to abolish hazing, which was only partially successful), served on the Billy Mitchell court-martial, commanded in the Philippines, and was chief of staff of the army in the early 1930s, violently suppressing the "Bonus March," apparently against orders from President Hoover. Despite this, Hoover's successor, FDR, kept MacArthur on for an extra year. In 1935 he went to the Philippines again to help organize the commonwealth's defense forces, and in 1938 resigned from the army in order to continue in the service of the commonwealth. When in mid-1941 the Philippine Armed Forces were activated by the president and merged into the US Armed Forces,

MacArthur was recalled to duty as a full general and placed in overall command. Caught napping by the onset of the war (he lost his entire air force on the ground nine hours after PEARL HARBOR), MacArthur seriously bungled the initial defense of the Philippines, but managed to salvage something from the disaster by a belated retreat to the BATAAN Peninsula.

In the closing days of the defense of Bataan, President ROOSEVELT awarded MacArthur a Medal of Honor and ordered him to turn command over to his principal subordinate, Jonathan WAINWRIGHT, and escape to Australia, to coordinate Allied efforts to carry on the war in the southwest Pacific. As a result, one night in February of 1942, MacArthur, some of his close aides, and a few others boarded several torpedo boats; the general himself was on *PT-41*, which successfully ran the Japanese blockade. Accompanying MacArthur were his wife, his son, and his son's nurse. Almost as soon as MacArthur had made good his escape, questions were raised as to why he brought along his family, albeit that the consequences of leaving them behind might have seriously impaired his abilities as a commander. Moreover, stories began to circulate that he had arranged to bring out not only members of his family, but also certain articles of furniture, including a refrigerator. The tale has proven extremely durable, but has no foundation in fact. None of those present, including the crews of the PT-BOATS, reported carrying anything unusual during the trip.

MacArthur assumed command of Allied forces in Australia, and shortly began an offensive that would eventually recover New Guinea and the

General Douglas MacArthur sports his twin trademarks, the cap of a Philippine field marshal and a corncob pipe, in a photograph taken during the Leyte landings, in October 1944.

Philippines. Army commander designate for the invasion of Japan, MacArthur instead commanded the occupation forces, and became virtual ruler of the country for several years.

In 1950 MacArthur assumed command of UN forces in Korea, planning the spectacularly successful Inchon Operation, but subsequently mismanaged the pursuit of the defeated North Korean Army and totally misread Chinese intentions, with disastrous results. After repeated warnings from President TRUMAN about unauthorized political statements, MacArthur was relieved of duty in April of 1951. Despite the belief by many that he would undertake a political career, he spent the rest of his life in retirement.

MacArthur was a commander of erratic capabilities. When he was good he was brilliant, but he was often careless and self-centered, which led to errors in planning. He also let his personal likes and dislikes, and particularly his love of publicity, interfere in his management of the war. From December of 1941 to March of 1942, 142 dispatches emanated from the headquarters of United States Army Forces in the Far East, of which 109 (76%) included the name of only one person, the theater commander, General Douglas MacArthur. MacArthur was so well known for his efforts to hog publicity that he once got an officer to undertake a difficult assignment by promising that if successful the man's name would appear in a press release.

He despised Marines and Australians, and made sure neither received any credit for operations in "his" theater. Even Robert EICHELBERGER, his most able subordinate, was almost fired after a newspaper accurately credited him with the victory at BUNA-GONA, and Eichelberger had to endure being on the shelf for almost a year.

MacArthur's reputation for being much more frugal with lives than Marine commanders is partially the product of the way in which CASUALTIES were classified. It was not uncommon for a campaign to be declared "over" in situations where the Marines would have declared the objective "secured," meaning that there was a lot of organized resistance still going on, but American control of the place was no longer in dispute. The protracted struggle for Luzon, for example, resulted in as many casualties as did OKINAWA, most of them after the campaign had been declared "over."

Although he despised the president, MacArthur seems never to have understood the extent to which FDR was responsible for creating his enormous reputation. It was Roosevelt who kept MacArthur on for an extra year as chief of staff of the army in 1934–35, who allowed him to accept the appointment as commander of the PHILIPPINE ARMY, who recalled him to active duty though overage in 1941, who made him commander of USAFFE, who ordered him out of CORREGIDOR, who awarded him the Medal of Honor, and so forth.

Although MacArthur was able to create the impression of intimacy with persons whom he wished to cultivate, he actually had no friends, merely a wide circle of acquaintances. His personality was such that people could not be indifferent to him; they either liked or hated him, attitudes often reflective of his purported political views. Generally regarded as a staunch conservative, MacArthur in fact appears to have had no genuine political principles, merely saying what seemed to please whomever he was speaking with (among other things he endorsed the American Civil Liberties Union). He was a masterful speaker, as can be seen from the proclamation he issued upon landing on Leyte on 20 October 1944:

> People of the Philippines, I have returned. By the Grace of Almighty God our forces stand on Philippine soil . . . Rally to me. Let the Indomitable spirit of Bataan and Corregidor lead on. As the lines of battle roll forward to bring you within the zone of operations, rise and strike! . . . For your homes and hearths, strike! For future generations of your sons and daughters, strike! In the name of your sacred dead, strike! Let no heart be faint. Let every arm be steeled. The guidance of divine God points the way. Follow in His name to the Holy Grail of righteous victory!

The MacArthurs are the only father and son to have both won the Medal of Honor. The "Defender of Australia, Liberator of the Philippines, Conqueror of Japan" is buried in a large monument at Norfolk, Virginia.

Ref: Rasor, *General Douglas MacArthur*; *Report of General MacArthur*.

Madras, India

A major commercial port, with a small naval base, Madras's location on the eastern coast of India made it vulnerable to Japanese carrier air raids in March 1942.

MAGIC

Completely independent of the ULTRA codebreaking project was an American effort to crack Japanese ciphers. This project was called MAGIC. Unlike the Germans, the Japanese did not use an Enigma machine, but rather a similar, but less capable device. They used older encryption methods, which could be (and constantly were) cracked by rooms full of clever and hardworking specialists. This was what American cryptanalysts did in the late 1930s and throughout the war. A US naval officer, Robert J. Rochefort, was the principal codebreaker for the Pacific Fleet for the entire war. Among his achievements was the breaking of the Japanese code JN25, which led to the American victory at MIDWAY. US naval officer Laurence F. Stafford and William Friedman were the two other men most responsible for breaking Japanese codes during the war. US Army codebreaker Friedman was head of the cryptanalysis bureau in the War Department. Friedman was chiefly responsible for breaking the Japanese PURPLE code. His wife, Elizabeth (1892–1980), was also a codebreaker of considerable ability.

As with ULTRA, MAGIC obtained timely results by reconstructing the Japanese cipher machine and automating the cracking of the coded messages. The Japanese, as a standard military practice, changed their codebooks from time to time, and this slowed down the deciphering of their messages by the Americans for several months. But, aside from that, secret Japanese radio messages were not very secret during the war. Some Japanese leaders were suspicious that their codes were compromised, but the American use of MAGIC information was done carefully, and the Japanese never took measures to completely change their cipher system.

MAGIC made possible two of the most crucial DECEPTIONS of the Pacific War. First, in June 1942 there was the ambush US carriers pulled off at Midway Island. A large Japanese fleet was headed for Midway, with the dual purpose of taking the island and drawing the remaining US fleet from HAWAII for a "decisive battle." Because of MAGIC intercepts, the Americans knew of the Japanese plans and set up an ambush with their outnumbered carriers. As a result, the Japanese were defeated. Having lost four of their large carriers, the Japanese were no longer able to do whatever they wanted in the Pacific.

The second deception involved yet another ambush. MAGIC intercepts informed the Americans of a visit to the SOLOMONS area by the commander of the Japanese Navy. This officer, Admiral Isoroku YAMAMOTO, was one of the most effective commanders the Japanese had. He had attended college in the United States and understood America better than most other Japanese leaders. Although opposed to war with the United States, Yamamoto nevertheless presided over the string of victories Japan enjoyed in the first seven months of the war. Yamamoto was known to be a superb leader and naval commander. While there was a risk that MAGIC would be compromised if Yamamoto's aircraft was attacked, the removal of Japan's best naval commander was considered worth the risk. So on April 18, 1943, long-range US P-38 fighters found and attacked Yamamoto's transport and its fighter escorts over the Solomons. The admiral died and with that Japan lost a naval commander who could have led Japanese forces in a much more effective defense. The Japanese did not suspect broken codes, but rather bad luck. There were many other lesser deceptions to come out of MAGIC. Knowledge of Japanese plans in many battles and preparations for battles enabled Allied forces to fight more effectively. MAGIC was particularly useful in the prosecution of the US submarine offensive against Japanese shipping. MAGIC intercepts indicated where valuable Japanese shipping would be, as well as the location of antisubmarine forces and other warships. Since subs depended on stealth and surprise for their success, MAGIC allowed US SUBMARINES to undertake their deceptions with maximum effectiveness and much less risk.

Ref: Boyd, *Hitler's Japanese Confidant*; Drea, *MacArthur's Ultra*; Lewin, *The American Magic*;

Prados, *Combined Fleet Decoded*; Van Der Rhoer, *Deadly Magic*.

Mahan Class, US Destroyers

The largest interwar class of US destroyers (18 ships), the Mahans, built 1934–37, were ordered partially to stimulate the economy during the Great Depression. This was a useful "economy of force" measure employed by President F. D. ROOSEVELT to get some REARMAMENT money out of a penny-pinching and isolationist nation. They embodied many innovative ideas, including extreme high pressure boilers and a greatly enhanced TORPEDO complement, while reverting to the 5"/38 dual-purpose main battery of the FARRAGUT CLASS. They were very good ships (indeed, three more were built for Brazil) and very stable, taking the weight of numerous wartime upgrades to their antiaircraft capability with little difficulty. Six were lost in action.

Maizuru, Honshu

One of the four principal bases of the Imperial Navy, and the only one on the Sea of Japan, Maizuru specialized in the construction of destroyers and other light forces. It was the site of the Imperial Navy's Engineering Academy (candidates for line commissions went to Eta Jima, at KURE, while paymasters—whose duties included personnel and administrative matters—attended a third academy in Tokyo). It was also one of the four bases of the Special Navy Landing Force (SNLF).

Majuro, Marshall Islands

Despite a fairly extensive atoll, Majuro was of only limited importance on the eve of the war. Like most of the atolls in the area, its potential as a base was considerable. The Japanese neglected to fortify Majuro, and in January 1944 the United States just moved in, turning it into a forward base for operations elsewhere in the MARSHALL ISLANDS.

Makassar, Celebes, Netherlands East Indies

A small port, accessible to tramp steamers and coastal shipping, with some potential as a base for local control via small ships and long-range aircraft. It served as local Japanese headquarters from its capture in early 1942 until the end of the war.

Makatea, Society Islands

A useful atoll in the Society Islands, with no facilities of any sort. Strategically, its location on the northern edge of the archipelago made it of potential value if a threat were to develop from that direction. It remained in Allied hands throughout the war.

Makin, Gilbert Islands

A desolate island, with a British residence, a boat landing, and some shelter for ships, and room for a small airfield. Of value because it was one of the easternmost of the GILBERTS. It was raided by Marines on August 17–18, 1942 and occupied by US forces in late 1943.

See also CENTRAL PACIFIC CAMPAIGN; GILBERT ISLANDS; SMITHS, WAR OF THE.

Makin Island Raid, 1942

The US landing on GUADALCANAL on 7 August 1942 is rightly considered the first Allied offensive operation of the Pacific War. Ten days later, on August 17th, 221 US Marine "Raiders" landed on the Japanese-held island of Makin. The Marines, including Capt. James ROOSEVELT, the president's son, came ashore from *Argonaut* (SS-166) and *Nautilus* (SS-168), two of the largest SUBMARINES in the fleet (respectively 2,878 and 2,987 tons standard when surfaced). Aided by some of the local natives, and despite the intervention of Japanese aircraft summoned by radio from nearby islands, they destroyed a new seaplane reconnaissance base and killed most of the 90-man Japanese garrison,

including three men originally taken prisoner. The Marines lost 21 dead and 14 wounded. The island was quickly evacuated before Japanese reinforcements could arrive. Although some of the Marines—including Roosevelt—ended up staying on the island overnight, their final departure was in such haste that nine men were inadvertently left behind, and the Japanese murdered them.

The raid was mainly for propaganda purposes, although it did serve some military function. But the raid had an enormous impact on the subsequent fighting in the Pacific. The Japanese were alarmed at the vulnerability of dozens of similar island bases throughout the Pacific. The decision was made to increase the garrisons of these islands and to build the fortifications with which the Marines became so intimately acquainted during the rest of the war.

This was not the only case in which the Japanese reacted strongly to a minor American operation. The DOOLITTLE Raid (April 18, 1942, when 16 B-25 bombers flew from a carrier to bomb Japan) caused the Japanese to keep hundreds of combat aircraft in the Home Islands to prevent another attack, thereby greatly easing the plight of Allied forces elsewhere in the Pacific.

Malaya, Campaign for

The conquest of Malaya and its principal city, SINGAPORE, in February 1942 was one of the most spectacularly successful victories the Japanese were to achieve during World War II. Against a larger number of defending enemy infantry, and advancing 1,100 kilometers through jungle against a heavily fortified city, the Japanese emerged victorious in 55 days. It was a notable conquest, but one that resulted from serious misconceptions on both sides. The port of Singapore ("Lion City"), situated at the end of the Malay Peninsula and controlling the vital Straits of Malacca, had been a British possession since its founding in 1819. During the 1930s, Britain installed considerable coastal artillery and fortifications. But this was not as important as it appears. During the 1930s, naval warfare changed, with aircraft replacing large guns as the deciding weapon at sea. Moreover, Singapore was always defended by British control of the surrounding waters. Thus the key to the Japanese plan of conquest was to use superior airpower to control the seas around Singapore. This done, Japanese amphibious operations could proceed unhindered.

The Japanese troops had more combat experience and training than their British opponents, and were better led. But the Japanese underestimated the number of British troops they faced, while the British commander overestimated how many Japanese were attacking him. The Japanese also knew more about the British situation than the British knew of the Japanese invasion force. The Germans supplied copies of British strategic plans for Singapore and the Far East. They were obtained by a German U-boat commander from a British ship. HITLER expected Japan to declare war on Russia eventually, and provided support like this to ensure that such a declaration of war came to pass (it didn't.)

The British knew that Japanese combat units were on ships headed for Malaya in early December 1941. The British deployed their troops in the Malay Peninsula to confront any Japanese amphibious operations. Indeed, the British plan was to send one division into Thailand to disrupt Japanese operations if it came to war. An hour before the PEARL HARBOR attack, Japanese troops began landing in northern Malaya. Two Japanese divisions were coming by sea, while a third was marching overland through Thailand (which had agreed to allow passage of Japanese troops). Total Japanese troops sent into battle were about 100,000.

What the British did not know was how decisive Japanese aircraft would be. While the Japanese had available 560 modern combat aircraft, Britain was able to muster only 158 older and much less effective aircraft. Japanese planes quickly established air superiority. The British aircraft were destroyed within the first few days of the campaign. The British had two battleships operating out of Singapore, and these were promptly sunk by Japanese aircraft on 10 December. This was the first time that bat-

tleships under way at sea had been destroyed solely by air power. The British did not expect this, and had no way to counteract the resulting loss of sea control. On the other hand, even if Japanese aircraft had not sunk the two ships, there were enough Japanese battleships on call in the region to have done the job within a couple of days anyway, so that the Japanese would still have secured command of the seas. In any case, with HMSs *Prince of Wales* and *Repulse* gone, Malaya was wide open to invasion by sea. Japanese infantrymen were soon advancing down the Malay Peninsula, a 400-mile trek they would accomplish in six weeks against stiff opposition.

The British troops (one Indian, one Australian, and one mixed British/Malay division, plus some miscellaneous brigades) were generally new, inexperienced, and poorly trained. There were 138,700 of them, 38% more than the attacking enemy. Two of the Japanese divisions, the Fifth and 18th Infantry Divisions, had years of experience fighting in China, while the Imperial Guards Division, which had no combat experience, had undergone special training for Malaya. The Japanese were prepared, the British were not. The result was that British units were constantly out-fought and out-maneuvered during the fighting down the peninsula toward Singapore. The number of things the Japanese did right during this campaign and the number of things the British did wrong provide an interesting list of what it takes to win, or lose, a campaign.

Experienced troops. This is not always possible, as there isn't always a way to provide combat experience. But Japan had been fighting in China throughout the 1930s and was able to withdraw two experienced divisions from China for the invasion of Malaya. The third division used for the operation, the Imperial Guards Division, had no combat experience, but the troops were carefully selected for membership in that prestigious division and they were given extra jungle training before being sent into combat. Still, the other two combat experienced divisions, even without the special jungle training, did much better.

Engineer and logistics support.   Knowing that the withdrawing forces would try to delay pursuit by destroying the bridges over Malaya's hundreds of rivers and streams, the attacking forces were given three independent engineer regiments, four bridging battalions, and seven bridging companies to supplement the engineer regiment each of the three divisions already had. Special exercises in early 1941 emphasized demolition and rebuilding of bridges. This attention to bridging paid off. River crossing and bridge repair units went with the forward elements all through the campaign and the ability to quickly get across river obstacles kept the British constantly off balance.

A railway rebuilding and maintenance brigade. This unit repaired and operated Malaya's main rail line, which ran north-south parallel to the Malay Peninsula's main hard-surface trunk road. There were also eight independent motor transport battalions and 10 independent motor transport companies. The railroad and truck units ensured that the advancing units did not have to halt because of a lack of fuel or ammunition. During the campaign's last act, the assault on Singapore Island, the supply units were able to provide the army's 440 artillery pieces with 1,000 rounds per field gun and 500 rounds per heavy gun. Once more, Japanese preparations had added speed to the assault and kept the British defense off balance.

Relentless pursuit of retreating units.   The Japanese assumed that they would be able to defeat British units when they met them, but only speedy pursuit would prevent the British from fighting a lengthy delaying action that would increase Japanese losses. The Japanese rotated fresh units into the lead so that the troops fighting along the road would not tire and falter. Japanese tactics had their lead units spreading out from the road whenever they encountered resistance and moving quickly through the jungle to outflank the defenders. Once back on the road, the Japanese troops would want to move quickly to the next British position before the defenders could construct a well prepared defense. To this end, they equipped the infantry with 6,000 bicycles. The bicycles were a brilliant touch, for each bike could carry 60–80 pounds of equipment, food, and ammunition. The bikes could be walked across streams and past destroyed portions of the road. On the clear portions of the road the infantry on bicycles could move quickly, with units making over 20 kilometers an hour. The bicycle infantry, armed with rifles, grenades, and machine guns, would overcome small enemy units. Anything requiring more firepower might have to wait a few hours until the artillery and TANKS caught up. The bridging engineers enabled the tanks and truck-drawn artillery to keep up. British forces were unable to deal with any of these tactics and were repeatedly surprised at how hard it was to break contact as they fell back.

Tanks.   While the Japanese were far behind the European nations in developing tanks, they did have them and used them to good effect in Malaya. Japan used two obsolescent tank models in Malaya, a light tank (with a 37mm gun) and a medium tank (with a 57mm gun). Although tanks could be used only on or near the one north-south road, and even though British forces had several effective antitank weapons, the Japanese tanks rampaged down the peninsula. Aggressive leadership by tank platoon commanders was the key. Junior lieutenants in several key engagements led a few tanks down the main road through the defenders, then pressed on without waiting for escorting infantry and shot up the defenders' rear areas. The tendency of junior armor officers to press on and exploit an initial breakthrough led to the rout of large British forces and cut weeks or months from the campaign. Timid use of tanks in Malaya would have made them practically useless.

The Japanese had one tank group of four regiments in Malaya. In effect, it was a tank division. Although the tank group was never used together as a single unit, it had over 200 tanks organized as follows:

ORGANIZATION OF THE 3RD TANK GROUP

Element	Medium Tanks	Light Tanks	Other MV
First Tank Regiment	37	20	91
Second Tank Regiment+	37	20	91
Sixth Tank Regiment	37	20	91
14th Tank Regiment	—	45	48
Tank Group Headquarters	5	5	(several)
Totals	116	110	321+

Other MV = Other motor vehicles. On January 29, 1942 this unit, less its light tank company, was sent to reinforce the units preparing to invade the Dutch East Indies.

The Japanese medium tank employed in Malaya was the Type 97 (1937), equipped with a 57mm low-velocity gun and two 7.7mm machine guns and had a crew of four. The light tank was the Type 95 (1935), mounting a short-barreled 37mm gun and one 7.7mm machine gun and had a crew of three. The armor on both tanks was quite light. The Type 95 tank could be shot up by heavy (12mm and up) machine guns. Both could easily be stopped by the standard British "2 pounder" (57mm) antitank gun.

The British had plenty of antitank guns and antitank MINES, but they did not use them properly. The antitank guns were largely organized into separate units that were constantly held in reserve while front-line units were overrun by Japanese tanks. The same was true of antitank mines; few were distributed to the front-line units. This was a command failure that, had it not occurred, would have made Japanese tanks much less effective.

Air force tactics. Making virtue of a necessity, Japanese combat aircraft did not operate in direct support of their ground units. The infantry and armor troops did not have enough radios to communicate with the aircraft and, because of all the jungle, it was difficult for pilots to tell friend from foe even if there was radio contact with the ground. So the Japanese initially used their qualitative and quantitative aircraft superiority to keep British aircraft out of action. After a week of pounding enemy air bases, Japanese fighters and bombers shifted much of their efforts to shooting up any British transport (road, rail, or sea) they spotted. This proved to be an excellent move, for the British found they could move safely only at night, while the Japanese could, and did, move around the clock.

Living off the land. Japanese forces traveled light. As a matter of policy, it was expected that enemy supplies and bases would be captured and immediately put to use. This was possible because of the high speed of the Japanese advance. In particular, several British air bases were overrun before they could be destroyed. In one case, the Japanese captured 100,000 gallons of aviation fuel. In several cases, Japanese aircraft were operating out of former British bases within 24 hours of capturing them, using British fuel and bombs. This allowed Japanese aircraft to operate closer to the fighting, making more sorties per day possible.

Amphibious operations. While we tend to think of World War II amphibious operations as US Marines storming ashore on some island, the more typical World War II example was putting a few hundred, or a few thousand, troops ashore on the mainland or on some large island. The Japanese had used these types of landings in China throughout the 1930s. The Japanese had a number of self-propelled 15-foot collapsible boats and 33-foot landing craft that were transported by truck and rail from southern Thailand to the west coast of Malaya right behind the advancing Japanese infantry. Along with a few boats captured on PENANG Island, this Japanese flotilla carried a reinforced infantry battalion of the Fifth Division (which had 20 years of experience with these landings) and made several landings behind the British front that disrupted the withdrawing enemy and made it easier to keep the Japanese advance moving. Later the Imperial Guards Division provided units for these landings and this led to the British abandoning Kuala Lumpur, the capital of the Federated Malay States. Thus, throughout the campaign the British had to worry about their open coastal flank.

One of the more decisive battles was on the Slim River, halfway down the Malay Peninsula and 80 miles north of Kuala Lumpur (the Malay capital). The British 11th Indian Division held the line with seven infantry battalions (three Indian, three Gurkha, and one British). On January 7, in a 24-hour battle starting shortly after midnight, one Japanese infantry regiment and less than 50 tanks took the 11th Indian Division apart. By the next day, only 1,150 of the troops in those seven infantry battalions were still available for action. The rest were dead, wounded, or for the most part either fleeing through the jungle or Japanese prisoners.

By the end of January, the Japanese were on the north shore of the narrow waterway that separates Malaya from Singapore Island. Despite the inevitability of the loss of Singapore, the British command insisted on pouring reinforcements into the island-city, including an entire new British division, the 18th. During the next two weeks, Japanese troops secured several beachheads on Singapore Island, and then fought their way toward the city, seizing the water reservoirs. At that point, with the Japanese beginning to penetrate the city itself, the British, deprived of drinking water, had no choice but to surrender. British losses were 8,000 killed in action and 130,000 taken prisoner, while Japanese dead totaled 10,000. Japan now possessed the best equipped port in Southeast Asia, complete with a system of coastal defense guns and shipyards that could repair any size ship.

The Japanese victory in Malaya had an enormous psychological impact on the British. For two years after this defeat, British commanders were extremely cautious, often overly cautious, in operations against the Japanese. In the longer term, the surrender of Singapore demonstrated to the local peoples that the Europeans were not invincible. This led to the rapid decolonialization of the region after the war.

Malaya, Federation of

Malaya is a peninsula about the size of Great Britain. For the most part covered by heavy jungles, its inhabitants were divided among native Malays, who were mostly Moslem, and Indians and Chinese who had settled there over the centuries. A British possession, Malaya was politically a federation of a number of semi-independent sultanates and several crown colonies.

It was rich in tin, as well as rubber and other tropical products, and the great port of Singapore was an important center of international commerce.

In 1941 the British were firmly in control. Although there was some nationalist sentiment among elements of the Malay population, the large Chinese and Indian communities were strongly committed to British rule.

The Japanese occupied Malaya in a swift campaign from December 1941 through February 1942, and ruthlessly exploited the country thereafter. By mid-1945, Allied—chiefly British—air raids and even naval raids were becoming common, in anticipation of a British plan to recover Malaya, with amphibious landings and an overland offensive from Siam, an operation that was scheduled to begin in late September.

Malaya, Resistance to the Japanese

This area, including SINGAPORE, was heavily garrisoned by the Japanese. A resistance movement sprang up anyway. GUERRILLA operations were most enthusiastically embraced by the Chinese population of Malaya, although there were also Malay and Indian (another local minority) guerrillas. The Chinese were the core of the resistance largely because of the depredations the Japanese were committing in China. The "overseas Chinese" maintained their language and traditions, as well as links with the homeland. Another item the Malay Chinese imported from China was communism, and the best disciplined partisans were communist led. Many native Malays and, to a lesser extent, Indians assisted the Japanese in fighting the guerrillas. This fighting continued after the war, when the Chinese communist guerrillas continued fighting. The British, like the Japanese, used Malay assistance to eventually put down the communist insurgency. This was something the Japanese were never able to do during the war. But the Japanese did manage to keep the guerrillas largely confined to the rural areas of Malaya.

Manchukuo

A Japanese puppet state established in 1932 comprising the region of Manchuria. From 1934 it was ostensibly ruled by Pu-yi, who as a boy had been deposed as the last emperor of China in 1911.

See also MANCHURIA.

Manchuria

The resource rich and industrially advanced northeastern regions of China, partially inhabited by the Manchu, a non-Chinese people who had given China its last imperial dynasty. In 1931 the Japanese invaded the region and set up the puppet "empire" of Manchukuo. Under Japanese rule, Manchuria was heavily exploited and settled by a surprisingly large number of Japanese, and even many migrants from China proper, who found peace under Japanese rule more attractive than the ongoing horrors of living in China. For most of the war it was a major training base for the Japanese Army, which maintained substantial forces there in anticipation of a Soviet invasion. Manchuria was more or less immune from the war, save for occasional bombing raids, until the Soviet Union invaded in August of 1945.

Manchuria, Campaign for, 1945

Japan and the Soviet Union had signed a nonaggression treaty in April 1941. But there was no love lost between the two, for Japan had defeated Russia in 1905 and taken a large chunk of Russian-controlled territory (actually, mostly Chinese territory that the Chinese were unable to control). The 1941 treaty was signed by the Japanese because they had found out, in several border battles during

1939, that they were outmatched by Soviet forces. The Soviets signed because they were preparing for a showdown with Germany and did not want any distractions in the Far East.

By 1945, the situation had changed. Over three years of war with America had left Japan weak. In May of 1945, Germany surrendered and the Soviet Union was free to use its armed forces elsewhere. In April 1945, Russia told Japan that the nonaggression treaty would not be renewed when it expired in April 1946. This led the Japanese to believe they were safe from a Soviet attack until that time. But in February 1945, Russia had promised its allies it would attack Japan three months after Germany surrendered. This promise was not made public. Germany surrendered on 8 May. It appeared that the Russian offensive would take place on or about 8 August 1945. It did.

A key factor in continued Japanese resistance was the forces Japan maintained in China and Manchuria. From early 1944 and into 1945, these forces had been on the offensive in China. The primary purpose of this fighting was to eliminate American air bases that could be used to bomb Japan, a moot point now that America had B-29 bases operating in the Mariana Islands. By the spring of 1945, Japanese forces deep inside China began to withdraw to Manchuria and Korea. Manchuria and Korea contained much of Japan's economic resources, as well as millions of Japanese colonists to see that the area stayed under Japanese control. Between the resources of Manchuria and Korea, and dogged resistance on the Japanese Home Islands, Japan felt it could keep fighting for years and eventually outlast the war-weary Allies. The key to all this was keeping the Russians from attacking. Diplomatic efforts to that end increased during 1945, but failed.

In early 1941 the Russians had 30 well equipped divisions in the Far East. This force contained 700,000 troops, 3,100 armored vehicles, and 4,100 combat aircraft. When Germany invaded in June of 1941, these divisions were quickly stripped of their best men and weapons and replaced, if at all, with less effective troops and equipment. For the rest of the war, the Russians used mainly older, younger, and less healthy local recruits to keep their Far East combat manpower at about one million troops. Artillery strength was increased, but armor strength averaged about 2,500 AFV and aircraft (mostly older models) strength fell to about 3,300. But once Germany was defeated, the Soviet troops went east again. Between May and August 1945, Russia sent 400,000 troops, 2,100 armored vehicles, and 17,000 trucks east. Combat aircraft strength was increased to some 4,600. By early August the Soviets had over 1.5 million troops (83 divisions) in the Far East. These were experienced soldiers who had defeated the Germans.

Japan's situation was rather less favorable. The army in Manchuria had 1.3 million troops, but a third of them were unreliable Korean and Chinese conscripts. These soldiers were organized into 37 infantry divisions and 40 independent regiments and brigades. There were only 1,200 TANKS, none of them anywhere near a match for Soviet armored vehicles. There were 1,900 Japanese combat aircraft available, and these matched Russian quality somewhat. But the Russians outnumbered the Japanese in the air two to one. Most of the Japanese troops were poorly trained and equipped. The best of them had been pulled back from China since June 1945. The Japanese had to defend a 4,500-kilometer front in Manchuria, and the math was against them. They had about 200 troops per kilometer of front and that wasn't going to be enough. Undaunted, the Japanese covered a thousand kilometers of this front with 17 fortified zones. This covered the routes that tanks were most likely to use. Some 8,000 bunkers and other fortifications were built in these zones. There was also a continuous series of bunkers and trenches along the entire border, but these were lightly manned and meant just to give a warning.

Although Japanese diplomats had noted the massive transfer of Russian combat units eastward since May 1945, Japan's leadership still thought they would be protected from a Russian attack until the non-aggression pact expired in April 1946. On August 8, 1945, Russia declared war on Japan.

Three Soviet Army groups invaded Manchuria and reached the Korean border in less than two weeks. Actually, a major part of the Russian attack took place on 6 August, as the Russian forces near the Pacific coast, faced with rather formidable Japanese defenses, got started early and achieved a high degree of surprise. Coming out of Mongolia and heading almost due east was the Russian Transbaikal Army Group, with 40 divisions, 654,000 troops and 2,400 tanks and assault guns, on a front of 580 kilometers. By August 14, units of this army group had advanced 250–450 kilometers into Japanese territory, making much headway once units were on the flat badlands of the Gobi Desert. By the end of August, this army group captured 220,000 Japanese troops. Next to the Transbaikal Army Group was the Second Far East Army Group, coming due south with 11 divisions, 337,000 troops and 1,200 armored vehicles, on a 480 kilometer front. By 14 August, units of this army group had advanced 50 to 200 kilometers through mountains and forests, and by the end of the month had captured 266,000 Japanese soldiers. Coming south along the Pacific coast was the First Far East Army Group with 32 divisions, 586,000 troops and 1,800 armored vehicles. By 14 August, units of this army group had advanced 120 to 150 kilometers and by the end of the month had captured 108,000 Japanese.

The Russian air force flew 14,000 combat sorties during August, and half as many noncombat sorties. Some 2,700 tons of bombs were dropped, plus 361 million cannon and a billion machine-gun rounds. Most of the Russian aircraft (2,497) were fighters, which, in addition to 808 ground attack aircraft and 1,364 bombers, spent most of their time pounding Japanese ground troops. The Japanese air force was swept from the skies during the first few days of the offensive. In support of parachute assaults, the 228 air force transports carried 16,000 troops, plus 4,800 tons of fuel, munitions, and other supplies.

RECORD COMBAT UNIT ADVANCES IN THE 20TH CENTURY

Force	War	Operation	Year	Advance	Duration	Rate
US 24th Inf.	Gulf	Iraq	1991	368 km.	4 days	92 km./day
British	WW I	Megiddo	1918	167 km.	3 days	56 km./day
Israeli	Six Day	Sinai	1967	220 km.	4 days	55 km./day
Russian	WW II	Manchuria	1945	300 km.	6 days	50 km./day
German	WW II	France	1940	368 km.	12 days	31 km./day
German	WW II	Russia	1941	700 km.	24 days	29 km./day
Allied	WW II	France	1944	880 km.	32 days	28 km./day

Note that smaller units have occasionally done even better over shorter periods.

It was surprise everywhere that hurt the Japanese the most. The Japanese generals mistakenly thought that the mountainous and wooded terrain along the border, as well as the immense size of Manchuria (500,000 square miles), would slow down the Russian attack. The combat-experienced Russian troops advanced over narrow mountain trails and through forests, avoiding the 17 Japanese fortified zones. For the most part, this shockingly fast advance paralyzed the Japanese troops on the border. Thus Russian armored units dashed past the border, leaving Japanese troops in their wake, to be captured or hunted down by following Soviet units.

But after a few days, resistance began to stiffen. Russian armored units were running out of fuel, and often had to halt and wait for supplies. Japanese units away from the border would barricade themselves within towns and fight it out to the last man. This type of resistance increased as the campaign went on. But the speed of the Russian advance made any kind of organized resistance useless. The Russian mechanized units were formidable, and these were the same units that had beaten the Germans at their own blitzkrieg game. The Japanese had nothing that could stop something like this, and only suicidal stubbornness with which to resist it.

Russian paratroopers landed on Japanese airfields to further paralyze resistance. After a week, Russian units were several hundred kilometers inside Manchuria. But the Russians were on a short leash because of resupply problems. It took them three weeks to traverse all of Manchuria (over 1,000 kilometers), and the Russians were unable to go much farther than Manchuria and northern Korea because of supply shortages. Most of the food and fuel for the troops had to come 4,500 miles over the Trans-Siberian Railroad. Nevertheless, the Russians did accomplish some record-breaking movement against armed opponents.

Although Japan announced its surrender on August 15, Japanese troops in Manchuria fought on for another week before their generals agreed to surrender. Even then, thousands of Japanese soldiers stayed in the woods, slowly making their way to the coast and what they hoped would be ships that would take them to Japan. Few ever got home.

The Soviet Union had ties to both major factions contending for primacy in China: the Nationalists and the Communists. Russia had signed a treaty with the Nationalists that called for the Soviets to evacuate Chinese territory within three weeks of the Japanese surrender. This the Russians did, but with a couple of twists. First, they left with all the industrial equipment they could carry off, and second, they gave most of the captured Japanese weapons to the Chinese communists. Meanwhile, the Chinese Red Army under Lin Piao took over villages and small towns, while CHIANG's Nationalist troops occupied the large cities in Manchuria. Chiang's Nationalist troops provided safe haven to Japanese civilians, which made great propaganda for the communists. Japanese civilians caught outside the safe havens were dealt with harshly by the Chinese. There were over 2 million Japanese civilians in Manchuria and many were never heard from again after 1945. Tens of thousands of Japanese refugees crossed the Yalu River trying to reach the ports farther south. Chinese mobs killed Japanese civilians by the thousands while many others died from starvation, disease, or exposure. Many more simply blended in with the local population.

On August 20, the Red Army moved into Korea. Within a week, Russian soldiers found themselves fighting Japanese stragglers moving down from Manchuria. The Japanese troops moved through the mountains, trying to reach the Sea of Japan and a ship for home. On August 24 Soviet troops occupied Pyongyang, the largest city in northern Korea, soon to become the capital of North Korea. On 1 September, the Korean People's Republic was established under Russian supervision. Russians also organized the roundup of Koreans who collaborated with the Japanese. Many were executed on the spot as crowds screamed "Kill the Jap lovers!" in reaction to 40 years of brutal Japanese occupation. On 8 September, US troops landed at CHEMULPO on the west coast. The US Military Government in Korea (USMGK) handed over police functions to former Japanese policemen. When word of this spread, nearly two million Koreans from the north (Japanese collaborators, landowners, Christians, and anti-communists) fled to South Korea.

There was a lot of settling of scores in the wake of the Manchurian Campaign. Hundreds of thousands of Japanese civilians, along with local collaborators, probably died from one cause (execution) or another (privation). The military costs were not that great, considering the size of the forces involved. Some two and a half million Russian and Japanese troops were in the area. There were another million Chinese troops who closed in as the campaign wound down and even Americans showed up toward the end. But the Soviets lost only 8,000 dead, one of their less bloody victories in World War II. Some 80,000 Japanese troops were killed in the fighting, plus many more Japanese civilians. Some 600,000 Japanese were taken prisoner, and nearly 100,000 of these died in captivity (the rest were returned to Japan from labor camps in Russia, in the 1950s).

See also KURILE ISLANDS.

Ref: DuPuy, *Great Battles of the Eastern Front*; Glantz, *August Storm*.

Mandalay, Burma

Although possessed of some facilities as a river port, Mandalay's chief importance lay in the fact that it dominated central Burma. As such it was the principal objective of the Japanese invasion of Burma in 1942 and the British counteroffensive of 1944.

Mandates

Prior to World War I, the Caroline, MARSHALL, and Mariana Islands (save for GUAM, which belonged to the United States) were owned by Germany, which had bought them from Spain in 1898. In 1914 the Japanese moved in. In the early 1920s the League of Nations assigned the islands to Japan as a "mandate." Under the terms of a league mandate, the mandatory power was required to promote local development with the ultimate intention of granting independence. There were actually three classes of mandates, of which the Pacific mandates fell into the lowest, on the assumption that they were so backward they would take generations to become self-governing. The phrase "the Mandates" became commonplace when referring to the islands mandated to Japan. Various members of the British Commonwealth also held mandates over other former German territories in the Pacific Northeast New Guinea, the Solomon Islands, NAURU, and SAMOA—but these were not included in the phrase "the Mandates."

The Mandates are very small places, spread over an enormous amount of water. Together with the GILBERT ISLANDS and Guam, the Mandates totaled only some 2,100 square miles, spread across about three million square miles of ocean. The MARIA-

NAS are the largest group in surface area, about 700 square miles, of which Guam is slightly more than 200 square miles.

During and after World War II it was common to accuse the Japanese of having violated the league mandate and the naval DISARMAMENT TREATIES by fortifying the Mandates. However, the islands were regularly subjected to inspection until Japan withdrew from the league in 1936, and it is now clear that the Japanese did not begin to develop military installations in the islands until after that date, albeit that they technically forfeited their mandate by doing so.

Manila Bay, Luzon, Philippines

Including not only Manila, but also CAVITE and several other small ports, Manila Bay was a major commercial port with an extensive sheltered anchorage and extensive facilities to service shipping. There was also a small but well equipped US naval base at Cavite, and several important air bases in the area. The war left this area devastated.

Manpower, the Division Slice

Although the division is the principal combat formation of an army, it represents a relatively small proportion of an army's total strength. For example, at peak strength the US Army totaled some nine million men and women in World War II, of whom about two-thirds were in the Army Ground Forces or the Army Service Forces. The 89 divisions—68 infantry, 5 airborne, and 16 armored—in the army averaged about 13,800 men each. This totals only about 1.2 million men. The balance were helping to keep the front-line troops fighting.

For each division there were:

In the division itself, 13,800 men (on average) plus another 13,000 men in combat support and service units, 10,000 men in communications zone troops, and 20,000 men in miscellaneous status.

Combat support and service units provided extra artillery fire, engineer services, tank support,

medical aid, and the like to the front-line troops, sometimes being on the front lines themselves.

Communications zone troops were the men and women (nurses, clerks) behind the front, who helped pass the ammunition and run the hospitals, as well as guard rear area installations, plus replacements, hospital patients, and the like. Miscellaneous status included troops in the United States in training, hospitals and headquarters personnel, and so forth.

Adding these troops to the division's brings the total up to about 56,800 men per division. This is referred to as a "division slice," the total number of troops in and supporting each division, all the way back to those in the recruiting stations back home. The US Army had the highest division slice in the war, partly because of its propensity for consuming enormous quantities of supplies, and partially because the Army Service Forces also supported Army Air Forces operations. In fact, if one includes the Army Air Forces, the US division slice rises to nearly 100,000.

The division slice varied by theater. That for troops in the Central Pacific was higher than that for those in the ETO. The six army divisions that took part in operations in the Central Pacific Theater had a division slice of about 76,000: 17,000 in the division, plus 28,000 in combat support and service units, and 11,000 in communications zone service forces, plus 20,000 in the United States.

The 60-odd divisions in Europe had a division slice of only about 60,000 men: 15,000 with the divisions (the 16 armored divisions were only about 60% the size of infantry divisions, and the airborne divisions even smaller), 15,000 in combat support and service units, 10,000 in communications zone forces, plus 20,000 in the United States.

Several other armies had problems with a burgeoning division slice. Initially, the Australian division slice was quite small, only 34,000 in the first half of 1942. However, during its mobilization in 1939–42, Australia had invested an inordinate amount of its manpower in combat units. A major part of these units served under British command in North Africa (Sixth, Seventh, and Ninth Divisions) and MALAYA (Eighth Division), and were supported by British combat support and service troops. The balance of the Australian divisions were serving in garrison in Australia into mid–1942, and thus needed little in the way of specialized support and service troops. Once the divisions in British service came home (less the eighth, lost at SINGAPORE) and, together with those at home, began to ship out to New Guinea and other operational theaters, Australia had to find support and service personnel for them. By mid–1945 the Australian division slice was 60,000.

The Japanese were very frugal with their division slice, preferring to put as many troops as possible in the front line. Early in the Pacific War it seems to have been as low as 25,000. Operationally, this proved to be a wasteful policy in the Pacific, as the troublesome geography and climate caused unsupported troops to waste away quickly in combat, which happened to the Japanese time after time. As the war went on the Japanese increased their division slice, until in the last year it was about 32,000 men, if one included the Imperial Army Air Force.

It's worth noting that the 173 divisions that Japan had, at least on paper, at the time of its surrender, amounted to only about as many combat troops as the 95 US divisions (89 army and 6 Marine) in existence at the time.

Ref: Greenberg, *The Ineffective Soldier*.

Manus, Admiralty Islands

A large island, with a modest anchorage and no port facilities. On paper, Manus was of great potential strategic value, being about 300 miles north of New Guinea and the same west of the BISMARCKS. It played a significant role in Operation CARTWHEEL and the NEW GUINEA campaign.

Mao Tse-tung (1893–1976)

Mao came from a prosperous peasant family in Hunan. He received an excellent traditional education but left school in 1911 to join Sun Yat-sen's revolutionary army. Discharged after about six months, Mao pursued a higher education, worked for a time as a librarian, and in 1921 helped found the Chinese Communist Party. For a time associated with the KOUMINTANG Party, Mao broke decisively with CHIANG KAI-SHEK in the late '20s and became a notable organizer and leader of GUERRILLA forces, and also an important theoretician of guerrilla warfare. Over the next 20 years Mao led communist forces in an on-again, off-again war against Chiang's Nationalist, pausing occasionally to fight the Japanese as well. After World War II the civil war resumed, to be concluded with a communist victory in 1949.

Maps

There were no reliable maps for many of the areas over which World War II was fought in Asia and the Pacific. Some regions, such as much of New Guinea, Burma, and BORNEO, had never been properly mapped. Others had been mapped years before, such as the Philippines, which were formally surveyed before World War I. So bad was the shortage of accurate maps and charts, that it was not uncommon for US forces in the South Pacific to operate with maps marked "U.S. Ex. Ex." This stood for the "United States Exploration Expedition," a major scientific survey conducted under the command of Lt. Charles Wilkes, USN, from 1838 to 1842. (Wilkes was later more famous for his precipitation of the "Trent Affair" during the Civil War; his great-grandson, RAdm John Wilkes, played a major role in the Normandy Invasion.) In the case of the BISMARCKS and SOLOMONS, despite several generations of German and British rule, many maps were barely updated versions of those produced by Bougainville, d'Entrecasteaux, La Perouse, Shortland, and other 18th century explorers. Needless to say, the available maps were often extremely inaccurate: To cite but one example, six different charts of Bougainville gave six different longitudes and latitudes for Cape Torokina, on the southwestern coast, not one of which was correct.

As the war went on, new maps were prepared and distributed and the situation improved. In addition to making use of traditional survey techniques, which could work only if a place was occupied by friendly personnel, cartographers employed a variety of innovative techniques in making new maps. Aerial photography using stereoscopic techniques was the principal tool used. However, since interpretation of the photographs was often difficult, the technique was supplemented in a variety of ways. Intelligence officers interviewed people who had visited or resided in the places being mapped, and also perused diaries, memoirs, and ship's logs. In some cases, SUBMARINES were used to survey coastal areas. On-site reconnaissance was also sometimes performed, with men landed from submarines to conduct investigations, often at some personal risk.

Initially, raw data was processed in the Pacific, and the resulting maps were then reproduced and distributed. It was later found to be more efficient, and the resulting product more accurate, if the data—and in some cases appropriate individuals—were shipped to Washington, to be processed by an increasingly efficient Hydrographic Office, which relied on hundreds of draughtsmen, or more often draughtswomen, to produce master maps. These maps could then be reproduced in the United States or in Australia, for final distribution.

One of the most interesting innovations during World War II was the preparation of three-dimensional maps and physical models of enemy-held islands. These were used to assist navy gunners and pilots to locate their assigned targets, and Marines and infantrymen to "see" up close what the ground would be like when they hit the beaches. Such maps and models were particularly popular with airmen, who were wont to "fly" their hands over them so that they could get a "feel" for the hills and valleys over which they would shortly be flying for real. By 1945, these relief maps and models had become a regular feature of island assaults. Even destroyers were supplied with them. This made sense, as destroyers often delivered vital fire support. Destroyers, because they drew less water, could get in closer and provide more immediate support with their five-inch (127mm) guns.

Marcus Island

Although it possessed no port facilities, not even an anchorage, Marcus was valuable to the Japanese as a forward air base, since reconnaissance aircraft based there could reach far into the central Pacific, being located about 800 miles east of IWO JIMA and 1,200 northwest of WAKE ISLAND.

In practical terms Marcus figured small in the global conflict. Its only offensive use by the Japanese occurred in late 1941, when reconnaissance aircraft based there took part in the Wake Island operation. Otherwise, save for an occasional raid by the Pacific Fleet, including one in March 1942 during which the island was worked over by carrier aircraft and heavy cruiser gunfire, Marcus was bypassed during the war. By early 1945 the island was completely isolated, and the garrison suffered considerable privation, with outright starvation averted only by the Japanese surrender.

Marianas, Campaign for

Also known as the "Ladrones" ("Thieves") Islands, the Marianas are a chain of islands in the western Pacific Ocean, about 1,400 miles south of Japan. The total land area is less than 700 square miles, of which 200 comprise GUAM proper. The other two large islands, SAIPAN and TINIAN, account for nearly half of the rest of the land area. Inhabited by Micronesians, the islands were for centuries Spanish, but Guam was taken by the United States in 1898, and the balance sold to Germany, which lost them to Japan in 1914, after which they became part of the MANDATES. A great many Japanese settled in the islands before World War II.

The Allies' GILBERTS and MARSHALLS campaigns were largely preliminaries for the capture of the Marianas, the main goal of the CENTRAL PACIFIC CAMPAIGN. By capturing islands in the Marianas, the B-29 bombers just entering service would have bases from which to bomb Japan's cities and ports. This bombing campaign would either end the war or pave the way for the final act: the invasion of Japan itself.

It was understood that the Marianas campaign would involve some of the bloodiest fighting of the war. The islands to be invaded were larger and more heavily defended than any in the Gilberts or Marshalls. Even though the Japanese bases in the CAROLINES (to the south) were to be stripped of their aircraft and isolated, Japan was expected to use most of its remaining warships and aircraft to defend the Marianas. And they did.

Of the 15 Mariana Islands, stretching in a 435-mile arc in the central Pacific, only four were large enough, and in the right location, to be useful as B-29 bases. These were Saipan, Tinian, Rota, and Guam.

In late February 1944, right after TRUK had been blasted into ineffectiveness, American warships steamed into the Marianas for the first time since Guam had fallen to the Japanese in late 1941. Their purpose was to bomb Japanese bases and scout. Recon aircraft went in and took a lot of pictures, for the assault on these islands would take place in four months.

By early June, 535 American ships were closing in on the Marianas. They came from HAWAII, 3,500 miles distant, and from the forward base at ENIWETOK, a thousand miles away. On board were 127,000 combat troops, most of them Marines. Starting on 11 June, carrier aircraft hit Saipan. On June 13 the battleships closed in and bombarded. On June 15 two Marine divisions (the Second and Fourth) hit Saipan. The Japanese garrison of 29,000 troops was dug in and cut off from reinforcement. It would be another fight to the death.

While the land battle was under way, Japan sent out what was left of its fleet. Nine carriers, 46 other warships, and 473 aircraft went up against a US force of 15 carriers, 97 other warships, and 956 aircraft. While outnumbered in quantity and quality of warships, the Japanese had a few advantages. The naval Battle of the PHILIPPINE SEA (the area just to the west of the Marianas) was fought within range of Japanese island air bases and land-based

aircraft. While US carriers had earlier destroyed most Japanese land-based aircraft, more were always being brought in. Japanese carrier aircraft had a longer range than their American counterparts (560 to 350 miles for searching and 300 to 200 miles for attack).

From June 19 to 21 the naval battle raged. The Japanese were decisively beaten and lost three carriers and 480 aircraft. The United States lost no ships and a hundred aircraft, nearly half of those from running out of fuel on their way back from the last strike on the retreating Japanese.

The ground combat on Saipan went on to the end of June, with the army's 27th Infantry Division brought in on June 20 to expedite matters. The result was the usual one. Only about 1,800 of the 29,000-man Japanese garrison were taken prisoner. The rest died, along with 3,426 Americans from the three divisions eventually sent into the battle. Thousands of Japanese civilians, also perished, mostly by suicide.

On 21 July Guam was invaded by the Third Marine Division, the army's 77th Infantry Division, and, as a later reinforcement, by the First Marine Brigade. The 11,000-man Japanese garrison died, along with 1,435 Americans.

Tinian was invaded on July 24 by the Second and Fourth Marine Divisions and taken in seven days. Nearly all of the 8,000-man Japanese garrison perished, along with 389 Americans. Rota was left in Japanese hands, isolated and starving.

The Marianas campaign was over by mid-August of 1944. The Japanese carrier fleet was broken, although surviving battleships and cruisers would make suicide raids over the next year. More importantly, airfields for B-29s were under construction in the Marianas through the summer of 1944. By the fall of that year, American bombers would appear over Japanese cities in large numbers.

Marine Corps, US

For most of the nation's history the Marines were a very small force. So small, in fact, that until a provisional Marine battalion landed at Guantanamo Bay in Cuba on 10 June 1898, during the Spanish-American War, most Americans had never even heard of the Marine Corps. Up until that time, US Marines had served as shipboard specialists, much like marines in the world's other major navies for the last few centuries. Of course, the Marines also occasionally provided provisional battalions for service ashore. Usually the Marines did well in this business. Thus, a detachment of Marines (eight of them, plus a Marine officer and a Navy midshipman) helped storm Derna, in North Africa, on April 26, 1805 (". . . To the shores of Tripoli . . ."). A brigade of Marines and sailors were the only American troops who didn't run at the Battle of Bladensburg, on August 24, 1814, a disgraceful affair that resulted in the British capture of Washington. A battalion of Marines helped storm Mexico City on September 13, 1847 ("From the halls of Montezuma . . ."). It wasn't all glory, however, as Marines did leave the field precipitously at Bull Run on July 21, 1861, an incident about which General VANDEGRIFT once said that the Marines must surely have been the last troops to flee the field.

Normally, Marines were organized as "detachments" on ships and at navy yards, only occasionally being formed into units of company-size and larger, on an ad hoc basis.

In 1911 all Marines not assigned to ships were formed into companies of 103 men (identical to US Army companies of that time). These companies were then organized into battalions (three companies) or regiments (10 companies) as needed. The cause of this reorganization was the Marines' fear of recurring bureaucratic and political efforts to abolish them by the army, and occasionally the navy. Thus the Marines began to seek a greater role for themselves than merely keeping order on warships, guarding naval bases, and occasionally landing in some remote place to "teach the natives a lesson." The Marines saw opportunities with the recent adoption of what became known as War Plan Orange, which envisioned the fleet advancing across the Pacific in the event of a war

with Japan. To effect such an advance islands would have to be occupied to serve as bases.

Although the Marines had previously never raised anything larger than a provisional regiment, quite early it was clear that the necessity of seizing islands from the Japanese as the fleet advanced across the Pacific in accordance with War Plan Orange would require the services of division-sized formations. As early as 1913 the Marines began to prepare for their role in War Plan Orange, creating the Advance Base Force. This was organized and trained to make amphibious landings. Over the years it did so several times, notably at Vera Cruz, in MEXICO, in Haiti, and in the Dominican Republic.

Still, on the eve of World War I the Marine Corps numbered only 13,700 men. During World War I the Corps grew rapidly, reaching 75,000 by late 1918. Two Marine brigades, about 25,000 men, served with the AEF in France. The Fourth Marine Brigade formed part of the Second Infantry Division, accumulating a distinguished record (Belleau Wood, for example). The other Marine brigade arrived later and, despite the efforts of Marine brass to create a Marine division, was used for rear-area security. After the Great War, the Corps was cut back to about 17,000 men. But the Advance Base Force, which had been redesignated a brigade, continued to exist, effecting occasional interventions but more importantly serving as a testbed for the development of amphibious doctrine, going through several name changes. Meanwhile, during the 1920s a regular Marine infantry regimental organization was developed. This was a small unit of only about 1,500 men.

The Marine Corps stayed small until the 1930s, when expansion began. On 1 February 1941 the Marines activated their first two divisions. By the end of the war they would have six.

As originally organized in 1941, a Marine division was quite similar to the army's contemporary infantry division. There were three rifle regiments of three battalions each, plus an artillery regiment (three battalions of 75mm guns and one of

105mm), plus supporting elements of reconnaissance, engineer, signal, service, and medical (supplied by the navy) troops. In addition, there were some formations specialized in amphibious warfare, like a US Navy "Beach and Shore" Battalion, to help get the troops ashore, and a "Defense" Battalion, intended to provided protection against attack from the sea and into a beachhead's rear.

A lot of changes in divisional organization took place even before the First Marine Division landed on GUADALCANAL on August 7, 1942. By then the on-paper 19,300 men of a Marine division had been reinforced by a tank battalion, a Navy Seabee battalion, and a 155mm artillery battalion, while the riflemen received an increased allocation of mortars (162) and light artillery (54 37mm antitank guns).

Although the basic organization of the division remained more or less unchanged for the rest of the war, equipment allocations continued to evolve, particularly in terms of automatic and semiautomatic weapons. By mid-1944 the division had over 16,000 M1 carbines or M1 rifles, 625 machine guns, and 45 submachine guns, not counting machine guns on TANKS and LVTs.

The Marines learned the hard way how useful it was to have many automatic weapons. When they first had to confront the reckless abandon of Japanese BANZAI attacks on Guadalcanal (1942), the Marines had to improvise. Some automatic weapons (machine guns and automatic rifles) were taken from all units and kept as a reserve in several trucks. When the signs of an imminent Japanese attack were detected (the Japanese were not always as stealthy as they could have been when preparing an attack), the trucks full of automatic weapons would be rushed to the threatened area and the troops promptly equipped with the needed additional firepower.

Although the number of mortars and 37mm guns fell slightly (to 153 and 36 respectively), the troops were lavishly provided with antitank rocket launchers (over 1,700) and flamethrowers, which had proven useful in "bunker busting."

As Marine Corps combat doctrine evolved, it was decided that each division should have an air wing associated with it (72 aircraft of various types) to provide air defense, ground support, and reconnaissance. In practice, however, only three air wings were fully formed and a fourth partially, so the "marriage" between ground and air elements was not as close as the Marine brass wished it to be, and Marines were often supported by navy airmen. On their own scale of evaluation, the Marine riflemen believed air support provided by Marines was best, followed by the navy, with the USAAF a distant third. There was something besides pride at work in this ranking. All Marine officers, including pilots, were trained as infantrymen. So Marine pilots supporting infantrymen were much more effective. Since these Marines trained the navy men in ground support, they were also pretty good. The Army Air Corps usually didn't want anything to do with ground support missions, and performed them only reluctantly, and thus with somewhat less effectiveness.

The Marines had the distinction of having most of the commando units in the Pacific. The army had formed six Ranger battalions, mostly for service in Europe, organized on the British model. The army Ranger units were not as successful as was hoped, and neither were their Marine counterparts in the Pacific. As good as these troops were, and they were very good, they were not supermen. Most of the fighting in the war required good infantry, not handpicked, highly trained COMMANDOS. The Marine commando units included several battal-

MARINE CASUALTIES IN WORLD WAR II	
Combat deaths	19,733
Wounds not mortal	67,207
Other deaths	4,778
*Prisoners of war	348
Total	92,066

*The prisoners of war figure omits c. 1,400 Marines captured by the Japanese in China in December 1941 and on Corregidor in May 1942.

STRENGTH OF THE MARINE CORPS			
Year	Officers	Enlisted	Total
1940	1,800	26,545	28,345
1941	3,339	51,020	54,359
1942	7,138	135,475	142,613
1943	21,384	287,139	308,523
1944	32,788	442,816	475,604
1945	37,067	437,613	474,680
1946	14,208	141,471	155,679

ions of "Raiders" and "Paramarines" (see MARINE CORPS, US, RAIDER BATTALIONS and MARINE CORPS US, PARAMARINES), but these were later disbanded and incorporated into the Sixth Marine Division.

The Marine Corps was a rather well-integrated force by the end of the war. There were many BLACK AMERICAN riflemen in its ranks by V-J Day. The Marines also used NAVAHO-speaking troops to provide a form of "code" the Japanese could not break. Many Japanese-speaking Japanese Americans also served in the ranks as translators. Both Navaho and Japanese-American Marines had to be provided with special bodyguards, lest overenthusiastic white Marines think they were enemy infiltrators, not to mention the necessity of preventing the capture of the Navahos by Japanese troops, since as communications personnel they knew quite a bit more than the average Marine.

In the 50 years since World War II, Marine Corps strength has never fallen below 150,000 troops. This, incidentally, was the size of the entire US Army in the late 1930s.

Ref: Heinl, *Soldiers of the Sea; History of United States Marine Corps Operations in World War II*; Sherrod, *History of Marine Corps Aviation in World War II*; Wood, *Fourth Marine Division*.

Marine Corps, US, Defense Battalions

Recognizing that isolated island outposts would need to be defended and beachheads protected from enemy attack by sea, long before PEARL HARBOR the Marine Corps created a number of specialized battalions of varied organization, tailored to the peculiar defense needs of particular islands. In effect, defense battalions were portable coast defense organizations. Altogether, 20 defense battalions were raised by the end of 1943, including two composed primarily of black personnel, and 18 of them saw active service in the Pacific. However, as the nature of the war changed, the need for the defense battalions passed. By mid-1944 only four remained on active duty, and only three by the end of the war.

Although there was no "typical" defense battalion, they usually ran about a thousand men, and had five or more companies. The companies were a mix of coast defense batteries, with 5-inch guns, antiaircraft batteries, 3-inch guns or automatic weapons, a couple of rifle companies, and a service element. Depending upon circumstances, a defense battalion occasionally found itself with one or two tank platoons, and occasionally even with a few combat aircraft. The more notable defense battalions were:

First Defense Battalion. Some of the battalion was at Pearl Harbor on December 7, 1941, with substantial elements on JOHNSTON ISLAND and Palmyra, and about 40% was under Maj. James Devereaux (who later served many years in the Senate) on WAKE ISLAND, where it put up an heroic defense, its 5-inch guns accounting for a Japanese destroyer.

Third Defense Battalion. Beginning the war at Pearl Harbor, and serving later on MIDWAY during the June battle, the Third Battalion held the beaches for the First Marine Division on GUADALCANAL, and went on to fight on BOUGAINVILLE.

Ninth Defense Battalion. Joining the Third on Guadalcanal in late 1942, the Ninth took part in the New Georgia operation, and then fought on GUAM.

Ref: *History of United States Marine Corps Operations in World War II*.

Marine Corps, US, Divisions and Other Notable Formations

Although some Marines had lobbied to create a Marine Division during World War I, Marine divisions were first seriously projected in War Plan Orange shortly after World War I, once it became obvious that the movement of the fleet across the Pacific would require amphibious assaults on Japanese-held islands. Aside from some theoretical planning on the basis of experience derived from exercises, no actual divisions were raised until early 1941. Note that the figures on divisional CASUALTIES found below can be better appreciated if you keep in mind that most of them took place in the 18,000–man division's nine infantry battalions, each of which contained about 600 actual infantry (or other specialists always at the front). Divide the casualties by 10 to get a rough idea of how many losses the 600 infantry in each of these infantry battalions took: A third of the troops were taking most of the casualties. Many troops were wounded more than once. In the course of the war, some battalions had to replace nearly all their infantry at least once because of incapacitating wounds and deaths.

First Marine Division. The division was activated in February 1941 from a brigade of prewar regulars, the "Old Breed." These were very good men, since the Corps could be highly selective during the Depression. When war came, the division was filled out and dispatched to the South Pacific, to be "bloodied" on GUADALCANAL, where it made a legend of itself reclaiming the first territory from the Japanese. After surviving that, it fought in eastern New Guinea and NEW BRITAIN, serving alongside army units in the unglamorous jungle fighting that characterized the war in the southwest Pacific (where they received little press coverage, it being General MACARTHUR'S bailiwick).

In September 1944, the division finally got a chance to make the kind of amphibious landing that the Marines made famous in the Pacific. Unfortunately, they were sent against PELELIU, a heavily fortified island southeast of the Philippines. The resistance was greater than anyone expected, and the terrain totally unlike anything the troops were prepared for. The result was a hard-fought battle. To make matters worse, it was later realized that Peleliu could have been bypassed. Later, the division ended its Pacific career in the OKINAWA assault in April 1945. This turned into a three-month slugging match, one of the most grueling island assaults of the Pacific War. Overall, the First Marine Division had a hard time of it in the Pacific. At war's end it was earmarked for the projected invasion of Honshu in early 1946. Three weeks after the surrender of Japan, the First Marine Division was transferred to northern China on occupation duty. It returned to the United States in 1947. Casualties for the war totaled 19,284, of whom 5,435 (28.2%) were killed in action or died of their wounds. The First Marine Division had the highest losses of any US division—army or Marines—in the Pacific. Although eight divisions in the ETO suffered equal or greater losses—First, Third, Fourth, Ninth, 29th, 36th, 45th, and 90th—only one had a greater number of men killed in action. Eighteen men in the division received the MEDAL OF HONOR.

Second Marine Division. Although it was also formed in February of 1941, the First Division got priority on men and equipment and went into action first. The Second Division relieved the battered First on Guadalcanal during late 1942 and worked with army troops to finish running the Japanese out. With the Guadalcanal campaign over in early 1943, the division was withdrawn for retraining. Thus prepared, it mounted the first genuine Marine Corps amphibious assault at TARAWA, in November 1943. After this tough fight, the division had to be rebuilt and retrained for the SAIPAN invasion during June of 1944. Right after that it went on to storm TINIAN during July of 1944. In April 1945, the division ended its Pacific War career with the attack on Okinawa, in April 1945. Had it become necessary to invade Japan, the division would have formed part of the V Amphibious Corps during Operation Olympic in November 1945. The Second Marine Division served on occupation duty in Japan until early 1946, when it returned to the United States. Casualties totaled 11,482, including 2,729 combat deaths (23.8%). Eight men won the Medal of Honor

Third Marine Division. Activated in September 1942 from drafts made on the veteran First and Second Marine Divisions, the first case in which these divisions became "parents." About 40% of the men in each succeeding Marine division were drawn from the combat-seasoned veterans of the older outfits, a much higher margin of experienced troops than was the norm in most army divisions. The division had its first combat experience longside army troops in the SOLOMONS (BOUGAINVILLE) during 1943. Its first real island invasion was at GUAM, in 1944. Its final assault was against IWO JIMA in February 1945. Thereafter the division was on Guam, preparing for its role in Operation Olympic, as part of the V Amphibious Corps. By the time the division was inactivated, on Guam at the end of 1945, nearly 40,000 men had served in its ranks. Total casualties were 8,676, of whom 1,932 (22.3%) were battle-related deaths. Nine men earned the Medal of Honor

Fourth Marine Division. The division was formed in August 1943 by splitting up the already formed Third Marine Division and drawing veterans from the First and Second Divisions. It first saw action in February 1944 against Roi-Namur islands in KWAJALEIN. After receiving replacements and more training, it went on to invade Saipan and Tinian during the summer of 1944. Finally, the division participated in the assault on Iwo Jima in February 1945. The end of the war found the division preparing for its role in Operation Coronet, the proposed invasion of Honshu in early 1946. The division was inactivated in California in November 1945. It had been in combat only 63 of the 835 days since its activation. Casualties totaled 16,323, including 3,317 (20.3%) men killed in action or died of their wounds. Twelve men with the

division won the Medal of Honor. There were also 111 Navy Crosses, 646 Silver Stars, and 2,517 Bronze Stars.

Fifth Marine Division. Formed in January 1944, the Fifth Division participated in the Iwo Jima assault during February 1945. At the end of the war the division was preparing to take part in Operation Olympic as part of the V Amphibious Corps. After a brief tour of occupation duty in Japan, it returned to the United States, where it was inactivated in early 1946. Casualties were 8,563, including 2,113 (24.7%) battle-related deaths. Seventeen men won the Medal of Honor.

Sixth Marine Division. Although the Sixth Marine Division was formed in August 1944, and its only combat as a division was during the Okinawa Campaign in April–June 1945, most of its component elements had seen combat and had unusual histories. The Fourth Marine Regiment (see also, below) had been formed from the old Raider Battalions, which had seen action on Makin, Guadalcanal, and Bougainville in 1942–43. The regiment served as an independent unit in the occupation of Emirau Island, and as part of the First Provisional Marine Brigade on Guam in June of 1944. A second regiment, the 22nd, raised in early 1942, had occupied ENIWETOK Atoll in the MARSHALL ISLANDS as an independent unit, and at Guam was also part of the First Provisional Marine Brigade. The third regiment, the 29th, was newly formed, but one battalion, the First had seen action on Saipan as an independent unit. As a result, the cadre of the division was unusually well seasoned. The end of the war found the division preparing to participate in the March 1946 invasion of Honshu. The division's Fourth Marines was the first US unit to take up occupation duties in Japan, landing at Yokosuka on August 29. The division served on occupation duty in Japan for a short time, and then was transferred to support the First Marine Division in China, arriving in October 1945. The division was inactivated in China in April 1946. Casualties for the division as a whole, excluding losses by component units before the division was formed,

Gunners of the 14th Marines, Fourth Marine Division, shelling Japanese positions on Iwo Jima, February 1945. The littered position suggests that their 105mm howitzer has seen heavy use. The man on the left appears to be leaning on a tractor, the one on the right is removing a shell from its packaging.

totaled 8,227, of whom 1,637 (19.9%) were battle-related deaths. Two men won the Medal of Honor.

Fourth Marine Regiment. For many years stationed in Japanese-occupied SHANGHAI, the Fourth Marines was transferred to the Philippines in November of 1941. At the time it had only 800 men, the Corps letting it run down to that figure rather than risk losing more men in China should war break out. In the Philippines it was beefed up to about 1,200 men through the assignment of Marines from CAVITE and other naval installations. Although a well-trained, well-equipped outfit (it had M1 rifles rather than Springfields), the regiment spent the entire PHILIPPINE campaign on

CORREGIDOR, MacArthur disliking Marines. As a result, it was surrendered to the Japanese after being only lightly engaged. The regiment was reformed in February 1944 from the old Marine Raiders (see Sixth Marine Division, above).

Ref: Heinl, *Soldiers of the Sea; History of United States Marine Corps Operations in World War II;* Wood, *Fourth Marine Division.*

Marine Corps, US, "Paramarines"

The Marine Corps became interested in creating a parachute element in 1940. By April of 1943 there were four battalions of "paramarines," three of which were fighting in the South Pacific as part of the First Marine Parachute Regiment. But by then the Marine brass had decided that "paramarines" were an unnecessary expense. Although the troops had performed well in combat, they never once made use of the parachute skills: All of the missions they performed could easily have been done by regular Marines. In December 1943 the First Marine Parachute Regiment was shipped to SAN DIEGO, where it was disbanded. In January of 1944 the paramarines were disbanded, and the men used to help form the Fifth Marine Division.

First Battalion: Organized in August 1941, it fought on GUADALCANAL in conjunction with the First Raider Battalion, and on Gavutu, Choiseul, and VELLA LAVELLA.

A patrol of Marines and scout dogs from the Second Raider Regiment somewhere on Bougainville, November or December 1943. Note the mud and jungle.

Second Battalion: Organized in August 1941, it fought in the central SOLOMONS and on Vella Lavella.

Third Battalion: Organized in 1942, it joined the other battalions on Vella Lavella.

Fourth Battalion: Organized in April 1943, it remained at San Diego until disbanded.

Ref: *History of United States Marine Corps Operations in World War II.*

Marine Corps, US, Raider Battalions

The notion of creating special battalions of Marines for the purpose of conducting lightning raids on isolated Japanese bases surfaced in 1941, inspired by the example of Britain's COMMANDOS and the effective use of small "hit-and-run" forces by the Chinese communists. The latter influence derived from the experience of Marine LTC Evans F. Carlson (1896–1947), who had been a US military observer in China with the communist Eighth Route Army in 1937–38. Carlson was a regular correspondent of President ROOSEVELT, having served as commander of the security detachment at Warm Springs, Georgia, and thus gained support at the highest levels. As a result, the Marine Corps began to organize what became known as Marine Raider Battalions. Eventually some 5,000 Marines were trained as raiders, and four battalions were raised. In March 1943 these were formed into the First Raider Regiment, which spun off its Second and Third Battalions to a provisional Second Regiment from September 1943.

First Raider Battalion: Organized in February 1942, from the First Separate Battalion, itself redesignated from the First Battalion, Fifth Marine Regiment, in January 1942, and commanded by LTC Merritt A. Edson. It spearheaded the assault on TULAGI at the onset of the GUADALCANAL Campaign, and went on to conduct many operations on Guadalcanal, usually combined with the First Parachute Battalion, most notably the Battle of Edson's Ridge (September 12–14, 1942), an action for which Edson and one of his men were awarded the MEDAL OF HONOR, and later fought on New Georgia in 1943.

Second Raider Battalion: Organized in February 1942 from the Second Separate Battalion, a newly created formation, and commanded by LTC Evans F. Carlson, with Capt. James Roosevelt as his executive officer. On August 17, 1942, about half the battalion, some 221 men, conducted a raid on MAKIN ISLAND, landing from two SUBMARINES. The battalion later served on Guadalcanal, conducting a grueling 30-day raid (November 4–December 4,

1942) which destroyed an entire Japanese regiment. Reinforced by the First Marine Dog Platoon, the first American canine unit to see action in the war, it supported the Third Marine Division landings on BOUGAINVILLE in late 1943. One man won the Medal of Honor.

Third Raider Battalion: Organized in SAMOA in September 1942 from individual volunteers, the Third Battalion took part in the unopposed occupation of the Russell Islands early in 1943, and went on to support the Third Marine Division's landings on Bougainville later that year. One man won the Medal of Honor.

Leathernecks of the Second Raider Regiment pose before a captured Japanese dugout at Cape Torokina, Bougainville, December 1943. Note the camouflage uniforms, which proved unsuitable for sustained wear.

Fourth Raider Battalion: Organized from volunteers in October 1942, under Maj. James Roosevelt, the Fourth Battalion fought on New Georgia in 1943.

By late 1943 the Marine brass were having second thoughts about the Raiders. Although they had performed well in combat, they had actually made only two raids, Carlson's raids on Makin and Guadalcanal. All their other missions could easily have been performed by regular Marine units. After thinking over the value of the investment in manpower, time, and training, the Marine brass decided to disband the Raiders. On February 1, 1944 the Raiders became the cadre of the reactivated Fourth Marine Regiment, which had been captured by the Japanese on CORREGIDOR in May 1942. The headquarters of the First Regiment became the headquarters of the new Fourth Marines, while the First, Third, and Fourth Raider Battalions became the First, Second, and Third Battalions, Fourth Marines, and the Second Raider Battalion became the Weapons Company, Fourth Marines.

Ref: *History of United States Marine Corps Operations in World War II.*

Marines, Japanese (Navy Ground Forces)

There was a bit of culture shock when America went to war with Japan. US troops knew little about Japan, and were forced to learn a lot in a short time once the shooting started. One of the "good news, bad news" surprises was the Special Naval Landing Forces (SNLF). Americans quickly assumed that these were Japanese marines, an elite force like the USMC; however, they were not as formidable as they were first thought to be.

As with most maritime powers, Japan had occasion to send troops ashore quickly when all they had available were warships sitting off the coast. In such cases the Japanese, like most navies, would simply arm sailors and have them land. If the warships involved were not going to move around or get into heavy combat themselves, a third or more of the crew could be sent ashore as infantry. For a

week or so, anyway. As recently as World War I (1914), America did the same thing, most obviously in MEXICO where sailors landed at Vera Cruz as infantry and seized the city. In continuation of this tradition, sailors still regularly train as riflemen. But the US Navy also had a few Marines on most major ships to send along with the sailors and contribute some expert advice on infantry operations. Marines (soldiers serving on board ships) were an ancient practice, as until the introduction of cannon, naval battles largely consisted of ships colliding and infantry fighting it out as if on land. When cannon came along, there was much less emphasis on infantry combat afloat. Some infantry troops remained on ships, and these evolved during the past few centuries into soldiers who served as guards on ships, helped man the big guns, and, when needed, went ashore to take care of infantry business. Since Japan got a late start in the navy business (in fact, it never owned a major sailing warship), it didn't develop marines in the traditional sense.

Yet Japan ran up against a need to land troops from warships along the Chinese coast in the 1920s their sailors worked relatively well because Japanese sailors were given infantry training as well as instruction in seamanship. However, the admirals were getting tired of seeing their ships stripped of sailors to take care of some emergency ashore and decided to do something about it. Thus was born the Special Naval Landing Forces in the late '20s. These were sailors trained and equipped to fight ashore. Their weapons were identical to those used by the army, and their uniforms were very similar. One of the differences, however, was the use of an anchor symbol on the steel HELMET instead of a star (which the army used.)

The SNLF was organized into large battalions (of 1,000 to 2,000 troops), containing a wide variety of weapons. Each of the four major Japanese naval bases (KURE, MAIZURU, SASEBO, and Yokosuka) was ordered to organize one or more of these units (called *Rikusentai* in Japanese). A dozen SNLF "battalions" were organized before and during the war, including a handful of parachute units. There were also several other types of specialized navy ground combat units. To put this in perspective, the US Marines during World War II organized some 100 battalion-sized combat units while only about three dozen (of all types) were created by the Japanese Navy's ground forces. Or, put another way, there were about five times as many American Marines as there were Japanese Navy ground troops.

After PEARL HARBOR, the SNLF spearheaded the Japanese Navy's offensive into the south and central Pacific. It was SNLF units that seized American islands such as Wake and the British GILBERTS. In cooperation with army troops, the SNLF, including paratroopers, also participated in the attacks on the Dutch East Indies (INDONESIA) and RABAUL (the major naval base just north of the SOLOMONS and Australia).

Because of the huge size of the Pacific battlefield, the Japanese Army and Navy had to divide the ground-fighting chores among themselves. In the wide open spaces (with few islands) of the central Pacific it was often an entirely navy show. The Japanese Navy had, in addition to all those warships, its own land-based aircraft and ground forces. But the navy was also forced to defend most of these islands against the expected American counterattack. For this purpose, the Japanese Navy organized special "island defense units." These were similar to the SNLF except that most of their weapons were antiaircraft guns for defending against air raids. The principal duty of these companies (100–200 men) and battalions (500–1,000 men) was the local defense of out of the way islands and their airfields. The Japanese had dozens of these islands garrisoned in this way. The aircraft they guarded were used to patrol the vast stretches of the Pacific that the Japanese held sway over early in the war.

The navy was also responsible for building these bases, or rebuilding ones they had captured. For this purpose they established naval construction battalions. These were similar in function to the US Navy's famed SEABEE battalions. The Japanese units were much less efficient, however, as they had little in the way of earth-moving equipment and special construction tools. Most work was done by

hand, and about 80% of the personnel were Koreans or Taiwanese conscripted for this purpose. Actually, there were two types of naval construction battalions. One, the *Setsueitai* (or Combat Engineers), was about 30% Japanese and did the skilled work. These units had 800–1,300 troops. The other type were basically labor battalions, and only 10% of their strength (the supervisors) were Japanese.

When America began its drive across the central Pacific in late 1943, the first Japanese garrisons it attacked consisted largely of SNLF and other Japanese Navy ground forces. The closer the US Marines got to Japan, the more Japanese Army troops they encountered. General MACARTHUR, meanwhile, fought largely against Japanese Army units in his campaign from New Guinea to the Philippines, as did the British in Burma and the Chinese in China. Even in 1942, when the Marines came ashore at GUADALCANAL, they encountered a Japanese Navy construction battalion (whose largely Korean troops fled into the jungle rather than fight). When the Japanese mustered forces for their counterattack on Guadalcanal, it was with army troops.

Thus the SNLF were largely found as garrisons on small islands in the Pacific. Like the US Marines, the SNLF's main purpose was seizing forward bases for the navy, and then holding on to them. Beyond that, there were several significant differences between the SNLF and the American Marines (USMC).

1. The USMC had a long tradition of highly trained and disciplined assault troops. The USMC was always distinct from the sailors it served with. The SNLF were sailors trained and equipped as infantry.

2. The SNLF officers were simply naval officers assigned to land combat duty. USMC officers were strictly Marine officers. Thus the USMC leaders were far more expert at commanding infantry operations than their SNLF counterparts.

3. USMC units were specially equipped for amphibious warfare. While their gear included much that was identical to what the army used, where necessary unique weapons or equipment was developed. The SNLF had very little special equipment. In particular, the SNLF never had anything like the array of specialized amphibious equipment used by the USMC.

4. The USMC was primarily an amphibious assault force while the SNLF spent most of its time guarding bases. The USMC also had "base defense units," but these were a handful of defense battalions compared to nearly a hundred assault units.

5. The USMC, by tradition and training, was an elite force that was expected to, and usually did, successfully undertake very difficult assignments. The SNLF, on the other hand, was not even considered as capable as its army counterparts.

In short, there never were any Japanese marines. The SNLF was composed of sailors serving ashore as infantry.

Marquesas Islands

Comprised of 14 island (c. 400 square miles) in the Pacific Ocean about 900 miles northeast of Tahiti. Part of French Polynesia, the Marquesas early fell under Free French control. During the war they had some value as Allied air and naval bases.

Marshall, George C. (1880–1959)

George Catlett Marshall graduated from Virginia Military Institute in 1902 and entered the infantry. He served in the Philippine Insurrection, on various staffs, attended several schools, rising to captain by the time the United States entered World War I. Among the first American soldiers to go to France, Marshall proved an extremely able staff officer, rising rapidly to colonel, and engineering the extraordinary shift of American forces from the St.

Mihiel front to the Meuse-Argonne front late in 1918. After the war he rose steadily in the army, despite the hostility of Douglas MACARTHUR (having John J. Pershing as a patron probably saved his career). Marshall was named chief of staff in 1938 and retained the post through 1945, during which period he oversaw the expansion of the US Army from 125,000 men to over eight million. A meticulous planner and strategist of great vision, he was one of the principal architects of victory. Marshall was a man of great character, reserve, and dignity. Even FDR—who called everyone, including the king of England, by his first name—never addressed Marshall by his first name (he tried once, but Marshall's reaction was such that the president never did it again). Marshall was the first professional soldier ever to win the Nobel Prize for peace, which he received in 1953 for the Marshall Plan, a massive postwar economic assistance program that helped rebuild European economies shattered by the war.

Marshall's stepson, Allen T. Brown, was killed in action in Italy in 1944.

Marshall Islands Campaign

An archipelago in the central Pacific, the Marshalls lie nearly 2,200 miles southwest of HAWAII in the Pacific Ocean. There are actually two chains of islands, about 125 miles apart, comprising only about 70 square miles. Japan took them from Germany in 1914, and they formed part of the Mandated territories.

There was little economic development, but the Japanese began building bases in the islands in the late 1930s. The more notable of the islands are Majuro, ENIWETOK, and Bikini.

Two months after the GILBERT ISLANDS were taken, American amphibious forces moved on to their next target, the Marshalls. This was a very ambitious schedule, as the same amphibious units could not be used for the November 1943 Gilberts operation and then the January 1944 Marshalls attack. Amphibious units, both men and equipment, had to be rested and rebuilt after each assault. But the warships and aircraft were another matter. In 1943, American commanders had decided to maintain two sets of amphibious assault divisions (and their amphibious shipping) to work with one set of warships. The Japanese were not expecting this sort of high-speed approach to amphibious operations, so the January assault on the Marshalls came as a bit of a surprise.

Less of a surprise was the prompt use of airfields in the Gilberts to attack the easternmost islands of the Marshalls. By the end of January, all the Japanese airfields on these heavily fortified and garrisoned islands were destroyed. The well entrenched infantry were ready for any invasion, although none was expected for at least another month or so. But then the Americans did the unexpected. The US fleet went right past the heavily defended easternmost Marshall Islands and headed to KWAJALEIN, which has the largest lagoon of any CORAL atoll in the world. Kwajalein is a string of small islands, 60 miles long and about 20 miles wide. On one end is Kwajalein island. About 40 miles north along the chain of coral islands are the islands of Roi and Namur, linked by a causeway. Along the way, supply and repair ships were dropped off at one of the few unoccupied atolls in the area—Majuro. This provided a fleet base for damaged ships, plus some dry land on which to stockpile supplies. Then, on January 31 the Fourth Marine Division assaulted Roi and Namur (defended by 3,500 Japanese) while the army's Seventh Infantry Division went after Kwajalein and its 5,000-man garrison. By February 2, Roi and Namur were conquered. By February 5, Kwajalein Island was taken. The 41,000 US troops suffered 372 fatalities. The Japanese did much worse, with 7,870 out of 8,675 being killed.

Before going on, the US task force went after TRUK Island, a carrier and bombardment raid meant to shut down the principal Japanese naval base in the central Pacific. There was also a raid on PONAPE Island (600 miles from Kwajalein,) which was being used as a refueling base for aircraft flying from the Caroline islands (including Truk) to bomb US forces in the Marshalls. Truk was found with nearly 400 aircraft on its airfields and dozens of merchant and war ships in its harbor and surrounding waters. For three days, US carrier aircraft pounded the island and, in cooperation with American warships, hunted down Japanese ships. For the first time in history, a major naval base was shut down by carrier aircraft. Even the Japanese raid on PEARL HARBOR had not shut down the base. But this 1944 raid on Truk shut down Japan's largest naval base in the Pacific. Subsequent raids kept Truk out of action, although, after the February 1944 raid, the Japanese never again stationed large naval or air forces there.

The final stage of the Marshall Islands Campaign was the capture of Eniwetok atoll. This was 326 miles northwest of Roi and only a thousand miles from the Mariana Islands. Six infantry battalions were used for this (four Marine, two army). The first landing took place on February 17, and within a week 2,677 Japanese were dead and less than a hundred taken prisoner. Typically, only 339 Americans were killed.

The Marshall Islands Campaign left a number of large Japanese garrisons bypassed. This surprised the Japanese, but they soon realized that the Americans could get away with it. By placing large numbers of aircraft on nearby captured islands, the Americans could constantly patrol the surrounding waters and prevent any supplies from getting through to the bypassed Japanese garrisons. The initial air raids destroyed Japanese aircraft and airbase facilities, and subsequent raids were largely a form of armed reconnaissance. The isolated Japanese garrisons remained where they were until the end of the war. Many of the troops died from starvation or disease before they could hear the emperor's message to surrender, which all of these isolated garrisons did.

Ref: Heinl and Crown, *The Marshalls.*

Marston Mat

Also known as Pierced Steel Planking or Steel Matting, Marston Mats were large perforated steel sheets, easily handled by one man, which could be used to pave roads, runways, and anything else quickly, even if the undersurface was less than ideal for such use. Matting sufficient for a 3,000-foot runway weighed only 1,200 tons and could be laid by 100 unskilled workers in about 96 hours of steady work. This produced front-line airfields far faster than the Japanese thought possible, a fact brought home to them when American aircraft operating out of these new airfields began attacking Japanese targets.

Marston Mat proved particularly useful in tropical areas where there was light sand, and in the arctic where there were quaking bogs and muskeg, or other surfaces unsuited to the construction of airstrips, roads, and the like.

In fact, Marston Mat was used for an enormous variety of tasks, from building runways to improving traction on muddy jungle roads, to making improvised docks, to flooring buildings, and just about anything else the troops could think of.

Maryland Class, US Battleships

Although designed during World War I, the completion of these ships, indeed the laying down of two of them, was delayed in order to incorporate lessons learned during the war. Virtually identical to the CALIFORNIAS, save for their main armament (eight 16-inch guns rather than 12 14-inchers), the Marylands were the most powerful of the prewar American battleships, and formed the core of the battlefleet in the Pacific.

Colorado, BB-45 (1919–1921–1923), was refitting at SAN DIEGO when PEARL HARBOR was attacked, and thus was the least modernized of the three sisters. She served with the battle force that was scraped together to backstop the carriers during the MIDWAY Campaign, and then went on to support landings throughout the Pacific. Scrapped in 1959.

Maryland, BB-46 (1917–1920–1921), was lightly injured at Pearl Harbor and returned to the fleet rather quickly. She supported amphibious operations to the end of the war, taking a TORPEDO off SAIPAN in June 1944, getting off 48 16-inch

rounds at SURIGAO STRAIT, shortly after which she took a KAMIKAZE. Scrapped in 1959.

West Virginia, BB-45 (1920–1921–1923), was heavily damaged at Pearl Harbor, and so extensively rebuilt as to be more a sister of the Californias than the Marylands, with a 114-foot beam, which prevented her from passing through the PANAMA CANAL. She did not return to the fleet until September of 1944. She played a critical role at Surigao Strait, getting off numerous salvos, and supported amphibious operations through OKINAWA. Scrapped in 1959.

Mason, Robert (1904–1995)

US naval officer and codebreaker. A 1925 graduate of the US Naval Academy, during the 1930s Mason learned Japanese while attached to the US Embassy in Tokyo. Although he served in a variety of capacities both ashore and afloat in a career that spanned 45 years, his most important service was as an intelligence officer in the Office of the Chief of Naval Operations, in which capacity he oversaw the breaking of numerous Japanese codes, including MAGIC and PURPLE, work so secret that when decorated for it, his citation was virtually incomprehensible. During the Korean War, Mason, by then a rear admiral, commanded naval support operations. Possessed of an éidetic memory, in 1956 he won $100,000 on the television quiz show "The Big Surprise." He retired as an admiral in 1966.

Matsu Class, Japanese Destroyer Escorts

Even before US SUBMARINES began destroying the Japanese merchant marine, the Imperial Navy seems to have become uneasy about the availability of escorts. As a result, in 1942 the Matsu class was ordered. Eighteen units were laid down in 1943–44, launched before the end of 1944, and completed between April 1944 and January 1945. Somewhat more heavily armed than US DEs, they took a long time to build, the first unit not completing until April of 1944 and the last in January of 1945. A further 11 were canceled. They proved reasonably satisfactory and saw considerable service, seven becoming war losses: one to a mine, one to a submarine, two to aircraft, and three to surface ships.

McMorris, Charles H. (1890–1954)

Charles H. McMorris graduated from Annapolis in 1912. Through 1919 his career was almost entirely in destroyers, and toward the end of World War I he commanded the destroyer *Walke*. Between the wars he alternated between sea, administrative, and school assignments, rising to captain. Assigned to the staff of CINCPAC shortly before PEARL HARBOR, in May 1942, he assumed command of the heavy cruiser *San Francisco*, skippering her through some of the toughest fights in the GUADALCANAL Campaign. In November 1942 he was promoted to rear admiral and sent to command Task Force 16.6, in Alaskan waters, fighting the Battle of the KOMANDORSKI ISLANDS, the only purely ship-to-ship daytime action in the Pacific War. In June 1943 he became chief of staff to CINCPAC, in which post he remained until the end of the war. After the war he held various posts until retirement. Bright (his nickname was "Soc," short for "Socrates"), McMorris was also tactless and critical, which probably impeded his rise.

Medal of Honor

The fighting in the Pacific was different from that in other theaters of World War II. Infantry combat was the most dangerous form of fighting worldwide, but in the Pacific it was particularly lethal. The vast majority of the amphibious operations (one of the most dangerous and desperate forms of infantry combat) in World War II took place in the Pacific. The Pacific Theater was also characterized by the KAMIKAZE attacks on naval vessels, which offered further opportunities for men to earn the Medal of Honor.

Although only about a quarter of the nation's military forces were committed to the Pacific, they earned Medals of Honor awarded during the Sec-

MEDAL OF HONOR AWARDS BY THEATER AND SERVICE

Branch	Total		(Post)	PTO	(Post)	ETO	(Post)
Army+		261	(128)	70	(44)	193	(84)
Army Air Forces		38	(18)	13	(6)	25	(12)
Coast Guard		1	(1)	1	(1)	0	(0)
Marine Corps		81	(47)	81	(47)	0	(0)
Navy		57	(27)	55	(26)	2	(1)
Total		441	(221)	220	124	220	(97)
Army	Artillery	1,688.4					
	Cavalry	594.4					
	Engineers	1,665.5					
	Infantry	800.4					
	Medical Corps	1,124.0					
Army Air Forces		861.0					
Coast Guard		574.0					
Navy		550.0					
Marines		368.9					

+ Excluding the Army Air Forces, listed separately; Post=Posthumous

ond World War. Moreover, where 43.5% of the awards in the European Theater of Operations were posthumous, 62.3% were in the Pacific Theater, in each case counting only those who died as a consequence of the action that caused them to receive the award (in both theaters there were men who were killed subsequent to their battlefield heroism, but before they were decorated).

A look at the relationship between the number of awards and casualty rates among the various branches of the service is interesting.

These figures are based on the number of men in each branch who were killed in action, divided by the number of Medals of Honor that were awarded to members of that branch. The ratios

INFANTRYMEN AS MEDAL OF HONOR WINNERS

Service	Theater	Awards	Infantry	(%)
Army	ETO	187	150	(80.2)
	PTO	69	60	(87.0)
Marines	PTO	81	64	(79.0)
Army and Marines	Both	337	274	(81.2)
All	Both	433	274	(63.3)

found on the two tables on page 413 were calculated in 1946, and so are not completely accurate, since several men have been awarded the Medal of Honor since then, in belated recognition of gallantry in action. The most dangerous job in the armed forces was infantryman, and it is worth recalling that most Marines were infantrymen.

Although the figures in the previous table do not suggest it, another very dangerous occupation was medic. Most medical personnel were more or less in the rear, and deaths among them were most likely to have been caused by artillery or air attacks, however, some medical personnel accompanied the troops, going right up to the front with the infantry. During World War II 16 medics earned the Medal of Honor, eight posthumously. Six recipients were with the army in the ETO, three of them posthumous. In the Pacific the army awarded three medics the Medal of Honor, one posthumously, and the navy, which supplied the medics for the Marines, decorated seven, four posthumously.

Both the oldest and the youngest winners of the Medal of Honor during World War II were in the Pacific. The oldest was General Douglas MACARTHUR, who was 64 when he was decorated for the heroic defense of the Philippines in early 1942. MacArthur was also the highest-ranking recipient in history, and the only one who was the son of a Medal of Honor winner, his father having received one for the Civil War. The youngest was PFC Jacklyn H. Lucas, who was just six days over 17 when he won the Medal of Honor on IWO JIMA, with the 26th Marines. Private Lucas had enlisted when UNDERAGE, and is apparently the youngest person to have won the Medal of Honor since the Civil War.

Other military specialties were much less dangerous. In the Army Air Forces the most common military specialty of Medal of Honor winners—pilot—represented 17 (44.4%) of the 38 recipients, all but three of them bomber pilots. It was not unusual for ACES to be awarded a Medal of Honor. The most common specialty in the navy—commanding officer—counted fully 22 (38.6%) of the

57 recipients, including commanders of squadrons, AIR GROUPS, ships, and SUBMARINES.

Incidentally, there is no absolute criteria for awarding the Medal of Honor. During World War II both services had different administrative mechanisms for processing Medal of Honor recommendations, and different regulations. Naval regulations permitted the award of the Medal of Honor for heroic deeds not connected with combat, and one man was so decorated during World War II.

See also BASILONE, JOHN; BONG, RICHARD I.; BOYINGTON, GREGORY; CALLAGHAN, DANIEL; DOOLITTLE, JAMES; DOSS, DESMOND; FLETCHER, FRANK; FRIENDLY FIRE, ALLIED PRISONER OF WAR DEATHS BY; JAPAN, ATTITUDE TOWARD THE ENEMY; KELLY, COLIN; MACARTHUR, DOUGLAS; MILLER, DORIE; O'CALLAGHAN, JOSEPH; PHILIPPINE SCOUTS; PORT CHICAGO MUTINY; ROOSEVELT FAMILY AT WAR; SCOTT, NORMAN; SHOUP, DAVID; VANDEGRIFT, ALEXANDER; WAINWRIGHT, JONATHAN; and divisional and unit entries under MARINE CORPS, US and UNITED STATES ARMY.

Medan, Sumatra, Netherlands East Indies

An important harbor, but lacking in extensive facilities and poorly sited for use as a base, Medan was occupied by the Japanese in early 1942. They used it as a local headquarters and transshipment point for the rest of the war.

Medical Service

Allied, and particularly American, medical services to the troops was extraordinarily extensive. Normally there was a medical battalion attached to every division, plus medical detachments in all elements of the division. Field treatment centers were set up just behind where heavy fighting was expected in order to render treatment quickly to badly wounded troops. It was known that speed was important, and throughout the Pacific War, procedures were improved to get intensive medical care to CASUALTIES faster and faster. This was accomplished by moving more medical personnel closer to the actual fighting.

Medics served with army and Marine infantry platoons. These first aid specialists were trained to give prompt care and make an accurate diagnosis of a wide range of battlefield injuries. That done, the wounded were quickly moved a few hundred meters (or less) to the rear and to an aid station manned by one or more MDs and more medics. Here the patient was given further diagnosis and treatment (including surgery, if needed). At that

point, the casualty went offshore to a hospital ship, by truck to a field hospital, or, once airfields were available, could be flown to islands with even more extensive medical facilities. Larger hospitals were always quickly established on newly conquered territory, and patients were usually driven to these, accompanied by medics or nurses to provide needed care en route. As a result, even in the most difficult environments, such as New Guinea or Burma, an Allied soldier who was wounded, even seriously, had a very good chance of pulling through.

Amphibious operations had their own special requirements, because there was usually a very large

A wounded man is transferred from the carrier Bunker Hill *(CV-17), seriously damaged by a kamikaze attack, to the cruiser* Wilkes-Barre *(CL-90), off Okinawa on May 11, 1945. Rapid evacuation of the wounded was an important factor in keeping US combat deaths low.*

An underground operating room, somewhere on Bougainville, December 13, 1943. Such facilities, though crude, permitted quick treatment of the wounded, which saved numerous lives.

number of casualties in a short time, and these were on a beach or a short distance inland at a place where there were few medical facilities set up. To overcome these problems, the engineer units that went ashore to set up the supply system for the invading troops also included transportation units equipped and trained to evacuate casualties rapidly.

The Allies also had an advantage in their numerous hospital ships. Every service had some, and they were an ideal way to bring the latest medical technology as close as possible to the fighting. The introduction of AMPHIBIOUS VEHICLES (DUKWs and LVPs) made it easier to take casualties from the battlefields to the beach and then directly out to a waiting hospital ship.

While the industrialized Allied nations (United States, Britain, etc.) were able to supply a high degree of medical care, their Chinese allies were not. The Chinese Army rarely had more than a few thousand doctors to treat several million troops. There was also a severe shortage of medical equipment and supplies. The Chinese made do by creating two or three medical officers (who where not MDs) for each MD and training even more medics and nurses to at least render first aid on a prompt basis. This approach saved many lives, although a wound that required complex surgery was still a problem.

Most of the Allied medical effort did not go into caring for combat casualties, but into dealing with the high incidence of disease in the Pacific. Disease borne by numerous local insects was a major problem, and the solution was to kill the bugs and provide drinkable water and clean living conditions as much as possible in a combat zone. To this end, army and navy engineers spent a lot of time killing insects (the first major use of insecticides like DDT) and purifying water. When necessary, swamps were drained and thousands of prefabricated buildings were shipped to the Pacific, to supplement the even greater number of tents. Additional quantities of clothing, especially socks and boots, were shipped. "Trench foot" and various other conditions arising from feet kept in the water too often, could be best treated by having dry socks available. Boots tended to rot faster than the feet, so they had to be replaced quickly. Many Japanese troops, not so well supplied, ended up barefoot. On tropical battlefields, a pair of boots would often last but a few weeks.

In contrast, Japanese medical arrangements left much to be desired. During the Russo-Japanese War (1904–05) the medical service of the Japanese Army had attracted widespread admiration, but by the 1930s it had seriously deteriorated. While in theory each division was assigned three field hospitals, each with 180 litters and 45 ambulances, many divisions lacked more than the most rudimentary medical services. It was not uncommon for wholly untrained soldiers to be assigned as medical orderlies and nurses, or even, as happened increasingly toward the end of the war, for whole schools of untrained teenaged girls to be conscripted and shipped abroad to serve as nurses. Moreover, the few trained medical personnel in a unit often found themselves in the firing line, or taking part in BANZAI CHARGES. Of course, the increasingly successful US submarine campaign against Japanese shipping cut off distant garrisons from medical supplies, as well as food and ammunition. As a result, a wounded Japanese soldier stood little chance, tens of thousands perishing from relatively minor injuries, which went untreated by trained personnel.

See also JAPAN, ATTITUDE TOWARD WARFARE.

Melbourne, Australia

One of the most important ports in Australia, with a considerable capacity to service shipping, but only limited utility as a naval base, being on the country's southern coast. Its principal value in the war was as a supply base and manufacturing center.

Merrill's Marauders

See US ARMY, OTHER NOTABLE UNITS.

Meteor, British Jet Fighter

The Meteor was the world's first operational jet combat aircraft. Entering British service in the summer of 1944, eight days before the German Me-262, the Meteor promptly went to work shooting down German cruise missiles (V-1s). Armed with four 20mm cannon and able to fly higher and faster than any other fighter, the Meteor was limited only by small numbers (100 produced during the war) and the heavy maintenance load its two jet engines put on the ground crew. No Meteors served in the Pacific, but had the war against Japan continued beyond the summer of 1945, the Meteor would have been involved.

See also AIRCRAFT TYPES, DEVELOPMENT.

Mexico

Although relations between the United States and Mexico were severely strained in the first third of the 20th century, the "Good Neighbor" policy instituted by the ROOSEVELT administration in the mid-1930s had led to a considerable measure of reconciliation. Mexico declared war on the Axis in March 1942, partially in response to US urgings and partially as a result of persistent Axis submarine attacks on Mexican shipping. Through LEND-LEASE the Mexican armed forces were modernized and expanded. Although this affected all branches of the service, the only element of the Mexican armed forces to see action in the war was the air force. In cooperation with the United States, Mexico organized a special air wing of three squadrons. The 201st Squadron was a combat squadron equipped with P-47s; the 202nd, a replacement training squadron; and the 203rd was a primary training squadron. The 201st Squadron ("*Aguilas Aztecas*"—Aztec Eagles) arrived in the United States for advanced flight training in July 1944 and departed for the Philippines in March 1945. Attached to the Fifth Air Force and based at Clark Field on Luzon, the 201st Squadron performed reconnaissance, ground attack, and close air support operations against Japanese forces in the Philippines and on Formosa until August, when it was reassigned to the 13th Air Force and transferred to OKINAWA in anticipation of the invasion of Japan. Nine Mexican airmen were killed in action.

In addition to the men who served in the Mexican Armed Forces, an unknown number of Mexican citizens joined the US Armed Forces (by one estimate as many as 250,000, a figure that cannot be substantiated).

Although there was some discrimination against Mexicans, Mexican Americans, and other Hispanic Americans in the US Armed Forces during the war, it was relatively marginal. In fact, a number of Hispanic Americans attained relatively high rank, the most notable being MG Pedro del Valle (USMC), who commanded the First Marine Division on Okinawa; MG Terry de la Mesa Allen, who commanded the First Infantry Division in North Africa and Sicily, and the 104th Division in France and Germany; and MG Elwood R. Quesada (USAAF), who commanded the XIX Tactical Air Corps under Patton in Europe.

Midway Campaign

Midway comprises two small islands enclosed in an atoll, for a total land area of only about two square miles. The group, about 1,300 miles northwest of PEARL HARBOR, had only a limited anchorage. The only facilities available at the outbreak of war were a cable station, lighthouse, and Pan Am seaplane base, with a US Navy seaplane base under construction. It was valuable as a reconnaissance base and as the northernmost anchor of the Hawaiian chain. During the war the US Navy developed it into a modest air base and home port for SUBMARINES and light craft.

The Japanese began planning for a decisive, June 1942 battle in the vicinity of Midway shortly after the DOOLITTLE Raid on Tokyo in April. Indeed, the CORAL SEA operation was actually an integral part of the overall strategic plan, which was to bring about this battle. The intention was to smash the remnants of American naval power in the Pacific, and advance Japan's outer defensive perimeter more than a thousand miles farther by seizing the western ALEUTIANS, Midway Island, and, ultimately, FIJI, SAMOA, and NEW CALEDONIA, simultaneously severing the Allied lifeline between the US West Coast and Australia. Like the Pearl Harbor operation, the Midway operation was the brainchild of Isoroku YAMAMOTO. But it was neither as well planned nor as well executed.

Yamamoto's plan for the Midway operation was complex. The principal striking force would be Chuichi NAGUMO's First Air Fleet (the Pearl Harbor Striking Force), down to four fleet carriers (due to losses at Coral Sea), and two fast battleships, two heavy cruisers, a light cruiser, a dozen destroyers. This would be supported by an Advanced Force of 16 submarines. The actual capture of the objective would be the responsibility of the Midway Occupation Force of 5,000 troops in a dozen transports, supported by two battleships, a light carrier, two seaplane carriers, eight heavy cruisers, two light cruisers, and 20 destroyers, plus a dozen smaller warships, organized into seven task groups. Giving deep support was the Main Body, three battleships, a light carrier, two seaplane carriers, a light cruiser, and 17 destroyers. Then there was the Northern Area Force, comprising a support group of four battleships and two light cruisers, plus two light carriers, three heavy cruisers, three light cruisers, a dozen destroyers, three submarines, and about a dozen miscellaneous small warships, grouped in no less than six task groups, including two troop transports. All of these task groups, of course, had supply ships and oilers assigned. The plan was for the Northern Area Force to make a demonstration against the Aleutians, grabbing a couple of islands in an effort to divert American attention from the principal objective. While the US Navy raced northward to cope with the threat to the Aleutians, perhaps suffering losses to the Advanced Force, the Midway Occupation Force would take its objective under the protection of the First Air Fleet. Presumably, then the Americans would race south to relieve Midway, once more running the gauntlet of the Advanced Force, and right into an aerial ambush by the First Air Fleet. Should the Americans try for a surface action, the Main Body would be ready to come up from its supporting position, several hundred miles behind the First Air Fleet.

This plan may have looked fine on paper, but was seriously flawed. Not only was Japanese organization very complex, scattering task forces across half of the western Pacific, but the Aleutians operation also consumed too many resources for a proper diversion (90 carrier aircraft, a quarter of the approximately 350 available). Moreover, by early May, American Pacific commander Chester W. NIMITZ had a pretty good notion as to the identity of the principal Japanese objective, partially as a result of good guessing and partially as a result of fortuitous code breaking. Nimitz intended to counter Yamamoto's offensive by a careful concentration of everything he had, which admittedly was not much. He had three carriers (233 aircraft, only about a dozen fewer than those on Nagumo's four carriers), including YORKTOWN (mostly repaired from her Coral Sea damage), seven heavy cruisers, one light cruiser, and 17 destroyers. These were organized into two task forces under RAdm Frank J. FLETCHER, and supported by 19 submarines, plus as much shore-based air power as could be jammed onto Midway's tiny surface (60 navy and Marine combat aircraft plus 23 army B-26s and B-17s, plus about 32 Catalina patrol bombers), plus some Ma-

rines for a total of some 3,000 men. There were also three destroyers, some PT-BOATS, and some miscellaneous smaller warships assigned to patrol portions of the long chain of islets and atolls linking Midway with HAWAII (where the Japanese had once planned, and now planned again, to establish a temporary flying boat base using submarines).

Aware of the "threat" to the Aleutians, Nimitz grudgingly assigned five cruisers, 13 destroyers, six submarines, and some seaplane tenders, patrol boats, and minesweepers. He also ordered the carrier *Saratoga*, completing repairs from a torpedo hit, up from SAN DIEGO with her escorts, and ordered the battle fleet, composed of the more lightly damaged Pearl Harbor survivors plus reinforcements from the Atlantic, with an escort carrier, to sortie from SAN FRANCISCO Bay, where it was temporarily housed.

With Nimitz's approval, Fletcher deployed his carriers northeast of Midway, reasoning that the Japanese would most likely come from the northwest, the west, or the southwest. This conceded the initiative to the Japanese. Normally, giving away the initiative is a bad idea in war. But in this case it was perfectly reasonable, since in order to hit the Japanese one had to find them. Locating the enemy could be done by patrol planes reaching out from Midway or, failing that, by letting them hit something first. In this case, the "something" was Midway. And that is precisely what took place.

The Japanese hit the Aleutians on 3 June 1942 and by the 7th had occupied Attu and KISKA, there being no one there to oppose them. But Frank Fletcher had not, in the interim, "raced north." On 3 June a Catalina patrol bomber had spotted the Midway Occupation Force. Early the next morning another PBY spotted the Japanese carriers. So Fletcher knew where the enemy was, while they were still in ignorance of his location. At 6:30 A.M. Fletcher ordered Raymond SPRUANCE, commander of TF 16, to prepare to launch a strike against the Japanese carriers from *Enterprise* and *Hornet*, holding back his own YORKTOWN for a follow-up strike. Even as this strike was getting into the air, Nagumo hit Midway with 108 aircraft. Spotted by radar, the Japanese air strike met resistance from Midway-based fighters.

Now came the critical moment of the battle. When dispatching his strike against Midway, Nagumo had ordered a second strike readied in the event American carriers had to be attacked. Meanwhile the leader of the Midway strike returned, ahead of his colleagues, and urged that a second strike be made against Midway, in order to destroy the island as a useful base. As Nagumo mulled over this suggestion, Midway-based bombers hit the fleet. Although the air strike was a failure, inflicting no loss on the Japanese carriers and suffering heavily itself, it seems to have helped convince Nagumo to have another go at Midway (he may also have recalled that his failure to authorize a third strike at Pearl Harbor had had unfortunate results). Confident that the American carriers were nowhere in the vicinity, Nagumo ordered the 93 fueled and armed aircraft to be rearmed for another go at Midway. Fifteen minutes into this operation, a reconnaissance plane reported spotting American ships to the northwest. Nagumo dithered for another 15 minutes, then ordered the rearmament reversed, so that the 93 aircraft could be dispatched to attack these American vessels. Soon the hangar decks of the Japanese carriers were littered with ammunition, as general-purpose bombs were being removed from the aircraft while TORPEDOES and armor-piercing bombs were being loaded. And on their flight decks the four carriers were recovering the aircraft returning from the Midway strike.

Meanwhile, Spruance's TF 16 airstrikes had lifted off at about 7:00 A.M.: 116 fighters, dive bombers, and torpedo bombers.

About two hours later, Fletcher put 35 of his own Yorktown planes into the air as well. Spruance had calculated the odds closely. Aware of the Japanese air raid on Midway, he had estimated the time it would take for the attackers to return to their carriers, and launched his strike with the intention of catching the Japanese aircraft as they were rearming on deck. But he had a run of bad luck. Nagumo ordered a course change at 0905, just

as the last of the Midway strike planes were returning. This caused the Hornet's fighters and dive bombers to miss the Japanese task force entirely. As a result, Torpedo Squadron 8—15 TBD1 DEVASTATORS—went in unsupported, with the loss of all the airplanes and all but one of the 45 crewmen to Zeros or antiaircraft fire. A similar fate awaited the Enterprise and Yorktown TBDs. Of 41 TBDs involved in attacks on the Japanese carriers only eight survived, and none scored a hit. By the time the Yorktown TBD strike had been beaten off, at 1024, the Japanese thought they had won the battle.

But within about 90 seconds the whole outcome of the battle was reversed. C. C. Wade McClusky arrived over Nagumo's carriers with 37 Enterprise dive bombers just as the last TBD was downed. With Nagumo's combat air patrol "on the deck" (at low altitude) from having annihilated the TBDs, McClusky's SBD DAUNTLESS attacks were largely unopposed and thus accurate. The SBD attack proved deadly. Within seconds KAGA and AKAGI took bombs to their hangar decks, which touched off ammunition and fueled aircraft, starting uncontrollable fires. Then, within seconds, Yorktown's 17 SBD Dauntlesses showed up and put three 1,000–pound bombs neatly into the center of fueled and armed aircraft on SORYU's deck, turning her into an inferno as well. By 1030 Nagumo had lost three carriers, all burning uncontrollably. He ordered his last carrier, HIRYU, to launch a strike on Yorktown, while bringing up all available escorts to cover the ship.

Hiryu's strike, 50 fighters and bombers, followed the American aircraft home, arriving over Yorktown at about 1440 hours. A furious action ensued, as Yorktown's CAP and escorts accounted for most of the Japanese attackers. But some got through, and the carrier took three bombs and two torpedoes. Not completely recovered from the damage she had taken at Coral Sea, Yorktown began to list dramatically and soon had to be abandoned. Admiral Fletcher shifted his flag to a cruiser and gallantly turned direction of the battle over to Spruance.

Having spotted *Hiryu*, at 1530 *Enterprise* launched 14 of her own and 10 of *Yorktown*'s SBDs. These jumped *Hiryu* at 1700. Nagumo's last carrier went down quickly after taking four hits. Apprised of the outcome of Midway within minutes of the loss of his carriers, Yamamoto reacted by ordering the Main Body and the light carriers in the Aleutians to the support of the now carrier-less First Air Fleet, a classic instance of "too little, too late." Save for some mopping up, the Battle of Midway was over, the Imperial Navy having lost four of its finest carriers and any chance to annihilate the US Navy in the Pacific.

Midway Campaign, Myths of

Midway, the second carrier battle of 1942, was the most decisive of the war. But not for the reasons the Japanese thought it would be, even if they had captured the place. In fact, the Battle of Midway would have turned into the "Siege of Midway" if the Americans had not known what the Japanese were up to or did not have forces available with which to ambush the Japanese. The Japanese plan was to seize Midway Island quickly and then advance down the chain of islands the thousand or so miles to HAWAII, forcing the US fleet to come out and do battle, so that it could then be decisively defeated. A base on Midway would provide an "unsinkable aircraft carrier" for the rest of the Japanese fleet to maneuver around, while the smaller US fleet was chopped to pieces. Midway was a massive operation, involving eight Japanese carriers plus numerous destroyers, cruisers, battleships, and SUBMARINES. The operation also involved landing Japanese troops on several undefended islands off Alaska as a diversion.

The US Navy had other ideas. If the Japanese had seized Midway, the United States would have put it under siege with long-range aircraft and submarines. Midway was over 2,000 miles from the Japanese Home Islands and quite isolated. It would have to be supplied by sea and the Japanese never fully grasped the problems of logistics in the Pacific War. A Japanese-held Midway Island would have

turned into another of many Japanese logistics disasters. While the Japanese played down logistics, they played up the importance of "military honor." They felt the Americans would come out to defend Midway no matter what. The Americans felt otherwise.

Because the United States had broken many Japanese codes, the United States knew most of the Japanese plan and had all three of its available Pacific carriers stationed off Midway to ambush the Japanese. The US force was lucky, the Japanese force was sloppy, and four Japanese carriers were sunk to the loss of only one US carrier. The Japanese Navy never recovered from this because the United States built new carriers much faster than Japan. American admirals knew they would have to deal with the Japanese carriers eventually, especially the six heavy carriers. In June 1942, the United States had only three heavy carriers available for operations in the Pacific and would not receive the first of the two dozen new ESSEX CLASS heavy carriers until after the new year. The Americans had already resigned themselves to fighting a defensive battle until then, emphasizing submarines and land-based aircraft. Midway was an opportunity the Americans could not pass up, but only because they had the drop on the Japanese. Without the advantage of reading the coded Japanese messages, the United States would not have risked its three carriers against the Japanese. Midway would have fallen to the Japanese, but the effect of this success on the course of the war may actually have been relatively minimal.

Midway Class, US Aircraft Carriers

The culmination of US wartime carrier development, *Midway* and her two sisters were huge ships (so big they were classified as "CVB—Large Aircraft Carriers"), yet fast, far better protected than any previous US carriers, and with an enormous aircraft capacity (over 130 planes). Although built with considerable speed (22–23 months each), they began to enter service only at about the time that Japan surrendered. Rebuilt from time to time, the last one was not withdrawn from service until the end of the Cold War.

Midway, CVB-41 (1943–1945–1945), was commissioned eight days after the surrender of Japan. Scrapped, after much service, in the 1990s.

Franklin D. Roosevelt, CVB-42 (1943–1945–1945), originally to have been named *Coral Sea,* but renamed after the president's death. She was commissioned 25 days after Japan surrendered. Scrapped after much service, in the 1980s.

Coral Sea, CVB-43 (1944–1946–1947). Withdrawn from service after much service, in the 1980s.

Three other units were authorized, but were canceled in early 1945 before being laid down.

Mikawa, Gunichi

Gunichi Mikawa graduated from Japan's naval academy in 1911. He had a very distinguished career, attending various schools, serving as naval attaché in Paris, on staffs, and in command of ships. Early in the Pacific War he commanded battleship divisions and cruiser squadrons (as a vice admiral). He commanded the forces that defeated the Allies at the Battle of SAVO ISLAND (the most lopsided naval defeat in American history) and commanded surface forces throughout the battles for GUADALCANAL in 1942. Relieved in late 1943, as someone had to take the fall for Japan's steadily declining fortunes in the area after Savo, he went on to command the South West Area Fleet in early 1944 until US naval forces seized the area in late 1944.

Military Economics, Japan, 1933–1945

Japan was a rather recent arrival on the world stage in 1941, and the rest of the world didn't quite know what to make of it. What garnered attention was Japan's growing military prowess. From a defenseless, insular nation in the 1850s, Japan had modernized itself to the point where it was making war on China with Western weapons and techniques by the end of the 19th century. In 1905 Japan went on to defeat a European power, Russia. Allying itself with the Western Allies during World War I, Japan entered the 1920s as a recognized and proven major military power.

But something was missing, and that vital something was an economy that could support a world-class military machine. Until the 1930s, Japan had spent more effort on its armed forces than it had on industrializing. But while the rest of the world wallowed in the Great Depression of the 1930s, Japan made great strides in expanding its manufacturing capacity. Between 1930 and 1940, truck PRODUCTION increased nearly a hundredfold. Aircraft production went up nearly 12 times, shipbuilding increased five times, and steel production nearly tripled.

But it wasn't enough. Japan made these great strides by concentrating on the production of military goods. Much less progress was made in the civilian sector. This can be seen by the amount of government income spent on the armed forces. In the early 1930s, 29% was spent on the military. By 1940, the armed forces were taking two-thirds of the national budget. Moreover, the government had grabbed much of the increased production wealth for its own use. Between 1931 and 1940, government income increased 16 times.

To put all this in perspective, consider what America and Japan spent on armaments.

ARMAMENTS SPENDING (1995 BILLIONS)		
Year	U.S.	Japan
1935–38	$13.6	$18.1
1939	5.4	4.5
1940	14.5	9.0
1941	40.6	18.1
1942	181.0	27.2
1943	344.0	43.0
1944	380.0	55.0

Much of what Japan spent in the late 1930s went to prosecute the war in China. The territories Japan conquered in 1942 were also ruthlessly plundered through 1944. By 1945, US production was decreasing at a rapid clip and Japan's had fallen even more precipitously.

About a third of US spending went to the Pacific, while nearly half of Japanese spending went into mainland Asia operations (China, Burma, and the huge garrison in MANCHURIA watching the Russians). Moreover, Japan also had to face Britain in the Indian Ocean and Burma. Britain's wartime armaments spending was twice that of Japan, although less than 10% of it went to the Pacific.

It was America that was literally the "Arsenal of Democracy." Throughout the war, the United States alone represented 52% of worldwide (Allies and Axis) aircraft production, 36% of all artillery, 48% of all vehicles, and 61% of all shipbuilding. Add Britain, Canada (which produced at 30% of Japan's level), and Russia and you can see what dire straights the Japanese were in. Japan's only major ally, Germany, had total a armaments production that was only 50% of America's and had to deal with Russia, which spent about half as much as America. The Japanese disadvantage in armaments spending manifested itself differently depending on the branch of the military. The Japanese Navy was carefully built up during the 30 years before the war. Well designed ships and weapons plus skillful crews gave Japan an advantage at the beginning of the war. But the lack of resources did not allow for the replacement of wartime losses. Japanese admirals went into the war expecting to take up to 50% losses. When they suffered far less in the first few months, they got ambitious, and the result was a string of devastating defeats from Midway onward through the end of 1942. Japan didn't have the ability to replace those losses.

The Japanese air forces (both navy and army) were in a similar, although more complex, situation. Japan could build a lot of aircraft, but air force leaders were unwilling to lower their prewar PILOT selection standards. The result was that aircraft were replaced after heavy losses in 1942, but pilots were not. US air commanders did adapt their pilot training to wartime needs and were thus able to achieve air superiority in the Pacific from 1943 on. But even if Japan had implemented more efficient pilot training, it would have done little more than cause more losses to the Americans. The United States would still have had air superiority by 1943.

The Japanese army was least affected by Japan's armaments disadvantage. The army was the largest of the services and its principal restriction was a lack of shipping to get the troops where they were needed in the Pacific. The Japanese style of warfare was heavy on spirit and manpower while light on equipment. Against poorly trained and equipped troops, like the Chinese, this was quite successful. Against the lavishly equipped Americans, it was disastrous.

In China, the Japanese had air superiority and the Chinese had little artillery. The situation was just the opposite against the Allies in the Pacific. Against US troops, the Japanese encountered artillery fire the likes of which they had never experienced. Actually, American artillery, as used in World War II, was a radical new form of artillery use. In addition to prodigious use of ammunition (first seen in World War I), the Americans developed communications techniques that allowed many guns to bring their fire down on a single target more quickly than ever seen in the past. Japanese attacks, even when they had the element of surprise, were regularly blown to pieces by artillery fire. The Japanese learned to use their shovels and skill at fortification to defeat this gunfire when they were defending. But there was no way for a Japanese attack to avoid the devastating effect of the Yankee guns.

American troops were also lavishly equipped with machine guns and used them skillfully. This, combined with their artillery, demolished the Japanese offensive capability. Deprived of their ability to control battles with their fearless attacks, the Japanese were forced to defend. Even defending to the death did little for them, except to provide a means to "die honorably in battle." This did not win wars and as a result Japan lost lives. It was possible to trade lives for a lack of guns and ammunition. Later analysis (during the Korean War) showed that a regularly supplied Chinese Army could stalemate American air and artillery superiority by suffering five CASUALTIES for every American one. This was no help for the Japanese, because, unlike the Chinese in Korea, the garrisons of Pacific islands were cut off from reinforcement and supply when the US invasion fleet showed up. The Americans not only had material superiority, but they also knew how to use it.

The civilian leaders and navy admirals were generally aware of American production superiority. Most army generals were either ignorant of these realities or chose to ignore them. Unfortunately for Japan, the generals were running the government from the mid-1930s, and it was their view of things that determined national policy.

While many civilian and navy leaders had studied in the United States, few generals had done so. Those educated Japanese who had spent time in America came away with a clear understanding that the United States was an industrial powerhouse and not likely to back down from a fight. While the generals ruling Japan might acknowledge American industrial superiority, they dismissed the idea that Americans would not back down and ask for peace if sufficiently pummeled by Japanese military might. It was on this misunderstanding that Japan went to war, and lost everything.

Ref: Barnhart, *Japan Prepares for Total War*; Harries and Harries, *Soldiers of the Sun*.

Miller, Dorie (1919–1943)

A native of Waco, Texas, Dorie (actually Doris, sometimes rendered Dory) Miller enlisted in the navy in 1939, and was a mess attendant (steward's mate) 2nd class aboard the battleship *West Virginia* on December 7, 1941. At the start of the Japanese attack Miller first rendered assistance to the ship's captain, Mervyn S. Bennion, who was mortally wounded. After carrying Bennion to a place of relative safety, Miller manned a machine gun through the balance of the attack, being officially credited with downing two Japanese aircraft (and unofficially with six, albeit that accepting all the unofficial claims would presuppose that few of the

Japanese got away). For his heroism under fire, Miller was promoted mess attendant 1st class and decorated with the Navy Cross by Chester W. NIMITZ.

Returning to duty, Miller was serving aboard the escort carrier *LISCOMBE BAY* when the Japanese submarine *I-175* TORPEDOED her in the GILBERTS on November 24, 1943. The ship sank with great loss of life, over 640 of her 840 crewmen perishing, among them Miller.

Over the years there have been occasional proposals to upgrade Miller's Navy Cross to a MEDAL OF HONOR, on the grounds that he was denied one because of his race. While it is true that several black soldiers have belatedly been awarded the Medal of Honor for service in World War II, Miller's deeds—for which he achieved nationwide fame—were certainly in keeping with the tradi-

Dorie Miller, as depicted in a recruiting poster released shortly after his death in action off Makin Island on November 24, 1943.

tional criteria for the Navy Cross. On the other hand, a number of awards of the Medal of Honor were made primarily for political reasons, such as that to Douglas MACARTHUR

Miller's job, mess attendant or steward's mate, was the most common navy job assigned to BLACK AMERICANS, even black submariners, until well after the war. Although the navy was desegregated in the early 1950s, black sailors for higher skilled rates were slow to show up on many ships. In some cases, especially on smaller ships like destroyers, a newly assigned black specialist, like a radioman, might be the only black sailor on the vessel aside from the messmen. Some captains, wanting to avoid any racial tensions among an otherwise white crew, would give the black radioman the option of bunking with the messmen rather than in the other bunk areas where the rest of the sailors lived. More than one black sailor, realizing that the separate messmen bunking area was rather more comfortable, albeit segregated, than the rest of the crew quarters, opted for the "separate but unequal" accommodations. Since the messmen took care of the food for the officers, this also meant they had access to better chow than the rest of the crew. This, in addition to the better quarters, passed into history in 1970, when the messman rating was abolished.

Milne Bay, Papua

Milne Bay is an inlet on the easternmost end of Papua. Although it had very limited port facilities, it had a considerable anchorage and several nearby areas very suitable for airfield construction that gave it enormous potential value as a base. In late August 1942 the Japanese decided to capture Milne Bay before some 9,500 Allied troops (1,400 Americans, mostly engineers, 8,100 Australians) could complete an air base. Allied aerial reconnaissance detected the approach of a Japanese convoy on August 25, and the American and Australian troops made hasty preparations to resist the landings. The first Japanese troops, "marines" of the SNLF, came ashore about six miles east of the Allied defensive perimeter on the night of Au-

gust 25–26, 1942. On the next night and that of the 28th–29th further contingents landed, until there were about 3,100 Japanese troops ashore. Surprisingly, the Japanese troops remained rather inactive, only a few skirmishes taking place, despite air strikes and naval shellings on the Allied positions. The first Japanese attack came at 0330 on 31 August, and it was easily beaten off, some 160 Japanese troops being killed as they attempted to cross one of the airfield clearings. Although the Allied command suspected that the Japanese would try again, they were wrong, for the Japanese troops essayed no further attacks. On September 5 the Japanese pulled out by sea. The Battle of Milne Bay was over. Milne Bay subsequently became an important air base for the Allies.

Minekaze Class, Japanese Destroyers

A Japanese World War I design, the Minekazes were comparable to the US "four stack" destroyers of the CLEMSON CLASS. Built 1918–23, they were obsolete even before the war. Two of the 15 ships in the class had been converted into high-speed transports, with reduced armament and speed, but able to carry 250 fully armed troops with landing craft, while a third had been fitted to serve as the command ship for a radio-controlled target vessel. All the units in the class saw considerable service in the war, 10 being lost in action.

Mines, Land

Land mines were one of the more feared weapons in the Pacific. Mines were usually detected only when victims stepped on them, and lost feet, legs, or lives. Mines were most frequently used on landing beaches and around heavily fortified Japanese positions. While the Japanese used a lot of mines, they did not have a very wide or sophisticated selection to choose from, compared with the Germans, or even the Americans. The most common mine was the 12-pound, saucer-shaped Model 93. It was used against both personnel and vehicles. This was done by varying the pressure device on the top of the mine to different degrees of sensitivity, from 7 to 250 pounds. More troublesome was the 107-pound, semi-spherical Model 96 mine. This was used on land or under a few feet of water, where it might encounter landing craft. Containing 46 pounds of explosive, the Model 96 would destroy any vehicle and most small landing craft. Another Japanese specialty was the Model 99 armor-piercing mine. However, this mine had to be placed against the side of a vehicle (or the metal door of a bunker) by a soldier who activated it, after which it would explode in five–six seconds. It was not entirely effective against heavier US TANKS and was often fatal to the user. The Model 99 weighed three pounds, contained 24 ounces of TNT, and had magnets on it to keep it attached to its intended target. The Japanese considered it a "grenade," and it was issued one per soldier when conditions warranted. The Japanese frequently improvised mines, using artillery shells, some even made from Russian stocks captured in 1905. These were relatively simple and not very effective, but could prove an annoyance to advancing Allied troops. One very odd antitank improvisation used relatively large-caliber naval shells (5–inch and up). A large hole was dug, into which the shell was placed. A Japanese soldier armed with a hammer then crouched down beside the shell and the whole was covered over with brush. The idea was that when an Allied tank drove over his position, the soldier was supposed to strike the detonator with the hammer. It is not known if any Allied vehicles were destroyed in this fashion, but Allied infantrymen caught a lot of Japanese troops assigned to this duty, and shot them before the hammer came down. The United States made only limited use of mines in the Pacific War.

Mines, Naval

Naval mines were first introduced during the mid-19th century. The TORPEDOES that Admiral David Glasgow Farragut "damned" at Mobile Bay in 1864 were actually mines. But for a long time the threat from mines was largely theoretical. Then came the Russo-Japanese War (1904–05), during which mines played a significant role. One battle was decided when the Russian flagship hit a mine and went down within minutes, taking with her the best Russian admiral of the day. Later the Japanese lost a third of their battleships to mines (their own mines) in one disastrous afternoon. Through and after World War I, mine technology developed steadily, so that during World War II a variety of mines was available. There were the original "contact mines," which go off when something hits them. New in World War II were magnetic mines, which detonate when large masses of steel pass by, and pressure mines, which go off if there is a change in water pressure, caused by a ship passing overhead. All of these could be delivered by surface ship, submarine, and, increasingly, by airplane.

Mines have generally been considered the weapon of the inferior naval power. And certainly no one has ever thought of them as a "warrior's weapon." In fact, many of the most perceptive naval commanders have tended to regard them with disdain. Despite this, the US Navy overcame its aversion to mines and used them extensively. Mines delivered by submarine and aircraft so effectively sealed off Japanese waters in 1945 as to completely shut down Japanese shipping, dealing the Japanese economy a deadly blow.

One reason that mines were so effective was that much Japanese shipping was actually carried by very small vessels, a response to Japan's long coastline and paucity of roads and railroads. Much of Japan's foodstuffs moved in small craft of 80 tons or less, which could easily run along coasts at night and hide in bays, rivers, and other inlets by day, where they could be CAMOUFLAGEd against American aircraft. Mines made this a problematic proposition. As a result, Japan began running short of food. Had Japan not surrendered in August 1945, many Japanese would have starved or frozen to death by the end of the next winter.

The Japanese also used mines effectively. Many US subs that never returned probably ran afoul of minefields planted off Japanese ports. The Japanese used mines extensively to defend their island bastions. These mines had to be cleared before the troops could hit the beach. This was dangerous work, with the minesweepers often operating under fire from Japanese shore batteries.

Some of the mines used against landing craft were planted like land mines. The 107-pound, Type 96 Japanese mine could be submerged under a few feet of water. Small landing craft and amphibious vehicles were the typical victims of this weapon. The only antidote was the UDT (Underwater Demolition Team) scuba divers the US Navy organized. UDT swimmers would go in at night, before an invasion, to disable mines and demolish other obstacles with explosives. This was, as one can imagine, very dangerous work. Sometimes the Japanese guarding the beaches were particularly alert and UDT CASUALTIES were very high. The UDT swimmers were an elite group and the only commando-type troops to be completely successful in the Pacific. The current US Navy SEAL teams are a direct descendant of the World War II-era UDTs.

Ref: Lott, *Most Dangerous Sea.*

Mitscher, Marc (1887–1947)

One of the most distinguished US naval officers in history, Marc Andrew Mitscher (1887–1947) graduated from Annapolis in 1910 and spent the next five years in battleships. In 1915 he took flight training, qualifying as a pilot the following year. During World War I he commanded various naval air stations. In 1919 he took part in an attempt to fly the Atlantic. Although his plane was forced down in the Azores by mechanical difficulties, another, *NC-4*, made it to Lisbon. Over the next few years he held various staff and air commands, and skippered a seaplane tender. In October of 1941 he became the first captain of the carrier *Hornet*, shortly rising to rear admiral in command of the *Hornet* task force, launching the DOOLITTLE bombers against Japan in April of 1942. After taking part in the Battle of MIDWAY, Mitscher for a time commanded a patrol wing, and in April of 1943 took command of all Allied air assets in the SOLOMONS.

The following January he was put in command of the newly formed Fast Carrier Task Force, TF 38/ 58. This he headed for most of the rest of the war, most notably in the Battle of the PHILIPPINE SEA, the Battle of LEYTE GULF, and ultimately in raids against the Japanese Home Islands. After the war Mitscher was promoted to full admiral. Continuing on active service, he died while in command of the Atlantic Fleet. Although overshadowed by HALSEY and, to a lesser extent, SPRUANCE, it was Mitscher who was responsible, under their overall direction, for the planning and execution of virtually all US carrier operations in the Pacific from January of 1944 onward.

Mogami Class, Japanese Heavy Cruisers.

Originally designed as light cruisers, mounting 15 6-inch guns ("A" on the light cruiser table), the Mogamis were refitted several times prior to being rebuilt in 1939–41. During this reconstruction they were converted to heavy cruisers mounting 10 8–inch guns ("B" on the heavy cruiser table). Despite shortcomings, they were tough ships.

Mogami (1931–1934–1935) helped cover operations in the East Indies early in the war, helping to sink *Houston* and PERTH in the Sunda Strait, and then escorted the First Air Fleet to Midway, where she was literally left a burning wreck after repeated US naval and marine air attacks. Remaining afloat, she managed to restore power, and returned to Japan for an extensive refit, lasting nearly a year, during which she was converted to something like the TONE CLASS, with six 8-inch guns in three turrets foreward, and a flight deck aft to operate a large number of floatplanes ("C" on the heavy cruiser table). She later accompanied Nishimura's squadron to SURIGAO STRAIT, where she was heavily damaged by gunfire and later sunk by dive bombers.

Mikuma (1931–1934–1935) was paired with *Mogami* from the start of the war until Midway, where on June 6, 1942 she was sunk by US Navy and Marine aircraft.

Suzuya (1933–1934–1937) operated with *Mogami* for much of the early part of the war, and then supported the battle force for most of the rest of the war, taking part in the action off SAMAR on 25 October 1944, during which she was sunk by carrier aircraft.

Kumano (1934–1936–1937) was paired with *Suzuya* until the action off Samar, in which she was severely damaged by air attack. She managed to escape, during which she took a TORPEDO from a submarine, and sought refuge in Dasoi Bay in the Philippines, where she was found and sunk by aircraft on 25 November 1944.

See also JAPAN, ATTITUDE TOWARD THE ENEMY; RECONNAISSANCE, NAVAL.

Mono, Bougainville

A small town with a sheltered anchorage but no facilities to supply or service ships; overshadowed as a potential base by RABAUL or KIETA, both nearby.

Montana Class, US Battleships

The five ships of the Montana Class were designed to succeed the IOWA CLASS battleships, being much larger and much more heavily armed, albeit at some sacrifice in speed. However, even before they were laid down it had become clear that the days of the battleship were numbered. Construction was suspended by order of President ROOSEVELT in April 1942, ostensibly as a result of a shortage of steel, and they were canceled in July 1943. Given the hull numbers BB-67 through BB-71, they were to have been named *Montana, Ohio, Maine, New Hampshire,* and *Louisiana.*

Morale

Happy, or less unhappy, troops are better fighters. Throughout history, military commanders have noted that cheering the troops up a bit improved their combat performance. At the very least, it reduced desertion and other forms of malingering. The Pacific War was no exception, even though the troops stuck on ships and sundry islands didn't

have the option of deserting. But the often horrendous physical conditions of this tropical battlefield did sap the will of the soldiers. Commanders quickly realized that they would have to cheer the lads up a bit from time to time in order to maintain morale and enthusiasm for the war.

As an example of what lengths American commanders would go to in the name of morale, consider that the US constructed on the 703.4 square miles of the MARIANA Islands and GUAM, 233 outdoor movie theaters, 65 staged theaters, 95 softball and 35 baseball fields, 225 volleyball and 30 basketball courts, and 35 boxing rings complete with seating for spectators, which works out to a total of 1.02 athletic facilities per square mile.

Danny Kaye entertains 4,000 leathernecks of the Fifth Marine Division on occupation duty at Sasebo, Japan. Literally hundreds of popular film and entertainment personalities made significant contributions to the war effort, promoting bond sales, making training films, and entertaining the troops in the field.

Using an improvised altar, a US Navy Roman Catholic chaplain conducts a field mass for Marines on Saipan, June 1944. Thousands of clergymen of all faiths were mobilized for service in the war, during which one earned a Medal of Honor.

The US Navy tried (and didn't always succeed) to provide a varied diet on board their ships. When possible, even ice cream was made on board. Army units were pulled out of battle when too many of their troops appeared to be getting punchy, and rear area rest facilities for the tired infantry were maintained. There were plenty of chaplains, entertainers, and other tangible evidence that the generals and admirals really cared.

America's allies also did what they could. To improve morale during the tedious New Guinea Campaign of World War II, an Australian officer offered a fortnight's home leave to whichever company in his brigade won a CAMOUFLAGE contest.

The result was an energetic competition, with the winners joyfully flying off for home. Unfortunately, upon arriving in Australia, the winning company, of the 39th Battalion, deserted almost to a man.

Japanese commanders tended to assume that morale was always high, regardless of circumstances, and that with their superior spirit Japanese troops could overcome all obstacles. As LG Renya Mutaguchi, commanding the Fifteenth Army in Burma put it shortly before his disastrous Imphal-Kohima Campaign in 1944, "Lack of weapons is no excuse for defeat." To be sure, raw courage and superior morale can win great victories against tremendous numerical and material odds. But as Inoguchi Rikihei, another Japanese soldier, observed, "Nothing is more destructive of morale than to learn of the enemy's superiority." As the war went on, the Japanese found themselves increasingly outclassed in material terms. No amount of élan could compensate for their inferiority. Toward the end of the war Japanese troops often went into action knowing that they could not possibly win. That they maintained their cohesion and discipline under such circumstances was extraordinary.

But the Japanese did make efforts to deal with troop morale. When there were foreigners about, they were preyed upon to provide more comfort for the troops. COMFORT WOMEN (non-Japanese women forced into prostitution) were one of the grimmer Japanese morale-building efforts, although the initial idea was to prevent the troops from rampaging and raping Chinese civilians in general.

The United States undertook a number of projects designed to undermine Japanese morale. Some of these were wholly impractical. For example, a study was made of the possibility of painting Mount Fuji red, which concluded that the project would consume so much paint, and so many aircraft that it might seriously impede the war effort.

Morotai, Moluccas, Netherlands East Indies

A small port, mostly suitable to coastal shipping, with no facilities. But it had some potential, and could be developed, particularly as an air base. The Japanese used it as a local base from 1942 onward.

Morison, Samuel Eliot (1887–1976)

Harvard scholar Morison became the principal historian of the US Navy in World War II when he suggested the assignment to fellow Harvard-man Franklin D. ROOSEVELT. He was well qualified for the job, being a seasoned sailor who had crossed the Atlantic under canvas, and a maritime historian of some note, his most famous work being a biography of Christopher Columbus, *Admiral of the Ocean Sea*. At one time or another Morison served in virtually all naval areas of operation, in eight different vessels, from battlewagons to Coast Guard cutters—though curiously never in a carrier—and was under fire often, as at KULA GULF, KOLOMBAN-GARA, and OKINAWA.

He began organizing and writing his 15-volume *History of United States Naval Operations in World War II* during the war, aided by a small staff, and later secured the cooperation of a number of former Japanese officers. The work is a remarkably literate, very complete treatment of the subject in sometimes extraordinary detail, which has stood the test of time rather well, despite the fact that he does not appear to have been privy to the existence of Ultra.

Quoque ipse miserrimi vidi, quorum pars magna fuit. ["These most grievous events I saw, and many of them I was."]

Mountbatten, Louis (1900–1979)

One of the youngest and most successful senior officers in the war, Louis Mountbatten's career was not harmed by his family connections. His father had been First Lord of the Admiralty for a time, and he himself was the uncle of Prince Philip of Greece and Denmark, during the war widely regarded as the prospective husband of Princess (later Queen) Elizabeth, which duly came to pass. A naval cadet and midshipman during World War I, by 1939 Mountbatten was a destroyer skipper. He commanded a British destroyer flotilla during the Norwegian Campaign and off Crete (Noel Coward's film *In Which We Serve* is loosely based on his exploits). In 1941 he was jumped several ranks and named head of Combined Operations, The Commandos. In order to enhance his already considerable clout he was simultaneously made a general and air marshal. In this role he oversaw numerous commando operations, and helped plan the raids on Dieppe and St.-Nazaire. From early 1943 he headed the Allied Southeast Asia Command, a post in which he rendered excellent service, being aided by a number of distinguished subordinates, most notably Bill SLIM. After the war he served as the last British viceroy of India, overseeing the British withdrawal and the partition. He later served in a variety of prominent military and civil posts, until his death by an IRA bomb in 1979. Mountbatten's abilities as a commander were considerable. Although his political connections helped smooth the way for him, he was an excellent administrator, could get along with the most sensitive egos, had a flair for the unusual, and possessed considerable charisma.

Munda, New Georgia, Solomon Islands

A well located peninsula off the island of New Georgia, in about the middle of the SOLOMONS, Munda had some plantation installations and a small port, of no particular importance. The plantation land was ideal for development into airfields. This the Japanese proceeded to do during the GUADALCANAL campaign, which led to US operations against New Georgia in 1943, Munda subsequently served as an Allied base.

Muskat, Oman

A small but decent harbor, with limited facilities and an important RAF base, Muskat, on the Persian Gulf of Oman, South Arabia, guarded the eastern approaches to the Persian Gulf, with its important oil resources and the Allied lifeline to Russia. It would have been the principal Japanese objective if the Imperial Navy had undertaken more extensive operations in the Indian Ocean. In October 1942 Japanese SUBMARINES briefly operated in the nearby Gulf of Oman, the farthest west in which the Imperial Navy conducted combat operations.

Mutsuki Class, Japanese Destroyers

The first Japanese destroyers designed after World War I, the Mutsukis were built 1923–27 and were refitted as fast transports early in the war. Despite this, they retained considerable antisubmarine and surface combat capability. All became war losses, most in the SOLOMONS.

MXY-7 Baka, Suicide Aircraft

The Japanese MXY-7 Baka was the ultimate KA-MIKAZE aircraft. It was a rocket-propelled flying bomb that was carried underneath a bomber for most of its flight. When about 50 miles from the target area, the MXY-7 was released. The PILOT then guided the aircraft into a steep glide toward a target (at about 300 MPH). When near the enemy ships, the pilot aimed the aircraft right at its target and ignited the rocket for the last 30 seconds of the suicide flight. The rocket provided high enough speed to get past any defending fighters and antiaircraft fire. While impressive on paper, the MXY-7 system didn't work. The lumbering bombers carrying the 1–1.5–ton rockets (there were two versions of the MXY-7) made easy targets for Allied interceptors. The high flying bombers (the MXY-7 needed some altitude before being dropped) were easily spotted by carrier radar. Those MXY-7s that did launch found that the new American proximity fuze shells, and heavy flak in general, presented a wall of exploding shells they had to fly through. But the Japanese had one thing right about the MXY-7. When it did hit a ship it was with devastating results. The speedy (over 500 MPH) rockets contained 1,300 or 2,600 pounds of explosive. It made quite a dent in whatever kind of ship it hit. Fortunately, only a few ships were hit by any of the 800 MXY-7s built.

See also KAMIKAZES, ROCKET POWERED.

N

N1K1 George, Japanese Fighter

The N1K1 George was originally developed as a Japanese floatplane fighter, but the floats were deleted and the N1K1 turned into a land-based naval fighter. The aircraft was fast, rugged, and extremely maneuverable. Entering combat in early 1944, it was quite a shock to Allied pilots. Like most other high-performance Japanese aircraft late in the war, the N1K1 suffered from repeated manufacturing defects and component failures. Only some 1,400 were produced.

See also AIRCRAFT TYPES, DEVELOPMENT.

Nachi Class, Japanese Heavy Cruisers

Good ships, designed with the experience of the FURUTAKAS and AOBAS in mind, the Nachis were much better protected, stabler, and somewhat faster vessels, being much larger (in violation of the 10,000–ton limit imposed by the naval limitation treaties). Despite this, like all Japanese ships they were rather cramped, having only 1.54 square meters of living space per man. Overall, they were tough ships, able to absorb considerable damage.

Nachi (1924–1927–1929) spent the early part of the war in the East Indies, where she fought in the JAVA SEA battles in February 1942, and operated against the British in the Indian Ocean later that year. She later fought in the KOMANDORSKI IS-LANDS and at SURIGAO STRAIT, where she got away despite taking some hits and a collision with MOGAMI. Eleven days later, on 5 November 1944, she was sunk by carrier aircraft in Manila Bay.

Myoko (1924–1927–1929) began the war with *Nachi* in the East Indies, served as TAKAGI's flag-

ship in the CORAL SEA, ran TOKYO EXPRESS bombardment missions to GUADALCANAL, fought at EMPRESS AUGUSTA BAY and LEYTE GULF, where she took a TORPEDO and made for SINGAPORE. In mid-December 1944 she attempted to get home to Japan, to effect repairs, and was torpedoed off INDO-CHINA by *Bergall* (SS-320). She limped back to Singapore, where she was surrendered—still unrepaired—at the end of the war, and was scuttled by the British in 1946.

Haguro (1925–1925–1929) was one of the busiest of Japan's heavy cruisers. She began the war with *Nachi* and *Myoko* in the East Indies, played a critical role in the JAVA SEA battles, fought at the Coral Sea, at Empress Augusta Bay, and in the action against the escort carriers off SAMAR. She operated out of Singapore thereafter, and sank shortly after midnight on 16 May 1945 after taking eight torpedoes from British destroyers off PENANG in the Malacca Straits, having thus taken part in both the first and the last surface actions of the Pacific War.

Ashigara (1925–1928–1929) helped cover the Japanese invasion of the Philippines and East Indies and took part in the Indian Ocean operations. She had a minor role in Leyte Gulf, and took part in an abortive attempt to attack the landing force at LINGAYEN Gulf in January 1945, before retiring to Singapore again. On 8 June 1945 she took five torpedoes from the British T-Class submarine *Trenchant*, near the Banka Strait, off Java.

Nagano, Osami (1880–1947)

Osami Nagano was one of the senior Japanese naval admirals who got the fleet behind the idea of going to war with Britain and America. Nagano served as a military attaché in the United States just before World War I, but this did not change his attitude as a staunch Japanese nationalist. He failed to get Japan parity with Britain and America during the second London naval DISARMAMENT CONFERENCE in 1936, and pulled Japan out of the naval disarmament agreement. He served as navy minister, and then commander of the Combined Fleet during the 1930s. In early 1941 he became chief of the Naval General Staff. He was an enthusiastic supporter of the "strike south" (against Dutch oil fields) STRATEGY. Nagano went ahead with plans for the PEARL HARBOR strike despite the Foreign Ministry's continued efforts at diplomacy. He was an advocate of taking SAMOA to cut the American supply line to Australia, but the MIDWAY operation was selected instead. He was deposed by General TOJO in early 1944 when the army seized control of the Naval General Staff. He was tried as a war criminal after the war, but died of pneumonia during the trial. Nagano was smart but not a hard worker. He preferred to get others to do the work while he concentrated on politics (at which he was pretty good). When the war began, he was already in his 60s and losing his energy. Unable to wheel and deal as he once had, he lost his support in the Naval Staff and the Imperial Household as the war went on.

Nagara Class, Japanese Light Cruisers

Like all older Japanese cruisers, the Nagaras were small, lightly built, fast, and very obsolete by World War II standards. They spent most of the war as flotilla leaders, though one was converted into an antiaircraft cruiser.

Nagara (1920–1921–1922) led a destroyer flotilla during operations in the Philippines and East Indies, 1941–42, then with the First Air Fleet at MIDWAY, where she took NAGUMO and his staff off the burning AKAGI. She later served with Combined Fleet, and was lost off Kyushu on 7 August 1944 to *Croaker* (SS-246).

Natori (1920–1921–1922) led destroyers during operations in the East Indies and SOLOMONS, until sunk 18 August 1944 by *Hardhead* (SS-365) off SAMAR in the Philippines.

Yuru (1920–1922–1923) led a destroyer flotilla in the East Indies in 1941–42, and went on to fight in the Solomons, where she was severely damaged by Marine aircraft on 25 October 1942 near GUADALCANAL, and had to be sunk by Japanese destroyers. She was the first Japanese light cruiser to be sunk in the war.

Isuzu (1920–1921–1923) led destroyers with Combined Fleet and in the East Indies, where she was lost on 7 April 1945 by TORPEDOES from *Charr* (SS-328) and *Gabilan* (SS-252).

Kinu (1921–1922–1922) led destroyer flotillas, particularly with Combined Fleet, and later with carrier task forces until sunk by carrier air attack on 26 October 1944, in the aftermath of LEYTE GULF.

Abukuma (1921–1923–1925) led the destroyer flotilla that accompanied the PEARL HARBOR Strike Force, and spent most the rest of the war with the battle fleet, though she did fight at the KOMANDORSKI ISLANDS. At SURIGAO STRAIT she was hit by a torpedo from *PT-137* on 25 October, and was sunk the next day off Los Negros, the Philippines, by air attack.

Nagasaki, Kyushu, Japan

Set at the head of a fine natural harbor, and partially surrounded by mountains, Nagasaki (population about 250,000 in 1940) was a major port and industrial city in western Kyushu, with extensive steel works and shipyards, the latter capable of building all classes of warships, up to carriers and battleships. The city was also the center of an important coal-mining area and was a major fishing port. The site of the local regional military district, in August 1945 Nagasaki was also the headquarters of an infantry brigade.

On 9 August 1945 Nagasaki was hit by the second ATOMIC BOMB. Some 65,000 to 75,000 people

Nagasaki, late 1945. The prominent structure is the Roman Catholic cathedral.

were killed or mortally wounded, and about a third of the city was left in ruins.

See also HIROSHIMA, THE PLOT.

Nagato Class, Japanese Battleships

Among the best older battleships in the world, the Nagatos were quite fast, well protected, and well armed. Under construction during the negotiations for the naval DISARMAMENT TREATIES, *Mutsu* was saved from the scrap heap when the Japanese negotiator observed that she had been paid for by the schoolchildren of Japan. The United States and Britain were allowed an increase in their battleship strength in compensation, the former retaining *Colorado* and *West Virginia*, originally slated to be scrapped, and the latter being allowed to build the two NELSON CLASS ships. Somewhat modernized

during the 1930s, like all Japanese battleships in the war, they saw little action.

Nagato (1917–1919–1920) spent most of the war with the battle force of Combined Fleet, initially as YAMAMOTO's flagship, until YAMATO became available. As a result, she was engaged only occasionally, taking some damage from a TORPEDO by *Skate* (SS-305) on Christmas Day, 1943. Her only serious action was against the escort carriers off SAMAR on October 25, 1944, during the Battle of LEYTE GULF. She ended the war relatively unscathed, the only surviving Japanese battleship, and was expended as a target during the 1946 Bikini atomic weapons trials.

Mutsu (1918–1920–1921) saw even less action than *Nagato*. On 8 June 1943 she was destroyed in HIROSHIMA harbor by an internal explosion, the nature of which has never been ascertained, but has generally been attributed to a new type of ammunition, the Mark 3 16–inch shell. This contained some 300 explosive submunitions (mini-bombs) and was designed for surface bombardment. It is believed that a Mark 3 round may have accidentally detonated in the ship's magazine, setting off a catastrophic explosion. The Mark 3 shell was withdrawn from service almost immediately after this incident.

Nagoya, Honshu, Japan

One of the principal bases of the Imperial Navy, a major port with extensive facilities to construct, repair, and service ships. Heavily bombed in 1944–1945.

Nagumo, Chuichi (1886–1944)

Chuichi Nagumo graduated from the Japanese naval academy in 1908, becoming a destroyerman and expert in TORPEDO warfare. During the 1920s he traveled in Europe and America, before returning to Japan to commence a series of increasingly important ship and squadron commands. Early in 1941 he was given the First Air Fleet, which he commanded in the attack on PEARL HARBOR. Although Japan's premier carrier admiral, Nagumo was not an able tactician or a bold leader. At Pearl Harbor his conservative nature caused him to refuse his staff's urging that a third strike be launched to hit the American fuel supplies and other targets at the now devastated base. However, in the following six months he added to his reputation by leading strikes against Allied bases in Australia and the Indian Ocean. His shortcomings didn't catch up with him until Midway, where his indecisiveness contributed to the loss of four Japanese carriers. He survived this debacle and continued to command carrier forces during 1942 as the Japanese attempted to retake GUADALCANAL. In these battles he again demonstrated a lack of drive and by the end of 1942 had been relegated to the command of the Sasebo Naval Base. In 1944, he was

given command of the forces defending SAIPAN. On July 7, 1944, he committed suicide as invading American forces completed their conquest of Saipan.

Naha, Okinawa

The principal port of Okinawa, Naha was small and cramped, and lacked important facilities, but did provide access to the island's several actual and many potential air bases. It was almost totally destroyed during the Okinawa Campaign.

Names, Battles, US versus Japanese

Many of the principal battles of the Pacific War have different names, depending upon whether the account is from the Allied side or the Japanese. Some examples are:

Allied Name of Battle	Japanese Name of Battle
Bandung Strait	Battle off Bali
Eastern Solomons	Second Battle of the Solomon Sea
Empress Augusta Bay	Gazelle Bay
Guadalcanal (Nov. '42)	Third Battle of the Solomon Sea
Komandorski Islands	Battle off Attu
Philippine Sea	Battle off the Marianas
Savo Island	First Battle of the Solomon Sea
Tassafaronga	Lunga Point
Unnamed	Battle of Horaniu

During the war there was occasionally more than one Allied name for a battle. The EASTERN SOLOMONS, for example, was sometimes referred to as the "Battle of the Stewart Islands." CAPE ESPERANCE was for a time officially known as the "Second Battle of Savo Island," the two November naval battles off GUADALCANAL being the "Third" and "Fourth," and TASSAFARONGA the "Fifth." But Santa Cruz is sometimes referred to as the "Third Battle of Savo Island," and Tassafaronga is also sometimes known as the Fourth or Sixth Battle of Savo Island. Similarly, the two naval battles of Guadalcanal (12–13 and 14–15 November 1942) are actually part of single air-sea battle that lasted

12–15 November, sometimes known to the Allies as the "Battle of the Solomons," and designated by the Japanese the "Third Battle of the Solomon Sea." The Battle of KOLOMBANGARA is sometimes referred to as the "Second Battle of Kolombangara," an otherwise unnamed engagement several weeks earlier in which several US cruisers and destroyers sank two Japanese destroyers off Vila, Kolombangara, being sometimes called the "First." To further complicate matters, Kolombangara is also occasionally referred to as the "Second Battle of KULA GULF" as well, since that took place in virtually the same waters!

National Guard

The National Guard constitutes the active militia of the individual states of the United States. Although neglected between the wars, it began to expand in the mid–1930s, and after the German invasion of Poland it was quietly expanded from 199,500 officers and men, so that by the summer of 1940 it comprised approximately 242,000 Guardsmen and was still growing. That September, the president began ordering National Guard units into federal service under special authority from Congress. This was accomplished in 22 increments, totaling as many as 63,646 officers and men in the first increment, down to as few as 362 in the last increment, in June 1941. A total of 297,754 National Guardsmen were taken into federal service, totaling 19,795 officers, 221 warrant officers, and 277,738 enlisted men. Only 1,032 of the prewar Guardsmen were refused induction. Although the accuracy of the figure is hard to confirm, by some estimates more than 75,000 (over 27%) of National Guard enlisted men eventually became officers during the war. In addition, Guard units won 148 Presidential Unit Citations, while individual Guardsmen were awarded 14 Medals of Honor, 50 Distinguished Service Crosses, 48 Distinguished Flying Crosses, and over 500 Silver Stars, testifying to the basic quality of National Guard manpower.

Although the preparedness, training, intelligence, and efficiency of the National Guard was generally—usually unjustly—denigrated by Regulars and the press, in fact it provided the nation with an immensely important pool of more or less trained men at a time when such were in short supply: The total Regular Army was only about 300,000 men at the time the Guard was federalized. It is worth noting that of the 12 divisions the army shipped overseas in 1942, eight were composed of National Guardsmen, and one included a National Guard regiment. Indeed, all seven of the divisions the army sent to the Pacific War in 1942 were composed at least partially of National Guardsmen (in order, the 27th, 41st, 32nd, Americal, 37th, and 43rd, which were followed by the 25th, which included a National Guard infantry regiment), as were two of the five divisions that went to the European Theater that year (the 34th and 29th, the others being the First, Third, and Ninth). By the end of the war, of 22 army divisions in the Pacific, 10.6 had their origins in the National Guard (48.2%), whereas of the 67 divisions that served in the European-Mediterranean-Middle Eastern Theater, only nine were from the National Guard (13.4%). Moreover, many of the so-called Regular Army and Reserve (i.e., draftee) divisions raised during the war were organized around cadres drawn from existing National Guard divisions. For example, the 30th Infantry Division (Guardsmen from the Carolinas, Georgia, and Tennessee), activated in September 1940, was actually down to only 2,100 officers and men exactly two years later, the balance of its manpower having been transferred to form the cadres of several new divisions. Of course, this meant that in fact much of the manpower of many ostensibly National Guard divisions was actually composed of draftees or volunteers, rather than Guardsmen.

To be sure, there were some problems with the National Guard units that first went into combat. Many of the troops were rather older than the optimal age for infantrymen, in their late 20s and early 30s or even older, rather than their late teens and early 20s. Then too, some National Guard personnel were not as well trained as they might have been. But then, as the disaster at Kasserine Pass in

North Africa in late 1942 demonstrated, neither were many old Regulars or new draftees. It's worth recalling that most armies—and most units—have problems upon first entering combat, and that the first US Army units to enter combat in the Pacific were National Guard units. Without the National Guard, getting ready would have taken longer.

Nauru Island, Central Pacific

Apart from some facilities to load phosphates, Nauru (8 square miles) lacked a port, although it could be said to have some value as a potential air base, lying south of the eastern CAROLINES and west of the GILBERTS, each only a few hundred miles distant. In 1942 it was under Australian administration when the Japanese walked in. Several times raided by U.S. naval aircraft, it remained under Japanese control until the end of the war.

Navaho Code Talkers, USMC

Early in 1942 the Marine Corps received a proposal to use Navaho Indians as communications technicians. By making use of their native tongue, an unwritten language virtually unknown by anyone but the Navaho, these men would be able to send radio and telephone messages without using codes, thereby facilitating communications. After tests, which demonstrated that this method of communication was faster than having to encode and then decode messages, the proposal was adopted. In September 1942 recruiting began for 200 Navaho to serve as communications specialists. The first group of recruits, 29 men, not only trained in radio and telephone communications, but also created a greatly expanded vocabulary for their language, inventing new words or adapting existing ones where the language lacked equivalent terms: Thus, Navaho for "turtle" was given the additional meaning of "tank."

The first Navaho code talkers reported for duty with Marine units in the Pacific in early 1943. That spring Marine commanders were asked their opinion of the program, and they universally praised it.

Navaho code talkers thereafter took part in every Marine operation for the rest of the war. Surprisingly, records as to the number of men so employed are imprecise. Estimates vary from about 375 to about 420. Attempts to determine the exact figure are futile, as many Navaho Marine veterans (altogether about 5,000 Navaho served in the armed forces during the war) subsequently claimed to have served as code talkers, but did not in fact do so.

Interestingly, before the outbreak of the war, Japanese intelligence suggested the possibility that the United States might use Indians as communications specialists. However, they decided that the language of choice was certain to be Lakota (Sioux), possibly because of the great military reputation of that nation. However, there were actually far more Navaho than Sioux, and they had proven pretty tough warriors as well, but had received less press coverage.

Naval Battles, Surface, in the Pacific

Before the Pacific War actually began, on 7 December 1941, surface combat was still expected to be the decisive form of naval action in the long-anticipated Japanese-American war. Certainly nothing that had occurred in the European war, which by then had been raging for more than two years, suggested otherwise.

However, PEARL HARBOR and the air-sea battles of CORAL SEA and MIDWAY in mid–1942 seemed to demonstrate that aircraft carriers now ruled the waves, rather than battleships and cruisers. But Coral Sea and Midway were followed by the EASTERN SOLOMONS and the SANTA CRUZ ISLANDS, which, together with some unfortunate torpedoings, effectively depleted everyone's carrier forces.

As a result, most of the naval actions from late 1942 until well into 1943 were surface engagements, occasionally influenced by the presence of aircraft. In fact, there were over a dozen major and several score minor engagements between battleships, cruisers, and destroyers during the Pacific War.

Aside from a number of surface actions in the Dutch East Indies in early 1942 and in the Philippines in 1944 virtually all of the remaining surface engagements took place in the Solomon Islands, notably in the vicinity of GUADALCANAL, where in the six months from August of 1942 through February of '43 there occurred five major and about 30 smaller surface engagements.

Before the war, the Japanese and the Americans had developed differing notions about surface combat. The Japanese, mindful of their probable numerical inferiority in a war with the United States, trained for night actions and stressed the use of TORPEDOES by both destroyers and cruisers. They preferred putting their heavier ships in the van, and were willing to use multiple columns, permitting the tactical independence of different squadrons operating together. All of these techniques were to make it easier for a smaller Japanese force to defeat a larger Allied one. And they worked.

The US Navy, in contrast, was fairly rigidly tied to the single line ahead formation, with destroyers at the van and rear and the heavier ships in the middle, all to operate under a single command. For all practical purposes, the US Navy saw no need to innovate or question what it was doing or what it was likely to face when surface naval combat occurred. Little attention was paid to Japanese preparations for the coming war, even though little effort would have been required to discover what the Japanese were doing to get ready. In fact, some military attachés in Tokyo did discern that the Japanese Navy was rather more effective than conventional wisdom in the West had it. These reports were generally ignored until it was too late.

When the two navies began to clash in surface actions, it quickly became apparent that the Japanese were superior. The battles did not conform to the USN's expectations. The extensive availability of land-based aircraft caused most surface battles to occur at night, since control of the air in daylight usually translated into victory. In night surface combat, the Japanese initially had an advantage. During peacetime they had trained hard for night

surface combat. They had evolved more realistic tactics for night combat and drilled their ships' crews relentlessly in all types of weather, regardless of CASUALTIES. In addition, they had developed superior optical equipment for range finding.

American sailors had received a more leisurely diet of daytime training exercises, marred by a contest-like atmosphere that resulted in training being conducted in the calmest possible weather, so that no ship would have an unfair advantage. Moreover, unlike their US counterparts, all Japanese cruisers carried torpedoes and many of them were provided with torpedo reloads. The cruiser crews were well trained in the use of torpedoes, something rare with torpedo equipped cruisers. The Japanese torpedoes were superior to all others in the world, being larger, more reliable, and longer ranged. The US admirals had generally neglected the use of the torpedo in surface combat, omitting it entirely from most cruisers, for example, and not getting enough practice in coordinating torpedo-armed destroyers with heavier ships during maneuvers.

So from the JAVA SEA battles (February 27– March 1, 1942) through the summer and fall battles around Guadalcanal, the Japanese were generally triumphant at night. American sailors had to undergo the same grueling training process as the Japanese before US surface ships could meet the Japanese on equal terms.

A lot of material changes in late 1942 helped the United States, but it was training that made the difference. Meanwhile, the USN gradually acquired superior ships, improved damage-control techniques, and found better communications methods. And it began to learn to use its torpedoes.

The torpedo was actually the most effective weapon used in the night battles, accounting for most of the ships lost. As it turned out, American destroyermen already knew how to make effective torpedo attacks, but had usually been kept on a tight leash by task force commanders intent on slugging it out. Given a chance to operate on their own they proved particularly effective in torpedo attacks, as at BALIKPAPAN (January 23–24, 1942) or CAPE ESPERANCE (October 11–12, 1942). Despite this, it was not until mid–1943 that US destroyers were routinely allowed to operate in conjunction with, rather than in line with, heavier ships.

Meanwhile, radar came along. Surprisingly, initially it may have actually handicapped US night fighting abilities. The first radars were inefficient, temperamental, and not at all understood by most senior officers. At times the presence of Japanese warships was first detected by lookouts, if it had not already been announced by the arrival of their shells, before they were detected by radar, at which point it was usually too late to do anything but die bravely. As radar improved and commanders who understood its capabilities and limitations (like Willis "Ching Chong China" LEE) came along, things began to improve, and American ships began to feel more comfortable in night actions. However, the Japanese remained formidable opponents. At KULA GULF (July 4–5, 1943) and KOLOMBANGARA (July 12–13, 1943) they gave better than they received, despite all the American ad-

vantages. But gradually they lost their edge, and in the last important surface actions of the war on anything like even terms, VELLA LAVELLA (August 6–7, 1943) and EMPRESS AUGUSTA BAY (November 2, 1943), the Japanese came off second best.

It had been a tough school, but the US Navy had learned, albeit the hard way. Learning how to fight while in combat is the hard way; learning during tough, realistic peacetime training is the easy way.

Naval War, World War II Outside the Pacific

Although Americans are wont to think that the naval war against Japan was where the seagoing action was during the Second World War, in fact the hottest maritime war was that against Germany and Italy, in terms of the loss not only of shipping, but also of major warships, destroyers, cruisers, carriers, and battlewagons.

Note, also, that the Axis actually inflicted and suffered losses in the Indian Ocean and the Pacific, where German and Italian SUBMARINES and surface raiders operated with some success against Allied shipping. The Axis accounted for a couple of warships in the Indian Ocean. For example, the German armed merchant raider *Kormoran* sank HMAS *Sydney* off Western Australia on Armistice Day, 1941, being sunk in turn as a result of damage

NAVAL FORCES IN THE PACIFIC, DECEMBER 1941

	Japanese	US	Allies	Totals
A/C: Carrier	545	280	—	280
A/C: Other	2,140	1,180	600	1,780
Carriers	10	3	0	3
Battleships	11	9	2	11
Heavy Cruisers	18	13	1	14
Light Cruisers	17	11	10	21
Destroyers	104	80	20	100
Submarines	67	73	13	86

Figures for carriers exclude ships working up (i.e., not yet fully operational) and escort carriers. Including these would raise the Japanese totals to 13 carriers with about 650 aircraft; US ships in these categories were all in the Atlantic. A/C indicates aircraft, with "Other" including non-naval land-based machines; US figures include aircraft in California, Washington, and Oregon. Allied battleship figures include one battlecruiser. The US allies were the British Commonwealth (Britain, Australia, New Zealand, Canada, and India) and the Netherlands. The United States also had its Atlantic Fleet, from which it quickly withdrew three carriers to improve the carrier odds in the Pacific, as well as a number of battleships and other vessels, but these were not available on 7 December 1941.

MAJOR WARSHIP LOSSES BY THEATER

Theater	Area	Number	Percent
European		856	58.9
	Atlantic	399	27.4
	Baltic/Black	126	8.7
	Mediterranean	331	22.8
Pacific		598	41.1
	Indian Ocean	25	1.7
	Pacific Ocean	573	39.4
Total		1,454	100.0

inflicted by her opponent. The Allies suffered no warship or merchant ship losses in the Atlantic at the hands of the Japanese.

See also GERMANY IN THE PACIFIC WAR; ITALY IN THE PACIFIC WAR.

Ref: Brown, *Warship Losses of World War Two.*

Ndeni, Santa Cruz Islands

Poorly suited to serve as a potential naval base, Ndeni did possess some possible value as an air base, helping to cover a wide area of the south-central Pacific, lying only about 400 miles east of GUADALCANAL and the same distance north of ESPIRITU SANTO. But the island was infected with a particularly virulent strain of malaria, which made it a dangerous place for foreigners. US forces reconnoitered the island for possible use as an air base in June 1942, and shortly thereafter the seaplane tender USS *Curtiss* arrived to establish a seaplane base. In October navy SEABEES laid out an airstrip, but construction never went beyond that stage, as malaria proved an insurmountable obstacle, causing numerous CASUALTIES and some deaths. Shortly after the Battle of the Santa Cruz Islands the project was abandoned. Not even COASTWATCHERS were left on the island, although Australian authorities did recruit men for labor service.

Nelson Class, British Battleships

Britain's Nelson Class had an odd design, to say the least. With three triple turrets forward of the superstructure ("C" turret, the third, was lower than "B" and could not fire ahead), intended to save weight, the Nelsons were the only battleships built during the "naval holiday" introduced by the DISARMAMENT TREATIES, and were actually rather successful. They were armored on the "Nevada" ("all or nothing") plan (See NEVADA CLASS, US BATTLESHIPS), which stressed enormous protection for vital areas and nothing at all elsewhere.

They were good ships, but very slow by World War II standards. They saw considerable service in the Indian Ocean.

Nelson (1922–1925–1927) spent most of the war in the North Sea, the Atlantic, and the Mediterranean. In late 1944 she joined the British Far Eastern Fleet, and supported British operations against Burma, MALAYA, and the Netherlands Indies until the surrender of Japan.

Rodney (1922–1925–1927) also spent most of the war in the ETO, the high point taking place on May 27, 1941 when, with HMS KING GEORGE V, she helped pound the German battleship *Bismarck* to destruction in the Atlantic. In late 1944 she accompanied *Nelson* to the Far East and served there until the end of the war.

Both ships were scrapped in 1948.

See also ROYAL NAVY.

Netherlands, The

Under German occupation from May 1940 to virtually the end of the war in Europe, the Netherlands could make only a limited contribution to the defense of its vast East Indian empire. There was a small army and air force in the NETHERLANDS EAST INDIES, but the main element of Dutch power in the region was the Royal Netherlands Navy, with three light cruisers, seven destroyers, and about 15 SUBMARINES. These put up a tough fight, only one light cruiser and seven submarines escaping the Japanese onslaught. Dutch influence on the Pacific War waned thereafter. Although a few Dutch ships always served with the British fleet in the Indian Ocean, while some reconnaissance aircraft as well as a small ground force operated out of Australia or those portions of Netherlands New Guinea not occupied by the Japanese, the Dutch played only a marginal military role in the Pacific. However, the large Dutch merchant marine proved of enormous value to the Allied cause. Of particular importance were the many small ships designed for inter-island trade in the East Indies, which escaped from the Japanese and helped support Australian and American operations in New Guinea waters.

Netherlands East Indies

Now called INDONESIA, these 3,000 islands stretch from Sumatra to western New Guinea, and total about 750,000 square miles. Some areas were well developed and densely populated (JAVA, Amboina, Bali), while others were thinly peopled, virtually virgin tropical forests (BORNEO, New Guinea). Rich in resources (oil, tin, rice, and more), the Netherlands East Indies constituted the core of the "Southern Resources Area" for which Japan was fighting.

When the Pacific War broke out the defense of the Netherlands East Indies was an impossible task. Although reinforced by some Australian and American troops and aircraft, the Dutch forces were greatly outnumbered by the Japanese. Moreover, the defense of the Indies was primarily a maritime problem, and the Allies could not commit ships and aircraft in numbers sufficient to do more than impede the Japanese advance. Nevertheless, Allied resistance was often fierce.

Under Japanese rule, the Netherlands East Indies were brutally exploited for their resources, to feed the Japanese economy. However, although they profited greatly from the tin and rubber produced in the Indies, the Japanese were never able to restore the oil fields to any sustained degree of PRODUCTION. In addition to material resources, the Japanese made extensive use of East Indians as slave laborers, many tens of thousands being shipped abroad. Most of these people did not survive the war.

In line with their "Asia for the Asiatics" policies, the Japanese supported local nationalist leaders, among them Sukarno, and promised eventual independence after the war. In fact, the nationalists who supported the Japanese were in league with those who took to the hills in presumed support of the Netherlands. The objective of both groups was the independence of the East Indies, not Japanese

or Dutch rule. Approximately 100,000 military and paramilitary personnel were organized by the collaborators ostensibly to support the Japanese. Shortly after the armistice of 15 August, these troops began clashing with Japanese forces, which were supposed to maintain "order" until relieved by Allied forces. When the British arrived, as surrogates for the Dutch, heavy fighting broke out as the erstwhile collaborationist troops began a full-scale insurrection against Dutch rule. This culminated in the eventual independence of Indonesia.

Netherlands East Indies Army

The bulk of the troops in the Dutch East Indian Army were locally raised. Organized, trained, and equipped primarily as a colonial constabulary, the army was badly scattered in numerous small garrisons, albeit that on paper two divisions and a division sized-task force existed. Total manpower was in the vicinity of 125,000, of whom about a fifth were Dutch, about as many more of mixed Dutch-Indonesian background or Indonesian Christians, and the rest natives of various cultural and ethnic backgrounds. When the Japanese came, the performance of the army was very uneven. Many units simply disintegrated, while others, particularly those with high proportions of Eurasian or native Christian troops, acquitted themselves well. Ultimately the difference didn't matter, as the defense of the Dutch East Indies was a naval problem; The destruction of the ABDA fleet at the end of February 1942 sealed the fate of the Netherlands East Indian Army.

Small elements of the Netherlands East Indies Army managed to maintain a GUERRILLA resistance on TIMOR with Australian assistance, before escaping to Australia in 1943, where they joined other elements that had escaped the collapse of Dutch power in the East Indies. Other detachments survived in the southern portions of Netherlands New Guinea, where the Japanese never reached. These enabled the Netherlands to maintain a token participation in the Pacific War. Although the Dutch government-in-exile authorized the creation of the First Netherlands East Indian Infantry Battalion for service on New Guinea, the primary role of the Netherlands ground forces (which included a lot of New Guineans and Indonesians under Dutch officers) was in providing scouts and guides for Australian troops. The only battalion-sized operation undertaken by the Netherlands East Indies Army was in support of the Australian landing at BALIKPAPAN.

Neutrality Acts, US

A series of laws enacted in the 1930s and designed to prevent the United States from being "dragged" into a war against its will. By the early 1930s a coterie of isolationist historians, political hacks of the far left and far right, and pacifists of various stripes, including many religious organizations, had established the notion that the American entry into World War I was due to a conspiracy on the part of the Allied powers and American bankers and munitions makers, the so-called "Merchants of Death." This theory attained its greatest influence as a result of the "Nye Commission." In 1934 Senator Gerald Nye headed an inquiry into the origins of American involvement in World War I. Calling only a handful of witnesses, all of them adherents of the "Merchants of Death" theory, the commission "proved conclusively" that Uncle Sam had been hustled into the war against his best interests. As a result, pacifist organizations applied pressure on Congress to enact a series of laws that would "insure" that the United States would never again go to war "against its will." These laws renounced the rights of neutrals in time of war, rights that had formed a cornerstone of American foreign policy since independence.

1935: Prohibited the sale or transport of munitions to belligerents by Americans, and withdrew American protection from citizens who traveled on belligerent ships or in war zones.
1936: Prohibited loans to belligerents.

1937: Modified the 1935 measure to permit "cash-and-carry" sales of certain goods to belligerents (i.e., they had to pay hard currency and take the goods away in their own ships).
1939: Authorized the president to prohibit US-flagships from entering "danger zones" in order to prevent international incidents likely to lead to war.

The Neutrality Acts were the culmination of the 1920s effort to legislate peace. Their primary effect was to encourage aggression. These laws helped convince both HITLER and the Japanese militarists that the United States lacked the moral courage for war.

The acts proved a serious impediment to assisting the Allies when World War II broke out. Only gradually, as the threat of Axis aggression grew, were the provisions of the law modified, culminating in LEND-LEASE.

Nevada Class, US Battleships

Old battleships, but well designed and a significant advance on the previous NEW YORK CLASS, they introduced a new armoring scheme, the "Nevada Plan," in which protection was on the "all or nothing" basis: Absolutely vital areas of the ship were given extremely heavy protection (13.5-inch side armor with 18 inches on the turret faces), while everything else was ignored. Both served with the ROYAL NAVY during World War I, although they saw no action. Between the wars they were extensively rebuilt.

Nevada, BB-36 (1912–1914–1916), was the only battleship to get underway during the PEARL HARBOR attack; she incurred heavy damage and was beached rather than risk having her sink in the narrow harbor entrance. Raised, she was extensively rebuilt and emerged as a very successful ship, in appearance surprisingly similar to the SOUTH DAKOTA CLASS. She saw action at Attu, then operated in the European Theater, helping support the Normandy invasion, and returned to the Pacific, where she continued to support amphibious operations. She took a KAMIKAZE off OKINAWA. After the war she was used as a target in the Bikini nuclear weapons tests, and finally sunk in weapons trials in 1948.

OKLAHOMA, BB-37 (1912–1914–1916), was struck hard below the waterline at Pearl Harbor and capsized. Hundreds of men trapped below were rescued through holes hastily cut in her bottom, but others could not be reached and died there. She became the object of one of the largest salvage operations in history, and after her hull was sealed while still under water, on 16 June 1943 she righted by a series of 21 bents, massive frames mounted right on her hull, linked to enormous winches ashore. It was determined that she was not worth repairing and she was sold for scrap. Shortly after the war she was being towed to the United States when she broke loose in a storm about 500 miles northwest of Hawaii, and was never seen again.

New Britain, Bismarck Archipelago

The largest of the BISMARCKS, an archipelago to the northeast of New Guinea, of which it was administratively a part under an Australian mandate dating from World War I. About 14,600 square miles, the island was very undeveloped and thinly inhabited, but RABAUL, the principal town, had a fine harbor, with numerous nearby sites suitable for airfields.

On January 26, 1942, Japanese troops landed on New Britain and seized the major anchorage at Simpson Harbor, Rabaul. The Japanese proceeded to make Rabaul a major military base. The Allies decided to bypass Rabaul rather than assault it directly. This approach, called operation CART-WHEEL required landing on New Britain Island to establish bases from which to isolate Rabaul. The first landings, by the US Army's 112th Cavalry Regiment, took place on 15 December 1943, 280 miles west of Rabaul itself. On December 26, the First Marine Division landed on the opposite side of the island from the army landing. The Japanese had a few thousand troops from their 17th Division on that part of New Britain, and these were either

killed or forced back to the eastern (Rabaul) end of New Britain. By April 1943, the fighting was over on New Britain. The original invading troops were withdrawn, and a variety of other US Army and Australian units were sent to maintain a presence on New Britain until the end of the war, keeping watch on the Japanese pocket at Rabaul.

New Britain was a terrible place to campaign. Hot, humid, full of jungle and swamp, it was an unhealthy and very uncomfortable place to live. At the time, and ever since, it was suggested that no invasion of New Britain take place, for there was little the Japanese could do on the island once supplies of fuel and munitions could no longer get through.

New Caledonia

A French colony, New Caledonia is a group of islands about 750 miles east of Australia and 870

Marines struggle with a 3-foot surf as they wade ashore at Cape Gloucester, New Britain, December 26, 1943.

Cape Gloucester, January 1944, Marines armed with the Browning .50 caliber heavy machine gun. During January the Japanese launched several determined counterattacks on the Marine positions at Cape Gloucester. These were beaten off by machine-gun and artillery fire, and the Japanese withdrew into the jungle, abandoning their efforts to eject the Marines.

north of New Zealand, totaling about 7,400 square miles, most of it in New Caledonia proper (c. 6,500 square miles). Mountainous, but pleasantly tropical, the islands were thinly inhabited. When the Pacific War broke out the Free French administration placed them at the disposal of the United States, which used them as a staging area for the offensive into the SOLOMONS during 1942, developing the capital of NOUMEA into a major base.

New Guinea

The second largest island in the world (after Greenland), lying in the southwest Pacific, north of Australia and east of the NETHERLANDS EAST INDIES. The rugged, wet, tropical, and jungle-clad island is about 300,000 square miles. The population was very sparse: By one estimate there were only about 6,000 persons of European stock and 500,000 Melanesians in Papua, the southeastern quarter of the island. Much of New Guinea was largely unexplored on the eve of World War II. Mostly covered by jungle, there were virtually no roads, with a few airfields here and there hacked out of the jungle by ambitious miners. A rugged chain of mountains more or less completely divides the northern side of the island from the southern.

Extremes of climate are common in highland areas, with steamy, tropical days and chilly temperate nights making for an interesting contrast. A great many poisonous plants and animals were to be found, as well as a variety of interesting tropical diseases. Most of the inhabitants were Melanesians, belonging to numerous warlike tribes more or less living in the Neolithic Age and enormously suspicious of outsiders (those miners had not always been peaceful).

The western half of the island was owned by the Netherlands and administered as part of the Netherlands East Indies, although it was ethnically and culturally distinct from the other Dutch holdings. With the Japanese invasion, the Dutch presence in the island virtually evaporated. Although US and Australian forces paid lip service to Netherlands' sovereignty, they generally conducted themselves with little regard for the token Dutch presence.

Australia owned Papua, the southeastern quarter of the island, which was organized as a territory of the Commonwealth. It also controlled the northeastern portion of the island through a League of Nations MANDATE, which required it to prepare the territory for eventual independence. With the Japanese invasion, the administrative differences between the two Australian territories tended to become blurred.

The Japanese invaders were ill-prepared for what they found in New Guinea. Relations with the natives deteriorated rapidly. The Japanese penchant for casual massacre and their efforts to recruit COMFORT WOMEN rapidly drove even the most anti-white Papuans and New Guineans to support the king's men over the emperor's. As a result, for most of the protracted New Guinea Campaign—and fighting on the enormous island was more or less continuous from mid-1942 to the end of the war—the natives were generally friendly to the allies.

Prior to the outbreak of the war, Australia had developed rudimentary armed forces in both Papua and New Guinea, which were later merged into the PACIFIC ISLANDS REGIMENT.

New Guinea, Campaign for, 1942–43

While GUADALCANAL is generally regarded as the pivotal land battle in the first year of the Pacific War, it was actually only an extension of operations in New Guinea, which was the main campaign in the South Pacific.

New Guinea, a large tropical island north of Australia, was, before the war, controlled by Holland (the western half) and Australia (the rest). Smaller groups of islands extended to the northeast (the BISMARCKS) and southeast (the SOLOMONS, at virtually the tail end of which was Guadalcanal). All these were considered vital parts of the Japanese defensive system.

New Guinea was the scene of some of the longest and toughest ground combat of the Pacific War. The Japanese landed on the north coast of in early March 1942. The Australians (and later Americans) were on the south coast. Fighting first raged in the OWEN STANLEY MOUNTAINS, which form the rugged spine of New Guinea. This fighting combined the worst aspects of jungle and mountain combat. The Japanese had managed to struggle over the mountains against Australian rearguard resistance, but had been halted literally a few dozen miles north of PORT MORESBY, the principal Allied base in New Guinea. Then they fell back, in an agonizing retreat that cost the lives of many men.

By late 1942, the fighting was concentrated on Japanese positions on the north coast. This fighting continued into 1944 as the Japanese continually reinforced their battered forces, while American and Australian forces "leap frogged" their way along the coast, isolating Japanese strongpoints. The Allied objective was to push the Japanese off New Guinea and keep advancing west to the nearby Japanese-controlled oil fields. Japanese pockets in New Guinea were still being guarded into 1945. The fighting and maneuvering was constant, with dozens of amphibious landings and hundreds of battles on land and in the air. It was during this campaign that the US Army Air Force developed the successful tactic of using the twin-engine B-25 bomber to attack Japanese shipping.

New Guinea was something of a forgotten battle. Partially this was because of the way the media worked. New Guinea was almost wholly an army affair with few Marines and relatively little naval action. In addition, even more than Guadalcanal, New Guinea was a protracted, grinding jungle campaign, characterized by mud, heat, and disease. New Guinea was a tropical meatgrinder of constant combat through steaming jungles and steep mountains. All the aircraft operated from primitive, often mud-soaked airfields. While Guadalcanal was over in six months, New Guinea went on for years. In the eyes of the American public, New Guinea soon became dreary. That attitude carried on in the public's memory after the war.

Although the New Guinea fighting did more to cripple the Japanese armed forces, Guadalcanal still rated higher in the pantheon of Pacific battles.

Ref: *Australia in the Second World War: Series I, Army*, vols. 4 and 6; Prefer, *MacArthur's New Guinea Campaign*.

New Hebrides

Now called Vanuatu, a group of about 75 islands, atolls, and islets in the southwest Pacific, about a

Troops of the 163rd Infantry, 41st Infantry Division, land at Wadke Island, May 18, 1944, increasing the isolation of Japanese forces on New Guinea.

A US Signal Corps cameraman, T4 Ernani d'Emidio, took this shot of two of his comrades, Sgt. Carl Weinke and PFC Marjoram, as they waded in a stream in New Guinea on April 22, 1944. The terrain is fairly typical of the coastal areas of New Guinea, where fighting continued throughout the war.

thousand miles northeast of Australia. Three of the islands (Efate, ESPIRITU SANTO, and Tana) were of importance, and they comprised most of the 5,700 square miles of the group. Thinly inhabited by Melanesians (Port Vila, the capital and largest settlement, on Efate, had only about 1,500 inhabitants in 1942), the islands were jointly owned by Britain and France, and made a poor living off of tropical produce and fishing.

A small US force landed at Efate from NOUMEA, in NEW CALEDONIA, in March 1942. From May 1942, Efate began to be developed as a major base, and by July 1942 US troops were developing airstrips on Espiritu Santo, the largest and most

northerly of the islands. With GUADALCANAL less than 600 miles to the northwest, Espiritu Santo soon became the most important US base in the South Pacific outside of Australia, and it remained so until the fighting moved up the chain of the SOLOMONS in 1943.

During the war there was no fighting in the New Hebrides. Japanese SUBMARINES were active in the area, however, and laid many MINES, which did cause some losses to Allied shipping. About 1,300 residents were recruited as labor troops. The war brought considerable prosperity to the islands, and a great deal of political and social change.

Ref: White and Lindstrom, *The Pacific Theater*.

New Mexico Class, US Battleships

The New Mexico Class battleships were substantially similar in design to the preceding PENNSYLVANIA CLASS, although much different in appearance. In the Atlantic in December of 1941, they were spared the trauma of PEARL HARBOR, and also the extensive modernization that the veterans of that disaster underwent, so that aside from numerous additions to their antiaircraft armament, they remained substantially unmodernized. All three were sent to the Pacific shortly after Pearl Harbor, where they formed part of the battle force that would have been all that remained had the Japanese won the carrier fight at MIDWAY. They spent the rest of the war supporting amphibious landings.

New Mexico, BB-40 (1915–1917–1918), was scrapped in 1947.

Mississippi, BB-41 (1915–1917–1917), fired one salvo at SURIGAO STRAIT, during the Battle of LEYTE GULF, and that the last one, after a cease-fire had been ordered. By some calculations these shells were the last rounds to strike *Yamashiro*, and so she has the distinction of being the last battlewagon to hit another in action. After the war she served as a test-bed for shipboard missile experimentation, until scrapped in 1957.

Idaho, BB-42 (1915–1917–1919), was scrapped in 1947.

New Orleans Class, US Heavy Cruisers

Representing a significant break with the earlier series of US heavy cruisers, the New Orleans Class were much better protected, among other things having a proper turret, rather than the turret-like gun shield that characterized earlier US heavy cruisers. In another divergence from earlier designs, the three 8–inch guns in each turret were mounted individually, rather than on a single sleeve. Although cramped, they were very good ships. They cost $14–15 million each. Despite their superior design, three of them became war losses in less than five minutes in the Battle of SAVO ISLAND on the night of August 9–10, 1942, no design being able to ensure against over-confidence, inexperience, bad luck, and a daring foe.

New Orleans, CA-32 (1931–1933–1934), escorted carrier task forces in the early months of the war, fighting at the CORAL SEA, Tassafaronga, (where she lost her bow), and Cape Engaño, among other actions. Scrapped in 1959.

Astoria, CA-34 (1930–1933–1934), escorted carrier task forces in the early months of the war, fighting at the Coral Sea, and later at Savo Island, where she was sunk.

Minneapolis, CA-36 (1931–1933–1934), helped escort carrier task forces in the early months of the war, was at the Coral Sea, Tassafaronga (like *New Orleans*, she lost her bow), and elsewhere. Scrapped in 1960.

Tuscaloosa, CA-37 (1931–1933–1934), served mostly in the Atlantic and ETO, supporting landings. Reached the Pacific in early 1945 and supported the fast carriers until the end of the war. Scrapped in 1959.

San Francisco, CA-38 (1931–1933–1934), survived Pearl Harbor with little damage, and went on to serve as Norman SCOTT's flagship at CAPE ESPERANCE, and Dan CALLAGHAN's in the First Naval Battle of GUADALCANAL, where the latter was killed, and the ship seriously damaged. Repaired, she returned to service and escorted fast carrier task forces until the end of the war. Scrapped in 1961.

Quincy, CA-39 (1933–1935–1936), was in the Atlantic at the start of the war. Shortly transferred to the Pacific, she supported the Guadalcanal landings and was sunk at Savo Island.

Vincennes, CA-44 (1934–1936–1937), was in the Atlantic when Pearl Harbor was attacked; she reached the Pacific in time to help cover the Guadalcanal landings and was sunk at Savo Island.

New York Class, US Battleships

America's first "super dreadnoughts," *New York* and *Texas* were a disappointment even when new. Although they served with Britain's Grand Fleet in 1917–18, they saw no combat in World War I. Modified somewhat between the world wars, by World War II they were not considered worth extensive reconstruction. Despite this, they saw considerable service. Until late 1944 both ships were in the European Theater, providing gunfire support for landings from North Africa to Normandy to the Riviera, *Texas* gaining the distinction of pounding a major coast defense installation at Cherbourg into rubble with only minor injury to herself, a rare occurrence in naval history. They then passed into the Pacific, where they rendered good service supporting the landings at IWO JIMA and OKINAWA.

New York (1911–1912–1914) was expended in the Bikini ATOMIC BOMB tests.

Texas (1911–1912–1914) is preserved as a war memorial near the San Jacinto battlefield in Texas.

New Zealand, Commonwealth of

Two large and numerous small islands about 1,200 miles east-southeast of Australia, New Zealand totals about 172,000 square miles. Possessed of an advanced agricultural economy, with some industry, in 1940 New Zealand was a self-governing member of the British Commonwealth. Despite having a population of only about 1.2 million, the New Zealand armed forces managed to reach a strength of 157,000 during the war, a remarkable 13.1% of the population under arms. Of these about 40,000 served in the Commonwealth, 75,000 in North Africa and Italy, and about 40,000 in the various Pacific campaigns.

Ref: Gillespie, *Official History of New Zealand in the Second World War, 1939–1945, The Pacific.*

New Zealand Army

On the outbreak of World War II, New Zealand, which had a very small regular army supported by a division's worth of militia (mostly World War I veterans), promptly raised a division of volunteers and dispatched it to the Mediterranean, where it covered itself with glory in North Africa and Italy. This left only the militia and some miscellaneous units to guard against invasion. Attempts to raise another field division were only partially successful. As a result, New Zealand's contribution to the ground war in the Pacific was small, ultimately involving a number of brigade-sized actions in which the Kiwis greatly distinguished themselves.

New Zealand also maintained small garrisons on numerous tiny Pacific islands, such as Fanning, Norfolk, and the like, as well as provided the cadres and advisers for Fijian and TONGAN forces.

First New Zealand Division. A militia unit composed of World War I veterans, the division performed security and garrison duties in New Zealand during the war.

Second New Zealand Division. Raised in late 1940, the division was sent to North Africa in the spring of 1941, and saw almost continuous combat there, in Greece, and in Italy until the end of the war. It was commonly referred to as "the New Zealand Division."

Third New Zealand Division. Raised from volunteers in mid–1942, the division was never completely formed. Comprising only two brigades, it was committed to operations on VELLA LAVELLA in September 1943, then went into action in the Treasury Islands in October-November 1943 and the Green Islands in February 1944. Shortly afterward the division was stood down, and disbanded in April 1944.

Eighth New Zealand Brigade. Formed in the spring of 1941, the brigade was on garrison duty in the FIJI ISLANDS at the outbreak of the Pacific War. It formed the core about which the Third Division was activated, and saw extensive service in the Solomon Islands and NEW GUINEA.

14th New Zealand Brigade. Formed in October 1942 on Fiji as part of the new Third New Zealand Division, the brigade saw extensive service in the SOLOMONS.

15th New Zealand Brigade. This was activated briefly in 1943, to be the third brigade of the Third New Zealand Division. A shortage of manpower

New Zealand Navy, Royal

caused the brigade to be disbanded on NEW CALE-
DONIA in early 1943.

Ref: Gillespie, *Official History of New Zealand in
the Second World War, 1939–1945, The Pacific.*

New Zealand Navy, Royal

The Royal New Zealand Navy was a small force,
never consisting of more than a few cruisers and
some corvettes (small destroyer-escort type vessels). It was a thoroughly professional force, however, and its ships fought in some of the toughest
actions of the war, HMNZS *Achilles* taking part in
the Battle of the River Plate in December 1939,
against the German "pocket battleship" *Graf Spee*,
while LEANDER was heavily damaged at Kolombangara in 1943. For most of the Pacific War the
RNZN served in the Solomons and East Indies, and
by the end of the war was operating virtually as an
integral part of the US Navy.

Ref: Gillespie, *Official History of New Zealand in
the Second World War, 1939–1945, The Pacific.*

Newcastle, Australia

A small but good harbor, with facilities to service
most merchant ships, albeit in limited numbers,
and an important air base, located on the northeastern coast of Australia, giving it some value as
a base for the domination of the CORAL SEA.

Nicobar Islands

South of the ANDAMANS and east of India, in the
Bay of Bengal. The 19 islands total only about 635
square miles. In 1940 they were a thinly inhabited,
primitive place, and were easily captured by the
Japanese, the British making no effort to defend
them. Nor did the British bother attempting to
eject the Japanese, so that their garrison was starving by the end of the war.

Niigata, Honshu, Japan

A small port, Niigata had a naval base suitable for
light forces and an air base.

Nimitz, Chester W., Sr. (1885–1966)

Chester W. Nimitz graduated from Annapolis in
1905 and embarked upon a career in SUBMARINES,
rising to command the Atlantic Fleet submarine
flotilla by 1912. The following year he toured various European nations, studying submarine development, and returned to build the first diesel
engine for the US Navy. During World War I he
served as chief of staff to the commander of Atlantic Fleet submarines. After the war he attended the
Naval War College, served on various staffs, and
rose steadily upward. At the time of PEARL HARBOR
he was chief of the Bureau of Navigation (i.e., personnel), from which post he was almost immedi-

*Admiral Chester W. Nimitz Sr., seen here decorating
Pearl Harbor hero Dorie Miller with the Navy Cross,
May 27, 1942.*

ately made commander of the Pacific Fleet, to which, in early 1942, he added command of all US forces in the central and North Pacific, as well as responsibility for coordinating operations with Douglas MACARTHUR in the southwest Pacific.

Nimitz oversaw all US operations in the Pacific for the entire war, approving STRATEGY, selecting personnel, ensuring the flow of men, ships, and materiel, and working with surprising smoothness with the egocentric MacArthur. After the war he was chief of naval operations until his retirement in late 1947. He later served as a special assistant to the secretary of the navy, as director of the UN plebiscite in Kashmir, and wrote a reasonably sound history of the Pacific War. A capable man, Nimitz was flexible in command and willing to listen to others, even when it annoyed him. Although a non-flyer, he recognized the logic behind John TOWERS' argument that all "black shoe" (non-aviation) officers should have a "brown shoe" (aviation) adviser and acted on it. His relaxed, almost informal style of command masked a great deal of toughness. Like his arch-foe YAMAMOTO, Nimitz had been injured in the service, and was missing the ring finger of his left hand. He had a schnauzer named Makalepa.

The admiral's son, LtCdr Chester W. Nimitz Jr., served in submarines in the Pacific, rising to command of *Hake* (SS-256), in which he accounted for a number of Japanese ships, including the destroyer *Kazagumo*. An occasional and forthcoming critic of his father's decisions, the younger Nimitz was also one of the officers instrumental in improving the malfunctioning US TORPEDO exploder during the war. After the war he rose to rear admiral.

Ning Hai Class, Chinese Light Cruisers

These Chinese light cruisers were to be built with Japanese assistance, which dried up during the project. Small for light cruisers, hardly larger than some oversized destroyers, and slow, their best trial speed only 24 knots, they were the largest, most modern, and most powerful ships in the Chinese Navy.

Both ships were sunk in the Yangtze River by Japanese air attacks on 23 September 1937. The sunken vessels were soon captured by the Japanese. Raised and repaired, they were turned over to the collaborationist Wang government in 1939. In 1943 the two ships were taken over by the Japanese Navy, and performed escort duties in the China Sea and in Japanese waters.

Ning Hai (1930–1931–1932) was built in a Japanese shipyard; after being transferred to the Japanese Navy in 1943 she was renamed *Ioshima*. She was sunk by the US submarine *Shad* (SS-235) while on convoy escort south of Honshu on 19 September 1944.

Ping Hai (1931–1935–1936) was built in a Chinese shipyard, initially with Japanese technical assistance, which was not forthcoming after 1933. The project languished until 1935, when the German Naval Mission to China took it over. As a result, she differed in some details from her sister, and had German antiaircraft guns, the Japanese having refused to deliver on the weapons originally ordered. She became *Yasoshima* in Japanese service and was sunk by US aircraft in Santa Cruz Bay, Luzon, on 25 November 1944.

Nishimura, Shoji (1889–1944)

Shoji Nishimura graduated from the Japanese naval academy in 1911. He had a satisfactory, but by no means distinguished career thereafter, rising slowly upward. At the beginning of the war he was a rear admiral. Nishimura commanded light cruiser and destroyer units through many of the 1941–42 operations, including the invasion of the Philippines and the East Indies. By 1944 he was a vice admiral and led the task force of two older battleships, one cruiser, and four destroyers that managed to avoid detection until it was in SURIGAO STRAIT and then headed for the American invasion force off Leyte. Nishimura kept coming despite enormous American fire. He went down with his flagship, the battleship *Yamashiro*, on 25 October 1944—". . . one of the least competent Japanese flag officers," according to Samuel Eliot MORISON.

Nixon, Richard M. (1913–1994)

A member of the Naval Reserve, Nixon went on active duty as a lieutenant junior grade in June 1942. He served in various administrative posts associated with naval aviation, and from January to June 1944 was commander of the South Pacific Combat Air Transport Command in the Northern SOLOMONS, in which capacity he earned a citation for "meritorious and efficient performance." He ended the war as a lieutenant commander on the staff of the Bureau of Aeronautics, in Washington. Entering politics, he became vice president under EISENHOWER (1953–61), lost the presidential election of 1960, won that of 1968 and that of 1972, but subsequently resigned due to the Watergate scandal in 1974.

Noemfoor Island

Just north of NEW GUINEA, Noemfoor had no port, but had a good anchorage and lots of room for airfields, which made it a valuable objective during MACARTHUR's drive up the New Guinea coast. The Allies developed it into an important base.

Norfolk Class, British Heavy Cruisers

The principal difference between the Norfolks and earlier British heavy cruisers lay in improved turret design and ammunition handling arrangements. The ships were involved in numerous actions in the Atlantic, including the final battle with the German battleship *Bismarck*, in May 1941, delivering the coup de grace with TORPEDOES.

Doresetshire (1927–1929–1930) joined the British Far Eastern Fleet in early 1942. On 5 April, while in company with HMS *Cornwall*, she was caught off CEYLON by Japanese carrier aircraft, who hit her with about 10 250–550 pound bombs, which caused a magazine explosion that sank her in about eight minutes.

Norfolk (1927–1928–1930) served in the ETO, once surviving two 11-inch rounds from the German battleship *Scharnhorst*. Scrapped in 1950.
See also ROYAL NAVY.

Normandie, SS

French ocean liner, a floating art deco palace, and at some 85,000 GRT matched in size only by QUEEN MARY and *Queen Elizabeth*. Interned in the United States upon the fall of France in 1940, she was taken over by the navy, renamed *Lafayette*, and converted into a troop transport (alternate proposals were to convert her into a carrier, a fate suggested for several other liners, until the army convinced the navy of the desperate need for troop transport). While completing her fitting out at the 44th Street dock on the North River in New York a fire began in the former ballroom when a welder's torch ignited one of 15,000 kapok life jackets stored there. Within hours she had been reduced to a burned out, sunken wreck. Although raised, she was never repaired and was sold for scrap.

Arguably, had she entered service she might have helped shorten the war appreciably, since like the Queens she could carry a division's worth of manpower overseas at very high speed.

North Carolina Class, US Battleships

Designed within the limitations imposed by the naval DISARMAMENT TREATIES, the two ships of the North Carolina Class were arguably technically superior to those of the succeeding SOUTH DAKOTA CLASS. They were good sea boats, handy, relatively fast, and had a tremendous main battery.

North Carolina, BB-55 (1937–1940–1941), was the first US battleship to enter service since *West Virginia* in 1923. Built at the Brooklyn Navy Yard, she was nicknamed the "Show Boat" almost as soon as she entered service. She saw some escort duty in the Atlantic before going to the Pacific in June 1942. Her first combat mission was supporting the carriers covering the GUADALCANAL landings, and helping defend the carriers during the Battle of the EASTERN SOLOMONS. She took a torpedo on September 15, 1942, in the same attack that sank the carrier WASP and destroyer *O'Brien*, and did not return to service until early December. Although often escorting carrier task forces or providing cover for operations, she did not see combat again until the MARSHALL ISLANDS Campaign in early 1944. Thereafter she bombarded shore targets in several invasions, fought in the Battle of the PHILIPPINE SEA, and helped bombard OKINAWA and the Japanese Home Islands. She was laid up after the war, and eventually preserved as a war memorial at Wilmington, North Carolina.

Washington, BB-56 (1938–1940–1941), served with the ROYAL NAVY, covering convoys to Iceland and Northern Russia in the spring of 1942, and passed into the Pacific in midsummer. She supported operations in the SOLOMONS, most notably in the shootout with a Japanese squadron off Guadalcanal on November 14–15, 1942, when, using radar fire control, she put nine 16-inch rounds (of 117 fired) and 55 5-inch rounds into the Japanese *Kirishima* in a few minutes, turning her into a burning wreck—the largest sustained series of broadsides ever fired by a US battlewagon. She thereafter escorted carrier task forces and bombarded Japanese installations until the end of the war, when she was pressed into service as a troop transport. She was scrapped in 1961.

See also GUADALCANAL, NAVAL BATTLES.

Northampton Class, US Heavy Cruisers

The second version of the US "Treaty Cruiser," the Northamptons were somewhat better protected than the PENSACOLAS. This was achieved by dispensing with one 8–inch gun, reducing the total to nine mounted in three turrets, the weight saved on the fourth turret and tenth gun being put into protection. They cost about $12 million, slightly more than their predecessors. Prewar modifications removed their TORPEDO tubes but enhanced their antiaircraft protection. All saw hard service, notably as escorts to the fast carriers and during the GUADALCANAL campaign in 1942–43, and three became war losses. Despite their rather light protection, they were tough ships.

Northampton, CA-26 (1928–1928–1930), escorted carrier task forces at MIDWAY and SANTA CRUZ, then served in the Solomons, where she was sunk off SAVO ISLAND on 30 November 1942, during the Battle of TASSAFARONGA.

Chester, CA-27 (1928–1929–1930), saw extensive service during the war, and was seriously damaged by a torpedo from the submarine *I-176* on 20 October 1942, in the Solomons. Survived the war to be scrapped in 1959.

Louisville, CA-28 (1928–1930–1931), spent most of the war escorting carriers, and was broken up in 1960.

Chicago, CA-29 (1928–1930–1931), was fitted as a flagship; she survived numerous actions, including Savo Island, where she took a torpedo. She was sunk on 30 January 1943, during the Battle of the Russell Islands.

Houston, CA-30 (1928–1929–1930), was fitted as a flagship, and was serving as such for the Asiatic Fleet when the war broke out. She was heavily engaged in the struggle for the NETHERLANDS EAST INDIES in the early months of the war, proving herself an enormously valuable asset to the ABDA command. During one action her antiaircraft fire was so intense some observers thought she was on fire. After fighting in the Battle of the JAVA SEA (February 27, 1942), she was sunk in the Sunda Strait early on March 1, 1942, having absorbed at least four torpedoes and scores of 8-inch and 5-inch rounds, in what Samuel Eliot MORISON called one of the most "gallant fights in the history of the United States Navy."

Augusta, CA-31 (1928–1930–1931), also fitted as a flagship, was President ROOSEVELT's favorite ship (the famous picture of him reviewing the fleet in his long cape was taken on her bridge), and she took him to Argentia Bay for a conference with CHURCHILL that resulted in the Atlantic Charter. The only US prewar heavy cruiser not to see action in the Pacific, she served throughout the European War, offering gunfire support to landings from North Africa to Normandy. She was broken up for scrap in 1960.

See also JAPAN, ATTITUDE TOWARD THE ENEMY.

Noumea, New Caledonia

The capital of New Caledonia, Noumea had a fairly good port for the region, and was located so as to give it potential as a naval and air base for control of the CORAL SEA and the southern SOL-OMONS. Though cramped and of limited capacity, there were extensive sheltered anchorages in the area. There was a small French naval and air base. Noumea served as a vital forward base early in the war.

O

O'Callaghan, Joseph (1904–1964)

A Roman Catholic priest and chaplain, O'Callaghan was aboard the USS *Franklin* (CV-13) when she was hit and suffered over 700 men killed in a few minutes off the coast of Honshu on March 19, 1945. Fr. O'Callaghan organized fire fighting parties, helped heave burning ammunition overboard, and rescued the wounded, while also finding time to administer the last rites to the dying. He was awarded a MEDAL OF HONOR.

Officer Training, Japanese

Throughout history, in most armies the officers were generally taller than the troops. This was because the officers were usually recruited from the wealthier classes, folk who could afford a better diet. As a result, the officers tended to be taller than the less well fed troops. This was not the case in the Japanese Army. Officers had to pass through the dreaded military academy at Ichigaya. Here the day began at 5:30 A.M. and went on relentlessly until 10 P.M. at night (unless there was night training, in which case the cadets would simply lose a night's sleep). Most officers began their officer training at special military grammar and high schools. All stressed the same dedication to "spirit" rather than the mundane matters of flesh and blood. Physical training was a minor religion and, even in the winter, it was done barechested. Worst of all was the bland and skimpy rations. As a result, teenage cadets grew only half an inch in their adolescence, and gained about three pounds. The resulting officers were indeed a tough bunch, but their average size was 5 feet four inches and 128 pounds. Allied officers averaged nearly 30 pounds heavier and six inches taller. Postwar Japanese military officers are nearly as tall as Allied officers of that era, mainly because they are now fed better during training.

Oil

The war in the Pacific was started over oil. The Allies, mainly the Dutch, controlled the local supplies in Borneo and the NETHERLANDS EAST INDIES. In 1940, these areas produced 65 million barrels a year. At the time, the major global producer was the United States, with over 1.3 billion barrels a year. America and the Dutch Borneo fields were Japan's sole source of oil. When this supply was cut off in the summer of 1941, in an attempt to stop Japanese aggression, Japan responded by attacking America and seizing the Dutch oil fields in Borneo and Sumatra. Because of the demolition of many of the oil facilities, the Japanese were able to pump only 25.9 million barrels in 1942. By 1943 they were getting 49.6. The major problem then became getting the oil refined and back to Japan. American SUBMARINES proved capable of sinking Japanese tankers faster than new oil transports could be built. While warships could use the Borneo oil right out of the ground, trucks and aircraft needed refined product. It was easier to carry the refined products back to Japan, than to haul larger quantities of crude oil back to Japan-based refineries. But the ultimate bottleneck was tankers.

PREWAR JAPANESE ESTIMATE OF OIL AVAILABILITY AND CONSUMPTION (MILLIONS OF BARRELS)			
War Year	Reserve	Production	Consumption*
1st	61.1	5.0	37.8
2nd	28.3	12.9	34.6
3rd	6.6	23.6	34.6
4th	4.4	30.0	34.6

*Note that the figures do not tally for the 3rd and 4th year, a "clerical error" the Japanese leadership appears to have overlooked.

JAPANESE COAL OIL PRODUCTION (MILLIONS OF BARRELS)	
Year	Output
1937	0.03 (The goal was .15 bbl)
1941	1.50
1942	N/A
1943	1.05
1944	1.20
1945	N/A

In December of 1941 the Japanese had about 61 million barrels stockpiled, enough to run the armed forces for about two years at peacetime levels of consumption. In mid-'41 they made what they considered careful calculations as to their oil needs and resources in the coming war.

Although the Japanese had made what they thought were conservative estimates of wartime oil PRODUCTION and consumption, these proved wildly optimistic. For example, peacetime imports from the Dutch East Indies were about 17.7 million barrels a year. The Japanese estimated that in the first year of the war they would be able to import only about 15.4 million barrels, due to destruction of the facilities and whatnot, but that by the third year they could crank it up to about 30.0 million barrels. In fact, they were never able to even approach the prewar figure. There were several reasons for this. The destruction of production and storage facilities was greater than expected, although it could have been worse. In addition, the Japanese do not seem to have understood the complexities of the oil industry.

They were short of technical personnel, various important chemicals, and spare parts, most of which were imported from Europe or America in the prewar period. Worse yet, one of the few cargo ships sunk early in the war was the one carrying Japanese refinery technicians and their equipment. As a result of all this they ran out of oil a lot faster than they expected.

The actual figures for oil production and consumption are quite interesting.

By the end of 1944 the Japanese had more or less run out of fuel. It is, however, interesting to note that their estimates for production in War Years 2 and 3 were not far off the mark. That they kept things going after 1944 is a testimony to their ability to scrounge unaccounted oil stocks. Where they failed was in estimating consumption, which was much higher than predicted. Surprisingly, there had been a minority opinion on this in the Japanese military. Although overruled before the war, this group had managed to convince the brass that an experimental coal oil production program might be useful in an emergency. Although the program was supposed to yield several million barrels a year, it never approached its goal, due largely to a lack of genuine interest and a shortage of resources.

In short, Japan began the war short of resources, and steadily fell further and further behind.

Okamura, Yasutsugu

Yasutsugu Okamura joined the Japanese Army in 1904. By the outbreak of the Pacific War he was

ACTUAL OIL AVAILABILITY AND CONSUMPTION (MILLIONS OF BARRELS)			
End of	Reserve	Production	Consumption
1941	61.1	—	—
1942	52.86	12.5	51.92
1943	14.47	20.1	41.7
1944	−8.1	9.6	29.5
1945	−28.0		

commander of the North China Area Army and a full general. At the end of 1944 Okamura took command of all Japanese forces in China. At the end of the war he surrendered to CHIANG KAI-SHEK and spent several years assisting the Nationalist Chinese in their civil war with the communists, whom he fervently hated. His postwar service in China allowed him to return to Japan in 1949 and become involved in the creation of Japan's "Self Defense Forces."

Okinawa, Battle of

On April 1, 1945, Easter Sunday, the last major battle of World War II began. This was the American invasion of the island of Okinawa, one of the smaller islands that were considered part of the Japanese Home Islands. Actually, it wasn't, as Okinawa had maintained itself as an independent kingdom until the 1870s, when the Japanese forcibly annexed it. Okinawa had a population of half a million at the time of the invasion, plus a garrison of 110,000 troops. The American force was 287,000 strong, of which over 60% were combat troops in four army infantry and three Marine divisions. The Japanese had learned from earlier island battles. They now realized that it was not wise to resist on the beaches, where American warships could deliver devastating firepower at point-blank range. Better to build defenses inland, where Japanese troops could do their usual "fight to the death" routine to maximum effect. So it was on Okinawa.

The initial landings, by 60,000 troops in two army and two Marine divisions, were essentially unopposed. Japanese air attacks were there from the beginning, however. On the second day a Japanese airfield was captured and friendly aircraft began operating from it. By 4 April Japanese resistance became more determined. US troops were now encountering the massive Japanese fortification system inland. The bloodbath had begun and would continue until 22 June, when the battle was declared over, though some Japanese holdout troops remained active even after the war ended.

On 6 April, the first major KAMIKAZE attack was launched. Only 24 of 355 suicide planes got through, but they caused a lot of damage. So much antiaircraft fire was put out that eight US ships were damaged by FRIENDLY FIRE. On 7 April, a Japanese task force was intercepted by 900 US aircraft before it could reach Okinawa. Japan's largest battleship, the 72,000-ton YAMATO, was sunk, along with a cruiser and four destroyers. The Japanese also lost 54 escorting aircraft. Only 10 US aircraft were lost. During the entire Okinawa campaign, Japan lost at least 180 ships, from small subchasers and transports up to major warships.

During the first two weeks of April, US forces on Okinawa probed Japanese defenses and prepared for a major offensive. On April 18, Ernie PYLE, one of the most famous World War II reporters, was killed by a sniper on an island off Okinawa. On 19 April, US forces made a major push, accompanied by heavy naval gunfire and air bombardment. For the rest of April the fighting raged. But the well-dug-in Japanese could be routed only with great effort. The fighting continued into May, with a small Japanese amphibious force making a landing behind US lines on 3 May. This was in conjunction with many Japanese counterattacks. As scary as this was to US troops, it was easier to kill Japanese troops out in the open than in their fortifications.

Throughout May, Japanese air attacks on US ships off Okinawa continued, with over 1,100 Japanese aircraft destroyed. On 5 May, the Japanese air attacks had their greatest success, sinking 17 US ships in 24 hours. The Japanese lost 131 aircraft in this effort. Their kamikaze tactics, first used six months earlier in the Philippines, were employed to maximum effect off Okinawa. Nearby airfields in Japan, as well as the supply of planes and pilots, also made it possible to use non-suicide aircraft attacks. Despite the hundreds of US carrier aircraft available, the Japanese did much damage to American shipping. Some 4,200 Japanese aircraft (1,900 of them kamikaze), went after the US fleet sinking 36 ships (all but two by kamikaze) and damaging 368 (only 164 by kamikaze). Overall, the Japanese

With the devastated ruins of recently captured Naha in the background, Sixth Marine Division commander, MG Lemuel Shepherd (1896–1990)—later the 22nd commandant of the Marine Corps—consults a map, late May 1945.

lost 7,830 aircraft during the Okinawa battle, versus US losses of some 800 planes.

The fighting on the ground remained intense for the first three weeks of May, but then two weeks of heavy rains came and this slowed operations down as US troops struggled to move supplies forward in the mud. Under cover of the rain, the Japanese landed paratroopers on 24 May. This desperate tactic was used against an American airfield on Okinawa, but succeeded in destroying only a few aircraft. On 28 May, the Japanese launched their last major air raid. Over a hundred Japanese aircraft were shot down and only one US ship was sunk.

On 5 June, a TYPHOON (Pacific hurricane) hit the US fleet off Okinawa. Severe damage was in-flicted on four battleships, eight carriers, seven cruisers, and 11 destroyers. Dozens of support ships were damaged. As the typhoon passed away, so did the rains. On 17 June, after two weeks of heavy fighting, the last line of Japanese fortifications was breached. The commander of the Japanese garrison, General KURIBAYASHI then committed suicide. On June 20, Japanese soldiers and civilians began to surrender in groups, something that had rarely happened before. In one case, a thousand Japanese gave up. Still, over 100,000 Japanese troops had fought to the death. On June 22, the battle for Okinawa was declared officially over.

The US Navy suffered its greatest number of CASUALTIES (some 10,000) in one operation while off Okinawa. Japanese deaths, including civilians, were well over 150,000. Some 7,000 Japanese troops surrendered, but thousands of civilians committed suicide rather than be captured. America suffered 12,281 combat deaths (including 4,907 navy). Over 50,000 Americans were wounded, plus over 14,000 combat fatigue casualties and nearly 30,000 noncombat casualties. It was the bloodiest campaign of the Pacific War. The high casualty rate of the Okinawa battle was a major factor in the decision to drop the ATOMIC BOMB on Japan. It was thought that an invasion of the main Japanese Home Islands would be even bloodier than Okinawa.

Okinawa, Ryukyu Islands

The largest of the RYUKYU ISLANDS (about 450 square miles) was the first victim of Japanese imperialism, the native dynasty being deposed in the 1870s and the islands forcibly incorporated into Japan. The site of important Japanese military installations by 1945, the principal reason for the American landings in the spring of that year was to seize the island as an advanced base for the pending invasion of Japan.

Olongapo, Luzon, Philippines

An important American naval base in the Philippines, Olongapo, on the northwestern side of Luzon, had a fair-sized harbor and considerable facilities to effect all but the most extensive repairs. It was also relatively isolated from Manila, the principal center of American military power in the islands, and only lightly defended. Hastily evacuated during the early stages of the Japanese invasion, whatever could not be withdrawn was sabotaged.

Omaha Class, US Light Cruisers

Although quite old, and no longer a match for contemporary light cruisers, the 10 Omahas, built 1918–25, were excellent ships, well designed, reliable, fast, maneuverable, and very seaworthy, even by World War II standards, albeit cramped. They gave excellent service in all theaters and, surprisingly, none became a war loss. Most served in the Atlantic and ETO, but several were heavily engaged in the Pacific:

Raleigh, CL-7 (1920–1922–1924), survived PEARL HARBOR with moderate damage and later served in the ALEUTIANS. Scrapped in 1946.

Richmond, CL-9 (1920–1921–1923), served in the Pacific for virtually the entire war, mostly in northern waters, where she took part in the Battle of the KOMANDORSKI ISLANDS. Scrapped in 1946.

Marblehead, CL-12 (1920–1923–1924), began the war with the Asiatic Fleet, and was so severely damaged off JAVA in February 1942 that she had to be sent home. She served thereafter in the Atlantic. Scrapped in 1945.

Onishi, Takejiro (1891–1945)

Takejiro Onishi, one of the militaristic "wild men" and the driving force behind Japanese carrier aviation, graduated from the naval academy in 1912. After flight training he was thrown out of the Naval College because of his enthusiasm for gambling and chasing women and went off to study in Britain and France for two years beginning in 1918. As one of the first Japanese naval aviators, he spent much of the 1920s and 1930s laying the foundation for the great carrier force that would forever change the nature of naval warfare, meanwhile finding time to become an ACE in China. Onishi not only

helped organize and train the carrier force, but was also instrumental in establishing much of the industrial base necessary to build and sustain it. He became a rear admiral in 1939, after having commanded land-based naval aviation units. In 1941 he worked on the plan for attacking PEARL HARBOR. His outspokenness about dumping battleships and building more aircraft and carriers prevented him from getting sea commands, and as a result he spent most of the war directing the construction of naval weapons and munitions. He became a vice admiral in 1944 and was given command of Japanese naval air forces in the Philippines. He went along with KAMIKAZE tactics because he was pragmatic, not because he believed the quasi-religious rhetoric. Onishi organized kamikaze operations in the Philippines through the end of 1944, when ordered to move himself and his staff to Taiwan. There he organized more kamikaze units, some of which operated during the battle for OKINAWA. When the emperor ordered the armed forces to surrender on August 15, 1945, Onishi chose suicide instead.

Order of Battle, Divisional, Outline

Although ground combat in the Pacific War was one of relatively small battles, the basic ground combat unit was still the division. Often the divisions were broken up to provide garrisons or assault forces for the many small islands fought over, but everyone still kept score by counting divisions. The divisions in the Pacific varied in size from about 4,500 men (Chinese) to as many as 20,000 (US Marines), depending upon their arm of service and nationality. Regardless of size, however, a division was supposed to be a more or less self-contained combat formation of all arms (infantry, armor, artillery, support troops) capable of some degree of sustained independent operations. The principal differences among the numerous types of division (infantry, armor, parachute, marine, and so forth) were due to the specialized missions to which they were dedicated. The vast majority of all divisions in the Pacific were infantry divisions. The US Marine division was basically an infantry division that was beefed up for amphibious assaults. There was a US parachute division in the Pacific and the Japanese had some armored divisions in China. But, overall, it was an infantry war.

This table summarizes the number of divisions available to each of the belligerent powers as of the beginning of the indicated year, regardless of location. "Pre" gives strength in September of 1939, and "End" at the end of the war (September 1945).

ASIATIC-PACIFIC THEATER OF OPERATIONS

	Pre	1940	1941	1942	1943	1944	1945	End
Australia	0	7	9	7	8	7	7	7
Britain	0	1	1	2	2	1	1	1
China				c. 250–300				
India	3	5	6	9	11	11	14	14
Japan	36	36	39	73	84	100	145	197
New Zealand	0	1	0	1	1	0	0	0
United States								
Army	2	2	3	3	9	13	21	21
Marine	0	0	2	3	5	6	6	6
USSR	32	30	30	25	25	35	45	65

By way of comparison with the rest of the war, here are the divisions involved elsewhere.

EUROPEAN-MEDITERRANEAN-MIDDLE EASTERN THEATER

	Pre	1940	1941	1942	1943	1944	1945	End
Australia	0	0	1	3	1	0	0	0
Brazil	0	0	0	0	0	1	1	1
Britain	9	33	34	36	37	36	30	30
Bulgaria	12	14	14	16	23	29	29	20
Canada	0	1	3	5	8	6	6	6
Finland	14	17	19	20	20	20	12	12
France	86	105	0	0	5	7	14	14
Germany	78	189	235	261	327	347	319	375
Hungary	6	7	10	16	19	22	23	30
India	0	0	4	5	5	5	4	4
Italy	66	73	64	89	86	2	9	10
New Zealand	0	0	1	1	1	1	1	1
Poland:								
Western Front	43	2	2	2	2	5	5	5
Eastern Front	–	0	0	0	0	1	12	17
Romania	11	28	33	31	33	32	24	24
S. Africa	0	0	3	3	3	4	3	1
US Army	0	0	0	0	8	17	57	68
USSR	170	180	210	240	340	390	478	411

Since several countries (e.g., the United States, the British Commonwealth, and the USSR) had forces in both theaters, their overall strength is summarized in the following table:

GLOBAL SUMMARY FOR THE TWO-THEATER ALLIES

	Pre-1940	1940	1941	1942	1943	1944	1945	End
Australia	0	7	10	10	9	7	7	7
Britain	9	34	35	38	39	37	31	31
India	3	5	10	14	16	16	18	18
New Zealand	0	1	1	2	2	1	1	1
United States								
Army	8	8	37	73	90	89	89	89
Marine	0	0	2	3	5	6	6	6
USSR	194	200	220	250	350	400	488	491

Figures for most countries are approximate, showing divisions active at the start of the indicated year. In some cases the figures include separate brigades, lumped together on the basis of three brigades per division. All types of divisions are included except training formations, depot divisions, militia, and territorial units. No attempt has been made to modify the figures on the basis of actual strength, degree of training, scales of equipment, or state of readiness. Japanese figures exclude "satellite" forces, but German and Soviet ones include them. For example, in January of 1943 German totals include one Serbian-manned division, two Bosnian-manned ones, eight Croatian ones, and four Slovakian ones, not to mention German divisions formed from troops of other nationalities. German figures include air force, navy, and Waffen-SS ground divisions. British figures include divisions composed primarily of African personnel. Polish "Western" figures include original forces raised in 1939 and those raised in exile in the Middle East, Mediterranean, and Britain, while "Eastern" figures are those raised under Soviet control. French figures after 1940 include only Free French units, omitting Vichy divisions, about 16 by mid-1941, including those in colonies that later went over to the Free French. Italian figures post–1943 omit units of Mussolini's Italian Social Republic, which numbered four by 1944 and six by 1945.

Romanian figures for 1945 reflect forces fighting under Allied control.

In 1939–41 the Netherlands had nine divisions (plus about three more in the East Indies, also not shown), the Belgians 22, the Danes two, the Greeks about 22, and the Yugoslavs 34, before being overrun by the Germans. The Dutch, Belgian, and Greek governments-in-exile were unable to raise any divisions. The Danish divisions were disbanded by the Germans. The Yugoslav partisans under Tito raised some 24 "divisions" (including one Italian-manned) from about mid-1943 onward, after Italy switched sides, opening up the Adriatic to Allied shipping (and easier resupply of the Yugoslav forces). US theater figures omit units within the 48 states, the 13 PHILIPPINE ARMY divisions, activated in late 1941 and destroyed by March of 1942, and the many GUERRILLA divisions formed in the Philippines during the Japanese occupation, but do include the Regular Army Philippine Division, which was also destroyed in March of 1942. SIAM maintained four divisions through the war, although these saw little service.

Organization, Ground Combat Divisions, 1942

The Chinese division shown here was more or less the paper T/O&E for regular divisions of the "Central Army," the forces directly under CHIANG KAI-SHEK's control, and only about 10 of those had full allocations of men and equipment. Most divisions were not so well equipped, often lacking artillery. There were also many variants in the divisional T/O&E. Shown here is a "square" division, one with two brigades of two regiments each. Several divisions had one or even two additional brigades (6–12 additional battalions), and some were on a triangular model (three regiments), and there was also a group of divisions organized and rather lavishly equipped on a triangular model by the United States. These were supposed to have about 12,000 troops, but generally operated with 8,000 or so. To further complicate matters, the Chinese Army had

several series of divisions, each with its own numbering system, so that there were, for example, at least eight different units designated "First Division": There were regular divisions, "new" divisions, "honor" divisions, reserve divisions, provisional divisions, guerrilla divisions, training divisions, "temporary" divisions, and even a "Salt Tax Division."

The British 1941 infantry division shown here was more or less similar to those of the other Imperial and Commonwealth forces throughout the war, albeit that Australian and New Zealand divisions, which had some minor differences in organization, tended to be composed of better manpower. Note that, particularly during the early part

DIVISIONS OF THE PACIFIC WAR, 1942

Army	Chinese	British	Phil.	U.S. Army	USMC	Japanese Type I	Japanese Type II
Men	10.9	17.5	8.2	15.5	19.3	15.5	12.0
Bns.:							
Inf.	12	10	9	9	9	9	6
Art.	1	5	3	4	6	3	1
Recon.	0	1	0.3	0.3	0.3	1	0
Engr.	1	1	1	1	2	1	1
Sig.	0	1	0.3	0.3	1	0.3	0.3
Equipment							
MG	54	867	54	280	680	412	270
Art.	24	72	36	72	60	70	16
A/T	0	48	0	109	54	8	0
Mtr.	24	218	24	138	162	108	72
Value	4	9	4	12	16	10	5

Key to the table: Under US, **Phil.** = units of the Philippine Commonwealth; **Army** = Army Divisions; **USMC** = Marine units; **Men** = the number of men in the division, in thousands; **Bns.** = the number of battalions of each type (.3 indicates a company): **Inf.** = infantry; **Art.** = artillery, including antitank and antiaircraft battalions; **Recon.** = reconnaissance; **Engr.** = Engineers; **Sig.** = signals, which in some armies were subsumed in the engineers; **Equipment** = excluding rifles: automatic rifles (BARs), carbines, submachine guns, pistols; **MG** = machine guns, excluding antiaircraft machine guns and automatic rifles, classed as light machine guns by the Chinese; **Art.** = artillery pieces, excluding antitank and antiaircraft pieces; **A/T** = antitank guns, also useful for "bunker busting"; **Mtr.** = mortars; **Value** = a rough mathematical calculation of the relative fighting power of each division, combining manpower, equipment, experience, organizational, and doctrinal factors.

of the war in Malaya and Burma, most of the British and Indian divisions committed to action were not at full strength, about 13,500 men being common, with equipment reduced in proportion. Commonwealth divisions often had some armored vehicles attached and were frequently supported by non-divisional resources.

Usually overlooked is the fact that the "American" troops defending the Philippines in 1941–42 were mostly locally recruited. Figures here are for the optimal paper strength of a Philippine Army division. The US Army division shown is on the basis of those that fought in New Guinea and GUADALCANAL during 1942, as is the Marine division. In general, it's important to keep in mind that the American divisions—both army and Marines—usually went into action with various attached combat and combat support units, such as tank battalions, with 72 light and medium TANKS, which are not shown in the table. The additional engineer battalion in the Marine division was a US Navy Seabee unit.

The Japanese Army had an extremely confusing organization. The two types of divisions (see page 461) didn't really exist at all. They are merely given to show some idea of the broad differences between divisions. Type I divisions were "triangular" formations (built around three regiments), while Type II divisions were "square" formations (four regiments). But in practice there were many variations in division strength. So many, in fact, that the Japanese themselves came to designate divisions in three classes: "A," overstrength and ready for action; "B," more or less at normal strength; and "C," weak, without artillery or other services. The actual details of each type (or of any of the half-dozen or so different varieties of brigades) could vary greatly. There were Type I divisions with as many as 26,000 men, and others as small as 12,000, and while some were fully motorized, such as the Fifth (15,340 men and over 1,000 motor vehicles, with no HORSES) or the Guards (12,650 men, over 900 motor vehicles, and no horses) when they spearheaded the conquest of MALAYA, most were "leg" outfits, in which the men walked and much of the equipment

was horse-drawn. There were Type II divisions as small as 8,000 men on occupation duty in China and as large as 22,000 men being used for offensive operations (the 18th Division in Malaya, which had just 33 motor vehicles and over 5,700 horses). In all armies, of course, there was some variation in divisional organization, but the Japanese were rather extreme in this regard.

Organization, Ground Combat Divisions, US, 1945

During the war a considerable evolution took place in divisional organization in all armies, sometimes formally and often informally. However, the changes to US units were greatest, partially because the increasing productivity of the "Arsenal of Democracy" permitted ever increasing upgrades of equipment. It would be impossible to trace all the changes in American divisional organization that took place during the war. For example, the US Army's standard infantry divisions underwent four official reorganizations between June of 1941 and September of 1945, with a fifth planned. The Marines went through seven reorganizations in roughly the same period. But some idea of the great changes that took place may be gained by comparing the official divisional tables of organization and equipment as they stood at the beginning of 1945 with the figures in the preceding entry.

Japanese divisions had not appreciably changed since 1942, save for an increased allocation of automatic weapons. British and Chinese divisions have been omitted, because there had been little change in their organization or equipment scales since 1942, albeit that the British divisions were more likely to be at full T/O&E rather than at about 70–75% and had a lot more light antitank weaponry. The PHILIPPINE ARMY, of course, had disappeared.

Changes in division manpower and weapons allocations were rooted in weapons developments, the growth in firepower, the increasing role of TANKS, and changes in the tactical situation, such as the greatly increased allocation of automatic

Type	Army	USMC
Men	14.0	17.5
Bns.:		
Tank	0	1
Inf.	9	9
Art.	4	6
Recon.	0.3	0.3
Engr.	1	2
Sig.	0.3	1
Equipment:		
MG	448	625
Art.	99	60
A/T	57	36
Mtr.	144	153
Tanks	0	46
Value	16	20

Key to the table: **Bns.** = battalions; **Inf.** = infantry; **Art.** = artillery; **Recon.** = reconnaissance; **Engr.** = engineer; **Sig.** = signal; **MG** = machine guns; **A/T** = antitank guns; **Mtr.** = mortar; **Value** = rough approximation of the relative combat value of the unit.

weapons. In addition, there was a desperate need to conserve manpower. By eliminating a single man from each infantry platoon, the US Army could realize a manpower savings of about 30 men per regiment, some 10,000 men on an army-wide basis. Similar small economies in the manpower of other elements could yield sufficient surplus personnel to allow the army to raise entire new divisions. Of course such changes often led to acrimonious disputes. Not every officer, for example, was sufficiently understanding as to want to lose a couple of clerks or drivers.

Note that equipment allocations were usually exceeded in the field, when units would scrounge up additional equipment, often adopting overrun enemy material. On GUADALCANAL and SAIPAN, for example, the US Marines made good use of some captured Japanese 37mm guns.

Organization, Higher Army Commands, Comparative

At the higher levels, US and British military organizational terminology differed from that employed by the Chinese and Japanese.

US/British	Chinese	Japanese
Army Group	War Area	General Army
Army	Army Group	Area Army
	Front Army	
	Route Army	
Corps	Army	Army
Division	Division	Division

Osaka, Honshu, Japan

One of the principal ports of Japan, with important naval and air base facilities.

Oshima, Hiroshi (1886–1975)

A former military officer, Oshima was the Japanese ambassador to Nazi Germany. Despite German racial attitudes (he was, after all, an "honorary Aryan"), Oshima was very well regarded by most senior German political and military leaders, including HITLER. As a result, he was privy to an enormous amount of critical information, which he shared with his superiors in Tokyo. As these were in the PURPLE diplomatic code, this proved of enormous value to the Allies, since the United States had broken the code. After the war Oshima, who was an enthusiastic supporter of Axis aggression, was tried as a war criminal. Sentenced to life imprisonment, he was released in 1955.

Ref: Boyd, *Hitler's Japanese Confidant*.

Otori Class, Japanese Fleet Torpedo Boats

Completed in the mid-1930s, the Otori class torpedo boats were much enlarged and improved versions of the unsuccessful TOMOZURU CLASS. When the American submarine warfare program began sinking Japanese shipping in enormous numbers they were pressed into service as improvised destroyer escorts. Like the Tomozurus they proved surprisingly effective in this role. Seven of the eight units of the class were lost in action.

Owen Stanley Mountains, Papua New Guinea

A spine of rugged mountains extending through the east-west axis of the easternmost portion of Papua New Guinea. With many peaks over 13,000 feet, the range is carved up into numerous valleys at all altitudes, plus occasional plateaus. The KO-KODA TRAIL, the principal track traversing the range from Papua to northeastern New Guinea, crossed the mountains at an altitude of 7,000 feet. All of this is covered by lush tropical vegetation, the product of a rain forest climate. Rainfall averages over 80 inches a year. High humidity, frequent thick mist, and winter (June-August) nighttime temperatures in the 50s make for one of the more unhealthy climates on the planet.

Oyodo, Japanese Antiaircraft Cruiser

An enlarged version of AGANO, *Oyodo* (1941–1942–1943) was intended to serve as a flagship for submarine flotillas, for which she was supposed to have a sizable complement of floatplanes on a plan similar to that of the TONE CLASS heavy cruisers. During construction plans were changed, and she emerged with enhanced antiaircraft defenses, which were constantly improved during the war, so that by its end she was effectively an antiaircraft cruiser. She saw little action, most notably while taking part in the "bait" squadron during the Battle of LEYTE GULF. She was sunk in KURE Harbor by US naval aircraft on 28 July 1945.

Ozawa, Jisaburo (1886–1966)

Jisaburo Ozawa graduated from the naval academy in 1909, served in destroyers, went on to various service schools, and then made his mark as a surface warfare expert in the 1920s and 1930s. He was particularly skillful in the use of TORPEDOES, a weapon the Japanese Navy became noted for during the 1942 battles. By 1941 he was a vice admiral and commanded the surface forces that supported the invasions in MALAYA and the Dutch East Indies from late 1941 through early 1942. He became the commander of the Third Fleet at TRUK in late 1942. In early 1943, he commanded an unsuccessful attempt to destroy Allied air power in the New Guinea/Solomons area. Commanded Japanese forces during the summer 1944 BATTLE OF THE PHILIPPINE SEA. The result was the GREAT MARIANAS TURKEY SHOOT. Offered to resign after this, but was instead put in charge of Japanese naval forces that sortied to resist the American invasion of the Philippines in late 1944. This led to another defeat, and he returned to Japan with the few surviving ships. He served on the Naval General Staff for the remainder of the war. He died in 1966, at age 80. Ozawa was a classic "fighting admiral," but even these capabilities were not able to overcome the quantity and quality of naval forces America was able to muster. He was several inches taller than the average Japanese, but was actually rather modest in demeanor.

P

P-26 Peashooter, US Fighter

The P-26 Peashooter played only a minor role in the Pacific War, with some being used in the US defense of the Philippines in late 1941. The P-26 was the US Army's first all-metal monoplane fighter. It was in US service between 1934 and 1938, being replaced by the P-36 (which was itself quickly replaced by the P-40). The P-26 was the last army fighter with an open cockpit. It was a good performer, by 1930s standards. The Chinese Air Force bought some and with these P-26s shot down many Japanese aircraft. The Philippine Army Air Force also scored some victories with its handful of P-26s during the opening weeks of the war. Fewer than 200 P-26s were produced. Several continued to serve in the Guatemalan Air Force until 1957.

See also AIRCRAFT TYPES, DEVELOPMENT.

P-35, US Fighter

The P-35 was one of the many fighters produced in America during the 1930s that eventually saw Pacific combat while serving with American allies. In this case, the P-35 flew with the newly formed Philippine Army Air Force. These P-35s had originally been ordered by Sweden, but events in Europe prevented delivery. In the summer of 1941, 40 were sent to the Philippines where they were quickly lost during the Japanese invasion later that year. Lacking any armor or self-sealing fuel tanks, the P-35s didn't last long against the more maneuverable and better armed Japanese fighters.

See also AIRCRAFT TYPES, DEVELOPMENT.

When introduced in 1934 the P-26 was one of the hottest fighters in the world, but it was hopelessly obsolete by 1941. The first all-metal monoplane fighter with an air-cooled engine in US service, it retained an open cockpit and fixed landing gear, as well as requiring wire stays, not visible in this silhouette.

P-36 Hawk, US Fighter

The US P-36 Curtiss Hawk was obsolete when the war began. Even so, P-36s opposed the Japanese attack on PEARL HARBOR and managed to shoot down two enemy aircraft. While it looked fairly modern, and was a contemporary of the German Me-109, the P-36 was not as well designed and its performance was lower than most of the aircraft it faced in combat. While a very maneuverable and sturdy aircraft, it was relatively slow. The P-36 was built largely for export, and many nations received them (China, Thailand, France, South Africa, Argentina). Fewer than 400 were built, with PRODUCTION ending in early 1941.

See also AIRCRAFT TYPES, DEVELOPMENT.

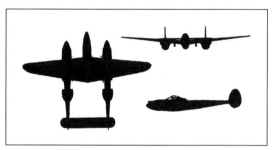

Arguably the most effective US fighter in the Pacific, the P-38 came in more than a dozen models, with numerous subvariants. Shown here is the P-38J, introduced in early 1944.

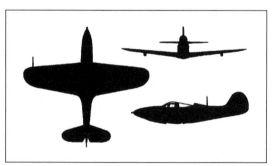

Although it proved a poor fighter, the P-39 Airacobra found its niche as a ground-attack aircraft, in which role it performed quite well.

P-38 Lightning, US Fighter

The Lockheed P-38 Lightning was one of the more successful American fighters, and the only one that was in PRODUCTION continuously from PEARL HARBOR through V-J Day. Over 9,000 were built. But the P-38 was unusual in many respects. It had twin engines, a characteristic that does not usually produce successful fighters. The P-38 succeeded by using its high speed and superior ceiling to dive on opponents with guns blazing. If this did not work, the P-38 was usually going fast enough to escape for another try. It was heavily armed, with 37mm or 20mm cannon, plus four .50 caliber machine guns. The twin engines were often a lifesaver, as the aircraft could fly on one engine. Large and sturdy, the P-38 could absorb more punishment than most other fighters. Lastly, the P-38 had exceptional range. Twelve-hour flights were not uncommon, at a time when most fighters carried only enough fuel to stay in the air for a few hours, which made the P-38 very useful as a reconnaissance aircraft. The major disadvantage of the P-38 was its lack of maneuverability at low altitudes. Despite this, there was always enough high-altitude work available to keep the P-38 busy throughout the war. By some reckoning the P-38 shot down more Japanese aircraft than any other fighter.

See also AIRCRAFT TYPES, DEVELOPMENT.

P-39 Airacobra, US Fighter

The P-39 Airacobra was another prewar US design that came up short when the shooting started. However, in this case it was the military's fault. The original 1936 design was for a speedy, heavily armed, and robust interceptor. But the generals insisted on a ground-support aircraft and the design was changed to meet those requirements. When fighters were desperately needed in the Pacific during 1942, the P-39 was among the few aircraft available. Pilots soon found out that if they could stay away from the Japanese Zeros, the P-39 was a very effective ground-attack aircraft. The 37mm cannon also made the P-39 an excellent "bomber buster." Over 7,000 were built, with PRODUCTION continuing into early 1943. Many were exported to allies, and the Russians were particularly fond of the P-39's ground-attack capabilities. A number of P-39s were produced in a special "export" version called the P-400, and some of these saw service with US Army pilots in the South Pacific.

See also AIRCRAFT TYPES, DEVELOPMENT.

P-40 Tomahawk, US Fighter

The US P-40 Tomahawk was a follow on to the P-36 Hawk and was a more effective aircraft. Actually, it was a P-36 with a more powerful engine and some other improvements. About 13,000 were built. Nevertheless, the P-40 was not quite as good as most of its opposition. The main reason that the P-40 was the most widely available fighter in 1942 was because America had waited so long to rearm. While not as capable as the contemporary Japanese Zero or German FW-190, the P-40 could hold its own if used properly. A sturdy aircraft, like its P-36 predecessor, P-40 PRODUCTION continued until late 1944. Most P-40s ended up being used as

fighter-bombers or as interceptors in secondary theaters (where first-line enemy fighters were unlikely to be encountered). Thousands were given to allies, for whom a P-40 was considered better than no fighter at all.

See also AIRCRAFT TYPES, DEVELOPMENT.

P-43, US Fighter

An experimental aircraft, similar in appearance to the P-47 and made by the same firm, Republic Aviation. First flew in 1940. Only 272 were built and some were supplied to Australia and China as part of the LEND-LEASE program.

See also AIRCRAFT TYPES, DEVELOPMENT.

P-47 Thunderbolt, US Fighter

The US P-47 Thunderbolt—nicknamed the "Jug"—was a very successful design, although it didn't enter service until late 1942 and didn't get to the Pacific until early 1944. Europe had priority on top-of-the-line air force aircraft, and European commitments had to be filled before any could be diverted to the Pacific. Over 15,000 were produced, and more were built after the war. Some were given

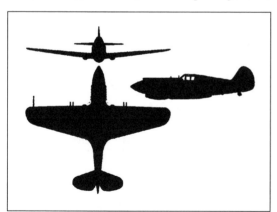

The P-40 Tomahawk was the US Army's principal fighter for most of the first year of the war. Although outclassed by many enemy fighters, it remained in production into 1944, fully 17 different models being developed: The P-40C is shown.

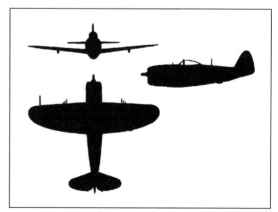

Introduced in 1942, the P-47D was the principal version of the Thunderbolt to see combat in the Pacific Theater, flying not only with USAAF squadrons, but also with the RAF in Burma and the Mexican Air Force in the Philippines.

to allies. The P-47 was one of the heaviest single-engine fighters of the war. It was quite modern in that the aircraft was literally designed around the most powerful engine available (2,000 horsepower initially, 2,300 and then 2,800 as the war went on). Most of those in the Pacific came with the more powerful engines. Its normal loaded weight of 7 to 8 tons was puny by modern standards, but it was a heavyweight in World War II. Carrying eight .50 caliber machine guns (and up to 3,000 pounds of bombs), the P-47 could inflict enormous damage on air or ground targets. Partly because of its own weight, the P-47 could take a lot of punishment and keep flying. It wasn't unusual for the P-47 to take dozens of machine gun and cannon shell hits and keep flying. Once pilots got used to the "heft" of the P-47, they loved it. At high altitudes, the P-47 was quite nimble. Its weight allowed it to dive away from trouble at high speed. With drop tanks, the P-47 was widely used as a bomber escort. The Japanese never came up with anything that could overwhelm the P-47.

See also AIRCRAFT TYPES, DEVELOPMENT.

P-51 Mustang, US Fighter

The US P-51 Mustang was the thoroughbred of World War II fighters. It was designed at the request of the British. An extraordinary airplane,

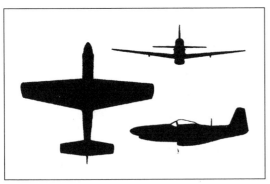

The final production version of the P-51, the P-51H, was introduced in 1945 and was primarily employed as an escort for B-29 missions over Japan.

many consider the P-51 the best of the lot. Unfortunately, few got to the Pacific. The P-51 arrived on the Pacific scene in late 1944, primarily to serve as an escort for long-range B-29 bombers. The P-51 was more agile than the P-47 and had a longer range. It weighed about half as much as the P-47 and had about half the firepower (six .50 caliber machine guns). Nevertheless, the P-51 could carry a 2,000-ton bombload. About 16,000 were delivered and PRODUCTION continued after the war. Mustang was the British name, the Americans originally calling it the Apache.

See also AIRCRAFT TYPES, DEVELOPMENT.

P-59 Airacomet, US Jet Fighter

The P-59 Airacomet was America's first jet fighter. Work began in 1941 using technology from the British. Although it performed satisfactorily, the design was never considered capable enough for combat use. Nearly 200 were built by late 1945 for use as trainers. The technology was transferred to Lockheed, which used it to produce the more successful postwar P-80 fighter. Had the design gone better, the P-59 could have been deployed by late 1944. Most would probably have ended up in Europe but, if the situation had warranted, could have appeared in the Pacific.

See also AIRCRAFT TYPES, DEVELOPMENT.

P-61 Black Widow, US Night Fighter

The US P-61 Black Widow was a night fighter, a 15-ton, two-engine aircraft designed specifically to carry a large radar and heavy armament (four 20mm cannon). The pilot and radar operator would seek out and destroy enemy bombers trying to hide in the darkness. Unfortunately, development only began after noting the problems the British were having with night bombers in late 1940. The first flight was just before PEARL HARBOR. Thus P-61s didn't reach the front until 1943, and the Pacific Theater didn't get them until the summer of 1944. While there were few German aircraft still operating at night, the Japanese were

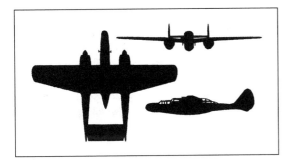

Introduced in mid-1944, the P-61B began to see service in the Pacific late that year, supplementing the older "A" model, which had been at the front since the spring of 1944.

another matter. Several Pacific P-61 pilots became aces for shooting five or more Japanese bombers trying to attack at night. Only about 700 were built.

See also AIRCRAFT TYPES, DEVELOPMENT.

P-63 Kingcobra, US Fighter

The P-63 Kingcobra was a much improved version of the earlier P-39. Some 3,300 were produced between 1943 and 1945. Most of them (2,400) were sent to Russia (already an enthusiastic user of the P-39) and another 300 were given to the French. US forces took the remainder but did not use them in combat. This was another of those aircraft that could have shown up in the Pacific. As it was, the P-63 did fly for the French in Vietnam in the late 1940s.

See also AIRCRAFT TYPES, DEVELOPMENT.

P-66, US Fighter

A prewar fighter made by the Vultee Corporation, it was not impressive and 129 of the 144 produced in 1939 and 1940 were sent to China. Originally ordered by Sweden, exports to that nation were prohibited by the US government.

See also AIRCRAFT TYPES, DEVELOPMENT.

P-80, US Jet Fighter

Test-flown in mid-1945, this was the US jet design most likely to have seen combat if the war had dragged into mid–1946. Army Air Force ACE Richard I. BONG was killed test-flying one in 1945.

See also AIRCRAFT TYPES, DEVELOPMENT.

P-400, US Fighter

A special "export" version of the P-39 designed for poverty-stricken countries. A number of them were shipped to the South Pacific in 1942 due to the desperate shortage of aircraft, and they performed with surprising effectiveness during the GUADAL-CANAL Campaign.

See also AIRCRAFT TYPES, DEVELOPMENT.

P1Y1 Frances, Japanese Bomber

The P1Y1 Frances was the Japanese Navy's most modern bomber, entering service during the summer of 1943. Faster, better armed and more robust than earlier models, the P1Y1 could outrun many Allied fighters at low altitudes. Hampered by shortages of fuel, spare parts, and skilled crews, about 1,100 were built (including night fighter versions).

See also AIRCRAFT TYPES, DEVELOPMENT.

Pacific Islanders, Japanese Subjects

Japan controlled most of the MARIANAS and all of the MARSHALL and CAROLINE ISLANDS from 1914, when it seized them from Germany. Under a League of Nations MANDATE from 1920, Japanese rule in the islands was surprisingly benevolent. For the most part Japanese exploitation of the larger islands was lightly supervised by the league until Japan withdrew from the organization in the mid–1930s. Japanese rule brought considerable economic prosperity to the natives of some islands, generally the larger, more fertile, and occasionally mineral-rich "high" islands (those of volcanic origins, such as SAIPAN or PONAPE, rather than the numerous "low" CORAL atolls). The Japanese also brought schools, hospitals, and other useful installations. Of course, the emphasis was on "Japanizing" the natives. On some islands this proved highly successful. For example, when the CHINA INCIDENT broke out in 1937, many men on Saipan, Rota, Ponape, and PALAU offered themselves for the emperor's service.

Although there was considerable recruiting of labor troops in the islands during World War II, the emperor never made any systematic attempt to recruit combat troops among his South Seas subjects. Nevertheless, small contingents of men from Palau and Ponape did enter imperial service as combat troops. Although the Palauans did not see active service, a platoon of Ponapans did. Some 20 men were sent to New Guinea in 1943, where they saw considerable action. Only three men survived.

However, with some exceptions, when US troops landed on one of the Japanese-mandated islands the local people either welcomed the invaders or maintained a certain distance. The principal exception was on Saipan, where many of the natives joined—voluntarily or otherwise—the thousands of Japanese residents who committed mass suicide rather than surrender.

Ref: White and Lindstrom, *The Pacific Theater*.

Pacific Islanders, Resistance to the Japanese

The Japanese overran most of the SOLOMONS, the BISMARCKS, many of the other islands in the southwest Pacific, and much of New Guinea rather easily, there being nothing much to oppose them. The local populations were Melanesian, stone age people with Negroid features, descended from Southeast Asians. Some of these peoples were Christians, and many spoke PIDGIN, a form of English. They had relatively long experience of colonial rule under the British, Dutch, Australians, or New Zealanders.

By the late 1930s many of the more educated elements, particularly clergymen and local tribal leaders, were expressing some dissatisfaction with the colonial powers. Despite this, for the most part

these "stout black fellows," cooperated quite freely with their Commonwealth overlords in resisting the Japanese. This was partially out of loyalty, but mostly out of self-interest. A few weeks of Japanese domination usually convinced even the most hardened anti-British islander that the king's men were easier to get along with than the emperor's.

To be sure, in a few instances the Japanese were able to recruit among the native peoples, notably on New Guinea and BOUGAINVILLE, where tribal rivalries were strong. And many of the islanders tried desperately to remain neutral, in some cases even returning downed pilots to their appropriate comrades with the deliberate intention of convincing both the Allies and the Japanese that they were friendly.

On several islands local hostility to colonial domination broke into open rebellion upon the withdrawal of most whites in the early months of 1942, even when there was no Japanese presence. In the LOUISIADES, for example, a local man named Buriga prophesied that if the people rose up and killed all the remaining whites and all persons of mixed race, the traditional gods of the islands would return, bringing with them many good things. The rebellion cost the lives of several whites, including representatives of the ANGAU. After the return of Australian forces in some strength, over 150 local people were arrested. Tried for treason to the Crown, nine men, including Buriga, were sentenced to be hanged, and many others to imprisonment. Buriga cheated the executioner by hanging himself in his cell, but the other eight men were publicly executed. The revolt, in fact, attracted few supporters, most of the people of the islands being much in terror of the rebels.

The peoples of the Pacific suffered severely during the war. Not only were many brutalized, killed and some even eaten by the Japanese, but others were also killed during the fighting, particularly by Allied air attacks, which often struck innocent villages that just happened to be behind Japanese lines.

Without the cooperation of these islanders, the task of ejecting the Japanese from the southwest

Pacific would have been far more difficult. Coast-watching operations, in which Commonwealth officers kept tabs on Japanese fleet and air movements from jungle-covered islands, would have been impossible without the assistance of the islanders. The islanders also reconnoitered Japanese positions, helped rescue downed flyers, and occasionally knocked off Japanese troops. The Allies offered a bounty for dead Japanese and live Allied pilots, a form of transaction the avid hunters among the islanders could appreciate. Many a downed Allied pilot was shocked to be confronted by a group of stone age warriors, one of whom would inquire in a British accent, "Are you all right, chap?" A great many islanders were killed, and many were subsequently decorated by the various Allied governments and awarded pensions for their wartime service.

The war had a profound effect on the peoples of the South Pacific in other ways. In addition to the devastation, it brought an extraordinary measure of prosperity and many luxury goods. At the same time, it undermined the authority of the colonial powers to an enormous extent.

One of the most pervasive influences on social change in Pacific societies was the US armed forces. Since the Americans had no vested interests to protect in the islands—they were there because the war was there, and they mostly wanted to be elsewhere—they tended to ignore the niceties of colonial hierarchy. The casual informality of Americans, their generosity (especially with regard to food, the sharing of which has an important religious meaning in many cultures), their tendency to treat everyone as an equal, their objections to calling grown men "boys," and the fact that Americans supervising native laborers never struck them (a common practice of British, Australian, or New Zealand foremen), all greatly impressed the islanders. That the US armed forces included many BLACK AMERICANS (not to mention some Chinese Americans, Hawaiian Americans, Native Americans, and even Japanese Americans) was a particularly important influence on the peoples of the South Pacific. If anything, the colonial powers had

maintained a stricter racial separation than was common in even the most segregated parts of the United States. On many islands the "boys" were not permitted to wear Western clothing, drink alcohol, or even eat European foods, let alone eat at the same table with whites. The apparent equality among the various types of Americans (the uniform clothing, similar occupations, common equipment, identical rations, and even the presence of nonwhite officers) caused many islanders to perceive a racial equality that, of course, did not actually exist. This had an important impact on postwar political developments on many of the South Pacific islands, where even today Americans are immensely popular.

See also GUERRILLA WARS; PACIFIC ISLANDS REGIMENT; SOLOMON ISLANDS DEFENCE FORCE.

Ref: White and Lindstrom, *The Pacific Theater*.

Pacific Islands Regiment

Shortly before the Pacific War broke out, the Australian colonial authorities created the Papua Light Infantry from local police forces in Papua. This force was composed of locally recruited enlisted men under Australian officers, with commands usually given in PIDGIN. By the outbreak of the war the Papua Light Infantry was at about the strength of a battalion. In addition, several companies had been raised in the mandated territory of Northeast NEW GUINEA. The New Guinea Defence Force ultimately totaled four battalions. These forces proved invaluable to the Allied cause, not merely as guides, scouts, and GUERRILLAS, but also as combat troops, the Papua Light Infantry taking a major part in the brutal KOKODA TRAIL Campaign in mid- and late 1942.

In February 1945 the two forces were united into the Pacific Islands Regiment. By then all of the NCOs and many warrant officers were Papua-New Guineans. The merger was not achieved without some acrimony. The Papua Light Infantry had worn European-style uniforms, shorts and shirts with insignia on the collars, in colonial terms symbolic of very high status. When the Pacific Islands

Regiment was formed, the prescribed uniform was that of the New Guinea Defence Force, kilt-like laplaps (lavalavas) with insignia of rank on the skirt. Many veterans of the Papua Light Infantry objected to this symbolic lowering of their status, and there was some indiscipline in the ranks, including an incident in which three Australian officers were injured in a riot. Tensions festered for several months, before order was restored, when the Australian military authorities acknowledged that they had made a mistake.

By the end of the war there were three active battalions in the Pacific Islands Regiment (one each was serving on BOUGAINVILLE, New Guinea, and NEW BRITAIN) plus two more being formed. A total of 3,500 Papuans and New Guineans served in the Pacific Islands Regiment during the war, and it accumulated 11 battle honors. Thousands of other Papua-New Guineans served as combatants in other organizations, including the ANGAU, the police, special operations forces, the Australian militia, and as guides for Allied troops. Although inactivated shortly after the war, the regiment was subsequently reactivated in the late 1940s, and became the basis of the Papua-New Guinea armed forces when the combined territories achieved their independence.

See also FIJI ISLANDS; TONGA.

Ref: Sinclair, *To Find a Path*; White and Lindstrom, *The Pacific Theater*.

Pacific War, the Course of the War

The Pacific War did not simply start at PEARL HARBOR, then move west until Japan was reached. The fighting took place over a third of the Earth's surface and often simultaneously, thousands of miles apart. Understanding how this came to be requires that we take a look at the reasons why Japan decided to start the war.

Many of Japan's top military leaders realized that they could not win a long war against the United States. But that was not enough to keep Japan from entering World War II. Since the 1920s, the government had been increasingly dom-

inated by army officers who had involved Japan in its aggressive war in China that had led to the oil embargo by the Western nations. This last action put the Japanese generals on the spot. They could not afford to abandon their operations in China, as that was their principal justification for running the government. But they could not ignore the oil embargo either, as the Western countries controlled the world's oil supply and without oil the Japanese armed forces would be largely crippled within a year.

For the military, it was a case of use it or lose it. The Japanese generals convinced themselves that some chance of military victory in the Pacific was preferable to guaranteed impotence from a lack of oil. The generals saw the embargo as an offensive move, and their military response as a defensive reaction. While the Imperial Navy's admirals did not exercise nearly as much control over the government, they went along with the generals. Japan was a maritime nation, it depended on control of the seas. The generals recognized this and the navy budget was relatively large throughout the 20 years preceding Pearl Harbor. But the generals were in firm control of the government and the admirals followed the generals' lead.

The basic plan for the Pacific War was to destroy the Allied forces in the region, seize all the Allied colonies and possessions, and then sue for peace on favorable terms. It was felt (though not all Japanese leaders believed it) that the Allies would prefer some kind of settlement to a long war in the Pacific. It was a desperate gamble, which at first appeared to be working.

The Japanese had a high opinion of their own military prowess. This attitude certainly helped, because the numbers didn't look quite so favorable. Most of the Japanese Army was tied down in China. Only about a quarter of a million ground troops could be scraped together for the Pacific offensive. Japan's target list was impressive: the Philippines, sundry central Pacific islands, the NETHERLANDS EAST INDIES (modern INDONESIA), NEW GUINEA and nearby island groups, INDOCHINA (Vietnam and environs), MALAYA (Malaysia and SINGAPORE), Thailand, Burma, and parts of India. In these territories there were over half a million Allied troops. But it was more than numbers that counted. Many of the Allied troops were either poorly trained, inexperienced or both, and many were locally recruited and were not necessarily completely happy with the rule of the "Mother Country."

The Vichy French troops in Indo-China were neutral (and, technically, allies of Japan, because of Vichy France's relationship with Japan's ally, Nazi Germany). SIAM (Thailand) was pro-Japanese, primarily out of fear rather than enthusiasm for the Japanese cause.

But the biggest asset the Japanese Army had was the Japanese Navy. The Pacific War began with the Allies and Japan having a rough parity in naval forces, and Japanese carrier superiority, as well as larger and more capable air forces.

The Japanese plan for conquering the Pacific was to be executed with naval superiority, and barely sufficient ground forces. Most of the Japanese target areas were not heavily garrisoned. The British had large forces in Singapore, as did the United States in the Philippines. But the nearby Japanese forces were better trained and led and had superior air support. Many Allied territories were held by token forces, and all the Japanese had to do was walk in and take over.

The initial Japanese attacks in December 1941 and January 1942 soon overwhelmed all resistance. The Japanese used their naval superiority to isolate Allied forces. This not only cut the Allied forces off from resupply and reinforcement, it also allowed the Japanese to take care of Allied forces one at a time. For example, Japanese troops took care of Malaya before going on to the Netherlands East Indies and Burma.

What stopped the Japanese eventually, and slowed them down in the meantime, was a lack of merchant shipping to move the troops and supplies forward. In the first six months of the war, Japan had seized all the central Pacific islands, all of what is now called Indonesia, all of southeast Asia except for western Burma and most of New Guinea

and the adjacent islands. In less than half a year, Japan's carriers attacked targets from the Hawaiian Islands to southern India, going almost halfway around the world in the process. Japan's fleet, and particularly its carriers, were what protected the relatively small Japanese ground forces from retribution by Allied land, air, or naval forces.

But in May, with more US carriers in the Pacific, Japan began to lose carriers. First, a light carrier was lost in the Battle of the CORAL SEA and a heavy carrier damaged. A month later, four heavy carriers were lost at MIDWAY. That essentially evened up the carrier situation in the Pacific, despite the United States's loss of two carriers (one each at Coral Sea and Midway). Equally important was the United States pouring land-based aircraft into the theater. This restricted where the Japanese carriers, and their ships in general, could operate with relative safety.

Had they not lost five carriers in the first seven months of the war, the Japanese planned to keep pushing their defensive perimeter outward. These planned conquests (as far south as the FIJI ISLANDS and, eventually, HAWAII to the east and India and the Persian Gulf in the west) would be garrisoned slowly (because of the lack of cargo ships) by troops withdrawn from China and new units raised in Japan. The Japanese Army had misgivings about these expansion plans, even though it agreed with the navy about the need to grab as much territory as possible as a prelude to the eventual peace negotiations with the Allies. The army did draw the line at an attempt to land in Australia. That nation was simply too large for the Japanese Army's scant resources to handle, particularly in light of the hostile population there.

But in the spring of 1942, there was much optimism and little clear thought at Japanese military headquarters. The early victories had been more spectacular than even the most enthusiastic Japanese militarists envisioned. For a few months, anything seemed possible. But after Midway, reality again set in. However, the worst news was not the loss of the carriers at Midway, but the refusal of the Allies to negotiate. Pearl Harbor had wakened the sleeping tiger (as many Japanese officers who had studied in America had warned) and America now wanted vengeance.

Japanese who knew a bit about world economics and US history knew that the Americans would not rest until Japan was a smoldering ruin, and the Americans were quite capable of Japan's destruction. No one in Tokyo would ever admit this publicly until near the end. But it was now clear, the Americans were on the offensive.

In August 1942, the United States landed a Marine division on GUADALCANAL and seized an unfinished Japanese airfield. Meanwhile, to the northwest the Japanese were continuing to fight over possession of NEW GUINEA. The Guadalcanal battle lasted six months and resulted in a Japanese defeat. This was but one of a series of battles in this area that took Allied troops right up the Solomon chain of islands, past RABAUL, across New Guinea, and on toward the Philippines by late 1944. Meanwhile, the fighting on New Guinea continued into 1945.

During late 1942 there were a series of carrier battles that demonstrated US capabilities in carrier warfare and killed many of Japan's hard-to-replace carrier pilots.

Meanwhile, two other fronts gave the Japanese still more trouble. In Burma, the Japanese offensive had stalled by mid–1942. Noting that the Allies were building railroad, truck, and air routes into China, the Japanese eventually tried in 1943–44 to push the British back into India and away from any access to China. But the forces were more evenly matched now and the Japanese offensives failed. By early 1945, the Allies were on the offensive and eventually pushed the Japanese out of most of Burma. While Burma was a stalemate the Japanese could afford, the third prong of the Allied counteroffensive led right to Tokyo. In late 1943, the United States began the series of amphibious operations in the Central Pacific that would, eight months later, seize islands close enough to Japan for B-29 bombers to reach Tokyo and other Home Island cities. Trying to defeat this offensive, in the summer of 1944, the rebuilt Japanese carrier force

was destroyed once and for all in the Battle of the PHILIPPINE SEA (the GREAT MARIANAS TURKEY SHOOT). In late 1944 the Philippines were retaken. In early 1945, islands even closer to Japan were taken and the bombing campaign against Japanese industry and population intensified.

By the summer of 1945, Japan was isolated and broken.

Ref: Collier, *The War in the Far East*; Cook and Cook, *Japan at War*; Dower, *War without Mercy*; Dunnigan and Nofi, *Victory at Sea*; Hoyt, *Japan's War*; Ienaga, *The Pacific War*; MacIntyre, *The Battle for the Pacific*; Ready, *Forgotten Allies*; Spector, *Eagle Against the Sun*; Van der Vat, *The Pacific Campaign*.

Palau Group, Caroline Islands

The westernmost group of the CAROLINE ISLANDS, about 600 miles east of the Philippines, the Palau Group are "high" islands, primarily volcanic in origin rather than CORAL atolls. There are hundreds of them, but they amount to only about 175 square miles. In Japanese hands since World War I, the Palaus were among the most developed of the MANDATES, and some 30,000 Japanese civilians set up residence there during the 1920s and 1930s, establishing a fairly modern community on Koror, in the central part of the archipelago. There were also about 5,000 Melanesian Palauans.

The Palaus figured early in US war planning, being one of the places earmarked for occupation under the various incarnations of War Plan Orange. In the 1920s the eccentric, and alcoholic, Colonel Pete Ellis (USMC) resided in the islands in disguise, attempting to spy on Japanese military installations, which he was convinced existed there in violation of the naval DISARMAMENT TREATIES and the League of Nations MANDATES. Ellis died of alcoholism in 1923 (though some attribute his death to poisoning by Japanese Intelligence). In fact, the Japanese did not begin intensive military development in the Palaus until the late 1930s, after they had left the League of Nations. The war initially had little impact on the islands. During it upward of 50,000 Japanese troops were stationed in the islands, most of whom were left to "wither on the vine" as US forces island-hopped across the Pacific. From March of 1944, the islands were subjected to American aerial and naval bombardment on numerous occasions, which succeeded in destroying several airfields and other military installations. The two southernmost large islands, Anguar and PELELIU, were invaded by US forces in late 1944, and there was particularly heavy fighting on the latter. During the last year of the war there was considerable privation and some starvation in the islands.

After nearly 30 years of Japanese rule, many of the Palauans were devoted to the emperor. A large number of men volunteered for labor service, and many were shipped to New Guinea, where they supervised work gangs composed of local natives. Late in the war some Palauans volunteered for military service, forming a "suicide commando" that saw no action.

Ironically, after the war, when the United States took control of the Palaus under a United Nations trusteeship, the islanders proved distinctly unhappy. Prosperous under Japanese rule, if only because the Japanese invested heavily in the islands, particularly after they began to develop them as military bases, the Palauans found the United States much less generous.

Ref: White and Lindstrom, *The Pacific Theater.*

Palau Islands, Campaign for

The Palaus, located midway between the CAROLINES and Philippines, were to be the target of the US central Pacific offensive, before the carriers and amphibious ships turned north and went after Japan itself. At the last minute, it was argued that invading the Palaus was no longer necessary, but Admiral NIMITZ ordered the operations to go ahead anyway. The campaign took place from September to October 1944, cost the lives of some 2,000 Americans, and centered largely around the Battle for PELELIU Island.

At the time, in late 1944, there was no unambiguous way to know that avoiding the Palaus would have been all right. As it turned out, the air bases in the Palaus were not needed because of ineffective Japanese airpower in the area and the unexpectedly rapid advance of Allied forces from the south and across the central Pacific. No one realized that the Japanese were particularly well fortified in Peleliu. This was one of the few campaigns that was fought unnecessarily.

The island of Anguar was not defended nearly as stoutly as Peleliu and was taken by an army division in three days (September 17–20) at a cost of 540 dead and 2,735 wounded. The Japanese garrison of 2,600 fought, as usual, to the death with only a handful of PRISONERS being taken. Peleliu (see also, PELELIU, BATTLE OF) proved much tougher.

Perhaps most importantly, as part of the Palau Campaign the unoccupied atoll of ULITHI was taken over as a fleet base to support future operations.

Palawan, Philippines

A local port, with a good anchorage but limited facilities, Palawan also had potential as an air base, given that it fronted on both the South China Sea and the Sulu Sea, as well as northern Borneo. Palawan was overrun by the Japanese in early 1942, and retaken by the United States three years later.

Palembang, Battle of, Sumatra, Netherlands East Indies

In early 1942 Palembang was a small upland city, the administrative center of much of Sumatra. It was the site of some recently discovered oil deposits, which were just being exploited. That made it a prime target for the Japanese.

The Japanese attacked Palembang in mid-February 1942. The Dutch garrison had two months warning that the Japanese were on the way, but did not destroy the oil facilities in time because they wanted to keep pumping oil for the revenue it would bring in for the cash-strapped Dutch government-in-exile.

The Japanese were aware that the Dutch had not yet destroyed the oil facilities and sought to capture them intact. They did this with an airborne assault, dropping in a battalion of SNLF paratroopers on February 14. A tough fight ensued, in which the Dutch got the upper hand. However, the airdrop so disrupted the defense that the Dutch were unable to effect demolition before substantial Japanese reinforcements arrived by sea, on the 15th. By the 16th the Japanese had secured the city and the substantially intact oil fields.

It was the speed of the assault that was the key to this battle, a classic example of airborne assault as a way to achieve surprise and a quick victory. The battle was over in two days.

Allied naval forces were still active in the area, but Japanese air and naval forces were too strong for these Allied efforts to have any effect on the campaign in the NETHERLANDS EAST INDIES.

Palmyra Island

One of the LINE ISLANDS. Like a number of other normally deserted places, Palmyra, a thousand miles south of HAWAII, had very great potential as an air base, helping to control extensive areas of the central Pacific, in which role it served as a US base throughout the war.

Panama Canal

Connecting the Atlantic Ocean with the Pacific, the Panama Canal was possibly the most important strategic place in the world in early 1942. So critical to US strategic thinking was the canal that until the Second World War all US warships were designed to pass through the canal, so that the Atlantic Fleet could quickly reinforce the Pacific, and vice versa. As a result, until 1940 no US warship was designed with a beam greater than the width of the canal locks (110 feet). The first vessels that exceeded that beam were the MONTANA CLASS battleships, authorized in 1940 but never laid down. The first ships to exceed the width of the

locks were several units of the MARYLAND and CALIFORNIA CLASSES, which emerged from their post-PEARL HARBOR refits in 1943–44 with a beam of some 114 feet. The first ships deliberately designed and built wider than the locks were the three units of the MIDWAY CLASS, which entered service after the war.

The US Navy had given considerable thought to the defense of the canal, and as early as 1929 (in Fleet Problem 9) had postulated a surprise carrier aviation attack to disable it. With this in mind, the canal was heavily fortified. Although the navy dismissed the possibility that the Japanese would attempt a carrier raid on the canal—with considerable reason, given limited Japanese logistical resources—there remained the constant fear that Japanese or other Axis saboteurs might try to disable it. The simplest way of doing this would have been to sink a merchant ship in one of the "cuts" or blow up one of the sets of locks. Although these scenarios were so obvious that they actually turned up in movies, the Japanese never attempted either.

During the war, recognizing that ships were going to become wider, construction began on a new, wider set of locks, but the project was abandoned after the war. Another Panama construction project, which did see completion, was that of an oil pipeline to run parallel to the canal. Originally planned as a single 20-inch line, even before completion a second pipeline began being laid. Completed in 1945, daily capacity on the 46-mile-long line was reportedly over 300,000 barrels.

Without the Panama Canal the war in the Pacific would certainly have dragged on into 1946, if not longer.

Panay Incident

The USS *Panay* (PR-5) was a small (450-ton) gunboat built in the 1920s for service on the Yangtze River in China. On Sunday, 12 December 1937, she was escorting three US flag tankers downriver to the sea from above Nanking. At about 1330 hours, *Panay* and the tankers were anchored near

Hoshein, upstream from Nanking. It was a clear, calm day. Although plainly marked as an American vessel, *Panay* was attacked by Japanese dive bombers, which sank her and machine-gunned the wreck. Two of the tankers were also hit but managed to survive. The attack took over 20 minutes and was conducted by three waves of aircraft. Two American sailors were killed, as well as an Italian journalist, and 11 others were wounded.

After a protest from the United States, the Japanese government issued an apology for the "accident" and paid some $2.2 million in compensation. The officer responsible for the attack, Col. Kingona Hashimoto, was reassigned. After PEARL HARBOR Hashimoto received a decoration for the sinking of *Panay*, which subsequent investigation has determined was a deliberate act, apparently inspired by orders from higher commanders.

See: TUTUILA, US RIVER GUNBOAT; WARSHIPS, US, CAPTURED.

Ref: Perry, *The Panay Incident*.

Paramushiro, Kuriles, Japan

Through perseverance and sacrifice the Japanese had developed a modest naval base and a surprisingly extensive air base at desolate Paramushiro, with an eye on operations toward Siberia and the ALEUTIANS. It was several times subject to US air raids from the Aleutians and was taken by the Russians in August 1945.

Patch, Alexander McC., III (1889–1945)

Alexander McCarrell Patch, an army brat, graduated from West Point in 1913. Commissioned in the infantry, he saw active service on the Mexican border and in combat as commander of a machine gun battalion during World War I. He afterward held various posts, attended several army schools, and rose slowly through the ranks. One of the officers who developed the "triangular" infantry division table of organization in 1936, PEARL HARBOR found him in a training command, from which he was sent in January of 1942 to prepare the defense of NEW CALEDONIA. Organizing the Americal Division from odd units he found in the South Pacific, Patch took the division to support the Marines on GUADALCANAL in October of 1942. Succeeding to command on Guadalcanal later that year, he oversaw the final reduction of the Japanese forces. In February of 1943 Patch was ordered home to the United States, where he assumed command of a corps. In March of 1944 he was given command of the Seventh Army for the invasion of Southern France, which he executed flawlessly. He led his army until the end of the war, which found his troops in Bavaria. During Patch's operations in Lorraine his son, Captain Alexander McCarrell Patch IV, was killed in action. After the war assigned to head a study of how best to organize the army for the postwar world, Patch died suddenly in late 1945.

PB2Y Coronado, US Flying Boat

The PB2Y Coronado was a four-engine US flying boat designed two years after the two-engine PBY. The PB2Y was a much larger aircraft, weighing 30 tons fully loaded. It was also faster than the PBY, with a max speed of 224 MPH and a cruise speed of 141 MPH. The PB2Y was so large, in fact, that it was used primarily as a transport, getting men and supplies to front-line bases quickly. Only 210 PB2Ys were built, and one was the personal plane of Admiral NIMITZ, enabling him to move across the vast Pacific comfortably, and to work with his staff while doing so.

See also AIRCRAFT TYPES, DEVELOPMENT; RECONNAISSANCE, NAVAL.

PBM Mariner, US Flying Boat

The US PBM Mariner was a follow on for the PBY Catalina. Although the Mariner was a generally better aircraft, it wasn't superior enough to cause cessation of PBY PRODUCTION. The Catalina was cheaper and easier to build and it did its job well. So the PBY did most of the naval reconnaissance during the war, with PBMs being added as they were available.

See also AIRCRAFT TYPES, DEVELOPMENT; RECONNAISSANCE, NAVAL.

PBY Catalina, US Flying Boat

The PBY Catalina was the most common US flying boat of the war, mainly because it was the first to enter service, in 1936. This aircraft served several purposes. Reconnaissance was the PBY's main job. But that could be done more effectively by B-17s and B-24s. What made the PBY unique was its ability to "land" on the water. This allowed PBYs to be stationed in places where there were no airfields, or where the local airfields were crammed with conventional bombers and fighters. Seaplane tenders (ships with fuel, repair facilities, and ground crews) would anchor in the same bays and inlets that the PBYs operated from. The ability to float

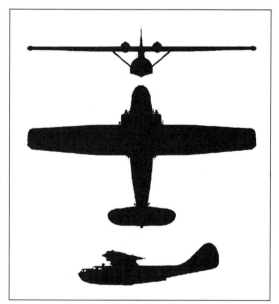

Although a mid-1930s design, the PBY Catalina was the most successful American flying boat of the war.

also made PBYs invaluable (and quite popular) for picking up the crews of downed aircraft. Thousands of airmen owed their lives to the timely arrival of a PBY. Unfortunately, the PBY was too slow (175 MPH top speed) to make an effective bomber. But it was effective against SUBMARINES, as they were less likely to shoot back and were more vulnerable to any damage. Nearly 3,300 PBYs were built during the war, about 40% of them being "amphibian" (with wheels allowing them to land on an airfield if available). Some 20% were given to allies. Although the PBY was slow (cruising speed of 110–115 MPH), it was well armed. Up to 4,000 pounds of bombs or depth charges could be carried, and the average PBY was equipped with five machine guns facing in various directions. PBY range was over 2,000 miles and the maximum weight was 16 tons. Normal patrols were 8 to 10 hours long. All in all, not too shabby for an ugly two-engine aircraft that could float.

See also AIRCRAFT TYPES, DEVELOPMENT; RECONNAISSANCE, NAVAL.

Peace Feelers, Japanese with Russia

By the late spring of 1945 the Japanese government was attempting to get the Soviets to use their good offices with the United States to bring about an end to the war. Somehow the message never got to the appropriate authorities. By the time the Japanese realized what the Russians were up to (stonewalling) and attempted to reach the United States through Sweden, it was too late to avoid the final horrors of HIROSHIMA and NAGASAKI. The extent to which Stalin deliberately impeded the peace process has never been established, although this may come out now that the old Soviet archives are opening up.

Pearl Harbor, The Campaign

Japan opened the war with three major attacks and several minor ones. The first strike (by a number of hours) was at Pearl Harbor. The objective was to cripple the only force (the US Pacific fleet, and particularly its battleships) in the Pacific that could interfere with the other two Japanese attacks (on the Philippines and MALAYA). Surprise was essential to the Pearl Harbor attack. This was so not only because surprise put the defender at a disadvantage, but also because attacking a major naval base with carrier aircraft in broad daylight had never been done before and no one was sure how successful it would be. On paper it appeared it would work, and the British had been rather successful in a night-time carrier air raid on the Italian fleet in Taranto Harbor on 11–12 November 1940. The experienced and history-savvy officers of the Japanese fleet knew that the first time anything is tried, particularly something risky, the unexpected can be expected.

The Pearl Harbor operation was the brainchild of Admiral Isoroku YAMAMOTO, who first suggested the idea in a conversation with another admiral in February 1941. That spring he ordered his staff to gather information about the proposal. Formal planning began in the summer, and was completed in November of 1941. The basic concept was to injure American military power in the Pacific to the extent that Japan would be able to overrun a territory so vast that the United States would ultimately decide on a negotiated peace rather than a protracted war. Japan could not grab a lot of territory in the Pacific if a large enemy fleet were in the same waters. America had the only other large fleet, and most of it was based at Pearl Harbor in the Hawaiian Islands. Cripple that fleet, and Japan could do whatever it wanted in the Pacific.

The Pearl Harbor Striking Force (six carriers, two fast battleships, two heavy cruisers, a light cruiser, nine destroyers, and three SUBMARINES, supported by eight tankers and supply ships) was concentrated in great secrecy at TANKAN BAY, a secure anchorage in the KURILE ISLANDS north of Japan. As part of the undertaking, another group of submarines was assigned to ferry five two-man midget subs tasked with penetrating Pearl Harbor from the sea at the same time the airmen attacked.

On 26 November 1941, the strike force sailed, under the command of VAdm Chuichi NAGUMO.

Maintaining total radio silence, the Strike Force took a route through the North Pacific, which had proven wholly devoid of shipping under normal circumstances. The progress of the strike force across the Pacific was relatively fast, despite the necessity of having to refuel by the inefficient tow method.

Although American and Allied intelligence were aware that war was increasingly imminent, the much less secretive concentration of Japanese forces for their offensive southward into the "Southern Resources Area" (Malaya, the NETHERLANDS EAST INDIES, the Philippines, and so on) attracted Allied attention. War warnings to Pacific Theater commanders only confirmed their expectations that something would soon happen in that quarter.

In December of 1941 the naval and air base at Pearl Harbor and other installations on Oahu, in the central Hawaiian Islands, represented the greatest concentration of American military power in the world. In normal circumstances the island was the home of nine or ten battleships, three carriers (with over 250 aircraft), a score or more cruisers, and literally dozens of destroyers, submarines, mine warfare vessels, and support ships, plus about 500 land-based aircraft and two understrength infantry divisions. On the morning of 7 December 1941, there were eight battleships, two heavy cruisers, six light cruisers, 29 destroyers, five submarines, one gunboat, nine minelayers, and 10 minesweepers, and 24 auxiliaries plus several ancient hulks being used for various purposes (including a cruiser so old she had fought at Manila Bay in 1898). In addition to combat forces, Oahu had elaborate maintenance and repair facilities, extensive warehouses, and a large fuel dump. Command of these forces was divided between Admiral Husband KIMMEL and LG Walter C. SHORT. Typical of the haphazard command structure that prevailed in the US armed forces before (and to some extent during) World War II, neither officer was in overall command. Short was responsible for the defense of HAWAII from attack, including air attack and the protection of the fleet when in port. Kimmel was responsible for all naval forces and for the direction of naval operations. Although the two socialized occasionally, and even played golf together, there was little professional communication between them, and they did not consult with each other very often on matters respecting their commands and missions.

As early as February of 1941, Short, newly arrived in Hawaii, had dismissed the possibility of a carrier air raid on the place, despite the fact that the navy had several times practiced such a strike against the PANAMA CANAL, SAN DIEGO, and Pearl Harbor itself. These practice raids had demonstrated that such operations were not all that difficult. Although air raid drills were held periodically—there was one at 0200 on December

6—Short's principal concern was the perceived threat of sabotage by members of Hawaii's large resident-Japanese and Japanese-American population.

The Japanese Strike Force arrived at a point some 230 miles north of Pearl Harbor late on 6 December. At 0600 the next morning Admiral Nagumo launched his first strike, of 49 high-level bombers, 40 torpedo bombers, and 51 dive bombers, escorted by 42 fighters. As these flew southward, they split up into different sections, each with its particular objective.

Two US Army enlisted men manning an experimental radar system spotted the incoming aircraft and called air defense headquarters twice. However, the duty officer at air defense headquarters

To cries of "Banzai!" from the ship's company, Japanese aircraft begin taking off from their carrier for the attack on Pearl Harbor at approximately 0600 hours, December 7, 1941.

As Hickam Field burns in the background, Japanese aircraft begin the attack on Battleship Row, off Ford Island, in Pearl Harbor. In the lower left is the battleship Nevada *(BB-36), with some lighters alongside. To her right in the picture is* Arizona *(BB-39), with the minelayer* Vestal *alongside. To her right are* West Virginia *(BB-48), which has just taken a torpedo, and* Tennessee *(BB-43). Foreward of them are* Maryland *(BB-46) and* Oklahoma *(BB-37). The large vessel foreward of them is the oiler* Neosho; *barely visible foreward of her is* California *(BB-44).*

—a very junior lieutenant without much military experience—twice dismissed the bogie, suggesting that it was a flight of B-17s due in from California.

At about the same time, a destroyer exercising outside the harbor entrance spotted a submarine periscope, made a vigorous attack, and confirmed a kill (getting one of the five Japanese midget subs that were trying to enter the harbor), but no one took the destroyer skipper's frantic messages seriously. As a result, the air raid achieved complete surprise, the first bombs falling at 0753. Air bases were hit first, to ensure no interference from American aircraft. Then the bombers went after the fleet, anchored neatly in the shallow and narrow waters of Pearl Harbor. Although it was a Sunday morning, and many of the ships' companies were understrength, having sent men ashore on weekend passes, fleet antiaircraft guns came into action quite quickly. The first strike worked the ships over heavily. The principal objective was the battleships, of which seven were tied up along "Battleship Row" and an eighth was in dry dock. These took an enormous pounding, notably the ships moored outboard of Ford Island. Within a half-hour, all eight battleships were damaged or sunk, as were 10 other warships. The strike ended at

UNITED STATES CASUALTIES AT PEARL HARBOR		
Service	Killed	Wounded
Army	233	364
Navy	1,998	710
Marines	109	69
Civilians	48	35

Note that the casualty figures are found with minor variations in different official sources.

0825. A second strike almost as strong as the first (36 high-level bombers, 78 dive bombers, and 54 fighters) came over at 0840, Nagumo having launched it at 0700. Hampered by dense smoke from the damage inflicted by the first strike, and by an increasingly voluminous antiaircraft fire, the second strike inflicted relatively little damage. It flew home at 0945.

Even as the second strike flew back to its carriers, a critical argument was going on aboard the Japanese flagship. Impressed by the success of their first strike, air-minded officers like Minoru GENDA and Mitsuo FUCHIDA tried to convince Nagumo to undertake a third strike, this time against the harbor installations, repair facilities, warehouses, and fuel dumps. Nagumo demurred, concerned over the whereabouts of the American carriers, which had not yet been located. As a result, as soon as the second strike had been recovered, the strike force turned back for Japan. No Japanese naval task force ever again penetrated so far eastward.

USS Shaw (DD-373), a Mahan-class ship, blows up in her floating dock. Despite extensive damage, the ship was repaired and returned to service.

USS Arizona *(BB-39), burning after the Japanese attack, during which she suffered a magazine explosion and lost about 1,177 of her 1,512 crewmen.*

Pearl Harbor was a devastating defeat for the United States. A total of 21 vessels were sunk or heavily damaged, including two battleships that were total losses, *Arizona* and *Oklahoma*. In addition, nearly 200 aircraft had been destroyed, virtually all on the ground. CASUALTIES were 2,388 killed and 1,178 wounded.

Japanese losses were five midget submarines and about 29 aircraft, for a total of 55 airmen and nine submarine crew members. Arguably, the defeat could have been worse. The three Pacific Fleet carriers escaped the debacle, the carriers were spared. (*Saratoga* was undergoing a refit at San Diego, while LEXINGTON and *Enterprise* were at sea, returning from delivering aircraft to Wake and other island garrisons).

A case can be made that Nagumo's decision not to undertake a third strike was in error, for it would have destroyed the fuel dumps, thereby crippling the remnants of the fleet, and so seriously damaged the harbor facilities that not even minor repairs would be practical—in effect, forcing the United States back to the West Coast. While such a possibility existed, it is important to note that Nagumo's second strike had been relatively ineffective in fact, most of the Japanese aircraft losses occurred during the second strike. Moreover, since his own pilots had just demonstrated the devastating effectiveness of carrier aviation, his concern over the location of the US carriers was by no means unreasonable.

See also DECEPTION.

Ref: Goldstein and Dillon, *The Pearl Harbor Papers: Inside the Japanese Plans*; Prange, Goldstein, and Dillon, *At Dawn We Slept* and *Pearl Harbor: The Verdict of History*.

Pearl Harbor, The Doomed Survivors

In the aftermath of the Japanese attack on Pearl Harbor, much was made of the heroic efforts to release men trapped in the hulls of the sunken ships. Nothing was said at the time, nor for some 25 years afterward, about the men who survived for days, and in some cases even weeks, trapped deep in the bowels of capsized battlewagons, beyond hope of rescue, who died of their injuries or slowly suffocated or starved to death. In virtually every case the identities of these men are known but have never been revealed, out of consideration for their families. Similarly, the navy has never revealed the number of Pearl Harbor survivors who were eventually classified as psychological CASUALTIES, some of whom remained in institutions for the rest of their lives.

Pearl Harbor, Oahu, Hawaii

The principal American naval and naval air base in the Pacific, Pearl Harbor had extensive repair and maintenance facilities, including large dry docks, enormous workshops, great ammunition magazines, and a very large oil tank farm, not to mention vast airfields. However, it had a very

Damage control parties coping with fires aboard USS West Virginia *(BB-48), burning after taking six or seven torpedoes and two bombs, as well as damage from the debris of* Arizona *(BB-39), which blew up astern.*

Although a devastating defeat, Pearl Harbor ultimately sealed the fate of the Japanese Empire, by dragging a hitherto isolationist America into World War II.

narrow and not easily navigated entrance, and was cramped, with barely three square miles of surface area. The biggest problem, in 1941, was that its defense was based on an assumption of army-navy cooperation, which was not always forthcoming.

Despite the devastating Japanese attack of 7 December 1941, the base facilities at Pearl Harbor were little harmed, and it almost immediately resumed its role as the main fleet base in the Pacific, a role that it never lost.

Pearl Harbor, The Plot

The most enduring World War II conspiracy theory contends that President ROOSEVELT and sundry other national political and military leaders "knew" that the Japanese were about to attack Pearl Harbor, and, indeed, even provoked the attack. There are numerous variations on the theme. For example, one suggests that Winston CHUR-

CHILL "knew" but refused to tell, so that the United States would be able to come to Britain's rescue against Germany. These theories are all based on "evidence," often "new" evidence that has "just come to light." Unfortunately, when all this evidence is examined, including the "new" evidence (which always turns out to be information of little value or relevance and long available to the public if it cared to inquire), the most charitable thing that can be said is "not proven."

Consider, for example, the statement of the US ambassador to Japan, Joseph C. Grew. Grew claimed that in January 1941 he forwarded to the State Department information from a "reliable source" to the effect that the Japanese were planning an attack on Pearl Harbor. There are two things wrong with this statement. To begin with, Grew was constantly forwarding rumors and tips from allegedly reliable sources. More importantly, however, in January 1941 there was no Japanese plan to attack Pearl Harbor, as it was not until February of that year that YAMAMOTO came up with the idea, having digested Minoru GENDA's report about the British attack on the Italian Fleet in Taranto Harbor on 11 November 1940, and serious planning did not begin until the summer.

Some of the "theories" about the attack are completely fantastical, including one contention that the attack was actually carried out by British aircraft based on one of the outlying islands of the Hawaiian group!

In fact, the disaster at Pearl Harbor was the result of a lot of audacity and luck on the part of the Japanese and numerous blunders by many American political and military leaders, with no particular person being criminally responsible. As historian Gordon Prange said, "There's enough blame for everyone."

See also KIMMEL, HUSBAND; LANIKAI, US SCHOONER; SHORT, WALTER C.

See also DECEPTION.

Ref: Goldstein and Dillon, *The Pearl Harbor Papers: Inside the Japanese Plans*; Prange, Goldstein, and Dillon, *At Dawn We Slept* and *Pearl Harbor: The Verdict of History*.

Pedang, Sumatra, Netherlands East Indies

A small coastal port, with a good harbor but limited resources, Pedang (or Padang) was potentially of value due to its location, on the western—mostly harborless—side of Sumatra, fronting on the Indian Ocean.

Peking, China

The capital of China, long in Japanese hands, Peking had some value as an industrial center and as a critical rail junction.

Peleliu, Battle of

One of the PALAU ISLANDS, Peleliu was in an excellent strategic location, about 500 miles east of the Philippines and a similar distance west of Japanese bases in the CAROLINES. A thick coat of jungle concealed the unusually rugged nature of this island. It had a small population, and neither port nor air facilities.

Peleliu was the setting of one of the toughest and perhaps least necessary battles of the Pacific War. It was suspected at the time, and confirmed shortly thereafter, that an invasion of Peleliu was not necessary. Other bases in the area were being captured more easily, and the Japanese lacked the airpower and shipping to keep Peleliu active as an air base.

What made the conquest of Peleliu such a bloody endeavor was it was where the Japanese first used their new tactic of defending off the beach. This was a technique later used effectively on IWO JIMA and OKINAWA. The Japanese had examined earlier American island assaults and decided that it was a wasteful proposition to resist on the beach. American ships were able to bombard beach defenses at point-blank range, and US aircraft had a simple run in over the water to beach-front targets. The Japanese knew how to build CAMOUFLAGED fortifications anywhere, and on larger islands, like Peleliu, there were plenty of places off the beach

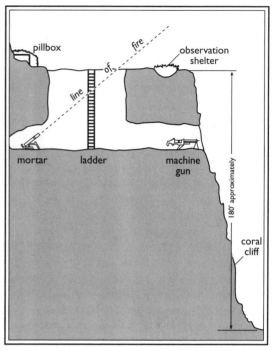

A "typical" Japanese defensive bunker in the latter period of the Pacific War, such as were found on Peleliu and numerous other islands. From MacArthur's New Guinea Campaign by Nathan Prefer (Conshohocken, Pa.: 1995); used with permission.

where defending troops could dig in, hide, and wait for the Americans to come after them. Thus it was on Peleliu. The First Marine Division lost 1,252 killed and 5,274 wounded before the 11,000-man Japanese garrison was wiped out. The fighting went on from September 15 to October 13, 1944, about three weeks longer than the original expectation.

Ref: Hallas, The Devil's Anvil.

Penang, Battle of

Late on May 15, 1945, the Japanese NACHI CLASS heavy cruiser Haguro and destroyer Kamikaze were returning from a voyage to supply Japanese troops in Burma when they were spotted in the Malacca Straits, between MALAYA and SUMATRA by carrier reconnaissance aircraft from a British task force.

Two Marines, PFC Gerald Churchby and PFC Douglas Lightheart, take a cigarette break on Peleliu, September 14, 1944. Note the Amphtrak in the background, and Lightheart's .30 caliber machine gun.

Fleet Air Arm aircraft succeeded in damaging *Haguro*, but lost her as darkness fell. A task group built around the French battleship RICHELIEU was not too far from the Japanese ships. Stripping away the battleship's escorting destroyers, which could make 36 knots to her 30, the task force commander sent them after the Japanese vessels. The destroyers, HMS SAUMAREZ and her near-sisterships *Venus*, *Verula*, *Virago*, and *Vigilant*, caught up with the Japanese ships northwest of Penang shortly after midnight on 15 May. A running fight ensued, as the Japanese ships tried to escape. The British destroyers gradually gained on them. At about 0150 hours the British executed a classic destroyer attack, and

put eight TORPEDOES into *Haguro*. She sank shortly afterward with considerable loss of life. The destroyer KAMIKAZE managed to escape. *Saumarez* was the only British ship damaged, when she took a shell from the Japanese cruiser, but CASUALTIES were light. This was the last surface action of the Pacific War.

Penang, Malaya

On an island off the west coast of Malaya, Penang had a good harbor, with good facilities and a small airport. It was overrun by Japanese forces in early

USS Pennsylvania (BB-38) steams into Lingayen Gulf in January 1945, followed by a battlewagon of the Colorado class and three heavy cruisers. Some of the ship's numerous antiaircraft guns can readily be seen.

1942, and served thereafter as a local military and naval base.

Pennsylvania Class, US Battleships

A good design, the Pennsylvanias were a derivative of the preceding NEVADA CLASS. They were among the strongest battleships in World War I, and both saw service with the ROYAL NAVY, although they were never in combat. Extensively reconstructed during the 1930s, they emerged with improved underwater protection and modernized engines, while modifications to their 14-inch turrets made for improvements in gunnery range.

Pennsylvania, BB-38 (1913–1915–1916), was flagship of the Pacific Fleet at the time of PEARL HARBOR. In dry dock during the attack, she was only lightly damaged and returned to service within a few days. With the transfer of the NEW MEXICO CLASS ships from the Atlantic in early 1942, she was sent to the West Coast for some modernization, but this was less than the extensive rebuilding the more heavily damaged battlewagons received. Back in service in August 1942, she served to the end of the war, providing fire support for amphibious landings. Present at SURIGAO STRAIT, she did not fire. One of the first American warships to be damaged by enemy action in the war, she was also the last, taking a Japanese aerial TORPEDO on August 12, 1945 while lying off OKINAWA. Since the war was at an end, she was not fully repaired. *Pennsylvania* was in the target fleet at the Bikini ATOMIC BOMB tests, and was finally sunk in naval gunnery tests in 1948.

Arizona, BB-39 (1914–1915–1916), was the most seriously hit ship at Pearl Harbor, blowing up apparently as a result of a magazine explosion caused by a Japanese bomb. Over a thousand men went down with *Arizona*. Her wreck is preserved as a war memorial.

Pensacola Class, US Heavy Cruisers

The first American "Treaty Cruisers," the Pensacolas were provided with a powerful offensive armament but were lightly protected. Their main batteries had an unusual arrangement, with two triple 8–inch gun turrets mounted above two double ones. The turrets were actually very lightly built, hardly armored at all, and the guns in each were mounted on a single sleeve, so that they had to be elevated together. "Wet" ships, taking a lot of water when under way, they rolled badly in heavy weather. They cost about $11 million each. Like all US heavy cruisers, they had their TORPEDO tubes removed before the war, a loss that would be felt during the numerous surface actions of the Pacific War.

Pensacola, CA-24 (1926–1929–1930), was escorting the PENSACOLA CONVOY to the Philippines when the Japanese attacked PEARL HARBOR. She took her charges to Australia, then joined the fleet, serving mostly in the southwest Pacific, fighting at TASSAFARONGA, where she took a torpedo, and in many other actions. She was sunk as a target in 1948.

Salt Lake City, CA-25 (1926–1929–1929), was nicknamed "Swayback Maru" and had a busy war. She began it at Pearl Harbor, where she got away to sea and took part in the abortive attempt to relieve WAKE ISLAND. She then joined the fast CARRIER raids on Japanese territories, shooting up

WOTJE and Wake in February 1942, took part in the DOOLITTLE Raid that April, supported the GUADALCANAL landings that August, and did in the Japanese heavy cruiser FURUTAKA at the battle of CAPE ESPERANCE (11 October 1942). As she took three hits in that action, she returned to the states for repairs and modernization, and in March 1943 headed north for the ALEUTIANS, where she served as the American flagship in the Battle of the KOMANDORSKI ISLANDS. Thereafter her life was less hectic, but she served through to the end, to be expended as a target in 1948.

Pensacola Convoy, The

The Pensacola Convoy, several transports carrying reinforcements to the Philippines, escorted by the heavy cruiser *Pensacola*, was transporting several thousand troops; in addition to the B-25s of the 27th Bombardment Group (the crews were already in the Philippines), the ships carried two battalions of 105mm howitzers (the 2nd/131st and one from the 147th Field Artillery), plus large supplies of ammunition.

The convoy was between HAWAII and Australia when the Japanese attack on PEARL HARBOR occurred. It was immediately ordered to Australia. None of the troops, equipment, or supplies ever reached the Philippines, but the 2nd/131st did get into action on JAVA, where it was captured by the Japanese.

See also FUJITA, FRANK, JR.

Percival, A. E. (1887–1966)

A British career army officer with limited service in World War I, Percival began World War II as chief of staff to the British I Corps, with which he saw service in France. After Dunkirk he served for a time as a division commander, and in July of 1941, by then a lieutenant general, he was sent to command in MALAYA and vicinity. There were many things wrong with Percival's command. His ground troops, mostly Indians and Australians, were mostly of less than the finest quality, poorly trained and very unseasoned, the best units of both nations being in the Middle East. His air force was composed primarily of obsolescent aircraft. However, when the Japanese did attack, in December, although they had some material superiority, notably in the air, they were otherwise greatly outnumbered by the defenders (about 60,000—later rising to 100,000—to 130,000). The Japanese didn't even realize they were outnumbered until the campaign was almost over, but had been operating on a shoestring even without that knowledge. Ultimately, Percival never developed an adequate plan of campaign, so that the Japanese retained the initiative throughout, repeatedly outflanking his many attempts to form defensive lines, until he was forced onto SINGAPORE Island, where he surrendered the remnants of his command, some 73,000 troops, to greatly inferior Japanese forces within 70 days of the beginning of the war. Percival spent the balance of the war in a Japanese prison camp, from which he was liberated in time to attend the surrender of Japan aboard USS *Missouri*. Although admittedly entrusted with a very flawed command, Percival certainly did not act with skill or determination. An inept, unlucky commander.

Perth Class, Australian Light Cruisers

Australia's Perth class was typical of British-designed light cruisers. Although lightly protected, they were rather resilient.

Sydney (1933–1934–1935, ex-HMS *Phaeton*) saw considerable service in the Mediterranean, where she sank the Italian light cruiser *Bartolomeo Colleoni*, 19 July 1940. On 19 November 1941 she engaged the German surface raider *Kormoran* in the Indian Ocean, northwest of Australia. After taking at least one TORPEDO and numerous 5.9-inch rounds she drifted away, burning and sinking, and was never seen again, but had meanwhile so heavily damaged *Kormoran* that the raider had to be abandoned.

Perth (1933–1934–1936, ex-HMS *Amphion*) served with the ABDA squadron at the beginning

of the war, fighting in the JAVA SEA and the Sunda Strait February 28–March 1, 1942), where after a long fight in company with USS *Houston* she succumbed to three Japanese torpedoes and several 8-inch rounds.

Hobart (1933–1934–1936, ex-HMS *Apollo*) spent most of the war in the southwest Pacific, fighting in the Battle of the CORAL SEA and in the GUADALCANAL, SOLOMONS, and New Guinea Campaigns, and during the liberation of the southern Philippines. She was scrapped in 1962.

See also GERMANY IN THE PACIFIC WAR; JAPAN, ATTITUDE TOWARD THE ENEMY.

Philippine Army

The Tydings-McDuffie Act of 1934 established an autonomous government for the Commonwealth of the Philippines, with the intention of granting full independence on July 4, 1946. Among the measures the new Philippine government adopted upon taking office was to hire the retired US Army chief of staff, General Douglas MACARTHUR, promote him to field marshal, and put him in charge of organizing a national military force.

Recognizing the financial and industrial limitations of the infant nation, MacArthur's staff, headed by Dwight D. EISENHOWER, developed a plan that by 1946 would have given the Philippines a Regular Army of about a thousand officers and 10,000 enlisted men, plus a large Reserve Army of some 400,000 men, supported by a coast defense navy of about 50 motor torpedo boats and an air force of some 250 airplanes, mostly fighters and light bombers. This force was to be built up gradually. An annual contingent of 35,000–40,000 20-year-old men was to be drafted in two batches for about 24 weeks of training, with short annual refresher courses thereafter. Once the system was properly established a new reserve division would be created in each of the 10 military districts every three years, toward a projected goal of one million men organized in 100 small divisions by 1966, plus the naval and air contingents.

There were many obstacles to creating armed forces for the Philippine Commonwealth. Money was an obvious one, and budgets remained very tight. Optimally about $24 million was needed annually, but the Commonwealth could afford only about $1 million. Both to save money and stimulate the local economy, an attempt was made to rely on locally manufactured substitutes for many items of equipment. For example, a fairly effective HELMET could be made from coconut fiber, while shoes and web gear were made from other native fibers. At one point a surprising problem arose in terms of relations with the War Department, which proved unwilling to sell surplus Springfield '03 rifles at a discount rate to the Philippines for fear they might be used in an insurrection!

By mid-1941 much had been accomplished. A small Regular Army had been established, totaling about 510 officers and 3,650 enlisted personnel, who could be supplemented by the Philippine Constabulary, with 350 officers and 4,500 men. Some equipment had been accumulated and 140,000 men had actually been called up and had received some basic training.

Providing officers for the new army was difficult. Since 1908 at least one Filipino had been admitted to West Point every year, and several others had gone to Annapolis. Some of these men were on duty with the PHILIPPINE SCOUTS, but a number had transferred over to the Philippine Army. The new Philippine Military Academy, modeled on West Point, had graduated a few hundred young officers, and ROTC programs at various colleges in the archipelago had produced a few thousand more. In addition, some senior NCOs from the Philippine Scouts had accepted commissions in the Philippine Army, as had some officers from the Constabulary. The most experienced officers had served either in the US Army or as reserve officers in the Philippine National Guard Division during World War I. (Authorized by the Philippine Territorial Legislature, this was raised in late 1918 and numbered about 14,000 men. Most of the junior officers were Filipino, as was one of the field grade officers, Vicente Lim, USMA 1912. It served for three

months, one of US expense and two at that of the Philippines. Although some Filipinos wished to maintain the division in the NATIONAL GUARD, there was little interest in doing so either in Manila or in Washington.) Nearly 6,000 men held regular or reserve commissions in the Philippine Army, which was not enough, particularly since most of these officers were quite junior. As a result, many of the senior positions in the Philippine Army were held by American officers.

With the threat of war rising, in late 1941 President ROOSEVELT federalized the entire Philippine Army, from Field Marshal MacArthur on down to the greenest private. In August 1941 the Philippine Army began mobilizing, a process only partially completed when the Japanese invaded in December.

Everything was in desperately short supply. In practice, most divisions were woefully lacking in everything, including rifles. There was also supposed to be a small contingent of army troops, including the Philippine Army Air Force, engineers (the equivalent of 18 battalions), heavy artillery (several regiments of 105mm howitzers and 155mm guns), and the like, to support the front-line troops, but they were short of everything as well. The PAAF, for example, had only 16 obsolete P-26 fighters, 12 equally obsolete B-10 bombers, and a handful of other aircraft, with only 500 men. Nevertheless, despite their lack of equipment and training, and ultimately the debilitating effects of hunger and disease, the hardy and brave Filipino troops did extremely well during the defense of BATAAN. Many of those who eluded capture by the Japanese later joined the resistance, where they proved particularly effective. The Filipinos were much encouraged in their war efforts by the prewar declaration that they would have their independence in 1946. This American decision was not made under any wartime duress, but in recognition of the desires of the Filipino people (and the desire to avoid another insurrection like the one at the turn of the century). America also had pretty good relations with Filipinos, and these emotional ties were further strengthened by the subsequent shared wartime experiences.

Had the outbreak of the war been delayed, MacArthur's mobilization timetable provided that by April of 1942 there would have been about 150,000 troops in the Philippine Army, and some 180,000 by mid-year, with each man having received at least three months of training. Moreover, by then there would have been more equipment, albeit still not enough to properly outfit all the divisions. And American troop strength in the archipelago would have reached some 50,000 men, nearly half in the Philippine Scouts. So, had the Japanese delayed their offensive into the spring, they would have found the Philippines a far tougher nut to crack than was actually the case. As it was, the Philippines took longer to conquer than any other of Japan's southeast Asian or Pacific targets. A better prepared Philippine Army could have made for a much more interesting first year of war.

The Philippine Army did not die with WAINWRIGHT's formal surrender in May 1942. In some areas only 25% of the Philippine Army troops turned themselves in to the Japanese. While in the Philippines the survivors of the Philippine Army organized GUERRILLA bands to fight the Japanese, the government of the Philippines in exile, under President Manuel Quezon, created a new Philippine Army. Working with a cadre of officers and men who had escaped the Japanese invasion or who were abroad at the time, the Commonwealth government reestablished the administrative core, of the army creating essential elements such as a military government branch, and managed to raise some combat troops among Filipinos living in the United states.

See also UNITED STATES ARMY, OTHER NOTABLE UNITS.

Ref: Baclagon, *Military History of the Philippines*; Salazar, Reyes, and Nuval, *Defense, Defeat, and Defiance*; Trota, *The Philippine Army*; Whittam, *Bataan*.

Philippine Army, Divisions and Other Major Formations

Under Douglas MACARTHUR's plan for the development of the Philippine Army, by independence in 1946 there were to have been 40 small (8,200-man) divisions, in an armed force of some 400,000. On paper each Philippine division was supposed to have 420 officers, 7,881 enlisted men, and about 40 US advisers, in three infantry regiments, plus an artillery regiment of 36 pieces (24 2.95–inch mountain guns of 1898–1903 vintage and 12 75mm Model 1917 field guns), a 500–man engineer battalion, and small reconnaissance, service, and medical contingents. By December of 1941 10 divisions had been formed, and several more were organized in the opening weeks of the war. However, none of these had completed training nor possessed their proper allocations of equipment. These divisions were all destroyed during the Japanese invasion.

Despite the general surrender of US and Philippine forces in May 1942, many men and some small units managed to escape into the mountains and jungles, to begin a GUERRILLA war against the invaders. The guerrillas soon began to reestablish the Philippine Army. A number of divisions were formed to oversee operations and prepare for the day that MacArthur would return.

First Division. Composed of most of the prewar regulars of the infant Philippine Army, reinforced by many new recruits, on paper the division was supposed to number about 10,000 men. However, the division never served as a unit, since some elements were rather widely dispersed (the Second Regiment was on Mindanao, the rest of the division on Luzon), and it had no artillery. Activated after the Japanese attack, the rump division entered combat on BATAAN in early January, as part of I Corps. It performed well, undertaking several successful counterattacks, but was eventually destroyed in the final Japanese offensive. The Second Regiment performed well in fighting on Mindanao, but surrendered upon receipt of WAINWRIGHT's instructions of 7 May 1942, although many of the men fled to the hills, where they shortly began a guerrilla campaign against the Japanese occupiers. The division was reactivated in mid–1945.

Second Division.   Hastily organized in December 1941–January 1942, the division was formed around the First and Second Regiments of the Philippine Constabulary, to which were added new recruits, for a total of about 6,000 men. It proved an excellent unit, although its lack of artillery was only partially compensated for by the presence of an antitank battalion, the only one in the Philippine Army. The division actually entered combat even before it was formed, when the First and Second Regiments were grouped into the 51st Provisional Brigade, and opposed the Japanese invaders in southeastern Luzon with the South Luzon Force. It joined the retirement to Bataan, where it performed well in numerous actions until the final disaster. The division was reactivated in August 1945.

Fifth Division.   Activated in April 1945, the Fifth Division was organized from the best of the guerrilla forces and the cadre of regular Filipino troops that was maintained throughout the war. Intended as the Philippines' contribution to the invasion of JAPAN, its officers and men were undergoing intensive training when the war ended.

11th Division.   Activated in October 1941, the division formed part of the North Luzon Force. It was one of the best PA divisions, performing well during the staged retreat from LINGAYEN Gulf and in several counterattacks on Bataan.

21st Division.   Activated in October 1941, the division formed part of the North Luzon Force, and anchored the left of the line during the retreat from Lingayen Gulf to Bataan. Well trained, by Philippine Army standards, albeit possessed of only 24 artillery pieces, the division served in reserve in II Corps, being committed to several counterattacks until overwhelmed during the final Japanese offensive.

31st Division.   Activated in October 1941 in North Luzon Force, the division saw little fighting until after the retreat to Bataan, where it was committed to the line in II Corps and was eventually overwhelmed.

41st Division.   Recruited from southwestern Luzon and activated in October 1941, the 41st was the best of the PA reserve divisions. Not only was it larger than most PA divisions, with some 8,000 men, but it also had a greater than average number of troops who had completed their prewar training, and most of its allotment of equipment, including, eventually, all of its artillery. Its commander was BG Vicente Lim (1889–1944), the first Filipino to attend West Point (Class of 1912), who had served as a temporary lieutenant colonel in the 1918 Philippine National Guard Division, and retired from the US Regular Army as a lieutenant colonel in the 1930s. Although reputed to be touchy, Lim was tough, and a good organizer. The division formed part of South Luzon Force, and defended the area southwest of Manila during the initial phases of the Japanese invasion. It entered the lines on Bataan as part of II Corps, and was thereafter continuously on the front until smashed by the Japanese Fourth Division and 65th Brigades on 3 April, the opening day of Japan's final offensive. (Lim was captured on Bataan. Subsequently released by the Japanese, he joined the guerrillas, was recaptured, and was executed in late 1944.)

51st Division.   Activated in October 1941, the division contested the Japanese advance northwestward up the Bicol Peninsula, thereby covering the retirement of the rest of the South Luzon Force to Bataan, which it reached on 7 January. The division was seriously injured in the Japanese assault on II Corps of January 10–25, and thereafter passed into reserve and was not again committed to serious combat until the final days of the defense.

61st Division.   Activated on Panay in October 1941, after the fighting began the division was forced to send two infantry regiments and its artillery to support operations on Mindanao, but managed to recruit some manpower locally. Left alone by the Japanese for several months, it eventually numbered some 7,000 men, who, although ill-equipped, were surprisingly well-trained. Upon the Japanese invasion of Panay, April 16, 1942, the division undertook a fighting withdrawal into the interior, where a base of sorts had been established and supplies stockpiled. Under COL Albert F. Christie it began a guerrilla campaign against the invaders. When MG Jonathan Wainwright issued his orders for all US forces in the Philippines to surrender, Christie initially refused, doing so only on 20 May, by which time some 90% of his men had deserted, fleeing to the hills. The division was reorganized as a guerrilla force under LTC (later BG) Macario Peralta Jr. in mid-1942. By late 1944 it had liberated most of the interior of Panay, the Japanese managing to hold only the principal coastal towns.

71st Division.   Activated in October 1941, in the central islands, the division was transferred to Luzon before hostilities began, leaving behind one infantry regiment. On Luzon it formed part of the North Luzon Force, and was committed to action against the Japanese landings at Lingayen Gulf. Elements were badly mauled during the retreat to Bataan, and the division was effectively broken up, its combat elements going to strengthen the 91st Division.

72nd Division.   Organized on Negros Island in late 1942 and engaged in guerilla operations against the Japanese, particularly in 1944–45.

81st Division.   Activated on CEBU and Bohol, in the central islands, in October 1941, the division was committed to action on Mindanao in April and May of 1942. It surrendered to the Japanese after confirmation of Wainwright's 7 May order to do so. Many of the troops slipped away, to eventually fight as guerrillas.

82nd Division.   A guerrilla command organized on Bohol in late 1942.

83rd Division.   A guerrilla command organized on Cebu in late 1942.

91st Division.   Activated in the central islands in October 1941, the division was shortly transferred to Luzon, leaving behind one infantry regiment. With the US Army's Philippine Division, it formed MacArthur's principal reserve. The division was committed to combat on December 23, on the right of the US-Philippine defensive line confronting the Japanese beachhead at Lingayen Gulf. It anchored the right of the line during the staged withdrawal toward Bataan with considerable success, but was severely handled by the Japanese. Once inside the Bataan lines, the division, greatly depleted and suffering from poor morale, was reinforced with the combat elements of the 71st Division and was for a time held in the rear. It eventually recovered sufficiently to occupy the lines in I Corps, but was destroyed in the last days of the campaign.

92nd Division.   A guerrilla force of about 3,000 raised on Leyte in late 1942, which performed very well during the liberation of the island late in 1944 and early 1945.

101st Division.   Activated on Mindanao in October 1941, the division benefited from the protracted Japanese inactivity in the south to recruit additional manpower and train all hands. As a result, when the Japanese finally undertook serious operations on Mindanao, in April and May, the division, reinforced by the 81st Division and the Philippine Regular Army's Second Infantry Regiment, offered rather stiff resistance, despite a shortage of equipment. The division surrendered upon receipt of Wainwright's order of 7 May.

102nd Division.   Formed in northeastern Mindanao from miscellaneous units and raw recruits in January 1942, the division was heavily attacked by Japanese forces on May 2, 1942, and virtually destroyed within a week.

105th–110th Divisions.   Guerrilla formations created on Mindanao from December 1942 through June 1943. The 105th, with about 4,300 men, was on the long, narrow western part of the island around ZAMBOANGA, while the other units, totaling 25,000 men were on the larger eastern part of the island. They made an important contribution to the liberation of Mindanao in early 1945.

First Filipino Regiment. Technically a unit of the United States Army, the regiment was activated in California in July 1942 from Filipinos who had escaped from the Philippines or were residents of the United States. It was intended as the cadre about which the Philippine Army would form a new division, to fight for the liberation of its homeland. The regiment shipped out to the South Pacific in early 1944. Meanwhile a Second Filipino Regiment had been raised in the United States. However, it proved difficult to recruit sufficient manpower to form a full division. As a result, it was never formed. The Second Regiment never left the United States, serving essentially as a training formation for the first. The First Filipino Regiment saw considerable action, fighting in New Guinea in mid-1944, on Leyte from October through May 1945, and then on Samar until the end of the war, shortly after which it was inactivated.

Ref: Baclagon, *Military History of the Philippines*; Salazar, Reyes, and Nuval, *Defense, Defeat, and Defiance.*

Philippine Constabulary

The Philippine Constabulary was a paramilitary national police force similar to Italy's Carabinieri or Spain's Guardia Civil. It had its origins in the early period of US rule in the Philippines. By the 1930s the Constabulary was entirely staffed by Filipino personnel, many of the enlisted men being retired PHILIPPINE SCOUTS.

Members of the Constabulary were the first troops in the Philippines to fight the Japanese invaders, when a patrol of the Fourth Regiment went into action against them near Vigon, in northern Luzon, shortly after 0200 hours on 10 December.

Throughout the Philippine Campaign of 1941–42, the Philippine Constabulary fought alongside US and Philippine troops, and two regiments were used to form the Second Division. After the Japanese conquest of the islands many of the men joined the GUERRILLAS.

See also PHILIPPINES, CAMPAIGN FOR, 1941–42.

Philippine Division

See PHILIPPINE SCOUTS.

Philippine Islands

An archipelago of over 7,000 islands, mostly of volcanic origin and most quite small (the 11 largest constitute over 90% of the land area), the Philippines encompass some 115,000 square miles (about the same as Britain or Italy). Although they spoke scores of different—albeit somewhat related—languages, the approximately 16 million inhabitants, for the most part Christian were more or less Westernized, though there were some Moslems in the southern areas. Long a Spanish colony, the islands came under US control in 1898. By 1941 they were internally self-governing and were slated for independence in 1946, which helps explain why the inhabitants put up the stiffest resistance of any colonial people to Japanese aggression. Although chiefly agricultural, there was some mining and manufacturing in the islands, as well as a number of excellent harbors, including Manila, which was a major world port.

Philippine Scouts (PS)

The Philippine Scouts had their origin in the numerous Filipinos who supported the United States during the Philippine Insurrection (1899–1902), when the primarily Tagalog-speaking anti-Spanish Philippine insurgents under Emilio Aguinaldo attempted to form an independent "Philippine Republic." Recruited initially from among the scores of non-Tagalog ethnic groups in the islands, with Aguinaldo's acceptance of US authority in 1901 the force was opened to all Filipinos. Authorized at a strength of 5,000 in 1902, the officers of the Philippine Scouts were at first entirely American, while the rank and file were Filipino. Many later prominent American officers, such as John J. Pershing, served in the Scouts during the ongoing Moro insurgency, a rebellion among the Moslem tribes of the southern islands, who had few ties to Aguinaldo's earlier movement.

Although initially companies were recruited on the basis of linguistic unity, in 1908, when battalions were authorized, this policy was abandoned, and Tagalog tended to become the common language of the Scouts. By the end of World War I there were five provisional regiments of Scouts, who had come to comprise the bulk of the US garrison in the islands. In 1920–21 the Scouts were formally incorporated into the Regular Army, forming several infantry regiments (43rd, 45th, and 57th), the 26th Cavalry Regiment, the 23rd and 24th Field Artillery Regiments, the 91st and 92nd Coast Artillery Regiments, the 14th Engineers, and various ancillary units. The infantry, field artillery, engineers, and signals formed the bulk of the Philippine Division, with the 31st Infantry, an American unit. The division had only about 10,000 men, mostly Filipinos, with American officers. It was the primary combat force in the islands.

When the Japanese came in 1941, the Philippine Scouts, numbering about 12,000 seasoned men, formed the backbone of the American-Filipino defense of the islands. During the desperate fighting that followed, Scout personnel won three MEDALS OF HONOR (Sgt. Jose Calugas, 6 January 1942; 2Lt Alexander R. Nininger, January 12, 1942, posthumously; and 1Lt Willibald Bianchi, 3 February 1942), some 40 Distinguished Service Crosses, and over 200 Silver Stars. The few detachments of the Scouts not involved in the surrender on BATAAN in April 1942, mostly surrendered in May, on orders from General WAINWRIGHT, but some men took to the hills to join GUERRILLA bands.

In late 1944 Douglas MACARTHUR and others began urging that the Philippine Scouts be reactivated. Tradition aside, it was hoped that the revived Scouts would be available for service during the invasion and subsequent occupation of Japan. The process was a lengthy one, and not until after the surrender of Japan was legislation enacted to permit the Scouts to be reactivated. By June 1946 there were some 25,000 men in the Scouts, which had been expanded from three infantry regiments to six, as well as CAVALRY, artillery, and service troops. Although the Philippines became independent a few weeks later, the Philippine Scouts continued in US service under a special agreement with the new republic. For a time it was planned to raise three divisions of Scouts (the reactivated Philippine Division, redesignated the 12th Infantry Division, plus the 14th and 16th Infantry Divisions), and strength reached over 30,000 officers and men by June 1947. At that point it was decided that the continued existence of the Philippine Scouts violated American sensibilities concerning mercenary forces. The Philippine Scouts were officially disbanded as of 30 September 1949. All surviving prewar Scouts were offered comparable rank in the Regular Army, an offer that many took. Other personnel were discharged. Although its existence was relatively short, and it fought in only two wars in its 50 years of service, the Philippine Scouts proved one of the premier fighting forces in history.

See also FRIENDLY FIRE, ALLIED PRISONER OF WAR DEATHS BY.

Ref: Stanton, *Order of Battle*.

Philippine Sea, Battle of

The greatest (and last) carrier battle of the war, at least in terms of the number of carriers and aircraft involved, the Battle of the Philippine Sea resulted from an effort by the Japanese Navy to reverse the fortunes of war in the Pacific. The Japanese plan was rather simpler than previous ones, a tribute to the direction and clear thinking of VAdm Jisaburo OZAWA.

Ozawa had assumed command of the First Mobile Fleet, comprising most of Japan's surface warships, in late 1943. Ordered by the chief of naval operations, Admiral Soemu TOYODA, to annihilate the American Fifth Fleet, Ozawa concentrated five battleships, nine carriers (with 430 aircraft), 11 heavy cruisers, two light cruisers, 34 destroyers, and several auxiliaries at TAWI TAWI, a small island group at the southeastern end of the Philippines, with a fine but rather open anchorage and great proximity to the Borneo oil fields, which produced a crude oil so light it could be burned by ships' boilers without refining.

While this fleet was concentrating, hundreds of aircraft were being ferried into the MARIANAS and CAROLINES, as also were 25 SUBMARINES, all intended as part a trap that Ozawa would spring on Raymond SPRUANCE's Fifth Fleet.

Ozawa's plan was simple. When word came that the Americans were hitting the Marianas, their next logical target for an amphibious landing, he would sortie from Tawi Tawi and head directly to intercept the attackers, deployed in such a fashion that three of his light carriers would act as "bait" about a hundred miles in advance of the main body, which was deployed in two task forces. Considering the circumstances, Ozawa's plan was probably the best he could do, and a lot better than most previous Japanese carrier battle plans.

Raymond Spruance, commanding Fifth Fleet, had enormous resources at hand for the Marianas operation. In addition to the fast carriers (Task Force 58, 15 carriers with over 890 aircraft embarked, plus seven battleships, eight heavy cruisers, 13 light cruisers, and 69 destroyers) assigned to defend the landings from interference by the Imperial Navy, he had available nearly a dozen escort carriers and numerous older battleships, cruisers, and destroyers assigned to actually support the landings. So Spruance was overwhelmingly superior to Ozawa.

On 15 June, learning that the Americans had landed on SAIPAN, Admiral Toyoda ordered Ozawa to implement "Operation A." For three days Ozawa steamed slowly northeastward. One reason for the lack of speed was that Ozawa had summoned the "Kon Force," a battleship-cruiser task force assigned to relieve BIAK, and it needed time to rejoin the main fleet

Spruance, apprised of Ozawa's coming by submarine reconnaissance, calmly laid his plans. One task group was dispatched on a scheduled raid to the BONIN ISLANDS, where it took out numerous aircraft assigned to assist Ozawa in the destruction of the Fifth Fleet. Meanwhile, Spruance borrowed a few additional ships from the invasion force to further bolster his defensive screen, and ordered the fleet to rendezvous about 140 miles west of TINIAN at 1800 hours on 15 June.

Marc MITSCHER, the actual Task Force 58 commander, formed his task groups into a "T" with its base pointing toward the enemy. Three task groups formed the cross bar, supported by another, forward and to their right, with the pointing base of the "T" formed by his fast battleship task group, closest to the enemy. Despite his great superiority, Spruance moved with caution, as Japanese aircraft were longer legged than American ones. This was a wise decision, as Ozawa knew where Spruance was, while Spruance did not know where Ozawa was.

On the morning of June 19, Task Force 58 made some air strikes at Japanese air bases on GUAM, usefully destroying aircraft intended to support Ozawa. Meanwhile, at about 0800 Ozawa launched 69 aircraft from his three "bait" light carriers against the American carriers. Spotted on radar at 0959, the strike was quickly intercepted and only about 16 of the attackers got through the swarm of F6F HELLCATS that met them, inflicting insignificant damage on the US fleet. Only 24 of the 69 Japanese aircraft made it back to their carriers.

Ozawa's second strike, 130 aircraft dispatched from the main body at about 0900, did even worse than the first, 98 falling after having inflicted only minor damage. Worse, even as this strike was getting off, a US submarine put a TORPEDO into Ozawa's newest and largest carrier, TAIHO, which shortly succumbed to a series of massive internal explosions.

Ozawa launched a third strike at 1000 hours, 47 aircraft, all but seven of which returned safely because they completely failed to intercept the American ships, the others falling to roving patrols of F6F Hellcats.

At 1100 hours Ozawa launched 82 aircraft from *Zuikaku*, RYUHO, and JUNYO. Although these also failed to intercept, the strike commander led them further and they managed to attack Task Group 58.2, but they inflicted no damage and only 28 made it back to the carriers, most badly shot up. Meanwhile Ozawa lost yet another carrier, SHO-KAKU, to an American submarine. By now night was falling. So far the battle had been one of Japanese air strikes on American ships, Mitscher having difficulties locating the enemy carriers.

During the night of June 19–20, Mitscher kept feeling for the enemy, while Ozawa maneuvered to keep within range, yet undetected. Not until 1540 on 20 June was Mitscher able to get a fix on the enemy, when Ozawa was about 275 miles southwest of Task Force 58. At 1620 Mitscher launched 216 planes from 10 carriers.

These reached Ozawa at about 1840. With darkness closing in, the aircraft attacked, sinking carrier *Hiyo*, damaging *Zuikaku* and some other ships, and disabling two fleet oilers. In this action Ozawa lost 65 more aircraft, while the United States lost only 20.

With night falling, the American aircraft hastened back to their carriers, and several were damaged or lost making night landings, despite the fact that Mitscher gallantly ordered the carriers to light up their flight decks (thus making it easy for potentially lurking Japanese subs to find targets).

The final count of Japanese losses on June 19–20, was three carriers sunk plus damage to another, and two oilers so badly damaged they had to be scuttled. The Japanese lost about 410 aircraft, and nearly 200 land-based planes, not to mention hundreds of men. All of this was done at the cost of 130 US aircraft lost, plus some slight damage to a few ships. Only 76 Americans had been killed.

During the night of June 20–21, Ozawa tried to put as much distance as possible between himself and Spruance. The latter undertook a pursuit, but then broke it off to rescue downed aircrewmen (59 of whom were fished out of the sea). The lopsided massacre of Japanese carrier aviation was promptly dubbed the GREAT MARIANAS TURKEY SHOOT. In the aftermath of the battle it seems clear that Spruance should have pursued Ozawa more vigorously, so that he might have inflicted a decisive defeat on the 21st. But Spruance had two missions, one to defeat the Imperial Navy and one to support the landings on Saipan.

See also CARRIER TASK FORCES, TACTICAL FORMATIONS, JAPANESE; CARRIER TASK FORCES, TACTICAL FORMATIONS, US.

Philippines, Campaign for, 1941–42

The Philippines had the grim distinction of suffering two major invasions during World War II.

While General Douglas MACARTHUR is generally considered one of the most capable military leaders America ever produced, he had his failures. One of the most devastating was his defense of the Philippines. In late 1941, the Philippines were defended by 25,000 US and Philippine regular troops and over 100,000 poorly trained Filipino reservists and conscripts. Using airbases on FORMOSA and some carrier forces, the Japanese first established air superiority over the Philippines, then their navy established maritime supremacy around the islands. The Japanese Army then invaded with 50,000 troops and, after five months of hard fighting, conquered the islands.

Despite ample warning of a Japanese attack, nearly a half-day after PEARL HARBOR MacArthur allowed his air force to be largely destroyed on the ground. Although the Japanese air bases were only 500 miles away, MacArthur did not order his aircraft dispersed nor did he take pains to resist the Japanese air attacks effectively. Similar errors were made with the ground forces. Although MacArthur had been in the Philippines for several years, he failed to take into account the low training levels of his Philippine troops when reacting to the actual Japanese invasion. Most of the PHILIPPINE

ARMY's troops had less than a month's training on December 7, 1941 (December 8 in the Philippines, Japan, and other places west of the International Date Line).

When the Japanese invaded, MacArthur, rather than implement the long-standing operational plan, which called for an immediate withdrawal to the rugged BATAAN Peninsula, decided to try to halt the Japanese in mobile operations on the North Luzon Plain, which has no significant natural obstacles aside from two small rivers. The results were disastrous. The American and Philippine troops fought bravely, if not skillfully, and actually managed to slow the Japanese advance. But on the whole the Japanese were almost always able to overwhelm the defenders with their more skillful manpower and leadership, and their material superiority. In the process many of the few experienced men and much of the best equipment of the Philippine Army was lost. Meanwhile, troop and supply movements were bungled before and during the land battles with the Japanese invasion force. As a result, 4.5 million tons of rice, about five months' rations, plus about 6 million gallons of gasoline and 500,000 artillery shells, were abandoned or destroyed. When the surviving US and Philippine troops finally did retreat to the Bataan Peninsula, they did so short of ammunition, food, and spare parts, all of which were available, but had not been ordered moved in time. Part of this was due to the usual bureaucratic sloth, but politics and incompetence played a part in it also. Overall, MacArthur performed in a decidedly lackluster manner, especially compared to his later accomplishments.

What prevented "MacArthur's Disaster" from becoming "The End of MacArthur's Career" was largely MacArthur's reputation, his skill at public relations, and the need for a presentable hero in the dark days of early 1942. MacArthur was one of the most famous American officers of the post–World War I period. A genuine hero of World War I, he had been the head of the US Army during the early 1930s and had accepted the job of leading the infant Philippine Army (which brought with it the title "field marshal") partially because the Japanese threat was recognized and everyone felt safer with someone of his caliber in charge. Although many military leaders in the United States could see that MacArthur was making significant mistakes in December of 1941, the political leaders looked at the bright side. While British and Dutch forces were collapsing in weeks all over the Pacific, MacArthur's forces were still holding out through the spring of 1942. Although the American situation was hopeless in the Philippines, MacArthur was declared a hero, and evacuated just before his army had to surrender and march off to four years of Japanese captivity. This gave MacArthur a chance for a rematch, with better results later. But the veterans of the campaign always remembered that "Dugout Doug" spent most of his time in a bunker (a "dugout") and then fled.

The 1942 Philippines campaign was not an unmitigated disaster for America. The Japanese had expected to conquer the Philippines by January 1942. The stout resistance of the American and Filipino troops kept additional Japanese troops engaged until May 1942. This had a serious impact on later fighting in New Guinea and GUADALCANAL. If one or two of the divisions tied down in the Philippines through the first week of May had been available for use in New Guinea earlier, the Japanese would have had more success against the Australian troops defending PORT MORESBY. An Allied defeat in New Guinea may well have hastened the assault on Guadalcanal. Such a result would have had serious consequences, for once the Japanese airfield there became operational, an invasion would have required more carriers than the United States had available in 1942. Seen in that light, MacArthur's defense of the Philippines was not so unsuccessful after all.

Nevertheless, the loss of the Philippines rankled. For the rest of the war Douglas MacArthur's headquarters bore the code designation "Bataan" as did his personal B-17. And on 19 August 1945 when a Japanese delegation arrived at Manila to negotiate the details of the surrender their aircraft had to broadcast "Bataan" as a recognition sign.

Ref: Beck, *MacArthur and Wainwright*; Whittam, *Bataan*.

Philippines, Campaign for, 1944–45

The Japanese put a lot more into defending the Philippines in late 1944 than the United States had in 1941. America had about 130,000 mostly untrained troops defending the islands in 1941. Japan had 350,000 troops as a garrison in 1944. The Japanese troops were also better trained, motivated, and equipped. Japan also had a larger air force and fleet to defend the islands. In turn, the United States went after the Philippines with far larger forces than Japan had used in 1941. During the 1941 invasion, the Japanese actually had fewer troops than the defending Americans. The Japanese went straight for the main island of Luzon (containing the capital, Manila), while in 1944 the United States first landed on Leyte, in the east-central part of the Philippines. In both cases, the area first invaded was dictated by the presence of friendly air bases. The 1941 Japanese invasion was staged out of Taiwan, which was a few hundred miles north of Luzon. In 1944, the Allies came from the south because they had just established air bases on recently captured islands northwest of New Guinea. In 1944 the Japanese were under far more pressure than the Americans had been in 1941. For Japan, the Philippines was the Allied staging area for an invasion of the Japanese Home Islands. This brought out the Japanese air and naval forces in large numbers, which the United States proceeded to destroy. After that, a series of amphibious landing extending into mid-1945 led to the liberation of all the Philippine islands. By early March of 1945, Manila was again in US hands. Although fighting continued in remote areas until Japan surrendered, the Philippines were effectively liberated. MacArthur had kept his promise to the Philippine people and "returned."

Philippines, Commonwealth of the

The "Territory of the Philippines" became the "Commonwealth of the Philippines" under the terms of the Tydings-McDuffie Act of 1934, which created it as an internally self-governing entity in preparation for independence. The president of the Commonwealth was Manuel Quezon y Molina (1878–1944). Quezon had been elected the first president of the Commonwealth in 1935, defeating the famous Philippine Insurrection leader, Emilio Aguinaldo. Reelected in November 1941, Quezon's inauguration took place in Manila on December 30, as the Japanese were closing in on the city. Initially somewhat inclined to try to make terms with the Japanese, at the "urging" of MacArthur, he fled with his cabinet, to the security of Bataan, and then CORREGIDOR. From there, he escaped by submarine to the United States. In the United States he represented Philippine interests as best he could, establishing a government-in-exile, which was financed by Philippine gold and silver reserves (20 tons), which had been brought out of the islands by submarine, and by a special reserve fund established under the terms of Tydings-McDuffie, into which duties on Philippine goods brought into the United States were deposited. President Quezon's health failed, and he died on 1 August 1944. Vice President Segismondo Osmeña (1878–1961) assumed the presidency. As the liberation of the Philippines proceeded in 1944–45 the Commonwealth government was prepared to reestablish itself, but a decision by MACARTHUR (who knew that Osmeña disliked him intensely) put the initial civil administration of liberated areas under US Army Civil Affairs personnel, a matter that rankled with the Philippine political leadership. Not until after the surrender of Japan was most of the Philippines returned to civil administration.

Philippines, Republic of the

On October 14, 1943 the Japanese declared the Philippines "independent," with José Laurel, a prominent politician and former official of the Commonwealth government, as president. The new government had limited power and served primarily as a means by which the Japanese occupa-

Work details unloading two LSTs on the beach at Leyte, October 1944.

tion forces could better control the populace. Laurel and the other officials of the government were by no means abject puppets of the Japanese, and clashed with the occupiers on numerous occasions. After the war most of the officials, including Laurel, were let off lightly by the Commonwealth of the Philippines.

Philippines, Resistance to the Japanese

Of all their early campaigns, the Japanese had the hardest time in the Philippines. It took six months to defeat the regular American and Filipino forces, far longer than any of their other early conquests. Most of the troops were Filipino and few had more than rudimentary training. While most of the fight-

ing was concentrated northwest of Manila, on the BATAAN Peninsula, there were thousands of American and Filipino troops elsewhere on the many islands that comprise the Philippines. Not all of these troops surrendered, and many simply took their weapons into the hills, there to continue the resistance. Because of the generally good relations between Americans and Filipinos (aided by the prewar promise to grant the islands their independence in 1946), the Japanese encountered a hostile population.

Bolstered by popular support, the first Philippine GUERRILLAS were able to recruit more fighters and withstand strenuous Japanese attempts to eradicate them. While there were some American officers and troops among these partisans, many of the units were led by patriotic Filipinos. Guerrilla operations actually began long before the formal surrender of regular US and Filipino troops in April and May 1942. By late December 1941 some troops on Luzon who had been unable to join the retreat to Bataan were already operating as guerrillas, and in one instance managed to kill a Japanese general in an ambush.

At first there was little the guerrilla bands could do but survive. Some of them did this badly, preying on local villagers who eventually turned them in to the Japanese. Other bands, with better leadership, formed more effective ties to local villagers. Gradually the many small bands coalesced into a few larger ones, not always peacefully.

Unfortunately, before the Americans came back, the guerrillas were isolated for two years deep inside Japanese-controlled territory. Until 1944, when physical contact with the outside world was reestablished, the guerrillas were pretty much on their own. Despite the regular radio contact with some of the guerrillas, Washington was rather surprised at the vigor and size of the anti-Japanese guerrilla movement. As early as February 1943, however, MACARTHUR was making efforts to strengthen the resistance movement. Operation Baus Au (Tagalog for "Get it back") was instituted, to send supplies, equipment, and even personnel in by submarine (62 missions) and aircraft. MacArthur also granted formal recognition and rank to guerrilla leaders, assigning them territorial commands on the basis of the 10 prewar military districts in the islands, and involving them in planning. Nevertheless, fearing that premature large-scale operations would lead to the destruction

Heavily laden with US Army assault troops, Coast Guard-manned LCVPs head into the beach at Lingayen Gulf, Luzon, shortly before 0930 on January 9, 1945.

of the guerrillas, MacArthur urged them to "lie low" until the day of liberation was at hand.

Constantly harassing the Japanese and supplying valuable information to the Allies, the guerrillas waited for the day when MacArthur would return. Meanwhile, the Japanese built up their forces in the Philippines in anticipation of a late 1944 American attack. The larger number of Japanese troops led to increased anti-guerrilla activity, simply because there were now more targets. The clumsy and brutal Japanese anti-guerrilla tactics served to increase the number of guerrillas and the desire for revenge by the much abused Filipinos.

Hardened by over two years of living and fighting in the jungles, the guerrillas became a substantial force. By the time MacArthur and his troops returned to the Philippines in late 1944, there were tens of thousands of organized guerrillas (estimates vary from 100,000 to 180,000) waiting to act as scouts and fighters. The arriving American troops were surprised at the quantity, and quality, of the guerrilla troops. Although later official accounts of the Philippines fighting played down the contributions of the guerrillas, at the time American units were glad to have these local troops available.

The guerrillas served the US forces in many ways. They provided valuable pre-invasion intelligence, conducted sabotage and harassment raids against the Japanese, made diversionary attacks, served as scouts, helped rescue downed pilots, performed security duties to prevent Japanese infiltration, and undertook mopping up operations. On more than one occasion, when a US unit had outrun its supplies, the guerrillas provided food and sometimes ammunition from their own stocks. Just about the only thing the guerrillas were not very good at was serving on the front lines in conventional combat, having neither the training nor the equipment for the role; they occasionally performed that function too, but not always successfully, a matter that became the basis for official denigration of their prowess.

There were a number of notable guerrilla leaders.

LTC Martin Moses and LTC Arthur Noble, formerly advisers to the Philippine 11th Division, had escaped to northern Luzon in early 1942 and were shortly in command of some 6,000 guerrilla fighters. Prone to daring, even foolhardy undertakings, they were eventually captured by the Japanese, tortured, and murdered. Their replacement, LTC R. W. Volkman, proved less rash and was probably a better administrator. By late 1944 Volkman's North Luzon Force had expanded to some 25,000 men, organized into five infantry regiments, an artillery battalion, and various support and service elements. The North Luzon Force proved a valuable asset to MacArthur in the early months of 1945.

On Leyte LTC Ruperto Kangelon organized about 3,000 guerrillas into the 92nd Division, which, supported by part-time guerrillas, proved highly effective. According to a Japanese account there were 561 clashes with Kangelon's men during the first eight months of 1944. Although the 92nd Division's support of the Leyte landings was immensely valuable, perhaps its most impressive achievement was the clandestine evacuation of thousands of villagers from the invasion area on the eve of the American landings.

On Panay, LTC Macario Peralta Jr. organized the 61st Division in mid-1942. A very effective administrator, Peralta had his division up to about 15,000 men and women by mid-1943, and over 21,000 by September 1944, albeit that only about a third of the troops were properly armed. The division suffered about 1,100 killed in action, died of wounds, or murdered by the Japanese, in the process of inflicting thousands of CASUALTIES on the enemy. So effective was Peralta as a commander, that when the Philippine Army created the Fifth Division in April 1945, he was given command of one of its regiments. Peralta served as deputy chief of staff of the Philippine Army from late 1945 until shortly after independence.

On Mindanao COL Wendell Fertig had some 30,000 regular guerrillas, forming six divisions, the 105th through 110th, plus perhaps 15,000 or more part-time guerrillas. By the time US troops landed in early 1945, Fertig's men had effectively liberated about 90% of the island, although the Japanese still held most of the major population centers.

In central Luzon, Luis Tarluc, a communist sympathizer, created the Hukbalahap (or Huk) movement. The name is an acronym for the Tagalog phrase *Hukbu Ng Bayan Laban Sa Hapones*, which may more or less be translated as "Patriotic Army for Killing the Japanese." The Huks appear to have mobilized some 10,000 to 15,000 guerrillas by late 1944, taking advantage of widespread peasant dissatisfaction with traditional landowning policies. The Huks were organized into regiments, military districts, and squadrons. The success of the Huks in fighting the Japanese is difficult to assess. They themselves claim to have killed more than 5,000 Japanese and some 10,000 Filipino collaborators, figures that cannot be reconciled with Japanese records. After the war the Huks refused to demobilize, went underground, and in 1948 emerged to begin an "armed struggle" to establish a communist regime in the Philippines, which was put down with some difficulty by the early 1950s.

Because many of the Japanese subsequently fled to the hills to fight on in early 1945, the Filipino guerrillas proved invaluable in hunting the Japanese down and limiting the damage the enemy irregulars could cause. There was a certain amount of payback involved here, as the Japanese had indulged in savage reprisals when confronted with the generally pro-American attitude of the Filipinos.

Ref: Baclagon, *Military History of the Philippines*; Manikan, *Guerrilla Warfare on Panay*; Salazar, Reyes, and Nuval, *Defense, Defeat, and Defiance*.

Philipps, Thomas (1891–1941)

Tom Philipps, the son of a colonel and an admiral's daughter, entered the ROYAL NAVY in 1904. During World War I he saw action in cruisers, notably at the Dardanelles and in the Atlantic. Between the wars he rose steadily, and on the outbreak of World War II was vice chief of the Naval Staff. He was still in this post in late 1941, when he was promoted two ranks and sent to command Force Z, the Royal Navy's squadron in the Far East. Philipps was wholly unsuited to his command, having spent most of his career as a staff officer. Although it is unlikely that any British admiral could have avoided defeat at the hands of the Japanese off MALAYA in December of 1941, Philipps' lack of understanding of the influence of air power turned defeat into disaster. A very short man, he was nicknamed "Tom Thumb."

Phoenix Islands

Eight uninhabited Pacific islands totaling 11 square miles, the Phoenix Islands are just south of the equator. Administered jointly by the United States and Britain (which considered them part of the GILBERT ISLANDS), on the eve of World War II several of the islands, (CANTON, Enderbury) had small air bases established to help guard the supply lines from the US West Coast to the South Pacific.

Pidgin

A language common among the peoples throughout much of the South Pacific, either as their primary tongue or as a second language. Its vocabulary derives mostly from English, so that, for example, World War II in some forms of Pidgin is referred to as *taemfaet* ("time-fight"), while woman is usually *mary* and man is *fella*. However, the grammatical structure is essentially Melanesian, so, for example, plurals are formed by repetition: *mary-mary* means "women." The prevalence of Pidgin (sometimes written as Pijin) made communication between Allied troops and the native peoples relatively easy.

Pilots, Quality and Quantity

On the eve of the Pacific War the Japanese Navy may have had the best pilots in the world, carefully selected men, intensively trained to extraordinarily

US Navy carrier pilots being briefed prior to a raid on Tokyo on February 17, 1945. American training produced such prodigious numbers of pilots that by mid-1944 the number of men in flight training was actually reduced.

exacting standards. However, an inability to maintain these standards in wartime was deleterious and ultimately disastrous to the Japanese war effort.

The Imperial Navy had about 1,500 pilots in late 1941, including men who had graduated flight school but not yet completed all their training. In fact, in December of 1941 there were not enough qualified pilots to man all available aircraft, which included about 550 on active carriers, plus another 100 or so on a new escort carrier and two light carriers still working up, plus some hundreds of floatplanes on battleships, cruisers, and seaplane carriers and tenders, as well as about 500 land-based aircraft, for a total of about 2,210 aircraft. In contrast, the US Navy had about 3,500 regular pilots, plus a pool of nearly 3,500 reservists, more than sufficient to man all available aircraft—about 600 on fleet carriers, 40 on escort carriers, about 150–200 floatplanes on battleships and cruisers, plus hundreds of flying boats and land-based aircraft, for a total of about 8,500 aircraft. The US Navy originally had a pilot training program almost as rigorous as that of the Japanese. But in the mid–1930s it was restructured to produce more pilots, albeit less spectacularly qualified ones than their older comrades.

On the eve of the war a man needed a minimum of 700 hours of flight time to qualify as a full-fledged pilot in the Imperial Navy, while his American counterpart needed only 305 hours. About half of the active duty pilots in the US Navy in late 1941 had between 300 and 600 hours flying experience, a quarter between 600 and 1,000 hours, and the balance more than 1,000 hours. So at the beginning of the war nearly 75% of the US Navy's pilots had fewer flying hours than did the least qualified of the Japanese Navy's pilots. And that was just in terms of flying hours: Many of the Imperial Navy's pilots had seen combat against the Chinese and the Russians, experiences that most US Navy pilots lacked.

However, the Japanese pilot training program was so rigorous that only about 100 men a year were being qualified, in a program that required 50 to 64 months to complete, depending upon education completed on entry (high school graduates vs. elementary school graduate). In January of 1940 some prescient officers had proposed reorganizing the Imperial Navy's pilot training program to make it shorter, less rigorous, and more productive, in order to build up the pool of available pilots to about 15,000. This was rejected as visionary.

As a result, as soon as the war began, the Imperial Navy started losing pilots faster than they could be replaced. For example, the 29 pilots lost at Pearl Harbor represented more than a quarter of the annual crop. Then came the losses at the Battles of the CORAL SEA and MIDWAY, and during the GUADALCANAL and SOLOMONS Campaigns—lit-

"Back to the barn": Fighter pilots aboard the second USS Lexington *(CV-16) celebrate shooting down 17 of 20 Japanese aircraft intent on attacking the Tarawa beachhead in November 1943. The airplane is an F6F Hellcat.*

erally hundreds of superb pilots. In a desperate attempt to replace the lost airmen, the Japanese began cutting corners on their pilot training programs. Initially the ground component of pilot training was cut from 14 or 28 months (high school/elementary school grads) to three, then to one, and then virtually eliminated. Soon afterward the flight, operational, and carrier training portions of the program were cut as well, from 12 months each to four, then three, then one month each. By 1945 men were being certified fit for combat duty with less than four months training. In contrast, the US Navy was actually increasing its flight time, while keeping pilot training programs to about 18 months.

Unlike the Japanese, the US Navy applied mass production techniques to pilot training, with the result that by mid-1944 it was qualifying about 8,000 pilots a month, at which point pilot training programs actually began to be cut. Altogether, the US Navy seems to have peaked at about 60,000 pilots. Total Japanese pilot strength may actually have approached this figure, albeit with men trained to decreasingly rigorous standards.

Aside from the Imperial Navy's initially overly exacting pilot training program, there were several other factors that contributed to the decline in the quality of Japanese naval pilots.

Lack of Rotation.   Pilots were kept with line units until killed or wounded. This had two negative effects. One, veteran pilots were not normally available to lend a hand with training, which deprived novice pilots of their valuable advice and experience. Two, experienced men soon became over-experienced, tired, and careless from excessive and continuous exposure to combat. The US Navy regularly rotated men from line to training units and back again, and pulled combat-weary units out of action for regular rests. This maintained skills and morale, and helped trainees learn the ropes from the best qualified instructors.

"Beaching" of Carrier Aircraft.   On several occasions, notably during the Solomons Campaign, the Imperial Navy transferred entire carrier AIR

FLYING HOURS TO QUALIFY FOR COMBAT		
Year	USN	IJN
1941	305	700
1942	305	700
1943	500	500
1944	525	275
1945	525	90

GROUPS to land bases to provide air support for ground operations. Carrier operations require constant training, and once committed to ongoing operations from a land base, carrier pilots quickly begin to lose the skills necessary to operate safely from carriers. The US Navy occasionally committed carrier pilots to land-based operations, but with great reluctance.

Lack of Search-and-Rescue.   As the war went on, the US Navy developed an elaborate search and rescue system, which used SUBMARINES, flying boats, and surface vessels to locate and rescue downed flyers. As a result, on average about 50% of US airmen who crash-landed or parachuted into the sea were rescued (among them George BUSH), a figure that was rising to 75% by the end of the war. The Japanese had no such system, which cost them the services of many valuable men.

Ill-trained pilots were not simply less effective against more experienced pilots, they were also a greater danger to themselves. Throughout the war, a quarter of the aircraft lost were due to accidents, most of them "pilot errors." More experienced pilots made fewer errors. When operating over the open ocean, things could get particularly complicated. Navigation skills were crucial when flying over open water, and the weather was different. In the northern Pacific, the weather and operating conditions in general were particularly horrendous. In this region, nearly 90% of American aircraft losses were due to noncombat causes. The Japanese had a similar experience. Experience was a valuable resource, and the Japanese learned the hard way how easy it is to lose and how difficult it is to regain. New pilots, of any nation, are most at risk, and if there are few experienced pilots to help the inexperienced pilots, the survival rate will remain dismal. American pilots had a 7% chance of getting shot down on their first mission. This went down to under 1% after about 10 missions.

Only 5% of pilots shot down five aircraft and became ACES. But most managed to keep going and survive. American pilots knew the importance of helping the new guys along to even the odds in combat. The Japanese had such a low ratio of experienced to inexperienced pilots by 1944 that they were slaughtered in lopsided battles with their American counterparts. After 1943, few Japanese pilots survived long enough to become aces. From 1944 on, American pilots had more to fear from mechanical problems or bad luck than from the skill of Japanese pilots. Meanwhile, the Japanese saw their aircraft losses from poor flying skills skyrocket. This was made worse by the increasing shortage of key raw materials for Japanese industry. Certain alloys were not available and this led to less than ideal substitutes when building aircraft engines. The Japanese aircraft engine industry was never top of the line in the best of times, and by 1944 their pilots had to be ever watchful of sudden engine problems. Inexperienced pilots were less able to coax a cranky engine into performing long enough to allow the aircraft to be landed and this produced ever more "noncombat" losses. It saved Allied pilots some work and not a little risk.

Poison Gas

While chemical weapons were not used in combat during World War II, they were used in other ways. Lieutenant General Suri Hasimoto ordered his First Army to use poison gas against civilians in China (Shansi Province) during 1939. The Germans and Japanese used PRISONERS to test the effects of existing and experimental chemicals. All nations used chemical weapons in tests (on volunteers) of their protective masks and clothing. While the Germans and Japanese caused thousands of deaths with their "experiments," there were also

hundreds of injuries and some fatalities in the more humane Allied tests as well. And then there were the accidents.

Thousands of tons of various chemical agents were produced and shipped to the front, by all nations. While no one wanted to use chemicals, no one wanted to be caught unprepared if the enemy decided to "go chemical." One of the worst of these accidents occurred in 1943, when a German air raid on the Italian port of Bari managed to hit an Allied cargo ship carrying mustard gas. Few people in the harbor knew what the ship was carrying. Mustard gas is basically an oily substance that, when it hits the skin (or lungs, if inhaled), begins to burn through the flesh. The poison got into the water of the harbor and floated to the surface along with oil from the fuel tanks of sunken ships. The survivors were hauled out of the water and wrapped in blankets, but were still covered with oil and mustard gas. Hours later, many of these victims began to die in agony. It took a while before the medical personnel could figure out what was going on. But even more quickly, the security people made sure that everyone was sworn to secrecy. This incident did not become generally know until many years after the war.

Beyond accidents, there were also the methods by which the thousands of tons of German chemical weapons, (including nerve gas, which the Nazis invented) were disposed of after the war. Most were dumped in the Baltic Sea, or deep lakes, or left in bunkers and deep mountain tunnels, and soon no one was around who knew where the substances were. Fish are still dying and occasionally people are seriously injured. In an incident during the mid-1980s a large number of Danish fishermen became ill after accidentally trawling up a number of gas canisters in their nets. In some parts of Germany, one is cautioned to be careful nosing around in the many World War II-era tunnels that still exist. Similarly, Japanese chemical weapons were dumped into the Sea of Japan, where some remain.

On at least three occasions during the Pacific War US military leaders seriously considered the possibility of using poison gas. The tenacity of the Japanese defense of BIAK, in June 1944, caused LG Robert L. EICHELBERGER to suggest the use of captured Japanese stocks of poison gas to kill Japanese troops ensconced in deep caves. The staff demurred, one officer observing that not only would it result in Eichelberger's removal from command within 24 hours, but it would also probably cost more in time and CASUALTIES than conventional methods.

During the preparations for the invasion of IWO JIMA, where it was known that there were no civilians, the subject again came up. On consideration, it was decided that the possible saving of American lives was not worth the bad press that was sure to result.

Planners for the invasion of JAPAN—operations Olympic and Coronet—also considered the use of poison gas, because of the extreme fanaticism that it was believed would characterize Japanese resistance. Although the proposal was formally rejected, it is likely that the matter would have arisen again had the invasion been undertaken.

There was one occasion during the New Guinea Campaign where poison gas was detected in the atmosphere, although it caused no significant harm. Initially attributed to the deliberate Japanese use of chemical weapons, upon investigation it was concluded that the incident was an accident, and no retaliation in kind was made. This was the only occasion on which poison gas was released in the Pacific War. However, the Japanese did use poison

American sailors stacking 6-inch shells at the Naval Ammunition Depot, Espiritu Santo, in the New Hebrides, thousands of miles from the disaster at Port Chicago, but only a second's misstep from a similar catastrophe.

gas many times during their war with China, including one reported incident on March 28, 1942, near Toungoo in Burma. The Japanese were also the only nation to use biological weapons in World War II, or in any war in this century. They made several such attacks in China before and after Pearl Harbor and were still developing such weapons at the end of the war.

See also BIOLOGICAL WARFARE.

Ponape, Caroline Islands

A large, high island with a fairly good lagoon, Ponape, in the eastern CAROLINES, had limited port facilities. The island had seen much Japanese investment before the war, and the Ponapans were relatively prosperous and moderately devoted to the empire.

In the late 1930s the Japanese began to fortify the island, installing some coast defense guns, establishing a seaplane base, and finally constructing two air fields.

During the Pacific War the Japanese recruited hundreds of workers on Ponape, many of whom served on distant islands. In May 1942 the Japanese drafted 20 men, five from each of the island's four tribes, for combat service. The men were sent to Japanese units at RABAUL and later took part in the BUNA-GONA CAMPAIGN in New Guinea. Only three of them survived.

Ponape figured in US war plans on several occasions, and was marked for invasion at least twice. But as American confidence in "island hopping" grew, the island was bypassed. Although it was bombed an estimate of 250 times from February 1944 to the end of the war, and subject to a naval bombardment in April of 1944, it remained in Japanese hands until their surrender.

Ref: White and Lindstrom, *The Pacific Theater*.

Port Arthur, Manchuria/Manchukuo, China

A major port, with important docking and service facilities, Port Arthur was also a major Japanese naval base, although one of limited strategic value.

Port Blair, Andaman Islands

The principal port of the ANDAMAN ISLANDS, a small miserable place with no particular facilities but some potential as an air or naval base, since it could be used to project power over a wide area of the Indian Ocean and Bay of Bengal. The Japanese occupied it in early 1942. Although they attempted to turn Port Blair into a base, this proved impossible in view of the increasingly effective presence of the British Far Eastern Fleet. Although the British contemplated recapturing the Andamans—and nearby NICOBAR—from the Japanese, in the end they were satisfied with neutralizing them. Over 40,000 Japanese troops were effectively isolated in the two island groups until the end of the war.

See also ROYAL NAVY.

Port Chicago Mutiny

On July 17, 1944, an explosion occurred at the ammunition depot at Port Chicago, California, on the Sacramento River about 40 miles northwest of SAN FRANCISCO. The resulting blast—estimated at five kilotons—killed 323 people and destroyed five ships, an entire train, and numerous buildings, in addition to causing considerable damage in a wide area surrounding the town.

Shortly after the explosion, one of the US Navy ammunition handling companies, which had lost about 200 men in the explosion, was ordered to load ammunition aboard a ship. Most of the men, virtually all of whom were BLACK AMERICANS, refused. Although the navy convinced a majority of the protesters to return to work soon afterward, about 50 flatly refused to do so. Subject to courts-martial for mutiny, most were sentenced to 15 years hard labor and a dishonorable discharge. Shortly after the war the sentences and discharges were revoked and the men issued honorable discharges. The question of whether there actually was a "mutiny" or whether racism was the principle reason for the prosecutions remains controversial.

The Port Chicago disaster was one of several noncombat-related ammunition explosions that have occurred in the United States or to US forces in the Pacific War. Some other notable incidents were:

April 14, 1944. The steamer *Fort Strikene*, a merchant ship carrying 1,300 tons of TNT, exploded in Bombay Harbor. This touched off another ammunition ship nearby. A total of 21 ships were destroyed and nearly a thousand people were killed, with hundreds of others injured.

May 21, 1944. *LST-553*, loaded with ammunition in preparation for operations in the MARIANAS, blew up in the West Loch at PEARL HARBOR. Five other LSTs were destroyed or sunk in the blast ((*LSTs-43, 69, 179, 353,* and *480*) and hundreds of men were killed, including 207 from the Fourth Marine Division, with hundreds more injured. The blast delayed the departure of the Fourth Marine Division for the Marianas by one day. Salvage operations on the sunken vessels resulted in the only noncombat-related award of the MEDAL OF HONOR during World War II, to US Navy diver Owen F. P. Hammerberg, who died on 17 February 1945 as a result of injuries sustained in rescuing two other divers who had been trapped by collapsing wreckage.

Port Moresby, New Guinea

A modest-sized town, with limited use as a port, although possessing a valuable, if small, airfield. As a potential base, Port Moresby would give anyone holding it easy entrée into either New Guinea or the CORAL SEA.

With the approach of the Japanese, in February 1942 all white civilians, government officials included, were evacuated from Port Moresby. This touched off a major disorder on the part of some green Australian troops stationed there, who rioted and looted until steadier troops were brought in.

Port Moresby was soon built up as the principal Allied base in New Guinea, serving as MacArthur's headquarters for much of the war.

Porter Class, US Destroyers

Designed to serve as flotilla leaders (i.e., flagships to squadrons of destroyers) the eight US Porters, built 1934–37, were large, benefiting from modifications to the naval DISARMAMENT TREATIES in this regard. However, they were badly armed, having only surface-capable main guns, rather the dual-purpose ones of the preceding FARRAGUT CLASS, albeit eight to the latter's five. They were rather cramped, but seaworthy, and saw considerable service in the war, during which they were several times modified and in which only *Porter* was lost in action. After the war several of the surviving units were retained for various experiments.

Portland Class, US Heavy Cruisers

Designed as follow-ons to the NORTHAMPTON CLASS, the Portlands were somewhat better protected. They cost about $13 million each but were still not very satisfactory, sharing the lightly protected turrets and sleeve-mounted 8–inch guns of earlier designs. They were fitted as flagships but designed without TORPEDOES, a flaw they shared with all US heavy cruisers.

Portland, CA-33 (1930–1932–1933), nicknamed "Sweet P," accompanied the fast carriers on numerous raids in early 1942, and fought to the end of the war, including such famous actions as the CORAL SEA, SANTA CRUZ, the First Naval Battle of GUADALCANAL and SURIGAO STRAIT. She was broken up in 1959.

Indianapolis, CA-35 (1930–1931–1932), accumulated 11 battle stars in 36 months of war, serving for a long time as SPRUANCE's flagship for the Fifth Fleet. She took a KAMIKAZE off OKINAWA in April 1945 and returned to the West Coast for repairs. Upon completion of these in July she was selected to carry the ATOMIC BOMBS from the West Coast to TINIAN. She then made a short voyage to GUAM to pick up ammunition, and left unescorted for LEYTE GULF where she was to engage in gunnery exercises. Shortly after midnight on 30 July 1945, while running at medium speed on a straight course across the PHILIPPINE SEA, she was torpedoed by the Japanese submarine *I-58*, skippered by Cdr. Mochitasura Hashimoto. The ship sank within 15 minutes. Remarkably, about 880 of the 1,197 men aboard survived the sinking and managed to cling to rafts and wreckage. Unfortunately, the ship had not gotten off a distress call. As no one at either Leyte or Guam bothered to notice that the vessel had not arrived (orders having been given that no communications should be made regarding the routine arrival of ships), the crewmen remained adrift four and a half days before a PBY on routine patrol chanced by. Only 317 of the ship's company survived, the rest succumbing to thirst, salt water poisoning, exposure, wounds, or shark attacks. She was the last major warship lost by the United States in the Pacific.

In December 1945 the ship's skipper, Capt. Charles B. McVay III, the son of an admiral, was subject to a court-martial, on the grounds that his failure to zigzag put the vessel at unnecessary risk. On 13 December McVay's defense counsel produced Cdr. Hashimoto as a witness, who testified that whether the cruiser had been zigzagging or not made no difference to his shot. This was the only time in US military history that a foreign enemy officer testified at a court-martial, and there is a possibility that Hashimoto lied when he said the Kaiten Weapon (see p. 622) was not used in the attack.

McVay later committed suicide

See TORPEDOES

Ref: Hashimoto, *Sunk*.

Pound, Alfred Dudley (1877–1943)

Alfred Pound entered the ROYAL NAVY as a very young boy in the late 1880s and rose steadily, if slowly, thereafter. During World War I he served as a staff officer, being present at Jutland. After the war he held a variety of posts and commanded the Mediterranean Fleet in the late 1930s, a trying time during which Italian SUBMARINES were illegally active against Spanish Republican shipping. In 1939 he was promoted Admiral of the Fleet and made

First Sea Lord, chief of staff of the Royal Navy. Pound had an enormous capacity for administrative work, and was totally devoted to his duties (even having a cot placed in his office so that he could sleep there rather than return home). Unfortunately, he tended to over-concentrate control of operations in his own hands, which often led to unfortunate results. By 1942 he was aware that he had a terminal brain tumor, but remained on active duty until almost the last.

Prisoners of War

While Japanese violations of the rights of prisoners of war under the terms of the GENEVA CONVENTION never reached the scale of the mutual violations of those rights by the Germans and Russians duringWorld War II, they were nevertheless very serious.

In addition to brutal treatment, as in the BATAAN DEATH MARCH, the Japanese generally failed to provide medical supplies to prisoners of war, used them in medical, chemical, and biological experiments, employed them in prohibited occupations (prisoners of war may not be employed in direct war work; they can, for example, be used as agricultural workers, but not in munitions factories, shipyards, or to dig trenches), and denied them pay for their work. Prisoners of the Japanese generally suffered from malnutrition, but this was a more difficult problem, not addressed by the Geneva Convention.

The rules of war prevailing at the time merely required the capturing power to feed prisoners of war a ration equal to that it normally provided its own personnel. This failed to take into account physical and cultural differences between various peoples regarding food, so that even in cases where the Japanese fed Allied prisoners strictly according to the Geneva Convention, the prisoners were likely to slowly starve to death. The Geneva Convention of 1949 adjusted the provisions governing prisoners of war to require the capturing power to take into account the normal diet of prisoners.

American prisoners of war holding a secret Independence Day party in the Japanese POW camp at Casisange, Malaybalay, Mindanao, the Philippines, 4 July 1942.

Excluding members of the PHILIPPINE ARMY, approximately 130,000 Americans were taken prisoner during World War II; about 22,000 fell into Japanese hands, some 80% in the Philippines. About a third of the American prisoners held by the Japanese—7,000 men—died. The number of dead was approximately the same as that among the nearly 110,000 American POWs held by the Germans and Italians, but the death rate among those troops was only about 15%.

The total number of western POWs held by Japan seems to have been about 170,000, of whom about 130,000 were British or Commonwealth troops, mostly Indian, 22,000 were Dutch, and 22,000 American. The Japanese rarely took Chinese prisoners, and no figures are available.

Until the collapse of Japanese resistance, only about 11,600 Japanese military personnel were held by the Western Allies. This was rooted mostly in the Japanese penchant to die rather than surrender. Moreover, Allied troops tended to be wary of taking Japanese prisoners. For one thing, a Japanese soldier who appeared to be surrendering often did so only to pull out a grenade or other weapon in order to go out gloriously, while "taking one with him," a practice in which even wounded Japanese often indulged. This was one reason why pictures of Japanese prisoners often show the men wearing only their loin cloths: Their captors were ensuring that the men were not carrying any concealed weapons. In addition, in war brutality breeds brutality. Very early it became clear that the Japanese tended to mistreat and even murder prisoners. As early as December of 1941 Filipino troops making local counterattacks during the retreat from Lingayen to Bataan often found comrades who had fallen into Japanese hands bound and murdered, often after being subject to torture and other ATROCITIES. These sorts of behavior quickly inclined all Allied troops against taking Japanese prisoners.

The Russians took over 600,000 Japanese prisoners in MANCHURIA, but most of these were taken after the Japanese surrender. Many were held in Siberian labor camps for over a decade. Many did not return.

The Japanese also captured many Western civilians. The fate of these people was hard. Those

Two Marines escort a Japanese prisoner off a US submarine, May 1945.

Gaunt Allied prisoners welcoming their liberators at the Aomori POW Camp, Honshu, 29 August 1945. Note the Dutch, American, and British flags.

who were not murdered outright (and after the war several Japanese officers and soldiers were punished for killing European civilians, including children, rather than be burdened by them), were treated as prisoners of war, not as internees, as prescribed by the Geneva Convention. For example, of some 1,100 civilian construction workers captured on Wake Island in December 1941, 400 did not survive the war: 47 were killed during the fighting, 98 were executed in October 1943 in "retaliation" for an American air raid on the island, and the rest died of disease, malnutrition, and casual brutality in labor camps and MINES in Japan, Manchuria, and China. Some Dutch women captured by the Japanese in the NETHERLANDS EAST INDIES were forced to become COMFORT WOMEN.

See also FRIENDLY FIRE, ALLIED PRISONER OF WAR DEATHS BY; FUJITA, FRANK, JR.; TOKYO WAR CRIMES TRIBUNAL.

Ref: Daws, *Prisoners of the Japanese*; Dower, *War without Mercy*; Fujita, *Foo*; Kerry, *Surrender and Survival*.

ARMAMENTS SPENDING, 1935–1945 (BILLIONS OF 1994 DOLLARS)							
Nation	1935–38	1939	1940	1941	1942	1943	1944
United States	13.5	5.4	13.5	40.5	180.0	342.0	378.0
Canada	?	?	?	4.5	9.0	13.5	13.5
Britain	22.5	9.0	31.5	58.5	81.0	99.0	100.0
USSR	72.0	30.0	45.0	76.0	104.0	125.0	144.0
Germany	108.0	31.0	54.0	54.0	77.0	124.0	153.0
Japan	18.0	4.5	9.0	18.0	27.0	42.0	54.0

Production, Spending

The war was won with courage and determination, and the help of those nations who possessed sufficient resources to arm and supply their troops. National economies and wealth were at the base of

A war bond poster, early 1942. American ability to mobilize enormous sums of money was a major factor in helping to win the production war.

each nation's military strength. Consider the money spent on armaments by each nation each year (left).

One explanation for Germany's initial success in the war can be found in the figures for 1935–38, when HITLER spent nearly as much as all the other powers indicated combined, and certainly outspent Britain, France, and Poland, his principal opponents in the first nine months of the war.

What kind of armaments were purchased and how efficiently money was spent were also important. American arms were more "expensive" than German arms because the United States paid its workers good wages while the Germans used millions of slave laborers—Jews, Poles, Czechs, Russians, Italians, and so forth—who didn't get paid at all. Russia paid its workers, but didn't give them much to buy, thus making the wages nearly worthless (to the workers). The US "bang for the buck" tended to get better as the war went on, due to increased efficiency, greater skill, and economies of scale. By 1945 a dollar spent on defense procurement was buying about 25% more than one spent in 1940, and that despite some wartime inflation.

Nations concentrated on different things. America spent over $300 billion (1996 value) on aircraft between 1941 and 1944. In that same period the United States also spent nearly as much on ships, but only half as much on vehicles and only about $80 billion on guns and artillery. Russia spent little on ships, not nearly as much on aircraft, and a lot more on artillery and TANKS. Even so, American production dwarfed all others, no matter how much the workers were paid. America came very close to matching its peak World War II defense spending in the late 1980s, and the Soviet Union began regularly exceeding its peak World War II spending in the 1970s.

Production, US

Enormous amounts of weapons and equipment were built during World War II. America was the most prodigious producer.

In addition, America contributed enormous (and significant) amounts of industrial material to its allies (particularly Britain and Russia). This aid ranged from raw materials (ores, fuel, etc.) to industrial machinery. Substantial supplies of food and medicines were also shipped. America provided the guns and the butter throughout the war, primarily through LEND-LEASE.

By the end of the war the United States was accounting for approximately 50% of the gross world product. At the beginning of the war, America was already the major industrial power in world, accounting for nearly 30% of world product, despite the Great Depression. By 1945, every other major industrial power (including Britain) had some, or most, of its industries wrecked. The dominant economic position of the United States from 1945 until the 1970s, while profitable for Americans, was not sustainable. Once the other industrial nations rebuilt their factories and infrastructures, America's share of gross world product fell back to a more "normal" 20–25%. This is still huge, for a nation containing less than 6% of the world's population.

PT-Boats, US Motor Torpedo Boats

The American version of motor torpedo boats, PT-boats were small, fast, combatant vessels whose primary weapon was supposed to be the TORPEDO, but they were eventually loaded down with all sorts of other weapons as well, usually heavy machine guns, light cannon, and depth charges, as the crews "customized" their boats. In fact, PT-boats used guns far more often than they used torpedoes.

Their hulls were made of shaped marine plywood, and they had four very powerful gasoline engines, with a very clumsy gearshift system (basically the skipper shouted commands down to two sailors in the engine compartment, each of whom was responsible for two of the four propeller shafts, using manual clutches and stick shifts). Most PT-boats served in the Pacific.

The distribution of PT-boats in the Pacific was dictated by the nature of the operations in which the three commands indicated engaged. The Third/Fifth Fleet operated primarily on the broad reaches of the Central Pacific, and its PT-boats were used mostly to patrol advanced bases and keep Japanese forces on bypassed islands entertained. The Seventh Fleet operated in the SOLOMONS, the BISMARCKS, NEW GUINEA, and the Philippines, where the numerous islands made the use of large numbers of small patrol craft necessary. The Hawaiian Sea Frontier used its PT-boats to patrol the small atolls and islets, which stretched northwest from the main islands, lest the Japanese use them as anchorages for SUBMARINES capable of launching floatplanes or refueling flying boats for airstrikes against HAWAII, as had been done once early in the war.

Most PT-boats listed under "All other commands" were in the Mediterranean.

Altogether, 70 PT-boats were lost during the war, all but six in the Pacific. A majority of the losses (39) were due to accidents, such as groundings, collisions, fires, and explosions; one was sunk by a KAMIKAZE.

See also HIGGINS, ANDREW JACKSON; KENNEDY, JOHN F.

Item	Worldwide	By U.S.	% U.S.
Aircraft	542,000	283,000	52%
Guns (all types)	49,300,000	17,500,000	36%
Vehicles	5,100,000	2,470,000	48%
Ships (tons)	79,000,000	54,000,000	68%

PT-BOATS ON HAND, 1 JAN. 1945	
Third/Fifth Fleets	75
Seventh Fleet	221
Hawaiian Sea Frontier	10
Total Pacific Commands	306
All Other Commands	165
Total Available	471

PT-boats on patrol off New Guinea, mid-1943. Although originally conceived as cheap weapons to use against major warships in narrow waters, PT-boats came into their own operating against Japanese coastal shipping that was attempting to supply isolated garrisons.

Publicity, False Reports

In modern war the demands of "propaganda" or "public information" to keep the folks back home happy have often led to rather extraordinary claims of success on the part of one's armed forces. Some apparently fraudulent claims are perfectly innocent of propagandistic intent, merely being made on the basis of honest mistakes. For example, on 20 October 1942 the Japanese submarine *I-175* claimed to have sunk a "battleship of the Texas Class" southeast of GUADALCANAL. In fact, the submarine had put a TORPEDO into the heavy cruiser *Chester*, damaging but not sinking her.

During the Pacific War a number of vessels achieved the distinction of having been claimed as sunk numerous times. The US submarine *Tang* (SS-306) seems to hold a world's record, being reported as sunk by Japanese forces no less than 25 times before she succumbed to a torpedo malfunction in October of 1944. The most frequently sunk American surface ship was "The Big E," the carrier *Enterprise*, claimed no less than six times, a record apparently matched by US claims of having sunk the Japanese battleship *Haruna*, including the one that really counted, when US carrier aircraft finally did her in at KURE on 28 July 1945.

The record for exaggerated claims of success is held by the Japanese. In early October 1944 the Third Fleet raided FORMOSA, the Philippines, and OKINAWA. This provoked an enormous air-sea battle, with the Japanese committing as many as a thousand aircraft, hundreds of which were shot down. On 10 October the Japanese claimed to have sunk 11 aircraft carriers, two battleships, three heavy cruisers, and one destroyer or light cruiser, as well as inflicting varying degrees of damage on 40 other vessels (including eight carriers and two battlewagons). Actually, although a number of ships in the Third Fleet were hit, only two suffered serious damage, heavy cruiser AUSTRALIA and light cruiser HOUSTON, both of which survived.

The business end of the twin .50 caliber machine-gun mount on a US PT-boat, somewhere off New Guinea, in July 1943. Although their primary weapon was supposed to be the torpedo, PT-boats did most of their work with machine guns and light cannon.

There was at least one occasion when the United States claimed to have sunk a non-existent ship. Because of different possible readings of Japanese characters, when the light carrier *Shoho* was sunk, during the Battle of the CORAL SEA in May 1942, the navy claimed to have sunk a carrier named *Ryukaku*.

Puller, Lewis B. (1898–1971)

Lewis "Chesty" Puller enlisted in the US Marines in mid-1918, after a brief stay at VMI. Although he secured a commission, he was shortly discharged in the post–World War I reorganization of the Corps. He reenlisted as a private. Puller's service was typical of a Marine of his generation, including tours in Haiti, Nicaragua, and China, and aboard ship, between which he attended various schools, was recommissioned, and was repeatedly decorated. On the eve of World War II he was a battalion commander in the Seventh Marines, with which he went to GUADALCANAL in August of 1942. Puller greatly distinguished himself on Guadalcanal, earning his third Navy Cross and sundry other decorations. He went on to command in several other operations, culminating in command of the First Marine Regiment on PELELIU, meanwhile earning a fourth Navy Cross. The end of the war found him in a training assignment at Camp Lejeune.

In the postwar years Puller held various assignments, and then in 1950 was once more given the First Marines, which he led with great élan during the Inchon landings and in the battle for Seoul, winning another Navy Cross.

Returning stateside, he rose to division command and assistant commandant before retiring for reasons of health in 1957. A short, tough, profane man, Puller, the most decorated Marine in history, was an ideal tactical commander.

Purple

The principal Japanese diplomatic code, purple was introduced in 1937. By 1941 the United States had broken the code through the efforts of the navy's

Laurence Stafford and the army's William Friedman. This enabled American intelligence to read Japanese diplomatic communications throughout the war. The Japanese never realized that the code had been broken, and continued to use it for the most sensitive messages between the Foreign Ministry and Japanese diplomatic officials overseas even after the surrender of Japan.

See also MAGIC.

PV-1 Ventura, US Patrol Bomber

The PV-1 Ventura was originally built by an American firm in response to a 1940 British order. After going into action in late 1942, it was found that the PV-1 (called the Vega 36 at the time) was not a very effective bomber. The US Army didn't want them and most of the 1,600 built (plus 535 improved PV-2s) were used by the US Navy for ocean reconnaissance. In this role, the PV-1 was quite good.

See also RECONNAISSANCE, NAVAL.

Pyle, Ernest T. (1900–1945)

The most respected American correspondent in the war, Ernie Pyle began his wartime career in London in 1941, and covered operations in North Africa, Sicily, Italy, and France before going to the Pacific, where he reported from IWO JIMA and OKINAWA. Unlike a great many war correspondents, Pyle spent most of his time up front with the troops, reporting on the common soldier's war. Rather than discuss grand matters of command and STRATEGY, he focused on the daily routine of the soldier's life, the stress of combat, the simple pleasures and pains. Although like all correspondents he left much of the misery and horror unsaid, it was clearly evident from the sensitivity expressed in his writings, for which he won a Pulitzer in 1943. Pyle was killed by a Japanese machine gunner on IE SHIMA, 18 April 1945. On the site was erected a simple monument, originally just of wood and paint but later replaced in stone: "On this spot the 77th Division Lost a Buddy, Ernie Pyle."

Queen Elizabeth Class, British Battleships

The "QEs" were the finest battleships of their generation, the most powerful and speediest of World War I, and the decade after as well. They were the first capital ships to burn oil fuel exclusively. Well protected, heavily armed, and relatively speedy (25 knots), they had excellent sea-keeping qualities. Though old by World War II, they were still of considerable value, not only for shore bombardment, but also in ship-to-ship action, as proven in several surface actions with German and Italian warships. Several saw service with the British Far Eastern Fleet, primarily as escorts for convoys and on bombardment duty.

Queen Elizabeth (1912–1913–1915) served in the Far East, 1944–45.

Malaya (1913–1915–1916) saw no service in the Far East.

Warspite (1912–1913–1915) served in the Far East, 1944–45.

Valiant (1913–1914–1916) served in the Far East, 1944–45.

One unit, *Barham* (1913–1915–1916), was sunk in the Mediterranean. The survivors were disposed of 1946–48.

See also ROYAL NAVY.

Queen Mary and *Queen Elizabeth*, RMSs

Two of the three largest and fastest ocean liners ever built, the third being the French NORMANDIE.

Queen Mary (80,000 GRT) entered transatlantic service in the spring of 1936, for a time holding the Blue Ribband for the fastest crossing. She was converted into a troop transport shortly after the German invasion of Poland in 1939.

Queen Elizabeth (83,000 GRT, later increased) was still under construction when the European War began. She made her maiden voyage in great secrecy in 1940, laying up for a time in New York (with *Queen Mary* and *Normandie*, the only occasion on which all three superliners were together). Although there was some discussion about converting her into an aircraft carrier, she entered service as a troop transport.

As both ships were fast, 28–29 knots, they could make high-speed crossings with minimal escorts, since SUBMARINES were much too slow to intercept them: On one such voyage *Queen Elizabeth* rammed and sank a light cruiser. As each could carry as many as 15,000 men at one time (50% more than any other ship, and more than three times the capacity of the average liner), they were the mainstay of Allied troop movements throughout the war, turning up in all theaters. By one calculation about 24% of US troops in Europe reached there aboard one of the Queens, which made a total of 37 Atlantic crossings.

At the time of the PEARL HARBOR attack they were engaged in transporting the Sixth and Seventh Australian Divisions home from the Middle East.

Unlike the United States, which took merchant ships into the navy or the army for use as transports, Britain permitted the ships to be run by their owners, a move that proved more economical than the American approach. Not only did the owners take better care of the ships, but they also operated them with sailors who were not necessarily fit for

With the Manhattan skyline behind her, RMS Queen Mary steams up the North River, crowded with over 10,000 homebound American troops, June 20, 1945.

military service, an important consideration given Britain's strained manpower resources.

After the war both were engaged in repatriating troops and were then overhauled for commercial service. Both plied the North Atlantic into the early 1960s when they were sold. *Queen Elizabeth* was destroyed by a fire in HONG KONG Harbor, while undergoing conversion into a floating university, and *Queen Mary* is preserved as a tourist attraction and movie set at LONG BEACH, California.

R

Rabaul, New Britain, Bismarck Archipelago

Rabaul, a modest settlement at the northern end of NEW BRITAIN, had a wonderful natural harbor, although very limited facilities for servicing and maintaining ships. Well suited for a naval or air base, being within easy reach of New Guinea and the SOLOMONS, in January 1942 the garrison of Rabaul was only some 1,500 Australians, comprising an infantry battalion and a few old coast defense guns, plus some Hudson reconnaissance aircraft. The Japanese undertook air strikes against Rabaul on 20 January, then landed troops. Australian resistance was stiff, but the situation was clearly hopeless. On 23–24 January the Australians fell back into the jungle.

The Japanese built Rabaul up into their largest base south of TRUK, concentrating very large ground, air, and naval forces there. When they arrived they found two dirt airstrips, to which they added three more, paving four of the five, which were capable of housing over 500 aircraft. It was from Rabaul that all Japanese operations in the Solomons were supported. Although initial Allied plans called for the capture of Rabaul (code named CARTWHEEL) some time in 1943, these were later changed. Subsequent operations against Rabaul were primarily intended to bypass it and let it "wither on the vine." This subjected well over 100,000 Japanese troops to increasing isolation and increasing ineffectiveness for the rest of the war.

See also JAPAN, FORCES ABROAD AT THE SURRENDER.

Range, Aircraft

The radius of air patrol shows the greatest extent to which aircraft at a land base are likely to spot ships or aircraft. No matter how many aircraft are stationed at a base, the chances of spotting something always decrease with distance. This is a matter of simple geometry; the farther away from the base, the more area there is to cover. Reconnaissance reaches out farther than air attacks because the recon aircraft do not have to carry large-weapons loads or conserve fuel for high-speed combat.

See also RECONNAISSANCE, NAVAL.

Ranger, US Aircraft Carrier

An unsuccessful ship, *Ranger* (1931–1933–1934) was America's first carrier designed as such from the keel up. However, this occurred before much experience had been gained in operating the LEXINGTONS. As a result, far too much was attempted on a limited hull. Her wartime career was confined to the Atlantic, where she rendered valuable service in support of the North African landings and in air strikes on German installations in Norway. She was eventually relegated to service as a training carrier, and scrapped in 1947.

Rangoon, Burma

A river port of some pretensions, but only limited facilities, albeit the nerve center of British power in Burma, with an important air base and other military installations. Captured by the Japanese in March 1942, it was liberated in June 1945.

RANKS, OFFICERS, ARMY, AIR FORCE, AND MARINE, COMPARATIVE TABLE

| United States | China | British Commonwealth | | Japan |
		Army	Air Force	
General of the Army	Chi Shang-Chiang	Field Marshal	Marshal of the RAF	Cen-Sui
General	Erh Chi Shang-Chiang	General	Air Chief Marshal	—
Lieutenant General	—	Lieutenant General	Air Marshal	Tai-Sho-gen+
Major General	Chun-Chiang+	Major General	Air Vice-Marshal	Chun-jo+
Brigadier General	Shao-Chiang+	Brigadier	Air Commodore	Sho-sho+
Colonel	Shang-hsiao	Colonel	Group Captain	Tai-sa
Lieutenant Colonel	Chung-hsiao	Lieutenant Colonel	Wing Commander	Chu-sa
Major	Shao-hsiao	Major	Squadron Leader	Sho-sa
Captain	Shang-wei	Captain	Flight Lieutenant	Tai-i
First Lieutenant	Chung-wei	Lieutenant	Flying Officer	Chu-i
Second Lieutenant	Shao-wei	Second Lieutenant	Pilot Officer	Sho-i

A British brigadier is not a general officer. The PHILIPPINE ARMY and the PHILIPPINE CONSTABULARY, which used US ranks, also had "third lieutenants," who ranked just below second lieutenants. As generalissimo of the Chinese armed forces, CHIANG KAI-SHEK appears to have borne the title T'e Chih Shang Chiang. The crossed (+) Chinese and Japanese ranks are usually translated into English at the next highest equivalent. In the Japanese Army field marshal was essentially an honorary distinction, rather than a rank. The comparison is easier to understand by looking at the normal commands held by the ranks in question, using US terminology.

NORMAL RANK OF MAJOR UNIT COMMANDERS

Unit	China	Japan	United States
Army Group	I Chi Sang-Chiang	Gen-Sui/Tai Sho-gen	General/Lieutenant General
Army	I Chi Sang-Chiang	Tai Sho-gen	General/Lieutenant General
Corps	Erh Chi Shang-Chiang	Tai Sho-gen/Chun-jo	Major General/Lieutenant General
Division	Chun-Chiang	Chun-jo	Major General
Brigade	Shao-Chiang	Sho-sho	Brigadier General
Regiment	Shang-hsiao	Tai-sa	Colonel

See also ORGANIZATION, HIGHER ARMY COMMANDS, COMPARATIVE.

Reagan, Ronald Wilson (1911–)

Despite very poor eyesight, Reagan, already a moderately prominent actor, was a prewar reserve officer in the CAVALRY. In April 1942 he went on active service as a second lieutenant. Reagan was initially assigned to the SAN FRANCISCO Port of Embarkation, where he helped oversee the loading of troopships and transports. He was subsequently transferred to the Army Air Force First Motion Picture Unit, with which he made numerous training films. He was discharged in July 1945 as a captain.

After the war he returned to acting, entered politics, and served as governor of California, 1967–75, and as president, 1981–89.

Rearmament, US, 1930s

US rearmament for the Second World War began in a modest way as a result of the ROOSEVELT administration's attempt to fight the Great Depression through economic pump priming. The preceding three Republican administrations had been rather tightfisted, and the Hoover administration's reaction to the onset of the Depression was to make severe cuts in already modest defense spending, and very deep reductions in manpower.

RANKS, OFFICERS, NAVY, COMPARATIVE TABLE

British Commonwealth	Japan	United States
Admiral of the Fleet		Fleet Admiral
Admiral	Taisho	Admiral
Vice Admiral	Chujo	Vice Admiral
Rear Admiral	Shosho	Rear Admiral (Upper Half)
Commodore		Rear Admiral (Lower Half)
Captain +	Taisa	Captain +
Commander	Chusa	Commander
Lieutenant Commander	Shosa	Lieutenant Commander
Lieutenant	Tai-i	Lieutenant
Sub-Lieutenant	Chu-i	Lieutenant, j.g. [junior grade]
Midshipman ++	Sho-i	Ensign

+A captain commanding a flotilla or the senior captain in a flotilla usually bore the courtesy title commodore. In the US Navy, commodore was also given to a small number of selected officers, such as the chief of naval history, who needed to outrank most other people but did not really need to be an admiral.

++Actually there is no rank equivalent to ensign in the Royal Navy, since the Royal Navy's midshipmen serve afloat while functionally filling the same role as ensigns.

Between 1921 and 1933 not a single destroyer had been added to the US Navy, and only three aircraft carriers, 15 heavy cruisers, and seven SUBMARINES had been built or ordered. In contrast, during Roosevelt's famous "Hundred Days" two aircraft carriers, four light cruisers, 20 destroyers, and six other vessels were ordered, in a package worth $238 million, a bit of economic "pump priming" that had beneficial effects in terms of modernizing the navy. Although the president had to cope with charges of warmongering, he was ably assisted by naval enthusiasts in Congress such as Carl Vinson, and by the time the European War broke out in September of 1939, the navy had four battleships, three carriers, two heavy, and nine light cruisers, 70 destroyers, and 27 submarines, newly built or under construction. It was the war in Europe that really sparked US rearmament, albeit that resistance to even modest measures intensified.

On 8 September 1939, with the war underway, the president proclaimed a "limited national emergency" and ordered an increase in the enlisted strength of the armed forces, permitting the addition of 130,000 men to the army (to about 280,000), some 35,000 more to the navy (to about 145,000), and about 7,000 more to the Marines (to 25,000), in addition authorizing the recall of retired personnel to active duty, while also authorizing a modest increase in the strength of the NATIONAL GUARD. This was possible because existing legislation authorized much larger forces than were actually in uniform.

In May 1940, the president requested military spending be increased to $1.1 billion, and declared that the nation's aircraft industry must be prepared to produce 50,000 new aircraft a year. The program was quickly approved in Congress, but not without acrimony. In mid-June, with the Germans having occupied Paris, the president signed "An Act to Expand the Navy by 11 Percent," which added 167,000 tons of combat ships and 75,000 tons of auxiliaries. This was followed by a bill expanding naval aviation, and a request by the chief of naval operations, Admiral H. R. Stark, for the creation of a "Two Ocean Navy," at a cost of $4 billion. Between 12 June and 1 July 1940 the navy awarded contracts for the construction of 66 new ships.

In July, in the face of fierce resistance by isolationists and pacifists of all political pursuations (from right-wing "America Firsters" to left-wing communists), Congress passed what became known as the "Two Ocean Navy" bill, part of a package of emergency defense measures that appropriated about $12 billion between June and October of 1940. Included in the Two Ocean Navy bill was $4 billion (nearly $43 billion in 1996 terms) for new ships: seven battleships, 18 aircraft carriers, 27 cruisers, 115 destroyers, and 43 submarines, plus many auxiliary vessels, this represented an increase in the fleet of 70%, with 1,325,000 tons of combat ships, 100,000 of auxiliary vessels, and 15,000 new aircraft. By early September the navy had awarded contracts for seven new battleships, a dozen new carriers, and nearly 200 other ships.

Much of the attention in American rearmament had hitherto been focused on the navy, although the strength of the army had been increased and it had been authorized 20,000 new aircraft. This was largely due to the fact that it requires years to build a fleet, while to some extent armies can be improvised in a much shorter time. However, by mid–1940 it was becoming clear that the expansion of the army could no longer be deferred. On 27 August Congress authorized the federalization of the National Guard, and three weeks later, on 19 September, passed the Selective Service Act.

This set the tempo for the military build-up over the next 14 months, until PEARL HARBOR, when even greater measures were undertaken.

It must not be forgotten that without the naval building begun in 1939 and 1940, America would not have been ready for a counteroffensive against the Japanese until 1944. Had the Japanese carrier fleet not been lost at MIDWAY in June 1942, the delay could have been another year. The prewar rearmament made more of a difference in the way the war was fought than any of the battles later fought.

See also CONSCRIPTION; LINDBERGH, CHARLES; NEUTRALITY ACTS; PRODUCTION, SPENDING.

Ref: Abbazia, *Mr. Roosevelt's Navy.*

Reconnaissance, Naval

The very first, and perhaps most important, role that aircraft had in warfare was that of reconnaissance—information gathering. Aircraft especially designed for reconnaissance were introduced in the decade before World War II. By the outbreak of the war there were essentially two types of reconnaissance aircraft, long-range and short-range.

Navies were particularly interested in long-range reconnaissance aircraft because of the need to patrol vast expanses of ocean and to escort convoys. Multi-engine aircraft were the norm, and flying boats were very popular, since they could operate with a minimum of basing facilities.

The ideal long-range reconnaissance airplane was not particularly fast but had a very high endurance, giving it a long "loiter" time, and was capable of attaining considerable altitude, to keep it safe from enemy fighters. Such aircraft usually had one or two machine guns for self-defense, and were often equipped to carry some small bombs or depth charges, to enable them to attack targets of opportunity. Bombers, particularly obsolete types, were often pressed into the role of maritime patrol, a duty for which they were generally satisfactory.

Short-range reconnaissance aircraft were designed to engage in tactical reconnaissance. Both armies and navies needed information on the enemy's local resources, information that could be obtained by relatively fast, small aircraft. During World War I navies began experimenting with catapult-launched seaplanes on major warships, and by World War II virtually all cruisers and battleships were equipped with such. Their duties were to help the ships' gunners find their targets. They proved valuable in this role, but by the end of the war were increasingly being dispensed with. There were two reasons for this. The increasing availability of carrier aircraft to support shore bombardment was an important factor, but perhaps even more significant was the extreme danger that the aircraft and their highly volatile fuel posed on the ships. Not a few battleships and cruisers suffered serious damage when their recon planes or the fuel for them caught fire, occasionally due to the blast effects of their own guns.

The US Navy developed a third type of reconnaissance aircraft, the blimp. The blimp was a "non-rigid" airship, essentially a collection of helium gas bags loosely held together by an aluminum frame. Blimps were very slow, 80–90 knots being their maximum speed. But they had enormous range and a wonderful ability to loiter in an area for hours on end. Armed with depth charges, they proved immensely useful in convoy defense in the Atlantic, but saw little service in the Pacific.

While ships have always conducted searches for other ships and landward obstacles, aircraft were the premier search methods in World War II. Nevertheless, aircraft could not do it all. At night and in bad weather, ships still had to rely on their own onboard resources.

Search by ships was, and still is, performed by sailors "on watch." While most sailors on watch are doing vital jobs like manning the engines, steering the ship, and monitoring the radio, others are lookouts. The Japanese in particular carefully trained their lookouts and equipped them with excellent optical devices (binoculars and telescopes). Drilled at night and in bad weather, Japanese lookouts often outperformed the crude radar that US ships had (and Japanese ships lacked) early in the war.

American radar soon improved and by the end of 1942, the Japanese had lost their lookout advantage. Radar was first used on ships in the late 1930s and saw rapid development during the first few years of World War II.

By 1943, it was increasingly common for large aircraft to carry radar. This was particularly important for naval reconnaissance. For army units on land radar was useless because of the "clutter" created by hills, forests and buildings, but ships at sea could be spotted clearly by airborne radar. The bigger the ship, the farther away it could be spotted. Since most warships traveled in groups, a spotter merely had to locate the largest ship in order to find the entire group.

SUBMARINES were another matter, as they are the smallest ships that operate on the high seas and are small enough to be hard to spot by ship's radar. But subs could still be spotted by airborne radar, and it was this vulnerability that eventually doomed the German U-boat threat in the Atlantic and made Japanese submarines much less lethal in the Pacific.

The Allies had the edge in radar development and in the number of long-range aircraft built during World War II, and this provided them with a considerable advantage. However, effective radar and abundant search aircraft did not give the Allies perfect knowledge of what was afloat on the vast Pacific since there were never enough aircraft to cover all the ocean areas simultaneously. It was never possible to equip all recon aircraft with radar and darkness and bad weather often made recon flights futile. What was possible was to increase the probability of spotting enemy ships depending on how many aircraft were at a particular base, or on a task force's carriers. Moreover, spotting was also

RANGES OF SEARCH METHODS

Method	Range in km.	
	Low	High
Lookout	12	22
Aircraft	30	40

The low range is for smaller ships (lower lookouts) and aircraft (fewer crew to keep a sharp lookout). These are clear weather ranges and don't show the lesser probability of spotting something that is farther away. Weather is also a factor, mist and fog severely limiting range. Night spotting is highly dependent on available moonlight, and even under the best of conditions is less than half the range of daylight.

more likely the closer you got to the base or carriers that the aircraft were flying from. As recon aircraft flew out from their own base, the area to be covered increased. Recon aircraft customarily flew a course that resembled a slice of pie. Often they would fly back and forth across an area in much the same way a lawnmower would cover an area of grass to be cut. Thus the range of the aircraft was critical not so much for the distance it traveled from its base as it was for the amount of sea area it could cover before it had to land. The farther from the aircraft's base, the less likely aircraft were to spot what was out there, since the area to be covered increased.

The sharp-eyed lookout is an old naval tradition. There are many dangers at sea that can be seen before you encounter them (including enemy ships), and there are always alert lookouts standing watch on ships. The 20th century brought with it a new vantage point for naval lookouts, the floatplane, an airplane with pontoons instead of wheels, to enable it to operate from water.

About the same time aircraft carriers came into use, battleships and cruisers began to carry floatplanes for reconnaissance purposes. The Japanese were quite fond of floatplanes, but they were popular with all nations possessing cruisers (which carried one or two aircraft each) or battleships (which carried two or more).

The Japanese relied heavily on their floatplanes for reconnaissance instead of their carrier aircraft. After 1942, the Japanese had little choice because most of their carriers were sunk. But in addition to floatplanes on warships, Japan formed floatplane units that operated from the coves and bays of Pacific islands.

The Japanese built special supply ships that could repair and maintain these floatplanes wherever their island base might be. Some of these support ships looked like carriers and could launch amphibious (with wheels and floats) planes from their decks. The Allies had sufficient engineering units to quickly build landing strips on islands. Moreover, the Allies also had thousands of larger (two- or four-engined) floatplanes that had larger range than the normally single-engine Japanese floatplane.

Radar gave a spotting range a bit farther than lookouts, but with greater probability of spotting something and considerable immunity from atmospheric and night effects. Radar early in the war was erratic, and it wasn't until late 1943 that Allied ship radar became routinely reliable. The Japanese were still struggling with radar technology when the war ended. A persistent problem with radar was the difficulty in using it close to land. It was very difficult to separate distant ships from islands and other landforms.

Renown Class, British Battlecruisers

As ships, the Renowns were speedy, maneuverable, and good sea boats. They had been hastily built during World War I, and saw considerable service against the German High Seas Fleet. Modernized between the wars, they—and the even larger and more famous *Hood*, which was lost to the German *Bismarck* in May 1941—were the only old big-gun ships able to keep up with modern battleships and aircraft carriers, and they saw extensive service during the war. However, they suffered from all the handicaps common to battlecruisers; they were virtually unprotected and rather lightly armed.

Repulse (1916–1916–1916) saw considerable service in the European War, before being sent with HMS *Prince of Wales* to the Far East, where they were both sunk by Japanese air attack on 10 December 1941. Her maneuverability helped *Repulse* survive for about an hour, but she could not escape and succumbed to five TORPEDOES. There were few survivors, among them the ship's chaplain, the Reverend J. T. Bezzent, who later returned to the war as fleet chaplain to the British Pacific Fleet.

Renown (1915–1916–1916) saw extensive service in the European War, and then in the Indian Ocean from 1944, where she supported offensive operations in Burma. She was retired in early 1945.

See also ROYAL NAVY.

Repatriation of Civilians and Diplomatic Personnel

Early in the war, acting in accordance with well established custom and international law, the United States, Japan, and other belligerents began negotiations to arrange for the repatriation of diplomatic and other personnel caught in each others' country. These negotiations were conducted through the good offices of the respective "protecting powers," neutrals who had assumed responsibility for overseeing the interests of the belligerents in each other's country. Eventually arrangements were made to transfer thousands of people. Among them were the Japanese ambassadors to the United States, with their staffs and families, US Ambassador to Japan Joseph C. Grew, with his staff and their families, and many civilians, including a number of Japanese residents in the United States. Among both the Japanese and American personnel repatriated were military officers who returned to active duty upon reaching their homelands, which was perfectly legitimate under the terms of the GENEVA CONVENTION.

The actual number of persons repatriated in this fashion is unknown. In addition to transporting personnel to be repatriated, the ships involved carried relief supplies and mail for PRISONERS OF WAR.

The process of repatriation was extremely difficult. Not only did ships have to be procured (the United States chartered the Swedish liner GRIP-SHOLM, while the Japanese used two of their precious merchantships, AWA MARU and *Asama Maru*), but safe conducts had to be arranged, special markings agreed upon, and notification made to military forces. The ships involved in such transactions usually sailed to neutral ports. This was one reason why the United States continued to maintain friendly relations with Vichy France, since Madagascar was the most conveniently "neutral" place for such exchanges.

By 1945 there still remained large numbers of people not yet repatriated. Those in Japanese hands were by this time suffering considerable privation. The process of repatriation broke down following the sinking of the Japanese transport *Awa Maru*, by a US submarine in March 1945.

Ref: Corbett, *Quiet Passages.*

Richelieu Class, French Battleships

The Richelieus were large vessels, of unusual design, carrying their main armament forward in two quadruple turrets. They were built in dry dock, rather than on a shipway, and took a long time to build due to technical problems, design changes, and the strains that France was undergoing in attempting to mobilize rapidly during the late 1930s. The Richelieus were very well protected. Like all World War II battleships except American and British ones, they had large-caliber secondary armament (nine 6" guns), which were of no use for antiaircraft purposes.

Richelieu (1935–1939–1940) while still only partially completed fled France in June 1940 to avoid being captured by the Germans, taking refuge in Dakar, West Africa. Under Vichy control at Dakar from 1940 to 1942, she took some damage in action against British and Free French forces on two occasions, one of which involved a clash with ROYAL NAVY battleships. In early 1943, now with the Free French, she was completed at the Brooklyn Navy Yard and served with the Royal Navy in the North Sea and Arctic Ocean from mid-1943 to early 1944. She then joined the British Far Eastern Fleet, serving with it until the end of the war, protecting carrier task forces and shelling Japanese

installations, and just missing the last surface action of the war, when her escorting Royal Navy destroyers sank HIJMS *Haguro* in May 1945. She saw some postwar service and was scrapped in 1968.

Jean Bart (1936–1940–1950) was very incomplete at the time of the fall of France to the Nazis. Heavily escorted, she was taken to Casablanca, where from her dockside in November of 1942 she traded shots with the USS *Massachusetts*, much to her loss. She saw no further service in the war. Finally completed in 1950, she was the last battleship ever built. Scrapped in 1970.

A sistership was broken incomplete on the ways.

Roosevelt, Franklin D. (1882–1945)

The scion of a very prosperous family, which had been prominent in New York society for generations, FDR was a Harvard man (he earned a "gentleman's C") and a graduate of Columbia Law School. Roosevelt had no formal military experience, although not for want of trying. The Spanish-American War broke out when he was a 16-year-old student in a posh boarding school. With another boy, he plotted to run away and join the navy, only to have their plans frustrated by an outbreak of scarlet fever, which imposed a quarantine on the school. After Columbia he worked at law for a time, and became involved in Democratic Party politics, earning him an appointment as assistant secretary of the navy in the Wilson administration When the United States entered World War I, he offered his resignation in the hope of securing a commission in the navy, but was prohibited from doing so by the president. Despite this, he did get to the front on several occasions, visiting the Marines while in France, once narrowly missing death in a German shelling. He ran unsuccessfully for vice president in 1920. Shortly afterward he contracted polio and spent several years in rehabilitation. Elected governor of New York in 1928 and again in 1930, in 1932 he was elected president.

Like his distant cousin Theodore Roosevelt, FDR was a close student of history, and particularly naval history. An able shiphandler himself (on several occasions he took the helm of destroyers, once bringing that of Lieutenant William HALSEY into port; the nervous young officer realized the assistant secretary knew his business when he saw Roosevelt glancing back to see if the ship's stern was clear), he identified so closely with the navy that he probably visited every major warship in the fleet during the 1930s (his particular favorite was the heavy cruiser *Augusta*). In conversation he often referred to the navy as "us" and to the army as "them," until George C. MARSHALL asked him to stop.

President Franklin D. Roosevelt signs the declaration of war against Japan, December 8, 1941. The strain of events can readily be seen in the president's face. The black armband was a sign of mourning due to a death in the family.

Roosevelt's pro-navy attitude was fortunate in many ways, for just at the moment when the Nation was fighting its most important sea war, it was led by a man who had a more intimate knowledge of the navy than any other chief executive ever.

Roosevelt took an active part in running the war. Not only did he involve himself in strategic decision making, but he was also instrumental in the introduction of the escort carrier and the light aircraft carrier. As he knew most of the senior officers in the navy and Marine Corps, some for as long as 30 years, and many of those in the army as well, he selected personnel for most senior positions personally, and it speaks well of his judgment that very few of his appointees proved wanting. His principal flaw as commander-in-chief was that he thought he'd be around to see the end.

Ref: Larrabee, *Commander in Chief.*

Roosevelt Family at War

The living male offspring of the two presidents Roosevelt (Theodore Roosevelt's son Quentin having been killed in action in France in World War I, in which his daughter Edith Roosevelt Derby served as a nurse) all served in World War II, mostly in the Pacific.

Theodore Roosevelt's sons were:

Theodore Roosevelt Jr. (1887–1944), who entered the army via the Plattsburg program in World War I, during which he was wounded. He returned to civilian life after the war, entering politics unsuccessfully. On the eve of the US entry into World War II he was recalled to active duty as a brigadier general. He fought in North Africa and Sicily, before earning a MEDAL OF HONOR for his work on Utah Beach on D-day. The only general to land in the first wave, upon discovering that he had been deposited on the wrong beach, Roosevelt signaled the troop ships to land the follow-up waves there anyway, saying "We'll start the war from here." He died in his sleep of a heart attack several weeks later. During his military career he earned every American decoration for ground combat.

Kermit Roosevelt (1889–1943) joined the British Army prior to American entry into World War I, later transferring to the US Army; he again joined the British Army in World War II, serving in Norway (Military Cross) and North Africa. Transferring to the US Army after PEARL HARBOR, he died of natural causes in Alaska in 1943, a lieutenant colonel.

Archibald Roosevelt (1894–1979) served as a captain in World War I, during which he was wounded and decorated (Croix de Guerre). He rejoined the army for World War II, winning a Silver Star while commanding a battalion on NEW GUINEA. Apparently the oldest battalion commander in the infantry, he was badly wounded on BIAK, and later discharged as disabled.

Presidential grandson Quentin Roosevelt (1918–1948) served as a captain in the army during the war, and was present on D-day in Normandy.

Franklin D. Roosevelt's sons were:

James Roosevelt (1907–1991), who served in the Marines, rising from captain to colonel. He won a Silver Star for his part in the Second Marine Raider Battalion (Carlson's Raiders) raid on MAKIN ISLAND in August 1942, and later commanded the Fourth Marine Raider Battalion, rose to colonel, and won a Navy Cross.

Elliott Roosevelt (1910–1990), who served in the Army Air Corps in Europe, rising from captain to brigadier general. A licensed pilot, though not a military flying officer, he was decorated for taking the controls of a damaged B-24 after both the pilot and copilot had been wounded, and landing the aircraft safely.

FDR Jr. (1914–1988), who served in the navy, distinguishing himself during the North African invasion, and later rising to command of the USS *Ulvert H. Moore* (DE-442) in the Pacific, aboard which he endured radar picket duty off OKINAWA. He ended the war as a commander, with a Silver Star and Purple Heart.

John Aspinwall Roosevelt (1916–1981), who served as a logistics officer, mostly aboard the second carrier WASP, being discharged as a lieutenant commander.

Royal Navy

Rich in tradition and experience, in 1941 the Royal Navy was still the largest in the world, although the US Navy was shortly to overtake it. Overstretched by the demands of the European War, the threat of war with Japan found the RN with only limited resources to commit to the Indian Ocean.

Force Z, a task force consisting of the battleship *Prince of Wales* and battlecruiser *Repulse* plus some destroyers, was scraped together and sent east in late 1941 (carrier INDOMITABLE was supposed to accompany them, but ran aground on her way to the Pacific and could not make it in time). Under Admiral Thomas PHILIPPS, these sortied from Singapore on the first day of the war, and were sunk by Japanese aircraft off MALAYA on 10 December. British fortunes in the Far East were long in recovering from the disaster.

By early 1942 a modest task force of old battleships, carriers, a few cruisers, and destroyers had been formed into the British Far Eastern Fleet under Admiral James SOMERVILLE. Apprised of Japanese movements through ULTRA, Somerville kept his fleet away from the Japanese First Air Fleet (the PEARL HARBOR strike force) when it sortied into the INDIAN OCEAN in March and April of 1942. Although he lost a few ships, including the old carrier HERMES, he preserved his fleet. Sommerville remained in the Indian Ocean until mid-1944, conducting raids on Japanese shore installations in Burma and the Netherlands Indies, blockading the Japanese garrisons in the ANDAMAN and NICOBAR ISLANDS, lending a hand in the capture of Madagascar, supporting amphibious operations against Burma, and even conducting some diversionary attacks in support of US operations in the Pacific. His Far Eastern Fleet was always a scratch force, made up of what could be scraped together by the Royal Navy, mostly older ships, plus some French vessels, including the battleship RICHELIEU, an occasional Dutch or Polish ship, and even, for a time, the US carrier *Saratoga*.

In 1944, as the strategic situation in Europe became increasingly favorable, the Royal Navy began transferring more modern vessels to the Far Eastern Fleet. Meanwhile CHURCHILL and First Sea Lord Sir Andrew CUNNINGHAM won from a reluctant US Navy consent to send a fleet to support operations against Japan. In November 1944 the British Pacific Fleet was created out of the enlarged Far Eastern Fleet, and placed under the administrative command of Admiral Bruce FRASER. Early in 1945, even as the Far Eastern Fleet continued operations in the Indian Ocean, the British Pacific Fleet joined the US Third/Fifth Fleet for operations against Japan.

Forming a distinct task group within TF 38/58, the British Pacific Fleet, under the immediate command of Sir Philip VIAN, operated against Okinawa, the Mandates, and the Japanese Home Islands until the end of the war, by which time battleships of the KING GEORGE V CLASS were joining their American counterparts in raiding Japanese coastal installations. A contingent of the British Pacific Fleet was present in Tokyo Bay for the surrender of Japan, while other elements accepted the surrender of Japanese forces in various British colonies, including HONG KONG.

In addition to providing task forces in the Indian Ocean and Pacific, the Royal Navy supplied many officers and technicians to the Commonwealth Navies, including most of the senior personnel.

See also AIRCRAFT CARRIERS; AUSTRALIAN NAVY, ROYAL; CARRIERS, DESIGNING AIRCRAFT FOR; CRUTCHLEY, V.A.C.; NEW ZEALAND NAVY, ROYAL.

Ref: Barnett, *Engage the Enemy More Closely*; Marder, *Old Friends, New Enemies*; Roskill, *White Ensign* and *The United Kingdom Military Series: The War at Sea*.

Royal Sovereign Class, British Battleships

Apparently having expended all their ideas on the QUEEN ELIZABETH CLASS, the ROYAL NAVY's de-

signers produced a very inferior battleship in the succeeding Royal Sovereign Class. They were poorly conceived and poorly designed, and, in a moment of panic over fuel oil supplies, were designed to burn coal. Although converted to oil during construction, they never matched the older class either in performance or sea keeping. Unlike the older "QEs," they were not extensively reconstructed between the wars. Their principal role in World War II was convoy escort. Many were sent to the Indian Ocean in early 1942, there being nothing else to spare. It is unlikely that they would have withstood the Imperial Japanese Navy had it taken a more aggressive role in the Indian Ocean in early 1942. The four ships in the class, *Royal Sovereign* (1914–1915–1916), *Revenge* (1913–1915–1916), *Resolution* (1913–1915–1916), and *Ramilles* (1913–1916–1917), were all scrapped in 1948–49. A fifth unit, *Royal Oak* (1914–1914–1916), had been sunk by a German submarine in 1939.

Rudderow/Butler Classes, US Destroyer Escorts

Derived from the BUCKLEY CLASS destroyer escorts, the Rudderows (the "TEV" Class) were about the same size (roughly comparable to the old FARRAGUT CLASS destroyers) and dimensions, but mounted two 5"/38 dual-purpose guns rather than three 3"/50 dual-purpose guns, with heavier antiaircraft and TORPEDO allotments as well (three tubes rather than two). This made the 22 Rudderows, as well as the 24 virtually identical John C. Butlers ("WGT"), the most successful American destroyer escorts in the war. "TEV" referred to turbo-electric drive DEs with 5-inch (hence the "V") guns, "WGT" to geared turbine engines using small gears.

Russia, Battles with Japan Before Pearl Harbor

In 1939 the Soviets and Japanese fought a series of battles in Mongolia, the most notable of which were at Khalkin-Gol (or Nomonhan). The Japanese got the worst of it, and this had a major impact on later battles in World War II. In this border dispute, the Japanese tested their army against the Russian forces. The Japanese failed the test, and as a result decided to leave the Russians alone during World War II. This had a considerable effect on the Russian battles with the Germans far to the west. In 1941, Russia had nearly 40 divisions facing a dozen Japanese divisions in MANCHURIA, and most of these Russian units were quickly shipped west when the Germans invaded in June. The Japanese, Germans, and Italians had signed a military alliance in 1936 (the "Axis"), but the terms were vague. The Germans hoped that the Japanese would attack Russian forces in Siberia if the Germans invaded Russia from the west. The outcome of Khalkin-Gol caused the Japanese to leave the Russians alone throughout World War II.

In the mid-1930s, Japan felt that it was militarily superior to the Russians. Having defeated the Russians on land and at sea in the 1904–05 war, they believed they still held a military edge. Then came the series of border clashes. The Japanese were defeated in a division-sized battle in eastern Manchuria in 1938. They rationalized this defeat and spoiled for another round with the Russians. While the Japanese had some success in smaller border skirmishes, they had yet to defeat the Russians in a deliberate battle. They sought to test their imagined advantage in May 1939 by forcibly redrawing the border between Japanese-held Manchuria and Russian-controlled Mongolia. A Japanese division advanced to the Khalkin-Gol (or Halha) River, and a reinforced Russian division threw it back. Undeterred, the Japanese planned a larger attack in July. This battle involved two major changes. The Japanese reinforced the division they had used in May by adding two tank regiments (70 TANKS) and a new infantry regiment. The Russians brought in General Georgy Zhukov (later to be the architect of the Russian defeat of the Germans) and a larger force (about three divisions, mostly motorized). Because the battlefield was 500 miles from the nearest railroad, the Japanese

thought the Russians incapable of reinforcing their forces so quickly and heavily. Despite their transportation problems, the Russians massed over 300 tanks against the Japanese. In the air, both sides were more evenly matched.

The July battles were another disaster for the Japanese. Their initial attack on July 3rd made some progress, but then the Russians attacked and forced the Japanese back. By July 14th, both sides halted. At this point, the Japanese decided that artillery was the key, and brought in heavy guns. The artillery duels during the last week of July went against the Japanese. The Russians were able to fire three times as many shells, and had generally heavier guns. In August, the Russians planned their own attack, an armored offensive that would settle this border dispute once and for all. Bringing up four divisions and 500 tanks (as well as 24,000 tons of ammunition), the Russians moved forward against the two Japanese divisions on August 20th. This was, in effect, the first real armored offensive of the 20th century and was a smashing success. Within four days, the Japanese had been pushed back to what the Russians considered the real border. There the Russians halted, although they could have kept chasing the shattered Japanese. Events back in Europe (Germany was about to invade Poland) made further involvement in Manchuria inadvisable. In September a cease-fire agreement was signed, thus ending the fighting.

As World War II battles go, the Khalkin-Gol fights were not big ones. The Japanese committed two divisions, plus replacements, and suffered 18,000 CASUALTIES (out of 40,000 troops involved). The Russians suffered 14,000 casualties, out of 70,000 troops sent in. Altogether, some hundred tanks were lost and nearly 200 aircraft.

The Japanese drew the correct conclusions from this three-month clash. They acknowledged that the Russians were superior, and discarded their pre Khalkin-Gol plan for assembling 45 divisions in 1943 in order to drive the Russians back to the Ural Mountains. At the same time the battle was ending, the Nazi-Soviet treaty was announced. This caused the Japanese to renounce their 1936 treaty with the Germans. These diplomatic and battlefield defeats hurt Germany the most, as the lack of an active ally in the Far East enabled the Russians to concentrate their full strength against the Germans. Many of the best Russian troops facing the Japanese were sent west to defend Moscow in late 1941. These divisions made a big difference, especially to the German troops who got close enough to Moscow in late 1941 that they could see the spires of the Kremlin. It was as close as the Germans ever got.

One of the most curious things about Khalkin-Gol is that the rest of the world knew virtually nothing about it, or any of the other smaller Russo-Japanese clashes, until several years afterward. The Japanese naturally were not inclined to spread the word about their unpleasant experience and the Russians were obsessed with secrecy. The Germans remained blissfully unaware of Japanese reluctance to take on the Russians, and attacked the Soviet Union with the idea that the Japanese could eventually get involved. Had the word got out about Khalkin-Gol, the course of World War II might have been rather different.

Russia, Relations with China

Soviet Russia had aligned itself politically with the Chinese Nationalists for a time in the 1920s and 1930s, much to the chagrin of the Chinese communists. This was a purely realpolitik arrangement, as the Soviets had territorial and political designs on China. Nevertheless, the arrangement greatly benefited the Chinese. Chinese military officers (including CHIANG KAI-SHEK), for a short time studied in Russia, while Russian military advisers helped train Chinese troops. Meanwhile, the Soviets urged a "popular front" behind Chiang Kai-shek against the Japanese. Although viewed by the Nationalists with suspicion, the proposal appears to have been made in the belief that Chiang was the man mostly likely to be able to sustain a united resistance against the Japanese. Certainly the Chinese communists were not particularly happy about it. When the CHINA INCIDENT broke out in 1937,

the Soviet Union sent "volunteer" aviation units to support the Nationalist war effort, although these were withdrawn by 1939.

During World War II the Soviets supplied some arms and equipment to the Chinese, mostly to the Nationalists. They also attempted to help themselves to some Chinese real estate. For example, in May 1943 the Russians engineered local uprisings in northwestern Sinkiang, which permitted them and their Mongolian surrogates to occupy two areas of the vast province (the "Altai Incident" and the "Eli Incident"). Not until the final year of the war did the Soviets more or less begin to support the Chinese communists, turning over to them vast amounts of Japanese military equipment captured when they overran Manchuria in August and September of 1945.

Russian attitudes toward China changed drastically once the Russo-Japanese neutrality treaty was signed in April 1941. When the Germans invaded Russia two months later, the Soviets were eager not to provide Japan with any incentives to break their truce. This meant that any assistance given to the Chinese had to be very discrete. As a result, there was little aid of any significance. Diplomatically, however, the Russians took a keen interest in the Chinese situation. As the Russian war with Germany reached its conclusion, it was obvious to the Russians that they could pick up some real estate in the Far East and play a large role in postwar Chinese affairs. With this in mind, Russia attacked Japanese forces in MANCHURIA and northern China with the intention of beefing up the strength of the Chinese communists. After 1941, the Chinese communists had remained away from the Chinese coast and Japanese troops. Rebuilding their military and political forces, the Chinese communists had, by 1945, created a core of support that controlled 65 million Chinese, 250,000 square miles of territory, and a disciplined army of half a million troops. Russia constantly pressured the United States to provide weapons and diplomatic support for the Chinese communists, and at the same time played down reports (substantially correct) that the Chinese communists had arranged truces with the Japanese, a situation that allowed Japanese forces to spend more time attacking Chinese Nationalist troops. Russia also encouraged the idea that the Chinese communists were not really communists at all, but rather social reformers who had been unfairly tagged as communists. While the Russian and Chinese communists had their doctrinal differences, there was no doubt that the Chinese communists were indeed Marxists, and arguably more doctrinaire ones than the Russian version. America did not catch on to this subterfuge until 1947, even though many Americans on the spot had long insisted that the Chinese communists were indeed communists and cut from the same ideological cloth as their Soviet counterparts.

The Russians, in particular Stalin, told American officials outright that the Soviet Union would support American policy in China after the war. In other words, the Russians said they would back the Chinese Nationalists after World War II. Despite reports that the conquering Russian armies in Manchuria were handing over captured Japanese weapons to the Chinese communists, America did not make any moves to counter this Russian support for the communist faction in the ongoing Chinese civil war. As a result of the shrewd Soviet diplomacy in China during World War II, America supported the Chinese Nationalists against the Japanese, while the Russians saw to it that the Chinese communists stayed out of most of the fighting, received most of the surrendered Japanese weapons and equipment, and were in a good position to quickly defeat the battered Chinese Nationalists when the Chinese civil war resumed in earnest after the Japanese surrender. The Russians followed the same STRATEGY in Korea when they occupied the northern part of that country during their Manchurian offensive in 1945. Korean communists were promptly installed in North Korea, a govern-

ment that went on to outlast the Soviet Union itself.

Ryuho, Japanese Light Aircraft Carrier

The submarine tender *Taigei* (1933–1933–1935) was built to a plan that permitted her to be converted rather quickly into an aircraft carrier. In 1941 she was taken in hand for conversion. Reengined and partially reconstructed, she emerged as a light carrier in late 1942. *Ryuho* was not as successful a vessel as *Zuiho,* being slow and poorly constructed. She served mostly as a training carrier. Severely damaged at KURE by a carrier air raid on 17 March 1945, she was not repaired and was scrapped in 1946.

Ryujo, Japanese Aircraft Carrier

Ryujo (1929–1931–1933) was a poor vessel, lightly constructed, unstable, and top-heavy, designed to squeeze the last few tons out of Japan's carrier quota under the terms of the naval DISARMAMENT TREATIES. Subjected to a virtual reconstruction in 1934–37, the ship emerged only little improved. She took part in a number of operations in the war against China, and began World War II by making some of the first attacks on the Philippines on 8 December 1941, before going on to support operations in the NETHERLANDS EAST INDIES and serve with the Combined Fleet. She was sunk by four bombs and a TORPEDO from US carrier aircraft in the Battle of the EASTERN SOLOMONS.

Ryukyu Islands, Japan

Stretch roughly southwestward for about 650 miles between Kyushu, the southernmost of the Japanese Home Islands, and Taiwan. Although the 143 islands total about 1,700 square miles, more than a third of the land area comprises OKINAWA.

S

Sabang, Sumatra

The westernmost important port in the NETHER-
LANDS EAST INDIES, Sabang, on Sumatra, had a
good harbor but only limited resources. If properly
developed, however, Sabang could have been used
to project power into the Indian Ocean, an undertaking beyond the capacity of the Japanese, who
occupied the place early in 1942 and remained in
possession until their surrender. It served as the
principal base for Italian and German submarine
operations in the Far East.

See also GERMANY IN THE PACIFIC WAR; ITALY
IN THE PACIFIC WAR.

SACO

See SINO-AMERICAN COOPERATIVE ORGANIZA-
TION.

Saguenay Class, Canadian Destroyers

Canada's Saguenay Class destroyers, built 1929–31,
were sisters to the British Acasta class. They saw
considerable service in the northeast Pacific.

Saigon, Indo-China

A major city, with a good river port, Saigon had
only limited facilities to service ships. There were
important French military installations there in
1940. It was several times bombed by US aircraft
in the closing months of the war.

Sailors, Homemade Alcohol

Sailors and strong drink have been an inseparable
combination since time immemorial. Unfortunately for Uncle Sam's bluejackets, potable alcohol
has been prohibited on US Navy ships since tee-
totaling Secretary of the Navy Josephus Daniels
banned it in 1914. The last night of legal booze
found the fleet lying off Vera Cruz, with parties of
officers rowing from ship to ship heroically trying
to drink up every last drop before the midnight
deadline. So the hardest stuff officially available on
American ships was coffee, of which endless gallons were consumed. Indeed, British officers often
complained of caffeine overdoses after staff conferences on American warships. This was one reason
why such conferences tended to be on the foreign
ships when US vessels were operating in conjunction with British or other Allied vessels. The Allies
avoided caffeine jags and the Americans could be
treated to some alcohol (in exchange, since the
British were on tight rations for the entire war, the
Americans always brought a few hams or some
other items to donate to the officers' mess).

Improvisations were commonplace in the US
Navy throughout the war. Given some rice and
raisins, the seamen would brew up a rather powerful homemade whiskey called "tuba" (after an
Asian plant used to make alcoholic drinks). This
was potent stuff, usually concocted by shipfitters,
cooks, or other below-deck types with access to the
tools and supplies needed for assembling, operating, and hiding a still.

Alcohol content varied, but was usually high
and unpredictable—"smoothness" varied from

harsh on up. Other improvisations were common. For example, the advent of alcohol-fueled TORPEDOES was shortly followed by the discovery that "torpedo juice" was drinkable, if strained through stale bread or some other dense material, which improved the taste. A few sailors are said to have rigged up stills to improve the character of torpedo juice, which was already 160 proof, and were reportedly able to boost it to 190 proof.

Some captains were more fanatical about eliminating tuba (and other such improvisations) than others. A few captains and even senior officers (like William HALSEY) winked at minor violations of the ban. Some officers even went out of their way to circumvent it, procuring hard liquor for "medicinal" purposes and issuing it to their men on special occasions. There was also quite a lot of beer shipped to the fleet, which was periodically issued for consumption "off the ship." The sailors would literally take one of the ship's boats a few hundred yards from their vessel, consume their two cans of brew, and then come back so the next batch of men could do the same.

On the whole, let's just say that a sailor was in a lot more trouble if he left his ship drunk than if he returned to it in that state.

Saipan, Battle of

A critical stage in the CENTRAL PACIFIC CAMPAIGN, the battle for Saipan began on 15 June 1944, when the US Second and Fourth Marine

Troops of the 27th Infantry Division land on Saipan from LSTs beached offshore, June–July 1944.

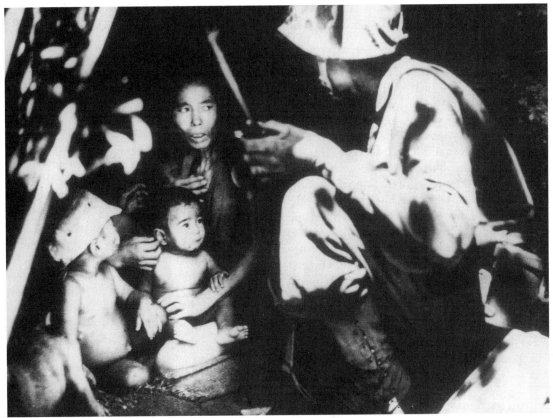

A Marine discovers a Japanese woman with four children and a dog, hiding in a cave on Saipan, June 21, 1944. This family was lucky. Thousands of Japanese civilians on Saipan committed suicide—willingly or otherwise—rather than fall prisoner to the Americans.

Divisions began what was the largest of the invasions in the MARIANAS Islands. Saipan had been controlled by the Japanese for 30 years, and they had garrisoned it with 30,000 troops (43rd Division, 47th Brigade, two separate infantry battalions, and a naval infantry brigade). The Japanese were determined to win. To this end, over a hundred TANKS were assembled on the island. On the second and third days of the battle the Japanese used these tanks to spearhead attacks on the Marines. These armored operations failed, as American tanks (M-4 Shermans) and antitank weapons were far more capable. The Japanese tanks were

annihilated in short order, as was the accompanying infantry. Nevertheless, these were the largest tank battles in the Pacific outside of China.

The aggressive Japanese tactics on Saipan made life exciting for the Marines, and led to more Japanese troops getting killed a lot sooner. But American firepower and infantry prevailed, and by early July the Japanese defenses were in tatters. On July 7, many of the surviving Japanese (about 3,000 troops) made a suicidal charge on American lines. The attack was stopped and after that there was only mopping up until the island was declared secure on 9 July. In the final stages of the fighting thousands of Japanese and Saipanese civilians committed suicide, voluntarily or under duress from Japanese troops.

In addition to the two Marine divisions, the army's 27th Infantry Division came ashore to help finish the job. This led to the "Battle of the SMITHS" as General Smith (USMC), commanding all forces on Saipan, relieved General Smith, commanding the army division. The dispute is still argued among army and Marine officers to this day and spotlights the differences in operating procedures between the two services. Nevertheless, the CASUALTIES were heavy on the American side. The Second Marine Division had 1,256 dead and 6,170 wounded. The Fourth Marine Division had 1,107 dead and 6,612 wounded (including the uncle of one of the authors), while the 27th Division suffered 1,034 dead and 3,566 wounded. While most of the Japanese garrison fought to the death, for the first time in the Pacific several hundred PRISONERS were taken. Not all of the Japanese prisoners were captured unconscious or while wounded. Many laid down their arms and gave up.

Saipan, Marianas

Long in Japanese hands, this island located about a thousand miles south of Tokyo had a large Japanese population, with an extensive system of air bases under construction in 1941. There were only limited port facilities, however.

Saipan Class, US Light Carriers

Inspired by the success of the INDEPENDENCE CLASS, CVL-48 *Saipan* (1944–1945–1946) and CVL-49 *Wright* (1944–1945–1947) were intended as light carriers based on the BALTIMORE CLASS heavy cruiser design. Unlike the Independence class, they were built from the keel up as carriers. Had the war continued into 1946 they would certainly have seen service. Two additional vessels were never laid down, and both ships saw only lim-

ited service before being relegated to the reserve. They were scrapped in the 1970s.

Sakai, Saburo (1916–)

A Japanese Navy enlisted fighter pilot, Sakai was the highest scoring Japanese naval ACE to survive the war (4th, with 64 victories). Educated in an American mission school, Sakai enlisted in the Imperial Navy in the 1930s and became a fighter pilot. He first saw combat during the CHINA INCIDENT, and was heavily engaged from then until he was wounded during the GUADALCANAL Campaign, losing an eye after he managed to fly the thousand miles to RABAUL, he was sent home to Japan to recuperate, and later became a flying instructor, his injuries presumably disqualifying him from further combat. However, late in the war he flew several interceptor missions against B-29s.

See also KELLY, COLIN.

Sakakida, Richard (1921–1996)

A Japanese American from HAWAII, Sakakida was drafted in early 1941. An honor graduate of high school ROTC, he skipped basic training and was trained as an intelligence agent. With another young Japanese American, he was sent to the Philippines to spy on resident Japanese. Disguised as merchant seamen who had jumped ship, Sakakida and his associate arrived in the Philippines in April 1941. They soon made contact with the local Japanese community, convincing them that they were unhappy with America. Information they provided proved useful in rounding up Japanese agents and freezing Japanese assets after PEARL HARBOR. Both men served on BATAAN and CORREGIDOR, as uniformed members of the army, interrogating prisoners of war, translating documents, and helping decrypt Japanese messages. Sakakida's associate was among those evacuated in the closing weeks of the first Philippine campaign (ending up on MacArthur's staff in Australia). However, Sakakida gave up his place on the aircraft to a married man and remained behind.

Captured by the Japanese, he managed to resume his "cover," even convincing them that his services as a translator and interrogator had been forced through torture. Although some Japanese officers were unconvinced, by mid–1943 he had been released, to become a civilian employee at Japanese headquarters in Manila. From this position he was able to supply information to Filipino GUERRILLAS, who passed it on to MACARTHUR's headquarters. In addition to supplying information that proved essential to the Allied victory in the Battle of the BISMARCK SEA, he once engineered the release of a large number of guerrillas by disguising himself as a Japanese officer. When Japanese headquarters withdrew from Manila into northern Luzon in early 1945, Sakakida went with them. Shortly after the surrender of Japan he made contact with American troops. Save for the period when he was on active duty on Bataan and Corregidor he had been undercover for over 1,600 days.

After the war Sakakida served as a prosecution witness in the trial of General YAMASHITA, and during the court-martial of at least one American collaborator. He remained in the army, retiring in 1975 as a heavily decorated lieutenant colonel.

Aside from Frank FUJITA, he was the only Japanese-American prisoner of the Japanese during the war.

Ref: Crost, *Honor by Fire*; Harrington, *Yankee Samurai*.

Samar, Battle off

One of the more dramatic naval battles of the war occurred during the Leyte Campaign in late 1944. On October 25, after several days of cat and mouse searching and fighting among the many small Philippine islands, a Japanese task force of four battleships, six cruisers, and 10 destroyers sneaked through the San Bernardino Strait at night and in the predawn hours appeared off the coast of Leyte,

and prepared to attack U.S. amphibious shipping in Leyte Gulf. The only American warships present were an escort carrier task force with the radio call sign "Taffy 3" (six escort carriers, three destroyers, and four destroyer escorts). There were 10 other escort carriers within flying distance (a hundred miles or so), and these sixteen carriers had available 235 fighters and 143 TBF AVENGER bombers. Although some of these aircraft were already on their way to attack land targets when the Japanese were discovered at dawn, all aircraft were soon turned against the Japanese ships. What followed was one of the wildest shootouts of the war. The Japanese could hardly believe their good fortune and immediately attacked what they believed were the American fleet carriers, beyond which presumably lay the scores of American transports and troopships standing off the Leyte shore. But after two and a half hours of combat, the combination of hundreds of American aircraft and desperate attacks by the handful of US destroyers convinced the Japanese that they were up against a strong opposition. The Japanese withdrew, still under attack by US aircraft. American losses were one carrier, two destroyers, and one destroyer escort. Some 1,130 US sailors were killed and 913 wounded. The Japanese lost three cruisers in the battle, and most of their remaining ships were damaged.

See also LEYTE GULF, BATTLE OF.

Samoa

An archipelago of 15 islands totaling c. 1,150 square miles in central Polynesia, Samoa was controlled mostly by Britain, but six of the easternmost islands, smaller, (c. 77 square miles) including the fine harbor at Tutuila, were in US hands. Until the late 1930s the islands were virtually bereft of military facilities, but with war raging in Europe, by 1940 the United States was developing air and naval stations there. Samoa formed a link in the chain of bases between the United States, Australia and New Zealand. Not attacked by the Japanese, the islands were on their list of "Far South

Pacific" objectives had they won the Battle of MID-WAY.

In their part of Samoa (eight major islands, c. 1,080 square miles), the British recruited many labor troops and raised a local defense force, which did not see combat.

American Samoa was under the administrative control of the navy from its acquisition in the late 1800s until after World War II. For local security, the navy raised the Fitafita Guards, composed of Samoan men under naval officers. Initially a mostly police and ceremonial force, the Fitafitas, who wore lavalavas, were reorganized as light infantry on the eve of the Pacific War, while the Marines recruited the First Samoan Battalion, USMC Reserve. During the war many Samoans also joined the navy. Well over a thousand men served in uniform, and many other people, women as well as men, in labor detachments.

Ref: White and Lindstrom, eds., *The Pacific Theater*.

San Diego, California, United States

With nearby Coronado, the second most important American naval base in the Pacific (after PEARL HARBOR), with enormous resources, extensively supported by several major air bases, and easy access by rail to the rest of the United States.

San Francisco, California, United States

Including not only the city of San Francisco, but also the extensive port facilities surrounding San Francisco Bay, one of the premier harbors of the world, with valuable naval and air bases at Alameda and Treasure Island, considerable industrial resources, and access by rail to the rest of the United States.

See also PORT CHICAGO MUTINY.

Sandakan, Borneo

A very small port, with limited capacity and no facilities, of some value as a local base for domi-nating the Sulu Sea and northern BORNEO. Japanese forces occupied it early in 1942, and remained there until the end of the war.

Sangamon Class, US Escort Carriers

These four ships were converted from incomplete tanker versions of the standard Maritime Commission C3 hull. The Sangamons (all 1939–1939–1942) were much superior to LONG ISLAND or BOGUE, being larger (23,800 tons full load), somewhat faster (18 knots), with slightly more aircraft (31), better defensive armament, and more internal space, making servicing the aircraft much easier. As an added bonus, they retained an enormous fuel capacity (over 12,000 tons), being, in effect, self-escorting tankers. They were among the best escort carriers, and reached the Pacific in early 1943, supporting operations in the SOLOMONS and helping to compensate for the desperate shortage of fleet carriers. They saw considerable service, and inspired the design of the COMMENCEMENT BAY CLASS.

The four, *Sangamon*, CVE-26; *Suwannee*, CVE-27; *Chenango*, CVE-28; and *Santee*, CVE-29 were all scrapped in 1960–62.

Sansapor, New Guinea

A good harbor, with no facilities, on the northwesternmost part of NEW GUINEA, with the possibility of being used as a base to dominate portions of the Philippine Sea, the entire "Vulture's Head" region of New Guinea, and surrounding regions.

Santa Cruz Islands

A small volcanic group about 400 miles north of ESPIRITU SANTO, in the NEW HEBRIDES. Under Australian control before the war, the small number of Europeans were evacuated in mid-1942, and the islands virtually ignored thereafter. Some recruiting for labor service occurred in 1943. Although well suited for an advanced base, only NDENI figured in the war, and then only marginally.

Santa Cruz Islands, Battle of

The late October 1942 Battle of the Santa Cruz Islands was the result of a Japanese effort to undertake a major ground offensive on GUADALCANAL supported by carrier aircraft. Unable to secure command of the sea through a naval engagement, the Japanese now decided to do so by capturing Henderson Field, through a combination of ground attack and naval air assault.

As YAMAMOTO was willing to commit a fleet of four battleships, five carriers (with 267 aircraft), eight heavy cruisers, three light cruisers, plus 38 destroyers, a dozen SUBMARINES, and a number of auxiliary vessels, as well as considerable land-based air power, this might have worked if the Japanese Army had not taken too long to "soften up" the Marines. The fleet was supposed to intervene in the ground action on October 22, but the army stretched out the softening up process until the 26th. This gave newly appointed Allied theater commander VAdm William F. HALSEY time to strengthen his forces, calling up the *Enterprise* Task Force, which was at NOUMEA, on the 22nd (thus giving him two carriers with 169 aircraft, plus one battleship, six cruisers, and 14 destroyers), while sending all available troops and aircraft to bolster Guadalcanal.

So while Halsey grew stronger during the protracted ground fighting for Henderson Field, Yamamoto grew weaker, as his ships kept to sea for days on end, consuming precious fuel, developing engine trouble (which forced one carrier back to TRUK), and exhausting their crews. The Japanese Army, of course, lost the battle for Henderson, which for a time was so desperate that US Army infantrymen were fed into the front-line Marine units. Had Yamamoto known this, there would never have been a Battle of the Santa Cruz Islands. But at 0126 on 25 October an Imperial Navy liaison officer with the troops on Guadalcanal signaled that the airfield was now in Japanese hands. So Yamamoto ordered the fleet south.

American PBYs spotted VAdm Chuichi NAGUMO's carriers, SHOKAKU and *Zuikaku*, at about noon on 25 October. RAdm Thomas KINKAID, commanding the *Enterprise* Task Force, attempted a strike that afternoon but failed to locate the enemy. Although each side groped for the other, neither was successful. During the night of 25–26 October Kinkaid maintained a steady course northwestward, toward the probable location of the Japanese. Before dawn he launched several scouts, and these soon apprised him of the location of the enemy carriers. Passing the word back to Halsey in Noumea, he received the order, "ATTACK—REPEAT—ATTACK!" Kinkaid was ahead of him, having already dispatched a scouting group, and at 0740 several dive bombers inflicted severe damage on the light carrier ZUIHO, knocking her out of battle.

However, Japanese fleet commander Nobutake KONDO's scouts had by this time spotted *Hornet* and ordered a major strike. Shortly afterward, *Hornet* and *Enterprise* both dispatched major strikes (by some accounts the two hostile air groups passed each other en route to their respective targets; it is unclear as to whether this actually occurred).

Kinkaid adopted the then-standard defensive formation, with his carriers each surrounded by a ring of escorts (later in the war it was found better to concentrate all carriers within a single ring of escorts), with a healthy CAP overhead. *Enterprise* was about 10 miles from *Hornet* when the Japanese struck, at just about 0900. A fortuitous rain squall sprang up, shielding "The Big E" from the enemy, who promptly concentrated on *Hornet*. The latter took several bombs, two suicidal crash dives, and two TORPEDOES, knocking her completely out of action, before the Japanese broke off the attack on her to work over *Enterprise* as she emerged from the rain squall. Superb ship handling, and voluminous fire from the battleship SOUTH DAKOTA and antiaircraft cruiser *San Juan*, kept *Enterprise* from serious harm. At just about the time *Hornet* was being battered, the American air strikes hit Nagumo's carriers, quickly inflicting damage on SHOKAKU, knocking her out of action and heavily damaging a cruiser as well. But the Japanese had more carriers than the Americans. Kondo ordered strikes from his two undamaged carriers, *Zuikaku* and JUNYO. Kondo's strike hit at 1101. Although *Enterprise's* escorts took some damage, she escaped unscathed. Not so the already severely battered *Hornet*, which took three more hits. She would later have to be abandoned after an unsuccessful attempt to sink her; Japanese destroyers sank her with torpedoes the next day. As Kondo's strike winged its way home, Kinkaid decided to break off the action and began steaming southward. Surprisingly, Kondo did not pursue. He might have essayed another air strike, still having two intact carriers and lots of pilots. Apparently unaware of the extent of the damage he had inflicted on the US Navy, Kondo believed that the action would be renewed the next day. It was not.

Santa Cruz was a tactical victory for the Japanese, for they inflicted greater losses than they suffered; indeed, it left them with the only undamaged carriers in the Pacific. But they had suffered about 100 pilots lost, and pilot replacement was becoming an increasingly serious problem. Strategically the battle was an American success, for the Japanese once again failed to crush the numerically inferior US Navy, thereby failing to secure control of the seas, thereby failing to retake Guadalcanal.

Sapwahfik (Ngatik), Caroline Islands

A small atoll southwest of PONAPE, in the CAROLINE ISLANDS. Although under Japanese control from World War I, Sapwahfik was little affected by Japanese rule, and preserved a unique cultural heritage. During the 1830s the entire male population of the atoll was massacred by British and American sailors, aided by some warriors from Ponape, who then settled down with the local women. Sapwahfik developed its own form of PIDGIN and became Christian, traits that survived Spanish, German, and finally Japanese rule, all of which touched the atoll only lightly, mostly in the form of increased trade and the recruitment of men for work on Ponape.

During the war, many men and women from Sapwahfik were recruited for work on Ponape, but the island was otherwise unaffected. It was, in fact, one of the few inhabited islands in the Carolines that was never bombed or subject to surface bombardment. The islanders attributed their good fortune to messages traced on beach sands in English saying things like "No Japanese on this Island" and "Help this island," and claims that US pilots dropped food, tobacco, and other valuable gifts, and that American flying boats and floatplanes occasionally landed in the lagoon bearing gifts. While the accuracy of these claims cannot be established beyond oral tradition, it is known that US seaplane and flying boat pilots made informal visits to other islands.

Ref: White and Lindstrom, eds., *The Pacific Theater*.

Sasakawa, Ryoicho (1899–1995)

Right-wing Japanese politician, industrialist, expansionist, and militarist, Sasakawa, a former army officer, formed the Patriotic Masses Party in 1931 to promote his ideas. He made an enormous fortune from investments in MANCHURIA during the Japanese occupation. Wealthy enough to maintain his own "air force" of some 20 bombers, in 1939 he flew one to Rome, where he met with Mussolini. During World War II he served in the Diet. After the war he was arrested, tried as a war criminal, and served four years in prison. He later recouped his wealth through a variety of schemes—including motorboat racing and gambling—and became a noted philanthropist, anticommunist, and ultranationalist. He was the last surviving prominent Japanese war criminal.

Sasebo, Honshu, Japan

A major port, with important naval and air installations, Sasebo was one of the four principal bases of the Imperial Navy. It specialized in the construction of destroyers and lighter warships, and was the headquarters of one of the four SNLF commands.

Saumarez Class, British Destroyers

A further evolution of Britain's TRIBAL CLASS, the Saumarez class—or S-class—destroyers were laid down 1941–1942, launched in 1942–1943, and entered service 1943–1944. Including the very similar T, U, V, and W classes, the ROYAL NAVY had some 80 ships of this design in service by the end of the war. Several were active with the British Far Eastern and Pacific Fleet in the latter part of the war. HMS *Saumarez* herself was one of the destroyers that took part in the last surface action of the war, the Battle of PENANG, during which they sank the heavy cruiser *Haguro*.

Savo Island, Battle of

On the night of 9 August 1942, a Japanese squadron steamed undetected into the waters north of GUADALCANAL and within a few minutes inflicted the most serious and most one-sided reverse ever suffered by the US Navy in a surface action, sinking four heavy cruisers (one of them Australian) and a destroyer, killing 1,270 men and wounding 709 others, all in about 30 minutes, with virtually no loss to themselves. These CASUALTIES amounted to about two-thirds the number of the US ground troops killed during the entire Guadalcanal campaign, which lasted from August of 1942 into February of 1943.

Savo Island is a small, conical island at the north end of the sound between Guadalcanal and Florida Island, which later became known as IRON BOTTOM SOUND.

The course of the battle may be told simply. The Japanese military headquarters in RABAUL was alarmed when it received word that its base on Guadalcanal had been invaded by US troops on 8 August 1942. Knowing that there would be American ships in the area for a while, a number of warships were sent south. An Allied reconnaissance plane actually detected the approaching squadron, but its report was misrouted. After 0100 hours on 9 August, a Japanese squadron of five heavy cruisers, two light cruisers, and a destroyer under Admiral MIKAWA slipped into Iron Bottom Sound to the south of Savo, evading a pair of US destroyers clumsily patrolling the western approaches to the sound. There were three Allied squadrons in the sound. One was posted at the eastern end of the southern channel around Savo, another at the eastern end of the northern channel around Savo, and the third much farther back, protecting the transports unloading supplies for the Marines. The battle took little more than a half hour. Superior Japanese night fighting training counted heavily in their favor. They spotted the southern group of Allied cruisers and destroyers at 0136, and fired TORPEDOES four minutes later, sinking a cruiser and a destroyer, and heavily damaging one more of each within minutes. Then the Japanese squadron turned north, splitting into two columns, with the heavy cruisers on the right, and passed on both sides of the Allied northern squadron, opening fire between 0150 and 0156. Despite the fact that they should have been alerted to the presence of the enemy by the fate of the southern force, the US cruisers were caught unprepared and were badly shot up; three were sunk, one of which did land some hits on the Japanese flagship, the only damage inflicted on the Japanese. At this point Mikawa ought to have pressed eastward, to shoot up the transports and their protective screen. However, at about 0200 he changed course to the northwest, and the Japanese drew off. Their victory had been won at the cost of fewer than 50 casualties, with no serious damage to any of their ships. Japanese reluctance to push on and go after the American transports denied them a decisive victory. The Japanese commander did not know how many warships the Allies had off Guadalcanal and did not want to risk running into a larger, and now fully alerted, enemy force.

The disastrous outcome of the Battle of Savo Island had several causes. The Japanese were clearly superior in night combat, for which they had trained intensively. Indeed, their lookouts spotted the Allied ships even before Allied radar detected the Japanese squadron. The pattern maintained by the US destroyers supposedly patrolling the channels around Savo Island left approaches to Iron Bottom Sound uncovered for long periods. The patrol sectors and deployment of the two squadrons near Savo Island were very poorly thought out. In addition, the Allies were over-confident, believing that they were definitely superior to the Japanese, and were excessively enamored of the abilities of radar, which most of the senior officers did not understand at all. Communications between the three squadrons were not well coordinated. There was also a disrupted chain of command; since the senior officer, Britain's Admiral CRUTCHLEY, was at a conference with his superior, Admiral Richmond Kelly TURNER (USN), it was unclear who was in overall command of the ships. Finally, the US and Australian sailors had been on full alert for several days, standing by their guns, even eating and sleeping by them, so that they were literally exhausted at their posts. Alert procedures were shortly modified to permit a less intense state of readiness.

Savo Island, the Cover-up

The commander of the Allied squadron defeated in the Battle of Savo Island, Britain's RAdm V. A. C. CRUTCHLEY, was not present during the engagement, having gone off to a staff conference with the overall local commander, RAdm Richmond Kelly TURNER (USN), taking his flagship, heavy cruiser HMAS *Australia,* with him. After the battle both Crutchley and Turner continued in command. As the 20th anniversary of the battle approached, a prominent conservative monthly advanced the theory that the ROOSEVELT administration had promoted a massive cover-up of Crutchley's incompetence in order to preserve good relations with the British.

In fact, aside from the general excellence of the Japanese at night naval combat, the disaster that befell the Australian and American ships off Savo Island was due more to failures of prewar doctrine and training, a continuing peacetime mindset, a surprisingly durable contempt for the enemy, and excessive confidence in the as-yet inadequate ra-

dar, than to command failures by Crutchley and Turner. If Crutchley had been present at the battle, the Japanese would probably have killed him and sunk his flagship as well.

SB2A Buccaneer, US Carrier Dive Bomber

The SB2A Buccaneer was an unsuccessful American dive bomber design. It first flew in June 1941, and 750 aircraft were produced in 1942 and 1943. None were used in combat, serving instead as trainers and target tugs.

See also AIRCRAFT TYPES, DEVELOPMENT; CARRIERS, DESIGNING AIRCRAFT FOR.

SB2C Helldiver, US Carrier Dive Bomber

The US SB2C Helldiver was a replacement for the SBD DAUNTLESS dive bomber. Unfortunately, the SB2C took so long to enter PRODUCTION that, by the time it arrived in 1943, the TBF AVENGER had already taken over many of its missions. The SB2C was a major improvement over the SBD Dauntless, but dedicated aircraft types for dive bombing and TORPEDO bombing were increasingly seen as unnecessary. It was obvious that carriers needed more fighters and, by 1944, many fighters were being equipped to carry bombs. The age of "multipurpose" aircraft was dawning, and the Helldiver simply arrived at the wrong time. Although some 5,000 were produced, they were not one of the favorite carrier aircraft.

See also AIRCRAFT TYPES, DEVELOPMENT; CARRIERS, DESIGNING AIRCRAFT FOR.

SBD Dauntless, US Carrier Dive Bomber

The US SBD Dauntless dive bomber entered service in 1941 and was considered obsolete even then. The prewar experts were wrong, as the SBD proved one of the most effective carrier bombers of the war. Its long range (1,200 miles for bombing, 20% more for scouting) and reliable operation enabled the SBD to rack up a credible war record. SBDs sunk 300,000 tons of enemy shipping, as well as 18 warships of all sizes, including six carriers. It could defend itself, shooting down 138 Japanese aircraft, while losing only 80 to enemy fighters. Nearly 6,000 were delivered, including 1,000 for the US Army as the A-24. Despite its excellent record, a replacement, the Helldiver, was already in the works when the war broke out. Moreover, the TBF AVENGER, the replacement for the hapless TBD1 DEVASTATOR torpedo bomber, proved to be a capable dive bomber also. TORPEDO bombing declined in importance as the war went on, and the TBF Avenger was used, quite successfully, as a regular bomber most of the time. What kept the SBD in service throughout the war was its versatility and delays in getting the Helldiver into service. Even

Navy ordnancemen loading belted .30 caliber machine-gun ammunition on an SBD Dauntless dive bomber, Norfolk Naval Air Station, Virginia, September 1942.

so, SBDs went from half of all carrier aircraft in mid-1942 to about 6% by mid-1944. Many SBDs were transferred to the Marines for land-based operations. A testimony of the SBD's worth can be seen in its use into the 1950s by many foreign air forces. The French used SBDs during the early stages of their war in Vietnam.

See also AIRCRAFT TYPES, DEVELOPMENT; CARRIERS, DESIGNING AIRCRAFT FOR.

SC Seahawk, US Reconnaissance Floatplane

The SC Seahawk was an American floatplane used on cruisers and battleships for scouting. It was a new design, to replace the 1930s models in use through most of the war. The first SC flew in early 1944, and only nine were built (out of 500 ordered) before the war ended. The SC had a top speed of 312 MPH and a range of 625 miles. Armament consisted of two .50 caliber machine guns and up to 500 pounds of bombs or depth charges.

See also AIRCRAFT TYPES, DEVELOPMENT; CARRIERS, DESIGNING AIRCRAFT FOR; RECONNAISSANCE, NAVAL.

Scott, Norman (1889–1942)

Norman Scott graduated from Annapolis in 1911 and served in destroyers during World War I, being decorated for heroic action when his ship was sunk by a U-boat in the Atlantic. Between the wars he served as a presidential aide, attended several navy schools, and held various staff and line assignments, including the heavy cruiser PENSACOLA. By 1941 he was on the staff of the chief of naval operations. From this post in June of 1942 he was promoted to temporary rear admiral and given command of various task forces in the South Pacific. A tough but very well liked commander, Scott drove his men hard, training them in night tactics to meet the Japanese, hitherto masters of the art. As a result, Scott neatly dished up an enemy squadron in the Battle of CAPE ESPERANCE (October 11–12 1942), for which he was named a permanent rear admiral. Scott might have gone on to greater things, but navy regulations intervened. In early November he was superseded in command by Dan CALLAGHAN, whose commission as a regular rear admiral antedated Scott's by a few days, despite the fact that Callaghan had been skippering a desk for most of the war. Scott was killed in the Japanese ambush of Callaghan's squadron during the night action off GUADALCANAL on November 12–13, 1942, a few minutes before Callaghan himself perished. Both men were awarded the MEDAL OF HONOR

Seabees, US Navy Construction Battalions

The impetus for the organization of the famous "Seabees" was the need for the navy to quickly prepare forward areas for use as bases. Prewar experience with contracted construction workers on outlying islands such as Wake and MIDWAY had demonstrated their probable unreliability in time of war. Not only did they insist on strict adherence to the terms of their union contracts, but they were also ineligible to serve in combat, not only for lack of training but also because of their civilian status. This problem was demonstrated most clearly during the Battle for WAKE ISLAND in December 1941, when the nearly 1,150 construction workers on the island proved more of a hindrance to the defense than a help, an impression reinforced by difficulties with construction workers on Midway in June of 1942.

Fortunately, RAdm Ben Moreell, chief of the Bureau of Yards and Docks, had devoted some thought to this problem before the war, and came up with the idea of creating a combat engineer corps for the navy, men organized, trained, equipped, and disciplined to serve as construction workers capable of defending themselves.

The first Seabee battalions—the name Seabee derived from the initials CB, for Construction Battalion—were organized in March of 1942. They were raised from construction workers, mostly men otherwise unsuited for normal combat duty by rea-

son of age, thereby economizing on manpower. In fact, many enlisted Seabees were World War I veterans. The average age of the enlisted men in the Seabees was 31, about five years older than the average for the armed forces as a whole. Enlisted men were recruited from professional specialists in virtually every civilian construction trade, with considerable cooperation from industry and unions. Their officers were recruited from the navy's Civil Engineering Corps, which normally builds docks and barracks, and from reservists with construction industry backgrounds. Such reservists made the best officers, since Seabees were notoriously careless about military propriety. As one admiral put it, "They're a rough, tough bunch of men who don't give a damn about anything but getting the job done, the war won, and going home."

About 350,000 men served in the Seabees, who were organized into battalions and regiments, and occasionally brigades.

The first Seabee unit to enter combat was the Sixth CB Battalion, which landed on GUADALCANAL on 1 September 1942. Using a lot of captured Japanese construction equipment, they completed Henderson Field under trying conditions, suffering attacks by Japanese air and naval units, and having to defend themselves against enemy snipers as well. Thereafter Seabees were active in every theater of the war, but were of particular importance in the Pacific, usually getting to work even before the troops were off the beaches. Seabees often developed enormously creative solutions to construction problems, frequently inventing new techniques that were subsequently applied to civilian construction.

Their motto was "Can Do!" and their mascot was a bee, wearing a sailor's cap and armed with a Tommy gun and various tools.

Seafire, British Carrier Fighter

The Seafire was a navalized version of Britain's SPITFIRE fighter. Some 2,000 were built. As the Spitfire went through its many wartime versions, the Seafires were produced to the same plans with the addition of folding wings and other modifications needed for carrier operation. The Seafire was an effective carrier aircraft, but had a weak undercarriage, so that the airframe tended to shake apart after too many carrier landings. PRODUCTION continued after the war.

See also AIRCRAFT TYPES, DEVELOPMENTS; CARRIERS, DESIGNING AIRCRAFT FOR.

Seaplane Tenders and Carriers

The enormous distances between land in the Pacific led both Japan and the United States to make considerable use of seaplanes and floatplanes for reconnaissance, since they could land on and take off from water. Smaller floatplanes could be carried on cruisers and battleships, but large seaplanes, which had much greater range, required special vessels to serve as home bases.

The US Navy had 74 seaplane tenders during the war, in 10 classes. Of these, 24 were prewar conversions from other types: the former carrier *Langley*, 14 old "four stacker" destroyers, and nine old minesweepers. The remaining classes were built 1940–45.

Seaplane tenders, most of which could make only about 20 knots, could support their charges from any convenient moderately sheltered waters, and it was not unusual for them to be more or less permanently stationed in an area.

In contrast to American practice, Japan did not have seaplane tenders. Instead, the Imperial Navy built seaplane carriers, a category of warship unknown to most navies. Seaplane tenders supported multi-engine aircraft, that took off from and landed on water. Japan's seaplane carriers were capable of launching small seaplanes from catapults. The Imperial Navy was keen on using non-carrier aircraft for reconnaissance purposes, thereby reserving all aircraft in an air group for combat missions. This was one reason for the existence of the TONE CLASS heavy cruisers, with their large complement of floatplanes, and also for the use of seaplane carriers, the idea being that they could accompany the fleet and conduct reconnaissance.

Secrecy

More than a half-century after its end there are still a surprising number of things about the Second

US SEAPLANE TENDERS						
Class	Launched	Displ.	Speed	Avgas	Number	Note
Langley (AV–3)	1912	11,000	15	30.0	1	A
"Bird" (AVP–1)	1917–19	950	13.5	40.0	9	
Clemson (AVD–4)	1918–21	1,200	24	50.0	14	B
Curtiss (AV–4)	1940	12,053	18	269.6	2	
Curritcuck (AV–7)	1943–44	15,000	19.2	278.0	4	
Barnegat (AVP–10)	1941–45	2,040	20	80.0	38	C
Tangier (AV–8)	1943	11,760	16	312.0	1	
Pocomoke (AV–9)	1943	11,760	17	291.0	1	
Chandeleur (AV–10)	1944	11,760	16	300.0	1	
Whiting (AV–14)	1944–45	12,000	16	312.0	4	D

Key: Class, name ship of the type; Launched, year of launching; Displ., standard displacement; Speed, in knots; Avgas, aviation fuel carried, in thousands of gallons; Number, units completed; Note, as below:

A. Sunk off Java, 27 February 1942, while ferrying aircraft.

B. Former Clemson Class destroyers, converted 1939–40. Many of them were converted to other uses beginning in 1943, as the Barnegat Class AVPs became available.

C. After the war they were turned over to the Coast Guard.

D. Properly the Kenneth Whiting Class, converted from standard C–3 merchant hulls requisitioned while still on the ways. Several additional units were canceled.

JAPANESE SEAPLANE CARRIERS AND TENDERS							
Class	Launched	Displ.	Speed	A/C	Avgas	Number	Note
Notoro	1920	14,050	12	10	??	1	A
Kamoi	1922	17,000	15	22	??	1	B
Chitose	1936–37	11,000	29	24	??	2	C
Mizuho	1938	10,929	22	24	??	1	D
Nisshin	1939	11,217	28	20	??	1	E
Akitsushima	1941	4,650	19	1	??	1	F
Maru Types	??	6,000 to 9,000	10–14	8	??	9	G

Key: As previous table; A/C, number of aircraft carried; Note, as below:

A. Converted from a tanker in 1924; reconverted to a tanker in 1942.

B. Converted from a tanker 1932–33 and reverted to same 1943. Sunk in Hong Kong Harbor by US carrier aircraft, April 5, 1945.

C. Built purposely to be converted to light carriers, which was done 1942–43.

D. A modified *Chitose*, she could carry midget submarines in lieu of some aircraft. Sunk 2 May 1942 by a US submarine, which probably prevented her from being converted into an escort carrier.

E. An improved *Mizuho*, able to carry 700 mines, in lieu of some aircraft, or midget submarines. Sunk by American aircraft in the southwest Pacific, July 22, 1943. Two somewhat larger sisters were projected but never begun.

F. Actually a seaplane tender, able to service one large flying boat. Sunk by US carrier aircraft on September 24, 1944. Several proposed sister ships were never begun.

G. Converted from merchant ships 1937–42, these ships were apparently not commissioned into the Imperial Navy, as they retained their "maru" names. The figure under Displacement is GRT. They varied greatly in size and speed but were outfitted and armed identically. One was lost 28 May 1943, in the South Pacific. Most of the rest reverted to transports during the war. See also RECONNAISSANCE, NAVAL.

World War that remain secret, or are at best only partially known. Some of these unrevealed items deal with minor matters, but others are of considerable importance. For a variety of reasons, most are unlikely to be revealed for many years to come, if ever. Some British documents dating back to the Armada (1588) allegedly have never been made public.

There are many reasons for this secrecy. Bureaucratic inertia is one. At other times, such policies are designed to protect the lives, or at least the reputations, of certain people, politicians, or officers who found themselves entrapped in enemy espionage, or foreign officials, even enemy politicians and officers, who collaborated in the defeat of their own nations. And some things really ought to remain classified. For example, revealing where the remains of Hermann Göring and other Nazi leaders were disposed of could turn the site into a Nazi shrine, grounds enough for perpetual secrecy. Many times it's politically expedient to keep certain things secret, rather than open the proverbial can of worms.

Human nature and modern media being what they are, it's not surprising that people have a tendency to come up with theories about conspiracies, treachery, cover-ups, and other nefarious Machiavellian plottings, particularly in cases where they learn of unpleasant things that occurred and were classified. In fact, most of the secrets of World War II were declassified long ago. But the volume of materials is enormous, so interesting or important stories sometimes do not come before the public eye until someone stumbles across them and begins hurling charges about a "cover-up."

Security Breaches, Critical

For a variety of reasons, on several occasions during the war serious breaches of security occurred. Some of the most notable were as follows.

In December 1941, days before PEARL HARBOR, several newspapers published details of the War Department's "Germany First" plans. The information was presented as an example of conspiratorial war planning on the part of the ROOSEVELT administration. The leak may have had some influence on HITLER'S decision to declare war on the United States shortly after Pearl Harbor. The leak was later traced to an isolationist captain in the War Department, but there were suggestions that other officers of isolationist bent may have been involved, including Albert WEDEMEYER, then a lieutenant colonel serving under EISENHOWER in the Office of War Plans.

As part of its coverage of the Battle of MIDWAY, in June 1942 the *Chicago Tribune* casually revealed that one reason for the American victory was that the United States was able to read Japanese naval codes—in effect, revealing MAGIC. By good fortune the Japanese never learned of it. President Roosevelt, General MARSHALL, and senior officials chose to ignore the breach, rather than act against the paper and thereby draw attention to the incident. The source of the leak has never been determined. The *Chicago Tribune* was a notoriously anti-Roosevelt paper, and it is possible that an anti-Roosevelt officer or official in the War Department or the Navy Department passed along the information.

At a press conference in May 1943 Representative Andrew Jackson May, a member of the House Military Affairs Committee, announced that the Japanese were setting their depth charges to detonate too shallowly, thereby saving many US SUBMARINES from destruction. The Japanese apparently caught on to this leak and began increasing the settings on their depth charges. VAdm Charles Lockwood, chief of Pacific submarines, later stated that at least 10 US submarines had been lost as a result of May's indiscretion. May appears to have been taken to the woodshed by the Speaker of the House.

At a diplomatic reception in Moscow in October 1944 the Soviet foreign minister "casually" mentioned to the Japanese ambassador that US heavy bombers based in China were about to undertake operations against the Philippines, alerting the Japanese as to the next US objective in the Pacific.

In February 1945, *Amerasia*, a semi-monthly journal of Asian affairs, published portions of a top secret report on China's internal political situation that had been prepared by the OSS. The leak was traced to a Foreign Service officer who believed that the United States should not support CHIANG KAI-SHEK as leader of China, and who had been passing secret documents to *Amerasia*'s publisher, a Soviet sympathizer. Surprisingly, although indictments were issued against several of the participants, the case dragged on into the early 1950s and eventually disappeared in a series of cover-ups. It had little effect on Chinese-American relations.

See also SOVIET UNION.

Ref: Klehr and Radosh, *The Amerasia Spy Case*.

Sendai Class, Japanese Light Cruisers

The best of the older Japanese cruisers, the Sendais served as flotilla leaders during the war. Although lightly built ships, they took a surprising amount of punishment.

Sendai (1922–1925–1925) served as a flotilla leader during operations in the Philippines and East Indies, and was later in the SOLOMONS, fighting in the Second Battle of GUADALCANAL, before being sunk November 2, 1943 at EMPRESS AUGUSTA BAY, having taken numerous 6-inch hits.

Jintsu (1922–1923–1925) led a destroyer flotilla during the conquest of the Philippines and East Indies, fighting in the JAVA SEA, and later at the EASTERN SOLOMONS and KOLOMBANGARA, where she was sunk July 13, 1943, having been repeatedly hit by 6-inch and 5-inch shells.

Naka (1922–1925–1925) led a destroyer flotilla during operations in the Philippines and East Indies, and then with the Combined Fleet until she was sunk at TRUK by carrier aircraft on 17 February 1944.

Shakishima Islands, Ryukyu Islands

The southernmost group of the RYUKYU chain, the Shakishima Islands contained an important Japanese naval and air station during World War II. Since aircraft there could threaten Allied forces operating against Okinawa, in the spring of 1945 the group received a thorough going over by the British Pacific Fleet.

See also ROYAL NAVY.

Shanghai, China

Before the outbreak of the Sino-Japanese War Shanghai was the most important city in China, the center of business, industry, and banking. It was also the largest port in China, with considerable resources to build and service all but the largest vessels. The Japanese occupied most of Shanghai in 1937, after a hard fight with the Chinese. The part they did not occupy was the so-called International Sector, a district with considerable extraterritoriality, ruled by a commission of representatives from the Great Powers, including Japan. This was occupied in December 1941. The city subsequently served as an important rear-area base for Japanese forces in China and as a port of embarkation for Japanese units being transferred to other areas.

Sherman, Forrest P. (1896–1951)

Forrest P. Sherman attended MIT for a time before entering Annapolis in 1914. He graduated second in the three-year class of 1917, and served aboard ship in European waters during World War I. After the war he took flight training, served variously in fighter squadrons, in training assignments, including a tour as an instructor at Annapolis, on various staffs, and attended the Naval War College. In December 1941 he was on the staff of the chief of naval operations. In May 1942 he was named captain of the carrier WASP. When *Wasp* was sunk that September, he was assigned as chief of staff to Admiral John TOWERS, the principal aviation officer

in the Pacific Fleet, and in November 1943 became deputy chief of staff to NIMITZ, in which post he helped plan operations from the CAROLINES to OKINAWA. Present at the surrender of Japan, after the war he had a very distinguished career, working to strengthen the navy's influence in the defense reorganization of 1947, and tirelessly struggling to increase, the fleet's carrier forces, a victory that he had won at the time of his death, which occurred while he was still on active duty, as chief of naval operations.

Sherman, Frederick C. (1888–1957)

Nicknamed "Ted," Frederick C. Sherman graduated from the Naval Academy in 1910, and served for several years in battleships and armored cruisers, before transferring to SUBMARINES in 1914. He commanded several submarines during World War I, and after the war transferred to Naval Aviation. In the 1920s and 1930s he held various line, staff, and training assignments, attended the Naval War College, and in June 1940 became captain of the carrier LEXINGTON. He commanded *Lexington* in all her operations from PEARL HARBOR to CORAL SEA, when she was lost. He was the last man to leave the ship. Promoted to rear admiral, he served for a time as assistant chief of staff to Admiral King, before returning to the Pacific in October 1942, to command various carrier divisions through March 1944, meanwhile taking part in operations in the SOLOMONS, against RABAUL and BOUGAINVILLE, and during the TARAWA invasion. For a time in 1944 he commanded all naval aviation on the West Coast but returned to sea as a task force commander, fighting from Leyte through OKINAWA and in operations off the Japanese coast. In July 1945 he was named a vice admiral and commander of the First Fast Carrier Task Force, in which post he ended the war. His service in the postwar period was cut short by his participation in the so-called "Revolt of the Admirals," a group of senior naval officers who fought to preserve the navy's air arm in the face of threats from the air force after the "unification" of the armed forces in 1947.

Shimakaze, Japanese Destroyer

Shimakaze (1941–1942–1943) was intended to be the prototype of a large class (18 ships) of a radically new destroyer design. She was very large (nearly 2,600 tons standard), very fast (over 40 knots on trials), and very well armed (six 5-inch guns, numerous AA guns, and 15 TORPEDO tubes). However, wartime strains on shipbuilding (she took from August 1941 to May 1943 to build) limited the class to the one ship. *Shimakaze* saw only limited service before she was sunk by U.S. naval aircraft in the Philippines in mid-November 1944. During her 17 months of operational life, she was rearmed twice, each time enhancing antiaircraft capabilities at the expense of her surface combat weaponry.

Shinano, Japanese Aircraft Carrier

Arguably the most poorly designed carrier built during the war, *Shinano* (1940–1944–1944) was laid down as a battleship of the YAMATO CLASS, and ordered converted while still on the building ways, when about 50% complete. She retained much of her battleship armor. As redesigned she was not intended to serve as a fleet carrier, but rather as a support carrier, providing aircraft repair facilities and replacement aircraft for other carriers, an idea adopted by the British with more success in HMS UNICORN. As a result, *Shinano* could store about 50% more aircraft than she could operate. She was sunk when *Archerfish* (SS-311) put four TORPEDOES into her on 29 November 1944, just 10 days after she had been completed and just a few hours into her maiden voyage. She required seven hours to sink, testimony to her excellent protection. The largest ship ever sunk by a submarine, *Shinano* was the largest aircraft carrier built until the nuclear-powered *Enterprise* was commissioned in 1960.

Shinyo, Japanese Escort Carrier

The German passenger liner *Scharnhorst* (1932–1934–1936) found refuge in Japan when the European War broke out in 1939. In early 1942 the Imperial Navy bought her for conversion into an escort carrier. *Shinyo* entered service at the end of 1943. The shortage of aircraft and trained airmen confined her to serving as an aircraft transport and training ship. She was TORPEDOED by *Spadefish* (SS-411) on 17 July 1944 off the coast of China (see table below).

Ship Sinkings, Accidental

The Soviet SUBMARINE sunk by *I-25* was in the mid-Pacific, en route from VLADIVOSTOK to Panama. As she went down with all hands, it was not until after the war that her correct identity was known. *I-19* may also have sunk two Soviet vessels.

The Soviet ships sunk by *Sawfish* (SS-276) and *Sandlance* (SS-381) were proceeding with lights

Flag	Vessel	Type	Date	Sinker	Locale
USSR	*L–16*	submarine	11 Oct. '42	HIJMS *I–25*	Mid-Pacific
USSR	*Ilmen*	merchantship	17 Feb. '43	USS *Sawfish*	Honshu
USSR	*Kola*	merchantship	17 Feb. '43	USS *Sawfish*	Tsushima Strait
USSR	*Belorussia*	merchantship	3 May '43	USS *Sandlance*	Tsushima Strait
USSR	*Seiner No. 20*	trawler	4 Jul. '43	USS *Permit*	North Pacific
US	*Seawolf*	submarine	4 Oct. '44	USS *Rowell*	Philippines
US	*Extractor*	salvor	3 Jan. '45	USS *Guardfish*	Marianas
Jap.	*Awa Maru*	transport	28 Mar. '45	USS *Queenfish*	China Seas
USSR	*Transbalt*	merchantship	13 Jun. '45	USS *Spadefish*	Sea of Japan

and neutrality markings, but were torpedoed because they were using Tsushima Strait, between Korea and Japan, rather than the more northern La Perouse Strait, between Japan and the Kuriles, having been rerouted due to severe icing. The United States acknowledged responsibility and paid an indemnity. The captain of the trawler sunk by *Permit* (SS-178) notified his government that the vessels had been damaged by Japanese attack, and that *Permit* had come to its rescue, thereby avoiding an international incident. In August 1944 *Tambor* (SS-198) fired upon but missed an unidentified Soviet vessel in the Sea of Japan.

The skipper of *Richard M. Rowell* (DE-403), LtCdr Harry A. Barnard Jr., was found at fault for having ignored recognition signals from *Seawolf* (SS-197) and also the safety zone in which she was operating (she was carrying supplies and personnel to Filipino GUERRILLAS. This was probably an unjust decision on the part of the navy. *Rowell* had been alerted to the presence of the submarine by naval aircraft off the escort carrier *Midway* (later renamed), and *Seawolf* was operating in an area in which a Japanese submarine had torpedoed a US ship only the day before. The loss of *Seawolf* seems, to have been the only occasion in the war of an American submarine being sunk by friendly fire.

A board of inquiry into the sinking of *Extractor* by *Guardfish* (SS-217) concluded that the skippers of both vessels were at fault. H. M. Babcock, of *Extractor*, was censured because he had not requested a repeat of a garbled transmission, which turned out to be a warning that *Guardfish* was in the area and he was to return to port immediately. Douglas Hammon, of *Guardfish*, was admonished for failing to properly identify his target, which he claimed looked like a Japanese submarine. The incident was the only one in the war in which a US submarine sank an American vessel. However, two US submarines are known to have been sunk by their own torpedoes, which malfunctioned: *Tuillbee* (SS-284) on 26 March 1944 and *Tang* (SS-306) on 24 October 1944, survivors living to tell the tale.

The AWA MARU incident is treated in a separate entry.

Shipbuilding, American Plans

During the 1930s the navy attempted to calculate its needs in the event of a future major war. Prewar construction programs were based on these estimates, as were the emergency programs that were adopted in 1940 and 1941. But the war came rather sooner than planned and was somewhat different than anticipated. As a result, the actual navy was quite different from the planned wartime strength of the navy.

The table gives a fair notion of the difference between the war that was expected and that which occurred. Clearly in the 1930s the navy's brass still believed the battleship would play a major role in the next war, and they planned to have an almost completely new battleline for the occasion. However, the exigencies of war resulted in fewer new

	Planned	Actual	Percent	Inc.	Canc.
Battleships: New	17	10	58.8	2	2
Old	5	15	300.0		
Carriers: Fleet	15	28	186.7	11	2
Light	0	9	—	2	0
Escort	5	85	1,700.0	11	4
A/C	1,600	4,500	281.3	1,920	310
Cruisers: Large	6	2	33.3	1	1
Heavy	26	38	146.2	14	0
Light	49	51	104.1	17	6
Destroyers: Fleet	450	620	133.8	65	5
Escort	0	337	—	0	0
Submarines	200	350	175.0	39	24

Key: "A/C" is the number of aircraft slots on the carriers, not the number of aircraft available; "Planned" is the number of ships that the navy expected to have available by the outbreak of war, sometime around 1944; "Actual" is the number of ships in commission during the Second World War (note that figures for destroyers and SUBMARINES have been rounded); "Percent" is the number of ships actually in commission as a proportion of the planned figures; "Inc." (incomplete) covers ships laid down but still not in commission by the summer of 1945, when the war was effectively over; "Canc." shows how many of these were canceled, the balance being completed postwar.

battleships being built, and all (except two demolished at Pearl Harbor) the older ones being upgraded and put to work. Note, too, that the navy certainly did not dismiss the aircraft carrier as a useful weapon, and planned to have about as many flattops as battlewagons. But it certainly greatly underestimated the need for carriers.

Of particular interest are the figures for escort carriers, which ultimately included about a quarter of all carrier-borne aircraft (listed under "A/C"). In fact, the escort carrier was an idea more or less foisted upon the navy by President ROOSEVELT. His enthusiasm was well rewarded, for their role in antisubmarine and amphibious operations was one of the more interesting developments of the war.

Figures for cruisers are also rather interesting. The so-called "large" cruisers were really light battleships, often erroneously called "battlecruisers," which were built on the erroneous assumption that the Japanese were building similar vessels. They turned out to be fine ships, but had even less of a role than did proper battleships. In contrast, the predicted need for heavy cruisers was rather lower than the demand, while that for light cruisers was pretty much on target.

It is interesting to note that despite the experience of World War I, the navy underestimated the need for destroyers to curb the submarine menace. Indeed, the average monthly completion rate for destroyers rose enormously during the war: 1.33 per month in 1941, 6.75 in 1942, and peaking at 10.83 in 1944. The shortage of destroyers was a critical factor in the creation of the destroyer escort, a sort of "second class" destroyer designed primarily for antisubmarine operations, rather than general fleet operations. In addition, considering that the navy's prewar plans were predicated upon a submarine campaign against Japanese shipping, the prewar estimate of the need for submarines was extremely low.

A great many ships that had been ordered were never laid down, including five battleships, three MIDWAY CLASS carriers, and three large cruisers. By mid–1944 the navy had begun to cancel orders for

ships that it considered no longer necessary for the war effort, including many already under construction.

Another area in which prewar estimates fell short was in terms of auxiliary and amphibious warfare vessels. The navy actually ordered very few of these before hostilities broke out, but by war's end they formed the greatest proportion of the navy's approximately 75,000 vessels, counting everything from battlewagons and aircraft carriers to lighters and "honey bucket" barges.

See also GIBBS, WILLIAM F.; REARMAMENT, US, 1930s.

Ref: Abbazia, *Mr. Roosevelt's Navy.*

Shipbuilding, Japanese Plans

The Imperial Navy projected its needs in the 1930s and adopted what it considered a realistic program for expansion. Between 1931 and the attack on PEARL HARBOR a large number of warships were ordered to be built, or converted from other types of vessels. When war came, additional orders were made, and changes authorized in existing orders, leading to a quite different fleet.

Shipbuilding, Warships, Japan vs. United States

From the mid–1930s both the United States and Japan began building warships at a rather prodigious rate, a pace that, at least in the case of the United States, did not slacken until the war was virtually over. Note particularly the sudden jump in United States launchings in 1942, a consequence of the "Two Ocean Navy" bill of 1940. In the end, Japan lost the war in the shipyards as much as on the high seas.

During the war both powers greatly reduced the time required to build ships.

Each navy required about 12 months to convert a ship to a light carrier, the United States using partially complete light cruiser hulls for this purpose, and the Japanese prewar seaplane carriers and

JAPAN: WARSHIPS ORDERED

	Older	1930s	1941–45	Total	Compl.	Fleet	Canc.	Inc.
Battleships:	10	4	0	4	2	12	1	0
Aircraft Carriers								
Fleet:	2	9	13	22	11	11	0	3
Light:	2	3	3	6	5	7	0	1
Escort:	0	3	4	7	5	5	0	0
A/C	200	800	960	1,760	970	1,170	0	200
Cruisers	25	17	8	25	14	39	1	0
Destroyers								
Fleet:	58	89	38	127	77	135	0	2
Escort:	0	0	113	113	32	32	0	9
Submarines:	53	90	642	732	151	204	1	18

Key: "Older" indicates pre-1930s vessels that were available for first-line service at the outbreak of the Pacific War. All completion figures include conversions from other types: one battleship was converted to an aircraft carrier; cruisers include six ordered as light cruisers in the 1930s and converted to heavy cruises, plus one ordered as a heavy cruiser during the war, and then taken in hand for conversion to a light carrier. "Warships Ordered" includes vessels not laid down; "Compl." covers only ships that entered service; "Fleet" is the total available to the Imperial Navy of each type during the war; "Canc." covers ships that were laid down but canceled during construction; "Inc." includes ships laid down but not completed by the end of the war. Escort carrier figures omit the so-called Japanese Army escort carriers; aircraft figures are approximate; cruisers omits two captured from the Chinese; submarine figures omit midget, suicide, and transport boats.

MAJOR WARSHIP LAUNCHINGS, 1937–45

Year		CV	CVE	BB	CA/CL	DD	DE	SS
1937–1940	Jap.	3	0	2	4	27	0	21
	U.S.	2	1	3	7	47	0	28
1941	Jap.	2	1	0	2	8	0	10
	U.S.	0	2	3	6	27	0	15
1942	Jap.	0	1	0	3	11	0	22
	U.S.	6	14	2	10	120	25	37
1943	Jap.	5	2	0	0	9	0	39
	U.S.	12	25	3	11	92	205	66
1944	Jap.	6	0	0	1	5	24	31
	U.S.	8	35	1	19	64	101	78
1945	Jap.	0	0	0	0	0	12	30
	U.S.	11	9	1	10	73	0	22
Total	Jap.	16	4	2	10	60	36	153
	U.S.	39	76	13	63	315	331	246

Figures for carriers (CV) include light carriers and, as with escort carriers (CVE), include conversions. Escort carrier figures exclude aircraft transports (the Japanese Army built several of these, which looked like carriers but could not operate combat aircraft). US battleship figures include three "large cruisers." Japanese submarine figures exclude numerous midgets and 28 cargo boats built by the Imperial Army. Note that not all vessels launched were actually completed, particularly in the case of the United States, which canceled numerous partially completed hulls.

AVERAGE CONSTRUCTION TIME IN MONTHS

	Prewar		Wartime	
Type	U.S.	Jap.	U.S.	Jap.
BB	35–42	53–61	32	—
CV	32–34	36–44	15–20	22–24
CVE	—	—	8	12
CA	32–38	40–50	24–30	—
CL	32–38	40–50	20–30	19–24
DD	13–14	24–30	5	12
SS	14–15	24–36	7	15
Liberty	12–14	20–30	1	18–24

other vessels especially built to be converted in an emergency. The US figure for escort carriers (CVE) is for new construction, but conversions took about the same time; the Japanese figure is for conversion.

LIBERTY SHIPS, the standard mass-produced US general purpose cargo vessels of the war, were based on a prewar Maritime Commission design. Although they were larger than the average prewar merchantmen (10,000–14,000 GRT vs. about 6,000), they are useful as a basis of comparison. The

Japanese, of course, did not build Liberty ships, but did produce some large marus (the Japanese word for merchantman) of similar concept, albeit smaller.

There were a number of factors that contributed to the considerable reduction in building times. Economies of scale were obviously one factor, since wartime orders were made in large numbers. The extensive use of welding and prefabrication were of great importance. The operation of shipyards on a 24-hour, seven-days-a-week, no-holidays basis also contributed. In the case of the United States modularization was a major factor: A lot of the equipment on US ships was interchangeable, regardless of type of vessel. The best example of this was the twin 5"/38 dual-purpose gun mount, which

Submarines under construction for the US Navy at Groton, Connecticut, in August 1943. These appear to be Balao-class boats, of which Groton produced 48 during the war.

appeared on battleships, carriers, cruisers, and destroyers, even being "retrofitted" on vessels undergoing refits.

It is interesting to note that even before the war the Japanese took much longer to build ships than the Americans, and that, although they improved considerably, it was not proportional to the reductions in time effected by US yards. In fact, US construction time figures for cruisers might actually have been lower but completion of many vessels was deliberately delayed in order to give priority to more desperately needed carriers, destroyers, and destroyer escorts.

See also GIBBS, WILLIAM F.

Shipping, War Against Japanese

While the Germans got most of the publicity for their spectacular U-boat (submarine) success in the Atlantic, less is said about America's successful campaign against Japanese shipping in the Pacific. US SUBMARINES accounted for over half of Japanese merchant shipping and were able to prowl every corner of Japan's maritime empire. Complementing this effort was the increasing reach and dominance of American carrier and land-based aviation at the front lines. Japanese shipping had to run an obstacle course from the time it left port (and promptly encountered waiting American subs) until it reached front-line bases and was pummeled by US bombers.

In 1945, US subs and B-29s began planting thousands of MINES in Japanese coastal waters. In addition to the shipping sunk, these mines virtually shut down Japanese ports. The mines worked day and night and in any weather. With the mines, Japanese ships had neither bad weather nor darkness as protection from enemy subs and aircraft.

Although the Allied anti-shipping campaign wiped out the Japanese merchant marine by the end of the war, the campaign had already severely crippled the latter by the end of 1943. This meant that Japan had less ability to meet the multiple Allied offensives during 1944. Japan began the war

The launching of the Gato Class submarine USS Robalo (SS-273), May 9, 1943, at Manitowoc, Wisconsin. The unusual sideways launch was one of many innovative construction techniques introduced during the war, in this case permitting vessels to be built on rivers and bays too narrow for normal launching. Robalo, skippered by Manning Kimmel, son of Admiral Husband Kimmel, was lost in mid-1944.

with about six and a half million tons of shipping. That amount steadily declined throughout the war, despite some captures and new construction.

Japan fought a poor man's fight for the entire war, using much less ammunition and fewer weapons. This lowered its combat capability and increased its CASUALTIES. The Japanese had little choice in the matter, as they were simply unable to move much over the water because they never had enough shipping.

The Japanese shipping crisis was made worse by the policies of their army and navy. At the begin-

ning of the war, each service appropriated large amounts of shipping (1.8 million tons for the navy, 2.1 million for the army) to support its offensive operations. This left the civilian economy about a million tons short of its minimum needs. Since the arms factories depended on imports for most of their raw materials, PRODUCTION took a beating from the beginning. To make matters worse, the army and navy would not cooperate with each other or with industry in the use of shipping. The army would send a supply ship to JAVA and, instead of coming back with raw materials, it would come

JAPANESE SHIPPING SUNK
(THOUSANDS OF GRT)

Sunk by	Total Lost	% lost in				Total
		1942	1943	1944	1945	
Submarines	5,880	69%	83%	69%	23%	62%
Naval Air	1,740	11%	2%	23%	28%	18%
Land Air	825	9%	11%	6%	12%	9%
Mines	600	0%	0%	0%	28%	6%
Misc.	450	11%	3%	2%	8%	5%
Total	9,495	875	2,175	4,330	2,115	
		9%	23%	46%	22%	

Note that these figures are not necessarily as authoritative as they may appear. Most statistics on shipping losses were compiled shortly after the war. Those compiling the figures were often not privy to certain secret information, notably Ultra and Magic. In recent years a number of additional sinkings of Japanese ships—about 120—have been credited to various submarines.

Misc. includes accidents at sea (storms, breakdowns, etc.) as well as losses to enemy surface warships. Naval air is primarily carrier-based aircraft but also includes land-based Navy planes.

back empty because moving raw materials was not an army responsibility. This situation was not rectified until 1944, when it was too late.

It got worse. Japan never developed an effective convoy system or antisubmarine techniques. But underlying all of this was the fact that Japan was still a minor industrial power. It was during the 1930s that Japan began to industrialize in a serious way. Even so, by 1940 Japan was producing only half a million tons of shipping a year. This was less than a tenth of US capability. Even with a massive effort, Japan was never able to produce more than

JAPANESE MERCHANT SHIPPING
(MILLIONS OF GRT)

Date	Available	Loss to Date
Dec. '41	6.4	0
Jan. '43	5.9	.9
Jan. '44	4.8	3.1
Jan. '45	2.4	7.4
Aug. '45	1.5	9.3

1.7 million tons of shipping a year. That was in 1944, the year that American subs and aircraft sunk 2.7 million tons.

Japan did have one item in its favor. For the first 18 months of the war American submarines were equipped with defective TORPEDOES. It wasn't until September 1943 that this problem was completely resolved, although by the end of 1942 many submarine crews had developed ways to get some use out of their torpedoes. Nevertheless, this gave the Japanese merchant marine something of a free ride through the middle of 1943. After that, Japanese shipping disappeared beneath the waves with great rapidity.

Oddly enough, Japanese submarines were never a menace to Allied shipping. The Japanese felt that the only proper target for their submarines was enemy warships. It was considered a waste of good torpedoes to shoot at merchant ships. However, the Japanese subs did have some success against Allied warships. Two carriers were sunk (one an escort carrier) as were two cruisers. Several other major warships (carriers and battleships) were put out of action for months by Japanese submarine torpedoes.

The Americans also went after Japanese warships, when there were merchant ships handy. Arguably, the US submariners were better at it than their Japanese counterparts.

American subs spent 31,671 days on patrol, about three weeks per patrol. Many patrols were cut short by mechanical problems and some were in support of fleet operations. These fleet patrols were much shorter. To attack 4,112 Japanese merchant ships, 14,748 torpedoes were used. This was 3.6 torpedoes per attack and indicates how the typical attack involved firing a "spread" of torpedoes to maximize the chances of hitting something. Even at that, only about a third of these attacks succeeded in sinking anything. Because of defective torpedoes, the odds were under 20% from 1941 to late 1943, but rose to over 50% thereafter. For the entire war, some 350 tons of enemy shipping was sunk for every torpedo fired.

US SUBMARINE ACTIVITY IN THE PACIFIC

	1941–42	1943	1944	1945	Total
Warships sunk	2	22	104	60	188
Merchantmen sunk	180	325	603	186	1,294
War Patrols	350	350	520	330	1,450
US Subs Lost	7	15	19	8	49

Note that a "war patrol" is one submarine going out looking for the enemy for up to two months, or until damaged or out of torpedoes. Not counted are enemy warships and merchantmen damaged by submarine attacks. These amounted to a smaller number than those sunk, mainly because warships attacked tended to be small escort types and Japanese shipping was, on average, rather smaller than Western ships. These smaller ships were much less likely to survive a torpedo hit. Not all of these ships sank from torpedo hits. When the opportunity presented itself (no enemy warships around), the sub would surface and use its deck gun, usually a 76mm–127mm piece (3-inch to 5-inch) to sink smaller ships. This would save torpedoes, as only about 24 to 30 were carried by an American sub.

Of 52 US submarines lost in World War II from all causes, 49 were lost in the Pacific War. The Japanese lost 130 subs during the war, most of them to aircraft attacks, while the Germans lost 11 in the Pacific Theater. The British also lost three subs and the Dutch five in the Pacific or Indian Oceans. Allied subs accounted for about 2% of the Japanese shipping sunk.

At the beginning of the war, Japan was the premier submarine user in the Pacific, with 67 boats. The United States had 56 in the Pacific, more in the Atlantic, and the ability to outproduce Japan in this area. This is precisely what America did, building over 200 new subs. Japan was able to build only 120.

Unrestricted submarine warfare was prohibited by the London Naval DISARMAMENT TREATY of 1930, of which both the United States and Japan were signatories. Unrestricted submarine warfare is the policy of deliberately attacking non-warships without warning. The traditional law of the sea, embodied in the GENEVA CONVENTION, required that regardless of flag, merchant vessels could not be attacked in wartime without giving them the opportunity to heave to and permit inspection and possible seizure. Although the initiation of unrestricted submarine warfare in the Pacific is generally attributed to the US Navy, it was in fact first employed by the Imperial Navy. Japanese attacks on merchant shipping began soon after the attack on PEARL HARBOR. On 7 December 1941, the USAT *Cynthia Olsen* was torpedoed and sunk by the Japanese submarine I-26, about a 700 miles northeast of Oahu. Before the end of December three other merchant ships were sunk by Japanese submarines between Hawaii and California, while five others were attacked unsuccessfully in the same area.

Had the Japanese Navy committed itself more vigorously to unrestricted submarine warfare it would have made the war longer and far more difficult for the United States, since considerable resources would have been committed to antisubmarine patrol. However, Japanese naval doctrine eschewed attacks on merchant shipping. The Japanese Navy viewed submarines as auxiliaries to the battlefleet. Their task was to scout for the battlewagons, to locate the enemy and perhaps whittle his strength down by successful torpedo attacks, rather than waste time with less honorable objectives such as merchant ships. Precisely why the attacks on US shipping in the eastern Pacific occurred is unclear. In their aftermath the US Navy began to organized a convoy system. However, once it became evident that there was not going to be an antisubmarine "Battle of the Pacific" similar to the Battle of the Atlantic, the US Navy began permitting merchant ships to proceed from the West Coast without escort. It was not long before US and allied merchant ships in rear areas were proceeding individually, without escort. By the end of 1942 the only shipping that moved in heavily escorted convoys in rear areas was troop movements.

But what principally defanged Japanese subs was American airpower and warships using effective antisubmarine weapons and tactics. Thousands of American patrol aircraft constantly crisscrossed the Pacific, making life decidedly uncomfortable for Japanese subs. America also produced over 600 destroyers and destroyer escorts. While over half of these initially went to the Atlantic (to confront German U-boats), plenty were left for the Pacific.

Japan produced fewer than a hundred destroyers and smaller antisubmarine ships during the war and used them much less efficiently.

Another serious Japanese shortcoming was many long and exposed sea routes. Many of these were outside the range of friendly aircraft, and the Japanese had far fewer long-range patrol aircraft anyway. Roundtrips for merchantmen from Japan to outlying bases took from 30 to 90 days. This was particularly true of bases in the central Pacific. By the end of the war, many of these bases could no longer be reached anyway because American forces had seized nearby islands and installed air bases. Japanese troops on these bypassed islands often starved before the war ended, though not before resorting to cannibalism. Even some shot down American pilots ended up in the stew pot.

As successful as they were, American sub crews still took high losses, with 22% of the US submariners being killed during the course of the war. This was the highest percentage loss of any arm of the US service.

Ref: Alden, *U.S. Submarine Attacks during World War II*; Blair, *Silent Victory*; Boyd and Yoshia, *The Japanese Submarine Force in World War II*; Friedman, *Submarine Design and Development*; Parillo, *The Japanese Merchant Marine in World War II*; Roscoe, *United States Submarine Operations in World War II*.

Ships, Classes

Warships are usually built in groups called "classes," with each vessel in the class being more or less identical to all the others. This saves money on design and during construction and repair, and makes it easier to create homogeneous squadrons. Some classes numbered in the hundreds, while others included only two or three ships.

Warships are occasionally built to unique designs for a variety of reasons. Parsimony is one. A navy without much money may be able to afford only one new ship of a particular type every few years. So it tries to build the most up-to-date one it can, each time it does so. Another reason for building a ship to a unique design is experimentation. When a new design incorporates a number of innovative, or perhaps revolutionary, ideas, it's best to build a single ship, rather than invest money in a fleet of potential lemons. A good case in point is the US heavy cruiser WICHITA, based on the BROOKLYN CLASS light cruiser design, the experience with which led to the creation of the more successful BALTIMORE CLASS. The naval DISARMAMENT TREATIES of 1922–30 provided yet a third reason for building a ship to an individual design. The treaties very clearly defined the total tonnage of the navies of the signatory powers. As a result, a number of navies discovered that if they built one ship, to a unique design, they could use up those last few thousand tons of their quota. In this way the US Navy acquired the carrier WASP and the Japanese Navy its RYUJO, both squeezing the last few tons out of their national quotas, and both rather unsatisfactory as a result.

Note, by the way, that even when built in classes, ships will differ from each other in numerous ways. These differences are usually minor. For example, only two of the four battleships of the IOWA CLASS had the same hull length, 887 feet 3 inches, *Iowa* being 887 feet 2.75 inches and *New Jersey* 887 feet 6.626 inches long, while the British DIDO CLASS antiaircraft cruisers differed so much among themselves that they are sometimes listed as five separate classes. The differences are caused by many factors: variations in the quality of materials, differing skills, modifications during construction, wartime shortages, unanticipated technical problems, and even weather (which affects the coefficient of expansion).

Ships, Naming Conventions

Most nations adopted systems for naming their warships.

The US Navy named battleships after states. Aircraft carriers were mostly named after famous ships of the "Old Navy" or famous battles, with a handful named after individuals (*Langley* and *Franklin D. Roosevelt*). Escort carriers were produced in such numbers that they were mostly named after bays or rivers, although as the war went on some were renamed after battles. Large cruisers were named after US territories, while heavy and light cruisers were named after large cities. Destroyers and destroyer escorts were mostly named after naval heroes or persons who made important contributions to the navy, including, in one case, a woman. This was the USS *Higbee* (DD-806) a GEARING CLASS ship named after Lenah Higbee, who had been the chief of the Navy Nurse Corps during World War I. The only other ships named after real women were the Coast Guard cutters *Harriet Lane*, a traditional name in the Coast Guard, after the daughter of a mid-19th-century secretary of the treasury, and *Spars*, after the Coast Guard's women's reserve. SUBMARINES received the names of "denizens of the deep," both real and mythical. There were also conventions for naming various types of smaller warships. Gunboats, for example, were named after small cities or islands. Hospital ships, were given "soothing" names, such as *Solace* or *Bountiful*, while ammunition ships were appropriately named after volcanoes.

The Imperial Navy named battleships after ancient provinces of Japan, or, in the case of the KONGO CLASS, which were converted from battlecruisers, after famous mountains. Aircraft carriers mostly were given picturesque names related to flying, to flying creatures, or to the sea, but this system was not always adhered to. Several carriers were converted from another type of ship, or for other reasons had different types of names. For example, KAGA and SHINANO were originally intended to be battleships, AKAGI a battlecruiser, IBUKI a heavy cruiser, and CHITOSE and *Chiyoda* seaplane carriers. In addition, several of the ships of the Unyu Class were named after famous cruisers of the Imperial Navy.

A complete list of Japanese carrier names: *Akagi*, "Red Castle," a mountain near Tokyo; *Amagi*, "Castle in the sky"; *Aso*, a volcano on Kyushu; *Chitose*, "A Thousand Years!"; *Chiyoda*, "A Thousand Generations!"; *Chuyo*, "Middle Sea"; *Hiryu*, "Flying Dragon"; *Hiyo*, "Bright Sea"; HOSHO, "Flying Bird" (see *Shoho*); *Ibuki*, a volcano on Kyushu; *Ikoma*, a mountain near Osaka; JUNYO, "Deep Sea"; *Kaga*, "Increased Joy," a former region around Ishikawa Prefecture; *Kasagi*, a mountain near Osaka; *Katsuragi*, a mountain; KAIYO, "Eternal Sea"; RYUHO, a mythological bird; RYUJO, "Sacred Dragon"; *Shinano*, ancient region of Honshu, as well as Japan's longest river; SHINYO, "Holy Sea"; *Shoho*, "Flying Bird" (see *Hosho*); SHOKAKU, "Flying Crane"; SORYU, "Blue Dragon"; TAIHO, a mythological bird; TAIYO, "Spirit of the Ocean"; UNRYU, "Cloud Dragon"; *Unyo*, "See of Clouds"; ZUIHO, "Auspicious Bird"; *Zuikaku*, "Auspicious Crane."

Battle cruisers and heavy cruisers were named after mountains, while light cruisers were named after rivers. Seaplane carriers were given inspiring names, which also happened to be the names of places, thus *Nisshin*, "Ever Advancing!" Destroyers received names related to meteorological or physical phenomena, for example: KAMIKAZE, "Divine Wind"; *Tanikaze*, "Valley Wind"; *Kasumi*, "Mist of Flowers"; *Shiranui*, "Phosphorescent Foam"; *Yagumo*, "Mountain Cloud"; *Asagumo*, "Morning Cloud"; *Murakumo*, "Gathering Clouds"; *Natsugumo*, "Summer Cloud"; *Akizuki*, "Autumn Moon"; *Shirayuki*, "White Snow"; FUBUKI, "Snowstorm"; *Katsuyuki*, "First Snowfall"; *Nenoni*, "New Years' Day"; *Katuharu*, "First Days of Spring"; *Wakaba*, "Fresh Green of Springtime"; *Hatusimo*, "First Frost"; *Akebono*, "Daybreak"; *Usugumo*, "Fleecy Clouds"; *Oboro*, "Moonlight Through Haze"; *Usio*, "Ocean Tide"; *Hibiki*, "Echo"; *Inazuma*, "Lightning"; *Ikazuchi*, "Thunder"; *Nozake*, "Wind in the Sails"; *Shiokaze*, "Wind Rising from the Turn of the Tide."

The ROYAL NAVY had a complex system for naming ships. In general, the names of famous old warships were used for battleships, battlecruisers, and aircraft carriers, but battleships were also given royal names or titles, and the names of famous commanders as well. Cruisers built after World War I were usually named after towns, counties, or colonies, but mythological and traditional names, including those of naval heroes, were also common.

There was little system to the name of smaller warships, which were sometimes named in bunches, after flowers, tribes, naval heroes, jewels, and so forth, there being so many of them.

Shiratsuyu Class, Japanese Destroyers

Built 1933–37, the Shiratsuyus were similar to the preceding HATSUHARU CLASS, but had a heavier TORPEDO armament. During the war they lost one of their 5-inch dual-purpose guns in order to accommodate additional antiaircraft armament. All 10 units became war losses: one in a collision, one by air attack, three in surface actions in the SOLOMONS, and five by submarine attack.

The most notable unit in the class was *Shigure* (1933–1935–1936). *Shigure*, which means "Drizzling Autumn Rain," was undoubtedly the luckiest ship in the Imperial Navy. Although repeatedly "in harm's way" from the start of the war, she led a charmed life. *Shigure*'s battle honors read like a record of the principal actions of the war. Escort for the battleships covering operations in the Philippines and East Indies early in the war, she later fought in Battle of the CORAL SEA without a scratch. Thereafter based at RABAUL, she fought through the GUADALCANAL Campaign, bombarding the beachhead on the night of 14–15 October 1942 without injury, taking part in the chaotic Second Battle of Guadalcanal, November 14–15, with no damage, then VELLA GULF (August 6–7, 1943), where she was the only one of the four Japanese destroyers involved to survive, and did so without any damage. Ten days later she joined with several other destroyers to successfully land reinforcements on VELLA LAVELLA despite a skirmish with American destroyers. At the Battle of Vella Lavella (October 6–7 1943) she was part of a squadron of nine destroyers and a number of lighter vessels assigned to evacuate Japanese troops, but apparently took no damage when six American destroyers attempted to intercept, coming off the worse for it. The "apparently" turned into an "almost" when, a few months later, it was discovered that a US torpedo had hit one of *Shigure*'s rudders,

but not detonated, leaving instead a rather neat 21-inch hole. During the Battle of EMPRESS AUGUSTA BAY (November 2, 1943) she was one of four cruisers and six destroyers that came off second best in an action with four American cruisers and eight destroyers while trying to disrupt the Allied landings at Cape Torokina on BOUGAINVILLE, but once again suffered not at all. During the Battle of BIAK (June 7, 1944), *Shigure*, one of several Japanese ships engaged in a long-range stern chase by some US destroyers, was near-missed five times, with no significant damage. In the Battle of the PHILIPPINE SEA (June 19–21, 1944) she was one of the escorts for Carrier Task Force B, but came away from the battle with no damage. During the Leyte Campaign she fought at SURIGAO STRAIT (October 25, 1944), being the only ship in her squadron to survive, with only slight damage from an 8-inch dud, despite tangling with a nest of US PT-BOATS and some cruisers in the midst of the biggest shoot-'em-up of the Pacific War.

Shigure's luck ran out on January 24, 1945, when she took a torpedo from the US submarine *Blackfin* (SS-322) while escorting a small convoy about 150 miles north of SINGAPORE. She sank with great loss of life. *Shigure*'s skipper—and perhaps her luck—for most of the war was Cdr. Tameichi Hara, who was promoted to captain in mid-1944 and given command of the new light cruiser *Yahagi*, of the AGANO CLASS.

Ref: Hara, Saito, and Pineau, *Japanese Destroyer Captain*.

Shokaku Class, Japanese Aircraft Carriers

The Shokakus were Japan's best prewar carriers, and the first Japanese carriers to be sisterships, all eight previous carriers having been single-ship designs. *Shokaku* and *Zuikaku* entered service only a few months before PEARL HARBOR (August and September 1941, respectively), and, indeed, the details of the attack were planned so that they could complete training. Much larger versions of HIRYU, they were better protected and had a greater avgas capacity, but could operate only about the same number of aircraft. They formed Carrier Division Five and were at Pearl Harbor, helped support Japanese operations in New Guinea in January 1942, then accompanied the First Air Fleet into the Indian Ocean. They went on to fight at CORAL SEA, where damage to *Shokaku* and losses among their air groups resulted in their missing MIDWAY. They were also together at EASTERN SOLOMONS, SANTA CRUZ, and the PHILIPPINE SEA.

Shokaku (1937–1939–1941) was so seriously damaged at the Coral Sea that she almost sank on the return voyage to Japan, but her aircraft had mortally wounded LEXINGTON. She took two bombs in the Battle of the Eastern Solomons and survived six during the Battle of the Santa Cruz Islands. She was sunk by three TORPEDOES from the submarine *Cavalla* (SS-244) on June 19, 1944 during the Battle of the Philippine Sea.

Zuikaku (1938–1939–1941) led a charmed life, apparently taking no injury despite being in numerous actions until the Battle of the Philippine Sea, when she was heavily damaged. She returned to service in time for the Battle of LEYTE GULF in October 1944, in which she took seven torpedoes and six or seven bombs from US naval aircraft before sinking off Cape Engaño. As the ship was going down, her crew stood to attention on her increasingly sloping flight deck to give several cries of "Banzai!" for the glory of the emperor. She was the last of the Pearl Harbor carriers to be sunk.

Short, Walter C. (1880–1949)

Short graduated from the University of Illinois in 1901 and accepted a direct commission in the US Army in 1902. He served in various garrisons, in the Philippines, and on the Pershing Expedition, before going to France in 1917. During World War I his service was entirely in staff and training posts, and he ended the war as chief of staff of the Third Army, on occupation duty in the Rhineland. From 1920 to 1940 he held various staff and line positions, attended several army schools, and rose to brigadier general. Short commanded a corps in the

maneuvers of 1940, and was promoted major general. Early in 1941 he was given command of the Hawaiian Department and promoted to temporary lieutenant general. He was in command at the time of the Pearl Harbor attack. Relieved about two weeks after the attack, Short was soon forcibly retired in his permanent rank of major general. He began hurling accusations as to responsibility for the attack. A congressional investigation in 1942 concluded that he—and his naval counterpart, Admiral Husband KIMMEL—had been derelict in his duty and had committed errors of judgment. A second investigation, in 1946, cleared him of charges of dereliction of duty, but confirmed that he had committed errors of judgment. He spent the rest of his life attempting to clear his name.

While some controversy still clings to the investigative conclusions concerning Short's responsibility (much of it motivated by anti-Roosevelt sentiments in some political circles), in fact at the very least he had committed serious errors of judgment. Like most army officers he believed that the main event in any future war would be with Germany, and viewed his posting to HAWAII as likely to keep him out of it, ending his chances for further advancement. He seems to have had little understanding of the capabilities of air power. In a memorandum available at the National Archives, dated in February of 1941, shortly after he assumed command in Hawaii, he dismissed the possibility of a serious Japanese carrier raid on the islands. Upon receiving the famous November 27, 1941 message from General MARSHALL that concluded with the line "This is to be considered a war warning," Short's initial reaction was to make preparations to cope with possible sabotage by Japanese Americans, but he instituted few changes in the daily routine or procedures of the troops under his command.

Shoup, David M. (1904–1983)

One of the controversial officers the Marines seem to produce from time to time, Shoup graduated from DePauw University in 1926 and was commissioned a second lieutenant in the Corps. He served afloat and in China, attended various schools, and at the outbreak of the Pacific War was commanding a battalion of the Sixth Marines in Iceland. In mid-1942 he was assigned to the staff of the Second Marine Division, and served in the New Georgia operation. Promoted to colonel, he commanded the Marines who assaulted Betio, the principal island comprising TARAWA Atoll, being awarded the MEDAL OF HONOR for refusing to be evacuated despite serious wounds. Later he was chief of staff of the Second Marine Division, serving during the Marianas Campaign in mid-1944 and until the end of the war, when he was assigned to an administrative command in Washington. After the war Shoup held various increasingly important posts, ending his career as commandant of the Corps in 1963. Afterward an outspoken critic of intervention in Vietnam, Shoup found himself vilified and ostracized by many formerly close associates.

Siam (Thailand)

A large kingdom in Southeast Asia, between Burma and French INDO-CHINA, Siam's population was mostly Buddhist. Its economy was primarily agricultural, with some export of timber and raw materials.

Siam had maintained a precarious independence during the Age of Imperialism. By the outbreak of the war in Europe, the Thais were ruled by a military dictatorship. The Fall of France led them into a brief, unsuccessful border war with the Vichyite forces in French Indo-China (see SIAMESE ARMED FORCES).

Despite some admiration for Japan, as an Asian nation that had modernized itself and risen to the status of a great power, the Thais decidedly wanted to remain neutral in the war.

Siam was in a most bizarre situation during World War II. The only independent nation in Southeast Asia, it had maintained its independence by deft diplomacy. Even before PEARL HARBOR, the Japanese made it known that they might call upon Siamese "cooperation." When a Japanese army showed up on its border, demanding passage through Siam to Burma, the Siamese did what they had learned to do in order to survive. After a token resistance, they concluded an armistice and let the Japanese march through. But the Japanese wanted more "cooperation" than that and soon had Siam under what amounted to military occupation. This did not make the Japanese popular with the Siamese people, or the government. So by late 1942 there was a typically Siamese "resistance movement." This was not a typical guerrilla resistance movement, although there were some armed people in the jungles and a few acts of sabotage during the war. The Siamese resistance had strong ties to the government. It maintained contact with the Allies and provided a steady stream of reliable information on Japanese activities in Siam. As a result, the Allies never declared Siam "hostile" and simply treated it as another victim of Japanese aggression after the war.

The name of the country was changed from Siam to Thailand in June 1939, back to Siam in September 1945, and then to Thailand once more in the late 1940s.

Siamese Armed Forces

Siam had a small, relatively well equipped military establishment, but it was not particularly efficient. The Siamese Army had four modestly equipped divisions. It performed rather well in the brief 1940–41 border war with French INDO-CHINA, but found itself hopelessly outclassed when the Japanese occupied the country in December 1941. An armistice was soon arranged. Although Siam subsequently formally allied herself with Japan, the Siamese Army saw little action. Had the Siamese gotten into more serious action, indications are that they would not have done well against first-line Allied or Japanese troops. Peak wartime strength was 127,000 troops, plus about 25,000 more in paramilitary forces.

The Siamese Air Force had about 150 aircraft in 1941, mostly older models, many of them more or less obsolete. It saw some action against the even weaker French Air Force during the Franco-Siamese Border War. In addition, it put up a token resistance against the Japanese for a few hours after the invasion on 8 December 1941. For most of the war, the Siamese Air Force remained largely inactive.

The Siamese Navy was a small force, consisting mostly of obsolete vessels until the early 1930s, when an ambitious expansion program was undertaken. This added two coast defense ships of 2,265 tons (with four 8-inch guns), two sloops, and two gunboats, plus torpedo boats and many smaller coastal craft by the late 1930s, by which time there were also two light cruisers on order from Italian shipyards, completion of which was prevented by the outbreak of the war in Europe. The Siamese Navy saw limited action in World War II, and that only against Vichy French forces during the brief Siamese-French War of 1941.

In a bid to grab some territory, the Siamese invaded French Indo-China in November 1940. The result was a war that lasted less than three months (November 1940–January 1941). Siamese land forces made some gains against Vichyite French forces on the Cambodian-Siamese frontier, and as a result the French Far Eastern Squadron sortied into the Gulf of Siam. This resulted in the principal action of the war, the Battle of the Gulf of Siam or Koh-Chang (16–17 January 1941), when the French light cruiser LAMOTTE-PICQUET and four gunboats had a running night action of about 105 minutes with a Siamese squadron, which included the coast defense ships *Sri Ayuthia* and *Dhonburi* and three torpedo boats, in the Koh-Chang Islands off the southwest coast of Cambodia. Both Siamese coast defense ships were heavily damaged and sank in shallow water, as did the three torpedo boats, with little loss to the French. Siam signed an armistice on 29 January 1941. Despite their victory, the Vichy French were forced by the Japanese to cede several provinces from Cambodia to the Siamese.

Sims Class, US Destroyers

The dozen destroyers of the Sims Class, built 1937–40, were intended to be a major evolutionary development over preceding designs, which had been restricted to 1,500 tons by the various DISARMAMENT TREATIES. As completed they turned out unsuccessfully, displacing much more than expected, and they had to be extensively redesigned and refitted before entering service. Redesigned, they proved rather successful, despite the loss of some armament, and they became the prototypes for the succeeding two classes. They saw considerable service. Five were lost in action. The surviving vessels were broken up or expended as targets in the late 1940s.

Singapore, Malaya

A major port, and the principal British naval and air base in the Far East. Although well appointed, Singapore was ill-suited to its role as the bastion of British power in Southeast Asia. It was a small island, bereft of industrial resources, very close to the Malayan mainland, and with no really open sea around it. Despite this, between the wars the British invested heavily in developing it as a major base. Not only was a first-class naval dockyard constructed, but there were also several airfields and an elaborate system of fortifications. Altogether some 60 million pounds sterling was spent (over $3 billion in money of 1997). Unfortunately, it was poorly spent. The installations at Singapore were all badly planned. The naval base, for example, was on the landward side of the island, approachable only through the narrow Straits of Johore, and within artillery range of the Malay Peninsula. Similarly, the coast defense facilities, which included five 15-inch naval guns (not 18-inch, as is often claimed), capable of firing upon targets on the landward side of the island fortress (claims to the contrary notwithstanding), and a half-dozen 9.2-inchers, were supplied only with armor-piercing ammunition that was of dubious value against infantrymen in jungles.

In the years before World War II the British buildup of Singapore as their principal military base in the Far East led to the place assuming considerable psychological importance. It was a formidable place, but by no means as impregnable as it was touted in the press. All the propagandizing about the fortifications was a little ploy to keep the colonials happy. Thus, when the fortress fell to the Japanese with very little fuss early in 1942, British prestige plummeted throughout Asia.

In reality, Singapore was virtually indefensible unless one commanded the skies and seas around it, and in 1941–42 the ROYAL NAVY did not have the ships nor the RAF the aircraft to secure such control. Moreover, the city was on an island and its water supply came from the mainland. Should a hostile force control the mainland water (as the Japanese did when they invaded), this tropical city and its thirsty population would quickly capitulate. This was precisely what happened to the British.

What might have saved Singapore was the Japanese supply situation, which provided for only a week's worth of food. The average Japanese infantryman had but a hundred bullets with him, to last the entire campaign. Moreover, the Japanese commander thought the British garrison comprised only 30,000 troops, not the nearly 90,000 that were there. The Japanese had to storm the island of Singapore and could not wait for the British to run out of water (there was a small reservoir on the island). The British didn't know of the precarious Japanese supply situation, not that it would have done much good. British leadership was so inept that they were unable to prevent the outnumbered and ill-supplied Japanese from getting across the water, onto the island, and into the city. The fall of Singapore unleashed a host of rumors and tall tales. There were numerous stories of treachery (always a reliable crutch when one doesn't want to admit to ineptitude or carelessness). Incompetence in high places was also a good target.

Despite their inability to hold Singapore, the British really had built it up into an extraordinary fortress. As a result, it turned into a valuable resource for the Japanese. They very quickly began to use bits and pieces of equipment captured at Singapore to bolster their defenses elsewhere. One result of this was that US Marines assaulting TARAWA found themselves being fired upon by 8-inch coast defense guns from Singapore, firing some of His Majesty's best munitions.

Sino-American Cooperative Organization (SACO)

Pronounced "Socko," SACO was formed on April 15, 1943 and was a collaborative effort between Chinese intelligence and the US Naval Group, China (NGC), a navy-Marine Corps-Coast Guard mission to China. Commanded by RAdm Milton E. Miles, the NGC was formed in mid-1942, initially to collect weather information and provide technical support and training to the Chinese armed forces. The NGC eventually comprised about 2,500 volunteers from the navy, Coast Guard, and Marine Corps. With Chinese auxiliaries, these men were organized into eight GUERRILLA training detachments, 27 medical teams, and numerous weather detachments.

Although their headquarters near CHUNGKING was designated Weather Central (and codenamed Happy Valley), NGC personnel actually performed a variety of duties in addition to operating weather stations. They trained Chinese guerrillas, conducted long-range reconnaissance, rescued downed fliers, mined Chinese rivers and coastal waters, and undertook special warfare missions against the Japanese.

SACO coastwatchers regularly communicated the movements of Japanese ships to US SUBMARINES in the China Seas and to American aircraft operating out of the Philippines in the last months of the war. By the armistice, SACO controlled about 200 miles of the Chinese coast.

SACO operated a dozen training camps for guerrillas, medical personnel, radio operators, and other technical specialties. An estimated 80,000 Chinese troops were trained in these camps, although only about 30,000 could be properly armed. By its own estimates, SACO guerrillas rescued 76 Allied airmen who had bailed out over Japanese-held territory, and destroyed 141 ships and other vessels, 209 bridges, 84 locomotives, and 97 Japanese depots, ammunition dumps, and arms warehouses, while killing nearly 24,000 Japanese, wounding about 10,000 more, and taking nearly 300 PRISONERS. SACO losses were reported as about 8,000 men killed, including a small number of Americans. Three Americans were also captured by the Japanese and subsequently put to death.

Nor was the NGC's official mission, weather reporting, neglected. By October 1944 there were some 150 American and 700 Chinese personnel operating more than a dozen weather stations all over China, which provided invaluable meteorological data for the Pacific Fleet. This mission took naval personnel to the most exotic locales, from the jungles of Yunan to the sands of Inner Mongolia.

The NGC had a number of truly unique achievements.

On 18 January 1944, the NGC established what will undoubtedly remain the most unusual naval station in history, when it set up shop in Suiyan, in the Gobi Desert of Mongolia, literally hundreds of miles from the sea. Under the command of Marine Maj. Victor R. Bisceglia, a dozen Americans and about 80 Chinese operated the station until the end of the war. To provide protection from Japanese patrols, Maj. Bisceglia organized about 600 local Mongol tribesmen into a mounted security detail, to whom he had the navy issue CAVALRY saddles. With these troops, he occasionally attacked Japanese installations, and once defeated a Japanese motorized column of about 500 men.

The NGC also conducted the last naval action of World War II, on August 20, 1945, nearly a week after the emperor's announcement that Japan would surrender. A SACO detail was patrolling in a sailing junk off Wenchow, on the Chinese coast, when it was attacked by several Japanese motorized junks, which the personnel proceeded to board and capture with pistol and cutlass in hand.

The NGC's operations were tinged with some controversy. It conducted a running feud with the OSS, which was constantly trying to assert control over its activities. In addition, SACO's ties with Chinese intelligence were quite controversial. Admiral Miles' Chinese contact was General Tai Li, chief of the Investigation and Statistics Bureau, which has been variously described as "China's FBI" or "China's Gestapo," depending upon one's political perspective. The truth is probably somewhere between the two. Tai did a lot of CHIANG's dirty work, but no one in China had particularly clean hands, and the fact that he made a tidy profit through corruption was hardly surprising in a Chinese official. He was a highly effective intelligence chief, and helped hold Chiang's fragile coalition together in China's most desperate hours.

Ref: Stratton, *SACO*.

Skull Island

Off the southwest coast of New Guinea, Skull Island was of little strategic value and only occasionally visited. The island lacked even the most rudimentary anchorage, was incapable of supporting airfields, was possessed of a hostile population, and was plagued by numerous dangerous and unpleasant animals.

Slim, William J. (1891–1970)

Of working-class background, William Slim enlisted in Britain's Indian Army during World War I, and by its end had earned a regular commission in the Gurkhas. By the outbreak of World War II he commanded a brigade, which he led with considerable distinction in East Africa in 1940–41, where he was wounded. During the Iraqi Revolt and the Syrian Campaign (spring 1941) he again proved himself. Promoted to lieutenant general in early 1942, he was sent by Sir Archibald WAVELL

(C-in-C India) to try to stem the Japanese invasion of Burma, commanding the I Burma Corps. With troops mostly of mediocre quality, Slim, ably supported by his superior, Sir Harold ALEXANDER, performed wonders. Although an attempted counteroffensive failed, Slim was able to effect a remarkably arduous retreat of some 900 miles back to India. Given command of XV Corps, he subjected it to an intensive regimen of physical toughening, jungle training, and irregular tactics. Appointed to command 14th Army in October of 1943, Slim directed the defense of India ably, and then went over to the offensive in late 1944. By the spring of 1945 Slim had liberated most of central Burma, having inflicted over 350,000 CASUALTIES on the Japanese Army. Shortly afterward appointed to command all Allied ground forces in Southeast Asia, at the end of the war he was poised to liberate MALAYA. After the war Slim served in several prominent military and civil posts. A simple man, Slim was a no-nonsense soldier with enormous regard for the welfare of his men. A meticulous planner, he was not averse to unconventional methods, employing irregular forces and air supply to a degree unprecedented in the war. One of the most successful, and least famous, of all World War II commanders.

Small Arms

The Pacific War was an infantry war, and the infantryman's personal weapons counted for more than in Europe. Most of the Pacific fighting was done in jungles and mountains, in general under conditions where the infantryman had to depend more on his personal weapons than in other theaters.

Most of the troops fighting in the Pacific used a combination of older (World War I-era) and newer weapons.

The Japanese used a bolt-action rifle that was literally a World War I weapon, being a 1905 design. This was not as surprising as it may seem, since most World War II armies used relatively older rifles, including the German Army. In 1941,

INFANTRY RIFLES OF THE PACIFIC WAR

	Name	Caliber	Weight	Action	Magazine
Chinese	Mauser 98	7.9mm	9.0 lbs.	bolt	5
Commonwealth	No. 14	7.7mm	9.4 lbs.	bolt	5
Japanese	Model 38	6.5mm	9.4 lbs.	bolt	5
	Model 99	7.7mm	8.8 lbs.	bolt	5
United States	M-1	7.62mm	9.5 lbs.	semi-auto	8
	M-1903	7.62mm	8.6 lbs.	bolt	5

Magazine: the number of bullets the weapon carried.

most Japanese troops were equipped with the original 6.5mm 1905 design rifle. Most other armies had long since upgraded to 7.5mm–8mm weapons, which had longer range, greater stopping power, and superior accuracy. Gradually throughout the war, Japanese infantry were reequipped with a newer, 7.7mm version of the 1905 "Arisaka" rifle, the model 99 of 1939

The Chinese Army actually used a great variety of infantry rifles, but the standard was the reliable old German Mauser, the *Infanterie Gewehr '98*, introduced in the late 19th century. A limited number of units eventually received the US M-1 Garand rifle.

British and other Commonwealth troops mostly fought using the No. 14 rifle. Although designed after 1919, it was essentially a World War I weapon. As time went by, however, light automatic weapons, such as Sten guns, came into wide usage.

US troops were much better off. While the troops who went into combat on WAKE ISLAND, GUAM and in the Philippines in late 1941 and early 1942 were still equipped mostly with the 1903 bolt-action (7.62mm/.30 caliber) Springfield rifle, the semi-automatic M-1 Garand (also 7.62mm) rapidly replaced the Springfield.

The semi-automatic M-1 could deliver about 30–36 aimed shots per minute, about twice as many as a bolt-action rifle. This was because the M-1 would fire as quickly as you pulled the trigger, while the bolt-action rifle required you to pull the bolt back to extract the shell casing and then move the

Two men of the First Marine Division in action against Japanese positions near Wana, Okinawa, May 1945. The Marine on the left wields a Thompson submachine gun, uncharacteristically taking aim with a weapon better suited for short bursts while advancing. His comrade carries an M-1 Garand semi-automatic rifle, the standard American infantry weapon of World War II. As this man is more elaborately equipped than the first, the two were probably working as a team.

bolt forward to load another round. In combat most fire was aimed in only a general sense. Thus the higher rate of fire of the M-1 (about 50 rounds per minute to about 20) gave it an edge. In a tight spot, which was normal for infantry combat, the ability to get off eight shots in a few seconds was decisive.

For well aimed fire, both sides had sniper versions of their rifles. The Japanese used Model 38 and 99 rifles manufactured to higher production standards and equipped with telescopic sights. The United States used special M-1903 "Springfield" bolt-action rifles equipped with telescopes. For well aimed fire, a bolt-action weapon had an intrinsic advantage over a semiautomatic one, although a good sniper was lethal with either type.

Japanese pistols came in a wide variety of types, both revolvers and automatics, most of which were 9mm. The principal US pistol was the .45 caliber (11.4mm), which was originally designed for close-in jungle combat in the Philippines at the turn of the century.

The Japanese had no submachine guns, while the United States had three. The most popular was the .30 caliber (7.62mm) M-2 carbine. This was actually a small rifle (weighing 5.3 pounds) firing a pistol-type cartridge. It came with a 20- or 30-

round magazine. The M-3 (or "grease gun") was .45 caliber (11.4mm), weighed six pounds, and had a 30-round magazine. US troops, particularly Marines, and SEABEES, also made use of the Thompson .45 submachine gun. None of these weapons was accurate beyond 100 meters. But at night, in the jungle, the action was commonly a lot closer than that. The carbine was comfortable to carry, but distrusted by combat troops for the low stopping power of its lightweight pistol cartridge. Japanese infantry attacks were carried out with much vigor, and a large bullet was often needed to stop the hard-charging Japanese troops. For that reason, the grease gun was preferred. But the M-3 was heavy and awkward to carry. It was also, because of its short barrel and pistol cartridge, accurate only at very short ranges. The carbine, because of its longer barrel, had greater accuracy when aimed and fired one shot short at a time at longer ranges. The "Tommy" gun was less accurate, but easier to carry. British and Commonwealth troops used the Sten M3, a cheaply produced, light (6.5 pounds) weapon firing 9mm pistol ammunition. The normal clip was 20 rounds, but it was physically impossible to manually load a clip beyond 18. It lacked a safety and was highly inaccurate.

Smith, Holland M. (1882–1967)

Holland "Howlin' Mad" Smith was a lawyer in Alabama when he received a commission in the US Marines in 1905. He served in the Philippines, PANAMA, and the Dominican Republic before going to France in 1917 as a machine gunner and later a staff officer, fighting in virtually all of the AEF's operations, Aisne-Marne, the Oise, St.-Mihiel, and the Meuse-Argonne. After occupation duty in Germany, he went through a series of staff and command assignments, helped develop the Corps' amphibious doctrine, and on the eve of the Pacific War was a major general in command of the newly formed First Marine Division. Smith trained not only the Marine Corps' amphibious forces, but also the army's, and was responsible for

training both the First and Third Infantry Divisions in amphibious operations. Promoted to command what would become the V Marine Amphibious Corps, and later commander of Fleet Marine Force, Pacific. Smith directed the assaults on TARAWA, ENIWETOK, SAIPAN, TINIAN, GUAM, IWO JIMA, and OKINAWA, several times personally leading the assault forces. Smith retired shortly after the war, in the rank of general. A non-nonsense commander, Smith's nickname came from his occasional bursts of temper. One of his most famous acts was the so-called "War of the SMITHS," in which he relieved an army division commander also named Smith during the Marianas Campaign.

Smith, Oliver P. (1893–1977)

Oliver Prince Smith graduated from Berkeley in 1916 and was commissioned in the US Marines the following year. He saw no action in World War I, being in the Pacific. His interwar service was typical of a Marine of the time, serving on shipboard, in Haiti, on various staffs, and attending several schools, including the army's Infantry School. In May of 1941 he took his Sixth Marine Regiment to Iceland, where the outbreak of the Pacific War found him. In March of 1942 he was transferred to Marine Corps headquarters. In January of 1944 he got into action, receiving command of the Fifth Marines, which he led on NEW BRITAIN. Shortly made brigadier general, he served on PELELIU as assistant commander of the First Marine Division and on OKINAWA as Marine deputy chief of staff to Simon B. BUCKNER's 10th Army. After Okinawa he returned stateside to command the Marine schools at Quantico, in which post peace found him. After the war he was assistant commandant for a time, and in 1950 was made commander of the newly reactivated First Marine Division, which he led at Inchon, in the fighting for Seoul, at the Chosin Reservoir, and in the retreat to the coast, one of the most distinguished episodes in the history of American arms. Smith afterward rose to lieutenant general and retired in 1955.

Smiths, War of the

Arguably the most long-enduring interservice wrangle of World War II, the "War of the Smiths" broke out when MG Holland M. Smith (USMC) relieved MG Ralph Smith (USA) on SAIPAN in June 1944.

Ralph Smith commanded the 27th Infantry Division, of the New York NATIONAL GUARD. He and his division had served under Holland Smith's V Amphibious Corps during operations against MAKIN in the GILBERT ISLANDS in late 1943 and on Saipan in the MARIANAS in mid–1944.

The 27th Division had come in for some criticism during the Makin operation, the Marines considering that it had taken too long to overcome what seemed to be relatively light Japanese opposition. (There were 6,500 US troops involved, against about 700 Japanese, including several hundred Korean laborers; CASUALTIES were 64 Americans killed, and virtually all of the Japanese.) When questioned about the matter, Ralph Smith appeared to have agreed that his division had not acted energetically on Makin. However, Makin was the division's baptism of fire. Moreover, the island had been designated the division's objective only a few weeks earlier, prior to which the division had been preparing for an invasion of NAURU. In addition, the landing had taken place after the division had spent 18 months on garrison duty in HAWAII. Some senior officers believed that it was stale from overtraining and inactivity, and considered the matter of little importance. Then, on Saipan, the division was assigned a sector between two Marine divisions. To the Marines, the division took much too long to get into position (some units were up to three hours late in reaching their assigned lines of departure) and then it attacked piecemeal. During the action, it appeared to be lagging behind the adjacent Marine units, creating a potentially dangerous situation as the flanks of these Marine units were exposed to the enemy. "Howling Mad" Smith took the matter up with Ralph Smith, with whom he was on fairly good personal terms. Ralph Smith seemed to agree that

the division was not progressing as fast as it might, and H. M. Smith ordered him to take care of the matter and get his front-line abreast of the Marine divisions. However, the performance of the division did not apparently improve. After consulting with MG Sandeford Jarman (USA), who was to become the commander of Saipan once it was secured, H. M. Smith took the matter up with VAdm Raymond SPRUANCE, his superior, requesting that Ralph Smith be relieved. After considering the matter, Spruance authorized H. M. Smith to effect the relief.

The relief of Ralph Smith was officially the result of poor performance on the part of his division. However, the problem was as much one of training, perception, and pride as it was of operational inefficiency. Ralph Smith was a likable, easygoing man, not a hard-driving, strong commander. Nor was he an effective communicator. He totally failed to apprise H. M. Smith of the nature of the opposition that his troops were facing. In fact, they had encountered the principal Japanese positions on the island, much stronger than those confronting the two Marine divisions. Indeed, the casualties borne by the 27th Division bear this out: Although the overall losses of each of the two Marine divisions were greater, the ratio of killed-to-wounded in the 27th Division was higher.

CASUALTIES ON SAIPAN			
Division	Killed	Total	Ratio
2nd Marine	1,256	6,170	1:4.9
4th Marine	1,107	6,612	1:5.9
27th Infantry	1,034	3,566	1:3.4

Further complicating the situation were differences in mindset between the army and the Marine Corps. Despite operating on islands, army commanders tended to think in continental terms. If you encounter difficult opposition, go around it. Unfortunately, on an island there is no room to go around. The only way to make progress is to go forward, using infiltration if possible, but in any case being prepared to take the losses. In addition, the Marine perception is essentially a naval one. The uppermost issue is the safety of the fleet. The quicker an island can be secured, the quicker the enormous concentration of ships lying off it to support the operation can disperse. Although unsaid at the time of Ralph Smith's relief, both H. M. Smith and Spruance believed that the delay in securing Makin in November 1943 was at least peripherally connected with the loss of the escort carrier *Liscome Bay*, TORPEDOED off the island on 24 November, with heavy loss of life.

The relief of an army general by a Marine struck a nerve in the army's high command, although some of the brass had also been critical of the 27th Division's performance. A number of senior army commanders in the Pacific undertook an investigation, bypassing the chain of command, which ran through Spruance and H. M. Smith. They concluded that there were no grounds for the relief, arguing that the operations of the 27th Infantry Division were conducted properly and with regard for conserving soldiers' lives, implying that the Marine Corps was not particularly concerned about that commodity. The relief of Ralph Smith still echoes in the US Army, specifically in the 27th Division, New York National Guard, where it remains a matter of "fighting words."

However, it seems reasonable to conclude that there would have been little furor if Ralph Smith had been relieved by an army officer. Four other army division commanders were relieved during the Pacific War. Little controversy, attended three of these reliefs, all effected by army superiors. The fourth case stirred up trouble because an admiral relieved the commander of the Seventh Infantry Division on Attu. In at least one case a relief by an Army officer was unjustified, that of MG Edward Herring of the 32nd Division. Herring was sacked by MACARTHUR for not taking BUNA quickly enough, despite the fact that he had no artillery, little air support, only half his manpower, few supplies, and a green division. No controversy resulted.

See also TARAWA, BATTLE OF.

Smoke

It has long been noted that fog, mist, and clouds can produce militarily useful concealment. Some parts of the world commonly have morning fog or mist, and the local troops have to learn to deal with it. Until artificial smoke devices were invented in this century, fog and the like would usually be a danger to defending troops, as they would allow attackers to get close without being exposed to missile fire (spears, arrows, muskets, cannon, etc.). Defenders derived some benefit from these natural obscurants because the attackers had to find their way partially blinded. One could always hope that the attacking troops would get lost, and this sometimes happened. But a well trained attacker knew how to find his way in the fog and usually didn't cover much more than a few hundred meters under these conditions anyway. Sometimes fires would be set to provide a smokescreen, but this was rather obvious, the enemy would thus be alerted, and was never commonly used. With the coming of gunpowder weapons in the past 500 years, battlefields often became obscured by the smoke of thousands of muskets and cannon being fired. Since these primitive weapons weren't all that accurate, and were fired in the general direction of the enemy, this black powder smoke screen was rarely a major factor for either side.

In this century, right about the time smokeless gunpowder appeared and cleared the battlefield somewhat, it was discovered that smoke grenades, smoke shells, and smoke pots could provide copious amounts of smoke on demand. This led to a new form of DECEPTION—blowing smoke. Rather than wait for nature to provide a convenient fog, artificial smoke could be used as needed. While a strong wind would rapidly disperse artificial smoke, average weather conditions were, quite naturally, the norm and no problem. Artificial smoke is delivered by three means: smoke grenades, smoke shells, and smoke pots. Smoke grenades are thrown like regular grenades. Smoke shells are like high-explosive shells, but contain smoke producing material instead of high explosive. Smoke pots are containers of various size that contain smoke producing material. The characteristics of these various items are as follows.

	Grenade	Shell	Pot
Weight (lbs.)	1–2	5–100	5–100
Time to Form (sec.)	10–20	1–3	10–30
Max. Length of Cloud (m.)	20–40	20–100	50–200
Duration of Smoke (sec.)	60–120	40–160	300–900

The variation in weight of the item results from different national designs as well as a variety of different sizes available for most items. Time to form reflects how long it takes to achieve a useful amount of smoke; the maximum length of cloud is in meters. The smoke is designed to stay close to the ground, so most smoke clouds are less than 10 meters high. Duration of smoke is the average time that the smoke cloud will last before dissipating into uselessness. In most cases, more than one of these items is used at once. Several grenades are tossed out to make sure there is sufficient smoke created. Smoke shells are fired in volleys, the number of shells depending on whether it's a battery volley (four to six guns) or a battalion volley (12–24 guns). The shells land in a line, quickly putting up a wall of smoke. Volleys may then be fired again and again to maintain the concealment provided by the smoke. Smoke pots have to be placed and ignited by hand, although in some rare cases the pots can be ignited by remote control. The normal use of artificial smoke is to hide troops from observation. If the enemy couldn't see troops, he couldn't accurately fire at them. While smoke did not stop bullets and shells, it made them much less accurate.

Infantry are very fond of smoke grenades, as they often find themselves in need of concealment, fast. But the infantry are also fond of using smoke as a pure deception. A knowledgeable enemy will expect something to be happening behind the cloud created by a few smoke grenades and will often fire into the cloud. For the smoke-using infantry, that enemy fire means the other guys are preoccupied with smoke, thus allowing for other maneuvers by the troops that tossed the grenades. In Vietnam, smoke grenades of various colors were used to mark targets for air strikes. Desperate troops could hurl colored smoke at the enemy even if there wasn't any friendly aircraft around. The enemy, not knowing about the absence of aircraft, but seeing the colored smoke that usually preceded the appearance of bombs and rockets, would take cover. The US troops could then make their escape.

Armored vehicles also use smoke. Most TANKS now have smoke-grenade launchers mounted on the turret. One or more of these grenades can be launched by the crew, putting an obscuring cloud of smoke to the front, thus ruining the aim of enemy gunners. Tank battles are often rather like chess games, with individual tanks moving to and fro trying to get a favorable firing position against any enemy tanks that might become visible. Smoke thus becomes a key tool in hiding tanks and their location or direction of movement. Smoke is so important that many older tanks had the ability to automatically pour oil over the hot engine manifold and create an impromptu smoke cloud that a tank could back up and retreat through. Along the same lines, some nations issue smoke grenades that put out black smoke. These are used to make a vehicle look like it's been hit by enemy fire. This usually fools pilots, and often ground troops as well. The most common use of black smoke grenades is to make a fake tank parking lot (full of inflated rubber tanks) look like the real thing after the bombs hit. But this trick is even used on the battlefield. The enemy will usually stop shooting at a target once it appears to be hit. A clever tank crew can stop their tank, pop a black smoke grenade out the hatch and then wait for the enemy artillery or antitank fire to shift.

Although SUBMARINES have little need for smoke grenades, they used a similar deception during World War II when they would release some oil (and perhaps debris from the torpedo tubes) when under attack. The destroyers topside would conclude that the sub had sunk and stop their attack. Unless, of course, the destroyer commander wasn't fooled. As always, a deception is only as good as its believability.

Smoke pots are most often used to hide rear area targets from observation or attack. Protecting a vital target like a bridge from air attack often involved the use of smoke pots. When it is known that enemy aircraft are in the area, the pots are ignited and the bridge covered with smoke. This will not stop the attack, but it will spoil the pilot's aim. Pots were also used to support major attacks. Crossing a river under enemy fire, for example, would often require the use of hundreds of smoke pots to hide the troops going across the water in assault boats. Most smoke pots can float, and can be released to flow with the current while emitting their protective cloud. Any attack across open ground benefits from smoke, and smoke pots are the best way to do it, given the time, and opportunity, to get the pots up front and ignited.

In the combat zone, smoke shells are the more common form of delivering large quantities of smoke. Everything from mortars to heavy artillery fire smoke shells. A particular favorite smoke shell type for Americans is White Phosphorus (WP, or "Willie Peter"). In addition to emitting a large quantity of shell, the phosphorus burns intensely, is difficult to extinguish, and provides a very unpleasant way to die. A little Willie Peter not only blinds the enemy, but also does a number on his morale as well.

Destroyers were also commonly equipped to make smoke, and both US and Japanese destroyes men made frequent use of it during the war.

SNLF

See MARINES, JAPANESE (NAVY GROUND FORCES).

SO3C Seamew, US Reconnaissance Floatplane

The SO3C Seamew was a US Navy floatplane used by cruisers and battleships for scouting. Although 800 SO3Cs were built between 1942 and 1944, it was an unsuccessful design that was withdrawn from service in 1944.

See also AIRCRAFT TYPES DEVELOPMENT; RECONNAISSANCE, NAVAL.

SOC Seagull, US Reconnaissance Floatplane

The SOC Seagull was a US Navy 1930s era biplane floatplane used for scouting by cruisers and battleships. It was a very successful design. The models entered service in 1935 and over 200 were built. The SOC continued in service until the end of the war.

See also AIRCRAFT TYPES DEVELOPMENT; RECONNAISSANCE.

Society Islands

Including Tahiti, these form the principal part of French Polynesia. Although they were too far to the east to experience any fighting, the islands were useful for air and naval bases. The Japanese never attacked the Society Islands, but they were on their list of objectives to be pursued after the expected victory at MIDWAY. In early 1942 the United States established a modest base at Bora Bora.

Soerabaya, Java, Netherlands East Indies

The principal Dutch naval base in the East Indies, Soerabaya had good, if limited facilities to service warships, even a decent dry dock, and was an important air base. Despite Allied efforts to sabotage the base, and the ships in it, the Japanese were able to put it, and them, into service. Soerabaya was several times bombed by carrier aircraft from the British Far Eastern Fleet, but remained in Japanese hands until the end of the war.

See also ROYAL NAVY.

Solomon Islands

The Solomon Islands comprise seven large and many small islands forming two chains that stretch about 900 miles southeastward from the BISMARCK ARCHIPELAGO in the southwest Pacific, totaling about 60,000 square miles. Very wet, the jungle-covered, mountainous islands were poor but supplied various tropical products to the world market (copra-dried coconut meat, for the soap trade, for example). In 1941 the islands had a thin population consisting mostly of Melanesians (c. 100,000) with a few Australians and Britons (c. 650), mostly managers of the copra plantations and colonial officials. Most of the Europeans were evacuated before the Japanese invaders arrived in early and mid-1942.

Solomon Islands, Campaign for

This was the longest campaign of the Pacific War and was still going on when the war ended. Japanese troops kept fighting in the Solomons until mid-1945, and for some years after that. The portion of the Solomon Islands campaign that is most often remembered is the initial battle for Guadalcanal. This American landing in August of 1942 led to three months of furious land, air, and naval battles that resulted in a Japanese decision to withdraw from the island by early 1943. But the Japanese were not giving up on the Solomons, but rather pulling back toward their major base to the north, at RABAUL.

Throughout 1943, two American divisions (one army and one Marine) moved up the Solomons from island to island. Hundreds of bombers and fighters supported these amphibious operations. Japanese warships in the area would give battle from time to time, usually in support of moving troops from an island or bringing in supplies. Having lost control of the air to the Allies, the Japanese could only resist the enemy advance, not stop it.

The Japanese ground forces involved were the Sixth Infantry Division, based on BOUGAINVILLE Island (the northernmost of the Solomons), and the equivalent of another division in various smaller army and navy infantry units. Because the Japanese were defending a lot of island, or trying to, their units were spread out, allowing the Amer-

icans to concentrate on one smaller Japanese garrison at a time. During the summer of 1943, American amphibious and air attacks destroyed Japanese defenders in the central Solomon islands. New Georgia and the surrounding islands were taken by September, although fight-to-the-death Japanese tactics kept the attacking American units occupied through the rest of 1943. In October of 1943, the NEW ZEALAND Third Infantry Division and the US Third Marine Division joined the operation for the assault on Bougainville. The fighting here died down by the end of 1943. But the shooting never stopped. The Allies built airfields on Guadalcanal, and sent troops to defend them. The aircraft then bombed Japanese bases on Bougainville and surrounding islands, while keeping Japanese ships from supplying their island garrisons. The Japanese were still fighting when the war ended. But because of American air superiority, Japanese troops never had sufficient ammunition or other supplies to launch serious attacks. After the war, the remaining Japanese troops were often hunted with tracking dogs. After a few years, all the remaining and defiant Japanese were either dead of natural causes or hunted down.

Considering the remaining Japanese resistance, the Solomons Campaign continued until after the war ended. But for all practical purposes, Japanese forces in the Solomons were no longer a threat by early 1944. It had taken the Allies some 20 months to retake the Solomons, once the campaign got under way in August 1942. New Zealand and Australian troops, for the most part, remained behind to harry the Japanese. The American units continued north for the invasion of the Philippines in late 1944.

Solomon Islands Defence Force

In 1939 the British colonial authorities in the Solomon Islands raised the small Solomon Islands Defence Force, composed of local enlisted men under British and Australian officers, using PIDGIN as the language of command. When the Japanese came, most of these troops took refuge in the rugged, jun-

Freshly landed troops of the 43rd Infantry Division take shelter among the trees on Rendova, June 30, 1943. The invasion of Rendova, in the central Solomons, was a further step toward the isolation of Rabaul. The landings occurred at daybreak in a rainstorm, and this may have contributed to light Japanese resistance to the initial assault

gle-covered interiors of the islands. Although it never numbered more than about 400 men, the Solomon Islands Defence Force proved invaluable to the Allies. Not only did its men collect information, rescue downed pilots, and act as guides for US and Commonwealth troops, but they also regularly ambushed Japanese troops and provided essential protection for COASTWATCHERS.

The most famous SIDF soldier was Sergeant Major Jacob Vouza. A former chief of police in the local constabulary and a native of GUADALCANAL, Vouza, a Christian, served with Coastwatcher Martin Clement. He had many heroic adventures during the war. For example, on the eve of the Japanese attack across the Tenaru River, on Guad-

alcanal, he was scouting behind Japanese lines when he was captured. Finding a small American flag on his person, the Japanese tied him to a tree, then beat him and bayoneted him several times. They then left, leaving him to die. Vouza managed to get loose from his bonds and crawl three miles through the jungle to warn the Marines of the impending attack. He later guided the MARINE Raiders on their month-long (4 November–4 December 1942) foray behind Japanese lines. For his efforts he received a Silver Star from the United States and a knighthood from Britain. So impressed by his courage were the Marines that they presented him with a sword of honor and made him an honorary sergeant major in the Corps. A national hero in the SOLOMONS, Vouza wore his Marine uniform on ceremonial occasions for the rest of his life, and was ever willing to talk over old times with old comrades.

In addition to the SIDF there was also a Solomon Islands Labour Corps, which had a peak strength of some 3,700 men who performed a variety of tasks, from unloading supplies to clearing brush, often under fire.

See also KENNEDY'S ARMY.

Ref: Ready, *Forgotten Allies*; White and Lindstrom, eds., *The Pacific Theater*.

Somers Class, US Destroyers

Designed as flotilla leaders, the five destroyers of the Somers class, built 1936–39, were about 10% larger and mounted 50% more TORPEDO tubes than the PORTERS, completed two or three years earlier. As their hull dimensions were virtually the same as that of the Porters, the Somers were rather top heavy. A disappointment in service, in order to increase their antiaircraft capability they had to lose four torpedo tubes and two 5-inch guns to retain their stability. One became a war loss.

Somerville, James (1882–1949)

James E. Somerville joined the ROYAL NAVY in 1897. After serving in gunboats on the Nile in the Sudan he became one of the Royal Navy's first radio specialists. During World War I he held various posts as a wireless officer, notably distinguishing himself during the Dardanelles Campaign. He rose through the ranks between the wars, and actually retired from the service for reasons of health shortly before World War II broke out.

Somerville remained inactive until Dunkirk, when he voluntarily offered his services to Admiral Bertram Ramsay, for whom he performed yeoman service in coordinating the movements of the numerous ships involved in the evacuation. He soon found himself back on active duty (his health problems meanwhile having been cleared up), assigned to command Force H, at Gibraltar, from June 1940

through March of 1942, one of the most demanding posts in the Royal Navy, during which period he commanded the attack on the French Fleet at Mirs-el-Kebir, and attempted with considerable success to keep the sea lanes open to Malta. In March of 1942, with the Japanese overrunning much of Southeast Asia, Somerville was transferred to command the hastily assembled British Far Eastern Fleet. Although his performance in this post was successful, Somerville was also quite lucky and he made the most of ULTRA information, so that in March and April of 1942, when the Japanese First Air Fleet (i.e., the PEARL HARBOR Strike Force, of six carriers) did considerable damage to shipping and port facilities in the Bay of Bengal (racking up a light carrier, two heavy cruisers, and much else besides), he was able to avoid a direct confrontation with the enemy.

In 1944 Somerville was sent as head of the British Naval Mission to the United States, in which capacity he ended the war, having meanwhile been promoted to admiral of the fleet. A good officer, Somerville was also lucky.

Sorge, Richard (1895–1944)

A German journalist, the Tokyo correspondent for the *Frankfurter Zeitung* from 1933, and a member of the Nazi Party, Sorge was actually a Russian agent, having been recruited by Soviet intelligence in the 1920s. An apparent admirer of Japanese culture, and married to a Japanese woman, Sorge had several links into the Japanese high command. One of his closest friends was Ozaki Hozumi, a closet communist sympathizer who was an aide to Prince Konoye, a kinsman of the emperor. Sorge also cultivated the German ambassador to Japan, General Eugene Ott. He provided Stalin with the critical information that the Japanese were going to attack the United States and Britain in December of 1941, not Russia. This enabled Stalin to safely shift troops from the Far East to undertake the Moscow counteroffensive the day after Pearl Harbor.

Sorge was arrested by the Japanese in October 1941 and hanged in 1944.

Ref: Prange, Goldstein, and Dillon, *Target Tokyo*.

Soryu, Japanese Aircraft Carrier

Soryu (1934–1935–1937) was a well-designed ship, lightly built and fast, with an aircraft operational capacity equal to that of AKAGI or KAGA, both of which were about twice her displacement. She took part in operations against China, 1937–39, and then, paired with HIRYU, which was sometimes classed as her sister, Soryu formed Carrier Division Two and served with the First Air Fleet from Pearl Harbor to MIDWAY, where she took three bombs, burst into flames, and blew up.

South Dakota Class, US Battleships

Although displacing slightly more than the NORTH CAROLINA CLASS battleships, the South Dakotas were shorter by about 50 feet and narrower by about 2 feet. They were also built with several innovative ideas in mind, none of which had been adequately tested, and not all of which proved satisfactory. As a result, they were not only rather cramped and uncomfortable, but were also slightly slower, less stable, and less maneuverable than were their predecessors. On the other hand, they were probably somewhat better protected.

South Dakota, BB-57 (1939–1941–1942), fitted as a flagship with four fewer 5"/38 dual-purpose guns than her sisters, was the only unit seriously engaged in the Pacific. Entering the Pacific in August of 1942, she provided antiaircraft protection for the carrier *Enterprise* at SANTA CRUZ ISLAND (26 October), repeatedly beating off Japanese air attacks. In one action she was attacked by 29 dive bombers, only one of which was able to plant a bomb on her, which caused one death, about 50 other injuries, and some serious damage to one 16-inch gun. She was more heavily damaged by Japanese shell fire on the night of 14–15 November 1942, taking 26 hits by 5-inch to 8-inch shells, plus one 14-inch, the only confirmed enemy battleship hit on an American battlewagon ever, suffering 38

killed and about 60 wounded. Repair, in Brooklyn, required 62 days of round-the-clock work. Upon being repaired she served with the ROYAL NAVY in Europe in 1943, before returning to the Pacific to support fast carrier operations and amphibious landings. Although the ship was scrapped in 1962, certain relics were preserved for display in South Dakota.

Indiana, BB-58 (1939–1941–1942), began active service off GUADALCANAL in early November 1942, but missed the ferocious night battles there on 12–15 November. Her career in the war was rather pedestrian, firing on shore targets (Guadalcanal, TARAWA, HOLLANDIA, TRUK, the MARIANAS, IWO JIMA, OKINAWA, and the Home Islands) and providing antiaircraft protection to the fleet. Her only damage due to enemy action (she suffered severely in a collision with the battleship *Washington* in 1944 and less so in the typhoon of 5 June 1945) occurred on 19 June 1944, during the Battle of the PHILIPPINE SEA, when a Japanese plane crashed into her, wounding several men but causing only a barely perceptible dent in her armor. Scrapped in 1964.

Massachusetts, BB-59 (1939–1941–1942), nicknamed "Big Mamie," first went into action at Casablanca on November 8, 1942, where 786 of her 16-inch and 221 of her 5-inch rounds put a partially completed French battleship (see RICHELIEU CLASS, FRENCH BATTLESHIP) out of action, helped sink two destroyers, and damaged another destroyer and a light cruiser, as well as various shore installations, while taking several hits in return, albeit without serious damage or any CASUALTIES. She entered the Pacific in early 1943, helping to bombard enemy-held islands and to protect the fleet from air attack. During the war she was in action against enemy forces 35 times, sinking or damaging five ships by gunfire and downing 18 Japanese aircraft, all while never losing a man to enemy action. In 1965 she became a war memorial at Fore River, Massachusetts.

Alabama, BB-60 (1940–1942–1942), served with the Royal Navy March–July 1943, helping to cover Arctic convoys to Russia. She began operations in the Pacific at Tarawa in November of 1943, and from then to the end of the war provided shore bombardment and antiaircraft defense to the fleet. She was never damaged by enemy action. In 1964 she became a war memorial at Mobile, Alabama.

Soviet Union

In 1941 the Soviet Union was the third most populous nation on the planet. With 199 million people, it was eclipsed only by India (controlled by Britain) and China. When Japan attacked in the Pacific, the Soviet Union was already six months into its war with Germany. The Nazis were within sight of Moscow and were about to be tossed back by the first successful Soviet counterattack. Germany expected Japan to attack Russia shortly after it conquered its objectives in the Pacific. But Japan refused to do so, and for good reason. Throughout the war, the Soviets always maintained at least a million troops in their Far East.

Despite the need to maintain enormous forces against the Germans, and in the face of over 10 million combat deaths, the Russians managed to maintain formidable combat forces facing the Japanese in northern China. In the chart (below), the "Military Situation" shows that, despite the fact that the German invasion in June 1941 was a major catastrophe for the Russians, their forces in the Far

East were nearly doubled in the following six months. The Russians did not discount the possibility that the Japanese might attack them, and this shows as the Soviets increased their Far East manpower through the summer of 1942. Two things happened that summer. First, the Japanese lost their naval advantage when four of their carriers were sunk at the Battle of MIDWAY. Then, in the fall, the German summer offensive stalled and the stage was set for the Battle of Stalingrad in late 1942. This battle became the first major decisive defeat for the Germans. At this point, any alliance of Japan with Germany seemed less likely, as did a Japanese attack on the Russian Far East. So Soviet troops strength declined in the Far East.

Although the number of Russian troops was large, the quality of these Far Eastern forces was not the same as those facing the Germans. Many of the Russian troops were lower quality local reservists. As long as they could move and hold a weapon, the Russians put them in uniform. The equipment, by and large, was not first rate. Secondline TANKS and aircraft could be safely sent to the Far East. While the Japanese had a lot of good aircraft in MANCHURIA, they were always outnumbered by Russian equipment. Moreover, the Japanese never developed world-class tanks, so even the older Russian models were superior.

Despite 30 million dead by early 1945, the Soviet Union still managed to have 11 million troops in the field by the time the Germans surrendered in May of that year. Millions of tons of weapons, equipment, and raw materials from the Western Allies (mainly the United States) kept the Russians going. The Germans had, by the fall of 1942, occupied areas containing 40% of Russia's population and over a third of its industry. This was not enough to knock the Soviet Union out of the war, nor tempt Japan to attack in the Far East.

The battles Russia and Japan fought on their borders in 1939 had left an impression on the Japanese Army. There was no desire to take on the Russians again unless the situation looked very favorable. Indeed, the Japanese went out of their way to maintain cordial relations with the Russians

SOVIET MILITARY FORCES IN THE FAR EAST

Date	Troops (x1000)	Armored Vehicles	Combat Aircraft	Military Situation
1941 June	703	3,100	4,100	German Invasion
1941 December	1,343	2,100	3,100	Battle of Moscow
1942 July	1,446	2,500	3,100	German Summer Offensive
1942 November	1,296	2,500	3,300	Battle of Stalingrad
1943 July	1,156	2,300	3,900	Battle of Kursk
1944 January	1,162	2,000	4,000	Russian Winter Offensive
1945 May	1,185	2,300	4,300	Germany Surrenders
1945 August	1,577	5,500	5,400	Attack on Japan

throughout the war. In April 1941, the Japanese signed a five-year non-aggression pact with the Soviet Union and were careful to avoid any incidents that might threaten this treaty. Thus Russian pilots were able to freely fly thousands of American LEND-LEASE aircraft from Alaska to airfields in the Soviet Far East throughout the war. In addition, Russian ships regularly carried American aid from US ports to Vladivostok throughout the war. The Japanese never molested these ships or aircraft.

The Soviets also made contributions to these good relations. In 1939, the Russians cut off their aid to the Nationalist Chinese. This was not insubstantial, as thousands of Russian military advisers, including combat pilots, worked with the Chinese. Aid continued to the communist Chinese, but this was not substantial and was done discreetly. On at least one occasion during the war, the Soviets deliberately leaked critical information about US war plans to the Japanese. Early in October 1944 the Japanese were still uncertain as to whether the next major US objective in the Pacific would be the Philippines, FORMOSA, or possibly even OKINAWA. At a diplomatic cocktail party, the Soviet foreign minister "casually" mentioned to the Japanese ambassador that US heavy bombers based in China were about to undertake operations against the Philippines, a matter that the ambassador dutifully communicated to his government. Soviet motivation for this leak is unclear, but may have represented a desire to ensure that the Pacific War lasted long enough for Russia to get involved.

The Japanese believed, once it was obvious that the Americans would keep on coming to Japan itself, that a deal could be made with the Russians. In early 1945, Japan offered to form a coalition with Russia and "rule Asia." The Russians strung the Japanese along, not letting on that the Soviet Union had promised Britain and America that Russian armies would invade Manchuria, "within three months of Germany surrendering." Germany gave up on 8 May and Russia attacked Japan on 8 August. Not only that, but the Russians began their invasion of Japanese-held Sakhalin Island on 16 August, a day after Japan surrendered. America

protested, but did nothing to interfere with the Soviet conquest of Sakhalin and the KURILE ISLANDS throughout late August.

Millions of Japanese colonists lived and worked in Korea and Manchuria. Moreover, most of the Japanese Army was still in Manchuria and China. The Japanese leadership expected to fall back on these mainland resources even if Japan itself was invaded. The only thing that could spoil this grand plan was the entry of Russia into the war. The Soviets, with advance knowledge of the American ATOMIC BOMB project, saw no reason whatsoever to ally themselves with the Japanese. Yet the senior people in Tokyo continued to believe a deal with Russia was possible until the Soviet Union invaded Manchuria on August 8, 1945.

See also ANTI-COMINTERN TREATY.

Ref: Glantz, *August Storm*.

Soviet Union, Internment of US Airmen

Although allied with the United States in the European War, the Soviet Union was formally neutral in the Pacific. As a result, US pilots who landed in Soviet territory after missions over Japan were interned.

The first internees were the crew of one of the B-25s that participated in the DOOLITTLE Raid, in April 1942. They were eventually joined by 242 US Army and Navy airmen who participated in missions from the ALEUTIANS to the KURILES and were forced to make emergency landings on Soviet territory. Still others became lost during air raids over Japan and were interned after landing B-29s.

US airmen interned in the USSR were treated according to the provisions of the GENEVA CONVENTION. Their aircraft were generally impounded by the Russians and used for experimentation and, in the case of B-29s, became the basis for the PRODUCTION of a line of Soviet postwar bombers. In a number of cases interned American airmen somehow managed to "escape" from Soviet internment, make their way to Iran, and turn themselves in to US occupation authorities. Of those not previously spirited out of the country, all known US internees in the Soviet Union were released beginning August 24, 1945.

Spitfire, British Fighter

The Spitfire, the principal British fighter throughout the war, went through continuous upgrades and modifications to keep it competitive with new enemy aircraft. This resulted in many Spitfire types, each having substantially different performance. The first (1938) Spitfire, the Mark 1, had a speed of 360 MPH and four .30 caliber machine guns. The last wartime version, the Mark 18, had a top speed of 448 MPH and was armed with two 20mm cannon and two .50 caliber machine guns. Loaded weight went from 2.6 tons to 4.6 tons. Ceiling, rate of climb, maneuverability, range, and bomb load all improved with the many different versions. Some 20,000 were produced during the war and several hundred more into the late 1940s. By 1943, the Spitfire was a common foe for Japanese aircraft over Burma. For service with the ROYAL NAVY there was a "navalized" version, the SEAFIRE.

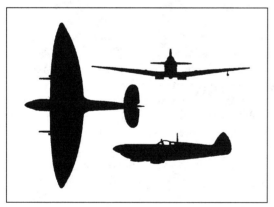

One of the finest fighter aircraft of all time, the Supermarine Spitfire was in continuous production from 1936 through 1947, 22 distinct models being produced, as well as eight models of the Seafire.

Spruance, Raymond (1886–1969)

One of the most successful American admirals of the war, Raymond Spruance graduated from Annapolis in 1906, made the Great White Fleet's world cruise, commanded a destroyer, and helped complete and commission the new battleship PENNSYLVANIA, all by 1916. During World War I he commanded the destroyer *Aaron Ward* in the Atlantic. After the war he held various command and staff positions, taught in several navy schools, and attended the Naval War College. Shortly after PEARL HARBOR he was given command of Cruiser Division 5, which served with Task Force 16 on the DOOLITTLE Raid. Due to William HALSEY's illness, Spruance was in temporary command of TF 16 at MIDWAY, and performed so well in this role that despite not being aviation qualified, he continued thereafter to command carrier task forces, being provided with a staff consisting mostly of aviators. For a time chief of staff to NIMITZ, Spruance was shortly put in command of what would become the Fifth Fleet (an assignment he rotated with Halsey, under whom it was called the Third Fleet). With Fifth Fleet Spruance commanded in the TARAWA Operation, at ENIWETOK, in the MARIANAS (during which he won the Battle of the PHILIPPINE SEA), IWO JIMA, and OKINAWA.

At the end of the war Spruance became president of the Naval War College. He retired in 1948, and served for a time as ambassador to the Philippines. Spruance proved surprisingly effective as a carrier commander. However, although he did everything right at Midway, his actions during the Philippine Sea were less effective. Failing to realize that he had the Japanese carriers at his mercy, he defeated but did not destroy them, despite the urging of several members of his staff. This was a failure without much penalty, as the Japanese force had been basically ruined during the battle, if not completely destroyed. But in other circumstances, such a lack of follow-through on Spruance's part might have had serious aftereffects. However, considering Halsey's more disastrous failure during the

Battle of LEYTE GULF, which led to the Japanese battleship attack on the escort carriers off SAMAR, it seems strange that Halsey was promoted to fleet admiral and Spruance was not.

Stilwell, Joseph W. (1883–1946)

One of the most controversial American officers of the war, Joseph "Vinegar Joe" Stilwell graduated from West Point in 1904 and soon afterward was in action against the Moro tribesmen in the Philippines. Over the next few years he rose through the ranks. The outbreak of World War I found him as an instructor at West Point, from which post he was sent to France to serve first as a liaison officer with the Allied armies and later as staff officer with the AEF. After the war he was an intelligence officer in China, attended various army schools, commanded the 15th Infantry in China, once again served on various staffs and as an instructor, was military attaché to China, and at the time of PEARL HARBOR was commanding the III Corps in California. Early in 1942 he was promoted to lieutenant general and sent to command all US forces in the CBI, while simultaneously serving as chief of staff to the Chinese Nationalist Army. Although reinforced by several Chinese divisions, the Allied position in Burma collapsed, and Stilwell led a remarkably arduous retreat to the security of India. In India he reorganized US forces, while training Chinese divisions that were then flown home over the Himalayas. Although he did well in these assignments, even when made deputy commander to Lord MOUNTBATTEN, Stilwell's personality was abrasive. A "tell it like it is" sort, Stilwell tended to irritate CHIANG. Although President ROOSEVELT attempted to get Chiang to place Stilwell in overall command of Chinese forces, in the end he had to recall the general. For a time chief of Army Ground Forces, in the spring of 1945 Stilwell was put in command of the 10th Army on OKINAWA. After the war he held an administrative command until his death, from stomach cancer. He was a brilliant officer, with excellent ideas that would probably have worked, but without much chance of getting them into practice due to Chinese resistance.

Strategic Planning, Average Speeds

Since different types of ships had different speeds, coordinating the movements of large forces for offensive undertakings was no easy task. Consider the difficulties a fleet commander would have if he was trying to effect an amphibious landing on a hostile shore, supported by appropriate naval forces.

The Landing Force probably could sustain 12 knots, which was very likely its maximum speed as well, because LSTS could make no more than that, albeit they could do so for over 3,500 miles without refueling.

The Bombardment Group, old battleships assigned to "soften up" the landing beaches, could sustain 15 knots, and in a pinch make 20 or so for a while.

The Escort Group, "jeep" carriers providing close air support to the assault force, could sustain about 15 knots for short periods, but 12 was more practical for extended voyages.

The Support Group, the cargo ships, tankers, hospital ships, repair vessels, and so forth, could sustain 15 knots, albeit not for very long periods, 12 being more practical.

The Carrier Task Forces supporting the landings could cruise at 15 to 25 knots for extended periods, and could maintain as much as 30 for days on end as well.

Now, making allowances for maneuvering, replenishment and the like, the Carrier Task Force could cover 300 to 500 miles a day, and the Bombardment and Escort Groups could probably manage 300, while the Landing Force and Support Group would be lucky to make 250. In addition, it was common to have SUBMARINES support operations, as a scouting screen and to pick up downed flyers, and these could cover only 200 to 250 miles a day. Note that on land, the average speed of a mechanized unit (when not fighting) was rarely more than a hundred miles a day.

So the admiral in command had to juggle his task groups. This was one factor that made life on the fast carriers a grueling experience. While the slower ships maintained relatively steady courses, the fast carriers ended up making frequent, irregular course changes, moving back and forth in irregular patterns, so as to provide cover for the slower moving ships. And in order to confuse the enemy as to location of the landings, the carriers would probably undertake air strikes at everything within range.

A knot is a unit of time and distance. Saying that a particular force "proceeded at 20 knots" is the equivalent of saying it "proceeded at 20 nautical miles an hour," which is the same as "23 miles per hour" in landlubberese, or "37 kilometers an hour" in metric.

Strategic Planning, Japanese Wishful Thinking

Military planners tend to be an optimistic lot. After all, there are so many things that can go wrong in war that one has to have a pretty positive outlook in order to have any faith whatsoever in success. But optimism can be taken to extremes. And perhaps never in military history has wishful thinking come to substitute for solid planning as much as in the Imperial Japanese Navy during World War II.

For example, during staff wargames (simulated operations on paper, using elaborate rules), it was not uncommon for umpires to allow "operations" to proceed despite an absence of supplies. They often permitted units to "refuel" from tankers the fleet did not possess, without any loss of time, so that the planned operations could proceed as scheduled.

But there were worse cases of cheating at wargames than the refueling gambit. The Japanese naval general staff held a major wargame as part of the planning for the MIDWAY Operation. Early in the game the American player managed to "sink" several of the attacking carriers, a matter that so upset the umpires that they restored the carriers to play. Even the subsequent disaster at Midway did not prove a salutary lesson.

Aware of the shortcomings of these earlier wargames, a new approach was decided on. Shortly after Midway, there was another wargame with even more interesting results, and some unusual players, namely Japanese diplomats just returned from the United States. During the early part of the war all the belligerents, including the United States and Japan, arranged for the REPATRIATION of diplomatic personnel (including military attachés) who had found themselves trapped in enemy countries by the outbreak of hostilities. As a result, a number of senior and middle-ranking Japanese naval personnel actually spent much of the first eight or nine months of the Pacific War living in relatively comfortable circumstances in the United States.

When the last batch of these officers returned to Japan, shortly after Midway, they were deliberately not briefed on the status of the war as understood by the Imperial Navy, and were then organized into a team to play the American side in a simulation game, which was to cover the next two years of the war. The idea was sound, as these officers, one of whom was a rear admiral had full access to the American press while awaiting repatriation, and might be expected to have a useful perspective on American notions of how the war should be fought.

The game was conducted around the time the Marines landed on GUADALCANAL. Despite rules that were generally favorable to the Japanese (such as reduced US industrial productivity), by October 1944 the "Americans" were landing in the Philippines, a matter that was extremely upsetting to the naval staff. The results of these games so shocked the Japanese High Command that no official notice of the game was circulated, all documentation was destroyed, and the officers who had taken the part of the Americans were scattered to various obscure posts, and told "Keep your mouth shut." This despite the fact the game could easily have been used to help develop more realistic industrial PRODUCTION and strategic plans.

The initial US landings in the Philippines occurred approximately three weeks later than those in the wargame.

Strategy, Multiple and the Japanese

An ancient bit of military wisdom is that it is unwise to fight a "two front" war. Japan went into World War II struggling to deal with five fronts.

Two of these are familiar to Americans, with General MACARTHUR's offensive in the southwest Pacific, from the SOLOMONS and NEW GUINEA and northwestward toward the Philippines, and Admiral NIMITZ's series of island assaults across the central Pacific.

A third campaign is rather less familiar to Americans—Burma and the Indian frontier—where sizable Japanese armies struggled with British and Indian soldiers for three years.

The fourth front was where most of the Japanese Army (which ultimately comprised 10% of Japan's adult population) was occupied, the war in China. Here, millions died during the war, mostly Chinese.

And finally, there was that potential fifth front, as tensions had existed between the Soviet Union and Japan for a long time. In 1939 the Japanese initiated several battles with Soviet forces on the Manchurian border. The Japanese lost, and decided to defer their plans to run the Soviets out of eastern Siberia. Japan had to maintain large forces in MANCHURIA to guard against an attack by the Soviet Union, an attack which did not come until literally the last week of the war.

Because Japan is an island, all these battlefronts had to be supplied by ship. Japan began the war with a shipping shortage and this only got worse. Japan's prospects of success on any of these fronts were dim. Indeed, even if Japan had had but one front, her shipping problems would have been enormously difficult. America opened two widely separated fronts in the Pacific because US industry was able to produce enough ships and aircraft to support two separate assaults on Japan.

The war in China had been dragging on since the early 1930s, with slim prospects for eventual Japanese success. The occupation of Burma and subsequent invasion of India was largely based on the assumption that if the Japanese got into India proper, the Indians would rise up and drive the British out. The British took the precaution of promising the Indians independence when the war was over; the Indians believed the British and most of the "British" fighting the Japanese were actually Indian.

Japan had long seen Russia, and later the Soviet Union, as its major enemy in Asia. The war with America and her allies was something Japan wanted to avoid, and believed she could avoid. But the Soviet Union bordered the Japanese colony of Manchuria. Through most of the war, there were at least 30 Soviet divisions in what the Russians called "the Far East" (Siberia is the region to the north and west). Japan had only a dozen divisions in Manchuria, but the Japanese believed they could eventually increase this force and successfully attack the Russians.

The Japanese kept the peace on their border with the Soviet Union from then on and assumed that all would be forgotten. Especially when the Japanese did not take advantage of Soviet weakness when most Russian divisions were sent west against the Germans in late 1941. In 1942, the Japanese made plans to rebuild their Manchurian forces. But defeats in the Pacific soon undercut these aspirations.

The Soviets did not forget, and in August 1945 the Soviets opened a fifth front with a massive invasion of Japanese-controlled Manchuria. Japan surrendered to the Allies on August 15 1945.

Strategy, US, FDR vs. MacArthur

Douglas MACARTHUR and his numerous sycophants often claimed that his command was starved of men and resources during the war because high-ranking military and political leaders feared that if he proved too successful against the Japanese, he would almost certainly win the presidency in 1944, unseating the jealous Franklin ROOSEVELT.

Actually, MacArthur's command was hardly "starved." Particularly in 1942, far more men and equipment were sent to him than to Europe. Both FDR and George C. MARSHALL, the army chief of staff, although committed to the "Germany first" strategy, recognized the desperate nature of the situation in the southwest Pacific. An examination of available figures on troop and materiel movements bears this out. Six of the first 10 divisions to ship out during the war went to the Pacific, where there were already two US divisions, not counting the forces in the Philippines.

What did give MacArthur some cause for concern was that, although massive amounts of shipping, troops, and supplies were sent to the Pacific, much was diverted to the ALEUTIANS. The Japanese occupation of several islands in the Aleutians during June 1942 caused consternation on the west coasts of Canada and the United States. It became politically imperative to get the Japanese out of there as soon as possible. But this took enormous amounts of materiel, and to this day it is little known that, for months at a time, over a third of the materiel sent to the Pacific went north to Alaska rather than west to New Guinea and the SOLOMONS. By spring of 1943, the Aleutians were cleared of Japanese and all supply efforts again went west.

See also NATIONAL GUARD.

Ref: Larrabee, *Commander in Chief.*

Strategy, US and Japanese

Strategy is the overall plan a nation has for winning a campaign or war. The United States and Japan had quite different strategies for winning in the Pacific.

The original, 1920s-era US plan for a war with Japan ("WAR PLAN ORANGE") was to advance across the central Pacific to the Philippines (whether those islands were under attack or not). Most of the central Pacific islands were under Japanese control and many were known to be heavily fortified. The principal weapon would be the battleship, with the aircraft carriers used for scouting and support. Once the enemy battleships were found, the decisive battle would be fought, the United States would win, and it would all be over within about six months or so. Not much attention was paid to Japanese aircraft that might be on their central Pacific islands, as aircraft had not yet demonstrated that they could demolish a large battle fleet.

By the late 1930s prescient naval officers were beginning to realize that War Plan Orange was unworkable, but it was not really formally replaced because other officers continued to argue that the plan would work. The pessimists were right, of course. The problem now was that all those Japanese-held islands had airfields, and an increasing number of naval officers were accepting the fact that warships on the high seas would be very vulnerable to enemy bombers. The optimists were not yet convinced, although they would be during December 1941. When the war came the Philippines were lost, along with nearly everything else west of HAWAII, and the battleships that were not sunk at PEARL HARBOR were now acknowledged to be quite vulnerable to carrier aircraft.

Forced to use Australia as the main forward base in the Pacific, the primary American advance initially was from the south, through New Guinea and on to the Philippines, which were reached after nearly three years of war. All this was supported by some carrier, but mostly land-based, aircraft.

The US Navy had built so many carriers and support ships by late 1943, that a second advance through the central Pacific was proposed. This was accomplished with massive carrier air power, huge amphibious operations, and admirals determined not to let the army run the show by itself.

This brings up another important point about Pacific war STRATEGY, the ongoing conflict between army and navy commanders. This was a problem in both Japan and America. It was worse for the Japanese, where there was no one like President ROOSEVELT or Admiral KING and General MARSHALL (the senior US officers) to resolve, or at least defuse, the disputes. It's ironic that the Japanese are now known for their devotion to consensus, for they were anything but during World War II. It was the Americans who managed to work out their different approaches to strategy during the war.

In both nations, the army and navy had long been quite separate worlds. But there were some unique aspects to the army-navy situation in America.

The United States was, and is, a maritime power. Normally, it does not need much of an army because there are no threatening armies on its land borders. But from its beginnings, America depended on overseas trade, and the protection of its shipping, in order to provide a livelihood for many of its people. In the century before Pearl Harbor:

The army and navy rarely operated together. The one major exception was the Civil War. But that was seen as a unique situation and no lasting wisdom was obtained from the experience.

The army had always seen itself as the senior service when it came to planning and directing military operations. Of course, this began to change with the Spanish-American War, where the navy had to go first, defeat the Spanish fleets, and then the army followed. The army was not happy about this new state of affairs, but it was obvious that any future war would see the army traveling by sea, under navy protection, to future battlefields.

While the president was commander in chief, nothing was done to create any organization to coordinate planning and operations by the army and navy. Early in World War II, something was cobbled together, but it was improvisation all through the war.

The Japanese army-navy situation was also characterized by some uniquely Japanese conditions:

The army was heavily involved in domestic, and foreign, politics. The navy was relatively apolitical and, as a result, kept its distance from army commanders.

Japan was, like America, a maritime power and even more dependent on overseas trade to sustain its people. Protecting sea lanes was, of course, a navy responsibility. But until the war began, the most crucial routes were short (between Japan and Korea and China) and could, in theory, be secured by army land-based air power. As a result, the army didn't pay as much attention to working with the navy as it should have. In effect, the army acted like it was doing the navy a favor by letting the navy help out in the China war.

When the Pacific war began, the army and navy had to improvise all their cooperation. In many cases, like the central Pacific, the navy often did everything with its own resources, including naval infantry (SNLF) to seize islands.

Keep in mind, that, relative to the squabbling between American generals and admirals, that between their Japanese counterparts was infinitely worse. Prominent examples of the damage done by Japanese army-navy rivalry were:

The refusal (until too late in the war) to coordinate the use of shipping. The Japanese had a shipping shortage from the beginning of the war, and the situation got worse as the war went on. The army and navy insisted on maintaining their own separate merchant fleets and not cooperating with each other or Japanese commercial interests. In other words, if an army cargo ship was leaving Japan for JAVA half-full, and the navy needed to get supplies to Java at the same time, the army would not allow the navy cargo in the empty space on its outgoing ship. Moreover, when these ships returned from places like Java, they would not carry commercial cargo back to Japan, they would come back empty. It was an absurd policy, but persisted for most of the war.

The army and navy would not consult with each other when they were planning operations in the same area. Part of this was the navy's fault, because what joint planning that did occur took place in Tokyo, where the army had the last word, since it ran the government. So the navy just went ahead and did what it thought best and hoped the army didn't find out until it was too late. The army-navy rivalry in Japan was a considerable asset for the Allied war effort. And it made similar army-navy conflicts in the American camp look trivial by comparison.

It's difficult to discern a coherent positive strategy on the part of the Japanese. In effect, their strategy was to seize as many islands as possible and fortify enough of them with so many ground troops and aircraft that the Allies would not be able to get through to Japan. This was the whole point behind Pearl Harbor, which was designed to gain as much time as possible for the Imperial Army and Navy to grab real estate that the United States would presumably eventually want to take back. If enough territory was seized, and if it was held with sufficient tenacity, the Japanese thinking went, the United States might eventually decide that the cost of recovering it wasn't acceptable, whereupon Japan would emerge with more than what it had at the start of the war. It didn't work. The keystone of Japanese strategy, however, was not so much grabbing real estate as it was gaining economic resources. The Japanese Home Islands had few natural resources, and nearly all the raw material for Japanese industry had to be imported. While China and Korea provided sufficient ores and food, the oil had to come from fields in INDONESIA. It was to obtain access to this oil that Japan went to war with America, the British Empire, and Holland. Japan's strategy was one of desperation, as it turned out that the Indonesian oil fields could not produce sufficient oil for Japanese needs. More to the point, Japan could not produce sufficient tankers to get the oil from Indonesia to Japan. Allied SUBMARINES kept sinking Japanese tankers, and shipping in general. Many senior Japanese military leaders recognized the futility of the war, but they carried out their orders anyway. Loyal unto death was more than just a catchphrase in the Japanese military.

Submarines

Historically, the submarine is a rather recent development. Submarines first became practical in the late 19th century. They were the first "stealth" weapons, being essentially torpedo boats with the capacity to operate underwater for limited periods, albeit with a considerable loss of speed and endurance. Submarines proved of considerable value during World War I, when Germany almost succeeded in severing Britain's maritime lifeline through an aggressive submarine campaign. This campaign ultimately failed, but attracted considerable attention. As a result, between the wars many navies invested rather heavily in submarines. By World War II there were essentially two types of submarine.

The "coastal" submarine, built in considerable numbers by many navies, was of modest dimensions, less than 800 tons surface displacement. It generally had a relatively low surface speed, 18 knots being at the high end. Coastal submarines usually carried four to six torpedo tubes, plus a deck gun and one or two antiaircraft machine guns. Despite their name, they were designed to roam the oceans and snipe at enemy shipping, or linger along the coast and ambush enemy warships.

Then there was the "fleet" submarine, to use its American name. The fleet submarine was large, 1,000 tons or more, and usually had a relatively high surface speed, 20 knots, from which came the term "fleet submarine," since it was able to keep up with the battlefleet. Being larger, the fleet submarine was better armed, usually with six to ten torpedo tubes, plus the usual deck armament, usually one gun of 3-inch to 5.5-inch caliber, plus one or two antiaircraft guns or machine guns. Fleet submarines also had more endurance than coastal submarines, since they could carry more diesel fuel and more batteries. When submerged there was little difference in speed between the two types, 8 knots being more or less the norm. The only other important technical difference was that the fleet submarine was slightly more habitable.

Most navies had a mix of coastal and fleet submarines, the idea being that the coastal types were supposed to raid enemy commerce, while the fleet types were supposed to serve as supports for the battlefleet, scouting for the enemy, harassing him before battle, mopping up fleeing enemy vessels after a victory, or covering the retreat of friendly vessels after a reverse. For various reasons, however,

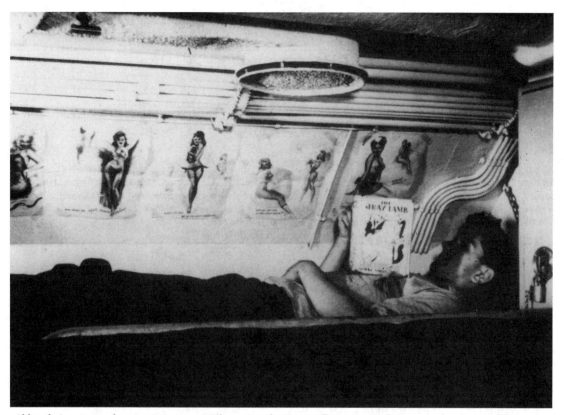

Although American submarines were roomier than most, they were still very cramped. Here a sailor aboard USS Capelin
(SS-289) reads in his bunk, which he probably shares with another sailor who is on duty.

the United States built only fleet submarines, since it intended to meet any enemy—specifically the Japanese—in a decisive surface clash as soon as possible. This proved of considerable benefit once the war began, because the main use of US subs was to attack Japanese merchant ships at great distances from American bases.

See also SHIPPING, WAR AGAINST JAPANESE.

Ref: Alden, *The Fleet Submarine in the U.S. Navy*;———, *U.S. Submarine Attacks during World War II*; Blair, *Silent Victory*; Boyd and Yoshida, *The Japanese Submarine Force*; Carpenter and Polmar, *Submarines of the Imperial Japanese Navy*; Friedman, *Submarine Design and Development*; Hezlet, *Submarines and Sea Power*; Roscoe, *United States Submarine Operations*.

Submarines, Appendectomies Aboard

A staple of several submarine films, the emergency appendectomy performed by a navy medic with improvised tools was by no means the figment of some scriptwriter's imagination. During the war three such operations are known to have been performed, all successfully.

Boat	Corpsman	Patient
Seadragon (SS–194)	Wheeler B. Lipes	Darnell Rector
Grayback (SS–208)	Harry B. Roby	W.R. Jones
Silversides (SS–236)	Thomas Moore	George Platter

ALLIED SUBMARINES OF THE PACIFIC WAR

Fleet	Class	Launched	Displ.	Speed	TT	Number	Lost	Note
British	Porpoise	1932	2,500/2,053	15.5/8.8	6	1	1	
British	S	1941–43	715/990	14.8/9	7	22	9	
British	T	1940–45	1,090/1,570	15.3/9	11	53	17	A
Neth.	K-VII	1922–23	573/712	15/8	4	3	1	B
Neth.	K-XI	1924	670/815	15/8	6	3	1	
Neth.	K-XIV	1932–33	771/1,008	17/9	8	5	3	
Neth.	O–16	1936	869/1,170	18/9	8	1	1	
Neth.	O–19	1938–39	998/1,536	19.3/9	8	2	2	

Key: Class, the official designation of the type; Launched, years in which the boats were launched; Displ., displacement, in tons, with standard followed by submerged; Speed, in knots, with surface and then submerged; TT, torpedo tubes carried; Number, units available during the war; Lost, units lost during the war, including losses in all theaters; Note, as indicated below:
    A. The class comprised five slightly differing groups, ordered prewar, 1939, 1940, 1941, and 1942.
    B. Laid down during World War I, the two surviving units were scrapped in Australia in 1942.

Submarines, British and Dutch

Although US submarines dominated the Pacific, British and Dutch boats did a great deal of work in the Indian Ocean and in East Indian waters.

The ROYAL NAVY lost *Porpoise*, two S Class boats, and one T Class to the Japanese, while all Royal Netherlands Navy losses shown were in the East Indies. One Dutch boat, *K-XVIII*, was scuttled while under repair in Soerabaya, to prevent her capture. She was partially salvaged by the Japanese, who used her hull as a picket boat until a British submarine sank her in July 1945. Surviving Dutch boats operated with the Royal Navy in the Indian Ocean and the East Indies until the end of the war. The Royal Navy also employed a number of midget submarines in the Pacific.

See also NACHI CLASS.

Ref: Alden, *U.S. Submarine Attacks during World War II*; Friedman, *Submarine Design and Development*; Hezlet, *Submarines and Sea Power*.

Submarines, Japanese

Japan had some of the finest submarines in the world. They were broadly classified into three groups:

JAPANESE SUBMARINE TYPES

Class	Designation	Surface Displacement	Completed
1st	I	1,000 tons or more	112
2nd	RO	500–1,000 tons	47
3rd	HA	under 500 tons	20

These designations had less to do with the missions the boats were designed to perform than with their size. So although I boats were supposed to be "first class" submarines, there were some that were designed to carry cargoes, others equipped to transport landing parties, and some to carry seaplanes for attacks on distant targets such as the PANAMA CANAL. While RO boats were "second class" submarines, they usually had enormous range, and were used for fleet operations interchangeably with I boats. Even the little "third class" HA boats had more than one mission: coast defense and the supply of isolated garrisons.

There were also some submarines designated "Yu," of which 14 were built of 200 proposed. Unlike I, RO, and HA boats, the two classes of Yu boats belonged to the Imperial Army. Quite small (273 and 392 tons surface displacement), slow, and lightly armed, they were intended to carry cargo to isolated garrisons

JAPANESE NAVY SUBMARINES

Class (Lead Boat)	Launched	Displ.	Speed	TT	Number	Lost	Note
L3 (RO-57)	1922–23	897/1,195	10/4	4	3	0	A
KT (RO-30)	1923–24	665/1,000	10/4	4	3	0	A
KD2 (I-52)	1922	1,390/2,500	22/10	8	1	0	A
L4 (RO-60)	1922–26	988/1,322	16.5/9	6	9	5	
J1 (I-1)	1924–28	1,970–1,791	18/8	6	4	4	B
KD3a (I-53)	1925–26	1,635/2,300	20/8	8	4	0	
KRS (I-21)	1926–27	1,142/1,768	14.5/7	4	4	3	C
KD3b (I-56)	1927–28	1,635/2,300	20/8	8	4	0	
KD4 (I-61)	1927–29	1,635/2,300	20/8.5	6	3	1	
J1M (I-5)	1931	2,080/2,921	18/8	6	1	1	C
KD5 (I-65)	1931	1,575/2,330	20.5/8.2	6	2	2	
KD6a (I-68)	1933–35	1,400/2,440	23/8.2	6	6	6	
J2 (I-6)	1934	1,900/3,061	20/7.5	6	1	1	
K5 (RO-33)	1934–35	700/1,200	19/8.3	4	2	2	
J3 (I-7)	1935–36	2,231/3,538	23/8	6	2	2	C
KD6b (I-74)	1936–37	1,420/2,564	23/8	6	2	2	
C1 (I-16)	1938–39	2,184/3,561	23.6/8	6	5	5	
A1 (I-9)	1939–41	2,434/4,149	23.5/8	6	3	3	C
B1 (I-15)	1939–42	2,198/3,654	23.6/8	6	20	20	C
KD7 (I-76)	1941–43	1,630/2,602	23/8	6	10	10	
KS (RO-100)	1941–43	525/782	14.2/8	4	18	18	
B2 (I-40)	1942–43	2,230/3,700	23.5/8	6	6	6	C
K6 (RO-35)	1942–44	960/1,447	19.7/8	4	18	17	
A2 (I-12)	1943	2,390/4,172	17.7/6.2	6	1	1	C
B3 (I-54)	1943–44	2,140/3,688	17.7/6.5	6	3	2	C
C2 (I-46)	1943	2,184/3,564	23.5/8	8	3	2	
C3 (I-52)	1943	2,095/3,644	17.7/6.5	6	3	2	
D1 (I-361)	1943–44	1,440/2,215	13/6.5	0	12	9	D
D2 (I-373)	1944	1,660/2,240	13/16.5	0	1	1	E
AM (I-13)	1944	2,620/4,762	16.7/5.5	6	2	1	F
ST (I-201)	1944	1,070/1,450	15.8/19	4	3	0	G
SH (I-351)	1944	2,650/4,290	15.8/6.3	4	1	1	
SS (HA-101)	1944–45	370/493	10/5	0	10	0	H
STO (I-400)	1944	3,530/6,560	18.7/6.5	8	3	0	I
STS (HA-201)	1944–45	320/440	10.5/13	2	10	0	J

Key: Class, the official designation of the type; Launched, years in which the boats were launched; Displ., displacement, in tons, with standard followed by submerged; Speed, in knots, with surface and then submerged; TT, torpedo tubes carried; Number, units available during the war; Lost, units lost during the war, including losses in all theaters; Note, as indicated below:

    A. Assigned to training duties.

    B. Carried a floatplane and had two 5.5-inch deck guns.

    C. Carried a floatplane.

    D. Transport submarines, able to carry 82 tons of cargo and 110 passengers.

    E. High-speed transport submarine, able to carry 150 tons of fuel and 110 of other cargo.

    F. Carried two floatplanes.

    G. Experimental high-speed boats.

    H. Transport submarines, able to carry 60 tons of cargo.

    I. Designed to attack the Panama Canal, they had a surface range of 30,000 nautical miles at 16 knots, and carried three aircraft.

    J. High-speed coast defense submarines.

Ref: Boyd and Yoshida, *The Japanese Submarine Force*; Carpenter and Polmar, *Submarines of the Imperial Japanese Navy*; Friedman, *Submarine Design and Development*; Hezlet, *Submarines and Sea Power*.

Submarines, US

The US Navy had over 20 different submarine designs during the war, several of which were represented by only a single unit, while some numbered scores of boats. Save for some old O, R, and S Class boats and two experimental units, all US submarines were large "fleet" boats, displacing more than a thousand tons on the surface. They were designed to keep up with the battle fleet, which they were intended to support as scouts, and had great range and a relatively high surface speed.

US SUBMARINES								
Class	(Lead Boat)	Launched	Displ.	Speed	TT	Number	Lost	Note
0-1	(SS-62)	1917–18	521/629	14/10.5	4	7	0	A
R-1	(SS-78)	1917–19	569/680	13.5/10.5	4	18	1	B
S-1	(SS-105)	1918–22	854/1,062	14/11	4	23	3	B
S-3	(SS-107)	1919–21	876/1,092	15/11	4	7	0	B
S-42	(SS-153)	1923–24	906/1,126	14.5/11	4	6	1	B
S-48	(SS-159)	1921	903/1,230	14.5/11	5	1	0	
Barracuda	(SS-163)	1923–25	2,119/2,506	18.7/9	6	3	0	
Argonaut	(SS-166)	1927	2,878/4,045	13.5/7.4	4	1	1	C
Narwal	(SS-167)	1927–30	2,987/3,960	17.5/8	6	2	0	C
Dolphin	(SS-169)	1932	1,688/2,215	17/8	6	1	0	
Cachalot	(SS-170)	1933	1,120/1,650	17/8	6	2	0	
Porpoise	(SS-172)	1935	1,316/1,934	19/10	6	2	0	
Shark	(SS-174)	1935	1,315/1,968	19.5/9	6	2	2	
Perch	(SS-176)	1936–37	1,330/1,997	19.3/8	6	6	3	
Salmon	(SS-182)	1937–38	1,449/2,210	21/9	8	6	0	
Sargo	(SS-188)	1938–39	1,450/2,350	20/8.5	8	6	2	
Seadragon	(SS-193)	1939	1,450/2,350	20/8.5	8	4	2	D
Tambor	(SS-198)	1939–40	1,475/2,370	20/8.5	10	6	2	
Gar	(SS–206)	1940–41	1,475/2,370	20/8.5	10	6	5	
Mackerel	(SS-204)	1940	825/1,190	16.2/11	6	1	0	E
Marlin	(SS-205)	1941	800/1,165	16.5/11	6	1	0	E
Gato	(SS-212)	1941–43	1,526/2,410	20/8.5	10	73	20	
Balao	(SS-285)	1942–45	1,525/2,415	20/8.5	10	116	13	
Tench	(SS-417)	1944	1,570/2,415	20/8.5	10	24	0	

Key: Class, the official designation of the type; Launched, years in which the boats were launched; Displ., displacement, in tons, with standard followed by submerged; Speed, in knots, with surface and then submerged; TT, torpedo tubes carried; Number, units available during the war; Lost, units lost during the war, including losses in all theaters; Note, as indicated below:

Notes:

A. Relegated to training duties.

B. Several transferred to the Royal Navy.

C. Large boats, designed as submarine cruisers, with two 6-inch guns. *Argonaut* (which was also equipped as a minelayer) and *Nautilus* (SS–168) carried 200 Marines for the Makin Raid.

D. *Squalus* (SS–192) of this class was sunk in a prewar accident. When salvaged, she was recommissioned as *Sailfish*, under the same number.

E. Experimental boats.

The most successful US submarines were those of the Gato Class and the closely related Balao and Tench Classes, which altogether totaled nearly 200 units completed during the war, and a number after it. Most saw extensive service against Japanese shipping. Of the 12 US submarines accredited with the highest amount of enemy tonnage sunk, eight were Gato Class boats and three others were Balao Class. Many of these boats were built inland, on rivers like the Ohio, using innovative techniques, including sideways launching. Submarines of these three classes formed the backbone of the US underwater fleet well into the 1950s, and many served in other navies long after that. Most were broken up for scrap in the 1960s, but four Gatos and eight Balaos are preserved as war memorials in various places.

Ref: Alden, *The Fleet Submarine in the U.S. Navy*; Blair, *Silent Victory*; Friedman, *Submarine Design and Development*; Roscoe, *United States Submarine Operations in World War II*.

Submarines, US, Highest Scoring

In terms of patrol scores, on her fifth patrol *Archerfish* (SS-311) attained the highest score for a single patrol, and for a single target, when she sank the Japanese carrier SHINANO, at 59,000 tons, the largest ship ever sunk by a submarine. While on her third patrol, *Tang* (SS–306) sank 10 ships, the maximum number ever, for a total of 39,100 tons. It is interesting to note that only one boat listed was commissioned before PEARL HARBOR—*Tautog*.

Ref: Alden, *U.S. Submarine Attacks During World War II*; Blair, *Silent Victory*; Roscoe, *United States Submarine Operations in World War II*.

SUBMARINES, US, HIGHEST SCORING				
Rank	Boat	Tonnage	Ships Sunk	Class
1.	*Flasher* (SS-249)	100.2	21	Gato
2.	*Rasher* (SS-269)	99.9	18	Gato
3.	*Barb* (SS-220)	96.6	17	Gato
4.	*Tang* (SS-306)	93.8	26	Balao
5.	*Silversides* (SS-236)	90.1	23	Gato
6.	*Spadefish* (SS-411)	88.1	21	Balao
7.	*Trigger* (SS-237)	86.5	18	Gato
8.	*Drum* (SS-228)	80.5	15	Gato
9.	*Jack* (SS-259)	76.7	15	Gato
10.	*Snook* (SS-279)	75.5	17	Gato
11.	*Tautog* (SS-199)	72.6	26	Tambor
12.	*Seahorse* (SS-304)	72.5	20	Balao
Tonnage is in thousands				

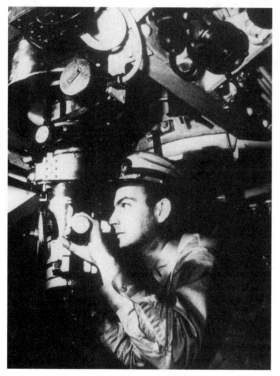

An American submariner at his periscope, sometime in 1942. Relatively ineffective in 1942, due to poor tactics, defective torpedoes, and a certain lack of aggressiveness on the part of older skippers, US submarines became more efficient with the introduction of better tactics, better torpedoes, and younger skippers.

Subversion, Japanese in America

In the years before Pearl Harbor the Japanese government is known to have provided covert financial assistance to a number of organizations in the United States. Most of this money went to Japa-

The Japanese destroyer Yamakaze *goes down, in a photograph taken through the periscope of the USS* Nautilus *(SS-168), June 25, 1942.*

nese-American social and cultural organizations, or to groups like the Society of the Black Dragon, ostensibly composed of veterans of the Russo-Japanese War, but actually a cover for Japanese nationalist activities in the United States. Some went to dissident American movements, such as certain radical black organizations including one religious group which has since gained considerable prominence. While the US government has never revealed the extent of such aid, nor even formally acknowledged that it existed, the National Archives contain a good deal of material on the subject, as some of the secret Japanese radio messages American codebreakers read related to such dealings.

See also AMERICAN CITIZENS, RELOCATION OF; JAPANESE AMERICANS, IMPERIAL ARMED FORCES.

Ref: Harries and Harries, *Soldiers of the Sun*; Stephan, *Hawaii under the Rising Sun*.

Sugiyama, Gen (1896–1945)

Gen Sugiyama joined the Japanese Army in 1911, commanded forces in China during the 1930s, and was promoted to full general in 1936. An enthusiastic supporter of Japanese expansion in China and the Pacific, he became chief of staff of the army in 1940 and presided over the planning for army operations in the Pacific during the initial expansion. Became field marshal in 1943 and lost chief of staff post to TOJO in 1944. Became commander of army forces in Eastern Japan until the end of the war. Committed suicide when Japan surrendered.

Suicide, US Officers

While the Japanese penchant for self-destruction is well known, a number of Americans also took their own lives during or after the war.

Capt. Howard Bode, former skipper of the USS *Chicago*, eventually killed himself, apparently because he believed he had commanded the ship badly at the Battle of SAVO ISLAND.

Capt. Charles B. McVay III, former skipper of the USS *Indianapolis*, killed himself several years after the war, apparently plagued by doubts concerning his performance in command at the time of the ship's loss.

LG George Moore, who commanded the CORREGIDOR garrison under Jonathan WAINWRIGHT, and had spent three years as a Japanese POW, killed himself shortly after the war.

See also KAMIKAZE; KELLY, COLIN.

Sullivan Brothers, The

The sons of Thomas Sullivan, an Irish-American railroad worker from Waterloo, Iowa, and his wife Alleta, who served and died together aboard the antiaircraft cruiser USS *Juneau*. Shortly after PEARL HARBOR, George (b. 1913) and Francis ("Frank," b. 1915), who had both served an enlistment in the navy 1937–41, as well as Joseph ("Red," b. 1918), Madison ("Matt," b. 1919), and Albert ("Al," b. 1921), volunteered for the navy. When told that they would not be allowed to serve together, they requested special permission to do so. This was granted, as well as a waiver of Al's exemption, he being the only one of the five who was married. Amid considerable publicity they were assigned to the newly commissioned *Juneau* at the Brooklyn Navy Yard in February 1942, after abbreviated boot camp at Great Lakes Naval Training Station. The ship's company was shortly augmented by another set of brothers, Patrick ("Pat,"

b. 1917) and Joseph ("Joey," b. 1920), both semi-pro boxers who had already served a year each in the army, plus Louis ("Louie," b. 1921) and James ("Jimmy," b. 1924) Rogers, of Italian and Irish descent (their father, had changed his name to Thomas Rogers), from Bridgeport, Connecticut, who had also received special permission to serve together, again with considerable publicity.

Shortly after arriving in the South Pacific, the ship acquired another set of brothers. When the survivors of the carrier WASP, sunk 15 September 1942, were brought into NOUMEA for reassignment, *Juneau*'s skipper, Capt. Lyman K. Swensen, agreed to the request Boatswain's Mate Russell Coombs that his brother Charles be signed on. The Sullivan, Rogers, and Coombs brothers served aboard *Juneau* in the Battle of SANTA CRUZ (26 October 1942), during which *Juneau* proved enormously effective in helping to beat off Japanese air attacks. Shortly afterward the navy had second thoughts about brothers serving together, and refused to permit siblings to do so in the future. While not ordering those brothers already serving together to be separated, the navy urged them to transfer voluntarily to other ships. The inherent wisdom of this suggestion, plus the opportunity to engage in amateur boxing, caused two of the Rogers brothers, Joey and Jimmy, to transfer to another ship, a move that they urged upon the Sullivans, who deferred a decision.

Soon afterward *Juneau* took part in the First Naval Battle of GUADALCANAL (12–13 November 1942), a ferocious night surface action in which three cruisers, including her sister ATLANTA, were sunk. *Juneau* survived, although with heavy damage to her hull. Early the next morning she was TORPEDOED by the Japanese submarine I-26. The torpedo struck her in a previously damaged part of the hull, and she blew up almost instantly. The Coombs brothers, Louie and Pat Rogers, and Frank, Matt, Red, and Al Sullivan all appear to have been killed instantly. George Sullivan was one of 140 to 150 men who escaped on rafts and floating debris, to watch the remnants of the US squadron steaming away, Capt. Gilbert Hoover of

USS *Helena*, the senior surviving officer, having decided that it was too risky to attempt to rescue the survivors. He was subsequently relieved of duty, perhaps unjustly, given that there were army aircraft overhead and that he attempted to signal the survivors' location and did have the safety of the remnants of the squadron to worry about. Due to failures in command, communications, and staff procedures the survivors were "lost" by the navy. AAF recon planes that spotted the survivors failed to make timely reports. Over the next few days their location was reported to higher headquarters several times, by recon aircraft and even by Capt. Hoover. However, a junior staff officer placed a low priority on the messages. He too was subsequently relieved of duty, with more justification than in the case of Capt. Hoover. Over the next week most of the survivors died of thirst, drowning, wounds, or shark attacks. Among them was George Sullivan, who was killed in a shark attack, a fact not revealed for more than 40 years. Only 10 of the scores of *Juneau*'s men who had taken to the water on the morning of November 13 were picked up on the 20th. Of nearly 700 men in the ship's company, 676 had perished.

Shortly after the loss of *Juneau*, the navy forcibly separated other siblings who had been serving together.

The last surviving Sullivan child, sister Genevieve, subsequently joined the Waves.

On April 4, 1943 the FLETCHER CLASS destroyer USS *The Sullivans* (DD-537) was christened by Alleta Sullivan. The ship had a distinguished career in the Pacific War, and served for many years after it. In 1974 she was designated a war memorial. A new USS *The Sullivans* has since joined the fleet.

Ref: Kurzman, *Left to Die*.

Sunglasses

World War II aviators, particularly fighter pilots, were a dashing bunch. "Aviator glasses" (sunglasses) certainly added to the slick appearance. But the sunglasses weren't there just to sustain a striking image. For fighter pilots in particular, sun-glasses were often a matter of life and death. Aircraft usually fought above the clouds, and a pilot who turned into the sun could be temporarily blinded. In the tropical Pacific the sunlight was particularly intense. Early in the war, more or less through the end of the GUADALCANAL Campaign, Allied pilots (at least those who didn't already know) learned the advantage of sunglasses. The aviator glasses were considered as important as a parachute, because having shades made it less likely a pilot would need his 'chute.

Surigao Strait, Battle of (24–25 October 1944)

During the Battle of LEYTE GULF, a US squadron including the refurbished old battleships *Mississippi*, MARYLAND, *West Virginia*, *Tennessee*, CALIFORNIA, and PENNSYLVANIA (all but the first, veterans of PEARL HARBOR), supported by numerous smaller warships, ambushed a Japanese force including the old battleships FUSO and *Yamashiro*, which were annihilated in an action so one-sided the *Pennsylvania* never got to fire. This was the last time battleships ever fired on each other. Considering that both the Imperial Navy and the US Navy had put so much emphasis on battleships in their prewar plans, it is worth noting that only two of the nine battleship slug-outs during World War II occurred in the Pacific.

See also BATTLESHIPS, ENCOUNTERS.

Surprise Attacks, Japanese

Imperial Japan's major foreign wars were all begun by surprise attacks without benefit of a declaration of war.

Sino-Japanese War (1894–95). By midsummer of 1894 relations between China and Japan had been deteriorating for some time, due to Japanese pressures on Korea, which China considered a dependency, but the possibility of war did not seem imminent. However, Japanese troops in Korea had engaged in some ATROCITIES, and even attacked the king's palace in Seoul. As a result, the Chinese had dispatched several shiploads of troops to Korea. At about 0600 on 25 July, two Chinese warships escorting a chartered British transport carrying about 1,200 troops in the Gulf of Korea, were approached by a Japanese squadron of considerably greater strength. Quite suddenly the Japanese opened fire (they, of course, charged that the Chinese made "threatening" moves). The Chinese warships were severely damaged, and the merchantship sunk, despite her British flag. Over 700 Chinese troops died in the water, many of them by machine-gun fire. This touched off the Sino-Japanese War (and almost caused Britain to break relations with Japan).

Russo-Japanese War (1904–05). Tensions between Japan and Russia had been rising for some time, over the status of MANCHURIA and Korea. On 6 February 1904 Japan recalled her ambassador, effectively breaking relations. Three days later, a Japanese squadron jumped two Russian warships lying off CHEMULPO (Inchon) in Korea without warning, both of which were scuttled in order to avoid capture. That same night the Japanese fleet conducted a surprise attack on the Russian fleet, at anchor outside of PORT ARTHUR, torpedo boats sinking a cruiser and a gunboat, and severely damaging two battleships and another cruiser. This gave the Japanese the initiative in the war, which they maintained through a series of bloody battles on both land and sea, until peace was concluded on highly favorable terms in 1905.

World War II (1941–45). Even as the First Air Fleet was steaming across the Pacific for Pearl Harbor, two Japanese officials with ambassadorial rank were in negotiations with the president and secretary of state concerning the possibility of cooling things off in the Far East; the surprise attack was so secret that the ambassadors themselves did not know it was imminent.

Suva, Fiji

An important harbor, with limited resources but a fine location, about 1,200 miles north of New Zealand. During the war Suva served as a staging area for US divisions being committed to the South Pacific, as an important link in the chain of air bases between the United States and the South Pacific, and as a naval base.

Suzuki, Sasaki (1893–1945)

Sasaki Suzuki joined the Japanese Army in 1912 and spent much of his early career as a staff officer and military attaché. This marked him for greater things in the future. He received troop commands in the 1930s and was chief of staff of the 25th Army during the invasion of MALAYA, then went back to a series of key staff jobs after that. In July 1944, given command of the 35th Army in the Philippines and told to prepare to defend against expected American invasion, he led his troops in a resourceful resistance, successfully moving troops to other islands. Suzuki was killed by US aircraft in June 1945, while moving by boat to another island.

Swordfish, British Carrier Torpedo Bomber

The Swordfish was the most successful biplane of the war. An early 1930s British design, with nearly 2,400 eventually built, the Swordfish was a torpedo bomber and had considerable success in that role in the European Theater. In the Pacific they were more commonly used as reconnaissance aircraft (often as floatplanes), but a few conducted combat missions in the Indian Ocean as late as 1944, attacking Japanese shipping. The Swordfish prototype flew in 1934 and PRODUCTION began shortly thereafter. The Swordfish was slow (top speed 139 MPH), but had a long range (about 1,000 miles) and could carry 1,500 pounds (a TORPEDO, or MINES, rockets, and bombs). The aircraft was very steady and maneuverable, and quite rugged. Its admirable qualities were the primary reason it survived the entire war. The Swordfish would have had a harder time if it had been involved in the 1942 Pacific carrier battles. Its slow speed would have been fatal in the face of carrier antiaircraft fire and Japanese fighters. Later in the war, at least the enemy fighter threat could be smothered. By then it was common to plaster Japanese ships with heavily escorted dive bombers and then bring in the torpedo bombers to finish off the stricken vessels. At this, the Swordfish would still be effective.

See also RECONNAISSANCE, NAVAL.

Sydney, Australia

One of the roomiest harbors in the world, with considerable port facilities, extensive industrial resources, a modest naval base, and several air bases, Sydney was the most important Allied base between Pearl Harbor and SINGAPORE.

Sydney was attacked once during the war. On the afternoon of 31 May 1942 a floatplane from a Japanese submarine reconnoitered Sydney Harbor. That night, Japanese SUBMARINES *I-12*, *I-22*, *I-24*, *I-27*, and *I-29* stood off the entrance to Sydney Harbor and each launched a midget submarine. At least two of the five midget subs managed to penetrate the harbor and fired several TORPEDOES. These caused little damage, missing entirely several transports, an American heavy cruiser, and several destroyers, but they did sink an old accommodation ship, killing several sailors who were sleeping aboard. In response to the attacks, shore batteries opened fire and antiaircraft guns began tearing up the sky, causing some CASUALTIES among civilians. Meanwhile, the warships present in the harbor got underway and attempted to hunt down the attackers. Although the Allied warships were completely unsuccessful in detecting them, none of the Japanese midget submarines survived the operation. Two were actually found inside the harbor, with no apparent damage, and it is believed that the crews scuttled them as a way of committing suicide.

Six nights later, on 7 June, another Japanese submarine surfaced off Sydney and fired several rounds into the city, with little effect, before getting completely away.

See also I-26

T

Tachibana Class, Japanese Destroyer Escorts

A follow-on to Japan's MATSU CLASS destroyer escorts, the Tachibanas were designed almost simultaneously with the former. They were larger and somewhat better armed, but easier to build, taking only about five or six months each. Only 23 of nearly 40 ordered were actually laid down, in late 1944–45, of which only 14 were completed between January and June of 1945, while four others were still fitting out when the war ended. Three of the ships became war losses. After the war most of the survivors were transferred to various Allied powers for disposal.

Taclaban, Leyte, Philippines

A fishing village with limited port facilities but a fine harbor. Occupied by the Japanese in early 1942, it was retaken by US forces in October 1944, and served as a major forward base during further operations in the Philippines.

Taiho, Japanese Aircraft Carrier

Taiho (1941–1943–1944) was arguably the culmination of Japanese carrier design. A large, fast, well protected ship, like all Japanese carriers, she suffered from a limited aircraft operating capacity. In *Taiho*'s case, however, the limitation was due to the installation of a 3-inch armored flight deck, the first in Japanese service. Displacing about 10% more than the American ESSEX, *Taiho* was rated at only about 75–85 aircraft, as against 100 on *Essex*.

Despite this impressive number of aircraft, she was actually apparently able to operate only about 50 to 60 airplanes, due to poorly designed facilities. Supposed to be the lead ship of a batch of seven carriers more or less on the same design, she was the only one ever laid down. *Taiho* was sunk just weeks after completing her training, on 29 June 1944, during the Battle of the PHILIPPINE SEA. The US submarine *Albacore* (SS-218) put a single torpedo into her. This caused an avgas leak, a leak with which inept damage control failed to cope, leading to the accumulation of volatile fumes in confined spaces, resulting in a fatal explosion.

Tainan, Formosa

A major port on the southwestern edge of FORMOSA, with good facilities to service and repair ships, Tainan had been developed by the Japanese as their principal base against the Philippines, only a few hundred miles to the south, and it was an important air base during the initial Japanese operations against Luzon in 1941. During the war it was subject to heavy attacks by carrier-based aircraft, and, after the liberation of Luzon, by land-based airplanes as well.

Taiyo Class, Japanese Escort Carriers

The Taiyo Class were converted 1941–42 from ocean liners under construction at the start of the war. They were much larger than comparable Allied escort carriers. Due to a shortage of aircraft and trained pilots, their primary service was not as escorts, but rather as aircraft transports and training ships. In this role they were quite busy.

Taiyo (?–1940–1941) (ex-*Kasuga Maru*) was TORPEDOED by USS *Trout* (SS-202) near TRUK on 28 August 1942, but did not sink. On 18 November 1944 she was sunk by USS *Rasher* (SS-269) in the Central Pacific.

Unyo (?–1939–1942) (ex-*Yawata Maru*) was sunk 16 September 1944 by USS *Barb* (SS-220) off the Coast of China.

Chuyo (?–1939–1942) (ex-*Nitta Maru*) was sunk by USS *Sailfish* (SS-192) off Honshu on 2 December 1943.

Takagi, Takeo (1892–1944)

A 1912 naval academy graduate, Takagi specialized in TORPEDO warfare and SUBMARINES, but also commanded various surface ships and served on a number of staffs over the following two decades. Late in 1941 he was given command of the Fifth Fleet as a rear admiral. He commanded the carrier strike force during the Battle of the CORAL SEA and assumed command of Sixth Fleet (submarines) in late 1943 as a vice admiral. Takagi was killed on Saipan in July 1944 during the American invasion.

Takao Class, Japanese Heavy Cruisers

An improvement on the NACHI CLASS heavy cruisers, the Takaos were bigger and better protected. All had extensive war service, *Atago* as a flagship. All became war losses, taking considerable punishment before succumbing. They formed the Fourth Cruiser Squadron and saw service in the NETHERLANDS EAST INDIES, during the GUADALCANAL Campaign, and with carrier task forces on several occasions. All four were hit, and three sunk, during the Battle of LEYTE GULF.

Takao (1927–1930–1932) accompanied *Atago* during early operations in the Philippines and Netherlands East Indies, but otherwise had a relatively quiet war. She was hit, but not sunk, by two TORPEDOES from *Darter* (SS-227) on 23 October 1944, during the preliminary phases of the Battle

of Leyte Gulf. This sent her back to SINGAPORE, where she remained until the British midget submarine *XE3* sank her in the harbor on 31 July 1945.

Atago (1927–1930–1932) was Admiral KONDO's favorite flagship, serving him in this capacity from the initial operations in the Philippines and Netherlands East Indies right on through the fighting off Guadalcanal, and later serving as such for Admiral KURITA, in which capacity she was sunk by two torpedoes from *Darter* (SS-227) October 23, 1944, on the eve of the Battle of Leyte Gulf.

Maya (1928–1932–1932) served with *Chokai* in the Netherlands East Indies and the Solomons, fought at the KOMANDORSKI ISLANDS. Severely damaged by US aircraft at RABAUL in November 1943, she lost her "C" turret, leaving her with only eight 8-inch guns. She was sunk by several torpedoes from the USS *Dace* (SS-247) on October 23, 1944 on the eve of the Battle of Leyte Gulf.

Chokai (1928–1931–1923) took part in operations against the Netherlands East Indies and in the SOLOMONS (SAVO ISLAND and the Tokyo Express), and attacked the US escort carriers off SAMAR on October 25, 1944, during which she was sunk by dive bombers and destroyer gunfire.

Tana, New Hebrides

A small port, with limited facilities, overshadowed as a potential base by ESPIRITU SANTO, a hundred miles or so to the north. The United States developed a modest base there during the SOLOMONS CAMPAIGN.

Tanaka, Raizo (1892–1969)

Raizo Tanaka graduated from the Japanese naval academy in 1913 and specialized in destroyers and TORPEDO warfare. He rose steadily, commanding a series of ships culminating with the battleship KONGO in 1939. Promoted to rear admiral in 1941, Tanaka led destroyer units on escort duties during the Dutch East Indies invasion and later during the MIDWAY operation. His main fame came when he organized and led the TOKYO EXPRESS that used de-

TANKS OF THE PACIFIC WAR								
Country	Model	Weight	Gun	MG	Armor	Crew	Speed	Year
Britain	Mk VI Light	5.2	—	1	15	3	35.0	'39
	Matilda	26.5	40	1	78	4	15.6	'39
	Valentine	17.0	40	1	65	3	15.6	'41
Japan	Type 95 Light	4.7	—	1	16	2	25.0	'37
	Type 97 Medium	15.0	57	2	25	4	23.5	'37
United States	M3 Medium (Grant)	29.5	75	1	76	6	20.0	'40
	M3 Light (Stuart)	12.5	37	2	44	4	36.3	'41
	M4 Medium (Sherman)	30.0	75	2	76	5	25.0	'42
	LVT A Amtrak	16.0	75	2–4	76	6	17.0	'44

Key: Model is a simplified form of the tank's official designation; some of these were quite intricate, such as M4A2, indicating the second variant of the A version of the Sherman. Weight, in tons, is that of the tank, loaded but unmanned. Gun is given in millimeters, for the principal cannon carried; MG, the number of machine guns carried. Armor is the thickest carried, in millimeters. Crew, the normal complement. Speed, in miles per hour on roads; cross-country would be much less. Year is that of introduction.

stroyers to supply and reinforce the Japanese troops on GUADALCANAL during 1942, his doggedness causing the Americans to bestow on him the nickname "Tenacious Tanaka." By the end of the year he was removed from command for his outspoken criticism of how the Guadalcanal operation was being run, and spent the rest of the war commanding naval bases in Burma. Promoted to vice admiral before the end of the war, Tanaka didn't get around to surrendering until January 1946. Tanaka was one of the most able Japanese commanders, a resourceful and wily tactician. He didn't get more important posts because he saw the situation as it was, not as many of his overly optimistic commanders wanted to see it.

Tanaka, Shimishi

Shimishi (or Shinichi) Tanaka graduated from the military academy in 1913. He held a variety of posts, primarily as a staff officer, and was one of those who believed Japan should take over all of China and attack the Soviet Union. The head of the army's Operations Division at the outbreak of the Pacific War, in 1942 he was sent as chief of staff to the Southern Area Army, which supervised operations in INDONESIA and Southeast Asia. In March of 1943 he received a division in Burma,

leading it with great ability in tenacious rearguard actions. In September 1944, he became chief of staff, and virtual commander, of the Burma Area Army headquarters and from there constantly urged defense of Burmese positions to the last man.

Tankan Bay, Kuriles, Japan

Plagued by subarctic weather, and with only limited facilities, Tankan Bay was roomy and isolated. It was the base from which the PEARL HARBOR Strike Force sortied in late November of 1941. Otherwise it played little role in the war.

Tanks in the Pacific War

Although ground combat in the Pacific Theater was very much an infantry show, tanks often played an important role in the fighting. Tanks, both Japanese and Allied, fought in virtually every land campaign, usually in an infantry support role but occasionally in tank-to-tank clashes.

By British or American standards, Japanese tanks and antitank weapons were not particularly good. Even the best Japanese tank, the Type 97 medium tank, was vulnerable to a 37mm antitank gun, while the British Matildas and Valentines were virtually impregnable to Japanese A/T weaponry, and the Sherman nearly so. As a result Allied tanks that were essentially obsolete in the European Theater were still useful in the Pacific. However, Japanese tanks proved effective and useful against infantry, or lighter Allied tanks, such as they encountered in Malaya, the Philippines, Burma, and the NETHERLANDS EAST INDIES in 1941–42

Although Australia organized two armored divisions in 1941–42 (to use Stuarts, Matildas, and Grants which were in short supply), these saw no active service and were eventually disbanded. The largest Allied armored units used in the Pacific War were several brigades employed by the British in

India and Burma, where the Sino-American First Tank Group also operated. For the most part Allied tank operations were conducted by separate battalions and even companies. The Japanese usually deployed their tanks in small regiments (about 40 medium tanks and a dozen lights, about the allotment of an American tank battalion), but did organize four tank divisions in MANCHURIA. The Third Tank Division conducted offensive operations in China as part of ICHI GO, and the Second Tank Division fought on Luzon in 1944–45, where any possibility of its use as a massed formation was lost when it was dispersed in small detachments to help hold back the advance of US forces while the

An M-4 Sherman medium tank supporting troops engaged in "mopping up" Japanese stragglers and infiltrators on Bougainville, March 1944. Note that the infantrymen have fixed bayonets, not normally used in combat but useful during mopping up. Tankers in the South Pacific suffered greatly from heat and dehydration, but had the comfort of knowing that Japanese antitank equipment was relatively ineffective.

An M-4 Sherman in action on Bougainville, 1944, accompanied by troops of the 25th Infantry Regiment.

bulk of the Japanese troops on the island retired to the mountains. The other two tank divisions were brought to Japan in 1944 as part of preparations for the expected Allied invasion.

The largest tank battle of the Pacific War occurred on SAIPAN, where three companies of the Japanese Ninth Tank Regiment, equipped with the 1943 version of the Type 97 medium tank, supported by a company of SNLF Type 95 light tanks, conducted two major tank attacks. At dawn on 16 June 1944, the Fourth Company of the regiment, and the SNLF company, took part in a major attack against the Marine beachhead, and were virtually wiped out by the Shermans of the Marines' Second and Fourth Tank Battalions. At 0200 the next morning, about 44 Japanese tanks from the Ninth Tank Regiment and SNLF undertook an at-

tack on the Marine lines carrying infantry, to be met by a storm of antitank fire, and then hit with an attack by Marine tanks and tank destroyers, with very heavy losses. This was the biggest Japanese tank attack of the war outside of China.

Had the war lasted until the spring of 1946, the United States would have committed two armored division to the invasion of Honshu, an endeavor that would almost certainly have led to a major clash with the Japanese First and Fourth Tank Divisions, deployed to defend Tokyo.

Note that in 1940 an upgraded version of the Japanese Type 97 medium tank was designed, with a superior model 47mm gun, but this did not enter large-scale PRODUCTION until 1943. The US M3 Grant tank carried its 75mm gun in a sponson on the right front of the hull, and also had a 37mm in a turret. These were employed in the Pacific on only one occasion, during the capture of Makin. Beginning in 1944 the M4 Sherman was equipped with a superior 76.2mm high-velocity gun. US forces also used the M5 light tank, a development of the Stuart. The LVT (A), or "Assault Amphtrak," was strictly speaking not a tank; some early models had a 37mm antitank gun, but the later LVT A4 had a Sherman turret.   The principal Allied tanks were the Sherman and Stuart, although the British and Australians made considerable use of the Matilda. While the obsolete Japanese Type 89 medium tank (introduced in 1929) saw considerable service in China, their principal battle tanks against the Allies were the Type 97 medium and Type 95 light.

In addition to the tanks shown, about 50 obsolete Vickers Carden-Lloyd and Marmon Herrington light tanks served with Dutch forces in the Netherlands East Indies in 1941–42, and Chinese forces used a number of older Soviet models brought in during the late 1930s.

See also AMPHIBIOUS VEHICLES; Malaya Campaign in

Tarakan, Borneo

An oil port, with limited facilities to service ships, but with a refinery of some value. Tarakan was strategically of some value for its location on the east coast of BORNEO, about halfway between BALIK-PAPAN and Sandikar.

Tarawa, Battle of

Although its atoll could protect a considerable number of ships, Tarawa had the barest port installations and no facilities to service or repair shipping. Despite its very limited land area, Tarawa was of great value as an air base, having the potential to dominate the GILBERTS.

In November 1943 Tarawa—and nearby MAKIN—became the object of the first US amphibious attack against heavily fortified Pacific atolls. Planning for this operation began in the summer of 1943, although such amphibious assaults had been discussed long before that. The GILBERT ISLANDS, particularly Tarawa and Makin atolls, were selected. These would be taken from their Japanese defenders and turned into air bases for the support of future island invasions to the west.   Makin was easy, the garrison was only 800 troops, of which only 300 were combat troops. Still, it took a reinforced regiment of the army's 27th Infantry Division four days to take the place. The US Army lost 64 dead, the Japanese nearly 800. Meanwhile, the Japanese brought up submarines and sank a US CVE, *Liscombe Bay*, killing 644 sailors. Had the army troops hustled, the carriers would have been gone by the time the Japanese subs showed up.

Tarawa would also be costly, especially to the Marines assaulting the principal island, Betio. The Japanese garrison was 4,836 troops. These had spent the last year fortifying an area only 3.7 kilometers long and about half a kilometer wide, smaller than New York's Central Park. The US Second Marine Division would do the invading. Since this was the first assault of its type, lots of things went wrong. The amount of pre-invasion shelling and bombing necessary was underestimated. The Japanese had bombproof shelters for all of their troops, and it would have taken extraordinary shelling and bombing to get at them. Most of the Japanese troops were unharmed by the shelling. Next, the CORAL reefs that comprise Tarawa atoll were of a typically complex nature, and this in combination with the tides made it difficult to predict when the landing craft could get across the reefs and right up to the beach on Betio Island, the "mainland" of sprawling Tarawa Atoll. Not knowing the exact layout of the reefs, nor the precise schedule of the local tides proved disastrous. On the first day, thousands of the troops had to wade through 400 to 500 meters of waist-high water. Of the 5,000 Marines landed that day, some 1,500 were killed or wounded. TANKS that tried to land stalled in water that flooded their engines before they could get ashore. On the second day, the reefs were located and the tides sorted out. The US landing craft were now able to get right onto the

Marines heavily engaged on Tarawa, amid the devastation wrought by the preliminary bombardment, November 1943.

beaches with more troops, equipment, and supplies, including tanks. At the end of day two there were enough Marines ashore to put the Japanese on the defensive. By day four, all but 146 of the Japanese garrison were dead. The Marines had 900 killed, and 3,300 wounded. Less than a hundred sailors were killed.

This was not the bloodiest of the Central Pacific assaults, nor the longest. But as far as intense fighting in a short time, Tarawa was the worst. There were also many, many mistakes made, and they were pretty obvious to all concerned. But this provided opportunities to fix things and this was done quickly. Tarawa was also the first of the modern island assaults, using the new landing craft designs. Much had to be learned in a short time and Tarawa

was the live test. Thus the next series of assaults in the MARSHALL ISLANDS went much more smoothly. Yet because Tarawa was the first of the Marine assaults, and a bloody one at that, it will always hold a special place in Marine history.

See also SHOUP, DAVID; SMITHS, WAR OF THE.

Task Force, Task Group, Task Unit

Task force is a US Navy term for squadron of ships given special mission. A task group is a substantial portion of a task force given a separate ancillary mission, while a task unit is a subdivision of a task group. During the war, task forces tended to get larger and larger. A carrier task force in 1942 was likely to include only one carrier, plus escorts, whereas by 1945 it might include a dozen carriers with their escorts, organized into several task groups. Task forces were usually named after the fleet under which they operated, thus TF 38 or TF 58. A task group was numbered as a fraction of its parent task force, thus TF 38.1, and a task unit similarly, TU 38.1.1. The US Fleets operating in the Pacific were: First (originally the whole Pacific Fleet, but later confined to the West Coast); Third/Fifth, in the Central Pacific; and Seventh, in the Southwest Pacific. Occasional task forces were given numbers outside the system, such as TF 44, which operated during the CORAL SEA Campaign.

Tassafaronga, Battle of

This naval action between US and Japanese ships on November 30, 1942, was fought off the north coast of GUADALCANAL, near Tassafaronga Point). During the battle for Guadalcanal, the Japanese kept their troops on the island supplied via fast transports (disarmed destroyers) escorted by destroyers running down the "Slot" (the north-south channel between the major islands). After the fierce naval battles off Guadalcanal in the first half of November, the Japanese seemed to be reeling. They were, but they still had plenty of fight in them. Admiral TANAKA, who ably led the "Tokyo Express" down the Slot throughout the Guadalcanal Campaign, was leading eight destroyers down the slot on the night of November 30. He was intercepted by a larger US force of five cruisers and seven destroyers. The battle was over quickly, as Tanaka's force promptly turned, launched TORPEDOES, and sank one cruiser and damaged three others. Some 400 Americans were killed. The Japanese were unhurt.

Tawi Tawi, Philippines

A roomy but exposed anchorage in the southern Philippines (virtually the southernmost place in the Philippines), Tawi Tawi—or Tawitawi—lacked even the most rudimentary facilities to serv-

ice ships, but was convenient to the oil producing areas of Borneo and had potential as a base for projecting naval power in a broad arc eastward, and that was how the Japanese used it, in preparation for the Battle of the PHILIPPINE SEA.

Tawi Tawi was reoccupied by US forces on 1 July 1945, in an operation sometimes called the "last amphibious landing of World War II," a distinction more correctly belonging to the Australian landings at Balikpapan.

TBD-1 Devastator, US Carrier Torpedo Bomber

The TBD-1 Devastator was the standard US Navy torpedo bomber at the start of World War II and was markedly ill-equipped for that role. The fatal flaw for the TBD was its slow speed and the low height from which it had to drop its TORPEDO. These characteristics caused TBDs to take very heavy losses from Japanese flak and interceptors. At MIDWAY, nearly all the attacking TBDs were shot down without scoring any hits. Because the TBF AVENGER was just entering service in 1942, it wasn't until early 1944 that all the TBD-1s could be withdrawn from combat units.

See also AIRCRAFT TYPES, DEVELOPMENT; CARRIERS, DESIGNING AIRCRAFT FOR.

TBF Avenger, US Carrier Bomber

The US TBF Avenger was originally designed as a new torpedo bomber, but proved so successful that it became the only bomber aircraft carriers needed. Nearly 10,000 TBFs were built from 1942 to 1945. Half a dozen participated in the Battle of MIDWAY, and by the end of 1943 the TBF was the most common bomber on carriers. The TBF was much better than the TBD-1 DEVASTATOR, with 50% more speed, nearly as much additional range, twice the bombload (2,000 pounds), and was more heavily armed. While outclassed in most categories by the new Helldiver, the TBF still had twice the bombload, which in the later stages of the war was most

Avenger TBM variants from USS Essex *(CV-9) in a bombing raid on Kokadate, late July 1945. The aircraft in the left background are SB2C Helldivers.*

important. Equally important was the ease with which the TBF could be equipped with radar, making it an optimal scout aircraft. The TBF was supplied to allies, particularly Britain, where it served well during the battle against German U-boats in the Atlantic. TBF Avengers served with foreign air forces into the 1960s. There were many variants, including a transport version.

See also AIRCRAFT TYPES, DEVELOPMENT; CARRIERS, DESIGNING AIRCRAFT FOR.

Tempest, British Fighter Bomber

The Tempest was Britain's second-generation fighter bomber (after the Typhoon). Entering service in the summer of 1943, it was fast (427 MPH) and heavily armed (four 20mm cannon and 2,000 pounds of bombs and rockets). It was also heavy (6.1 tons loaded) and not as nimble as fighters like the SPITFIRE. Nevertheless, it was a terror to Japanese ground troops in Burma. Nearly 1,000 were produced.

See also AIRCRAFT TYPES, DEVELOPMENT.

Tenryu Class, Japanese Light Cruisers

Japan's oldest light cruisers, the Tenryus were designed during World War I to serve as squadron leaders for destroyer flotillas. They were very small by World War II standards, indeed not much bigger than some destroyers, and no better armed. Beyond the addition of some antiaircraft armament, they were not modernized between the wars.

Tenryu (1917–1918–1919) served as a flotilla leader in the South Pacific, at the CORAL SEA and in the SOLOMONS, fighting at SAVO ISLAND. She was sunk by *Albacore* (SS-218) on 18 December 1942, in the BISMARCK SEA.

Tatsuta (1917–1918–1919) served as a flotilla leader in the South Pacific, including the Coral Sea. She was sunk by *Sundance* (SS-381) off Honshu on 13 March 1944.

Terauchi, Hisaichi (1879–1946)

Count Hisaichi Terauchi, the son of Field Marshal Count Masakata Terauchi (who started his military career as a samurai, rose to army command during the Russo-Japanese War, and later held important government posts), graduated from the military academy in 1899. He fought in the Russo-Japanese War, attended various schools, and spent several years as an attaché and student in Germany and Austria before World War I. Between 1914 and 1936 he rose to general and war minister, in which role he crushed the last vestiges of parliamentary authority over the military. In 1937 he commanded the forces that invaded China from MANCHURIA, and in 1941 was given the Southern Area Army, which controlled all army operations in Southeast Asia and the South Pacific. Made a field marshal in June 1943, Terauchi suffered a mild stroke in April 1945, but remained in command until the end of the war because his staff did not report his ill-health to Tokyo. That he did not stand trial for war crimes was due to his illness, which proved terminal. Surprisingly, he was looked after by Lord MOUNTBATTEN once the war was over. Terauchi was a soldier of the old school and did not agree with all the army involvement in politics. His noble rank and personal ability allowed him to retain his command despite these attitudes. Despite this, he gave orders that all PRISONERS OF WAR in his command were to be executed if Allied forces landed in Japan.

Tientsin, China

The port of PEKING, Tientsin had limited, but adequate facilities to fulfill its primary function. It was held by the Japanese for the entire war. In 1945 it was for a time occupied by the US Marines.

Timor

An island in the East Indies, Timor was divided between the Dutch, on the western side, and the Portuguese, on the east, which included Dili, the largest town and principal port of the island. On the outbreak of the Pacific War, Dutch and Australian troops occupied Portuguese Timor. Allied GUERRILLA forces, mostly Australian but with some

Five TBF Avengers on a training flight near Norfolk, Virginia, in September 1942. Introduced in early 1942 and intended as a torpedo bomber, the Avenger soon proved itself an immensely versatile airplane, and quickly became the navy's primary carrier-based bomber.

Dutch troops, were active on Timor from December 1941 through February 1943, when they were withdrawn due to increasing enemy pressure.

Ref: *Australia in the Second World War*, series I, vol. 5.

Tinian, Marianas

Shortly before the war began the Japanese had started to develop Tinian as a major base, despite the fact that it lacked a proper port. Strategically, Tinian, one of the MARIANAS, shared with SAIPAN and GUAM an excellent location that could act either as an outlying bastion of Japan or an offensive base against Japan (with Tokyo only a bit more than a thousand miles to the north). It figured prominently in the CENTRAL PACIFIC CAMPAIGN.

Tinker, Clarence L. (1887–1942)

Clarence L. Tinker entered the US armed forces as a third lieutenant in the PHILIPPINE CONSTABULARY before World War I. Later transferring to the Regular Army, he took flight training in 1921. Over the next 20 years he performed a variety of line and staff duties in the Air Corps, attended various army schools, rose to brigadier general, and managed to acquire an army life saving medal as well. Promoted to major general shortly after PEARL HARBOR, in March 1942 he was sent to HAWAII to command the Seventh Air Force, which controlled all Army Air Corps units in the central Pacific. Tinker directed Army Air Corps operations during the Battle of MIDWAY, from Midway Island. Late on June 6, 1942, he took part in a very-long-range raid intended to bomb WAKE ISLAND using four specially-prepared B-24 LIBERATORS. Sometime during the night his aircraft developed engine trouble and disappeared at sea. He was the first Regular Army general killed in the war. He was also probably the highest ranking person of American Indian descent killed in the war, being one-eighth Osage.

Tjilatjap, Java

A small port on the south coast of JAVA, of some value as a base for projecting power into the eastern Indian Ocean. It served the allies as a base until overrun by the Japanese in early 1942. They made some use of it for naval and air operations in the Indian Ocean.

Tojo, Hideki (1884–1948)

General Hideki Tojo was not a field commander during World War II, but he was the most important Japanese army commander because he ran the government for most of the war and was generally considered the one man most responsible for getting Japan into a war that many senior Japanese military officers knew Japan could not win. He graduated from the military academy in 1905. Most of his early career was spent in staff assignments and at the war college. From 1919 through 1922 he served with the Japanese Embassy in Berlin. Considered bright, but not among the brightest, Tojo made up for this with a workaholic dedication to whatever he was doing and an intense nationalism and ambition. Tojo was posted to the Kwantung (Manchurian) Army in the summer of 1934, as the head of the army military police. The Kwantung Army was a hotbed of army enthusiasm for Japanese expansion, and Tojo was caught up in what was, to him, a very congenial cause. In 1937 he became chief of staff of the Kwantung Army. He actively participated in operations against Chinese troops and, in 1938, went back to Japan to become vice minister of war. He offended so many senior officials with his ultra-nationalist attitudes that he was removed to the more obscure post of inspector of army aviation at the end of 1938.

By hard work and much politicking, he worked himself into the job of minister of war by the summer of 1940. By late 1941 he had gotten the post of prime minister and, in effect, control of the government. He retained his rank in the army. While Japan never became a military dictatorship in the classic sense, by the end of October 1941 the army was calling the shots. (Tojo was also both the minister of home affairs and minister of war.) The decision to go to war was already made when Tojo took over, and he heartily supported it. Through 1942 and 1943, he became the head of more ministries (foreign affairs, education, commerce and industry, munitions). By late 1943 he capped all this by becoming the chief of staff (commander) of both the army and the navy. For the first six months of 1944, Tojo was a one-man government. But he was not a complete dictator. In July 1944, the Privy Council (composed of older, semi-retired senior officials) agreed that he should go and forced him to retire. The main reason for this vote of no-confidence was that Japan was losing the war and Tojo refused to face reality. Although Tojo was then given a place on the Privy Council, he spent the rest of the war writing and (literally) tending his garden.

At the end of the war, he attempted suicide, but an American doctor was able to save his life. During his incarceration pending trial as a war criminal, a US Army dentist is alleged to have engraved the Morse Code for "Remember Pearl Harbor" on his teeth. Tried by the TOKYO WAR CRIMES TRIBUNAL, he was condemned and hanged. Although Tojo's body was burned and the ashes secretly buried by the Allies, Japanese crematorium workers stole some of the ashes and turned them over to the government after the occupation had ended. In 1960 an impressive tomb was constructed at the YASUKUNI SHRINE to contain these ashes (mixed in with six other war criminals). The monument is inscribed, "The Tomb of the Seven Martyrs."

Ref: Butow, *Tojo and the Coming of the War*.

Tokyo, Honshu, Japan

Including the nearby cities of Yokohama and Yokosuka, in 1940 there were more than 10 million people in the Tokyo area, concentrated around an extensive bay on the east coast of Honshu.

Tokyo was a major industrial and commercial center, as well as the seat of the Japanese government and armed forces. Tokyo was also the site of

the Imperial Navy's Paymasters' Academy, which trained officers for the administrative branches of the service; other officer candidates went to Eta Jima, at KURE, or MAIZURU.

Nearby Yokohama was a major industrial city and port, with extensive shipbuilding facilities, suitable for merchantships and cruisers. Yokosuka was one of the four main bases of the Imperial Navy, with facilities to build any kind of warship. It was the headquarters of the Yokosuka SNLF.

Tokyo Express

In October 1942 the Japanese established a standing force of destroyers converted to carry troops and cargo. These high-speed transports were intended to take troops and supplies to GUADALCANAL, an island American troops had taken from the Japanese the previous August. The United States had promptly established an airfield and the bombers stationed there would spot Japanese transports during daylight and attack the ships before nightfall provided any protection. The faster destroyer transports could wait until nightfall and then move into range of US aircraft, land their cargo on Guadalcanal, and be back out of range of American aircraft before the sun came up. For the second half of 1942, as the battle for Guadalcanal raged, this Japanese force was called the "Cactus Express" ("Cactus" was the US code word for Japanese forces on Guadalcanal).

But even after the Japanese were forced out of Guadalcanal in early 1943, the Japanese fast transports continued to supply Japanese garrisons in the adjacent islands. At that point, these fast transports came to be known as the "Tokyo Express," and continued to operate in 1944 from bases like RABAUL. The original organizer of the Tokyo Express, Raizo TANAKA, was an able destroyerman and an outspoken naval officer. By early 1943 he had been transferred elsewhere for being too outspoken on how Japanese commanders were mismanaging the war effort. In the summer of 1943 the Tokyo Express took such a hammering in a series of losing battles with American ships that its operations were greatly reduced. Japan was running out of destroyers. There were several dozen available for the Tokyo Express in late 1942, but after a year, nearly two-thirds of these were sunk or under repair. Few replacements were forthcoming, and the destroyer component of the Tokyo Express eventually faded away because of attrition.

There were, however, other types of transport running the same routes. While traditional merchant ships proved too slow and vulnerable, slow-moving barges and smaller ships found ways to survive. They did this by running up on a beach before dawn and camouflaging themselves so Allied aircraft could not spot them. Some were spotted anyway, but most made it down to Japanese garrisons, unloaded their cargo at night, and returned north time and again. For special missions the Japanese would also use submarines and parachute drops. By late 1944, Rabaul, the northern terminus for the Tokyo Express, was itself cut off from Japan. With nothing to send south, the dogged supply service faded away in early 1945.

Tokyo Rose

The name given to several women who made English-language broadcasts for the Japanese in an effort to weaken US morale. The troops often listened because, between propaganda pitches, it was common to play American popular music. Senior US officers wisely did nothing to prevent their troops from listening, and there were no noticeable morale problems due to these broadcasts.

The only "Tokyo Rose" who was an American citizen was Iva Toguri (1916–   ). Pearl Harbor found her visiting Japan, where she secured employment as a disc jockey with an English-language radio station. Although she apparently did not broadcast propaganda, after the war she was arrested by the US Army and tried on treason charges. She received a 10–year sentence and a $10,000 fine. After her release she worked for many years to clear her name, meanwhile marrying and

"Tokyo Rose," Iva Toguri, being interviewed by war correspondents in Tokyo, September 1945.

becoming Iva d'Aquino. In January 1977 President Gerald FORD issued her a full pardon.

Ref: Duus, *Tokyo Rose*.

Tokyo War Crimes Tribunal

The International Military Tribunal for the Far East convened in 1946 to try the highest-ranking Japanese officials charged with war crimes. The court consisted of representatives from the various Allied powers. The trials lasted from 3 May 1946 to 12 November 1948, and were held in the former Japanese War Ministry building. The charges were various, including both general and specific counts of conspiracy to make war, violations of international law, and countenancing ATROCITIES. In deference to the claim that while Japan had signed the 1929 GENEVA CONVENTION it had never ratified the signature and was thus not bound by it, the charges were brought under the terms of the 1899 Hague Convention, which Japan had signed and ratified.

Altogether 28 men were tried. Two of them died during the trial. Seven were sentenced to death, 16 to life, one to 20 years in prison, and one to seven years in prison. One was found mentally unfit to stand trial and was relegated to an insane asylum. By one reckoning the Tokyo trial cost $9 million and used 100 tons of paper.

Those sentenced to death were:

Gen. Kenji DOHIHARA

Koki Hirota, prime minister during the CHINA INCIDENT

Gen. Seishiro ITAGAKI, former war minister

Gen. Heitaro KIMURA

Gen. Iwane Matsui, commander of the Japanese forces during the "Rape of Nanking"

Gen. Akira Muto, chief of staff of the occupation forces in the Philippines

Gen. Hideki TOJO, head of the Japanese government for much of the war

This trial dealt with the principal war criminals. Other trials took up the cases involving persons of lesser importance, such as those involving generals HOMMA and YAMASHITA.

Only a handful of Japanese war criminals were ever tried. Most of those sentenced had their sentences reduced and few served for very long, and even those who had been sentenced to death had their sentences commuted to life. By the mid-1950s there were no Japanese war criminals still in jail.

Tomozuru Class, Japanese Torpedo Boats

Like several nations, Japan continued to build so-called "ocean-going" or fleet TORPEDO boats, basically very small destroyers specialized for torpedo attack. They were poorly designed, being unstable (*Tomozuru* once capsized in a storm, later to be salvaged and returned to service) and unsuited to their original purpose—coordinated high-speed torpedo attacks in fleet actions. They were pressed into service as convoy escorts after extensive modifications to their armament, a role in which they proved surprisingly effective, as they could carry 48 depth charges each, far more than most fleet destroyers. Three were lost in action.

Tone Class, Japanese Heavy Cruisers

The two Tones were designed as light cruisers with a dozen 6–inch guns, in four turrets all forward, but converted to four 8-inch guns while still building. Grouping the main armament forward gave the cruisers an odd appearance, but permitted them to carry a very large complement of floatplanes. As a result, the Tones were the best Japanese heavy

	Nation Holding Trial					
	Australia	Britain	France	Netherlands	United States	Total
Cases	296	306	39	448	474	1,563
Defendants	924	920	230	1,038	1,409	4,521
Convictions	644	811	198	969	1,229	3,851
Acquittals	280	106	31	55	180	652
Prison Terms	369	532	134	719	1,066	2,820
Death Sentences	148	279	63	236	163	889
Executed	148	265	26	226	92	757
Commuted	0	14	37	10	71	132
Other	0	3	1	14	0	18

RESULTS OF WAR CRIMES TRIALS IN THE FAR EAST

Trials by China and Russia unknown. "Other" includes persons who died during trial or who were found unfit to stand trial for reasons of mental or physical health.

cruisers, combining high speed, heavy armament, extensive protections, good sea-keeping qualities, excellent maneuverability, and all those floatplanes that enhanced their role as fleet scouts. Although rated at six aircraft, they apparently never carried more than five.

The two ships served together for virtually the entire war, helping escort the First Air Fleet to PEARL HARBOR, and serving with it in the Indian Ocean and at MIDWAY (where one of *Tone*'s scout planes located the US carriers). They were with the Japanese carriers from then to the PHILIPPINE SEA, fighting in virtually all of the carrier battles. During the Battle of LEYTE GULF they took part in the attack on the US escort carriers off SAMAR on 25 October 1944.

Tone (1934–1937–1938) was damaged during Leyte Gulf, and retired to Japan for repairs, which were never fully effected. She was sunk in shallow water by US carrier aircraft in KURE Harbor on 24 July 1945, and broken up postwar.

Chikuma (1935–1938–1939) was sunk by US carrier aircraft bombs and a TORPEDO off Samar on October 25, 1944.

Tonga

A Polynesian kingdom in the South Pacific, under British protection, Tonga provided useful naval and air basing sites. In addition, the kingdom raised a small brigade group, composed of two infantry battalions, with a small artillery and engineer element, plus support troops, which was supplemented by a NEW ZEALAND infantry battalion. Although most of the Tongan Brigade did not see action, a special infantry platoon did.

Usually attached to Fijian forces, the Tongan contingent occasionally served independently. Attached to US forces during the New Georgia landings in mid-1943, the Tongans performed so well that one was awarded a Silver Star.

Ref: Gillespie, *Official History of New Zealand in the Second World War, 1939–1945, The Pacific*; Ready, *Forgotten Allies*.

Torpedoes

World War II was the golden age of torpedo warfare. This was the only conflict in which torpedoes were used extensively by SUBMARINES, aircraft, and surface ships. The Japanese had a significant advantage in torpedo warfare for the first two years of the war. This was because their principal surface ship torpedo was larger and more capable than anyone else's and because the prinicipal US submarine torpedo was defective. The Japanese aerial torpedo was also superior during this period, giving the Japanese an advantage in every torpedo category. This was a particularly decided edge for the Japanese during the first year of the war.

In the early part of the war Japanese surface ships used their so-called "Long Lance" torpedoes to destroy far more Allied ships than their opponents could using the same technique. US carrier aircraft caused less damage with their less capable torpedoes, and US submarines were practically disarmed because of their defective torpedoes. The entries below shows the torpedo situation in detail.

Torpedo Types Range and speed are given, when needed, as the two extreme settings for the torpedo, with range in kilometers and speed in knots (1 knot = 1 nautical mile or 1.9 kilometers per hour).

The Japanese Type 8 was a 24–inch surface weapon that weighed 5,207 pounds and had a 761–pound warhead. The range (kilometers) and speed (knots) were from 10 and 38 to 15 and 32. The Type 8 was a 1920s design that was still being used by older destroyers and light cruisers early in the war. An effective torpedo similar to the US Mark 15.

The Japanese Type 89 was a 21–inch submarine weapon that weighed 3,677 pounds and had a 661-pound warhead. The range (kilometers) and speed (knots) were from 5.5 and 45 to 10 and 35. The Type 89 was a 1920s design for SUBMARINES and was widely used during the first year of the war. During that period, it was much more effective than the newer US Mark 14.

The Japanese Type 90 was a 21-inch submarine weapon that weighed 5,743 pounds and had an 827-pound warhead. The range (kilometers) and speed (knots) were from 7 and 46 to 15 and 35. The Type 90 was a 1930s design for cruisers. Used extensively early in the war.

The Japanese Type 93 (nicknamed Long Lance by the Allies) was a 24-inch surface weapon that weighed 5,952 pounds and had a warhead of 1,080 pounds. The range (kilometers) and speed (knots) were from 20 and 49 to 40 and 36. The Japanese were way ahead of everyone else with this 24-inch surface ship torpedo. Very reliable, fast, and deadly. Widely used throughout the war, especially in the first year.

The Japanese Type 95 was a 21-inch submarine weapon that weighed 3,671 pounds and had an 893-pound warhead. The range (kilometers) and speed (knots) were from 9 and 50 to 12 and 46. The Type 95 was a smaller, submarine version of the Type 93 Long Lance and was quite effective. There was also a Type 92 electric torpedo that was produced from 1942 on in small quantities (650) to supplement the more widely used Type 95.

The Japanese Type 97 was a 17.7-inch submarine weapon weighing 2,094 pounds with a 772-pound warhead. The range (kilometers) and speed (knots) were 5.5 and 45. The Type 97 was an even smaller version of the Long Lance, for use in midget submarines. Only 100 Type 97s were built, and it was used only by the midget subs at PEARL HARBOR, where recent evidence suggests one may actually have struck a battleship. The Type 97 was not very reliable in any event.

The Japanese Type 91-1 was a 17.7-inch aircraft weapon weighing 1,728 pounds and having a 331-pound warhead. The range (kilometers) and speed (knots) were two and 42. The Type 91-1 was the standard aircraft torpedo in the first year of the war. This was an early 1930s design and was being replaced by the Type 91-2 in 1941. All Type 91s could be launched at over 200 knots (twice the launch speed of early US airborne torpedoes) early in the war and 350 knots by 1944. Launch altitude was, for tactical reasons, rarely more than a few hundred feet.

The Japanese Type 91-2 was a 17.7-inch aircraft weapon weighing 1,841 pounds with a 452-pound warhead. The range (kilometers) and speed (knots) were two and 42. The Type 91-2 replaced the 91-1 in 1942.

The Japanese Type 91-3 was a 17.7-inch aircraft weapon weighing 1,872 pounds with a 529-pound warhead. The range (kilometers) and speed (knots) was two and 42. The Type 91-3 replaced the 91-2 in 1943.

The Japanese Type 04 was a 17.7-inch aircraft weapon that weighed 2,169 pounds and had a 670-pound warhead. The range (kilometers) and speed (knots) were 1.5 and 42. The Type 04 was a further development of the Type 91 that could be launched at speeds over 400 knots. In service by late 1944.

The Japanese Kaiten was a 39.4-inch submarine weapon that weighed 18,300 pounds and had a 3,420-pound warhead. The range (kilometers) and speed (knots) varied from 23 and 30 to 78 and 12. The Kaiten was a manned suicide torpedo. Although 330 were put into service, only one US ship (fleet oil tanker *Mississinewa* at ULITHI Atoll in the CAROLINE ISLANDS, in November 1944) is known for certain to have been sunk by one, although it has been suggested that the heavy cruiser *Indianapolis* was actually sunk by a Kaiten and not a torpedo, as *I-58* skipper C. Mochitasura Hashimoto stated at the court-martial of Capt. Charles B. McVay III and in his memoirs.

The US Mark 10 was a 21-inch submarine weapon weighing 2,215 pounds with a 497-pound warhead. The range (kilometers) and speed (knots) were 3.2 and 36. The Mark 10 was a World War I torpedo still in use on "S" class US submarines early in World War II.

The U.S. Mark 15 was a 21-inch surface weapon weighing 3,841 pounds with an 825-pound warhead. The range (kilometers) and speed (knots) varied from 5.5 and 45 to 13.7 and 26. The Mark 15 was the standard destroyer torpedo throughout the war. Compared to the Japanese Type 93 Long

Lance, the Mark 15 was decidedly inferior. But the Type 93 was arguably the most effective torpedo used by any navy during the entire war. The Mark 15 was reliable and effective, even though it was slower and had a 20% smaller warhead than the Type 93.

The US Mark 14 was a 21-inch submarine weapon weighing 3,280 pounds and with a 643-pound warhead. The range (kilometers) and speed (knots) varied from 4.1 and 46 to 8.2 and 31. The Mark 14 was the 1930s replacement for the Mark 10 and got off to a rocky start. It was designed to explode under its target using a magnetic field-detecting detonator. In this way it would do maximum damage ("breaking the ship's back," or generally breaking up the internal structure of the ship). It worked during tests in the Atlantic Ocean. But the conditions in the Pacific turned out to be different enough to make the Mark 14 almost useless. It seems that the magnetic field of ships, because of the Earth's own magnetic influence, took a different shape nearer to the equator. In effect, the magnetic field of metal ships flattened out and extended farther from the ship when near the equator. Thus the magnetic detonator caused the torpedo to explode prematurely. Moreover, the depth-setting mechanism reacted differently to the different water conditions in the Pacific to the extent that the torpedo ran 10 or more feet deeper than it was supposed to. It took nearly a year for submarine captains to convince the navy's torpedo establishment that there was a problem. A new detonator of more conventional design was then put on the Mark 14, but this one also turned out to be unreliable, the "firing pins" being made of relatively cheap metal, which bent at the critical moment. It wasn't until the middle of 1943 that the Mark 14 finally became a reliable torpedo. With more modifications, Mark 14s continued in use until the late 1970s.

The US Mark 13 was a 17.7-inch aircraft weapon that weighed 2,216 pounds and had a 600-pound warhead. The range (kilometers) and speed (knots) were 6.7 and 33. The Mark 13 was the standard US airborne torpedo for most of the war.

While not a bad design, it suffered from the need for low and slow launching speed (50 feet and 110 knots). This caused many lost aircraft, as at that altitude and speed the torpedo bombers were perfect targets for enemy fighters or ships' antiaircraft guns. At MIDWAY, an entire squadron of torpedo bombers carrying Mark 13s was shot down while approaching their targets. In early 1944, some simple modifications were made to the Mark 13 that allowed it to be dropped at a thousand feet and speeds of over 200 knots. By the end of the war, the configuration of the Mark 13 had been tweaked to the point that it could be dropped at 2,400 feet while traveling at over 400 knots. Aside from the height and speed problems, the Mark turned out to be an effective weapon, with 40% of those launched actually hitting a target. The Mark 13 was also used successfully on PT BOATS.

The US Mark 18 was a 21-inch submarine weapon weighing 3,154 pounds and having a 575-pound warhead. The range (kilometers) and speed (knots) were 3.6 and 29. The Mark 18 was an unsuccessful copy of the more effective German G7e submarine torpedo. This model did not leave a track and was a lot cheaper to build than the Mark 14. But while the design could be copied, the reliability of the German original could not. Many Mark 18s were fired late in the war, but submarine captains tended to prefer the older Mark 14.

The US Mark 24 was a 19-inch aircraft weapon weighing 680 pounds and with a 92-pound warhead. The range (kilometers) and speed (knots) were 3.6 and 12. The Mark 24 was the first effective homing torpedo. Four sensors steered it toward the noise of a diving or snorkeling (running on diesel engines via a periscope-type air vent) submarine. The Mark 24 was quite effective, with 346 used and 101 obtaining hits (two-thirds resulting in destroyed subs, the others were badly damaged). Only about 10% of subs attacked with air-dropped depth charges would be sunk or damaged. The Mark 24 was first used in the summer of 1943 against German subs in the Atlantic.

The US Mark 27 was a 19-inch submarine weapon weighing 720 pounds and having a 95–

pound warhead. The range (kilometers) and speed (knots) were 4.5 and 12. The Mark 27 was a submarine version of the Mark 24. Rails were added so that it would fit the submarine's 21–inch torpedo tubes. The Mark 27 was used only against Japanese escorts. It was quite effective, with 106 fired to obtain 33 hits (73% of which were fatal to the surface ship, usually something smaller than a destroyer). First used in mid-1944.

One reason that the flaws in several US torpedo designs were not detected earlier was that they were not fully tested before the war under wartime conditions. This was a way to cut costs, as it saved $8,000–$10,000 for each torpedo not expended, but it would have been money well spent.

As good as tested torpedoes were they all had a "wander" problem. "Wander" is the maximum distance a torpedo will "wander" off course at different ranges. The "wander" of the Japanese Type 93 was typical of all torpedoes. At 15 kilometers, a Type 93 would wander off a straight-line course as much as 500 meters right or left. At 25 kilometers wander was 700 meters and at 30 kilometers it was 1,000 meters. Even at range of a few kilometers, wander could be as much as 100 meters. For this reason, you usually launched a "spread" of torpedoes. Because of "wander" and the fact that they carried only one weapon per aircraft, which had very short ranges, torpedo bombers were a risky proposition.

Ref: Hashimoto, *Sunk*.

Torpedoes, Malfunctions

On at least two occasions US SUBMARINES were sunk by their own torpedoes, which malfunctioned and ran in a circular pattern.

Date	Boat	Area
March 3, 1944	USS *Tulibee* (SS–284)	Palau
October 24, 1944	USS *Tang* (SS–306)	Philippines

Towers, John H. (1885–1955)

Among the most important molders of the US Navy's carrier forces in World War II, John Henry Towers is one of the most unsung heroes of the Pacific War, a man so forgotten that he is often overlooked in most standard works on naval history: He is mentioned barely a dozen times in Samuel Eliot MORISON's 15–volume *History of U.S. Naval Operations in World War II*. A 1906 graduate of the naval Academy, Towers was taught to fly by Glenn Curtis in 1911 and was thereafter closely involved with the development of naval air power, among other feats, taking part in the navy's 1919 transatlantic flight as pilot of *NC-3*. From the early 1920s until 1939 he served as assistant director of naval aviation, as assistant chief of the Bureau of Aeronautics, and as skipper of the carrier *Saratoga*; during breaks he served as an aviation adviser for the London Naval DISARMAMENT Conference Treaty. Chief of the Bureau of Aeronautics from 1939 to 1942, from early 1942 until the end of the war, Towers was the principal naval air officer in the Pacific, serving first as commanding officer, Air Forces, Pacific Fleet, later as deputy commander in chief, Pacific, and once again as chief of the Bureau of Aeronautics. Instrumental in the development of the fast carrier task force, the evolution of AIR GROUP composition, the coordination of carriers with escorts, and the assignment of flying officers as chiefs of staff to non-flying commanders (and vice-versa), Towers' enormous intellectual and administrative powers kept him from active command until virtually the end of the war, when, in August of 1945, he was named commanding officer of the newly formed Second Fast Carrier Force, and later CINCPAC after the surrender of Japan.

Townsville, Australia

Although possessed of only a modest port, Townsville had the distinction of being one of the principal air transport centers in Australia, making it an important air base, of considerable strategic value, as it lay on the northeastern coast of the country.

Toyoda, Soemu (1885–1957)

Soemu Toyoda graduated from the naval academy in 1905. A naval gunnery specialist, his career was impressive, including numerous special assignments and duty as an admiral's aide, along with the usual run of ship and staff posts. In the late 1930s, as a vice admiral, he commanded naval forces during the heavy fighting in China. Opposed to the idea of war with America, Toyoda had little respect for the militant army officers running the government. He spent the early part of the Pacific War commanding naval bases in Japan. In early 1944 he became commander of the Combined Fleet and was ordered to gather his forces for a "decisive battle" against the approaching American naval might. Despite his earlier attitudes toward war with America, he proposed that Japan fight on even after most of the Japanese fleet was destroyed by early 1945. Nevertheless, he accepted the emperor's surrender order. Arrested as a war criminal, he was cleared of culpability for war crimes committed by naval personnel. He had given his sword to Admiral NIMITZ at the end of the war, but Nimitz returned it as a gesture of goodwill in 1952.

Tradition

Tradition is one of the mainstays of a military service. Some customs practiced during the Second World War go back centuries. For example, as late as World War II it was common for old chiefs (chief petty officers, the most senior enlisted men) to say that upon retirement they were going to put an anchor over their shoulder and begin walking inland. When someone asked "Where'd you get the funny fishhook?" they planned to settle down to raise chickens, as far from blue water as physically possible. This is a seaman's joke so old that it is virtually identical to one Homer told in *The Odyssey* nearly 3,000 years ago.

Several other old customs were (and are) still common in the navy. For example, by early 1945 an astute observer aboard a US Navy ship might have gotten a good sense of how soon the war was going to end by noticing that many of the sailors were working on "homecoming" pennants. These are long multicolored streamers that are flown from the mainmast as ships return victorious from a war. It's an ancient tradition, maintained by the old salts since time immemorial. By early 1945, with the fleet operating off Japan, sailors on many ships began sewing homecoming pennants. Most ships had one by the time Japan surrendered in August of 1945, and they can be seen streaming astern from the mainmasts in pictures of ships returning home after the war. By tradition, a homecoming pennant is one foot long for every man aboard who had been away from home a year or more. The longest belonged to "The Big E," the carrier *Enterprise*, which, upon her return to the United States in late 1945, had been continuously away from the 48 states for well over 500 days. Her streamer was so long, in fact, that helium balloons were needed to keep it aloft.

The submarine service preserved another very old maritime tradition. Boats returning from successful war patrols customarily wore a broom at the top of their mainmast. This custom dates back to the 17th century, when the Dutch seadog Michael DeRuyter tied a broom to his mainmast to let everyone know that he had "swept" the seas of enemy ships.

One tradition common to all navies was continued during the war, whenever practical. This was the initiation of pollywogs into Neptune's Kingdom. During these ceremonies, in which men who had never crossed the equator (Pollywogs) were made loyal subjects of King Neptune (the senior enlisted men on the ship), many a fuzz-cheeked seaman and ensign found himself far more worried about the shave that the Shellbacks (old salts) were preparing for him than anything that the enemy was likely to throw his way. Among those so initiated during the war was Secretary of the Navy

Frank Knox. FDR had been initiated during the 1930s.

The Japanese Armed Forces had one interesting custom. When a man was killed in action he was automatically promoted two grades. This, as well as traditional obligations to honor the dead, is one reason why the families of missing Japanese servicemen have often traveled to distant islands in an effort to find the remains of their loved ones. If they prove the guy died in action they receive a better pension.

There was one hoary naval tradition that was not practiced in the US Navy, the awarding of prize money, upon the successful conclusion of a war. Originally a way to organize the division of loot, prize had passed out of fashion in the US Navy shortly after the Spanish-American War. It was a wonderful custom, about which the Civil War Union admiral, David Dixon Porter, who greatly profited from prize, remarked, "Armies loot, Navies take prize." Prize was, however, still awarded in the ROYAL NAVY, and shortly after the end of World War II His Majesty's tars and jollies (sailors and marines) received a rather nice little bonus, amounting to several hundred dollars each for the common seamen, and proportionately more as one went up the ranks.

Tribal Class, British Destroyers

The Tribal Class (named after the great native tribes of the British Empire) marked a significant increase in British destroyer size, being about 30% larger than the previous classes, and set the model for subsequent British destroyer construction. The initial run of 16 ships was built 1936–39. A repeat run of 11 more for Australia and Canada were ordered in 1939, but not all were completed before the end of the war. Several of the Canadian ships and the three Australian ones saw extensive service in the Pacific.

Trincomalee, Ceylon

The principal British naval and air base in the eastern Indian Ocean, in 1942 Trincomalee lacked ex-

tensive facilities, making it of only limited utility. It was raided by the Japanese during their Indian Ocean foray, March–April 1942. The British later expended its facilities.

Trobriand Islands

A small island group off the east coast of NEW GUINEA, the Trobriands (of which Kiriwana is the largest) were noted before the war chiefly for the interesting sexual practices of the natives, made known to the world by various anthropologists. Militarily, their position provided potentially useful sites for air bases from which to dominate the BISMARCKS, and eastern Papua-New Guinea. The Japanese occupied them briefly in mid-1942, but withdrew in September. The Allies ignored them until June of 1943, when they were occupied by the US 158th Regimental Combat Team.

Truk, Carolines

A fine natural harbor in a roomy atoll, with the surrounding islands and islets suitable for several airfields, by late 1941 Truk was well on its way toward becoming one of the most important military bases in the Pacific, being roughly equidistant from New Guinea, GUADALCANAL, and the GILBERT ISLANDS. It was the principal Japanese military base in the South Pacific. Truk was raided repeatedly by US naval aircraft and surface vessels during the course of the war. Although there were initially plans to take the place, these were dropped in favor of neutralizing it, and it remained in Japanese hands throughout the war, though increasingly on starvation rations. Today it possesses one of the most extensive collections of sunken ships in the world.

Truman, Harry S (1884–1972)

Harry S Truman came from a modest background in his native Missouri. Entering retail trade, he sub-

President Harry S Truman makes the formal announcement of the Japanese surrender, Washington, D.C., August 14, 1945.

sequently joined the NATIONAL GUARD in order to improve his business connections. Activated during World War I, Truman proved a very able artillery captain, reputedly the best mule skinner in the war, and, after acquiring that skill, among the best "cussers" in the AEF. After the war he remained in trade and in the National Guard, and entered politics. He did well in the latter two (his partner managed the business quite successfully, however), and by 1939 was a National Guard colonel and a senator. Although he volunteered for active service when the Missouri National Guard was federalized, General George C. MARSHALL urged him to remain in the Senate, where he was a staunch supporter of REARMAMENT. Truman's

chairmanship of one of the numerous congressional committees investigating the war brought him to the attention of President ROOSEVELT, with the result that he was elected vice president in 1944. Although not a member of FDR's inner circle, when Roosevelt died in April of 1945, Truman very quickly assumed control, proving an effective president in the final months of the war.

Truman's decision to use the ATOMIC BOMB is considered in some circles highly controversial, although among military historians it is generally regarded as a logical response to the strategic situation confronting the nation at the time.

Truman's nephew, Louis W. Truman, was a Regular Army officer, and served in the ETO.

Tsuji, Masanohu (1901–1961?)

Probably the most notorious Pacific War criminal to escape justice, Tsuji was a military academy graduate, and one of the most belligerent and nationalistic officers in the emperor's service. A distinguished intelligence officer, he served as a fixer and troubleshooter on numerous fronts: Before the war he helped engineer the takeover of MANCHURIA in 1931, was deeply involved in the CHINA INCIDENT in the mid- and late 1930s, and helped provoke the clash with Russia at Nomonhan in 1939. In anticipation of a general war, he conducted extensive intelligence missions in Southeast Asia and Burma. His meticulous intelligence work and planning were critically important to the Japanese victory in MALAYA. He later served on GUADALCANAL and in Burma.

At the time Japan surrendered he was in Siam, where he joined a Japanese monastery under an assumed name, and later reportedly worked as an adviser to CHIANG KAI-SHEK during the Chinese Civil War. In the late 1940s he returned to Japan, where he managed to avoid trial for, among other things, the murder of an American PILOT in Burma. He subsequently became involved in various nationalist and veterans organizations, and wrote a memoir, *Underground Escape* (1952). In 1961 he took a still unexplained trip to North Vietnam and was never heard from again. He was declared legally dead in 1968.

Tulagi, Solomons

A modest island group off the much larger Florida Island, just a few miles north of GUADALCANAL, Tulagi was the administrative center of the Solomon Islands. It had a fine anchorage, but otherwise had only very rudimentary port facilities. It was the scene of some bitter fighting on 7 August 1942, when the Marines landed there preparatory to their landing on Guadalcanal.

Turner, Richmond Kelly (1885–1961)

The unquestioned master of amphibious warfare during the Second World War, Richmond Kelly Turner graduated from the US Naval Academy in 1908. His early career was typical of that of a junior naval officer of his generation, including sea duty, some staff time, and some schooltime. During World War I he served in battleships, but did not get overseas. After the war he continued in the peacetime routine of the navy until he took flight training in the late 1920s. Thereupon his career began to blossom. He commanded several aviation squadrons, was involved in planning the future of naval aviation, was an adviser to the US delegation at the Geneva Disarmament Conference of 1932, saw some more sea time and staff duty, and in October of 1940 was named director of war plans. In this post he was deeply involved not only in planning the navy's war, but also in developing amphibious doctrine in cooperation with Marines such as Alexander A. VANDEGRIFT. As a result, in mid-1942 he was ordered to the South Pacific to assume command of the task force that landed Vandegrift's First Marine Division on GUADALCANAL. Despite SAVO ISLAND and other setbacks, Turner's tenacity and determination helped keep the Marines on Guadalcanal and they kept Henderson Field in American hands. Thereafter Turner directed numerous amphibious operations with increasing skill and success. In April of 1945 he was named commander, Amphibious Forces, Pacific, comprising the III and V Marine Amphibious Corps, in anticipation of the invasion of Japan, which he would have directed. When peace came he briefly held some minor diplomatic posts, retiring in 1947.

Ref: Dyer, *The Amphibians Came to Conquer.*

Tutuila, U.S. River Gunboat

A small (150-ton) US gunboat on the Yangtze in China, *Tutuila* (PR-4) was caught well up the river when the Japanese invaded China in 1937. In violation of the treaties governing foreign gunboats in Chinese waters, the Japanese refused to permit her to pass through their lines, and she remained upriver thereafter. In air raids on Chungking on July 6–7, 1939 she was almost struck by several Japanese bombs. The same air raids had resulted in the bombing of an American mission church. Despite a Japanese apology, President ROOSEVELT used these two incidents as a pretext not to renew the 1911 United States-Japan commercial treaty, which meant that after January 26, 1940 Japan had to negotiate every transaction with the US government separately.

The ship was again struck by Japanese bombs at Chungking on July 30, 1941. The Japanese government apologized the next day.

Tutuila was eventually turned over to the Chinese Navy as part of LEND-LEASE.

See also PANAY INCIDENT; WARSHIPS U.S., CAPTURED.

Typhoon, British Fighter Bomber

The Typhoon was Britain's first-generation fighter bomber. It entered service in the summer of 1941. Teething problems limited its effectiveness for about a year, but by 1943 the Typhoon was the terror of any enemy ground forces within range. Initially armed with eight .50 caliber machine guns and 1,000 pounds of bombs, this was soon changed to four 20mm cannon and 2,000 pounds of bombs and rockets. Top speed was 410 MPH, and loaded weight was six tons. Typhoons eventually went to the Far East, where they were found to be particularly effective against Japanese shipping. Some 3,300 were produced.

See also AIRCRAFT TYPES, DEVELOPMENT.

Typhoons and Tropical Storms

As if the normal hazards of war were not enough, war at sea adds a few extra. One enemy encountered often during the Pacific War were the ty-phoons ("cyclonic storms," or hurricanes) that regularly sweep across the ocean.

The Pacific Fleet was hit by several typhoons of unusual force during 1944–45.

October 10–18, 1944.   The Third Fleet was operating in the western Pacific, conducting raids on FORMOSA and OKINAWA, when a typhoon passed through the central CAROLINES, battering ULITHI Atoll. Although damage to the fleet was slight, since the eye of the storm passed to its east, heavy seas made some operations difficult, and almost resulted in the abandonment of the light cruiser *Houston* and heavy cruiser AUSTRALIA, both of which were under tow, having just been heavily damaged by enemy action.

December 17–18, 1944.   A small, fast-moving (9 knot) storm blindsided Task Force 38 off the Philippines on December 17, 1944. Over 800 sailors were killed, three destroyers were sunk, and 20 other ships severely damaged, while many aircraft were damaged or destroyed. One reason for the seriousness of this incident may be that Admiral HALSEY—though a "brown shoe" (i.e., flying) admiral—used a battlewagon for his flagship, which was very stable in foul weather, and it has been charged that he underestimated the danger of this storm, because the seas didn't seem so rough to him as he stood on the bridge of his battleship. In addition, the three destroyers lost appear to have been riding high, having pumped out ballast in anticipation of refueling. Another complicating factor may have been that many skippers were relatively young, and had not had years of experience in coping with heavy seas.

January 8–10, 1945.   A typhoon passing nearby in the western Pacific interfered with Task Force 38 air operations against Formosa, the Pescadores, and the RYUKYU ISLANDS.

June 4–5, 1945.   Task Group 38.1 was hit square by a typhoon northeast of the Philippines, and had to lie to until the eye passed over it. Two carriers (*Hornet* and *Bennington*), three cruisers, and several smaller ships were damaged, while 76 aircraft were destroyed and 16 damaged, but only six men lost (swept overboard) and four injured. Having had ample warning, all ships were riding deep, with full ballast.

September 9–10, 1945. Occurring after the surrender of Japan, this was probably the worst of the major storms to hit the fleet, Typhoon Louisa passed 15 miles east of Okinawa. It sank 12 small ships and landing craft, beaching 222 more, and damaging a further 32. Loss of life was considerable. Of the beached and damaged vessels, 52 were considered not worth repairing. Over the next few days, as the storm passed east of Japan and gradually lost force, a number of ships of the Third Fleet were damaged, none seriously. The vessels destroyed had originally been earmarked for Operation Olympic, but were now engaged in preparing to transport troops from Okinawa to Japan for occupation duties. Had the war lasted just a few more days, losses might readily have been far greater.

The "nursery" for Pacific typhoons north of the equator is between 155 and 165 degrees east longitude, and from the equator to about 20 degrees north, at least for most of the year. From January through March it's between 145 and 155 degrees east. Further complicating matters, some ferocious storms form west of Japan in the Sea of Japan and a few even farther north, over land in northeast Siberia, and then gain typhoon-strength as they move out over the water. Most of these "northern" typhoons don't get beyond storm strength (over 34 knots wind), but some do. For every typhoon, there are several storms of (somewhat) lesser ferocity, which can be almost as disruptive as a typhoon, as carrier operations were not possible during most storms, and this made it easier for enemy SUBMARINES to get close to the carriers. All of this storm activity happens smack in the middle of the Central Pacific Theater of Operations. Interestingly, the Great White Fleet had a rough time with a typhoon in about the same area during its around-the-world voyage in 1908, but the navy seems not to have remembered this, despite the fact that some later senior admirals had been on that cruise as junior officers.

Making life even more difficult was the fact that since the Japanese held so many of the central Pacific islands, there was often insufficient meteorological information on the formation of new storms or the paths of existing ones. For this reason the US Navy regularly used submarines to report the weather, and maintained weather stations in China, including several in the Gobi Desert in Inner Mongolia, probably about as far from blue water—perhaps from open water—as the navy has ever operated, until the Apollo Program. The Japanese were not the only enemy ready to hit you while you weren't looking.

U

UDT (Underwater Demolition Team)

Many technological advances in the 1920s and '30s led to unique new weapons systems in World War II. Perhaps the most curious was scuba-diving gear. The use of an air tank and mask allowed a swimmer to stay underwater for an hour or more. This led to two "special weapons": underwater COMMANDOS and manned TORPEDOES. The underwater commandos' primary function was gathering information on beaches to be invaded and clearing some obstacles. This latter task was achieved by having the swimmers attach explosives to man-made obstacles and blow them up. This was particularly useful for obstacles lying on the bottom, but not protruding above the surface. These obstacles were designed to rip the bottoms off landing craft. The UDTs first had to find these (although many were visible at low tide) and then destroy them. The UDTs also went ashore at night to check the condition of the beach, sometimes taking sand samples (which, after analysis, would show what types of vehicles could safely traverse the beach).

Being able to stay underwater for long periods gave these intruders an enormous advantage. With the primitive radars available during World War II, it was possible for small boats or SUBMARINES to get close to heavily defended areas. Naval minefields could be crossed by rubber boats before the divers made their final approach underwater. So the UDTs played an important role in the amphibious war. Realizing, of course, that the Germans and Japanese would take the presence of UDTs as portending an American landing, the US

Navy began using them as part of DECEPTION plans. Special UDTs ("Beach Jumpers") were deliberately sent to explore beaches that no one had any intention of hitting, so that the enemy would believe a landing was imminent. On several occasions the UDTs were particularly successful in diverting enemy attention and resources from a genuine objective.

It was the Italian Navy that first made extensive use of underwater commandos. Transported off an enemy port by submarine or small craft, the divers would swim inside, place MINES on ships' bottoms, and then make their getaway. This technique was particularly successful at Gibraltar, for the Italians were able to turn a merchant ship, interned at a Spanish dock across the Bay of Algeciras, and a nearby villa into secret underwater assault team bases. Divers would enter the water through a secret airlock cut into the ship's bottom, swim across to the British side of the bay, and plant mines on the bottoms of various ships. By timing the mines so that they went off when the ships were far out at sea, the Italians were able to confuse the British as to the causes of various sinkings. The secret base was never detected, and closed down only when Italy joined the Allies.

The US Navy did not get into the UDT business until quite late. Its UDT force was largely the creation of LtCdr Draper L. Kaufman. The first teams were organized in early 1943. They were first used in action in Sicily that July. But it was TARAWA that convinced the navy of the need for UDT. No UDTs served at Tarawa, but it was clear that had they been used to conduct pre-invasion reconnaissance, the Marines would have had a much easier time getting ashore.

UDTs were organized in platoons of three officers and 15 men, with four platoons plus a headquarters platoon (four officers and 20 men) forming a company totaling 96 officers and enlisted men.

The other development that made use of scuba gear was the so-called "human torpedo." These came in two varieties, but both were essentially miniature submarines. One type might best be called an "underwater motorcycle," able to carry two men astride. The Italian Navy developed these shortly before the war, as a vehicle for its UDT teams. Called *Maielli* ("Pigs"), they were used with considerable success to damage British warships in heavily defended ports, the most notable being when two battleships were sunk at their moorings in Alexandria harbor. These devices were so effective that the ROYAL NAVY began its own experiments with "human torpedoes," giving them the more dignified name "Chariots." These were used with some success to sink several ships in Axis-controlled ports in the Mediterranean later in the war. The Japanese also developed a manned torpedo, in the literal sense, a one-man suicide submarine called the "Kaiten Weapon." Over 300 of these were sent to sea to take on Allied shipping. However, they were very inefficient and not particularly useful on the high seas, so that only one Allied ship was sunk. On the other hand, some hundreds of kaiten were available to attack the invasion fleet if the United States had undertaken Operation Olympic, the invasion of Japan. Supporting them would have been thousands of suicide swimmers, men equipped with a simple breathing apparatus who were supposed to walk along the sea floor and hit the bottom of landing craft with bomb-tipped poles. The direct descendant of these World War II scuba warriors is the US Navy SEAL force, and similar commando units in many nations. The adventure continues.

See also TORPEDOES.

Ref: Dwyer, *Seaborne Deception*; Hashimoto, *Sunk*.

Uganda Class, British Light Cruisers

The three Ugandas, sometimes referred to as the "Second Group" of the "Colony Class," were a rather successful attempt by the ROYAL NAVY to improve the stability of the FIJI CLASS light cruisers by reducing the number of 6-inch guns from 12 to nine to save weight. They were actually all laid down in 1939, as part of the original order. Launched in 1941–42, their completion was delayed due to the pressures of war. As a result, the stability problems of the original eight Fijis having become evident, they were redesigned and completed in 1943. All accompanied the Royal Navy's carrier task force in the Pacific during 1945. *Uganda* (1939–1941–1943) and *Newfoundland* (1939–1941–1943) accompanied the British Pacific Fleet in 1945, the former manned by a Canadian crew. *Uganda* was scrapped in 1961, *Newfoundland* and *Ceylon* (1939–1942–1943) were sold to Peru in 1959, and later scrapped 1979–80.

The Swiftsure Class, built 1941–45, was quite similar, being a few hundred tons heavier and a foot wider, to improve stability still further. *HMS Swiftsure* (1941–1943–1944) served with the British Pacific Fleet in 1945. She was scrapped in 1962.

Ujeland, Carolines

One of many atolls in the CAROLINES with a roomy anchorage, but otherwise unprovided with port facilities. The war passed it by.

Ulithi, Carolines

A large atoll, providing an enormous protected anchorage for ships and some land for support facilities and air bases, Ulithi had been wholly neglected by the Japanese, who had owned it for over 25 years. It had, however, come to the notice of US Navy planners as a potential advanced base for even more years than that. Ulithi became the major forward fleet base for the final US advance against Japan.

Underage Soldiers, Sailors, and Marines

It is estimated that several hundred boys under the age of 17 managed to enlist during World War II using false documents. The youngest combatant in the armed forces during World War II (and probably the youngest since the Spanish-American War, if not the Civil War) was Calvin Graham (1930–1992) of Fort Worth, Texas. Early in 1942 12–year-old Graham forged his mother's name to enlistment papers, and joined the navy. He served in the battleship SOUTH DAKOTA during the GUADALCANAL Campaign, in which he was wounded and decorated. His correct age having meanwhile been established to the satisfaction of the ship's skipper, Capt. T. L. Gatch, when *South Dakota* returned to the United States for repairs, Graham was given a one-way pass to his original recruiting station, which didn't know what to do with him. Meanwhile, Gatch having been transferred from the ship, when Graham failed to return, he was classed as a deserter, arrested, and jailed. Released after he finally managed to convince the navy that he was only 13, Graham was promptly stripped of his decorations and campaign ribbons, given a dishonorable discharge, and denied medical benefits because he had enlisted under false premises. Graham, who later reenlisted for a time in the navy after attaining the proper age, was eventually the beneficiary of special legislation in May 1978, which restored pay, decorations, and benefits lost upon his original discharge. By a curious twist of fate, Graham's division officer while aboard *South Dakota* was Sargent Shriver, who was later President John F. Kennedy's brother-in-law, while another of his shipmates was a future English teacher of one of the authors of this work, serving as a steersman.

The shabby treatment accorded Graham by the navy stands in contrast to that accorded Jimmy Baker (1931–   ). At 12 Baker enlisted in the Marine Corps. He served eight months, fortunately not in combat, before being discovered, and was promptly issued an honorable discharge. Another Marine, PFC Jacklyn H. Lucas (1928–   ) had enlisted when just 16, and was only six days over 17 when he won the MEDAL OF HONOR on IWO JIMA.

The actual number of underaged American boys who served in the war will never be known, as many of them were never detected. Nor can the number killed in action be determined.

Unicorn, British Light Aircraft Carrier

Although they built her as an aircraft maintenance and depot ship, intended to support fleet carriers by servicing and supplying aircraft, the British soon found that *Unicorn* (1939–1941–1943) was eminently suitable as a light, if slow, carrier. Lacking the extensive protection preferred by British carrier designers, her aircraft capacity was equal to that of the ILLUSTRIOUS CLASS fleet carriers. She began her wartime service during the Salerno landings in September 1943, later served as a convoy escort in the Atlantic, and then went to the Pacific in early 1945, where she supported the OKINAWA landings and operations against the Japanese Home Islands. Scrapped in 1959.

Uniforms, Sailors

Anyone who has read the book or seen the film *Mister Roberts* will recall that one of the captain's hobbyhorses was that all men had to wear their shirts at all times, even when working in the ship's stifling hold. This was not a figment of the author's imagination. One of the numerous petty naval regulations during the Pacific War was the mandatory wearing of shirts, with sleeves rolled down at all times. US sailors were also prohibited from wearing short pants, unlike their Commonwealth comrades. As a result, while Australian and New Zealand sailors generally sported terrific tans, being practically naked while on duty and most of the rest of the time as well, American bluejackets tended to be rather pale. This may seem to have been a manifestation of militaristic authoritarian bureaucraticism, but it was actually a very intelligent and reasonable measure.

Quite early in the war some prescient US Navy medical personnel noted that there were significant differences in the severity of burns suffered by men who had been wearing shirts and those who had not, despite the fact that they had come through the same infernos. A little experimentation soon determined that the navy's standard blue cotton denim work shirts and jeans actually offered considerable protection from burns, especially "flash" burns from onboard explosions. If flames touched a man's bare skin, it quickly began to burn, but if they licked at his shirt, that burned first, and the additional few seconds were often enough to save a man's life, not to mention a good deal of his skin. Also, the shirt offered some protection against short but intense bursts of high, searing heat. So the orders went out and American sailors sweated through the rest of the war. Hotter and paler than their Commonwealth counterparts, they also tended to get burned less often.

By the way, the flash protection works only with cotton. Polyester burns hotter and faster, and in the process adheres to human flesh, causing extremely serious burns. But then, during World War II the navy issued only cotton uniforms.

The one common exception to these dress regulations was on board destroyers. The "tin can sailors" tended to dress any way they pleased, at least when not in immediate danger of engaging the enemy (at which point the long pants and long-sleeve shirts went on). Their workaday "uniforms" consisted of regulation dungarees cut down to shorts, homemade sandals, and sundry improvised headgear. Earrings and pigtails were often quite popular, as were beards. Since senior officers rarely visited destroyers, the bohemian lifestyle was maintained until the ships returned to port, at which point a certain amount of dress discipline was restored. For a time a similar regime prevailed under Captain T. L. Gatch on the battleship SOUTH DAKOTA. Gatch, a wonderfully eccentric fellow (he used to read the lesson at divine services every Sunday), was allowed to get away with this because his "wild men" proved the best shots in the fleet, even if they happened to be virtually—and sometimes

literally—naked at times. But after he was promoted upstairs a less understanding skipper came aboard and the men had to tidy up.

See also UNDERAGE SOLDIERS, SAILORS, AND MARINES.

United States Army

Although the main event for the US Army was the war against Germany, nearly a quarter of the army's total divisional strength (21 of 89) ended up in the Pacific. Army units served in all parts of the Pacific Theater, some even getting into action in Burma and the NETHERLANDS EAST INDIES. The army conducted 17 division-sized assault landings, plus many others on a smaller scale (the Eighth Army alone conducted 58 amphibious landings), so that the army actually "hit the beach" more often than the Marine Corps.

Initially, army units were not well prepared for the unique kind of fighting they encountered in the Pacific. The army had been focused on affairs in Europe for a long time, and unit organization, doctrine, equipment, and training were not always well suited to the terrain most typical in the Pacific (jungle and swamp), nor to Japanese tactics. In addition, several of the first units to go into action were from the NATIONAL GUARD, and these sometimes experienced leadership, manpower, and training problems, some of them caused by the character of the Guard itself, but many by the Regulars' lack of confidence in the Guardsmen. The army's attitude toward infantry also created difficulties, as it was assumed that the infantry had the least need for quality manpower.

In time, many of these problems were ironed out (albeit that the manpower procurement and replacement problem was never properly resolved), and army units generally did well. Special training programs were set up in the Pacific, to get new troops in shape for the unique kind of fighting encountered in the tropics. Although the Pacific is generally regarded as a maritime theater, an awful lot of ground fighting went on. Aside from China, which tied up more Japanese troops than all the other areas of the theater combined, there was considerable ground combat in Burma and on many of the islands, from the Philippines in 1941–42 to OKINAWA in 1945.

Ref: Perret, *There's a War to Be Won; United States Army in World War II*.

United States Army, Divisions

Some prewar estimates by military planners placed the maximum possible mobilization effort of the United States at 334 divisions. In September 1941 less optimistic army planners projected that the nation would be able to mobilize 215 divisions, exclusive of the Marine Corps. As late as October 1943 they were estimating as many as 105. In fact, the maximum number of divisions in the army was 90, a figure attained in January 1944, which dropped to 89 when the Second Cavalry Division was disbanded a few months later. Even after including the six Marine divisions, in relative terms this was a very low number. With nearly 140 million people by the end of the war, the US Army and Marines managed to create 95 divisions at peak strength, while Australia, with 7.2 million people (5% of the United States), for a time maintained 10 divisions (10.4% of the US division total).

There were several reasons why the number of divisions raised by the United States was relatively low. Unlike most countries, the United States maintained not only a very large army (c. eight million men), but also a large air force (c. three million), and very large sea services (c. three million—navy, Coast Guard, and Marines taken together). In addition, the US Army put a lot of manpower into non-divisional formations. There were, for example, about 50 independent infantry regiments, 20 separate tank groups, 16 cavalry reconnaissance groups, and two separate cavalry regiments, not to mention numerous independent battalions of all arms. Altogether, in mid-1944 there were nearly 1,300 non-divisional combat battalions of infantry, armor, cavalry, and artillery, which, if organized into proper divisions, would have almost doubled the number available. In fact,

about 45% of US combat forces were in non-divisional formations, a figure that greatly exceeded that of other armies (the Soviets maintained about 20% of their combat strength in independent units, and the Germans only about 10%) but was more or less matched by the Marine Corps. Another factor in reducing the number of American divisions available, was the insistence by the army that all divisions be maintained at full strength. In most other armies, particularly those of the totalitarian states (Germany, Russia, and Japan), divisions fought until they had exhausted their manpower, whereupon they were disbanded or rebuilt. US divisions received a continuous flow of "replacements," which kept them at relatively full strength even in the most serious circumstances.

In any case, the 89 divisions the US Army did field gave a good account of themselves. The following descriptions cover those that served in the Pacific. Note that the divisional CASUALTIES can be better appreciated if you keep in mind that most of them were incurred by a division's nine infantry battalions, each of which contained only about 500 to 600 actual infantrymen (or other specialists always at the front). Divide the casualties by ten to get a rough idea of how many losses the infantry in each of these infantry battalions took. Infantry divisions took over two-thirds of all US casualties in World War II. Many troops were wounded more than once. In the course of the war, some battalions had to replace nearly all their infantry at least once because of incapacitating wounds and deaths.

First Cavalry Division. Active as a mounted outfit in the Regular Army since 1921, the division was dismounted in 1942 and reorganized as an infantry division on a special T/O&E (two brigades, each of two dismounted cavalry regiments, totaling 12 infantry battalions, plus four battalions of 105mm howitzers, a medium tank battalion, a reconnaissance troop, an engineer battalion, and sundry service and support units). It was the "lightest" infantry division in the army, with only about 11,000 men. Reaching Australia in July of 1943, the division fought in NEW GUINEA, the BIS-

MARCKS, and the Philippines, before going to Japan on occupation duty, where it remained after the war. Casualties totaled 4,055, including 970 (23.9%) combat fatalities. Two men from the division won the MEDAL OF HONOR.

Sixth Infantry Division. Activated in the Regular Army in October 1939, the division arrived in HAWAII in July 1943. From January 1944 it saw action in New Guinea and the Philippines, and afterward served on occupation duty in Korea, where it was inactivated in 1949. Casualties were 2,370, including 514 (21.7%) dead. Two men earned the Medal of Honor.

Seventh Infantry Division. Activated in July 1940 from Regular Army personnel, to whom were added a regiment of National Guardsmen from California. The division undertook the first opposed US Army amphibious landing of the Pacific War when it took Attu from the Japanese, May 11–29, 1943. Subsequently served in the Marshall Islands, the Philippines, and OKINAWA, ending the war on occupation duty in Japan and Korea, where it remained. Combat casualties were 9,212, of whom 2,334 (25.3%) were killed in action or mortally wounded. It had the highest losses of any army division in the Pacific, but more than 20 divisions in the ETO had higher losses. Three men won the Medal of Honor.

11th Airborne Division. The only one of five US airborne divisions to serve in the Pacific, the division was activated in February 1943 from volunteers. It shipped out for the South Pacific in May 1944, and served in New Guinea and the Philippines, where it earned the unique distinction of being the only airborne division to undertake an amphibious assault, landing at Nasugubu, Luzon, the Philippines, on 31 January 1945. Although individual battalions and regiments made a number of combat jumps, it never made a division-sized jump. It incurred 2,431 casualties, of whom 614 (25.3%) were killed or died of wounds. The division remained on active duty for many years after the war. Two men won the Medal of Honor.

12th Infantry Division. A postwar redesignation of the old "Philippine Division" (See PHILIPPINE SCOUTS). Two other Scout divisions were planned postwar, to have been designated the 14th and 16th Infantry Divisions.

23rd Infantry Division. A postwar redesignation of the "Americal Division" (see page 629).

24th Infantry Division. A Regular Army unit organized as the garrison of Hawaii in 1921, the division was known as the Hawaiian Division until "triangularized" and redesignated as the 24th Infantry Division in the summer of 1941, surplus personnel going to form the 25th Infantry Division. The division lost some personnel in the Japanese attack on PEARL HARBOR. It remained on garrison duty in Hawaii until transferred to Australia, arriving in September 1943. The division saw action in New Guinea, the Caroline Islands, and the Philippines, before going to Japan on occupation duty, where it remained after the war. Casualties totaled 7,012, including 1,689 (24.1%) deaths by combat. Three men won the Medal of Honor.

25th Infantry Division. Activated in Hawaii in July 1940, from elements of the old Regular Army Hawaiian Division (the balance becoming the 24th Infantry Division), to which a NATIONAL GUARD regiment from the state of Washington was added. Headquartered at Schofield Barracks, the division incurred some casualties during the Japanese attack on Pearl Harbor. It served as part of the garrison of Hawaii until December 1942, when it went to GUADALCANAL, subsequently seeing action in the Northern SOLOMONS and the Philippines, suffering 5,432 casualties, 1,497 (27.6%) of them battle deaths. The division remained in Japan on occupation duty after the war. Six men won the Medal of Honor.

27th Infantry Division. National Guardsmen from New York, federalized in October 1940, this division was the first to ship out for the Pacific Theater, arriving in Hawaii from the West Coast in March 1942, while still based on a "square" T/O&E. It was the last in the army to retain a "square" T/O&E, not being triangularized until September 1942. When the division invaded MAKIN ISLAND in the GILBERTS in late 1943, some Marine officers suggested that its performance was not optimal. The division subsequently took part in the capture of SAIPAN in June 1944, and fought on Okinawa the following spring. On Saipan the division became the focus of the "War of the SMITHS," when MG Holland "Howling Mad" SMITH (SMC), in overall command of the landing force, relieved division commander MG Ralph Smith. The division suffered 6,533 battle casualties, of whom 1,844 (28.2%) were deaths from combat. The division was inactivated at the end of 1945. Three men won the Medal of Honor.

31st Infantry Division. A National Guard unit (Alabama, Florida, Louisiana, and Mississippi) federalized in November 1940, the division saw action in New Guinea and the Philippines, incurring 1,733 casualties, of whom 414 (23.9%) were killed or mortally wounded, before being inactivated at the end of 1945.

32nd Infantry Division. A National Guard division (Michigan and Wisconsin), the 32nd arrived in Australia in May 1942, and served in New Guinea, the Philippines, and Japan, incurring 7,268 casualties, of whom 1,985 (27.3%) were combat deaths. Inactivated in Japan at the end of 1945.

The 32nd Division, called into federal service in October 1940, was the first army division to enter combat in the Pacific, after the surrender in the Philippines, during the BUNA-GONA CAMPAIGN in New Guinea in late 1942. The division's performance was denigrated by many senior personnel, but considering the state of its training, the failure of American supply service, the unwillingness of higher headquarters (i.e., Douglas MACARTHUR) to understand the character of the terrain or the nature of Japanese resistance, and the excessive optimism about American martial skills, it appears that the division performed about as well as any could have in the circumstances. The division went on to be one of the best fighting divisions in the Pacific. Japanese LG Tomoyuki YAMASHITA, "The Tiger of Malaya," probably Japan's best field commander, who commanded the Japanese defense of Luzon in 1945, rated it as the best American division in that campaign. This outfit took a beating. Eleven of its men won the Medal of Honor.

33rd Infantry Division. National Guardsmen from Illinois, the division was federalized in March 1941. It reached Hawaii in July 1943 and went on to the South Pacific in May 1944, seeing action in New Guinea and the Philippines. It suffered 2,426 casualties, including 497 (20.5%) deaths. Inactivated in Japan in February 1946. Three men earned the Medal of Honor.

37th Infantry Division. National Guardsmen from Ohio, federalized in October 1940. Arrived in FIJI, then considered a possible Japanese objective, in June 1942, thereafter seeing combat in the Northern Solomons and the Philippines. The division suffered 5,960 casualties, of whom 1,344 (22.6%) were battle deaths. Inactivated at the end of 1945. Seven men were awarded the Medal of Honor.

38th Infantry Division. A National Guard organization (Indiana, Kentucky, and West Virginia) federalized in January 1941, the division saw action in New Guinea and the Philippines, suffering 3,464 battle casualties, including 784 (22.6%) deaths, before being released from federal service in November 1945. One man won the Medal of Honor.

40th Infantry Division. Composed of California National Guardsmen called into federal service in March 1941, the 40th Infantry Division deployed to Hawaii in September 1942. In April 1944 it went into action on NEW BRITAIN, in the Bismarcks, fighting thereafter in the Philippines. Combat casualties were 3,052, of whom 748 (24.7%) were killed in action or mortally wounded. Inactivated in April of 1946. One man won the Medal of Honor.

41st Infantry Division. A National Guard unit (Washington, Montana, Oregon, and Idaho), federalized in September 1940. In the summer of 1941 Gen. MARSHALL considered this division sufficiently well trained for overseas deployment and offered it to Gen. MacArthur, in the Philippines. The latter rejected the offer, although it would have more than doubled the number of active troops under his command. This saved the division from defeat and captivity, and probably would not have slowed the Japanese down that much, as US troops defending the Philippines were brought down more by supply problems than anything else. The division deployed to Australia in April 1942. It served in New Guinea and the Philippines, and helped occupy Japan, suffering 4,260 casualties, 960 (22.5%) of them combat fatalities. Inactivated in Japan at the end of 1945. Two men won the Medal of Honor.

43rd Infantry Division. National Guardsmen from New England (Maine, Vermont, Rhode Island, and Connecticut), the division was federalized in February 1941. It reached NEW ZEALAND in October 1942, and fought thereafter in New Guinea, the Solomons, where it was granted the army's first "Assault Arrowhead" (awarded to units making amphibious or airborne assault), for its landing on Rendova, 30 June 1943, and the Philippines. Casualties were 6,026, of whom 1,406 (23.3%) were combat-related fatalities. Inactivated in October 1945. Two men won the Medal of Honor.

77th Infantry Division. Activated from New York State reservists and draftees in March 1942, the division was shipped to newly liberated GUAM in July 1944, and thereafter saw combat in the Philippines and Okinawa. Casualties were 7,461, of whom 1,850 (24.8%) were battle-related deaths. The division performed occupation duties in Japan until it was inactivated in March 1946. Six men won the Medal of Honor.

81st Infantry Division. Activated in June 1942 from draftees, the division reached the central Pacific in September 1944, fighting in the PALAU ISLANDS and the Philippines. It incurred 2,314 casualties, of whom 515 (22.3%) were killed in action or died of wounds.

86th Infantry Division. Activated from draftees in December 1942, the Battle of the Bulge caused the army to cancel plans to ship the division to the Pacific virtually as it was ready to board the transports in SAN FRANCISCO. It arrived in Europe in March 1945, the last US infantry division to reach the ETO, and saw action during the final drive into Germany. Upon the surrender of Germany, the division was shipped back to the United States, given 30 days leave, and then sent to the Pacific. The troops learned of Japan's surrender aboard their transports. The division landed in the Philippines in early September 1945, and it remained there until inactivated at the end of 1945. Casualties in Europe had been 785, of whom 161 (20.5%) had been killed in action or mortally wounded. With the 97th Infantry Division, this was the only US division to serve in both theaters of war.

93rd Infantry Division. Activated in May 1942, mostly from black draftees but including the Regular Army's 25th Infantry Regiment. The division arrived in the South Pacific in February 1944 and saw some action in New Guinea and the Northern Solomons, mostly in "mopping up" operations. At no time did the division serve as a unit. Combat casualties were 135 officers and men, including 17 (12.6%) killed in action (12) or died of wounds (5), the smallest loss of any US division committed to combat. The division was inactivated in February 1946.

96th Infantry Division. Activated from draftees in August 1942, the division reached the Pacific in mid–1944 and saw action in the Philippines and Okinawa. Casualties totaled 8,812, including 2,036 (23.1%) deaths. It was inactivated in February 1946. Five men won the Medal of Honor.

97th Infantry Division. Activated from draftees in February 1943, in December 1944 the Battle of the Bulge caused the army to cancel plans to ship the division to the Pacific. Sent to Europe in February 1945, it saw action in the final offensive into

Germany. Upon the surrender of Germany, the division was shipped back to the United States, given 30 days leave, and then shipped to the Pacific, arriving in Japan for occupation duty in late September 1945, where it remained until inactivated at the end of March 1946. Casualties in Europe had been 979, of whom 217 (22.2%) had been killed in action or mortally wounded. With the 86th Infantry Division, this was the only US division to serve in both theaters of war.

98th Infantry Division. Activated from draftees in September 1942, the division shipped to the Pacific in mid–1944 but remained on garrison duty in Hawaii thereafter, one of only three US divisions that did not see combat in the war (the others were the Second Cavalry Division, disbanded in North Africa in 1944, and the 13th Airborne Division, in Europe). In August of 1945 the division went to Japan on occupation duty, and was inactivated there in February 1946.

Americal Division. Activated in NEW CALEDONIA during May 1942 from elements of Task Force 6814, a conglomeration of mostly miscellaneous National Guard units (primarily from Illinois, Massachusetts, and North Dakota), under MG Alexander PATCH. Taking its name from "America" and "New Caledonia," it was the only American division not activated on US soil. Saw action on Guadalcanal, in the Northern Solomons, and the Philippines, suffering 4,050 casualties, of whom 1,157 (28.7%) were killed in action or died of wounds. Inactivated in late 1945, the division was subsequently given the numerical designation "23rd Infantry Division" and assigned to the Regular Army. One man won the Medal of Honor.

CAM (Combined Army-Marine) Division. A provisional division-sized task force created in January 1943 to facilitate the pursuit of the Japanese in the final weeks of the Guadalcanal Campaign. It incorporated the army's 147th Infantry Regiment (Separate) and 182nd Infantry (Americal Division), plus the Sixth Marine Regiment (Second Marine Division), with the artillery of the Amer-

ical Division, under the control of the headquarters of the Second Marine Division. The CAM Division was disbanded in February 1943.

Hawaiian Division. See 24th Infantry Division, page 626.

Philippine Division. See PHILIPPINE SCOUTS, separate entry.

Ref: Stanton, *Order of Battle.*

United States Army, Army Air Forces, Numbered Air Forces

A numbered air force was the administrative equivalent of a numbered army, usually operating directly under an army group or theater commander. The USAAF organized 16 numbered air forces in the war (the First through 15th, plus the 20th), 10 of which had some connection to the Pacific Theater.

Air Force	Operational Area
Second	Washington, Oregon, Northern California
Fourth	Central and Southern California
Fifth	Southwest Pacific, under MacArthur
Sixth	Panama Canal Zone
Seventh	Central Pacific, under Nimitz
Tenth	India and Burma
Eleventh	Alaska and the Aleutians
Thirteenth	Southeast Pacific, under MacArthur
Fourteenth	China
Twentieth	Marianas and Japan (B–29s)

Ref: Craven and Cate, eds., *The Army Air Forces in World War II.*

United States Army, Engineer Special Brigades

Engineer Special Brigades, initially designated Engineer Amphibious Brigades, were very large formations (initially about 7,350 men, later reduced to some 7,100) designed to facilitate landings on enemy-held beaches. Each brigade was capable of supporting the landing of one or more divisions. Their particular utility was in a shore-to-shore landing, where troops could be loaded into landing craft on a beach, escorted a short distance, and then landed on a hostile beach. The US Army raised seven Engineer Special Brigades during World War II, including a provisional one for the Normandy Invasion. One of the brigades served in both the ETO and the Pacific, three others operated only in the Pacific, while the other two regular ones served in the ETO and were en route to the Pacific when Japan surrendered.

An Engineer Special Brigade consisted of three Engineer Boat and Shore Regiments, which had two battalions, one a "boat" battalion, operating landing craft to get troops and equipment ashore, and the other a "shore" battalion, which organized the beach. In addition, each brigade had an artillery battery (for self-defense), two ordnance companies (to repair weapons), a maintenance battalion (to repair other equipment), a quartermaster battalion (to organize and move supplies), and an Amphtrac company (to facilitate the movement of supplies from transports offshore or from one point on the beach to another). During an operation it was not at all unusual for an ESB to be reinforced with as many as four or five independent Boat and Shore regiments or individual battalions. Each brigade had 540 landing craft, 32 command boats, and 72 miscellaneous craft, such as patrol boats, fire support boats, salvage boats, floating workshops, and so forth. Those serving in the Pacific were:

The First Engineer Special Brigade. Activated in Massachusetts in January 1942, the brigade served in North Africa, December 1942–July 1943, supported the landings in Sicily and at Salerno, June-September 1943, and then those at Utah Beach, Normandy, from D-day through September 1944. The brigade was then transferred to the Pacific via the United States from December 1944 to February 1945 (the troops being given 30 days leave during the movement), and supported the landings on OKINAWA in the spring of 1945. Preparing to support the invasion of Japan when the war ended, the brigade served for a time as part of the occupation force in Japan before being inacti-

vated there in February 1946. No other ESB saw such extensive service.

Second Engineer Special Brigade. Formed in June 1942 in Massachusetts, the brigade arrived in Australia in April 1943, and supported the landings at Oro Bay, New Guinea, October 1943, and on Leyte, October 1944. Preparing for the invasion of Japan when the war ended, it facilitated the occupation of Japan, and was inactivated in California in late 1946.

Third Engineer Special Brigade. Organized in Massachusetts in August 1942, the brigade deployed to the South Pacific in June 1944, and supported landings in New Guinea, July 1944, BIAK, September 1944, and in the southern Philippines in early 1945, where it ended the war. It was inactivated in Oregon in December 1945.

Fourth Engineer Special Brigade. Activated in February 1943 in Massachusetts, the brigade deployed to New Guinea in May 1944, and supported the landings on Morotai, in September 1944, and at Lingayen Gulf, Luzon, in January 1945. Preparing to support the invasion of Japan when the war ended, it took part in the occupation of Japan, where it was inactivated in April 1946.

See also AMPHIBIOUS OPERATIONS, LOGISTICAL ARRANGEMENTS; UNITED STATES ARMY, FORCES IN TRANSIT, 12 AUGUST 1945.

Ref: Stanton, *Order of Battle*.

United States Army, Forces in Transit, August 12, 1945

At the time Japan surrendered the United States was in the midst of redeploying large forces from the European Theater to the Pacific, for use in the second phase of the projected invasion of Japan. Two divisions that had served in the ETO, the 86th and 97th Infantry, were already in the Pacific at the time of the surrender, although neither had seen active service.

Army Headquarters. First Army headquarters, staff, and service elements were reorganizing to

Some of the happiest people at the news of the surrender of Japan were US troops in Europe and America scheduled to ship to the Pacific for the invasion of Japan. In Paris, soldiers at the "Rainbow Corner Red Cross Club" celebrate.

take part in Operation Coronet. Fifth and Ninth Army headquarters, staff, and service elements were preparing for redeployment to China, where they were to command mostly Chinese forces against the Japanese.

Armored Divisions. The 13th and 20th, which been only lightly engaged in the ETO, were training in California.

Engineer Special Brigades. The Fifth and Sixth, which had taken part in several invasions, including Normandy, were training in Florida when Japan surrendered.

Infantry Divisions. The Second, Fourth, Fifth, Eighth, 44th, 87th, 95th, and 104th Infantry Divisions were all training in the United States.

Mountain Division. The 10th Mountain Division was on trains bound from Virginia to Colorado, where it was to train for operations on Honshu.

Ref: Stanton, *Order of Battle.*

United States Army, Other Notable Units

In addition to divisions, the US Army raised a large number of non-divisional and specialized units for various duties. Some of the more notable were:

First Provisional Tank Group. Organized in the Philippines in November 1941; supported US and Philippine troops in the defense of Luzon, during the retreat to BATAAN, and in the defense of Bataan, until the surrender in April 1942. The group comprised two tank battalions and an ordnance company. The 192nd Light Tank Battalion consisted of four companies, and had been activated in the United States in December 1940 from NATIONAL GUARD light tank companies from Wisconsin, Illinois, Ohio, and Kentucky. The 194th Light Tank Battalion, of three companies, was activated in the United States in March 1941, from National Guard tank companies from Minnesota, Missouri, and California (a fourth company was created, but did not ship out with the battalion). Both battalions reached the Philippines in late September 1941. They had a total of 108 Stuart M-3 TANKS. The group repeatedly engaged the Japanese during the retreat to Bataan, and was virtually destroyed in combat.

First Special Reconnaissance Battalion. Organized as the 5217th Recon Battalion in October 1943, from Filipino personnel in Australia. Initially based in NEW GUINEA, and later on Leyte, the battalion sent special reconnaissance details into the Philippines by air and submarine. It was disbanded in Manila in August 1945.

First Special Service Force. Organized in 1942, from American and Canadian personnel, the 1st SSF was essentially a stripped-down division of three specialized regiments, with very small contingents of artillery, combat support, and service forces, totaling about 7,000 men. It was trained to fight in deep winter, in jungles, mountains, and swamps, in amphibious and airborne operations, and as COMMANDOS. Committed to action in the unopposed KISKA landings in mid–1943, later that year the First SFF was shipped to Europe, where it took part in the Anzio operation, turning in an heroic performance securing the right flank during the protracted struggle for the beachhead. After the Anzio breakout, however, both US and Canadian brass concluded that the First SFF consumed too much quality manpower, which might otherwise serve to boost the performance of regular formations, and it was broken up. The battle honors of the First SSF were later assigned to the 474th Infantry Regiment.

Sixth Ranger Battalion. Organized at HOLLANDIA, New Guinea, from the 98th Field Artillery Battalion in September 1944, the battalion saw action in New Guinea and in the liberation of Leyte and Luzon. It was inactivated in late 1945.

24th Infantry Regiment. A non-divisional regiment, the regiment was one of the army's four regiments of "Colored" regulars organized after the Civil War. Forming the core of the 24th RCT, the regiment was sent to the Pacific in early 1944. It performed mopping up and occupation duties on BOUGAINVILLE in March-May 1944, on SAIPAN and TINIAN from December 1944 to March 1945, and on OKINAWA in July-August 1945, seeing some action against Japanese holdouts. The regiment returned to the United States from Okinawa in 1946.

112th Cavalry Regiment. A Texas National Guard unit, the regiment was federalized in November 1940 and deployed without its HORSES to NEW CALEDONIA in August 1942. The regiment performed garrison duties as horse CAVALRY, using livestock procured in Australia, which the men had to train themselves. Dismounted and converted to infantry in Australia May–June 1943. With the 148th Field Artillery Battalion attached, the 112th Cavalry RCT occupied Woodlark Island and fought elsewhere in the northern SOLOMONS and on New Guinea, before being attached to the First Cavalry Division, with which it remained through the Philippine Campaign. Because the regiment consisted of dismounted cavalry, it had only some 1,500 men, about half that of an infantry regiment, a matter that commanders sometimes forgot, leading them to give it tasks for which it was too weak. It was inactivated in Japan in January 1946. Two of its men won the MEDAL OF HONOR.

124th Cavalry Regiment. Part of the Texas National Guard, the regiment was federalized in November 1940 and deployed to India as an infantry unit in mid–1942. Attached to Task Force Mars in mid–1944, it was flown into Myitkyina, Burma, in

October of that year and served with TF Mars until inactivated in southern China in July 1945. At times during the campaign elements served mounted. One of its men won the Medal of Honor.

147th Infantry Regiment.   A unit of the Ohio National Guard, the regiment was activated in October 1940 as part of the 37th Infantry Division, becoming a separate infantry regiment when the division was "triangularized"; deployed to FIJI in May 1942. It entered combat for the first time on Guadalcanal in November 1942, literally shoulder-to-shoulder with the Marines (the situation being so critical that the Guardsmen were sent into the Marine ranks), and fought to the end of the campaign. Thereafter the regiment served entirely as a garrison or mopping-up force on various islands, including IWO JIMA and Okinawa. It was inactivated in Washington State in December 1945.

158th Infantry Regiment.   A unit of the Arizona National Guard, the regiment was federalized along with the rest of the 45th Infantry Division in the "First Increment," September 1940. When the division was triangularized, the regiment became a non-divisional one. There were an unusual number of Native Americans in the regiment, and Company F was reputedly composed mostly of Pueblo Indians. Shipped to the PANAMA CANAL for jungle training in December 1941. Shipped to the South Pacific in early 1943, the regiment formed the core of the 158th RCT (with the 147th Field Artillery Battalion), occupied the TROBRIAND ISLANDS and fought on NEW BRITAIN in 1943, and on New Guinea from May through July 1944, before going on to fight in the Philippines, where it ended the war. Nicknamed the "Bushmasters," it was inactivated in Japan in January 1946.

475th Infantry Regiment.   See 5307th Composite Unit, Provisional, below.

503rd Parachute Infantry Regiment.   A separate regiment, the 503rd Infantry was organized in February 1942 from two independent parachute battalions raised earlier. It arrived in Australia in November 1942 and was shipped to New Guinea in August 1943, where it served for over a year, and later fought in the Philippines. It made three operational air drops, at Nadzab, New Guinea, in September 1943, and at Noemfoor, a small island north of New Guinea, in July 1944—both of which were unopposed—and on CORREGIDOR, in Manila Bay, the Philippines, in February 1945, against stout resistance. This was the only US combat jump of the Pacific War. The regiment was inactivated in California at the end of 1945. Two men won the Medal of Honor.

5332nd Brigade.   See Task Force Mars, below.

5307th Composite Unit, Provisional.   Better known as Galahad Force or "MERRILL'S MARAUDERS," the 5307th CUP was organized in India in October 1943. Configured for special operations, it had three long-range penetration battalions, which operated more or less on the model of Orde WINGATE's CHINDITS. Merrill's Marauders—a name bestowed by the press, and not used by the troops—served in Burma from February 1944. In May 1944 the unit captured the airport at Myitkyina, in central Burma, which paved the way for the eventual capture of the town itself by the Marauders and STILWELL's Chinese forces in early August 1944. By then the troops had been in continuous action for six months, under the most trying conditions. Pushed beyond their physical and spiritual limits, the men were having serious morale and discipline problems, particularly after their commander, BG Frank D. Merrill (1903–1955), was evacuated for medical reasons (he had suffered several heart attacks during the grueling campaign, and was ill with malaria as well). Shortly afterward the 5307th CUP was withdrawn to Ledo, India, where it was disbanded, and the troops reorganized as the 475th Infantry. The 475th joined Task Force Mars in October 1944, and served with it until inactivated in China in July 1945. In the early 1960s the battle honors of the 475th were granted to the newly raised 75th Infantry, the Special Forces.

Alamo Scouts. Ten long-range reconnaissance teams organized from Sixth Army personnel beginning in December 1943. From then until the end of the war, the Alamo Scouts conducted over 60 special, deep-penetration intelligence, reconnaissance, and combat missions in New Guinea and the Philippines.

Kachin Rangers. Organized in 1944 from among Kachin tribesmen in northern Burma by the OSS, with the help of Dr. Gordon Seagraves, a US medical missionary in northern Burma, who was serving on Stilwell's staff. The Kachin Rangers specialized in long-range reconnaissance and raiding operations, and were particularly useful during the liberation of northern and central Burma.

Mars, Task Force. Organized in Burma in July 1944, and officially known as the 5332nd Brigade, TF Mars initially comprised the partially mounted 124th Cavalry plus two US field artillery battalions and the Chinese First Separate Regiment, to which was added the 475th Infantry in October 1944. TF Mars took part in operations to clear the BURMA ROAD in January–February 1945. In April 1945 it was transferred by air to south China, where it was inactivated in June 1945.

Merrill's Marauders. See 5307th Composite Unit, Provisional, above.

See also PHILIPPINE ARMY; PHILIPPINE SCOUTS.
Ref: Stanton, *Order of Battle*.

United States Strategic Bombing Survey

Interservice squabbling over the effectiveness of strategic bombing led to the creation of the Strategic Bombing Survey. The USSBS was staffed by military personnel and civilian specialists (such as economist John Galbraith), assisted, after the war ended, by former enemy officers as technical advisers. They were charged with investigating the consequences of strategic bombing. The USSBS began to work during the war, and several staffers were actually killed by enemy action. Preliminary studies revealed that this job would mean investi-

gating just about every aspect of the war. With the help of former Japanese and German military personnel the USSBS produced an enormous series of reports on everything from battle analyses to the production of soft coal in Japan. These were published in over 300 volumes.

Not surprisingly, the USSBS confirmed that air power had played a vital role in the war. However, this role was not necessarily the one that prewar air enthusiasts had predicted. For example, the USSBS concluded that one of the most important consequences of the strategic bombing of Germany was not so much that it had a negative impact on German war PRODUCTION as that it forced the Luftwaffe to concentrate resources for the defense of Germany, thereby rendering it less able to support ground forces, particularly on the Eastern Front. Likewise, it concluded that bombing from high altitude was unprofitable.

Unfortunately, the USSBS is like Holy Writ— in that what it says can be subject to misquotation and interpretation. The air power mavens argued— and continue to argue—that the USSBS vindicated their prewar position that strategic bombing could win the war.

Unryu Class, Japanese Aircraft Carriers

Essentially a modified version of HIJMS HIRYU, *Unryu* and her half-sisters were built quickly (22 to 24 months from keel to completion). The initial order, placed in 1941, was for two ships, *Unryu* and an identical sister. However, the sistership was canceled before being laid down, since Japanese naval architects had convinced the brass that a modification to the original design would be superior. Eight ships were ordered to this slightly different design, of which only five were laid down. In practice, all the ships differed considerably in design detail. Only two actually were commissioned. Good ships, they saw little service, the Imperial Navy being unable to provide AIR GROUPS for them.

Unryu (1942–1943–1944) actually went to sea with a small air group, and was sunk by two TOR-

PEDOES from the US submarine *Reldfin* (SS-272) in the South China Sea off SHANGHAI on December 19, 1944.

Amagi (1942–1943–1944) never saw active service. She capsized in sheltered waters near KURE on July 24, 1945 after being pounded by US naval aircraft, and was later scraped in situ.

Katsuragi (1942–1944–1944) never saw active service. Damaged in US carrier air strikes against Kure in July 1945, after the surrender of Japan she was found sufficiently reparable to be used as a transport, and served to repatriate Japanese troops before being scrapped in 1947.

Three other units were begun—*Kasagi* (1943–1944–), *Aso* (1943–1944–), and *Ikoma* (1943–1944–)—but were never completed and were all scrapped in 1947.

Ushijima, Mitsuru (1887–1945)

Mitsuru Ushijima graduated from the military academy in 1908. A regimental officer during World War I, in 1918–19 he was on the staff of the Siberian Expedition. His later career included staff, line, and school duty, and in 1939 he was given command of a division, which he led in Burma with some distinction in early 1942. There followed a tour as commandant of the military academy, from which post he was sent in mid-1943 to command the Thirty-second Army on OKINAWA, an island considered part of Japan proper and populated by Japanese. With nearly two years to organize the defenses, Ushijima put up a tenacious and bloody resistance to the American invasion in April 1945. About 100,000 Japanese troops were killed or captured (10,755, an unusually high number) in this battle. Many Okinawan civilians also died, with estimates ranging from 40,000 to 110,000. The battle saw the highest American losses for any single operation in the Pacific, between the ferocity of the resistance and the dedication of the KAMIKAZE. It was these high losses that convinced American commanders and troops that resistance on the Japanese Home Islands would be equally fanatic and costly. After leading the stubborn defense, Ushijima committed suicide on 21 June when he saw that further resistance was futile.

V

Van Ghent and Van Galen Classes, Netherlands Destroyers

These two closely related classes formed the Royal Netherlands Navy's destroyer force in the East Indies at the outbreak of the Pacific War. The four Van Ghents were built 1924–28 in Dutch shipyards, to a British design with British technical assistance, while the three surviving Van Galens (one having been sunk by the Luftwaffe in 1940) were built 1927–31 on the basis of experience gained from the construction and operation of their predecessors. The principal differences between the two classes were subtle. Although identical in displacement, dimensions, and appearance, the Van Galens carried slightly different antiaircraft armament (one 75mm AA gun and two 40mm guns, rather than two 75s). Both classes were obsolescent by 1941. All seven ships were lost in the last two weeks of February 1942. *Van Ghent* was wrecked on the 15th in Banka Strait, *Piet Hein* was sunk by the destroyers *Oshio* and *Asashio* in the Bandung Strait on the 19th, *Kortenaer* by destroyer TORPEDOES in the Battle of the JAVA SEA on the 27th, and *Evertsen*, set afire in a clash with Japanese cruisers and destroyers on the 28th, had to be abandoned the next day. Of the Van Galens, *Van Ness* was sunk by Japanese air attack in Banka Strait on the 17th, *Banckert* was scuttled in a dry dock at Soerabaya on 2 March, while under repair for bomb damage received earlier, and *Witte de With* had to be scuttled after being bombed at Soerabaya on 2 March. *Banckert* was partially salvaged by the Japanese, as *Patrol Boat Number 106*. Never fully operational, she returned to Dutch control in 1945 and was sunk as a target in 1949.

Vancouver, British Columbia, Canada

A major port, Vancouver had extensive facilities to service and maintain ships, but was of limited value as a naval base.

Vandegrift, Alexander A. (1887–1973)

The first US Marine to rise to four-star rank while on active duty, Alexander A. Vandegrift enlisted in the Marine Corps in 1908 rather than complete college. Commissioned the following year, he had an active career before World War I, serving in Cuba, Nicaragua, PANAMA, MEXICO, and Haiti by 1915, where, with some minor interruptions, he remained until 1923. After teaching or attending several advanced courses, he was in China for a time, and then on staff assignments at Marine headquarters. In the mid- and late 1930s he was again in China, later becoming secretary to the commandant of the Corps. When the Pacific War broke out he was assistant commander of the First Marine Division, assuming command in April of 1942. On August 7, 1942, Vandegrift undertook the first American amphibious operation of the war, landing his division on GUADALCANAL, beginning an arduous campaign that ended six months later, by which time his division had been relieved. Awarded a MEDAL OF HONOR, promoted to lieutenant general, and given command of I Marine Amphibious Corps in the spring of 1943, Vandegrift undertook the landings on BOUGAINVILLE in later 1943. He was shortly afterward named commandant of the Marine Corps. Promoted to full general in March of 1945, Vandegrift retired in 1949.

Vanguard, British Battleship

Britain's last battleship, Vanguard (1941–1944–1946) was not ready for sea until after the war. Although equal in size and protection to contemporary foreign battlewagons, Vanguard's main battery dated from World War I, her turrets and guns being those removed from the "large light cruisers" Glorious and Courageous when they were converted to aircraft carriers during World War I. The decision to complete her was a tremendous waste of resources, given Britain's strained situation during the war.

Vella Gulf, Battle of

Naval battle fought on the night of 6–7 August 1943, in the SOLOMONS, between the islands of VELLA LAVELLA and KOLOMBANGARA. During the battle for the Solomons, the Japanese kept their troops on the islands supplied via fast transports (converted from old destroyers) escorted by destroyers running down the "Slot" (the northwest-southeast channel between the major islands). At first, the United States responded with cruiser and destroyer task forces. But many American naval commanders felt that the cruisers got in the way and that pure destroyer forces would be more effective. In the summer of 1943, it was decided to try the "destroyers only" approach. After all, the Japanese had been successful with this method. The first test came in Vella Gulf 6–7 August, when a force of six American destroyers caught four Japanese destroyers and sank three of them without loss to themselves. The American commander, Commander Rodger Moosbugger, was a genuine ace as a destroyer commander, and he managed to surprise the Japanese as well as deploy his own ships handily. This battle threw the TOKYO EXPRESS off track for a while, if only because the Japanese were starting to run out of destroyers.

Vella Lavella, Battle of

Naval battle in the SOLOMONS off Vella Lavella Island on the night of October, 6–7, 1943. The battle was brought about by a Japanese attempt to evacuate the survivors of their garrison on Vella Lavella. After three weeks of fighting against American and NEW ZEALAND troops, there were only about 600 Japanese troops left. A force of nine destroyers and a dozen smaller ships were sent to get these soldiers away from certain destruction at the hands of the Allied troops. Six American destroyers were sent in when the Japanese evacuation effort was detected. In the ensuing battle, one Japanese and two American destroyers were sunk, and other American ships were damaged. The Japanese evacuated their troops.

This was the last Japanese naval success in the Solomons and was the last battle fought for the central Solomons. In three months of naval battles, the United States had lost six warships and the Japanese 17. The Americans could afford these losses, the Japanese could not.

Venereal Disease

Venereal disease has long been recognized as a major cause of non-battle-related military non-effectiveness in wartime. Through World War II the problem was of significant, but declining, importance. During World War I the VD rate for men

VD CASES PER 1,000 MEN PER YEAR		
War	Rate	Ratio
World War I	87	100.0%
World War II	49	56.3
Korea	146	171.3
Vietnam	325	373.6

Ratio compares the World World II, Korea, and Vietnam rates as a percent of that for World War I

in the US Army was quite high, about 87 cases per 1,000 men per year, higher than that prevailing in the French Army. During World War II the VD rate in the US Army decreased markedly, to about 56% of that of the earlier war, due largely to an intensive educational program to alert the troops to the dangers of venereal infections, plus the introduction of penicillin, and, not incidentally, to the fact that many troops campaigned in areas where there were few opportunities to contract VD (e.g., the ALEUTIANS, NEW GUINEA, most atolls, etc.). Despite this, VD cases still accounted for over a third of all infectious and parasitical disease cases among US Army personnel in World War II. It is interesting to note that in American military operations since World War II (with the exception of the 1990–91 Gulf War) the VD non-effectiveness rate has actually increased. In fact, while the World War I rate was considered disastrous, that for the Korean War was much worse, and that for Vietnam worse still. The rate for the Gulf War was a fraction of the World War I incidence. There were strong religious and social prohibitions against extramarital sex in Saudi Arabia. There was VD among US troops in the Gulf, but the exact data was kept confidential for diplomatic reasons.

Veterans, Pacific War

An enormous number of people served in uniform during World War II, by one estimate over 100 million. What follows is a random sample of some of those who served in the Pacific who were, or later became, famous for reasons other than being warriors.

Eddie Albert (1908–), the actor, served as an officer aboard an amphibious transport in the navy, and commanded a casualty evacuation landing craft at TARAWA.

Idi Amin (1925–), repressive dictator of Uganda for many years during the 1960s and 1970s, served as a sergeant in the King's African Rifles

during the Burma Campaign of 1944–45, during which he was actually disciplined for mistreating enemy prisoners, a rare event considering the general brutality of the campaign.

Howard Baker (1925–), later a senator and White House chief of staff under RONALD REAGAN, was a PT-BOAT skipper in the South Pacific.

Hank Bauer (1922–), major league baseball player, served as a platoon sergeant in the Marines, winning two Bronze Stars, two Purple Hearts, and 11 battle stars.

Arthur A. Benline (1903–1995), a distinguished architect and public official in New York, served in the SEABEES during the war, rising to captain in the navy and battalion commander. Wounded at OKINAWA, he was awarded the Bronze Star.

Richard Boone (1917–1981), the actor ("Have Gun, Will Travel," etc.), was a tail gunner on TBF AVENGERS in the Pacific.

Vincent L. Broderick (1921–1995), for several years police commissioner of New York, and later a highly regarded federal judge, served in the army's Amphibious Engineers in New Guinea and the Philippines during the war, and on occupation duty after it, rising to captain.

Art Buchwald (1925–), the humorist and columnist, joined the Marines while UNDERAGE, at 16, and served with an aviation unit in the CAROLINE ISLANDS.

Johnny Carson (1925–), the noted television personality, served in the US Navy, managing to survive a TORPEDO that severely damaged his ship off Okinawa in 1945.

John Connally (1917–1994), Navy secretary and Texas governor who was riding with President Kennedy when he was assassinated, served in the navy during the war, initially as a member of EISENHOWER's staff in Europe, and later aboard carriers in the Pacific, earning a Bronze Star and Legion of Merit.

Jackie Coogan (1914–), the actor, was an army glider pilot in Burma, and landed the first glider at Myitkyina during the March 1944 invasion of Burma.

Tony Curtis (1925–), the actor, was a submariner from 1943 to the end of the war.

Jack Dempsey (1895–1983), former heavyweight champion of the world, served in the Coast Guard, taking part in the Okinawa invasion.

Joseph B. DiMaggio (1914–), Yankee baseball star, served as a USAAF physical training instructor in HAWAII for a time during the war, despite persistent ill-health.

Kirk Douglas (1916–), the actor, served in the navy in the Pacific, until discharged due to injuries incurred in the service.

Melvyn Douglas (1901–1981), already a well-known actor and over-age to boot, joined the army in 1942 and eventually served in the CBI.

Paul H. Douglas (1892–1976), although a politician of some note, and a pacifist, joined the Marines at age 50, made it through boot camp, and served in the First Marine Division on Peleliu and Okinawa, being so severely wounded that he spent 18 months in hospitals before being discharged as a lieutenant colonel.

Eddy Duchin (1909–1951), the band leader, served in the navy, taking part in the IWO JIMA and Okinawa invasions as a antisubmarine warfare officer.

Buddy Ebsen (1908–), the actor, served as a junior officer in the Coast Guard, in the ALEUTIANS.

Henry Fonda (1905–1982), already a noted actor, enlisted in the navy in mid-1942, was later commissioned, and served as an intelligence officer in the central Pacific.

George MacDonald Fraser (1925–), the novelist (*Flashman*) and critic, served as an enlisted man in the British Army during the Burma Campaign.

John Glenn (1921–), the astronaut and senator, was a Marine pilot during the war, flying F4U CORSAIRS in the MARSHALL ISLANDS. Between World War II and Korea he had a total of 149 combat missions, accumulating four DFCs and 18 Air Medals.

John Gorton (1911–), for several years prime minister of Australia, served as a fighter pilot in the RAAF from 1940 to 1944, when he was discharged as a result of injuries received in combat.

Alex Haley (1921–1992), author of *Roots,* served as a messman in the Coast Guard in the southwest Pacific.

Mark Hatfield (1922–), for many years a prominent Republican senator from Oregon, several times suggested for the presidency in the 1960s and 1970s, served in the navy in the Pacific and was present during the Okinawa Campaign.

Charlton Heston (1924–), the actor, served in the AAF 1942–45, mostly as a radioman on medium bombers in the Aleutians.

Gil Hodges (1924–1972), the famous baseball player, served as a sergeant in the Marines, in antiaircraft units in the central Pacific.

Edmund Hillary (1919–), who with Tenzing Norgay became the first man to climb Mt. Everest in 1953, was wounded serving in the RNZAF in the South Pacific.

Jim Lee Howell (1915–1995), coach of the football Giants for their 1954–60 winning streak, served as a company commander in the Marine Corps for three years in the South Pacific.

William Kunstler (1919–1995), the famous attorney and champion of leftist causes, served as an army officer during the war, for a time in the Pacific, where he received a Bronze Star, and was later at the Battle of the Bulge, rising to major.

Norman Mailer (1923–), American novelist, served as an enlisted man in the army's intelligence service on Luzon in 1945.

William Manchester (1922–), noted historian and author, served as a Marine rifleman on Okinawa.

Lee Marvin (1924–1987), the actor, joined the Marines at 17 and served in the Fourth Marine Division in the Marshalls and MARIANAS, until severely wounded on SAIPAN, requiring 13 months to recuperate. He is buried in Arlington National Cemetery, next to Joe Louis, who served in the Army.

Ed McMahon (1923–), the television and sweepstakes personality, served as a Marine fighter pilot for most of the war.

Raymond Meek (1897–1995), noted pioneer eye surgeon, served in the US Navy Medical Corps during the war, including a tour aboard the hospital ship *Bountiful*, off Okinawa.

Joseph Papp (1921–1991), noted theatrical producer, staged his first play while a sailor aboard the escort carrier USS *Solomons Sea* in the Pacific.

Philip, H. R. H. the Duke of Edinburgh (1921–), a career officer in the ROYAL NAVY, served on a destroyer in the Pacific from late 1944 to the end of the war, and was present aboard the USS *Missouri* when the Japanese surrendered.

Jason Robards Jr. (1922–), the distinguished actor, served in the navy during the war, from PEARL HARBOR, where as a radioman he received the famous message, "Air Raid Pearl Harbor, This is no drill," to V-J Day, during which he survived the loss of two cruisers and won a Navy Cross.

George Lincoln Rockwell (1918–1967), founder and leader of the American Nazi Party (1958–67), served as a fighter pilot in the navy.

Barney Ross (1909–1967), world middleweight boxing champion in the 1930s, served as a Marine, winning a DSC and Silver Star on GUADALCANAL.

Sabu (1924–1963), star of the *The Elephant Boy* and *Jungle Book* (his full name was Sabu Dastagir), served in the Army Air Forces in the Pacific, flying 42 missions as a B-29 tail gunner, and winning the Distinguished Flying Cross and four Air Medals, in a squadron that earned the Presidential Unit Citation.

Rod Serling (1925–1975), author and television producer ("The Twilight Zone"), served in the 11th Airborne Division, in the Philippines, where he was wounded during the Battle for Manila.

Sargent Shriver (1915–) the first head of the Peace Corps, and a brother-in-law to President John F. Kennedy, was a gunnery officer aboard the battleship SOUTH DAKOTA in the South Pacific during the great naval battles of late 1942.

George Stafford (1915–1995), chairman of the Interstate Commerce Commission from 1970 to 1977, was an infantryman in the southwest Pacific, rising to captain and earning a Bronze Star and Purple Heart.

Harold Stassen (1907–), perennial Republican presidential candidate in the 1950s and 1960s, was governor of Wisconsin when the war broke out, whereupon he resigned the state house to serve as a staff officer with the navy in the Pacific for the entire war. After the emperor's surrender proclamation, Stassen parachuted into Japan, virtually the first US officer to land there. He was also present at the founding meeting of the United Nations.

Leon Uris (1924–1980), the novelist, served in the Marine Corps on Guadalcanal and Tarawa, but was later discharged due to malaria.

Gore Vidal (1925–), author and critic, served as a warrant officer on an army transport in the Aleutians.

Mike Wallace (1918–), the television journalist, served as a navy communications officer in the Pacific.

James Whitmore (1921–), the actor, enlisted in the Marines in 1942 and took part in several amphibious landings, winning a commission.

Ted Williams (1918–), the baseball star, joined the Marines in 1942, took flight training (George BUSH was in the same class), and became a fighter pilot, logging over a thousand hours in the air before the end of the war.

Veterans, Warships, in the War

A number of the warships in service during the Pacific War were already seasoned veterans.

USS *Baltimore* (C-3), a cruiser so old she had fought at Manila Bay in 1898, was present as a storage hulk during the Japanese attack on Pearl Harbor. By 1944 the ship was in such bad shape that the navy towed her out to sea and scuttled her.

USS *Rochester* (CA-2), which as the armored cruiser *New York* had fought at the Battle of Santiago in 1898, was a station ship (a floating office and workship) at OLONGAPO in the Philippines when the war began. She was scuttled on Christmas Eve of 1941, to prevent her from falling into Japanese hands.

USS *IX-25*, the erstwhile Spanish unprotected cruiser *Reina Mercedes*, built for the Royal Spanish Navy in the 1880s and captured in 1898, served throughout the war as a receiving ship at the Naval Academy. She was scrapped in 1957.

USS *Oregon* (BB-3), the battlewagon famous for her voyage around South America during the Spanish-American War, had entered service in the mid-1890s. Preserved as a relic since the 1920s, she was to have gone to the scrap yard in a recycling drive when the navy converted her into an ammunition barge. Towed to the MARIANAS, she supplied the newer battlewagons. *Oregon* remained there after the war. On one occasion she was wrested from her anchorage by a typhoon and not found until several days later—some 500 miles away. Towed back to GUAM, in 1956 she was scrapped in Japan.

USS *Kearsarge* (BB-5), the only American battleship not named for a state, had been completed under Theodore Roosevelt. Demilitarized in the 1920s, she was converted to a "crane ship,"

equipped with an extremely heavy lift crane. The most powerful crane afloat at the time, it could lift a 16-inch gun. She served in various navy yards throughout the war, helping to build and repair warships of all types. She was disposed of in the 1950s.

USS *Arkansas* (BB-31), commissioned in 1912, served more or less continuously for over 33 years, until decommissioned after the war and later expended as a target at Bikini. She had the longest active life of any major modern American warship until the 1970s, when she was surpassed by the carrier *Midway*.

The old Japanese battleship *Asashi*, which had fought at the Battle of Tsushima Strait in May 1905, was serving as a submarine tender when she was sunk by USS *Salmon* (SS-182) in Vietnamese waters on May 25, 1942. Her sistership *Shikishima* served as an accommodation ship at Sasebo until scrapped after the war. Another old battlewagon that had been at Tsushima, *Fuji*, served as an accommodation ship at Yokosuka. The flagship of the Japanese fleet at Tsushima, *Mikasa*, was preserved as an historical relic. Damaged by US aircraft, she survived the war and was restored in the 1960s, primarily by donations from Americans.

The old armored cruisers *Asama, Tokiwa, Idzumo, Iwate, Yakumo, Adzuma,* and *Kasuga,* which had all served in the Russo-Japanese War (1904–05), were re-rated as "coast defense ships" in the early 1920s. In this guise, they continued in service, some seeing action supporting Japanese operations in China in the 1930s and during World War II. *Iwate* and *Idsumo* were sunk in KURE Harbor by carrier aircraft on 28 July 1945, *Tokiwa* was sunk by carrier aircraft on 9 August 1945, and the others were scrapped 1945–47. The old light cruiser *Yahagi*, completed in 1912, served as a training ship at the Eta Jima Naval Academy during the war.

The oldest warship to have a role in the war was undoubtedly the wooden ship of the line HMS *Victory*, Nelson's flagship at Trafalgar, which, although preserved as an historic relic in Portsmouth Harbor, was used for staff conferences by senior

ROYAL NAVY officers from time to time, apparently in the hope that Nelson's ghost might provide some inspiration.

Veterans, Warships, of the War

Many of the ships that served in the war continued to do so for many years afterward. From 1945 until well into the 1970s, the huge US World War II fleet provided the bulk of the secondhand warships for thrifty fleets around the world. Some of these ships will still be in service into the 21st century.

Several units of the BROOKLYN CLASS were transferred to various Latin American navies in the 1950s, including *Brooklyn* herself, which became the Chilean *O'Higgins*. The only one to see any action was *Phoenix*, which, as the Argentine *General Belgrano*, was TORPEDOED by HMS *Conqueror* on 2 May 1982, during the Argentine-British War, thereby gaining the dubious distinction of being the first, and so far only, ship ever to have been sunk in action by a nuclear submarine.

The Indian Navy acquired HMS *Achilles*, a veteran of the Royal New Zealand Navy, which had fought in the Battle of the River Plate and in several of the most heated actions in the SOLOMONS. As INS *Delhi* she saw some action during the brief Indian-Portuguese War of 1961. She was scrapped in 1978.

The Circle Line, which conducts boat rides around New York's Manhattan Island, does so in former LCIs, which performed yeoman service at numerous amphibious landings throughout the Pacific. *Circle Line X* was originally *LCI-758*, which made five combat landings in the Philippines, shot down two Japanese aircraft, and was under fire many more times. *LCI-758*'s adventures did not end on V-J Day. In September 1945, the ship survived a typhoon off OKINAWA, the same typhoon that was featured so prominently in the book and movie *The Caine Mutiny*. In October 1945, *LCI-758* was sent to China to take part in US operations on the Yangtze River. During two years of war service, *LCI-758* received three battle stars. After 1945, *LCI-758* was retired from military serv-

ice and purchased as war surplus by Circle Lines. Rebuilt and reengined, *LCI-758* became *Circle Line X*. In a fitting retirement for a warship, the former *LCI-758* now spends its time running in circles around Manhattan Island, still within the sound of gunfire and aircraft (and at least one blimp) falling from the skies.

USS *Prairie*, the last of the prewar US Navy ships that fought in World War II, was decommissioned on March 27, 1993. A destroyer tender, providing maintenance and support for destroyers while far from base, *Prairie* was built in Camden, New Jersey, and entered service in late 1939. She was for a time the flagship for the Atlantic Fleet support forces, but during the war the ship was assigned to the Pacific, and stayed there afterward. Over 10,000 sailors served on *Prairie* including, since 1982, many women. Traditionally, the oldest serving ship flies the "Don't Tread on Me" pennant. Upon *Prairie*'s retirement this was transferred to USS *Orion*, another tender that entered service during the war, in 1944.

The last major combatant ship in continuous commission in the US Navy to have seen action in World War II was USS *Lexington* (CV-16), an ESSEX CLASS carrier that served as a training ship into the late 1980s, before becoming a war memorial at Corpus Christi, Texas.

The last World War II ship to serve in the Japanese Maritime Self-Defense Force was the TACHIBANA CLASS DE *Nashii*. Sunk by air attack at KURE on 28 July 1945, in 1955 she was raised, refurbished, and put into service as one of the first ships in the new Japanese Maritime Self-Defense Force. The revived *Nashi* was taken out of service in the 1960s, after more than half a century of service above, and below, the waves.

Vian, Philip (1894–1968)

Sir Philip Vian entered the ROYAL NAVY as an officer cadet shortly before World War I. During the war he served in destroyers, mostly in the Mediterranean. By World War II he was skipper of HMS *Cossack*, which he took into neutral Norwegian waters on the night of 16 February 1940, to liberate British PRISONERS OF WAR held in the German ship *Altmarck*. During the hunt for the German *Bismarck* he commanded a destroyer flotilla, and may have put several TORPEDOES into the battle-wagon on the night of 26–27 May 1940. He commanded a cruiser squadron in the Mediterranean in 1941–42, several times running supplies into Malta, for which he was knighted. Although a non-flyer, he was given command of a carrier task force in 1943 and helped cover the Salerno landings. The following year he commanded the Eastern Task Force during the Normandy invasion. In late 1944 he was given tactical command of the British Pacific Fleet, under Adm Bruce FRASER, leading it until V-J Day. After the war he held several high military and civil posts until his retirement.

Victoria, Australia

A major city, with a major port, possessed of important facilities to service and repair ships, though by no means a major naval base.

Vietnam, Resistance to the Japanese

There was already GUERRILLA activity in Vietnam before World War II. In this case it was against the French, who had controlled Vietnam (and neighboring Cambodia and Laos) since late in the 19th century. The Japanese relationship with Vietnam proved to be a curious one. As a French colony, Vietnam had to answer to the pro-German Vichy French government established after the Germans defeated France in June of 1940. This technically made Vietnam an "ally" of Japan (because Japan and Germany were tied by treaties). Britain and America protested when the French, under Japanese pressure, shut down Allied supply routes to China through Vietnam in late 1940. In July 1941, the local Vichy officials gave into Japanese demands for access to Vietnamese ports and airfields and the right to station an unlimited number of troops in Vietnam. The local resistance then shifted its operations to oppose the Japanese, and

because of this received Allied aid. The Vietnamese resistance, dominated by communists, did not get help in keeping the French out after the war and this led to prolonged fighting that eventually dragged in the United States in the 1960s. The guerrillas were quite bitter about their treatment by the Allies. Immediately after the war, British troops moved in and rearmed Japanese soldiers to fight the communist guerrillas for few months.

Vildebeeste, British Torpedo Bomber

The Vildebeeste was an early 1930s British torpedo bomber that was quickly superseded by the SWORD-FISH. Only 200 Vildebeestes were built, and only 30 aircraft—owned by New Zealand—were in the Pacific during the first year of the war. The aircraft had about the same speed, range, and bombload as the Swordfish.

Vladivostok, Soviet Union

The largest and most important Russian military and naval base in the Pacific, with extensive industrial facilities, ample repair and maintenance establishments, and a number of air bases in support. It was one of the ports through which American Lend-Lease aid reached Russia from West Coast ports and carried in Soviet-flag vessels, which were themselves often supplied by the United States.

Volcano Islands

The Volcano Islands are a chain of actively volcanic islands, islets, and reefs lying about 650 miles south of Tokyo, and about the same distance north of SAIPAN. Total land area is about 11 square miles, most of them barren. The principal ones, Chichi Jima and IWO JIMA, were important Japanese outposts in the final defenses of the Home Islands.

Interestingly, the few inhabitants were of mixed American, Hawaiian, and Japanese descent. In 1830 two Americans, one Italian, and about 25 Hawaiians set up a trading post on Chichi Jima, then uninhabited. Other Americans later settled there, mostly whalers jumping ship and survivors of ships, including several African Americans. After his visit to Japan in 1853, Commodore Peary urged the United States to annex the islands, but to no avail. The Japanese occupied them in 1861, and moved some settlers in about 25 years later. By the 1940s the population was rather mixed. During 1944 the civilian inhabitants were evacuated.

W

Wadke, New Guinea

Aside from a roomy harbor, and its location on the north side of New Guinea between HOLLANDIA and BIAK, Wadke had little to recommend it in 1941. Later, the Japanese turned it into a base, which was expanded considerably when taken by the Americans.

Wainwright, Jonathan M., IV (1883–1953)

Jonathan M. Wainwright came from a family with a long military tradition: His father and grandfather both died while on active service, the latter in action during the Civil War. He graduated from West Point in 1906 and was commissioned in the CAVALRY. Aside from serving on a number of famous old posts in the West and Southwest, he saw action in the Philippines against the Moros, some staff time, and some school time. On the eve of World War I he was an instructor at the Plattsburg Officer's Training Camp, where he remained until early 1918, when he went to France. In France, Wainwright served as a division chief of staff during the St. Mihiel and Meuse-Argonne Offensives, and later on occupation duty in Germany, not returning to the United States until 1920. His peacetime service was a mixture of troop duty, staff time, and school time. In late 1940 he was promoted to major general and sent to command the Philippine Division, a Regular Army outfit composed primarily of Philippine troops (see PHILIPPINE SCOUTS). Upon the Japanese invasion of the Philippines, Wainwright's command formed the backbone of the defense. Given command of a corps by MAC-ARTHUR, he did well on BATAAN. When MacArthur was ordered to Australia in February of 1942, Wainwright assumed command of US forces in the Philippines. Following the surrender of Bataan he withdrew to CORREGIDOR, which in turn surrendered on May 6, 1942. Wainwright spent the rest of the war in various Japanese prisoner of war camps, ending up in a Manchurian camp reserved for senior Allied officers. Convinced that he would be court-martialed upon his release, Wainwright was surprised to learn that he had been awarded a MEDAL OF HONOR and promoted to general for the tenacity with which he had held on in the Philippines. He retired in 1947.

Wake Island, Battle for

Wake Island, some 2,000 miles west of PEARL HARBOR, is actually a small atoll (three square miles of land on three islets) with limited port facilities and no particular value, except as a base for reconnaissance aircraft, being some 2,300 miles west by southwest from Pearl Harbor. The island has no ground water and is covered by scrub, which often grows to 10 feet despite infrequent rain. In 1941 it was a stopover on the Pan American Clipper route to the Far East, and a small naval air station was under construction.

In December 1941 the Wake garrison consisted of elements of the First Marine Defense Battalion (449 men under Maj. James P. Devereaux, later a senator), who manned various coast defense installations and supported a dozen old-model F4F WILDCAT fighters. There were also some sailors

(68) and soldiers (5), plus 70 employees of Pan American and 1,146 construction workers.

The Japanese occupation of Wake Island was a subsidiary aspect of the Pearl Harbor operation. The island first came under attack by Japanese surface ships and aircraft operating out of the MANDATES on 8 December. These severely punished the garrison, destroying many of the handful of fighters available. Three days later a detachment of the Special Naval Landing Force (the SNLF or "Imperial Marines") essayed a landing, only to be beaten off with considerable loss, the defenders sinking two destroyers in the process, *Kisaragi* by air attack and *Hayate* by coast defense gunnery, an almost unique occurrence in the war, while inflicting serious damage to several other ships. At least 500 Japanese personnel were killed, but only one American.

Carriers SORYU and HIRYU, returning from the Pearl Harbor Operation, were detached from the Pearl Harbor strike force and called in to work over the island's defenses by air attacks. These carriers lingered in the vicinity of Wake for most of three days, December 21–23, on the last of which the Japanese attempted another landing, which was successful in putting about 1,200 SNLF troops ashore. Shortly afterward the garrison surrendered. US losses in the two attacks were 49 Marines, three sailors, and about 70 civilians killed. Japanese losses were at least 820 killed. Historically, that was the end of the struggle for Wake.

But there might have been more.

As the US Navy began picking up the pieces from the Pearl Harbor disaster, Admiral Husband KIMMEL, still commanding the Pacific Fleet, decided to strike back at the Japanese, and ordered the three carriers in the Pacific to the support of Wake. One, *Saratoga*, under RAdm Frank Jack FLETCHER, was in position to intercept the Japanese carriers before the island fell. At dawn on 23 December *Saratoga* was about 425 miles northeast of the island, and about the same distance due east of the Japanese carriers. Moreover, at that moment the LEXINGTON and her escorts were less than 750 miles southeast of Wake and the *Enterprise* group

a little more than a thousand miles east of the island. In the event, the attempted relief of Wake was called off by VAdm W. S. Pye, who had just replaced Kimmel in an acting capacity pending the arrival of Chester W. NIMITZ. Had Pye not called off the operation, it is perfectly possible that the first carrier battle of the war would have taken place off Wake. And the outcome of that engagement would certainly have dramatically altered the entire course of the Pacific War.

Had the US carriers succeeded in sinking both Japanese carriers at Wake, the sudden loss of a third of their first-line carriers might have seriously injured Japanese morale, provoking a major offensive against HAWAII early in 1942, rather than the MIDWAY operation in June of that year. The resulting battle for Hawaii might have been fought on even better terms for the United States than was historically the case, with perhaps five first-line US carriers against four Japanese.

But it is also possible that the Japanese could have won the battle of Wake. One US carrier air group was still equipped with Brewster F2A BUFFALOS, an older aircraft even more outclassed by the Zeros than were the F4F Wildcats on the other two flattops. A Japanese victory at Wake, with the attendant loss of one or maybe two carriers, would have seriously crippled the US war effort in the Pacific. Such a victory might also have brought on a much earlier Japanese offensive against the Hawaiian Islands than was actually the case, at a time when American resources would have been much slenderer than they were at Midway.

After they seized Wake, the Japanese renamed it Otori Shima, "Bird Island," and developed it as a modest base. Although the US Navy several times struck the island with air raids or surface attack, it made no serious plans to recapture Wake, a possibility that gave the Japanese some concern.

Ref: Cressman, "A *Magnificent Fight*."

War Plans, US, Color Plans

In peacetime, armies and navies are supposed to consider possible threats and make plans accordingly. Of course such matters have to be kept secret, lest a journalistic leak lead to embarrassment or even an international incident. As a result, from quite early in the 20th century the US Armed Forces began referring to potential opponents, allies, locations, and objectives by various colors. Thus, while discussing a hypothetical operation, the brass could refer to "War Plan Indigo," knowing that it was the plan for the occupation of Iceland in the event that Denmark fell under the control of an unfriendly power. Similarly, they could discuss our options if we had to assist "Lemon" in the event that it was attacked by "Olive," or were allied with "Red" against "Black," all the while confident that outsiders would be thoroughly confused by the "cover names" for the countries involved. This was the origin of the famous "War Plan Orange," the scheme (actually a successive series of blueprints developed over nearly 40 years) for war with Japan, designated "Orange." Altogether there were more than 20 color plans. The accompanying list indicates the countries and other places represented by the various colors, so far as is known today.

The origin of the colors is unclear. In some cases there is an obvious link, such as Britain and red (and variations of red for the Commonwealth), perhaps deriving from the reddish tint traditionally used to indicate British territories on maps. Gray for the Azores probably comes from an old poem about Columbus, which includes the line "Behind him lay the gray Azores." And "Yellow" for China seems rooted in blatant racism. But others are more obscure. Orange, for example, might refer to the color of the Japanese flag, and olive might refer to one of the principal products of Spain, but what was the connection of purple to Russia or indigo to Iceland?

Although the first version of War Plan Orange was developed quite early in the century, all versions envisioned a systematic island-hopping advance across the Pacific, so that the plan remained the principal guide for the conduct of the war in the Pacific.

Color	Country
Black	Germany
Blue	USA (foreign involvement)
Brown	Netherlands East Indies; also used for local plans to cope with insurgencies in the Philippines and other US colonies
Citron	Brazil
Crimson	Canada
Emerald	Ireland
Garnet	New Zealand
Gold	France
Gray	The Azores
Green	Mexico
Indigo	Iceland
Lemon	Portugal
Olive	Spain
Orange	Japan
Purple	Russia
Red	Britain
Ruby	India
Scarlet	Australia
Silver	Italy
Tan	Cuba
Violet	China (internal problems)
White	USA (domestic disorders, e.g., race war, communist putsch, etc.)
Yellow	China (international conflict)

Beginning in 1939 the army and navy began to develop a new series of war plans, the "Rainbow" plans, based on the assumption that the United States would participate in a war against the Axis. There were five different Rainbow plans.

Rainbow 1: A US defense of the Americas north of 10 degrees south latitude, without any European allies.

Rainbow 2: The United States allied with Britain and France, with American power free to be used primarily in the Pacific.

Rainbow 3: A United States-Japan war, without European involvement.

Rainbow 4: A US defense of all of the Americas, without European allies.

Rainbow 5: The United States allied with Britain and France, in a "Germany First" situation.

In view of the changing international situation, in mid–1941 versions 2 and 3 were explicitly rejected as they no longer reflected likely possibilities. "Rainbow Five" became the basis of US STRATEGY after PEARL HARBOR. Although it incorporated the final version of War Plan Orange, its basic assumption was the "Germany first" strategy, that is, that in the event of war with both Germany and Japan, the Allies would concentrate their efforts on defeating Germany first, as the more dangerous of the two.

Ref: Miller, *War Plan Orange.*

Warships, Fuel Consumption

Warships are notorious fuel hogs. A "typical" 1944–45 US carrier task force of three fleet carriers, a light carrier, a couple of heavy cruisers, several light cruisers, and a dozen destroyers would consume nearly 50 tons of fuel oil an hour at 15 knots, or 1,200 tons a day. Even at this very economical speed, the task force would require a tanker loaded with fuel about every eight days. And at full speed, around 30 knots, consumption would more than triple. Some figures based on US and Japanese ships are of interest.

Aside from the battleships NAGATO, TENNESSEE, and YAMATO, and the escort carrier CASABLANCA all of the ships on this table could do 30 knots or better at full speed, at the cost of skyrocketing fuel consumption. At full steam an American destroyer's fuel consumption roughly quadrupled. This was the main reason destroyers always seemed to be refueling: At 30 knots they ran out of fuel in about four days.

Being short of fuel not only put a ship at an operational disadvantage, but also created safety problems, particularly in a smaller vessel, since it affected stability. At full load (c. 2,900 tons), fuel constituted about 17% of the displacement of a FLETCHER CLASS destroyer. The three destroyers lost in the typhoon of 17 December 1944 all appear to have been low on fuel, and unballasted with sea water in anticipation of refueling.

The most "fuel efficient" ship on the list is the battleship IOWA, burning only 6.5 tons of fuel an hour to move some 57,000 tons of warship, or about one ton of fuel for each 8,800 displacement

Type	Year	Displacement	Fuel	Usage	Efficiency
Battleships					
Nagato	1919	42,750	5,600	8.4	5.8
Tennessee	1919	40,345	4,700	5.8	7.0
Yamato	1940	69,990	6,300	9.5	7.3
Iowa	1942	57,540	6,250	6.5	8.9
Alaska	1943	34,250	4,619	4.5	7.6
Aircraft Carriers					
Lexington	1925	43,055	3,600	4.9	8.8
Ranger	1933	17,577	2,350	3.1	5.7
Soryu	1935	19,800	3,670	5.5	3.6
Shokaku	1939	32,100	4,100	6.2	5.2
Essex	1942	34,881	6,330	6.2	5.6
Independence	1942	14,751	2,600	3.0	4.9
Taiho	1943	37,700	5,700	8.6	4.4
Casablanca	1943	10,902	2,200	3.2	3.4
Cruisers					
Aoba	1926	10,650	1,800	3.0	3.0
Mogami	1934	10,990	2,163	3.2	3.4
Brooklyn	1936	12,200	1,800	2.7	4.5
Atlanta	1941	8,350	1,360	2.4	3.5
Agano	1941	8,535	1,400	2.1	4.1
Baltimore	1942	17,030	2,000	3.0	5.7
Destroyers					
Fubuki	1927	2,057	500	0.8	2.6
Somers	1937	2,765	400	0.8	3.5
Akitsuki	1941	3,700	1,097	1.6	2.3
Fletcher	1942	2,925	492	1.1	2.7

Ships are grouped by type (with the "Large Cruiser" *Alaska* placed among the battleships due to her size) and according to year of launching, which more or less puts together vessels of comparable age and levels of engine technology. Displacement is full load, in standard tons. Fuel is full load capacity, in tons. Usage is hourly consumption in tons at 15 knots, a quite common speed for long voyages, even by ships capable of much better. Efficiency is the number of tons of displacement (in thousands) each ton of fuel can move at 15 knots, so the higher the figure the more efficient the ship.

tons, followed by the carrier LEXINGTON, burning only 4.9 tons of oil an hour to move some 43,000 tons of warship, or little more than one ton of fuel per hour for each 8,700 tons of displacement—extraordinarily economical vessels. In general, larger ships were more fuel efficient than smaller ones, longer ones more than shorter ones (speed in a ship is partially a factor of hull length), and newer ones more than older ones. The prime exception to the last point, about age, was *Lexington*. Although she had been commissioned in 1927, she possessed unusually powerful engines (180,000 shp) and an experimental electric drive. Other factors influencing fuel consumption were type of engines (reciprocating vs. turbine), time between engine overhauls, condition of the hull (clean or foul), weather, and crew training, not to mention basic design. Note also that US ships were consistently more fuel efficient than Japanese ones, a matter of superior technology.

Warships, Small

In addition to the major warship types there were numerous classes of "small boys."

Gunboats (PGs), a catchall designation that included vessels that ranged in size from 100 to 2,000 tons, were highly specialized vessels designed to impress the various "natives" in peacetime. The smaller ones were mostly used on rivers, especially in China. Larger ones were usually oceangoing, designed to patrol distant colonial outposts.

Frigates (PFs) were essentially cut-rate destroyer escorts of about 500 to 1,000 tons; in some navies called sloops.

TORPEDO boats (TBs) were speedy vessels much smaller than destroyers (600–800 tons) and designed primarily to deliver torpedo attacks against surface vessels.

Motor torpedo boats (MTBs) were very small (50–60 tons), high-speed motor boats (35–40 knots) armed with a small number of torpedoes; called PT-BOATS in the US Navy.

Mine warfare vessels (AMs) were small ships specializing in the planting and clearing of MINES.

Corvettes and submarine chasers (PCs) were very small (300–800 tons), very uncomfortable, slow vessels, which could be produced cheaply in great numbers and sent out to escort convoys.

Mine warfare vessels aside, most of the "small boys" were of only marginal value and were at best expedients.

Although some navies continued to build torpedo boats, by World War II they had long been supplanted by destroyers. Gunboats, frigates, sloops, torpedo boats, and the like were all pressed into service as antisubmarine escort vessels when the war came, to be quickly joined by submarine chasers and corvettes, and anything else that could be adapted to the role. Motor torpedo boats had some value for coastal operations, but on balance they were probably not worth the money, resources, and manpower invested in them.

Several navies, including the Japanese and US, converted obsolescent warships for use as minor combatants, such as old destroyers to minelayers (DMs) and sweepers (DMSs), patrol boats, and the like. This was an economical use of available resources in a wartime emergency.

Warships, US, Captured

Since the War of 1812, only one US warship has ever struck its colors, the river gunboat USS *Wake* (PR-3). A sister to the equally ill-fortuned TUTUILA, *Wake* surrendered without firing a shot at SHANGHAI on 8 December 1941, being then in a hopeless situation, tied up at a dock and surrounded by Japanese troops. *Wake* saw service with the Imperial Army and was eventually turned over to the Chinese. Note that in December 1968 the US Navy electronic intelligence gathering ship *Pueblo* surrendered to North Korean warships off the coast of North Korea. *Pueblo* was not a warship, possessed minimal armament, and was not trained or intended to fight. However, some consider this a "warship surrender."

The Imperial Navy also acquired a US destroyer, albeit not by surrender. USS *Stewart* (DD-224), an old CLEMSON CLASS four-stacker, had been damaged during the fighting in the NETHER-LANDS EAST INDIES early in 1942. She was put into a dry dock at Soerabaya, in JAVA, but was still undergoing repairs when the Japanese overran the island. Although demolition charges were set, these only slightly damaged the ship, and she was captured by Japanese troops on 2 March 1942. Repaired, *Stewart* was commissioned as an escort in the Imperial Navy, and occasionally caused the radio waves to heat up when spotted by American or Allied long-range reconnaissance aircraft. After a relatively uneventful career in the emperor's service, *Stewart* was returned to American control in 1945 and expended as a target during the nuclear weapons trials at Bikini in 1946.

Wasp, US Aircraft Carrier

Wasp, CV-7 (1936–1939–1940), was designed so that the navy could use the last 15,000 tons remaining from America's carrier allocation under the terms of the naval DISARMAMENT TREATIES, which became a dead letter even before she was launched. A greatly improved RANGER, with better protection and stability, she was still too small to be considered a fully useful fleet carrier. In the Atlantic early in the war, she made two trips to bring British fighter aircraft to Malta through the Axis siege. Entering the Pacific in mid-June of 1942, she took part in the operations against GUADAL-CANAL, but was refueling during the Battle of the EASTERN SOLOMONS. On 15 September 1942, while escorting a troop convoy from ESPIRITU SANTO to Guadalcanal, she was hit by three TOR-PEDOES from the Japanese submarine *I-19,* which also torpedoed the battleship NORTH CAROLINA and a destroyer. These started fires that proved uncontrollable, probably due to design flaws, and she was sunk by torpedoes from the destroyer *Lansdowne* (DD-486).

Wavell, Archibald (1883–1950)

One of the few British officers to hold important commands throughout the war, Wavell joined the British Army in time to see service in the South African War (1898–1902). He ended World War I as a brigade commander, and rose slowly to high command between the wars. Appointed commander in chief, Middle East, shortly before World War II broke out, he oversaw operations on as many as four fronts simultaneously: East Africa, the Western Desert, Greece, and Iraq/Syria. This disparate array of responsibilities was a critical factor in explaining the general success of Rommel's spring offensive in 1941 and the failure of British counteroffensives in the desert, for which Wavell nevertheless bore the blame. Transferred as commander in chief in India in late 1941, Wavell shortly found himself Allied supreme commander of the ABDA Theater in the Far East, when the Japanese launched the Pacific War. In this capacity he oversaw a succession of Allied disasters: Malaya, SINGAPORE, the NETHERLANDS EAST INDIES, and Burma. By the time the situation had stabilized, Wavell's troops were confronting the Japanese along the Indo-Burmese frontier. Although he attempted an offensive on the Arakan front in late 1942, Wavell was convinced that the Allies had little hope of recovering Burma by a ground offensive, considering the manpower and logistic difficulties, not to mention the political ones (i.e., India was restive, Nationalist China unreliable, and the United States uncooperative). At American urging, CHURCHILL jumped Wavell up to viceroy of India, in which post he exercised no control over military operations. After the war Wavell almost immediately passed into retirement. A good officer, with considerable administrative abilities, Wavell, who had only one eye as a result of an old wound, had the bad luck to always be given hopeless tasks. A man of great intellectual power, he was the author of nearly a dozen books, including *Generals and Generalship,* which Rommel found interesting, and an anthology of poems, *Other Men's Flowers.*

Wedemeyer, Albert C. (1897–1990)

A 1918 West Point graduate, Wedemeyer saw no combat service in World War I. In the 1920s he served in troop units, on various staffs, and attended several army schools. From 1930 to 1932 he was assigned to the 15th Infantry, at Tientsin, China, where he learned the language. After various other assignments, from 1936 to 1938, Wedemeyer, a German American, attended the German Kriegsakademie as an exchange student, during the Nazi regime. He later held several school and command posts in the United States. Wedemeyer served on the War Department general staff as an expert on war plans from 1941 to 1943. An isolationist, he is thought by some scholars to have been involved in several "leaks" of preliminary war plans to the press in the period before PEARL HARBOR, and in his memoirs charged that such contingency planning "proved" the ROOSEVELT administration was "plotting" to bring the United States into the war. For a time in 1943 he served as an observer in the ETO. In August 1943, as a major general, he was appointed as deputy chief of staff of Allied forces in Southeast Asia, under Lord Mountbatten. In October 1944 he was sent to replace General STILWELL as CHIANG KAISHEK's chief of staff. This appointment signaled President Roosevelt's displeasure with Chiang's handling of the situation in China. Wedemeyer continued in this post until May 1946, rising to (temporary) lieutenant general in the process. He afterward held various administrative posts until retiring in 1951.

Wellington, New Zealand

The capital of New Zealand, Wellington was an important city and port, though with only limited facilities to service vessels. It served as an important supply port during the war.

Wewak, New Guinea

A good harbor, with no facilities but a good location on the north coast of NEW GUINEA, east of AITAPE.

Whampoa Military Academy

Created by Sun Yat-sen in the spring of 1924, at Whampoa, near CANTON, to train junior officers for the KUOMINTANG army. The academy's first president was CHIANG KAI-SHEK, and the faculty included a number of Soviet military advisers, as well as many Chinese officers who had formal military training at foreign military academies, including Chou En-lai, the later Chinese communist defense minister.

The academy was created on a Soviet model. It provided a six-month course for secondary school graduates. The program was based on the principles of ideological purity, rigid discipline, practical knowledge, flexibility of thought, thoroughness of training, and individual responsibility. The curriculum included not only modern Western military theory, but also some innovative Soviet notions, particularly as introduced by Leon Trotsky to the Red Army's officer training programs, and the Chinese military classics, which were edited and annotated by Chiang himself.

The academy trained officers not only for the army, but also for the air force, the navy, and the national police. All candidates took basic training together, and then passed on to specialized programs. In addition to the six-month course at Whampoa, there was a series of post-graduate courses in various specialities, which were attended by many of the graduates.

The course was as much practical as academic. The first class, in May 1924, numbered 960 young cadets in a single training regiment. They alternated among classroom, drill field, and battlefield. By November 1925 the cadet corps was serving as part of the cadre of a training corps of some 30,000 men, learning as they led troops in battle against warlord armies. The communists were ousted from the academy staff in 1926. The academy rapidly became the source of the best officers in the Chinese Army. By 1929 there were already some 5,000 graduates, of whom about 2,600 were serving in the Northern Expedition. The number of graduates rose to about 3,000 a year, where it remained through 1945.

When the capital of Republican China was established at Nanking, the academy was moved there and renamed the Central Military Academy. When the capital moved to Chungking, the academy followed.

See also CHINA, ARMIES.

Ref: Liu, *A Military History of Modern China.*

Wichita, US Heavy Cruiser

An experimental design, *Wichita* (1935–1937–1939) was essentially a heavy cruiser version of the light cruiser BROOKLYN. As ships of that class were by no means wholly successful, neither was she, being a bit top-heavy. She was however, much better protected than earlier American heavy cruisers and had an improved 8-inch turret. Experience gained from *Wichita* proved enormously valuable in the design of the BALTIMORE CLASS. She saw considerable service during the war but was rarely in heavy action. Scrapped in 1959.

Wingate, Orde C. (1903–1944)

One of the most unconventional soldiers of the 20th century, Orde Wingate entered the British Army between the wars. Assigned to the Palestine garrison during the Arab Revolt in the mid–1930s, he developed a passion for the Zionist cause, and soon went beyond his authority to train Jewish settlers for self-defense. Shortly after Italy's entry into World War II, Wingate was sent to East Africa, where he commanded Gideon Force, a GUERRILLA column that had enormous success in disrupting Italian defenses in Ethiopia in 1940–41.

Sent to the Far East shortly after the Japanese overran Burma, Wingate organized and led numerous guerrilla raids into the Japanese rear, dis-rupting the enemy at a time when regular British Empire forces were in desperate shape. A pioneer in the use of air supply, Wingate's basic strategy was to use air supply to support raids by his specially trained troops (the CHINDITS). He would parachute troops into inaccessible areas behind Japanese lines, where they would hack out an airstrip, be joined by additional troops and supplies brought in by air, and then cut their way back toward British lines. His two most successful operations (February '43 and March '44) were very deep penetrations, literally hundreds of miles into the enemy rear. Although enormously disruptive of Japanese logistics and communications, and although they tied down considerable Japanese forces at a critical juncture, the cost of the operations in manpower was extraordinary. Despite retaining influence with CHURCHILL and other unorthodox thinkers, Wingate would probably have been replaced had he not died in an aircraft accident. As the airplane was an American one, and none of the recovered bodies could be positively identified, Wingate lies in a group grave in Arlington National Cemetery. (He is one of only two foreign soldiers buried at Arlington, the other being Sir John Dill, British representative to the Combined Chiefs of Staff, who died in Washington in 1944.) Like many other successful commanders, Wingate was an eccentric, fond of quoting the Old Testament, eating raw onions, and the like, and was certainly mentally unstable (he attempted suicide after the East African Campaign)—never by itself a disqualification for military genius.

Wirraway, Australian Trainer/Fighter

The Wirraway was an American design built under license in Australia. Originally intended as a two-seat trainer, the aircraft was also used as a fighter (with disastrous results) and as a light bomber (a few hundred pounds of bombs, at most) in the early days of the war. Some 750 were built between 1939 and 1946.

Women, American, In the Pacific War

On the eve of World War II there were very few American women in uniform, and all of them were in either the Army Nurse Corps or the Navy Nurse Corps, old institutions founded in the early years of the century. Down to only a few hundred women each by the early 1930s, these had begun recruiting again during the gradual buildup of US forces that preceded PEARL HARBOR.

When the war actually broke out the armed forces did not at first express any interest in putting women in uniform, save for nurses. However, as manpower became increasingly scarce, the idea of enrolling large numbers of women became increasingly attractive. In 1942 the enlistment of women began in earnest, under the slogan "Free a man to fight." By the end of the war some 350,000 American women had served in uniform.

Army. Over 210,000 women served, including about 4,000 black women, who served in segregated units. There were three distinct ways in which women could serve.

Army Nurse Corps. Some 60,000 women served as officer nurses in all theaters, more than a 50-fold increase in numbers over those of 1939.

Women's Army Auxiliary Corps (WAAC). About 150,000 women were enrolled in a new separate emergency branch of the army. These women served in numerous ways, such as truck driver, hospital orderly, and aviation mechanic, and in all theaters. Before the war ended this became the Women's Army Corps (WAC), a part of the regular establishment.

Women Air Service Pilots (WASPS). Under the leadership of famed aviatrix Jacqueline Cochrane, who had earlier served as a ferry pilot for the RAF, about a thousand women were enrolled as pilots, ferrying aircraft of all types (including B-17s) throughout the United States and occasionally overseas as well.

Navy. About 115,000 women served in the navy during the war.

A 1944 poster by artist Steele Savage, urging women to enlist. From left to right, the WAACs, WAVES, Women Marines, and SPARS.

Navy Nurse Corps. Some 14,000 women served, a substantial increase over the 442 who had been on duty in 1939.

Women Accepted for Volunteer Emergency Service (WAVES). About 100,000 women served in a variety of duties, much as did their sisters in the WAAC. Several women served as air navigators, and as such became the first women permitted to serve in airplane crews on what were theoretically combat missions, in patrols off both coasts. At the war's end, by which time the "Emergency" had been dropped from their title, WAVES comprised 55% of the personnel at Headquarters, Department of the Navy.

Marine Corps. The Marines were the last service to enlist women, creating the Women's Reserve, which had no "cute" acronym, in 1943. About 23,000 women served. Although women Marines endured a more difficult regimen than their sisters in the other services ("They *will* be Marines," as the Corps put it), their duties differed little.

Coast Guard. The SPARS (from the motto of the Coast Guard, "Semper Paratus," Latin for "Always Prepared") enrolled a total of 12,000 women in the course of the war. They performed what was perhaps the broadest range of duties of any of the women in uniform, from radar operators to carpenter's mates, with some even serving afloat. So pleased was the Coast Guard brass with its women that they honored them by naming a cutter *Spars*.

While a large proportion of the women in the two nurse corps served outside the continental United States, relatively few of the other women in uniform got overseas. For example, only 4,000 WAVES served outside the United States, all in the Pacific and most of them in HAWAII, and only 450 SPARS in Hawaii and Alaska. A handful of women Marines also served in Hawaii. About 8,000 WACs served in Europe, and about 5,500 in the Pacific, with small numbers in the CBI. Douglas MACARTHUR was probably the most enthusiastic supporter of women in uniform, and openly sought to increase the number of women troops in his command. By the end of the war there were more American women serving in his theater than in any other.

Figures on CASUALTIES among American military women are indeterminate. An estimated 300 died in the service, counting all theaters and including deaths from disease and accident, as well as a number by enemy action. The Army Nurse Corps had 16 women killed in action, five others missing in action, and 26 wounded. At least five navy nurses were killed in action when a KAMIKAZE hit the hospital ship *Comfort* on 25 April 1945. The number of women killed in action in the other branches is not clear. A number of American military women became PRISONERS OF WAR, 68 in the Philippines (and one other in the ETO). Although mistreated, they were not subjected to the mass rape and murder that was inflicted on the Canadian nurses captured at HONG KONG or the British nurses captured at SINGAPORE.

Ref: Larsen, " *'Till I Come Marching Home*."

Women's Voluntary Service Corps

A Japanese organization that conscripted women age 16 and above for service as factory workers, clerical employees, and nurses, depending upon their education. Service was under quasi-military conditions, with the women having little say in their assignments, which could take them considerable distances. Pay was minimal. In Korea the WVSC served as an agency for the recruitment of COMFORT WOMEN.

Worcester Class, US Light Cruisers

Designed with wartime experience in mind, *Worcester* (1945–1947–1948) and *Roanoke* (1945–1947–1948) were very large light cruisers equipped with a new double turret that permitted their 6-inch guns to be used in both an antiship and an antiaircraft role. These, and their 24 new-pattern 3-inch secondary dual-purpose guns, made them the most powerful antiaircraft cruisers ever built, but they were never used in their designed role. They were scrapped in the 1970s.

Wotje, Caroline Islands

Although potentially useful as both a naval or air base, Wotje had facilities for neither in 1941. During the war the Japanese developed it in a modest way, even using it as a base for flying boat raids on Pearl Harbor, via FRENCH FRIGATE SHOAL. It was repeatedly raided by carrier aircraft during the war, but remained in Japanese hands throughout.

Y

Yamada, Otozo (1881–1965)

Otozo Yamada graduated from the military academy in 1903 and entered the CAVALRY. Surprisingly, Yamada appears to have seen no service during the Russo-Japanese War. Over the years he passed through a variety of command, staff, and school assignments, all of which demonstrated his considerable abilities. In 1938 he was appointed to a senior command in China. At the start of the Pacific War he was a full general commanding the General Defense Command in Japan. He served on the Supreme War Council for most of the war, and was given command of the Kwantung Army in mid–1944, which was crushed by the Soviets in August 1945. Tried for war crimes by the Russians and sentenced to 25 years in labor camps, he was released in 1956 (he was 75 years old and in ill health) and sent back to Japan.

See also TOKYO WAR CRIMES TRIBUNAL.

Yamaguchi, Tamon (1892–1942)

One of Japan's most talented carrier admirals, Tamon Yamaguchi graduated from the naval academy in 1912. Over the years he held various posts, studied at Princeton (1921–23), served on the naval general staff, was a delegate to the London disarmament conference, and naval attaché in Washington (1934–37). Although a non-flyer, in 1940 he was promoted rear admiral and given the Second Carrier Division, HIRYU and SORYU. With his command he participated in the PEARL HARBOR operation, the subsequent operations in the Dutch East Indies and, finally, MIDWAY. There he committed suicide by going down with his flagship, *Hiryu.* Yamaguchi was known to criticize his superiors for their narrow-minded handling of carriers. He would have been a formidable opponent had he survived Midway.

Yamamoto, Isoruku (1884–1943)

Isoruku (or Isoroku) Yamamoto—born Takano—was among the outstanding admirals of World War II. He graduated from the Japanese Naval Academy in 1904 and saw action during the Russo-Japanese War, losing several fingers while commanding a TORPEDO boat in the Battle of Tsushima Strait in 1905 (his principal opponent in the Pacific War, Chester W. NIMITZ, was also missing a finger). During World War I he served as a staff lieutenant commander, but saw no action. He later attended Harvard for two years, and then Yale as a graduate student in the 1920s, where he became well acquainted with the military and industrial potential of the United States. It was this experience that caused him to constantly counsel against war with America.

The commander of the Japanese Combined Fleet since 1939, Yamamoto was recognized by Americans and Japanese alike as the most capable Japanese commander, architect of the spectacular success that attended Japanese efforts early in 1942. Yamamoto's undoing was the American success at breaking the Japanese naval codes. His staff suspected that their secret communication codes had been broken, but Yamamoto never believed it to be the case, at least he didn't believe it sufficiently to do much about it. As a result, American P-38 fighters ambushed Yamamoto's aircraft and its seven escorts on April 18, 1943, killing Yamamoto in the process.

Beyond being an excellent leader and combat admiral, Yamamoto spoke English. He was quite an independent thinker and, by Japanese standards, something of an eccentric. For example, Yamamoto had a Bible with him wherever he traveled and regularly consulted it, even though he was not a Christian. What made Yamamoto dangerous to America was his pragmatism. He knew that Japan could not defeat America, but he had the skill and rank to cause maximum CASUALTIES to American troops. The Midway operation was a workable plan, if only Yamamoto had known that his codes were compromised and been able to change the codes (thus keeping the enemy in the dark for at least a few months). The Pearl Harbor attack was his doing, and he had many other bold plans to make the American advance across the Pacific as costly as possible.

The other obstacle Yamamoto faced was the Japanese Army, which saw him as a dangerous free-thinker. If Yamamoto had had his way, Japan would never have gotten involved in World War II in the first place. As early as 1940 he had told senior Japanese officials that war with America would be futile and disastrous for Japan. But Yamamoto was still very Japanese. He allowed himself to be adopted into the Yamamoto clan when he was 32 years old and already a distinguished naval officer because the higher status Yamamotos would help him overcome the stigma of his original family's lower social status (and because the Yamamotos wanted someone already famous like Isoruku Takano to be the leader of their clan). Yamamoto also believed in the emperor, whom he was obliged to serve as a sailor unto death. Yamamoto was typical of the many (but not nearly all) Japanese admirals who saw the army's policy in China (and eventual takeover of the government) as not in Japan's best interests. But because the army managed to get the emperor to agree (or at least remain silent) to their plans, there was nothing other Japanese could do but follow "the Emperor's wishes."

Yamashita, Tomoyuki (1888–1946)

Tomoyuki Yamashita joined the Japanese Army in 1906. In 1914 he saw action during the capture of the German colony of Kai-chow, China. Noted as an able officer, he spent most of the 1920s and 1930s in staff and school positions, rising rapidly in rank. By 1941 he was a lieutenant general and in command of the Twenty-fifth Army. His task was to invade MALAYA and take SINGAPORE. This he did in a stunning operation. In the summer of 1942 he moved to a command in MANCHURIA and in the summer of 1944 was put in charge of all the forces defending the Philippines. He commanded his forces on Luzon until ordered to surrender on August 19, 1945. He still had 50,000 troops left, even though completely cut off from outside assistance. After the war he was tried for ATROCITIES in Singapore and Manila, convicted, and hanged in 1946. Yamashita was considered the most able of all Japanese generals, and his final campaign in the Philippines bears this out. However, he did not get along with other Japanese leaders and was paranoid, among other things believing that TOJO was trying to have him killed. Tojo was jealous and afraid of Yamashita, but there is no evidence to support Yamashita's assassination fears.

Yamato Class, Japanese Battleships

The largest battleships ever built, and the largest warships ever until the commissioning of the nuclear-powered carrier USS *Enterprise* in 1960, *Yamato* and *Musashi* were enormous yet graceful looking behemoths, mounting the heaviest guns afloat and impressively protected. Nevertheless, they were probably a bad investment. Neither ship saw much service in the war. They were rather slow by World War II standards, lacked maneuverability, and were probably no better than an even match for US battleships of the IOWA CLASS. They were also expensive, and their construction limited the expansion of the Japanese Navy in terms of other, more vital types of vessels, such as aircraft carriers or destroyers. Construction of this class entailed construction of a special 13,000–ton GRT ship to transport their guns to the shipyards and several enormous floating cranes to help mount the guns. For the same investment in time, money, steel, shipyard facilities, and manpower, two or three SHOKAKU CLASS carriers (including aircraft) might have been built for each *Yamato* completed, and the carriers would have been available in considerably less time. The Japanese appear to have recognized this, for the third ship in the class was converted to a carrier while still on the ways and the fourth was canceled.

Yamato (1937–1940–1941) became the flagship of Combined Fleet in February of 1942, but her first war mission occurred during the MIDWAY Campaign, in which she saw no combat. On August 29 she led Combined Fleet into TRUK Lagoon, which was to serve as the main base for operations in the South Pacific. Save for one day when she changed her location, she spent the next 253 days swinging at anchor in the lagoon. On May 9, 1943 she departed for KURE, where she was refitted, returning to Truk Lagoon in mid-August, to once again swing at anchor, this time until mid-October, when US carrier raids on WAKE prompted an abortive sortie of Combined Fleet in the belief that a landing on the island was imminent. Sent to Japan to escort troop convoys to the South Pacific, in December 1943 she was TORPEDOED by USS *Skate* (SS-305), which revealed serious flaws in her construction. She did not return to Combined Fleet until April 1944. She took part in the Battle of the PHILIPPINE SEA and during the Battle of LEYTE GULF, absorbing some bomb damage in the Sibuyan Sea on October 24 1944; the next day she fired her 18.11–inch guns for the only time in anger, when she attacked the US escort carriers off SAMAR. Returning to Japan for repairs, she was damaged in the 19 March 1945, Task Force 58 carrier air strikes on Japanese ports, but was soon repaired. In April she was sent to attack American shipping off OKINAWA, and on April 7, 1945 was sunk by carrier aircraft, after absorbing about a baker's dozen torpedoes and at least eight bombs.

Musashi (1938–1940–1942) had an even less distinguished career than her sistership. Her first war mission was in early 1943, when she relieved *Yamato* as flagship of Combined Fleet at Truk. She brought Admiral YAMAMOTO's ashes back to Japan in May 1943, and then returned to Truk as Admiral Koga's flagship on August 5, not leaving the anchorage again until November, when she conducted a patrol east of the CAROLINES, before returning to stay at anchor until early February 1944, when she was withdrawn to Japan out of fear of US naval airpower (a prescient decision, given that Truk was subjected to a devastating air and surface raid in mid-February). In March 1944 she was torpedoed by *Tunny* (SS-282), with the resulting damage paralleling that to *Yamato* the previous December. She later took part in the Battle of the Philippine Sea, and was sunk in the Sibuyan Sea on October 24, 1944, during the early phases of the Battle of Leyte Gulf: She absorbed an estimated 20 torpedoes and 17 bombs, plus 18 near-misses before sinking. She had never fired her main battery at an enemy vessel.

SHINANO, the third ship of the class, was completed as an aircraft carrier. The fourth vessel, designated *Number 111*, was laid down in 1940 but broken up on the ways when about 30% completed. A fifth vessel was proposed in 1942, but never begun, as were two similar ships with six 20-inch guns in lieu of the 18.11-inchers.

Yap, Carolines

Although of limited potential as a naval base, Yap, one of the large, "high" islands of the CAROLINES, was well located for an air base, which the Japanese proceeded to construct. By mid-1944 US strategic plans envisioned capturing the island in October. In a reassessment of US plans, the operation was canceled several weeks before it was to have taken place, and the forces assigned to it was committed to the Leyte landings. The island remained in Japanese hands until the end of the war.

Yasukuni Shrine

A Shinto temple in Tokyo where the 2.46 million Japanese who died in battle—though not those killed in air raids—during the Japanese Empire's wars from the 1850s through 1945 are worshiped as *kami*, demi-gods. World War II accounts for the bulk of those memorialized, some 2.3 million, including virtually all of the 56,000 female nurses and auxiliaries commemorated. The shrine, which occupies 24 acres, includes numerous war memorials, such as the tomb of the "Seven Martyrs," the principal Japanese war criminals executed by the Allies at the end of World War II, and a museum dedicated to the KAMIKAZE. In 1965 a small memorial, named Chinreisha, was added to commemorate the war dead of all nations.

Once closely identified with the Imperial Government, since World War II the shrine has been maintained by private contributions. Informal ties to government, however, are strong; Japanese premiers and cabinet members regularly make formal pilgrimages.

Yorktown Class, US Aircraft Carriers

Arguably the most successful class of warship ever built, and certainly one of the most decorated, the Yorktowns were the model for all future US carrier designs. Relatively large, fast, very seaworthy vessels with excellent protection and large aircraft complements, they played an enormous part in the Pacific War, garnering great distinction in the process.

Yorktown, CV-5 (1934–1936–1937), was in the Atlantic when PEARL HARBOR was bombed, and was shortly transferred to the Pacific. She took part in several raids, and then fought in the Battle of the CORAL SEA, where she was severely damaged. Rushing to Pearl Harbor, she was partially repaired in order to get her into action in time for the Battle of MIDWAY. At Midway she took several bombs and two TORPEDOES on 4 June and was temporarily abandoned. Still afloat the next day, she was taken in tow. On 6 June the Japanese submarine *I-168*

put two more torpedoes into her and she finally went down.

Enterprise, CV-6 (1934–1936–1938), was flagship of the HALSEY Task Force at the time of Pearl Harbor, delivering reinforcements to WAKE ISLAND. She took part in the early raids on Japanese islands, escorted *Hornet* on the DOOLITTLE Raid, fought at Midway, EASTERN SOLOMONS, and the SANTA CRUZ ISLANDS, covered numerous landings throughout 1942–44, and fought on through to the end of the war, suffering frequent damage in action. By the end of the war she was the most decorated ship in American history. Despite a campaign to preserve her as a war memorial, "The Big E" was scrapped in 1958.

Hornet, CV-8 (1939–1940–1941), was laid down after the final collapse of naval limitations. Rather than wait for a new and better design, the navy decided to repeat the successful *Yorktown* design. Shaking down in the Atlantic when the war began, she shortly passed into the Pacific. Her first wartime mission was transporting Jimmy Doolittle's B-25s to within bombing range of Japan, in April 1942. She subsequently took part in several raids, fought at the Battle of Midway, the Eastern Solomons, and the Santa Cruz Islands, where on 24 October 1942 she took four Japanese bombs and three aerial torpedoes plus two suicide crashes by damaged Japanese aircraft, which caused considerable damage and engine failure. Since her hull remained sound, she was taken in tow, only to absorb three more Japanese bombs the following morning. As Japanese surface units were known to be closing in, it was decided to scuttle the ship. Despite about 300 rounds of 5-inch shells and nine torpedoes from US destroyers (not all of which detonated), she refused to sink. Abandoned, her burned out hulk was later found still afloat by Japanese surface forces, who finished her off with four 24-inch "Long Lance" torpedoes.

Yubari, Japanese Light Cruiser

An experimental vessel, the smallest cruiser in the war, *Yubari* (1922–1923–1923) was perhaps the most graceful looking vessel in the Japanese Navy, a service noted for some particularly graceful ships. On the whole, however, the ship was a failure. She was quite overloaded and unstable. On a hull designed to displace about 2,900 tons she mounted virtually the same armament as the 5,900-ton SEN-DAI. The principal difference was six rather than seven 5.5-inch guns and four rather than eight 24-inch torpedo tubes, but in compensation she carried three reload sets of TORPEDOES, where most ships carried two. She had a busy war as a flotilla leader, mostly in the southwest Pacific. She fought at the CORAL SEA and SAVO ISLAND, among other actions. Near PALAU on 27 April 1944 she was hit by a torpedo from *Bluegill* (SS-242) and sank the next day.

Yugumo Class, Japanese Destroyers

Japan ordered 36 Yugumo Class destroyers between 1939 and 1942, of which only 20 were completed, the last not until May of 1941. Closely resembling the KAGERO CLASS, they were better designed and their main armament had a superior elevation, on virtually the same displacement and with the same speed. Extensively modified during the war, they saw considerable service. All were lost in action, one to MINES, four to surface ships, one in a surface and air attack, nine to aircraft, and five to SUB-MARINES.

Z

Zamboanga, Philippines

A small port, with limited resources and an airstrip occasionally frequented by the USAAF before the war. During the war it served as Japanese HQ for eastern Mindanao.

Zuiho Class, Japanese Light Aircraft Carriers

These two ships were designed as submarine tenders readily convertible into aircraft carriers, in a covert effort to expand Japan's carrier tonnage beyond that allowed by the naval DISARMAMENT TREATIES. *Tsurugisaki* actually entered service in that role in early 1939, while the second, *Takasaki*, was completed as a carrier while still building. Rather successful ships, fast and with a reasonable aircraft operating capacity, they were surprisingly tough.

Shoho (1934–1935–1942, ex-*Tsurugisaki*) was converted from a submarine tender 1941–42. Commissioned in February 1942, her only war mission ended in the CORAL SEA on 7 May 1942, when she was hit by aircraft from USS YORKTOWN, absorbing 11 bombs and about seven TORPEDOES in a few minutes, which turned her into a burning wreck that soon plunged to the bottom. She was the first Japanese carrier lost in the war.

Zuiho (1935–1936–1940, ex-*Takasaki*) helped support operations in the East Indies in early 1942, was damaged in the Battle of the SANTA CRUZ ISLANDS in October of that year, supported several attempts to run supplies into GUADALCANAL in December, served in the central Pacific in 1943, formed the core of one of the "bait" task forces in the PHILIPPINE SEA in mid-1944, and went down off Cape Engaño on October 25, 1944, having taken numerous bombs and torpedoes.

CHRONOLOGY

This Chronology is designed to give a sense of the day-to-day flow of events during the Pacific War. It outlines the principal developments in the Pacific Theater for each month of the war, with an occasional reference to critical events in the European War. Each month is treated separately. There is a brief summary of the general trend of the action that month, followed by daily detail. Of course, not everything that occurred each day can be summarized. Moreover, for all its vast size and scope, even the Pacific War tended to have long periods during which nothing spectacular happened. When there was action, there was a lot of it. But at other times there was little of note going on. Of course, there was always the tedium of patrolling, maintaining equipment, moving supplies, and getting ready for the next operation. For most of the soldiers, sailors, airmen, and Marines this was how they spent most of their time.

In addition to the material on the great events, this Chronology also covers the key dates in the military career of one of the millions of people who participated in the Pacific War.

Bill Howell (b. 1920) was a civilian on December 7, 1941. He soon volunteered for the navy and went to war. Howell survived the war and went on to live a normal life indistinguishable from that of the other 16 million Americans who had served in World War II. Like most of them, he hasn't gotten any mention in the history books, until now. But it should be remembered that without the Bill Howells, there would be no history to write about. It's easy to overlook the details of history, but it is in the details that the real work is done. So consider well the experiences of Bill Howell. You are more likely to find yourself in his situation than in that of Douglas MACARTHUR or Bill HALSEY.

Note: The dating of events in the Pacific War is somewhat confused by the presence of the International Date Line, running roughly through the middle of the Pacific Ocean. For example, the Japanese attack on PEARL HARBOR occurred on the morning of December 7, 1941 in HAWAII, while the Japanese attacks in the Philippines and MALAYA later that same morning are dated 8 December.

Outline History of World War II. While putting this together, it occurred to us that the history of World War II could be aptly summed up in three short quotations:

September 1, 1939: Adolf HITLER orders his troops to "Close your hearts to pity," as he sends them into Poland and starts World War II.

December 7, 1941: Mitsuo FUCHIDA cries "*Tora! Tora! Tora!*" from the cockpit of his aircraft over Pearl Harbor. His radio carries the message—"Tiger! Tiger! Tiger!"—back to the Japanese carriers, to let them know the sneak attack was a success.

September 2, 1945: The Japanese surrender documents having been signed on the US battleship *Missouri*, Douglas MacArthur says "These proceedings are closed," bringing World War II to an end after 2,193 days.

November 1941

The Pacific War began before the bombs fell on Pearl Harbor on December 7, 1941. For China the war began in 1931, when the Japanese seized Manchuria, or perhaps in 1932, when the Japanese briefly seized Shanghai, or maybe 1933, when they grabbed Jehol Province. Certainly for China the war was in progress by 1937, when the Japanese began a sustained campaign to conquer the entire country, the CHINA INCIDENT. But, however many Americans may have sympathized with the sufferings of the Chinese people, they did not think of China's war as an American war. For Americans the war began at Pearl Harbor. But even that date is erroneous.

Military operations actually began on November 26, 1941, when the Japanese First Air Fleet sailed from the KURILE ISLANDS for HAWAII unbeknownst to anyone, except a few Japanese. All anyone else noted that November was the frantic diplomatic activity between Japan and America.

If it is necessary to pick a date for the start of the Pacific War, it's either November 26, when the Japanese fleet set off for Pearl Harbor, or a few days before the attack, when the Japanese committed to the bombing raid no matter what their diplomats in Washington worked out with the Americans.

So, on November 26 the Japanese First Air Fleet sorties from TANKAN BAY in the Kurile Islands at a cruising speed suitable for a long voyage, destination—Pearl Harbor. The next day, the 27th, an official communiqué from the US Army chief of staff, issued with the concurrence of the chief of naval operations, goes out to all major US headquarters in the Pacific, concluding "this is to be considered a war warning." That same day HMAS *Parramatta*, a patrol vessel, is sunk by an unknown agent off Australia. On the 28th, the US chief of naval operations informs Adm Husband KIMMEL, at Pearl Harbor, "Hostile action is possible at any moment . . ." Carrier *Enterprise* sails from Pearl Harbor with aircraft for Wake; RAdm William HALSEY, the task force commander, orders the crew to full wartime alert, a measure also adopted by Adm Thomas HART, commanding the Asiatic Fleet, and LG John L. DEWITT, commanding US Army forces on the West Coast. But LG Walter SHORT, commanding in Hawaii, takes less vigorous measures, as does Adm Kimmel. On the 29th, Hi-

deki TOJO, a general and prime minister of Japan, announces that "Nothing can be allowed to interfere in Japan's sphere of influence in the Pacific, because it has been decreed by Divine Providence." By the 30th it appears that Japanese diplomatic efforts with the Americans are going nowhere, but both sides keep trying, the Japanese diplomats in Washington being unaware of the imminent attack on Pearl Harbor.

December 1941

December began with Japanese warships and troopships scurrying all over the Pacific. This activity did not go unnoticed, and Allied headquarters were alerted that something was up. It was obvious that the Japanese had decided upon war. Not until 7 December did it become obvious how bold their planning was. The rest of the month saw Japanese forces running amok all over the Pacific. The Japanese appeared unstoppable and, in December of 1941, they were.

The coming of war was not a complete surprise to many American military men. On the first of the month, the US SUBMARINES *Argonaut* and *Trout* take station off MIDWAY, *Triton* and *Tambor* off WAKE, as a defensive measure against any approaching Japanese vessels. On the 2nd, President ROOSEVELT asks Japan to clarify its intents with regard to French INDO-CHINA, where the Japanese show signs of taking over the entire region. That same day the British declare a state of emergency in MALAYA, where "Force Z" (battleship *Prince of Wales*, battlecruiser *Repulse,* and four destroyers) has just arrived at SINGAPORE. Reconnaissance aircraft on HAWAII are ordered to search out as far as 400 miles, in an arc from the northwest to the south. At 43 degrees north latitudes, 158 degrees 30 minutes east longitude, about 3,200 miles northwest of Pearl Harbor, the Japanese First Air Fleet alters course due east. To thunderous cheers, the officers and crewmen of the First Air Fleet are informed that their objective is Pearl Harbor. On the 3rd, reconnaissance aircraft on Hawaii are ordered to search out to 400 miles in an arc from the northwest to the south. Meanwhile, the First Air Fleet refuels, 45 degrees north latitude, 170 degrees east longitude, about 2,400 miles northwest of Pearl Harbor. Upon completion of the refueling, the tankers return to Japan and the fleet resumes its eastward course, increasing speed. It crosses the International Date Line during the night, so the next day for the First Air Fleet is the 5th. The Japanese carrier fleet is now committed to the attack, no matter what. On the 4th, heavily escorted Japanese invasion forces begin to sail for their objectives in Southeast Asia. At the same time, US carrier *Enterprise* flys off reinforcements for Wake Island. Reconnaissance aircraft on Hawaii are ordered to search up to 400 miles from the northwestward to the south. On the 5th, additional Japanese invasion forces sail from CAM RANH BAY and SAIGON. Carrier LEXINGTON steams from Pearl Harbor to deliver aircraft to Midway. At 45 degrees north latitude, 178 degrees west longitude, about 1,200 miles northwest of Pearl Harbor, the Japanese First Air Fleet alters course from due east to southeast. On the 6th, President Roosevelt makes a personal appeal to Emperor HIROHITO asking him to use his influence to help preserve peace in the Pacific. Reconnaissance aircraft on Hawaii are ordered to concentrate their efforts to the west and south. At 2100 hours the Japanese First Air Fleet arrives at 31 degrees north latitude, 158 degrees east longitude, about 500 miles north of Pearl Harbor. On the 7th, the First Air Fleet attacks the US Pacific Fleet at its anchorage in Pearl Harbor, inflicting heavy damage at little loss to itself. Japanese destroyers shell Midway Island. Later that same day, west of the International Date Line, and therefore officially the 8th, Japanese aircraft destroy US air power in the Philippines in a massive raid on Clark and Iba airfields on Luzon. Japanese destroyers attack Wake. Japanese troops begin landing in Malaya, attack HONG KONG, occupy the International Settlement in SHANGHAI, and invade Siam. The United States and Britain declare war on Japan, and British "Force Z" sails from Singapore. An Australian independent infantry company lands on western TIMOR, in the NETHERLANDS EAST INDIES. A Dutch submarine sinks the Japanese destroyer *Isonami* off Celebes, the first Japanese warship to be sunk in the war. Japanese troops land on GUAM. Bill Howell, age 21, a resident of New City, in New York's Hudson Valley, is having a beer with friends at the local Knights of Columbus hall when the Pearl Harbor attack is announced. Bill works 40 miles south in New York City. At a time when as many people graduated from high school as today finish college, Bill had used his high school diploma to get a job with McCann-Erickson, a major advertising agency. The Great Depression was still going on and for a 21-year-old to snag a job like that, even if it was mainly because of skill at the typewriter, was quite an accomplishment. Bill knew how to type and take stenography, skills that he would find very useful during the war. And on hearing about Pearl Harbor, it was obvious that America was now in the war. Bill Howell's life, and the lives of millions of other young men, would never be the same. On the 9th, Japanese troops from KWAJALEIN occupy TARAWA in the GILBERTS. SIAM agrees to a cease-fire with Japan. Japanese bomb Nichols Field in the Philippines. Japanese capture KHOTA BARU airfield in northern Malaya. China declares war on Japan, after four years of "unofficial" warfare. On the 10th, Japanese aircraft sink *Prince of Wales* and *Repulse* in the South China Sea. Guam surrenders to a Japanese landing force after a two-day battle. Japanese troops begin landings in northern Luzon. Japanese naval aircraft bomb the CAVITE Navy Yard, Manila Bay. On the 11th, Marines on Wake Island beat off a Japanese landing, sinking destroyers *Hayate* and *Kisaragi*. This was rare during World War II, in which nearly all amphibious assaults succeeded. US submarines commence war patrols against Japanese shipping. Germany and Italy declare war on the United States. On the 12th, Japanese troops land at Legaspi, southeastern Luzon. In northern Luzon, Japanese troops advancing from Vigan and Aparri capture two airstrips. Japanese troops complete the occupation of southern Thailand, crossing the Burmese frontier. The British decide to abandon northern Malaya. Bill Howell acts on a decision he—and many other Americans—made on 7 December, and enlists in the navy. Because so many young men enlisted right after the Pearl Harbor attack, the day on which these new recruits are to report is set for a later date. Bill is ordered to report to the Brooklyn Navy Yard (40 miles down the Hudson River, in New York City) on 26 December. On the 13th, British and Canadian troops abandon the mainland portions of Hong Kong. The Japanese temporarily abandon the attempt to capture Wake, returning to base but continuing to subject the island to air attacks from the MANDATES. On the 14th, Japanese forces in Malaya occupy Kroh, and Japanese air units begin repairing northern Luzon airfields for their own use. On the 15th, Congress votes an additional $10.1 billion (some $60 billion in 1997 dollars) for the war effort. The surviving B-17s in the Philippines are ordered to Australia. Japanese forces in Malaya occupy Gurun. On the 16th Japanese troops land at Miri, in Sarawak, on BORNEO. Carriers HIRYU and SORYU, with escorts, separate from the homeward bound First Air Fleet to attack Wake Island. In Malaya Japanese forces land at PENANG. A carrier task force sails from PEARL HARBOR to relieve Wake Island. On the 17th, Adm Husband KIMMEL is relieved of command of the Pacific Fleet. VAdm W. S. Pye is in temporary command until Adm Chester W. NIMITZ arrives. LG Walter C. Short, commanding the Hawaiian Department, is also relieved. Japanese troops land in British North Borneo. On the 18th the Japanese 38th Division lands on Hong Kong Island. Japanese aircraft begin operating from strips in northern Luzon. Japanese destroyer *Shinonome* mined and sunk off Borneo. In Malaya the British reorganize forces and prepare for further withdrawal. British and Dutch troops occupy Portuguese Timor. On the 19th, Japanese attack Del Monte Field, Mindanao. In Malaya the Japanese occupy Penang Island, while the British continue withdrawal. Congress authorizes the president to draft men up to 44 years of age. On the 20th, Adm Ernest J. KING is named commander-in-chief, US Fleet. The American Volunteer

Group (FLYING TIGERS) goes into action for the first time, shooting down six Japanese bombers over Kunming, China. On the 21st, heavily reinforced and supported by carriers *Hiryu* and *Soryu*, the Japanese renew their attempt to capture Wake Island. Japanese land on Mindanao, rapidly occupy DAVAO. Siam allies itself with Japan. On the 22nd, Japanese task forces arrives off Wake, begin intensive bombardment. Japanese troops begin a major landing on Luzon, at Lingayen Gulf in the northwest. B-17s based in Australia attack Japanese shipping off Mindanao. The PENSACOLA CONVOY lands the first US troops in Australia. On the 23rd, Japanese begin air raids on RANGOON, Burma. Japanese troops land on Wake, which surrenders. US carriers speeding to support Wake Island are recalled when 400 miles east of the island. Heavy fighting on Luzon as US and Philippine troops attempt to hold the Japanese to their beachhead. Gen. Douglas MACARTHUR decides to withdraw to BATAAN. On the 24th, Japanese troops land at KUCHING, Sarawak. Japanese troops land at Lamon Bay, in east-central Luzon, and on Jolo, in the southern Philippines. Manila is bombed severely by Japanese aircraft. At the Arcadia Conference, in Washington, Roosevelt, CHURCHILL, and their principal advisers plan Allied STRATEGY. The Italian BLOCKADE RUNNER *Orseolo* departs KOBE for Bordeaux. On the 25th, Hong Kong surrenders to the Japanese 38th Division. On Luzon the Japanese dislocate a US-Philippine temporary defense line, while the South Luzon Force begins withdrawing northward. Manila is heavily bombed by Japanese aircraft. British attempt to stabilize their lines in Malaya north of Johore. On the 26th the Japanese continue to press the defenders on Luzon, the Philippines, from the north and the southeast. Manila is declared an open city. Japanese columns advancing down the west coast of Malaya merge near Taiping. The day after Christmas, Bill Howell reports for basic training at 52nd Street and First Avenue, the Brooklyn Navy Yard's Bay Ridge annex. He is told that because of the need to train sailors quickly he will receive an abbreviated three weeks of training, rather than the usual eight. It is cold and the accelerated training goes by as a blur. On the 27th, under heavy Japanese pressure US/Philippine troops occupy a temporary line running through Gerona and San Jose on Luzon. On the 28th, Japanese forces in Malaya capture Ipoh, having advanced about 150 miles since landing, with 200 more to Singapore. On Luzon, US/Philippine troops fall back to the Tarlac-Cabanatuan phase line. The US Navy authorizes the raising of special construction battalions (the SEABEES). On the 29th, Japanese troops eject US/Philippine troops from the Tarlac-Cabanatuan line on Luzon. First Japanese air raid on CORREGIDOR. On the 30th, Japanese troops occupy Kuantan, on the east coast of Malaya. On Luzon, US/Philippine troops occupy the Bambam-Gapan line, but the Japanese unhinge the line's right flank by capturing Gapan as the Philippine 91st Division collapses. On the 31st in the Philippines, by denying his right flank, Major General Jonathan Wainwright manages to preserve portions of the old Tarlac-Gapan line, hanging his right on Mt. Arayat while other forces cover the Paridel and Calumpit positions, vital for the withdrawal of the South Luzon Force to Bataan. In Malaya, British forces maintain a relatively stable line.

January 1942

If December 1941 was bad for the Allies, January 1942 was worse. At the beginning of 1942, the Allies still possessed considerable military forces in the Western Pacific, but the Japanese appeared more and more irresistible. The year opened with the Japanese advancing everywhere. Fighting continued in MALAYA and the Philippines, but it was clear that the Japanese would eventually prevail. The Japanese also moved into the NETHERLANDS EAST INDIES, the islands northwest of Australia, and Burma. Things looked grim. Yet there was some hope, the United Nations Pact was signed, as representatives of 26 nations meeting in Washington adopted the principles of the Atlantic Charter

and declared that none of them would make a separate peace.

On the 1st, PHILIPPINE ARMY units begin holding the Borac-Guagua line, to cover the final withdrawal into BATAAN. Japan is temporarily halted in Malaya. On the 2nd, on Luzon, the Japanese Army occupies MANILA and CAVITE from the south, but the Borac-Guagua line, farther north, holds. Japanese forces in Malaya occupy Kampar. On the 3rd, the ABDA Command is formed to unite Allied efforts in Southeast Asia and the Netherlands East Indies, under the overall command of Sir Archibald WAVELL. The Borac-Guagua line holds on Luzon. British once again withdraw under pressure in Malaya. On the 4th US aircraft attack Japanese shipping in DAVAO harbor, damaging the cruiser *Myoko*. The Philippine Army abandons the Borac-Guagua line, and the withdrawal to Bataan is nearly completed: Japanese troops continue to advance in Malaya. On the 5th, the Japanese 48th Division begins withdrawing from the Philippines for duty on JAVA. US/Philippine troops begin consolidating the defenses of Bataan. Japanese troops continue to advance in Malaya. First British reinforcements (elements of 17th Indian Division) arrive in Burma. On the 6th, Philippine Army units hold the Dinalupihan-Orani line, last defensive position before Bataan. In Malaya the British manage to hold the Japanese north of Kuala Lumpur. On the 7th, US and Philippine troops complete occupation of the Bataan position: 15,000 US and 65,000 Philippine troops are immediately put on half-rations. In Malaya the Japanese turn the British defenses north of Kuala Lumpur. On the 8th, British troops in Malaya are ordered to fall back on the "Johore Line," about 50 miles north of SINGAPORE. On Bataan, US/Philippine troops continue to organize their defenses as Japanese units close with them. On the 9th, Japanese SUBMARINES begin operating in the Indian Ocean. First Japanese offensive against the Bataan defenses. In Malaya the Japanese make an amphibious "end run" around the British left and occupy Port Settenham on the Strait of Malacca. On the 10th Japanese troops continue pressure on Bataan, begin landing at Tarakan Bay, BORNEO. Sir Archibald Wavell arrives at Bandung, near BATAVIA, to take over the ABDA Command. On the 11th Japanese Navy airborne troops land on Celebes, in coordination with an amphibious attack. US carrier *Saratoga* is TORPEDOED south of HAWAII. Heavy fighting on Bataan. In Malaya the Japanese capture Kuala Lumpur. A Japanese submarine shells Pago Pago, in American SAMOA. On the 12th the Japanese in Malaya begin to advance on Malacca. Dutch coast-defense battery sinks two Japanese minesweepers off Tarakan, Borneo. Heavy fighting on Bataan. On the 13th heavy fighting continues on Bataan, as Philippine troops counterattack. Elements of British 18th Division reach Singapore, as forces in Malaya complete withdrawal to the Johore line. On the 14th, the Japanese capture Malacca in Malaya. Heavy fighting on Bataan. Arcadia Conference ends. On the 15th, Chinese troops halt a Japanese offensive near CHANGSHA in Hunan Province. The Japanese Southern Army invades Burma from the Isthmus of Kra in Thailand. In Malaya the Japanese make several small "end run" amphibious landings to dislocate the British left. On Bataan, Japanese troops penetrate US/Philippine defenses. As Bill Howell's navy basic training comes to an end, he is told that he will be kept at the training center to help out with the processing of new recruits: His typing and stenographic skills are proving more useful than he had anticipated. On the 16th the British in Malaya attempt to hold the line of the Muar River against Japanese forces advancing down the west coast. Heavy fighting on Bataan. Rio Conference begins, as 21 American republics discuss hemispheric defense. On the 17th the British are under heavy pressure on the Muar River line in Malaya. Heavy fighting on Bataan continues. On the 18th British troops in Malaya heavily engaged on the Muar River Line. Heavy fighting continues on Bataan, as attempts to restore original lines fail. On the 19th US/Philippine troops continue to try to restore lines, under increasing Japanese pressure. In Malaya British troops abandon the Muar River

line; all forces are now within the Johore line. On the 20th Japanese aircraft carriers raid RABAUL and KAVIENG, in the BISMARCKS. The Japanese 55th Division invades Burma from central Thailand. On the 21st a British task force built around the carrier INDOMITABLE arrives at ADDU ATOLL, in the Indian Ocean southwest of India. Heavy fighting continues on Bataan. Rabaul and Kavieng again raided by Japanese aircraft. In Malaya, the Japanese begin to dislocate the Johore line. On the 22nd, Japanese troops begin landings on New Ireland and NEW BRITAIN. Japanese air strikes on LAE and Salamaua, in NEW GUINEA. CHIANG KAI-SHEK agrees to let USLG Joseph STILWELL serve as his chief of staff, authorizes movement of Chinese troops into Burma. Heavy fighting on the Johore line in Malaya. US Army Task Force 6814 (later the Americal Division) sails from New York for the South Pacific. On the 23rd, US destroyers and a Dutch submarine attack Japanese shipping off BALIKPAPAN, Borneo. Heavy fighting on Bataan, and US/Philippine troops begin to fall back to secondary defensive positions, while Japanese troops land at Quinauan and Longoskayan Points in the American rear but are contained. In Burma the Japanese capture the Sittang River bridge, in the British rear, causing the collapse of the understrength and green 17th Indian Division. In Malaya the Johore line crumbles. British reinforce Singapore with an additional new Indian brigade. On the 24th, Australian resistance at Rabaul ends. Japanese begin landings at Balikpapan, Borneo, and Keita, BOUGAINVILLE. In Malaya, British plan for withdrawal to Singapore. On the 25th, US task forces built around carriers *Enterprise* and YORKTOWN rendezvous off Samoa and proceed on raid into the MANDATES. In the Philippines, the American/Filipino troops complete their withdrawal to secondary positions. On the 26th, US and Philippine troops consolidate the Bagac-Orion line on Bataan; Japanese troops land at Canas Point, and other headlands, in their rear but are contained. In Malaya the Japanese make major inroads into the Johore line position. On the 27th, HMS *Indomitable* flies off 48 aircraft to reinforce the defense of Java. *En-*

terprise and YORKTOWN task forces raid the MARSHALL ISLANDS. US submarines begin supply runs to CORREGIDOR. On the 28th the Japanese attack the new US/Philippine line on Bataan. Under heavy pressure, the British forces in Malaya begin to withdraw toward Singapore. On the 29th Japanese pressure continues on Bataan, but the lines hold. The first US troops arrive on FIJI. An additional brigade of the British 18th Division reaches Singapore from India, as British troops in Malaya continue withdrawing into the island city. On the 30th, Japanese undertake a surprise attack on Moulmein, Burma. On Bataan, US/Philippine troops begin clearing Japanese pockets along the coast. Japanese attack AMBOINA, in the Netherlands East Indies. On the 31st, the British abandon Moulmein, Burma, and retire across the Salween River. British troops in Malaya are withdrawn to Singapore Island. Japanese pressure on Bataan eases.

February 1942

February saw the situation beginning to turn around for the Allies, or at least become less grim. American forces continued to hold off the Japanese in the Philippines and the British were still holding out against the Japanese in Burma. U.S. carrier groups began raiding Japanese island bases and interfering with Japanese invasion operations. Otherwise, the Japanese advance kept moving forward. February demonstrated that the Japanese could be slowed down, but not that they could be stopped.

On the 1st, US carriers *Enterprise* and *Hornet* raid Japanese bases in the GILBERT and MARSHALL ISLANDS. On the 2nd, the British carrier INDOMITABLE arrives at TRINCOMALEE, on CEYLON. US and Philippine troops counterattack in BATAAN. On the 3rd, US and Philippine troops successfully restore the Bagac-Orion line on Bataan, despite Japanese counterattacks. On the 4th, Japanese aircraft catch the ABDA cruiser-destroyer squadron in Madoera Strait, north of Bali, inflicting heavy damage on US cruisers *Marblehead* and *Houston*. The last Allied (Australian) troops on AMBOINA

surrender. On the 5th, Japanese artillery begins bombarding Singapore from across the Strait of Johore, while the final elements of the British 18th Division arrive by sea. On the 6th, Japanese make local attacks on Bataan but are beaten off. On the 7th, US/Philippine troops begin clearing Japanese pockets and beachheads on Bataan. On the 8th, Japanese troops begin crossing the Strait of Johore, to land on Singapore Island. Japanese land at MAKASSAR, Celebes. Philippine troops eliminate Japanese troops holding Quinauan Point. On the 9th, Japanese troops effect a second beachhead on Singapore Island, which is subject to a heavy air raid. Japanese troops on Bataan suspend offensive operations and begin a long period of rest and reorganization; for the first time since the Pacific War began in early December the Japanese have been stopped cold. On the 10th, Gen. WAVELL visits Singapore, orders continued resistance, despite Japanese presence on the island. On the 11th Japanese overrun elements of the Indian 46th Brigade as it retreats from the Salween River. Japanese demand surrender of Singapore. On the 12th, US/Philippine troops on Bataan mop up isolated Japanese pockets in their rear. On the 13th, US and Philippine troops eliminate Japanese forces at Canas Point beachhead on Bataan, eliminating the last Japanese pockets in their rear. Japanese light surface forces sink the British gunboat *Scorpion* in Banka Strait, prompting the ABDA cruiser-destroyer force to sortie from BATAVIA. United States and Canada agree to construct the ALCAN HIGHWAY. That night the Japanese submarine *I-17* shells an oil depot at Goleta, California, with little serious effect. On the 14th, Japanese Navy paratroopers land near PALEMBANG. Attempting to intercept a convoy proceeding through Banka Strait, ABDA cruisers and destroyers are attacked by Japanese aircraft and break off the effort. On the 15th, Singapore surrenders to the Japanese, depriving the Allies of the major British naval base in Asia. Japanese amphibious troops land at Palembang, where there is heavy fighting. Dutch destroyer VAN GHENT runs aground in Banka Strait and must be abandoned. The Japanese First Air

Fleet departs PALAU for the Dutch East Indies. On the 16th, Japanese secure Palembang. An Australian and American convoy attempting to reach TIMOR is turned back by Japanese air attack. On the 17th, the Dutch destroyer *Van Ness* is sunk by Japanese aircraft in Banka Strait. On the 18th, the Dutch coast defense ship *Soerabaya* and a submarine are destroyed by air attack on Soerabaya Naval Base. On the 19th, Japanese naval- and land-based aircraft raid the port at DARWIN, northwestern Australia, inflicting heavy damage. Japanese troops begin landing on Bali. Later that night the ABDA cruiser-destroyer force engages Japanese shipping, losing Dutch destroyer *Piet Hein* and suffering a cruiser and two destroyers damaged while damaging two Japanese destroyers (Battle of Lombok Strait). On the 20th, the USS LEXINGTON beats off a Japanese air attack some 300 miles east-northeast of RABAUL, but is forced to abandon a planned raid on that place. In a combined amphibious and airborne attack, Japanese troops land on Timor. On the 21st, on Timor, Dutch and Australian troops begin GUERRILLA resistance. British Seventh Armoured Brigade reaches RANGOON, in Burma, while the 17th Indian Division begins defending the Sittang River bridgehead. On the 22nd, the Japanese 48th Division arrives at BALIKPAPAN from the Philippines. President ROOSEVELT orders MACARTHUR to leave the Philippines for Australia to assume command of all Allied forces in the southwest Pacific. On the 23rd, Japanese submarine *I-17* shells Elwood, California. B-17s from Australia raid Rabaul. On the 24th, USS *Enterprise* raids WAKE ISLAND. Heavy fighting for the Sittang River bridgehead in Burma. On the 25th the ABDA Command is formally dissolved; US, British, and Commonwealth forces pass under Dutch control in the NETHERLANDS EAST INDIES. In Burma the Japanese threaten to flank the 17th Indian Division, penetrating between it and the First Burma Division. On the 26th the aircraft transport USS *Langley* is sunk off Java with 32 aircraft aboard. Heavy fighting by the 17th Indian Division in Burma. On the 27th, the Battle of the JAVA SEA: Under VAdm Karel DOORMAN, an Al-

lied cruiser-destroyer force attempts to intercept a Java-bound Japanese invasion force, only to be intercepted by a superior Japanese squadron, losing two light cruisers and three destroyers, with heavy damage to other ships. On the 28th, the Battle of Sunda Strait: After nightfall, as Japanese troops begin landing on Java, USS *Houston* and HMAS *Perth* attempt to escape from the Java Sea by way of Sunda Strait. En route they encounter a Japanese convoy and attempt to attack it, only to be sunk, along with three of the accompanying destroyers, by overwhelming Japanese naval forces.

March 1942

Allied resistance began to stiffen in places like Burma and New Guinea, but Japanese forces continued to advance everywhere. Allied prospects were still in free fall, and the bottom wasn't even in sight.

On the 1st, Japanese troops continue landing on Java. Battle off Soerabaya: HMS EXETER and an American and a British destroyer are intercepted and sunk by Japanese naval and air forces while trying to escape eastward from Java. Japanese battleship *Hiei*, supported by cruisers and destroyers, sinks two US destroyers south of Java. Chinese troops reach the front in Burma, where Japanese pressure remains steady. On the 2nd, Japanese troops occupy ZAMBOANGA, on Mindanao in the Philippines. Japanese encounter heavy fighting on Java. On the 3rd, heavy fighting on Java, while Japanese cruisers and destroyers sink destroyer HMS *Stronghold*, several smaller warships, and a merchant ship south of Java. Japanese aircraft raid Broome, Australia, inflicting heavy damage. On the 4th, the USS *Enterprise* raids MARCUS ISLAND. In the Netherlands East Indies, heavy fighting continues on Java, while three damaged Allied destroyers and other vessels in the SOERABAYA navy yard are scuttled. Refueling from a submarine at FRENCH FRIGATE SHOAL, two Japanese flying boats raid Pearl Harbor, inflicting no damage. On the 5th, the Japanese First Air Fleet raids TJILATJAP, sinking several vessels. Japanese troops land at Salamaua, in northeastern New Guinea. General Harold ALEXANDER is appointed British commander in Burma. On the 6th, Dutch resistance on Java becomes fragmented; the Dutch Navy begins scuttling its last vessels in Javan ports. In Burma, after an unsuccessful counterattack, Gen. Alexander orders RANGOON evacuated. On the 7th, Japanese surface units shell CHRISTMAS ISLAND (Indian Ocean), sinking one ship. Having only recently arrived, the US Americal Division sails from MELBOURNE, Australia, for NOUMEA. Japanese troops land at Lae and Salamaua, in northeastern New Guinea. Japanese naval units reconnoiter Buka, north of BOUGAINVILLE. Japanese troops depart SINGAPORE for northern Sumatra. On the 8th, Japanese troops occupy Rangoon. On the 9th, Allied forces on Java (c. 20,000) surrender. Adm Ernest J. KING, commander-in-chief, U.S. Fleet, is also named chief of naval operations, replacing Adm Harold Stark. British withdrawal in Burma proceeds smoothly. On the 10th, Adm Wilson BROWN's carriers LEXINGTON and YORKTOWN make a daring raid over the OWEN STANLEYS in New Guinea, to hit Japanese shipping at Lae and Salamaua, sinking an auxiliary cruiser and two merchant ships, and damaging four warships and several merchantmen. MacArthur appoints MG Johnathan WAINWRIGHT commander of forces on Luzon. US 27th Infantry Division sails from SAN FRANCISCO for HAWAII. On the 11th, over two weeks after receiving orders to proceed to Australia, MACARTHUR leaves CORREGIDOR on a PT-BOAT bound for Mindanao. In Burma British and newly arrived Chinese forces prepare to defend the central region of the country. On the 12th, the US Americal Division lands at Noumea. Japanese troops land at SABANG, in northern Sumatra. General Joseph STILWELL arrives in Burma to assist Sir Harold Alexander as combined US and Chinese commander. On the 13th, Japanese troops land at Buka, north of Bougainville, and begin building an airfield. British Commonwealth and Chinese troops establish the Prome-Toungoo line in Burma. On the 14th, the Japanese forces in Burma halt in order to rest and reorganize, as the British and Chi-

nese hold on the Prome-Toungoo line. The Joint Chiefs of Staff reaffirms the "Germany first" policy. MacArthur arrives on Mindanao. On the 15th, the US 27th Infantry Division arrives in Hawaii. In the Philippines, the Japanese begin an intensive bombardment of the island forts guarding Manila Bay. On the 16th, a small task force from the US Americal Division sails from Noumea bound for Efate, in the NEW HEBRIDES. On the 17th, MacArthur leaves Mindanao by B-17, and arrives in Australia. On the 18th, a task force from the Americal Division occupies Efate, in the New Hebrides. On the 19th, British LG William SLIM takes command of the British Burma Corps. In central Burma the Japanese attack the Chinese 200th Division. US 41st Infantry Division sails from San Francisco for Australia. On the 20th, elements of the Japanese 18th Division sail from PENANG, MALAYA, for the ANDAMAN ISLANDS. On the 21st, in Burma, a massive Japanese air raid on Magwe seriously damages airfield facilities and aircraft, as the Japanese prepare a new offensive to break the Prome-Toungoo line. On the 22nd, the Japanese complete the destruction of the Magwe air base, forcing British and American aircraft to withdraw to fields closer to India and China. The British Fifth Division departs from Britain bound for Madagascar. On the 23rd, troops of the Japanese 18th Division occupy PORT BLAIR, in the Andamans, without opposition (the small British garrison withdrew on the 12th). On the 24th, the US-British Combined Chiefs of Staff declares the Pacific Theater a US responsibility. Japanese forces begin an intensive air and artillery bombardment of BATAAN. Japanese troops conduct "mopping up" operations throughout the Netherlands East Indies, landing troops at numerous small ports bypassed during the invasion. In Burma the Japanese open an offensive up the Sittang, Irrawaddy, and Chindwin Rivers. On the 25th, US Task Force 39 (carrier WASP, a fast battleship, two heavy cruisers, and eight destroyers) steams from the East Coast bound for Scapa Flow, northern Scotland, where it will relieve British forces earmarked for operations in the Indian Ocean. US troops (162nd Infantry, 41st Division) occupy Bora

Bora, in the SOCIETY ISLANDS. On the 26th, the Japanese First Air Fleet departs the Celebes bound for the Indian Ocean. Heavy Japanese pressure against Chinese forces near Toungoo, in central Burma. On the 27th, British Adm James SOMERVILLE assumes command of the British Far Eastern Fleet (three carriers, five battleships, seven cruisers, including one Dutch, and 14 British, Dutch, and Australian destroyers, divided into a "fast" division able to make 24 knots, and a "slow" one able to make 18), based on CEYLON. A Japanese submarine flotilla (six boats) departs Penang for the Indian Ocean. Chinese 200th Division beats off Japanese attacks on Toungoo, Burma. On the 28th, in preparation for a major offensive, the Japanese undertake a probe against US lines on Bataan. On the 29th, the British Burma Corps attacks to support Chinese troops at Toungoo. After reconnaissance reports the presence of the Japanese First Air Fleet in the Indian Ocean, Admiral Somerville concludes it will attack his bases in Ceylon and orders his ships to deploy so as to ambush them. On the 30th, the Joint Chiefs of Staff issues directives dividing the Pacific Theater into the Southwest Pacific Area, under MacArthur, and the Pacific Ocean Areas, under Adm Chester W. NIMITZ, further dividing the latter's command into North, Central, and South Pacific areas. In Burma Japanese pressure forces the Chinese 200th Division to withdraw from Toungoo, as the Burma Corps falls back as well. On the 31st, Japanese troops in Burma occupy Toungoo, thus unhinging the Prome-Toungoo line.

April 1942

The Allied situation hits rock bottom, although this wouldn't be clear until the following month. At the beginning of the month, American troops in the Philippines were barely hanging on, the British were falling back toward the Indian frontier in Burma, and a Japanese carrier fleet was raiding into the Indian Ocean. By month's end, BATAAN had fallen, the British had virtually abandoned Burma, and the Japanese seemed everywhere triumphant.

But American bombers, flying off a carrier, had bombed Tokyo.

On the 1st, US/Philippine troops on Bataan go on quarter-rations because of the inability to get supplies through the Japanese naval blockade. The British Far Eastern Fleet continues to search for the Japanese First Air Fleet south and east of CEYLON. The First Air Fleet refuels south of JAVA. A Japanese cruiser-destroyer force departs Megui for operations in the Bay of Bengal. On the 2nd, the US carrier *Hornet*, carrying 16 Army B-25 medium bombers, sails from SAN FRANCISCO. Low on fuel, the British Far Eastern Fleet is ordered to retire to ADDU ATOLL in the Maldive Islands, as the whereabouts of the Japanese First Air Fleet is still unknown, making Ceylon too dangerous. The Japanese 18th Division sails from SINGAPORE for RANGOON. US bombers operating from India attack Japanese shipping in the ANDAMAN ISLANDS. In Burma, the British abandon Prome. On the 3rd, heavily reinforced with fresh troops, heavy artillery, and lots of ammunition, the Japanese launch a major offensive on Bataan. In Burma, as the British withdraw from Prome, STILWELL orders the Chinese to make a stand at Pyinamana. On the 4th, the Japanese succeed in dislocating the front on Bataan, and US and Philippine troops fall back to a reserve line. The British detect the Japanese First Air Fleet south of Ceylon, where all operational ships are ordered to put to sea. Japanese carrier aircraft sink the British heavy cruisers *Cornwall* and *Dorsetshire*, at sea off Ceylon, as well as several other vessels. On the 5th, the British Far Eastern Fleet hastily sorties from Addu Atoll in an attempt to intercept the Japanese First Air Fleet. Japanese aircraft from the First Air Fleet strike COLOMBO, Ceylon, sinking a destroyer, an auxiliary cruiser, and another minor warship as well as many auxiliaries and merchant ships, downing 27 British aircraft, while losing only seven airplanes. The British and Japanese fleets in the Indian Ocean fail to spot each other, although coming within 200 miles of each other. On Bataan, Japanese troops capture Mt. Samat, unhinging the defenses. When a counterattack by US/Philippine troops fails to throw them back, a withdrawal is ordered. On the 6th, elements of the Japanese First Air Fleet begin a raid into the Bay of Bengal. CHIANG KAI-SHEK agrees to provide additional forces for Burma, as Stilwell's Chinese forces prepare to defend Pyinamana. On the 7th, US/Philippine troops fail to form a new defensive line, as the Japanese advance continues. Japanese troops land on BOUGAINVILLE, in the Solomon Islands. The Japanese 18th Division lands at Rangoon. In the Indian Ocean the British Far Eastern Fleet is ordered to return to Addu Atoll. On the 8th, as US/Philippine resistance on Bataan begins disintegrating, the decision to surrender is made. US carrier *Enterprise* and her escorts, under RAdm William F. HALSEY, sail from PEARL HARBOR. On the 9th, aircraft from the Japanese First Air Fleet sink nine merchant ships off the coast of India, while cruisers raid commerce in the Bay of Bengal, accounting for three more ships, for a total of about 92,000 tons. Japanese carrier aircraft raid Trincomalee, inflicting little damage save to defending aircraft, but sink carrier HERMES, two smaller warships, and two tankers in nearby waters. US/Philippine forces on Bataan (c. 75,000) surrender to the Japanese, ending the desperate resistance of the "Battling Bastards of Bataan." US troops still hold CORREGIDOR, which lies in the entrance to Manila Bay. On the 10th, the British Far Eastern Fleet (mostly older battleships and cruisers, plus carriers INDOMITABLE and *Formidable*) retires to Bombay and East Africa. Japanese troops land on CEBU, in the central Philippines. Japanese renew their offensive in Burma. In the Philippines the Japanese begin bombardment of Corregidor and the smaller island forts in Manila Bay. On the 11th the Japanese begin a major offensive against the British in Burma. The Japanese rapidly overrun the settled portions of Cebu. On the 12th US/Philippine forces on Cebu retire to the interior to begin GUERRILLA warfare. Japanese heavy bombardment of Corregidor and the Manila harbor forts continues. In Burma the British Burma Corps requires support from Chinese troops to hold off Japanese attacks. Bill Howell achieves the rank of petty officer third class, as a yeoman. Because of his clerical

skills and hard work, it was decided earlier that he would "strike" for the navy rating of yeoman (clerk, handling the paperwork). This means that he underwent on-the-job-training in navy administrative procedures. Successful completion of that training resulted in the rank yeoman third class. On the 13th VAdm Robert L. GHORMLEY is designated commander, South Pacific Area. In Burma the front of the Burma Corps breaks. On the 14th in Burma the Yenangyaung oil field is ordered destroyed. Australia approves the appointment of MACARTHUR as commander, Southwest Pacific. On the 15th, Japanese troops threaten to encircle the British Burma Division. On the 16th, Japanese troops land on Panay, in the southern Philippines, as the defenders retire to the interior to begin guerrilla warfare. Japanese troops occupy Magwe, in central Burma. On the 17th, British, Indian, and Chinese forces are unable to hold the Japanese advance; Stilwell abandons plans to make a stand at Pyinamana. On the 18th, the DOOLITTLE Raid: From little more than 650 miles east of Honshu, carrier *Hornet* launches 16 B-25 medium bombers against Tokyo and other targets, which comes as quite a shock to the Japanese, even though the damage is slight. In Burma, despite some local success by Allied forces, the Chinese 55th Division collapses under Japanese pressure, breaking the Allied front and uncovering the road to Lashio, in northern Burma. On the 19th, the British abandon the Yenangyaung oil fields in Burma, despite a partially successful Chinese counterattack. On the 20th British forces in Burma begin a general withdrawal. On the 21st the Japanese close up on the retiring Allied forces in Burma. On the 22nd, the US 32nd Infantry Division sails from San Francisco for Australia. In Burma Stilwell attempts to reorganize Chinese forces to better hold the Japanese. On the 23rd, uncovered by the British withdrawal to their west, Chinese troops in central Burma begin to pull out northward to avoid being outflanked by the Japanese. On the 24th, Japanese troops advance on all fronts in Burma. On the 25th, ALEXANDER orders Allied forces to retire to the north bank of the Irrawaddy River, as Chinese counterattacks fail to halt Japanese advance toward Lashio. Task Force 16 returns to Pearl Harbor; its mission (the Tokyo Raid) remains a closely guarded secret for months. Japanese reaction to the raid is to recall some fighter groups from the front, while Adm Isoroku YAMAMOTO is inspired to propose a plan to expand Japan's defensive perimeter to the ALEUTIANS and MIDWAY. On the 26th, Alexander decides that Burma is lost, and all efforts must be concentrated on the defense of India. On the 27th Stilwell proposes to CHIANG that a new Chinese army be organized and trained in India. On the 28th Stilwell orders the Chinese 28th Division to defend Lashio, which the Japanese are rapidly approaching. On the 29th, Japanese troops begin a systematic campaign to clear Mindanao of US and Philippine forces. In Burma, the Japanese capture Lashio, arriving before the Chinese 28th Division. China is now completely isolated from overland contact with the outside world. On the 30th, British troops evacuate MANDALAY in Burma, retiring to the north side of the Irrawaddy, abandoning all central Burma to the Japanese. On Mindanao the Japanese continue pressing the defenders back, while on Luzon the bombardment of Corregidor and the harbor forts continues.

May 1942

The Allies finally began to slow down the Japanese advance. Although the British and Chinese continued to fall back in Burma, and organized resistance in the Philippines ceased with the surrender of CORREGIDOR, the Japanese were stopped in New Guinea and suffered their first naval reverse in the Battle of the CORAL SEA. Moreover, the scene was set for the climactic Battle of Midway in June.

On the 1st, Japanese troops occupy MANDALAY, Burma, and press on toward India, while on Mindanao Japanese troops press their advance and the bombardment of CORREGIDOR continues. On the 2nd, US submarine *Drum* TORPEDOES the Japanese seaplane carrier *Mizuho* off Honshu. On Mindanao, Philippine troops make a stand in the north, briefly holding the Japanese. The small Australian garrison at TULAGI near GUADALCANAL in the eastern SOLOMONS, is withdrawn. On the 3rd, Japanese troops land on Tulagi, near Guadalcanal. Japanese troops land at Cagayan, Mindanao, last important town in the Philippines still in US hands. Despite fierce resistance US/Philippine troops on Mindanao fall back. A US submarine evacuates a few key personnel from Corregidor as the Japanese continue to bombard the island. On the 4th, the US carrier YORKTOWN attacks Japanese at Tulagi, seriously damaging a destroyer, which has to be beached and abandoned. Corregidor subject to an intense artillery and aerial bombardment. US and Philippine troops on Mindanao regroup as Japanese pressure lets up. On the 5th, Japanese carriers *Zuikaku* and SHOKAKU enter the Solomons Sea from the north, intent upon supporting operations against the eastern Solomons and PORT MORESBY, while the *Yorktown* and LEXINGTON task forces rendezvous in the Coral Sea. Japanese troops land on Corregidor, in the Philippines. British troops land at Diego Suarez, a Vichy-held naval base in northern Madagascar. British forces evacuate Akyab in Burma. Japanese Imperial General Headquarters orders the Combined Fleet to prepare for an attack on Midway and the ALEUTIANS. On the 6th, on Corregidor, LG Johnathan WAINWRIGHT surrenders all US and Philippine forces in the Philippines. Japanese resume their advance on Mindanao. Chinese forces in northern Burma are ordered to retire to China. In the Coral Sea, US and Japanese carrier task forces search for each other. On the 7th, Battle of the Coral Sea begins: US carrier aircraft sink carrier *Shoho*, while Japanese carrier aircraft sink a US oiler and destroyer. Japanese submarine-borne aircraft reconnoiter Aden. The British capture Diego Suarez, Madagascar, from the Vichy French. On the 8th, the Battle of the Coral Sea continues: US and Japanese carrier task forces trade blows, the United States losing *Lexington* while the Japanese suffer heavy damage to *Shokaku* and severe aircraft loss. This is the first setback for the Japanese Navy since the war began. Japanese SUBMARINES begin reconnaissance operations off East Africa. In Burma, Japanese troops close on Myitkyina, in the far north, held by the Chinese. MACARTHUR urges the Joint Chiefs of Staff to authorize an offensive in the Solomons, under his command, to stop the Japanese from advancing any farther. On the 9th the Japanese abandon the Port Moresby operation, the first time since the war began that Allied resistance has forced them to cancel their plans. US troops arrive on TONGA and the Galapagos. On the 10th, US troops on Mindanao surrender to the Japanese, ending formal resistance, but some flee to the interior to conduct GUERRILLA operations. In Burma the Japanese attack the British rear guard near Shwegyin. On the 11th, US submarine *S-42* sinks Japanese merchant cruiser *Okinoshima* in St. George's Channel, NEW BRITAIN. On the 12th, in revenge for the DOOLITTLE Raid on Tokyo, and Chinese assistance in getting the American airmen safely away, the Japanese launch a punitive expedition in China, eventually killing thousands of Chinese. In Burma Japanese troops cross the Salween River. On the 13th, other US forces relieve New Zealand troops holding FIJI. On the 14th, US troops in the mountains of north Luzon surrender to the Japanese, but some resort to guerrilla warfare. In Burma the Japanese reach the foothills of the Arakan Mountains near Shwegyin, leaving the British in control of only small areas of the country along the Indian frontier, the Burma Army having been completely shattered, although small groups (including STILWELL and his staff) make their way out of Japanese-held territory in the following months. The US 32nd Infantry Division arrives in Australia. On the 15th, the US 41st Infantry Division completes its movement to Australia. British headquarters for the Burma front is established at Imphal, in the mountainous eastern portion of Assam, in the extreme northeast of India. Australian troops in Papua begin fortifying Port Moresby. On the 16th, the first US service troops arrive in India, to be greeted with hostile demonstrations by Indian nationalists. On the 17th, US submarines sink two of their Japanese counterparts, *I-28* by *Tautog* (SS-199) off TRUK, in the CAROLINES, and *I-164* by *Triton* (SS-201) southeast of Kyushu. On the

18th, US/Philippine troops on Panay surrender to the Japanese, ending formal resistance in the Philippines, but some desert and form guerrilla bands that fight on until MacArthur returns in 30 months. US intelligence begins detecting evidence of an imminent Japanese attack on MIDWAY. On the 19th, in accordance with orders from NIMITZ, as of 20 May all air forces in the South Pacific are to be under the command of RAdm John S. McCain. On the 20th, the United States begins sending reinforcements to Midway and Alaska. Japanese submarine-borne aircraft reconnoiter Durban, in South Africa. The last organized British forces retire from Burma, as Japanese troops assume a defensive posture along the Indo-Burmese frontier, but some Chinese forces are still in retreat toward China, and the Japanese never overrun the rugged northern parts of the country, where Kachin tribesmen engage in a guerrilla war against them. The Burma Campaign has cost the Japanese only about 7,000 CASUALTIES, while British Empire forces have suffered 18,000–20,000 and the Chinese almost as many, with losses among the civilian population undetermined. On the 21st Japanese troops occupy SAMAR and Leyte, in the eastern Philippines. US RAdm Robert Theobold assumes command of all US and Canadian forces in Alaska, in anticipation of a Japanese offensive. On the 22nd, US aircraft begin airlifting small contingents of troops to Wau, in northeastern New Guinea, to support the local Australian forces. On the 23rd US fighter aircraft use a new airfield at Unmak, in the Aleutians, for the first time. On the 24th, Japanese submarine-borne reconnaissance aircraft scout Kodiak Island, south of Alaska. On the 25th Japanese submarine-borne reconnaissance aircraft scout KISKA, in the Aleutians. Japanese carriers sortie from Onimato, Hokkaido, for the Aleutians. On the 26th, Japanese submarine-borne reconnaissance aircraft again scout Kiska. U.S. Task Force 16 (*Enterprise* and *Hornet*) arrives at PEARL HARBOR. The Japanese First Air Fleet sorties from the INLAND SEA, bound for Midway, while the Midway occupation force sails from SAIPAN and GUAM. The US 37th Infantry Division sails from

SAN FRANCISCO for the Fiji Islands. In North Africa, Rommel attacks the Gazala Line. On the 27th, USS *Yorktown* arrives at Pearl Harbor and immediately goes into dry dock for emergency repairs. Japanese troop convoy and escorts leave Onimato bound for the Aleutians. On the 28th, the Main Body of the Japanese Combined Fleet sorties from the Inland Sea for Midway. US Task Force 16 puts to sea from Pearl Harbor, followed later in the day by TF 17, with *Yorktown* still under repair. US Army and Navy personnel from Efate begin to establish a base on ESPIRITU SANTO. On the 29th, a Japanese submarine-borne reconnaissance plane scouts Diego Suarez, in northern Madagascar. Japanese and US naval forces begin converging on Midway. On the 30th, a Japanese midget submarine torpedoes the British battleship *Ramilles* and a tanker at Diego Suarez. First US troops reach New Zealand. Last elements of Chinese New 38th Division cross the Chindwin River, into India. On the 31st, a squadron of old US battleships sorties from San Francisco to support the carriers in the Central Pacific. Japanese and US fleets converge on Midway. That night Japanese midget submarines penetrate SYDNEY harbor, sinking one old vessel and causing considerable panic.

June 1942

This was the month that the tide turned in favor of the Allies. The US victory at Midway crippled the Japanese carrier fleet. Meanwhile, planning went ahead for the first Allied amphibious operation, the attack on GUADALCANAL in the SOLOMON ISLANDS.

On the 1st, Japanese SUBMARINES begin taking station off Midway and the Hawaiian Islands. On the 2nd, US TFs 16 and 17 unite 350 miles northeast of MIDWAY. The Japanese Main Body nears Midway from the west and south. The Japanese ALEUTIANS task force is about 400 miles south of KISKA. On the 3rd, Japanese carriers RYUJO and JUNYO raid DUTCH HARBOR in the Aleutians. Battle of Midway begins: Japanese invasion force is attacked southeast of Midway by B-17s and PBY CA-

TALINAS, the latter sinking a tanker. TFs 16 and 17 keep station northeast of Midway as the Japanese Main Body approaches. On the 4th, the Battle of Midway: Japanese aircraft raid Midway, sparking a daylong action that costs Japan four carriers sunk and one US carrier, YORKTOWN, so badly damaged as to have to be towed. Japanese carrier aircraft bomb Dutch Harbor in the Aleutians. On the 5th, the Battle of Midway: B-17s attack damaged Japanese cruisers retiring from Midway with no effect. Damaged carrier *Yorktown* remains afloat and under tow. Admiral Isoroku YAMAMOTO orders the Combined Fleet to retire. Japanese submarines operating in Mozambique Strait. On the 6th, the Battle of Midway: US carrier aircraft attack damaged Japanese cruisers retiring from Midway, sinking *Mikuma* and severely damaging MOGAMI; USS *Yorktown*, still under tow, is TORPEDOED by Japanese submarine *I-168*, along with an escorting destroyer, which sinks. Japanese troops land on Kiska in the Aleutians. On the 7th, the Battle of Midway: *Yorktown* sinks, other US carriers retire from Midway. Japanese fleet retires from Midway. Japanese troops land on Attu in the Aleutians. In China, the Japanese continue their offensive in Chenkiang. On the 8th MACARTHUR again urges the Joint Chiefs of Staff to undertake an offensive in the Solomon Islands. On the 9th there is consternation in Imperial Navy circles at Tokyo as the scale of the Midway disaster becomes clear: While an attempt is make to keep it secret, details are soon circulating throughout the navy's officer corps, although the army is not informed until much later. On the 10th, as damaged US ships from Midway begin reaching PEARL HARBOR, major reinforcements to the US fleet enter the Pacific via the PANAMA CANAL (carrier WASP, a fast battleship, a heavy cruiser, and eight destroyers). Lead elements of the US 37th Infantry Division reach FIJI. Chinese fall back in Chenkiang. On the 11th, Japanese ships from the Midway operation begin returning to bases in the MARIANAS. US and Canadian aircraft begin attacks on Kiska. On the 12th, Japanese submarines withdraw from Mozambique Strait. MacArthur authorizes construction of air bases at MILNE BAY, New Guinea. On the 13th, nothing much happened. On the 14th, German merchant cruiser *Thor* begins operating in the Indian Ocean. Headquarters and first echelon of the First Marine Division debark in New Zealand. On the 15th, US and Australian Pacific Fleets reorganized into TF 1 (battleships) at SAN FRANCISCO, TF 8 (cruisers and destroyers) in the Aleutians, TF 11 (*Saratoga* and escorts), TF 16 (*Enterprise* group), and TF 17 (*Hornet* group) at Pearl Harbor, and TF 18 (*Wasp* group) temporarily at SAN DIEGO, plus TF 44 (cruisers and destroyers) in Australian waters. On the 16th, Japanese submarine-borne airplane reconnoiters Mauritius in the Indian Ocean. On the 17th, the Japanese deploy six submarines in the Aleutians. On the 18th Prime Minister CHURCHILL arrives in Washington for consultations with President ROOSEVELT. On the 19th, US submarine *S-27* is lost by grounding in the Aleutians. On the 20th, Japanese submarine *I-26* shells Port Estevan, near VANCOUVER. On the 21st, Allied intelligence estimates Japanese land-based air forces in the Solomons, BISMARCKS, and northeastern New Guinea at 126 combat and reconnaissance aircraft, with a further 33 two-engined bombers at TIMOR believed capable of intervening in operations around the Solomon Sea. On the 22nd, the Japanese are estimated by Allied intelligence as having about two brigades at RABAUL, two companies on New Ireland, a battalion in the Admiralties, a regiment at TULAGI, and a few companies on BOUGAINVILLE, plus air base and service personnel. An estimated 1,000 SNLF troops are believed at LAE and Salamaua. MG Robert L. EICHELBERGER assigned to command the US I Corps in Australia. On the 23rd, Rommel's success in breaking the Gazala line leads to a drive on Egypt, disrupting Allied plans: 24 B-17s crossing Africa bound for China and some Air Corps officers in India are ordered to Egypt. On the 24th, Japanese submarine *I-25* shells Port Stevens, Oregon. Chief of Naval Operations KING suggests to the army's Chief of Staff MARSHALL that an amphibious offensive be undertaken in the Solomon Islands on 1 August, to be under navy control. On the 25th, in New Guinea

the Australians activate Maroubra Force (most of the Australian 39th Battalion, plus the Papua Light Infantry) to defend the KOKODA TRAIL across the OWEN STANLEYS. A small Australian force reaches Milne Bay, eastern Papua. US submarine *Nautilus* (SS-168) sinks the Japanese destroyer *Yamakaze* about 50 miles southeast of Tokyo Bay. On the 26th, Germans begin unrestricted submarine warfare off the east coast of the United States (limited attacks had begun earlier); the resulting carnage puts a further strain on US naval resources and makes it more difficult to divert ships to the Pacific. On the 27th, reactions to Japanese shellings by submarine of US and Canadian coastal installations in the past week bring calls for more naval resources to guard the west coast of North America. On the 28th, MacArthur unfolds his plans for undertaking an offensive in the New Guinea-Bismarcks-Solomons area. On the 29th, CNO KING suggests MacArthur control offensive operations in New Guinea and GHORMLEY in the Solomons, a compromise that is shortly adopted. US airfield construction engineers arrive at Milne Bay and begin work. On the 30th, Congress votes $42 billion (over $400 billion in 1997 dollars) for defense for the next fiscal year. Australian Kanga Force, in northeastern New Guinea, raids Salamaua.

July 1942

Not much combat took place in July, but there was a lot of activity. The Japanese were busy taking control of the vast areas they had conquered in the last six months. But there was vicious fighting in New Guinea, and some action in China. Meanwhile, the British were still hanging on by the Burma-India border and the Americans were massing forces for their invasion of GUADALCANAL in the SOLOMON ISLANDS.

On the 1st, Task Force 18 (WASP group) sorties from SAN DIEGO, bound for the South Pacific and escorting the Second Marines, to complete the First Marine Division already at New Zealand. On the 2nd, the US Joint Chiefs of Staff finally adopts a compromise plan to begin driving back the Japanese in the South Pacific: the navy to drive up the Solomon Islands while MACARTHUR recovers northeastern New Guinea and then drives on RABAUL. The JCS authorize "Operation Watchtower," the seizure of Guadalcanal. CHIANG names STILWELL commander of Chinese forces in India. On the 3rd, Japanese troops land on Guadalcanal from TULAGI and begin constructing an airfield (expecting to complete it by 15 August). On the 4th, Australian COASTWATCHERS report Japanese airfield construction on Guadalcanal. Japanese destroyer *Nehoni* is sunk in the ALEUTIANS by US submarine *Triton* (SS-201). The AVG (FLYING TIGERS) is inducted into the US Army Air Force, passing from the Chinese payroll to the American. On the 5th, aerial reconnaissance confirms Japanese airfield construction on Guadalcanal. US submarine *Growler* (SS-215) sinks Japanese destroyer *Arare* in the Aleutians, near KISKA. On the 6th, based on reconnaissance information, CNO KING orders "Operation Watchtower" (the capture of Guadalcanal) implemented immediately. On the 7th, US Task Forces 11 (*Saratoga*) and 16 (*Enterprise*) sortie from PEARL HARBOR to support the Guadalcanal operation. In Papua, Maroubra Force begins its march to Kokoda. On the 8th VAdm GHORMLEY and General MacArthur confer in MELBOURNE over details of "Operation Watchtower." On the 9th, the general plans for "Watchtower" take shape, as the First Marine Division practices amphibious landings in New Zealand, between which it helps load and unload ships due to local labor union problems. Advanced elements of the Australian Seventh Brigade sail from TOWNSVILLE for MILNE BAY. On the 10th, USAAF agrees to increase the allocation of aircraft to the Pacific Theater, thereby slowing its planned buildup in Britain. Allied aircraft land a small party near BUNA, northeastern Papua, to reconnoiter airfield sites. On the 11th, Japanese Imperial General Headquarters acknowledges the results of the Battle of MIDWAY (the destruction of Japanese carrier superiority) and cancels its orders of 5 May to capture Midway and other outlying islands. Second

echelon of the First Marine Division debarks in New Zealand. On the 12th, the US Joint Chiefs of Staff proposes that, following the completion of an offensive up the Solomons to Rabaul, the logical course of action would be to proceed northward along the axis Truk-Guam-Saipan "and/or" through the Dutch East Indies to the Philippines. The first elements of the Australian Maroubra Force reach Kokoda, in central New Guinea, pressing on toward the north coast. On the 13th, Allied ground combat forces potentially available for offensive operations in the Pacific total more than four divisions: US 37th Infantry Division, in the FIJI ISLANDS; US American Division, on NEW CALEDONIA; Australian Seventh Division, in Australia; US First Marine Division (understrength), in New Zealand; Fourth New Zealand Brigade, in the Fijis; US Seventh Marine Regiment (of the First Marine Division), SAMOA; 147th Infantry Regiment, Tongatabu. Additional US and Australian divisions are available in Australia, but are either committed to the defense of the western and northern portions of the country or not yet trained. On the 14th, Japan's Admiral YAMAMOTO reorganizes the Combined Fleet as a consequence of Midway, among other things creating the Eighth Fleet, at Rabaul under VAdm Gunichi MIKAWA, to oversee operations in the Solomons and New Guinea. On the 15th, US submarine *Grunion* (SS-216) sinks three Japanese submarine chasers and a large merchant ship (c. 8,600 tons) in the Aleutians, beginning the interdiction of Japanese forces in the Aleutians. On the 16th, the Allies postpone the target date for the Guadalcanal operation from August 1 to August 7, as the convoy transporting the Seventh Marines is delayed. The Japanese push preparations for operations in New Guinea. On the 17th, massive amounts of manpower are committed to building up military strength in Alaska, and the west coast of North America in general, putting a considerable drain on resources for the Pacific Theater and slowing offensive operations farther west. MacArthur issues orders to occupy Buna, northeastern Papua. The Amphibious Force, South

Pacific Area, is established under RAdm Richmond Kelly TURNER. On the 18th, US planners see reconquest of Japanese bases in the Aleutians in 1943, it being politically impractical (due to public fears) to simply cut off the Japanese and leave them there. On the 19th, US naval forces available to support "Operation Watchtower" total three aircraft carriers, one fast battleship, nine heavy cruisers, two antiaircraft cruisers, 31 destroyers, six SUBMARINES, and numerous smaller vessels. Australian naval forces total two heavy cruisers and a light cruiser. At Rabaul, escorted by cruisers and destroyers, 1,800 Japanese troops take ship for GONA, to capture nearby Buna. On the 20th, all but one of six Japanese submarines in the Aleutians are withdrawn, having sunk only one ship in 34 days of patrolling. The German merchant cruiser *Thor* sinks a British freighter in the Indian Ocean. On the 21st, Japanese troops land at Gona, northeastern Papua, despite Allied air attacks, while Japanese warships shell Buna, and several nearby villages. On the 22nd, Japanese troops at Gona advance on Buna and Giruwa, and begin to move up the KOKODA TRAIL toward PORT MORESBY on the southern coast. Allied aircraft attack Japanese shipping off Buna and Gona, inflicting some damage. The First Marine Division sails from AUCKLAND, New Zealand, for the Fiji Islands. In North Africa, the British halt Rommel on the Alamein line. On the 23rd, Japanese ships at Buna and Gona depart for Rabaul. Japanese troops advancing up the Kokoda Trail clash with elements of the Australian Maroubra Force at Awala, which falls back. On the 24th, US submarines being operating in the KURILE ISLANDS. US carrier aircraft available to support "Operation Watchtower" total 230 (99 fighters, 102 dive bombers, and 39 torpedo bombers) aboard carriers *Saratoga*, *Enterprise*, and *Wasp*. This is the bulk of US carrier assets in the Pacific. In Papua, the outnumbered Australian Maroubra Force is again forced back by the Japanese. On the 25th the Japanese outflank the Maroubra Force in Papua, to come within six miles of Kokoda. On the 26th Japanese reinforcements land at Buna. Desperate

fighting near Kokoda in Papua; Australians fall back to Deniki. The First Marine Division arrives at Fiji for amphibious landing rehearsal; virtually all navy and Marine elements involved in "Operation Watchtower" are now concentrated. Allied land-based or amphibian combat and reconnaissance aircraft concentrated for "Watchtower" total 321 (196 US Navy or Marine, 95 US Army, and 30 Royal New Zealand Air Force), organized into TF 63 and deployed mostly in the NEW HEBRIDES and on New Caledonia. In addition, about 175 aircraft (c. 120 USAAF, 30 RAF, 20 RAAF) based in Australia and New Guinea are capable of supporting operations at Guadalcanal by air attacks on Rabaul and on surrounding Japanese-held areas. On the 27th Australian forces continue to hold Deniki, south of Kokoda in Papua. The First Marine Division continues amphibious exercises at Fiji. On the 28th, US RAdm Frank Jack FLETCHER, overall commander of the landing forces and covering forces in "Operation Watchtower," issues his operational orders, detailing the courses and duties of all forces for the invasion of Guadalcanal. US forces continue amphibious assault rehearsals at Fiji. In Papua, the Australians retake Kokoda in a counterattack. On the 29th, some Japanese reinforcements land at Buna, despite the loss of one of two transports to Allied air attack. In Papua the Japanese retake Kokoda from the Australians, who again fall back on Deniki. On the 30th, US submarine *Grunion* (SS-216) declared "over due" from a patrol in the Aleutians, probably lost to hazards of the sea. VAdm Gunichi Mikawa arrives at Rabaul to assume command of the Eighth Fleet. An additional Australian company reaches Deniki. On the 31st, TF 62 (the First Marine Division) sails from Fiji toward Guadalcanal, escorted by TF 61 (TFs 16, 17, and 18). Fast division of the British Far Eastern Fleet returns to COLOMBO from East Africa. US aircraft carrier ESSEX is launched at Newport News, Virginia, the first of an order of 26 to the same design. A Japanese convoy bound for Buna (New Guinea) with reinforcements is forced to return to Rabaul by intensive Allied air attack, although no vessels are lost. Another company reinforces the Australians at Deniki.

August 1942

The Allies begin their counterattack as US Marines land on Japanese-held GUADALCANAL Island in the Solomons. This begins a six-month campaign that will see heavy use of air, naval, and ground forces. Fighting continues in Burma and NEW GUINEA, but attention is focused on Guadalcanal.

On the 1st, Allied fleet units are moved around to mask the Guadalcanal operation: The US Pacific Fleet battleline (seven old battleships, 10 destroyers) is transferred from SAN FRANCISCO to PEARL HARBOR, while the British "Force A" (two carriers, one battleship, several cruisers and destroyers) sorties from COLOMBO toward the ANDAMANS. On the 2nd, the new US battleship SOUTH DAKOTA begins operating in the Pacific. On the 3rd, the Japanese Army begins the formation of three tank divisions in Manchuria. On the 4th, MG George C. KENNEY assumes command of Allied air forces in the southwest Pacific, under MACARTHUR. US destroyer *Tucker* is mined at ESPIRITU SANTO. On the 5th, blockade-running Japanese submarine *I-30* arrives at Lorient, France. Japanese superbattleship *Musashi* is commissioned. A Japanese convoy leaves Rabaul with reinforcements for BUNA. On the 6th, MacArthur brings all forces on New Guinea under control of the New Guinea Force, unifying command under Australian General Thomas BLAMEY. On the 7th, Watchtower begins as the First Marine Division is landed on Guadalcanal, TULAGI, and some smaller islands by TF 62, finding spotty resistance. A Japanese convoy bound for Buna with reinforcements from Rabaul is recalled. US warships bombard KISKA for the first time. On the 8th, Marines on Guadalcanal advance westward from their landing beaches, capture the unfinished Japanese airstrip. The first Japanese air raids on Guadalcanal occur. On the 9th, the Battle of SAVO ISLAND: Shortly after midnight seven Japanese cruisers and one destroyer smash an Allied squadron in the waters north of Guadalcanal, sinking four heavy cruisers (one Australian) and one destroyer with minor loss to themselves, the worst defeat in a surface naval action in US history. The Marines on Guadalcanal consolidate their hold on Henderson Field and occupy several small islands near Tulagi. Chinese forces defeat a Japanese offensive in Kiangsi Province. On the 10th, TF 62 pulls out of Guadalcanal waters. A US submarine sinks the Japanese heavy cruiser *Kako* as she retires from the Battle of Savo Island. Marines on Guadalcanal are put on two-thirds rations because many of the supply ships withdrew before they could be unloaded. The British Far Eastern Fleet returns to COLOMBO from its diversionary mission near the Andaman Islands. Maroubra Force (c. 500 men) counterattacks along the KOKODA TRAIL in Papua. On the 11th, the Japanese Combined Fleet begins to move from the ISLAND SEA to TRUK, in order to support operations at Guadalcanal. On the 12th, Japanese convoys land reinforcements at Buna, in northwestern New Guinea. US destroyer-transports land supplies on Guadalcanal. First US airplane lands at Henderson Field, Guadalcanal. Japanese troops reach Kokoda, the principal pass across the OWEN STANLEY MOUNTAINS on New Guinea. On the 13th, the Japanese seize the main pass in the Owen Stanley Mountains, on the Buna-Kokoda Trail in New Guinea, as the Australians fall back on Isurava. On the 14th, the Japanese complete the landing of 3,000 construction troops near GONA, in New Guinea. On the 15th, US transports land supplies at Guadalcanal, but Marine rations remain cut to conserve supplies. The last Japanese submarine in the ALEUTIANS, *I-6*, is withdrawn. On the 16th, heavily escorted, the Ichiki Detachment (c. 1,000 infantry) sails from Truk for Guadalcanal. Japanese convoys land reinforcements at Buna, in northwestern New Guinea. On the 17th, the Marine Second Raider Battalion, landed from SUBMARINES, begins two-day raid on MAKIN ISLAND in the GILBERTS: An unfortunate aftereffect of this raid is that the Japanese decide to heavily fortify the many small islands they occupy in the central Pacific, which comes back to haunt the Marines when they storm TARAWA in the following year. After nightfall the Japanese land the Ichiki Detachment on Guadalcanal, at Taivu and Kokumbona. On the 18th, Japanese troops land unnoticed at Basabura, New Guinea. On the 19th, Japanese convoys land reinforcements at Buna, in northwestern New Guinea. On Guadalcanal the Fifth Marines conducts a sweep eastward from the beachhead, skirmishing with the Ichiki Detachment. Japanese dispatch 1,500 troops from RABAUL in a convoy bound for Guadalcanal. Australian 21st Brigade (Seventh Division) arrives at PORT MORESBY by air, immediately begins marching to support the Maroubra Force. On the 20th, Henderson Field on Guadalcanal is completed; 31 Marine Corps fighters are landed from CVE LONG ISLAND. Japanese order landing of 1,500 troops at MILNE BAY, southeastern Papua. On the 21st, before dawn the Japanese Ichiki Detachment attacks the eastern face of the Guadalcanal beachhead, and is crushed by the defenders, who envelop their rear (Battle of the Tenaru River). US destroyers and fast transports deliver supplies to Guadalcanal, at the cost of one escorting destroyer. On New Guinea the Japanese land reinforcements at Basabura, while the Australian 18th Brigade reinforces Milne Bay. On the 22nd, Marines continue to consolidate their hold on Guadalcanal and Tulagi. US Army fighters begin landing at Henderson Field (five P-400s) from NEW CALEDONIA. Off Savo Island, Japanese destroyer *Kawakaze* TORPEDOES US destroyer *Blue*, which is towed to Tulagi. On the 23rd, Japanese cruisers and destroyers shell NAURU. US recon aircraft spot a Japanese force intent on reinforcing Guadalcanal. That night Japanese destroyers shell the Marines on Guadalcanal. US destroyer *Blue* (damaged on the 22nd) is scuttled at Tulagi. The US 40th Infantry Division begins leaving San Francisco for HAWAII. On the 24th, the Battle of the EASTERN SOLOMONS: Aircraft from carrier *Saratoga* sink Japanese carrier RYUJO, while Japanese carrier aircraft damage *Enterprise*. Before she retires for repairs, *Enterprise* lands 11 dive bombers at Henderson Field. That night Japanese destroyers

shell Henderson Field, while Japanese SNLF troops land on the Goodenough Islands, off northeastern New Guinea. On the 25th, Marine and navy aircraft attack Japanese reinforcing squadrons near Guadalcanal. Japanese SNLF troops land at Milne Bay, in southeastern New Guinea, but are contained by Australian defenders. North of the Solomons, army B-17s sink the Japanese destroyer MUTSUKI with high-altitude bombing, the first and only time this tactic works against an underway warship. On the 26th, Japanese troops occupy Nauru Island against no resistance. Australian troops at Milne Bay stoutly resist the Japanese landing force. At Ramgarh, in India, the US Army opens a training center for Chinese troops. On the 27th, Japanese reinforcements are landed at Milne Bay, where Australian and US troops put up heavy resistance. On Guadalcanal, elements of the Fifth Marines make an overland and amphibious raid against Kokumbona On the 28th, Australian and American troops at Milne Bay beat off determined but ill-planned Japanese attacks. Off Guadalcanal, several Japanese destroyer transports are intercepted by US aircraft and sunk or damaged, but others manage to land reinforcements later that night. Battleship *Washington* and several destroyers enter the Pacific via the PANAMA CANAL. On the 29th, initial elements of the Japanese Kawaguchi Detachment are landed on Guadalcanal from destroyers and high-speed transports. A Japanese cruiser squadron attempts to support SNLF troops at Milne Bay with little success, but reinforcements are landed. The Australian 21st Brigade relieves the Maroubra Force confronting the Japanese on the Kokoda Trail in the Owen Stanley Mountains. Japanese battleship YAMATO arrives at TRUK as flagship to Adm YAMAMOTO; save for one day, when she changes her mooring, she will swing at anchor for the next seven months. On the 30th, Japanese aircraft sink a US destroyer transport attempting to reinforce Guadalcanal. US troops land on unoccupied Adak Island, in the Aleutians. Japanese make another attack on Milne Bay and press forward along the Kokoda Trail. On the 31st, US carrier *Saratoga* is torpedoed by Japanese submarine

I-26 west of the SANTA CRUZ ISLANDS. US destroyers and fast transports land reinforcements on Guadalcanal. The Japanese decide to abandon their landing at Milne Bay. In Egypt, Rommel begins the Battle of Alam Halfa.

September 1942

Most of the action was in the SOLOMON ISLANDS, particularly on, around, and above GUADALCANAL. American and Japanese forces struggled for control of the island, with the Allied troops getting the upper hand, as was also the case on NEW GUINEA. But more hard fighting was to come as the Japanese sent more ground, naval, and air forces into action.

On the 1st, "Tokyo Express" destroyers en route to resupply Guadalcanal are slightly damaged by US B-17s. US fast transports run supplies and reinforcements into Guadalcanal. Japanese press on along the KOKODA TRAIL in Papua. On the 2nd, Marines on Guadalcanal consolidate beachfront defenses, deploying the Third Defense Battalion. Japanese land reinforcements at Basabura, New Guinea, and press on along the Kokoda Trail. On the 3rd, the US Fifth Air Force is given responsibility for operations over the SOLOMONS and New Guinea. On the 4th, the "TOKYO EXPRESS" lands the last elements of the Kawaguchi Detachment on Guadalcanal. Off Lunga Point Japanese destroyers sink two US destroyer transports. Japanese aircraft also threaten US daytime supply efforts. Marine First Raider Battalion scouts SAVO ISLAND, which is free of Japanese. On the 5th, Japanese troops withdraw by sea from MILNE BAY, in eastern Papua-New Guinea. On the 6th, Japanese troops on New Guinea occupy Efogi on the Kokoda Trail, about 50 miles north of PORT MORESBY. On the 7th, US transports land supplies on Guadalcanal. In Egypt the Battle of Alam Halfa ends; Rommel's attempt to reach the Nile is frustrated. In Russia, the German Stalingrad offensive is virtually halted. On the 8th, on Guadalcanal, some 700 Raiders and Paramarines effect a landing at Tasimboko, in the rear of the Kawaguchi Detachment, disrupting Jap-

anese preparations for an offensive, and then withdraw. Japanese air raids on Guadalcanal. That night a Japanese destroyer squadron shells TULAGI. In Papua, five Japanese battalions open a fresh attack on the Australians at Efogi on the Kokoda Trail, driving back or encircling the three defending battalions. On the 9th, major elements of the Japanese Combined Fleet sortie from TRUK to cover reinforcements to Guadalcanal from Rabaul and support an offensive planned for the 12th. That night Japanese Navy pilot Nobuo Fujita, in an airplane from the submarine I-25, drops incendiary bombs on a wooded area of Mt. Emily, Oregon, with little effect. The Australian 25th Brigade is rushed up the Kokoda Trail to support troops engaged near Efogi. On the 10th, British troops effect a landing on the west coast of Vichy French-controlled Madagascar. On the 11th, having failed to secure a lodgment at Milne Bay, the Japanese also withdraw from the nearby TROBRIAND ISLANDS. Australian forces disengage at Efogi, on the Kokoda Trail, and fall back to a position near Oribawiba. On the 12th, an Australian ship steams from DARWIN to reinforce GUERRILLAS on TIMOR. On Guadalcanal, the Battle of BLOODY RIDGE: The Kawaguchi Detachment attacks the southeastern face of the beachhead with heavy losses; on the 13th, after the Kawaguchi Detachment is beaten off, Raiders and Paramarines attempt to probe the Japanese positions but are driven back. On the 14th, the Japanese retire from Bloody Ridge on Guadalcanal, but make small attacks at other points on the Marine perimeter. The WASP and *Hornet* task forces join south of the Solomons to support a convoy carrying the Seventh Marines to Guadalcanal from ESPIRITU SANTO. KISKA is bombed for the first time, by US aircraft based on Adak. In Papua, despite reinforcements, the Australians fall back along the Kokoda Trail, taking up positions on the Imita Ridge, just 32 miles north of Port Moresby. On the 15th, US carrier *Wasp*, battleship NORTH CAROLINA, and destroyer *O'Brien* are TORPEDOED south of the Solomons ("Torpedo Alley"), the carrier sinking. US reinforcements reach Guadalcanal, where the

Marines extend their perimeter. Elements of the 126th Infantry (32nd Division). Are flown into Port Moresby, the first US infantry to arrive on New Guinea. On the 16th, the Third Marine Division is activated at SAN DIEGO. On New Guinea the Australians hold along Imita Ridge, which marks the high point of the Japanese offensive over the OWEN STANLEY MOUNTAINS. On the 17th, US reconnaissance parties in Papua begin looking for sites for airfields and possible trails around Japanese positions. An Australian ship lands reinforcements on TIMOR. On the 18th, the Seventh Marine Regiment is landed on Guadalcanal with a large quantity of ammunition, fuel, and other supplies. British troops land at Tamatave, on the east coast of Madagascar. On the 19th, Marine lines on Guadalcanal are reorganized and consolidated, while full rations are restored because of the improved supply situation. On the 20th, the Japanese Combined Fleet is ordered back to Truk. Japanese intelligence estimates that there are only 7,500 US troops on Guadalcanal; the actual figure is over 19,000. On the 21st, British Commonwealth forces undertake an offensive on the Arakan coast of Burma. On the 22nd, confronted by advancing British and Free French forces, Vichy French troops on Madagascar abandon the capital, Tananarive, and withdraw south. On the 23rd, British troops occupy Tananarive, capital of Madagascar. On Guadalcanal, the First Battalion, Seventh Marines (LTC Lewis "Chesty" PULLER), infiltrates through the Japanese lines and advances on Mt. Austen, deep in the interior. On the 24th, Puller's battalion engages Japanese troops on Mt. Austen. On the 25th, Marines on Guadalcanal are heavily engaged on Mt. Austen and in the Matanikau-Kokumbona area. Australian troops open an offensive along the Kokoda Trail. While attempting to run supplies to Dutch and Australian guerrillas on Timor, the Australian destroyer *Voyager* goes aground, to be scuttled when she is attacked by Japanese aircraft. On the 26th, Marines press limited offensives on Guadalcanal. Stealthily entering SINGAPORE harbor in three canoes, British raiders manage to sink or damage about 40,000 tons of shipping. On the

27th, frustrated in an attempt to attack across the Matanikau River on Guadalcanal, one attacking Marine battalion is sealifted to Point Cruz, where it is hoped this will enable the other two battalions to break across the Matanikau, but the Japanese counterattack in a double envelopment, pocketing the battalion, which nevertheless manages to cut its way back to the coast. Japanese aircraft bomb Guadalcanal. Japanese fall back from Oribawiba on the Kokoda Trail. On the 28th, the last regiment of the US 32nd Division arrives at Port Moresby. On the 29th, South African troops land at Tulear, in southwestern Madagascar. US troop strength on Guadalcanal is slightly over 19,000, with nearly 3,300 more on Tulagi; Japanese troop strength is about 12,000. On the 30th, the Japanese make their first air strike against Adak, in the ALEUTIANS.

October 1942

Again, most action in the Pacific was in the SOLOMONS, particularly at GUADALCANAL. In America and Japan, it was obvious that this was a crucial battle. The outcome was in doubt. A victory for Japan would prolong the war, an Allied victory would demonstrate to all that Japanese arms were no longer triumphant and that Japanese defeat was at hand.

On the 1st, US and Australian forces prepare a three-pronged offensive to throw the Japanese out of Papua. In Russia, the Germans are virtually halted in heavy fighting at Stalingrad. The Italian BLOCKADE RUNNER *Orseolo* departs Bordeaux for KOBE. On the 2nd, a US air raid on RABAUL damages the Japanese cruiser YUBARI and other shipping. Marines occupy Funafuti, in the ELLICE ISLANDS, southeast of the Japanese-held GILBERTS. On the 3rd, US troops occupy the Andreanof Islands, in the Aleutians. On the 4th, a US submarine sinks the Japanese merchantman *Setsuyo Maru* (c. 4,150 GRT) just east of Tokyo: Since the war began Japan has lost 156 merchant ships for a total of over 700,000 tons of shipping, a loss of about 11% of her prewar merchant tonnage. On the 5th,

US Navy and Marine aircraft raid Japanese shipping in the Shortland Islands (north end of Solomons chain). On the 6th, despite being urged to concentrate all available efforts on securing Guadalcanal, Admiral GHORMLEY orders the 147th Infantry to occupy NDENI in the SANTA CRUZ ISLANDS. On the 7th, the First Marine Division begins a new offensive on Guadalcanal to clear Japanese troops from within artillery range of Henderson Field, the Fifth Marines advancing westward along the coast against some resistance from the Japanese Fourth Infantry, while elements of the Second and the Seventh Marines advance across country farther inland against little opposition. On the 8th, heavy rains impede the Marine offensive on Guadalcanal, but some gains are made, and Japanese counterattack plans are captured. On the 9th, Japanese destroyers land elements of their Second Division on Guadalcanal. As the Fifth Marines hold Japanese attention on the Matanikau River, the Second and Seventh Marines advance westward and then northward, trapping the Japanese Fourth Infantry and inflicting heavy CASUALTIES before falling back eastward across the Matanikau in the afternoon. On the 10th, the Marines on Guadalcanal prepare to meet the expected Japanese counteroffensive. On the 11th, the Battle of CAPE ESPERANCE: US cruisers and destroyers ambush the "Tokyo Express" off Guadalcanal, sinking a heavy cruiser and destroyer, while losing one destroyer, in the first surface action in which US ships defeat their Japanese counterparts. On the 12th, US aircraft sink two Japanese destroyers, one near SAVO ISLAND and the other nearly 90 miles to the northwest. Japanese submarine begin operations in the Gulf of Oman, threatening Allied oil being shipped from the Persian Gulf. On the 13th, US destroyers shell Japanese positions on Guadalcanal during the day, while Japanese aircraft and artillery join battleships and other naval forces to shell Marine positions on Guadalcanal after dark. The 164th Infantry (Americal Division) lands on Guadalcanal, raising the garrison to over 23,000. On the 14th, Japanese cruisers shell Marine positions on Guadalcanal,

temporarily knocking Henderson Field out of action, while covering the landing of reinforcements. Australians advancing along the KOKODA TRAIL encounter stiff Japanese resistance near Templeton's Crossing. On the 15th, before dawn, four Japanese transports have to beach on Guadalcanal under US air attack, but about 3,000 to 4,000 troops and tons of supplies are landed. That night Japanese cruisers again shell Henderson Field. US destroyer *Meredith* sunk by *Zuikaku* aircraft off San Cristobal. On the 16th, USAAF sink a Japanese destroyer near KISKA, off Alaska. US destroyer *O'Brien* (damaged by a TORPEDO on the 15th) founders off SAMOA, en route to PEARL HARBOR. Japanese submarines, ignoring plentiful Allied supply ships, concentrate on attacking warships (as was their custom) to increasing effect, and the area south of Guadalcanal is nicknamed "Torpedo Alley" because of all the Japanese subs lurking there. On the 17th, there is heavy fighting on the Kokoda Trail, at Eorea Creek in Papua. On the 18th, VAdm Ghormley is replaced by HALSEY as Allied commander in the South Pacific; Halsey immediately cancels ancillary operations, including the movement of the 147th Infantry to Santa Cruz, to concentrate all forces for the battle for Guadalcanal. A US submarine damages a Japanese "Tokyo Express" light cruiser off Guadalcanal. Heavy fighting continues at Eorea Creek, Papua. On the 19th, US aircraft damage a Japanese destroyer off Guadalcanal. On the 20th, the Australian 16th Brigade relieves the 25th in the fighting at Eorea Creek. Troops are flown over "the HUMP" to strengthen Chinese divisions training at Ramgarh, India. On the 21st, US destroyers land supplies on Guadalcanal, where the Marines beat off a limited Japanese tank attack across the Matanikau. On the 22nd, Australian troops land on Goodenough Island to find only about 300 Japanese troops. On the 23rd, Battle of Edson's Ridge begins: A fierce Japanese assault against the southern face of the Guadalcanal beachhead is stopped, while the Marines beat off an attack across the Matanikau. The US 43rd Infantry Division begins arriving in New Zealand. In North Africa, the Battle of El Alamein begins. On the 24th, US carriers *Enterprise* and *Hornet* rendezvous northeast of ESPIRITU SANTO to block a move by a Japanese carrier force known to be to the northwest. On Guadalcanal, the Battle of Edson's Ridge ends, as fierce Japanese attacks are thrown back. Japanese destroyers evacuate the 250 surviving troops on Goodenough Island. On the 25th, Battle of Lunga Point, Guadalcanal: Japanese cruisers and destroyers engaged in daylight bombardment of Henderson Field, chase two US destroyers and sink two small US harbor craft, before being attacked by Marine and army aircraft, suffering one destroyer lost and damage to other vessels. Battle of the Santa Cruz Islands: US and Japanese carriers search for each other northeast of the Solomons. After nightfall a Japanese attempt to flank the Marine Matanikau line is defeated. On the 26th, Battle of the Santa Cruz Islands: USS *Hornet* is put out of action, eventually to be sunk by Japanese destroyers, while Japanese carriers are heavily damaged, in an action that frustrates a Japanese attempt to use carrier aviation to support efforts on Guadalcanal. Elements of the US 43rd Infantry Division arrive at Espiritu Santo. On Guadalcanal the Marines begin preparing for a new offensive westward toward Kokumbona. At Espiritu Santo the liner *President Coolidge* sinks after hitting a mine: Only two of the thousands of troops aboard are killed, but all their equipment is lost. On the 27th, Britain's General WAVELL and American-Chinese commander STILWELL agree that US and Chinese troops will begin an offensive in northern Burma shortly in order to reopen the BURMA ROAD, which will be linked to a new "Ledo Road." On the 28th, Japanese "Tokyo Express" uses its destroyer transports to land troops on Guadalcanal from Kokumbona to Cape Esperance. On the 29th, the ALCAN HIGHWAY is opened, the only motor road to Alaska, freeing shipping for service in the Western Pacific. On Guadalcanal the Japanese withdraw toward Koli Point and Kokumbona, disengaging from the Marines' front. On the 30th, the Marines on Guadalcanal prepare to assume the offensive. On the 31st, America announces that 800,000 US troops are now serving overseas. After nightfall, the Marines on Guadalcanal begin establishing outposts west of the Matanikau River.

November 1942

The campaign for GUADALCANAL reached a climax, with the Japanese getting the worst of it. A stalemate on New Guinea favored the Allies. Germany suffered major setbacks in Russia (Stalingrad) and Africa (Alamein), which demoralized the Japanese, who were expecting the Germans to keep advancing east to link up with Japanese forces in India. From this point on, the War in the Pacific was all downhill for the Japanese.

On the 1st, on Guadalcanal, supported by heavy naval, air, and artillery bombardments, the Marines attack across the Matanikau River. On the 2nd, the Australian 25th Brigade captures Kokoda and its airfield from the Japanese. On Guadalcanal, the Marine offensive gains ground against heavy resistance, while after nightfall the "Tokyo Express" lands about 1,500 troops and supplies at Tetere, about 15 miles east of the main beachhead on Guadalcanal. On the 3rd, Marines on Guadalcanal clear Point Cruz of Japanese troops. In North Africa, Rommel begins pulling out of the Alamein line, conceding victory to the British. On the 4th, additional Marines arrive on Guadalcanal, where the offensive is halted to regroup and consolidate gains. In Papua, the 16th Australian Brigade begins an attack on Oivi, on the KOKODA TRAIL. On the 5th, the 164th Infantry makes a limited attack on Guadalcanal to support the Seventh Marines, threatened by a Japanese concentration on their flank. In Papua, Australian troops on the Kokoda Trail continue their attack on Oivi, while also moving against Gorari. Vichy French troops on Madagascar surrender to the British at Fort Dauphin in southeastern Madagascar. On the 6th, the Seventh Marines resumes the offensive, supported by the 164th Infantry. MacArthur establishes his headquarters at PORT MORESBY. Heavy fighting on the Kokoda Trail. On the 7th, while the Japanese land reinforcements on Guadalcanal, Marines and army troops press them back from Koli Point. On the 8th, the Japanese land reinforcements on Guadalcanal, but east of Koli Point the Marines and army troops make an amphibious "end run" around them, pocketing them at the mouth of Gavaga Creek. A large US reinforcement convoy sails from NOUMEA for Guadalcanal, supported by a heavy escort (*Enterprise*, two battleships, eight cruisers, 23 destroyers). Operation Torch begins as US and British forces land in northwestern Africa, an operation that has caused the Pacific to be somewhat starved of amphibious shipping and, to a lesser extent, warships. On the 9th, the Japanese Second Fleet sorties from TRUK to support a planned major naval offensive at Guadalcanal on November 12–13. On Guadalcanal, the Marines and army troops encircle some Japanese forces. On the 10th, the Japanese land reinforcements on Guadalcanal, where US troops begin reduction of the Gavaga pocket. On the Kokoda Trial, in Papua, the Australians eject the Japanese from Oivi. On the 11th, United States lands reinforcements on Guadalcanal, but halts offensive moves in anticipation of a Japanese assault. Japanese aircraft raid Henderson Field. West of Australia, Royal Indian Navy minesweeper *Bengal*, escorting a tanker, beats off an attack by two Japanese auxiliary cruisers, sinking one. In Papua, elements of the US 32nd Division are firmly established at Pongani, having flown in over the last few days. On the 12th, the Australians take Gorari, on the Kokoda Trail in Papua, while the US 32nd Division begins moving overland toward the BUNA-GONA area. US reinforcements land on Guadalcanal, where Marines and army troops eliminate the Gavaga pocket. Japanese aircraft raid Henderson Field. Protracted Naval Battle of Guadalcanal begins: Shortly before midnight Japanese cruisers and destroyers inflict a severe defeat on US Navy, which loses several cruisers and destroyers, plus several more damaged, at a cost to the Japanese of one destroyer sunk, plus severe damage to battleship *Hiei* and several destroyers. On the 13th, Naval Battle of Guadalcanal continues: US aircraft further damage Japanese battleship *Hiei*, which has to be scuttled, while a US cruiser sinks a disabled Jap-

anese destroyer and a Japanese submarine sinks CLAA *Juneau*, on which the five SULLIVAN BROTHERS perish. In Papua, the Australians drive the Japanese across the Kumusi River. On the 14th, Naval Battle of Guadalcanal continues. In "The Slot" *Enterprise* and Marine aircraft from Henderson Field batter Japanese ships, sinking a cruiser and two transports, and damaging several others. Japanese transports beach on Guadalcanal in order to land reinforcements. During the night, large Japanese forces (one battleship, two heavy cruisers, two light cruisers, and eight destroyers) try to bombard Henderson Field, to be ambushed around midnight by US battleships *Washington* and SOUTH DAKOTA with four destroyers. *South Dakota* is badly damaged, but the Japanese lose a destroyer and battleship *Kirishima* is reduced to a burning wreck, in the first fleet action by US battleships against enemy warships since the Spanish-American War (1898). On the 15th, unable to provide air cover for a tow, the Japanese scuttle *Kirishima* off Guadalcanal. On the 16th, in Papua, the US 32nd and Australian Seventh Divisions close on Buna Gona, and Sananada, against increasing resistance. On the 17th, the Japanese commit aircraft and land reinforcement to support their troops at Buna and Gona, in Papua. On the 18th, an army infantry battalion advances west of the Matanikau River, on Guadalcanal; although resistance is slight, the troops make slow progress, being green and unacclimated. In Papua, US and Australian troops begin encountering Japanese outposts around Buna and Gona. On the 19th, on Guadalcanal the drive westward is strengthened with seasoned troops, but resistance remains slight; during the night Japanese troops move up. At Buna and Gona, US and Australian troops come up against the Japanese main line of resistance and are soon bogged down. The Soviet Stalingrad offensive begins, heralding a major turning point of the war in Russia, and comes as a blow to Japanese morale, as they had expected eventual assistance from the Germans once the Nazis had conquered southern Russia and driven on into the Persian Gulf area. On the 20th, on Guadalcanal the Japanese launch a surprise attack at the two battalions west of the Matanikau River, but US troops hold with air and artillery support, as reinforcements begin moving toward them. On the 21st, on Guadalcanal, US Army troops of the 164th and 182nd Infantry Regiments make some gains against the Japanese but are held by skillfully constructed defenses. In Papua, US and Australian troops make unsuccessful attacks on Japanese positions at Sanananda, near Buna, which is holding back an attack by the US 32nd Division. On the 22nd, army troops again make small gains against the Japanese on Guadalcanal, while the Eighth Marines prepares to attack through their lines. In Papua, the Japanese hold US and Australian troops before Buna and Gona, making skillful counterattacks. On the 23rd, the Eighth Marines attempts to attack through the 164th Infantry, on Guadalcanal, but meets with no success; offensive operations are called off. In Papua, US and Australian troops make no gains against the Japanese at Buna-Gona, suffering heavy losses. On the 24th, US aircraft sink a Japanese destroyer attempting to reinforce Guadalcanal. Allied troops continue unsuccessful attacks at Buna-Gona in Papua. On the 25th, the fighting at Buna-Gona eases, as both sides exchange artillery fire and engage in patrolling. On the 26th, cruisers HNMS JACOB VAN HEEMSKERCK and HMAS ADELAIDE intercept a German BLOCKADE RUNNER bound for France from the NETHERLANDS EAST INDIES. In Papua, Allied troops make some gains at Buna-Gona. On the 27th, US and Australian troops cease offensive efforts at Buna-Gona, to regroup. US troops on Guadalcanal also regroup, giving the Japanese some respite. On the 28th, Teheran Conference begins, as FDR, Prime Minister CHURCHILL, and General Secretary Stalin discuss policy and STRATEGY for three days, while celebrating their victories at Stalingrad, El Alamein, Northwest Africa, and Guadalcanal: After years of Axis success, the tide has turned. On the 29th, Japanese troop strength on Guadalcanal peaks, 30,000 men (about equal to US strength), then rapidly declines to about 20,000 in the next two months due to lack of food and medicine,

while US strength rises to 40,000 well-supplied troops in December. Allied aircraft prevent four Japanese destroyers from landing reinforcements at Gona. On the 30th, Battle of Tassafaronga: In a night action, eight Japanese destroyers attempting to reinforce Guadalcanal get the better of five U.S. cruisers and six destroyers trying to stop them, sinking one heavy cruiser and damaging three others while losing one destroyer, but are forced to break off their mission. German merchant cruiser *Thor* destroyed in a fire while docked at Yokohama. At Teheran, the "Big Three" reach tentative agreements on strategy. In Papua, Australian and US troops resume the offensive at Buna and Gona, making small gains.

December 1942

Fighting continued on GUADALCANAL, NEW GUINEA, and in Burma. Superior Allied resources had began to make their presence felt on the battlefield. Japan began adopting a defensive posture, falling back from one defeat after another, a trend that will continue until the end of the war.

On the 1st, LG EICHELBERGER is put in command of the BUNA-GONA operation in Papua, where the Australians capture GONA village. On Guadalcanal, staff officers from the US Americal Division assume control of supply functions from Marine Corps personnel. In Burma, having completed a long refit of their forces, the Japanese begin moving into offensive positions. On the 2nd, in Papua, despite Allied air interference, the Japanese land reinforcements about 12 miles behind their forces in the BUNA area, and beat off another American attack. Eichelberger relieves the commanders of the 32nd Division and several of its subordinate units. The Italian BLOCKADE RUNNER *Orseolo* arrives at KOBE from Bordeaux. On the 3rd, Japanese destroyers land reinforcements on Guadalcanal, where the First Marine Division is preparing to be withdrawn. US aerial reconnaissance discovers that the Japanese are building an airstrip on MUNDA, in the central Solomons. On the 4th, Carlson's Marine Raiders complete a month-long raid through Japanese-controlled portions of Guadalcanal, having killed 400 of the enemy, for the loss of only 17 dead. In Papua, Eichelberger reorganizes US forces before Buna. On the 5th, Australian troops at Gona put pressure on Japanese troops at nearby Gona Mission, while other Australian troops move westward to prevent the arrival of reinforcements, and US troops make a major attack against Buna, which, although only partially successful, does isolate the village. On the 6th, US aircraft bomb Munda to slow Japanese work on a new airbase. In Papua, US forces employ "time on target" artillery tactics for the first time, against Buna. On the 7th, Japanese destroyers attempting to land reinforcements on Guadalcanal are beaten off by a combination of aircraft and PT-BOATS, among them *PT-109*, skippered by John F. KENNEDY. On the 8th, the 132nd Infantry (Americal Division) lands on Guadalcanal, where the division assumes full control of all staff duties. US aircraft turn back a Japanese attempt to land more troops to support the Buna area, in northeastern Papua, while Japanese troops withdrawing from Gona sustain heavy losses. On the 9th, in Papua, Australian troops complete capture of the Gona area in hand-to-hand fighting. On Guadalcanal, MG Alexander A. VANDEGRIFT and the First Marine Division are officially relieved and MG Alexander PATCH (USA) assumes command. The Fifth Marines boards transports and sails away that afternoon, with the balance of the division to follow over the next few days: Guadalcanal was the first major Marine operation of the Pacific War and one of the longest, lasting four months. British prepare an offensive from India into Arakan, the westernmost coastal province of Burma. On the 10th, Australian troops land at Oro Bay, New Guinea, near Buna, into which Japanese aircraft manage to airdrop supplies. US aircraft bomb Munda. British offensive into Arakan gets underway, moving between the sea and the mountains. On the 11th, Japanese destroyers land reinforcements on Guadalcanal, but lose one of their number to PT-boat attacks. US aircraft bomb Munda. The overstrength 14th Indian Division advances slowly in

Arakan region of Burma. On the 12th, Japanese destroyer *Teruzuki* is sunk by US *PT-45* northeast of KOLOMBANGARA. On Guadalcanal, Japanese infiltrators destroy a P-39 and a fuel truck, while the Second Marine Division begins taking up positions west of the Matanikau. On the 13th, Australian troops prepare to make an "end run" around Buna, which is subjected to a heavy artillery barrage: That night the surviving Japanese defenders (c. 100 men) evacuate the village and escape across the Giruwa River. US aircraft bomb Munda. The British advance cautiously in Arakan region of Burma. On the 14th, Australian reinforcements land at Oro Bay, near Buna. Japanese destroyers land 800 troops at the Mambare River, near Buna, which Allied troops occupy after discovering it has been abandoned by the enemy. The British advance cautiously in Arakan region of Burma; rather than resist, weaker Japanese forces begin to retire. On the 15th, on Guadalcanal, US reconnaissance patrols scout Mt. Austen. US aircraft bomb Munda. The British advance cautiously in Arakan region of Burma, even though the Japanese are beginning to fall back. On the 16th, the British offensive on the Arakan coast takes Maungdaw only to discover that it has been abandoned by the Japanese. In Papua, Eichelberger takes direct command of the 32nd Division, after two commanders in succession have been wounded in action. On the 17th, US Americal Division attacks toward Mt. Austen on Guadalcanal. Elements of US 25th Division land on Guadalcanal. US aircraft bomb Munda. On the 18th, Japanese cruiser TENRYU is sunk by US submarine *Albacore* (SS-218) near the BISMARCKS. In Papua, US and Australian troops begin a major assault on Sanananda, while elsewhere Allied forces make limited but important gains. On the 19th, the CASUALTY rate from malaria among US troops on Guadalcanal reaches a statistical rate of 972 cases in every thousand men per year, and it is even worse for the Japanese, who have lost most of their troops on the island to disease and malnutrition. The British advance in Arakan, Burma, but the outnumbered Japanese begin to develop a major defensive position in front of Akyab, more than a hundred miles to their rear, giving themselves time to bring up reinforcements. In Papua, the Allied assault on Sanananda moves forward. On the 20th, the new US policy of using SUBMARINES to mine the waters off major Japanese ports finds its first victim, as an 8,000-ton Japanese transport goes down off Tokyo. In Papua, Allied forces make important gains in the Sanananda area. On the 21st, Australians make major gains in the Sanananda area. On Guadalcanal, the Americal Division's attack on Mt. Austen falters. US aircraft bomb MUNDA. On the 22nd, Australian and American troops overcome the last Japanese resistance in the Buna area, in northeastern Papua, but are brought to a halt on the Sanananda Front. On Guadalcanal the Americal Division's Mt. Austen offensive continues to run into problems. On the 23rd, the US 41st Infantry Division ships out from Australia for New Guinea. On Guadalcanal, the Americal Division's attack on Mt. Austen is temporarily halted. On the 24th, on Guadalcanal, the Americal Division encounters the main Japanese defenses, the "Gifu," in the Mt. Austen area. On the 25th, US aircraft continue their incessant bombing of Munda Island, slowing Japanese efforts to build a base there. On Guadalcanal the Americal Division can make no gains against the Gifu position. On the 26th, the Japanese 20th Division movement from Korea to New Guinea is underway. The Americal Division makes limited gains against the Gifu on Guadalcanal. On the 27th, lead elements of the US 41st Infantry Division land at PORT MORESBY, Papua-New Guinea, while to the northeast Allied forces continue to make gains in the Buna area but are held before Sanananda. Heavy fighting around the Gifu, on Guadalcanal. On the 28th despite constant US bombing, Japanese begin using new airstrip on Munda, in the Central Solomons. In Papua, Japanese forces in the Buna area begin withdrawing to Giruwa. On the 29th, the US destroyer-minesweeper *Wasmuth* sinks off the ALEUTIANS, after a gale causes two of her depth charges to detonate, causing extensive damage. In Papua, Japanese forces near Buna Mission are cut off by US troops. On the 30th, on Guadalcanal,

the Americal Division rotates fresh units into the line and prepares for a renewed attack on the Gifu. On the 31st, Japan's Prime Minister TOJO decides to abandon Guadalcanal. US aircraft carrier ESSEX is commissioned.

January 1943

Fighting entered its final phase on GUADALCANAL, as the United States set out to clear the island of Japanese forces. As a foretaste of things to come, the Japanese put up a desperate resistance, fighting to the death. Even so, the Japanese high command had already decided to abandon Guadalcanal. The aircraft and ship losses were too great to support ground combat that far south in the SOLOMONS. Allied ground forces also succeeded in clearing out Japanese forces in eastern Papua, New Guinea. In Burma, the British offensive stalled.

On the 1st, Japanese destroyers run supplies into Guadalcanal, despite attempts by US aircraft and PT-BOATS to interfere. Additional elements of the US 25th Infantry Division land on Guadalcanal, where the Americal Division resumes its assault on Mt. Austen. In Papua, US and Australian forces make steady if slow gains in the BUNA Mission area. On the 2nd, the US I Corps captures Buna Mission in Papua: Fighting for Buna has cost the Japanese about 1,400 troops, mostly killed, and the Australians and Americans 2,817 CASUALTIES, 620 of whom were killed. US forces on Guadalcanal (Second Marine, Americal, and 25th Infantry Divisions) are reorganized as XIV Corps under MG PATCH. The British continue their advance in the Arakan region of Burma, but Japanese resistance stiffens. On the 3rd, the Americal Division succeeds in partially surrounding the Japanese Gifu position on Mt. Austen, Guadalcanal. US and Australian forces mop up in the Buna area of Papua. On the 4th, Japanese Imperial General Headquarters issues orders for the evacuation of forces from Guadalcanal to New Georgia. Additional elements of the Second Marine Division and the last echelon of the 25th Infantry Division land on Guadalcanal. A US-Australian cruiser-destroyer force shells MUNDA, suffering slight damage in a Japanese air attack, during which the USS *Helena* introduces the use of proximity-fuzed anti-aircraft ammunition for the first time in the Pacific. On the 5th, on Guadalcanal, US Army engineers complete a truck bridge across the Matanikau River, greatly easing supply problems. In Arakan, Burma, a stalemate begins to develop, as the Japanese hold the British before Akyab. On the 6th, on Guadalcanal, General Patch lays plans for a major offensive that will drive the Japanese from the island. In Papua, American and Australian troops mass for a final assault on Sanananda. On the 7th, US strength on Guadalcanal reaches 50,000 men (Marine, army, and navy); Japanese strength is less than 25,000. On Guadalcanal, small detachments of soldiers and Marines begin to be sealifted to strategic locations along the coast in the rear of the Japanese, to establish "block" positions should the enemy attempt to retreat. A stalemate develops in Arakan, Burma, where the British will take heavy losses in several major attacks over the next weeks. On the 8th, British occupation forces turn control of Madagascar over to the Free French. Allied aircraft attack Japanese transports landing 4,000 troops at LAE, in northeastern NEW GUINEA. In Papua, US troops make limited attacks to prepare for a major assault on Sanananda. On the 9th, an Australian brigade is airlifted to a jungle airstrip at Wau, near Salamaua in northeastern New Guinea, where it begins to build a major base. On the 10th, Japanese destroyers bringing supplies to Guadalcanal are ambushed by US PT-boats, which sink two of the Japanese ships with slight damage to themselves. US forces on Guadalcanal begin a general offensive to eliminate Japanese forces. Henderson Field now usable in all weather due to a paved runway. Limited Allied attacks continue in the Sanananda area of Papua. On the 11th, the US 35th Infantry succeeds in encircling the Gifu, but Japanese resistance remains fierce. In northeastern New Guinea, the Australian Kanga Force undertakes a three-day raid against Japanese-held Mubo, inflicting considerable damage. On the 12th, losing the destroyer *Worden* to the hazards of the sea, US

troops land on unoccupied Amchitka in the ALEUTIANS and commence building an airstrip. On Guadalcanal US forces encounter heavy fighting at the Gifu and Galloping Horse positions. On the 13th, US submarine *Guardfish* TORPEDOES a Japanese patrol vessel off New Ireland. On Guadalcanal, the US 25th Division, in a daring attack, breaks Japanese resistance and occupies the Galloping Horse area, clearing the entire western flank of the American beachhead, while the Second Marine Division attacks westward along the coast. On the 14th, Japanese destroyers bringing about 600 men and supplies to Guadalcanal are attacked by US aircraft and PT-boats with little effect, while on the island the US offensive is temporarily held to limited gains. Casablanca Conference opens, as President ROOSEVELT and Prime Minister CHURCHILL begin 10 days of meetings, enunciating the "unconditional surrender" policy and outlining future Allied global STRATEGY, with Chinese leader CHIANG present. On the 15th, Japanese superbattleship *Musashi* arrives at TRUK. On Guadalcanal and in the Sanananda area of Papua, Allied forces make only limited gains. On the 16th, the Second Marine Division cautiously clears Japanese troops out of "the Ravine" on Guadalcanal, while other US forces make only limited gains. Near Sanananda, US and Australian forces clear outlying areas of Japanese holdouts. On the 17th, XIV Corps on Guadalcanal forms the CAM (Combined Army-Marine) Division, which attacks westward along the coast. In Papua, Allied forces begin a major offensive against Sanananda. On the 18th, a US cruiser-destroyer force bombards Japanese-held Attu, in the Aleutians. On Guadalcanal, having gained only 1,500 yards in five days of fighting, the Second Marine Division halts its offensive against the last Japanese stronghold in the interior, while the CAM Division offensive gains ground. On the northeast coast of Papua, Sanananda, falls to Allied troops, who press the Japanese westward. On the 19th, US destroyers shell Japanese positions on Guadalcanal, while the CAM Division presses westward. Fierce Japanese resistance on the Sanananda front, in Papua. In Burma, the British attempt a renewed attack at Japanese forces before Akyab, with little success. On the 20th, on Guadalcanal, the US 25th Infantry Division tightens its hold on the Gifu, as Japanese resistance weakens all along the front. In Papua, Japanese resistance on the Sanananda front collapses. On the 21st, US troops on Guadalcanal pause to resupply. In Papua, Allied troops mop up Japanese remnants in the Sanananda area. On the 22nd on Guadalcanal, the US 25th Infantry Division tightens its hold on the Gifu, despite a Japanese BANZAI attack after nightfall, while the CAM Division renews its offensive westward along the coast, making surprising gains. In Papua the last organized Japanese resistance ends in the Buna-Gona-Sanananda area: Of 16,000 Japanese troops committed to the area at least 7,000 have been killed or died of disease (the Allies buried that many) and many others wounded or seriously ill, while Allied casualties (about two-thirds Australian) are 8,500, with some 2,000 dead from all causes. On the 23rd, US cruisers and destroyers, supported by aircraft from the carrier *Saratoga*, bombard Japanese positions on Guadalcanal, in support of the CAM Division, which overruns Kokumbona. Casablanca Conference of Allied leaders agrees on strong offensive in Burma, a "dual" approach to the Philippines, from the central and southwest Pacific, and "unconditional surrender" for Axis. On the 24th, the Japanese on Attu begin a series of air raids against Amchitka, in the Aleutians. The US offensive on Guadalcanal continues to gain ground. On the 25th, the Japanese are in full retreat on Guadalcanal, closely pursued by US forces. In Papua the US 41st Division relieves the 32nd and the Seventh Australian Divisions. The Italian BLOCKADE RUNNER *Orseolo* departs KOBE for Bordeaux. On the 26th, the 25th Infantry Division is pulled out of the line on Guadalcanal, as the CAM Division sweeps the Japanese westward. On the 27th, a US submarine sinks the Japanese merchantman *Shoan Maru* (c. 5,600 GRT): Since PEARL HARBOR Japan has lost 273 merchant ships, for a total of about 1.3 million GRT, roughly 20% of her prewar merchant tonnage. On the 28th, the Japanese make a final at-

tempt to reach PORT MORESBY by an overland offensive, attacking the Australian Kanga Force at Wau, northeastern New Guinea. On Guadalcanal, the CAM Division advances across the Nueha River. On the 29th, Japanese submarine *I-1* is sunk off Cape Esperance by two New Zealand corvettes, which salvage important cryptographic equipment, greatly assisting American experts who have been cracking Japanese codes since before the war began. At Wau in northeastern New Guinea the Australian Kanga Force holds the Japanese to limited gains. On the 30th, the United States lands reinforcements and supplies on Guadalcanal. Air-Sea Battle of the Rennell Islands: Japanese aircraft sink heavy cruiser *Chicago*. In northeastern New Guinea, the Australian Kanga Force, reinforced by air with the Australian 17th Brigade, decisively defeats attacking Japanese forces. On the 31st, the CAM Division on Guadalcanal advances to the Bonegi River, against light resistance. The Japanese 20th Division completes its concentration at WEWAK in New Guinea. At Wau, in northeast New Guinea, Australian troops mop up Japanese forces.

February 1943

The Japanese abandoned GUADALCANAL, successfully evacuating almost 13,000 troops by sea. American troops took the Russell Islands and both sides continued to reinforce their positions in NEW GUINEA. Stalemate developed in Burma. Most of 1943 will see low-level activity in the SOLOMONS and New Guinea, as both sides rebuild their forces for larger campaigns in 1944.

On the 1st, US Marine regiment lands on the west coast of Guadalcanal, in an attempt to outflank the defending Japanese. Twenty Japanese destroyers sortie from RABAUL to evacuate remaining troops on Guadalcanal, and are virtually uninjured in a running fight with US aircraft and PT-BOATS, but lose one of their number to a mine, while sinking three PT-boats. On the 2nd, 19 Japanese destroyers evacuate thousands of Japanese troops from Guadalcanal before dawn, while the US

CAM Division captures Cape Tassafaronga. In the NETHERLANDS EAST INDIES the last Australian GUERRILLAS on TIMOR (operating there since 8 December 1941) are withdrawn by sea. On the 3rd, US battleship *Massachusetts* begins operating in the Pacific. Heavy skirmishing between Allied and Japanese troops along the Indo-Burmese frontier. In northeastern New Guinea, the Australian Kanga Force counterattacks from Wau, driving the Japanese back on Mubo. On the 4th, the United States lands reinforcements and supplies on Guadalcanal. Japanese light cruiser *Isuzu* and 22 destroyers sortie from Rabaul to evacuate troops from Guadalcanal, suffering serious damage from US aircraft. Heavily escorted, the battle-hardened Australian Ninth Division sails home from Suez after two years of service in North Africa. On the 5th, Japanese light cruiser *Isuzu* and escorts evacuate thousands of Japanese troops from Guadalcanal, where the US CAM Division continues to advance along the northern coast. On the 6th, additional US reinforcements arrive on Guadalcanal, while the CAM Division reaches the Umasani River. In northeastern New Guinea, the Japanese lose 24 aircraft in an attack on the Wau airfield, while no Allied aircraft are lost. On the 7th, 18 Japanese destroyers sortie from Rabaul to evacuate troops from Guadalcanal, suffering some damage from US air attacks. On Guadalcanal, US troops advance on both the northern and the northwestern coasts. Admiral HALSEY authorizes "Operation Cleanslate," the occupation of the Russell Islands. CHIANG-KAI SHEK commits China to a new offensive in Burma. On the 8th, 18 Japanese destroyers evacuate more Japanese troops from Guadalcanal; altogether the Imperial Navy manages to pull nearly 12,000 army and about a thousand navy personnel out of Guadalcanal. In Burma Orde WINGATE's 77th Indian Brigade, the CHINDITS, undertakes its first operation against the Japanese: Over the next few weeks its seven columns will spread out over central Burma inflicting great destruction on bridges, roads, and isolated Japanese installations before the survivors return to India. On the 9th, no organized Japanese forces remain on Guadalcanal, as US

troops advancing along the northwestern and northern coasts make contact at CAPE ESPERANCE. CNO KING "invites" CINCPAC NIMITZ to consider capturing the GILBERT ISLANDS. On the 10th, Guadalcanal is secure, at the cost of 1,600 US Army and Marine Corps troops killed and 4,245 wounded, plus thousands of CASUALTIES from disease, while Japan lost at least 14,800 killed, 9,000 dead of disease, and about a thousand as PRISONERS, many of them Korean labor troops. While the naval battles off Guadalcanal and in the general area were far more numerous and, for the Allies at least, caused far more casualties than the fighting on the island, it was the land battle that decided the issue. Guadalcanal was a sobering experience for the Japanese, who had never been so decisively defeated on land. Some Japanese leaders realized that Guadalcanal would be the pattern in the future. Bill Howell leaves his billet (navy job) at the Brooklyn Armed Guard Center and reports to the Philadelphia Navy Yard to join the crew of the new light carrier *Monterey*. He is the first enlisted member of the crew to report to the ship, which already has two officers: Commander Silvius Gazze, the air officer, and Commander R. M. Oliver, the executive officer. *Monterey* (CVL-26) was originally laid down as a light cruiser (*Dayton*, CL-78) on December 29, 1941, at the New York Shipbuilding Company's yard in Camden, New Jersey. But President ROOSEVELT pressured the navy to convert nine incomplete light cruisers to light carriers and this was done. So on February 23, 1943, the converted cruiser was launched as a light carrier. Bill Howell's ship carried about a third as many aircraft (33) as the standard ESSEX CLASS carrier, and displaced a little less than a half as much at full load, about 14,000 tons to 32,000. She was a cramped ship, but an effective one. Crew size was 1,569 men, including 159 officers. On the 11th, at NOUMEA, preparations for "Operation Cleanslate," the occupation of the Russell Islands, proceed. On Guadalcanal, Marine and army troops mop up Japanese stragglers. Heavy skirmishing between Allied and Japanese troops along the Indo-Burmese frontier. On the 12th, at Noumea, a small naval task force is organized to support "Operation Cleanslate," four destroyers, four destroyer-transports, five minesweepers, and 12 LSTS, plus some smaller vessels. MACARTHUR issues plans for operations against NEW BRITAIN, New Ireland, and northeastern New Guinea. On the 13th, the Japanese 41st Division arrives at WEWAK, New Guinea, from China. On the 14th, at Noumea, elements of the US 43rd Infantry Division are embarked for Guadalcanal. On the 15th, Admiral Halsey consolidates his aircraft resources under a joint Aircraft, Solomons Command (AIRSOLS). On the 16th, US fighter aircraft begin using the new airstrip on Amchitka in the Aleutians, ending Japanese air strikes against the island. About two-thirds of the US 43rd Infantry Division lands at Koli Point, Guadalcanal, to prepare for the occupation of the Russell Islands. On the 17th, the 55th Indian Brigade attempts to capture a Japanese strongpoint on the Arakan front but is unsuccessful, and the stalemate in western Burma continues. After nightfall the New Zealand corvette *Moa* lands a small American reconnaissance team on Banika, the easternmost large island in the Russell group. On the 18th, US cruisers and destroyers shell Japanese positions on Attu, the Aleutians, for the first time. The New Zealand corvette *Moa* lands an American reconnaissance team on Pavuvu, the largest of the Russell Islands: Allied intelligence concludes that the Japanese have evacuated the island group. On the 19th, US cruisers and destroyers again shell Japanese positions on Attu. The naval forces under MacArthur are designated the Seventh Fleet. On the 20th, US submarine *Albacore* (SS-218) sinks the Japanese destroyer *Oshio* near the ADMIRALTY ISLANDS. Continued stalemate in the Arakan region of Burma. On the 21st, the first RCT of the US 43rd Infantry Division lands in the Russell Islands, the unopposed operation being treated as a large-scale training exercise. After nightfall the Royal Indian Navy lands raiding parties on the Burmese coast southwest of Akyab; they successfully raid Japanese positions before pulling out. On the 22nd, the United States commissions the battleship IOWA, the most powerful in the world, at the Brooklyn

Navy Yard. On the 23rd, on Guadalcanal, the army and Marines are still coping with Japanese stragglers, most of whom refuse to surrender and fight on as snipers. On the 24th, US troops in the Russell Islands begin construction of an airfield. Heavy skirmishing between Allied and Japanese troops along the Indo-Burmese frontier; the Japanese decide to withdraw to the Burmese side of the mountains because of their tenuous logistical situation. On the 25th, the US Navy establishes a motor torpedo boat base in the Russell Islands. On the 26th, US construction projects in the Russell Islands include an airfield, three landing craft bases and repair facilities, and a base for the First Marine Division: Pavuvu becomes the division's "home" when it is not engaged in operations. Off the Burma coast light forces of the Royal Indian Navy engage a small Japanese troop convoy, sinking one vessel and damaging another. On the 27th, the veteran Ninth Australian Division arrives at SYDNEY from the Middle East, after 23 days at sea. On the 28th, escorted by cruisers and destroyers, eight Japanese transports (c. 7,000 troops) sail from Rabaul bound for LAE, in eastern New Guinea. In northern Burma the Japanese begin operations to eject small British garrisons supporting Kachin guerrillas.

March 1943

The fighting swung back and forth in Burma, as it would until nearly the end of the war. Superior Allied airpower began to assert itself in the SOLOMONS and NEW GUINEA. Japanese forces were isolated in the ALEUTIANS, where the Allies planned to clear them out in the next few months, diverting tremendous naval and air resources and slowing down buildups in the rest of the Pacific. In China, the Japanese launched a major offensive. Heavy fighting would continue in China until the end of the war.

On the 1st, aided by unusually hazy weather in the BISMARCK SEA, a Japanese troop convoy bound from Rabaul for LAE, on Huon Gulf, northeastern New Guinea, is undetected by US aerial reconnaissance. In northern Burma, British garrisons and

Kachin GUERRILLAS fall back. On the 2nd, the Battle of the Bismarck Sea: A Japanese convoy bound for Lae is attacked by USAAF aircraft, losing one transport. On the 3rd, the Battle of the Bismarck Sea continues: Off Huon Gulf, New Guinea, the Japanese convoy is attacked by over 350 US and Australian aircraft, plus light surface forces, with the loss of all transports and four destroyers, at a cost of 21 Allied aircraft. On the 4th, the Battle of the Bismarck Sea ends: In a three-day running fight, Allied air and naval forces have sunk eight Japanese transports and four destroyers, while shooting down many enemy aircraft and killing thousands of Japanese troops. In an official report to army units throughout the South and southwest Pacific, a senior Japanese staff officer criticizes American combat methods on GUADALCANAL, concluding that the Americans have many admirable qualities ("they are quite brave"), but many faults as well ("infantry forces do not engage in night attacks"), and that leadership is poor ("officers of middle rank and below possess little tactical ability"). On the 5th, the Japanese 54th Division arrives at JAVA from Japan. After nightfall, US destroyers shell Japanese positions at Vila and MUNDA, in the central Solomons. On the 6th, in the Solomon Islands US cruisers and destroyers ambush and sink two Japanese destroyers attempting to reinforce Vila, while Japanese aircraft raid the Russell Islands. Stalemate in Arakan region of Burma, but the Japanese begin preparing for an offensive. On the 7th, US and Japanese forces conduct regular naval and air patrols throughout the Solomons. The Japanese refuse a German request to join the war against Russia. On the 8th, US commanders assess the lessons of Guadalcanal; the Marines call for more firepower and special training. In China, the Japanese begin an attack across the Yangtze River between Ichang and Yoyang. On the 9th, British CHINDIT commandos in Burma advance to the Irrawaddy River. In northeastern New Guinea, Japanese aircraft conduct a major raid on Wau. On the 10th the Chinese resist the new Japanese offensive. On the 11th, the "American Volunteer Group" (FLYING TIGERS) in China is

redesignated the 14th Air Force, under Claire CHENNAULT. Adm YAMAMOTO transfers his flag to battleship *Musashi*, at TRUK. On the 12th, senior US military officials open a "Pacific Military Conference" in Washington to discuss plans. In Burma, the Japanese begin a counteroffensive against the British. On the 13th, in the Arakan region of Burma, the Japanese 55th Division undertakes an attack against the British 14th Indian Division. In northeastern New Guinea, the Australian Kanga Force presses the Japanese back to the vicinity of Guadagasel. On the 14th, there is heavy fighting in Arakan region of Burma; Japanese forces begin an arduous crossing of "impassable" mountains, which will bring them into the British rear. On the 15th, US Navy forces in the central Pacific are designated the Fifth Fleet. In New Guinea, the Japanese offer no resistance as the US 162nd Infantry occupies positions at the mouth of the Mambare River. On the 16th, US destroyers shell Vila in the central Solomons. In the Arakan region of Burma, the 55th Indian Brigade is outflanked by the Japanese, who attack across "impassable" mountains. On the 17th, in the Arakan the 71st Indian Brigade assists 55th in retiring from its outflanked positions, exposing the entire British left. On the 18th, in central Burma, the "Chindits," having already cut several rail lines, make several raids across the Irrawaddy River, while the British Sixth Brigade makes a final attempt to break the Japanese lines before Akyab; their failure, combined with increased Japanese infiltration and encirclement attacks, forces the British to begin a retreat. On the 19th, US naval forces in MACARTHUR's Southwest Pacific Theater are designated the Seventh Fleet. On the 20th, US submarine *Pollack* (SS-180) sinks Japanese merchant cruiser *Bangkok Maru* in the MARSHALL ISLANDS. On the 21st, the British rush reinforcements to their forces in the Arakan, Burma. On the 22nd, the Japanese, alarmed at their deteriorating position in the Aleutians, decide to be more aggressive with their naval patrols off the Alaskan coast, to facilitate supply of their forces there. US SUBMARINES *Grampus* (SS-207) and *Amberjack* (SS-219) are declared overdue and presumed lost in the southwest Pacific. On the 23rd, the British retreat from the Arakan region of Burma shows signs of turning into a rout, as the Japanese turn or infiltrate every position the British attempt to hold. On the 24th, the US Joint Chiefs of Staff approves a plan to retake Attu. On the 25th, US naval aircraft raid NAURU in the central Pacific, north of the SANTA CRUZ ISLANDS. On the 26th, the Battle of the KOMANDORSKI ISLANDS: In the last daylight naval shoot-out in history without interference from aircraft or submarines, US cruisers and destroyers barely beat off a stronger Japanese squadron (two cruisers and four destroyers versus four cruisers and four destroyers, with a transport) attempting to reinforce Japanese garrisons in the ALEUTIANS. On the 27th, Orde WINGATE's Chindits are ordered back to their Indian base after nearly two months of rampaging in the Japanese rear area in central Burma, where they made over 70 cuts in Japanese rail lines. On the 28th, the Japanese squadron defeated at the Komandorski Islands returns to PARAMUSHIRO, where its commander is sacked. In Washington, the Joint Chiefs of Staff directs MacArthur and HALSEY to occupy the TROBRIAND ISLANDS. On the 29th, Japanese gather hundreds of aircraft in bases throughout the northern Solomons and RABAUL, in order to launch decisive attacks on the growing Allied base on Guadalcanal. On the 30th, a US submarine sinks the Japanese cargo ship *Kurohime Maru* (c. 4,700 GRT) off MANUS, north of New Guinea: Since PEARL HARBOR the Japanese merchant marine has lost 330 ships, for a total of 1.5 million GRT, a full quarter million tons since late January, as US submarines begin to operate with greater effectiveness. On the 31st, MacKechnie Force, a task force of the US 41st Division, moves by water to secure the mouth of the Waria River and an airstrip at Dona.

April 1943

The Japanese launched a massive air offensive from RABAUL against Allied bases in New Guinea and the Solomons, which didn't do them much good. Their offensive in China was more successful, and in Burma they continued to push British forces back toward India. Allied forces were massed in Alaska to push out Japanese bases in the ALEUTIAN ISLANDS.

On the 1st, Japanese aircraft attack the Russell Islands. On the 2nd, although TORPEDOED on the previous day by a British submarine, the Italian BLOCKADE RUNNER *Orseolo* reaches Bordeaux from KOBE. On the 3rd, elements of MacKechnie Force land at Morobe, northeastern New Guinea, near the Waria River, without opposition and begin to establish a beachhead. On the 4th, the Fourth Marine Division is activated at SAN DIEGO, using cadres drawn from the Third Marine Division. On the 5th, the British Sixth Brigade headquarters is overrun by advancing Japanese in Arakan region of Burma, who occupy the Mayu Peninsula. On the 6th, US submarine *Trout* (SS-202) begins laying MINES near Sarawak, BORNEO, late at night. On the 7th, nearly 190 Japanese aircraft from Rabaul (including aircraft landed from four carriers) attack Allied shipping at GUADALCANAL and TULAGI, sinking the US destroyer *Aaron Ward*, the New Zealand corvette *Moa*, and a tanker, damaging other vessels as well, while losing 21 of their number to the Allies, who lose seven aircraft. On the 8th, the Japanese press on with their offensive in the Arakan region of Burma. This, coupled with their recent success in the air over the Solomons and their continued hold on bases in the Aleutians, gives some Japanese cause to believe that the war is going their way. On the 9th, Japanese destroyer *Isonami* is sunk southeast of Celebes by the US submarine *Tautog* (SS-199). On the 10th, the US submarine *Triton* (SS-201) is reported as overdue and presumed lost near the ADMIRALTY ISLANDS; she is the twelfth US submarine lost in the war. On the 11th, Japanese aircraft from Rabaul raid Oro Bay, near BUNA in northeastern New Guinea, burning two merchant ships. On the 12th, Japanese aircraft from Rabaul make a major raid on PORT MORESBY in southern New Guinea, but cause little damage. On the 13th, nothing much happened. On the 14th, Japanese aircraft from Rabaul make a major raid on MILNE BAY, sinking two transports. Japanese submarine *Ro-102* is sunk by *PT-150* and *PT-152*, off LAE in eastern New Guinea. On the 15th, US convoys begin converging on Attu, in the Aleutians. The United States completes a major airfield on Banika, Russell Islands, which, with a second strip still under construction, will allow more effective use of American air power in the central and northern Solomons. On the 16th, American codebreakers discover that Japanese Navy commander-in-chief YAMAMOTO will be flying to visit bases in the Solomons: Acting on this information, senior US officers decide to attempt to shoot down Yamamoto's airplane, thereby depriving Japan of one of her most capable admirals, a risky decision since the Japanese may conclude that their codes are being broken, and change them, leaving the Allies unable to read secret Japanese transmissions, for months, at least. On the 17th, the British situation in the Arakan region of Burma is becoming hopeless, as nothing seems able to stop the Japanese, not even their increasingly difficult logistical situation. On the 18th, US P-38 fighters intercept two airplanes carrying Japanese Admiral Isoruku Yamamoto and his staff, shooting down both and killing the admiral, at Buin, BOUGAINVILLE. On the 19th, the US submarine *Scorpion* (SS-278) lays mines in Japanese waters, the beginning of an operation that will eventually prove more lethal than torpedoes or aircraft bombs in shutting down Japanese shipping. On the 20th, US submarine *Runner* lays mines off HONG KONG. On the 21st, the US submarine *Stingray* lays mines in Chinese waters. On the 22nd, Australians complain to their Allies that "Germany First" policy is putting a severe strain on their depleted resources. On the 23rd, US submarine *Seawolf* (SS-197) sinks a Japanese patrol vessel in the Yellow Sea. In northeastern New Guinea, on the Mubo front where the fighting has developed into a stalemate, the Australian Kanga Force is relieved by the Australian Third Division. On the 24th, the US Seventh Infantry Division sails from SAN FRANCISCO for Alaska, for the final assault on Japanese bases in the Aleutians. On the 25th, the US Navy launches the submarine *Dace*

(SS-247) at Groton, Connecticut: Since PEARL HARBOR 67 new American SUBMARINES have slid down the ways. While on leave, Petty Officer Bill Howell, knowing he is about to ship out for a long, long tour in the Pacific, gets married to his high school sweetheart Catherine. It will be a year and a half and several naval battles before Bill and Catherine see each other again. On the 26th, US cruisers and destroyers shell Japanese positions on Attu in the Aleutians. Off Mauritius the German submarine *U-180* transfers Indian radical nationalist leader Subhas Chandra BOSE to the Japanese submarine *I-29*. On the 27th, Chinese resistance to the Japanese advance in Huphe Province begins to stiffen. The Japanese are attacking with scant resources and depend on marginal Chinese performance to keep the offensive going. On the 28th, US submarine *Scamp* (SS-277) sinks Japanese seaplane carrier *Kamikawa Maru* off New Ireland. On the 29th, the US submarine *Gato* (SS-212) lands COASTWATCHERS on Teop, in the Solomon Islands, and evacuates missionaries. On the 30th, the submarine *Gudgeon* (SS-211) lands supplies and personnel on Panay, in the Philippines, to assist Filipino GUERRILLAS. On the 31st, after heavy fighting, Chinese troops halt a Japanese offensive in Huphe Province, ending a threat to Chungking.

May 1943

The most significant event of the Pacific War for this month occurred in the Atlantic. By May of 1943, it had become clear to the Allies that the Battle of the Atlantic had been won. From this point on, German U-boat activity declined markedly, making greater naval and shipping resources available for the Pacific. The large, increasing concentration of Allied antisubmarine forces in the North Atlantic caused the Germans to redeploy their U-boats, and they began stationing some in the Indian Ocean, where they operated in conjunction with several Italian SUBMARINES from bases in the Dutch East Indies. Meanwhile, fighting continued in New Guinea and the Solomons, and Japan launched another offensive in China, while the United States and Canada finally invaded Japanese-held islands in the ALEUTIANS.

On the 1st, the escort carrier *Coral Sea* (CVE-57, later renamed *Anzio*) is launched at VANCOUVER: Since PEARL HARBOR the US Navy has commissioned or launched 31 fleet carriers, light carriers, and escort carriers. On the 2nd, DARWIN, Australia, is bombed by Japanese aircraft based at Salamaua, New Guinea. On the 3rd, Chief of Staff MARSHALL (USA) informs General STILWELL that the United States plans to base B-29s in China for attacks on Japanese-held territory and Japan itself. On the 4th, the US Seventh Division sets sail for Attu from Cold Bay, Alaska. On the 5th, US submarines sink three small Japanese freighters, for a total of less than 7,000 GRT, but this brings the loss of Japanese merchant shipping to over 1.7 million tons since Pearl Harbor. On the 6th, Japanese hopes of a German advance into the Middle East (to meet Japanese troops moving through India) are dashed as the Allies launch their final offensive in North Africa. Within a week, all Axis troops in North Africa surrender. This will be followed by an invasion of Sicily and, before the end of the year, the surrender of Italy, one of the charter members of "the Axis." On the 7th, US destroyers mine the Blackett Strait, under cover of a cruiser-destroyer raid into VELLA GULF. In the Arakan, Burma, British forces once again withdraw, as the Japanese continue their infiltration and encirclement tactics. On the 8th, three Japanese destroyers are lost on a US minefield in Blackett Strait, near New Georgia. The Japanese battleship YAMATO puts to sea for Japan from TRUK, her first movement out of anchorage since 29 August 1942. The US Seventh Infantry Division arrives off Attu, but cannot land due to poor weather. On the 9th, foul weather continues to delay a US landing on Attu. On the 10th, Japanese intelligence informs Attu that a US assault is not imminent, and the garrison there lets down its guard, while the American invasion force rides out bad weather just over the horizon and a destroyer and a destroyer-minelayer are damaged in a collision. On the 11th, the US Seventh Division commences landings on two beaches on Attu in the Aleutians. The Japanese battleship *Yamato* arrives at KURE for a refit. Italian submarine *Cappellini* departs La Pallice, France, on a BLOCKADE RUNNING mission to Japan. On the 12th, US cruisers and destroyers shell Vila and MUNDA and mine KULA GULF in the central SOLOMONS. In the Arakan, having driven the British back roughly to the line of the front in mid-December, the Japanese halt their advance. The Trident Conference begins in Washington, as ROOSEVELT, CHURCHILL, and the Combined Chiefs of Staff confer on STRATEGY. On the 13th, Axis troops in Tunisia, North Africa, surrender. There is very heavy fighting on Attu, as US troops are unable to advance out of their beachheads. On the 14th, Japanese minesweepers clear Kula Gulf. On the 15th, heavy fighting continues on Attu in the Aleutians, as the Japanese defenders fight to the death. Chinese troops assigned to a planned Allied offensive in Burma are diverted to the Ichang area, in the light of a Japanese offensive across the Yangtze. On the 16th, Italian submarine *Tazzoli* departs La Pallice, France, on a blockade running mission to Japan and is never heard from again (probably sunk by British aircraft in the Bay of Biscay later that day). On the 17th, Japanese forces on Attu surprisingly abandon their forward positions and withdraw into the rugged interior of the island. On the 18th, the two US beachheads on Attu link up, as additional troops land on the island. On the 19th, US troops on Attu reestablish contact with Japanese forces, and heavy fighting resumes. On the 20th, the US Joint Chiefs of Staff approves a plan for the defeat of Japan, to include simultaneous offensives through the GILBERT and MARSHALL ISLANDS, the BISMARCK ARCHIPELAGO, and Burma, preparatory to further advances, and ultimately an air and sea blockade of Japan and possible invasion. In Burma, the main body of the CHINDITS manages to return to British lines, after a three-month operation during which it lost about a third of its strength; stragglers continue coming in through early June. On the 21st, the Japanese battleship *Musashi* and a strong escort arrive at Tokyo Bay, for a possible sortie to the Aleutians, but the mission is abandoned. The Japanese open a new offensive across the Yangtze River in China. On the 22nd, the US destroyer *Caperton* (DD-650) is launched at the Bath Iron Works, Maine: Since Pearl Harbor the US Navy has lost 27 destroyers but has added nearly 160; in the same period the Imperial Navy has lost 35 destroyers and has added barely a dozen. On the 23rd, Italian submarine *Giuliani* departs La Pallice, France, on a blockade running mission to Japan. Heavy fighting continues on Attu. On the 24th, Churchill and Roosevelt agree to increase aid to China and adopt an "island hopping" strategy in the Pacific. On the 25th, elements of the Japanese Fifth Fleet (Northern Pacific) are at sea for a possible rescue of the Attu garrison. In Washington, the Trident Conference ends, having decided, among other things, to undertake a landing in France in the spring of 1944, and a major increase in Allied air supply to China. On the 26th, Japanese commence covert submarine evacuation of troops on KISKA, in the Aleutians. Elements of the Japanese Fifth Fleet go to sea for a possible rescue of the Attu garrison, which is heavily engaged with US troops. On the 27th, US forces on Attu begin building an airfield, as heavy fighting continues. On the 28th, aircraft drop surrender leaflets on remaining Japanese troops of the Attu Island garrison, with no perceptible effect. On the 29th, the Japanese abandon plans to evacuate the Attu garrison, which undertakes a major BANZAI attack in recognition of its desperate position. On the 30th, organized Japanese resistance on Attu ends. On the 31st, Chinese troops in Hopen Province halt a Japanese drive on Chungking, but the Japanese offensive gains ground elsewhere.

June 1943

The fighting in NEW GUINEA and the SOLOMONS heated up as MACARTHUR executed Operation CARTWHEEL. This plan landed US, Australian, and New Zealand troops on lightly defended islands and places, where air bases could be built. In this way, aircraft will be used to surround and neutralize the huge Japanese base at RABAUL, isolating it and its 100,000-man garrison, which will slowly starve, as Japanese ships carrying fuel, ammunition, and food will be unable to get through. By the end of the war Rabaul will be a de facto POW camp for its malnourished garrison. Cartwheel was initially planned as a preliminary maneuver before invading Rabaul. But it was soon decided that the huge base could simply be left surrounded and bypassed. Many other Japanese island garrisons were bypassed in a similar fashion throughout the Pacific. This saved many lives, both Allied and Japanese. But the Cartwheel operation was the first, and largest, of these bypass operations.

On the 1st, the Japanese Army reorganizes the Imperial Guard, forming a second division at Tokyo, which is designated the "First," while the original Imperial Guards Division, in Sumatra since early 1942, is redesignated the "Second." US forces in the Aleutians and California begin training for the invasion of KISKA. On the 2nd, Pope Pius XII denounces air bombardment, which does not in any way delay US plans to deploy the B-29 bomber in the Pacific in 1944. On the 3rd, the Japanese offensive in China succeeds after hard campaigning, as they take control of all shipping on the upper Yangtze in western Hopeh Province, after which they will begin a voluntary withdrawal. On the 4th, the German auxiliary cruiser *Michel* sails from BATAVIA, JAVA, to raid Allied shipping in the Indian Ocean. On the 5th, the Air Battle of the Russell Islands: Over 80 Japanese aircraft from Rabaul tangle with over 100 US aircraft from Henderson (GUADALCANAL) and other fields, losing 24 aircraft to seven American ones. On the 6th, the Japanese assess their situation on Kiska, Aleutians, conclude that it is hopeless, and decide that evacuation is the only option. On the 7th, the Japanese resume air attacks on Guadalcanal, losing 23 aircraft to the Allies' nine. On the 8th, the Japanese battleship *Mutsu* is destroyed by an internal explosion while lying in HIROSHIMA harbor. In the ALEUTIANS, the United States completes an airfield on Attu, while Kiska is subjected to air and naval bombardment whenever the weather will allow. On the 9th, on convoy duty off FREMANTLE, an Australian minesweeper is sunk in a collision with a merchant ship. On the 10th, US submarine *Trigger* (SS-237) TORPEDOES the Japanese carrier *Hiyo* off Japan, but the carrier does not sink. The Japanese submarine *I-24* is sunk off Kiska by a US patrol boat. On the 11th, Japanese submarine *I-9* is sunk off Kiska by US destroyer *Frazier*. On the 12th Japan's Prime Minister TOJO grapples with the problem of how to present Japan's declining fortunes to the rest of the national leadership. It is decided to simply make an announcement to the Diet (parliament): So far in 1943, Japan has had to abandon Guadalcanal, the Aleutians, and an offensive in China, finding success only in Burma, and there only as a matter of throwing back a British offensive. Allied aircraft intercept a large Japanese raid on Guadalcanal, shooting down 31 enemy planes while losing six. On the 13th, Japanese forces in China complete their withdrawal from western Hopeh, returning to their lines of 21 May. On the 14th, Tojo meets with Indian nationalist leader Subhas Chandra BOSE and agrees to allow him to set up an Indian government and raise an Indian army, to assist Japanese forces in Burma in the "liberation" of India. On the 15th, the German merchant cruiser *Michel* sinks a 7,700–ton merchant ship west of Australia. The Italian submarine *Barbarigo* departs La Pallice, France, with critical materials and electronic equipment for Japan, and is never heard from again. On the 16th, 120 Japanese aircraft from Rabaul and New Georgia attack Allied ships in the vicinity of Guadalcanal, damaging three ships, two of which must be beached, but losing nearly 100 of their number to 104 intercepting Allied aircraft, who suffer only six planes lost. On the 17th, Italian BLOCKADE-RUNNING submarine *Giuliani* reaches the East Indies, bringing critical materials and documents for the Japanese. West of Australia, the German merchant cruiser *Michel* sinks a 9,900–ton tanker. In China, LG STILWELL briefs CHIANG KAI-SHEK on the Trident Conference. Bill Howell's skipper, Captain Lester T. Hundt, assumes command of CVL *Monterey* as the ship is commissioned into active service. Bill works with the executive officer, keeping track of personnel records and things like the Plan of the Day (the daily schedule) and legal paperwork (Captain's Mast and any courts-martial that came around). It is an important job, for Yeoman Howell handles the paperwork on everything of importance that happens on the ship. On the 18th, the 43rd Infantry Division issues its final orders for operations on Rendova and New Georgia, as part of Cartwheel. The Italian submarine *Torelli* departs La Pallice, France, on a blockade-running mission to Japan. On the 19th, Allied preparations for Cartwheel concluding, convoys begin sailing for New Georgia. On the 20th, the Japanese undertake a series of sharp attacks against the Australian 17th Brigade, on the Mubo-Lababia Ridge front in northwestern New Guinea, making little headway. The blockade-running Italian submarine *Capellini* enters the Indian Ocean, bound for the Japanese-held NETHERLANDS EAST INDIES. Gen. Claude Auchinleck succeeds Gen. Archibald WAVELL as British commander-in-chief India. On the 21st, Operation Cartwheel begins, as fast transports covertly land the US Marine Fourth Raider Battalion at Segi Point, New Georgia, to deny it to the enemy: For the next year, virtually all operations in the Solomons, BISMARCKS, and northeastern New Guinea will be related to Operation Cartwheel. On the 22nd, fast transports covertly land two companies of the US 43rd Division, and some engineers, at Segi Point, New Georgia, to reinforce the Marines, reconnoiter, and select a site for an airfield, while the US 112th Cavalry RCT (dismounted) begins landing on Woodlark Island, off eastern New Guinea, which is unoccupied by the Japanese. The Japanese submarine *I-7* is damaged off Kiska by US destroyer *Monaghan*, and puts in to Kiska harbor. On the 23rd, the US 158th RCT begins landing on Kirwina Island, in the TROBRIANDS, between Woodlark and New Guinea, which is unoccupied by the Japanese. The Japanese submarine *Ro-103* sinks two transports off Guadalcanal. In New Guinea, Japanese pressure on the

Australian 17th Brigade on the Mubo-Lababia Front eases. On the 24th, in a radio broadcast from Tokyo, Indian nationalist Subhas Chandra Bose calls for the Indian people to rise up in armed revolt against British rule, an appeal that is largely unheeded. On the 25th, US submariners finally convince the navy that there is something wrong with American torpedoes, and the brass agree to correct the problem, while authorizing temporary fixes: This, and more effective tactics, results in US subs beginning to make big inroads against the Japanese merchant marine. On the 26th the MacKechnie Force (elements of the 162nd RCT plus some Australian forces) begins moving from Morobe in preparation for an amphibious assault at Nassau Bay. On the 26th, with the sinking of three cargo ships, Japanese merchant marine losses reach approximately two million GRT. On the 27th, the US First Cavalry Division (dismounted, organized as an infantry division) sails from SAN FRANCISCO for Australia. On New Georgia, the Fourth Marine Raiders is sealifted from Segi Point to the Lambeti Plantation. On the 28th, the Marine Raiders on New Georgia begin a cross-country reconnaissance from the Lambeti Plantation to Viru Harbor, on the opposite side of the island. On the 29th, US cruisers and destroyers shell Japanese installations in the Shortlands, at MUNDA, and at Vila, to cover the movement of troop convoys. The Japanese submarine Ro-103 encounters the troop convoys and reports them, but the report is dismissed by higher headquarters. On the 30th, Operation Cartwheel begins in earnest as, in New Guinea, Allied troops feint an offensive against Salamaua with a US amphibious landing at nearby Nassau Bay while Australian troops advance from Wau, to cover Allied occupation of the Trobriand and Woodlark Islands, east of New Guinea; heavily supported by naval and air forces, elements of the US 43rd Infantry Division land at Rendova against slight resistance, while small detachments begin landing on New Georgia. In New Guinea, MacKechnie Force lands at Nassau Bay, while elements of the Australian Third Division attack overland in support.

July 1943

Japanese completed their evacuation of ALEUTIAN Island bases in Alaskan waters. Fighting continued as the noose was tightened around RABAUL.

On the 1st, Operation CARTWEEL United States lands reinforcements at Rendova; Marine Fourth Raider Battalion captures Viru Harbor on New Georgia. Japanese destroyer *Hokaze* is damaged by US submarine *Thresher* (SS-200) in the southwest Pacific. On the 2nd, Operation Cartwheel: Japanese cruisers and destroyers shell US positions at Rendova; the US 37th and 43rd Divisions and Marines, supported by artillery fire from Rendova and large naval and air forces, land on both sides of MUNDA on New Georgia. On the 3rd, Operation Cartwheel: Japanese destroyers on a resupply mission depart Rabaul; heavy fighting on New Georgia. In NEW GUINEA, the Australian Third Division links up with MacKechnie Force at Nassau Bay. On the 4th, Operation Cartwheel: Elements of the US 37th Infantry Division land at Bairoko, on KULA GULF; Japanese destroyers, landing reinforcements at Vila, on Kula Gulf, sink a US destroyer. Heavy fighting on New Georgia. On the 5th, Japan cedes five provinces of MALAYA to Siam, in order to strengthen Siamese loyalty. Operation Cartwheel: Major "Tokyo Express" supply mission departs Rabaul; heavy fighting on New Georgia. At KISKA, damaged Japanese submarine *I-7* is scuttled. On the 6th, US cruisers and destroyers shell Japanese positions on Kiska in the Aleutians, a mission that is repeated several times over the next two weeks. Operation Cartwheels, Battle of Kula Gulf: Japanese destroyers attempting to land troops at Vila, on Kula Gulf, are ambushed by a US cruiser-destroyer force, but sink cruiser *Helena*, while losing destroyer *Nagatsuki*, grounded and then attacked by Allied aircraft; heavy fighting on New Georgia. On the 7th, a Japanese destroyer force sets out from PARAMUSHIRO in the KURILES to evacuate the remaining garrison on Kiska. On the 8th, heavy fighting continues on New Georgia, as US units make gains against stout resistance. On the 9th, Operation Cartwheel: US destroyers shelling

Japanese positions at Munda beat off attacks by about 100 enemy aircraft. Italian submarine *Capellini* reaches SABANG, Sumatra, bringing mercury, electronic equipment, and other items for the Japanese. On the 10th, B-25 bombers from Attu attack Paramushiro in the Kuriles for the first time. On the 11th, Operation Cartwheel: US cruisers and destroyers shell Munda. On the 12th, Operation Cartwheel, Battle of KOLOMBANGARA: eight Japanese destroyers and a light cruiser attempting to land reinforcements on New Georgia are ambushed by three cruisers (one New Zealander) and 10 destroyers, losing light cruiser *Jintsu*, while sinking a destroyer and heavily damaging all three Allied cruisers. Heavy fighting on New Georgia, where US troops are bogged down and one isolated battalion out of food. On the 13th, HALSEY reorganizes the higher command of the New Georgia operation. On New Guinea the Australian Third Division clears the Japanese from the Mubo area. On the 14th, Japanese submarine *I-179* is lost to an accident in Japanese home waters. On the 15th, a new commander takes over on New Georgia, as additional forces are landed. Major daylight air battle in the central SOLOMONS, as 74 Japanese aircraft attempt to interfere in the New Georgia battle, losing 45 of their number against three US planes shot down. On the 16th, unable to reach Kiska due to adverse weather, Japanese destroyers that sailed on 7 July return to Paramushiro. Two Australian cruisers and four US destroyers are ordered from ESPIRITU SANTO to join Seventh Fleet forces engaged off New Guinea. On the 17th, US aircraft from Henderson Field and other bases in the Solomons attack Japanese shipping off Buin, BOUGAINVILLE, sinking a destroyer and damaging several other vessels. US destroyers shell Kiska. Late in the day, the Japanese begin a series of offensive moves on New Georgia. On the 18th, desperate fighting continues on New Georgia, as the Japanese counterattacks are beaten off, while additional US forces land. On the 19th, heavily escorted, three Japanese destroyers land supplies at Vila, on Kula Gulf. On the 20th, retiring from Kula Gulf, a Japanese cruiser-destroyer force is attacked by US aircraft, with two destroyers lost and a cruiser damaged. A Japanese submarine TORPEDOES, but does not sink, Australian light cruiser *Hobart* in the Solomons. On New Georgia, US forces relieve a battalion that had been isolated for days. The Joint Chiefs of Staff issues orders for "Operation Galvanic," the seizure of the GILBERT ISLANDS. On the 21st, the US Navy cancels an order for five new battleships. Chief of Staff George C. MARSHALL (USA) proposes bypassing Rabaul, leaving the large garrison isolated and ineffective because of a lack of supplies of fuel and ammunition. On the 22nd US battleships, cruisers, and destroyers shell Kiska and nearby islets in the Aleutians. Japanese cruisers, destroyers, and support ships sail from Paramushiro, in the Kuriles, to complete the evacuation of Kiska. Japanese seaplane carrier *Nisshin* sunk by US aircraft off Bougainville. On the 23rd, US forces on New Georgia begin a drive to capture the airfield at Munda, as a Japanese attempt to land troops by using motorized barges is frustrated by US PT-BOATS. On the 24th, US destroyers land supplies at Bairoko, on Kula Gulf. Adm NIMITZ orders US submarines to deactivate magnetic exploders on their SUBMARINES, as these are finally admitted to be defective. On the 25th, retiring from Kula Gulf, US destroyers shell Munda and Lailand. The US 25th Infantry Division reinforces New Georgia, where heavy fighting continues. Mussolini is deposed as dictator of Italy, effectively taking Italy out of the Axis. On the 26th, two ships of the Japanese Kiska evacuation squadron collide in heavy seas and are forced to turn back to Paramushiro. US destroyers shell Munda. On the 27th, "The Battle of the Pips": US battleships, cruisers, and destroyers expend hundreds of rounds against false radar blips ("pips") west of Kiska. Japanese destroyers *Ariake* and *Mikazuki* are sunk off NEW BRITAIN by US Army aircraft. In Chinese waters US submarine *Sawfish* (SS-276) sinks the Japanese minelayer *Hiroshima* and a merchantship. On the 28th after nightfall, the Japanese Kiska evacuation squadron withdraws over 5,000 troops in less than an hour and departs for Paramushiro. On the 29th, the commander of the 43rd Division on New Georgia is relieved, as his troops press on slowly. On the 30th, US destroyers shell suspected Japanese positions on Kiska. Heavy fighting continues on New Georgia, and Japanese counterattacks isolate much of an American regiment. On the 31st, the Japanese 17th Division begins moving to Rabaul from central China. Experienced troops are being steadily withdrawn from China for service in the Pacific and Burma, to be replaced (if at all) by green troops from Japan.

August 1943

The Allies poured more troops, aircraft, and ships into the New Guinea and SOLOMONS fighting. The Japanese doggedly hung on in this jungle fighting. In many parts of New Guinea and the Solomons, the Japanese will continue resisting until the end of the war.

On the 1st the Japanese KISKA evacuation squadron returns to Paramushiro in the KURILES, having suffered no losses due to enemy action. In the Blackett Strait, off New Georgia, five Japanese destroyers intent upon resupplying KOLOMBAN-GARA tangle with 15 US PT-BOATS, sinking one, *PT-109*, skippered by John F. KENNEDY. On the 2nd US battleships, cruisers, and destroyers shell suspected Japanese positions on Kiska. The US 27th RCT reinforces troops on New Georgia. On the 3rd, Fijian and Solomon Island troops join US forces in action on New Georgia, serving as scouts. On the 4th, US troops close in on Japanese airfield at Munda, New Georgia. USAAF bombers drop 152 tons of bombs on Kiska. On the 5th, US troops on New Georgia capture the Japanese airfield at Munda, after 12 days of heavy fighting. Battleship *Musashi* and her escorts return to TRUK. On the 6th, Battle of VELLA GULF: Four Japanese destroyers attempting to land troops on Kolombangara are ambushed by six US destroyers, with only lucky *Shigure* getting away. US troops on New Georgia pursue Japanese forces into the interior, as engineers begin to repair the Munda air strip. On the 7th, US troops on New Georgia break Japanese

resistance. On the 8th, fighting continues around Munda, New Georgia, the struggle for which has cost 93 US and 350 Japanese aircraft. On the 9th, the American 35th Division is ordered to make an amphibious landing on VELLA LAVELLA. On the 10th, Japanese troops on New Georgia become, effectively, GUERRILLAS, fighting on in the wild interior of the island. On the 11th, Adm NIMITZ proposes to VAdm HALSEY that Kolombangara be isolated and bypassed, a plan that is adopted. On the 12th, while the USAAF drops tons of bombs, US battleships, cruisers, and destroyers shell suspected Japanese positions on Kiska. On the 13th, flying from Australia, US B-24s bomb the oil fields at BALIKPAPAN, in Borneo. Reconnaissance parties landed on Vella Lavella determine that there are few Japanese on the island. On the 14th, Quadrant Conference: ROOSEVELT and CHURCHILL meet at Quebec for 10 days of talks concerning Allied policy and STRATEGY, definitively setting "Operation Overlord" (the landings in France) for the spring of 1944. It is agreed that the Pacific offensive will be on two fronts, one an island-hopping drive through the central Pacific, the other the ongoing advance up the Solomons toward the Philippines. On the 15th, US and Canadian troops begin landings on Kiska, heavily supported by naval and air bombardments. Five days pass before it is established that the Japanese have definitely evacuated the island. Allied CASUALTIES are a score of deaths from FRIENDLY FIRE and 75 killed on a destroyer damaged by a mine. Elements of the US 25th Infantry Division begin landing on Vella Lavella in the central Solomons, unopposed save by Japanese aircraft. On the 16th, the Fourth Marine Division is activated at Camp Pendleton. Having completed a refit, battleship YAMATO arrives at Truk. On Vella Lavella the 25th Infantry Division encounters moderate resistance. US troops who have landed on Baanga, a small island near New Georgia, encounter stiff resistance. On the 17th, Japanese light forces land reinforcements on Vella Lavella, while their covering force of four destroyers beats off an attempt by four US destroyers to intervene, with little effect on either side. Major

US/Australian air raid on Japanese installations at WEWAK, northern New Guinea, destroys over 100 aircraft. On the 18th, Nationalist Chinese complain of being left out of decision making by the Allies. China had been acknowledged as one of the "Big Four" (United States, Britain, Russia, China) Allies, but only for propaganda purposes. China wanted real power among the Big Four, but lacked the military or political clout to obtain it. US forces on Baanga Island capture Japanese guns that had been shelling Munda airfield on nearby New Georgia. On the 19th, off ESPIRITU SANTO, Japanese submarine *I-17* is sunk by US aircraft and New Zealand corvette *Moa*. Heavy Allied air raids on Wewak, New Guinea. On the 20th, Baanga Island is finally secured, at a cost of 52 Americans killed and 110 wounded, while hundreds of Japanese have been killed. On the 21st, heavy Allied air raids on Wewak, New Guinea. Japanese air raids against shipping off Vella Lavella, with little effect. On the 22nd, US destroyers shell Finschhafen, in eastern New Guinea. US Marines occupy undefended Nukufetau in the ELLICE ISLANDS. On the 23rd, Japanese submarine *I-25* reconnoiters Espiritu Santo with a small scout plane. On the 24th, British decide to appoint Lord Louis MOUNTBATTEN supreme Allied commander for Southeast Asia. On the 25th, Inter-Allied Quebec Conference ends with a recommendation that MACARTHUR and Halsey leap-frog RABAUL, occupying outlying portions of NEW BRITAIN and New Ireland to isolate the enormous (over 100,000 troops) base at Rabaul. Australian Fifth Division goes into action on the Salamaua front in New Guinea. On the 26th, operating from bases in China, US bombers attack Japanese installations in HONG KONG. Italian submarine *Torelli* reaches SABANG, Sumatra, bringing critical materials, documents, and a Japanese intelligence officer. On the 27th, elements of the 43rd Infantry Division land on Arundel Island in the Solomons unopposed. On the 28th, US Marines occupy Nanomea in the Ellice Islands unopposed, while men of the 43rd Division advance on Arundel against light Japanese resistance. On the 29th, on Vella Lavella the 25th Infantry Division

advances slowly against moderate resistance. On the 30th, US Navy Fast Carrier Task Force approaches Marcus Island to stage a raid. This type of operation is an opportunity to train pilots and ship crews under combat conditions without a great deal of risk. On the 31st, escorted by elements of the Seventh Fleet, the Australian Ninth Division sails from MILNE BAY for a landing near LAE, in northeastern New Guinea. A small task force lands US Army personnel on BAKER ISLAND, in the Central Pacific, which is not held by the Japanese.

September 1943

More fighting in New Guinea and the Solomons. First bombing raids on TARAWA (in the GILBERT ISLANDS, 1,600 miles from HAWAII), the newly designated target of a late 1943 amphibious attack. More Allied aircraft, ships and infantry entered the Pacific, increasing the pressure on the Japanese.

On the 1st, the US Fast Carrier Task Force hits MARCUS ISLAND, in the west-central Pacific, with both air and gunnery attacks. Japanese submarine *I-182* is sunk by US destroyer *Wadsworth* off ESPIRITU SANTO. On the 2nd, USAAF aircraft bomb LAE, in northeastern New Guinea, sinking a patrol vessel, while another patrol vessel is TORPEDOED near TRUK by US submarine *Snapper* (SS-185). On the 3rd, Japanese submarine *I-25* is sunk near Espiritu Santo by US destroyer *Ellet*, *I-20* in the NEW HEBRIDES by US destroyer *Patterson*. On the 4th, elements of the Australian Ninth Division land near Lae, in New Guinea. On VELLA LAVELLA the 25th Infantry Division makes gains against Japanese resistance. On the 5th, Japanese resistance on Arundel has stiffened, and the US advance is slow. On the 6th, the US 503rd Parachute Regiment airdrops 1,700 men at Nadzab, northwest of Lae, securing the airstrip, into which is flown the Australian Seventh Division. US submarine *Halibut* (SS-232) torpedoes but does not sink Japanese heavy cruiser NACHI off Japan. On the 7th, heavy fighting around Lae and on Vella Lavella. The Japanese 54th Division moves from JAVA to Burma. On the 8th, US destroyers bombard Lae in support of operations of the Australian Ninth Division. On the 9th, formal announcement is made of the surrender of Italy. The Italian sloop *Eritrea*, in Japanese-controlled SABANG, escapes to sea, eludes pursuit, and eventually reaches CEYLON, but Italian SUBMARINES *Capellini*, *Giuliani*, and *Torelli* are captured by the Japanese and turned over to the Germans, who commission them as *UIt-24*, *UIt-23*, and *UIt-25*. On the 10th, a German merchant cruiser sinks a tanker (c. 10,000 tons) in the eastern Pacific. On the 11th, the 27th Division lands on Arundel to help break Japanese resistance. Japanese minesweeper *W-16* sinks while attempting to clear MINES off MAKASSAR, in the Celebes. Japanese submarine I-26 reconnoiters FIJI. On the 12th, Australian and US troops capture Salamaua, in northeastern New Guinea, while the Australian Seventh and Ninth Divisions close in on Lae. On the 13th, Nationalist Chinese leader CHIANG consolidates his power by becoming president of China. While not an important post, it adds to Chiang's stature. On the 14th, heavy fighting around Lae. On the 15th, Japanese submarine *Ro-101* is sunk by US destroyer *Saufley* aided by two aircraft, in the South Pacific. On the 16th, Australian troops capture Lae, in northeastern New Guinea. Additional US forces are ordered to Arundel. On the 17th, US B-24s bomb Tarawa in the Gilbert Islands, from air bases on CANTON and Funafuti. On the 18th, B-24s bomb Tarawa. On Vella Lavella the US 25th Infantry Division is officially relieved by the New Zealand Third Division. On the 19th, aircraft of the US Fast Carrier Task Force and US B-24s raid Tarawa. On the 20th, in the aftermath of the previous day's attack by US carrier aircraft on their base at Tarawa, the Japanese redouble their efforts to fortify the island against amphibious attack. On the 21st, Australian raiders in six canoes enter SINGAPORE harbor, to sink two ships with limpet mines. On the 22nd, the Australian 20th Brigade Group (Ninth Division) lands near Finschhafen, New Guinea, against light resistance. On the 23rd, Allied aircraft begin operating from Vella Lavella, while in New Guinea the Australian Ninth Division presses on toward

Finschhafen. On the 24th, US submarine *Cabrilla* (SS-288) damages Japanese escort carrier TAIYO near Japan. On the 25th, the Japanese begin concentrating light craft on the north coast of KOLOMBANGARA in order to evacuate the garrison. On the 26th, Japanese counterattacks against the Australian Ninth Division before Finschhafen are beaten off. Japanese oceangoing torpedo boat *Kasasagi* is sunk off Flores, NETHERLANDS EAST INDIES. On the 27th, heavy fighting near Finschhafen, as the Australians defend against fierce Japanese attacks. On the 28th, Japanese naval forces begin evacuating troops from Kolombangara. The Japanese minelayer *Hoko* is sunk east of Buka by US Army aircraft. On the 29th STILWELL proposes that 60 Chinese divisions be reorganized, retrained, and reequipped under American auspices. On the 30th, on Vella Lavella the New Zealanders confine (c. 600) Japanese to a small pocket on the northwestern tip of the island. US submarine *Barb* (SS-220) departs PEARL HARBOR carrying the new Mark-18 torpedo.

October 1943

American carriers newly deployed to the Pacific were given training by raiding Japanese-held islands. Once such series of raids, on Wake, caused the Japanese to suspect an invasion of Wake would follow. They put the Combined Fleet to sea from TRUK. The Japanese soon realized their error and returned to Truk. The six remaining Japanese carriers were taken out of action by transferring their aircraft to RABAUL, a base attracting ever more Allied bombing raids. The Japanese carriers steamed back to Japan, there to spend nearly a year training new carrier pilots. Meanwhile, fighting continued in New Guinea and the SOLOMONS, while NIMITZ completed plans for the opening of a second drive against the enemy, across the central Pacific.

On the 1st, on VELLA LAVELLA the New Zealanders suspend offensive operations, containing the Japanese pocket on the northwest of the island. On the 2nd, Australian 20th Brigade secures Finschhafen, in eastern New Guinea. US destroyer

Henley sunk off Finschhafen, New Guinea, by Japanese submarine *Ro-103*. On the 3rd, some 9,500 Japanese troops complete withdrawing from KOLOMBANGARA. In central China, the Japanese begin another offensive, to grab as much of the local rice harvest as possible. On the 4th, in the Indian Ocean, Japanese submarine *I-37* scouts the Chagos Islands with a small reconnaissance plane. On the 5th, US carrier aircraft raid WAKE ISLAND in the central Pacific, while cruisers shell Japanese installations there; in retaliation, the Japanese execute US civilians interned on the island. On the 6th, Japanese small craft succeed in getting most of the surviving Japanese troops off Vella Lavella, leaving the central Solomons firmly under Allied control. Late that night occurs the naval Battle of Vella Lavella, as the US destroyers intercept a flotilla of Japanese destroyers trying to evacuate troops; each side loses one destroyer, and three more American ones are damaged. On the 7th, US carriers and cruisers raid Wake Island; on the 8th, Japanese leader TOJO assumes more power by taking over as minister of commerce and industry. In New Guinea the exhausted Australian I Corps is relieved by the II Corps. On the 9th, the first Allied airfield on Ellice Island becomes operational. On the 10th, the Japanese naval command concludes that the United States plans a landing at Wake Island. In the Indian Ocean, Japanese submarine *I-37* scouts Diego Suarez with a small reconnaissance plane. On the 11th, Japanese Combined Fleet is ordered to prepare for action if the United States attacks Wake Island. US submarine *Wahoo* (SS-238) is sunk by Japanese aircraft in La Perouse Strait. On the 12th, the Fifth Air Force begins heavy bombardment raids on Rabaul. On the 13th, several Japanese SUBMARINES converge on HAWAII on reconnaissance missions, but are unable to ascertain the presence of the bulk of the US fleet. On the 14th, the Fifth Air Force subjects Rabaul to a major air raid. On the 15th, Admiral Sir Andrew CUNNINGHAM is appointed first sea lord of the British Admiralty (chief of naval operations). In the Pacific final orders are issued for operations in the northern Solomons. On the 16th, the Japanese declare the Philippines an independent republic under "temporary Japanese supervision." Filipinos continue their GUERRILLA war against the Japanese. In New Guinea the Japanese begin a series of major counterattacks against the Ninth Australian Division before Finschhafen, which beats them off over the next few days. On the 17th, in the Indian Ocean, Japanese submarine *I-37* scouts Kilindini, East Africa, with a small reconnaissance plane. Japanese submarine *I-36* scouts PEARL HARBOR with a reconnaissance plane, determining that the fleet is at sea. Based on this evidence, and the heavy pounding to which Wake has been subject in recent weeks, Japanese naval headquarters feels certain the US Navy is about to conduct a landing at Wake and orders the Combined Fleet to sea. US submarine *Tarpon* (SS-175) sinks the German merchant cruiser *Michel* in the BONIN ISLANDS. On the 18th, the Japanese Combined Fleet steams northward from Truk, bound for Wake. Japanese submarine *I-19* is reported overdue. On the 19th, British, American, and Russian foreign ministers meet in Moscow and agree that Russia will enter the war against Japan once Germany has been defeated. The Japanese are not informed. On the 20th, aircraft from six Japanese carriers based at Truk are transferred to bases at Rabaul, the carriers then steam for Japan to pick up new air groups. Thus there are no operational Japanese carriers available in the Pacific, and none will be available until the new air groups are trained. This will take at least six months. The Japanese Combined Fleet steams northward from Truk, bound for Wake. On the 21st, Operation Galvanic (invasion of the GILBERTS) gets underway, as transports and escorts begin movements toward troop concentration areas. On the 22nd, Sir Archibald WAVELL is made viceroy of India, with the urgent mission of keeping India loyal and in the war. On the 23rd, the Japanese conclude that there is no American threat to Wake Island, and recall the Combined Fleet to Truk. On the 24th, the Japanese destroyer *Mochizuki* is sunk by Marine aircraft southwest of Rabaul. On the 25th, USAAF bombers based in China raid Japanese airfields in FORMOSA for the first time.

Battle of CAPE ST. GEORGE: Six US destroyers intercept six Japanese destroyers carrying reinforcements for BOUGAINVILLE, sinking three. On the 26th, Chandra BOSE proclaims a provisional Indian government in SINGAPORE and declares war on Britain. On the 27th, the New Zealand Eighth Brigade (c. 8,000 men) occupies Mono and Stirling in the Treasury Islands and the USMC Second Parachute Battalion lands amphibiously on Choiseul, against no resistance, as a deceptive measure designed to mask operations against Bougainville. The Japanese Combined Fleet returns to Truk after its abortive sortie toward Wake Island. On the 28th, the Japanese evacuation of Kolombangara ends, only about 1,000 out of nearly 11,000 men of the garrison failing to get away safely. On the 29th, USAAF subjects Rabaul to a major air raid. The newly activated Japanese 31st Division reaches Burma. On the 30th, US subs mine the waters off Indochina. Before long, Hainan Strait and the waters off SAIGON are heavily mined. On the 31st, the Japanese Second Division, withdrawn from GUADALCANAL in February 1942 for rest, reinforcement, and reorganization in the Philippines, is deployed to MALAYA.

November 1943

The drive across the central Pacific began with Operation Galvanic, the assault on TARAWA in the GILBERTS. Heavy fighting in China and Burma. On the 1st, the Third Marine Division lands at Cape Torokina, at EMPRESS AUGUSTA BAY, BOUGAINVILLE, easily overcoming initial resistance on the ground (the local Japanese garrison was only 270 men and one 75mm gun) and in the air. US destroyers shell the Japanese air base at Buka. Japanese surface forces sortie from Rabaul. US carrier aircraft raid Japanese installations at Buin and Buka. On the 2nd, Battle of Empress Augusta Bay: In a nighttime attempt to interfere in the landings at Cape Torokina four Japanese cruisers and six destroyers are intercepted by four US cruisers and nine destroyers, the Japanese being beaten off after losing a light cruiser and a destroyer and incurring

heavy damage to two cruisers and two destroyers, the United States suffering two damaged destroyers. Marine Second Parachute Battalion withdraws from Choiseul. US ships off Empress Augusta Bay are subject to a Japanese air attack, with little damage. US carrier aircraft raid Japanese installations at Buin and Buka. In China the Japanese undertake a "rice offensive" (to steal the recent harvest for their own troops) in Hunan Province. On the 3rd, major elements of the Japanese Combined Fleet (10 cruisers and about a dozen destroyers) set sail from TRUK to reinforce ships at RABAUL. Marines on Bougainville meet little resistance, since Japanese are as yet on the wrong (i.e., northern and southern) parts of the island. On the 4th, the Japanese concentrate a strong cruiser-destroyer force at Rabaul to threaten the Bougainville beachhead, and HALSEY orders air strikes. On the 5th, US submarine *Halibut* (SS–232) sinks the Japanese carrier JUNYO en route to Japan from Truk. Massive US Navy and Army air strikes at Rabaul severely damages six cruisers and several destroyers; most damaged ships promptly depart for Truk. On the 6th, the New Zealand Eighth Brigade is withdrawn from the Treasury Islands. Light action on Bougainville, where a Japanese "Tokyo Express" from Rabaul lands over 1,000 troops. On the 7th, Japanese cruisers and destroyers damaged at Rabaul on November 5 reach Truk. Japanese troops make a weak attack on Marine positions at Cape Torokina, Bougainville. On the 8th, despite Rabaul-based air strikes on its transports, US 37th Infantry Division beings reinforcing Marines at Cape Torokina, Bougainville, where VANDEGRIFT has just assumed command. On the 9th, Japanese 36th Division reaches Halmahera, northwest of New Guinea. On the 10th, Task Force 52 sails from PEARL HARBOR bound for the Gilbert Islands. The Fifth Air Force makes a major attack on Rabaul. On the 11th, major US carrier air strikes are added to Fifth Air Force attacks on Japanese at Rabaul, sinking one destroyer and damaging a cruiser and a destroyer; 41 Japanese aircraft attack US carriers with no success, only eight returning to base. Desultory action on Bougainville. On the 12th, Japanese carrier air groups landed at Rabaul on October 20 are withdrawn for reorganization after loss of 121 of their 173 aircraft. Light combat on Bougainville, while the United States lands additional Marine and army troops at Cape Torokina, despite Japanese air strikes on covering force, which cause some damage. On the 13th, Operation Galvanic (invasion of Tarawa) underway; Task Force 53 sails from the NEW HEBRIDES bound for the Gilbert Islands. US Army and Navy B-24s from Funafuti and CANTON bomb Tarawa and Makin, in the Gilberts. On the 14th, moderate fighting on Bougainville continues; US forces at Empress Augusta Bay total nearly 34,000, while Japanese forces on Bougainville and surrounding islands may total 40,000 but are unable to concentrate effectively. On the 15th, Task Force 74 (two Australian cruisers and two destroyers, plus two US destroyers) arrives at the New Hebrides from MILNE BAY. US bombers based in China attack harbor installations in HONG KONG. Operation Galvanic: Task Force 52 refuels near Baker and Howland Islands in the central Pacific, while Task Force 53 refuels near Funafuti, before resuming course for the Gilbert Islands. US Army and Navy B-24s from Funafuti again bomb Tarawa and Makin. On the 16th, Japanese minelayer *Ukishima* lost to an unknown cause near Hatsushima (possibly sunk by a US submarine later lost). US submarine *Corvina* (SS-26) sunk by Japanese submarine *I-179* near Truk. On the 17th, US destroyer transport *McKean* is sunk off EMPRESS AUGUSTA BAY by Japanese aircraft. Operation Galvanic: Task Forces 52 and 53 unite about 500 miles east of the Gilbert Islands and begin "softening up" air strikes on MAKIN and Tarawa, supported by battleship and cruiser gunfire. On the 18th, Japanese destroyer escort *Sanae* is sunk by US submarine *Bluefish* (SS-222) in the Philippines. Operation Galvanic: Makin and Tarawa are subject to intense air and sea bombardment. On the 19th, fighting continues on Bougainville. Operation Galvanic: Fast Carrier Task Force raids Japanese-held islands in the Gilberts and NAURU. US Army and Navy B-24s from Funafuti bomb Tarawa and Makin Atolls, in the Gilberts. Japanese light

cruisers *Isuzu* and NAGARA sail from Truk for Mili, in the MARSHALLS, while *Naka* departs for KWAJALIEN. Bill Howell and his ship (CVL-26, *Monterey*) see combat for the first time as they launch aircraft against Japanese forces during the Gilbert Islands (Tarawa, Makin) operation. This continues until 18 December. Bill's battle station is on the bridge, where he and another petty officer man the TBS (Talk Between Ships) radio. This short-range radio is for short commands that must be sent quickly between ships in the task force. As a short-range radio, its signals are not likely to be picked up by the enemy. Petty Officer Howell's job is to listen carefully to this radio for messages, usually course changes to ensure that the fast moving ships of the task force don't collide while rapidly maneuvering during combat or bad weather. The other petty officer manning the TBS handles the outgoing messages. When Bill is not attending to his administrative duties with the ships personnel records, he stands a four-hour "watch" each day, often in the wee hours of the morning, manning the TBS radio and listening for messages from nearby ships. On the 20th, Operation Galvanic goes into high gear: The Second Marine Division lands on Betio Island, Tarawa, while elements of the 27th Infantry Division land on Makin Island, in the Gilberts. Heavy fighting on Tarawa. Japanese air attacks on the fleet cause damage to carrier INDEPENDENCE. On the 21st, Operation Galvanic: Heavy fighting on Tarawa, troops advance on Makin, 78 Marines land on Abemama Atoll, about 75 miles southeast of Tarawa. On the 22nd, Operation Galvanic: Heavy fighting on Tarawa, where the Japanese make a BANZAI CHARGE after dark. On Makin, army personnel advance slowly; SEABEES begin construction of an air base at Abemama. On the 23rd, Operation Galvanic continues: Makin Island is secured by the US 27th Infantry Division; Marines secure Betio. In India, the Chinese New 38th Division essays an offensive into Burma across the Assamese Mountains. Chinese troops in Hunan begin stout resistance to a Japanese "rice offensive" at Changteh. Japanese light cruisers *Isuzu* and *Nagara* arrive at Mili in the Marshalls, the former then proceeds to Kwajalein, while the latter returns to Truk. Japanese light cruiser *Naka* arrives at Kwajalien from Truk. In the Indian Ocean Japanese submarine *I-37* scouts the Seychelles with a small reconnaissance plane. On the 24th, US escort carrier *Liscombe Bay* is TORPEDOED by Japanese submarine I-175 in the Gilbert Islands, sinking with heavy loss of life (including Pearl Harbor hero Dorie MILLER). Three Japanese heavy cruisers plus a destroyer squadron depart Truk for Kwajalein. The Chinese 38th Division advances across the mountains on the Burma-India frontier. On the 25th, first major Japanese operation on Bougainville, as a Japanese infantry regiment attacks the US defense perimeter, to be beaten off with heavy losses. Battle of CAPE ST. GEORGE: Five US destroyers intercept five Japanese destroyers near New Georgia, sinking three. Operation Galvanic: Japanese aircraft from Kwajalein make two unsuccessful attempts to raid the US fleet off Tarawa and Makin (one a "spectacular" night attack), as Marines eliminate final Japanese pockets on outlying islets of Tarawa Atoll. The Chinese New 38th Division continues its attack into Burma from India. On the 26th, Marines mop up Japanese pockets on outlying islets of Tarawa Atoll. Japanese submarine *I-39* is sunk near Makin by US destroyer *Boyd*. The Japanese cruiser-destroyer force that had departed Truk on the 24th arrives at Kwajalein. In Burma the Chinese New 38th Division advances into the Hukawng Valley. On the 27th, Marines eliminate final Japanese pockets on outlying islets of Tarawa Atoll. Japanese light cruiser *Isuzu* arrives at Kwajalein from Mili. The Japanese cruiser-destroyer force departs Kwajalein for ENIWETOK. On the 28th, Japanese light cruiser *Nagara* departs Truk for Maloelap. The Japanese cruiser-destroyer force arrives at Eniwetok from Kwajalein. On the 29th, US and Australian destroyers bombard Japanese positions on NEW BRITAIN US destroyer *Perkins* sunk off Cape Vogelkopf in New Guinea in a collision with an Australian troop transport. US submarine *Sculpin* (SS-191) sunk by a Japanese destroyer near Truk. Aircraft from US escort carrier *Chenango* sink Japanese submarine I-

21 in the Gilberts. The Japanese cruiser-destroyer force departs Eniwetok for Kwajalein. On the 30th, US destroyers bombard Japanese positions near Cape Torokina on Bougainville, where heavy fighting continues. The Japanese cruiser-destroyer force arrives at Kwajalein from Eniwetok. In Burma, the Japanese begin to counterattack the Chinese New 38th Division.

December 1943

Fighting continued in Burma, raids in the Pacific intensified, and Allied forces were being built up for the really big push in late 1944. For the moment, amphibious resources were being shifted to Europe to support the D-day invasion of France in June (or, as it was put at the time, "in the spring of 1944"). During November-December 1943, to release troops for combat elsewhere while still maintaining local control, the Japanese Army activated 10 "Independent Mixed Brigades" (each of four to five infantry battalions, an artillery battalion, an engineer battalion, and some services) by reorganizing occupation forces in the NETHERLANDS EAST INDIES (four new brigades), the Philippines (four), Thailand (one), and Indochina (one).

On the 1st, the Fifth Marine Division begins organizing at Camp Pendleton, California. On the 2nd, nothing much happens, except the steady grind of combat on numerous fronts, and the tedium of getting ready for more. On the 3rd, Third Phase of the Sextant Conference begins, as US and British delegates meet at Cairo; among other things, they agree to postpone an amphibious invasion of Burma. On the 4th, US Fast Carrier Task Force raids KWAJALEIN and WOTJE, sinking six transports while damaging three more plus two light cruisers and destroying 55 aircraft, at a cost of five US planes lost and an aerial TORPEDO hit on carrier *Lexington*. Japanese escort carrier *Chuyo* sunk and carrier RYUHO damaged about 250 miles southeast of Tokyo Bay by US submarine *Sailfish* (SS-192). Japanese light cruiser *Nagara* arrives Kwajalein from Maloelap, joining a light cruiser, three heavy cruisers, and a destroyer squadron, which have been there for several days. On the 5th, major Japanese air raid on port facilities at CALCUTTA, India. On the 6th, major revision of Allied plans in Burma leads to cancellation of amphibious operation designed to support Operation Tarzan, leading to concerns about Chinese reaction. On the 7th, the Japanese cruiser-destroyer force arrives at TRUK from Kwajalein, having spent a month at sea without accomplishing anything against US forces. The Sextant Conference ends in Cairo. On the 8th, a US fast battleship task force bombards Japanese positions on NAURU. Australian troops capture Wareo in New Guinea. Japanese air raids on British airfields in Assam. On the 9th, SEABEES complete an airstrip at Torokina, BOUGAINVILLE, which becomes operational. CHIANG KAI-SHEK responds to cancellation of major operations in Burma by requesting increased US financial and air assistance. On the 10th, on Bougainville, army and Marine personnel push their defensive perimeter outward, as Japanese resistance stiffens (resistance is so dogged that Japanese troops will still be fighting on Bougainville at the end of the war). On the 11th, hitherto separate British and American air forces in Southeast Asia are combined under one commander, in the Eastern Air Command. On the 12th, US and Nationalist Chinese governments cannot agree on the extent to which Chinese troops should get involved in Burmese fighting; United States wants more action, China wants more aid. On the 13th, a US Army amphibious task force sails from Goodenough bound for a landing on Arawe Peninsula off NEW BRITAIN, nearly 300 miles west of RABAUL. In Burma the Chinese New 38th Division reaches Bhamo. On the 14th, Japanese destroyer *Numakaze* is sunk by US submarine *Grayback* (SS-208) about 50 miles east of OKINAWA. Chinese New 38th Division encounters heavy fighting around *Bhamo*. On the 15th, after a major aerial bombardment the US 112th Cavalry RCT lands at Arawe, New Britain. In Burma, the Chinese New 38th Division is driven back in the Bhamo area. On the 16th, Japanese submarine *I-29* departs PENANG for France. On the 17th, Allies

battle last Japanese defenders on the Arawe Peninsula of New Britain. On the 18th, Japanese stage air raids in southern China (Kunming) to cripple Chinese forces advancing into Burma. Chiang Kai-shek gives STILWELL direct command of all Chinese forces in India and Burma. On the 20th, Japanese destroyer *Fuyo* is sunk about 60 miles west of Manila by US submarine *Puffer* (SS-268). On the 21st, the Third Marine Division begins pulling out of the Bougainville beachhead. In Burma, Stilwell arrives at Ledo to assume personal direction of operations. On the 22nd, Japanese bombers again hit Kunming in China. On the 23rd, USAAF aircraft operating from bases in China sink a Japanese gunboat about 35 miles south of FORMOSA, while other army aircraft begin operating from MUNDA, New Georgia. On the 24th, in northern Burma, General Joseph Stilwell undertakes an offensive to rescue elements of the Chinese New 38th Division, which have been bottled up by the Japanese. On the 25th, US carrier aircraft raid KAVIENG, New Ireland, sinking or damaging several ships. Battleship YAMATO is damaged by a torpedo from US submarine *Skate* (SS-305) about 180 miles north of Truk. Japanese submarine *I-29*, bound for France, replenishes from the German supply ship *Bogota* in the Indian Ocean. Bill Howell's ship, *Monterey* (CVL-26), is part of a task force that launches air strikes against Japanese bases and shipping lanes in the Bismarck Islands. On 4 January 1944, *Monterey* completes its combat duty in the BISMARCKS, having accounted for an enemy destroyer and cruiser. On the 26th, the First Marine Division lands at Cape Gloucester, New Britain. US destroyer *Brownson* sunk by Japanese Army aircraft off Cape Gloucester, New Ireland. On the 27th, the First Marine Division makes a 3-mile advance at Cape Gloucester, despite monsoon rains. In Burma the Chinese New 38th Division remains heavily engaged in the Hukawng Valley. On the 28th, the US Americal Division completes relief of the Third Marine Division on Bougainville. On New Britain a Japanese attack against Arawe is repulsed. On the 29th, at Cape Gloucester, First Marine Division captures Japanese airfield. In Burma the Chinese New 38th Division begins breaking Japanese defenses along the Tarung River. On the 30th, the ROYAL NAVY dispatches two carriers, two battleships, a battle cruiser, and seven destroyers from Britain for the British Far Eastern Fleet. On Bougainville, FIJIAN troops reconnoiter behind Japanese lines. On the 31st, in northern Burma the Chinese New 38th Division breaks through to isolated elements and clears the Japanese from much of the Tarung River line.

January 1944

RABAUL was increasingly isolated. At the end of the month, the MARSHALL ISLANDS were invaded, only two months after TARAWA was taken. The speed of this island-hopping campaign unnerved the Japanese. Some Allied progress was made in Burma, but not enough to open the BURMA ROAD once more.

On the 1st, fighting in Cape Gloucester, on New Britain, ceases as all Japanese resistance is overcome. Allies now control western New Britain, further isolating Rabaul, at the eastern end of the island. On the 2nd, Allied troops land on Saidor, New Guinea. This isolates 12,000 Japanese troops at Sio. On the 3rd, the Chinese New 38th Division struggles to overcome last Japanese positions along the Tarung River in Burma. On the 4th, Australian forces struggle to reach Kelanoa in New Guinea, bringing them within 60 miles of linking up with US forces. On the 5th, on New Guinea, American and Australian offensives (now separated by 60 miles of jungle) struggle on to combine at Kelanoa. This juncture will greatly increase the Allied position in New Guinea, and render the Japanese position strategically hopeless. On the 6th, Nationalist Chinese government faces crisis because President ROOSEVELT demands greater Chinese operations against Japan. NIMITZ issues plan for the capture of the Marshall Islands. On the 7th, Imperial General Headquarters orders the Japanese Southern Army, in Burma, to capture the Imphal area of India. On the 8th, US Navy ships bombard Japanese base at Shortlands in the Solo-

mon Islands. On the 9th, in the Arakan area of Burma, British troops recapture Maungdaw. Heavy fighting along the Tarung River in Burma. On the 10th, British bombers begin dropping naval MINES at the mouth of the Salween River in Burma. Major Japanese counterattacks on New Britain. On the 11th, airfield at Saidor, New Guinea, becomes operational. On the 12th, reinforcements arrive on New Britain to strengthen the Arawe beachhead. On the 13th, Chinese forces complete their operation to secure the Tarung River line in northern Burma. Nimitz issues an outline plan for operations in the central Pacific through November 1944. On the 14th, President Roosevelt threatens Chinese with loss of Lend-Lease aid if more Chinese forces are not committed to fight against Japan. On the 15th, Australian troops reach the north coast of the Huon Peninsula in New Guinea near Sio. On the 16th, Chinese reply to US threats of LEND-LEASE loss by threatening to halt all Chinese aid for US forces unless America comes across with a billion dollars in new aid. On the 17th, after desperate last ditch resistance, Allied troops subdue last organized Japanese defenders at Arawe on the southern coast of New Britain. On the 18th, the Saidor beachhead, New Guinea, is heavily reinforced. Heavy patrolling necessary on New Britain, as Japanese stragglers require mopping up. On the 19th, the Chinese New 38th Division and Japanese troops struggle for control of Taro Plain in northern Burma. On the 20th, Allies prepare to unleash thousands of commandos in northern Burma against Japanese rear-area installations. This, combined with the advance of US, British and Chinese troops, is to reopen the Burma Road to allow supply of China overland from India. On the 21st, the Chinese New 38th Division advances slowly in Burma. On the 22nd, heavy US air raids on the ADMIRALTY ISLANDS. Preparations for the occupation of the Marshall Islands end as convoys sail from HAWAII. On the 23rd, the Chinese government is caught in a quandary. Americans insist that China commit its strategic reserve of capable divisions to fighting in Burma, but this would leave

China without any reserve if the Japanese in eastern China attack again. On the 24th, US aircraft conduct long-range reconnaissance over the Marshalls, from the GILBERTS. On the 25th, major Allied air raid on main Japanese base at Rabaul results in destruction of 83 enemy aircraft. In Burma the bulk of the Chinese New 22nd Division begins supporting the 38th. On the 26th, minor diplomatic coup for the Allies. Liberia declares war on Germany and Japan while Argentina severs diplomatic relations with Germany and Japan. US bombers raid the Marshalls. On the 27th, United States issues a report on Japanese ATROCITIES (the BATAAN DEATH MARCH) against US and Filipino troops after the surrender of BATAAN in early 1942: This is the first formal public announcement of the atrocity. On the 28th, US Navy Task Force 58 (nine carriers, several battleships, many cruisers and destroyers) steams within striking distance of the Marshall Islands. On the 29th, major US Navy air offensive against Japanese bases in the Marshall Islands begins. Bill Howell's ship, *Monterey* (CVL-26) is part of the vast armada supporting the invasion of the Marshall Islands, or at least the KWAJALEIN part of the operation. This operation ends on 8 February. Between this operation and their next one, there is some time for rest and recreation on board. Along these lines, a basketball game is arranged between officers and chief petty officers (CPOs). Bill Howell is on the CPO team and he literally runs into one of the officer players during the game. The officer is Jerry FORD, later to become the president of the United States. Note that it's only in wartime that you have a lot of young men in their twenties achieving the rank of chief petty officer; in peacetime, the youngest CPOs are in their thirties. CPO Bill Howell is 24 when he makes CPO, and was doing a CPO's job soon after he arrived on *Monterey*. On the 30th, Chinese forces oust Japanese from Taro Plain in northern Burma. On the 31st, US troops land in Japanese-held Kwajalein Atoll and other nearby islands in the Marshalls. These are the first of Japan's prewar territories to fall to the Allies.

February 1944

MARSHALL ISLANDS were conquered. British won their first pitched battle in Burma. Japanese Home Islands were shelled, RABAUL and TRUK surrounded and cut off. US carrier task forces rampaged across the Pacific, pounding Japanese targets at will.

On the 1st, Japanese leadership learns that Australia has formed a commission to investigate Japanese war crimes. On the 2nd, American troops advance rapidly against light resistance on KWAJALEIN and other Marshall islands. The Soviets agree to permit US bombers to be based in Russia, "later"; nothing ever comes of this. On the 3rd, in a daring raid, US warships based in Alaska bombard the northern Japanese island of PARAMUSHIRO in the northern KURILES. This was the first time any of the Japanese Home Islands was shelled by Allied ships. On the 4th, Japanese troops launch a major offensive against British forces in the Arakan region of Burma. On the 5th, except for a few isolated holdouts, Kwajalein Atoll is conquered. The Japanese lost 5,100 troops (all dead, save for 200 POWs); American losses were 142 dead. On the 6th, Chinese troops advance from the north in Burma, while British CHINDIT irregulars to the south try to distract and delay Japanese reinforcements. On the 7th, the United States and China come to a tentative agreement on financial arrangements for Chinese support of US forces in Burma. On the 8th, STILWELL informs Washington that a major Japanese offensive in Burma is imminent. On the 9th, Americans ask Nationalist Chinese permission to send a military mission to the Chinese communists (to try to get the communists to help against the Japanese, or to frighten the Nationalists into doing so). On the 10th, Australian troops complete their takeover of the Huon Peninsula in New Guinea, and make contact with US forces near Saidor. In the Arakan region of Burma, the Japanese launch an offensive, isolating some British and Indian units that must be supplied by air. On the 11th, Japan stops using Truk (in the

CAROLINES) as a major naval base, as it has become too difficult to keep the fleet supplied there. Japanese continue heavy attacks against the Seventh Indian Division in the Arakan. On the 12th, US Marines occupy Umboi Island (off the western end of NEW BRITAIN). In Burma, the British begin moving reinforcements to support the Seventh Indian Division. On the 13th, US Marines take possession of Arno Atoll in the Marshall Islands. On the 14th, MOUNTBATTEN warns that a further Japanese offensive is likely if they win the Arakan battle. On the 15th, New Zealand troops land on Green Island in the northern SOLOMONS. On the 16th, elements of TF 58 conduct air attacks and reconnaissance of ENIWETOK. Bill Howell's ship, *Monterey* (CVL-26), takes part in a series of raids that now begin against Japanese-held islands. On 16–17 February, *Monterey*'s aircraft hit Truk. On 21–22 February, the Mariana Islands are hit, and from 30 March to 1 April, PALAU, Yap, ULITHI, and Woleai islands are all hit. On the 17th, Allies complete massive (six battleships and nine carriers) two-day attack on main Japanese base on Truk Island. Although most Japanese warships had earlier been withdrawn, Allied ships and aircraft still sink two cruisers, three destroyers, and over 200,000 tons of merchant shipping (including several tankers). The island's airstrips are destroyed. Truk is now neutralized and bypassed, leaving many of its garrison to starve before the war will end. Meanwhile, other elements of TF 58 land on Eniwetok and Engebi. On the 18th, Allied destroyers shell Japanese bases at Rabaul and KAVIENG. On the 19th, fighting continues on the Marshall Islands of Engebi and Eniwetok. On the 20th, New Zealand troops complete their conquest of Green Island. This cuts off all remaining Japanese troops in the Solomon Islands. The Allies now have an air base only 117 miles from the main Japanese base at Rabaul. This short distance permits steady aerial bombing of Rabaul, escorted by fighters. Air power on Rabaul will soon be neutralized. On the 21st, Japanese resistance on Engebi and Eniwetok ends. TOJO takes over direct control of the Japanese Army by assuming the position of army chief of staff. On the 22nd, US Navy Task Force 58 approaches the MARIANA Islands, and is attacked by Japanese aircraft, which are easily beaten off with heavy losses. On the 23rd, for the first time in the Burma war, British forces defeat the Japanese in a pitched battle; Japanese forces at Sinzweya, in the Arakan, withdraw after their attacks on the Seventh Indian Division fail. The Japanese style of warfare has been difficult for the British to deal with. The dramatic Japanese victories over the British early in the war (particularly the fall of SINGAPORE) have played a part, as has the British use of a variety of different troops (Indian and British). But there has also been the Japanese soldier's fatalistic perseverance and refusal to surrender when beaten. Eventually, the British will learn to cope. On the 24th, US carrier aircraft complete a series of attacks against Japanese positions in the Marianas (SAIPAN, TINIAN, Rota, and GUAM), the first such attacks of the war. On the 25th, British, US, and Chinese forces all advance in Burma. On the 26th, US fleet carrier *Bennington* and escort carrier *Steamer Bay* are launched. Since PEARL HARBOR the US Navy has commissioned eight fleet carriers (700–800 total aircraft capacity), nine light carriers (370 aircraft), and 43 escort carriers (729 aircraft) to its fleet, while the Imperial Navy has commissioned only three fleet carriers (c. 160 aircraft), four light carriers (121 aircraft), and five escort carriers (138 aircraft). On the 27th, US amphibious task force approaches the ADMIRALTY ISLANDS, while elements of the Alamo Scouts land on Los Negros, the Admiralties, to conduct a covert reconnaissance, and Allied aircraft attack Japanese targets there. On the 28th, the Alamo Scouts are withdrawn from Los Negros, while air attacks continue. In Burma, the British restore their earlier positions in the Arakan. On the 29th, US Army troops invade Los Negros (the Admiralty Islands) to complete the encirclement of Rabaul.

March 1944

The Japanese surprise offensive in Burma drove the British back into India. US carrier raids continued to pummel Japanese bases in the Pacific. Japanese leadership announced to the Japanese people that the war situation was not good—a bit of understatement.

On the 1st, American troops on Los Negros Island defeat Japanese attacks on their beachhead. On the 2nd, in Burma, the US MERRILL'S MARAUDERS and the British Special Air Service begin an offensive from the Ledo area, supporting Chinese troops in a drive to reopen the BURMA ROAD. The Japanese airfield at Momote on Los Negros Island is seized by US troops. On the 3rd, Japanese make a final effort to force US troops off Los Negros, which fails, a defeat involving most of the remaining Japanese combat capability. On the 4th, an airfield becomes operational on Green Island, off New Guinea. Allied forces in northern Burma continue their advance. On the 5th, US Navy ships bombard MANUS, in the ADMIRALTY ISLANDS. On the 6th, US Marines make a new landing on New Britain and establish a beachhead over a mile-deep near Talasea. US forces in Burma repel a major Japanese counterattack. On the 7th, three brigades of British COMMANDOS (CHINDITS) begin attacking Japanese rear-area installations in northern Burma; the Chindits had been dropped behind the Japanese lines two days earlier. On the 8th, while part of the Japanese force desperately struggles against Chinese regulars and British and American commandos, another Japanese force launches an offensive against British forces near Imphal in eastern India. On the 9th, US Marines seize the Talasea airstrip in New Britain, against no resistance. On the 10th, Chinese troops and Merrill's Marauders seize full control of the Walawbum Valley in northern Burma. On the 11th, Japanese counterattacks on BOUGAINVILLE threaten several airfields. On the 12th, Ireland refuses to oust Axis (Japanese and German) diplomats (who act, in effect, as spies). Britain enacts sanctions. The Joint Chiefs of Staff approaches a "dual advance" in the Pacific. On the 13th, British launch an outflanking amphibious operation in the Arakan area of Burma. On the 14th, attacking Japanese forces at Imphal (eastern India) threaten to surround re-

treating British units. On the 15th, US Army troops invade Manus Island in the Admiralties. On the 16th, Japanese destroyer *Shirakumo* is TORPEDOED east of Hokkaido by US submarine *Tautog* (SS-199): Since Pearl Harbor, Japan has lost 62 of her 129 destroyers. On the 17th, elements of the First Cavalry Division capture Lorengau airfield, the principal US objective on Manus. On the 18th, US Task Group 50.1 bombards Mili Atoll in the MARSHALL ISLANDS. On the 19th, TOJO and his aides debate whether to announce to the Japanese people that the outlook for the war is dire. Several days later, the announcement is made. On the 20th, US Marines occupy Emirau Island in the BISMARCK ARCHIPELAGO, without opposition. The island completes the isolation and neutralization of RABAUL. On the 21st, in northern Burma, US and Chinese forces advance toward road junctions at Inkangahrawng and Kamaing. On the 22nd, Japan's offensive in Burma gains momentum as its troops approach the Indian border. On the 23rd, Japanese troops launch attacks on Bougainville (in the SOLOMONS), which are halted by US artillery. This is the last major battle in the Solomons. On the 24th, Britain's Major General Orde WINGATE is killed in a plane crash in Burma; he had developed the commando tactics and organization used with much success against the Japanese in Burma. On the 25th, last organized Japanese resistance on Manus Island is put down. On the 26th, USS *Tullibee* (SS-284) sinks itself when one of its torpedoes circles and hits the sub; one survivor lives to tell the tale. On the 27th, the British move reinforcements to Imphal. On Bougainville, the Japanese withdraw from the EMPRESS AUGUSTA BAY beachhead. On the 28th, Merrill's Marauders and Chinese troops continue their advance. On the 29th, advancing Japanese troops in eastern India cut the road between Imphal and Kohima, threatening the entire British position in the area. On the 30th, US Task Force 58 begins several days of raids into the western CAROLINES (PALAU, YAP, and ULITHI). For a cost of 20 aircraft, the US forces destroy 150 enemy aircraft, six warships, and over 100,000 tons of shipping. On the 31st, Admiral Koga, commander of the Japanese Combined Fleet, dies in an airplane crash in the Philippines, to be succeeded by Admiral TOYODA. HOLLANDIA is bombed by the Fifth Air Force.

April 1944

US carrier raids continued across the Pacific. Japanese invasion of India faltered. Fighting intensified in New Guinea and in the SOLOMONS. TRUK was pounded into uselessness after being cut off.

On the 1st, US Navy Task Force 58's raid into the western CAROLINES enters its third and final day, with the Japanese unable to offer any effective resistance. Elements of the First Cavalry Division begin mop-up of outlying islands of the Admiralty Group, which are found to be mostly undefended. On the 2nd, US Fifth Air Force raids Hansa Bay, New Guinea. MERRILL'S MARAUDERS are heavily engaged at Nhpum Ga, Burma, where one battalion has been cut off. On the 3rd, US Fifth Air Force launches large raid on major Japanese base at HOLLANDIA, New Guinea. Over 300 Japanese aircraft are destroyed, most of them on the ground before they can take off. British juggle forces in Burma to stem the Japanese drive on Imphal, while Allied forces in northern Burma remain heavily engaged. On the 4th, in eastern India, the Japanese move on Kohima, after having cut the road from Kohima to Imphal. Heavy fighting around Nhpum Ga, Burma. On the 5th, heavy fighting continues in northern Burma, as British reinforcements reach the Kohima-Imphal front. On the 6th, after several days of US air raids, the Japanese have only 25 flyable aircraft at Hollandia. On the 7th, British forces at Kohima are brought under more pressure as advancing Japanese cut off the town's water supply. On the 8th, in a skillful, and lucky, bit of bombing, B-24s bring down the Sittang bridge in Burma, crippling Japanese railroad traffic to crucial battle areas for two months. On the 9th, Japanese offer to mediate a peace agreement between Germany and Russia. The Germans are perplexed (it was a Japanese idea) and the Russians turn down the offer. In Burma the Japanese abandon Nhpum

Ga, while the Japanese complete the encirclement of Imphal, which must be supplied by air, despite the onset of the monsoon season. On the 10th, British forces on the Imphal-Kohima front in eastern India take the offensive. The Japanese gamble everything on their offensive and soon run out of resources. The Japanese troops are left largely without food, ammunition, or other supplies. Bill Howell's ship, *Monterey* (CVL-26), gets a new skipper, with Captain Stuart Ingersoll taking over from Captain Lester Hundt. On the 11th, Japanese destroyer *Akigumo* is sunk off ZAMBOANGA, the Philippines, by US submarine *Redfin* (SS-272). On the 12th, US, British, and Chinese forces in northern Burma halt their advance, but the British airlift a West African CHINDIT brigade into central Burma. Australian light forces depart Finschhafen, New Guinea, to escort convoys carrying reinforcements to the ADMIRALTY ISLANDS and to shell bypassed Japanese positions. On the 13th, heavy fighting on the Imphal-Kohima front. On the 14th, in one of those all too common wartime accidents, the SS *Fort Stikene*, carrying 1,300 tons of TNT, explodes in Bombay. Another ammunition ship nearby explodes, and in the ensuing blast a total of 21 ships are destroyed. Nearly a thousand people are killed. On the 15th, reflecting the decreased importance of the area since the ejection of the Japanese from the ALEUTIANS, US command arrangements in the north and northeastern Pacific are reorganized. In heavy fighting, the British and Indians make important gains on the Kohima Front, in India. On the 16th, senior American military planners address the question of what must be done to defeat Japan and whether an invasion of Japan itself will be necessary, leading to preliminary studies for "Operation Olympic," the invasion of Japan. On the 17th, Japan begins its last major offensive in China as one division crosses the Yellow River. The objective is the US airfields in China that are supporting raids by long-range bombers as far as Japan itself. Chinese forces in northern Burma resume the offensive. On the 18th, fighting in NEW BRITAIN begins to die down and, by the end of the month is over save for some sporadic Japanese holdout activity. On the 19th, Japan sends two more divisions south from PEKING toward US air bases in China. On the 20th, a British division lifts the Japanese siege of Kohima in eastern India; the Japanese still hold the key road to Imphal. In northern Burma the Chinese New 38th Division ejects the Japanese from critical terrain near Kamaing. On the 21st US Task Force 58 raids Hollandia, and other points in northern New Guinea with aircraft and gunfire in preparation for the Hollandia landings. In central Burma, Allied forces are ordered to begin a drive on Myitkyina. Bill Howell's ship, *Monterey* (CVL-26), moves as far west as it will ever get, as it takes part in supporting General MACARTHUR's army troops in western New Guinea. From 21 April to 1 June, *Monterey* aircraft operate around Hollandia. On the 22nd, US Army troops make an amphibious landing near Hollandia in New Guinea. On the 23rd, staff officers at the US War Department conclude that Japan can be defeated only with an invasion of the Home Islands. This becomes an objective for the rest of the war, until the unexpected success of the ATOMIC BOMB test in July 1945 provides an alternative. On the 24th, Australian troops occupy Madang in New Guinea. This provides another airfield for the Allies, and Australian aircraft promptly begin using it. On the 25th, the First Marine Division turns over responsibility for New Britain to the 40th Infantry Division, and begins moving to Paavu, in the Solomons, for rest, recuperation, and retraining in anticipation of the PELELIU operation. On the 26th, more Allied gains in New Guinea. Australians take Alexishafen; US troops take the airfield at Hollandia. On the 27th, heavy fighting continues at Imphal, India, as the Japanese attempt to defeat the British before the start of the rainy season. On the 28th, Japanese advance in China continues. US Army Air Force planes attack Yellow River bridges in an attempt to slow down the Japanese by cutting off their supply lines. On the 29th, in Burma the 16th Brigade, Third Indian Division, a Chindit formation, is evacuated from the front, having completed a long raid behind enemy lines. On the 30th, US Navy carrier aircraft begin a two-day raid on Truk Island naval base, destroying over 120 aircraft and most of remaining fuel supplies. This effectively completes the neutralization of Truk as a naval or air base against Allied forces. US and Chinese forces begin a drive on Myitkyina, Burma.

May 1944

Heavy fighting in Burma and China. US carrier raids continued to smash Japanese bases in the Pacific.

On the 1st, PONAPE Island in the CAROLINES is worked over by US battleships and carrier aircraft. On the 2nd, STILWELL is ordered to build up supplies in China for future operations. On the 3rd, Allied aircraft begin mining river approaches to RANGOON and BANGKOK, making it nearly impossible for the Japanese to bring merchant shipping into those ports. On the 4th, Chinese troops battle to the vicinity of Kamaing in northern Burma. On the 5th, the British, feeling their military position in Burma and political position in India is now stable, release nationalist leader Mahatma Ghandi (who had been imprisoned since August 1942). On the 6th, fighting in the AITAPE area of New Guinea goes poorly for the Japanese, who, in several weeks of fighting, have lost over 500 dead to only 19 Americans killed. Allied reinforcements and supplies continue to land amphibiously. On the 7th, Allied air raids against the sea routes off Rangoon and Bangkok virtually drive Japanese shipping from the Bay of Bengal. On the 8th, heavy fighting continues in northern Burma, where the Chinese New 38th Division, supported by the 30th, presses the advance on Kamaing. On the 9th, the Japanese offensive in China succeeds in capturing Lushan, thus securing complete control of the Peking-Hankow railroad. On the 10th, Chinese launch major offensive in north Burma, the 198th, 36th, and 116th Divisions cross the Salween River and advance on a hundred-mile front. On the 11th, the new Chinese offensive across the Salween River meets little Japanese opposition. Indian troops advance on Kohima. On the 12th, Japanese troops counterattack against the Chinese forces crossing the Salween River, in northern Burma. On the 13th, one of several Japanese SUBMARINES operating outside the Pacific is sunk in mid-Atlantic by a US destroyer escort. A Japanese counterattack on the Salween front, in Burma, almost wipes out a Chinese battalion until reinforcements arrive. On the 14th, in Burma, MERRILL'S MARAUDERS begin a surprise attack on the Japanese airport at Myitkyina. On New Guinea, Japanese counterattacks briefly isolate elements of the US 127th Infantry, which are withdrawn. On the 15th, Merrill's Marauders reach within 15 miles of Myitkyina. British Indian troops finally break down the Japanese defenses of Kohima in eastern India. On the 16th, the siege of Kohima in eastern India is finally ended, with the last Japanese resistance crushed. On the 17th, US and British aircraft attack Soerabaya, in JAVA, and sink 10 enemy ships. In Burma, Merrill's Marauders capture the Myitkyina airfield in a coup de main. Preliminary phase of the WADKE Operation begin, as US troops land at Arare, Netherlands New Guinea. On the 17th, in an unusual example of inter-theater cooperation, carrier aircraft of the British Far Eastern Fleet raid the naval base at Soerabaya, Java, during the day, followed with a nighttime raid by B-24s from MACARTHUR's Southwest Pacific Theater. On the 18th, Japanese and Chinese forces engage in street fighting in the Chinese city of Loyang. Heavy fighting at Myitkyina, Burma. US Army troops make an amphibious assault on Wadke Island, off the north coast of New Guinea. On the 19th, US troops overrun most of Wadke and begin repairing the airfield. Chinese troops join battle for Myitkyina. On the 20th, US carrier aircraft begin a two-day raid on Japanese-held MARCUS ISLAND. On the 21st, Japanese resistance on Wadke Island is crushed, with over 750 dead and only four PRISONERS; US losses are 43 killed and 139 wounded. The island will support an air base that will provide air cover for the coming Allied invasion of Mindanao in the Philippines. At PEARL HARBOR, where preparations are underway for the SAIPAN landings in June, an LST loaded with fuel and ammunition inexplicably

blows up in the West Loch, near an ammunition depot. Five other LSTs alongside are destroyed and CASUALTIES are heavy—207 Marines killed and nearly 400 wounded, not to mention losses among sailors and civilians. The blast delays the movement of the Fourth Marine Division by 24 hours. On the 22nd, the campaign in the ADMIRALTY ISLANDS ends, Japan having lost over 3,000 dead, the United States 326. On the 23rd, the Japanese offensive in China is hit by a Chinese counteroffensive. In Burma, the Japanese counterattack on both the Myitkyina and Salween fronts. On the 24th, US Navy carrier aircraft attack WAKE ISLAND. On the 25th, the Japanese lose ground in fighting around Myitkyina in Burma, but reinforce their troops for a counteroffensive. On the 26th, heavy fighting develops along the Tirfoam River, on the New Guinea coast opposite Wadke. Japanese counterattacks continue on the Myitkyina and Salween fronts in Burma. On the 27th, the US Army 41st Division meets only token resistance when it lands on BIAK Island. This brings Allied troops to within 900 miles of the Philippines. On the 28th, the Chinese commit all available forces to their advance across the Salween River in north Burma, but their supplies are limited and must be supplemented by airdrops. Heavy fighting develops on Biak. On the 29th, the first tank battle of the Pacific War takes place as Japanese and American armor clash on Biak. The Japanese lose. On the 30th, despite increased Chinese resistance, two Japanese divisions force their way across the Hsiang River in their attempt to shut down Allied air bases in China. Japanese attack Arare, Netherlands New Guinea. On the 31st, Allied air attacks and air-dropped MINES keep nearly all Japanese ships out of the Bay of Bengal. Heavy fighting in the Arare, Aitape, and Tirfoam areas of New Guinea.

June 1944

The British defeated the Japanese invasion of India. US Marines invaded SAIPAN, in the MARIANA Islands, providing bases from which B-29s could bomb Japan. Fighting in Burma stalled as monsoon rains began. Japanese offensive in China continued, reaching some US airbases there.

On the 1st, monsoon rains in Burma begin. Most military operations begin to slow down because of the reduced mobility, a situation that endangers Allied forces, who are far from their sources of supply. Heavy fighting continues on BIAK. On the 2nd, Japanese forces in Honan Province of China halt their operations, having achieved all of their objectives. Allied forces before Myitkyina begin to besiege the place, with Chinese troops attempting to tunnel under Japanese defenses. On the 3rd, the Battle of Kohima in eastern India ends in a British victory. Japanese forces on Biak break contact. On the 4th, US forces on Biak halt their advance after two days without serious resistance, in anticipation of a Japanese counterattack. Chinese forces on the Salween front make significant gains. On the 5th, the Japanese not having undertaken a counterattack, US forces on Biak resume the advance but still meet no resistance. In Burma, the British and Indians clear the Japanese from the vicinity of Kohima and begin operations to open the Kohima-Imphal road. On the 6th, Pentagon planners decide on 1 October 1945 as the date for the first landings on the Japanese Home Islands, setting in motion vast logistical preparations for the operation. In Europe, the Allies land in Normandy. On the 7th, Chinese forces on the Salween front in Burma reach Lung-ling, an important regional center. US forces on Biak capture the airfield unopposed, but then face intense fire from Japanese forces ensconced in the hills beyond it. On the 8th, a desperate Japanese attempt to resupply Biak Island with five heavily laden destroyers ends with one ship sunk and the other four turned back. On the 9th, heavy fighting at Lung-ling. On the 10th, the US and Chinese assault on Myitkyina, Burma, resumes. On the 11th, US Navy ships and aircraft attack the Marianas (GUAM, SAIPAN, and TINIAN), losing a dozen aircraft but destroying 200 Japanese planes and damaging installations.

On the 12th, the Chinese communists, fearful of the recent Japanese offensive, pledge support of the Chinese Nationalists in the fight against the Japanese. On the 13th, heavy fighting continues at Myitkyina, Burma. US aircraft begin limited operations from Biak, where the Japanese are still resisting. On the 14th, the Japanese offensive in China rolls on, as the city of Liu-yang falls. Heavy fighting on all fronts in Burma. On the 15th, Saipan, in the Marianas, is stormed by two US Marine divisions. The 27,000 Japanese defenders are hit by the firepower of seven battleships and 11 cruisers. Saipan, and other islands in the Marianas, will be bases for B-29 attacks on Japan. On the 16th, returning to their China bases, US B-29s have made the first air attack on Japan since the DOOLITTLE raid in early 1942. On the 17th, US Navy carrier aircraft attack IWO JIMA and the BONIN ISLANDS. On the 18th, in China, the Japanese offensive takes the city of CHANGSHA, an area the Japanese had twice reached earlier in the war and failed to take. On the 19th, the three-day Battle of the PHILIPPINE SEA begins, to end in a defeat for the Japanese, who will lose three carriers and 426 of their 473 aircraft, with no US ships lost and only a handful of US aircraft. This is a major Japanese attempt to slow the American advance across the Pacific. After their failure in this battle, Japanese senior leaders know that the war is lost. Bill Howell's ship, *Monterey* (CVL-26), takes part. In the days before the battle, CVL *Monterey* aircraft support the assault on Saipan. On the 20th, heavy fighting continues on Biak. British and Indian forces approach Imphal, in eastern India. On the 21st, US aircraft begin using Owi airfield, New Guinea; no Japanese airfields are operational anywhere on New Guinea. On the 22nd, and after 10 weeks of fighting, the battle for Imphal comes to an end as British and Indian troops open the road from Kohima to Imphal; the Japanese find they have suffered nearly 44,000 CASUALTIES, mostly dead, compared to 14,000 British Empire losses, including 2,700 dead. Chinese forces on the Salween front make significant gains. On the 23rd, Japanese forces at Sarmi, near WADKE in New Guinea, attack Allied lines. Heavy fighting on Biak. On the 24th, fighting continues at Sarmi, New Guinea, as US forces try to outflank Japanese positions. On the 25th, Emperor HIROHITO calls a conference of senior generals and admirals to discuss Japan's worsening situation. The military admit that "outer" defenses like Saipan can not be held and that emphasis must be placed on bases closer to Japan. Japanese troops begin withdrawing at Sarmi, New Guinea. On the 26th, US air base at Hengyang, China, is overrun by Japanese troops. On the 27th, Japanese forces halt the Chinese advance on the Salween front, northern Burma. On the 28th, around Hengyang, Chinese forces put up stiff resistance to advancing Japanese. On the 29th, US submarine *Archerfish* (SS-311) sinks Japanese *Patrol Boat Number 24* off IWO JIMA, while *Darter* (SS-227) sinks minelayer *Tsugaru* off Morotai: During June of 1944 US SUBMARINES in the Pacific sink about 260,000 tons of Japanese merchant shipping, exclusive of vessels under 500 tons, not to mention two aircraft carriers, six destroyers, and these two smaller warships. On the 30th, operations on Biak enter the mopping up phase, as they do at Sarmi, on New Guinea.

July 1944

US troops battled all month to eliminate Japanese resistance in the Mariana Islands and prepare airfields for B-29 bombers. Japanese situation in Burma collapsed, mainly because of poor supply arrangements. Only in China did a Japanese offensive continue to advance.

On the 1st, as Japanese resistance on Saipan crumbles, Admiral NAGUMO commits suicide. He had led Japanese fleets to victory early in the war, until defeated at MIDWAY. He was then demoted to command of the naval forces in the Saipan area, which is how he came to end his life in a bunker surrounded by US Marines. On the 2nd, surviving Japanese forces fall back to the north end of Saipan to make a last stand. US troops land on Noemfoor, off New Guinea. On the 3rd, US Navy ships bombard IWO JIMA and the BONIN ISLANDS. Several Japanese transports are sunk. Bill Howell's ship, *Monterey* (CVL-26), takes part. A week later, *Monterey* assists in the capture of GUAM and remains in

the Marianas until 15 August. On the 4th, elements of the 503rd Parachute Infantry drop on Noemfoor to reinforce US troops already engaged there. On the 5th, Japanese commanders on the Imphal front in eastern India, discuss calling off the operation, and after several days of debate decide to withdraw: They have lost 53,000 out of the 85,000 troops committed, many due to disease and starvation caused by inadequate logistical arrangements. On the 6th, US troops make an amphibious "end run" around Japanese positions on Noemfoor, breaking enemy resistance. On the 7th, surviving Japanese troops on Saipan make a final BANZAI CHARGE, in which most of the 3,000 attackers are killed but not before inflicting heavy CASUALTIES on the defending troops. US B-29s from Chinese bases again attack targets in Japan. On the 8th, Guam is bombarded by US Navy ships, beginning a series of daily attacks in preparation for landings later in the month. On the 9th, Saipan finally falls to American forces. The Japanese lose nearly 27,000 troops, almost all dead save for a few hundred taken prisoner, while US losses are 3,200 killed, for a total of 14,200—3,700 army and 10,500 Marine. In addition, thousands of Japanese civilians commit suicide. On the 10th, cut off from supply and air support, desperate Japanese troops launch a counterattack at AITAPE, New Guinea. Heavy fighting on the Salween front in Burma, as the Chinese press their attacks. On the 11th, US vice president Henry Wallace, having been sent to China to investigate the situation, reports that Nationalist leader CHIANG KAI-SHEK is more interested in fighting the communists than the Japanese. Wallace suggests that the United States try to mediate the disputes between the Nationalists and communists. On the 12th, another Allied attempt to capture Myitkyina, Burma, fails, because Allied aircraft mistakenly bomb their own troops. On the 13th, fighting continues on Noemfoor. Japanese make small local attacks on several fronts in New Guinea. On the 14th, senior members of the Japanese government suggest that in the wake of the loss of SAIPAN it might be a good idea if General TOJO resigned as prime minister. On the 15th, heavy fighting in the Aitape area of New Guinea. On the 16th, Australian cruisers and destroyers shell Japanese positions near Aitape, New Guinea. On the 17th, the Japanese minister of the navy, Admiral Shimada, resigns, bringing down the Tojo government. Heavy fighting in the Aitape area. On the 18th, pressure from senior members of the government and from the "elders" (retired politicians and senior officers) forces General Tojo to resign his government posts (prime minister, minister of the army and army chief of staff, minister of the interior, minister of munitions, etc). A new government is formed under Kuniaki Koiso, with much the same policies as the old one. On the 19th, heavy fighting continues in the Aitape area of New Guinea, as Allied and Japanese forces make numerous small attacks and counterattacks against each other. On the 20th, American invasion force approaches Guam and begins shelling and bombing the island intensively. On the 21st, two divisions (one Marine, one army) storm ashore on Japanese-held Guam in the MARIANAS, while a pre-invasion bombardment of TINIAN commences. On the 22nd, after allowing American troops to advance a mile or so inland on Guam, Japanese launch a fierce counterattack, which is defeated. On the 23rd, from Saipan, a Marine invasion force puts to sea for nearby Tinian. Heavy fighting on Guam. Chinese troops renew their offensive on the Salween front, Burma. On the 24th, after two weeks to recuperate from the Saipan fighting, two Marine divisions land on Tinian. Only one Japanese regiment is defending. On Saipan, each US division suffers a thousand dead and over 4,000 wounded. On Tinian, each division averages less than 200 dead and 900 wounded—tough fighting, but not nearly as severe as on Saipan. In large part, the lower losses are the result of a successful DECEPTION. There was one large beach in the southern part of Tinian but only two smaller ones (65 and 130 yards wide) in the north. Going ashore on Saipan, there were heavy losses from Japanese machine guns and mortars just approaching and crossing the beach. On Tinian the Japanese were fooled, as each of these small beaches were hit by

a Marine regiment that quickly pushed past the few Japanese stationed there. On the 25th, US Army and Marine units are still four miles away from linking up their separate beachheads on Guam, with Japanese resistance stiffening. On the 26th, President ROOSEVELT holds a conference in HAWAII with MACARTHUR and NIMITZ. The navy wants to take FORMOSA in order to cut Japan off from its oil and resource supplies in the Dutch East Indies (and to make it easier to supply the Chinese). MacArthur proposes retaking the Philippines, and wins the argument, even though he offers a larger and more difficult operation. On the 27th, US Marines clear most of northern Tinian and begin rebuilding the airfield they find there. On the 28th the Japanese commander at Myitkyina, Burma, orders his troops to withdraw but decides to commit hara-kiri to atone for the shame of withdrawing in the face of the enemy: The fighting has caused the Japanese nearly 2,000 casualties, including 790 dead. On the 29th, US Marines capture the Orote airstrip on Guam, despite fierce Japanese resistance. On the 30th, the US Sixth Infantry Division lands on the Vogelkop Peninsula on the northwest coast of New Guinea, as well as on the nearby islands of Amsterdam and Middleberg. On the 31st, the British assist in forming an anti-Japanese, Burmese government in exile in India.

August 1944

Japanese resistance in New Guinea and the SOLOMONS crumbled, particularly since they could no longer supply their forces there. Japanese resistance in the MARIANA Islands was crushed. Preparations moved ahead for the invasion of the Philippines. In the course of the month, US SUBMARINES sank 245,000 tons of Japanese merchant shipping, not counting vessels of under 500 tons, plus an escort carrier, two light cruisers, two destroyers, and six smaller warships, while another 50,000 tons of shipping was sunk by aircraft and surface ships.

On the 1st, US Marines crush Japanese resistance on TINIAN. Heavy fighting before Hengyang, in China, as the Japanese try to take the city. Bill Howell is promoted to chief petty officer, the top of the food chain as far as enlisted navy ranks go. For over a year before he became a "Chief," Bill did a CPO's work and took care of personnel matters for the ship's executive officer (Lieutenant Commander Frank B. Miller) and supervised six sailors (all yeomen, like himself, but of less exalted rank). On the 2nd, Chinese troops on the Salween front in northern Burma are heavily engaged before Teng-chung, to which the Japanese cling tenaciously. On the 3rd, the key town of Myitkyina in northern Burma finally falls to US and Chinese troops. This permits the reopening of the BURMA ROAD, providing a land route into China for military aid. The fierce fighting deep in the jungle costs the Allies over 5,400 CASUALTIES (including 972 Chinese and 272 Americans killed). On the 4th, US Army and Marine divisions link up on GUAM, cutting the Japanese defenders into two groups. On the Salween front in northern Burma, Chinese troops finally break into Teng-chung. On the 5th, elements of Task Force 58 attack IWO JIMA and Chichi Jima with air strikes and shellings, sinking one destroyer and two transports, and destroying or damaging many aircraft. On the 6th, Japanese troops in China advance toward Hengyang, in the face of heavy Chinese resistance. US aircraft begin raiding the Philippines from bases in New Guinea. On the 7th, Japanese light cruiser NAGARA is sunk in Japanese waters by US submarine *Croaker* (SS-246): Since PEARL HARBOR Japan has lost 16 of her 44 cruisers. On the 8th, Japanese troops finally take Hengyang, despite stiff Chinese resistance. On the 9th, the fall of Hengyang in China causes some of the warlords in the Nationalist coalition to seek to replace CHIANG KAI-SHEK as leader of the Nationalist cause. On the 10th, organized Japanese resistance on Guam is stamped out: Some 10,000 Japanese defenders have died; American casualties are 5,000, including 1,400 killed. The United States now had an island large enough, and close enough, to support hundreds of B-29 bombers with which to bomb Japan. On the 11th, US B-29s flying out of bases in India

complete the first of over 150 missions to drop marine MINES in rivers and ports in China, Indochina, MALAYA, and Sumatra. On the 12th, "mopping up" proceeds on Guam, continuing until the end of the war. On the 13th, the 14th Air Force reconnoiters Manila from Chinese bases, but MAC-ARTHUR prohibits air attacks on the Philippines capital. On the 14th, surviving Japanese forces on New Guinea and nearby islands break contact and try to fall back. On the 15th, US troops in various parts of New Guinea and nearby islands (AITAPE, Noemfoor, the Vogelkopf) are unable to find the Japanese. On the 16th, Japanese forces on New Guinea continue to fall back on all fronts. On the 17th, the last Japanese troops to have entered Indian territory during the Imphal-Kohima offensive are killed or driven over the border into Burma. On Noemfoor, off New Guinea, US troops manage to regain contact with retiring Japanese. On the 18th, US submarine *Rasher* (SS-269) sinks the Japanese escort carrier TAIYO off Luzon: Since Pearl Harbor the Imperial Navy has lost 12 aircraft carriers of all types, out of a total of 23, with a total capacity of 525 aircraft. On the 19th, the White House announces that President ROOSEVELT has appointed a special envoy to China in order to effect a military alliance between Nationalist and communist forces. On the 20th, after three months of fighting in the jungle, BIAK ISLAND, northwest of New Guinea, is finally cleared of Japanese forces: The US Army has suffered 2,400 casualties (including 400 dead); the Japanese have lost nearly 5,000 dead, although an unprecedented 220 PRISONERS are taken. On the 21st, US B-29s operating out of bases in CEYLON begin a series of raids on Japanese installations on Sumatra. On the 22nd, the Japanese voluntarily abandon ULITHI in the western CAROLINES, not realizing that the Americans want the atoll as a forward base. Japanese troops on the Salween front in northern Burma attempt a counterattack, which is handily repelled by Chinese forces. On the 23rd, formation of the new Sixth Marine Division begins on GUADAL-CANAL. On the 24th, the British Far Eastern Fleet makes a carrier raid on Padang, in southwestern

Sumatra. On the 25th, US Army troops finally overcome all Japanese resistance in the Aitape region of New Guinea, in an operation that has cost the Japanese 8,800 dead and 98 surrendered; US dead number 440. On the 26th, in anticipation of the liberation of the Philippines, Filipino GUERRILLA organizations begin to receive their orders for the coming battle. On the 27th, the ROYAL NAVY doubles its submarine strength in the Far East with the arrival of the Second Submarine Flotilla at Ceylon. On the 28th, during a B-24 raid on the KURILES, Japanese *Submarine Chaser No. 77* is sunk. On the 29th, the Japanese offensive in China continues, as 11 divisions advance from Hengyang toward the major US air bases at Kweilin and Liuchow. On the 30th, the US 96th Infantry Division completes its movement from SAN FRANCISCO to HAWAII: Allied ground forces in the Pacific (Pacific Ocean Areas and Southwest Pacific) total 34 divisions (seven Australian, 21 US Army, and six US Marine divisions, plus a large New Zealand brigade and numerous independent brigades, regiments, and battalions). In these same areas Japanese ground forces total 30 divisions and about as many independent brigades, plus numerous separate regiments and battalions, plus large numbers of troops in the Home Islands. On the 31st, Chinese forces in north Burma and south China approach a linkup and re-establishment of access between the two nations severed by the Japanese in 1942. Off New Guinea, Noemfoor is declared secured by US forces.

September 1944

The BURMA ROAD was reopened, providing land access to China for the first time since early 1942. The Japanese offensive in China rampaged on. The last landing of the US Marines' cross-Pacific campaign occurred in the PALAU ISLANDS. US Army troops made more landings, bringing them closer to the Philippines.

On the 1st, the Fourth Marine Division arrives at Maui, after having invaded and conquered SAIPAN and TINIAN. The division has a 28% casualty rate (5,981 killed or wounded), most of them in the 27 240-man rifle companies. The 6,500 Marine infantry have suffered over 50% CASUALTIES. It will take several months to train the replacements up to the level of the experienced survivors of Saipan and Tinian. On the 2nd, Task Group 38.4 raids the BONIN ISLANDS. On the 3rd, US Navy ships attack the Japanese base on WAKE ISLAND. On the 4th, US Army forces on New Guinea rehearse for the Morotai operation, while the First Marine Division sails from the Solomons for Palau. On the 5th, Chinese forces moving from Burma reach the Kaolingkung Pass, to link up with Chinese forces from Yunan Province in China and reestablish the land link that had been severed by the Japanese in 1942. On the 6th, the US Navy uses 16 carriers to launch air strikes against Japanese-held islands in the western CAROLINES (YAP, ULITHI and PALAU). Bill Howell's ship, *Monterey* (CVL-26), is part of this operation. The Philippines are right to the west of the Palaus, and toward the end of September, aircraft from the *Monterey* operate in that direction. On the 7th, Chinese forces on the Salween front in Burma finally clear out all resistance, killing most of the 2,000 Japanese defenders, having lost 7,700 dead since 10 May in clearing another vital area that had to be secured in order to reopen the Burma Road. On the 8th, two and a half Japanese divisions stationed in south China join the attack on the US airfields at Kweilin and Liuchow. On the 9th, a dozen carriers of Task Force 38 begin two days of raids against Japanese bases on Mindanao. On the 10th, elements of TG 38.4 raid the Palau Islands. On the 11th, US SUBMARINES sink two Japanese transports on their way from SINGAPORE to FORMOSA. The transports carry 1,274 Allied POWs; over 300 of the POWs die, with 159 rescued by the subs and the rest by the Japanese. On the 12th, Allied leaders hold a conference in Canada where CHURCHILL and ROOSEVELT agree that emphasis should be shifted to the Pacific now that the Germans appear to be at the end of their rope. It is also reaffirmed that the first invasion of the Japanese Home Islands will take place in October 1945. On the 13th, US

Navy ships and aircraft pound PELELIU Island (in the Palaus) preparatory to an invasion. On the 14th, Japanese abandon their efforts at a counter-offensive in the Salween area of Burma; this eliminates a major threat to the reopening of the Burma Road. The United States agrees to the participation of the Royal Navy and RAF heavy bombers in the Pacific War. On the 15th, a US one-two punch as Marines land on Japanese-held island of Peleliu, 450 miles east of the Philippines (Mindanao), while the Army's 31st Division lands on Morotai in the ADMIRALTY ISLANDS, about 350 miles southeast of Mindanao, in preparation for the scheduled liberation of the Philippines. On the 16th, aided by the terrain, Japanese troops on Peleliu offer fierce resistance, although greatly outnumbered by US Marines. On the 17th, the US Army Air Force abandons major air base at Kweilin, China, as the Japanese close in. Elements of the 81st Division land on Anguar, near Peleliu. On the 18th, the Marines encounter very heavy resistance on Peleliu; army troops advance on Anguar. On the 19th, heavy fighting continues on Peleliu; army troops advance on Anguar. On the 19th, heavy fighting continues on Peleliu and Anguar. On the 20th, US troops on Morotai expand their perimeter and begin building an airfield. On the 21st, US Navy Task Force 38 launches air strikes from a dozen aircraft carriers against Japanese targets in the Luzon (Philippines) area. On the 22nd, a US Army regiment lands unopposed on Ulithi Atoll in the western Carolines. On the 23rd, the airfield on Peleliu is repaired and US Marine aircraft begin operating from it. On the 24th, elements of the army's 81st Division are sent to reinforce the Marines on Peleliu; the Japanese promptly counterattack. On the 25th, Admiral HALSEY proposes, and NIMITZ and MACARTHUR accept, changing the operational agenda and canceling the landings on Mindanao scheduled for 10 October in favor of a landing on Leyte at that date. On the 26th, Marines and soldiers make gains on Peleliu, Anguar, and Morotai, against stiff resistance. On the 27th, very heavy fighting on Peleliu. On the 28th, the British XV Corps in Burma is ordered to resume the offensive in the Arakan. On the 29th, heeding a message from Filipino GUERRILLAS, US sub *Narwhal* (SS-167) arrives at Mindanao to pick up 81 Allied POWs who have survived the sinking of a Japanese transport (sunk by another US sub). On the 30th, US and Filipino guerrillas complete preparations to support expected American landings, having mobilized their entire strength and deployed to do maximum damage to the Japanese once the invasion gets underway.

October 1944

The Philippines were invaded by US troops, starting a battle that would still be going on when the war ended. The Japanese used KAMIKAZE attacks for the first time. Chinese troops continued to hunt down Japanese troops in northern Burma. During October Allied (mainly US) SUBMARINES in the Pacific had their best month of the war, sending 328,000 tons of Japanese shipping to the bottom. Allied aircraft and ships sunk another 186,000 tons. From this point on, the sinking of Japanese merchant shipping declined simply because there weren't many Japanese ships left to sink.

On the 1st, heavy fighting continues on PELELIU, as Allied commanders begin to realize they have seriously underestimated the number of Japanese troops on the island. On the 2nd, an American-built pipeline reaches Myitkyina from northern India, greatly easing the supply of POLs to Allied troops in northern Burma. On the 3rd, the US Joint Chiefs of Staff instructs NIMITZ and MACARTHUR that, after the landings on Leyte in October, operations are planned for Luzon in January, IWO JIMA in February, and OKINAWA two months after that. On the 4th, Task Force 38 completes replenishment and rest at ULITHI, which has been turned into an enormous navy logistical base. On the 5th, Japanese troops continue to resist on Peleliu, a battle that is turning out to be more difficult than the Marines had first thought. On the 6th, operations on Anguar enter the mopping-up phase, as the last major Japanese forces are broken.

On the 7th, US fighters begin operating from Morotai in raids against Japanese positions in the Philippines. On the 8th, Chinese forces in northern Burma begin regrouping for a renewed offensive. On the 9th, elements of the Third Fleet shell MARCUS ISLAND. On the 10th, moving ever closer to Japan itself, the US Navy launches air strikes from 17 carriers, to hit targets in the RYUKYUS (especially Okinawa). Bill Howell's ship, the *Monterey* (CVL-26), takes part in bombing Japanese bases on Okinawa. Then, attention shifts south to the Philippines and FORMOSA, where the *Monterey*'s aircraft spend most of October hitting Japanese targets on Luzon and Formosa. These operations go on into December of 1944. On the 11th, the Japanese military leadership develops a series of plans for "Operation Victory" ("Sho-Go"). These plans spell out the desperate measures Japan will take when the Home Islands are threatened. Basically it comes down to, "fight to the last man, woman, child, weapon and piece of equipment." On the 12th, US Navy carrier task forces launches air strikes against Formosa, in order to destroy Japanese air power in the area. The Japanese commanders are shocked at the ineffectiveness of their air forces against the better trained and equipped Americans. On the 13th, the US Navy carrier task force launches second day of the air strikes against major Japanese air strength in Formosa. On the 14th, U.S. Navy carrier task forces completes three days of air strikes against Formosa, breaking the back of Japanese air power in the area (destroying 280 aircraft). On the 15th, Peleliu (in the PALAU ISLANDS) is finally secured after a month of heavy fighting, though some Japanese troops hold out for months longer. Japanese loses are nearly 12,000 troops killed, US over 1,200. On the 16th, Chinese forces in Burma launch another offensive to clear remaining Japanese forces that might block the BURMA ROAD between India and China. On the 17th, Admiral Nimitz announces that, during the second week of October, Allied forces had destroyed nearly 700 Japanese aircraft and over 70 Japanese ships. On the 18th, in preparation for the coming invasion of the Philippines, U.S. Army Rangers begin landing on islands off LEYTE GULF. On the 19th, General STILWELL is relieved of his posts in China, as a result of CHIANG KAI-SHEK seeing Stilwell as the cause of all the problems with the Nationalist, American and communist leadership. On the 20th, General MacArthur returns to the Philippines, as he had promised two and a half years earlier: In the first 24 hours of the invasion, nearly 200,000 troops land on the east coast of Leyte. On the 21st, Japanese forces on Leyte counterattack, although their long-term STRATEGY is to defend, not attack. On the 22nd, Japanese naval forces close in on Leyte in order to oppose the American invasion. On the 23rd, three-day air-sea Battle of LEYTE GULF begins, as the Japanese meet the American invasion of the Philippines with a naval attack, in what becomes the greatest naval action in history. On the 24th, as US and Japanese forces close in the Philippines, the Japanese split their remaining warships between the INLAND SEA (between Honshu, Shikoku, and Kyushu) and the waters off SINGAPORE. Bill Howell's ship, *Monterey* (CVL-26), takes part in the key battles for the Philippine Islands, including the Battle of Leyte Gulf from 24 to 26 October. On the 25th, it is the decisive day of the Battle of Leyte Gulf, as Japanese forces are defeated in SURIGAO STRAIT, off SAMAR (with some difficulty), and off Cape Engaño. During the battle and the subsequent "mopping up," the Japanese fleet is smashed, losing three battleships, four carriers, 10 cruisers, and 17 other warships, while US losses are three escort carriers and three destroyers. On the 16th, the Japanese offensive in China, stalled because of logistical problems and increased Chinese resistance, starts rolling again toward the US air bases at Kweilin and Liuchow. On the 27th, the Japanese begin launching kamikaze suicide plane attacks at US ships off the Philippines. On the 28th, kamikazes draw first blood, when a US cruiser is damaged by suicide aircraft. On the 29th, heavy fighting continues on Leyte. On the 30th, covering the troops on Leyte, US Task Group 38.4 is attacked by kamikaze aircraft, which severely damage two carriers. On the 31st, Chinese troops continue to battle the Japanese in the border area of China and Burma. By the end of the year, the area will be clear.

November 1944

The Allies advanced everywhere in the Pacific, except in China, where the Japanese offensive kept moving deeper into the heartland.

On the 1st, despite the enormous US naval and air forces in the area, the Japanese are able to land reinforcements on Leyte. On the 2nd, the US Army clears Japanese troops from the central valley on Leyte. On the 3rd, the Japanese Army's "Special Balloon Regiment" begins releasing the first of over 9,000 hydrogen-filled balloons; these are expected to float with the prevailing westerly winds all the way from Japan to the west coast of North America. Each carries a 40-pound bomb that will explode on landing, injuring anyone in the vicinity or starting a fire. Over 300 of the balloons actually do reach North America, but only three are known to have caused any damage (six dead and two brush fires). On the 4th, the Japanese launch air attacks against SAIPAN and TINIAN (in the MARIANAS) to disrupt preparations for further attacks against Japan. On the 5th, B-29's, fly from Chinese bases to bomb SINGAPORE. On the 6th, the Soviet Union accuses Japan of aggression, a prelude to eventually declaring war on Japan. On the 7th, the Chinese New 22nd Division takes Shwego in northern Burma. On the 8th, Japanese transports get through US naval and air blockade to land another division as reinforcements for their troops on Leyte. On the 9th, another reinforcement landing by Japanese troops on Leyte is only partially successful: The troops get ashore, but US Navy aircraft sink the transports before the ammunition and supplies can be unloaded. On the 10th, the Japanese offensive in China finally captures the two major US air bases at Kweilin and Liuchow. The strategic situation in China is now considered critical. On the 11th, in response to the vast number of US aircraft carriers, Japan commissions its newest carrier, SHINANO, but she will be sunk in just 17 days by a US sub, giving her the shortest combat life of

any major ship in the war On the 12th, Task Force 38 refuels and resupplies in the PHILIPPINE SEA, after supporting the Leyte operation and having raiding the VOLCANO ISLANDS. On the 12th, Allied forces in Burma and India are reorganized to put all ground troops—Commonwealth, American, and Chinese—under a single command, to improve operational coordination. On the 13th, US Task Force 38 begins two days of air strikes on Luzon, concentrating on Japanese shipping in Manila Bay; the Japanese will lose a light cruiser, four destroyers, and 10 transports sunk, plus a destroyer and five transports damaged. On the 14th, the Chinese New 22nd Division takes Mantha, in northern Burma, as other Chinese forces advance as well. On the 15th, escorted by US and Commonwealth warships, an American infantry regiment storms Pegun Island, near Morotai. On the 16th, US Task Force 38 refuels and resupplies in the Philippine Sea. By this time in the war, US ships are staying at sea for months on end, being replenished by fleets of cargo ships and oilers, while hospital ships and special repair ships tend to injured sailors and equipment. On the 17th, the Japanese offensive in China continues, with the next objectives being Kweiyang, then the key cities of Kunming and Chungking. On the 18th, a British carrier task force raids oil facilities, air bases, and port installations in Sumatra. On the 19th, Indian troops begin crossing the Chindwin River in Burma, opening an unusual monsoon season offensive. US troops make an amphibious landing on Asia Island (off the northwest coast of New Guinea). On the 20th, Chinese forces on the Salween front in northern Burma capture Mangshih and its airfield. On the 21st, General WEDEMEYER presents a plan to CHIANG KAI-SHEK designed to stem the Japanese drive on Kunming. On the 22nd, the British Far Eastern Fleet in the Indian Ocean is reorganized; the British Pacific Fleet is formed (four new carriers, two new battleships, plus cruisers and destroyers) for operations with the US Third/Fifth Fleet. On the 23rd, Japanese troops from Indochina move north to link up with Japanese troops approaching the Chinese city of Nanning. On the 24th, the first

B-29 raid from bases in the Marianas (Saipan) sees 111 B-29s hit Tokyo. On the 25th, Japanese KA-MIKAZE launch more attacks at US Navy carriers off the Philippines, damaging four. On the 26th, Japanese troops in central Burma begin to with-draw. On the 27th, B-29s from the Marianas hit Tokyo; B-29s from India hit BANGKOK. On the 28th, Japanese resistance on PELELIU in the PALAU ISLANDS finally ends: 14,000 Japanese troops have been killed and 400 captured, with US ground forces suffering nearly 10,000 CASUALTIES, includ-ing 1,800 dead, more than at GUADALCANAL. On the 29th, Chinese Nationalist leader Chiang Kai-shek refuses to allow US ammunition to be shipped through his territory to communist forces. On the 30th, with the Japanese closing in, most Nation-alist Chinese divisions on the Salween front in Burma are ordered north to aid in the defense of Kunming.

December 1944

The Japanese advance in China slowed from lack of supplies, and exhaustion. Fighting continued in the Philippines. Allied forces advanced in Burma. IWO JIMA was pounded in preparation for an am-phibious assault.

On the 1st, Japanese troops on Leyte exhaust their food supplies. The US blockade prevents everything except supply SUBMARINES from getting through. On the 2nd, Chiang Kai-shek again re-jects US proposals to arm some communist units for service against the Japanese. On the 3rd, the Japanese 11th Army, which had advanced into south China against orders from Tokyo, runs out of supplies and slows down. On the 4th, the new US military representative in China, General WED-EMEYER (who replaced STILWELL), requests that re-maining B-29s in China be withdrawn, since the BURMA ROAD is not yet functional and all supplies for the bombers have to be flown in over the Him-alaya Mountains. On the 5th, Chinese forces on the Salween front in northern Burma continue their advance, as the Japanese try to extricate their garrison from Bhamo. On the 6th, despite a lack

of supply, Japanese forces on Leyte continue to re-sist and even launch counterattacks. On the 7th, the Japanese attempt to resupply their forces on Leyte, but 13 transports are sunk by US aircraft. The US 77th Division lands in the Japanese rear, at Ormoc, Leyte. On the 8th, US land-based bombers and carrier aircraft begin a 72-day pound-ing of Iwo Jima in preparation for an amphibious assault. On the 9th, British troops continue ad-vancing into central Burma as they realize that the Japanese are pulling out without much of a fight. On the 10th, Japanese forces advancing north from INDO-CHINA make contact with Japanese forces ad-vancing south in southern China, a linkup that later permits the transfer of two divisions from the Indo-China garrison to southern China. On the 11th, US forces capture Ormoc, on Leyte in the Philippines, and discover the reason for the stub-born Japanese defense of the city: It was the main supply dump for the Japanese troops on Leyte; with Ormoc gone, the remaining 35,000 Japanese troops on Leyte are short on ammo and food. On the 12th, US forces on Leyte consolidate their positions. On the 13th, Chinese forces in northern Burma enter outskirts of Bhamo. On the 14th, the Third Fleet begins carrier air attacks on Japanese positions on Luzon, in preparation for the liberation of the prin-cipal island in the Philippines. On the 15th, US troops land on the Philippine island of Mindoro, meeting no resistance on the beach, but KAMIKA-ZES attack landing ships, damaging several and sinking two LSTS. On the 16th, Chinese forces in northern Burma capture town of Bhamo. On the 17th, 500 miles east of the Philippines, the US Third Fleet is caught in a mighty typhoon for two days, with losses greater than those in many naval battles. Three destroyers are sunk, over 140 aircraft destroyed, and severe damage inflicted on eight carriers, a cruiser, seven destroyers, and many sup-port ships, while nearly 800 sailors lose their lives and many more are injured. On the 18th, nearly 300 US aircraft, including over 75 B-29s, raid the Japanese base at Hankow, China, in an effort to disrupt the Japanese offensive. Bill Howell's ship, *Monterey* (CVL-26), undergoes its most harrowing moments of the war—due not to Japanese attack, but to the gigantic typhoon that pounds her and the other ships in the fleet for two days. The sustained winds are over a hundred miles an hour. There is some warning of the storm, and the crew lashes everything down with additional cables, especially *Monterey*'s aircraft. But the storm is so violent that, on 19 December, several aircraft tear loose from their ¾-inch steel cables. Before the crew can secure the aircraft, the constant movement of the planes sets off sparks, which start fires. Soon, most of the hangar deck is aflame and nearby ships think *Monterey* is done for. On the bridge, Lieutenant Commander Attard is standing watch when the fire breaks out. Bill Howell watches as Attard immediately orders the *Monterey* helmsman to turn the ship into the wind. While this will take the *Monterey* out of formation, and possibly cause a collision with another ship, it is the right decision. Heaving into the wind stabilizes the ship sufficiently so that the fire-fighting crews can do their work and the wayward aircraft can be lashed down again. There are dozens of injuries, and Lieutenant Jerry FORD will later receive a medal for his heroic actions in leading sailors in the damage control operations. On the 19th, foul weather forces postponement of a major Third Fleet carrier raid on Japanese bases on Luzon. British Commonwealth forces in Burma make steady gains. On the 20th, Japanese troops on Leyte are told by Tokyo that they can expect no further reinforcements or supplies. Bill Howell's ship, *Monterey*, damaged from the typhoon, is sent back to BREMERTON, Washington, for repairs and upgrades. *Monterey* arrives in Bremerton in early January and stays two months. On the 21st, British troops in Burma capture Kawlin. On the 22nd, the Vietnamese Liberation Army is formed in Vietnam by Vo Nguyen Giap, the core of the communist army that will eventually overcome Japanese, French, and American forces. Bill Howell manages to get word back to his wife that he is going to be on the West Coast soon. A meeting is arranged in Seattle for 22 January and despite wartime censorship and a shortage

of transportation, the reunion comes off. Another minor wartime miracle. On the 23rd, the United States opens an airfield on newly liberated Mindoro, in the Philippines. On the 24th, US cruisers and destroyers bombard Iwo Jima. On the 25th, British troops move into the Akyab Peninsula of Burma, as the Japanese withdraw. On the 26th, Japanese ships attack US beachhead on Mindoro, the Philippines. On the 27th, B-29s from SAIPAN, the MARIANAS, make their fifth major raid on Tokyo. On the 28th, Japanese assess the after-effects of five B-29s raids and find that the damage being done is not crippling. Soon the Americans realize the same thing and this leads to a switch to fire-bomb raids and a much less favorable outcome for the Japanese. On the 29th, stepping up their attack against Japanese forces on Leyte (now low on food and ammo), in less than two weeks US Army troops kill nearly 6,000 Japanese while losing only 11 of their own troops. Bill Howell's ship, *Monterey*, while undergoing repairs at Bremerton, Washington, gets her third skipper, as the executive officer, Commander Frank B. Miller, replaces Captain Stuart Ingersoll—but only on a temporary basis, as a new commanding officer is on the way. On the 30th, US Army aircraft attack Japanese shipping in the Manila Bay area. On the 31st, heavy Japanese air attacks on US shipping off Mindoro sink a PT-BOAT tender and damage a destroyer.

January 1945

The Japanese offensive continued in China, albeit less vigorously. More US landings took place in the Philippines. American carriers battled and destroyed Japanese airpower in FORMOSA and on the Asian mainland.

On the 1st, the US Eighth Army on the Philippine island of Leyte begins a campaign to clear still active Japanese troops, an effort that will continue until the end of the war. On the 2nd, as US Navy ships leave Leyte for the invasion of Luzon, they are forced to beat off attacks by KAMIKAZE.

On the 3rd, the US Third fleet stages raids on OKI-NAWA, Formosa, and the Pescadores, losing 18 aircraft, while the Japanese lose a dozen ships and over a hundred aircraft. On the 4th, the US amphibious invasion force approaching the main Philippine island of Luzon suffers heavy Japanese air attack, the CVE *Ommaney Bay* being so badly damaged by a kamikaze that she has to be sunk. On the 5th, although weakened by transfers of several divisions to China, Chinese forces in northern Burma continue to advance, with US support, crossing the Shweli River. On the 6th, the Japanese Air Force on Luzon is reduced to only 35 aircraft, down from 150 at the end of 1944. On the 7th, British troops occupy Akyab, in the Arakan area of Burma, as the Japanese situation continues to deteriorate in the region. On the 8th, heavy air strikes continue against Luzon, with a concentration on the Lingayen Gulf area, followed up during the night by the arrival of surface vessels to make the final preparations for the liberation of the island. On the 9th, the US Sixth Army lands on Luzon. Nearly 100,000 troops are landed at Lingayen Gulf, a hundred miles north of Manila in the first 24 hours. On the 10th, US forces on Luzon enlarge their beachhead. Chinese and American forces in northern Burma continue their advance. British and Indian forces capture Shwego, in the Arakan. On the 11th, the Japanese leadership examines their situation and decides to put all their remaining resources into kamikaze-type weapons. By the end of the month, all industrial and military organizations will have channeled their energies to building suicide weapons, and providing crews to man them. On the 12th, US Navy Task Force 38 sweeps the Indo-Chinese coast, its carrier aircraft sinking over three dozen Japanese ships. On the 13th, Japanese forces in the Philippines launch their few remaining aircraft against recently landed US troops on Luzon. On the 14th, British troops crossing the Irrawaddy River in Burma are hit by a Japanese counterattack, which results in a month-long battle. On the 15th, the Japanese offensive in China continues, with Japanese forces advancing

on the US air base at Suichuan. On the 16th, US carrier aircraft attack Japanese-held HONG KONG. The Japanese defenses are found to be meager, having been stripped for other fronts. On the 17th, US Sixth Army on Luzon steps up its drive on Manila. On the 18th, although "secured," fighting on PELELIU continues, with Japanese stragglers forming raiding parties to attack US ammo dumps and the air base. On the 19th, in China, Japanese troops seize control of the CANTON-Hankow rail line. On the 20th, first convoy navigates the BURMA ROAD, but the route needs repair and rebuilding before full-scale use is possible. On the 21st, US carrier aircraft attack Japanese air bases on Okinawa and Formosa, destroying some 100 enemy aircraft in the process. On the 22nd, CORREGIDOR, the island fortress guarding Japanese-held Manila Bay, is attacked by US aircraft. On the 23rd, the Burma Road is declared open, but small, scattered Japanese units in the area make travel on the route dangerous. On the 24th, in China, advancing Japanese troops cause the US air base at Suichuan to be evacuated. On the 25th, US B-29s undertake a major mining effort in the waters off the ports of SINGAPORE, SAIGON, CAM RANH BAY, and PENANG. This is the largest mining operation of the war, with 366 MINES dropped off Singapore alone. On the 26th, the Japanese government orders its troops in China to call off their offensive and concentrate on defending the China coast and key installations in north China. As is customary, the commanders in China do not instantly or consistently comply. On the 27th, US forces on Luzon are reinforced by the First Cavalry and 32nd Infantry Divisions, plus the 122nd Cavalry RCT. On the 28th, the Philippine island of Mindoro is declared free of organized Japanese resistance and under US control. On the 29th, the US 38th Division lands northwest of Subic Bay, on the Philippine island of Luzon, and promptly moves southward toward BATAAN. On the 30th, Task Force 63, the British Pacific Fleet (four carriers, a fast battleship, four cruisers, and 11 destroyers), refuels at sea in the Indian Ocean and then proceeds eastward to join the US Pacific Fleet. On the 31st, the US 11th Airborne Division lands—by amphibious craft—at the south entrance to Manila Bay.

February 1945

U.S. liberation of the Philippines continued. Japanese-held IWO JIMA was invaded by US Marines. The BURMA ROAD was reopened. Japanese offensive in China continued to advance toward remaining US air bases.

On the 1st, Japanese offensive in China captures Kukong, the last Chinese stronghold on the Hankow rail line. This cuts off Chinese forces to the east from the rest of China. On the 2nd, major combat operations come to a halt on Leyte Island in the Philippines, although small pockets of Japanese resistance remain. On the 3rd, on the Philippine main island of Luzon, the US Sixth Army is poised to fight its way into the Philippine capital of Manila. On the 4th, the first large supply convoy makes it from Ledo in India to Kunming in China along the full length of the BURMA ROAD. On the 5th, Australian troops effect a new landing on NEW BRITAIN, further sealing the RABAUL pocket. On the 6th, the Battle for Manila, Luzon, begins in earnest, while over 4,000 American POWs are freed from prison camps in the area, after nearly three years' imprisonment. On the 7th, the Japanese offensive in China captures another US air base, this one at Kanchow. On the 8th, Japanese resistance in Manila stiffens. On the 9th, heavy fighting continues on Luzon, particularly at Manila, Nichols Field, and the Val Verde Trail. On the 10th, Tokyo is hit with a severe earthquake shortly before a raid by nearly a hundred B-29 bombers. On the 11th, heavy fighting continues on Luzon. On the 12th, off the Philippine coast, the US sub *Batfish* (SS-113) sinks its third Japanese submarine in four days (*I-41*, *Ro-112*, and *Ro-113*). On the 14th, US troops reach the BATAAN Peninsula outside Manila as US PT-BOATS enter Manila Bay. On the 15th, US troops make a landing on the southern tip of Bataan. Japanese troops in nearby Manila are surrounded. On the 16th,

American troops make a surprise attack on CORREGIDOR Island (guarding the entrance to Manila Bay on Luzon, the Philippines), using paratroopers and troops coming ashore from nearby Bataan. Over 4,000 Japanese defenders on Corregidor are killed, with the loss of only 136 American dead. On the 17th, attempts to clear beach defenses on Japanese-held Iwo Jima encounter unexpected problems and nearly 200 US Navy frogmen are killed. On the 18th, British troops land on the Burmese coast in the Arakan region and cut off the retreat of Japanese forces. On the 19th, nearly 800 miles south of the Japanese Home Islands, 30,000 US Marines land on Iwo Jima. The Japanese have planned to use Iwo Jima to launch suicide aircraft attacks against Allied forces attempting to invade the Japanese Home Islands and also as a forward fighter base to oppose B-29 raids from the MARIANA ISLANDS. Three US Marine divisions are involved in this assault on this eight-square-mile island defended by 22,000 fanatical Japanese. Most of the Japanese are still sitting in fortified positions away from the beaches. Even so, the resistance on the beach is fierce. On the 20th, US Army troops land on SAMAR and Capul islands, giving them control of the vital San Bernardino Strait in the Philippines. On the 21st, Japanese resistance on Iwo Jima is fierce, with the invading Marines already losing half their TANKS. The fighting increases in intensity. On the 22nd, Marines on Iwo Jima make slow gains against heavy resistance. On the 23rd, on Iwo Jima, elements of the 28th Marines raise the US flag on Mount Suribachi. On the 24th, most of the Manila area on Luzon is under US control. On the 25th, in a major change in tactics against Japanese cities, US B-29 bombers switch from high-altitude daylight raids with high explosive bombs, to low-level night raids with incendiary bombs. The first raid against Tokyo, with 334 B-29s, burns out nearly 10,000 acres of the city. On the 26th, in Burma, the British begin an offensive against MANDALAY and Meiktila. On the 27th, even as heavy fighting continues on Iwo Jima, the US Navy opens a seaplane base on the island. On the 28th, US forces land on PALAWAN

Island in the Philippines. Occupation of this island effectively completes cutting off Japan from its resource areas in the East Indies.

March 1945

Japanese cities were pounded by US bombers. Japanese offensive in China slowed almost to a crawl. Recognizing its inability to provide fuel or pilots for them, the Imperial Navy laid up the last of its aircraft carriers, transferring the men to other duties.

On the 1st, US Navy ships and aircraft attack the Japanese-held RYUKYU ISLANDS. On the 2nd, Japanese resistance on CORREGIDOR Island, at the entrance of Manila Bay, ends, less than three years after the Japanese first took the island fortress from American defenders. On the 3rd, Japanese resistance in the Philippine capital of Manila ends. On the 4th, advancing British troops cut off Japanese forces in central Burma. On the 5th, US Marines have cleared most of IWO JIMA and US fighters begin operating from a captured airstrip. On the 6th, on Luzon, the US First Cavalry Division is relieved by the 43rd, as the Sixth Army reorganizes. On the 7th, trapped Japanese troops in central Burma counterattack to break out, bringing British advance to a halt. On the 8th, British troops fight their way into Japanese-held MANDALAY, Burma. In eastern Luzon the Sixth Army begins a major offensive against the Japanese Shimbu Defensive Line. On the 9th, the Japanese, having concluded a temporary armistice with Ho Chi-minh's communists, attack French garrisons in Indo-China, thus eliminating the last remnant of pro-German Vichy French rule. The Japanese fear that Free French troops will be landed (via the Allied-controlled waters around Indochina) and the Vichy troops will join the Free French. On the 10th, dawn over Tokyo reveals a manmade hell. The previous night, 279 low-flying B-29 bombers dropped 1,665 tons of incendiary bombs, which created a firestorm that killed 84,000 Japanese. This is a greater death toll than either of the later A-bomb raids. On the 11th, Emperor Bao-Dai of Vietnam,

a puppet of the French, and later the Japanese, declares Vietnam's independence from France. The Japanese ignore this and remain in control. On the 12th, heavy fighting on the Shimbu Line on Luzon. On the 13th, elements of the Indian 26th Division make an amphibious "end run" to trap Japanese forces on the Arakan coast. On the 14th, US B-29s raid the Japanese city of Osaka, inflicting 13,000 CASUALTIES. On the 15th, the British complete the recapture of Mandalay, though Japanese resistance continues in some suburban areas. On the 16th, Iwo Jima is declared free of organized Japanese resistance, but some mopping up continues for weeks. On the 17th, US B-29s raid the Japanese city of KOBE, inflicting 15,000 casualties. Bill Howell's ship, Monterey (CVL-26), spends the next 12 weeks operating off OKINAWA, dodging KAMIKAZE and providing air support for the American infantry on Okinawa. On the 18th, US troops land on the Philippine island of Panay and push inland. On the 19th, US Navy aircraft attack the KURE naval base area in the Japanese Home Islands. On the 20th, the last ship of a 21-vessel Japanese convoy is hunted down and destroyed. The convoy has attempted, for 10 weeks, to carry supplies from Japan to its beleaguered forces in Southeast Asia. None of the ships make it as far as SINGAPORE, being constantly harried by US aircraft and SUBMARINES. Bill Howell's ship, Monterey, gets its last wartime skipper, with Captain John B. Lyons taking over from Commander Frank B. Miller. On the 21st, British forces take control of Mandalay, with surviving Japanese troops in the area retreating toward SIAM. On the 22nd, Japanese offensive in China continues, with an attack toward the US air base at Laohokow. On the 23rd, a British carrier task force joins the US fleet for operations against the Japanese Home Islands. On the 24th, the last pocket of 200 Japanese troops on Iwo Jima is cornered in an area about 50 yards square. The Japanese eventually launch an attack from this position and nearly all are killed. On the 25th, the US air base at Laohokow in China is destroyed as the Japanese close in. This is the last US air base in China that the Japanese will capture. On the 26th, a US

Army division lands on Philippine island of CEBU. On the 27th, B-29s begin mining operation in the waters around Japan. In the space of a few weeks, the mining brings Japanese shipping to a standstill and makes the blockade of Japan nearly complete. On the 28th, a US Army division lands on Kerama Island, the Ryukyu Islands, providing a forward base to support an assault on Okinawa Island. On the 29th, US troops clearing Kerama Island discover 350 suicide boats, held there for use against any force that might attempt to land on Okinawa. That same day the United States informs Britain that it will probably have a usable ATOMIC BOMB in the near future. On the 30th, the British 14th Army advances against crumbling resistance. On the 31st, heavy fighting continues on eastern Luzon.

April 1945

The last major battle of World War II began, as OKINAWA was invaded. The amphibious assault was on the same scale as the one at Normandy (D-day). Okinawa turned out to be the bloodiest of the Pacific island battles. The British retook Burma from the Japanese.

On the 1st (Easter Sunday), Okinawa is assaulted by 60,000 US Army and Marine troops (two divisions of each). The island is only 360 miles south of the Japanese Home Islands. The landings on Okinawa are the last major assault of the war, and the bloodiest. On the 2nd, on Okinawa, the Japanese pull back rather than oppose the invading American troops on the beach, to await the American in fortifications farther inland. On the 3rd, Soviet Union decides to renounce the five-year Soviet-Japan neutrality pact signed in April 1941. On the 4th, US troops on Okinawa finally encounter dug-in Japanese garrison, and the bloody battle for the island ensues. The Fourth Marine Division arrives back at Maui after the IWO JIMA operation. The Marines are ordered to start training for the invasion of Japan, the first operation to take place in October 1945. The Marines will lead the way. But first the damage from Iwo

Jima has to be repaired. The division has suffered over 8,000 CASUALTIES. Over half of these are wounded who gradually returned from hospitals. The rest of the losses have to be made up by fresh replacements. While the war in Europe looks close to ending, the Marines on Maui begin retraining for the invasion of Japan. On the 5th, in the wake of the Soviet abrogation of the April 1941, five-year neutrality pact with Japan, the Japanese cabinet resigns. On the 6th, Japanese launch mass KAMIKAZE attacks on US ships off Okinawa. The 355 aircraft fly from the Home Islands (Kyushu) and only 24 of them hit anything. Six smaller ships (destroyers and support vessels) are sunk, but many more are damaged by FRIENDLY FIRE as all US ships in the area open up to stop the kamikaze. On the 7th, the Japanese Second ("suicide") Fleet is intercepted by US carrier aircraft before it can reach Okinawa: Some 900 US aircraft are involved in this battle, of which 10 are lost, while Japanese losses include the superbattleship YAMATO, a cruiser, four destroyers, and 54 aircraft. On the 8th, the battle for the Motobu Peninsula on northern Okinawa begins, as Marines probe the Japanese lines, while other Marines and soldiers on the island push southward. On the 9th, US forces land on the island of Jolo in the Sulu Sea (off the Philippines). On the 10th, British carrier aircraft attack Japanese air bases on FORMOSA to stop Japanese air raids on US ships off Okinawa. On the 11th, British forces in Burma hustle toward RANGOON (300 miles) in order to take the city before the monsoon rains begin. On the 12th, over 150 Japanese kamikaze are shot down off Okinawa, although a Baka flying bomb hits and sinks a US destroyer. On the 13th, Chinese and Japanese forces both begin offensives in different parts of China. President ROOSEVELT dies of a cerebral hemorrhage (April 12th in North America). Radio Tokyo broadcasts a dignified notice. On the 14th, Japanese forces in China are again ordered to withdraw troops for the defense of the Chinese coast and this time they comply, abandoning several captured US air bases in the process. B-29 air raid on Tokyo damages the Imperial Palace. On the 15th, in Burma, the first use of HELICOPTERS in a rescue takes place. The crew of a transport has to bail out high in the mountain jungles, then a search plane crashes during the search. When a patrol reaches an injured search plane survivor on foot, they radio back that he is too ill to move. The nearest US air base has an experimental Sikorsky YR-4 helicopter on hand for testing, and the helicopter PILOT decides to attempt the risky mission in an area where no aircraft can land. He succeeds, and thus effects the first use of a helicopter as a rescue aircraft. On the 16th, IE SHIMA, a smaller island off Okinawa, is invaded by a US Army division. On the 17th begins the last invasion of the Philippines Campaign, as US forces land on Mindanao Island. On the 18th, popular American war correspondent Ernie PYLE is killed by Japanese fire on Ie Shima. On the 19th, assisted by an enormous amount of naval gunfire and aircraft support, US Army forces launch a major offensive to break Japanese resistance on Okinawa. On the 20th, Japanese troops in Burma continue to be hunted down or trapped by advancing British forces. The British are closing in on the Yenangyaung oil fields, the largest in Burma. On the 21st, advancing British forces move to within 200 miles of Rangoon in Burma. The Japanese decide to abandon Rangoon and pull back farther to reorganize their forces. On the 22nd, the island of PALAWAN (the Philippines) is declared secure. On the 23rd, the battle for the central Philippines ends as Japanese resistance is crushed on the island of CEBU. On the 24th, around Japan, Allied airpower, SUBMARINES, and especially naval MINES begin to shut down Japanese ports. By the end of April, the port of NAGOYA becomes the first of many to cease operations. On the 25th, the Japanese Army in China still has fight left in it. At Wukang, a Chinese division is routed by Japanese forces. On the 26th, Japanese resistance on Okinawa intensifies, stalling US efforts to secure the island. On the 27th, US and Australian warships begin four days of bombarding the Japanese-held oil facilities on TARAKAN Island (off the northeast coast of BORNEO). On the 28th, Japanese kamikaze attacks on US ships off Okinawa continue. During the month

of April, over 1,000 Japanese aircraft are destroyed. But 20 Allied ships are sunk and 157 damaged, mostly by kamikaze. On the 29th, fighting is so intense on Okinawa that one US Army division has to be pulled out of the line because of heavy losses. On the 30th, the large minelayer *Terror* (CM-5) and destroyer *Bennion* (DD-662) are damaged by kamikaze aircraft off Okinawa: Since late March US naval losses off Okinawa total 20 ships sunk (14 by kamikaze) and 157 damaged (90 by kamikaze), but the Japanese have lost nearly 1,200 aircraft in attacks on the fleet. In Europe, as soldiers of the Red Army encircle his bunker, HITLER commits suicide.

May 1945

Germany surrendered. Japan was now alone against the world. Battle for OKINAWA raged. Last surface naval battle took place. Chinese counterattacked as the Japanese withdrew troops for defense of the Home Islands.

On the 1st, Australian forces land on TARAKAN, off BORNEO. The island has been held by the Japanese since early 1942. On the 2nd, advancing British troops discover that Rangoon, Burma, has been abandoned by the Japanese. On the 3rd, the Japanese attempt to reverse their declining position on Okinawa by making a pair of amphibious landings behind American lines. Nearly a thousand Japanese troops are involved, and most are quickly killed or captured. On the 4th, British warships bombard Japanese installations in the Sakishima Islands of the southern RYUKYUS. On the 5th, Japanese KAMIKAZE score a major success off Okinawa, sinking 17 ships at a loss of only 131 aircraft. On the 6th, the British declare the Burma Campaign over, although isolated Japanese units will fight on for several more weeks. On the 7th, British forces in southern Burma advance to link up with Allied units in the interior. On the 8th, the war in Europe ends with the surrender of Germany. Japan now stands alone against the massed military might of the Allied powers. With the defeat of Germany comes the announcement of a "leave plan" to determine who will get some relief now that only Japan is left and not as many troops are needed at the front. What this meant to many troops is that those who have seen the most action are eligible for transfer back to the mainland for six months of easier duty. On the 9th, as German forces lay down their arms, in the Pacific, ferocious Japanese resistance continues in Burma, China, the Philippines, and on Okinawa. On the 10th, assisted by Filipino GUERRILLAS, the US Eighth Army expands its hold on Mindanao. On the 11th, Australian troops land in the WEWAK area of New Guinea. On the 12th, heavy Japanese kamikaze attacks on US and British ships off Okinawa; battleship NEW MEXICO is badly hit. On the 13th, the US Fast Carrier Task Force begins a two-day raid against Japanese airfields on Kyushu. On the 14th, US Task Force Mars completes its concentration in China, having taken over a month to move from Burma. On the 15th, British warships and aircraft attack Japanese installations on the ANDAMAN ISLANDS. On the 16th, the most intensive use of napalm in the war occurs near the Philippine capital of Manila, where Japanese troops threaten the city's water supply. Over 300 tons of napalm are dropped over several days. US troops are then able to go in and mop up remaining Japanese resistance. On the 17th, the last surface battle of the war takes place, as the Japanese cruiser *Haguro* is sunk by five British destroyers in the Malacca Strait. On the 18th, Chinese troops take the port of FOOCHOW on the China coast. On the 19th, on Okinawa, another US Army division has to be pulled out of combat because of high casualty rates. Even the Marines are suffering an exceptionally high rate of combat fatigue losses. On the 20th, Japanese begin withdrawing divisions from China to shore up the defenses of the Home Islands. On the 21st, Marines and soldiers make small gains on Okinawa, as fighting for Shuri Castle begins. On the 22nd, Okinawa is hit with heavy rains, which stall offensive operations for nearly two weeks. On the 23rd, Japan's largest port, Yokohama, ceases operations because of Allied air and naval activity, as well as MINES offshore. On the 24th, in addition to kamikaze at-

tacks, Japanese suicide paratroopers land on US airfield on Okinawa. Several US aircraft are destroyed before the paratroopers are all killed. On the 25th, US military planners set 1 November as the date of the first invasion of the Japanese Home Islands. On the 26th, Chinese troops reoccupy Nanning, cutting off 200,000 Japanese troops in Indo-China (who no longer have access to the sea). On the 27th, the port of Tokyo is closed because of damage to port installations and Allied military activity in the surrounding waters On the 28th, Japanese make a last attempt to reverse their situation on Okinawa with kamikaze attacks. Over a hundred Japanese aircraft are destroyed, but only one US destroyer is sunk. On the 29th, organized Japanese resistance on the Philippine island of Negros collapses. On the 30th, the Okinawan capital of NAHA is almost completely under US control. On the 31st, the United States withdraws its forces from MOUNTBATTEN's Southeast Asia Command to concentrate on supporting China, while SEAC, now entirely British Commonwealth in composition, is to concentrate on the liberation of MALAYA.

June 1945

Australian amphibious forces liberated numerous islands west of New Guinea. Japanese resistance was not as stubborn as before, a result of poor Japanese logistics and veteran Australian troops. Fighting in the Philippines wound down, but Japanese resistance went on for several more months. The battle for OKINAWA ended.

On the 1st, Japanese resistance on Luzon in the Philippines is reduced to small-unit actions. Without supplies of food or ammunition, the surviving Japanese troops begin acting like GUERRILLAS. On the 2nd, Nationalist Chinese leader CHIANG KAI-SHEK gives up his title of premier of the Nationalist government but remains the president and strongman. On the 3rd, in eastern Luzon the Japanese attempt to break contact and regroup. On the 4th, heavy fighting continues on Okinawa. On the 5th, a typhoon hits Okinawa, damaging four battleships, eight carriers, seven cruisers, 11 destroyers, and dozens of support ships. On the 6th, US Marines on Okinawa clear the NAHA airfield of Japanese resistance. On the 7th, in China, the Japanese are forced back to the starting point of their spring offensive. On the 8th, on Luzon in the Philippines, US Army patrols reach deep into the back country, finding only scattered Japanese resistance. On the 9th, the Sixth Army manages to isolate some Japanese forces in eastern Luzon. On the 10th, Australian troops land at BRUNEI Bay, BORNEO. On the 11th, British warships steam into the Caroline Islands to attack the Japanese base at TRUK. On the 12th, the southeastern end of the main Japanese line on Okinawa is pierced by a surprise attack by elements of the Seventh Infantry Division. On the 13th, Japanese resistance on the Visayan Islands ends. Nearly 10,000 Japanese have died, compared to 3,200 US CASUALTIES (including 835 dead). On the 14th, the Pentagon orders commanders in the Pacific to prepare plans to deal with a sudden surrender by the Japanese. On the 15th, in China, Chinese forces advance on a broad front into territory formerly held by Japanese troops (most of whom have been pulled back to MANCHURIA or Japan itself). On the 16th, British warships bombard Truk, in the CAROLINES. On the 17th, on Okinawa, US Army troops breach the final defensive line of the Japanese forces. The Japanese commander commits suicide. On the 18th, having burned out Japan's major cities, US B-29s begin attacking the smaller ones. On the 19th, British forces move out of Burma into Thailand. On the 20th, in an unprecedented event in the war, over a thousand Japanese soldiers surrender on Okinawa. Civilians, who so far have actively assisted the soldiers, also begin to surrender in great numbers. On the 21st, all of the islands in the southern Philippines are declared clear of organized Japanese resistance. On the 22nd, the United States declares the battle for Okinawa over. In 81 days of fighting, the 118,000-man Japanese garrison has been killed, except for 7,400 who have been captured (usually while wounded or otherwise incapacitated) or

have surrendered. US casualties are 49,000, of whom 12,520 are dead. Japan has lost 7,800 aircraft in KAMIKAZE attacks, as well as many ships. Allied forces have lost 800 aircraft, nearly 5,000 sailors dead and 36 ships sunk (none larger than a destroyer). Deaths among the Okinawan civilian population may have reached 150,000; we will never know for sure. It is the ferocity of this battle, more than anything else, that makes the use of ATOMIC BOMBS against Japan preferable to attempting a landing on the Home Islands. On the 23rd, on Luzon, the United States uses paratroopers, glider troops, Filipino guerrillas, and US Army troops to close the net around surviving Japanese troops. On the 24th, Australian forces capture Sarawak. On the 25th, in support of the principal operations on Okinawa, Marines land on Kume Shima, a small nearby island, meeting light resistance. On the 26th, B-29s begin night raids on Japanese oil refining facilities (to deny then aviation fuel for their remaining aircraft). On the 27th, the campaign against the Japanese on Luzon (the Philippines) is declared over, although 50,000 Japanese soldiers still hold out in the mountains of the northeast of Luzon. On the 28th, Australian troops capture Kuala Belait in the East Indies. On the 29th, President TRUMAN approves plans for Operation Olympic, to take place about 1 November. Chinese forces begin advancing into Indochina. On the 30th, although many Japanese soldiers continue to resist on Luzon, these troops pose no threat to the US hold on the island. Japanese losses in the Philippines total 317,000 troops killed, plus 7,236 captured. Total US casualties are 60,000. Philippine losses (including civilians) are far higher.

July 1945

Australian troops conquered Borneo and seized the oil fields Japan originally went to war for. Dozens of US and British carriers rampaged up and down the Japanese coast, sinking ships and bombing land targets. Chinese troops continued to push Japanese troops out of China. Japan was told to surrender or be destroyed. Already, most of Japan's cities had been largely burned out.

On the 1st, Australian troops invade BALIKPAPAN, Borneo, the largest oil field in Asia. Japanese troops resist. On the 2nd, Japan announces that over five million of its citizens have been killed or injured in the US air raids so far; the actual figure is about 672,000 killed, with several million more injured, depending on how you count "war related injuries." On the 3rd, Australian troops take over oil fields at Balikpapan, Borneo. On the 4th, US troops in the southern islands of the Philippines, working with Filipino GUERRILLA units, continue to track down and kill isolated, but still resisting, Japanese troops, few of whom express a willingness to surrender. On the 5th, Australian troops continue their conquest of Borneo. On the 6th, Chinese forces continue moving north toward MANCHURIA. Japanese troops offer less resistance. On the 7th, Dutch troops enter the fighting in Borneo. On the 8th, Filipino troops take a major role in completing the liberation of Mindanao. On the 9th, Task Force 38 arrives off Japan; except for the rotation of individual ships to rear areas for rest, refit, or repair, the fleet (16 US carriers with escorting vessels, joined by four British carriers and escorts) will remain in Japanese waters until the war is over. On the 10th, in the largest air assault of the Pacific War to date, over a thousand US and British carrier aircraft bomb airfields and industrial installations in the Tokyo area. On the 11th, Allied bombers turn their attention to the Japanese Home Islands of Shikoku and Honshu. On the 12th, Japan asks the Soviets to assist in negotiating a cease-fire with the Allies; somehow the message doesn't get through. On the 13th, Italy declares war on Japan. Mopping up continues on Mindanao and scores of other places throughout the Pacific Theater. On the 14th, US battleships shell Kamamishi, Japan, in the first surface attack on the Home Islands. On the 16th, the first ATOMIC BOMB is tested in New Mexico. It works. On the 17th, the US Third Fleet, with the British carrier task force, engages in surface and air attacks on targets in the Tokyo area. On the 18th, Australian troops take the Sambodja oil fields in Borneo. On the 19th, surrounded Japanese units in Burma make a coordinated attack to break out of their encirclement. On the 20th, the USS *Threadfish* (SS-410) sinks Japanese *Minesweeper No. 39* in the Yellow Sea. On the 21st, US radio broadcasts demand that Japan surrender or be destroyed. On the 22nd, British troops in Burma generally defeat Japanese attempts to break out. On the 23rd, US Navy and British Commonwealth warships sweep past Japanese Home Islands of Shikoku and Kyushu, sinking over a hundred Japanese transports as they go. The first US troops land in Japan, as a raiding party off the USS *Barb* (SS-220) blows up a train on the east coast of Sakhalin Island. On the 24th, over 1,500 Allied carrier aircraft attack the Japanese naval base at KURE (on the INLAND SEA), sinking three of Japan's four remaining battleships. On the 25th, in response to a call from the Allies to surrender, Japan says it will surrender, but not unconditionally. On the 26th, British warships and aircraft attack Japanese installations on the west coast of MALAYA. On the 27th, Japan's cities are "bombed" with leaflets telling them that Japan must surrender or be destroyed. On the 28th, around midnight, KAMIKAZE sink their last ship, US destroyer *Callaghan* (DD-792) named after RAdm Dan CALLAGHAN, off Okinawa. On the 29th, US warships shell naval and air bases on Honshu. On the 30th, two British midget SUBMARINES sneak into SINGAPORE harbor and sink a Japanese cruiser by attaching MINES to it. On the 31st, malnutrition grows rampant in Japan, with the average citizen getting only 1,680 calories a day (22% less than the minimum to survive).

August 1945

Two ATOMIC BOMBS were dropped. Although these bombs killed fewer people than the earlier fire-bomb raid on Tokyo, the appearance of this new weapon, and the expectation that America has many more, made an impression on the Japanese. The Soviet Union declared war on Japan and invaded Japanese-held MANCHURIA, Sakhalin, and the KURILES. Japan surrendered.

On the 1st, mines air-dropped by the United States on the Japanese-controlled Yangtze river sink 36 Japanese transports and damage another 11. On the 2nd, B-29s drop 6,600 tons of bombs on five Japanese cities. There are few Japanese cities left to bomb. On the 3rd, the blockade of Japan is complete. Nothing gets in, nothing gets out. On the 4th, the last organized Japanese troops in Burma are killed or captured, with only 10,000 Japanese troops escaping to fight on individually or in small groups. On the 5th, Chinese forces recapture Tanchuk and Hsinning, in central China. On the 6th, a 4.5-ton atomic bomb is dropped on the Japanese city of HIROSHIMA. Over 80,000 Japanese die, with many more injured. A quarter of the dead are military personnel. On the 7th, elements of Headquarters, U.S. First Army, arrive on Luzon from Europe to begin planning for Operation Coronet, the second phase of the proposed invasion of Japan. On the 8th, the Soviet Union declares war on Japan. On the 9th a second atomic bomb is dropped on NAGASAKI, killing over 30,000 Japanese. The Red Army begins a massive offensive in Manchuria. Aircraft of the Third Fleet raid northern Honshu and Hokkaido. On the 10th, Allied carrier aircraft continue raids on northern Honshu and Hokkaido, destroying 400 Japanese aircraft and damaging over 300. The Allies lose 34 of their own planes. Bill Howell's ship, *Monterey* (CVL-26), takes part in the operations off the coast of Japan, hitting installations ashore and running down any surviving Japanese shipping at sea. In Japan, the war minister reminds senior officers of their obligation to obey the emperor's orders, whatever they might be. On the 11th, US and British warships shell Japanese steel mills, factories, and other installations along the eastern coasts of the Kuriles and Honshu. On the 12th, leaflets are dropped on Japanese cities calling for surrender or face "utter devastation." On the 13th, Japan's leaders offer to surrender unconditionally if the em-

peror's status is left unchanged. This is refused and the debate rages on in the Japanese government about what to do. The demand for unconditional surrender is made to avoid the mistakes made after World War I, when the German military was left intact and became the crucial factor in Germany's World War II success. Air raids on Tokyo. USS *LaGrange* (APA-124) is damaged by a KAMIKAZE off OKINAWA, the last US vessel damaged by direct enemy action. On the 14th, the emperor agrees to surrender unconditionally. In Tokyo, elements of the First Imperial Guard Division attempt a coup, which is put down after some bloodshed. Bill Howell leaves his ship, via a bosun's chair, a wood and canvas seat slung from a line between *Monterey* and a tanker. Bill has more time in service than anyone else in the crew and is eligible for rotation back to the States. The tanker is headed that way, but slowly. On the 15th, HIROHITO's surrender message is broadcast. Task Force 38 is approximately 100 miles east of Tokyo, where it beats off an attack by Japanese aircraft at 1100 hours, nearly a half-day after the emperor's surrender message. On the 16th, Soviet troops land on South Sakhalin. On the 17th, B-32 bombers on reconnaissance over Tokyo are attacked by Japanese aircraft but suffer no CASUALTIES. A new Japanese cabinet is formed under Prince Higashikuni, a general and kinsman of the emperor. On the 18th, two B-32 bombers on reconnaissance over Tokyo are again jumped by Japanese aircraft, suffering one man killed and several wounded, while knocking down three of the attackers. Soviet troops land in the Kuriles. On the 19th, a Japanese delegation arrives by air at Manila (via IE SHIMA) to negotiate details of Allied occupation of the Home Islands and of the surrender. On the 20th Japanese military authorities suppress an attempt to stage a coup and establish a "Government of National Resistance." British reconnaissance aircraft in Burma are fired upon by Japanese antiaircraft batteries. Japanese forces in China cease fire. Red Chinese forces occupy Kalgan, northwest of PEKING. Having met with MACARTHUR, a Japanese delegation leaves Manila by air for Tokyo, via Ie Shima, with instructions from the Allies on the details of the surrender. On the 21st the Asiatic Wing, Naval Air Transport Service, is established at Oakland, California, as part of preparations for the REPATRIATION of American personnel from the Pacific. On the 22nd, Mili Atoll, in the MARSHALLS, becomes the first island garrison to surrender, to the USS *Levy* (DE-162). On the 23rd, Soviet troops occupy PARAMUSHIRO, in the Kuriles. On the 24th, Red Chinese forces occupy CHEFOO and Wei-hai-wei. Nationalist China and Russia conclude an alliance. On the 25th, the last day on which specially marked Japanese aircraft are permitted to fly, US aircraft begin routine patrols over Japan to monitor compliance with terms of the armistice, and to locate prisoner-of-war camps. Nationalist Chinese forces occupy NANKING. On the 26th, Soviet troops occupy Matsuma, in the southern Kuriles. On the 27th, the Third Fleet enters Sagami Bay, south of Tokyo Bay. On Morotai and Halmahea, Japanese forces totaling over 36,000 troops and 5,000 civilians surrender to the US 93rd Division. On the 28th, a party of US personnel lands at Atsugi Airfield near Tokyo, to be greeted by a sign reading "Welcome to the U.S. Army from the Third Fleet"—erected the previous evening by a pilot from the USS YORKTOWN who had made an unofficial landing there. On the 29th, the Fourth Marine Regiment lands at Yokosuka Naval Base, near Tokyo. Japanese forces in Southeast Asia surrender to the British. On the 30th, surface combatants of TF 38 enter Tokyo Bay. The 11th Airborne Division lands at Atsugi Airfield. On the 31st, MARCUS ISLAND surrenders to the USS BAGLEY (DD-386), which has been in the Pacific since PEARL HARBOR. Additional US troops land in Japan.

September 1945

Japan formally surrendered. However, it was six months before the last of the far-flung Japanese gar-

risons actually laid down their arms. Indeed, Japanese troops were used as local police in many areas through late 1945, until the Allies could get their own troops in place. The REPATRIATION of former Japanese soldiers to Japan continued through 1947. And some holdouts didn't return until the 1970s.

On the 1st: Since December 7, 1941 Japan has lost nearly 700 warships of 100 tons or more, for over two million tons of warships, as well as over 2,300 merchant vessels of 500 tons or more, for some 8.5 million tons, both totals exceeding the tonnage of the Imperial Navy and Merchant Marine on PEARL HARBOR Day. On the 2nd, Japan formally signs an instrument of surrender aboard the battleship USS *Missouri* in Tokyo Harbor, as the crews of 257 other Allied warships look on. World War II is over.

Although Japan has surrendered, Bill Howell's former ship, *Monterey* (CVL-26), spends the first half of September patrolling off Japan to make sure that any Japanese ships that have not surrendered, are not tempted to go back to war.

On 19 October, Chief Petty Officer Bill Howell, after 44 months of service, is given his Honorable Discharge at Lido Beach, Long Island (New York State).

After the war, Bill Howell and his wife Catherine will have four children. Two of his sons will serve in the Far East (Vietnam and Korea) as army helicopter pilots, and survive the experience. Although the *Monterey* was scrapped in the early 1960s, the 3,000 or so sailors who served on the ship have not forgotten her and reunions are held periodically. Bill Howell begins attending some of these in the early 1980s. Although the *Monterey* is gone, the memories of wartime service on her are not. The crew remembers, and so does anyone who has ever taken any interest in the Pacific War.

Appendix 1

MODERN EQUIVALENTS OF NOTABLE PACIFIC WAR PLACE-NAMES

One consequence of decolonialization and of other political changes in the half-century since the end of World War II is that many places prominent to the war now bear different names, or names spelled in a radically different fashion according to new transliterations, than was the case between 1941 and 1945. This list is limited to places that figured somewhat prominently in the war. Omitted are numerous places where the modern form is a recognizable variant of the original spelling (e.g., Lungga Point rather than Lunga Point). Note that political changes in some of these areas are fairly constant, and names have a tendency to change on short notice.

Old Name	New Name
Amboina	Ambon
Amoy	Xiamen

Old Name	New Name
Batavia	Jakarta
Bonin Islands	Ogasawara Gunto
British North Borneo	Sabah (part of Malaysia)
Burma	Myanmar
Canton	Guangzhou
Celebes	Sulawesi
Ceram	Seram
Ceylon	Sri Lanka
Charar Province	region abolished
Chengtu	Chengdu
Chosen	Korea
Chungking	Chongqing
Dalny (Dairen)	Dalian
Diego Suarez	Anteranana
Dutch Borneo	Kalimantan
Ellice Islands	Tuvalua
Efate	Vate

Old Name	New Name	Old Name	New Name
Florida Island, Solomons	Nggela	Moulmein	Mawlamyine
Formosa	Taiwan	Mukden (Fengtien, 1932–45)	Shenyang
Fusan	Pusan	Nanking	Nanjing
Gilbert Islands	Kiribati	Ndeni	Nidu
Gona	Garara	Netherlands East Indies	Indonesia
Hankow	Kankou	Netherlands New Guinea	Irian Jaya
Honan	Henan	New Hebrides	Vanuatu
Hopeh	Hebei	Noemfoor	Numfor
Hupeh	Hubei	Palau	Balau
Indo-China	Cambodia, Laos, Vietnam	Parece Vela Island	Okina Daito
Irrawaddy River	Ayeyarwady River	Pegu	Bago
Java	Jawa	Peking (Peiping)	Beijing
Jehol Province	region abolished	Ponape	Pohnpei
Karafuto (Russian: Sakhalin)	Sakhalin	Port Arthur	Lushun
Karen	Kayin	Rangoon	Yangon
Kingsu	Jiangu	Salween River	Thanlwin River
Kurile Islands	Kurilskiye Ostrova	Sapwahfik	Ngatik
Kwantung	Guangdong	Sian	Xian
Makin Island	Butaritari Island	Sumatra	Sumatera
Malacca	Melaka	Szechuan	Sichuan
Malaya	part of Malaysia, with Sarawak and the former British Borneo	Taierchwang	Teierzhuang
		Tassafaronga Point	Tasivarongo
Manchuria (Manchukuo, 1932–45)	region abolished	Timor	Nusa Tenggara
		Truk Island	Chuuck Island
Marcus Island	Minamitori Island	Volcano Islands	Kaman Retie
Moluccas Islands	Maluku Islands	Yangtze River	Joint Jung

CODE WORDS AND CODE NAMES OF IMPORTANCE IN THE PACIFIC WAR

By one account the Allies used over 10,000 code words during World War II, for everything from operations to secret weapons, and from politicians to islands. And the Axis used thousands as well. Code words were coined not only for major operations and territorial features, such as islands, but also for various individuals, such as politicians and senior commanders, smaller operations, rivers, towns, military units, even different sides of the same island. For example, the Awi River in New Guinea was code-named Colabar; McGrath, Alaska, was Hacksaw; Kavieng was Forearm, later changed to Fosdick;

while the Japanese Fourth Division was the Aoba Detachment. To further complicate matters, code names were sometimes changed. In addition, during combat it was not unusual for front-line forces to give code names to local features. So the total number of code names that were used during the war must surely have been in the tens of thousands. And in fact there could easily have been more, were it not for the frequent use of numerals, both Roman and Arabic, the letters of the military alphabet (Able, Baker, etc.), and even colors (such as Beach Easy Red 2) to indicate minor geographic features or to distinguish among different versions or aspects of particular plans.

Although code names were supposed to mask the identity of a person, place, or thing, they sometimes were rather transparent, such as "Gateway" for the Marianas, "Jackfrost" for Canada, and "Hotrocks" for Mount Suribachi. Occasionally they were frivolous, a practice against which Winston Churchill railed at one point, observing that it not only trivialized the importance of the operation, but was also bad for morale, both military and civilian.

What follows are some of the more important, or at least more interesting, code names. By the way, the Japanese for operation is "Go."

Allied code names were ultimately decided by the Combined Chiefs of Staff. Their working staffs drew up lists of acceptable names. Words likely to have a double meaning or deemed to be "too frivolous" were generally avoided. These lists were then distributed to theater commanders who could assign names as needed.

Ref: Faldella, *Operazioni Segrete*; Ruffner and Thomas, eds., *The Codenames Dictionary*.

Word	Code Name For
1	See Ichi Go
3	See HA Go
157	Japanese New Guinea reinforcement, Jan. 1943
A	Japanese plan for the Battle of the Philippine Sea, June 1944; used previously for a plan for a decisive air battle in the Solomons, Apr. 1943; also the designation given the Japanese atomic bomb development project
Abattoir	Netherlands New Guinea
Accumulation	Leyte
Acorn	Small USN base development unit (see Cub)
Admiral Q	Occasional name for President Roosevelt
AF	Japanese code name for Midway
Air Mica	Admiral Marc Mitscher
Alamo	US Sixth Army
Alligator	Makin Island
Amnesia	Attu
Amoeba	Goodenough Island, New Guinea
Amount	Kyushu

Word	Code Name For
Ampersand	Espiritu Santo
Anaconda	Truk
Anakim	Proposed operations in Burma, 1943
Annuity	New Guinea operations after Hotplate
Aoba Detachment	Japanese Fourth Infantry Division
Aphorism	Nauru
Apothecary	Samoa
Arabic	New Britain
Arcadia	Washington Conference, Dec. 1941–Jan. 1942
Archbishop	Jaluit, Caroline Islands
Argonaut	Malta (Cricket) and Yalta (Magneto) conferences
Artist	Ponape, Caroline Islands
Ash	Vella Lavella
B	Japanese secret radar development project
Babacoute	Eniwetok
Bamboo	Proposed operation against the upper part of the Kra Peninsula, Siam (see Clinch)
Barney	US submarine missions in the Sea of Japan, June 1945
Bataan	Headquarters of Gen. Douglas MacArthur
Baus Au	Submarine supply missions to the Filipino guerrillas, 1942–45 ("Get it back," in Tagalog)
Beefsteak	Emirau Island
Bequest	Yap, Carolina Islands
Berry	Phases in the occupation of Japan (see Blacklist); also US plan to capture Wake Island
Blacklist	Plan for the peaceful occupation of Japan, drawn up in parallel with Olympic and implemented after the surrender
Bonus	Proposed Madagascar operation, early 1942
Braid	Occasional code name for Gen. G. C. Marshall
Brewer	Admiralty Islands operation, Feb.–May 1944
Broadway	Airborne invasion of Burma, Mar. 1944
Bronx Shipment	Movement of atomic bombs to Tinian
Bu	Japanese plan for an offensive across the Chindwin River, Burma, late 1944
Buccaneer	Plan to take the Andaman Islands, 1943
Bunkum	RN recon landing on Sumatra, 23–24 Apr. 1944
Button	Major rear base on Espiritu Santo
Byproduct	Trobriand Islands Task Force
C	Japanese plan to invade India, Feb. 1944

Word	Code Name For
Cactus	Guadalcanal
Cannibal	Akyab Operation, Jan. 1945
Capital	Operations in Central Burma, June 1944–Mar. 1945
Carillon	Kwajalein
Cartwheel	Encirclement of Rabaul, Aug. 1943–mid-1944.
Cast	USN codebreaking team at Cavite, the Philippines, 1941–42; later, Frumel (see Negat, Hypo)
Catchpole	Eniwetok operation, Feb. 1944
Champion	Plan to invade Burma from the north (see Capital, Copilot)
Chervil	Fiji Islands
Chronicle	Trobriand Islands Operation, summer 1943
Clinch	Proposed operation against the lower part of the Kra Peninsula, Siam (see Bamboo)
Colleen	Occasional code name for Adm E. J. King
Collodion	Secretary of State E. R. Stimson
Copilot	Original name for Champion
Corollary	Shanghai
Coronet	Proposed invasion of Honshu, Mar. 1946
Crasher	Proposed Formosa-China Coast Operation, late 1944
Cricket	Malta Conference (see Argonaut)
Crossroads	Bikini nuclear weapons tests, July 1946
Cub	Medium USN base development unit (see Lion)
Cudgel	Operations in the Arakan, late 1943
Culverin	Plans to invade Sumatra and Malaya, 1944
Detachment	Iwo Jima operation, Feb. 1945
Downfall	Proposed invasion of Japan (see Olympic, Coronet)
Dowser	Rendova Island, the Solomons
Dracula	Plan to capture Rangoon from the sea, early 1944
Drake	Early proposal to bomb Japan from China
Dumbo	Allied program to rescue pilots downed at sea
Ebon	Espiritu Santo
Elkton	Northeastern New Guinea operations, mid-1943
Eureka	Teheran Conference, Nov. 1943
Excelsior	The Philippines
Fall River	Gili Gili, Milne Bay, Papua
Falsehood	Tinian

Word	Code Name For
Fantan	Fiji
Fat Boy	The Hiroshima atomic bomb
Ferdinand	Australian coastwatcher program
Filbert	Russell Islands
Firebreak	West Coast defensive plan against Japanese carrier raids, 1942–43
Flintlock	Marshall Islands operations, Jan.–Feb. 1944
Forager	Marianas operations, June–July 1944
Forerun	Zamboanga
Foresquare	The Panama Canal
Fourfold	Gen. G. C. Marshall
Frumel	USN codebreaking team, Australia, 1942–45 (see Cast)
Galahad	5307th CPU (Merrill's Marauders)
Galvanic	Gilbert Islands operation, Nov. 1943
Gastronomy	Schouten Islands
Gateway	The Marianas
General Lyon	King George VI
Glyptic	Soviet leader J. V. Stalin
Goodtime	Treasury Islands
Granite	Admiral Nimitz's operation plans for 1944, issued January, March (Granite I), and June (Granite II)
Granny	Manila
Gratitude	Third Fleet raid into the South China Sea, early 1945
Grew	Australia
Gymnast	A modification of Tarzan
HA Go	Japanese feint in the Arakan, Feb. 1944, to mask U Go
Hailstone	Truk Island raid, Feb. 1944
Halfterm	Manchukuo
Happy Valley	SACO HQ, near Chungking
Helen	Makin Island during Galvanic
Horror	Ulithi Atoll
Horse	Bututari Island, Tarawa
Hotfoot	Proposed carrier raid on Japan, Oct. 1944
Hypo	USN codebreaking team at Pearl Harbor (see Negat, Cast)
Hypocrite	Japan
I Go	Yamamoto's plan for Midway
Iceberg	Okinawa Operation, spring 1945
Ichi Go	"Operation One," Japanese offensive in China, mid–1944 onward
Incredible	Tarawa
Insurgent	Proposed Mindanao operation, Oct. 1944
Integer	Visayan Island, the Philippines

Word	Code Name For
Inwall	Gen. J. W. Stilwell
Ironclad	British occupation of Madagascar, Apr.–Sept. 1942
Ironhorse	Artificial harbor for Operation Coronet
Isolator	Proposed landing in southeastern China, late 1944
Jackboot	Attu Island
Jackfrost	Canada
Jacodet	Munda Island, the Solomons
Jeroboam	Wake Island
Ka Go	Japanese reinforcement of Guadalcanal, August 1942 (Battle of the Eastern Solomons)
Kan	Japanese plan to defend Burma from amphibious attack, 1944
KE	Evacuation operations for Guadalcanal, Feb. 1943, and Kiska, July 1943
Kilting	Harry S Truman
King	Plans for the liberation of the Philippines (e.g., King II, the Leyte operation, Oct. 1944)
KO Go	First phase of Ichi Go, Apr. 1944
Kon	Japanese plan to reinforce Biak, June 1944
Kourbash	Makin Island
Kutzu	Japanese defense plan for Kyushu and Shokaku
L	Prewar Japanese espionage ring run out of Mexico
Landcrab	Attu operation, May 1943
Lawlord	Jaluit Island, the Carolines
Lawmaking	Karafuto
Leadmine	Singapore
Leech	Sunda Straits
Leguminous	Plan to develop Okinawa as a base for Olympic
Little Boy	Alternative name for Thin Man
Longchop	Manus operation
Longsuit	Tarawa operation, within Galvanic, Nov. 1943
Love I-V	Phases in liberation of central Philippines, Dec. 1944–Apr. 1945
Lucius	Ho Chi Minh
Magic	US intelligence derived from Purple
Magnet	British plan for an offensive into Siam, if Japan entered that country, 1941
Magneto	Yalta Conference (see Argonaut)

Word	Code Name For
Mailfist	Tentative plan to capture Singapore, fall 1945
Mainyard	Guadalcanal, after its capture
Majestic	Alternative name for Olympic, early Aug. 1945
Manhattan Project	Nuclear weapons research program
Manhole	Hawaii
Matterhorn	B-29 missions to Japan from China
Mike I-VII	Phases of Luzon operation, Jan. 1945
Millet	RAF raids in Southeast Asia as a diversion for the Leyte operation, Oct. 1944
Miss Kimiko	Japanese code name for President Roosevelt
Miss Umeko	Japanese code name for Cordell Hull
MO	Japanese plan to occupy Port Moresby and Guadalcanal, which led to the Battle of the Coral Sea, May 1942
Montclair	Operations in SW Pacific Theater, 1945
Mr. P	Churchill, during the Casablanca Conference
Musketeer	Overall plan for the liberation of the Philippines, Oct. 1944 onward
Mythology	Canton Island
Negat	USN codebreaking team in Washington (see Cast, Hypo)
Nutcracker	Panama Canal
Nutpine	Corregidor
Oboe	Netherlands Indies Operations, Apr.–June 1945
Octagon	Quebec Conference, Sept. 1944
Olympic	Proposed invasion of Kyushu, Nov. 1945
Orange	US series of prewar plans for war with Japan
Oxygen	Cebu Island, the Philippines
Pastel	Deception plan for Operation Olympic
Peanut	Chiang Kai-shek (not a nickname, as often said)
Peon	Samoa
Petersburg	Allied contingency plan to abandon New Guinea, should the Japanese secure the Solomons, 1942
Pigstick	Proposed landing on the Magu Peninsula, Burma
Postern	Lae-Salamaua Operation, Papua, 1943
Privilege	Eniwetok, the Carolines
Propulsion	Nagasaki
Purple	Top Japanese code broken by the United States before the war
Quadrant	Quebec Conference, Aug. 1943

Word	Code Name For
Quinine	Arawe, New Britain
Rainbow	Chinese Salween offensive, Burma, 1943–44
Rainbow I-V	US prewar plans for war
Ravenous	Proposed operation in northern Burma, fall 1943
Reckless	Hollandia operation, New Guinea, Apr. 1944
Recuperate	Ellice Islands
Red	US designation for an early Japanese naval code
Reno I-V	Preliminary proposals for the liberation of the Philippines, Feb. 1943–June 1944
RO Go	Japanese reinforcement of Rabaul with carrier aircraft, Oct.–Nov. 1943
Roger	Proposed operations against the Kra Peninsula
Romulus	Plans to occupy the Arakan and Akyab, Dec. 1944
Roses	Efate
Rover	Eleanor Roosevelt
Ruth	Siamese regent, Nai Pridi Bhanangang
San Antonio	B-29 missions against Tokyo from the Marianas
Sawbuck	Stalin
Schoolboy	Lae, Papua-New Guinea
Schoolgirl	Palau Islands
Screwdriver I-II	Landings in the Arakan, Nov. 1944
Seclusion	Bonin Islands
Seizure	Bikini Atoll
Sextant	Cairo Conference
Sho Go	"Operation Victory," the Japanese defense plans for the Philippines (Sho-1), Formosa (Sho-2), and the Home Islands (Sho-3, etc.), mid- to late 1944; Sho-1 culminated in Leyte Gulf
Shrimp	Saigon
Silverplate	Training of B-29 crews to drop the atomic bomb
Silversand	Mindanao; also Silverware
Snapshot	USN reconnaissance operations in the western Carolines, July 1944
Snow White	Madam Chiang
Spider	Sasebo

Word	Code Name For
Stalemate I-II	Palau operation, Sep.–Oct. 1944: I, Anguar; II, Peleliu
Starlit	Iwo Jima
Starvation	B-29 mining of Japanese waters, from March 1945 on
Steamroller	Manila
Stepsister	Repatriation of Australian troops from the Middle East, late 1941 to early 1942
Stevedore	Guam
Straightline	Wadke Operation, Apr. 1944
Suzu	Japanese defense plan for the Visayas and Mindanao, the Philippines, 1944–1945
Symbol	Casablanca Conference
Talon	Amphibious operations against Akyab, Jan. 1945
Tarzan	Advance on Indow-Katha area, Burma
Ten Go	Japanese plan for the defense of the Home Islands, 1944–45
Ten Ichi	Yamato's "suicide" mission, Apr. 1945
Terminal	Potsdam Conference, July 1945
Thin Man	Nagasaki atomic bomb (see Little Boy)
Thorn	Rabaul
Thunder	Chindit Operations in Burma, from March 1944
Thursday	Allied special warfare operations in Burma, 1944
TIGAR 1C	Ledo Road project
Tiger Force	RAF heavy bomber force for the Pacific, 1946
TO	Japanese Navy plan for the seaward defense of the Home Islands, mid-1944
Toenails	New Georgia Operation, mid-1943
TOGO	Second phase of Ichi Go, from May 1944
Tolstoy	Churchill-Stalin summit, Oct. 1944
Trident	Washington Conference, May 1943
U Go	Japanese Imphal Offensive, Mar. 1944
Vanguard	Similar to Dracula
Z	Japanese plan for a naval clash in the central Pacific in early 1944; evolved into A Go
Zero Zero	Adm Chester W. Nimitz
Zipper	British plan for Malaya offensive, late 1945

RECOMMENDED READING AND REFERENCES

This does not purport to be an exhaustive, or even extensive bibliography of materials on the Pacific War. There are literally thousands of books on the subject, and even a work the size of the present one would not be enough to cover items in English alone. However, some works are more important, or at least more unusual, than others, and make for particularly rewarding reading. We have omitted biographies, memoirs, most treatments of individual battles and campaigns, and "technoporn," to focus on broader topics, darker corners, and unusual perspectives.

Most of the works listed here have extensive bibliographies of their own.

Abbazia, Patrick, *Mr. Roosevelt's Navy* (Annapolis: Naval Institute Press, 1975).

Albee, Parker Bishop, Jr., and Freeman, Keller Cushing, *Shadow of Suribachi: Raising the Flag on Iwo Jima* (Westport, Conn. Greenwood: 1995).

Alden, John D., *The Fleet Submarine in the U.S. Navy* (Annapolis: Naval Institute Press, 1979).

———, *U.S. Submarine Attacks During World War II* (Annapolis: Naval Institute Press, 1989). Includes all US attacks, worldwide, as far as can be determined, whether successful or not, plus British and Dutch attacks in the Pacific Theater.

Allen, Louis, *The End of the War in Asia* (London: Beekman, 1976). An excellent summary treatment of the final phase of the war in India, Burma, Siam, Indo-China, the Netherlands East Indies, China, and Korea, stressing political developments.

Allen, Thomas B., and Polmar, Norman, *Code-Name Downfall: The Secret Plan to Invade Japan and Why Truman Dropped the Bomb* (New York: Simon and Schuster, 1995).

Angelucci, Enzo, *The American Fighter* (New York: Outlet, 1987).

Armstrong, Anne, *Unconditional Surrender: The Impact of the Casablanca Policy Upon World War II* (Westport, Conn.: Greenwood, 1974).

Australia in the Second World War (Canberra: Australian War Memorial, 1957–63). A very good, very detailed work, in five series: Army, Navy, Air Force, Medical, and Civil. The operational volumes for the Pacific War are:

Series I (Army): IV, *The Japanese Thrust*, by Lionel Wigmore; V, *Southwest Pacific Area: Kokoda to Wau*, by Dudley McCarthy; VI, *The New Guinea Offensive*, by David Dexter; VII, *The Final Campaigns*, by Gavin Long.

Series II (Navy): II, *The Royal Australian Navy, 1942–1945*, by G. Herman Gill.

Series III (Air): II, *Air War Against Japan, 1943–1945*, by George Odgers.

Baclagon, Uladrico S., *Military History of the Philippines* (Manila: St. Mary's, 1975). A very good treatment of a neglected subject.

Barnett, Corelli, *Engage the Enemy More Closely: The Royal Navy in the Second World War* (New York: W. W. Norton, 1991).

Barnhart, Michael A., *Japan Prepares for Total War: The Search for Economic Security, 1919–1941* (Ithaca, N.Y.: Cornell University Press, 1987).

Beck, John Jacob, *MacArthur and Wainwright: Surrender of the Philippines* (Albuquerque: University of New Mexico Press, 1974).

Becton, F. Julian, *The Ship That Would Not Die* (Englewood Cliffs, N.J.: Prentice Hall, 1980). An account of the USS *Laffey* and her struggle against the kamikaze, by her skipper.

Bergamini, David, *Japan's Imperial Conspiracy* (New York: William Morrow, 1971). A controversial book, not without its faults, but one that raises important questions about the role of Hirohito that have never been properly answered.

Blair, Clay, Jr., *Silent Victory: The U.S. Submarine War Against Japan* (Philadelphia: Lippincott, 1975).

Borf, Dorothy, and Okamoto, Shumpei, eds., *Pearl Harbor as History: Japanese-American Relations, 1931–1941* (New York: Columbia University Press, 1973). A multifaceted look at a complex subject.

Boyd, Carl, *Hitler's Japanese Confidant: General Oshima Hiroshi and MAGIC Intelligence, 1941–1945* (Lawrence, K.: University Press of Kansas, 1993). Hitler told Hiroshi, and Hiroshi radioed the information to Tokyo, and courtesy of MAGIC, Pearl Harbor.

Boyd, Carl, and Yoshida, Akihiko, *The Japanese Submarine Force and World War II* (Annapolis: Naval Institute Press, 1995).

Boyington, Gregory, *Baa, Baa, Black Sheep* (New York: Bantam, 1990).

Brice, Martin, *Axis Blockade Runners of World War II* (Annapolis: Naval Institute Press, 1981). Unsatisfactory, but the only work available on the subject.

Brown, Robert, *Warship Losses of World War Two* (Annapolis: Naval Institute Press, 1995). A valuable compendium of all warship losses during the war, including those of neutrals. In addition to the basic chronological presentation of ship losses, with location, circumstances, and often extensive explanatory notes, there are statistical tables and sometimes extensive analysis of the causes of ship loss. Very handy for the serious student of World War II at sea.

Butow, Robert J., *Japan's Decision to Surrender* (Stanford: Stanford University Press, 1954).

———, *Tojo and the Coming of the War* (Stanford: Stanford University Press, 1961).

Carpenter, Dorr, and Polmar, Norman, *Submarines of the Imperial Japanese Navy* (Annapolis: Naval Institute Press, 1986).

Chesneua, Roger, *Aircraft Carriers of the World, 1914 to the Present: An Illustrated Encyclopedia* (Annapolis: Naval Institute Press, 1984).

Ch'i, Hsi-Sheng, *Nationalist China at War* (Ann Arbor: University of Michigan Press, 1982). The best short account of the Sino-Japanese War, with a good balance of political, diplomatic, military, and economic treatment.

Collier, Basil, *The War in the Far East, 1941–1945* (New York: Heineman, 1969).

Collins, Donald E., *Native American Aliens: Disloyalty and the Renunciation of Citizenship by Japanese-Americans during World War II* (Westport, Conn.: Greenwood, 1985).

Conway's All the World's Fighting Ships, 1922–1946 (Annapolis: Naval Institute Press, 1980).

Cook, Charles, *The Battle of Cape Esperance: Encounter at Guadalcanal* (Annapolis: Naval Institute Press, 1968).

Cook, Haruko Taya, and Cook, Theodore F., *Japan at War: An Oral History* (New York: The New Press, 1992).

Corbett, P. Scott, *Quiet Passages: The Exchange of Civilians between the United States and Japan during the Second World War* (Kent, Ohio: Kent State University Press, 1987).

Couffer, Jack, *Bat Bomb* (Austin: University of Texas Press, 1992). Worth reading.

Craven, Wesley E., and Cate, James L., eds., *The Army Air Forces in World War II*, 7 vols. (Chicago: University of Chicago Press, 1948–55).

Cressman, Robert J., *"A Magnificent Fight"; The Battle for Wake Island* (Annapolis: Naval Institute Press, 1995).

Crost, Lyn, *Honor by Fire: Japanese Americans at War in Europe and the Pacific* (Novato, Calif.: Presidio Press, 1994).

Daws, Gavin, *Prisoners of the Japanese* (New York: William Morrow, 1995).

Department of the Army, *Army Battle Casualties and Nonbattle Deaths in World War II, Final Report* (Washington: DA, 1953).

Door, Robert F., *U.S. Bombers of World War II* (London: Ian Alan, 1989).

Dorrance, William H., *Fort Kamehameha: The Story of the Harbor Defense of Pearl Harbor* (Shippensburg, Pa.: White Mane, 1993).

Dower, John W., *War Without Mercy: Race and Power in the Pacific War* (New York: Pantheon, 1986). Overstates the case, and neglects Japanese racism toward other Asians and their response in kind.

Drea, Edward J., *MacArthur's Ultra: Codebreaking and the War Against Japan, 1942–1945* (Lawrence, K.: University Press of Kansas, 1992).

Dull, Paul S., *A Battle History of the Imperial Japanese Navy, 1941–1945* (Annapolis: Naval Institute Press, 1978).

Dunnigan, James F., *How to Make War*, 3rd ed. (New York: William Morrow, 1993). Focuses on the theory and practice of warfare in the late 20th century, but contains much that is useful in helping to understand the conduct of the Second World War as well.

Dunnigan, James F., and Nofi, Albert A., *Dirty Little Secrets of World War II* (New York: William Morrow, 1994).

———, *Shooting Blanks: Warmaking that Doesn't Work* (New York: William Morrow, 1991).

———, *Victory and Deceit: Dirty Tricks at War* (New York: William Morrow, 1995).

———, *Victory at Sea: World War II in the Pacific* (New York: William Morrow, 1995).

DuPuy, Trevor N., *Great Battles of the Eastern Front, 1941–1945* New York: Macmillan, 1982).

———. *Numbers, Predictions, and War* (Indianapolis: Bobbs, Merrill 1978). A discussion of the Quantified Judgment Model, an attempt to develop a mathematical model capable of comparing the military capabilities of various military forces, based on the experience of several dozen battles during the Second World War.

Duus, Masayo, *Tokyo Rose: Orphan of the Pacific War* (New York/Tokyo: Kodansha, 1979).

Dwyer, John B., *Seaborne Deception: The History of U.S. Beach Jumpers* (New York: Greenwood, 1992). US "frogman" operations.

Eastman, Lloyd E., "Nationalist China during the Sino-Japanese War, 1937–1945," in *The Cambridge History of China* (Cambridge: Cambridge University Press, 1986), vol. 13, pt. 2.

Edoin, Hoito, *The Night Tokyo Burned* (New York: St. Martin's, 1987).

Ellis, John, *World War II, A Statistical Survey: Essential Facts and Figures for All the Combatants* (New York: Facts On File, 1993).

Feis, Herbert, *The Atomic Bomb and the End of World War II* (Princeton: Princeton University Press, 1965). Revised and expanded version of his *Japan Subdued: The Atomic Bomb and the end of the War* (Princeton: Princeton University Press, 1961).

Feldt, Eric A., *The Coastwatchers* (Oxford: Oxford University Press, 1959).

Ford, Daniel, *Flying Tigers* (Washington: Smithsonian, 1991).

Fox, Stephen, *The Unknown Internment: An Oral History of the Relocation of Italian-Americans During World War II* (Boston: Macmillan, 1990).

Francillon, Rene J., *Japanese Aircraft of the Pacific War* (Annapolis: Naval Institute Press, 1987).

Frank, Richard B., *Guadalcanal* (New York: Random House, 1990).

Friedman, Norman, *Submarine Design and Development* (Annapolis: Naval Institute Press, 1984).

———, *United States Aircraft Carriers: An Illustrated Design History* (Annapolis: Naval Institute Press, 1983).

————, *United States Battleships: An Illustrated Design History* (Annapolis: Naval Institute Press, 1988).

————, *United States Destroyers: An Illustrated Design History* (Annapolis: Naval Institute Press, 1982).

Fujita, Frank, Jr., *Foo: A Japanese-American Prisoner of the Rising Sun* (Dexter, Tex.: University of North Texas Press, 1993).

Fukui, Shizuo, *Japanese Naval Vessels at the End of the War* (Annopolis: Naval Institute Press, 1992).

Fuller, Richard, *Shokan: Hirohito's Samurai, Leaders of the Japanese Armed Forces, 1926–1945* (London: Arms and Armour Press, 1992). Though limited, this is the only biographical guide to the Japanese military available in English.

Furer, Julius A., *Administration of the Navy Department* (Washington: Government Printing Office, 1959).

Gailey, Harry A., *Bougainville, 1943–1945: The Forgotten Campaign* (Lexington, Ky.: University Press of Kentucky, 1991).

Garfield, Brian, *The Thousand Mile War* (Fairbanks: University of Alaska Press, 1995).

Garzke, William H., Jr., and Dulin, Robert O., Jr., *Battleships: Allied Battleships in World War II* (Annapolis: Naval Institute Press, 1980).

————, *Battleships: Axis and Neutral Battleships in World War II* (Annapolis: Naval Institute Press, 1985).

————, *Battleships: United States Battleships in World War II* (Annapolis: Naval Institute Press, 1976).

Giangreco, D. M., "Casualty Projections for the U.S. Invasion of Japan, 1945–1946: Planning and Policy Implications," *Journal of Military History* 61, no. 3 (June 1997), pp. 521–81.

Glantz, David, *August Storm: The Soviet 1945 Strategic Offensive in Manchuria* (Ft. Leavenworth: Combat Studies Institute, 1983).

Goldstein, Donald M., and Dillon, Katherine V., eds., *The Pearl Harbor Papers: Inside the Japanese Plans* (New York: Viking, 1993).

Greenberg, Eli, and associates, *The Ineffective Soldier: Lessons for Management and the Nation*, 3 vols. (Westport Conn.: Greenwood, 1975). Analyzes where and how the U.S. Armed Forces mismanaged its manpower, one volume is subtitled *The Lost Divisions*.

Grover, David H., *U.S. Army Ships and Watercraft of World War II* (Annapolis: Naval Institute Press, 1987).

Hallas, James H., *The Devil's Anvil: The Assault on Peleliu* (Westport, Conn.: Praeger, 1994).

————, *Killing Ground on Okinawa: The Battle for Sugar Loaf Hill* (Westport, Conn.: Praeger, 1996).

Handbook on Japanese Military Forces (London: Greenhill, 1991). Originally published by the US War Department during World War II, this should be used with that reservation in mind. A valuable source nonetheless.

Hara, Tameichi, Saito, Fred, and Pineau, Roger, *Japanese Destroyer Captain* (New York: Ballantine, 1983).

Harries, Merion, and Harries, Susie, *Soldiers of the Sun: The Rise and Fall of the Japanese Imperial Army* (New York: Random House, 1991). Although not entirely successful as a history of the Imperial Army, this comes into its own in a series of chapters that analyze the doctrine, character, equipment, and philosophy of the Japanese Army in the period of World War II.

Harrington, Joseph D., *Yankee Samurai: The Secret Role of Nisei in America's Pacific Victory* (Detroit: Nicholas Books, 1979).

Hashimoto, Mochitasura, *Sunk!* (New York: Ballantine, 1954).

Hayashi, Saburo, and Coox, Alvin D., *Kogun: The Japanese Army in the Pacific War* (Westport, Conn: Greenwood, 1979).

Heinl, Robert Debs, Jr., *Soldiers of the Sea: The United States Marine Corps, 1775–1962* (Annapolis: Naval Institute Press, 1962).

Heinl, Robert Debs, Jr., and Crown, John A., *The Marshalls: Increasing the Tempo* (Washington: US MC, 1954).

Hezlet, Arthur, R. *Aircraft and Sea Power* (New York: Stein and Day, 1970).

——, *Electronics and Sea Power.* (New York: Stein and Day, 1975).

——, *Submarines and Sea Power* (New York: Stein and Day, 1972).

Hicks, George, *The Comfort Women: Japan's Brutal Regime of Enforced Prostitution in the Second World War* (New York: W. W. Norton, 1995).

History of United States Marine Corps Operations in World War II (Washington: Government Printing Office,1956–1971): I, *Pearl Harbor to Guadalcanal*, by Frank O. Hugh, Verle E. Ludwig, and Henry I Shaw; II, *The Isolation of Rabaul*, by Henry I. Shaw, Jr., and Douglas T. Kim; III, *The Central Pacific Drive*, by Henry I. Shaw, Jr., Bernard C. Nalty, and Edwin J. Turnblodh; IV, *Western Pacific Operations*, by George W. Garond and Truman R. Strobridge; V, *Victory and Occupation*, by Benis M. Frank and Henry I. Shaw, Jr.

Hough, Richard, *The Hunting of Force Z* (London: Collins, 1963).

Howarth, Stephen, *To Shining Sea* (New York: Random House, 1991).

Hoyt, Edwin P., *Hirohito: The Emperor and the Man* (Westport, Conn.: Bergin and Garvey, 1992).

——, *Japan's War: The Great Pacific Conflict, 1853–1952* (New York: McGraw-Hill, 1986).

——, *The Last Kamikaze: The Story of Admiral Matome Ugaki* (Westport: Praeger, 1993).

Hutchison, Kevin Don, *World War II in the North Pacific: Chronology and Fact Book* (Westport, Conn.: Greenwood, 1994).

Ienaga, Saburo, *The Pacific War: World War II and the Japanese, 1931–1945*, tr. Frank Baldwin (New York: Random House, 1978).

Iriye, Akira, "Japanese Aggression and China's International Position, 1931–1945," in *The Cambridge History of China* (Cambridge: Cambridge University Press, 1986), vol. 13, pt. 2.

Irokawa, Daikichi, *The Age of Hirohito: In Search of Modern Japan*, tr. Mikiso Hano (New York: The Free Press, 1995).

Isely, Jeter A., and Crowl, Philip A. *The U.S. Marines and Amphibious War* (Princeton: Princeton University Press, 1951).

Ito, Masanori, with Roger Pineau, *The End of the Imperial Japanese Navy*, tr. Andrew Y. Kuroda and Roger Pineau (Westport, Conn.: Greenwood, 1984).

Janes Encyclopedia of Aviation (London: Janes, 1980).

Jentschura, Hansgeorg, Jung, Dieter, and Michel, Peter, *Warships of the Imperial Japanese Navy, 1869–1945*, tr. Anthony Preston and J. D. Brown (Annapolis: Naval Institute Press, 1992).

Kerr, E. Bartlett, *Flames Over Tokyo* (New York: Donald I. Fine, 1991).

——., *Surrender and Survival: The Experience of American POWs in the Pacific, 1941–1945* (New York: William Morrow, 1985).

Kirby, Stanley Woodburn, *The United Kingdom Military Series: The War Against Japan*, 5 vols. (London: HMSO, 1957–70).

Klehr, Harvey, and Radosh, Ronald, *The Amerasia Spy Case: Prelude to McCarthyism* (Chapel Hill, N.C.: University of North Carolina Press, 1996).

Koburger, Charles W., Jr., *Pacific Turning Point: The Solomons Campaign, 1942–1943* (Westport, Conn.: Praeger, 1995).

Kurzman, Dan, *Left to Die: The Tragedy of the* USS *Juneau* (New York: Pocket Books, 1994).

Lane, Frederic, *Ships for Victory: A History of Shipbuilding Under the U.S. Maritime Commission in World War II* (Baltimore: Johns Hopkins, 1950).

Larrabee, Eric, *Commander in Chief: Franklin Delano Roosevelt, His Lieutenants, and Their War* (New York: Simon and Schuster, 1987). The handiest treatment of the principal players in the US war effort during World War II, with excellent, and sometimes groundbreaking, word portraits of FDR, and his commanders, including MacArthur, Nimitz, and all the rest.

Larsen, C. Kay, " 'Till I Come Marching Home": A Brief History of American Women in World War II (Pasadena, Maryland: The Minerva Center, 1996).

Leasor, James, Boarding Party: The Last Action of the Calcutta Light Horse (Annopolis: Naval Institute Press, 1995).

Lewin, Ronald, The American Magic: Codes, Ciphers and the Defeat of Japan. (New York: Viking, 1982).

Liu, Frederick Fu (Liu Chih-pu), A Military History of Modern China, 1924–1947 (Princeton: Princeton University Press, 1956). Despite its age, still the best treatment of the subject.

Long, Gavin, The Six Years War: A Concise History of Australia in the 1939–1945 War (Canberra: Australian War Memorial, 1973). An excellent one-volume treatment of the Australian contribution to the war.

Lord, Walter, Lonely Vigil: Coastwatchers of the Solomons (New York: Viking, 1977). Although not entirely accurate, this remains the most available treatment of the subject.

Lorelli, John A., The Battle of the Komandorski Islands, March 1943 (Annapolis: Naval Institute Press, 1984).

Lott, Arnold S., Most Dangerous Sea: A History of Mine Warfare (Annapolis: Naval Institute Press, 1959).

MacGregor, Morris J., Jr., Integration of the Armed Forces, 1940–1965 (Washington: Department of Defense, 1981).

MacIntyre, David, The Battle for the Pacific (London: Batsford, 1966).

Marder, Arthur J., Jacobsen, Mark, and Horsfield, John, Old Friends, New Enemies: The Royal Navy and the Imperial Japanese Navy, 2 vols. (Oxford: Oxford University Press, 1990).

Masters, John, Bugles and a Tiger (New York: Viking, 1956).

———, The Road Past Mandalay (New York: Bantam, 1961). Perhaps the best book ever written about men and war. Period.

Mayo, Lida, Bloody Buna (Garden City, N.Y.: Doubleday, 1974).

Mikesh, Robert C., Japan's World War II Balloon Bomb Attack on North America (Washington: Smithsonian Institute Press, 1973).

Miller, Edward S., War Plan Orange: The U.S. Strategy to Defeat Japan, 1897–1945 (Annapolis: Naval Institute Press, 1991). Presents a superbly detailed analysis of US planning for a war with Japan, with an examination of the personalities involved and the ways in which changing world events influenced such planning; plus a look at the ways in which the various prewar plans influenced the actual development of US strategy in the Pacific War.

Millett, Allan Reid, and Murray, Williamson, eds., Military Effectiveness, 3 vols. (New York: Routledge, Chapman & Hall, 1988). A collection of essays by noted specialists on the military capabilities and limitations of the armed forces of each of the great powers during World War I, the interwar period, and World War II, with many valuable insights and much food for thought. Their Calculations: Net Assessment and the Coming of World War II (New York: Allan and Unwin, 1992) contains a series of essays on how each of the great powers dealt with the problem of evaluating the military capabilities and limitations of their opponents.

Morison, Samuel Eliot, History of United States Naval Operations in World War II, 15 vols. (Boston: Little, Brown, 1947–62). The volumes of particular interest to the Pacific War are: III, The Rising Sun in the Pacific, 1931–April 1942; IV, Coral Sea, Midway, and Submarine Actions, May 1942–August 1942; V, The Struggle for Guadalcanal, August 1942–February 1943; VI, Breaking the Bismarcks Barrier, 22 July 1942–1 May 1944; VII, Aleutians, Gilberts, and Marshalls, June 1942–April 1944; VIII, New Guinea and the Marianas, March 1944–August 1944; XII, Leyte, June 1944–January 1945; XIII, The Liberation of the Philippines: Luzon, Mindanao, the Visayas, 1944–1945; and XIV, Victory in the Pa-

cific, 1945. For those short of the leisure to read 15 volumes, Morison's *The Two Ocean War* (Boston: Little Brown, 1963) presents a shorter treatment of the subject. On Morison himself, see the entry in the main text.

Nelson, Dennis D., *The Integration of the Negro into the United States Navy* (New York: Ferrar-Strauss, 1982).

Niven, John, *The American President Line and Its Forebears, 1848–1984* (Newark, Del.: University of Delaware Press, 1987).

O'Connell, Robert L., *Sacred Vessels* (New York: Westview Press, 1991).

Ogburn, Charlton, Jr., *The Marauders* (New York: William Morrow, 1982).

Overy, R. J., *The Air War, 1939–1945* (New York: Stein and Day, 1981). A critical analytic look at the nature of the war in the air, with many valuable perspectives, such as the importance not merely of aircraft production, but also of the production of spare parts. One of the most incisive thinkers on the war, Overy's most recent volume, *Why the Allies Won* (New York: W. W. Norton, 1996), takes some startling positions on the causes of the Allied victory, an outcome that, as he effectively points out, was by no means as obvious in 1941–42 as it seems today.

Parillo, Mark P., *The Japanese Merchant Marine in World War II* (Annapolis: Naval Institute Press, 1993).

Pelz, Stephen E., *Race to Pearl Harbor: The Failure of the Second London Naval Conference and the Onset of World War II* (Cambridge, Mass.: Harvard University Press, 1974).

Perret, Geoffrey, *There's a War to Be Won: The United States Army in World War II* (New York: Ballantine, 1992). Presents a pretty good look at the US Army in the late 1930s and 1940s, weaving together the diverse trends in doctrine, organization, equipment, and planning that ultimately led to the army with which the United States fought World War II, while looking into everything from the personalities of the army's leaders, problems and surprises in weapons development, racial policies, the medical corps, the famous maneuvers of 1940–41, and, of course, the experience of battle.

Perry, Hamilton D., *The Panay Incident* (New York: Macmillan, 1969).

Polmar, Norman, and Allen, Thomas B., *America at War, 1941–1945* (New York: Random House, 1991).

Prados, John, *Combined Fleet Decoded: The Secret History of American Intelligence and the Japanese Navy in World War II* (New York: Random House, 1995). Takes a look at US codebreaking activities as they influenced the war against Japan, covering much new ground. Moreover, although the focus of the work is on cryptography, there is much material on other forms of intelligence gathering as well.

Prange, Gordon R., Goldstein, Donald M., and Dillon, Katherine V., *At Dawn We Slept* (New York: Viking, 1981).

———, *Miracle At Midway* (New York: Viking, 1982).

———, *Pearl Harbor: The Verdict of History* (New York: Viking, 1986).

———, *Target Tokyo: The Story of the Sorge Spy Ring* (New York: Viking, 1984).

At Dawn We Slept and *Pearl Harbor* provide the most detailed and exhaustive inquiry into the American disaster at Pearl Harbor, along with Goldstein and Dillon's *The Pearl Harbor Papers Inside the Japanese Plans*. Going to considerable lengths to examine the numerous conspiracy theories (some of which—such as, the attack was actually carried out by British pilots operating from a secret base on one of the other Hawaiian islands as a result of a deal between Roosevelt and Churchill—are remarkable indeed), the authors conclude that "There is enough blame for everyone," and not a little credit for the Japanese. *Miracle at Midway* carries the story forward to the series of Japanese blunders and American successes that led to the Japanese disaster just seven months later, while *Target Tokyo* looks at that intriguing aspect of the Pacific War.

Prefer, Nathan, *MacArthur's New Guinea Campaign: March–August 1944* (Conshohocken, Pa.: Combined Publishing, 1995).

Rasor, Eugene L., *General Douglas MacArthur, 1880–1964: Historiography and Annotated Bibliography* (Westport, Conn.: Greenwood, 1994).

Ravuvu, Asesela, *Fijians at War* (Suva: Institute of Pacific Studies, 1974).

Ready, J. Lee, *Forgotten Allies* (New York: McFarland, 1985). Takes an in-depth look at the role in the war of the minor powers and the numerous resistance movements, with one volume for the war against Germany and the other that against Japan. A valuable and very neglected book.

Reit, Seymour, *Masquerade: The Amazing Camouflage Deceptions of World War II* (New York: Dutton, 1978).

Reynolds, Clark G., *The Fast Carriers* (Annapolis: Naval Institute Press, 1992). Although relatively old (originally published in 1962), and rather focused on the American point of view, still the best overall treatment of the carrier war in the Pacific.

Rigelman, Harold, *Caves of Biak: An American Officer's Experience In the Southwest Pacific* (New York: Dial, 1955). Up close, and very personal.

Roscoe, Theodore, *On the Seas and in the Skies: A History of the U.S. Navy's Air Power* (New York: Hawthorne, 1970).

———, *United States Destroyer Operations in World War II* (Annapolis: Naval Institute Press, 1953).

———, *United States Submarine Operations in World War II* (Annapolis: Naval Institute Press, 1949).

Roskill, S. W., *The United Kingdom Military Series: The War At Sea, 1939–1945* Nashville: Battery Press, 1994.

———, *White Ensign: The British Navy in World War II* (Annapolis: Naval Institute Press, 1960).

Ruffner, Frederick G., Jr., and Thomas, Robert C., eds., *The Codenames Dictionary* (Detroit: Gale, 1963). A good start.

Salazar, Generoso P., Reyes, Fernando R., and Nuval, Leonardo Q., *Defense, Defeat, and Defiance:* *World War II in the Philippines* (Manila: Veterans Federation of the Philippines, 1993). A somewhat disorganized but very detailed treatment of the war in the Philippines, with emphasis on the guerrilla resistance.

Seagrave, Sterling, *The Soong Dynasty* (New York: HarperCollins, 1986).

Sherrod, Robert, *History of Marine Corps Aviation in WWII* (Baltimore: Nautical and Naval, 1987).

Sigal, Leon, *Fighting to the Finish: The Politics of War Termination in the United States and Japan, 1945* (Ithaca, N.Y.: Cornell University Press, 1988).

Sinclair, Thomas, *To Find a Path: The Life and Times of the Royal Pacific Islands Regiment*, 2 vols. (Brisbane: Boolarong Publications, 1990).

Skates, John Ray, *The Invasion of Japan: Alternative to the Bomb* (Columbia, S.C.: University of South Carolina 1994). The most complete treatment of Allied and Japanese preparations for an invasion of Japan. Very detailed, and with a careful analysis of casualty predictions.

Smith, Page, *Democracy on Trial: The Japanese-American Evacuation and Relocation in World War II* (New York: Simon and Schuster, 1995).

Spector, Ronald H., *Eagle Against the Sun: The American War with Japan* (New York: Random House, 1985).

Stanton, Shelby L., *Order of Battle, U.S. Army, World War II* (Novato, Calif.: Presidio, 1984). Everything you ever wanted to know about the organization of the US Army in the war. And more.

Stephen, John J., *Hawaii under the Rising Sun: Japan's Plans for Conquest after Pearl Harbor* (Honolulu: University of Hawaii Press, 1984).

Stone, James, ed., *Crisis Fleeting: Original Reports on Military Medicine in India and Burma in the Second World War* (Washington: Government Printing Office, 1969).

Stouffer, Samuel A., et al., *The American Soldier: Studies in Social Psychology in World War II* (Princeton: Princeton University Press, 1949). Summarizes the army's massive series of surveys of the common soldier's view on everything from army chow to race relations to the nature of the enemy. The volumes are subtitled: *Adjustment During Army Life, Combat and Its Aftermath, Experiments in Mass Communication,* and *Measurement and Prediction.*

Stratton, Roy O., *SACO: The Rice Paddy Navy* (Pleasantville, N.Y.: C.S. Palmer, 1950).

Tokayer, Marvin, *The Fugu Plan: The Untold Story of the Japanese and the Jews During World War II* (New York: Grosset and Dunlop, 1996).

Trota, Ricardo Jose, *The Philippine Army, 1935–1942* (Manila: Ateneo de Manila, 1992). A short, but valuable look at the organization and history of this much neglected force.

Tuchman, Barbara, *Stilwell and the American Experience in China, 1911–1945* (New York: Macmillan, 1970).

The United States Army in World War II (Washington: Government Printing Office, 1947–). The official account of the US Army in the war is probably the best official history ever written, running to about 80 volumes thus far (excluding the clinical medical history, which has been published separately in about 20 additional volumes). This is an often highly detailed account of how the war was organized, supplied, and fought. While the operational volumes are literate, well reasoned, critical, and worth reading, the really good stuff is in the technical volumes, on matters from the procurement of ammunition and aircraft to providing boots and bread for the troops. No other major-power official history comes even close to the objectivity, scholarship, and readability of this series.

The United States Strategic Bombing Survey (Washington: USSBS, 1945–1949). A 320-volume look at the war, focusing on the influence of strategic bombing, with many valuable insights.

Van Der Rhoer, E., *Deadly Magic* (New York: Time-Life, 1978).

Van der Vat, Dan, *The Pacific Campaign: World War II, the U.S.-Japanese Naval War, 1941–1945* (New York: Touchstone, 1991).

Van Slyle, Lyman, "The Chinese Communist Movement during the Sino-Japanese War, 1937–1945," in *The Cambridge History of China* (Cambridge: Cambridge University Press, 1986), vol. 13, pt. 2.

Warship International, a quarterly published for many years now by the International Naval Research Organization (5905 Reinwood Dr., Toledo, OH, 43613), is an extraordinary source of detailed historical, technical, and operational information about fighting ships, with frequent articles, letters, and reviews related to the naval war in the Pacific, marred only by lack of an index.

Webber, Bert, *Retaliation: Japanese Attacks and Allied Countermeasures on the Pacific Coast in World War II* (Corvallis, Oreg.: Oregon State University Press, 1975).

———, *Silent Siege: Japanese Attacks Against North America in World War II* (Fairfield, Wash.: Webb Research Group, 1983).

White, Geoffrey M., and Lindstrom, Lamont, eds., *The Pacific Theater: Island Representations of World War II* (Honolulu: University of Hawaii Press, 1989). For most of the Pacific islands, this is the best treatment of the effects of the war on the local peoples.

Whitman, John W., *Bataan: Our Last Ditch* (New York: Hippocrene, 1990).

Wilcox, Robert K., *Japan's Secret War.* (New York: Marlowe, 1975).

Y'Blood, William T., *Little Giants: Escort Carriers at War* (Annapolis: Naval Institute Press, 1987).

Yoshimura, Akira, *Zero Fighter*, tr. Retsu Kaiho and Michael Gregson (Westport, Conn.: Praeger, 1996).

Cyberography: World Wide Web Sites of Interest

Material dealing with World War II in general and the Pacific War in particular is beginning to become available online. The sites noted below are of special interest. Be warned that World Wide Web sites have a tendency to appear and disappear with some frequency, but the list on page 751

shows that the information you may want is out
there. All you have to do is look.

Sites of Special Interest

Bibliography:	http://www.sonic.net/~bstone
Armies:	http://www.infinet.com/~nafziger/wwii.html
Hiroshima:	http://www.cs.umn.edu/~dyue/wiihist/hiroshima/
Images:	http://www.azc.com/client/page/military.html
Japan:	http://www.cs.umn.edu/~dyue/wiihist/
Pearl Harbor:	http://www.execpc.com/~dschaaf/other.html
South Pacific:	http://life.csu.edu.au/~dspennem/MILARCH/MILARCH.HTM
USAF:	http://www.usaf.com/past.htm
USMC:	http://www.hpa.edu/CampTarawa.html
U.S. Military	
All Branches:	htt://www.dtic.mil/defenselink
US Navy:	http://www.sealion.com/
	http://www.wpi.edu/~elmer/navy.html
	http://www.history.navy.mil

INDEX